*When should I travel to get the best airfare?*
*Where do I go for answers to my travel questions?*
*What's the best and easiest way to plan and book my trip?*

# frommers.travelocity.com

**Frommer's**, the travel guide leader, has teamed up with **Travelocity.com**, the leader in online travel, to bring you an in-depth, easy-to-use resource designed to help you plan and book your trip online.

At **frommers.travelocity.com**, you'll find free online updates about your destination from the experts at Frommer's plus the outstanding travel planning and purchasing features of Travelocity.com. Travelocity.com provides reservations capabilities for 95 percent of all airline seats sold, more than 47,000 hotels, and over 50 car rental companies. In addition, Travelocity.com offers more than 2,000 exciting vacation and cruise packages. Travelocity.com puts you in complete control of your travel planning with these and other great features:

**Expert travel guidance from Frommer's** - over 150 writers reporting from around the world!

**Best Fare Finder** - an interactive calendar tells you when to travel to get the best airfare

**Fare Watcher** - we'll track airfare changes to your favorite destinations

**Dream Maps** - a mapping feature that suggests travel opportunities based on your budget

**Shop Safe Guarantee** - 24 hours a day / 7 days a week live customer service, and more!

Whether traveling on a tight budget, looking for a quick weekend getaway, or planning the trip of a lifetime, Frommer's guides and Travelocity.com will make your travel dreams a reality. You've bought the book, now book the trip!

# A New Star-Rating System & Other Exciting News from Frommer's!

In our continuing effort to publish the savviest, most up-to-date, and most appealing travel guides available, we've added some great new features.

Frommer's guides now include a new **star-rating system.** Every hotel, restaurant, and attraction is rated from 0 to 3 stars to help you set priorities and organize your time.

We've also added **seven brand-new features** that point you to the great deals, in-the-know advice, and unique experiences that separate travelers from tourists. Throughout the guide, look for:

***Finds*** Special finds—those places only insiders know about

***Fun Fact*** Fun facts—details that make travelers more informed and their trips more fun

***Kids*** Best bets for kids—advice for the whole family

***Moments*** Special moments—those experiences that memories are made of

***Overrated*** Places or experiences not worth your time or money

***Tips*** Insider tips—some great ways to save time and money

***Value*** Great values—where to get the best deals

We've also added a **"What's New"** section in every guide—a timely crash course in what's hot and what's not in every destination we cover.

# Canada

## 12th Edition

by Shawn Blore, Hilary Davidson, Paul Karr, Herbert Bailey Livesey, and Bill McRae



**Here's what the critics say about Frommer's:**

**"Amazingly easy to use. Very portable, very complete."**

—*Booklist*

**"The only mainstream guide to list specific prices. The Walter Cronkite of guidebooks—with all that implies."**

—*Travel & Leisure*

**"Complete, concise, and filled with useful information."**

—*New York Daily News*

**"Hotel information is close to encyclopedic."**

—*Des Moines Sunday Register*

**"Detailed, accurate, and easy-to-read information for all price ranges."**

—*Glamour Magazine*



Hungry Minds™

Best-Selling Books • Digital Downloads • e-Books • Answer Networks

e- ... ning

N

Published by:

**Hungry Minds, Inc.**
909 Third Ave.
New York, NY 10022



ISBN 0-7645-6606-7
ISSN 1044-2251

Editor: Matthew X. Kiernan
Production Editor: Bethany André
Photo Editor: Richard Fox
Cartographer: Elizabeth Puhl
Production by Hungry Minds Indianapolis Production Services

Front and back cover photos: Alberta, Moraine Lake in Banff National Park.

**Special Sales**
For general information on Hungry Minds' products and services, please contact our Customer Care department; within the U.S. at 800-762-2974, outside the U.S. at 317-572-3993, or fax 317-572-4002. For sales inquiries and reseller information, including discounts, bulk sales, customized editions, and premium sales, please contact our Customer Care department at 800-434-3422.

Manufactured in the United States of America

5 4 3 2 1

# Contents

## 7 Montréal 198

*by Herbert Bailey Livesey*



## 8 Québec City & the Gaspé Peninsula 256

*by Herbert Bailey Livesey*



## 9 Ottawa & Eastern Ontario 307

*by Herbert Bailey Livesey*



## 10 Toronto & the Golden Horseshoe 348

*By Hilary Davidson*

## 11 Southwestern Ontario 420

*by Hilary Davidson*



## 12 North to Ontario's Lakelands & Beyond 439

*by Hilary Davidson*



## 13 Manitoba & Saskatchewan 471

*by Bill McRae*

## 17 The Yukon, the Northwest Territories & Nunavut: The Great Northern Wilderness 733

*by Bill McRae*



## Appendix: Canada in Depth 779

*by Bill McRae*



## Index 789

# List of Maps

## About the Authors

A native of California and resident by turns of Ottawa, Amsterdam, Moscow, and (for the past half-decade) Vancouver, **Shawn Blore** is an award-winning magazine writer and the best-selling author of *Vancouver: Secrets of the City.* He's also the author of *Frommer's Vancouver & Victoria.*

**Hilary Davidson** divides her time between her hometown of Toronto and New York City. She's a restaurant critic for *Toronto Life* and has worked for *Harper's*, the *Globe and Mail, Chatelaine, Profit*, and *Equinox.* She's also the author of *Frommer's Toronto.* Her recent travels have taken her to Northern Ireland, Spain, and Thailand, though her most exciting trips have been of the aquatic variety—since learning to scuba dive she has explored shipwrecks in Eastern Ontario and swum with reef sharks in The Bahamas. She can be reached at hilary.davidson@usa.net.

**Paul Karr** has written, co-authored, or edited more than 25 guidebooks, icluding *Vancouver & Victoria For Dummies* and *Frommer's Nova Scotia, New Brunswick & Prince Edward Island.* He has also contributed to *Discovery Channer/Insight Guides' Montréal, Atlanta, Vienna, Austria*, and *Switzerland*; Avalon Publishing's *Irreverant Guides to Rome* and *Vancouver*, and *Scandinavia: The Rough Guide.* In addition, he has written articles for *Sierra* and *Sports Illustrated*, among other publications. He divides his time among New England, both coasts of Canada, and Europe.

**Herbert Bailey Livesey** has written about travel and food for many publications, including *Travel & Leisure, Food & Wine*, and *Playboy.* He's the author or coauthor of several guidebooks, including *Frommer's Montréal & Québec City, Frommer's Europe from $60 a Day*, and *Frommer's New England.*

**Bill McRae** was born and raised in rural eastern Montana, though he spent the better years of his youth attending university in Great Britain, France, and Canada. He has previously written about Montana and Utah for Moon Publications and about the Pacific Northwest and Seattle for Lonely Planet. Other publications he has written for include *National Geographic* and *Microsoft Expedia.* Bill is also coauthor of *Frommer's British Columbia & the Canadian Rockies.* He makes his home in Portland, Oregon.

## An Invitation to the Reader

In researching this book, we discovered many wonderful places—hotels, restaurants, shops, and more. We're sure you'll find others. Please tell us about them so that we can share the information with your fellow travelers in upcoming editions. If you were disappointed with a recommendation, we'd love to know that, too. Please write to:

*Frommer's Canada, 12th Edition*
Hungry Minds, Inc. • 909 Third Ave. • New York, NY 10022

## An Additional Note

Please be advised that travel information is subject to change at any time—and this is especially true of prices. We therefore suggest that you write or call ahead for confirmation when making your travel plans. The authors, editors, and publisher cannot be held responsible for the experiences of readers while traveling. Your safety is important to us, however, so we encourage you to stay alert and be aware of your surroundings. Keep a close eye on cameras, purses, and wallets, all favorite targets of thieves and pickpockets.

### New! Frommer's Star Ratings & Icons

Every hotel, restaurant, and attraction listing in this guide has been ranked for quality, value, service, amenities, and special features using a star-rating scale. In country, state, and regional guides, we also rate towns and regions to help you narrow down your choices and budget your time accordingly. Hotels and restaurants in the Very Expensive and Expensive categories are rated on a scale of one (highly recommended) to three stars (exceptional). Those in the Moderate and Inexpensive categories rate from zero (recommended) to two stars (very highly recommended). Attractions, towns, and regions are rated according to the following scale: zero stars (recommended), one star (highly recommended), two stars (very highly recommended), and three stars (must-see).

In addition to the rating system, we also use seven icons to highlight insider information, useful tips, special bargains, hidden gems, memorable experiences, kid-friendly venues, places to avoid, and other useful information:

*Finds* *Fun Fact* *Kids* *Moments* *Overrated* *Tips* *Value*

The following abbreviations are used for credit cards:

| | | | | | |
|---|---|---|---|---|---|
| AE | American Express | DISC | Discover | V | Visa |
| DC | Diners Club | MC | MasterCard | | |

## FROMMERS.COM

Now that you have the guidebook to a great trip, visit our website at **www.frommers.com** for travel information on nearly 2,500 destinations. With features updated regularly, we give you instant access to the most current trip-planning information available. At Frommers.com, you'll also find the best prices on airfares, accommodations, and car rentals—and you can even book travel online through our travel booking partners. At Frommers.com, you'll also find the following:

- Online updates to our most popular guidebooks
- Vacation sweepstakes and contest giveaways
- Newsletter highlighting the hottest travel trends
- Online travel message boards with featured travel discussions

# What's New in Canada

The strength of the U.S. dollar against the Canadian version, despite the events of September 11, 2001, continues to make Canada a bargain for American travelers. **Montréal** has roared back. Optimism and prosperity have returned after a decade of urban malaise, and a billion-dollar construction boom is filling downtown's empty spaces.

**MONTREAL Where to Stay** A perhaps excessive exuberance has caused a surge in hotel construction, notably in the oldest riverside district known as Vieux Montréal. Most notable is the hyper-stylish new **Hôtel Place d'Armes,** 701 Côte de la Place d'Armes (© **888/450-1887**) which opened last year with 48 rooms.

**Where to Dine** Quebecers were a little slow to embrace the food revolution that swept the continent in the 1980s and 90s. Montréal's better restaurants were good to excellent, but they were French, with a few Italians. That's changed, with a vengeance. Eat at a place like **Area,** 1429 rue Amherst (© **514/890-6691**) and see. The "Fusion" umbrella is about the only label that will contain its cuisine, which hops around the world for inspiration, with ingredients and techniques from several continents piled high on each plate. A thriving local taste for Thai cookery has promoted the success of **Chao Phraya,** 50 av. Laurier Ouest (© **514/272-5339**) and the need for reservations to partake in dishes that range from slightly peppery to incendiary, but invariably flavorful.

**Seeing the Sights** Utilizing a variety of technological tricks and displays, the **Interactive Science Centre,** King Edward Pier, Vieux-Port (© **514/496-4724**) intends to enlighten visitors, especially young ones, about science. Its most popular component by far is its IMAX Theater, with powerful images on a screen at least four stories high. **La Ronde,** Parc des Iles, Ile Ste-Hélène (© **514/872-4537**), home to 35 rides and the annual international fireworks competition, was teetering on the edge of bankruptcy when it was rescued in 2001 by the Six Flags empire. Improvements in maintenance and attractions should start to become apparent soon.

**Montréal After Dark** During the 2001 Formula One car race, native son and driver, Jacques Villenueve, opened **Newtown,** 1476 rue Crescent (© **514/284-6555**). The instantly trendy nightspot contains a disco, a big barroom, and a restaurant.

For more deatails, see chapter 7, "Montréal."

**QUEBEC CITY & THE GASPE PENINSULA Where to Stay** In a trend similar to that in Montréal, the Lower Town has experienced a surge in the recycling of older buildings into boutique hotels. One of the first, the superb **Hôtel Dominion 1912,** 126 rue Saint-Pierre (© **888/833-5253**) has been so successful the owners purchased the building next door, adding a bistro and 20 more bedrooms.

**Where to Dine** For the *hot-hot-hottest* new entry, make time for the

**Voodoo Grill,** 575 Grande-Allée (© **418/647-2000**). Geopolitical references are a little confused, with a decor of African masks and food from around the Pacific Rim—hardly "voodoo"—but the eats are surprisingly good, and assuming you don't require quietude with your dinner, you'll enjoy the energy of the good-looking young clientele.

**Québec City After Dark** On the boisterous Grande Allée, two grungy new bar/dance clubs are the **Liquid Bar,** 580 Grande Allée (© **418/524-1367**) and the **Living Lounge,** 690 Grande Allée (no phone). Crowds are in their late teens and early twenties, and T-shirts and jeans or the cold-weather equivalent are the dress.

For more great information, see chapter 8, "Québec & the Gaspé Peninsula."

**OTTAWA & EASTERN ONTARIO**
**Where to Stay** The hotel situation in the capital region has remained fairly stable, unlike that in Montréal and Toronto. An expanding mid-priced division of the Sheraton empire has brought to Hull the shiny new **Four Points Sheraton,** 35 rue Laurier (© **800/567-9607**), directly opposite the Canadian Museum of Civilization. It equals pricier competitors in most regards, and give management a gold star for restoring the rectory of the adjacent 19th-century Notre-Dame Church, now serving as an annex to the hotel. A sister entry in Kingston, also opened in 2001, is the **Four Points Hotel & Suites,** 285 King St. East, (© **888/478-4333**). Whisker-clean and sturdy, its downtown location is excellent, with unobstructed views of the town and Lake Ontario from the upper floors.

**Where to Dine** In Kingston, **Casa Dominico,** 35 Brock St. (© **613/542-0870**) aspires to and achieves a higher order of quality. The front windows open in summer, a fireplace blazes in winter, and this upscale rendezvous blissfully chatters away almost every night of the year. No red-sauce-and-spag joint, its Italian classics are cuts above the norm, making it popular with large celebratory parties as well as amatory couples.

**Ottawa After Dark** The biggest news in Ottawa's nightlife offerings is the opening of the **Casino de Hull,** 1 bd. du Casino (© **800/665-2274** or 819/772-2100). It has over 1,300 slot machines and more than 50 gambling tables, while a dance-and-music revue provides respite from losing. A connected 23-floor hotel opened for business in late 2001.

See chapter 9, "Ottawa & Eastern Ontario," for more information.

**ALBERTA & THE ROCKIES**
**Where to Dine** One of Banff's newest and most fashionable restaurants is **Saltlik,** 221 Bear St. (© **403/760-2467**). The setting is as cool as the grills are scorching: Industrial chic—concrete and steel—isn't exactly what you expect in an Alpine setting, but in summer the glass walls fold back and nearly the entire restaurant turns al fresco.

For complete details, see chapter 14, "Alberta & the Rockies."

**VANCOUVER** Waterfront renewal is a big issue across North America, and nobody does it better than Vancouver—at least to judge by the legions of architects and planners from Baltimore to San Francisco who come to town to gawk at what we've done and then scribble away in little notebooks. The latest phase of waterfront Reno is at **Coal Harbour,** where a new park and community center flank a 9m (30-ft.) wide seawall with benches, bike paths, and the occasional outdoor cafe. With this section in place, it's now possible to hop on the seawall near Canada Place in downtown and stay on past Coal Harbour, around Stanley Park, back to English Bay, and all the way east along False Creek to Science World: a 30km (18-mile) waterfront stroll. Bring your walking shoes.

See chapter 15, "Vancouver," for more information.

**VICTORIA & BRITISH COLUMBIA The Okanagan Valley: A Taste of the Grape Where to Dine in Kalowna** In a city with a big reputation for fine dining, people notice when someone opens a new restaurant. Especially when that person is Rod Butters, a young chef who previously led the kitchen at such famous hotel as the Chateau Whistler, the Wickaninnish Inn in Tofino, and the Pacific Palisades in Vancouver. **Fresco,** 1560 Water St. (**© 250/868-8805**), is Butters' first venture as a chef entrepreneur, and the results are stellar. Expect hearty though refined cuisine based on regional meats and produce.

For complete information, see chapter 16, "Victoria & British Columbia."

# 1

# The Best of Canada

Planning a trip to such a vast and diverse country can present you with a bewildering array of choices. We've scoured all of Canada in search of the best places and experiences, and in this chapter, we share our very personal and opinionated choices. We hope they'll give you some ideas and get you started.

## 1 The Best Travel Experiences

- **Exploring the Cabot Trail** (Nova Scotia): This wildly scenic driving loop around Cape Breton Highlands National Park delivers a surplus of dramatic coastal scenery. Take a few days to explore the area. You can hike along blustery headlands, search for whales on a tour boat, and dabble around a cove or two in a sea kayak. See chapter 3, "Nova Scotia."
- **Hiking Gros Morne National Park** (Newfoundland): When the earth's land masses broke apart and shifted 500 million years ago, a piece of the mantle, the very shell of the planet, was thrust upward to form tableland mountains of rock here. Spend a week or more trekking along the coastal trails, venturing to scenic waterfalls, and strolling alongside landlocked fjords. See chapter 6, "Newfoundland & Labrador."
- **Watching the World Go By in a Québec City Cafe** (Québec): On a sunny summer Saturday, sit outside at Le Marie-Clarisse restaurant in the Quartier Petit-Champlain at the foot of the Breakneck Stairs. From there you can watch the goings-on in one of the oldest European communities in the New World while enjoying some of the best seafood in town. A folksinger may do a half-hour set, then be followed by a classical guitarist. See chapter 8, "Quebec City & the Gaspé Peninsula."
- **Seeing the Polar Bears in Churchill** (Manitoba): In October or November, travel by train or plane to Churchill and the shores of Hudson Bay to view hundreds of magnificent polar bear, who migrate to the bay's icy shores and even lope into Churchill itself. In the evening, you can glimpse the famous aurora borealis (northern lights). Either take **VIA Rail**'s *Hudson Bay* train (✆ **888/VIA-RAIL** in Canada, 800/561-3949 in the U.S.), a 2-night/1-day trip from Winnipeg, or fly in on **Air Canada** (✆ **888/247-2262;** www.aircanada.ca). See chapter 13, "Manitoba & Saskatchewan."
- **Horseback Riding in the Rockies** (Alberta): Rent a cabin on a rural guest ranch and get back in the saddle again. Spend a day fishing, then return to the lodge for a country dance or barbecue. Ride a horse to a backcountry chalet in the rugged mountain wilderness. Forget the crowded park highways and commercialized resort towns and just relax. **Brewster's Kananaskis Guest Ranch** (✆ **800/691-5085** or

403/673-3737) in Kananaskis Village, near Banff, Alberta, offers a variety of guided horseback trips, from C$125 to C$140 (US$78–US$87) per day, including food, lodging, and the horse you ride in on. See chapter 14, "Alberta & the Rockies."

- **Sailing the Great Bear Rain Forest** (British Columbia): About halfway up BC's west coast is an isolated region of mountains, fjords, bays, rivers, and inlets. It's one of the last places where grizzly bear are still found in large numbers, plus salmon, killer whales, otters, and porpoises. You need a boat to get there, so why not take the gorgeous 100-year-old schooner *Maple Leaf*? **Maple Leaf Adventures** (**© 888/599-5323** or 250/715-0906; fax 250/715-0912) runs a number of trips to the area, from 4 days to 2 weeks, all including gourmet meals and comfortable accommodation aboard the *Maple Leaf.* See chapter 16, "Victoria & British Columbia."
- **Dog-Sledding Through Baffin Island** (Nunavut): Spectacular fjords, knife-edged mountains draped with glaciers, and friendly craft-oriented Inuit villages make this rarely visited island—the world's fifth largest—a great off-the-beaten-path destination. Arrange a dogsled tour to the floe edge, where the protected harbor ice meets the open sea and where seals, polar bears, and bowhead whales converge. A weeklong dog-sledding trip with **NorthWinds Arctic Adventures** (**© 800/549-0551** or 867/979-0551) costs C$2,300 (US$1,426). See chapter 17, "The Yukon, the Northwest Territories & Nunavut: The Great Northern Wilderness."

## 2 The Best Family Vacations

- **Fundy National Park and Vicinity** (New Brunswick): You'll find swimming, hiking, and kayaking at this extraordinary national park. And don't overlook biking in the hills east of the park or rappelling and rock climbing at Cape Enrage. See chapter 4, "New Brunswick."
- **Prince Edward Island's Beaches:** The red-sand beaches will turn white swim trunks a bit pinkish, but it's hard to beat a day or two splashing around these tepid waters while admiring pastoral island landscapes. See chapter 5, "Prince Edward Island."
- **Ottawa** (Ontario): In this family-friendly city, you and your kids can watch soldiers strut their stuff and red-coated Mounties polish their equestrian and musical skills. Canoeing or skating on the canal is lots of fun, and Ottawa boasts a host of live museums to explore—like the Canada Aviation Museum, the Canadian Museum of Civilization, and the Canada Museum of Science and Technology. See chapter 9, "Ottawa & Eastern Ontario."
- **The Muskoka Lakes** (Ontario): This region is filled with resorts that welcome families. Kids can swim, canoe, bike, fish, and more. Since most resorts offer children's programs, parents can enjoy a rest as well. See chapter 12, "North to Ontario's Lakelands & Beyond."
- **Whistler/Blackcomb Ski Resorts** (British Columbia): Whistler and Blackcomb's twin ski resorts offer lots of family-oriented activities. You'll find everything from downhill and cross-country skiing, snowboarding, snowshoeing, and snowmobiling lessons in winter to horseback riding, mountain

biking, golfing, in-line skating, paragliding, heli-skiing, swimming, kayaking, and rafting summer trips designed for families with school-age children. See chapter 16, "Victoria & British Columbia."

## 3 The Best Nature & Wildlife Viewing

- **Whales at Digby Neck** (Nova Scotia): For a chance to see fin, minke, or humpback whales, choose from a dozen whale-watching outfitters located along this narrow peninsula of remote fishing villages. Right, sperm, blue, and pilot whales, along with the infrequent orcas, have also been seen over the years. Getting to the tip of the peninsula is half the fun—it requires two ferries. See chapter 3, "Nova Scotia."
- **Birds and Caribou on the Avalon Peninsula** (Newfoundland): In one busy day you can see a herd of caribou, the largest puffin colony in North America, and an extraordinary gannet colony visible from the mainland cliffs. See chapter 6, "Newfoundland & Labrador."
- **Whales at Baie Ste-Catherine** (Québec): At Baie Ste-Catherine, about a 2-hour drive northeast of Québec City, and along the northern shore to the resort area of La Malbaie, hundreds of resident beluga and minke whales are joined by several additional species of their migratory cousins, including humpbacks and blues. Mid-June to early October, you can spot the graceful giants from land, but whale-watching cruises depart from Baie Ste-Catherine for closer looks. See chapter 8, "Quebec City & the Gaspé Peninsula."
- **Pelicans in Prince Albert National Park** (Saskatchewan): On Lavallee Lake roosts the second-largest pelican colony in North America. Bison, moose, elk, caribou, black bear, and red fox also roam free in this 400,000ha (million-acre) wilderness. See chapter 13, "Manitoba & Saskatchewan."
- **Orcas off Vancouver Island** (British Columbia): The waters surrounding Vancouver Island teem with orcas (killer whales), as well as harbor seals, sea lions, bald eagles, and harbour and Dahl's porpoises. At the island's southern tip, **Victoria Marine Adventure Centre** (**© 250/995-2211**) is one of many companies offering whale-watching tours in Zodiacs and covered boats. See chapter 16, "Victoria & British Columbia."
- **Rare Seabirds, Beluga Whales, and Narwhals near Bylot Island** (Nunavut): Spend a week in August rounding Bylot Island (soon to be called North Baffin National Park) on sea kayaks. Off the northern tip of Baffin Island, Bylot's soaring mountain peaks choked with ancient glaciers don't look hospitable, but during the short summer season they're the nesting grounds of rare gulls, puffins, and other seabirds. In addition, you may come kayak-to-tusk with a narwhal, the unicorn-like cousin of the whale and walrus that sports a twisted horn in its forehead. And watch for the noses of creamy white Beluga whales as they gather to breathe holes in the ice. **Polar Sea Adventures** (**© 867/899-8870**) offers guided sea kayak tours to Bylot Island. See chapter 17, "The Yukon, the Northwest Territories & Nunavut: The Great Northern Wilderness."

## 4 The Best Views

- **Cape Enrage** (New Brunswick): Just east of Fundy National Park, you'll find surprisingly harsh coastal terrain of high rocky cliffs pounded by the sea. Route 915 offers a wonderful detour off the beaten path. See chapter 4, "New Brunswick."
- **Signal Hill** (Newfoundland): Signal Hill marks the entrance to St. John's harbor. Never mind the history that was made here; it's uncommonly scenic, with views of a coast that hasn't changed in 500 years. The North Head Trail is one of Newfoundland's most dramatic, and it's entirely in city limits. See chapter 6, "Newfoundland & Labrador."
- **Bonavista Peninsula** (Newfoundland): The peninsula's northernmost tip offers a superb vantage point for spotting icebergs, even into midsummer. You'll also see puffins, whales, and one of the most scenic lighthouses in eastern Canada. See chapter 6, "Newfoundland & Labrador."
- **Terrasse Dufferin in Québec City** (Québec): This boardwalk promenade with benches and green-and-white-roofed gazebos runs along the cusp of the bluff rearing up behind the original colonial settlement. At its back is the landmark Château Frontenac, and out front is the long silvery sweep of the St. Lawrence, where ferries glide back and forth and cruise ships and Great Lakes freighters and tankers put in at the port. To the east is the trailing edge of the Adirondacks, and downriver you can see the last of the Laurentian Mountains. See chapter 8, "Quebec City & the Gaspé Peninsula."
- **Niagara Falls** (Ontario): This is still a wonder of nature despite its commercial exploitation. You can experience the falls from the decks of the *Maid of the Mist,* which takes you into the roaring maelstrom, or look down from the cockpit of a helicopter. The least scary view is from the Skylon Tower. See chapter 10, "Toronto & the Golden Horseshoe."
- **Agawa Canyon** (Ontario): To see the northern Ontario wilderness that inspired the Group of Seven, take the Agawa Canyon Train Tour on a 184km (114-mile) trip from the Soo to Hearst through the Agawa Canyon, where you can spend a few hours exploring scenic waterfalls and vistas. The train snakes through a vista of deep ravines and lakes, hugging the hillsides and crossing gorges on skeletal trestle bridges. See chapter 12, "North to Ontario's Lakelands & Beyond."
- **Moraine Lake in Banff National Park** (Alberta): Ten snow-clad peaks towering more than 3,030m (10,000 ft.) rear up dramatically behind this eerily green tiny lake. Rent a canoe and paddle to the mountains' base. See chapter 14, "Alberta & the Rockies."

## 5 The Most Dramatic Drives

- **Cape Breton's Cabot Trail** (Nova Scotia): This 280km (174-mile) loop through the uplands of Cape Breton Highlands National Park is a world-class excursion. You'll see Acadian fishing ports, pristine valleys, and some of the most picturesque coastline anywhere. See chapter 3, "Nova Scotia."
- **Viking Trail** (Newfoundland): Travelers looking to leave the crowds behind needn't look any

further. This beautiful drive to Newfoundland's northern tip is wild and solitary, with views of curious geology and a wind-raked coast. And you'll end up at one of the world's great historic sites—L'Anse aux Meadows. See chapter 6, "Newfoundland & Labrador."

- **Icefields Parkway** (Highway 93 through Banff and Jasper national parks, Alberta): This is one of the world's grandest mountain drives. Cruising along it is like a trip back to the ice ages. The parkway climbs past glacier-notched peaks to the Columbia Icefields, a sprawling cap of snow, ice, and glacier at the very crest of the Rockies. See chapter 14, "Alberta & the Rockies."
- **Highway 99** (British Columbia): The Sea to Sky Highway from Vancouver to Lillooet takes you from a dramatic seacoast past glaciers, pine forests, and a waterfall that cascades from a mountaintop and through Whistler's majestic glacial mountains. The next leg of the 4-hour drive winds up a series of switchbacks to the thickly forested Cayoosh Creek valley and on to the craggy mountains surrounding the Fraser River gold-rush town of Lillooet. See chapter 16, "Victoria & British Columbia."
- **Dempster Highway** (from Dawson City to Inuvik, Northwest Territories): Canada's most northerly highway, the Dempster is a year-round gravel road across the top of the world. From Dawson City, the road winds over the Continental Divide three times, crosses the Arctic Circle, and fords the Peel and Mackenzie rivers by ferry before reaching Inuvik, a native community on the mighty Mackenzie River delta. See chapter 17, "The Yukon, the Northwest Territories & Nunavut: The Great Northern Wilderness."

## 6 The Best Walks & Rambles

- **Halifax's Waterfront** (Nova Scotia): Take your time strolling along Halifax's working waterfront. You can visit museums, board a historic ship or two, enjoy a snack, and take an inexpensive ferry ride across the harbor and back. Come evening, there's fiddle and guitar playing at the pubs. See chapter 3, "Nova Scotia."
- **Cape Breton Highlands National Park** (Nova Scotia): You'll find bog and woodland walks aplenty at Cape Breton, but the best trails follow rugged cliffs along the open ocean. The Skyline Trail is among the most dramatic pathways in the province. See chapter 3, "Nova Scotia."
- **Green Gardens Trail** (Gros Morne, Newfoundland): This demanding hike at Gros Morne National Park takes you on a 16km (10-mile) loop, much of which follows coastal meadows atop fractured cliffs. It's demanding but worth every step of the way. See chapter 6, "Newfoundland & Labrador."
- **Old Montréal** (Québec): Wander the cobblestone streets, where you'll find some remains—above and below the streets—of what founder Paul de Chomedey, sieur de Maisonneuve, christened Ville-Marie in 1642. Aboveground, buildings have been restored into homes, stores, restaurants, and nightclubs. Horse-drawn carriages clop and creak along the streets, past the heart of the district, place Jacques-Cartier, which is lined with cafes. Below ground, a tunnel leads from the new

Museum of Archaeology to the old Custom House. See chapter 7, "Montréal."

- **Lake Superior Provincial Park** (Ontario): Follow any trail in this park to a rewarding vista. The 16km (10-mile) Peat Mountain Trail leads to a panoramic view close to 152m (500 ft.) above the surrounding lakes and forests. The moderate Orphan Lake Trail offers views over the Orphan Lake and Lake Superior, plus a pebble beach and Baldhead River falls. The 26km (16-mile) Toawab Trail takes you through the Agawa Valley to the 25m (81-ft.) Agawa Falls. See chapter 12, "North to Ontario's Lakelands & Beyond."
- **Johnston Canyon** (Banff National Park, Alberta): Just 24km (15 miles) west of Banff, Johnson Creek cuts a deep, very narrow canyon through limestone cliffs. The trail winds through tunnels, passes waterfalls, edges by shaded rock faces, and crosses the chasm on footbridges before reaching a series of iridescent pools, formed by springs that bubble up through highly colored rock. See chapter 14, "Alberta & the Rockies."
- **Plain of Six Glaciers Trail** (Lake Louise, Alberta): From Chateau Lake Louise, a lakeside trail rambles along the edge of emerald-green Lake Louise, then climbs up to the base of Victoria Glacier. At a rustic teahouse you can order a cup of tea and a scone—each made over a wood-burning stove—and gaze up at the rumpled face of the glacier. See chapter 14, "Alberta & the Rockies."
- **Long Beach** (Vancouver Island, British Columbia): Part of Pacific Rim National Park, Long Beach is more than 16km (10 miles) long and hundreds of meters wide and is flanked by awe-inspiring rain forests of cedar, fir and Sitka Spruce. Beyond the roaring surf you'll see soaring eagles, basking sea lions, and occasionally even migrating gray whales. See chapter 16, "Victoria & British Columbia."

## 7 The Best Biking Routes

- **Nova Scotia's South Shore:** Not in a hurry to get anywhere? Peddling the peninsulas and coasting along placid inlets is a great tonic for a weary soul. You'll pass through graceful villages like Shelburne, Lunenburg, and Chester and rediscover a quiet way of life. See chapter 3, "Nova Scotia."
- **Prince Edward Island:** This island province sometimes seems like it was created specifically for bike touring. The villages are reasonably spaced, the hills are virtually nonexistent, the coastal roads are picturesque in the extreme, and a new island-wide bike path offers detours through marshes and quiet woodlands. See chapter 5, "Prince Edward Island."
- **Old Port Route** (Montréal): The city has 239km (148 miles) of biking paths, and the Métro permits bicycles in the last car of its trains. One popular route is from the Old Port west along the side of the Lachine Canal. A little under 11km (7 miles) one-way, it's tranquil, vehicle-free, and mostly flat. You can rent bikes at the Old Port. See chapter 7, "Montréal."
- **Ile d'Orléans** (Québec): You can enjoy a day or two of biking around this bucolic island 15 minutes downriver from Québec City. A main road runs around the island, never far from the water's edge. You can stop at a pick-your-own orchard or strawberry field or

in a tiny village with 18th- and 19th-century houses and churches. Two roads cut across the island at the southern end, and a third does the same a little beyond midpoint. You can rent bikes on the island. See chapter 8, "Quebec City & the Gaspé Peninsula."

- **Niagara Region** (Ontario): The flatlands here make for terrific biking terrain. A bike path runs along the Niagara Parkway, which follows the Niagara River. You'll bike past fruit farms, vineyards, and gardens with picnicking spots. See chapter 10, "Toronto & the Golden Horseshoe."
- **Highways 1 and 93 Through Banff and Jasper National Parks** (Alberta): This well-maintained wide highway winds through some of the world's most dramatic mountain scenery. Take the Bow Valley Parkway, between Banff and Lake Louise, and Parkway 93A between Athabasca Falls and Jasper for slightly quieter peddling. Best of all, there are seven hostels (either rustic or fancy) at some of the most beautiful sights along the route, so you don't have to weigh yourself down with camping gear. See chapter 14, "Alberta & the Rockies."
- **Stanley Park Seawall** (Vancouver, British Columbia): Vancouver's Seawall surrounds the Stanley Park shoreline on the Burrard Inlet and English Bay. Built just above the high-tide mark, it offers nonstop breathtaking views, no hills, and no cars. See chapter 15, "Vancouver."

## 8 The Best Culinary Experiences

- **Fresh Lobster** (Nova Scotia & New Brunswick): Wherever you see the wooden lobster traps piled on a wharf, you'll know a fresh lobster meal isn't far away. The most productive lobster fisheries are around Shediac, New Brunswick, and all along Nova Scotia's Atlantic coast. Sunny days are ideal for cracking open a crustacean while sitting at a wharf-side picnic table, preferably with a locally brewed beer close at hand. See chapters 3, "Nova Scotia," and 4, "New Brunswick."
- **Newfoundland Berries:** The unforgiving rocky and boggy soil of this blustery island resists most crops but produces some of the most delicious berries you can imagine. Look for roadside stands in midsummer or pick your own blueberries, strawberries, partridgeberries, or bakeapples. Many restaurants add berries (on cheesecake, in custard) when they're in season. See chapter 6, "Newfoundland & Labrador."
- **Dining at the Best in Montréal** (Québec): Montréal boasts one of the hottest dining scenes in Canada. The current favorite is **Toqué!** (**© 514/499-2084**), the kind of restaurant that raises the gastronomic expectations of an entire city. The silky greeting-to-tab performance of the kitchen and waitstaff is a pleasure to observe, and the postnouvelle presentations are visually winning and completely filling. No restaurant in eastern Canada surpasses this contemporary French gem. See chapter 7, "Montréal."
- **Sampling Smoked Meat in Montréal** (Québec): Somewhere between pastrami and corned beef, this deli delight appears to have had its origins with the immigrations of eastern Europeans during the late 19th century. Meat eaters are ravenous at

the sight and aroma of it, and *the* place to inhale smoked meat is **Chez Schwartz** on The Main (✆ **514/842-4813**). Elegant it's not; immensely satisfying it is. See chapter 7, "Montréal."

- **Eating Ethnic in Toronto** (Ontario): If you explore the city's neighborhoods, you'll find ethnic dining spots in Little Italy and Greek sections of the Danforth. Order seafood pasta at **Veni Vidi Vici** (✆ **416/536-8550**); or imaginatively updated Greek at **Pan on the Danforth** (✆ **416/466-8158**). Each is at the heart of its ethnic neighborhood. See chapter 10, "Toronto & the Golden Horseshoe."
- **Feasting on Danish Specialties** (Saskatchewan): Enjoy seven superlative dishes, from *frikadeller* (Danish meat patties served with red cabbage and potato salad) to *aeggekage* (a Danish omelette served with home-baked bread) at the warmly inviting **Bistro Dansk,** Winnipeg (✆ **204/775-5662**). See chapter 13, "Manitoba & Saskatchewan."
- **Going Organic in Calgary** (Alberta): You'll walk through a quiet tree-filled park on an island in the Bow River to reach the bustling **River Café** (✆ **403/261-7670**). An immense wood-fired oven and grill produces soft, chewy flat breads and smoky grilled meats and vegetables, all organically grown and freshly harvested. On warm summer evenings, picnickers loll in the grassy shade, nibbling this and that from the cafe's picnic-like menu. See chapter 14, "Alberta & the Rockies."
- **Dining at a Hotel in Lake Louise** (Alberta): At its cozy dining room in an old log lodge, the **Post Hotel** (✆ **800/661-1586** or 403/522-3989) serves up the kind of sophisticated yet robust cuisine that perfectly fits the backdrop of glaciered peaks, deep forest, and glassy streams. Both the wine list and the cooking are French and hearty, with the chef focusing on the best of local ingredients—lamb, salmon, and Alberta beef. After spending time out on the trail, a meal here will top off a quintessential day in the Rockies. See chapter 14, "Alberta & the Rockies."
- **Enjoying Dim Sum in Vancouver's Chinatown** (British Columbia): With its burgeoning Chinese population, Vancouver's Chinatown has more than half a dozen dim-sum parlors where you can try steamed or baked barbecued-pork buns, dumplings filled with fresh prawns and vegetables, or steamed rice-flour crêpes filled with spicy beef. One favorite is **Sun Sui Wah** (✆ **604/872-8822**). See chapter 15, "Vancouver."
- **Eating Local in Lotus Land** (British Columbia): Self-sufficiency is the new watchword on the West Coast, with top chefs sourcing all their ingredients locally. On Vancouver Island, the **Sooke Harbour House** (✆ **250/642-3421**) offers lamb from nearby Saltspring Island, seasoned with herbs from the chef's own garden. In Vancouver, the **Raincity Grill** (✆ **604/685-7337**) makes a specialty of fresh-caught seafood, while the vast selection of BC wines by the glass makes dinner an extended road trip through the West Coast wine country, with no need for a designated driver. See chapters 15, "Vancouver," and 16, "Victoria & British Columbia."

## 9 The Best Festivals & Special Events

- **International Busker Festival** (Halifax, Nova Scotia): In early August, the 10-day International Busker Festival brings together talented street performers from around the world, performing in their natural habitat. Best of all, it's free. See chapter 3, "Nova Scotia."
- **Newfoundland and Labrador Folk Festival** (St. John's, Newfoundland): How did such a remote island develop such a deep talent pool? That's one of the questions you'll ponder while tapping your feet at this 3-day festival, which is laden with local talent. It's cheap, folksy, and fun. See chapter 6, "Newfoundland & Labrador."
- **Winter Carnival** (Québec City, Québec): Think Mardi Gras in New Orleans, without the nudity (well, maybe a little). Ice sculptures, parades, a canoe race across the frozen St. Lawrence, and an impressive castle of ice are among the principal features. The general jollity is fueled by a nasty drink called Caribou, whiskey sloshed with red wine. See chapter 8, "Quebec City & the Gaspé Peninsula."
- **Toronto International Film Festival** (Ontario): Second only to Cannes, this film festival draws Hollywood's leading luminaries to town for 10 days in early September; more than 250 films are on show. See chapter 10, "Toronto & the Golden Horseshoe."
- **Stratford Festival** (Ontario): This world-famous festival of superb repertory theater, launched by Tyrone Guthrie in 1953, has featured major players like the late Sir Alec Guinness, Christopher Plummer, Dame Maggie Smith, and Sir Peter Ustinov. Productions, which run from May to October or early November on three stages, range from classic to contemporary. You can also participate in informal discussions with company members. See chapter 11, "Southwestern Ontario."
- **Northern Manitoba Trappers' Festival** (The Pas, Manitoba): This festival celebrates the traditions of the frontier pioneers each February with world-championship dogsled races, ice fishing, beer fests, bannock baking, moose calling, and more. See chapter 13, "Manitoba & Saskatchewan."
- **Calgary Stampede** (Alberta): In all North America, there's nothing quite like the Calgary Stampede. Of course it's the world's largest rodeo, but it's also a series of concerts, an art show, an open-air casino, a carnival, a street dance—you name it, it's undoubtedly going on somewhere. In July, all of Calgary is converted into a party and everyone's invited. See chapter 14, "Alberta & the Rockies."
- **Celebration of Light** (Vancouver, British Columbia): This 4-night fireworks extravaganza takes place over English Bay. Three of the world's leading manufacturers are invited to represent their countries in competition against one another, setting their best displays to music. On the fourth night, all three companies launch their finales. Last year more than 500,000 people showed up each night. The best seats are at the "Bard on the Beach" Shakespeare festival across False Creek. See chapter 15, "Vancouver."

## 10 The Best Luxury Hotels & Resorts

- **Keltic Lodge** (Cape Breton Island, Nova Scotia; ✆ **800/565-0444** or 902/285-2880): It's got grand natural drama in the sea-pounded cliffs that surround it, plus a generous measure of high culture. (Jackets on men at dinner, please!) The adjacent golf course is stupendous, and some of the national park's best hikes are close at hand. See chapter 3, "Nova Scotia."
- **Kingsbrae Arms Relais & Chateaux** (St. Andrews, New Brunswick; ✆ **506/529-1897**): This new deluxe inn manages the trick of being opulent and comfortable at the same time. The shingled manse is lavishly appointed, beautifully landscaped, and well situated for exploring charming St. Andrews. See chapter 4, "New Brunswick."
- **Dalvay-by-the-Sea** (Grand Tracadie, Prince Edward Island; ✆ **902/672-2048**). This intimate resort (just 30 rooms and cottages) is on a quiet stretch of beach. The Tudor mansion was built by a business partner of John D. Rockefeller, and the woodwork alone is enough to keep you entertained for your stay. Bring your bike. See chapter 5, "Prince Edward Island."
- **Loews Hôtel Vogue** (Montréal, Québec; ✆ **800/465-6654** or 514/285-5555): What was just an anonymous mid-rise office building has turned into the king of the hill of Montréal hotels. The Vogue targeted international executives on the go, and little was left to chance. Even the standard rooms come with fax machines, four phones, computer ports, bathroom TVs, and whirlpool bathtubs. Tins of caviar are tucked into the minibars. People with cell phones at the ready fill the lobby espresso bar and adjacent dining room. Even after two changes in management, the Vogue remains steady on its course. See chapter 7, "Montréal."
- **Langdon Hall** (Cambridge, Ontario; ✆ **800/268-1898** or 519/740-2100): This quintessential English country house, built in 1902 for the granddaughter of John Jacob Astor, is now a small hotel where you can enjoy 80ha (200 acres) of lawns, gardens, and woodlands. The guest rooms feature the finest amenities, fabrics, and furnishings. Facilities include a full spa, a pool, a tennis court, a croquet lawn, and an exercise room. The airy dining room overlooking the lily pond offers fine continental cuisine. See chapter 11, "Southwestern Ontario."
- **Manitowaning Lodge Golf & Tennis Resort** (Manitowaning, Ontario; ✆ **705/859-3136**): This resort on Manitoulin Island is an idyllic island retreat. A lodge and cottages are set on 4.5ha (11 acres) of beautiful gardens. The lodge, with its huge hand-hewn beams, a mask of the Spirit of Manitowaning, and images of the Native-American protective spirit, provides a serene setting to restore the spirit. See chapter 12, "North to Ontario's Lakelands & Beyond."
- The **Fairmont Chateau Lake Louise** (Banff National Park, Alberta; ✆ **800/441-1414** or 403/522-3511): First of all, there's the view. Across a tiny gem-green lake rise massive cliffs shrouded in glacial ice. And then there's the hotel. Part hunting lodge, part European palace, the Chateau is its own community, with sumptuous boutiques, sports rental

facilities, seven dining areas, two bars, magnificent lobby areas, and beautifully furnished guest rooms. See chapter 14, "Alberta & the Rockies."

- **Hotel Macdonald** (Edmonton, Alberta; ✆ **800/441-1414** or 780/424-5181): When the Canadian Pacific bought and refurbished this landmark hotel in the 1980s, all the charming period details were preserved, while all the inner workings were modernized and brought up to snuff. The result is a regally elegant but friendly small hotel. From the kilted bellman to the gargoyles on the walls, this is a real class act. See chapter 14, "Alberta & the Rockies."
- **Wickaninnish Inn** (Tofino, British Columbia; ✆ **800/333-4604** in North America, or 250/725-3100): No matter which room you book in this beautiful new lodge, you'll wake to a magnificent view of the untamed Pacific. The inn is on a rocky promontory, surrounded by an old-growth spruce and cedar rain forest and the sprawling sands of Long Beach. In summer, try golfing, fishing, or whale-watching. In winter, shelter by the fire in the Pointe restaurant and watch the wild Pacific storms roll in. See chapter 16, "Victoria & British Columbia."

## 11 The Best Bed & Breakfasts

- **The Manse** (Mahone Bay, Nova Scotia; ✆ **902/624-1121**): There's not a bad room in this four-room B&B, built in 1870 on a low hill in the picturesque village of Mahone Bay. Spend the day browsing local shops, then retreat in the evening to the casual luxury of this top-rated lodge. See chapter 3, "Nova Scotia."
- **Shipwright Inn** (Charlottetown, Prince Edward Island; ✆ **888/306-9966** or 902/368-1905): This in-town seven-room B&B is within easy walking distance of all the city's attractions yet has a settled and pastoral feel. It's informed by a Victorian sensibility without being over-the-top about it. See chapter 5, "Prince Edward Island."
- **At Wit's Inn** (St. John's, Newfoundland; ✆ **877/739-7420** or 709/739-7420): The centrally located B&B is bright, cheerful, and whimsical. Opened in 1999 by a restaurateur from Toronto, the inn preserves the best of the historical elements in this century-old home while graciously updating it for modern tastes. See chapter 6, "Newfoundland & Labrador."
- **Clifton Manor Inn** (Bayfield, Ontario; ✆ **519/565-2282**): You'll find romance at this elegant house, built in 1895 for the reve (bailiff or governor) of Bayfield. All the bathrooms have candles and bubble bath, and one has a deep tub for two. Four comfortable rooms are each named after an artist or a composer. All the rooms have cozy touches like mohair throws, sheepskin rugs, wingback chairs, and fresh flowers. Breakfast consists of omelettes or crêpes, plus fresh fruit often plucked from the trees in the garden. See chapter 11, "Southwestern Ontario."
- **Beild House** (Collingwood, Ontario; ✆ **888-322-3453** or 705/444-1522): On Fridays, you can sit down to a splendid five-course dinner before retiring to

the bed that belonged to the duke and duchess of Windsor. A sumptuous breakfast will follow the next morning. This handsome 1909 house contains 17 rooms, 7 with private bathroom. See chapter 12, "North to Ontario's Lakelands & Beyond."

- **Abigail's Hotel** (Victoria, British Columbia; ✆ **800/561-6565** or 250/388-5363): Abigail's began as a 1920s luxury apartment house, then was converted to an elegant boutique hotel. The rooms are bright and beautiful, with fresh flowers and Mission-style beds with goose-down comforters. Some boast soaker tubs and double-sided fireplaces, so you can relax in the tub by the firelight and later slip on a robe and lounge on the sofa by the fire's other side. A gourmet breakfast is served in the dining room, and in the evening cider and sherry are poured in the comfy library. See chapter 16, "Victoria & British Columbia."
- **Pearson's Arctic Home Stay** (Baffin Island, Nunavut; ✆ **867/979-6408**): Staying at this lovely private home overlooking Frobisher Bay is like staying at a museum of Inuit Arts and Crafts. The innkeeper is the town's former mayor and currently the island's public coroner, so you also get a real insight into life and death on Baffin Island. See chapter 17, "The Yukon, the Northwest Territories & Nunavut: The Great Northern Wilderness."

## 12 The Best Camping & Wilderness Lodges

- **Green Provincial Park** (Tyne Valley, Prince Edward Island; ✆ **902/831-7912**): Can't afford your own well-maintained estates? This provincial campground makes a decent substitute. Set on a quiet inlet, the 88ha (219-acre) park is built around an extravagant gingerbread mansion that's open to the public. See chapter 5, "Prince Edward Island."
- **Gros Morne National Park** (Newfoundland): Backpackers will find wild, spectacular campsites in coastal meadows along the remarkable Green Gardens Trail. Car campers should head to Trout River Pond, at the foot of one of Gros Morne's dramatic landlocked fjords. See chapter 6, "Newfoundland & Labrador."
- **Sir Sam's Inn** (Eagle Lake, Ontario; ✆ **705/754-2188**): You'll have to search a bit for this remote stone-and-timber lodge, built in 1917 in the woods above Eagle Lake for politician/militarist Sir Sam Hughes. You can stay in the inn or in new chalets or lakefront suites. At this friendly yet sophisticated place, you can play tennis, swim, sail, windsurf, water-ski, canoe, or mountain bike. See chapter 12, "North to Ontario's Lakelands & Beyond."
- **Arowhon Pines** (Algonquin Park, Ontario; ✆ **705/633-5661** in summer, 416/483-4393 in winter): Located 13km (8 miles) off the highway down a dirt road, this is one of the most entrancing places anywhere. You can enjoy peace, seclusion, and natural beauty, plus comfortable accommodations and good fresh food. There are no TVs or phones—just the call of the loons, the gentle lapping of the water, the croaking of the frogs, and the splash of canoe paddles cutting the surface of the lake. See chapter 12, "North to Ontario's Lakelands & Beyond."
- **Tunnel Mountain** (Banff, Alberta; ✆ **403/762-1500**): If you find Banff too expensive and

too crowded, these campgrounds—three within 5km (3 miles) of town—are a great antidote. There are showers and real toilets, and most sites have full hookups. And you'll pay just one-tenth of what hotel dwellers are paying for equally good access to the Rockies. See chapter 14, "Alberta & the Rockies."

- **Clayoquot Wilderness Resort** (British Columbia; © **888/333-5405** in North America, or 250/725-2688): Recently designated a World Heritage Site, Clayoquot Sound boasts fjords and rain forests best discovered by sea kayak. The preferred route leaves Tofino and travels for 2 or 3 days to the bubbling Hot Springs Cove. For a bit of comfort, try staying at this resort, floating in splendid isolation on Quoit Bay. From here you can set out on fishing or whale-watching expeditions and go horseback riding or mountain biking. See chapter 16, "Victoria & British Columbia.

# Planning Your Trip to Canada

*by Bill McRae*

This chapter can save you money, time, and headaches. Here's where you'll find travel know-how, such as when to visit, what documents you'll need, and where to get more information. These basics can make the difference between a smooth ride and a bumpy one.

## 1 Visitor Information

### TOURIST OFFICES

The various provincial offices below dispense visitor information. Canadian consulates do not.

- **Nova Scotia Dept. of Tourism & Culture,** P.O. Box 456, 1800 Argyle St., Halifax, NS B3J 2R5 (✆ **800/565-0000,** or [local] 902/424-5000; explore.gov.ns.ca).
- **Tourism New Brunswick,** P.O. Box 12345, Campbellton, NB E3N 3T6 (✆ **800/561-0123;** www.tourismnbcanada.com).
- **Tourism Prince Edward Island,** P.O. Box 2000 Charlottetown, PEI C1A 7N8 (✆ **888/734-7529;** www.peiplay.com or www.gov.pe.ca/visitorsguide)
- **Newfoundland and Labrador Dept. of Tourism, Culture and Recreation,** P.O. Box 8700, St. John's, NF A1B 4J6 (✆ **800/563-6353,** [local] 709/729-0862, or [local toll-free line access] 709/729-2830; www.gov.nf.ca/tourism).
- **Tourisme Québec,** P.O. Box 979, Montréal, QC H3C 2W3 (✆ **800/363-7777;** www.bonjourquebec.com or www.tourisme.gouv.qc.ca).
- **Ontario Travel,** Hearst Block, 900 Bay St., Toronto, ON M7A 2E1 (✆ **800/668-2746;** www.ontariotravel.net).
- **Travel Manitoba,** (mailing) 7th Floor, 155 Carlton St., Winnipeg, MB R3C 3H8; (visitors ctr.) Explore Manitoba Ctr., 1 Forks Market Rd., Winnipeg, MB R3C 4T7 (✆ **800/665-0040;** www.travelmanitoba.com).
- **Tourism Saskatchewan,** 1922 Park St., Regina, SK S4P 3V7 (✆ **877/237-2273;** www.sasktourism.com).
- **Travel Alberta,** Box 2500, Edmonton, AB T5J 2Z1 / Eau Claire Mkt., 200 Barclay Sq., Calgary, AB T2P 1K1 (✆ **800/661-8888;** www.travelalberta.com).
- **Alberta Economic Development and Tourism,** Commerce Place, 10155 102nd St., Edmonton, AB T5J 4L6 (✆ **800/661-8888;** www.travelalberta.com).
- **Tourism British Columbia,** P.O. Box 9830, Stn. Prov. Govt., 1803 Douglas St., 3rd Floor, Victoria, BC V8W 9W5 (✆ **800/435-5622** or 250/356-6363; www.hellobc.com).
- **Tourism Yukon,** P.O. Box 2703, Whitehorse, YT Y1A 2C6 (✆ **867/ 667-5340;** www.touryukon.com).

## Canada

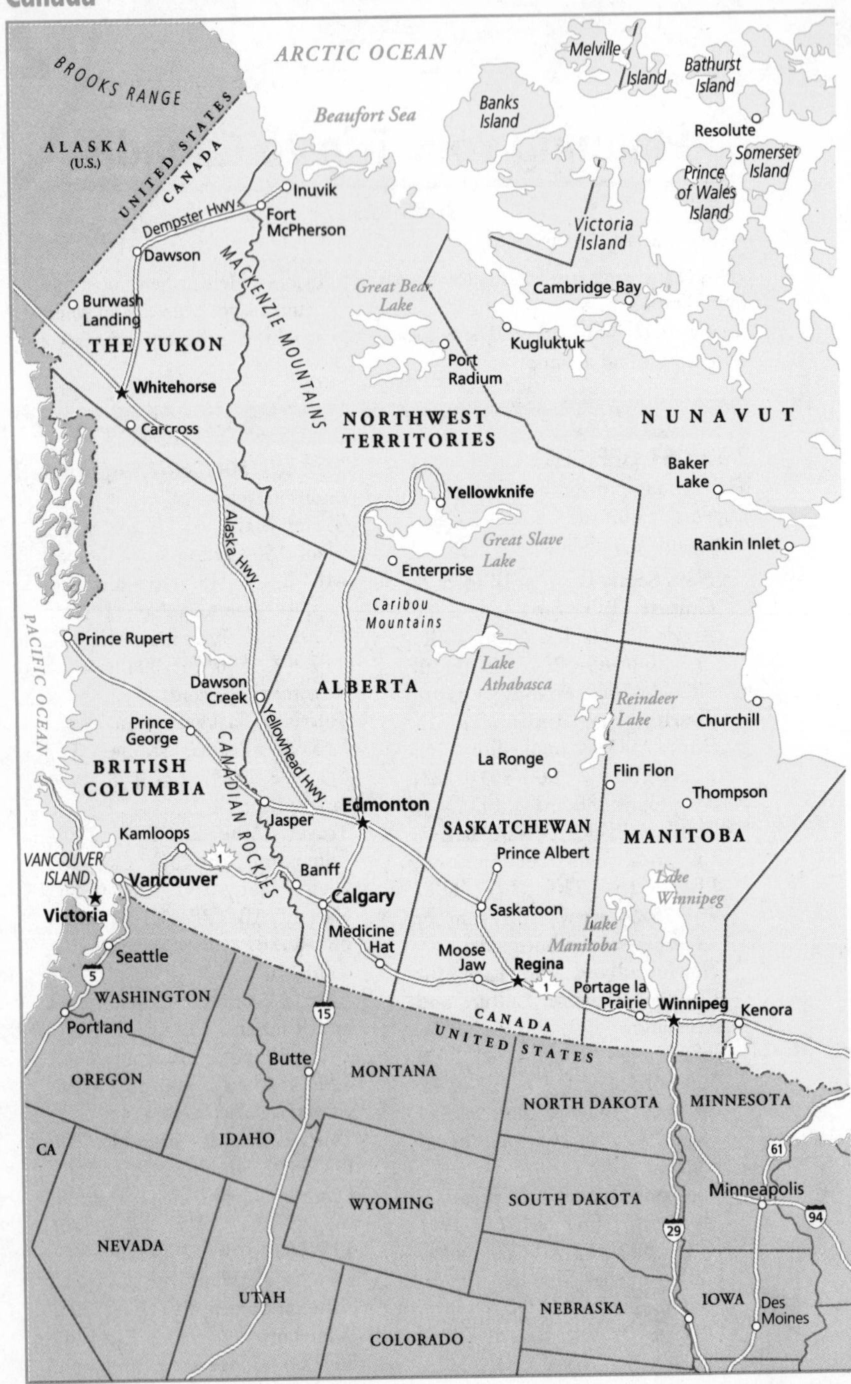
ARCTIC OCEAN
Beaufort Sea
BROOKS RANGE
ALASKA (U.S.)
UNITED STATES
CANADA
Melville Island
Bathurst Island
Banks Island
Resolute
Somerset Island
Prince of Wales Island
Victoria Island
Inuvik
Fort McPherson
Dempster Hwy.
Dawson
MACKENZIE MOUNTAINS
Great Bear Lake
Cambridge Bay
Burwash Landing
Kugluktuk
THE YUKON
Port Radium
Whitehorse
Carcross
NORTHWEST TERRITORIES
NUNAVUT
Baker Lake
Yellowknife
Alaska Hwy.
Great Slave Lake
Rankin Inlet
Enterprise
Caribou Mountains
PACIFIC OCEAN
Prince Rupert
Lake Athabasca
Dawson Creek
ALBERTA
Reindeer Lake
Churchill
Prince George
Yellowhead Hwy.
CANADIAN ROCKIES
La Ronge
Flin Flon
BRITISH COLUMBIA
Thompson
Edmonton
Jasper
SASKATCHEWAN
MANITOBA
Kamloops
Prince Albert
VANCOUVER ISLAND
Vancouver
Banff
Lake Winnipeg
Victoria
Calgary
Saskatoon
Medicine Hat
Lake Manitoba
Seattle
Moose Jaw
Regina
Portage la Prairie
Winnipeg
Kenora
WASHINGTON
Portland
CANADA
UNITED STATES
Butte
MONTANA
OREGON
NORTH DAKOTA
MINNESOTA
IDAHO
CA
Minneapolis
WYOMING
SOUTH DAKOTA
NEVADA
UTAH
IOWA
Des Moines
NEBRASKA
COLORADO
1
5
15
29
61
94

0
500 mi
0
500 km
N
National capital
Provincial capital
Provincial boundary
Devon Island
Baffin Bay
GREENLAND
(DENMARK)
Davis Strait
Baffin Island
NUNAVUT
Melville Peninsula
Prince Charles Island
Foxe Basin
Lake Amadjuak
Iqaluit
Southampton Island
Lake Harbour
Hudson Strait
Labrador Sea
Ivujivik
Coats Island
Mansel Island
NEWFOUNDLAND AND LABRADOR
Nairn
Hudson Bay
LABRADOR
Battle Harbour
Schefferville
Goose Bay
OTISH MOUNTAINS
Labrador City
Gander
St. John's
NEWFOUNDLAND
James Bay
Fort George
Anticosti Island
Sept-Iles
QUÉBEC
Moosonee
ONTARIO
Gaspé Peninsula
PRINCE EDWARD ISLAND
Cape Breton Island
Lake Nipigon
NEW BRUNSWICK
Sydney
Moncton
Thunder Bay
Cochrane
Ste-Agathe-des-Monts
Québec City
Fredericton
Halifax
Lake Superior
Timmins
Trois-Rivières
Saint John
North Bay
Montréal
MAINE
NOVA SCOTIA
Sudbury
Sault Ste. Marie
Ottawa
MICHIGAN
VT
NH
Lake Huron
Lake Ontario
Syracuse
Boston
Toronto
MA
Hamilton
MICHIGAN
Lake Michigan
NEW YORK
ATLANTIC OCEAN
Detroit
Windsor
Buffalo
Lake Erie
Chicago
PENNSYLVANIA
New York
INDIANA
OHIO
Philadelphia
ILLINOIS
1
81
95
94

- **NWT Arctic Tourism,** P.O. Box 610, Yellowknife, NWT X1A 2N5 (© **800/661-0788;** www.nwttravel.nt.ca).
- **Nunavut Tourism,** P.O. Box 1450, Iqaluit, NT X0A 0H0, (© **866/NUNAVUT** or 867/979-1261; www.nunatour.nt.ca).

For general information about Canada's national parks, contact **Parks Canada National Office** 25 Eddy Street Hull, Quebec Canada K1A 0M5 (© **888/773-8888;** www.parkscanada.gc.ca), or **Canadian Heritage,** 15 Eddy St, Hull, QC K1A 0M5 (© **819/997-0055;** www. zpch.gc.ca).

## THE INTERNET

**GENERAL SITES** Most major Internet (World Wide Web) directories contain subcategories on travel, country/regional information, and culture. Several directories have Canadian versions—try **Yahoo! (http://ca.yahoo.com)**, Excite (**www.excite.ca**), Sympatico-Lycos (**www.sympatico.ca**), and Altavista (**http://dir.altavista.com/cadir**). For U.S.-based Web directories, such as **http://directory.google.com**, search for links to websites specializing in Canada.

The excellent, all-Canada Web travel directories **www.canadatravel.ca** and **www.canada.worldweb.com** have thousands of links to official websites for destinations and activities across the country. Also, take a look at the official tourism and travel site for Canada at **www.travelcanada.ca**. Here are some general provincial sites:

- Parks Canada: **www.parcscanada.gc.ca**
- Nova Scotia: **www.destination-ns.com** or **explore.gov.ns.ca**
- New Brunswick: **www.tourismnbcanada.com**
- Prince Edward Island: **www.peiplay.com** or **www.gov.pe.ca/visitorsguide**
- Newfoundland and Labrador: **www.gov.nf.ca/tourism**
- Québec: **www.bonjourquebec.com** or **www.tourisme.gouv.qc.ca**
- Ontario: **www.ontariotravel.net**
- Manitoba: **www.travelmanitoba.com**
- Saskatchewan: **www.sasktourism.com**
- Alberta: **www.travelalberta.com**, **www.explorealberta.com** or **www.discoveralberta.com**
- British Columbia: **www.hellobc.com, www.discoverbc.com** or **www.travel.bc.ca**
- Yukon: **www.touryukon.com** or **www.discoveryukon.com**
- Northwest Territories: **www.nwttravel.nt.ca**
- Nunavut: **www.nunatour.nt.ca** or **www.arctic-travel.com**

**CITY SITES** Internet city guides are a good way to navigate without getting lost in the virtual countryside. Here are some to check out for Canada's top cities:

- Montréal: **www.tourism-montreal.org** (Bonjour à la Montréal), **www.gaycanada.com/cities/qc/montreal** (Gay Canada: Montréal), **www.vehiculepress.com/montreal** (Montréal: A Celebration), **http://english.montrealplus.ca** (Montréal Plus), or **www.montreal.worldweb.com** (Montréal Worldweb)
- Québec: **www.quebecregion.com** (Québec City and Area: Une Histoire d'Amour), **www.quebecplus.ca** (Québec Plus), or **www.quebec.worldweb.com** (Québec Worldweb)
- Ottawa: **www.ottawakiosk.com** (Ottawa Kiosk), **www.tourottawa.org** (Tour Ottawa), or **www.ottawaplus.ca** (Ottawa Plus)
- Toronto: **www.toronto.com** (Toronto.com), **www.toronto**

**Tips** **Site-seeing**

Besides the websites listed in this chapter, you'll find others given throughout this guide, whether they be general sites for the provinces or specific sites for the cities and their attractions.

tourism.com (Tourism Toronto), **www.toronto.worldweb.com** (Toronto Worldweb), **www.gaytoronto.com** (Gay Toronto), **www.rickym.com/cityguide** (Ricky McMountain Toronto City Guide), or **www.outsidetoronto.com** (Outside Toronto)

- Calgary: **www.visitor.calgary.ab.ca** (Tourism Calgary), **www.discovercalgary.com** (Discover Calgary), **www.calgaryplus.ca** (Calgary Plus), or **www.calgarywow.com** (Calgarywow.com)
- Edmonton: **www.gov.edmonton.ab.ca/enjoying_edmonton.html** (Enjoying Edmonton), **www.discoveredmonton.com** (Discover Edmonton), **www.edmontonplus.ca** (Edmonton Plus), **www.tourism.ede.org** (Edmonton Tourism)
- Vancouver: **www.tourism-vancouver.org** (Tourism Vancouver), **www.vancouverplus.ca** (Vancouver Plus), or **www.vancouverwow.com** (Vancouver-wow.com). Also see **www.whistler.com** (Whistler Resort Guide)
- Victoria: **www.city.victoria.bc.ca** (City of Victoria), **www.victoriabc.com** (Victoria BC), or **www.greatervictoria.com/directory.htm** (Greater Victoria)

## 2 Entry Requirements & Customs

### ENTRY REQUIREMENTS

All visitors to Canada must be able to provide proof of citizenship. A passport is not required for U.S. citizens and permanent U.S. residents, though it is the easiest and most convenient method of proving citizenship. If you don't have a passport, you'll need to carry other forms of proof of citizenship, such as a certificate of naturalization, a certificate of citizenship, a birth certificate with photo ID, a certificate of birth abroad with a photo ID, or a voter's registration card with photo ID or social security card. Some form of photo ID is usually a good idea. Although officers at border control are allowed to ask for any of these forms of identity, in most cases they request only a U.S. driver's license. Permanent U.S. residents who aren't U.S. citizens must have their Alien Registration Cards (green cards). If you plan to drive into Canada, be sure to bring your car's registration papers.

Citizens of most European countries and of former British colonies and certain other countries (Israel, Korea, and Japan for instance) do not need visas but must carry passports. Entry visas are required for citizens of more than 130 countries. Entry visas must be applied for and received from the Canadian embassy in your home country. For more information on entry requirements to Canada, see the Citizenship and Immigration website visitors' services page at **http://cicnet.ci.gc.ca/english/visit/index.html**.

*An important point:* Any person under 18 requires a letter from a parent or guardian granting him or her permission to travel to Canada. The letter must state the traveler's name and the duration of the trip. It's essential that teenagers carry proof of identity; otherwise, their letter is useless at the border.

## CUSTOMS

### WHAT YOU CAN BRING IN

Customs regulations are very generous in most respects but get pretty complicated when it comes to firearms, plants, meats, and pets. Fishing tackle poses no problems, but the bearer must possess a nonresident license for the province or territory where he or she plans to use it. You can bring in free of duty up to 50 cigars, 200 cigarettes, and 200g (about a half-pound) of tobacco, providing you're over 18. Those of age (18 or 19, depending on the province) are also allowed about 1.15l (40 ounces) of liquor, 1.5l (50 ounces) of wine, or 24 355ml (12-ounce) containers of beer or ale. Dogs, cats, and most pets can enter Canada with their owners, though you must have proof of rabies vaccinations within the last 36 months for pets over 3 months old.

For more details concerning customs regulations, contact the **Customs and Revenue Agency,** 1st Fl., 2265 St. Laurent Blvd., Ottawa, ON K1G 4K3 (✆ **204/983-3500,** or 506/636-5064 within the U.S., or 800/461-9999 within Canada; www.ccra-adrc.gc.ca).

### WHAT YOU CAN BRING HOME

**For U.S. Citizens** Contact the **U.S. Customs Service,** P.O. Box 7407, Washington, DC 20044 or Executive Director, Passenger Programs, U.S. Customs Service, 1300 Pennsylvania Ave., NW, Room 5.4D, Washington, DC 20229 (✆ **877/287-8667;** www.customs.gov), and request the free pamphlet, *Know Before You Go.* The pamphlet and lots of other useful customs information are also available on the Web at **www.customs.gov/know.htm**.

**For U.K. Citizens** Contact **HM Customs & Excise,** Passenger Enquiry Point, 2nd Floor, Wayfarer House, Great South West Road, Feltham, Middlesex TW14 8NP (✆ **020/8910-3744,** or consult their website at www.hmce.gov.uk).

**For Australian Citizens** A helpful brochure, available from Australian consulates or Customs offices, is *Know Before You Go* (www.customs.gov.au/bizlink/TRAVEL/know.htm). For more information, contact the **Australian Customs Services,** Customs House, 5 Constitution Ave, Canberra ACT 2601 / G.P.O. Box 8, Sydney, NSW 2001 (✆ **1300/363-263** or 02/6275-6666; www.customs.gov.au).

**For New Zealand Citizens** Contact **New Zealand Customs,** 50 Anzac Ave., P.O. Box 29, AUCKLAND (✆ **0800/428-786,** 09/300-5399, or 09/359-6515; www.customs.govt.nz). See the page **www.customs.govt.nz/travhome/advice1.htm** for advice to travelers.

## 3 Money

### CURRENCY

Canadians use dollars and cents, but with a very pleasing balance: The **Canadian dollar** is worth around 60¢ in U.S. money, give or take a couple of points' daily variation. (The Internet has many currency converters that provide current exchange rates and perform up-to-date conversions—try the Bank of Canada's at www.bankofcanada.ca/en/exchange.htm or another at www.oanda.com/convert/classic.) So your American money gets you roughly 50% more the moment you exchange it for local currency. And since the price of many goods is roughly on a par with that in the United States, the difference is real, not imaginary. (Before you get too excited, however, remember that sales taxes are astronomical. See "Taxes" in the "Fast Facts: Canada" section, later) You can bring in or take out any amount, but if you're importing or exporting sums of $5,000 or more, you must file a report of the transaction with U.S. Customs. Most tourist places in Canada will take U.S. cash, but for the best rate you should change your funds into Canadian currency. Customary tipping in restaurants is 15%, give or take a bit depending on your satisfaction with the service, and small tips on other services are a nice idea.

Note that Canada has no $1 bills. The lowest paper denomination is $5. Single bucks come in bronze-plated coins bearing the picture of a loon—hence their nickname "loonies." There's also a two-toned $2 coin sometimes referred to as a "twoonie."

If you do spend American money at Canadian establishments, you should understand how the conversion is done. Often by the cash register there'll be a sign reading U.S. CURRENCY __%, with some percentage in the blank. This percentage, say 25%, is the "premium"—it means that for every U.S. greenback you hand over, the cashier will see it as $1.25 in Canadian dollars. Thus, for an $8 tab you need pay only $6 in U.S. bills. However, 25% (or 125% on the U.S. dollar) is a bad exchange rate premium, so shop around to get the best rate. In fact, best of all, exchange your money at a bank.

## TRAVELER'S CHECKS

These days, traveler's checks seem less necessary than they once were, since abundant 24-hour ATMs allow you to withdraw cash as needed. But you may pay fees for each ATM withdrawal, so if you plan to need cash frequently, or if you're not sure you'll always be near an ATM, you might be better off with traveler's checks—provided you don't mind showing ID every time you want to redeem one. You can get traveler's checks at almost any bank, and most issuing companies run their own service centers where checks can be obtained and redeemed. Some banks will waive standard issuance fees, however, so shop around if you want to save some money. Most banks will also charge you a small fee per transaction (not per check) when you redeem U.S. dollar traveler's checks. You may be able to avoid such fees if you redeem at a bank affiliated with the issuer of your checks. Hotels, restaurants, and shops don't charge fees as a rule, but their exchange rate will usually be lower than the current official figure.

**American Express** (Amex) offers their Traveler's Cheques (the British spelling is favored by all issuers) and Cheques for Two (redeemable by two individuals) in denominations of $20, $50, $100, $500, and $1,000. See if your bank issues them, and whether you can get any fees reduced or eliminated. If not, American Express also operates travel service locations that issue and redeem their cheques. Fees at these locations generally range from 1% to 4%, and American Express platinum cardholders are exempt. If you're an AmEx cardholder, you can get their cheques over the phone at ✆ **800/721-9768.** Gold and platinum cardholders are exempt from a 1% fee for phone orders. For a standard per-order fee, plus shipping, anyone can buy AmEx cheques online at www31.americanexpress.com/tconline/phase2/urls/BuyTC.asp. American Automobile Association members can obtain AmEx cheques without a fee at most AAA offices.

**Visa** offers their Traveller's Cheques (the spelling becomes yet more British) and Dual-Signature Cheques at various banks and other locations nationwide. To find an issuer near you, call ✆ **800/227-6811.** The

### Value The Canadian Dollar & the U.S. Dollar

The prices cited in this guide are given first in Canadian dollars (C$), then in US dollars (US$); amounts over $5 have been rounded to the nearest dollar. Note that the Canadian dollar is worth significantly less than the American dollar but buys nearly as much in the way of goods and services. As we go to press, US$1 is worth about C$1.62 or C$1 is worth about US62¢, and those were the equivalencies used to figure the approximate prices in this guide.

service charge ranges from 1.5% to 2%, and cheques come in denominations of $20, $50, $100, $500, and $1,000.

Be sure to sign your traveler's checks before you travel and keep a record of their **serial numbers** (separately from the checks, of course). You must provide the serial numbers to the issuing company to get a refund if your checks are lost or stolen.

### ATMS

You can generally get the best rate of exchange using an ATM with a bank (ATM or ATM/debit) card. It's also convenient not to have to carry cash and checks. Some banks, however, impose a fee every time you use an ATM in a different city or bank, and you may also be charged twice, once by your own bank and once by the bank whose ATM you use. Also, if you plan to rely on ATMs for your cash, remember to bring in sufficient Canadian cash to pay for an initial cab or bus and a meal.

ATMs are linked to a national system of networks that most likely includes your bank at home. Most combination ATM/debit cards are branded either Visa or MasterCard, and the back of your card should also sport symbols of the networks with which your card will work. Both the **Cirrus** (✆ **800/424-7787**; www.mastercard.com/cardholderservices/atm) and **Plus** (✆ **800/843-7587**; www.visa.com/pd/atm/main.htm) networks have automated ATM locators listing the banks in Canada that'll accept your card. Or just search out any machine with your network's symbol emblazoned on it.

You can also get a cash advance at an ATM using a credit card. Be aware, however, that credit-card companies will begin charging you interest immediately, and many have begun assessing a fee for each cash advance. Visa or MasterCard cardholders should contact the issuing bank to enable this feature and get a PIN. American Express cardholders can get cash advances from AmEx travel service locations and designated Axis ATMs (find these at http://maps.americanexpress.com/expresscash/mqinterconnect?link=home) after signing up for their Express Cash program (✆ **800/ 227-4669**).

### CREDIT CARDS

Credit cards are invaluable when traveling, providing a safe way to carry money and a convenient record of all your expenses. You can also withdraw cash advances from your cards at any bank, although you'll start paying hefty interest the moment you receive the cash and won't receive frequent-flyer miles on an airline credit card.

Almost all credit-card companies have emergency toll-free numbers you can call if your wallet or purse is stolen. They may be able to immediately wire you a cash advance from your credit card account, and in many places they can deliver an emergency card in a day or two. The issuing bank's number is usually on the back of the credit card (though that doesn't help you much if the card was stolen). A toll-free information directory at ✆ **800/555-1212** will provide the number for you (as long as you know the name of that bank, so keep a record of it on your trip). You can also call your card company's hotline for help. In Canada or the U.S., call **Visa** at ✆ **800/847-2911, American Express** at ✆ **800/992-3404,** and **MasterCard** at ✆ **800/622-7747.**

### WIRE SERVICES

If you find yourself out of money, a wire service can help you tap willing friends and family for funds. The fees and options listed are for sending funds from the U.S. Through **MoneyGram,** 7401 W. Mansfield, Lakewood, CO 80232 (✆ **800/926-9400;** www.moneygram.com), you can get money sent to you often in less than 10 minutes. Cash is the only acceptable form of payment. Fees range on a sliding scale, from $12 for the first $100, to $17 for between $100 and $200, to $24 for between $200 and $300, and so on.

A similar service is offered by **Western Union** (✆ **800/235-0000** in Canada or 800/325-6000 in the U.S.; www.westernunion.com), which accepts cash and Visa, MasterCard, or Discover (in the U.S. only). You can arrange for the service over the phone, on the Web, or at a Western Union office. A sliding scale begins at $15 for sums paid for by cash ($25 when paid by credit card) for the first $100.

## 4 When to Go

### THE WEATHER

In southern and central Canada, the weather is the same as that in the northern United States. As you head north, the climate becomes Arctic, meaning long and extremely cold winters, brief and surprisingly warm summers (with lots of insects), and magical springs.

As a general rule, **spring** runs mid-March to mid-May, **summer** mid-May to mid-September, **fall** mid-September to mid-November, and **winter** mid-November to mid-March. Pick the season best suited to your tastes and temperament, and remember that your car should be winterized through March and that snow sometimes falls as late as April (in 1995 a foot of snow blanketed Prince Edward Island in May). September and October bring autumn foliage and great opportunities for photographers.

Evenings tend to be cool everywhere, particularly on or near water. In late spring and early summer, you'll need a supply of insect repellent if you're planning bush travel or camping.

With the huge size of some provinces and territories, you naturally get considerable climate variations inside their borders. Québec, for instance, sprawls all the way from the temperate south to the Arctic, and the weather varies accordingly. For up-to-date weather conditions and forecasts for any Canadian destination, check out Environment Canada's weather center on the Web at http://weatheroffice.ec.gc.ca.

### HOLIDAYS

**National holidays** are celebrated throughout the country; all government facilities and banks are closed, but some department stores and a scattering of smaller shops stay open. If the holiday falls on a weekend, the following Monday is observed.

Canadian national holidays include New Year's Day, Good Friday, Easter Monday, Victoria Day (in mid- to late May, the weekend before U.S.

Memorial Day), Canada Day (July 1), Labour Day (first Mon in Sept), Thanksgiving (in mid-Oct), Remembrance Day (Nov 11), Christmas Day, and Boxing Day (Dec 26).

Many provinces also celebrate a **provincial holiday,** usually on the first Monday of August. In addition, you may run into other provincial or local holidays, some of which are listed in each provincial, regional, or city section.

**Festivals & Special Events** Canada has some wonderfully unique festivals and events, from the Vancouver Folk Festival to the Calgary Stampede to the Stratford Festival Theatre to the Québec Winter Carnival. The best of each province's, region's, or community's special events are listed in the following chapters. As the dates for events often change from year to year, it's a good idea to check the events calendar at each destination's website. These Web calendars are the easiest way to get the most up-to-date information.

## 5 The Outdoor Adventure Planner

### SPORTS A TO Z

See the individual chapters for specific details on how and where to enjoy the activities below.

**BIKING** Most of Canada's highways are wide and well maintained, and thus well suited for long-distance bicycle touring. Most resort areas have ample supplies of rentals, so you don't have to worry about transporting your own (it's a good idea to call ahead and reserve a bike). You'll need to be in good shape to embark on a long bike trip and be able to deal with minor bike repairs.

While most hiking trails are closed to mountain bikes, other trails are developed specifically for backcountry biking. Ask at national-park and national-forest info centers for a map of mountain-bike trails.

Probably the most rewarding biking anywhere is in Banff and Jasper national parks. The Icefields Parkway, running between the parks, is an eye-popping route past soaring peaks and glaciers and is wide and well graded.

**CANOEING & KAYAKING** Much of Canada was first explored by canoe, as low-lying lakes and slow rivers form vast waterway systems across the central and northern regions. Canoes are still excellent for exploring the backcountry. Several-day canoe/camping trips through wilderness waterways make popular summer and early-fall expeditions for small groups; you'll see lots of wildlife (especially mosquitoes) and keep as gentle a pace as you like. Generally speaking, the longer the trip, the more experience you should have with a canoe and with wilderness conditions (weather, wildlife, and chance of injury). Lake-filled Manitoba is a good place to plan a canoe trip.

**DIVING** Both coasts of Canada, and several places in between, are worthy if not top scuba diving destinations. In the east, the Atlantic coast of Nova Scotia, including Halifax Harbour, there are excellent places to view shipwrecks—the province has the highest density of shipwrecks per linear mile of any location in the world, and almost 150 lie beneath the harbor of the capital city. Plenty of beautiful marine life lurks in and about those wrecks, as well. Another favorite diving site in the east is Québec's Les Escoumins, on the north side of the St. Lawrence River, not far from its confluence with the Saguenay. The nutrient-rich waters of this spot host a dazzling variety of marine species. The spot where the rivers meet is also a prime feeding area for many kinds of whales during the summer.

In the west, an amazing array of colorful marine life flourishes amid the 2,000 shipwrecks that have become artificial reefs off the coast of British Columbia. Divers from around the world visit the area year-round to see the Pacific Northwest's unique underwater fauna and flora, and to swim among the ghostly remains of 19th-century whaling ships and 20th-century schooners. The Pacific Rim National Park's Broken Group Islands is home to a multitude of sea life, while the waters off the park's West Coast Trail are known throughout the world as "the graveyard of the Pacific" for the hundreds of 19th- and 20th-century shipwrecks. Nanaimo and Campbell River, on Vancouver Island, are both centers for numerous dive outfitters.

**DOG-SLEDDING** Just imagine taking a traditional dogsled out into the Arctic ice floes and snowy tundra. Outfitters in the North run several-day trips to see the aurora borealis in early spring, and in late spring they offer trips to the floe edge, where wildlife viewing is great (this is your best chance to see a polar bear). You'll get a turn at driving the dog team and will sleep in comfort in special room-size tents heated with small stoves (no igloos!). Outfitters will usually provide all the gear necessary for the weather, though you should be prepared to get a little cold. Outfitters on Baffin Island provide dogsled trips ranging from part-day to a week out on the tundra amid dramatic mountain and fjord scenery; February to May is the best time.

**FISHING** Angling is another sport enjoyed across the entire country. The famed salmon fisheries along the Atlantic and Pacific coasts face highly restricted catch limits in most areas, and outright bans on fishing in others. However, not all salmon species on all rivers are threatened, and rules governing fishing change quickly; so check locally with fishing outfitters to find out if a season will open while you're visiting. Other species aren't so heavily restricted and probably make a better focus for a fishing-oriented vacation. Trout are found throughout Canada, some reaching great size in the thousands of lakes in the north country; northern pike and walleye are also wary fish that grow to massive size in the North. The Arctic char, a cousin of the salmon, is an anadromous fish running in the mighty rivers that feed into the Arctic Ocean; char fishing is often combined with other backcountry adventures by Arctic outfitters.

Fishing in Canada is regulated either by local government or by tribes, and appropriate licenses are necessary. Angling for some fish is regulated by season; in some areas, catch-and-release fishing is enforced. Be sure to check with local authorities before casting your line.

Perhaps Canada's most famous fishing hole is Great Slave Lake. This deep and massive lake is home to enormous lake trout and northern pike; the latter can reach lengths over 2m (6 ft.). You'll want to plan a trip with an outfitter, because weather conditions change rapidly and maneuvering small craft can be dangerous.

**HIKING** Almost every national and provincial park in Canada is webbed with hiking trails, ranging from easy interpretive nature hikes to long-distance trails into the backcountry. Late summer and early fall are good times to plan a walking holiday, since spring comes late to much of Canada—trails in the high country may be snowbound until July.

Most parks have developed free hiking and trail information, as well as details on accessible trails for people with mobility concerns. Before setting out, be sure to request this info and buy a good map. If you're taking a long trip, evaluate your fitness and equipment before you leave; once in the backcountry, there's no way out except on foot, so make sure your boots fit and you understand the risks you're undertaking.

Though there are great trails and magnificent scenery across Canada, for many people the Canadian Rockies, with their abundance of parks and developed trail systems, provide the country's finest hiking.

**HORSEBACK RIDING** Holidays on horseback have a long pedigree in western Canada, and most outfitters and guest ranches offer a variety of options. Easiest are short rides that take a morning or an afternoon; you'll be given an easygoing horse and sufficient instruction to make you feel comfortable no matter what your previous riding ability. Longer pack trips take riders off into the backcountry on a several-day guided expedition, with lodging in tents or at rustic camps. These trips are best for those who don't mind "roughing it": You'll probably go a day or two without showers or flush toilets and end up saddle sore and sunburned. While these trips are generally open to riders with varying degrees of experience, it's a good idea to spend some time on horseback before heading out: You get very sore if you haven't been in a saddle for a while. The Canadian Rockies in Alberta are filled with guest ranches offering a wide range of horseback activities.

**SEA KAYAKING** Though it may seem like a newer sport, sea kayaking is an ancient activity: The Inuit have used hide-covered kayaks for centuries. New lightweight kayaks make it possible to transport these crafts to remote areas and explore previously inaccessible areas along sheltered coasts; kayaks are especially good for wildlife viewing. Most coastal towns in British Columbia will have both kayak rentals and instruction, as well as guided trips. Handling a kayak isn't as easy as it looks, and you'll want to have plenty of experience in sheltered coves before heading out onto the surf. Be sure to know the tide schedule and weather forecast before setting out, as well as what the coastal rock formations are. You'll need to be comfortable on the water and ready to get wet, as well as be a strong swimmer. One of the best places in the world to practice sea kayaking is in the sheltered bays, islands, and inlets along the coast of British Columbia.

**SKIING** It's no wonder that Canada, a mountainous country with heavy snowfall, is one of the world's top ski destinations. If you've never skied before, you've got a basic choice between the speed and thrills of downhill skiing and the more Zen-like pleasure of cross-country skiing. Both sports are open to all ages, though downhill skiing is less forgiving of older bones and joints and carries a higher price tag: A day on the slopes, with rental gear and lift ticket, can easily top C$90 (US$56).

For **downhill skiing,** the Canadian Rockies and Whistler-Blackcomb resort near Vancouver are the primary destinations. The 1988 Winter Olympics were held at Nakiska, just outside Banff National Park, and the park itself is home to three other ski areas, including Lake Louise, the country's largest. If you're just learning to ski or are skiing with the family, then the easier slopes at Banff Mount Norquay are made to order. Readers of *Condé Nast Traveler* repeatedly award Whistler-Blackcomb the title of Best Ski Resort in North America. At all these ski areas, instruction, rentals, and day care are available, and world-class lodging is available at Banff, Lake Louise and Whistler. The slopes are usually open November to May.

The dry, heavy snows of eastern Canada make this the best destination for a **cross-country skiing** vacation.

The Laurentians, north of Québec, are a range of low mountains with many ski trails and small resort towns with rural French-Canadian charm. The best skiing is January to March.

**WHITE-WATER RAFTING** Charging down a mountain river in a rubber raft is one of the most popular adventures for many people visiting Canada's western mountains. Trips range from daylong excursions that demand little of a participant other than sitting tight to long-distance trips through remote backcountry where all members of the crew are expected to hoist a paddle through the rapids. Risk doesn't correspond to length of trip: Individual rapids and water conditions can make even a short trip a real adventure. On long trips, you'll be camping in tents and spending evenings by a campfire. Even on short trips, plan on getting wet; it's not unusual to get thrown out of a raft, so you should be comfortable in water and a good swimmer if you're floating an adventurous river (outfitters will always provide life jackets).

Jasper National Park is a major center for short yet thrilling white-water trips. For a weeklong white-water adventure in a wilderness setting, contact an outfitter about trips through Nahanni National Park.

## USING AN OUTFITTER VS. PLANNING YOUR OWN TRIP?

A basic consideration for most people who embark on an adventure vacation is time versus money. If you have time on your hands and have basic skills in dealing with sports and the outdoors, then planning your own trip can be fun. On the other hand, making one phone call and writing one check makes a lot more sense if you don't have a lot of time and lack the background to safely get you where you want to go.

**TRANSPORTATION & EQUIPMENT** In general, the more remote the destination, the more you should consider an outfitter. In many parts of Canada, simply getting to the area where your trip begins requires a great deal of planning. Frequently, outfitters will have their own airplanes or boats or work in conjunction with someone who does. These transportation costs are usually included in the price of an excursion and are usually cheaper than the same flight or boat trip on a chartered basis.

The same rule applies to equipment rental. Getting your raft or canoe to an out-of-the-way lake can be an adventure in itself. But hire an outfitter and they'll take care of the hassle.

Another option is to use an outfitter to "package" your trip. Some outfitters offer their services to organize air charters and provide equipment for a fee but leave you to mastermind the trip.

**SAFETY** Much of Canada is remote and given to weather extremes. What might be considered a casual camping trip or boating excursion in more populated or temperate areas can become life-threatening in the Canadian backcountry—which often starts right at the edge of town. Almost all outfitters are certified as first-aid providers, and most carry two-way radios in case there's a need to call for help. Local outfitters also know the particular hazards of the areas where they lead trips. In some areas, like the Arctic, where hazards range from freakish weather to ice-floe movements and polar bears, outfitters are nearly mandatory.

**OTHER PEOPLE** Most outfitters will lead groups on excursions only after signing up a minimum number of participants. This is usually a financial consideration for the outfitter, but for participants this can be both good and bad news. Traveling with the right people can add to the trip's enjoyment, but the wrong companions can lead to exasperation and disappointment. If you're sensitive to other peoples' idiosyncrasies, ask the potential outfitter specific questions regarding who else is going on the trip.

## SELECTING AN OUTFITTER

An outfitter will be responsible for your safety and your enjoyment of the trip, so make certain you choose one wisely. All outfitters should be licensed or accredited by the province and should be happy to provide you with proof. This means they're bonded, carry the necessary insurance, and have the money and organizational wherewithal to register with the province. This rules out fly-by-night operations and college students who've decided to set up business for the summer. If you're just starting to plan an excursion, ask the provincial tourist authority for its complete list of licensed outfitters.

Often a number of outfitters offer similar trips. When you've narrowed down your choice, call and talk to those outfitters. Ask questions and try to get a sense of who these people are; you'll be spending a lot of time with them, so make sure you feel comfortable. If you have special interests, like bird or wildlife watching, be sure to mention them. A good outfitter will also take your interests into account when planning a trip.

If there's a wide disparity in prices between outfitters for the same trip, find out what makes the difference. Some companies economize on food. If you don't mind having cold cuts for each meal of your weeklong canoe expedition, then perhaps the least expensive outfitter is okay. However, if you prefer a cooked meal, alcoholic beverages, or a choice of entrees, then be prepared to pay more. On a long trip, it might be worth it to you.

Ask how many years an outfitter has been in business and how long your particular escort has guided this trip. While a start-up outfitting service can be perfectly fine, you should know what level of experience you're buying. If you have questions, especially for longer or more dangerous trips, ask for referrals.

## OUTFITTERS & ADVENTURE-TRAVEL OPERATORS

Most outfitters offer trips in specific geographic areas only, though some larger outfitters package trips across the country. In the chapters that follow, we'll recommend lots of local operators and tell you about the outings they run. We've found a few, though, that operate in more than one region of Canada.

**The Great Canadian Adventure Company,** #300, 10190 104 Street, Edmonton Alberta T5J 1A7 (© **888/285-1676** or 780/414-1676; fax 780/424-9034; www.adventures.ca), offers over 40 different types of guided activities and expeditions—including all of the standards plus such options as native (First Nations and Inuit) cultural tours, helicopter- or snowcat-transported backcountry snowboarding, and a submersible excursion—in every province and just about every nook of the country.

**Nahanni River Adventures and Whitewolf Adventure Expeditions,** P.O. Box 4869, Whitehorse, YT Y1A 4N6 (© **800/297-6927** or 867/668-3180; fax 867/668-3056; www.nahanni.com), offers whitewater and naturalist float trips in rivers across western and northern Canada, with the Nahanni River a specialty.

**Canusa Cycle Tours,** Box 35104, Sarcee RPO, Calgary, AB T3E 7C7 (© **800/938-7986;** fax 403/254-8361; www.canusacycletours.com), offers guided cycle tours along some of Canada's most scenic highways.

**Ecosummer Expeditions,** P.O. Box 1765, Clearwater, BC V0E 1N0 CANADA, or 936 Peace Portal Dr. #240, Blaine, WA 98231 U.S.A.

**Tips A Warning**

All outfitters should be licensed by their province, and local tourist offices can provide listings of outfitters licensed to operate in the areas you intend to visit.

(© **800/465-8884** or 250-674-0102; fax 250-674-2197; www.ecosummer.com), offers a wide variety of sea kayaking, whitewater rafting, dogsledding, photography, and other expeditions in British Columbia, the Yukon, the Northwest Territories, and Nunavut. Ecosummer also offers trips to Greenland, as well as destinations in South and Central America.

**Black Feather Wilderness Adventures,** 1960 Scott St., Ottawa, ON K1Z 8L8 (© **800/574-8375;** fax 613/722-0245; www.blackfeather.com), leads kayaking, canoeing, and hiking trips in British Columbia, the Northwest Territories, Nunavut, Ontario, and Labrador.

## WHAT TO PACK

Be sure that it's clearly established between you and your outfitter what you're responsible for bringing along. If you need to bring a sleeping bag, find out what weight of bag is suggested for the conditions you'll encounter. If you have any special dietary requirements, find out whether you can be accommodated or need to pack and prepare accordingly.

While it's fun and relatively easy to amass the equipment for a backcountry expedition, none of it will do you any good if you don't know how to use it. Even though compasses aren't particularly accurate in the North, bring one along and know how to use it (or maybe consider using a GPS device). Detailed maps are always a good idea. If you're trekking without guidance, make sure you have the skills appropriate to your type of expedition, plan your packing well (with contingencies for changes in weather), and bring along a good first-aid kit.

For all summer trips in Canada, make sure to bring along insect repellent, as mosquitoes are particularly numerous and hungry in the North. If you know you're heading into bad mosquito country, consider buying specialized hats with mosquito netting attached. Sunglasses are a must, even above the Arctic Circle. The farther north you go in summer, the longer the sun stays up; the low angle of the sun can be particularly annoying. In winter, the glare off snow can cause sun blindness. For the same reasons, sunscreen is a surprising necessity.

Summer weather is changeable in Canada. If you're planning outdoor activities, be sure to bring along wet-weather gear, even in high summer. The more exposure you'll have to the elements, the more you should consider bringing high-end Gortex and artificial-fleece outerwear. The proper gear can make the difference between a miserable time and a great adventure.

If you're traveling in Canada in winter, you'll want to have the best winter coat, gloves, and boots you can afford. A coat with a hood is especially important, as Arctic winds can blow for days at a time.

# 6 Tips for Travelers with Special Needs

## FOR TRAVELERS WITH DISABILITIES

For information on disability travel in British Columbia, contact the **BC Accessibility Advisor,** Accessibility Program, Ministry of Municipal Affairs, Box 9490 Stn. Prov. Govt., Victoria, BC V8W 9N7

(✆ **250/387-7908**). In Alberta or BC, the **Canadian Paraplegic Association** (✆ **888/654-5444** or 780/424-6312 in Alberta; ✆ **877/324-3611** or 604/324-3611 in BC; www.canparaplegic.org) can offer advice for mobility-challenged travelers. Both the official British Columbia and Alberta accommodations guides provide information about accessibility options at lodgings throughout Canada.

*A World of Options,* a 658-page book of resources for travelers with disabilities, covers everything from biking trips to scuba outfitters. It costs US$35 (US$30 for members) and is available from **Mobility International USA,** P.O. Box 10767, Eugene, OR, 97440 (✆ **541/343-1284** voice and TDD; www.miusa.org). Annual membership for Mobility International is US$35, which includes the quarterly newsletter *Over the Rainbow.*

In addition, **Twin Peaks Press,** P.O. Box 129, Vancouver, WA 98666 (✆ **360/694-2462;** home.pacifier.com/~twinpeak), publishes travel-related books for people with disabilities.

You can join the **Society for the Advancement of Travel for the Handicapped (SATH),** 347 Fifth Ave., Suite 610, New York, NY 10016 (✆ **212/447-7284;** fax 212/725-8253; www.sath.org), for US$45 annually, $30 for seniors and students, to gain access to its vast network of connections in the travel industry. SATH provides information sheets on travel destinations and referrals to tour operators that specialize in traveling with disabilities. Its quarterly magazine, *Open World for Disability and Mature Travel* (www.sath.org/openworld/openworld.html), is full of good information and resources. A year's subscription is US$18 (US$35 outside the U.S.).

## FOR GAY & LESBIAN TRAVELERS

The larger cities of Canada—Québec, Winnipeg, Edmonton, Calgary, Victoria, and especially Montréal, Toronto, and Vancouver—are generally gay tolerant, though, with the exception of Montréal and Toronto, you'll find less openly gay visibility and nonchalance here than in comparably sized U.S. cities. Each of these cities has a number of gay bars and gay-owned businesses, as well as a small gay newspaper. In smaller cities and towns, gay and lesbian travelers are advised to be more cautious about overt displays of affection.

The **International Gay & Lesbian Travel Association** (IGLTA; ✆ **800/448-8550** or 954/776-2626; fax 954/776-3303; www.iglta.org) links travelers up with the appropriate gay-friendly service organization or tour specialist. With around 1,200 members, it offers quarterly newsletters, marketing mailings, and a membership directory that's updated quarterly. Membership is open to individuals for US$200 yearly, plus a US$100 administration fee for new members. Members are kept informed of gay and gay-friendly hoteliers, tour operators, and airline and cruise-line representatives. Contact the IGLTA for a list of its member agencies, who will be tied into IGLTA's information resources. Note that you do not need to be a member to use this service, and that the newsletter, travel information, and accommodations guide are available on the website at no charge.

There are also two good, biannual English-language gay guidebooks, both focused on gay men but include information for lesbians as well. You can get the ***Spartacus International Gay Guide*** or ***Odysseus*** from most gay and lesbian bookstores, or order them online. Both lesbians and gays might want to pick up a copy of ***Gay***

***Travel A to Z*** (US$16). The ***Ferrari Guides*** is yet another very good series of gay and lesbian guidebooks.

***Out and About,*** 995 Market St., 14th Fl., San Francisco, CA 94103 (© **800/929-2268** or 415/644-8044; www.outandabout.com), offers guidebooks and a monthly newsletter packed with good information on the global gay and lesbian scene. A year's subscription to the newsletter costs US$49. ***Our World,*** 1104 North Nova Rd., Suite 251, Daytona Beach, FL 32117 (© **904/441-5367;** www.ourworldpublishing.com), is a slicker monthly magazine promoting and highlighting travel bargains and opportunities. Annual subscription rates are US$25 in the United States (or US$12 for online access only), and US$50 for outside the United States.

## FOR SENIORS

Don't be shy about asking for discounts, but always carry some kind of identification, such as a driver's license, that shows your date of birth. Also, mention the fact that you're a senior citizen when you first make your travel reservations; many hotels offer senior discounts. In most cities, people over the age of 60 qualify for reduced admission to theaters, museums, and other attractions, as well as discounted fares on public transportation. A venerable resource for seniors interested in educational, arranged travel programs is **Elderhostel,** 11 Avenue de Lafayette, Boston, MA 02111-1746 (© **877/426-8056;** www.elderhostel.org). They offer numerous programs in Canada, but since the trips are popular, you must enter a lottery well in advance of traveling. The monthly newsletter ***Mature Traveler*** offers tips and news, and is available for US$30 annually from G E M Publishing Group, PO Box 50400, Reno, NV 89513-0400. Other good information for traveling seniors can be found at *Arthur Frommer's Budget Travel Online,* starting at the page www.frommers.com/vacations/special_travelers/senior.

## FOR FAMILIES

Several books on the market offer tips to help you travel with kids. Most concentrate on the United States, but two, ***Family Travel*** (Lanier Publishing International; also see www.familytravelguides.com) and ***How to Take Great Trips with Your Kids*** (The Harvard Common Press), are full of good general advice that can apply to travel anywhere. Another reliable tome, with a worldwide focus, is ***Adventuring with Children*** (Alpenbooks).

***Family Travel Times*** is published six times a year by TWYCH (Travel with Your Children; © **888/822-4388** or 212/477-5524; www.familytraveltimes.com) and includes a weekly call-in service for subscribers. Subscriptions are US$39 a year for quarterly editions. A free publication list and a sample issue are available by calling the above number or visiting the website.

## FOR STUDENTS

The best resource for students is the Council on International Educational Exchange, or CIEE (**www.ciee.org**). It can set you up with an ID card (see below), and its travel branch, Council Travel Service (© **800/226-8624;** www.counciltravel.com), is the biggest student travel-agency operation in the world. It can get you discounts on plane tickets, rail passes, and the like. Ask for a list of CTS offices in major cities so you can keep the discounts flowing (and aid lines open) as you travel.

CIEE, through Council Travel, offers the student traveler's best friend, the **International Student Identity Card (ISIC),** available for US$22. It's the only officially acceptable form of student identification, good for cut rates on rail passes, plane tickets, and more. It also provides you with basic health and life insurance and a 24-hour help line. If you're no longer a student but are still under 26, you can get a GO 25 card from the same organization; it gets you the insurance and some of the discounts, but not student admission prices in museums.

In Canada, **Travel CUTS,** 200 Ronson St., Suite 320, Etobicoke, ON, M9W 5Z9 (© **800/667-2887** or 416/614-2887, or 866/246-9762 for reservations; www.travelcuts.com), offers similar services, and its offices sell the ISIC card for C$16 (US$10). Worldwide, you can also find student travel options at **STA Travel** (© **800/781-4040** in the US; www.statravel.com).

### FOR WOMEN TRAVELERS

Canada is one of the most polite and nonviolent places on earth, and most women will have no problems traveling here, either alone or with other women. A little common sense should prevent dangerous or uncomfortable situations. It's never a good idea to hitchhike alone, and walking alone late at night in cities isn't recommended. You may want to hook up with a buddy if you're planning on an extensive hiking or camping trip. A number of western Canadian outfitters offer women-only adventure tours.

Several websites offer women advice on how to travel safely and happily, but there's a lot of chaff mixed in with the wheat. You might check out **www.journeywoman.com**, which offers a newsletter and lots of travel tips, stories, and links to other websites, all with an eye towards what women traveling might want or need to know.

## 7 Getting There

### BY PLANE

**THE MAJOR AIRLINES** Canada is served by almost all the international air carriers. The major international airports in the east are in Halifax, Toronto, and Montréal; in the west they're in Winnipeg, Edmonton, Calgary, and Vancouver.

**Air Canada** (© **888/247-2262;** www.aircanada.ca), Canada's dominant airline, has by far the most flights between the United States and Canada (including 18 daily from New York to Toronto). Most major U.S. carriers also fly daily between major cities in Canada and the states,—these include **America West** (© **800/235-9292** or **800/363-2597** in Canada; www.americawest.com), **American Airlines** (© **800/433-7300;** www.aa.com), **Continental** (© **800/525-0280;** www.continental.com), **Delta** (© **800/221-1212;** www.delta.com), **Northwest** (© **800/447-4747;** www.nwa.com), **United** (© **800/241-6522** or 538-2929; www.ual.com), and **US Airways** (© **800/428-4322;** www.usair.com). Canada's primary discount airline, **Canada 3000** (© **888/300-0669** or 416/674-3000; www.canada3000.com), has a more limited number of routes between the U.S. and Canada.

International airlines with non-stop service to Canada include **Air France** (© **800/237-2747** in the U.S., 800/667-2747 in Canada; www.airfrance.com), **British Air** (© **800/247-9297** in the U.S. or Canada, **0845/773-3377** in the U.K.; www.british-airways.com), **KLM** (© **800/447-7747** connects to KLM partner Northwest Airlines in the U.S. and Canada or 020/474-7747 for KLM in the Netherlands; www.klm.com), **Lufthansa** (© **800/563-5954** in the U.S., 800/581-6400 in Canada, or 0803/803-803 in Germany; www.lufthansa.com), **Qantas** (✆ **800/227-4500** in the U.S. and Canada, 131-313 in Australia; www.qantas.com), and **SAS** (✆ **800/221-2350** in the U.S. or Canada, check online for Scandinavian contacts; www.scandinavian.net). Additionally, **Air Canada** and **Canada 3000**, as well as **Air Transat** (✆ **866/847-1112**; www.airtransat.com), have international flights to and from many cities in Europe and Latin America. Air Canada and Canada 3000 also connect to Australia and New Zealand, but **Air Canada** has by far more connections to centers in the rest of Asia.

**USING THE INTERNET** Booking flights on the Internet has become the method of choice for many travelers. On airline websites, you can spend as much time as you like searching different options for flight dates, times, and airports, as well as sale fares and Internet-only advertised specials. You can also take advantage of a slew of virtual travel agents on the Web, which compare offerings and prices from multiple airlines. Be aware, however, that both individual airlines and most of the major Internet booking sites will provide you with a very limited list of options. The cheapest options may be available only through traditional or discounter travel agencies (some of which can also be found on the Internet; see below). For up-to-date information about your best bets for finding airfare deals, check out both *Arthur Frommer's Budget Travel Online* (www.frommers.com) and *The Practical Nomad* (www.hasbrouck.org, and particularly the FAQ on international airfares).

On Wednesdays, the **Air Canada** website (www.aircanada.ca) publishes highly discounted flights, or Web-Savers, for the following weekend. You need to reserve these flights a day in advance to depart anytime Thursday through Saturday and return anytime Monday through Wednesday. You can either check the WebSaver section of the Air Canada site weekly (early Wednesday is best) or sign up to have notices of these and other discounted fares e-mailed to you. Most major airlines offer similar discounted Web-only fares, often called E-savers or something equally gimmicky—check any airline's website for details.

Probably the most used virtual travel agents are **Travelocity** (✆ **888/709-5983** in the U.S., 877/282-2925 in Canada; www.travelocity.com) and **Microsoft Expedia** (✆ **800/EXPEDIA;** www.expedia.com). For basic searches on just about any travel reservation website, you simply enter your preferred dates and cities (and maybe times or time frames) and the computer will look for the lowest fares. (In many cases, you can also adjust the search parameters to prioritize specific airlines, numbers of connections, or times.) These sites also publish selected sale fares and will e-mail you weekly with low fares for chosen departure and destination cities. **Smarter Living** (www.smarterliving.com) features a more comprehensive automated e-mail service, alerting you weekly to discount fares offered by as many as 15 or more airlines from your chosen departure city.

## BY CAR

Hopping across the border by car is no problem, since the U.S. freeway system leads directly into Canada at 13 points. Canadian customs agents do have the right, however, to search your vehicle if they suspect you may be in violation of any customs codes, such as carrying illegal goods. Check with Canadian customs (✆ **204/983-3500** or 506/636-5064 within the U.S., or 800/461-9999 within Canada; www.ccra-adrc.gc.ca) to make sure you're in compliance with the law before you go. Also, be sure to bring

## *Tips* Flying for Less: Getting the Best Airfares

- **Take advantage of APEX fares. Advance-purchase excursion** or **APEX** fares are often the key to getting the lowest fare. You generally must be willing to make your plans and buy your tickets as far ahead as possible: The **21-day APEX** is seconded only by the **14-day APEX,** with a stay of 7 to 30 days. Since the number of seats allocated to APEX fares is sometimes less than 25% of plane capacity, the early bird gets the low-cost seat. There's often a surcharge for flying on a weekend, and cancellation and refund policies can be strict.
- **Watch for sales.** You'll almost never see them during July and August or the Thanksgiving or Christmas seasons, but at other times you can get good deals. If you already hold a ticket when a sale breaks, it may even pay to exchange it, which usually incurs a charge of between US$50 and US$100. Just about all airlines now post sale fares on their websites, and a variety of sale fares are listed on Internet travel booking sites, such as **Travelocity, Expedia,** and **Orbitz** (**© 888/656-4546;** www.orbitz.com). Note that airlines' published sale fares are by no means necessarily the lowest fares available (see consolidators, below).
- **Find out if you can secure a cheaper fare by staying an extra day or flying midweek.** If your schedule is flexible, you can definitely save money this way. Many airlines won't volunteer this information.
- **Be aware that consolidators (a.k.a. bucket shops) are good places to find low fares.** They buy seats in bulk from airlines and sell them to the public at prices below the airlines' published discounted rates. Their small, boxed ads usually run in Sunday newspaper travel sections. If you have time to do some research, go to the library or get online and search for consolidators in the Yellow Pages of San Francisco and New York City, two major centers of consolidator businesses.

  The Internet has become a center of consolidator offerings. It's a mystery exactly where these services source their fares, so you'll do best to shop around. However, the friendlier consolidator reservation systems will tell you up front what days you will travel and for how much, before you buy a ticket. This is not the case for one of the best-known Web consolidators, **Priceline** (www.priceline.com), which solicits your general flight preferences (days, times, and

your car's registration papers. At the border you'll usually be asked a few questions about where you've come from, where you're going, for what purpose, and for how long. Assuming what you say isn't incriminating, you should be through in no time. Once across the border, you can link up with the Trans-Canada Highway, which runs from St. John's, Newfoundland, to Victoria, British Columbia—a total of 8,000km (5,000 miles)—with some ferries along the way.

### BY BUS

**Greyhound Canada** (**© 800/661-8747** in Canada; www.greyhound.ca)

airports), takes your bid on a ticket, and then tells you whether the bid's been accepted, and when and how you'll be flying, only after you've agreed to buy. **Expedia** offers a similar bidding option, in addition to its separate search of published fares, and other published-fare search engines have begun or may begin to offer some consolidator fares. If you decide to use a bidding consolidator service, shop around first. If you aren't going to try to beat a fare offered up front, there's no reason to bother with bidding.

The consolidator **OneTravel** (www.onetravel.com) allows you to see the lowest published fares it can find, with airline and time information, before searching its consolidator fares (and it won't give you exact times until you buy the tickets). Other consolidators, such as **CheapTickets** (✆ **888/922-8849;** www.cheaptickets.com), search a variety of both published and unpublished fares. Yet others, such as **Hotwire** (✆ **877/HOTWIRE**; www.hotwire.com), search only their own network of consolidator fares, so for comparison, and specific flight options, you have to check published fares elsewhere.

Some other consolidators include **FlyCheap** (✆ **800/FLY-CHEAP;** www.flycheap.com) and **TFI Tours International** (✆ **800/745-8000** or 212/736-1140; www.lowestairprice.com), a clearinghouse for unused seats. **Council Travel** (✆ **800/226-8624;** www.counciltravel.com) and **STA Travel** (✆ **800/781-4040;** www.statravel.com) cater especially to young travelers, but some bargain prices are available to all ages. With all of the options available for consolidator fares, keep in mind that it may pay to call or visit some agencies, rather than just shop online.

- **Book a seat on a charter flight.** Most charter operators advertise and sell their seats through travel agents. Before deciding to take a charter, however, check the ticket restrictions: You may be asked to buy a tour package, pay in advance, be amenable if the departure day is changed, pay a service charge, fly on an airline you're not familiar with (unusual), and pay harsh penalties if you cancel (but be understanding if the charter doesn't fill up and is canceled up to 10 days before departure). Summer charters fill up more quickly than others and are almost sure to fly, but if you decide on a charter, seriously consider cancellation and baggage insurance.

operates the major intercity bus system in Canada, with frequent cross-border links to cities in the U.S. northern tier (many more than what's offered by Greyhound USA). Greyhound's routes also link up with those of smaller carriers, such as Voyageur (✆ **613/238-5900** in Ottawa, 514/842-2281 in Montréal; www.voyageur.com) and SMT (✆ **800/567-5151;** www.smtbus.com).

## BY TRAIN

**Amtrak** (✆ **800/USA-RAIL;** www.amtrak.com) can get you into Canada at a few border points, where you can connect up with Canada's **VIA Rail** (✆ **888/VIARAIL** within Canada or 416/236-2029; www. viarail.ca) system. On the East Coast, Amtrak's *Adirondack* starts at New York City's Pennsylvania Station and travels daily via Albany and upstate New York to Montréal. Round-trip fares are US$106 to US$132. The *Maple Leaf* links New York City and Toronto via Albany, Rochester, Buffalo, and Niagara Falls, departing daily from Penn Station. Round-trip fares run from US$130 to US$198. On the West Coast, the *Cascades* runs from Eugene, Oregon, to Vancouver, British Columbia, with stops in Portland and Seattle. Round-trip fares from Portland are US$66 to US$128 and fares from Seattle run between US$46 and US$68. Amtrak-operated buses may also connect segments of these routes.

Connecting services are available from other major cities along the border in addition to these direct routes. Call **Amtrak** or **VIA Rail** or see their websites for details. Amtrak and VIA Rail both offer a North American Railpass, which gives you 30 days of unlimited economy-class travel in the U.S. and Canada. In 2001, fares for this pass through Amtrak range from US$471 to US$674, with a 10% discount for seniors and students. Tickets for this offer must be purchased by phone, at a rail station, or through a travel agent. Remember that the prices don't include meals; you can buy meals on the train or carry your own food.

### BY FERRY

Ocean ferries operate from Maine to Nova Scotia and New Brunswick, and from Seattle and Port Angeles, Washington, to Victoria and Vancouver, British Columbia. For details, see the relevant chapters.

## 8 Package Tours & Escorted Tours

Tour packages divide into two main categories: escorted tours, which take care of all the details, and independent tours, which simply give you a package price on the big ticket items and leave you free to find your own way. Independent tours give you much more flexibility but require more effort on your part. Those who prefer not to drive and don't relish the notion of getting from train or bus stations to hotels on their own might prefer an escorted tour. But if you're the kind of traveler who doesn't like to be herded around in a group and wants to be able to linger at various sights at your leisure, an escorted tour will drive you to distraction. The samples below will give you an idea of your choices.

### INDEPENDENT PACKAGES

**Air Canada** offers an array of package deals specially tailored to trim the costs of your vacation. Collectively, these packages come under the title "Air Canada's Canada." This term covers a whole series of travel bargains ranging from city packages to fly/drive tours, escorted tours, motor-home travel, and ski holidays. For details, pick up the brochure from an Air Canada office, or have it sent to you by calling ✆ **800/254-1000.**

One of Canada's largest tour operators (mostly for vacations outside of Canada), **World of Vacations,** operates a number of independent package tours (flexible getaways, in their words) that include western destinations, including a number of fly/rail packages. Contact them at 191 The West Mall, Suite 600, Etobicoke, Ontario M9C 5K8 (✆ **800/661-1312;** www.wov.com).

**Collette Tours,** 162 Middle St., Pawtucket, RI 02860 (✆ **800/340-5158;** www.collettevacations.com), offers both independent and escorted tours. Their independent tours include visits to many cities across Canada, as well as some selected wilderness destinations.

### ESCORTED TOUR PACKAGES

**Collette Tours** also offers a wide variety of escorted trips by bus and train, including several in the Atlantic Provinces, the Pacific Northwest, and the Rockies. A 10-day tour of Newfoundland includes the seldom-visited northern peninsula and the Viking site at L'Anse aux Meadows, as well as a visit to Labrador. Shorter trips explore the Toronto/Niagara area, and some combine Atlantic Canada with New England or Western Canada with Alaska. An escorted train tour goes from Vancouver to Banff aboard the *Rocky Mountaineer* (see below). Order any of Collette's tour brochures by phone or on their website.

**Brewster Transportation and Tours,** P.O. Box 1140, Banff, Alberta T0L 0C0 (✆ **800/661-1152;** www.brewster.ca) offers a wide variety of tours throughout Canada, both escorted and independent. Their offerings include motor coach and train excursions, ski and other winter vacations, city and resort combination packages, chartered day tours by bus, and independent driving tours. Highlights include a visit to the Columbia Icefield in Jasper National Park, Alberta, and one to Yellowknife, Northwest Territories, to view the aurora borealis. Many packages in the Rockies include stays at guest ranches.

Travel by train lets you see the Rockies as you never would in a bus or behind the wheel of a car. The **Great Canadian Railtour Company,** 1150 Station St., 1st Fl., Vancouver, BC V6A 2X7 (✆ **800/665-7245;** www.rockymountaineer.com) bills its *Rocky Mountaineer* as "The Most Spectacular Train Trip in the World." During daylight hours between mid-April and mid-October, this sleek blue-and-white train winds past foaming waterfalls, ancient glaciers, towering snowcapped peaks, and roaring mountain streams. The *Rocky Mountaineer* gives you the options of traveling east from Vancouver; traveling west from Jasper, Calgary, or Banff; or taking round-trips. There's also a tour offering a VIA Rail connection from Toronto. Tours range from 2 to 12 days, with stays in both the mountains and cities.

John Steel Railtours (✆ **800/988-5778** or fax 604/886-2100, www.johnsteel.com) offers both escorted and independent tour packages, many through the Rockies and the west and a few in other regions, which combine train and other forms of travel. VIA Rail and BC Rail operate the train portions of John Steel tours. Packages run from 5 to 12 days, at all times of year, depending on the route, and combine stays in major cities and national parks.

## 9 Getting Around

Canada is a land of immense distances, so transportation from point A to point B forms a prime item in your travel budget as well as your timetable.

### BY PLANE

Canada's largest transcontinental airline is **Air Canada** (✆ **888/247-2262;** www.aircanada.ca). Most of Canada is also served by the major discount airline **Canada 3000** (✆ **888/300-0669** or 416/674-3000; www.canada3000.com). Other large carriers include **Air Transat** (✆ **866/847-1112;** www.airtransat.com) and **WestJet** (✆ **888/937-8538;** www.westjet.com). Together with its regional partner companies, Air Canada handles a great deal of Canada's air transport. There are also numerous small local outfits, but these will concern you only when you get into their particular territories.

Within Canada, Air Canada operates daily service among all major cities and many smaller destinations, and its schedules dovetail with a string of allied connector carriers like Air Nova, Air Ontario, and NWT Air to serve scores of smaller Canadian towns. Bookings for flights on these and other smaller airlines are made automatically through Air Canada, by phone or on their website. Canada 3000, WestJet, and Air Transat all serve many major Canadian cities, as well as some smaller ones. In general, expect to find the most travel options through Air Canada, but in some cases, some significantly lower fares can be found through its competitors.

## BY CAR

Canada has scores of rental-car companies, including **Hertz** (© **800/654-3131** in the U.S. or 800/263-0600 in Canada; www.hertz.com), **Avis** (© **800/331-1212** in the U.S. or 800/331-1084 in Canada; www.avis.com), **Dollar** (© **800/800-4000;** www.dollar.com), **Thrifty** (© **800/THRIFTY;** www.thrifty.com), **Budget** (© **800/527-0700** in the U.S. or 800/472-3325 in Canada; www.rent.drivebudget.com), **Enterprise** (© **800/RENTACAR** in the U.S. or 800/268-8900 in Canada; www.enterprise.com), and **National Car Rental** (© **800/CAR-RENT** in the U.S. or 800/387-4747 in Canada; www.nationalcar.com). Nevertheless, rental vehicles tend to get tight during the tourist season, from around mid-May to summer. It's a good idea to reserve a car as soon as you decide on your vacation.

Several rental car agencies offer roadside assistance programs in Canada. In case of an accident, a breakdown, a dead battery, a flat tire, a dry gas tank, getting stuck, or locking yourself out of your car, call your agency's 24-hour number. For **Hertz** call © **800/654-5060,** for **Avis** call © **800/354-2847,** for **Dollar** call © **800/800-4000,** for **Budget** call © **800/858-5377,** for **National** call © **800/268-9711** or 800/227-7368, and for **Enterprise** call © **800/307-6666.**

Members of the **American Automobile Association** (AAA) should remember to take their membership cards since the **Canadian Automobile Association** (CAA) (© **800/222-4357,** www.caa.ca) extends privileges to them in Canada.

**GASOLINE** As in the United States, the trend in Canada is toward self-service stations, and in some areas you may have difficulty finding the full-service kind. Though Canada (specifically Alberta) is a major oil producer, gasoline isn't particularly cheap. Gas sells by the liter and pumps for anywhere from about

### *Tips* Sample Driving Distances Between Major Cities

Here are some sample driving distances between major Canadian cities. The distances are calculated based on a particular route, possibly the fastest, but not necessarily the shortest: Montréal to Vancouver, 4,910km (3,041 miles); Vancouver to Halifax, 6,295km (3,897 miles); Toronto to Victoria, 4,700km (2,911 miles); Winnipeg to St. John's, 5,100km (3,159 miles); Calgary to Montréal, 3,710km (2,299 miles); St. John's to Vancouver, 7,625km (4,723 miles); Ottawa to Victoria, 4,810km (2,979 miles). To get driving directions online, check MapQuest (www.mapquest.com) or Yahoo! Canada Maps (http://ca.maps.yahoo.com) and select driving directions.

C50¢ to C80¢ (US35¢–US50¢) per liter, or about C$1.90 to C$3.00 (about US$1.25–US$1.95) per U.S. gallon. (Note that the term "gallon" in Canada usually refers to the imperial gallon, which amounts to about 1.2 U.S. gallons.) Gasoline prices will vary from region to region.

**DRIVING RULES** Canadian driving rules are similar to regulations in the United States. Wearing seat belts is compulsory (and enforced) in all provinces, for all passengers. Children under 5 must be in child restraints. Motorcyclists must wear helmets. Throughout the country, pedestrians have the right-of-way and crosswalks are sacrosanct. The speed limit on the autoroutes (limited-access highways) is usually 100kmph (62 mph). In all provinces but Québec, right turns on red are permitted after a full stop, unless another rule is posted. Drivers must carry proof of insurance in Canada at all times.

## BY TRAIN

Most of Canada's passenger rail traffic is carried by the government-owned **VIA Rail** (© **888/VIARAIL** within Canada or 416/236-2029; www.viarail.ca). You can traverse the continent very comfortably in sleeping cars, parlor coaches, bedrooms, and roomettes. Virtually all of Canada's major cities (save Calgary) are connected by rail, though service is less frequent than it used to be. Some luxury trains, like *The Canadian,* boast dome cars with panoramic picture windows, hot showers, and elegant dining cars. Reduced regular fares are available for students, seniors, and children traveling with adults.

You can buy a **Canrailpass,** C$658 (US$408) in high season and C$411 (US$255) in low season, giving you 12 days of unlimited economy class travel in one 30-day period throughout the VIA national network. Seniors 60 and over, students, and youths 17 or under receive a 10% discount on all fares. Class upgrades are available for a fee each time you ride. A similar, but less expensive package is available for 10 days of unlimited travel on the Québec-Windsor corridor, serving Toronto, Niagara Falls, Ottawa, Montréal, and Québec City.

## *FAST FACTS:* Canada

*American Express* See the city chapters that follow for the locations of individual American Express offices. To report lost or stolen traveler's checks, call © **800/221-7282.**

*Car Rentals* See "Getting Around," above.

*Climate* See "When to Go," earlier in this chapter.

*Driving Rules* See "Getting Around," above.

*Drugstores* Drugstores and pharmacies are found throughout Canada. In fact, many prescription-only drugs in the United States are available over the counter in Canada, and pharmacists are more likely to offer casual medical advice than their counterparts in the States. If you're not feeling well, a trip to see a pharmacist might save you a trip to the doctor.

*Electricity* Canada uses the same electrical plug configuration and current as the United States: 110 to 115 volts, 60 cycles.

*Embassies & Consulates* All embassies are in Ottawa, the national capital; the **U.S. embassy** is at 490 Sussex Dr., Ottawa, Ontario K1N 1G8

(© **613/238-5335;** www.usembassycanada.gov). The mailing address for the embassy's consular services is P.O. Box 866, Station B, Ottawa, Ontario K1P 5T1. For the other embassies in Ottawa, see "Fast Facts: Ottawa," in chapter 9, "Ottawa & Eastern Ontario."

You'll find **U.S. consulates** in the following locations: **Nova Scotia, Newfoundland, New Brunswick,** and **Prince Edward Island**—Suite 910, Cogswell Tower, Scotia Sq., 2000 Barrington St., Halifax, Nova Scotia B3J 3K1 (© **902/429-2480**); **Québec**—2 place Terrasse-Dufferin (behind Château Frontenac), PO Box 939, Québec City, QC G1R 4T9 (© **418/692-2095**), and 1155 St. Alexander St., P.O. Box 65, Postal Station Desjardins, Montréal, QC H5B 1G1 (© **514/398-9695**); **Ontario**—360 University Ave., Toronto, ON M5G 1S4 (© **416/595-1700** or 416/201-4100 for emergency after-hours calls); **Alberta, Saskatchewan, Manitoba,** and the **Northwest Territories**—615 Macleod Trail S.E., 10th Fl., Calgary, AB T2G 4T8 (© **403/266-8962**); **British Columbia** and the **Yukon**—Mezzanine, 1095 W. Pender St., Vancouver, BC V6E 2M6 (© **604/685-4311**). Visit the American Citizen Information Services website (www.amcits.com) for further U.S. consular services information.

There's a **British consulate general** at 777 Bay St., Ste. 2800, Toronto, ON M5G 2G2(© **416/593-1290;** for more information see www.britain-in-canada.org), and an **Australian consulate general** at Ste. 316, 175 Bloor St. E., Toronto, ON M4W 3R8 (© **416/323-1155;** for more information see www.ahc-ottawa.org).

*Emergencies* In life-threatening situations, call © **911.**

*Holidays* See "When To Go," earlier in this chapter.

*Liquor Laws* Laws regarding beer, wine, and liquor vary from province to province. In some provinces all beer, wine, and spirits are sold only in government liquor stores, which keep very restricted hours. Only Alberta and Québec have liquor laws that resemble those in the United States. In those provinces and Manitoba, the minimum drinking age is 18; in all others it's 19.

*Mail* Standard mail in Canada is carried by **Canada Post** (© **800/267-1177** within Canada or 416/979-8822 from the U.S.; www.canadapost.ca). At press time, it costs C45¢ (US30¢) to send a first-class letter or postcard within Canada and C60¢ (US40¢) to send a first-class letter or postcard from Canada to the United States. First-class airmail service to other countries is C$1.05 (US70¢) for the first 20 grams. Rates go up frequently. If you put a return address on your letter, make sure it's Canadian, otherwise leave it without. Delivery time is unaccountably slow between Canada and the States, and all U.S. letter mail travels by air: Expect a letter from Calgary to take a week to reach Seattle.

*Maps* Most provincial tourism offices produce excellent and up-to-date road maps, which you should request when you call to ask for information. Official tourism websites also often have downloadable maps. See specific chapters for tourism office contact information.

*Pets* Your pets can accompany you on your vacation to Canada. All you need to prove is that your dog or cat has had its rabies shots in the last 36 months.

***Pharmacies*** See "Drugstores" above.

***Smoking*** Smoking in restaurants and public places is more prevalent in Canada than in many places in the United States, but less so than in Europe. Most restaurants will have no-smoking sections; hotels will have no-smoking rooms, and many inns and B&Bs don't permit it at all.

***Taxes*** In January 1991, the Canadian government imposed the **goods and service tax (GST),** a 7% federal tax on virtually all goods and services. Some provinces (the maritimes) instead levy a 15% harmonized sales tax (**HST**), which combines their provincial sales taxes with the GST. Some hotels and shops include the GST or HST in their prices; others add it on separately. When included, the tax accounts for the odd hotel rates, such as C$66.05 per day, that you might find on your final bill. The GST is also the reason you may pay C50¢ (US35¢) for a newspaper at a vending machine, but C55¢ (US35¢) over a shop counter: The machine hasn't been adjusted to account for the tax.

Thanks to a government provision designed to encourage tourism, you can **reclaim the GST** or **HST** portion of your hotel bills (or one-half of tour package bills) and the price of goods you've purchased in Canada—in due course. The minimum rebate is C$14 (US$9.10, the tax on C$200/US$130) and the claim must be filed within a year of purchase. The rebate doesn't apply to car rentals or restaurant meals. And the GST isn't levied on airline tickets to Canada bought in the United States. To obtain GST or HST refunds, you must submit all your original receipts (which will be returned) with an application form. You can get the forms in some of the larger hotels, in some duty-free shops, or by phone at ✆ **613/991-3346** outside Canada or 800/66-VISIT in Canada.

Receipts from several trips during the same year may be submitted together. Claims of less than C$500 (US$310) can be made at certain designated duty-free shops at international airports and border crossings. You will need to present your receipts for validation, have your purchased goods available for inspection by customs officers, and have proof that you are leaving Canada (such as departing plane tickets, and you may need proof of your date of entry into Canada). Otherwise, you can mail the forms to **Visitor Rebate Program,** Canada Customs and Revenue Agency, Summerside Tax Centre, 275 Pope Rd., Suite 104, Summerside, PE C1N 6C6.

***Telephone*** The Canadian phone system is exactly the same as the system in the United States. Canadian phone numbers have 10 digits: The first three numbers are the area code, which corresponds to a province or division thereof, plus a seven-digit local number. To call a number within the same locality, usually all you have to dial is the seven-digit local number. If you're making a long-distance call (out of the area or province), you need to precede the local number with "1" plus the area code.

For **directory assistance,** dial ✆ **411.** If that doesn't work, dial 1 + area code + 555-1212. Many public phones are set up to accept phone cards, which are readily available at drugstores, tobacco shops, and other shops

***Time*** Six time zones are observed in Canada. In winter, when it's 7:30pm Newfoundland standard time, it's 6pm Atlantic standard time (Labrador,

Prince Edward Island, New Brunswick, and Nova Scotia); 5pm eastern standard time (Québec and most of Ontario); 4pm central standard time (western Ontario, Manitoba, and most of Saskatchewan); 3pm mountain standard time (northwestern Saskatchewan, Alberta, eastern British Columbia, and the Northwest Territories); and 2pm Pacific standard time (the Yukon and most of British Columbia).

Each year, on the first Sunday in April, daylight saving time comes into effect in most of Canada and clocks are advanced by 1 hour. On the last Sunday in October, Canada reverts to standard time. During these summer months, all of Saskatchewan observes the same time zone as Alberta.

*Tipping* The rules for tipping in Canada parallel those in the United States. For good service in a restaurant, tip 15% to 20%. Tip hairdressers or taxi drivers 10%. Bellhops get C$1 (US60¢) per bag for luggage taken to your room; for valets who fetch your car, a C$2 (US$1.20) tip should suffice.

*Water* The water in Canada is legendary for its purity. You can drink water directly from the tap anywhere in the country. Bottled water is also widely available.

3

# Nova Scotia

*by Wayne Curtis & Paul Karr*

Nova Scotia proves cagey to characterize. It generally feels more cultured than wild . . . but then you stumble upon those blustery, boggy uplands at Cape Breton Highlands National Park, which seem a good home for Druids and trolls. It's a province full of rolling hills and cultivated farms, especially near the Northumberland Straits on the northern shore . . . but then you find the vibrant, edgy, and lively arts and entertainment scene in Halifax, a city that's got more intriguing street life than many cities three times its size. It's a place that earned its name—Nova Scotia is Latin for "New Scotland"—with Highland games and kilts and a touch of a brogue hear and there . . . but then suddenly you're amid the enclaves of rich Acadian culture along the coast between Digby and Yarmouth. The place resists characterization at every turn.

This picturesque and historic province is an ideal destination for travelers who are quick to hit the remote control when parked on the couch back home. There's an extravagant variety of landscapes and low-key attractions, and the scene seems to change kaleidoscopically as you travel along the winding roads: from dense forests to bucolic farmlands, from ragged coast to melancholy bogs, and from historic villages to dynamic downtowns. About the only terrain it doesn't offer? Towering mountain peaks.

## 1 Exploring the Province

Visitors to Nova Scotia would do well to spend some time poring over a map and this travel guide before leaving home. The hardest chore will be to narrow your options before you set off. Numerous loops and circuits are available, made more complicated by ferry links to the United States, New Brunswick, Prince Edward Island, and Newfoundland. Figuring out where to go and how to get there is the hardest part.

### VISITOR INFORMATION

Be sure to pick up a free copy of the massive (350+ page) official tourism guide, which is the province's best effort to put travel-guide writers like us out of business. This comprehensive, colorful, well-organized and free guide lists all hotels, campgrounds, and attractions within the province, with brief descriptions and current prices. (Restaurants are given only limited coverage.)

The guide, entitled *Nova Scotia: Compete Guide for Doers and Dreamers,* is available starting each March from **Nova Scotia Tourism** (P.O. Box 130, Halifax, NS B3J 2M7; ✆ **800/565-0000** in North America or 902/425-5781 outside North America; fax 902/453-8401; www.gov.ns.ca/tourism.htm). If you wait until you arrive in the province before obtaining a copy, ask for one at the numerous visitor information centers, where you can also request the excellent free road map.

**TOURIST OFFICES** The provincial government administers about a dozen official Visitor Information Centres throughout the province, as well as in Portland, Maine, Bar Harbor, Maine, and Wood Islands, PEI. These mostly seasonal centers are amply stocked with brochures and tended by knowledgeable staffers. In addition, virtually every town of any note has a local tourist information center filled with racks of brochures covering the entire province, staffed with local people who know the area.

For general questions about travel in the province, call Nova Scotia's information hotline (✆ **800/565-0000** in North America, or 902/425-5781 outside North America).

**WEBSITES** For the best information, visit Nova Scotia Tourism (**www.gov.ns.ca/tourism.htm**) and Destination: Nova Scotia (**http://destination-ns.com**).

## GETTING THERE

**BY CAR & FERRY** Most travelers reach Nova Scotia overland by car from New Brunswick. Plan on 4 or more hours driving from the U.S. border at Calais, Maine, to Amherst (at the New Brunswick-Nova Scotia border). Incorporating ferries into your itinerary can significantly reduce time behind the wheel. Daily seasonal ferries connect both Portland and Bar Harbor, Maine, to Yarmouth, Nova Scotia, at the peninsula's southwest end.

The **Portland-Yarmouth ferry** trip is about 11 hours and costs around US$86 one-way for each adult passenger, US$43 for children, and US$105 for each vehicle. Cabins are available for an additional fare, ranging from about US$35 for a day cabin to US$100 for an overnight suite; small additional charges also sometimes apply for fuel prices and federal departure taxes. Reservations are essential. Contact **Prince of Fundy Cruises** (✆ **800/341-7540** or 207/775-5616; www.princeoffundy.com).

**Bay Ferries** (✆ **888/249-7245;** www.nfl-bay.com) operates the **Bar Harbor-Yarmouth ferry.** The Cat (short for catamaran) claims to be the fastest ferry in North America and since going into service in 1998 has cut the crossing time from 6 to 2¾ hours, zipping along at up to 80kmph (50 mph). Summer season rates are US$55 for adults, US$50 for seniors, US$25 for children (5–12), and US$90 to US$120 per vehicle. Off-season and family rates are available. Reservations are vital during summer.

To shorten the slog around the Bay of Fundy, Bay Ferries operates the 3-hour **Saint John, N.B. to Digby, N.S. ferry.** The ferry sails year-round, with as many as three crossings daily in summer. Summer fares are C$35 (US$22) for adults, C$30 (US$19) for seniors, C$15 (US$9) for children, and C$70 to C$150 (US$43–US$93) per vehicle.

**BY PLANE** Halifax is the air hub of the Atlantic Provinces. **Air Canada** (✆ **888/AIR-CANA;** www.aircanada.ca) provides direct service from New York and Boston, and its commuter partner **Air Nova** serves Sydney and Yarmouth plus about a dozen other Atlantic Canada destinations. Routes that involve connections at Montréal or Toronto can turn a short hop into an all-day excursion.

**BY TRAIN** **VIA Rail** (✆ **800/561-3949** in the U.S. or 888/842-7245 in Canada; www.viarail.ca) offers train service 6 days a week between Halifax and Montréal (trip time: 18–21 hrs.). The fare is about C$150 to C$200

# Nova Scotia & Prince Edward Island

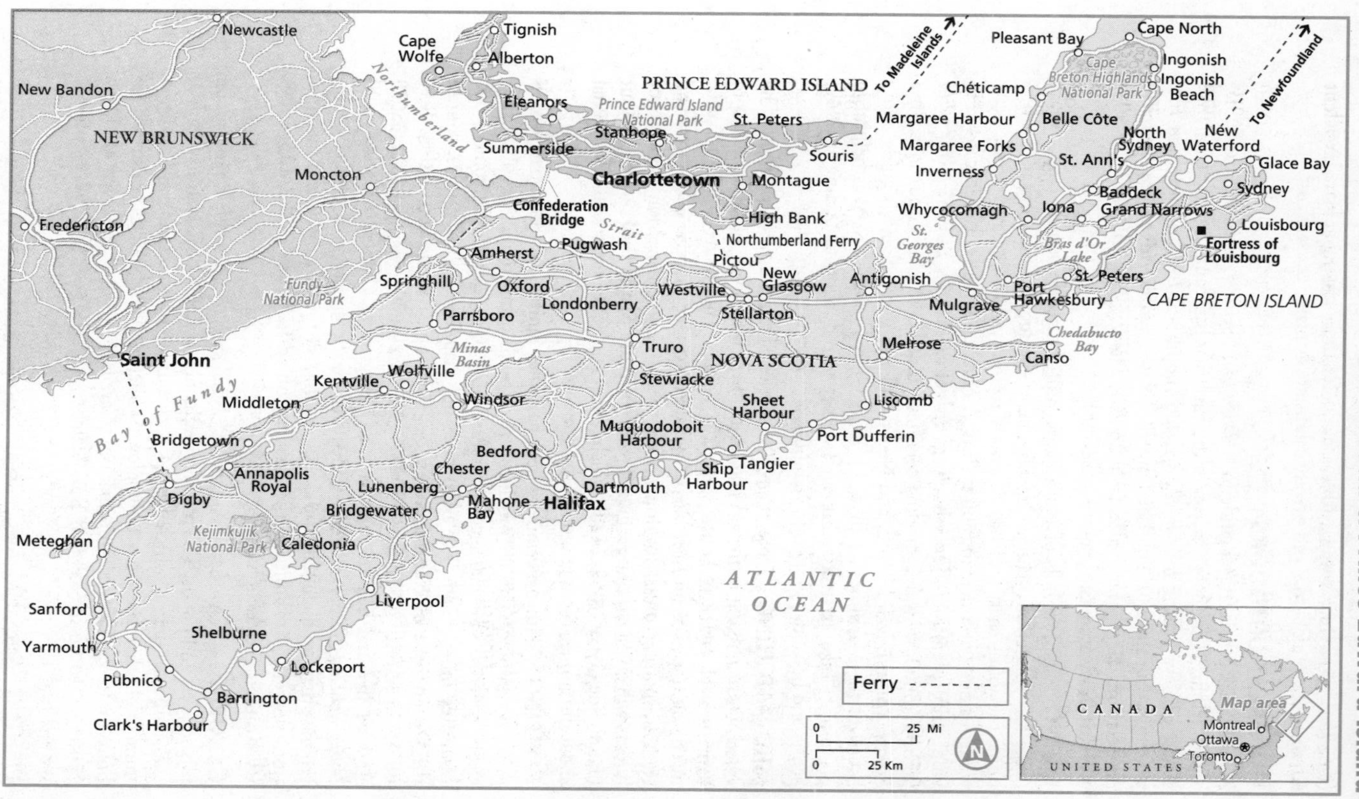

(US$93–US$124) each way, with discounts for those buying at least 1 week in advance. Sleeping berths and private cabins are available at extra cost.

## THE GREAT OUTDOORS

Nova Scotia's official travel guide (*The Doers and Dreamers Complete Guide*) has a very helpful "Outdoors" section in the back that lists camping outfitters, bike shops, whale-watching tour operators, and the like. A free brochure that lists adventure outfitters is published by the **Nova Scotia Adventure Tourism Association,** 1099 Marginal Rd., Suite 201, Halifax, NS B3H 4P7 (✆ **902/423-4480;** www.adventurenovascotia.com).

**BIKING** The low hills of Nova Scotia and the gentle, largely empty roads make for wonderful cycling. Cape Breton is the most challenging of destinations; the south coast and Bay of Fundy regions yield wonderful ocean views while making fewer demands on cyclists. A number of bike outfitters can aid in your trip planning. **Freewheeling Adventures** (✆ **800/672-0775** or 902/857-3600; www.freewheeling.ca) offers guided bike tours throughout Nova Scotia, Prince Edward Island, and Newfoundland. Walter Sienko's guide, Nova Scotia & the Maritimes by Bike: 21 Tours Geared for Discovery, is helpful in planning a bike excursion. For an Internet introduction to cycling in Nova Scotia and beyond, point your Web browser to www.atl-canadacycling.com.

**BIRD-WATCHING** More than 400 species of birds have been spotted in Nova Scotia, ranging from odd and exotic birds blown off course in storms to majestic bald eagles, of which some 250 nesting pairs reside in Nova Scotia, mostly on Cape Breton Island. Many whale-watching tours also offer specialized sea bird-spotting tours, including trips to puffin colonies. More-experienced birders will enjoy checking regularly with the **Nova Scotia Bird Society's** information line (✆ **902/852-2428**), which features up-to-date recorded information about intriguing sightings around the province.

**CAMPING** With backcountry options rather limited, Nova Scotia's forte is drive-in camping. The 20 provincial parks with campgrounds are uniformly clean, friendly, well managed, and reasonably priced, and offer some 1,500 campsites among them. For a brochure and map listing all campsites, contact the **Department of Natural Resources,** Parks and Recreation Division, R.R. no. 1, Belmont, NS B0M 1C0 (✆ **902/662-3030;** www.gov.ns.ca/natr/). Another free and helpful guide is the **Campground Owners Association of Nova Scotia's** *Campers Guide,* which includes a directory of private campgrounds that are members of the association. Ask for it at the visitor information centers, or contact the association directly (✆ **902/423-4480;** www.campingnovascotia.com).

**CANOEING** Nova Scotia offers an abundance of accessible canoeing on inland lakes and ponds. The premier destination is Kejimkujik National Park in the southern interior, which has 44 backcountry sites accessible by canoe. A number of other fine canoe trails allow paddlers and portagers to venture off for hours or days. General information is available from **Canoe Kayak Nova Scotia,** 5516 Spring Garden Rd., Halifax, NS B3J 3G6 (✆ **902/425-5450;** www.ckns.ca).

**FISHING** Saltwater fishing tours are easily arranged on charter boats berthed at many of the province's harbors. Inquire locally at the visitor information centers, or consult the "Boat Tours & Charters" section of the *Doers & Dreamers Guide.* No fishing license is needed for those on charters.

Committed freshwater anglers come to Nova Scotia in pursuit of the tragically dwindling Atlantic salmon, which requires a license separate from that for other freshwater fish. They can be obtained from a provincial office, campground, or licensed outfitter. For information, contact the **Department of Agriculture and Fisheries** (✆ **902/424-4560;** www.gov.ns.ca/nsaf/).

**GOLF** More than 50 golf courses are located throughout Nova Scotia. Among the most memorable: the **Cape Breton Highland Links** (✆ **800/441-1118** or 902/285-2600) in Ingonish, which features a dramatic oceanside setting, and **Bell Bay Golf Club** (✆ **800/565-3077**) near Baddeck, which is also wonderfully scenic, and was voted "Best New Canadian Golf Course" by Golf Digest in 1998. For one-stop shoppers, **Golf Nova Scotia** (✆ **800/565-0001;** www.golfnovascotia.com) represents 18 well-regarded properties around the province and can arrange customized golfing packages at its member courses. A handy directory of Nova Scotia's golf courses (with phone numbers) is published in the "Outdoors" section of *the Doers and Dreamers Guide.*

**HIKING & WALKING** Serious hikers make tracks for **Cape Breton Highlands National Park,** which is home to the most dramatic terrain in the province. But you're certainly not limited to here. Trails are found throughout Nova Scotia, although in many cases they're a matter of local knowledge. (Ask at the visitor information centers.) Published hiking guides are widely available at local bookstores. Especially helpful are the back-pocket-size guides published by **Nimbus Publishing** of Halifax (✆ **800/646-2879** or 902/455-4286; www.nimbus.ns.ca).

**SAILING** Any area with so much convoluted coastline is clearly inviting to sailors and gunkholers. Tours and charters are available almost everywhere there's a decent-size harbor. Those with the inclination and skills to venture out on their own can rent 5m (16-ft.) Wayfarers, or one of several slightly larger boats, by the hour and maneuver among beautiful islands at **Sail Mahone Bay** (✆ **902/624-8864**) on the south shore near Lunenburg. The province's premier sailing experience is an excursion aboard the *Bluenose II,* which is virtually an icon for Atlantic Canada. See the "Lunenburg" section later in this chapter.

**SEA KAYAKING** Nova Scotia is increasingly attracting the attention of kayakers worldwide. Kayakers traveling on their own should be especially cautious on the Bay of Fundy side, since the massive tides create strong currents that overmatch even the fittest of paddlers. Nearly 40 kayak outfitters (and growing) do business in Nova Scotia, and they offer everything from 1-hour introductory paddles to intensive week-long trips; consult the directory in *Doers and Dreamers.* Among the more respected outfitters is **Coastal Adventures,** P.O. Box 77, Tangier, NS B0J 3H0 (✆ **902/772-2774;** www.coastaladventures.com).

**WHALE-WATCHING** If you're on the coast, it's likely you're not far from a whale-watching operation. Around 12 whale-watching outfits offer trips in search of finback, humpback, pilot, and minke whales, among others. The richest waters for whale-watching are found on the **Fundy Coast,** where the endangered right whale is often seen feeding in summer. **Digby Neck** ★ has the highest concentration of whale-watching excursions, but you'll find them in many other coves and harbors. Just ask the staff at visitor information centers to direct you to the whales.

## 2 Wolfville: Introduction to the Annapolis Valley ★

### WOLFVILLE

The trim Victorian village of Wolfville (pop. 3,500)—the first major community as you move south into the gentle, orchard-filled Annapolis Valley—has a distinctly New England feel to it, both in its handsome architecture and its layout. It's not hard to trace that sensibility to a source: The area was largely populated in the wake of the American Revolution by transplanted New Englanders, who forced off the Acadian settlers who had earlier done so much to tame the wilds.

The town has emerged in recent years as a popular destination for weekending Halifax residents, who come to relax at the many fine inns, wander the leafy streets, and explore the countryside. Also a consistent draw is the **Atlantic Theatre Festival** (✆ **800/337-6661** or 902/542-4242; www.atf.ns.ca), which has attracted plaudits in the few years it has been presenting shows. Performances are staged throughout the summer season in a comfortable 500-seat theater. Reservations are encouraged; ticket prices are C$10 to C$37 (US$6–US$23).

### EXPLORING WOLFVILLE

The town's mainstay these days is handsome Acadia University, which has nearly as many full-time students as there are residents of Wolfville. The university's presence gives the small village an edgier, more youthful air. Don't miss the university's Art Gallery at the **Beveridge Arts Center** (✆ **902/585-1373**), which showcases both contemporary and historic Nova Scotian art; it's open daily from 1 to 4pm and admission is free.

Strolling the village is the activity of choice. The towering elms and maples that shade the extravagant Victorian architecture provide the dappled light and rustling sounds for an ideal walk. A good place to start is the **Wolfville Tourist Bureau** at Willow Park (✆ **902/542-7000**) on the north edge of the downtown. If you'd prefer to cover more ground, you can rent a mountain or touring bike at **Valley Stove and Cycle,** 232 Main St. (✆ **902/542-7280**); cost is C$30 (US$19) for a full-day rental or C$20 (US$12) for a half-day rental and includes locks and helmets.

One of the more intriguing sights in town occurs each summer day at dusk, in an unprepossessing park surrounded by a parking lot a block off Main Street. At **Robie Swift Park,** a lone chimney (dating from a long-gone dairy plant) rises straight up like a stumpy finger pointed at the heavens. Around sunset, between 25 and 100 chimney swifts flit about and then descend into the chimney for the night. Alas, the swifts have been declining in number in recent years, ever since some predatory merlins started nesting nearby. But you'll learn a lot by browsing the informational plaques posted here, where you can read interesting tidbits such as this: No one knew where swifts migrated in winter until 1943, when explorers in the Peruvian jungle found natives wearing necklaces adorned with small aluminum rings. These, it turned out, were tracking bands placed on swifts by North American ornithologists.

At **Blomidon Provincial Park** (✆ **902/582-7319** or 902/424-5937), 25km (15 miles) north of Route 101 (Exit 11), some 14km (8½ miles) of trail at the park take walkers through forest and along the coast. Among the most dramatic trails is the 6km (4-mile) Jodrey Trail, which follows towering cliffs that offer broad views over the Minas Basin.

**Grand-Pré National Historic Site** ★ Long before roving New Englanders arrived in this region, hardworking Acadians had vastly altered the local landscape.

They did this in large part by constructing a series of dikes outfitted with ingenious log valves, which allowed farmers to convert the saltwater marshes to productive farmland. At Grand-Pré, a short drive east of Wolfville and just off Route 1, you can learn about these dikes along with the tragic history of the Acadians, who populated the Minas Basin between 1680 and their expulsion in 1755.

More a memorial park than a living history exhibit, Grand-Pré (which means "great meadow") has superbly tended grounds that are excellent for idling, a picnic lunch, or simple contemplation. Among the handful of buildings on the grounds is a graceful stone church, built in 1922 on the presumed site of the original church. Evangeline Bellefontaine, the revered (albeit fictional) heroine of Longfellow's epic poem, was said to have been born here; look for the statue of this tragic heroine in the garden. It was created in 1920 by Canadian sculptor Philippe Hérbert, and the image has been reproduced widely since.

2241 Grand-Pré Rd., Grand-Pré. ✆ **902/542-3631.** Admission C$2.50 (US$1.55) adults, C$2 (US$1.20) seniors, C$1.10 (US70¢) ages 6–16, C$7 (US$4.35) family. Daily 9am–6pm. Closed Nov–May.

## WHERE TO STAY

**Gingerbread House Inn** ★ The ornate Gingerbread House Inn was originally the carriage house for the building now housing Victoria's Historic Inn (see below). A former owner went woodshop-wild, adding all manner of swirly accouterments and giving the place a convincingly authentic air. Guest rooms are a modern interpretation of the gingerbread style and are generally quite comfortable, although the two rooms in the back are dark and small. The floral Carriage House Suite features luxe touches like a propane fireplace and two-person Jacuzzi; the Garden House has the most space, plus a spa and a wet bar. The budget choice is the lovely Terrace Room, which is somewhat minuscule but has a lovely private deck on the second floor under a gracefully arching tree. Breakfasts tend toward the elaborate and are served by candlelight.

8 Robie Tufts Dr. (P.O. Box 819), Wolfville, NS B0P 1X0. ✆ **888/542-1458** or 902/542-1458. Fax 902/542-4718. www.gingerbreadhouse.ca. 6 units. C$79–C$169 (US$49–US$105) double, includes breakfast. Ask about golf packages. AE, MC, V. **Amenities:** Dinner service. *In room:* A/C, no phone.

**Tattingstone Inn** ★★ "We sell romance and relaxation," says innkeeper Betsy Harwood. And that pretty well sums it up. This handsome Italianate-Georgian mansion dates back to 1874 and overlooks the village's main artery. The inn is furnished with a mix of reproductions and antiques, and traditional and modern art blend well. The attitude isn't over-the-top Victorian as one might guess by looking at the manse, but decorated with a deft touch that mixes informal country antiques and regal Empire pieces. Rooms in the Carriage House are a bit smaller, but they are still pleasant. Two rooms have fireplaces and some have Jacuzzis. The spacious semiformal dining room is rather refined, and diners sup amid white tablecloths and stern Doric columns. Dinner is served nightly in summer from 5:30 to 9pm. Ask for a seat on the enclosed porch, which captures the lambent early evening light to good effect. House specialties include the rack of lamb and chicken served with pear and ginger sauce; the latter incorporates pears grown right on the property.

434 Main St. (P.O. Box 98), Wolfville, NS B0P 1X0. ✆ **800/565-7696** or 902/542-7696. Fax 902/542-4427. tattingstone@ns.sympatico.ca. 10 units. C$128–C$148 (US$79–US$92) double; cottage C$189 (US$117). AE. Children 12 and up. **Amenities:** Restaurant; heated outdoor pool; steam room; tennis court. *In room:* A/C, TV.

**Victoria's Historic Inn** ★★ Victoria's Historic Inn was constructed by apple mogul William Chase in 1893 and is architecturally elaborate. This sturdy Queen Anne-style building features bold pediments and massed pavilions, which have been adorned with balusters and ornate Stick-style trim. Inside, the effect seems a bit as if you'd wandered into one of those stereoscopic views of a Victorian parlor. Whereas the nearby Tattingstone Inn resists theme decor, Victoria's Historic Inn embraces it. There's dense mahogany and cherry woodwork throughout, along with exceptionally intricate ceilings. The deluxe Chase Suite features a large sitting room with a gas fireplace and an oak mantle. The less-expensive third-floor rooms are smaller and somewhat less historic in flavor. Four of the inn's suites have fireplaces and Jacuzzis.

416 Main St., Wolfville, NS B0P 1X0. © **800/556-5744** or 902/542-5744. Fax 902/542-7794. 15 units. C$95–C$175 (US$59–US$109) double C$160–C$225 (US$99–US$140), including full breakfast. AE, MC, V. **Amenities:** Laundry service; afternoon tea; meals. *In room:* A/C, TV.

## WHERE TO DINE

**Al's Homestyle Deli** *Value* DELI Randy and Linda Davidson now operate this place in the nearby hamlet of Canning, but Al Waddell's popular recipes for sausages live on: choose from Polish, German, hot Italian, and honey garlic sausages. Buy some links to cook later, or order up a quick road meal. You won't find a better cheap lunch: A sausage on a bun with a cup of soup will run you less than C$5 (US$3.10).

314 Main St., Canning. © **902/582-7270.** No reservations. All selections C$2–C$4 (US$1.20–US$2.50). V. Mon–Sat 8am–6pm, Sun 11am–5pm.

**Chez la Vigne** INTERNATIONAL Chez la Vigne is on a quiet side street a few steps off Main Street. The place is informal and comfortable, and the chef maintains the welcome philosophy that everyone should be able to afford a good meal. Dishes range from country simple (penne with vegetables) to rather more complex (rabbit stuffed with herbs and rice, roasted boar or venison). The quality varies, but more often than not, it's very good.

117 Front St. © **902/542-5077.** Reservations suggested. Lunch C$9.50–C$14.50 (US$6–US$9); dinner C$12.95–C$26 (US$8–US$16). Daily 11am–11pm (until 8 or 9pm in winter). AE, DC, MC, V.

# 3 Annapolis Royal: Nova Scotia's Most Historic Town ★★

Annapolis Royal is arguably Nova Scotia's most historic town—it even bills itself, with justification, as "Canada's birthplace." The nation's first permanent settlement was established at Port Royal, just across the river from the present-day Annapolis Royal, in 1605 by a group of doughty settlers that included Samuel de Champlain. (Champlain called the beautiful Annapolis Basin "one of the finest harbours that I have seen on all these coasts.") The strategic importance of this well-protected harbor was proven in the tumultuous later years, when a series of forts was constructed on the low hills overlooking the water.

Annapolis Royal today is truly a treat to visit. Because the region was largely overlooked by later economic growth (trade and fishing moved to the Atlantic side of the peninsula), it requires little in the way of imagination to see Annapolis Royal as it once was. (The current population is just 700.) The original settlement was rebuilt on the presumed site. Fort Anne overlooks the upper reaches of the basin, much as it did when abandoned in 1854. And the village itself maintains much of its original historic charm, with narrow streets and historic buildings fronting the now-placid waterfront. For anyone curious about Canada's early history, Annapolis Royal is one of Nova Scotia's don't-miss destinations.

## ESSENTIALS

**GETTING THERE** Annapolis is located at Exit 22 of Route 101. It is 206km (124 miles) from Halifax, and 133km (80 miles) from Yarmouth.

**VISITOR INFORMATION** The **Annapolis District Tourist Bureau** (✆ **902/532-5454** or 902/ 532-5769) is 1km (½ mile) north of the town center (follow Prince Albert Road and look for the Annapolis Royal Tidal Generating Station). It's open daily in summer 8am to 8pm, and 10am to 6pm in spring and fall.

## EXPLORING THE TOWN

Start at the tourist bureau (above), which is located at the **Annapolis Royal Tidal Generating Station**, where the extreme tides have been harnessed to produce electricity. It's the only tidal generator in North America, and the world's largest straight-flow turbine. Learn about the generator at the free exhibit center upstairs from the visitor center.

Before leaving the center, be sure to request a copy of the free "Footprints with Footnotes" walking-tour brochure. The annotated map provides architectural and historic context for a stroll around the downtown and waterfront. Take a moment to note that as you walk down lower St. George Street, you're walking down the oldest street in Canada.

**Fort Anne National Historic Site** ★ What you'll likely remember most from a visit here are the impressive grassy earthworks that cover some 14ha (35 acres) of high ground overlooking the confluence of the Annapolis River and Allains Creek. The French built the first fort here around 1643. Since then, dozens of buildings and fortifications have occupied this site. You can visit the 1708 gunpowder magazine (the oldest building of any Canadian National Historic Site), then peruse the museum located in the 1797 British field officer's quarters. The model of the site as it appeared in 1710 is particularly intriguing. If you find all the history a bit tedious, ask a guide for a croquet set and practice your technique on the lush rolling lawns.

Entrance on St. George St. ✆ **902/532-2321.** Admission to grounds is free; museum is C$2.75 (US$1.70) adult, C$2.25 (US$1.40) senior, C$1.35 (US85¢) child, C$7 (US$4.35) family. May 15–Oct 15 9am–6pm; off-season by appointment only (grounds open year-round).

**Historic Gardens** ★ You don't need to be a flower nut to enjoy an hour or two at these exceptional gardens. Created in 1981, the 4ha (10-acre) grounds are uncommonly beautiful, with a mix of formal and informal gardens dating from varied epochs. Set on a gentle hill, the plantings overlook a beautiful salt marsh (now diked and farmed), and they include a geometric Victorian garden, a knot garden, a rock garden, and a colorful perennial border garden. Rose fanciers should allow plenty of time—some 2,000 rose bushes track the history of rose cultivation from the earliest days through the Victorian era to the present day. A garden cafe (see below) offers an enticing spot for lunch.

***Moments*** **Sunset at Fort Anne**

A good strategy for visiting Fort Anne is to come during the day to tour the museum and get a feel for the lay of the land. Then return for the evening sunset, long after the bus tours have departed, to walk the Perimeter Trail with its river and valley vistas.

441 St. George St. ✆ **902/532-7018.** Admission C$6 (US$3.70) adult, C$5 (US$3.10) seniors and students, C$15 (US$9) family. July–Aug daily 8am–dusk, May–June and Sept–Oct 9am–5pm; closed remainder of year.

**Port Royal National Historic Site** ★ Canada's first permanent settlement, Port Royal was located on an attractive point with sweeping views of the Annapolis Basin. Those settlers who survived the dreadful winter of 1604 on an island in the St. Croix River (along the current Maine-New Brunswick border) moved to this better protected location and lived here for 8 years in a high style that approached decadent given the harsh surroundings. Many of the handsome, compact French-style farmhouse buildings were designed by Samuel de Champlain to re-create the comfort they might have enjoyed at home. Though the original settlement was abandoned and eventually destroyed, this 1939 re-creation is convincing in all the details. You'll find a handful of costumed interpreters engaged in traditional handicrafts like woodworking, and they're happy to fill you in on life in the colony during those difficult early years, an "age of innocence" when the French first forged an alliance with local natives.

10km (6 miles) south of Route 1, Granville Ferry (turn left shortly after passing the tidal generating station). ✆ **902/532-2321.** Admission C$2.75 (US$1.70) adult, C$2.25 (US$1.40) senior, C$1.35 (US85¢) child, C$7 (US$4.35) family. Daily May 15–Oct 15 9am–6pm.

## WHERE TO STAY

**Garrison House Inn** ★ The historic Garrison House sits across from Fort Anne in the town center and has bedded and fed guests since it first opened to accommodate officers at Fort Anne in 1854. Flowers make the inn welcoming, and the rooms are nicely appointed with antiques, some worn, some pristine. There's no air conditioning but fans are provided; the top floor can still get a bit stuffy on warm days. Room 2 is appealing, with wide pine floors, braided rug, and settee, though it faces the street and at times can be a bit noisy. Room 7 is tucked in the back of the house, away from the hubbub of St. George Street, and it has two skylights to let in a wonderfully dappled light. A recent addition is a screened-in verandah with food (fish and lobster, mostly) and drink service. Note that there are no TVs or phones, which could be a blessing, and that full breakfast is quirkily only served during the shoulder seasons (mid-May to July 1 and mid-October to mid-November).

350 St. George St., Annapolis Royal, NS B0S 1A0. ✆ **902/532-5750.** Fax 902/532-5501. www.come.to/garrison. 7 units. C$72–C$139 (US$45–US$86) double, sometimes including full breakfast. AE, MC, V. Street parking. Open May–Nov; call in advance for weekends rest of year. **Amenities:** Restaurant (see "Where to Dine," below), bar. *In room:* No phone.

**King George Inn** ★ *Kids* The handsome King George Inn was built as a sea captain's mansion in 1868, and served a stint as a rectory before becoming an inn. It's befittingly busy and cluttered for its era; guest rooms are furnished entirely with antiques, mostly of the country Victorian ilk. (Those who prefer clean lines might find a surplus of decor here.) All rooms have queen-size beds; two family suites have separate bedrooms and a bathroom that's shared between them. The best in the house is Room 7, with a Jacuzzi and a small private deck off the back of the house; a second Jacuzzi room was recently added.

548 St. George St., Annapolis Royal, NS B0S 1A0. ✆ **888/799-5464** or 902/532-5286. Fax 902/532-0144. 8 units. C$69–C$169 (US$43–US$105) double. AE, DC, MC, V. Closed mid-Nov to April. **Amenities:** Free bikes. *In room:* hair dryer, A/C, no phone.

**The Moorings** *Value* Just across the river from Annapolis Royal is the personable and appealing Moorings, a three-room B&B with great views of the town and Fort Anne across the water. This spot is much less "historic" compared to the high-Victorian inns in Annapolis, but is comfortably decorated with brushed walls and an attractive mix of antique furniture and modern art. Guests have the run of two downstairs parlors, one of which has a television. One room has a private bathroom, but this was actually my least favorite. The two others face the water and are brighter and more cheerful. The yellow room is flooded with afternoon light and has a half-bathroom in the room; showers are in the shared bathroom in the hallway.

P.O. Box 118, Granville Ferry, NS B0S 1K0. ✆ **902/532-2146.** tileston@tartannet.ns.ca. 3 units (2 share 1 bathroom). C$40–C$55 (US$25–US$34) double, including full breakfast. MC, V. Closed Oct 31–May 15. *In room:* No phone.

**Queen Anne Inn** ★ This Second Empire mansion, built in 1865, looks like the city hall of a small city. You won't miss it driving into town. Like the Hillsdale House across the street, the Queen Anne (built for the sister of the Hillsdale's owner) has benefited from a preservation-minded owner, who restored the Victorian detailing to its former luster. There's a zebra-striped dining-room floor (alternating planks of oak and maple) and the grand central staircase. Guest rooms are quite elegant, and furnished appropriately to the Victorian era. With their towering elms, the parklike grounds are shady and inviting. New ownership recently took over, converting breakfast to a three-course affair.

494 St. George St., Annapolis Royal, NS B0S 1A0. ✆ **902/532-7850.** Fax 902/532-2078. www.queenanneinn.ns.ca. 10 units. C$100–C$135 (US$62–US$84) double, family room C$140–C$175 (US$87–US$109), off-season C$80–C$100 (US$50–US$62), includes full breakfast. MC, V. Closed Nov to mid-April. *In room:* No phone.

## WHERE TO DINE

**Garrison House** ★ ECLECTIC The Garrison House is the most intimate and attractive of the village's restaurants. The three cozy dining rooms in this historic home each have a different feel, some with colonial colors, some contemporary, most with black Windsor chairs and modern piscine art. (My favorite room is the one with the green floors and the humpback whale.) The menu is also tricky to categorize, with starters like an Acadian seafood chowder and carrot vichyssoise with coconut, and entrees ranging from jambalaya to scallops in a Vietnamese curry to a simple pasta with garden vegetables; it leans mostly heavily toward seafood and reliable lobster. You can get individual-serving pizzas here, as well.

350 St. George St. (in the Garrison House Inn). ✆ **902/532-5750.** Reservations recommended in summer. Main courses C$14–C$27 (US$9–US$17). AE, MC, V. Daily 5:30–8:30pm.

**Newman's** ★ SEAFOOD Newman's is an informal spot located in an oddly out-of-place pink Spanish Revival building on Annapolis Royal's historic waterfront. But don't let that confuse you. Inside, you'll find some of the most carefully prepared food in Nova Scotia, with an eye to fresh produce and meats. The place has been run by the same folks for 20 years, and they haven't let standards slip. It's hard to nail down a specialty—the kitchen does so much so very well. The seafood is especially delectable (grilled Atlantic salmon with tarragon sauce, halibut sautéed with sliced almonds), as are the generous, old-fashioned desserts (bananas with chocolate and whipped cream, homemade strawberry shortcake).

218 St. George St. ✆ **902/532-5502.** Reservations recommended. Main courses C$11–C$19 (US$7–US$12). V. May–Oct Tues–Sun noon–9pm.

**Secret Garden** ★ Value Kids LIGHT FARE Located at the edge of the Historic Gardens, the Secret Garden is the ideal location for a light lunch on one of those beguilingly warm days touched with a mild breeze. The best seats are on the patio, which occupies a shady spot under a huge American elm overlooking the knot garden. The selections are tasty and light, with fare like tuna sandwiches and penne in a spicy tomato sauce. It's managed by the same folks who run the Garrison House, and the food quality is similarly high. There's also a children's menu.

471 St. George St. ✆ **902/532-2200.** Reservations not needed. Lunch C$6–C$16 (US$3.70–US$10). MC, V. Daily May–Oct 11:30am–4:30pm, weather permitting. Closed Oct–May.

**Sunshine Cafe** Value Kids CAFE You can get a reliably tasty lunch at this unpretentious place, which delivers seafood chowders featuring local haddock, scallops, clams or salmon, plus a savory tuna melt on a bagel. Management is justifiably proud of the homemade breads, which are mostly of the multigrain and rye variety; finish up with a cappuccino, latte, or espresso—and maybe a piece of carrot cake or Linzer torte.

272 St. George St. ✆ **902/532-5596.** Reservations not necessary. Lunch items C$3.50–C$9.95 (US$2.15–US$6). AE, MC, V. July–mid-Oct daily 9am–6pm; rest of the year, daily 10am–4pm.

## 4 Kejimkujik National Park ★

About 46km (28 miles) southeast of Annapolis Royal is a popular national park that's a world apart from coastal Nova Scotia. Kejimkujik National Park, founded in 1968, is located in the heart of south-central Nova Scotia, and it is to lakes and bogs what the south coast is to fishing villages and fog. Bear and moose are the full-time residents here; park visitors are the transients. The park, which was largely scooped and shaped during the last glacial epoch, is about 20 percent water, which makes it especially popular with canoeists. A few trails also weave through the park but hiking is limited; the longest hike in the park can be done in 2 hours. Bird watchers are also drawn to the park in search of the 205 species that have been seen both here and at the Seaside Adjunct of the park, a $22km^2$ (14-sq.-mile) coastal holding west of Liverpool. Among the more commonly seen species are pileated woodpeckers and loons, and at night you can listen for the raspy call of the barred owl.

### ESSENTIALS

**GETTING THERE** Kejimkujik National Park is approximately midway on Kejimkujik Scenic Drive (Route 8), which extends 115km (71 miles) between Annapolis Royal and Liverpool. The village of Maitland Bridge (pop. 130) is near the park's entrance. Plan on about a 2-hour drive from Halifax.

**VISITOR INFORMATION Tourist Office** The park's **visitor center** (✆ **902/682-2772**) is open daily and features slide programs and exhibits about the park's natural history.

**Website** Look for Kejimkujik National Park information on the Parks Canada website (**www.parcscanada.gc.ca**)

**FEES** Entrance fees are charged from mid-May to the middle of October. Daily fees are C$3.25 (US$2) adults, C$2.50 (US$1.55) seniors, C$1.75 (US$1.10) ages 6 to 16, and C$7.50 (US$5) for families; 4-day passes are available in all categories for the price of 3 days.

## EXPLORING THE PARK

The park's 381km$^2$ (237 sq. miles) of forest, lake, and bog are peaceful and remote. Part of what makes the terrain so appealing is the lack of access by car. One short, forked park road from Route 8 gets you partway into the park. Then you need to continue by foot or canoe. A stop at the visitor center is worthwhile, both for the exhibits on the region's natural history and for a preliminary walk on one of the three short trails. The Beech Grove loop (2km/1½ miles) takes you around a glacial hill called a *drumlin.* The park has a taped walking tour available for use; ask at the information center.

Canoeing is the optimal means of traversing the park. Bring your own, or rent a canoe at Jake's Landing for C$5 (US$3.10) per hour, or C$24 (US$15) per day. (The same rate applies to rentals of bikes, paddleboats, kayaks, and rowboats.) Canoeists can cobble together wilderness excursions from one lake to the other, some involving slight portaging. Multi-day trips are easily arranged to backcountry campsites and are the best way to get to know the park. Canoe route maps are provided at the visitor center. Rangers also lead short guided canoe trips for novices.

The park also has 15 walking trails, ranging from short easy strolls to, well, longer easy strolls. (There's no elevation gain to speak of.) The 6km (4-mile) Hemlocks and Hardwoods Trail loops through stately groves of 300-year-old hemlocks; the 3km (1¾-mile) Merrymakedge Beach Trail skirts a lakeshore to end at a beach. A free map that describes the trails is available at the visitor center.

## CAMPING

Backcountry camping is the park's chief draw. The canoe-in and hike-in sites are assigned individually, which means you needn't worry about noisy neighbors. Backcountry rangers keep the sites in top shape, and each is stocked with firewood for the night; the wood is included in the campsite fee. Most sites can handle a maximum of six campers. Naturally, there's high demand for the best sites; you're better off here midweek, when fewer weekenders are down from Halifax. You can also reserve backcountry sites up to 60 days in advance for an additional fee of C$4.25 (US$2.65); call the visitor center (© **902/682-2772**). The backcountry camping fee is C$16.25 (US$10) per night.

The park's drive-in campground at Jeremys Bay offers 360 sites, a few quite close to the water's edge. Campground rates are C$14 (US$9) per night. (During the shoulder seasons in spring and fall, you get a sixth night free after five nights; winter camping costs C$9.50/US$6). Starting early each April reservations at the drive-in campground may be made for an additional fee of C$7.50 (US$5) by calling © **800/414-6765.**

# 5 From Digby to Yarmouth: A Taste of the Other Nova Scotia

Two towns serving as gateways to Nova Scotia bracket this 113km (70-mile) stretch of coast. Whereas the South Shore—the stretch between Yarmouth and Halifax—serves to confirm popular conceptions of Nova Scotia (small fishing villages, shingled homes), the Digby-to-Yarmouth route seems determined to confound them. Look for Acadian enclaves, fishing villages with more corrugated steel than weathered shingle, miles of sandy beaches, and spruce-topped basalt cliffs that seem transplanted from Labrador.

## DIGBY

The unassuming port town of Digby (pop. 2,300) is located on the water at Digby Gap—where the Annapolis River finally forces an egress through the North Mountain coastal range. Set at the south end of the broad watery expanse of the Annapolis Basin, Digby is home to the world's largest inshore scallop fleet, which drags the ocean bottom for tasty and succulent Digby scallops. Ferries to Saint John, N.B., sail year-round from a dock a few miles west of downtown.

The town is named after Admiral Sir Robert Digby, who arrived here from New England in 1783. He led a group of loyalists who found relations with their neighbors somewhat strained following the unfortunate outcome of the War of Independence. Today, Digby is an active community where life centers on fishing boats, neighborhoods of wood-frame houses, and no-frills seafood restaurants. It's certainly worth a brief stopover when you're heading to or from the ferry.

### ESSENTIALS

**GETTING THERE** Digby is Nova Scotia's gateway for those arriving from Saint John, N.B., via ferry. The ferry terminal is on Route 303 west of Digby. If you're arriving by ferry and want to visit the town before pushing on, watch for signs directing you downtown from the bypass. Otherwise, you'll end up on Route 101 before you know it. From other parts of Nova Scotia, Digby is accessible via Exit 26 off Route 101.

**VISITOR INFORMATION** The province maintains a **visitor information center** (© **902/245-2201**) on Route 303 (on your right shortly after you disembark from the Saint John ferry). There's also the municipal **Visitor Information Centre** (© **902/245-5714**), located on the harbor at 110 Montague Row. It's open daily 8:30am to 8:30pm May to mid-October, and daily 9am to 5pm during spring and fall.

### EXPLORING DIGBY

Water Street runs along the water (of course), with views of the scallop fleet from various points. A narrow grassy promenade extends from the visitor information center to the small downtown; parking is usually plentiful.

Near the information center is the **Admiral Digby Museum,** 95 Montague Row (© **902/245-6322**). The Georgian home dates to the mid-19th century; inside you'll find a wide-ranging selection of artifacts, ranging from documentary photos of a Mi'kmaq porpoise hunt in the 1930s, to ship models and early Victorian fashions. Also on display are 2 of the 100 toy stuffed dogs made of old coats by local craftsperson Alma Melanson. It's open Tuesday to Sunday 9am to 5pm June to August; 9am to 5pm Monday to Friday September to mid-October, by appointment the rest of the year. Admission is by donation.

You can learn about the scallop industry at the **Lady Vanessa** fisheries exhibit, 34 Water St. (© **902/245-4555**). Set in a 30m (98-ft.) scallop dragger, it features videos and exhibits about the prized local catch. It's open daily 9am to 7pm June to late September during good weather; admission is C$1.75 (US$1.10).

### WHERE TO STAY

Digby is an entryway for those arriving or departing by ferry, and as such it has a number of basic motels. Two within walking distance of the promenade and downtown are the cottage-style efficiency units of **Seawinds Motel,** 90 Montague Row (© **902/245-2573**), offering good sea views and charging C$75 to

## Whale-Watching at Digby Neck ★

Look at a map of Nova Scotia and you'll see the thin strand of **Digby Neck** extending southwest from Annapolis Basin. You might guess from its appearance on the map that it's a low, scrubby sandspit. You would be wrong. In fact, it's a long, bony finger of high ridges, spongy bogs, dense forest, and expansive ocean views. The last two knuckles of this narrow peninsula are islands, both of which are connected via 10-minute ferries across straits swept with currents as strong as 9 knots.

In the Bay of Fundy just offshore, ocean currents mingle and the vigorous tides cause upwelling, which brings a rich assortment of plankton to the surface. That makes it an all-you-can-eat buffet for whales, which feed on these minuscule bits of plant and animal. As the fishing industry has declined, the number of fishermen offering whale-watching tours has boomed. Most are down-home operations on converted lobster boats—don't expect the gleaming whale-watch ships with comfy seats and full-service cafeterias that you find in larger cities or on the New England coast.

Declining inshore herring stocks means tours need to head farther out into the bay to find whales than in years past, but you'll almost always have sightings of fin, minke, or humpback whales. Right, sperm, blue, and pilot whales, along with the seldom-seen orcas, have also been spotted over the years. Plan on spending around C$35 to C$45 (US$22–US$28) for a 3- to 4-hour cruise. **Mariner Cruises** (✆ **800/239-2189** or 902/839-2346) in Westport on Brier Island sails aboard the 14m (45-ft.) *Chad and Sisters Two,* which is equipped with a heated cabin. Both whale- and bird-watching tours are offered. **Pirate's Cove Whale Cruises** (✆ **888/480-0004** or 902/839-2242), located in Tiverton, offers three tours daily aboard the 10m (34-ft.) *M/V Todd.* **Petite Passage Whale Watch** (✆ **902/834-2226** or 902/245-6132) sails out of East Ferry aboard a 11m (37-ft.), 20-passenger boat with a partially covered deck.

For a saltier adventure, **Ocean Explorations** (✆ **902/839-2417**) offers tours on rigid-hulled inflatable Zodiacs. The largest boat holds up to a dozen passengers and moves with tremendous speed and dampness through the fast currents and frequent chop around the islands and the open bay. Guests are provided with survival suits for warmth and safety.

C$90 (US$47 to US$56) double; and the more basic **Siesta Motel,** 81 Montague Row (✆ **902/245-2568**) just across the street, charging C$53 to C$80 (US$33 to US$50) double.

**Brier Island Lodge** ★ *Finds* Built to jump-start local eco-tourism, the Brier Island Lodge has a rustic-modern motif, with log-cabin construction and soaring glass windows overlooking the Grand Passage 40m (130 ft.) below. The rooms on two floors all have great views, the usual motel amenities, and some unexpected touches (double Jacuzzis in the pricier rooms). There's a well-regarded dining room that serves up traditional favorites, and an airy lounge where local fishermen congregate in the evening to play cards and watch the satellite TV. There's a small but good selection of field guides near the upholstered chairs in the corner of the lounge; hiking trails connect directly from the lodge to the Fundy shore.

Westport, Brier Island. ✆ **800/662-8355** or 902/839-2300. Fax 902/839-2006. www.brierisland.com. 40 units. C$60–C$129 (US$37–US$80) double. MC, V. **Amenities:** Television lounge; bike rental; game room. *In room:* A/C, TV.

**The Pines** ★★ *Kids* The Pines, situated on 120ha (300 acres) with marvelous views of the Annapolis Basin, is redolent of an earlier era when old money headed to fashionable resorts for an entire summer. Built in 1929 in a Norman château style, the inn today is owned and operated by the province of Nova Scotia. The imposing building of stucco and stone is surrounded by the eponymous pines, which rustle softly in the wind. Throughout, the emphasis is more on comfort than historical verisimilitude, although the gracious lobby features old-world touches. Guest rooms vary slightly as to size and views (ask for a water-view room; there's no extra charge), and all now have ceiling fans, although air-conditioning is said to be on the way. The cottages have one to three bedrooms and most feature wood fireplaces.

The resort's **Annapolis Dining Room** is open for all three meals, and the cuisine might best be described as Nova Scotian with a French flair. Look for entrees like roasted pork tenderloin with apples and a cider sauce, or poached char infused with green Chinese tea. Dinner reservations are advised.

Shore Rd., P.O. Box 70, Digby, NS B0V 1A0. ✆ **877/375-6343** or 902/245-2511. Fax 902/245-6133. www.signatureresorts.com. 84 units, 30 cottages. C$150–C$300 (US$93–US$186) double, cottages C$315 (US$195) and up. AE, DC, DISC, MC, V. Closed late Oct to early May. **Amenities:** Restaurant; pool; golf course; 2 night-lit tennis courts; fitness center; sauna; bike rental; concierge; courtesy car to ferry; shopping arcade; babysitting; children's center; laundry; dry cleaning. *In room:* TV.

**Thistle Down Country Inn** This personable Edwardian inn on the harbor has a dozen rooms evenly divided between the main house (built in 1904) and a two-story motel-style annex in the back. In the older house you get the charm of the oak staircase, banister and trim, the eclectic antiques in the rooms, and a sitting parlor in front. But the bathrooms are small, the views limited, and the front rooms noisy. The more modern units (built in 1996) are larger; and the two end units (the most expensive) have great views of the basin and hills beyond. The innkeepers—Ed Reid and Lester Bartson—know the region well and are generous with their time in helping guests plan day trips and excursions further afield. (They also own the local Digby's Cafe & Bookstore on Water Street.) Dinners in the intimate dining room are among the best in Digby, too, with an emphasis on the local scallops prepared both creatively and simply.

98 Montague Row (P.O. Box 508), Digby, NS B0V 1A0. ✆ **800/565-8081** or 902/245-4490. Fax 902/245-6717. 12 units (2 w/private hallway bathroom). C$75–C$120 (US$47–US$74) double, includes full breakfast. AE, DC, MC, V. Closed Nov 1–May 1. Pets accepted with prior permission. **Amenities:** Restaurant; laundry service; gift shop. *In room:* Fridge (some rooms).

## WHERE TO DINE

A meal at **The Pines** (above) offers a grand setting. Otherwise, the few downtown seafood restaurants are more or less interchangeable, serving up heaps of fried scallops. Of these, the spot with the best harbor view is the **Fundy Restaurant,** 34 Water St. (✆ **902/245-4950**); ask for a seat in the solarium. If you'd like your scallops with a more exotic tang, head to **Kaywin Restaurant,**

51 Water St. (✆ **902/245-5543**), an above-average Chinese-Canadian restaurant that serves scallops stir-fried with vegetables, as well as the more common fried variant.

**Red Raven Pub** ★ *Value* SEAFOOD This locally popular hangout serves up well-prepared seafood in a publike atmosphere with a fine harbor view, especially from the upstairs lounge and outdoor deck. You can find the usual suspects on the menu, like sautéed or fried scallops, and fish and chips. Or try the local favorite: creamed lobster on toast. There's also commendable seafood chowder and a great coconut cream pie. Scenes from Stephen King's *Dolores Claiborne* were filmed here.

100 Water St. ✆ **902/245-5533.** Sandwiches C$3.50–C$7 (US$2.15–US$4.35); main courses C$8–C$16 (US$5–US$10). AE, DISC, MC, V. May–Oct, Tues–Sat 11am–10am, Sun–Mon 11am–9pm. Closed Nov–May.

## YARMOUTH

The constant lament of Yarmouth restaurateurs and shopkeepers is this: The summer tourists who steadily stream off the incoming ferries rarely linger long enough to appreciate the city before they mash the accelerator and speed off to higher-marquee venues along the coast. There might be a reason for that. Yarmouth is a pleasant burg that offers some noteworthy historic architecture dating from the golden age of seafaring. But the town's not terribly unique, and thus not high on my list of places I'd choose to spend a few days. It's too big (pop. 7,800) to be charming; too small to generate urban buzz and vitality. It has more the flavor of a handy pit stop than a destination, though recent redevelopment efforts have spruced up the waterfront a bit and added evening entertainment during the summer months, a very welcome sign.

### ESSENTIALS

**GETTING THERE** Yarmouth is at the convergence of two of the province's principal highways, Route 101 and Route 103. It's approximately 300km (180 miles) from Halifax. Yarmouth is the gateway for two daily ferries (seasonal) connecting to Maine. **Air Nova** (✆ **888/247-2262** or 902/742-2450) serves Yarmouth with infrequent flights. The airport is located a few minutes' drive east of town on Starrs Road.

**VISITOR INFORMATION** The **Yarmouth Visitor Centre** (✆ **902/742-6639** or 902/742-5033) is at 228 Main St., just up the hill from the ferry in a modern, shingled building you simply can't miss. Both the provincial and municipal tourist offices are located here; open May to October daily 8am to 7pm.

### EXPLORING THE TOWN

The tourist bureau and the local historical society publish a very informative **walking tour brochure** covering downtown Yarmouth, which is well worth requesting at the visitor information center. The guide offers general tips on what to look for in local architectural styles (how do you tell the difference between Georgian and Classic Revival?), as well as brief histories of significant buildings. The whole tour is 4km (2½ miles) long.

The most scenic side trip—and an ideal excursion by bike or car—is to **Cape Forchu** and the **Yarmouth Light** ★. Head west on Main Street (Route 1) for 2km (1¼ miles) from the visitor center, then turn left at the horse statue. The road winds picturesquely out to the cape, past seawalls and working lobster wharves, meadows, and old homes. When the road finally ends, you'll be at the red-and-white-striped concrete lighthouse that marks the harbor's entrance. (This modern lighthouse dates to the early 1960s, when it replaced a much older octagonal light that succumbed to wind and time.) There's a tiny photographic exhibit on the cape's history in the visitor center in the keeper's house. Leave enough time to ramble around the dramatic rock-and-grass bluffs—part of Leif Eriksson Picnic Park—that surround the lighthouse. Don't miss the short trail out to the point below the light. Bright red picnic tables and benches are scattered about; bring lunch or dinner if the weather is right.

**Firefighters Museum of Nova Scotia** *Kids* This two-story museum will appeal mostly to confirmed fire buffs, historians, and impressionable young children. The museum is home to a varied collection of early fire-fighting equipment, with hand-drawn pumpers as the centerpiece of the collection. Also showcased here are uniforms, badges, helmets, and pennants. Look for the photos of notable Nova Scotian fires ("Hot Shots").

451 Main St. © **902/742-5525.** Admission C$2.50 (US$1.55) adult, C$2 (US$1.20) seniors, C$1 children (US60¢), C$5 (US$3.10) family. July and August Mon–Sat 9am–9pm, Sun 10am–5pm; rest of year, Mon–Fri 9am–4pm, Sat 1–4pm.

## WHERE TO STAY

Yarmouth is home to a number of chain motels. Among them are the **Best Western Mermaid Motel,** 545 Main St. (© **800/772-2774** or 902/742-7821), with rates of C$99 to C$140 (US$61–US$87) double; **Comfort Inn,** 96 Starrs Rd. (© **902/742-1119**), at C$75 to C$140 (US$47–US$87) double; and the **Rodd Grand Hotel,** 417 Main St. (© **902/742-2446**), C$80 to C$180 (US$50–US$112) double.

**Churchill Mansion Inn** Between 1891 and 1920, the Churchill Mansion was occupied just 6 weeks a year, when Aaron Flint Churchill, a Yarmouth native who amassed a shipping fortune in Atlanta, Georgia, returned to Nova Scotia for summer. This extravagant mansion with its garish furnishings, situated on a low bluff overlooking the highway and a lake, was converted to an inn in 1981 by Bob Benson, who is likely to be found on a ladder or with a hammer in hand when you arrive ("It never ends," he sighs). The mansion boasts some original carpeting, lamps, and woodwork, although it can be a little threadbare, flaky, or water-stained in other spots. One room has a Jacuzzi.

Route 1 (14.5km/9 miles west of Yarmouth), Yarmouth, NS B5A 4A5. © **888/453-5565** or 902/649-2818. 10 units. C$54–C$140 (US$36–US$93) double. DISC, MC, V. Closed mid-Nov to May. **Amenities:** TV room. *In room:* No phone.

**Harbour's Edge B&B** This exceptionally attractive early Victorian home (1864) sits on 2 leafy acres and 75m (250 ft.) of harbor frontage. You can lounge on the lawn while watching herons and kingfishers below, making it hard to believe you're right in town and only a few minutes from the ferry terminal. Harbour's Edge opened in 1997 after 3 years of intensive restoration (it had previously been abandoned for 5 years). Rooms are lightly furnished, which nicely highlights the architectural integrity of the design. The very attractive Audrey Kenney Room is the largest; the Ellen Brown Room is my favorite: it has fine oak furniture and a great view of the harbor, although the private bathroom is down the hall.

12 Vancouver St., Yarmouth NS B5A 2N8. © **902/742-2387.** Fax 902/742-4471. www.harboursedge.ns.ca. 3 units (1 with private hallway bathroom). C$90–C$125 (US$56–US$78) double, including full breakfast. MC, V. Head toward Cape Forchu (see above); watch for the inn shortly after turning at the horse statue. *In room:* No phone.

**Lakelawn Motel** The clean, well-kept Lakelawn Motel offers basic motel rooms done up in freshened bluish colors, newer carpeting, and so forth. It's been a downtown Yarmouth mainstay since the 1950s, when the centerpiece Victorian house (where the office is located) was moved back from the road to make room for the motel wings. Looking for something a bit cozier? The house also has four B&B-style guest rooms upstairs, each furnished simply with antiques.

641 Main St., Yarmouth, NS B5A 1K2. ✆ **877/664-0664** or 902/742-3588. mackie@auracom.com. 31 units. C$54–C$79 (US$33–US$49) double. AE, DC, DISC, MC, V. Closed Nov–Apr. **Amenities:** Meals available. *In room:* TV.

### WHERE TO DINE

**Harris Quick-N-Tasty** SEAFOOD The name about says it all. This vintage 1960s restaurant has no pretensions (it's the kind of place that still lists cocktails on the menu) and is hugely popular with locals. The restaurant is adorned with that sort of paneling that was rather au courant about 30 years back, and the meals are likewise old-fashioned and generous. The emphasis is on seafood, and you can order your fish either fried or broiled; the "Scarlet O'Harris" lobster club sandwich is notable, as is the seafood casserole. There's now a second, very handy location in a converted rail car at 75 Water St., just across the street from the international ferry terminal. Buzz through the drive-through window, or hang at the picnic tables, before tackling the rest of Nova Scotia.

75 Water St., Yarmouth & Route 1, Dayton. ✆ **902/742-3467.** No reservations. Sandwiches C$2.95–C$12 (US$1.80–US$7); main courses C$7–C$18 (US$4.35–US$11). AE, DC, MC, V. Daily 7:30am–9pm (until 8pm in winter). Closed mid-Dec to Feb. Original location just east of Yarmouth on the north side of Route 1; second location across from ferry terminal.

**Rudder's Seafood Restaurant & Brewpub** ★ BREWPUB Yarmouth's first (and Nova Scotia's fourth) brewpub opened in 1997 on the newly spiffed-up waterfront. It occupies an old warehouse dating to the mid-1800s, and you can see the wear and tear of the decades on the battered floor and the stout beams and rafters. The place has been nicely spruced up, and the menu features creative pub fare, with additions including Acadian and Cajun specialties, like rappie pie and jambalaya. The steaks are quite good, as is the beer, especially the best bitter. In summer, there's outdoor seating on a deck with a view of the harbor across the parking lot.

96 Water St. ✆ **902/742-6008.** Reservations not needed. Sandwiches, C$5.95–C$8.75 (US$3.70–US$5), entrees C$10.95–C$14.95 (US$7–US$9). AE, DC, MC, V. Daily 11am–11pm (shorter hours in off-season).

## 6 The South Shore: Quintessential Nova Scotia ★★

The Atlantic coast between Yarmouth and Halifax is that quaint, maritime Nova Scotia you see on laminated place mats and calendars. It's all lighthouses and weathered, shingled buildings perched at the rocky edge of the sea, as if tenuously trespassing on the good graces of the sea. If your heart is set on exploring this fabled landscape, be sure to leave enough time to poke in all the nooks and crannies along this stretch of the coast.

As rustic and beautiful as this area is, you might find it a bit stultifying to visit every quaint village along the entire coastline—involving about 350km (210 miles) of twisting road along the water's edge. A more sane strategy would be to sit down with a map and target two or three villages, then stitch together selected coastal drives near the chosen villages with speedier links on Route 103, which runs straight and fast a short distance inland.

**Tips A Fog Alert**

When driving along the south shore, allow extra time because of fog. When the cool waters of the Arctic currents mix with the warm summer air over land, the results are predictable and soupy. The fog certainly adds atmosphere, but it can also slow driving to a crawl.

## SHELBURNE

Shelburne is a historic town with an unimpeachable pedigree. Settled in 1783 by United Empire Loyalists fleeing New England after the unfortunate outcome of the late war, the town swelled with newcomers and by 1784 was believed to have a population of 10,000—larger than Montréal, Halifax, or Québec. With the decline of boat building and fishing in this century, the town edged into that dim economic twilight familiar to other seaside villages (it now has a population of about 3,000), and the waterfront began to deteriorate, despite valiant preservation efforts.

And then Hollywood came calling, hat in hand. In 1992 the film *Mary Silliman's War* was filmed here. The producers found the waterfront to be a reasonable facsimile of Fairfield, CT, dated around 1776. The crew spruced up the town a bit and buried power lines along the waterfront. Two years later director Roland Joffe arrived to film the spectacularly miscast *Scarlet Letter,* starring Demi Moore, Gary Oldman, and Robert Duvall. The film crew buried more power lines, built some 15 "historic" structures near the waterfront (most of which were demolished after filming), dumped tons of rubble to create dirt lanes (since removed), and generally made the place look like 17th-century Boston.

When the crew departed, it left behind three buildings and an impressive shingled steeple you can see from all over town. Among the "new old" buildings is the waterfront cooperage across from the Cooper's Inn. The original structure, clad in asphalt shingles, was generally considered an eyesore and was torn down, replaced by the faux-17th-century building. Today, barrel makers painstakingly make and sell traditional handcrafted wooden barrels in what amounts to a souvenir of a notable Hollywood flop.

### ESSENTIALS

**GETTING THERE** Shelburne is 223km (134 miles) southwest of Halifax on Route 3. It's a short hop from Route 103 via either Exit 25 (southbound) or Exit 26 (northbound).

**VISITOR INFORMATION** The **Shelburne Tourist Bureau** (**© 902/875-4547**) is located in a tidy waterfront building at the corner of King and Dock Streets. It's open daily mid-May to October; hours are 9am to 8pm during peak season, 10am to 6pm off-season.

### EXPLORING SHELBURNE

The central historic district runs along the waterfront, where you can see legitimately old buildings, Hollywood fakes (see above), and spectacular views of the harbor from small, grassy parks. A block inland from the water is Shelburne's more commercial stretch, where you can find services that include banks, shops, and a wonderful bakery (see "Where to Dine," below).

**Shelburne Historic Complex** ★ *Kids* The historic complex is an association of four local museums located within steps of one another. The most engaging is the **Dory Shop,** right on the waterfront. On the first floor you can admire examples of the simple, elegant craft (said to be invented in Shelburne) and view videos about the late Sidney Mahaney, a master builder who worked in this shop from the time he was 17 until he was 96. Then head upstairs, where all the banging is going on. There you'll meet Sidney's son and grandson, still building the classic boats using traditional methods. While you're there, ask about the difference between a Shelburne dory and a Lunenburg dory.

The **Shelburne County Museum** features a potpourri of locally significant artifacts from the town's Loyalist past. Most intriguing is the 1740 fire pumper; it was made in London and imported here in 1783. Behind the museum is the austerely handsome **Ross-Thomson House** (✆ **902/875-3141**), built in 1784 through 1785. The first floor contains a general store as it might have looked in 1784, with bolts of cloth and cast-iron teakettles. Upstairs is a militia room with displays of antique and reproduction weaponry. The fourth museum, the **Muir-Cox Shipbuilding Interpretive Centre** (✆ **902/875-1114**), was recently added and features, as you might guess, maritime displays of barques, sailboats, yachts and more.

Dock St. (P.O. Box 39), Shelburne, NS B0T 1W0. ✆ **902/875-3219** or 902/875-3141. Admission to all 4 museums, C$8 (US$5) adult, under 16 free; individual museums C$3 (US$1.85) adult. June–mid-Oct, Mon–Sat 9:30am–noon and 2–5pm. Closed mid-Oct to May (Dory Shop closes at the end of Sept).

## WHERE TO STAY

**Cooper's Inn** ★ Located facing the harbor in the Dock Street historic area, the impeccably historic Cooper's Inn was originally built by Loyalist merchant George Gracie in 1785. Subsequent additions and updating have been historically sympathetic. The downstairs sitting and dining rooms set the mood nicely, with worn wood floors, muted wall colors, and classical music in the background. Rooms in the main building mostly feature painted wood floors (they're carpeted in the cooper-shop annex), and they're decorated in a comfortably historic-country style. The third-floor suite features wonderful detailing, two sleeping alcoves, and harbor views and is worth stretching your budget for. The George Gracie Room has a four-poster bed and water view; the small Roderick Morrison Room has a wonderful claw-foot tub perfect for a late-evening soak. The two small, elegant dining rooms here serve the best meals in town. Dinner is served nightly from 6 to 9pm, and reservations are strongly recommended.

36 Dock St., Shelburne, NS B0T 1W0. ✆ **800/688-2011** or 902/875-4656. Fax: 902/875-4656. coopers@ns.sympatico.ca. 7 units. C$85–C$135 (US$53–US$84) double; C$165–C$175 (US$102–US$109) suite. Rates include full breakfast. MC, V. **Amenities:** Restaurant. *In room:* Hair dryers, no phone.

## WHERE TO DINE

For a full dinner out, see **Cooper's Inn,** above.

**Mr. Fish** ★ *Value* SEAFOOD You can't miss this little fried-fish stand on the side of busy Route 3, near a shopping center; what the place lacks in location, it more than makes up for in character and good simple seafood. The matronly line cooks fry up messes of haddock, scallops, shrimp, perfectly jacketed in a light crust, then add great fries and crunchy coleslaw on the side—plus a smile. You eat outside on picnic tables (but watch out for bees); if it's raining, you'll have to eat in your car.

Route 3 north of town center. ✆ **902/875-3474.** Meals C$2.60–C$12.60 (US$1.60–US$8). V. Mon–Sat 10am–7pm (Fri until 9pm), Sun noon–7pm.

**Shelburne Pastry & Coffee** *Value* BAKERY/CAFE When a family of German chefs set about to open the Shelburne Pastry shop in 1995, the idea was to sell fancy pastries. But everyone who stopped by during the restoration of the Water Street building asked whether they would be selling bread. So they added bread, and today it's among the best you'll taste in the province—especially the delectable Nova Scotian oatmeal brown bread. The simple cafe also offers great pastries (try the pinwheels), as well as sandwiches served on their own bread, and filling meals from a limited menu that includes German bratwurst and chicken cordon bleu. Everything is made from scratch, and everything (except the marked-down day-old goods) is just-baked fresh. You'll find good value for your dollar here.

151 Water St. © **902/875-1164.** Sandwiches C$3.50–C$4.25 (US$2.15–US$2.60); main courses C$7–C$10 (US$4.35–US$6). V. Mon–Sat 9:30am–7pm.

## LUNENBURG ★★

Lunenburg is one of Nova Scotia's most historic and appealing villages, a fact recognized in 1995 when UNESCO declared the old downtown a World Heritage Site. The town was first settled in 1753, primarily by German, Swiss, and French colonists. It was laid out on the "model town" plan then in vogue (Savannah, GA, and Philadelphia, PA, were also set out along these lines), which meant seven north-south streets intersected by nine east-west streets. Such a plan worked quite well in the coastal plains. Lunenburg, however, is located on a harbor flanked by steep hills, and implementers of the model town plan saw no reason to bend around these. As a result, some of the streets can be exhausting to walk.

About 70% of the downtown buildings date from the 18th and 19th centuries, and many of these are possessed of a distinctive style and are painted in bright colors. Looming over all is the architecturally unique Lunenburg Academy, with its exaggerated mansard roof, pointy towers, and extravagant use of ornamental brackets. It sets the tone for the town the way the Citadel does for Halifax. The first two floors are still used as a public school (the top floor was deemed a fire hazard some years ago), and the building is open to the public only on special occasions.

### ESSENTIALS

**GETTING THERE** Lunenburg is 103km (62 miles) southwest of Halifax on Route 3.

**VISITOR INFORMATION Tourist Office** The **Lunenburg Tourist Bureau** (© **902/634-8100**) is located at the top of Blockhouse Hill Road. It's open daily in summer from 9am to 8pm. It's not in an obvious place, but the brown "?" signs posted around town will lead you there. The staff here is especially good at helping you find a place to spend the night if you've arrived without reservations. You can also call up local information at **www.town.lunenburg.ns.ca**.

### EXPLORING LUNENBURG

Leave plenty of time to explore Lunenburg by foot. An excellent **walking tour brochure** is available at the tourist office on Blockhouse Hill Road, though supplies are getting limited. If that's gone, contact the **Lunenburg Board of Trade** (© **902/634-3170**) for the excellent local and regional map.

Before beginning, a sad note. Until the night of October 31, 2001, **St. John's Anglican Church** at the corner of Duke and Cumberland Streets had been one of the most impressive architectural sights in all of Eastern Canada. The original structure was rendered in simple New England meetinghouse style, built in

1754 of oak timbers shipped from Boston; between 1840 and 1880 the church went through a number of additions and was overlaid with ornamentation and shingles to create an amazing example of the "carpenter Gothic" style—one in which many local residents were baptized, and attended services throughout their adult lives. All this changed on that Halloween night, however: Vandals set fire to the place, gutting its precious interior and much of the ornate exterior as well. It is now closed to the public while heartbroken preservationists figure out whether a replica will be possible; you can sit in the pretty park beside it and pay your respects.

While exploring the steep streets of the town, note the architectural influence of later European settlers—especially Germans. Some local folks undoubtedly made their fortunes from the sea, but real money was also made by carpenters who specialized in the ornamental brackets which elaborately adorn dozens of

## The Dauntless Bluenose

Take an old Canadian dime—one minted before 2001, that is—out of your pocket and have a close look. That graceful schooner on one side? That's the ***Bluenose,*** Canada's most-recognized and most-storied ship.

The *Bluenose* was built in Lunenburg in 1921 as a fishing schooner. But it wasn't just any schooner. It was an exceptionally fast schooner. U.S. and Canadian fishing fleets had raced informally for years. Starting in 1920 the *Halifax Herald* sponsored the International Fisherman's Trophy, which was captured that first year by Americans sailing out of Massachusetts. Peeved, the Nova Scotians set about taking it back. And did they ever. The *Bluenose* retained the trophy for 18 years running, despite the best efforts of Americans to recapture it. The race was shelved as World War II loomed; in the years after the war, fishing schooners were displaced by long-haul, steel-hulled fishing ships, and the schooners sailed into the footnotes of history. The *Bluenose* was sold in 1942 to labor as a freighter in the West Indies. Four years later it foundered and sank off Haiti.

What made the *Bluenose* so unbeatable? A number of theories exist. Some said it was because of last-minute hull design changes. Some said it was frost "setting" the timbers as the ship was being built. Still others claim it was blessed with an unusually talented captain and crew.

The replica *Bluenose II* was built in 1963 from the same plans as the original, in the same shipyard, and even by some of the same workers. It's been owned by the province since 1971, and it sails throughout Canada and beyond as Nova Scotia's seafaring ambassador. The *Bluenose*'s location varies from year to year, and it schedules visits to ports from Labrador to the United States. In midsummer it typically alternates between Lunenburg and Halifax, during which visitors can sign up for 2-hour harbor sailings C$20 (US$12) adult, C$10 (US$6) children 12 and under). To hear about the ship's schedule, call the **Bluenose II Preservation Trust** (✆ **800/763-1963** or 902/634-1963; www.bluenose2.ns.ca).

homes here. Many of these same homes similarly feature a distinctive architectural element that's known as the "Lunenburg bump"—a five-sided dormer and bay window combo installed directly over an extended front door. Other homes feature the more common Scottish dormer. Also look for the double or triple roofs on some projecting dormers, which serve absolutely no function other than to give the home the vague appearance of a wedding cake.

Guided 1½-hour **walking tours** (✆ **902/634-3848** or 902/527-8555) that include lore about local architecture and legends are hosted daily by Eric Croft, a knowledgeable Lunenburg native who's in possession of a sizeable store of good stories. Tours depart at 10am, 2pm, and 9pm from Bluenose Drive (across from the parking lot for the Atlantic Fisheries Museum); the cost is C$10 (US$6).

Several **boat tours** also operate from the waterfront, most tied up near the Fisheries Museum. **Lunenburg Whale-watching Tours** (✆ **902/527-7175**) sails in pursuit of several species of whales, along with seals and seabirds on 3-hour excursions. There are four departures daily at 8:30am, 11am, 2:30pm and 5:30pm, with reservations recommended. The ***Harbour Star*** (✆ **902/634-3535**) takes visitors on a mellow, 45-minute tour of Lunenburg's inner harbor (no swells!) in a converted fishing boat. The same folks also offer 1½-hour sailing trips on the ***Eastern Star,*** a 15m (48-ft.) wooden ketch, with several sailings daily.

**Blue Rocks** ★ is a tiny, picturesque harbor a short drive from Lunenburg. It's every bit as scenic as Peggy's Cove, but without the tour buses. Head out of town on Pelham Street, and keep driving east. Look for signs indicating either THE POINT or THE LANE and steer in that direction; the winding roadway gets narrower as the homes get more humble. Eventually, you'll reach the tip, where it's just fishing shacks, bright boats and rocks, with views of spruce- and heath-covered islands offshore. The rocks are said to glow in a blue hue in certain light, hence the name.

**Fisheries Museum of the Atlantic** ★ *Kids* The sprawling Fisheries Museum is professionally designed and curated, and it manages to take a topic that some might consider a little, well, dull and make it fun and exciting. You'll find aquarium exhibits on the first floor, including a touch-tank for kids. (Look also for the massive 6.8kg/15-pound lobster, estimated to be 25–30 years old.) Detailed dioramas depict the whys and hows of fishing from dories, colonial schooners, and other historic vessels. You'll also learn a whole bunch about the *Bluenose,* a replica of which ties up in Lunenburg when it's not touring elsewhere (see "The Dauntless Bluenose" box). Outside, you can tour two other ships—a trawler and a salt-bank schooner—and visit a working boat shop.

On the waterfront. ✆ **902/634-4794.** Admission C$8 (US$5) adult, C$6.50 (US$4) seniors, C$2.50 (US$1.55) children, C$19 (US$12) family. June to late Oct daily 9:30am–5:30pm; late Oct to May Mon–Fri 8:30am–4:30pm.

## WHERE TO STAY

For budget travelers, a great little municipal **campground** is located next to (and managed by) the visitor center on Blockhouse Hill. It has wonderful views and hookups for RVs. Be aware that the sites are packed in tightly, but the location is well situated for exploring the town.

**Boscawen Inn** ★ This imposing 1888 mansion occupies a prime hillside site just a block from the heart of town. It's almost worth it just to get access to the main-floor deck and its views of the harbor. Most of the rooms are in the main building, which had a newer wing added in 1945. The decor is Victorian, but not aggressively so. Some of the rooms, including two spacious suites, are located in the 1905 MacLachlan House, just below the main house. A few things to know: Room 6 lacks a shower but has a nice tub. Guests on the third floor will need to navigate steep steps. Two rooms have televisions, and in-room phones are available on request. The inn's restaurant serves reliable, sometimes imaginative dinners nightly in season from 5:30 to 9pm.

150 Cumberland St., Lunenburg, NS B0J 2C0. ✆ **800/354-5009** or 902/634-3325. Fax 902/634-9293. boscawen@ns.sympatico.ca. 20 units (1 w/private hallway bathroom). C$85–C$185 (US$53–US$115), including continental breakfast. AE, DISC, MC, V. **Amenities:** 2 restaurants, bar; laundry service. *In room:* TV (2 rooms), irons, hair dryers.

**Kaulbach House Historic Inn** ★ The in-town Kaulbach House is decorated appropriately for its elaborate architecture: in high Victorian style, although rendered somewhat less oppressive with un-Victorian colors, like pink and green. The house also reflects the era's prevailing class structure, since the nicest room (the tower room) is on top. It features two sitting areas and a great view. (The least intriguing rooms are the former servants' quarters on street level.) Recent renovations have spruced up the building a good bit, with new rain gutters, windows, mattresses, comforters and hot water heating, and the huge breakfast is worth coming for alone. It's a unique property in another regard: this is one of the few small Lunenburg inns in which all the guest rooms have their own private bathrooms.

75 Pelham St., Lunenburg, NS B0J 2C0. ✆ **800/568-8818** or 902/634-8818. Fax 902/634-8818. www.kaulbachhouse.com. 7 units. C$80–C$139 (US$50–US$86) double, including full breakfast. MC, V. Closed mid-Dec to mid-Mar. **Amenities:** Laundry service. *In room:* A/C (1 room), hair dryers, no phone.

**Lennox Inn** In 1991, this strikingly handsome but simple house in a quiet residential area of Lunenburg was condemned and slated for demolition. Robert Cram didn't want to see it go, so he bought it and spent several years restoring it back to its original 1791 appearance, filling it with antiques and period reproduction furniture. It's more rustic than opulent, but this fine inn should still be high on the list for anyone fond of authentically historic houses. In fact, it claims, quite plausibly, to be the oldest unchanged inn in Canada. Three of the four spacious second-floor rooms have the original plaster, and all four have the original fireplaces (nonworking). A country breakfast is served in the former tavern; be sure to note the ingenious old bar.

69 Fox St. (P.O. Box 254), Lunenburg, NS B0J 2C0. ✆ **888/379-7605** or 902/634-4043. 5 units. (2 share 1 bathroom.) C$65–C$110 (US$40–US$68) double, including full breakfast. MC, V. Open year-round; by appointment only mid-Oct to April. *In room:* No phone.

## WHERE TO DINE

**Hillcroft Café** INTERNATIONAL The cozy Hillcroft, operated on the first floor of the guesthouse by the same name, is run by two globetrotters, Rafel Albo and Peter Fleischmann. The restaurant is adorned with the gleanings of their trips, lending the place a fun atmosphere and a sort of parlor-game amusement while waiting for dinner ("I bet that's from Bali. Or maybe Thailand.") The menu is equally eclectic, with starters ranging from baba ghannouj and hummus to Greek salad and local favorite clam chowder. Dinner entrees include Thai chicken (with green beans and baby corn in a coconut curry), roasted lamb topped with a mild cheese and green peppercorn sauce, and penne with local scallops and mussels in a Mediterranean sauce. Desserts feature fresh Italian ices, along with apple crisp and a shortbread-crust cheesecake.

53 Montague St. ✆ **902/634-8031.** Reservations recommended. Entrees C$12.95–C$19.95 (US$8–US$12). MC, V. Daily 5:30–9pm. Closed Nov to mid-April.

**Historic Grounds Coffee House** ★ *Value* CAFE More than just great coffee drinks, this youthful place in decidedly un-hip Lunenburg serves up hearty breakfasts, good chowders, sandwiches, salads and fish cakes throughout most of the day. Wash 'em down with real Italian espresso, something called a frappé (which is not an American-style frappe, but rather more like a frozen espresso), smoothies, or sodas. Ice cream and interesting dessert items are also available. Go for a table on the tiny balcony if you can snag one—they've got the best dining view in town, at a fraction of the cost of what you'd pay for a meal anywhere else.

100 Montague St. ✆ **902/634-9995.** Reservations not necessary. Lunch items C$3.95–C$8.95 (US$2.45–C$6). Jun–mid-Sept Mon–Fri 7:30am–9pm Sat–Sun 8am–9pm, rest of the year daily 7:30am–6pm.

**The Knot** ★ *Value* PUB FARE Good beer on tap and a convivial English atmosphere make this pub a great place to take a break from more upscale eateries in town. Located smack in the center of a tiny commercial district, it serves surprisingly good pub fare—think juicy burgers, fried fish, local sausage, and a warming mussel soup—plus a selection of bitters and ales, some of them brewed locally in Halifax. The crowd is an agreeable mixture of fishermen, local families, and tourists, and bar staff are all too happy to help you decide what's good that day.

4 Dufferin St. ✆ **902/634-3334.** Reservations not necessary. Meals C$6–C$10 (US$3.70–US$6). AE, MC, V. Daily 10am–12pm; kitchen closes at 9pm in summer, 8:30pm in winter.

**Lion Inn** ★★ CONTINENTAL The tiny Lion Inn seats just 24 diners in two compact dining rooms in an 1835 home on a Lunenburg side street; the interior is simply appointed with Windsor chairs and pale walls, and while it's all a bit snug, this is still the most elegant, enjoyable eating experience in town. The reliable menu, which more often than not is prepared with sophistication and flair, features seafood but also a great rack of lamb in summer. Other entrees include baked salmon with a white wine and dill sauce, and peppercorn steak served with a Madeira sauce.

33 Cornwallis St. ✆ **888/634-8988** or 902/634-8988. Reservations suggested. Main courses C$15.95–C$24.95 (US$10–US$16). AE, MC, V. Mon–Sat 5:30–8:30pm (open Fri–Sun only Nov–Apr).

**Magnolia's Grill** ★ SEAFOOD/ECLECTIC This is a bright, cheerful, funky storefront with a checkerboard linoleum floor, lively rock playing in the background, and walls adorned with old Elvis and Beatles iconography. It also serves some of the most delectable food in town. Look for rotating seafood specials, chicken tostadas, and sesame-ginger shrimp stir-fry—or whatever else the kitchen feels like scrawling on the blackboard. The restaurant is especially famed for its fishcakes (served with homemade rhubarb chutney) and, for dessert, Mrs. Zinck's Chocolate Sloppy (don't ask; it's terrific). No reservations are accepted, so come at off-peak hours or come expecting a wait.

128 Montague St. ✆ **902/634-3287.** Reservations not accepted. Main courses C$6.50–C$14 (US$4–US$9). AE, MC, V. Daily 11:30am–10pm. Closed Nov–Mar.

**Old Fish Factory Restaurant** ★ *Kids* SEAFOOD The Old Fish Factory Restaurant is—no surprise—located in a huge old fish-processing plant, which it shares with the Fisheries Museum. This large and popular restaurant can swallow whole bus tours at once; come early and angle for a window seat or a spot on the patio. Also no surprise: The specialty is seafood, which tends to involve medleys of varied fish. At lunch you might order a fish sandwich or a salmon filet. At dinner, lobster is served four different ways, along with bouillabaisse, snow crab, local haddock and scallops, and curried mango seafood pasta. There's steak, lamb, and chicken for more terrestrial tastes.

68 Bluenose Dr. (at the Fisheries Museum). ✆ **800/533-9336** or 902/634-3333. www.oldfishfactory.com. Reservations recommended (ask for a window seat). Lunch C$8–C$19 (US$5–US$12), dinner C$14–C$35 (US$9–US$22). AE, DC, DISC, MC, V. Daily 11am–9pm. Closed late Oct–early May.

## MAHONE BAY ★★

Mahone Bay, first settled in 1754 by European Protestants, is postcard-perfect Nova Scotia. It's tidy and trim with an eclectic Main Street that snakes along the bay and is lined with inviting shops. This is a town that's remarkably well cared for by its 1,100 residents, a growing number of whom live here and commute to work in Halifax.

### ESSENTIALS

**GETTING THERE** Mahone Bay lies 10km (6 miles) east of Lunenburg on Route 3.

**VISITOR INFORMATION** A **visitor information center** (✆ **888/624-6151** or 902/624-6151; www.mahonebay.com) is located at 165 Edgewater St., near the three church steeples. It's open daily in summer 9am to 7:30pm.

### EXPLORING THE TOWN

The free **Mahone Bay Settlers Museum,** 578 Main St. (✆ **902/624-6263**), provides historic context for your explorations from early May through early September (closed Mondays). A good selection of historic decorative arts is on display. Before leaving, be sure to request a copy of "Three Walking Tours of Mahone Bay," a handy brochure that outlines easy historic walks around the compact downtown.

Thanks to the looping waterside routes nearby, this is a popular destination for bikers. And the deep, protected harbor offers superb sea kayaking. If you'd like to give kayaking a go, stop by **Mahone Bay Kayak Adventures,** 618 Main St. (✆ **902/624-0334**). They offer everything from half-day introductory classes to a 5-day coastal tour. Among the more popular adventures is the day-long introductory tour, in which paddlers explore the complex shoreline nearby and learn about kayaking in the process. The price is C$85 (US$53) per person, including lunch. Rentals are also available, starting at C$30 (US$19) half day for a single kayak.

Another appealing means of exploring the harbor and islands beyond is aboard the ***Spirit,*** a 36-passenger sailing ship built in 1998 using traditional means and materials (✆ **902/624-8443**). Four sailings daily are offered during the peak summer sailing season from the town wharf. Cruises are C$20 (US$12) adult, C$10 (US$6) children 6 to 12, under 6 free.

### WHERE TO STAY

**The Manse** ★ Innkeepers Rose and Allan O'Brien have made a cozy retreat of their 1870 home, tucked off on a side street that's at once removed from and close to the activity in Mahone Bay. Guest rooms are bright and uncluttered, and are tastefully appointed with furniture that's both modern and classic. I'd be happy in any of the rooms, but if it were available, I'd opt for the Loft, a former hayloft on the second floor of the barn. With its whitewashed barn-board walls, large sitting area, small balcony, queen-size bed, and CD player, it's hard to imagine not enjoying a few days hidden away here. The rest of the house is equally attractive, and a morning spent with a cup of coffee in one of the oversize Adirondack chairs on the front deck is a morning well spent indeed.

88 Orchard St. (P.O. Box 475), Mahone Bay, NS B0J 2E0. ✆ **902/624-1121.** Fax 902/624-1182. 4 units. C$95–C$135 (US$59–US$84) double, including full breakfast. MC, V. **Amenities:** Bar. *In room:* Hair dryers.

## WHERE TO DINE

The seasonally open **Organic Cafe** ★★ at 567 Main St. (✆ **902/624-6484**) is my favorite—an affordable waterside cafe dishing up filling, healthy sandwiches and thick bowls of what might be the best seafood chowder in the Maritimes. Almost everything here is organic, and they also do juices, smoothies, and top-flight coffee. Fresh desserts are delivered several times weekly.

**Innlet Café** ★★ SEAFOOD/GRILL Jack and Katherine Sorensen have been serving up great meals here for two decades, and they've styled a menu that's brought back legions of devoted customers. Everything is good, especially the seafood. The menu is all over the place (oven-braised lamb shank to scallop stir-fry), but the smart money hones in on the unadorned seafood. Notable are the "smoked and garlicked mackerel" and the mixed seafood grill. The best seats are on the stone patio, which has a view of the harbor and the famous three-steepled townscape of Mahone Bay. If you end up inside, nothing lost. The clean lines and lack of clutter make it an inviting spot, and the atmosphere is informal and relaxed.

Edgewater St. ✆ **902/624-6363.** Reservations suggested for dinner. Main courses C$12–C$21 (US$7–US$13). MC, V. Daily 11:30am–9pm.

**Mimi's Ocean Grill** ★ CANADIAN Set under an overarching tree in a historic Colonial-style home painted a rich Cherokee red, Mimi's offers some of the region's most wonderful cooking amid a relaxed and informal atmosphere. The whimsical wall paintings put you immediately at ease, and the servers are jovial without overdoing it. The menu changes every 6 weeks or so to reflect available ingredients. For lunch you might opt for the fish and mussel chowder, Baja fish tacos, or a vegetarian muffuletta (a kind of Italian sandwich). For dinner, how about the restaurant's famous bayou haddock (with a spicy cornmeal crust), Thai noodles, scallops in Pernod and cream, or a grilled steak topped with cognac and mustard demiglaze? If the weather's right, angle for a table on the narrow front porch, where you can enjoy a glimpse of the bay and the ongoing parade of Main Street.

662 Main St. ✆ **902/624-1342.** Main courses, lunch C$8–C$10 (US$5–US$6), dinner C$13.95–C$20 (US$9–US$12). MC, V. Summer open daily noon–9pm; limited hours in the off-season. Closed Jan–Mar.

## CHESTER ★★

Chester has the feel of an old-money summer colony, perhaps somewhere along the New England coast dated around 1920. It was first settled in 1759 by immigrants from New England and Great Britain, and today it has a population of 1,250. The village is noted for its regal homes and quiet streets, along with the picturesque islands offshore. The atmosphere here is un-crowded, untrammeled, lazy, and slow—the way life used to be in summer resorts throughout the world. Change may be on the horizon: actors and authors have discovered the place, and are snapping up waterfront homes in town and on the islands as private retreats, giving a bit of an edge to the lazy feel of the spot.

## ESSENTIALS

**GETTING THERE** Chester is located on Route 3 and is a short drive off Route 103, 21km (13 miles) east of Mahone Bay.

**VISITOR INFORMATION** The **Chester Visitor Information Center** (© **902/275-4616;** www.chester-ns-ca.com) is in the old train station on Route 3 on the south side of town. It's open daily 9am to 7pm in July and August, 10am to 5pm in spring and fall.

## EXPLORING THE TOWN

Like so many other towns in Nova Scotia, Chester is best seen out of your car. But unlike other towns, where the center of gravity seems to be in the commercial district, here the focus is on the graceful, shady residential areas that radiate out from the Lilliputian village.

Some creative shops are beginning to find a receptive audience in and around Chester, and right now there's good browsing for new goods and antiques both downtown and in the outlying areas. One such shop is **Fiasco,** 54 Queen St. (© **902/275-2173**), which has an appealing selection of funky and fun home accessories and clothing. Another good stop is **Juwil By the Sea,** 33 Queen St. (© **902/275-4773**), an eclectic store of clothing, antiques, carpets, fine art, wood carvings, dolls, and pearl jewelry straight from China.

For an even slower pace, plan an excursion out to the **Tancook Islands** ★, a pair of lost-in-time islands with a couple hundred year-round residents. The islands, accessible via a short ferry ride, are good for walking the lanes and trails. There's a small cafe on Big Tancook, but little else to cater to travelers. Several ferry trips are scheduled daily between 6am and around 6pm. The ferry ties up on the island, however, so don't count on a last trip back to the mainland. Tickets are C$5 (US$3.10) round-trip, children under 12 go free.

In the evening, the intimate **Chester Playhouse,** 22 Pleasant St. (© **800/363-7529** or 902/275-3933), hosts plays, concerts, and other high-quality performances throughout the summer season. Tickets are usually C$17 (US$11) adult. Call for a schedule or reservations.

## WHERE TO STAY

**Graves Island Provincial Park** ★ (© **902/275-4425**) is 3km (1¾ miles) north of the village on Route 3. The 50ha (125-acre) estate-like park is one of the province's more elegant campgrounds, as befits moneyed Chester. The park has 73 sites, many dotting a high grassy bluff with views out to the spruce-clad islands of Mahone Bay. No hookups are available; the camping fee is C$14 (US$9) per night.

**Gray Gables** *Value* This spacious, modern Cape-Cod-style home north of the village (on the road to the provincial park) is tidy and trim in a Better Homes and Garden kind of way, with colonial reproduction furniture and great views of the bay from the wraparound porch. There's nothing rustic about it: the three guest rooms each have private bathrooms, and there's a sitting area with a television upstairs. Dutch innkeepers David and Jeanette Tomsett are quite helpful in directing you to activities in the area.

19 Graves Island Rd., East Chester, NS B0J 1J0. © **902/275-3983,** off-season 757/584-7506. 3 units. C$90 (US$56) double, including full breakfast. MC, V. **Amenities:** TV lounge; laundry. *In room:* VCR (some rooms).

**Haddon Hall** ★★ If there's no fog, Haddon Hall has the best view of any inn in Atlantic Canada, bar none. Perched atop an open hill with panoramic views of island-studded Mahone Bay, this very distinctive inn dates to 1905. It was built in what might be called "heroic Arts and Crafts" style. You'll recognize the bungalow form of the main house, but it's rendered in an outsized manner. Three stylish guest rooms are located in the main house; the remaining six are scattered in cottages around the property. Three rooms have wood fireplaces, four have Jacuzzis, several have kitchenettes; two plush suites, the Ohap and Sajoda, were renovated in 2001. The styling is eclectic—a woodstove and twig furniture mark the rustic log cabin, spare continental lines are featured in the main house—but everything is united by understated good taste. The inn's dining room is open April to mid-October, serving dinner nightly. Make reservations early, and ask for a table on the front porch with its sweeping vistas. The creative menu might include grilled lamb and papaya, or vegetable strudel with basil and feta.

67 Haddon Hill Rd., Chester NS B0J 1J0. © **902/275-3577.** Fax 902/275-5159. www.haddonhallinn.com. 9 units. C$150–C$400 (US$93–US$248) double, suites C$358–C$508 (US$222–US$315). Breakfast C$18 (US$11). DC, MC, V. **Amenities:** Restaurant (seasonal); outdoor pool; tennis court; boat tours; free bikes. *In room:* TV.

**Mecklenburgh Inn** *Value* This wonderfully funky and appealing inn, built around 1890, is located on a low hill in one of Chester's residential neighborhoods. The building is dominated by broad porches on the first and second floors, which invariably are populated with guests sitting and rocking and watching the town wander by. (Which it does: the post office is just next door.) Innkeeper Suzi Fraser has been running the place with casual bonhomie since the late 1980s, and she's a great breakfast cook to boot. Rooms are modern Victorian and generally quite bright. What's the catch? The four rooms share two hallway bathrooms, but guests often end up feeling like family, so it's usually not much of a bother.

78 Queen St., Chester, NS B0J 1J0. © **902/275-4638.** meckinn@auracom.com. 4 units (all share 2 bathrooms). C$65–C$85 (US$40–US$53) double, including full breakfast. AE, V. Closed Nov 1–June 1. Children 10 and up. *In room:* No phone.

### WHERE TO DINE

**Carta** GLOBAL Carta opened in 1999 in an odd sort of mini-mall hidden away in Chester's mini-downtown, and the proprietors did great and colorful things with their tiny space. They also concocted an appealing menu that's equally colorful and far-ranging, with offerings like a bento box, fish and chips, and green Thai curry; for more traditional appetites, they cooked big, meaty hamburgers. Now new owners, of Middle Eastern descent, have taken over and added their own Mediterranean cuisine as well. It's hard to conceive of any craving that won't be satisfied here.

54 Queen St. (behind Fiasco). © **902/275-5131.** Reservations helpful in summer. Main courses, C$5.95–C$13.95 (US$3.70–US$9). DC, MC, V. Tues–Sun 11:30am–10pm. Closed Jan–April.

## 7 Halifax: More Than a Natural Harbor ★★

Halifax's unusually pleasing harborside setting, now home to a city of some 115,000 (about three times as many in the greater metro area), first attracted Europeans in 1749, when Col. Edward Cornwallis established a military outpost here. (The site was named after George Montagu Dunk, 2nd Earl of Halifax. Residents tend to agree that it was a great stroke of luck that the city avoided the name Dunk, Nova Scotia.) The city plodded along as a colonial backwater for

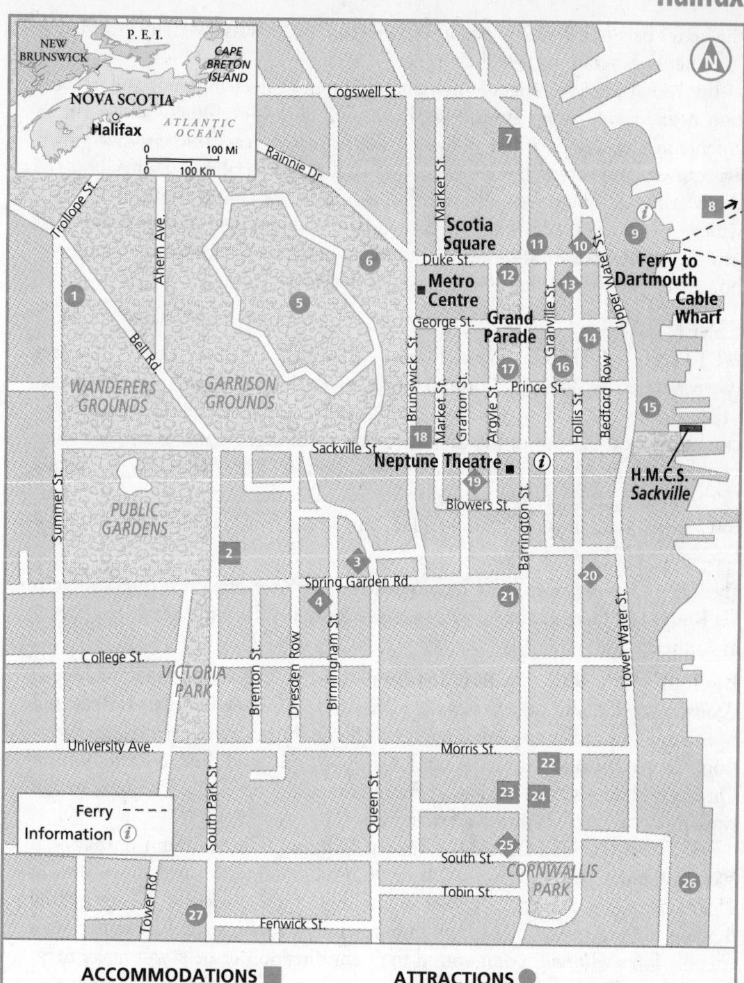


**ACCOMMODATIONS**

Cambridge Suites **19**
Delta Halifax **7**
Halliburton House Inn **23**
Halifax Heritage House Hostel **25**
Halifaxes Waverley Inn **24**
Lord Nelson Hotel and Suites **2**
Maranova Suites **8**

**DINING**

Cheapside Café **14**
deMaurizio **21**
Granite Brewery **25**
Il Mercato **3**
Maple **13**
Ryan Duffy's Steak and Seafood **4**
Satisfaction Feast **20**
Sweet Basil Bistro **10**

**ATTRACTIONS**

Art Gallery of Nova Scotia **14**
Barrington Place **11**
Halifax Citadel National Historic Park **5**
Historic Properties **9**
Maritime Museum of the Atlantic **15**
Nova Scotia Museum of National History **1**
Old Burying Ground **22**
Old City Hall **12**
Old Town Clock **6**
Pier 21 **21**
Point Pleasant Park **27**
Province House **16**
St. Paul's Church **17**

the better part of a century; one historian wrote that it was generally regarded as "a rather degenerate little seaport town."

But its natural advantages—including that well-protected harbor and its location near major fishing grounds and shipping lanes—eventually allowed it to emerge as a major port and military base. In recent years, the city has grown aggressively and carved out a niche as the vital commercial and financial hub of the Maritimes. The city is also home to a number of colleges and universities, which gives it a youthful, edgy air. Skateboards and bicycles often seem to be the vehicles of choice. In addition to the many attractions, downtown Halifax is home to a number of fine restaurants and hotels.

## ESSENTIALS

**GETTING THERE By Plane Halifax International Airport** (www.hiaa.ca) is 35km (21 miles) north of downtown Halifax in Elmsdale. (Take Route 102 to Exit 6.) Nova Scotia's notorious fogs make it advisable to call before heading out to the airport to reconfirm flight times. Airlines serving Halifax include **Air Canada** and **Air Nova** (both ✆ **888/AIR-CANA**). **Airbus** (✆ **902/873-2091**) offers frequent shuttles from the airport to major downtown hotels daily from 6:30am to 11:15pm. The rate is C$12 (US$7) one-way, C$20 (US$12) round-trip.

**By Car** Coming from New Brunswick and the west, the most direct route is via Route 102 from Truro; allow about 2 to 2½ hours from the provincial border at Amherst.

**By Rail VIA Rail** (✆ **800/561-3949** in the U.S. or 888/842-7245 in Canada; www.viarail.ca) offers train service 6 days a week between Halifax and Montréal. The entire trip takes between 18 and 21 hours, depending on direction. Stops include Moncton and Campbellton (and bus connections to Québec). Halifax's train station, at Barrington and Cornwallis Streets, is within walking distance of downtown attractions.

**VISITOR INFORMATION Tourist Offices** The **Halifax International Visitor Centre** (✆ **800/565-0000** or 902/490-5946) is located downtown at 1595 Barrington St., at the corner of Barrington and Sackville. It's open daily 8:30am to 9pm in summer (until 5pm in winter), it's huge, and it's staffed with friendly folks who will point you in the right direction or help you make room reservations. If you're on the waterfront, there's a helpful provincial center at **Red Store Visitor Information Centre** (✆ **902/424-4248**) at Historic Properties.

**Website** For information on the Web, visit **www.halifaxinfo.com**.

**GETTING AROUND** Parking in Halifax can be problematic. Long-term metered spaces are in high demand downtown, and many of the parking lots and garages fill up fast. If you're headed downtown for a brief visit, you can usually find a 2-hour meter. But if you're looking to spend a day, I'd suggest venturing out early to ensure a spot at a parking lot. The city's most extensive parking (fee charged) is available near Sackville Landing. Or try along Lower Water Street, south of the Maritime Museum of the Atlantic, where you can park all day for around C$6 (US$3.70).

**Metro Transit** (✆ **902/490-6600;** www.region.halifax.ns.ca/metrotransit/) operates buses throughout the city. Route and timetable information is also available at the information centers. Bus fare is C$1.65 (US$1) for adults and C$1.15 (US70¢) for seniors and children. Monday to Saturday throughout the summer a bright yellow bus named **Fred** (✆ **902/423-6658**) cruises a loop through the downtown, passing each stop about every 20 minutes. It's free. Stops include the Maritime Museum, the Grand Parade, and Barrington Place Shops. Request a schedule and map at the visitor center.

**SPECIAL EVENTS & FESTIVALS** The annual **Nova Scotia International Tattoo** (© **902/420-1114;** www.nstattoo.ca) features military and marching bands totaling some 2,000 plus military and civilian performers. This rousing event takes place over the course of a week in early July and is held indoors at the Halifax Metro Center. Tickets are C$12 to C$26 (US$8–US$17). The annual **Atlantic Jazz Festival Halifax** (© **902/492-2225;** www.jazzeast.com) has performances ranging from global and avant-garde to local and traditional music. Venues include area nightclubs and outdoor stages, and prices vary considerably.

In early August expect to see a profusion of street performers ranging from fire-eaters to comic jugglers. They descend on Halifax each summer for the 10-day **International Busker Festival** ★ (© **902/429-3910**). Performances take place along the waterfront walkway all day long and are often quite remarkable. The festival is free, with donations requested. Finally, the **Atlantic Film Festival** (© **902/465-2725;** www.atlanticfilm.com) offers screenings of more than 150 films in mid-September. The focus is largely on Canadian filmmaking, with an emphasis on independent productions and shorts. Panel discussions with industry players are also part of the festival. Most films cost about C$8 (US$5).

## EXPLORING HALIFAX

Halifax is fairly compact and easily reconnoitered on foot or by mass transportation. The major landmark is the Citadel—the stone fortress that looms over downtown from its grassy perch. From the ramparts, you can look into the windows of the tenth floor of downtown skyscrapers. The Citadel is only 9 blocks from the waterfront—albeit 9 sometimes steep blocks—and you can easily roam both areas in a day.

A lively neighborhood worth seeking out runs along Spring Garden Road, between the Public Gardens and the library (at Grafton St.). You'll find intriguing boutiques, bars, and restaurants along these 6 blocks, set amid a mildly Bohemian street scene. If you have strong legs and a stout constitution, you can start on the waterfront, stroll up and over the Citadel to descend to the Public Gardens, and then return via Spring Garden to downtown, perhaps enjoying a meal or two along the way.

### THE WATERFRONT ★

Halifax's rehabilitated waterfront is at its most inviting and vibrant between Sackville Landing (at the foot of Sackville St.) and the Sheraton Casino, near Purdy Wharf. (You could keep walking, but north of here the waterfront lapses into an agglomeration of charmless modern towers with sidewalk-level vents that assail the passersby with unusual odors.) On sunny summer afternoons, the waterfront is bustling with tourists enjoying the harbor, business-folks playing hooky while sneaking an ice cream cone, and baggy-panted skateboarders striving to stay out of trouble. Plan on about 2 to 3 hours to tour and gawk from end to end.

In addition to the other attractions listed below, the waterfront walkway is studded with small diversions, intriguing shops, take-out food emporia, and minor monuments. The waterfront's **shopping** core is located in and around the 3-block **Historic Properties,** near the Sheraton. These stout buildings of wood and stone are Canada's oldest surviving warehouses and were once the center of the city's booming shipping industry. Today, the historic architecture is stern enough to provide ballast for the somewhat precious boutiques and restaurants they now house. Especially appealing is the granite-and-ironstone Privateers' Warehouse, which dates to 1813.

A number of boat tours depart from the Halifax waterfront. You can browse the offerings on **Cable Wharf,** near the foot of George Street, where many tour boats are based. On-the-water adventures range from 1-hour harbor tours (about C$12/US$7) to 5-hour deep-sea fishing trips (about C$40/US$25). **Murphy's on the Water** (© **902/420-1015**) runs the most extensive tour operation, with three boats and a choice of tours, ranging from a cocktail sailing cruise to whale-watching to tours of historic McNab's Island, located near the mouth of the harbor (see below).

**Maritime Museum of the Atlantic** ★★ *Kids* All visitors to Nova Scotia owe themselves a stop at this standout museum on a prime waterfront location. The exhibits are involving and well executed, and you'll be astounded at how fast 2 hours can fly by. Visitors are greeted by a 3m (10-ft.) lighthouse lens from 1906, and then proceed through a parade of shipbuilding and sea-going eras. Visit the deckhouse of a coastal steamer (ca. 1940), or learn the colorful history of Samuel Cunard, a Nova Scotia native (born 1787) who founded the Cunard Steam Ship Co. to carry the royal mail and along the way established an ocean dynasty. Another highlight is the exhibit on the tragic Halifax Explosion of 1917, when two warships collided in Halifax harbor not far from the museum, detonating tons of TNT. More than 1,700 people died, and windows were shattered 100km (60 miles) away. But perhaps the most poignant exhibit is the lone deck chair from the *Titanic*—150 victims of the Titanic disaster are buried in Halifax, where rescue efforts were centered. Also memorable are the Age of Steam exhibit, Queen Victoria's barge, and the interesting new Shipwreck Treasures of Nova Scotia section with its stories and artifacts from more than a dozen local shipwrecks.

1675 Lower Water St. © **902/424-7490.** www.maritime.museum.gov.ns.ca. Admission charged May 1–Oct 15: C$6 (US$3.70) adult, C$5 (US$3.10) senior, C$2 (US$1.20) children, C$15 (US$9) family. Free admission Oct 16–May 31. May to Oct Mon–Sat 9:30am–5:30pm (until 8pm Tues), Sun 10:30am–5:30pm (opens at 1pm Sun May and Oct). Nov to April Tues–Sat 9:30am–5:30pm, Sun 1–5pm.

**C.S.S. Acadia** This unusually handsome 1913 vessel is part of the Maritime Museum ("our largest artifact"), but it can be viewed independently for a small fee. The Acadia was used by the Canadian government to chart the ocean floor for 56 years, until its retirement in 1969. Much of the ship is open for self-guided tours, including the captain's quarters, upper decks, wheelhouse, and oak-paneled chart room. If you want to see more of the ship, ask about the guided half-hour tours (four times daily), which offer access to the engine room and more.

On the water, in front of the Maritime Museum, 1675 Lower Water St. © **902/424-7490.** Free admission with museum ticket, or C$1 (US60¢) (can be applied to museum admission). Mon–Sat 9:30am–5:30pm, Sun 1–5:30pm. Closed mid-Oct to May 1.

**HMCS Sackville** This blue-and-white corvette (a speedy warship smaller than a destroyer) is tied up along a wood-planked wharf behind a small visitor center. There's a short multimedia presentation to provide some background. The ship is outfitted as it was in 1944, and it is now maintained as a memorial to the Canadians who served in World War II.

Lower Water St. (near the Maritime Museum). ✆ **902/429-5600** or 902/427-0550. Free admission. Open early June–early Sept, Mon–Sat 10am–5pm, Sun 1–5pm.

**Pier 21** ★ *Kids* Between 1928 and 1971 more than one million immigrants arrived in Canada by disembarking at Pier 21, Canada's version of New York's Ellis Island. In 1999 the pier was restored and reopened, filled with engaging interpretive exhibits, which aid visitors in vividly imagining the confusion and anxiety of the immigration experience. The pier is divided roughly into three sections, which recapture the boarding of the ship amid the cacophony of many languages, the Atlantic crossing (a 26-minute multimedia show recaptures the voyage in a ship-like theater), and the dispersal of the recent arrivals throughout Canada via passenger train.

1055 Marginal Rd. (on the waterfront behind the Westin Hotel). ✆ **902/425-7770.** Fax 902/423-4045. C$6.50 (US$4) adult, C$5.50 (US$3.40), seniors, C$3.50 (US$2.15) children 6–16, family C$15.50 (US$10). Daily mid-May to Oct 9am–5pm, Nov to mid-May Wed–Sun 9am–5pm.

## THE CITADEL & DOWNTOWN

Downtown Halifax cascades 9 blocks down a slope between the imposing stone Citadel and the waterfront. There's no fast-and-ready tour route; don't hesitate to follow your own desultory course, alternately ducking down quiet streets and striding along busy arteries. A good spot to regain your bearings periodically is the Grand Parade, where military recruits once practiced their drills. It's a lovely urban landscape—a broad terrace carved into the hill, presided over on either end by St. Paul's and City Hall.

**Halifax Citadel National Historic Site** ★★ Even if the stalwart stone fort weren't here, it would be worth the uphill trek for the astounding views alone. The panoramic sweep across downtown and the harbor finishes up with vistas out toward the broad Atlantic beyond. At any rate, an ascent makes it obvious why this spot was chosen for the harbor's most formidable defenses: There's simply no sneaking up on the place. Four forts have occupied the summit since Col. Edward Cornwallis was posted to the colony in 1749. The Citadel has been restored to look much as it did in 1856, when the fourth fort was built out of concern over bellicose Americans. The fort has never been attacked.

The site is impressive to say the least: sturdy granite walls topped by grassy embankments form a rough star; in the sprawling gravel and cobblestone courtyard you'll find convincingly costumed interpreters in kilts and bearskin hats marching in unison, playing bagpipes, and firing the noon cannon. The former barracks and other chambers are home to exhibits about life at the fort. If you still have questions, stop a soldier, bagpiper, or washerwoman and ask.

Citadel Hill. ✆ **902/426-5080.** Admission June to mid-Sept C$6 (US$3.70) adult, C$4.50 (US$2.80) senior, C$3 (US$1.85) youth (6–16), C$14.75 (US$9) family. Rest of the year, C$3.75 (US$2.30) adult, C$2.75 (US$1.70) senior, C$2 (US$1.20) youth (6–16), C$9.50 (US$6) family. July–Aug 9am–6pm; Sept–July 9am–5pm. Limited parking at site C$2.75 (US$1.70); no guides in fall or winter.

**Art Gallery of Nova Scotia** Located in a pair of sandstone buildings between the waterfront and the Grand Parade, the Art Gallery is arguably the premier gallery in the Maritimes, with a focus on local and regional art. You'll also find a selection of other works by Canadian, British, and European artists, with a well-chosen selection of folk and Inuit art. In 1998 the gallery expanded to include the Provincial Building next door, where the entire house (it's tiny) of Nova Scotian folk artist Maud Lewis has been reassembled and is on display. The museum can be comfortably perused in 60 to 90 minutes.

1723 Hollis St. (at Cheapside). ✆ **902/424-7542.** www.agns.gov.ns.ca. Admission C$5 (US$3.10) adults, C$4 (US$2.50) seniors, C$2 (US$1.20) students, C$8 (US$5) family. Tues–Fri 10am–6pm, Sat and Sun noon–5pm.

**Province House** Canada's oldest seat of government, Province House has been home to the Nova Scotian legislature since 1819. This exceptional Georgian building is a superb example of the rigorously symmetrical Palladian style. And like a jewel box, its dour stone exterior hides gems of ornamental detailing and artwork inside; note especially the fine plasterwork, rare for a Canadian building of this era. A well-written free booklet is available when you enter, and provides helpful background about the building's history and architecture. If the legislature is in session, you can obtain a visitor's pass and sit up in the gallery and watch the business of the province take place.

Hollis St. (near Prince St.). ✆ **902/424-4661.** Free admission. July and August Mon–Fri 9am–5pm; Sat, Sun, and holidays 10am–4pm. Rest of year Mon–Fri 9am–4pm.

**Nova Scotia Museum of Natural History** Situated on the far side of the Citadel from downtown, this modern, mid-size museum offers a good introduction to the flora and fauna of Nova Scotia. Galleries include geology, botany, mammals, and birds, plus exhibits of archaeology and Mi'kmaq culture.

1747 Summer St. ✆ **902/424-7353.** www.museum.gov.ns.ca. C$4 (US$2.50) adult, C$3.50 (US$2.15) senior, C$2 (US$1.20) children 6 and up, C$8 (US$5) family, free Wed nights. June to mid-Oct Mon–Sat 9:30am–5:30pm (until 8pm Wed), Sun 1–5:30pm; mid-Oct to May Tues–Sat 9:30am–5pm (until 8pm Wed), Sun 1–5pm.

**St. Paul's Church** ★ Forming one end of the Grand Parade, St. Paul's was the first Anglican cathedral established outside of England and is Canada's oldest Protestant place of worship. Part of the building, which dates from 1750, was fabricated in Boston and erected in Halifax with the help of a royal endowment from King George II. A classic white Georgian building, St. Paul's has fine stained-glass windows. A piece of flying debris from the explosion of 1917 (see Maritime Museum of the Atlantic, above) is lodged in the wall over the doors to the nave.

1749 Argyle St. (on the Grand Parade near Barrington St.). ✆ **902/429-2240.** Mon–Sat 9am–6pm; Sun services 8, 9:15, and 11am. Free guided tours Mon–Sat from June–Aug.

## GARDENS & OPEN SPACE

**Fairview Lawn Cemetery** ★ When the *Titanic* went down on April 15, 1912, nearly 2,000 people died. Ship captains from Halifax were recruited to help retrieve the corpses (you'll learn about this grim episode at the Maritime Museum). Some 121 victims, mostly crew members, were buried at this quiet cemetery located a short drive north of downtown Halifax. Some of the simple graves have names; others just numbers. Interpretive signs highlight some of the stories that survived the tragedy. A brochure with driving directions to this and two other *Titanic* cemeteries may be found at the Maritime Museum and visitor information centers.

Chisholm Ave. off Connaught Ave. ✆ **902/490-4883.** Open daylight hours year-round.

**Public Gardens** ★★ *Kids* The Public Gardens literally took seed in 1753, when they were founded as a private garden. It was acquired by the Nova Scotia Horticultural Society in 1836, and it assumed its present look in 1875, during the peak of the Victorian era. As such, the garden is one of the nation's Victorian masterpieces, more rare and evocative than any mansard-roofed mansion. You'll find wonderful examples of many of last century's dominant trends in outdoor

## A Side Trip to Peggy's Cove ★★

About 43km (26 miles) southwest of Halifax is the picturesque fishing village of Peggy's Cove (pop. 120). The village offers a postcard-perfect tableau: an octagonal lighthouse (surely one of the most photographed in the world), tiny fishing shacks, and graceful fishing boats bobbing in the postage-stamp-size harbor. The bonsai-like perfection hasn't gone unnoticed by the big tour operators, however, so it's a rare summer day when you're not sharing the experience with a few hundred of your close, personal, bus-tour friends. The village is home to a handful of B&Bs, boutiques (Wood 'n' Wool, The Christmas Shoppe), and a gallery, but scenic values draw the day-trippers with cameras and lots of film. While there, make sure to check out the touching **Swissair Flight 111 Memorial** ★ among the rocks just before the turnoff to the cove; this site memorializes the passengers of that flight, which crashed into the Atlantic just off this coast. For more information, visit **www.peggyscove.ca.**

landscaping, from the "natural" winding walks and ornate fountains to the duck ponds and fussy Victorian bandstand. (Stop by at 2pm on Sundays in summer for a free concert.) There are lots of leafy trees, lush lawns, cranky ducks who have long since lost their fear of humans, and tiny ponds. The overseers have been commendably stingy with memorial statues and plaques. You'll usually find dowagers and kids feeding pigeons, and smartly uniformed guards slowly walking the grounds.

Spring Garden and South Park St. Free admission. Spring to late fall 8am–dusk.

**Point Pleasant Park** ★ Point Pleasant is one of Canada's finer urban parks, and there's no better place for a walk along the water on a balmy day. This 75ha (186-acre) park occupies a wooded peninsular point, and it served for years as one of the linchpins in the city's military defense. You'll find the ruins of early forts and a nicely preserved Martello Tower. You'll also find a lovely gravel carriage road around the point, a small swimming beach, miles of walking trails, and groves of graceful fir trees. The park is located about 2km (1½ miles) south of the Public Gardens. No bikes are allowed on weekends or holidays.

Point Pleasant Dr. (south end of Halifax; head south on South Park St. near Public Gardens and continue on Young). Free admission. Open during daylight hours.

## WHERE TO STAY

### EXPENSIVE

**Cambridge Suites** ★ *Kids* The attractive, modern Cambridge Suites is nicely located near the foot of the Citadel and is well positioned for exploring Halifax. It's perfect for families—40 of the units are two-room suites featuring kitchenettes with microwaves. Expect comfortable, inoffensive decor, and above-average service; everything in the place was freshened up in 2001, too. Dofsky's Grill on the first floor is open for all three meals, which are palatable if not exciting. Look for pasta, blackened haddock, burgers, and jerked chicken.

1583 Brunswick St., Halifax, NS B3J 3P5. ✆ **888/417-8483** or 902/420-0555. Fax 902/420-9379. www.cambridgesuiteshotel.com. 200 units. C$129–C$189 (US$80–US$117). Children under 18 free with parents.

AE, DC, MC, V. Parking C$11 (US$7). **Amenities:** Restaurant, bar; fitness center with whirlpool, sauna, weights, and exercise bikes; rooftop sun deck with barbecue grill; concierge; room service; babysitting; self-service laundry; dry cleaning. *In room:* A/C, TV, minibar, coffeemaker, hair dryer.

**Delta Halifax** ★ The Delta Halifax (formerly the Hotel Halifax, more formerly the Chateau Halifax) is a slick and modern (built in 1972) downtown hotel that offers premium service. It's located just a block off the waterfront, to which it's connected via skyway, but navigating it involves an annoying labyrinth of parking garages and charmless concrete structures. The lobby is street-side; guests take elevators up above a six-floor parking garage to reach their rooms. The hotel is frequented largely by business travelers during the week. Ask for a room in the so-called "resort wing" near the pool, which feels a bit further away from the chatter of downtown and the press of business. A number of rooms have balconies and many have harbor views; ask when you book. Rooms are in two classes—either 300 or 500 square feet—and all are furnished simply and unexceptionably with standard-issue hotel furniture. The Crown Bistrot restaurant offers informal continental cuisine, while the Sam Slick Lounge next door is "cigar friendly."

1990 Barrington St., Halifax, NS B3J 1P2. ✆ **800/268-1133** or 902/425-6700. Fax 902/425-6214. www.deltahotels.com. 296 units. C$129–C$200 (US$80–US$124) double. AE, MC, V. Parking C$18.95/US$12 (valet), C$15.95/US$9 (self). **Amenities:** Restaurant, bar; fitness center with indoor pool, sun deck, sauna, and whirlpool; concierge; shopping arcade; car-rental desk; limited room service; babysitting; laundry; dry cleaning. *In room:* A/C, TV, minibar, coffeemaker, hair dryer.

**Halliburton House Inn** ★ The Halliburton House is a well-appointed, well-run, and elegant country inn located in the heart of downtown. Named after former resident Sir Brenton Halliburton (Nova Scotia's first chief justice), the inn is spread among three town house-style buildings, connected via gardens and sun decks in the rear but not internally. The main building was constructed in 1809 and was converted to an inn in 1995, when it was modernized without any loss of its native charm. Guest rooms are subtly furnished with fine antiques. Some have fireplaces and Jacuzzis. Among my favorites: Room 113, which is relatively small but has a lovely working fireplace and unique skylighted bathroom. Rooms 102 and 109 are both suites with wet bars and fireplaces; there's also one studio apartment. Halliburton is popular with business travelers, but it's also a romantic spot for couples. The intimate first-floor dining room, which serves from 5:30pm nightly, is dusky and wonderful with a menu that's small and inventive. The seafood is always reliable.

5184 Morris St., Halifax, NS B3J 1B3. ✆ **902/420-0658.** Fax 902/423-2324. www.halliburton.ns.ca. 29 units. C$135–C$325 (US$84–US$202) double and suite, including continental breakfast and parking (limited), off-season rates C$100–C$250 (US$62–US$155). AE, MC, V. **Amenities:** Restaurant; room service; babysitting; dry cleaning. *In room:* A/C, TV, hair dryer.

**The Lord Nelson Hotel and Suites** ★★ The Lord Nelson was built in 1928, and was for years the city's preeminent hostelry. It gradually sank in esteem and eventually ended up as a flophouse. In 1998 it was purchased and received a long-overdue top-to-bottom renovation. Today, it's back near the top of the heap as one of the city's better hotels. For starters, it has location: it's right across from the lovely Public Gardens, and abuts lively Spring Garden Road. The standard rooms are furnished with Georgian reproductions; some 40 have kitchenettes, and more than 100 have fax machines. The business-class Flagship Rooms also feature desks, chairs, robes, morning newspapers, ironing boards, and free local phone calls. The hotel charges a C$15 to C$20 (US$9–US$12) premium for a room that faces the street or the gardens. It's worth it: the others face into the rather bleak courtyard filled with service equipment.

The Victory Arms is a cozy and convincing English-style pub located off the handsome coffered lobby. There's British pub fare like steak and kidney pie, fish and chips, and liver with bacon and onions, along with a daily roast.

1515 South Park St., Halifax, NS B3J 2L2. ✆ **800/565-2020** or 902/423-6331. Fax 902/491-6148. www.lordnelsonhotel.com. 243 units. C$149–C$219 (US$92–US$136) peak season, C$99–C$114 (US$61–US$71) off-peak. Parking C$7 (US$4.35) per day. AE, DC, DISC, MC, V. Pets allowed with C$100 (US$62) deposit. **Amenities:** Restaurant, bar; fitness room; sauna; concierge; limited room service; babysitting; coin-op washers and dryers; dry cleaning. *In room:* A/C, TV.

## MODERATE

**Halifax's Waverley Inn** ★ The Waverley is adorned in high Victorian style, as befits its 1866 provenance. Flamboyant playwright Oscar Wilde was a guest in 1882, and one suspects he had a hand in the decorating scheme. There's walnut trim, red upholstered furniture, and portraits of sourpuss Victorians at every turn. The headboards in the guest rooms are especially elaborate—some look like props from Gothic horror movies. Room 130 has a unique Chinese wedding bed and a Jacuzzi (nine rooms have private Jacuzzis). Newly added is a two-bedroom suite in an annex; with its own kitchen and laundry, it's good for families or extended stays. There's a common deck on which to enjoy sunny afternoons; a first-floor hospitality room stocks complimentary snacks and beverages.

1266 Barrington St., Halifax, NS B3J 1Y5. ✆ **800/565-9346** or 902/423-9346. Fax 902/425-0167. www.waverleyinn.com. 32 units. June–Oct C$99–C$259 (US$61–US$161), Nov–May C$79–C$209 (US$49–US$130). Rates include continental breakfast and parking. DC, MC, V. *In room:* A/C, TV.

**Maranova Suites** *Value* *Kids* Located across the harbor from Halifax and a 2-minute walk to frequent ferry service to downtown, the Maranova Suites is one of the better options for travelers on a ginger-ale budget. Housed in a modern concrete building, it features rooms that are large and tidy. Guest rooms have sitting areas, kitchenettes, and balconies, and two penthouse suites come with full kitchens. Don't expect anything fancy; the rooms are basic, simple, and clean. Some have wonderful views of the harbor—ask when you book.

65 King St., Dartmouth, NS B2Y 4C2. ✆ **888/798-5558** or 902/463-9520. Fax 902/463-2631. maranova@istar.ca. 35 units. C$77–C$215 (US$48–US$133) double. AE, DC, MC, V. Underground parking available. **Amenities:** Restaurant; access to fitness center; coin-op washers and dryers; dry cleaning. *In room:* A/C, TV, kitchenettes, iron.

## INEXPENSIVE

**The Halifax Heritage House Hostel,** 1253 Barrington St. (✆ **902/422-3863**), is within walking distance of downtown attractions. You'll usually share rooms with other travelers (several private and family rooms are available); there are lockers in each room, shared bathrooms, and a shared, fully equipped kitchen. Rates are C$22 (US$14) per person in dormitories, C$40 (US$25) for a double bed in a private room.

A short way from downtown but convenient to bus lines are university dorm rooms open to travelers during the summer, when school isn't in session. **Dalhousie University** (✆ **902/494-8840**) has one-, two- and three-bedroom units furnished with plain single beds, many with private bathrooms and kitchenettes (you rent the dishes for a small fee). Single rooms go for C$38 (US$24), two-bedroom units for C$57 (US$35), and three-bedroom units are C$55 to C$78 (US$34–US$48).

## WHERE TO DINE

### EXPENSIVE

**daMaurizio** ★★★ ITALIAN Possibly Halifax's best restaurant, daMaurizio does everything right. Located in a cleverly adapted former brewery, the vast space has been divided into a complex of hives with columns and exposed brick that add to the atmosphere and heighten the anticipation of the meal. The decor shuns decorative doodads for clean lines and simple class. Much the same might be said of the menu. You could start with an appetizer of squid quick-fried with olive oil, tomato, and chiles or order ravioli with sausage. The main courses tax even the most decisive of diners: There's veal scaloppine with lobster, cream and tomato, roasted duck with cherries, honey and Grand Marnier, and grilled rack of lamb, among many other inspired choices. Desserts run beyond tiramisu and gelati to panetto cake, panna cotta, and a fruit, nut and cheese plate. The kitchen doesn't try to dazzle with creativity but relies instead on the best ingredients and a close eye on perfect preparation.

1496 Lower Water St. (in The Brewery). ✆ **902/423-0859.** Reservations highly recommended. Main courses C$24.95–C$29.95 (US$15–US$19), pasta dishes C$10.95–C$16.95 (US$7–US$11). AE, DC, MC, V. Mon–Sat 5:30–10pm.

**Maple** ★★★ NOUVEAU CANADIAN New chef Kevin Ouellette has brought his talents to this, one of Halifax's top restaurants. It's located on three levels, with the open kitchen center stage on the middle level; the menu changes seasonally, but diners can always rely on such favorites as beef tenderloin with oxtail gravy, sautéed onions and Portobello mushrooms, crisp-skinned salmon with grapefruit tarragon vinaigrette and market vegetables, and lobster ravioli served carrot lobster sauce and crispy dulse.

1813 Granville St., ✆ **902/425-9100.** Reservations recommended. Main courses, lunch C$9–C$15 (US$6–US$9), dinner C$23–C$30 (US$14–US$19). AE, DC, MC, V. Mon–Fri 11:30am–2pm, daily 5:30–11pm.

### MODERATE

**Ryan Duffy's Steak and Seafood** ★ STEAKHOUSE Located on the upper level of a small shopping mall on Spring Garden, Ryan Duffy's may at first strike diners as a knockoff of a middle-brow chain, like T.G.I. Friday's. It's not. It's a couple of notches above. The house specialty is steak, for which the place is justly famous. The beef comes from corn-fed Hereford, Black Angus, and Shorthorn, and it is nicely tender. Steaks are grilled over a natural wood charcoal and can be prepared with garlic, cilantro butter, or other extras upon request. The more expensive cuts, such as the striploin, are trimmed right at the table. If you move away from steak on the menu, expect less consistency—the shrimp cocktail is disappointing; the Caesar salad is wonderful. Americans who are disappointed that they can't order rare steak much anymore owing to liability concerns will like it here—you can even order it "blue-rare."

5640 Spring Garden Rd. ✆ **902/421-1116.** Reservations helpful. Main courses, lunch C$9–C$15 (US$6–US$9), dinner C$15.95–C$27.50 (US$10–US$17). AE, DC, MC, V. Dining room: Mon–Wed 11:30am–10pm, Thurs–Sat 11:30am–midnight, Sun 5–11pm.

**Sweet Basil Bistro** UPMARKET PASTA If hunger overtakes you while you're snooping around the waterfront's shopping district, this should be your destination. It has the casual feel of a favorite trattoria, but the menu transcends the limited regional offerings that implies. Pastas are well represented (especially good is the squash ravioli with Parmesan and hazelnut sauce), but you'll also find seared scallops with five-spice broth and Asian vegetables, crusted lamb chops with a demi glace, and a selection of stir-fries.

1866 Upper Water St. ✆ **902/425-2133.** Reservations recommended. Sandwiches C$8–C$15 (US$5–US$9); main courses C$10–C$19 (US$6–US$12). AE, DC, MC, V. Daily 11:30am–9:30pm.

## INEXPENSIVE

**Cheapside Café** *Value* *Kids* CAFE The cheerful and lively Cheapside Café is tucked inside the Provincial Building, one of two structures housing the Art Gallery of Nova Scotia. A whole groaning board of sandwiches and other delectables features choices like chicken breast with avocado and mango chutney, roast beef with fried onions, and smoked salmon served with an egg pancake and asparagus. Other fare includes fish cakes, quiche, and poached salmon with sun-dried tomato chutney. For kids, there's peanut butter and jelly and egg salad with carrot sticks. Desserts are delicious—especially notable is the Cheapside Café Torte.

1723 Hollis St. (inside the Art Gallery of Nova Scotia). ✆ **902/425-4494.** Sandwiches and entrees C$8.95–C$10.95 (US$6–US$7). MC, V. Tues–Sat 10am–5pm, Sun noon–5pm.

**Granite Brewery** ★ BREWPUB Eastern Canada's pioneer brewpub—this was the first—is housed in an austere building far down Barrington Street. The starkly handsome 1834 stone building has a medium-fancy dining room upstairs with red tablecloths and captain's chairs. (The pub downstairs is more boisterous and informal.) You can order off the same menu at either spot, and it's what you'd expect at a brewpub, only better-tasting: Entrees include beer-battered fish, steak sandwiches, an excellent smoked salmon club sandwich, burgers, beef-and-beer stew, salads, and meat loaf. The beer here is fresh and good; they also do Sunday brunches.

1222 Barrington St. ✆ **902/423-5660.** www.granitebrewery.ca. Reservations usually not needed. Main courses C$7–C$14 (US$4.35–US$9). AE, DC, MC, V. Mon–Sat 11:30am–12:30am, Sun noon–11pm.

**Il Mercato** ★ NORTHERN ITALIAN Light-colored Tuscan sponged walls and big rustic terra-cotta tiles on the floor set an appropriate mood at this popular spot amid the clamor of Spring Garden. Come early or late or expect to wait a bit (no reservations accepted), but it's worth making the effort. You'll find a great selection of meals at prices that approach bargain level. Start by selecting antipasti from the deli-counter in the front (you point; the waitstaff will bring them to your table). The focaccias are superb and come with a pleasing salad, while the ravioli with roast chicken and wild mushrooms is sublime. Non-Italian entrees include a seafood medley and grilled striploin with wild mushroom sauce. For dessert, repeat the antipasto routine: head to the counter and ogle the luscious offerings under glass, then point and sit, awaiting a fine gelato finale. If you are just passing by, order a cone or dish to go.

5475 Spring Garden Rd. ✆ **902/422-2866.** Reservations not accepted. Main courses C$10–C$17 (US$6–US$11). AE, DC, MC, V. Mon–Sat 11am–11pm.

**Satisfaction Feast** VEGETARIAN Located along the newly cool stretch of Grafton Street, Satisfaction Feast is Halifax's original vegetarian restaurant (it turned 20 in 2001), has been voted one of the top 10 veggie restaurants in Canada by the *Globe and Mail.* It's funky and fun, with a certain spare grace inside and a canopy and sidewalk tables for summer lounging. Entrees include lasagna, bean burritos, pesto pasta, veggie burgers, and a macrobiotic rice casserole. There's also "neatloaf" and tofu-and-rice based "peace burgers" for those who like their food with cute names. The vegan fruit crisp is the dessert to hold out for. They also do take-out; consider a hummus-and-pita picnic atop nearby Citadel Hill.

1581 Grafton St. ✆ **902/422-3540.** Main courses C$5–C$12 (US$3.10–US$7). AE, DC, MC, V. Daily 11am–10pm (until 8:30 or 9pm in winter).

## HALIFAX BY NIGHT

**THE PERFORMING ARTS** **Shakespeare by the Sea** (✆ **888/759-1516** or 902/422-0295) stages a whole line of Bardic and non-Bardic productions July to August at several alfresco venues around the city. Most are held at Point Pleasant Park, where the ruins of old forts and buildings are used as the stage settings for delightful performances, with the audience sprawled on the grass, many enjoying picnic dinners. Most shows ask for a suggested donation of C$8 (US$5). The more elaborate productions (past shows have included *King Lear* at the Citadel and *Titus Andronicus* at the park's Martello Tower) have limited seating, with tickets ranging from C$25 to C$27 (US$16–US$17).

The **Neptune Theatre,** 1593 Argyle St. (✆ **902/429-7070**), benefited from a C$13.5 million renovation and now also includes an intimate 200-seat studio theater. Top-notch dramatic productions are offered throughout the year. (The main season runs Oct–May, with a summer season filling in the gap with eclectic performances.) Main-stage tickets range from C$15 to C$35 (US$9–US$22).

**THE CLUB & BAR SCENE** The young and restless tend to congregate in pubs, in nightclubs, and at street corners along two axes that converge at the public library: **Grafton Street** and **Spring Garden Road.** If you're thirsty, wander the neighborhoods around here, and you're likely to find a spot that could serve as a temporary home for the evening.

In the evening there's usually lively Maritime music and good beer at the **Lower Deck** (✆ **902/425-1501**), one of the popular restaurants in the Historic Properties complex on the waterfront. There's music nightly at 9:30pm, and late afternoons on Saturdays. Among the clubs offering local rock, ska, and the like are **The Marquee Club,** 2037 Gottingen St. (✆ **902-429-3020**), and **The Attic,** 1741 Grafton St. (✆ **902/423-0909**).

Check *The Coast,* Halifax's free weekly newspaper (widely available), for listings of upcoming performances.

# 8 The Eastern Shore: Rugged Coastline from Halifax to Cape Breton Island

Heading from Halifax toward Cape Breton Island (or vice versa), you have to choose between two basic routes. If you're burning to get to your destination, take the main roads of Route 102 connecting to Route 104 (the Trans-Canada Highway). If you're in no particular hurry and are most content venturing down narrow lanes, destination unknown, by all means allow a couple of days to wind along the Eastern Shore, mostly along Route 7. Along the way you'll be rewarded with glimpses of a rugged coastline that's wilder and more remote than the coast south of Halifax. Communities tend to be farther apart, less genteel, and those that you come upon have fewer services and fewer tourists. With its rugged terrain and remote locales, this region is a good bet for those drawn to the outdoors and seeking coastal solitude.

## ESSENTIALS

**GETTING THERE** Route 107 and Route 7 run along or near the coast from Dartmouth to Stillwater (near Sherbrooke). A patchwork of other routes—including 211, 316, 16, and 344—continues onward along the coast to the causeway to Cape Breton. (It's all pretty obvious on a map.) An excursion along the entire coastal route—from Dartmouth to Cape Breton Island with a detour to Canso—is 422km (253 miles).

**VISITOR INFORMATION** Several tourist information centers are staffed along the route. You'll find the best-stocked and most-helpful centers at **Sheet Harbour,** next to the waterfall (✆ **902/885-2595;** open daily in summer 10am–7pm); **Sherbrooke Village,** at the museum (✆ 902/522-2400), open daily in summer 9:30am to 5:30pm); and **Canso,** 1297 Union St. (✆ **902/366-2170**), open daily in summer 9am–6pm).

## EXPLORING THE EASTERN SHORE

This section assumes travel northeastward from Halifax toward Cape Breton. If you're traveling the opposite direction, hold this book upside down (just kidding).

Between Halifax and Sheet Harbour the route plays hide-and-seek with the coast, touching the water periodically before veering inland. The most scenic areas are around wild and open **Ship Harbour,** as well as **Spry Harbour,** noted for its attractive older homes and islands looming offshore.

Between Ship and Spry Harbours is the town of Tangier, home to **Coastal Adventures** (✆ **902/772-2774**), which specializes in kayak tours. It's run by Scott Cunningham, who literally wrote the book on Nova Scotia kayaking (he's the author of the definitive guide to paddling the coast). This well-run operation is situated on a beautiful island-dotted part of the coast, but it specializes in multi-day trips throughout Atlantic Canada. You're best off writing (P.O. Box 77, Tangier, NS B0J 3H0) or calling for a brochure well in advance of your trip.

There's also a terrific little fish-smoking business just outside Tangier, **Willie Krauch & Sons Smokehouse** ★ (✆ **800/758-4412** or 902/772-2188). Krauch (pronounced "craw") and family sell wood-smoked Atlantic salmon, mackerel, and eel in an unpretentious little store; they'll also give you a tour of the premises, if you like, where you can check out the old-style smoking process in action. Take some to go for a picnic.

Adjacent to the well-marked Liscomb Lodge (see below), and just over the main bridge, is the **Liscomb River Trail** system. Trails follow the river both north and south of Route 7. The main hiking trail follows the river upstream for 5km (3 miles), crosses it on a suspension bridge, and then returns on the other side. The Mayflower Point Trail follows the river southward toward the coast, then loops back inland.

Continuing on Route 211 beyond historic **Sherbrooke Village** (below), you'll drive through a wonderful landscape of lakes, ocean inlets, and upland bogs and soon come to the scenic **Country Harbour Ferry.** The 12-car cable ferry crosses each direction every half hour; it's a picturesque crossing of a broad river encased by rounded and wooded bluffs. The fare is C$1.75 (US$1.10) per car, which includes driver and passengers. The ferry isn't always running, so it's wise to check at the Canso or Sherbrooke visitor centers before detouring down this way.

Further along (you'll be on Route 316 after the ferry), you'll come to **Tor Bay Provincial Park.** It's 4km (2½ miles) off the main road, but well worth the detour on a sunny day. The park features three sandy, crescent beaches backed by grassy dunes and small ponds that are slowly being taken over by bog and spruce forest. The short boardwalk loop is especially picturesque.

Way out on the eastern tip of Nova Scotia's mainland is the end-of-the-world town of **Canso** (pop. 1,200). It's a rough-edged fishing and oil-shipping town, often windswept and foggy. (If you're coming to Canso in summer, watch out for the annual folk music festival created to honor Nova Scotia's own Stan Rogers.) The chief attraction here is **Grassy Island National Historic Site** (**© 902/366-3136**). First stop by the small interpretive center on the waterfront and ask about the boat schedule. A park-run boat will take you out to the island, which once housed a bustling community of fishermen and traders from New England. The boat serves the island from May to mid-August from 10am to 6pm daily. Fares are C$2.25 (US$1.40) adult, C$1.75 (US$1.10) seniors, and C$1.25 (US80¢) children 6 to 16.

**Sherbrooke Village** ★ *Kids* About half of the town of Sherbrooke comprises Sherbrooke Village, a historic section surrounded by low fences, water, and fields. (It's managed as part of the Nova Scotia Museum.) You'll have to pay admission to wander around, but the price is well worth it. This is the largest restored village in Nova Scotia. Some 25 buildings have been restored and opened to the public, ranging from a convincing general store to the operating blacksmith shop and post office. Look also for the temperance hall, courthouse, printery, boat-building shop, drugstore, and schoolhouse. These are staffed by genial, costumed interpreters, who can tell you about life in the 1860s. Be sure to ask about the source of the town's early prosperity. The village is unique in several respects. Almost all of the buildings are on their original sites (only two have been moved), many homes are still occupied by local residents, and private homes are interspersed with the buildings open to visitors. The church is still used for services on Sundays, and you can order a meal at the old Sherbrooke Hotel. (The fish cakes and oven-baked beans are good.)

Route 7, Sherbrooke. **© 902/522-2400.** Admission C$7.25 (US$4.50) adult, C$6 (US$3.70) senior, C$3.75 (US$2.30) child, C$21 (US$13) family. Daily 9:30am–5:30pm. Closed mid-Oct to June 1.

## WHERE TO STAY & DINE

Other than a handful of motels and B&Bs, few accommodations are available on the Eastern Shore.

**Liscombe Lodge** ★★ This modern complex, owned and operated by the province, consists of a central lodge and a series of smaller cottages and outbuildings. It's situated in a remote part of the coast, adjacent to hiking trails and a popular boating area at the mouth of the Liscomb River. The lodge bills itself as "the nature lover's resort," and indeed it offers good access to both forest and water. But it's not exactly rustic, with well-tended lawns, bland modern architecture, shuffleboard, a marina, and even an oversize outdoor chessboard. (It's a popular stop for bus tours.) Rooms are modern and motel-like; cottages and chalets have multiple bedrooms and are good for families. The dining room serves resort fare.

Route 7, Liscomb Mills, NS B0J 2A0. **© 877/375-6343** or 902/779-2307. Fax 902/779-2700. 65 units. C$135–C$145 (US$84–US$90) double, suite C$199 (US$123); inquire about packages. AE, DISC, MC, V. Pets allowed in chalets. **Amenities:** Restaurant; indoor pool; fitness center; tennis court; shuffleboard; free bikes; room service; laundry. *In room:* TV, hair dryer, iron.

**Seawind Landing Country Inn** ★ What to do when your boat-building business plummets as the fisheries decline? How about opening an inn? That's what Lorraine and Jim Colvin did, and their 8ha (20-acre) oceanfront compound is delightful and inviting. Half of the guest rooms are in the 130-year-old main house, which has been tastefully modernized and updated. The others are in a more recent outbuilding—what you lose in historic charm, you make up for in brightness, ocean views, and double Jacuzzis. The innkeepers are especially knowledgeable about local artists (much of the work on display here was produced nearby), and they have compiled an unusually literate and helpful guide to the region for guests to peruse. The property has three private sand beaches, and coastal boat tours and picnic lunches can be easily arranged. The inn also serves dinner nightly (inn guests only), featuring local products prepared in a country-French style.

1 Wharf Rd., Charlos Cove, NS B0H 1T0. © 800/563-4667. Fax 902/525-2108. www.seawind.ns.ca. 13 units. C$80–C$120 (US$53–US$80). AE, MC, V. **Amenities:** Beach; laundry service. *In room:* Hair dryer, Jacuzzi (some rooms).

## 9 Cape Breton Island ★★★

Isolated and craggy Cape Breton Island—Nova Scotia's northernmost land mass—should be high on the list of don't-miss destinations for travelers, especially those with an adventurous bent. The island's chief draw is **Cape Breton Highlands National Park,** far north on the island's western lobe. But there's also the historic fort at Louisbourg and scenic Bras d'Or Lake, the inland saltwater lake that nearly cleaves the island in two. Above all, there are the picturesque drives. It's hard to find a road that's not a scenic route in Cape Breton. By turns the vistas are wild and dramatic, then settled and pastoral.

When traveling on the island, be alert to the cultural richness. Just as southern Nova Scotia was largely settled by English Loyalists fleeing the United States after they lost the War of Independence, Cape Breton was principally settled by Highland Scots whose families had come out on the wrong side of rebellions against the Crown. You can still see that heritage in the accents of elders in some of the more remote villages, and in the great popularity of Scottish-style folk music.

You'll often hear references to the **Cabot Trail** ★★★ when on the island. This is the official designation for the 300km (185-mile) roadway around the northwest part of the island, which encompasses the national park. It's named after John Cabot, who many believe first set foot on North American soil near Cape North. (Many disagree, however, especially those in Newfoundland.)

*Note:* we've divided Cape Breton into two sections: Cape Breton Island and Cape Breton Highlands National Park. Jump ahead to the next section for information on adventures in the park itself.

### ESSENTIALS

**GETTING THERE** Cape Breton is connected to the mainland via the Canso Causeway, which is a 24m (80 ft.) wide, 66m (217 ft.) deep, and 1,300m (4,300 ft.) long. It was built in 1955 with 10 million tons of rock. (You can see a half-mountain, the other half of which was sacrificed for the cause, as you approach the island on the Trans-Canada Highway.) The causeway is 271km (168 miles) from the New Brunswick border at Amherst, 282km (175 miles) from Halifax.

**VISITOR INFORMATION** Nine tourist information centers dot the island. The best stocked (and a much recommended first stop) is the bustling **Port Hastings Info Centre** (**© 902/625-4201**), located on your right just after crossing the Canso Causeway. It's open daily 8am to 8:30pm mid-May to mid-October.

**SPECIAL EVENTS** **Celtic Colours** (**© 902/295-1414;** www.celtic-colours.com) is a big annual music shindig timed to approximate the peak of the lovely highland foliage. Few tourists know about it—well, until now, that is—and the concentration of local Celtic musicians getting together for good times and music is simply astounding if you're into that sort of thing. It usually begins around the second week of October and lasts a full foot-stompin', penny-whistlin', fiddle-playin' week.

## MABOU & VICINITY ★

Mabou (pop. 400) is situated on a deep and protected inlet along the island's picturesque west shore. Scenic drives and bike rides are a dime a dozen hereabouts; few roads fail to yield up opportunities to break out the camera or just lean against your vehicle and enjoy the panorama. The residents are strongly oriented toward music in their activities, unusually so even for musical Cape Breton Island. Evening entertainment tends to revolve around fiddle playing, square dancing, or a traditional gathering of musicians and storytellers called a *ceilidh* ★ (pronounced kay-lee). To find out where things are going on, stop by the village grocery store or The Mull across the road (see below) and scope out the bulletin boards.

In a handsome valley between Mabou and Inverness is the distinctive post-and-beam **Glenora Distillery** ★ (✆ **800/839-0491** or 902/258-2662; www.glenoradistillery.com). This modern distillery began producing single-malt whisky from a pure local stream in 1990 and began selling it in 2000. (The owner can't call it Scotch, because it isn't made in Scotland.) He has modified the process slightly to use Kentucky bourbon casks, which the distillers here believe imparts a mellower taste to the spirit than traditional sherry casks. Production runs take place later in the fall, but tours of the facility are offered throughout the summer. Tours cost C$5 (US$3.10) and last about a half-hour (offered daily 9am to 5pm; closed November to mid-June); they conveniently end near the gift shop, where you can buy local music CDs, gift glasses and even bottles of the whisky itself for C$75 (US$47) a pop. The distillery has an adjoining restaurant and nine-room hotel, plus some spiffy new chalets with knockout views (below); traditional music is often scheduled for weekends or evenings in the contemporary pub.

### WHERE TO STAY

**Mabou River Guest House & Hostel** ★ Located not far from the river and adjacent to the Mother of Sorrows Pioneer Shrine, this hostel is not comprised of dorm rooms full of bunk beds. The homey hostel has private and semi-private rooms and two bedroom apartments available with both nightly and weekly rates. Recent renovations have resulted in both en-suite and private bathroom facilities, as well as a full size kitchen for guests. Nature lovers will appreciate the opportunity to hike, kayak, fish, and mountain bike on the scenic Ceilidh Trail. Reservations recommended, particularly in summer months.

19 Mabou Ridge Rd., Mabou, NS B0E 1X0, (✆ **888/627-9744** or 902/945-2356). www.mabouriverhostel.com. 10 units. Private rooms C$75–C$85 (US$46–US$53); shared rooms C$20 (US$12.35); apartments C$95–C$105 (US$59–US$65) nightly, C$550–C$625 (US$340–US$386) weekly. MC, V. **Amenities:** Restaurant; game room; deck; equipment rental. *In room:* No phone.

**Glenora Inn & Distillery Resort** ★★ So, when was the last time you spent the night at a distillery? This distiller of single-malt whiskey added nine modern rooms in a building next to the pub, which in turn is located next to the actual distillery. The contemporary yet rustic architecture has a pleasant feel to it, but the real attraction is easy access to the pub and restaurant on the premises, which

often features live performers from the area. The distillery has the feel of being in a remote vale in the Scottish highlands. Honeymooners will appreciate the half-dozen modern chalets, located on the hills overlooking the distillery: each has a kitchen, fireplace, Jacuzzi, satellite TV, and a wonderful view of the mist-covered valley below. (Be prepared for a bone-rattling ride up the hill on a gravel road.) These chalets are available in one-, two- or three-bedroom configurations. Route 19, Glenville, NS B0E 1X0. ✆ **800/839-0491** or 902/258-2662. www.glenoradistillery.com. Fax 902/258-3572. 15 units. C$100–C$120 (US$62–US$74); chalets C$148–C$210 (US$92–US$130). AE, MC, V. **Amenities:** Restaurant, bar.

## WHERE TO DINE

**The Red Shoe Pub** *Finds* PUB FARE You won't find a more local pub than this one, yet a constant stream of summer tourists keeps the mix interesting. The menu here features basic pub fare like buffalo wings, fried fish, salads and burgers; there are a few beers on tap, plus all the obvious bottles. The real highlight, though, is the frequent musical performances in the pub—the next area Celtic music star might be playing for peanuts on the night you swing by. The place is small and, when crowded, can get quite claustrophobic and smoky. Also, the kitchen closes promptly at 8pm.

Main Street (Hwy 19), Mabou. ✆ **902/945-2626.** www.redshoepub.com. Reservations not necessary. Meals C$5–C$12 (US$3.10–US$7). MC, V. Daily July–Sept noon–1am; rest of the year, shorter hours.

## MARGAREE VALLEY ★

West of Baddeck and south of Chéticamp, the Margaree Valley region loosely consists of the area from the village of Margaree Valley near the headwaters of the Margaree River, down the river to Margaree Harbor on Cape Breton's west coast. Some seven small communities are clustered in along the valley floor, and it's a world apart from the rugged drama of the surf-battered coast; it's vaguely reminiscent of the farm country of upstate New York. The Cabot Trail gently rises and falls on the shoulders of the gently rounded hills flanking the valley, offering views of the farmed floodplains and glimpses of the river.

The **Margaree River** has been accorded celebrity status in fishing circles—it's widely regarded as one of the most productive Atlantic salmon rivers in North America, and salmon have continued to return to spawn here in recent years, which is unfortunately not the case in many other waterways of Atlantic Canada. The river has been open to fly-fishing only since the 1880s, and in 1991 it was designated a Canadian Heritage River.

Learn about the river's heritage at the **Margaree Salmon Museum** ★ (✆ **902/248-2848**) in Northeast Margaree. The handsome building features a brief video about the life cycle of the salmon, and exhibits include fisherman photos by the score as well as antique rods (including one impressive 18-footer), examples of poaching equipment, and hundreds of hand-tied salmon flies. Museum docents can help you find a guide to try your hand on the water. (Mid-June to mid-July and September and early October are the best times.) The museum is open mid-June to mid-October daily 9am to 5pm. Admission is C$1 (US60¢) per adult and C25¢ (US15¢) per child.

### WHERE TO STAY

**Normaway Inn** ★★ From the moment you turn down the drive lined with tall Scotch pines, you'll feel you're in another world. And that world is a sort of 1920s Bertie Wooster world, both elegant and rustic at the same time. The lodge is located on some 200ha (500 acres), was built in 1928, and has been run by the MacDonald family since the 1940s. While it's the sort of place you might imagine running into gentlemen anglers dressed in tweed, it's not a true fishing resort. It appeals to both families and honeymooners and is spread out enough to accommodate all. Nine rooms are in the main lodge and have a timeless quality, with a vague 1920s character. I'd opt for one of the three first-floor rooms, which are larger and have corner windows for better ventilation. The cottages are spread around the property an easy walk to the main lodge, and have hardwood floors and a clean, almost Scandinavian quality. The older cottages were built in the 1940s and are a bit smaller and more sparse. Eight newer cottages have Jacuzzis, all but two have woodstoves, and some have two bedrooms. The dining room, decorated in pleasingly simple country farm style, is known for its Atlantic salmon and its lamb, which is raised for the inn about 16km (10 miles) away. (Don't fret: the sheep wandering the property are breed stock and won't appear on your dinner plate.)

P.O. Box 121, Margaree Valley, NS B0E 2C0. © **800/565-9463** or 902/248-2987. Fax 902/248-2600. www.normaway.com. 9 units, 20 cottages. C$89–C$199 (US$55–US$123) double. Breakfast C$10.50 (US$7) extra. DC, MC, V. Closed late Oct–May 31. Pets allowed in cottages only. **Amenities:** Restaurant; tennis courts; bikes. *In room:* No phone

## CHETICAMP

The Acadian town of **Chéticamp** ★ (pop. 1,000) is the western gateway to Cape Breton Highlands National Park and the center for French-speaking culture on Cape Breton. The change is striking as you drive northward from Margaree Harbour—the family names suddenly go from MacDonald to Doucet, and the whole culture and cuisine change.

The town itself consists of an assortment of restaurants, boutiques, and tourist establishments spread along Main Street, which closely hugs the harbor. A winding boardwalk follows the harbor's edge through much of town, and offers a good spot to stretch your legs and get your bearings. (That's Chéticamp Island just across the water; the tall coastal hills of the national park are visible up the coast.) Chéticamp is a good stop for provisioning, topping off the gas tank, and finding shelter.

Chéticamp is noted worldwide for its hooked rugs, a craft perfected by early Acadian settlers. Those curious about the craft should allow time for a stop at Les Trois Pignons, which houses the **Elizabeth LeFort Gallery and Museum.** It is located on Main Street (north end of town), © **902/224-2642,** and displays 20 of the 300 fine tapestries created by Dr. LeFort, along with a number of other rugs made by local craftspeople. It's open daily 8am to 6pm in July and August; 9am to 5pm spring and fall. Closed November to April. Admission is C$3.50 (US$2.15) adult, C$3 (US$1.85) senior, free for ages 12 and under. In the 1930s artisans formed the **Co-operative Artisanale de Chéticamp,** located at 774 Main St. (© **902/224-2170**). A selection of hooked rugs—from the size of a drink coaster on up—are sold here, along with other trinkets and souvenirs. There's often a weaver or other craftsperson at work in the shop. A small museum downstairs (free) chronicles the life and times of the early Acadian settlers and their descendents. It is closed mid-October to May 1.

Page ahead to the next section for more details on national park activities.

### WHERE TO STAY

A handful of motels service the thousands of travelers who pass through each summer. **Laurie's Motor Inn,** Main Street (© **800/959-4253** or 902/224-2400), has more than 50 motel rooms in three buildings well situated right in town, with rates of C$85 to C$135 (US$53–US$84) double.

**Pilot Whale Lodge** ★ These spare, modern cottages (constructed in 1997) each have two bedrooms and full housekeeping facilities, including microwaves. They may have a bit of an antiseptic, condo air, but they all have decks; some even have Jacuzzis and fireplaces. The best feature, though, is the grand view northward toward the coastal mountains. (Cottages 1, 2, 4, and 5 have the best vistas.) The lodge added apartments to the walk-out basements beneath two of the cottages in 1999, which impinges slightly on the privacy of those both upstairs and down.

Route 19, Chéticamp, NS B0E 1H0. © **902/224-2592** or 902/224-1040. Fax 902/224-1540. www.pilotwhalechalets.com. 8 units. C$90–C$159 (US$56–US$99) double (each additional guest C$10/US$6; no charge for children 6 and under). AE, MC, V. Closed Nov to mid-May. *In room:* TV/VCR, coffeemaker, grill, woodstove, kitchenette.

## WHERE TO DINE

For last minute snack food before setting off into the park, stop by **La Boulangerie Aucoin** (✆ **902/224-3220**)—a staple of Chéticamp life since 1959. Located just off the Cabot Trail between town and the national park (look for signs), the bakery is constantly restocking its shelves with fresh-baked goods; ask what's still warm when you order at the counter. Among the options: croissants, scones, loaves of fresh bread, and berry pies.

**Harbour Restaurant and Bar** ★ SEAFOOD The Harbour is Chéticamp's sleekest restaurant, located in a easy-to-pass-by building on the waterfront. The water views are excellent, and the food well above average for the region. The light fare menu consists of pub favorites (hamburgers, club sandwich, fish and chips), along with an Acadian specialty or two. The dinner menu favors seafood, with options like an East Coast casserole (scallops, lobster, shrimp, and haddock in a cheese sauce), broiled salmon, and farm-raised Margaree trout, served charbroiled and finished with a tarragon butter; there's also Alberta beef. The bar, which serves a good selection of single-malt Scotches, stays open until midnight.

15299 Cabot Trail (Main St.). ✆ **902/224-2042.** Reservations recommended in peak season. Light fare C$5.99–C$11.95 (US$3.70–US$7), dinner entrees C$9.95–C$18.95 (US$6–US$12). AE, MC, V. Daily 11am–10pm. Closed mid-Oct to mid-May.

**Restaurant Acadien** ACADIAN This restaurant is attached to a crafts shop on the south side of town and has the uncluttered feel of a cafeteria. The servers wear costumes inspired by traditional Acadian dress, and the menu also draws on local Acadian traditions. Look for fricot (a kind of chicken-potato soup), stewed potatoes, and the meat pies for which the region is renown. Also on the menu: blood pudding and butterscotch pie, for the brave and carefree.

774 Main St. ✆ **902/224-3207.** Reservations recommended. Breakfast C$3.50–C$5 (US$2.15–US$3.10), lunch and dinner C$1.95–C$16.95 (US$1.20–US$11). AE, MC, V. Daily 7am–9pm. Closed Nov–April.

## INGONISH ★

This area includes a number of similarly named towns (Ingonish Centre, Ingonish Ferry, South Ingonish Harbor), which together have a population of about 1,300. Like Chéticamp on the peninsula's east side, Ingonish serves as a gateway to the national park and is home to a park visitor information center and a handful of motels and restaurants. Oddly, there's really no critical mass here—the services are spread along a lengthy stretch of the Cabot Trail, and there's never any sense of arrival. You pass a liquor store, some shops, a bank, a post office, and a handful of cottages. Then you're suddenly in the park.

Highlights in the area include a **sandy beach,** good for chilly splashing around (near Keltic Lodge), and a number of shorter **hiking trails.** (See "Cape Breton Highlands National Park," later.) For golfers, windswept **Highland Links** course ★ (✆ **800/441-1118**), located adjacent to the Keltic Lodge (below) but under separate management, is considered one of the best in Nova Scotia, if not all of Atlantic Canada. South of Ingonish the **Cabot Trail** ★★ climbs and descends the hairy 300m (1,000-ft.) high promontory of Cape Smokey, which explodes into panoramic views from the top. At the highest point, there's a provincial park where you can cool your engine and admire the views. An 11km (7-mile) hiking trail leads to the tip of the cape along the high bluffs, with unforgettable viewpoints along the way.

## WHERE TO STAY

**Cape Breton Highlands Bungalows** *Value* *Kids* This attractive cluster of vintage cottages boasts a Cape Breton rarity: it's located on the shore of a freshwater lake rather than the ocean. But the ocean, at Ingonish Beach, is a short walk or paddle away. The green-trimmed white cottages were built in the 1940s and are pleasantly rustic. Two styles are offered: one- and two-room, the latter of which are suitable for families, who make up much of the clientele. All but one cottage have kitchenettes. Numbers 1 through 10 are located in an open grassy area, some with views across the lake to the Keltic Lodge. The rest are tucked away in a grove of birches and hardwoods; no. 11 and no. 12 are nicely sited at the edge of the lake. In the evening, there's a good chance you'll be serenaded by loons.

Cabot Trail, Ingonish Beach, NS B0C 1L0. ✆ **888/469-4816** or 902/285-2000. 25 cottages. C$69–C$75 (US$43–US$47) double. MC, V. Closed early Oct–June 1. **Amenities:** Laundry; playground. *In room:* TV, kitchenettes, no phone.

**Keltic Lodge** ★ The Keltic Lodge is reached after a series of dramatic flourishes: You pass through a grove of white birches, cross an isthmus atop angular cliffs, and then arrive at the stunning, vaguely Tudor resort that dominates the narrow peninsula. The views are extraordinary. Owned and operated by the province, the resort is comfortable without being slick and nicely worn without being threadbare. Most guest rooms are furnished rather plainly with run-of-the-mill motel furniture. (You might expect more for the price.) The cottages are set amid birches and have four bedrooms; you can rent just one bedroom and share a common living room with other guests. Be aware that some of the guest rooms are located at the more modern Inn at the Keltic building a couple hundred meters away, which has better views but a more sterile character. One Frommer's reader wrote to lament the inadequate soundproofing in the modern annex, and recommended an upstairs room here to avoid hearing heavy footfalls. The food in the main dining room is among the best on the island; the excellent C$40 (US$25) fixed-price dinner menu (included in room rates) offers several selections, with prime rib and lemon-pepper salmon filet among the favorites. A less formal option is the new Atlantic Restaurant, specializing in lighter fare like grilled salmon and pasta.

Middle Head Peninsula, Ingonish Beach, NS B0C 1L0. ✆ **800/565-0444** or 902/285-2880. Fax 902/285-2859. www.signatureresorts.com. 101 units. C$213–C$304 (US$132–US$188) double, including breakfast and dinner. AE, DC, DISC, MC, V. Closed late Oct–late May). **Amenities:** 2 restaurants; heated oceanside pool; golf course; game room; laundry service. *In room:* TV, fridge (some rooms), hair dryer, iron.

## BADDECK

Though Baddeck (pronounced *Bah-deck*) is at a distance from the national park, it's often considered the de facto "capital" of the Cabot Trail. The town offers the widest selection of hotels and accommodations along the whole loop, an assortment of restaurants, and a handful of useful services like grocery stores and Laundromats. Baddeck is also famed as the summer home of revered inventor Alexander Graham Bell, who is memorialized at a national historic site. It's also compact and easy to reconnoiter by foot, scenically located on the shores of Bras d'Or Lake, and within striking distance of the Fortress at Louisbourg. That makes it the most practical base for those with limited vacation time planning to drive the Cabot Trail in 1 day (figure on 6–8 hours). If, however, your intention is to spend a few days exploring the hiking trails, bold headlands, and remote coves of the national park (which I'd recommend!), you're better off finding a base farther north.

The useful **Baddeck Welcome Center** (✆ **902/295-1911**) is located just south of the village at the intersection of Route 105 and Route 205. It's open daily June to mid-October from 9am to 7pm.

## EXPLORING THE TOWN

Baddeck is much like a modern New England village, skinny and centered around a single commercial boulevard (Chebucto Street) just off the lake. Ask for a free **walking tour brochure** at the welcome center. A complete tour of the village's architectural highlights won't take much more than 15 or 20 minutes.

**Government Wharf** (head down Jones Street from the Yellow Cello restaurant) is home to three boat tours, which offer the best way to experience Bras d'Or Lake. **Amoeba Sailing Tours** (✆ **902/295-2481** or 902/295-1426) offers a mellow cruise on a 15m (50-ft.) sailboat, from which you'll likely spot bald eagles and other birds, and watch Baddeck's fine lakeshore drift past. Four sailings daily are offered in peak season; the cost is C$17.25 (US$11) per person. **Fan-A-Sea** (✆ **902/295-1900** or 902/295-7899) runs charter fishing trips from Baddeck, and with some luck you may land cod, haddock, or trout. Bait and rods are supplied; the rate is C$35 (US$22) per person, and a minimum of two people are required per tour. **Loch Bhreagh Boat Tours** (✆ **902/295-2016**) offers motorboat tours that pass Alexander Graham Bell's palatial former estate and other attractions at this end of the lake.

About 180m (200 yd.) offshore from the downtown wharf is **Kidston Island,** owned by the town. It has a wonderful sand beach with lifeguards and an old lighthouse to explore. The Lion's Club offers frequent pontoon boat shuttles between 10am and 6pm (noon to 6pm on weekends) across St. Patrick's Channel; the crossing is free, but donations are encouraged.

**Alexander Graham Bell National Historic Site** ★ *Kids* Each summer for much of his life, noted inventor Alexander Graham Bell fled the heat of Washington, D.C., for a hillside retreat high above Bras d'Or Lake. The mansion, which is still owned and occupied by the Bell family, is visible across the harbor from various spots around town. But to learn more about Bell's career and restless mind, you should visit this modern exhibit center, perched on a grassy hillside at the north edge of the village. You'll find extensive exhibits about Bell's invention of the telephone at age 29, as well as considerable information about Bell's less-lauded contraptions, like his ingenious kites, hydrofoils, and airplanes. There's an extensive discovery area, where kids are encouraged to apply their intuition and creativity in solving problems.

Chebucto St., Baddeck. ✆ **902/295-2069.** Admission C$4.25 (US$2.65) adult, C$3.25 (US$2) senior, C$2.25 (US$1.40) student, C$10.75 (US$7) family. Daily June 9am–6pm, July–August 8:30am–7:30pm, Sept to mid-Oct 8:30am–6pm, mid-Oct to May 9am–5pm.

## WHERE TO STAY

If the places below are booked, try **Auberge Gisele's,** 387 Shore Rd. (✆ **800/304-0466** or 902/295-2849), a modern 63-room hotel that's popular with bus tours, or the **Cabot Trail Motel,** Route 105, 1.5km (1 mile) west of Baddeck (✆ **902/295-2580**), with 40 rooms overlooking the lake and a heated outdoor pool. Doubles run around C$90 to C$100 (US$56–US$62) at either location.

**Duffus House Inn** ★ A visit to the Duffus House is like a visit to the grandmother's house everyone wished they had. These two adjacent buildings, constructed in 1820 and 1885, overlook the channel and are cozy and very tastefully furnished with a mix of antiques (the Cunard Room is decorated with memorabilia from the cruise line of the same name). The Duffus House is located far enough from Baddeck's downtown to keep the commotion at arm's length, yet you can still walk everywhere in a few minutes' time. (The inn also has its own dock, recently fixed up, where you can swim or just sit peacefully.) The several cozy common areas are comfortably furnished and offer great places to chat with the other guests, as does the intimate garden. The inn doesn't charge bargain room rates, but delivers fair value for the cost.

Water St. (P.O. Box 427), Baddeck, NS B0E 1B0. ✆ **902/295-2172.** 7 units (including 3 suites). C$105–C$150 (US$65–US$93) double, suites C$145–C$165 (US$90–US$102). Rates include continental breakfast. V. Closed mid-Oct to mid-May. **Amenities:** Dock; gardens.

**Green Highlander Lodge** The Green Highlander is located atop the Yellow Cello, a popular in-town eatery. The three rooms are nicely decorated in a sort of Abercrombie & Fitch gentleman's fishing camp motif. (Rooms are named after Atlantic salmon flies.) Blue Charm has a private sitting room. Rosie Dawn and Lady Amherst have private decks that look out to Kidston Island. Ask about the moonlight paddle trips, kayak rentals, and the private beach located a mile away.

525 Chebucto St., Baddeck, NS B0E 1B0. ✆ **902/295-2303** or 902/295-2240. Fax 902/295-1592. yellow@atcom.com. 3 units. C$90–C$120 (US$56–US$74) double, including full breakfast. AE, MC, V. Closed Dec–May. **Amenities:** Private beach; kayak rentals. *In room:* hair dryer.

**Inverary Resort** ★ *Kids* This sprawling resort, located lakeside on 5ha (12 acres) within walking distance of town, is a good choice for families with active kids. The slew of activities run the gamut from fishing and paddleboats to nightly bonfires on the beach. Guest rooms and facilities are spread all over the well-maintained grounds, mostly in buildings a dark-chocolate brown with white trim and green roofs. The rooms vary in size and style, but all are quite comfortable, even the snug motel-style units in the cottages; five two-bedroom units are offered, and four units have kitchens. The resort has two dining rooms: the Lakeside Cafe overlooks the resort's small marina and serves informal fare like penne with pesto and vegetable lasagna. The more formal Flora's, in the main lodge, has more upscale fare served in a sun-porch setting.

Shore Rd. (P.O. Box 190), Baddeck, NS B0E 1B0. ✆ **800/565-5660** or 902/295-3500. Fax 902/295-3527. www.inveraryresort.com. 138 units. C$95–C$150 (US$59–US$93) double, C$195 (US$121) suites, off-season C$80–C$200 (US$50–US$124). AE, DC, MC, V. Closed Dec–May. **Amenities:** 2 restaurants; indoor pool; 3 tennis courts; volleyball court; shuffleboard; sauna; boat tours; boat rentals (canoes, kayaks, paddleboats, surf bikes, Zodiacs); marina; playground; room service. *In room:* A/C, TV.

**Telegraph House** The rooms in this 1861 hotel right on Baddeck's bustling main street are divided between the original inn and two motel units on a rise behind the inn. This is where Alexander Graham Bell stayed when he first visited Baddeck, and the rooms are still rooming-house small. Four rooms on the top floor share two bathrooms between them, an arrangement that works well with families. Guests can linger on the front or side porch (there are several sitting nooks) and watch commerce happen on the main drag. I actually prefer the larger if unexciting motel rooms in back; ask for rooms 22 to 32, which have small sitting decks outside their front doors with glimpses of the lake. The dining room serves traditional favorites for both lunch and dinner. Expect shepherd's pie, ham plate, meat loaf, roast turkey, fish cakes—and big, sloppy, wonderfully nasty desserts.

Chebucto Street (P.O. Box 8), Baddeck, NS B0E 1B0. ✆ **902/295-1100.** Fax 902/295-1136. 43 units (4 share 2 bathrooms). C$65–C$130 (US$40–US$81) double. AE, MC, V. **Amenities:** Restaurant. *In room:* TV.

## LOUISBOURG ★★

In the early 18th century, Louisbourg on Cape Breton's remote and windswept easternmost coast was home to an ambitious French fortress and settlement. Despite its brief prosperity and durable construction of rock, it virtually disappeared after the British finally forced the French out (for the second time) in 1760. Through the miracle of archaeology and historic reconstruction, much of the imposing settlement has been re-created, and today Louisbourg is among Canada's most ambitious national historic parks. It's an attraction everyone coming to Cape Breton Island should make an effort to visit.

### EXPLORING THE VILLAGE

The hamlet of Louisbourg—which you'll pass through en route to the historic park—is pleasantly low-key, still scouting for ways to rebound from one devastating economic loss after another, including the cessation of the railway, the decline in boat building, and the loss of the fisheries. Louisbourg is now striving to gear its economy more toward tourism, and you can see the progress year by year.

A short **boardwalk** with interpretive signs fronts the town's tiny waterfront. (You'll get a glimpse of the national historic site across the water.) Nearby is a faux-Elizabethan theater, the **Louisbourg Playhouse** (✆ **888/733-2787** or 902/733-2996; www.artscapebreton.com). This was originally built near the old town by Disney for filming the movie *Squanto.* After the production wrapped up, Disney donated it to the village, which dismantled it and moved it to a side street near the harbor.

**Fortress of Louisbourg National Historic Park** ★★ *Kids* The historic French village of Louisbourg has had three lives. The first was early in the 18th century, when the French first colonized this area—aggressively—in a bid to stake their claim in the New World. They built an imposing fortress of stone. Imposing but not impregnable, as the British were to prove when they captured the fort in 1745. The fortress had a second, if short-lived, heyday after it was returned to the French following negotiations in Europe. War soon broke out again, however, and the British recaptured it in 1758; this time they blew it up for good measure. The final resurrection came during the 1960s, when the Canadian government decided to rebuild one-fourth of the stone-walled town—virtually creating from whole cloth a settlement from some grass hummocks and a few scattered documents about what once had been. The park was built to re-create life as it looked in 1744, when this was an important French military capital and seaport; visitors today arrive at the site after walking through an interpretive center and boarding a bus for the short ride to the site. (Keeping cars at a distance does much to enhance the historic flavor.)

You will wander through the impressive gatehouse—perhaps being challenged by a costumed guard on the lookout for English spies—and then begin wandering the narrow lanes and poking around the faux-historic buildings, some of which contain informative exhibits, others of which are restored and furnished with convincingly worn reproductions. Chicken, geese, and other barnyard animals peck and cluck as vendors hawk freshly baked bread out of wood-fired ovens. Allow at least 4 hours to explore. It's an extraordinary destination, as picturesque as it is historic.

✆ **902/733-2280.** www.parcscanada.gc.ca. Admission June–Sept C$11 (US$7) adult, C$8 (US$5.10) senior, C$5.50 (US$3.40) child, C$27.50 (US$17) family. Discounts in May and Oct. July and Aug daily 9am–6pm; May, June, Sept, and Oct daily 9:30am–5pm. Costumed interpreters limited in off-season. Closed Nov 1–Apr 30.

## WHERE TO STAY

**Cranberry Cove** ★ You won't miss this attractive, in-town inn when en route to the fortress—it's a three-story Victorian farmhouse painted a boisterous cranberry red with cranberry-tinged meals to match. Inside it's decorated with a light Victorian motif. The upstairs rooms are carpeted and furnished around themes—Anne's Hideaway is the smallest but has a nice old tub and butterfly collection; Isle Royale is done up in Cape Breton tartan. My favorite room is also the quirkiest: Field and Stream, with a twig headboard, and mounted deer head and pheasant. Breakfast includes cran-apple sauce and "cran-bran" muffins; dinner is served nightly from 5 to 8:30pm in the handsome first-floor dining room, which has a polished wood floor and cherry-wood tables and chairs. Entrees range from charbroiled Atlantic salmon to (you guessed it) cranberry-marinated breast of chicken. A "cranberry cottage" is said to be coming in the near future.

12 Wolfe St., Louisbourg, NS B1C 2J2. ✆ **800/929-0222** or 902/733-2171. Fax 902/733-2171. www.louisbourg.com/cranberrycove. 7 units. C$85–C$145 (US$53–US$90) double, including breakfast. MC, V. Closed Nov 1 to mid-May. **Amenities:** Restaurant. *In room:* TV (some rooms), Jacuzzi (some rooms), hair dryer.

**Louisbourg Harbour Inn** ★ This golden-yellow, century-old clapboard home is conveniently located in the village, a block off the main street and overlooking fishing wharves, the blue waters of the harbor, and, across the way, the Fortress of Louisbourg. The inn's lustrous pine floors have been nicely restored, and all the guest rooms are tidy and attractive, with some fussier than others. The best rooms are on the third floor, requiring a bit of a trek; Room 6 is bright and cheerful, Room 7 is very spacious and boasts an in-room Jacuzzi and a pair of rockers from which to monitor the happenings at the fish pier. A nice touch: All rooms facing the harbor have Jacuzzis. Room 1 and Room 3 also have private balconies. Dinner is occasionally available by advance reservations to guests in the first-floor dining room. A three-course meal (entree choices typically includes steak, lobster, or crab) runs C$20 to C$30 (US$12–US$19), depending on what's being offered.

9 Lower Warren St., Louisbourg, NS B1C 1G6. ✆ **888/888-8466** or 902/733-3222. louisbourg@sprint.ca. 8 units. C$95–C$155 (US$59–US$96) double, including breakfast. MC, V. Closed mid-Oct to June 1. **Amenities:** Dinner service by request. *In room:* fridge (some rooms).

# 10 Cape Breton Highlands National Park ★★★

Cape Breton Highlands National Park is one of the two crown-jewel national parks in Atlantic Canada (Gros Morne in Newfoundland is the other). Covering some 950km² (365 sq. miles) and stretching across a rugged peninsula from the Atlantic to the Gulf of St. Lawrence, the park is famous for its starkly beautiful terrain. It also features one of the most dramatic coastal drives east of Big Sur, California. The park holds something for everyone, from tourists who prefer to sightsee from the comfort of their car, to those who prefer backcountry hiking in the company of bear and moose.

The mountains of Cape Breton are probably unlike those you're familiar with elsewhere. The heart of the park is fundamentally a huge plateau. In the vast interior, you'll find a flat and melancholy landscape of wind-stunted evergreens, bogs, and barrens. This is called the taiga, a name that refers to the zone between tundra and the northernmost forest. In this largely untracked area (which is also Nova Scotia's largest remaining wilderness), you might find 150-year-old trees that are only knee-high.

But it's the park's edges that capture the attention. On the western side of the peninsula, the tableland has eroded into the sea, creating a dramatic landscape of ravines and ragged, rust-colored cliffs pounded by the ocean. The Cabot Trail, a paved road built in 1939, winds dramatically along the flanks of the mountains, offering extraordinary vistas at every turn. On the park's other coastal flank—the eastern, Atlantic side—the terrain is less dramatic, with a coastal plain interposed between mountains and sea. But the lush green hills still offer a backdrop that's exceptionally picturesque.

*Note:* This section focuses only on the park proper, which offers no lodging or services other than camping. You will find limited lodging and restaurants in the handful of villages that ring the park. See "Cape Breton Island," above.

## ESSENTIALS

**GETTING THERE** Access to the park is via the Cabot Trail, one of several tourist routes well marked by provincial authorities. The entire loop is 300km (185 miles). The distance from the park entrance at Chéticamp to the park entrance at Ingonish is 106km (65 miles). Although the loop can be done in either direction, I would encourage visitors to drive it in a clockwise direction solely because the visitor center in Chéticamp offers a far more detailed introduction to the park.

**VISITOR INFORMATION** Visitor information centers are located at both Chéticamp and Ingonish and are open daily summers from 8am to 7pm. The Chéticamp center has more extensive information about the park, including a 10-minute slide presentation, natural history exhibits, a large-scale relief map, and a very good bookstore specializing in natural and cultural history. The park's main phone number is ✆ **888/773-8888** or 902/224-2306. In winter, you can also call ✆ 902/285-2691. You can find the park online at www.parcscanada.gc.ca.

**FEES** Entrance permits can be purchased either at information centers or at toll houses at the two main park entrances. Permits are required for any activity along the route, even stopping to admire the view. Daily fees are C$3.50 (US$2.15) for adults, C$2.50 (US$1.55) for seniors, C$1.50 (US95¢) for children (6–16), and C$8 (US$5) for families; 4-day passes are C$10.50 (US$7) for adults, C$7.50 (US$4.65) for seniors, C$4.50 (US$2.80) for children, and C$24 for (US$15) families.

## CAMPING

The park has five drive-in campgrounds. The largest are at **Chéticamp** (on the west side) and **Broad Cove** (on the east), both of which have the commendable policy of never turning campers away. Even if all regular sites are full, they'll find a place for you to pitch a tent or park an RV at an overflow area. All the national park campgrounds are well run and well maintained. Chéticamp and Broad Cove offer three-way hookups for RVs. Rates are C$15 (US$9) for an unserviced site, C$17 (US$11) for electric only, C$21 (US$13) for fully serviced. It costs C$2 (US$1.25) more for a site with a fire pit (otherwise you must build fires at picnic areas within the campground). Camp more than 4 days and you get 25% off the daily rate. Remember that you're also required to buy a day-use permit when camping at Cape Breton.

Cape Breton also has two backcountry campsites. **Fishing Cove** ★ is especially attractive, set on a pristine cove an 8km (5-mile) hike from the Cabot

## A Scenic Drive

Cape Breton Highlands National Park offers basically one drive, and with few lapses it's scenic along the entire route. The most breathtaking stretch is the 44km (27-mile) jaunt from **Chéticamp to Pleasant Bay** along the western coast. Double the time you figure you'll need to drive this route, because you'll want to spend time at the pullouts admiring the views and perusing informational signboards. If it's foggy, save yourself the entrance fee and gas money. Without the views, there's little reason to travel and you'd be well advised to wait until the fog lifts. Until then, you could hike in the foggy forest or across the upland bogs, or explore some of the nearby villages in the atmospheric mist.

You'll want to be very confident in your car's brakes before setting out on the Cabot Trail. The road rises and falls with considerable drama, and when cresting some ridges you might feel mildly afflicted with vertigo. Especially stressful on the brakes (when traveling the Cabot Trail clockwise) are the descents to Pleasant Bay, into the Aspy Valley, and off Cape Smokey.

Trail. Watch for pilot whales at sunset from the cliffs. **Lake of Islands,** the other backcountry site, is 13km (8 miles) from the trail head on a remote lake in the interior; it's accessible by mountain bike. Fees are C$15 (US$9) per night; make arrangements at one of the visitor information centers.

## HIKING

The park has 27 hiking trails departing from the Cabot Trail. Many excursions are quite short and have the feel of a casual stroll rather than a vigorous tromp, but those determined to be challenged will find suitable destinations. All trails are listed with brief descriptions on the reverse side of the map you'll receive when you pay your entry fee.

The **Skyline Trail** ★ offers all the altitude with none of the climbing. You ascend the tableland from Chéticamp by car, then follow a 7km (4¼-mile) hiking loop out along dramatic bluffs and through wind-stunted spruce and fir. A spur trail descends to a high, exposed point overlooking the surf; it's capped with blueberry bushes. Moose are often spotted along this trail. On the downside: It's a very popular trek and often crowded.

Further along the Cabot Trail, the half-mile-long **Bog Trail** offers a glimpse of the tableland's unique bogs from a dry boardwalk. **Lone Shieling** is an easy half-mile loop through a verdant hardwood forest in a lush valley that includes 350-year-old sugar maples. A re-creation of a hut of a Scottish crofter (shepherd) is a feature along this trail.

On the eastern shore, a superb hike is out to **Middle Head,** beyond the Keltic Lodge resort. This dramatic, rocky peninsula thrusts well out into the Atlantic. The trail is wide and relatively flat, you'll cross open meadows with wonderful views north and south. The tip is grassy and open, and it offers a fine spot to scan for whales or watch the waves crash in following a storm. Allow an hour or two for a relaxed excursion out and back.

# 4

# New Brunswick

by Wayne Curtis & Paul Karr

Think of New Brunswick as the Rodney Dangerfield of Atlantic Canada—it just gets no respect. Among many Canadians, it has a reputation more for pulp mills, industrial forests, cargo ports, and oil refineries (the huge Irving Oil conglomerate is based here) than for quaint villages and charming byways. As such, travelers tend to view New Brunswick as a place you need to drive through—preferably really fast—en route from Québec or Maine to the rest of Atlantic Canada.

Granted, there's a grain of truth behind the province's reputation. But rest assured, New Brunswick has pockets of wilderness and scenic beauty that are unrivaled anywhere in eastern Canada. You'll find sandy beaches on warm ocean waters that hold their own to anything on Prince Edward Island. Not to mention rocky, surf-pounded headlands that could be in the farthest reaches of Newfoundland. The province's appeal tends to be more hidden than that of other locales. But with a little bit of homework—and by making inquiries at the innovative Day Adventure Centres the province has established—you can quite easily cobble together memorable excursions through an exquisite landscape.

## 1 Exploring the Province

Visitors drawn to rugged beauty should plan to focus on the Fundy Coast with its stupendous tides, rocky cliffs, and boreal landscape. (The south coast actually feels more remote and northerly than the more densely settled northeast coast.) Those interested in Acadian history or sandy beaches should veer toward the Gulf of St. Lawrence. Those interested in hurrying through the province to get to Prince Edward Island or Nova Scotia should at least detour down through Fundy National Park and visit Cape Enrage and Hopewell Rocks, which number among eastern Canada's more dramatic attractions.

### ESSENTIALS

**VISITOR INFORMATION** New Brunswick publishes several free annual directories and guides that are helpful in planning a trip to the province, including *Welcome to New Brunswick,* with listings of attractions, accommodations, and campgrounds, and the *Travel Planner,* which includes a catalog of multi-day and daylong adventure packages. Contact **Tourism New Brunswick,** P.O. Box 12345, Fredericton, NB E7M 5C3 (© **800/561-0123;** www.tourismnewbrunswick.ca).

**TOURIST OFFICES** The province staffs five visitor information centers; most cities and larger towns also have their own municipal information centers. A complete listing of phone numbers for these centers can be found in the *Travel Planner* guide, or look for "?" direction signs on the highway. Phone numbers and addresses for the appropriate visitor information centers are

# New Brunswick & the Gaspé Peninsula

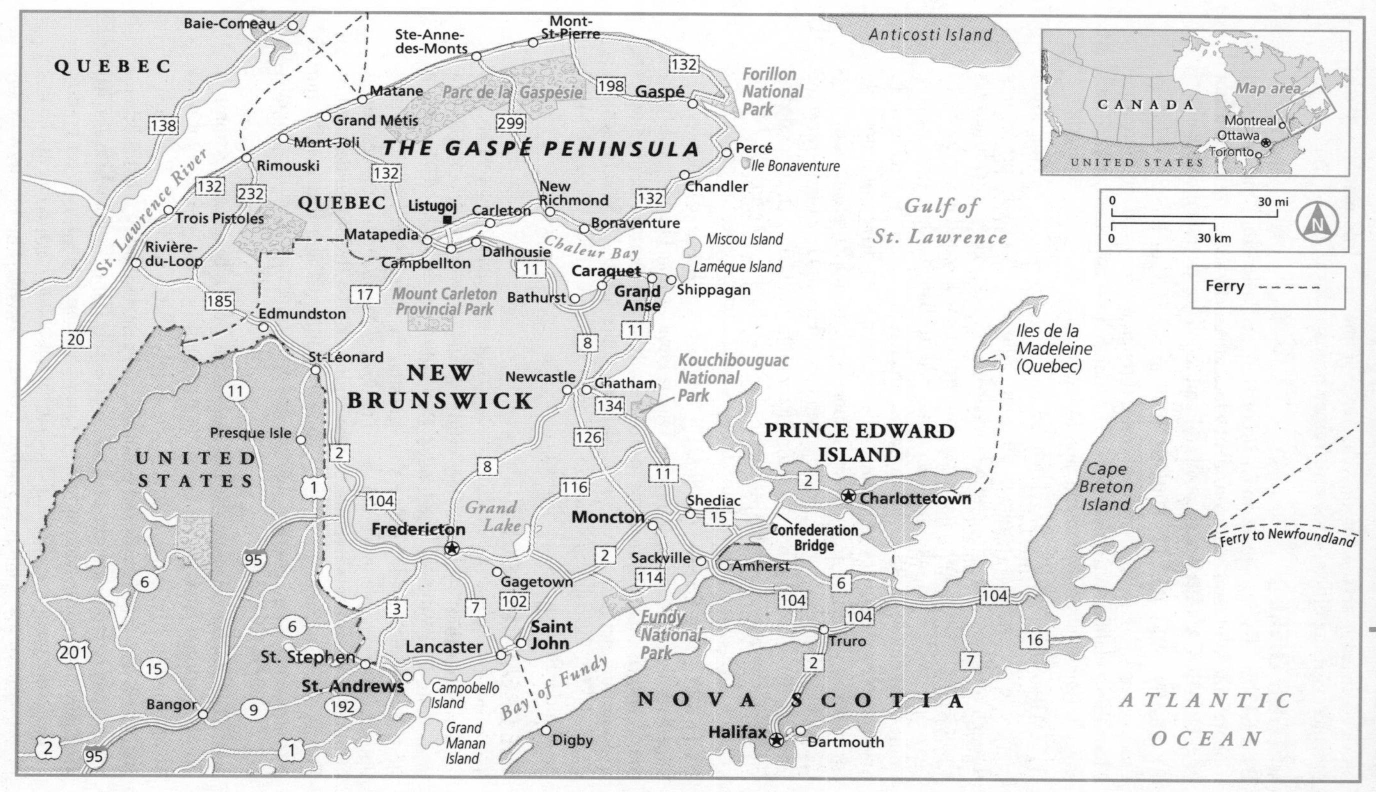

provided in each section of this chapter. For the best information on the province, visit the official **www.tourismnewbrunswick.ca**.

## GETTING THERE

**BY PLANE** The province's main airports are at Fredericton, the provincial capital, Saint John, and Moncton, all of which are chiefly served by **Air Canada** (✆ **888/AIR-CANA;** www.aircanada.ca) and the major car-rental companies.

**BY TRAIN** **VIA Rail** (✆ **800/561-3949** in the U.S. or 888/842-7245 in Canada; www.viarail.ca) offers train service through the province (en route from Montréal to Halifax) 6 days per week. The train follows a northerly route, with stops in Campbellton, Miramichi, and Moncton.

**BY CAR** The Trans-Canada Highway bisects the province, entering from Québec at St. Jacques. It follows the Saint John River Valley before veering through Moncton and exiting into Nova Scotia at Aulac. The entire distance is about 550km (330 miles). The fastest route from New England to southwestern New Brunswick is to take the Maine turnpike to Bangor, then head east on Route 9 to connect to Route 1 into Calais, which is just across the river from St. Stephen, New Brunswick. A more scenic variation is to drive to Campobello Island across the bridge from Lubec, Maine (see "Around Passamaquoddy Bay: Campobello Island & More", below), then take a ferry to Deer Island, drive the length of the island, and board a second ferry to the mainland. Those headed to Fredericton or Moncton will speed their trip somewhat by following US I-95 to Houlton then connecting with the Trans-Canada after crossing the border.

**BY FERRY** **Bay Ferries** (✆ **888/249-7245;** www.nfl-bay.com) operates a 3-hour ferry that links Saint John with Digby, Nova Scotia. The ferry sails year-round, with as many as three crossings daily each way in summer, taking 3 hours to do so. Summer fares are C$35 (US$22) for adults, C$30 (US$19) for seniors, C$15 (US$9) for children ages 5 to 14, and C$70 to C$150 (US$43–US$93) per vehicle. Reservations are advised.

## THE GREAT OUTDOORS

The province has put together a well-conceived campaign—called **"The New Tide of Adventure"**—to encourage visitors of all budgets to explore its outdoor attractions. The province has funded **Day Adventure Centers** (well marked from most major roads), where you can stop in, peruse the local adventure options, and then sign up on the spot. The ***Travel Planner*** also outlines dozens of multi-day and day adventures ranging from a C$10 (US$6) guided hike at Fundy National Park to C$389 (US$241) biking packages that include inn accommodations and gourmet dinners. For more information on the program, call ✆ **800/561-0123.**

**BACKPACKING** Among the best destinations for a backcountry tromp is **Fundy National Park,** which maintains backcountry sites. See below for more information.

**BICYCLING** The islands and peninsulas of **Passamaquoddy Bay** lend themselves nicely to cruising in the slow lane—especially Campobello, which also has good dirt roads for mountain biking. **Grand Manan** holds appeal for cyclists, although the main road (Route 776) has narrow shoulders and fast cars. Some of the best coastal biking is around **Fundy National Park**—especially the back-roads to Cape Enrage, and the Fundy Trail Parkway, an 11km (6½-mile), multi-use trail that hugs the coast west of the national park. Along the Acadian

Coast, **Kouchibouguac National Park** has limited but unusually nice biking trails through mixed terrain (rentals available).

A handy guide is ***Biking to Blissville,*** by Kent Thompson. It covers 35 rides in the Maritimes, and costs C$14.95 (US$9). Contact **Goose Lane Editions,** 469 King St., Fredericton, NB E3B 1E5 (✆ **888/926-8377** or 506/450-4251; www.gooselane.com).

**BIRD-WATCHING** **Grand Manan** is among the province's most noted destinations for birders, located smack on the Atlantic flyway. (Ur-birder John James Audubon lodged here when studying local bird life more than 150 years ago.) Over the course of a year, as many as 275 species are observed on the island, with September typically the best month for sightings. It's not hard to swap information with other birders. On the ferry, look for excitable folks with binoculars and Tilley hats dashing from port to starboard and back. Talk to them. Boat tours from Grand Manan will bring you to Machias Seal Island, with its colonies of puffins, arctic terns, and razorbills.

On **Campobello Island,** the mixed terrain also attracts a good mix of birds, including sharp-shinned hawk, common eider, and black guillemot. Ask for a checklist and map at the visitor center. Shorebird enthusiasts flock to **Shepody Bay National Wildlife Area,** which maintains preserves in the mudflats between Alma (near Fundy National Park) and Hopewell Cape. Also offering excellent birding is the marsh that surrounds Sackville, near the Nova Scotia border.

**CANOEING** New Brunswick has 3,600km (2,200 miles) of inland waterways, plus lakes and protected bays. Canoeists can find everything from glass-smooth waters to daunting rapids. Novices might enjoy the half-day trips run by **Kayakouch** (✆ **506/876-1199**) in Kouchibouguac National Park; they cost C$25 (US$16). More experienced canoeists looking for a longer expedition should head to the **St. Croix River** on the U.S. border, where you can embark on a multi-day paddle trip and get lost in the woods, spiritually if not in fact.

**FISHING** The **Miramichi River** has long attracted anglers both famous and obscure, lured by the wily Atlantic salmon. In some considered opinions, this ranks among the best salmon rivers in the world, although diminished runs have plagued this river in recent years as they have all rivers in the Maritimes. Salmon must be caught on flies, and nonresidents need to hire a guide to go after salmon. For other freshwater species, like bass, and saltwater angling, the restrictions are less onerous. Get up to date on the rules and regulations by requesting copies of two brochures: "Sport Fishing Summary" and "Atlantic Salmon Angling." These are available from **Fish and Wildlife,** P.O. Box 6000, Fredericton, NB E3B 5H1 (✆ **506/453-2440**).

**GOLF** In **St. Andrews,** the Algonquin hotel's newly expanded golf course is a beauty—easily among Eastern Canada's top ten, right behind the bigger-name stars on Cape Breton Island and Prince Edward Island. It features nine newer inland holes (the front nine), and then nine older seaside holes that become increasingly spectacular as you approach the point of land separating New Brunswick from Maine. (All 18 of them are challenging, so bring your "A" game.) Service and upkeep are impeccable here, and there's both a snack bar on premises and a roving club car with sandwiches and drinks. Greens fees are C$115 (US$71) for 18 holes, lessons are offered, and there's a short-game practice area in addition to a driving range; call (✆ **506/529-7142)** for tee times.

**HIKING** There's superb hiking at **Fundy National Park,** with a mix of coastal and woodland hikes on well-marked trails. The multi-use, 11km (6½-mile) Fundy

Trail Parkway has terrific views of the coast and is wheelchair accessible. Grand Manan is a good destination for independent-minded hikers who enjoy the challenge of finding the trail as much as the hike itself. An excellent resource is *A Hiking Guide to New Brunswick.* It's C$14.95 (US$9) and available in bookstores around the province, or directly from the Goose Lane Editions, 469 King St., Fredericton, NB E3B 1E5 (© **888/926-8377** or 506/450-4251; www.gooselane.com).

**SEA KAYAKING** The huge tides that make kayaking so fascinating along the Bay of Fundy also make it exceptionally dangerous—even the strongest kayakers are no match for a fierce ebb tide if they're in the wrong place. Fortunately, the number of skilled sea-kayaking guides has boomed in recent years. Among the most extraordinary places to explore is **Hopewell Rocks.** The rocks stand like Brancusi statues on the ocean floor at low tide but offer sea caves and narrow channels to explore at high tide. **Baymount Outdoor Adventures** (© **506/734-2660**) offers 90-minute sea kayak tours of Hopewell Rocks for C$45 (US$28) adult, C$40 (US$25) youth. Other kayak outfitters along the Fundy Coast include the **Outdoor Adventure Company** (© **800/365-3855** or 506/755-6415) in St. George, **Fresh Air Adventure** (© **800/545-0020** or 506/887-2249) in Alma, and **Seascape** (© **506/747-1884**) in Deer Island.

**SWIMMING** Parts of New Brunswick offer wonderful ocean swimming. The best beaches are along the **Acadian Coast,** especially near Shediac and in Kouchibouguac National Park. The water is much warmer and the terrain more forgiving along the Gulf of St. Lawrence than the Bay of Fundy.

**WHALE-WATCHING** The **Bay of Fundy** is rich with plankton, and therefore rich with whales. Some 15 types of whales can be spotted in the bay, including finback, minke, humpback, the infrequent orca, and the endangered right whale. Whale-watching expeditions sail throughout the summer from Campobello Island, Deer Island, Grand Manan, St. Andrews, and St. George. Any visitor information center can point you in the right direction; the province's travel guide also lists many of the tours, which typically cost around C$40 (US$25) or C$50 (US$31) for 2 to 4 hours of whale-watching.

## 2 Around Passamaquoddy Bay: Campobello Island & More

The Passamaquoddy Bay region is often the first point of entry for those arriving overland from the United States. The deeply indented bay is wracked with massive tides that produce currents powerful enough to stymie even doughty fishing boats. It's a place of lasting fogs, spruce-clad islands, bald eagles, and widely scattered development. It's also home to a grand old summer colony and a peninsula that boasts two five-star inns and a rambling turn-of-the-last-century resort.

### CAMPOBELLO ISLAND ★

Campobello is a compact island—about 16km long and 5km wide—(10 miles by 3 miles) at the mouth of Passamaquoddy Bay. Among its other distinctions, it's connected by a graceful modern bridge to Lubec, Maine, and is thus easier to get to from the United States than from Canada. To get here from the Canadian mainland without driving through the United States requires two ferries, one of which operates only during the summer. Campobello has been home to both humble fishermen and wealthy families over the years, and both have coexisted quite nicely. (Locals approved when summer folks built golf courses in the early 20th century, since it gave them a place to graze their sheep.) Today, the island is a mix of elegant summer homes and less-interesting tract homes of a more recent vintage.

## ESSENTIALS

**GETTING THERE** Campobello Island is accessible year-round from the United States. From Route 1 in Whiting, Maine, take Route 189 to Lubec, where a bridge links Lubec with Campobello. In the summer, there's another option. From the Canadian mainland, take the free ferry to Deer Island, drive the length of the island, and then board the small seasonal ferry to Campobello. The ferry is operated by **East Coast Ferries** (✆ **506/747-2159**) and runs from late June to early September. The fare is C$13 (US$8) for car and driver, C$2 (US$1.20) for each additional passenger, with a maximum of C$17 (US$11) per car.

**VISITOR INFORMATION** The **Campobello Welcome Center,** 44 Route 774, Welshpool, NB E5E 1A3 (✆ **506/752-7043**), is on the right side just after you cross the bridge from Lubec. It's open mid-May to early September 9am to 7pm, then 10am to 6pm until mid-October.

## EXPLORING THE ISLAND

**Roosevelt Campobello International Park** ★ Like a number of other affluent Americans, the family of Franklin Delano Roosevelt made an annual trek to the prosperous summer colony at Campobello Island. The island lured folks from the sultry cities with a promise of cool air and a salubrious effect on the circulatory system. The future U.S. president came to this island every summer between 1883, the year after he was born, and 1921, when he was stricken with polio. Franklin and his siblings spent those summers exploring the coves and sailing around the bay, and he always recalled his time here fondly. You'll learn much about Roosevelt and his early life at the visitor center, where you can watch a brief film, and during a self-guided tour of the elaborate mansion, covered in cranberry-colored shingles. For a "cottage" this huge, it's surprisingly comfortable and intimate.

Be sure to save some time to explore farther afield in the 1,130ha (2,800-acre) park, which offers scenic coastline and 14km (8½ miles) of walking trails. While the Park's Visitor Centre closes on Canada's Thanksgiving Day in late October, these extensive grounds and parklands remain open to the public year-round. Maps and walk suggestions are available at the visitor center.

459 Route 774, Welshpool. ✆ **506/752-2922.** www.fdr.net. Free admission. Daily 10am–6pm, last tour at 5:45pm. Closed mid-Oct to mid-May.

## WHERE TO STAY & DINE

**Lupine Lodge** *Value* In 1915, cousins of the Roosevelt's built this handsome compound of log buildings not far from the Roosevelt cottage. A busy road runs between the lodge and the water, but the buildings are located on a slight rise and have the feel of being removed from the traffic. Guest rooms are in two long lodges adjacent to the main building and restaurant. Rooms with bay views cost a bit more but are worth it—they're slightly bigger and better furnished in a log-rustic style. All guests have access to a deck that overlooks the bay. The lodge's attractive restaurant exudes rustic summer ease with log walls, a double stone fireplace, bay views, and mounted moose-head and swordfish. Three meals are served daily. Dinner entrees include favorites like salmon, T-bone, turkey, and steamed lobster.

610 Route 774, Welshpool, Campobello Island NB E5E 1A5. ✆ **506/752-2555.** www.lupinelodge.com. 11 units. C$50–C$95 (US$31–US$59) double. MC, V. Closed mid-Oct to mid-June. Pets accepted (C$15/US$9 additional). **Amenities:** Restaurant.

**Owen House, A Country Inn & Gallery** This clapboard captain's house dates to 1835 and sits on 4ha (10 acres) of tree-filled land at the edge of the bay. The first-floor common rooms are nicely decorated in a busy Victorian manner with Persian and braided carpets and mahogany furniture. The guest rooms are a mixed lot, furnished with an eclectic mélange of antique and modern furniture that sometimes blends nicely. Likewise, some rooms are bright and airy and filled with the smell of salty air (Room 1 is the largest, with waterfront views on two sides); others, like Room 5, are tucked under stairs and are rather dark, but the Owens are slowly renovating the old house with bigger bathrooms and new showers. The third-floor rooms share a single bathroom but also have excellent views. A filling breakfast, served family-style, is included in the room rates.

11 Welshpool St., Welshpool, Campobello, NB E5E 1G3. ✆ **506/752-2977.** www.owenhouse.ca. 9 units (2 share 1 bathroom). C$104–C$186 (US$64–US$115) double, including breakfast. MC, V. Closed mid-Oct to late May. No children under 6 in August.

## ST. ANDREWS ★★

The lovely village of St. Andrews—or St. Andrews By-The-Sea, as the chamber of commerce likes to call it—traces its roots back to the days of the Loyalists. After the American Revolution, New Englanders who supported the British were made to feel unwelcome. They decamped first to Castine, Maine, which they presumed was safely on British soil. It wasn't; the St. Croix River was later determined to be the border between Canada and the United States. Uprooted again, the Loyalists dismantled their houses, loaded the pieces aboard ships, and rebuilt them on the welcoming peninsula of St. Andrews. Some of these saltbox houses still stand today.

Thanks to its location off the beaten track, the village hasn't been spoiled much by modern development, and walking the wide, shady streets—especially those around the Algonquin hotel—invokes a more genteel era. Some 250 homes around the village are more than a century old. A number of appealing boutiques and shops are spread along Water Street, which stretches for some distance along the town's shoreline. Also don't miss the weekly **farmer's market,** held Thursdays in the summer from 9am to about 1pm on the waterfront.

### ESSENTIALS

**GETTING THERE** St. Andrews is located at the apex of Route 127, which dips southward from Route 1 between St. Stephen and St. George. The turnoff is well marked from either direction. **SMT** bus lines (✆ **800/567-5151** or 506/859-5060) runs one bus daily between St. Andrews and Saint John; the one-way fare is approximately C$15 (US$9).

**VISITOR INFORMATION** **Tourist offices** St. Andrews has two information centers. At the western intersection of Route 1 and Route 127 is the seasonal **St. Andrews Tourist Bureau** (✆ **506/466-4858**), which is staffed by local volunteers from May to September. A second facility, the **Welcome Centre** (✆ **506/529-3556**), is located at 46 Reed Ave., on your left as you enter the village. It's in a handsome 1914 home overarched by broad-crowned trees. It's open daily 9am to 6pm in May and September, and to 8pm in July and August. The rest of the year, contact the **Chamber of Commerce** in the same building, P.O. Box 89, St. Andrews, NB E0G 2X0 (✆ **800/563-7397** or 506/529-3555; stachmb@nbnet.nb.ca). For information online, go to **www.town.standrews.nb.ca.**

## EXPLORING ST. ANDREWS

The chamber of commerce produces two brochures, the *Town Map and Directory* and the *St. Andrews by-the-Sea Historic Guide,* both of which are free and can be found at the two visitor information centers. Also look for *A Guide to Historic St. Andrews,* produced by the St. Andrews Civic Trust. With these in hand you'll be able to launch an informed exploration. To make it even easier, many of the private dwellings in St. Andrews feature plaques with information on their origins. Look in particular for the saltbox-style homes, some of which are thought to be the original Loyalist structures that traveled here by barge.

The village's compact and handsome downtown flanks **Water Street,** a lengthy commercial street that parallels the bay. You'll find low, understated commercial architecture, much of it from the turn of the last century, that encompasses a gamut of styles. Allow an hour or so for browsing at boutiques and art galleries. There's also a mix of restaurants and inns. Two blocks inland on **King Street,** you'll get a dose of local history at the **Ross Memorial Museum,** 188 Montague St. (✆ **506/529-5124**), open late June to mid-October, Tuesday to Saturday 10am to 4:30pm; in July and August, it's also open Mondays. Admission is by donation.

St. Andrews is an excellent spot to launch an exploration of the bay, which is very much alive, biologically speaking. On the water you'll look for whales, porpoises, seals, and bald eagles, no matter which trip you select; numerous tour outfits cluster on the waterfront.

**Kingsbrae Garden** *Kids* This 11ha (27-acre) public garden opened in 1998, using the former grounds of a long-gone estate. The designers incorporated the existing high hedges and trees, and have ambitiously planted open space around the mature plants. The grounds include almost 2,000 varieties of trees (including old-growth forest), shrubs, and plants. Among the notable features: a day lily collection, an extensive rose garden, a small maze, a fully functional Dutch windmill that circulates water through the two duck ponds, and a children's garden with an elaborate Victorian-mansion playhouse. With views over the lush lawns to the bay below, the on-site Garden Cafe is a pleasant place to stop for lunch.

220 King St. ✆ **506/529-3335.** www.kingsbraegarden.com. Admission C$7.50 (US$4.65) adult; C$6 (US$3.70) students and seniors; free under 6. Daily 9am–6pm. Closed early Oct to mid-May.

**Ministers Island Historic Site/Covenhoven** ★★ This rugged, 200ha (500-acre) island is linked to the mainland by a sandbar at low tide, and the 2-hour tours are scheduled around the tides. (Call for upcoming times.) You'll meet your tour guide on the mainland side, then drive your car out convoy-style across the ocean floor to the magical island estate created in 1890 by Sir William Van Horne, president of the Canadian Pacific Railway and the person behind the extension of the rail line to St. Andrews. He then built a sandstone mansion (Covenhoven) with some 50 rooms (including 17 bedrooms), a circular bathhouse (where he indulged his passion for landscape painting), and one of Canada's largest and most impressive barns. The estate also features heated greenhouses, which produced grapes and mushrooms, along with peaches that weighed up to 1kg (2 pounds) each.

Route 127 (northeast of St. Andrews), Chamcook. ✆ **506/529-5081** (recorded tour schedule). C$5 (US$3.10) adult, C$2.50 (US$1.55) youth (13–18), under 12 free. Closed late October–May 31.

## WHERE TO STAY

Those traveling on a budget should head for the **Picket Fence Motel,** 102 Reed Ave. (✆ **506/529-8985**). This trim and tidy motel is near the handsome, newly expanded Algonquin golf course (see "Golf," above), and within walking distance of the village center. Rooms are C$55 to C$65 (US$34–US$40) in peak season.

**The Fairmont Algonquin** ★★ The Algonquin's distinguished pedigree dates back to 1889, when it first opened its doors to wealthy vacationers seeking respite from city heat. The original structure was destroyed by fire in 1914, but the surviving annexes were rebuilt in sumptuous Tudor style; in 1993 an architecturally sympathetic addition was built across the road, linked by a gatehouse-inspired bridge. The red-tile-roofed resort commands one's attention through its sheer size and aristocratic bearing (not to mention through its kilt-wearing, bagpipe-playing staff); rooms were recently redecorated and are comfortable and tasteful. One caveat: The hotel happily markets itself to bus tours and conferences, and if your timing is unfortunate you might feel a bit overwhelmed and small. The resort's main dining room is one of the more enjoyable spots in town—it's often bustling (great people-watching) and the kitchen produces some surprisingly creative meals.

184 Adolphus St., St. Andrews, NB E0G 2X0. ✆ **888/460-8999** or 506/529-8823. Fax 506/529-7162. www.fairmont.com. 250 units. May–Oct: C$99–C$239 (US$61–US$148) double. Meal package C$45 (US$28) per person per day. Other packages available. Nov–Apr: (limited operations w/51 units) C$85–C$145 (US$53–US$90), including continental breakfast. AE, DC, DISC, MC, V. Pets accepted, first floor only. **Amenities:** 5 restaurants; outdoor heated pool; golf course; 2 outdoor tennis courts; squash court; fitness center; sauna; whirlpool; bike rental; shuttle to Saint John airport; salon; massage; babysitting; laundry; dry cleaning; children's programs. *In room:* TV, minibar, coffeemaker, hair dryer.

**Inn on the Hiram Walker Estate** ★★ Innkeeper Elizabeth Cooney has put her indelible stamp on this exceptionally romantic getaway, a former home to the scion of the Walker distilling empire (which still makes Canadian Club whiskey). Rooms are filled with period antiques and furnished with four-poster beds and fireplaces; room 1 comes with a double Jacuzzi and views of lawn and sea, room 2 has a claw-foot tub and also looks out on the ocean—for half the price. Cooney cooks sumptuous prix-fixe dinners, for guests only, for about C$60 (US$37) per person; breakfast is also available.

109 Reed Avenue, St. Andrews, NB E5B 2J6. ✆ **800/470-4088** or 506/529-4210. Fax 506/529-4311. www.walkerestate.com. 10 units. Rates: May–Oct C$175–C$400 (US$109–US$248) double, off-season lower. **Amenities:** Meals; bar; heated outdoor pool; hot tub. *In room:* Fireplace.

**Kingsbrae Arms Relais & Chateaux** ★★★ Kingsbrae Arms, part of the upscale Relais & Chateaux network, is a five-star inn informed by an upscale European elegance. Kingsbrae brings to mind a rustic elegance—a bit of Tuscany, perhaps, melded with a genteel London town house. Located atop King Street, this intimate inn occupies an 1897 manor house, where the furnishings—from the gracefully worn leather chesterfield to the Delft-tiled fireplace—all seem to have a story to tell. A heated pool sits amid rose gardens at the foot of a lawn, and immediately next door is the Kingsbrae Horticultural Garden (some guest rooms have wonderful views of the garden, others a panoramic sweep of the bay; one has both). Guests will feel pampered here, with a complete guest-services suite stocked with complimentary snacks and refreshments. Five rooms have Jacuzzis; all have gas fireplaces. Guests can also enjoy a four-course meal around a stately table in the dining room during peak season. (This dining room is not open to the public.)

219 King St., St. Andrews, NB E0G 2X0. ✆ **506/529-1897.** Fax 506/529-1197. www.kingsbrae.com. 8 units. C$250–C$600 (US$155–US$372) doubles and suites, C$480–C$900 (US$298–US$743) including breakfast and dinner. 2-night minimum; 3 nights July and Aug weekends. 5% room service charge additional. AE, MC, V.

Children 10 and up. Pets allowed w/advance permission. **Amenities:** Dinner (peak season only); babysitting; laundry; dry cleaning. *In room:* A/C, TV, hair dryer.

**Salty Towers** Behind this somewhat staid Queen Anne home on Water Street lurks the soul of a wild eccentric. Salty Towers is equal parts 1900s home, 1940s boarding house, and 1960s commune. Overseen with great affability by artist-naturalist Jamie Steel, this is a world of wondrous clutter—from the early European landscapes with overly wrought gilt frames to exuberant modern pieces. Guest rooms lack the visual chaos of the public spaces and are nicely done up, furnished with eclectic antiques and old magazines. The top floor is largely given over to single rooms; these are a bargain at C$30 (US$19) with shared bathroom. Don't be surprised to find musicians strumming on the porch, artists lounging in the living room, and others of uncertain provenance swapping jokes around the stove.

340 Water St., St. Andrews, NB E5B 2R3. ✆ **506/529-4585.** steeljm@nbnet.nb.ca. 17 units (12 shared bathrooms). C$50 (US$31) double w/shared bathroom, C$65 (US$40) double w/private bathroom. V. **Amenities:** Babysitting.

**The Windsor House** ★ Located in the middle of the village on busy Water Street, the lovely Windsor House offers guests a quiet retreat amid lustrous antiques in a top-rate restoration. The home was originally built in 1798 by a ship captain. It's served almost every purpose since then, including stagecoach stop, oil company office, and family home, before reopening its doors as a luxury inn in 1999. Rooms are superbly appointed, most with detailed etchings of animals adorning the walls; four have working fireplaces. The best two are the suites on the third floor, with peaceful sitting areas, exposed beams, Asian carpets, handsome armoires, and limited views of the bay. (Both also have claw-foot tubs and glass shower stalls.) The basement features an appealing terracotta-floored billiard room; the first-floor pub is the perfect spot for an early evening libation or after-dinner drink.

132 Water St., St. Andrews, NB E0G 2X0. ✆ **888/890-9463** or 506/529-3330. Fax 506/529-4063. 6 units. Mid-June to Oct, C$225–C$300 (US$140–US$186), off-season C$150–C$250 (US$93–US$155). AE, DC, MC, V. Restaurant closed Jan–April. **Amenities:** Restaurant (see "Where to Dine," below), bar. *In room:* TV.

## WHERE TO DINE

**The Gables** SEAFOOD/PUB FARE This informal eatery is located in a trim home with prominent gables fronting Water Street, but you enter down a narrow alley where sky and water views suddenly blossom through a soaring window from a spacious outside deck. Inside, expect a bright and lively spot with a casual maritime decor; outside there's a plastic-porch-furniture informality. Breakfast is served during peak season, with homemade baked goods and rosemary potatoes. Lunch and dinner options include burgers, steaks, and seafood entrees like breaded haddock, daily specials, and a lobster clubhouse—a chopped lobster salad served with cheese, cucumber, lettuce, and tomato; there's a kid's menu, as well. Margaritas and sangria are available by the pitcher. The view here tends to outclass the menu, but those ordering simpler fare will be satisfied.

143 Water St. ✆ **506/529-3440.** Reservations not necessary. Breakfast C$3.95–C$6.95 (US$2.50–US$4.30), lunch and dinner C$7.50–C$24.50 (US$4.65–US$15). MC, V. July and Aug, open daily 8am–11pm, Sept–June daily 11am–9pm.

**Lighthouse Restaurant** SEAFOOD Located on the water at the eastern edge of the village, this spot rewards diners with a great view while they enjoy fresh-from-the-boat seafood. It's a bustling, popular place that seems to attract families and those who crave lobster. Look for a good selection of fish and lobster served with little fanfare or pomp. The menu includes sautéed scallops, seafood pasta, and lobster prepared any number of ways.

Patrick St. (drive eastward on Water St. toward Indian Point; look for signs). ✆ **506/529-3082.** Reservations helpful. Lunch C$5.50–C$11 (US$3.40–US$7.), dinner main courses C$14.50–C$36 (US$9–US$22); most C$18–C$24 (US$11–US$15). AE, DC, MC, V. Daily mid-May to mid-Oct, 11:30am–2pm and 5–9pm. Closed Labor Day to mid-May.

**The Windsor House** ★★ FRENCH/CONTINENTAL Guests are seated in one of two intimate dining rooms on the first floor of this historic home, which serves only dinner on weekdays. The setting is formal, the guests are dressed with a bit more starch than you'll find elsewhere in town, and the service is excellent. The weekend brunches are somewhat less formal and very delectable, including such treats as Windsor gravlax, omelettes, crepes, and Neptune's bounty (a kind of seafood chowder), while dinner offerings might include beef Oscar, cedar-planked salmon or a host of other entrées.

132 Water St., ✆ **506/529-3330.** Reservations recommended. Brunch Sat–Sun, C$4–C$12 (US$2.50–US$7), dinner C$26–C$35 (US$16–US$22). AE, DC, MC, V. Mon–Fri 5:30–9:30pm, Sat–Sun 11:30am–2pm and 5:30–9:30pm. Closed Mon–Tues during spring and fall; closed Jan–April.

## 3 Grand Manan Island ★

Geologically rugged, profoundly peaceable, and indisputably remote, this handsome island of 2,800 year-round residents is a 90-minute ferry ride from Blacks Harbour, southeast of St. George. For adventurous travelers Grand Manan is a much-prized destination and a highlight of their vacation. Yet the island remains a mystifying puzzle for others who fail to be smitten by its rough-edged charm. "Either this is your kind of place, or it isn't," said one island resident. "There's no in between." The only way to find out is to visit.

Grand Manan is a special favorite among serious **birders** and enthusiasts of novelist Willa Cather. Hiking the island's noted trails, don't be surprised to come across knots of very quiet people peering intently through binoculars. These are the birders. Nearly 300 different species of birds either nest here or stop by the island during their long migrations, and it's a good place to add to one's life list, with birds ranging from bald eagles to puffins (you'll need to sign up for a boat tour for the latter).

**Willa Cather** kept a cottage here and wrote many of her most beloved books while living on the island. Her fans are as easy to spot as the birders, say locals. In fact, islanders are still talking about a Willa Cather conference some summers ago, when 40 participants wrapped themselves in sheets and danced around a bonfire during the summer solstice. "Cather people, they're a wild breed," one innkeeper intoned gravely.

### ESSENTIALS

**GETTING THERE** Grand Manan is connected to Blacks Harbour on the mainland via frequent ferry service in summer. **Coastal Transport** ferries (✆ **506/662-3724**), each capable of hauling 60 cars, depart from the mainland and the island every 2 hours between 7:30am and 5:30pm during July and August; a ferry makes three to four trips the rest of the year. The round-trip fare is C$8.75 (US$5) per passenger (C$4.40/US$2.75 ages 5–12), C$26.20 (US$16) per car. Boarding the ferry on the mainland is free; tickets are purchased when you leave the island.

No reservations are accepted (although you can buy an advance ticket for the first trip each day off the island); get in line early to secure a spot. A good strategy for departing from Blacks Harbour is to bring a picnic lunch, arrive an hour or two early, put your car in line, and head to the grassy waterfront park adjacent to the wharf. It's an attractive spot; there's even an island to explore at low tide.

**VISITOR INFORMATION** The island's **Visitor Information Centre,** P.O. Box 193, Grand Manan, NB E0G 2M0 (© **506/662-3442**) is open daily in summer (10am–4pm except Sundays, when it's open 1–5pm) in the town of Grand Harbour. It's beneath the museum, across from the elementary school. If the center is closed, ask around at island stores or inns for one of the free island maps published by the **Grand Manan Tourism Association** (© **888/525-1655;** www.grandmanannb.com), which includes a listing of key island phone numbers.

## EXPLORING THE ISLAND

Start your explorations before you arrive. As you come abreast of the island aboard the ferry, head to the starboard side. You'll soon see **Seven Day's Work** in the rocky cliffs of Whale's Cove, where seven layers of hardened lava and sill (intrusive igneous rock) have come together in a sort of geological Dagwood sandwich.

You can begin to open the Japanese puzzle box that is local geology at the **Grand Manan Museum** (© **506/662-3524**) in Grand Harbour, one of three villages on the island's eastern shore. The museum's geology exhibit, located in the basement, offers pointers about what to look for as you roam the island. Birders will enjoy the Allan Moses collection upstairs, which features 230 stuffed and mounted birds in glass cases. The museum also has an impressive lighthouse lens from the Gannet Rock Lighthouse, and a collection of stuff that's washed ashore from the frequent shipwrecks. The museum is open mid-June to October from Monday to Saturday 10:30am to 4:30pm, Sunday 1 to 5pm. Admission is C$2 (US$1.20) per adult, C$1 (US60¢) for seniors and students, and is free for under 12s.

Numerous hiking trails lace the island, and they offer a popular diversion throughout the summer. Trails can be found just about everywhere, but most are a matter of local knowledge. Don't hesitate to ask at your inn or the tourist information center, or to ask anyone you might meet on the street. ***A Hiking Guide to New Brunswick*** (Goose Lane Editions, © **506/450-4251;** www.gooselane.com) lists 12 hikes with maps; this handy book is often sold on the ferry. The most accessible clusters of trails are at the island's northern and southern tips. Head north up Whistle Road to Whistle Beach, and you'll find both the Northwestern Coastal Trail and the Seven Day's Work Trail, both of which track along the rocky shoreline. Near the low lighthouse and towering radio antennae at Southwest Head (follow Route 776 to the end), trails radiate out along cliffs topped with scrappy forest; the views are remarkable when the fog's not in.

## WHALE-WATCHING & BOAT TOURS

A fine way to experience island ecology is to mosey offshore. Several outfitters offer complete nature tours, providing a nice sampling of the world above and beneath the sea. **Island Coast Boat Tours** (© **506/662-8181**) sets out for 4- to 5-hour expeditions in search of whales and birds; they cost C$48 (US$30) per adult and C$26 (US$16) per child. **SeaView Adventures** (© **800/586-1922** in Canada or 506/662-3211) offers 3½-hour educational tours with a unique twist: Divers provide a live underwater video feed to an onboard monitor. Prices are C$45 (US$28) adult, C$40 (US$25) seniors, and C$24 (US$15) children. **Sea**

**Watch Tours** (✆ **506/662-8552**) runs 5-hour excursions with whales guaranteed aboard a 17m (42-ft.) vessel with canopy. The rate is C$48 (US$30) per adult, and C$11 to C$38 (US$7–US$24) per child, depending on age.

## WHERE TO STAY

**Anchorage Provincial Park** (✆ **506/662-7022**) has 100 campsites scattered about forest and field. There's a small beach and a hiking trail on the property, and it's well situated for exploring the southern part of the island. It's very popular midsummer; call before you board the ferry to ask about campsite availability. Sites are C$24 (US$15) with hookups for RVs, C$21.50 (US$13) for a tent.

**Inn at Whale Cove Cottages** ★ The Inn at Whale Cove is a delightful, family-run compound set in a grassy meadow overlooking a quiet and picturesque cove. The original building is a cozy farmhouse that dates to 1816. It's been restored rustically with a nice selection of simple country antiques. The guest rooms are comfortable (Sally's Attic has a small deck and a large view); the living room has a couple years' worth of good reading and a welcoming fireplace. The cottages are scattered about the property, and they vary from one to four bedrooms. The 4ha (10-acre) grounds, especially the path down to the quiet cove-side beach, are wonderful to explore. Innkeeper Laura Buckley received her culinary training in Toronto, and she demonstrates a deft touch with local ingredients.

Whistle Rd. (P.O. Box 233), North Head, Grand Manan, NB E0G 2M0. ✆ **506/662-3181.** 3 units, 4 cottages. C$100 (US$62) double, including full breakfast; cottages rent by the week only, C$600–C$700 (US$372–US$434). MC, V. Closed Nov–Apr. Pets accepted. **Amenities:** Restaurant. *In room:* Kitchenette.

**Shorecrest Lodge** ★ *Value* *Kids* This century-old inn is a fine place to put your feet up and unwind. Located just a few hundred yards from the ferry, the inn is nicely decorated with a mix of modern furniture and eclectic country antiques. Most of the guest rooms have private bathrooms (a rarity for Grand Manan). The best is Room 8 with burgundy leather chairs and a great harbor view. Kids like the spacious TV room in the back, which also has games and a library that's strong in local natural history. The homey country-style dining room has a fireplace and hardwood floors, and a menu that includes local fresh seafood and filet mignon. It's open daily 5 to 9pm during peak season; hours are limited during the shoulder season.

North Head, Grand Manan, NB E0G 2M0. ✆ **506/662-3216.** shorcres@nbnet.nb.ca. 10 units (2 w/shared bathroom). C$65–C$99 (US$40–US$61) double, including continental breakfast. MC, V. Closed Dec–March. **Amenities:** Restaurant; fitness equipment; TV room.

## WHERE TO DINE

Options for dining out aren't exactly extravagant on Grand Manan. The two inns listed above offer appetizing meals and decent value.

In the mood for a dare? Try walking into **North Head Bakery** (✆ **506/662-8862**) and walking out without buying anything. It cannot be done. This superb bakery (open Tues–Sat, 6am–6pm) has used traditional baking methods and whole grains since it opened in 1990. Breads made daily include a crusty, seven-grain Saint John Valley bread and a delightful egg-and-butter bread. Nor should the chocolate-chip cookies be overlooked. The bakery is on Route 776 on the left when you're heading south from the ferry.

For a ready-made picnic, detour to **Cove Cuisine** (open Mon–Sat, 11am–5pm) at the Inn at Whale Cove (see above). Laura Buckley offers a limited but tasty selection of "new traditional" fixin's, like hummus, tabouli, and curried chicken salad to go.

## 4 Saint John: New Brunswick's Largest City ★

Centered on a sizeable commercial harbor, Saint John is the center of much of the province's industry. Spread over a low hill, the downtown boasts wonderfully elaborate Victorian flourishes on the rows of commercial buildings. (Be sure to look high along the cornices to appreciate the intricate brickwork.) A handful of impressive mansions lord over side streets, their interiors a forest of intricate wood carving—appropriate for the timber barons who built them.

There's a certain industrial grittiness to Saint John; some find this raw and unappealing, and others find in it a certain ragged raffishness. It all depends on your outlook. Just don't expect a tidy garden city with lots of neat homes. Saint John's got a surfeit of brick architecture in various states of repair, and from throughout the downtown you'll get glimpses of industry: large shipping terminals, oil storage facilities, paper mills, of the sort that was so popular with the Ashcan artists.

Don't let this put you off—make the effort to detour from the highway to downtown. (And it does take some effort; the traffic engineers have been very mischievous here.) When you finally arrive, you'll discover an intriguing place to stroll around for an afternoon while awaiting the ferry to Digby, to grab a delicious bite to eat, or to break up village-hopping with an urban overnight. The streets often bustle with everyone from skateboarders sporting nose rings to impeccably coiffed dowagers shopping at the public market.

### ESSENTIALS

**GETTING THERE** **By Plane** **Saint John Airport** (✆ **506/636-4904**) has regular flights to Toronto, Halifax, and other Canadian points; contact **Air Canada** (✆ **888/AIR-CANA**; www.aircanada.ca) for more information. Since September 1999 the airport has levied a C$10 (US$6) fee on all departing passengers to finance improvements.

**By Ferry** Year-round ferry service connects Saint John to Digby, NS. See "Exploring the Province" at the beginning of this chapter for information.

**By Car** Saint John is located on Route 1. It's 107km (66 miles) from the U.S. border at St. Stephens, and 424km (265 miles) from Halifax, NS.

**VISITOR INFORMATION** **Tourist offices** Saint John has three visitor information centers. Arriving from the west, look for a contemporary triangular building just off the **Route 1 West off-ramp** (open mid-May to mid-October), where you'll find a trove of information and brochures (✆ **506/658-2940**). A smaller seasonal information center, reached by exits 119A and 119B, is located inside the observation building overlooking the **Reversing Falls** on Route 100 (✆ **506/658-2937**).

If you've already made your way downtown, look for the **City Centre Tourist Information Centre** (✆ **888/364-4444** or 506/658-2855) inside Market Square, a downtown shopping mall just off the waterfront reached via exit 22. Find the info center by entering the square at street level at the corner of St. Patrick and

---

**Fun Fact** **Spell It Out**

Saint John is always spelled out, just like that. It's never abbreviated as St. John. That's to keep mail aimed for Saint John's in Newfoundland from ending up here, and vice versa.

---

Water Streets. During peak season (mid-June to mid-September) the center is open daily from 9am to 8pm. The rest of the year it's open daily 9am to 6pm. Visit Saint John's official site at **www.city.saint-john.nb.ca.**

**SPECIAL EVENTS & FESTIVALS** The **Saint John Jazz & Blues Festival** (✆ **506/642-JAZZ;** www.saintjohnjazzandblues.com) is held in July. In August, **Festival by the Sea** (✆ **506/632-0086;** www.festivalbythesea.com) offers a variety of performances.

## EXPLORING SAINT JOHN

If the weather's cooperative, start by wandering around near the **waterfront.** The Visitor and Convention Bureau has published three walking tour brochures that offer plenty of history and architectural trivia. Saint John is noted for the odd and interesting gargoyles and sculpted heads that adorn the brick and stone 19th-century buildings downtown. If you have time for only one tour, I'd opt for **"Prince William's Walk,"** an hour-long, self-guided tour of the impressive commercial buildings. Request the free tour brochures at the Market Square information center.

If the weather's disagreeable, head indoors. Over the past decade, Saint John has been busy linking its downtown malls and shops with an elaborate network of underground and overhead pedestrian walkways, dubbed **"The Inside Connection."** It's not just for shopping—two major hotels, the provincial museum, the city library, the city market, the sports arena, and the aquatic center are all part of the network.

**Loyalist House** A mandatory destination for serious antique buffs, this stately Georgian home was built in 1817 for the Merritt family, who were wealthy Loyalists from Rye, New York. Inside is an extraordinary collection of furniture dating from before 1833, most pieces of which were original to the house and have never left. Especially notable are the extensive holdings of Duncan Phyfe Sheraton furniture and a rare piano-organ combination. Other unusual detailing includes the doors steamed and bent to fit into the curved sweep of the stairway, and the carvings on the wooden chair rails. Tours last 30 to 45 minutes, depending on the number of questions you muster.

120 Union St. ✆ **506/652-3590.** C$3 (US$1.85) adult, C$1 (US60¢) children, C$7 (US$4.35) family. Daily 10am–5pm in July and August; Mon–Fri only in May and June. By appt. only mid-Sept to Apr.

**New Brunswick Museum** ★ The New Brunswick Museum opened in modern, downtown quarters in 1996, and is an excellent stop for anyone who is the least bit curious about the province's natural or cultural history. The collections are displayed on three open floors, and they offer a nice mix of traditional artifacts and quirky objects. (Among the more memorable items is a frightful looking "permanent wave" machine from a 1930s beauty parlor.) The exhaustive exhibits include the complete interior of Sullivan's Bar (where long-shoremen used to slake their thirst a few blocks away), a massive section of a ship frame, a wonderful geological exhibit, and even a sporty white Bricklin from a failed New Brunswick automobile manufacturing venture in the mid-1970s. New also in 2001 is Wind, Wood and Sail, an exhibit describing 19th-century shipbuilding in the province. Allow at least 2 hours to enjoy these eclectic and uncommonly well-displayed exhibits.

Market Square. ✆ **506/643-2300.** www.gnb.ca/0130/. Admission C$6 (US$3.70) adult, C$4.75 (US$2.95) senior, C$3.25 (US$2) student and youth ages 4–18, C$13 (US$8) families. Mid-May–Nov Mon–Fri 9am–5pm (until 9pm Thurs), Sat 10am–5pm, Sun noon–5pm, rest of the year Tues–Fri 9am–9pm (until 8pm Thurs), Sat–Sun noon–5pm.

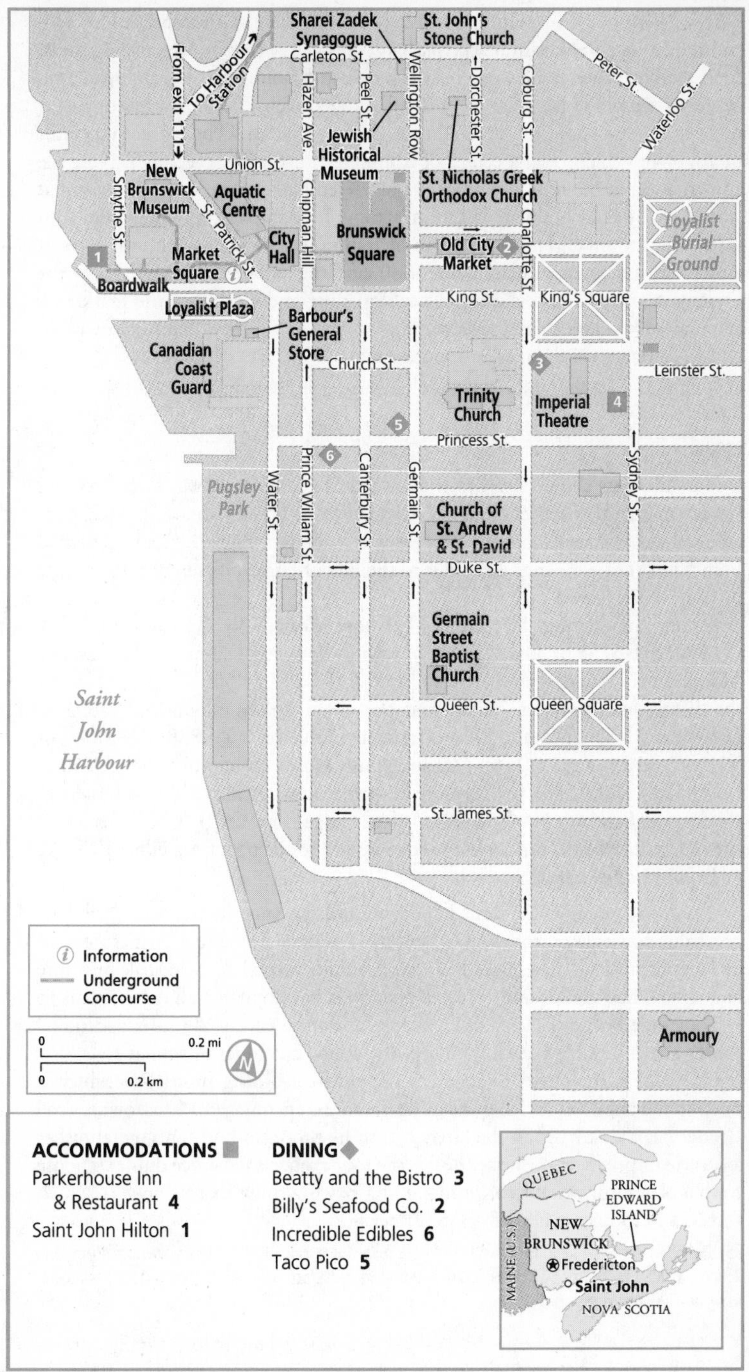
Sharei Zadek Synagogue
St. John's Stone Church
Carleton St.
Peter St.
Waterloo St.
From exit 111
To Harbour Station
Hazen Ave.
Peel St.
Wellington Row
Dorchester St.
Coburg St.
Jewish Historical Museum
Union St.
New Brunswick Museum
Smythe St.
Aquatic Centre
St. Patrick St.
Chipman Hill
St. Nicholas Greek Orthodox Church
Loyalist Burial Ground
Brunswick Square
City Hall
Market Square
Old City Market
Charlotte St.
Boardwalk
King St.
King's Square
Loyalist Plaza
Barbour's General Store
Canadian Coast Guard
Church St.
Leinster St.
Trinity Church
Imperial Theatre
Princess St.
Sydney St.
Pugsley Park
Water St.
Prince William St.
Canterbury St.
Germain St.
Church of St. Andrew & St. David
Duke St.
Germain Street Baptist Church
Queen St.
Queen Square
Saint John Harbour
St. James St.
Information
Underground Concourse
0
0.2 mi
0
0.2 km
N
Armoury
ACCOMMODATIONS
Parkerhouse Inn & Restaurant 4
Saint John Hilton 1
DINING
Beatty and the Bistro 3
Billy's Seafood Co. 2
Incredible Edibles 6
Taco Pico 5
QUEBEC
PRINCE EDWARD ISLAND
NEW BRUNSWICK
MAINE (U.S.)
Fredericton
Saint John
NOVA SCOTIA

**Old City Market** ★ Hungry travelers venture here at their peril! This spacious, bustling, and bright marketplace is crammed with vendors hawking meat, fresh seafood, cheeses, flowers, baked goods, and bountiful fresh produce. You can even sample dulse, a snack of dried seaweed from the Bay of Fundy. (One traveler has compared the experience to licking a wharf.) The market was built in 1876, and it has been a center of commerce for the city ever since. Note the construction of the roof—local lore says it resembles an inverted ship because it was made by boat builders who didn't know how to build anything else. And watch for the small, enduring traces of tradition: The handsome iron gates at either end have been in place since 1880, and the loud bell is rung daily by the Deputy Market Clerk, who signals the opening and closing of the market. A number of vendors offer meals to go, and there's a bright seating area in an enclosed terrace on the market's south side.

47 Charlotte St. ✆ **506/658-2820.** Mon–Thurs 7:30am–6pm, Fri 7:30am–7pm, Sat 7:30am–5pm. Closed Sundays and holidays.

## WHERE TO STAY

Budget travelers should head to Manawagonish Road for lower-priced motels. Unlike many other motel strips, which tend to be notably unlovely, Manawagonish Road is reasonably attractive. It winds along a high ridge of residential homes west of town, with views out to the Bay of Fundy. It's about a 10-minute drive into downtown.

Among the offerings here are the **Fairport Motel,** 1360 Manawagonish Rd. (✆ **800/251-6158** or 506/672-9700), with its home-cooked-meals; the **Seacoast Motel,** 1441 Manawagonish Rd. (✆ **800/541-0277** or 506/635-8700), where the rooms have sweeping views; and the clean, well-lit rooms and cabins at **Balmoral Court Motel,** 1284 Manawagonish Rd. (✆ **888/463-3779** or 506/672-3019). Rates at most Manawagonish motels are approximately C$60 to C$70 (US$37–US$43) peak season. In-town camping is available summers at **Rockwood Park** (✆ **506/652-4050**); fates range from C$15 (US$9) for a tent site to C$20 (US$12) for hookups. Follow signs to the park from either Exit 111 or Exit 113 off Route 1.

**Dufferin Inn** ★★ *Finds* This handsome Queen Anne house, across the harbor from downtown near the Digby ferry, was once home to a former premier of New Brunswick. The place has a wonderfully settled air, with oak furniture and overstuffed chairs, and recent renovations have updated all three rooms to now include both a Jacuzzi and a fireplace. By the end of 2002 six additional rooms are to be added, each with top-of-the-line amenities in similar style.

Guests often stay here for access to the excellent **dining room** ★★, which is open to the public as well as guests. (Reservations encouraged.) Chef/owner Axel Begner has a deft hand in the kitchen, and he produces fine continental dishes à la carte or prix fixe; the better deal is the four-course fixed-price dinner (choose from a New Brunswick-themed menu or a Bay of Fundy-themed menu), which runs C$45 to C$52 (US$28–US$32) per person.

357 Dufferin Row, Saint John, NB E2M 2J7. ✆ **506/635-5968.** Fax 506/674-2396. www.dufferininn.com. 3 units. C$80–C$160 (US$50–US$99) double, including breakfast. DC, MC, V. **Amenities:** Restaurant. *In room:* Hair dryer, iron.

**Homeport Historic Bed & Breakfast** ★★ *Kids* This architecturally impressive Italianate home sits high atop a rocky ridge on the north side of Route 1, overlooking downtown and the harbor. Built around 1858, the home opened its doors to guests in 1997, and is one of Saint John's more gracious options for staying overnight. Rooms are furnished eclectically with furniture gleaned from area auctions and shops; all have individually controlled heat. Ask for the Veranda Room; it's spacious, has fine harbor views, and gets superb afternoon sun. (I'm also partial to the pink-tiled bathroom.) The Harbour Master Suite has a small separate sitting room, which is ideal for those traveling with a child. Five more rooms were recently added in the twin house next door. "Come-hungry" breakfasts are served family-style around a long antique table in the formal dining room.

80 Douglas Ave., Saint John, NB E2K 1E4. ✆ **888/678-7678** or 506/672-7255. Fax 506/672-7250. www.homeport.nb.ca. 10 units. C$80–C$150 (US$50–US$93), includes breakfast. AE, MC, V. **Amenities:** Dry cleaning. *In room:* A/C, TV.

**Inn on the Cove** ★★ Inns like to tout celebrity connections, but the Inn on the Cove has the thinnest link to fame I've yet found: It was built by Alexander Graham Bell's gardener. Nevertheless, it's in a lovely setting, on a quiet road overlooking the water about 15 minutes' drive from downtown. The Irving Nature Park is next door; guests can hike right from the inn to dramatic Sheldon's Point. The house was once a classic late Victorian, built in 1910. In the 1950s it suffered from "improvements." Architectural preservationists will wince, but the changes did make for bright, spacious rooms that take advantage of the views. Some have Jacuzzis, some fireplaces, one a kitchen, and one a private laundry. Meals here are excellent—the owners host a local cooking show on TV—and there's a new day spa as well, offering mud wraps, facials, and more for an extra charge. Working? There's a small business center with a fax machine.

1371 Sand Cove Rd. (mailing address: P.O. Box 3113, Station B, Saint John, NB E2M 4X7). ✆ **877/257-8080** or 506/672-7799. Fax 506/635-5455. www.innonthecove.com. 5 units. C$95–C$195 (US$59–US$121) double peak season, lower in shoulder season. Rates include full breakfast. MC, V. Children 12 and up. Small dogs allowed in kennels. **Amenities:** Restaurant; day spa; business center. *In room:* Hair dryer.

**Parkerhouse Inn & Restaurant** ★ The Parkerhouse is a grand 1890 in-town mansion designed in high Victorian style by a wealthy timber merchant. The attention to architectural detail is above and beyond the usual, from the beveled leaded glass in the front doorway to the exquisite carved staircase of regal mahogany. Much of the downstairs is given over to a restaurant, and there's a bright sitting area fronting the street. Guest rooms are decorated in a light Victorian country style, several feature gas fireplaces. Among the best rooms are no. 5, with its sitting room, wood floors, pine armoire, and wonderful morning light; and no. 3 with maple floors, bay window, old-fashioned shutters, and a handsome birds-eye mahogany bed (alas, the bathroom is small). One of Saint John's better **restaurants** ★ is located on the ground floor. Angle for a seat in the Victorian solarium with its mosaic floor, although the two other dining rooms are both cozy and romantic.

71 Sydney St., Saint John, NB E2L 2L5. ✆ **888/457-2520** or 506/652-5054. Fax 506/636-8076. 9 units. C$99 (US$61) and up double. AE, DC, MC, V. Children 10 and up. **Amenities:** 3 restaurants. *In room:* Hair dryer.

**Saint John Hilton** ★ This waterfront hotel was built in 1984 and has the amenities one would expect from an upscale chain hotel; rooms on the top two Plaza Floors have even been repainted, redecorated, and upgraded to include perks such as electronic safes, cordless phones, bigger desks, and robes. This property boasts the best location in Saint John, overlooking the harbor yet just steps from the rest of downtown by street or indoor walkway. Windows in all guest rooms open, a nice touch when the breeze is coming from the sea, but not when it's blowing in from the paper mill to the west. The Hilton is connected to the convention center and attracts major events; ask whether anything's scheduled before you book if you don't want to be overwhelmed by conventioneers.

1 Market Sq., Saint John, NB E2L 4Z6. ✆ **800/561-8282** (in Canada), 800/445-8667 (in the U.S.), or 506/693-8484. Fax 509/657-6610. www.hilton.nb.ca. 197 units. Summer to mid-Oct C$99–C$165 (US$61–US$102) double, off-season C$99–C$115 (US$61–US$71). AE, DC, DISC, MC, V. Free parking weekends, otherwise C$12.95 (US$8) per day. Pets allowed. **Amenities:** 2 restaurants, bar; small indoor pool; fitness room; Jacuzzi; sauna; concierge; business center; 24-hour room service; babysitting; laundry. *In room:* A/C, TV, minibar, coffeemaker, hair dryer, iron.

## WHERE TO DINE

For lunch, don't overlook the **Old City Market,** mentioned above. With a little snooping you can turn up tasty light meals and fresh juices in the market, then enjoy your finds in the alley atrium.

**Beatty and the Beastro** ★ BISTRO/CONTINENTAL The small, simple, and attractive interior of this large-windowed establishment fronting King's Square features a mild European-moderne look, and is the most handsome eatery in Saint John. The service is cordial and efficient, and the meals are among the best in the city, always good, sometimes excellent. Lunch includes soups, salads, omelets, curry wraps, and elaborate sandwiches. At dinner, the restaurant is noted for its lamb, the preparation of which varies nightly according to the chef's desire; the curry dish is also recommended, as is chicken parmigiana and almost anything else. When dessert time rolls around, be aware that both the butterscotch pie and the lemon chess pie have large local followings.

60 Charlotte St. (on King's Square). ✆ **506/652-3888.** Reservations recommended weekends and when shows are slated at the Imperial Theatre. Lunch C$5.95–C$9.95 (US$3.70–US$6), dinner C$19.95–C$22.95 (US$12–US$14). AE, DC, MC, V. Mon–Fri 11:30am–3pm; Mon–Sat 5:30–9pm (until 10pm Fri and Sat). Closed weekends Sept–July.

**Billy's Seafood Co.** ★ SEAFOOD Billy Grant's restaurant off King's Square boasts a congenial staff, exceptionally fresh seafood (they sell to City Market customers by day), and slightly better prices than the more tourist-oriented waterfront seafood restaurants. The chef knows how to prepare fish without overcooking. This classy but casual restaurant is cozy and comfortable, painted a soothing deep, deep blue, with the likes of Ella Fitzgerald and Dinah Washington crooning in the background. Specialties include cedar-planked salmon, and Billy's bouillabaisse is also quite good. Lunch entrées are surprisingly versatile, too, including Thai curried mussels and seafood crepes among other choices. Offerings of beef, veal, and pasta fill out the menu for those not in the mood for fish.

Fish Market & Oyster Bar. 49–51 Charlotte St. (at City Market). ✆ **506/672-3474.** Reservations suggested. Light meals C$5.95–C$10.95 (US$3.70–US$7), dinner entrees C$15.95–C$28.95 (US$10–US$18). AE, DC, MC, V. Mon–Thurs 11am–10pm, Fri and Sat 11am–11pm, Sun 4–10pm.

**Incredible Edibles** ★ ECLECTIC This is another fine Saint John restaurant with a regrettably cutesy name. Located in the Brodie Building a block off King St., this relaxed and casual spot has four cozy dining rooms (three nonsmoking), high tin ceilings, mix-and-match seating, and little sand-and-rock Zen gardens on each table to while away the time. The menu is appealingly eclectic. Lunch ranges from omelets to pizza and pad thai. At dinner, there's Yorkshire pudding and a revolving set of specials. The service is friendly, and the food consistently good.

42 Princess St. ✆ **506/633-7554.** Reservations advised. Lunch C$5.75–C$13 (US$3.55–US$8), dinner C$10.50–C$23.95 (US$7–US$15). Daily 11am–11pm.

**Taco Pica** LATINO This worker-owned cooperative is owned and run by a group of Guatemalans and their friends. It's bright, festive, and just a short stroll off King Street. The restaurant has developed a devoted local following since it opened in 1994, and features a menu that's a notch above the usually dreary Canadian adaptations of Mexican or Latin American fare. Among the most reliably popular dishes are pepian (a spicy beef stew with chayote), garlic shrimp, and shrimp taco with potatoes, peppers, and cheese. Vegetarian offerings are available, as well. There's also a good selection of fresh juices, and the restaurant now possesses a liquor license—which means you can quaff any of a variety of fruit margaritas.

96 Germain St. ✆ **506/633-8492.** Reservations suggested on weekends. Main courses C$7.95–C$17.25 (US$5–US$11); same menu lunch and dinner. AE, MC, V. Mon–Sat 10am–10pm, closed Sun and holidays.

## 5 Fredericton

New Brunswick's provincial capital is a compact and historic city of brick and concrete that unfolds lazily along the banks of the wide St. John River. The handsome buildings, broad streets, and wide sidewalks make the place feel more like a big, tidy village than a small city. Keep an eye out for the two icons that mark Fredericton: the stately, stubborn elm trees that have resisted Dutch elm disease and still shade the occasional park and byway, and the Union Jack, which you'll occasionally see fluttering from various buildings, attesting to long-standing historic ties with the Loyalists who shaped the city.

For travelers, the city can be seen as divided into three zones: the malls and motels atop the hills and near the link to the Trans-Canada Highway; the impressive, Georgian-style University of New Brunswick on the hillside just south of downtown; and the downtown proper, with its casual blend of modern and historic buildings. Most visitors focus on downtown. The main artery—where you'll find the majority of the attractions and many restaurants—is Queen Street, which parallels the river between 1 and 2 blocks inland. An ill-considered, limited-access, four-lane bypass separates much of downtown from the river, but you can still reach the water's edge via the Green or by crossing a pedestrian bridge at the foot of Carleton Street.

### ESSENTIALS

**GETTING THERE By Plane Fredericton Airport** (✆ **506/444-6100**) is located 10 minutes southeast of downtown on Route 102 and is served by cab and rental car companies. Direct service is available to Toronto, Montréal, Ottawa, and Halifax. For flight information, contact **Air Canada** (✆ **888/AIR-CANA;** www.aircanada.ca).

**By Car** A major relocation and widening of the Trans-Canada Highway near Fredericton has relieved traffic congestion somewhat. Look for signs directing you to downtown; from the west, follow Woodstock Road, which tracks along the river to downtown. From Saint John, look for Route 7 to Regent Street, then turn right down the hill.

**VISITOR INFORMATION Tourist Offices** Always careful to cater to visitors, Fredericton maintains no less than two center-city tourism centers: the original in **City Hall** at 397 Queen St., and a second, newer one at **11 Carleton St.** Call ✆ **888/888-4768** or 506/460-2129 to reach either. Then there's a third information center at **King's Landing** (✆ **506/460-2191**), just west of town. No matter which one you find first, ask for a Visitor Parking Pass, which allows

**Tips** **What's Your Passion?**

If eastern Canada's allure for you is the shimmering sea, deep woods, and wide open spaces, you won't miss much by bypassing Fredericton. If your passions include history—especially the history of British settlement in North America—then it's well worth the detour.

visitors from outside the province to park free at city lots and meters in town for up to 3 days without penalty. You can request travel information in advance by visiting the city's website at **www.city.fredericton.nb.ca.**

**SPECIAL EVENTS & FESTIVALS** The **New Brunswick Highland Games & Scottish Festival** (**© 888/366-4444;** www.nbhighlandgames.com) is held in late July. The **Harvest Jazz & Blues Festival** (**© 888/NB-BLUES;** www.harvestjazzblues.nb.ca) livens mid-September.

## EXPLORING FREDERICTON

The free *Fredericton Visitor Guide,* available at the information centers and many hotels around town, contains a well-written and informative walking tour of the downtown. It's worth tracking down before launching an exploration of the city.

**City Hall,** 397 Queen St., is an elaborate Victorian building with a prominent brick tower and 2.5m (8-ft.) clock dial. The second-floor City Council Chamber occupies what was the opera house until the 1940s. Small, folksy tapestries adorn the visitor's gallery and tell the town's history. Learn about these and the rest of the building during the free building tours, which are offered daily from mid-May to mid-October on the hour (on the half hour in French). In the off-season, call **© 506/460-2129** to schedule a tour.

**Officer's Square,** on Queen Street between Carleton and Regent, is now a handsome city park. In 1785, the park was the center of military activity and used for drills, first as part of the British garrison, and later (until 1914) by the Canadian Army. Today, the only soldiers are local actors who put on a show for the tourists. Look also for music and dramatic events staged at the square in the warmer months. The handsome colonnaded stone building facing the parade grounds is the former officer's quarters, now the York-Sunbury Historical Society Museum.

Two blocks upriver of Officer's Square is the **Soldier's Barracks,** housed in a similarly grand stone building. Check your watch against the sundial high on the end of the barracks, a replica of the original timepiece. A small exhibit shows the life of the enlisted man in the 18th century. Along the ground floor, local craftspeople sell their wares from small shops carved out of former barracks.

One entertaining and enlightening way to learn about the city's history is to sign up for a **walking tour** with the Calithumpians of Fredericton's Outdoor Summer Theatre (**© 506/457-1975**). Costumed guides offer free tours daily in July and August, pointing out highlights with anecdotes and dramatic tales. Recommended is the evening "Haunted Hike" tour, which runs 3 nights each week. The evening tour is about 2 hours and costs C$12 (US$7) per adult and C$8 (US$5) per child.

Fredericton recently expanded its trail system for walkers and bikers. The centerpiece of the system is The Green, a 5km (3-mile) pathway that follows the river from the Sheraton hotel to near the Princess Margaret Bridge. It's a lovely

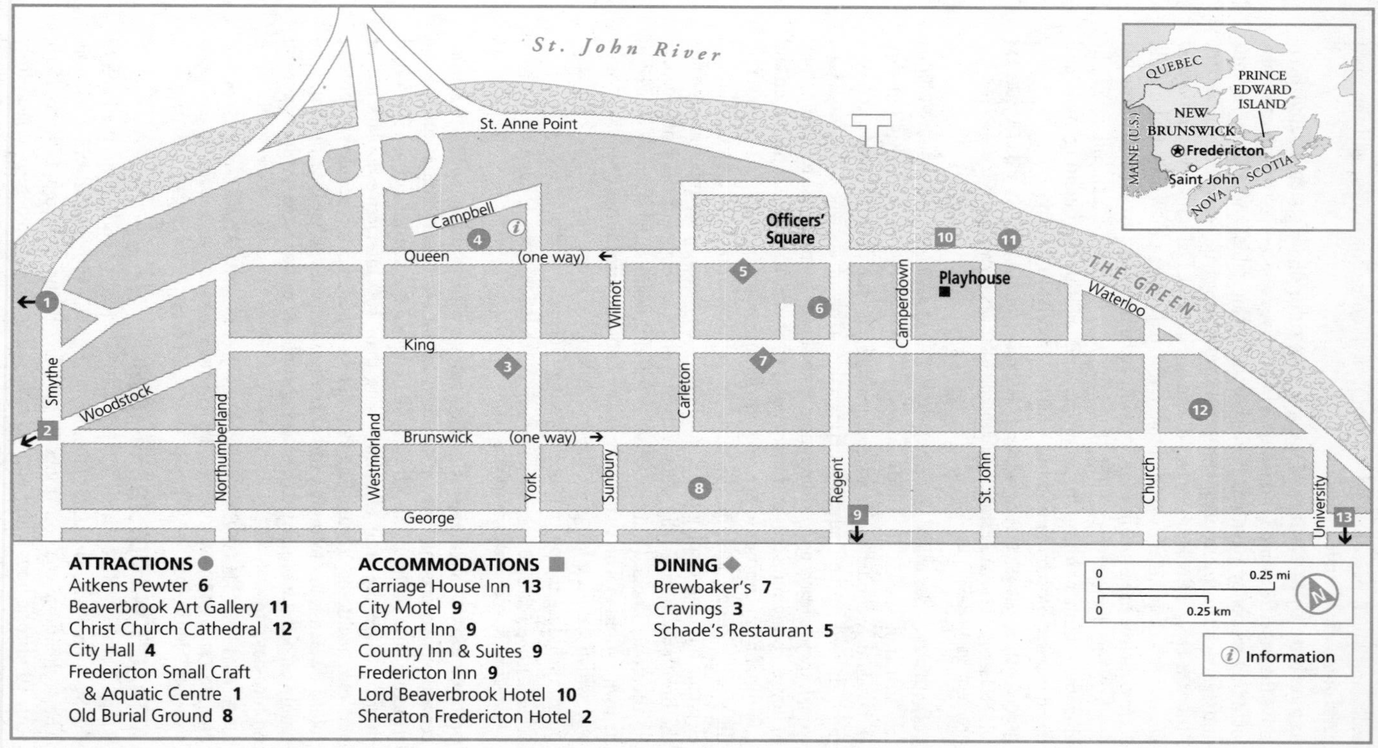
St. John River
St. Anne Point
QUEBEC
PRINCE EDWARD ISLAND
NEW BRUNSWICK
MAINE (U.S.)
Fredericton
Saint John
NOVA SCOTIA
Campbell
Officers' Square
Queen
(one way)
Wilmot
Playhouse
Camperdown
THE GREEN
Waterloo
Smythe
King
Woodstock
Northumberland
Westmorland
Carleton
Brunswick
(one way)
York
Sunbury
Regent
St. John
Church
University
George
ATTRACTIONS
Aitkens Pewter 6
Beaverbrook Art Gallery 11
Christ Church Cathedral 12
City Hall 4
Fredericton Small Craft & Aquatic Centre 1
Old Burial Ground 8
ACCOMMODATIONS
Carriage House Inn 13
City Motel 9
Comfort Inn 9
Country Inn & Suites 9
Fredericton Inn 9
Lord Beaverbrook Hotel 10
Sheraton Fredericton Hotel 2
DINING
Brewbaker's 7
Cravings 3
Schade's Restaurant 5
0
0.25 mi
0
0.25 km
N
Information

walk, and you'll pass the Old Government House, downtown, and the open parklands near Waterloo Row.

**Beaverbrook Art Gallery** ★ *Value* This surprisingly good museum overlooks the waterfront and is home to an impressive collection of British paintings, including works by Reynolds, Gainsborough, Constable, and Turner. Antique buffs gravitate to the rooms with period furnishings and early decorative arts. Almost everyone finds themselves drawn to Salvador Dali's massive *Santiago El Grande* as well as his early studies for an ill-fated portrait of Winston Churchill. A new curator has brought in more controversial modern art exhibits in the last 2 years; one focused on nudity, featuring various artistic perceptions of the unclothed human form, for example, and another highlighting provincial female artists. Stop by to find out what's currently on display.

703 Queen St. ✆ **506/458-8545.** www.beaverbrookartgallery.org. Admission C$5 (US$3.10) adults, C$4 (US$2.50) seniors, C$2 (US$1.20) students, children under 6 free; Tues, pay what you wish. Mon–Fri 9am–6pm (Thurs until 8pm), Sat–Sun 10am–5pm.

**Legislative Assembly Building** ★ The Legislative Assembly Building (construction started in 1880) boasts an exterior designed in that bulbous, extravagant Second Empire style. But that's just the prelude. Inside, it's even more dressed up and fancy. Entering takes a bit of courage if the doors are closed; they're heavy and intimidating, with slits of beveled glass for peering out. (They're a bit reminiscent of the gates of Oz.) Inside, it's creaky and wooden and comfortable, in contrast to the cold, unyielding stone of many seats of power. In the small rotunda, look for the razor-sharp prints from John James Audubon's elephant folio, on display in a special case. The assembly chamber nearly takes the breath away, especially when viewed from the heights of the visitor gallery on the upper floors. (You ascend via a graceful wood spiral stairway housed in its own rotunda.) The chamber is ornate and draperied in that fussy Victorian way, which is quite a feat given the vast scale of the room. Note all the regal trappings, including the portrait of the young Queen Elizabeth.

Queen St. (across from the Beaverbrook Art Gallery). ✆ **506/453-2527.** Free admission. May–Sept daily 8:45am–7pm; off-season weekdays 9am–4pm.

**Science East** ★ *Value* *Kids* Children enjoy a visit to this new (1999) science center for two reasons. First, it's located in the old county jail, a sturdy stone structure built in the 1840s. (It was still being used as a jail as late as 1996.) And then there are the great exhibits—more than 100 interactive displays indoor and out, including a huge kaleidoscope, a periscope for people-watching, a solar-powered water fountain, and a mini-tornado. It's an ideal destination for a family on a chilly or rainy day, and there's plenty to do in the outdoors portion on nice days, too.

668 Brunswick St. ✆ **506/457-2340.** www.scienceeast.nb.ca. C$3 (US$1.85) adult or child, C$2 students, (US$1.20), C$7 (US$4.35) family. May–Oct, Mon–Sat 10am–5pm, Sun 1–4pm, rest of the year Tues–Fri noon–5pm, Sat 10am–5pm.

## ATTRACTIONS OUTSIDE OF TOWN

**Kings Landing Historical Settlement** ★ Kings Landing, on the bank of the St. John River, is 34km (21 miles) and about 150 years from Fredericton. The authentic re-creation brings to life New Brunswick from 1790 to 1910, with 10 historic houses and nine other buildings relocated here and saved from destruction by the flooding during the Mactaquac hydro project. The aroma of freshly baked bread mixes with the smell of horses and livestock, and the sound of the blacksmith's hammer alternates with that of the church bell. More than

160 costumed "early settlers" chat about their lives. You could easily spend a day exploring the 60ha (150 acres), but if you haven't that much time, focus on the Hagerman House (with furniture by Victorian cabinetmaker John Warren Moore), the Ingraham House with its fine New Brunswick furniture and formal English garden, the Morehouse House (where you'll see a clock Benedict Arnold left behind), and the Victorian Perley House.

Exit 259 off the Trans-Canada Hwy. (Route 2 west). ✆ **506/363-4999** or 506/363-4959 for recorded information. www.kingslanding.nb.ca. Admission C$12 (US$7) adults, C$10 (US$6) seniors, C$8 (US$5) students over 16, C$6 (US$3.70) children 6–16, C$30 (US$19) family pass. June to mid-Oct daily 10am–5pm.

## WHERE TO STAY

A handful of motels and chain hotels are located in the bustling mall zone on the hill above town, mostly along Regent and Prospect Streets. Allow about 10 minutes to drive downtown from here. Among the classiest of the bunch is the **Fredericton Inn** 1315 Regent St. (✆ **800/561-8777** or 506/455-1430), situated between two malls. Peak season rates are C$89 to C$139 (US$55–US$86) and up to C$189 (US$117) for suites. Also near the malls are the **Comfort Inn,** 255 Prospect St. (✆ **506/453-0800**), at C$95 to C$125 (US$59–US$78) for a double room; **City Motel,** 1216 Regent St. (✆ **800/268-2858** or 506/459-9900), with rooms for C$75 to C$100 (US$47–US$62); and the **Country Inn and Suites,** 655 Prospect St. (✆ **506/459-0035**), C$100 to C$116 (US$62–US$72).

**Carriage House Inn** Fredericton's premier bed-and-breakfast is located a short stroll from the riverfront pathway in a quiet residential neighborhood. A former mayor built this imposing three-story Victorian manse in 1875. Inside, it's a bit somber in that heavy Victorian way, with dark wood trim and deep colors, and feels solid enough to resist glaciers. Rooms are eclectically furnished and comfortable without being opulent. Delicious and elaborate breakfasts are served in a sunny room in the rear of the house. Dinner is available at the inn with 48-hour advance notice; ask about the menu when you book. A complete dinner runs around C$25 (US$16) per person.

230 University Ave., Fredericton, NB E3B 4H7. ✆ **800/267-6068** or 506/452-9924. Fax 506/458-0799. chinn@nbnet.nb.ca. 11 units (2 w/private hall bathrooms). C$80–C$90 (US$50–US$56) double, includes breakfast. AE, DC, MC, V. "Small, well-trained pets" allowed. **Amenities:** Dinners by request; laundry. *In room:* Hair dryer.

**Lord Beaverbrook Hotel** This stern and hulking 1947 waterfront hotel is severe and boxy in an early deco kind of way, a look that may at first suggest that it houses the Ministry of Dourness. Inside, the mood lightens considerably, with composite stone floors, Georgian pilasters, and chandeliers. The downstairs pool and recreation area are positively whimsical, a sort of tiki-room grotto that kids adore. Guest rooms are nicely appointed with traditional reproduction furniture in dark wood. Standard rooms can be somewhat dim, and most of the windows don't open (ask for a room with opening windows when you book). Suites are spacious and many have excellent river views. This is the best accommodation for those who want the convenience of a downtown location and who enjoy the solid architectural touches of an old-fashioned hotel.

659 Queen St., Fredericton, NB E3B 5A6. ✆ **800/561-7666** (Canada and New England only) or 506/455-3371. Fax 506/455-1441. lbhotel@nbnet.nb.ca. 165 units. C$110–C$140 (US$68–US$87) double; suites to C$225 (US$140). AE, DC, MC, V. **Amenities:** 3 restaurants; small indoor pool; Jacuzzi; limited fitness equipment; airport shuttle; business center; babysitting; laundry; dry cleaning. *In room:* A/C, TV.

**On the Pond Lodge** ★ *Finds* In 1999, Donna Evans opened On the Pond, which is about 15 minutes west of Fredericton, with the idea of creating a comfortable retreat where guests could be pampered with spa treatments after indulging in soft adventure at the adjacent provincial park and surrounding countryside. The lodge is lovely, constructed in a strong sort of William Morris-inspired style with dark wood trim and fieldstone fireplaces. The two downstairs common rooms—one with wood fireplace and one lined with bookshelves—invite lingering and chatting with the other guests. The upstairs guest rooms each feature a queen and a double bed, and are slightly larger than the average hotel room. The lodge is developing a series of packages (golf, spa treatments, outdoor adventures) that makes good use of the Mactaquac area, which isn't wilderness but a rolling river valley of open farms and suburban homes.

20 Route 615, Mactaquac, NB E6L 1M2. ✆ **506/363-3420.** www.onthepond.com. 8 units. C$125–C$145 (US$78–US$90) double, including full breakfast. MC, V. Drive west of Fredericton on Woodstock Rd.; cross the Mactaquac Dam and continue to the Esso station; turn right and look for sign on right. **Amenities:** Meals; spa w/fitness center, sauna, hot tub, massage; free canoes and kayaks; mountain bikes. *In room:* A/C.

**Sheraton Fredericton Hotel** ★ This modern resort hotel, built in 1992, occupies a prime location along the river about 10 minutes' walk from downtown via the riverfront pathway. Much of summer life revolves around the outdoor pool on the deck overlooking the river, and on Sunday the lobby is surrendered to an over-the-top breakfast buffet. Although decidedly up to date, the interior is done with classical styling and is comfortable and well-appointed. The hotel lounge is an active and popular spot on many nights, especially weekends. Across the lobby is Bruno's Seafood Cafe, which offers a good alternative to the restaurants downtown. Look also for seasonal and regional specialties, including fiddleheads in early summer.

225 Woodstock Rd., Fredericton, NB E3B 2H8. ✆ **800/325-3535** or 506/457-7000. Fax 506/457-4000. www.sheraton.com. 222 units. C$180–C$234 (US$112–US$145) double. AE, DC, MC, V. **Amenities:** Restaurant; indoor and outdoor pools; fitness room. *In room:* A/C, TV, minibar, hair dryer.

## WHERE TO DINE

A popular local downtown spot for a quick and easy lunch is **Cravings,** 348 King St. (✆ **506/452-7482**), which features generous sandwiches and pita pockets.

**Brewbakers** ★ ITALIAN/PUB FARE Brewbakers is a convivial pub, cafe, and restaurant, located on three levels in a cleverly adapted downtown building. It's a bustling and informal spot, creatively cluttered with artifacts and artworks, and does boomtown business during lunch hours and early evenings. The cafe section is quieter, as is the mezzanine dining room above the cafe. The third floor bustles, with an open kitchen and folks lined up for the popular build-your-own pasta buffet. And pasta is the main attraction here, served up with the usual array of sauces. Also good are the personal pizzas, the roasted chicken, the grilled striploin, and the herb-crusted tenderloin. The lunch buffet is one of the better deals in town—bring a large appetite. For a meal on the go, the cafe offers a creative selection of boxed lunches.

546 King St. ✆ **506/459-0067.** Reservations recommended. Lunch C$6–C$10 (US$3.70–US$6), dinner C$12–C$26 (US$7–US$16). AE, DC, MC, V. Mon–Wed 11:30am–10pm, Thurs–Fri 11:30am–midnight, Sat 4pm–midnight, Sun 4–10pm.

**Schade's Restaurant** GERMAN This German-owned and -run restaurant features traditional meals from the mid-continent, including a variety of schnitzels (schnitzel specials change daily), beef stroganoff, and beef with broccoli, mushrooms, and spaetzle. The decor at this relaxed storefront restaurant isn't overly fussy (note the attractive tin ceiling), making it an appealing spot for a casual meal over a tall glass of DAB (northern German) beer. More rarified specialties (like sauerbraten and schweinehaxe) are offered with advance notice for groups of four or more.

536 Queen St. ✆ **506/450-3340.** Reservations recommended. Lunch C$3.99–C$7.99 (US$2.50–US$5), dinner C$9.95–C$18 (US$6–US$11). AE, MC, V. Tues–Fri 11:30am–2pm and 5–9pm; Sat 5–9pm.

## 6 Fundy National Park: Exploring the Wild Coast ★★

The Fundy Coast between Saint John and Alma is for the most part wild, remote, and unpopulated. It's plumbed by few roads other than the new Fundy Drive (see "Saint John: New Brunswick's Largest City," earlier), making it difficult to explore unless you have a boat. The best access to the wild coast is through Fundy National Park, a gem of a destination that's hugely popular with travelers with an outdoor bent. Families often settle in here for a week or so, filling their days with activities in and around the park that include hiking, sea kayaking, biking, and splashing around a seaside pool. Nearby are lovely drives and an innovative adventure center at Cape Enrage. If a muffling fog moves in to smother the coast, head inland for a hike to a waterfall or through lush forest. If it's a day of brilliant sunshine, venture along the rocky shores by foot or boat.

### ESSENTIALS

**GETTING THERE** Route 114 runs through the center of Fundy National Park. If you're coming from the west, follow the prominent national park signs just east of Sussex. If you're coming from Prince Edward Island or Nova Scotia, head southward on Route 114 from Moncton.

One word of warning for travel from Moncton: Beware the signs at the Route 15 rotary directing you to Fundy National Park. Moncton's traffic czars send tourists on a silly, Mr. Toad's wild ride around the city's outskirts, apparently to avoid downtown traffic; after 16km (10 miles) of driving you'll end up within sight of the rotary again, just across the river. It's far more sensible to head downtown via Main Street, cross the river on the first steel bridge (you can see it from about everywhere), and then turn left on Route 114.

**VISITOR INFORMATION** **Tourist offices** The park's main **Visitor Centre** (✆ **506/887-6000**) is located just inside the Alma (eastern) entrance to the park. The stone building is open daily during peak season 8am to 10pm (with limited hours in the off-season). You can watch a video presentation, peruse a handful of exhibits on wildlife and tides, and shop at the nicely stocked nature bookstore. The smaller **Wolfe Lake Information Centre** (✆ **506/432-6026**) is at the park's western entrance and is open daily in summer, weekdays only in spring and fall; hours are 8am to 4:30pm weekdays and 9am to 5pm weekends. Information on Fundy and all of Canada's national parks can be found at **www.parcscanada.gc.ca**.

**FEES** Park entry fees are charged from mid-May to mid-October. The fee is C$3.50 (US$2.15) per adult, C$2.75 (US$1.70) per senior, C$1.75 (US$1.10) for children ages 6 to 16, and C$7 (US$4.35) per family. Four-day passes are available for the price of 3 days.

### EXPLORING THE PARK

Most national park activities are centered around the **Alma** (east) side of the park, where the park entrance has a cultivated and manicured air, as if part of a landed estate. Here you'll find stone walls, well-tended lawns, and attractive landscaping, along with a golf course, amphitheater, lawn bowling, and tennis.

Also in this area is a **heated saltwater pool,** set near the bay with a sweeping ocean view. There's a lifeguard on duty, and it's a popular destination for families. The pool is open late June to August. The cost is C$2 (US$1) per adult, C$1.50 (US95¢) per child, and C$5 (US$3.10) for a family.

Sea kayaking tours are a way to get a good, close look at the ocean landscape and the tides. **Fresh Air Adventure** (✆ **800/545-0020** or 506/887-2249) in Alma offers tours that range from 2 hours to several days. The half-day tours explore marsh and coastline (C$60/US$37 including lunch); the full-day adventure includes a hot meal and 6 hours of exploring the wild shores (C$100/US$62).

The park maintains 104km (65 miles) of trails for hikers and walkers. These range from a 20-minute loop to a 4-hour trek, and they pass through varied terrain. The trails are arranged such that several can be linked into a 50km (30-mile) backpacker's loop, dubbed the **Fundy Circuit,** which typically requires 3 nights in the backcountry. Preregistration is required for the overnight trek, so ask at the visitor center.

Among the most accessible hikes is the **Caribou Plain Trail,** a 3km (2-mile) loop that provides a wonderful introduction to the local terrain. You'll hike along a beaver pond, on a boardwalk across a raised peat bog, and through lovely temperate forest. Read the interpretive signs to learn about deadly "flarks," which lurk in bogs and can kill a moose. The **Third Vault Falls Trail** is a 7km (4½-mile) in-and-back hike that takes you to the park's highest waterfall, about 14m (45 ft.) high. The trail is largely a flat stroll through leafy woodlands until you begin a steady descent into a mossy gorge. You round a corner and there you are, suddenly facing the cataract.

All the park's trails are covered in the pullout trail guide you'll find in *Salt & Fir,* the booklet you'll receive when you pay your entry fee.

**CAMPING** The national park maintains four drive-in campgrounds and 15 backcountry sites. The two main campgrounds are near the Alma entrance. **Headquarters Campground** is within walking distance of Alma, the saltwater pool, and numerous other attractions. Since it overlooks the bay, this campground tends to be cool and subject to fogs. **Chignecto North Campground** is higher on the hillside, sunnier, and warmer. You can hike down to Alma on an attractive hiking trail in 1 to 2 hours. Both campgrounds have hookups for RVs, flush toilets, and showers, and sites can be reserved in advance (✆ **800/213-7275** or 506/887-6000).

The **Point Wolfe** and **Wolfe Lake** campgrounds lack RV hookups and are slightly more primitive (Wolfe Lake lacks showers), but they are the preferred destinations for campers seeking a quieter camping experience. Rates at all campgrounds are C$12 to C$19 (US$7–US$12), depending on services required; Wolfe Lake has pit toilets only and is C$10 (US$6) per night.

Backcountry sites are scattered throughout the park, with only one located directly on the coast (at the confluence of the coast and Goose River). Ask at the visitor centers for more information or to reserve a site (mandatory). Backcountry camping fees are C$3 (US$1.85) per person per night.

## A SIDE TRIP TO HOPEWELL ROCKS

There's no better place to witness the extraordinary power of the Fundy tides than at **Hopewell Rocks** ★ (✆ **506/734-3429**), located about 40km (24 miles) northeast of Fundy National Park on Route 114. Think of it as a natural sculpture garden. At low tide (the best time to visit), eroded columns as high as 15m (50 ft.) tower above the ocean floor. They're sometimes called the "flowerpots," on account of the trees and plants that still flourish on their narrowing summits.

## Seeking Adventure on Cape Enrage

Cape Enrage is a blustery and bold cape that juts impertinently out into Chignecto Bay. It's also home to a wonderful adventure center that could be a model for similar centers worldwide.

**Cape Enrage Adventures** ★ traces its roots back to 1993, when a group of Harrison Trimble High School students in Moncton decided to do something about the decay of the cape's historic lighthouse, which had been abandoned in 1988. They put together a plan to restore the light and keeper's quarters and establish an adventure center. It worked. Today, with the help of experts in kayaking, rock climbing, rappelling, and other rugged sports, a couple dozen high-school students staff and run this program throughout the summer months. The program closes in late August, when the student-managers head back to school.

Part of what makes the program so notable is its flexibility. Day adventures are scheduled throughout the summer, from which you can pick and choose, as if from a menu. These include rappelling workshops, rock-climbing lessons, kayak trips, and canoeing excursions. Prices are C$50 (US$31) per person for a 2-hour rock climbing or rappelling workshop, C$54.50 (US$34) for a half-day kayak trip. (*Note to parents:* This is an ideal spot to drop off restless teens while you indulge in scenic drives or a trip to Hopewell Rocks.)

As if running the center didn't keep the students busy enough, they also operate a restaurant (open to the public), called **The Keeper's Lunchroom.** Light but tasty meals include a notable fish chowder made with fresh haddock from a recipe provided by a local fisherman's wife, served with hot biscuits. A few other selections are offered—like grilled cheese and cheesecake—but the smart money gets the chowder.

You park at the new visitor center and restaurant and wander down to the shore. (There's also a shuttle service that runs from the interpretive center to the rocks; it costs C$1/US60¢ per ride.) Signboards fill you in on the natural history. If you're here at the bottom half of the tide, you can descend the steel staircase to the sea floor and admire these wondrous freestanding rock sculptures, chiseled by waves and tides. The site can be crowded, but that's understandable. If your schedule allows it, come early in the day when the sun is fresh over Nova Scotia across the bay, the dew is still on the ground, and most travelers are still sacked out in bed. The park charges an entry fee of C$5 (US$3.10) per adult, C$3 (US$1.85) for children ages 4 to 18, and C$12 (US$7) for a family.

If you arrive at the top half of the tide, consider a sea kayak tour around the islands and caves. **Baymount Outdoor Adventures** (© **506/734-2660**) runs 90-minute tours daily for C$45 (US$28) per adult and C$40 (US$25) per youth. (Caving tours at nearby caverns are also offered; inquire for details.)

## WHERE TO STAY

**Broadleaf Guest Ranch** ★ *Kids* The 2-bedroom cottages at this homey, family-operated ranch are a great choice for families or couples traveling together, particularly those with an interest in horses: The ranch offers trail rides of varying duration, cattle checks, and some basic spa packages. The cottages feature full kitchens, a small sitting area with gas stove, TV and VCR, and lovely, sweeping views of the ranch's 600ha (1,500 acres) and the bay. Bedrooms are furnished with bunk beds (a single over a double) plus a single bed. You won't mistake these lodgings for a five-star luxury experience, but staying here is like sinking into a favorite armchair at the end of the day: supremely comforting and satisfying. The same could be said of the hearty, simple home-cooking Broadleaf dishes up in their large, cafeteria-style dining area. Some rooms have TV/VCRs, fireplaces, and kitchenettes.

Hopewell Hill, Fundy, Albert County, E4H 3N5. ✆ **800/226-5405** or 506/882-2349. Fax 506/882-2075. www.broadleafranch.com. 50 dorm beds (groups only) w/shared bathroom C$10–C$15 (US$6–US$9). 3 2-bedroom cottages sleep up to 8, C$120–C$150 (US$74–C$93). 5-bedroom trail lodge sleeps up to 16, C$700 (US$434). V, MC. **Amenities:** Restaurant; spa; canoe and bike rental; business center; 24-hour room service; laundry.

**Fundy Park Chalets** These storybook-like cabins are set amid birch and pines just inside the park's eastern entrance and will have immediate appeal to fans of classic motor courts. The steeply gabled white clapboard cabins have interiors that will bring to mind a national park vacation, dated around 1950—painted wood floors, pine paneling, metal shower stalls, small kitchenettes. Two beds are located in the main rooms, separated by a hospital-style track curtain that pulls around one bed. What the cabins lack in privacy they more than make up for in convenience and retro charm. The golf course, playground, tennis courts, lawn bowling, and saltwater pool are all within walking distance.

Route 114 (P.O. Box 72), Alma, NB E4H 4Y8. ✆ **506/887-2808.** 29 cabins. C$50–C$78 (US$31–US$48) double; discounts in spring and fall. MC, V. Closed Oct to mid-May. *In room:* TV.

### WHERE TO DINE

**Seawinds Dining Room** PUB FARE/CANADIAN Seawinds overlooks the park golf course, and it serves as a de facto clubhouse for hungry duffers. The handsome and open dining room is decorated in rich forest green and mahogany hues, and it has hardwood floors, a flagstone fireplace, and wrought-iron chandeliers. The menu offers enough variations to please most anyone. Lunches include a variety of hamburgers, fish and chips, and bacon and cheese dogs. Dinner is somewhat more refined, with main courses like grilled trout, roast beef, and fried clams.

Route 114 (near park headquarters), Alma, NB E0A 1B0. ✆ **506/887-2098.** Reservations helpful. Sandwiches C$3–C$7 (US$1.85–US$4.35), main courses C$9–C$16 (US$6–US$10). AE, MC, V. Daily 8am–9:30pm in summer. Closed Oct–May.

## 7 Moncton: A Rival to Saint John

Moncton, a city of some 113,500 residents, has been butting heads with Saint John in recent years as it strives to overtake the older port city as the province's economic powerhouse. As such, it's more notable as a regional commercial center than as a vacation destination. Travelers who detour off the Trans-Canada will find a mix of the antique and the modern. Brick buildings with elaborate facades and cornices exist cheek by jowl with boxy office towers of a less ornamental era. Moncton's low and unobtrusive skyline is dominated by an unfortunate concrete tower that houses a cluster of microwave antennae. It looks like a project designed by a former Soviet bureaucrat in a bad mood but serves as a good landmark.

The residents are also a mix of old and new. Moncton makes the plausible claim that it's at the crossroads of the Maritimes, and it hasn't been bashful about using its geographic advantage to promote itself as a business hub. As such, much of the hotel and restaurant trade caters to people-in-suits, at least on weekdays. But walk along Main Street in the evening or on weekends, and you're likely to spot spiked hair, grunge flannel, skateboards, and other youthful fashion statements from current and lapsed eras. There's life here.

## ESSENTIALS

**GETTING THERE** **By Plane** **Greater Moncton Airport** (www.gma.ca) is about 10 minutes from downtown on Route 132 (head northeast on Main St. from Moncton and keep driving). The city is served by daily flights on **Air Canada** (✆ **888/AIR-CANA**), although the upstart carrier **WestJet** (✆ **888/WEST-JET** or 800/538-5696; www.westjet.com) flies once daily from Hamilton, Ontario (near Niagara).

**By Rail** **VIA Rail** (✆ **800/561-3949** in the U.S. or 888/842-7245 in Canada; www.viarail.ca) trains from Montréal to Halifax stop in Moncton 6 days a week. The rail station is downtown on Main Street, next to Highfield Square.

**By Car** Moncton is at the crossroads of several major routes through New Brunswick, including Route 2 (the Trans-Canada Highway) and Route 15.

**VISITOR INFORMATION** **Tourist offices** Moncton's primary visitor information center is at **Magnetic Hill,** Exit 488 off the Trans-Canada Highway (✆ **506/853-3540**). It's located in the Wharf Village section, and isn't particularly convenient—you're required to walk from the parking lot through the faux "village" of shops and boutiques to reach the center. It's open 8am to 8pm daily, late May to early September; weekdays 9am to 5pm, weekends 10am to 6pm through mid-October (closed the rest of the year). Another visitor information center is **downtown** at 655 Main St. (✆ **506/853-3590**) in the lobby of modern City Hall. It's open daily from 8:30am to 8pm from the end of May to early September. It closes at 4:30pm on weekdays the rest of the year. The city's website is **www.gomoncton.com**.

## EXPLORING MONCTON

Moncton's downtown can be easily reconnoitered on foot—once you find parking, which can be vexing. (Look for the paid lots a block or so north and south of Main St.) **Downtown Moncton Inc.** (✆ **506/857-2991**) publishes a nicely designed *"Historic Walking Tour"* brochure that touches on some of the more locally significant buildings; ask for it at either visitor center.

The most active stretch of **Main Street** is the few blocks between City Hall (home to the visitor center) and the train underpass. Here you'll find cafes, newsstands, hotels, and restaurants, along with a handful of intriguing shops. Note the sometimes-jarring mix of architectural styles, the earlier examples of which testify to Moncton's historic prosperity as a commercial center.

The indoor amusement park at **Crystal Palace,** Champlain Place Shopping Centre, Trans-Canada Highway Exit 504-A West, Dieppe (✆ **877/856-4386** or 506/859-4386), will make an otherwise endless rainy day go by quickly. The spacious enclosed park includes a four-screen cinema, shooting arcades, numerous games (ranging from old-fashioned SkeeBall to cutting-edge video games), a medium-size roller coaster, a carousel, a swing ride, laser tag, bumper cars, mini-airplane and mini-semi-truck rides, mini-golf, batting cages, and a virtual-reality ride. From late June to early September, outdoor activities include go-karts and bumper boats. The park will particularly appeal to kids under the age of 12, although teens will likely find a video game to occupy them. The park is open daily in summer 10am to 10pm, the rest of the year Monday to Thursday noon to 8pm, Friday and Saturday noon to 9pm, and Sunday 10am to 8pm. Admission is free; rides cost 1 to 4 tickets each (C$1/US60¢ per ticket or 20 for C$16/US$10). Unlimited ride passes cost C$13.25 (US$8) for adults, C$11.95 to C$13.95 (US$7–US$9) for children and C$46 to C$56 (US$29–US$35) for a family.

## WHERE TO STAY

Several chain hotels have set up shop near Magnetic Hill (Trans-Canada Highway Exit 488). These include **Comfort Inn,** 2495 Mountain Rd. (✆ **800/228-5150** or 506/384-3175); **Country Inn & Suites,** 2475 Mountain Rd. (✆ **800/456-4000** or 506/852-7000); and **Holiday Inn Express,** also just off the exit at 2515 Mountain Rd. (✆ **506/384-1050**). At these clean, convenient hotels, rooms range from C$85 to C$180 (US$53–US$112).

**Best Western Crystal Palace** *Overrated* This modern chain hotel (built in 1990) adjoins the Crystal Palace amusement park and is a short walk from the region's largest mall. As such, it's surrounded by acres of asphalt and has little in the way of native charm. Most rooms are modern but unexceptional—not counting the 12 fantasy suites that go over the top with themes like "Deserted Island" (sleep in a thatched hut) or "Rock 'n' Roll" (sleep in a 1959 replica pink Cadillac bed). Some rooms face the indoor pool; others look out over the vast parking lot. For entertainment nearby, there's the amusement park, obviously. Also within the amusement complex is the hotel's restaurant, McGinnis Landing, which offers basic pub fare. Prices are high for what you get for main dinner courses; but specials are always available, and the restaurant caters well to younger appetites.

499 Paul St., Dieppe, NB E1A 6S5. ✆ **800/528-1234** or 506/858-8584. Fax 506/858-5486. 115 units. C$90–C$175 (US$56–US$109) double. Ask about value packages, which include amusement-park passes. AE, DC, DISC, MC, V. **Amenities:** Restaurant, bar; indoor pool; hot tub; sauna; limited room service; babysitting; dry cleaning weekdays. *In room:* A/C, TV, minibar, coffeemaker.

**Delta Beauséjour** ★ The downtown Delta Beauséjour, constructed in 1972, is boxy, bland, and concrete, and the entrance courtyard is sterile and off-putting in a Cold War Berlin sort of way. But inside, the decor is inviting in a spare, International Modern manner. The property is well maintained, with rooms and public areas recently renovated. The third-floor indoor pool offers year-round swimming. (There's also a pleasant outdoor deck overlooking the distant marshes of the Petitcodiac River.) The hotel is a favorite among business travelers, but in summer and on weekends, leisure travelers largely have it to themselves. In addition to the elegant Windjammer (see below), the hotel has a basic cafe/snack bar, a piano bar and lounge, and a rustic, informal restaurant.

750 Main St., Moncton, NB E1C 1E6. ✆ **800/268-1133** or 506/854-4344. Fax 506/858-0957. 310 units. C$92–C$169 (US$57–US$105) double summer and weekends; higher midweek in off-season. AE, DC, MC, V. **Amenities:** 3 restaurants, piano bar; indoor pool; health club; business center; shopping arcade; salon; 24-hour room service; babysitting; laundry; dry cleaning. *In room:* A/C, TV, minibar.

**Victoria Bed & Breakfast** ★ *Value* This vaguely Craftsman-style 1910 home in a reasonably quiet neighborhood across from a church offers three comfortable rooms, all with private bathrooms. All rooms are mid-sized, and feature stucco walls, lustrous maple floors, and a relaxed country styling. Room 1 is the best of the bunch: it faces Park Street, is brighter and slightly larger than the other two, and is decorated in dark and soothing tones. Guests often linger in the attractive downstairs common, noodling around on the baby grand piano.

For multi-night stays, ask about the corporate suites in a separate building around the corner.

71 Park St., Moncton, NB E1C 2B2. ✆ **506/389-8296.** 3 units (1 w/private bathroom across hall). C$95 (US$63) double, includes breakfast. MC, V. **Amenities:** Piano lounge. *In room:* A/C, TV/VCR.

## WHERE TO DINE

**Boomerang's Steakhouse** STEAKHOUSE Boomerang's is likely to remind diners of the Aussie-themed Outback Steakhouse chain, right down to the oversize knives. But since this is the only Boomerang's (it's not a chain), the service is rather more personal, and the Aussie-whimsical decor is done with a lighter hand. It's a handsome spot with three dining rooms, all quite dim with slatted dividers, drawn shades, and ceiling fans, which create the impression that it's blazingly hot outside. (That's a real trick in February in New Brunswick.) The menu features the usual stuff from the "barbie", including grilled chicken breasts and ribs. The steak selection is grand, ranging from an 8-ounce bacon-wrapped tenderloin to a 14-ounce porterhouse. The burgers are also excellent.

130 Westmoreland St. ✆ **506/857-8325.** Call-ahead seating in lieu of reservations. Hamburgers and grilled sandwiches C$9–C$11 (US$6–US$7), dinners C$14–C$20 (US$9–US$12). AE, DC, DISC, MC, V. Sun–Wed 4–10pm, Thurs–Sat 4–11:30pm.

**The Windjammer** ★★ CONTINENTAL Tucked off the lobby of Moncton's best hotel is The Windjammer, an intimate dining room that serves the city's best meals. With its heavy wood and nautical theme, it resembles the private officer's mess of an exclusive ship. The menu is ambitious, and the dining room has garnered an excellent reputation for its seafood, including an appetizer of scallops served with a truffle jus, and entree of pan-fried salmon marinated in molasses and ginger. Despite the seafaring decor, the chef also serves up treats for carnivores, including tournedos of caribou with jus and blueberries, served with a fricassée of wild mushrooms.

750 Main St. (in the Delta Beauséjour). ✆ **506/854-4344.** Reservations recommended. Main courses C$25–C$37 (US$16–US$33). AE, DC, MC, V. Mon–Sat 5:30–11pm.

# 8 Kouchibouguac National Park ★

Much is made of the fact that sprawling Kouchibouguac National Park has all sorts of ecosystems worth studying, from sandy barrier islands to ancient peat bogs. But that's a little bit like saying Disney World has nice lakes. It causes one's eyes to glaze over, and it entirely misses the point. In fact, this artfully designed national park is a wonderful destination for relaxing biking, hiking, and beach going. If you can, plan to spend a couple of days here doing a whole lot of nothing. The varied ecosystems (which, incidentally, are spectacular) are just an added attraction.

## ESSENTIALS

**GETTING THERE** Kouchibouguac National Park is between Moncton and Miramichi. The exit for the park off Route 11 is well marked.

---

*Tips* **A Weather Warning**

Be aware that Kouchibouguac is a fair-weather destination. If it's blustery and rainy, there's little to do except take damp and melancholy strolls on the beach. It's best to save a visit here for more cooperative days.

---

**VISITOR INFORMATION** **Tourist office** The park is open from mid-May to mid-October. The **Visitors Centre** (✆ **888/773-8888** or 506/876-2443) is just off Route 134, a short drive past the park entrance. It's open from 8am to 8pm during peak season, with shorter hours in the off-season. There's a slide show to introduce you to the park's attractions, and a small collection of field guides to peruse. Information on Kouchibouguac and all of Canada's national parks can be found at **www.parcscanada.gc.ca**.

**FEES** A daily pass is C$3.50 (US$2.15) adult, C$1.75 (US$1.10) children (6–16), C$2.75 (US$1.70) senior, and C$7 (US$4.35) family. Four-day passes are also available. A map of the park (helpful) costs C$1 (US60¢) at the information center. You should have permits for everyone in your car when you enter the park. There are no formal checkpoints, only occasional roadblocks during the summer to ensure compliance.

## EXPLORING THE PARK

Kouchibouguac is, above all, a place for bikers and families. (By the way, the ungainly name is a Mi'kmaq Indian word meaning "River of the Long Tides." It's pronounced "*Koosh*-uh-*boog*-oo-*whack*." If you don't get it right, don't worry. Few do.) The park is laced with well-groomed bike trails made of finely crushed cinders that traverse forest and field and meander along rivers and lagoons. Where bikes aren't permitted (such as on boardwalks and beaches), there are usually clusters of bike racks for locking them up while you continue on foot. If you camp here and bring a bike, there's no need to ever use your car.

The **hiking and biking trails** are as short and undemanding as they are appealing. The one hiking trail that requires slightly more fortitude is the **Kouchibouguac River Trail,** running for some 13km (8 miles) along the banks of the river. **The Bog Trail** ★ is just 2km (1¼ miles) each way, but it opens the door to a wonderfully alien world. The 4,500-year-old classic domed bog is made of peat originating from decaying shrubs and other plants. At the bog's edge is a wooden tower ascended by a spiral staircase that affords a panoramic view of this eerie habitat.

The boardwalk crosses to the thickest, middle part of the bog. Where the boardwalk stops, you can feel the bouncy surface—you're actually standing on a mat of thick vegetation that's floating atop water. Look for the pitcher plant, a carnivorous species that lures flies into its bell-shaped leaves, where downward-pointed hairs prevent them from fleeing. Eventually, the plant's enzymes digest the insect, providing nutrients for growth in this hostile environment.

**Callanders Beach** and **Cedar Trail** are at the end of a short dirt road. There is an open field with picnic tables, a small protected beach on the lagoon (with fine views of dunes across the way), and a 1km (½-mile) hiking trail on a boardwalk that passes through a cedar forest, past a salt marsh, and through a mixed forest. This is a good alternative for those who'd prefer to avoid the larger crowds at Kellys Beach (below).

## BEACHES

The park features some 15km (9 miles) of sandy beaches, mostly along barrier islands of sandy dunes, delicate grasses and flowers, and nesting plovers and sandpipers. **Kellys** ★ is the principal beach, and it's one of the best-designed and best-executed recreation areas I've come across in Eastern Canada. At the forest's edge, a short walk from the main parking area, you'll find showers, changing rooms, a snack bar, and some interpretive exhibits. From here, you walk some

540m (600 yd.) across a winding boardwalk that's plenty fascinating on its own. It crosses a salt marsh, lagoons, and some of the best-preserved dunes in the province.

The long, sandy beach features water that's comfortably warm, with waves that are usually quite mellow—they lap rather than roar, unless a storm's offshore. Lifeguards oversee a roped-off section of about 90m (100 yd.); elsewhere, you're on your own. For very young children who still equate waves with certain death, there's supervised swimming on a sandy stretch of the quiet lagoon.

**Ryans**—a cluster of buildings between the campground and Kellys Beach—is the place for renting bikes, kayaks, paddleboats, and canoes. Bikes rent for C$4.60 (US$2.85) per hour. Most of the watersports equipment (including canoes and pedal boats) rent for about C$7 (US$4.35) per hour, with double kayaks at C$12 (US$7) per hour. Canoes may be rented for longer excursions; it's C$29.90 (US$19) daily and C$41.75 (US$26) for 2 days. Ryans is located on the lagoon, so you can explore up toward the dunes or upstream on the winding river.

## WHERE TO STAY & DINE

Kouchibouguac is at heart a camper's park, best enjoyed by those who plan to spend at least a night. **South Kouchibouguac,** the main campground, is centrally located and very nicely laid out with 311 sites, most rather large and private. The 46 sites with electricity are nearer the river and somewhat more open. The newest sites (1–35) lack grassy areas for pitching a tent, and campers have to pitch tents on gravel pads. It's best to bring a good sleeping pad or ask for another site. Sites are C$22 (US$14) per night. Reservations are accepted for about half of the campsites; call ✆ **800/414-6765** starting in late April. The remaining sites are doled out first-come-first-served.

Across the river on Kouchibouguac Lagoon is the more remote, semi-primitive **Côte-à-Fabien.** It lacks showers and some sites require a short walk, but it's more appealing for tenters. The cost is C$14 (US$9) per night. The park also maintains three backcountry sites, which cost C$10 (US$6) per night for two, including firewood.

**Habitant Motel and Restaurant** ★ *Value* At about 15km (9 miles) from the park entrance, Habitant is the best choice for staying overnight if you're exploring Kouchibouguac by day. It's a modern, mansard-roofed, Tudor-style complex—well, let's just say "architecturally mystifying"—with a restaurant and small campground on the premises. The rooms are decorated in a contemporary motel style and are very clean. The restaurant next door is informal, comfortable, and reasonably priced. Seafood dinners are the specialty, including a heaping "fisherman's feast" for C$23 (US$14). One nice touch: There's a self-serve wine cellar, where wines are sold at liquor-store prices, many under C$20 (US$12).

Route 134 (RR no. 1, Box 2, Site 30), Richibucto, NB E0A 2M0. ✆ **888/442-7222** or 506/523-4421. Fax 506/523-9155. habitant@nbnet.nb.ca. 28 units. C$60–C$80 (US$37–US$50) double. AE, DC, DISC, MC, V. "Small, well-trained pets" allowed. **Amenities:** Restaurant; wine cellar; indoor pool; fitness center; sauna. *In room:* A/C, TV.

## 9 The Acadian Peninsula

The Acadian Peninsula is that bulge on the northeast corner of New Brunswick, forming one of the arms of the Baie des Chaleurs (Québec's Gaspé Peninsula forms the other). It's a land of tidy if generally nondescript houses, miles of shoreline (much of it beaches), modern concrete harbors filled with commercial fishing boats, and residents proud of their Acadian heritage. (You'll see everywhere the *stella maris* flag—the French tricolor with a single gold star in the field of blue.)

On a map it looks like much of the coastline would be wild and remote here. It's not. Although a number of picturesque farmhouses dot the route and you'll come upon brilliant meadows of hawkweed and lupine, the coast is more defined by manufactured housing that's been erected on squarish lots between the sea and fast two-lane highways. Other than the superb Acadian Village historical museum near Caraquet, there are few organized attractions in the region. It's more a place to unwind while walking on a beach, or sitting along harbors watching fishing boats come and go.

## ESSENTIALS

**VISITOR INFORMATION** Each of the areas mentioned below maintains a visitor information center. **Caraquet Tourism Information** is at 51 bd. St-Pierre Est (✆ **506/726-2727**). This office offers convenient access to other activities in the harbor, and there's plenty of parking. Shippagan dispenses information from a wooden lighthouse near the Marine Centre.

**GETTING THERE** Route 11 is the main highway serving the Acadian Peninsula.

## CARAQUET ★

The historic beach town of Caraquet—widely regarded as the spiritual capital of Acadian New Brunswick—just keeps on going and going, geographically speaking. It's spread thinly along a commercial boulevard parallel to the beach. Caraquet once claimed the honorific "longest village in the world" when it ran to some 22km (13 miles) long. As a result of its length, Caraquet lacks a well-defined downtown or any sort of urban center of gravity; there's one stoplight, and that's where Boulevard St-Pierre Est changes to Boulevard St-Pierre Ouest. (Most establishments mentioned below are somewhere along this boulevard.)

A good place to start a tour is the **Callefour de la Mer,** 51 bd. St-Pierre Est, a modern complex overlooking the man-made harbor. It has a spare, Scandinavian feel to it, and you'll find the tourist information office (see above), a seafood restaurant, a snack bar, a children's playground, and two short strolls that lead to picnic tables on jetties with fine harbor views.

While you're here you can consider your options for viewing the bay. Half-hour boat tours aboard the ***Ile Caramer*** (✆ **506/727-0813**), cost C$17.25 (US$11) per adult, C$15 (US$11) per senior, and C$10 (US$6) per child 12 and under. An exhilarating and fun 3-hour whale-watch tour with **Sea of Adventure** (✆ **506/727-2727**), aboard a high-speed Zodiac costs C$50 (US$31) per adult, and C$30 (US$19) per child 12 and under. You can also rent a kayak from **Tours Kayaket** (✆ **506/727-6309**) for C$15 (US$9) per 1½ hours (C$25/US$16 for a double kayak) and putter around inside the sea wall, or venture out into the bay if conditions are agreeable.

**Village Historique Acadien** ★ New Brunswick sometimes seems awash in Acadian museums and historic villages. If you're interested in visiting just one such site, this is the place to hold out for. Some 45 buildings—most of which were dismantled and transported here from other villages on the peninsula—depict life as it was lived in an Acadian settlement between the years 1770 and 1890. The historic buildings are set throughout 185ha (458 acres) of woodland, marsh, and field. You'll learn all about the exodus and settlement of the Acadians from costumed guides, who are also adept at skills ranging from letterpress printing to blacksmithing. Plan on spending at least 2 to 3 hours exploring the village.

In June 2002, the village is scheduled to open a major addition, which focuses on a more recent era. Some 26 buildings (all but one are replicas) will be devoted to continuing the saga, showing Acadian life from 1890 to 1939, with a special focus on industry. Among the new buildings will be a traditional hotel, which will house students enrolled in multi-day workshops in traditional Acadian arts and crafts.

Route 11 (10km/6 miles west of Caraquet). © **506/726-2600.** www.villagehistoriqueacadien.com. Admission C$12 (US$7) adult, C$10 (US$6) senior, C$7 (US$4.35) ages 6–16, C$30 (US$19) family. Daily in summer 10am–6pm (until 5pm in Sept and Oct). Closed mid-Oct to early June.

### WHERE TO STAY

**Hotel Paulin** ★ *Value* This attractive Victorian hotel, built in 1891, has been operated by the Paulin family for the past three generations. It's a three-story red clapboard building with a green-shingled mansard roof, located just off the main boulevard and overlooking the bay. (Some of the charm has been compromised by encroaching buildings nearby.) The lobby puts one immediately in mind of summer relaxation, with royal blue wainscotting, canary yellow walls, and stuffed furniture upholstered in white with blue piping. The rooms were extensively renovated in 1999; six rooms were combined into three suites, and all rooms now have private bathrooms. (The original suite has the only ocean view.) Expect rooms comfortably but sparely furnished with antiques. The hotel's first floor also houses a handsome, well-regarded **restaurant** ★. Specialties include a delectable crab mousse and a cure for the sweet tooth: brown-sugar pie.

143 bd. St-Pierre Ouest. © **506/727-9981.** Fax 506/727-3300. 8 units. C$95–C$150 (US$59–US$93) double. MC, V. **Amenities:** Restaurant. *In room:* A/C, TV.

### WHERE TO DINE

Caraquet is a good place for seafood, naturally. Our preference is still with the **Hotel Paulin's restaurant** for its charm, but the several inexpensive-to-moderate spots along the main drag all serve fresh seafood nicely, if simply prepared.

For a delicious and sophisticated snack, head to **Les Blancs d'Arcadie** ★, 340-A bd. St-Pierre Est (© **506/727-5952**), en route to Bas Caraquet on Route 145 (watch for the goat sign on the right shortly after you pass the road to St-Simon). This handsome compound of yellow farm buildings is set back hard against the forest just east of town. The specialties here are cheese and yogurt from the milk of a Swiss breed of goats called Saanen. The goats are raised indoors year-round; you can learn about the goats and the cheese- and yogurt-making process on a tour of the operation, which includes tastings. The 90-minute tour is C$6 (US$3.70). There's also a small shop to buy fresh cheeses and milk. We recommend both the peppercorn and the garlic soft cheeses.

## GRANDE-ANSE

Grande-Anse is a wide-spot-in-the-road village of low, modern homes near bluffs overlooking the bay. The town is lorded over by the stern **Saint Jude Church.** The best view of the village, and a good spot for a picnic, is along the bluffs just below the church. (Look for the sign indicating quai 50 yards west of the church.) Here you'll find a small man-made harbor with a fleet of fishing boats, a tiny sand beach, and some grassy bluffs where you can park overlooking the bay.

**Pope Museum** *Finds* Deep vermilion hues and liturgical strains piped into all the rooms mark the modern Pope Museum, founded in 1985—the year after the Pope visited Moncton. The devout will enjoy the portrait gallery featuring portraits of all 264 popes. But all will be fascinated by the intricate model of the Vatican, which occupies much of the central hall (the top of the dome stands about 2m/6 ft. high). Other models of houses of worship include a smaller Florence Cathedral, Bourges Cathedral, Cheops pyramid, and the Great El Hakim Mosque. Head upstairs for displays of various Roman Catholic artifacts and contemporary religious accouterment, including vestments and chalices. Most descriptions are bilingual, but a handful are in French only.

184 Acadie St., Grande-Anse. ✆ **506/732-3003.** www.museedespapes.com. Admission C$5 (US$3.10) adults, C$2 (US$1.20) children, C$2.50 (US$1.55) seniors, C$10 (US$6) family. Daily July and Aug 10am–6pm (tickets sold until 5pm). Closed Sept–June.

5

# Prince Edward Island

*by Wayne Curtis & Paul Karr*

Prince Edward Island might not be the world's leading manufacturer of relaxation and repose, but it's certainly a major distribution center. Visitors soon suspect there's something about the richly colored landscape of azure seas and henna-tinged cliffs capped with lush farm fields that triggers an obscure relaxation hormone, resulting in a pleasant ennui. It's hard to conceive that verdant and green Prince Edward Island (PEI) and boggy, blustery Newfoundland share a planet, never mind the same gulf.

The north coast is lined with red-sand beaches, washed with the warmish waters of the Gulf of St. Lawrence. Swimming here isn't quite like taking a tepid dip in North Carolina, but it's quite a bit warmer than in Maine or New Hampshire, farther down the Eastern seaboard. Away from the beaches you'll find low, rolling hills blanketed in trees and crops, especially potatoes, for which the island is justly famous. Small farms make up the island's backbone—one-quarter of the island is dedicated to agriculture, with that land cultivated by more than 2,300 individual farms.

The island is compact and its roads are unusually well marked. It's difficult to become disoriented and confused. But do try. I can think of few joys in life as simple and pleasurable as getting lost on some of PEI's back roads. The island has, somewhat remarkably, managed to retain its bucolic flavor of a century ago, and pockets of kitsch and sprawl are still happily few. But the handwriting is on the wall; in coming years, more and more of the island is certain to be claimed by subdivisions and shopping plazas. The sooner you can visit the better.

## 1 Exploring the Island

**VISITOR INFORMATION** Tourism PEI publishes a comprehensive free guide to island attractions and lodgings that's well worth picking up. The *Visitors Guide* is available at all information centers on the island or can be secured in advance by contacting **Tourism PEI,** P.O. Box 940, Charlottetown, PEI C1A 7M5 (✆ **888/734-7529** or 902/368-4444; fax 902/629-2428; www.peiplay.com).

### GETTING THERE

**BY PLANE** **Charlottetown Airport** (www.charlottetownairport.pe.ca) is the island's main airport. Commuter flights to Halifax take just a half-hour; direct flights from Toronto are offered daily.

**BY CAR** If you're coming from the west by car, you'll arrive via the Confederation Bridge, which opened with great fanfare in June 1997. Sometimes you'll hear it referred to as the "fixed link," a reference to the guarantee Canada made in 1873 to provide a permanent link from the mainland. The dramatic 13km

(8-mile) bridge is open 24 hours a day and takes about 10 to 12 minutes to cross. Unless you're high up in a van, a truck, or an RV, the views are mostly obstructed by the concrete Jersey barriers that form the guardrails along the sides.

The bridge toll is C$37 (US$23) round-trip. No fare is paid when you travel to the island; the entire toll is collected when you leave. Credit cards are accepted. Call ✆ **888/437-6565** for details.

**BY FERRY** For those arriving from Cape Breton Island or other points east, **Northumberland Ferries Limited** (✆ **888/249-7245** or 902/566-3838) provides seasonal service between Caribou, NS (just north of Pictou), and Woods Island, PEI. Ferries with a 250-car capacity run from May to mid-December. During peak season (June to mid-October), ferries depart each port approximately every 90 minutes throughout the day, with the last ferry departing at 8pm. The crossing takes about 75 minutes.

No reservations are accepted; it's best to arrive at least an hour before departure to boost your odds of securing a berth on the next boat. Early morning ferries tend to be less crowded. Fares are C$47 (US$29) for a car and all its passengers. Major credit cards are honored. As with the bridge, fares are paid upon exiting the island; the ferry to the island is free.

## THE GREAT OUTDOORS

**BICYCLING** The main off-road bike trail is the **Confederation Trail** ★. Eventually, the trail will cover some 350km (210 miles) along the old path of the ill-fated provincial railway from Tignish to Souris. At present, about half the trail has been completed, mostly in Prince and Kings Counties; Queens County is still largely under development. The pathway is covered mostly in rolled stone dust, which makes for good travel with a mountain bike or hybrid. Services are slowly developing along the route, with bike rentals and inns cropping up. Ask at the local tourist bureaus for updated information on completed segments. An excellent place to base for exploring the trail is the Trailside Cafe in Mount Stewart, where several spurs of the trail converge. The cafe can arrange for return shuttles if you'd prefer one-way cycling. **MacQueen's Island Tours & Bike Shop,** 430 Queen St., Charlottetown (✆ **800/969-2822**), organizes bicycle tour packages, with prices including bike rentals, accommodations, route cards, maps, luggage transfers, and emergency road repair service. At **Cycle Smooth,** 172 Prince St., Charlottetown (✆ **800/310-6550** or 902/566-5530), rentals include helmet, water bottle, and a lock and cost C$24 (US$15) per day.

**FISHING** For a taste of deep-sea fishing, head to the north coast, where you'll find plenty of outfitters happy to take you out on the big swells. The greatest concentrations of services are at **North Rustico** and **Covehead Bay** (see "Queens County: The Land of Anne" below). Rates are quite reasonable, generally about C$20 (US$12) for 3 hours or so.

**GOLF** PEI's reputation for golf has soared in the last few years. That's due in part to a slew of new and expanded courses—three opened in 1999 alone: Countryview Golf Course, Dundarave Golf Course, and St. Felix Golf and Country Club—and in part because the greens fees haven't followed the same sharply upward trajectory that has afflicted many courses in the United States. One of the best-regarded courses is the **Links at Crowbush Cove** ★★ (✆ **800/377-8337** or 902/961-7300). Sand dunes and persistent winds off the gulf add to the challenge at this relatively young (1994) course, which is on the

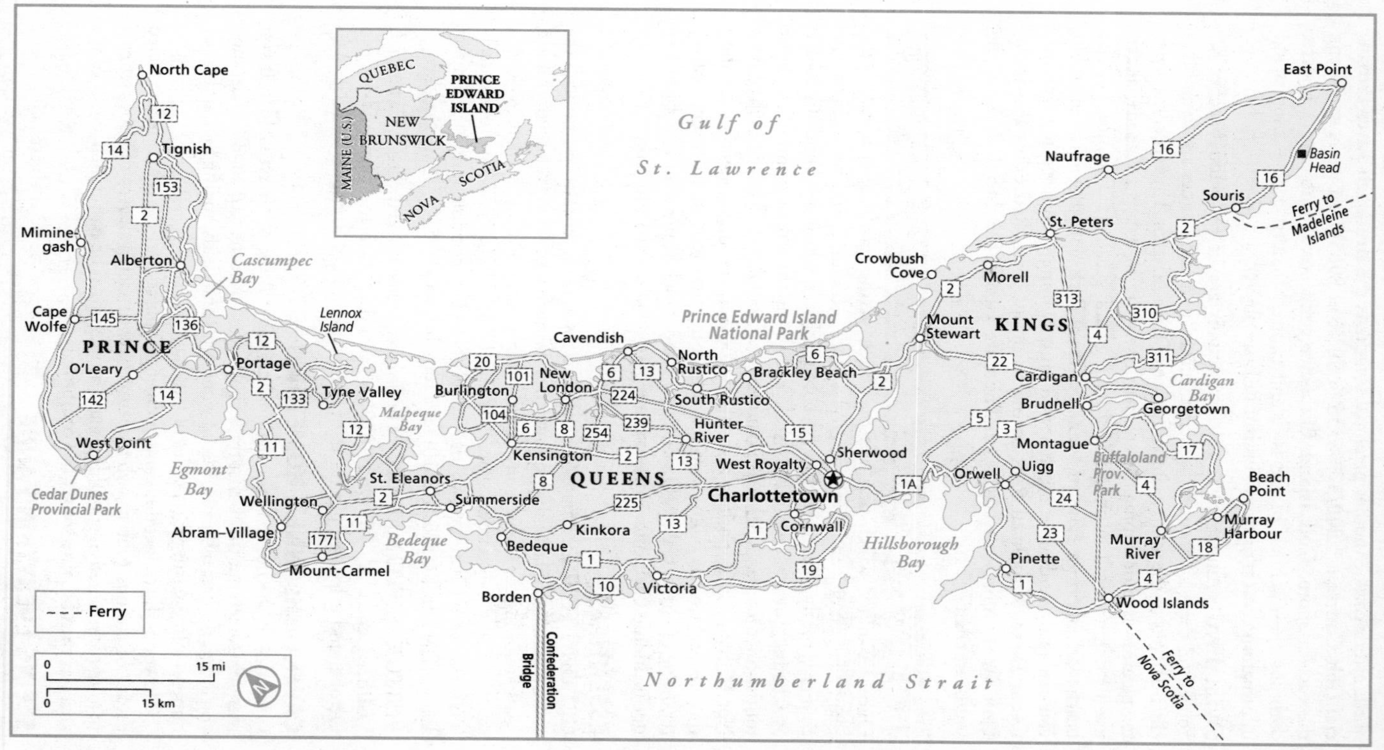
Gulf of
St. Lawrence
Northumberland Strait
QUEBEC
PRINCE EDWARD ISLAND
NEW BRUNSWICK
MAINE (U.S.)
NOVA SCOTIA
North Cape
Tignish
Miminegash
Alberton
Cascumpec Bay
Cape Wolfe
PRINCE
O'Leary
West Point
Cedar Dunes Provincial Park
Egmont Bay
Lennox Island
Portage
Tyne Valley
Malpeque Bay
Wellington
Abram–Village
Mount-Carmel
St. Eleanors
Summerside
Bedeque Bay
Burlington
New London
Cavendish
Kensington
Bedeque
Kinkora
Borden
Confederation Bridge
QUEENS
North Rustico
South Rustico
Brackley Beach
Prince Edward Island National Park
Hunter River
West Royalty
Sherwood
Charlottetown
Cornwall
Victoria
Hillsborough Bay
Crowbush Cove
Morell
Mount Stewart
KINGS
St. Peters
Naufrage
Souris
East Point
Basin Head
Ferry to Madeleine Islands
Cardigan
Brudnell
Georgetown
Cardigan Bay
Montague
Orwell
Uigg
Buffaloland Prov. Park
Pinette
Murray River
Murray Harbour
Beach Point
Wood Islands
Ferry to Nova Scotia
Ferry
0
15 mi
15 km

northeastern coast. Another perennial favorite is the **Brudenell River Provincial Golf Course** (✆ **800/377-8336** or 902/652-8965) near Montague along the eastern shore. **Golf Island PEI** (www.golfpei.com) publishes a booklet outlining the essentials of the 16 island courses. Request a copy from island information centers or from Tourism PEI (see above).

**SWIMMING** Among PEI's chief attractions are its **red sand beaches** ★. You'll find them all around the island, tucked in among dunes and crumbling cliffs. Thanks to the moderating influence of the Gulf of St. Lawrence, the water temperature is more humane here than elsewhere in Atlantic Canada, and it usually doesn't result in unbridled shrieking among bathers. The most popular beaches are at **Prince Edward Island National Park** along the north coast, but you can easily find other beaches with great swimming. Among my favorites: **Cedar Dunes Provincial Park** on the southwest coast, **Red Point Provincial Park** on the northeast coast, and **Panmure Island Provincial Park** on the southeast coast.

## 2 Queens County: The Land of Anne

Queens County, which occupies the center of the province, is home to the island's largest city and hosts the greatest concentration of traveler services. The county is neatly cleaved by the Hillsborough River, which is spanned by bridge at Charlottetown. Be aware that Cavendish on the north shore is the most tourist-oriented part of the entire province; if the phrase "Ripley's Believe It or Not Museum" lacks positive associations for you, you might consider avoiding this area, which has built a vigorous tourist industry around a fictional character, Anne of Green Gables. On the other hand, much of the rest of the county—not including Charlottetown—is quite pastoral and untrammeled.

### ESSENTIALS

**GETTING THERE** Route 2 is the fastest way to travel east-west through the county, although it lacks charm. Route 6 is the main route along the county's north coast; following the highway involves a number of turns at intersections, so keep a sharp eye on the directional signs. **The Shuttle** (✆ **902/566-3243**) provides daily service between Charlottetown and several points in Cavendish during the summer season. The rate is C$16 (US$10) for a round-trip and C$10 (US$6) one-way.

**VISITOR INFORMATION** The snazzy, well-stocked little **Cavendish Visitors Centre** (✆ **902/963-7830**) is open daily 8am to 10pm mid-May to October and is located just north of the intersection of Route 13 and Route 6.

### CAVENDISH: ANNE'S HOMETOWN

Cavendish is the home of the fictional character Anne of Green Gables. If you mentally screen out the tourist traps constructed over the past couple of decades, you'll find the area a bucolic mix of woodlands and fields, rolling hills and sandy dunes—a fine setting for a series of pastoral novels.

However, the tremendous and enduring popularity of the novels has attracted droves of curious tourists, who in turn have attracted droves of entrepreneurs who've constructed new buildings and attractions. The pastoral character of the area has thus become somewhat compromised.

### SEEING EVERYTHING ANNE

**Green Gables** ★ *Overrated* The best place to start an Anne tour is at Green Gables itself. The house is operated by Parks Canada, which also operates a

## The Birth of Anne Shirley

All visitors to Prince Edward Island owe it to themselves to read *Anne of Green Gables* at some point. Not that you won't enjoy your stay here without doing this, but if you don't, you might feel a bit out of touch, unable to understand the inside references that seep into many aspects of PEI culture.

Some background: Lucy Maud Montgomery wrote *Anne of Green Gables* in 1908. It's a fictional account of Anne Shirley, a precocious and bright 11-year-old who's mistakenly sent from Nova Scotia to the farm of the taciturn and dour Matthew and Marilla Cuthbert. (The mistake? The Cuthberts had requested a boy orphan to help with farm chores.) Anne's vivid imagination and outsized vocabulary get her into a series of pickles, from which she generally emerges beloved by everyone who encounters her. It's a bright, bittersweet story, and it went on to huge popular success, spawning a number of sequels.

The story has proven especially enduring in Japan, where it's taught in schools and where the cheeky heroine seems to have boundless appeal. This enduring fascination explains why you'll often see billboards and brochures hereabouts printed with Japanese translations.

helpful visitor's center on the site. You can watch a 7-minute video presentation about Montgomery, view a handful of exhibits, and then head out to explore the farm and trails. The farmhouse dates to the mid-19th century and belonged to cousins of Montgomery's grandfather. It was the inspiration for the Cuthbert farm, and it has been furnished according to descriptions in the books.

Route 6, Cavendish (just west of intersection with Route 13). ✆ **902/672-6350.** Admission: C$5 (US$3.10) adult, C$3 (US$1,85) senior, C$2 (US$1.20) children, and C$9 (US$6) family. Open daily May–Oct; mid-June to Sept 9am–8pm (until 5pm shoulder seasons).

**Cavendish Cemetery** This historic cemetery was founded in 1835, but it's best known now as the final resting spot for author Lucy Maud Montgomery. It's not hard to find her gravesite: Follow the pavement blocks from the arched entryway, which is across from the Anne Shirley Motel.

Intersection of Route 13 and Route 6, Cavendish. Open daily.

**Avonlea** *Kids* This new development of faux historic buildings was opened in the summer of 1999 with the idea of creating the sort of a village center you might find in reading the Anne novels. It's located on a large lot amid amusement parks and motels, and the new buildings have been constructed with an eye to historical accuracy. Several Anne-related buildings and artifacts are located on the site, including the schoolhouse in which Montgomery taught (moved here from Belmont), and a Presbyterian church (moved from Long River), which Montgomery occasionally attended. There's also a variety show, hayrides, staff in period dress, restaurant, several stores (including an art gallery and music shop), and a spot for ice cream and candy.

Route 6 (across from Rainbow Valley amusement park), Cavendish. ✆ **902/963-3050.** C$8.50 (US$5) adult, C$7.50 (US$5) senior, C$6.50 (US$4) ages 6–16. Musical variety show C$3 (US$1.85) extra. Daily mid-June to Sept, 9am–8:30pm. Closed Sept to mid-June.

**Anne of Green Gables Museum at Silver Bush** About 20km (12 miles) west of Cavendish near the intersection of Route 6 and Route 20 is the Anne of Green Gables Museum at Silver Bush. It's located in the home of Montgomery's aunt and uncle; the author was married here in 1911. For the best view of the "Lake of Shining Waters," take the wagon ride.

Route 20, Park Corner. © **902/436-7329.** C$2.35 (US$1.45) adults, C75¢ (US45¢) children under 16. Open daily mid-May to Oct 9am–6pm.

**Lucy Maud Montgomery Birthplace** Very near the Anne of Green Gables museum is the Lucy Maud Montgomery Birthplace, where the author was born in 1874. The house is decorated in the Victorian style of the era, and it includes Montgomery mementos like her wedding dress and scrapbook.

Intersection of Route 6 and Route 20, New London. © **902/886-2099** or 902/436-7329. Admission C$2 (US$1.20) adult, C50¢ (US30¢) ages 6–12. Open daily July and Aug 9am–7pm, June and Sept to mid-Oct 10am–5pm. Closed Nov–June 1.

**Lucy Maud Montgomery Heritage Museum** This museum is located in the 1879 home of Montgomery's grandfather—perhaps. (Its lineage is a bit unclear.) Attractions include antiques from the family, along with artifacts mentioned in her books. Three times weekly, special day-long events are held, which include readings, picnics by the lake, and the creation of flower-adorned straw hats. (C$80/US$50).

Route 20, Park Corner. © **902/886-2807** or 902/886-2752. C$2.50 (US$1.55) adults, C$1 (US 60¢). Daily July and Aug 9am–7pm; June and Sept 9am–5pm. Closed Oct 1–May 31.

**Anne of Green Gables—The Musical** This spritely, professional musical has been playing for years at the downtown arts center and brings to the stage many of Montgomery's stories and characters.

Confederation Arts Centre, Charlottetown. © **800/565-0278** or 902/566-1267. Tickets C$20–C$36 (US$12–US$22).

## WHERE TO STAY

Cottage courts are to Cavendish what 19th-century inns are to Vermont—they're everywhere and vary tremendously as to quality. Be aware that many of the cottage courts and motels are more interested in high volume and rapid turnover than personal attention to guests. A number also believe that hanging a straw hat or two on a door allows them to boast of "country charm," when they have anything but.

**Cavendish Beach Cottages** Location, location, location. This compound of 13 cottages is located on a grassy rise within the national park, just past the gatehouse into the park. The pine-paneled cottages are available in one, two, or three-bedroom configurations, and all feature ocean views, kitchenettes with microwaves, outdoor propane barbecue grills, and new pine floors. Some of the better-equipped cottages have dishwashers, and all are a 2-minute walk from the beach. There's also easy access to Gulf Shore Drive, where you'll find some of the island's premier biking.

Gulf Shore Dr., Cavendish (mailing address: 166 York Lane, Charlottetown, PEI C1A 7W5). © **902/963-2025.** Fax 902/963-2025. 13 units. C$135–C$185 (US$84–US$115) double. MC, V. Closed early Oct–late May. **Amenities:** Laundry. *In room:* TV, VCRs by request, kitchenettes, grills.

**Green Gables Bungalow Court** Located next to the Green Gables house, this pleasant cluster of one- and two-bedroom cottages began as a government project promoting tourism in the 1940s. As a result, they're quite sturdily built, and nicely arrayed among lawn and pines. Many have outdoor gas grills for an evening barbecue. The linoleum floors and Spartan furnishings take on a certain retro charm after a few hours of settling in. Some cabins were trimmed with cheap sheet paneling, others have the original pine paneling; ask for one with the latter. The beach is about 1km (½ mile) away.

Route 6 (Hunter River RR no. 2), Cavendish, PEI C0A 1N0. ✆ **800/965-3334** or 902/892-3542. www.greengablesbungalowcourt.com. 40 cottages. C$85–C$120 (US$53–US$74) for up to 4 people. AE, MC, V. Closed mid-Sept to June. **Amenities:** Heated outdoor pool. *In room:* TV, kitchenettes, fridge, coffeemaker.

**Red Road Country Inn** ★ Located 20 minutes west of Cavendish, this cream-colored inn sits on 13ha (33 acres) atop a lovely knoll. Rooms have unobstructed views down a long and rustling hayfield to Harding Creek, which widens and flows into the gulf. (Rowboats are tied up at a dock for guests.) The inn, which doesn't promise much from outside, was built in 1994 and '95, but adopts a more historic character inside thanks to pine floors, large beams, and the handiwork of the owner, who is also a furniture maker—the guest rooms are each tastefully furnished with his Shaker reproductions and Windsor chairs. (One also even has its own balcony and a Jacuzzi.) A buffet-style breakfast featuring homemade breads is included in the rates.

Route 6, Clinton, PEI C0B 1M0. ✆ **800/249-1344** or 902/886-3154. Fax 902/886-2267. 9 units. C$115–C$189 (US$71–US$78), including full breakfast. MC, V. *In room:* TV (some rooms).

### WHERE TO DINE

Cavendish itself offers limited opportunities for creative dining, although it's well stocked with restaurants offering hamburgers, fried clams, and the like. **Café on the Clyde,** at the intersection of Routes 224 and 258 in New Glasgow (✆ **902/964-4300**), serves light meals in a bright and modern dining room.

**Old Glasgow Mill Restaurant** ★ REGIONAL/CANADIAN This casual restaurant, formerly a 19th-century feed mill in twee little New Glasgow, is nicely shielded from the tourist throngs at Cavendish. The place overlooks a small pond and features an eclectic assortment of regional food. Appetizers include seafood chowder and a chilled strawberry and wine soup along with salads and PEI mussels. Lunch entrees are uncomplicated, with seafood crêpes and Cajun chicken pizza being typical, but dinner is more serious: Besides Atlantic salmon and scallops, you'll find rack of lamb swabbed in Dijon mustard and rosemary herb-crust served with a rosemary peppercorn sauce, or chicken breast served with a cranberry confit. There's a leisurely brunch on the weekends.

Route 13, New Glasgow. ✆ **902/964-3313.** Reservations recommended. Lunch C$4.95–C$10.95 (US$3.10–US$7), dinner C$14.95–C$29.95 (US$9–US$18). AE, MC, V. Daily 11:30am–10pm May–Oct, shorter hours in winter.

## NORTH & SOUTH RUSTICO TO BRACKLEY BEACH

A few miles east of Cavendish are the Rusticos, of which there are five: North Rustico, South Rustico, Rusticoville, Rustico Harbour, and Anglo Rustico. The region was settled by Acadians in 1790 and many residents are descendants of the original settlers. North and South Rustico are both attractive villages that have fewer tourist traps and are more amenable to exploring by foot or bike than Cavendish. Although out of the hubbub, they still provide easy access to the national park and Anne-land, with beaches virtually at your doorstep.

**North Rustico** clusters around a scenic harbor with views out toward Rustico Bay. Plan to park and walk around, peeking in the shops. The village curves around Rustico Bay to end at North Rustico Harbour, a sand-spit with fishing wharfs, summer cottages and a couple of informal restaurants.

In **South Rustico** ★, turn off Route 6 and ascend the low hill overlooking the bay. Here you'll find a handsome cluster of buildings that were home to some of the more prosperous Acadian settlers. Among the structures is the sandstone **Farmer's Bank of Rustico** (✆ **902/963-3168** or 902/963-2304), established with the help of a visionary local cleric in 1864 to help farmers get ahead of the hand-to-mouth cycle. Renovations have been ongoing for several years; it is open for tours from June to mid-September, Monday to Saturday from 9:30am to 5:30pm and Sunday from 1 to 5:30pm. Next door is handsome **St. Augustine's Parish Church** (1838) and a cemetery beyond. If the church's door is open, head in for a look at this graceful structure.

**Brackley Beach** is the gateway to the eastern section of the national park, and has the fewest services of all. It's a quiet area, with no village center to speak of, that will be best appreciated by those who prefer their beach vacations unadulterated.

## WHERE TO STAY

**Barachois Inn** ★★ *Finds* The proudly Victorian Barachois Inn was built in 1870, and it is a soothing retreat for road-weary travelers. It's topped with a lovely mansard roof adorned with pedimented dormers, and it boasts a fine garden and historic furnishings throughout. Innkeepers Judy and Gary MacDonald bought the place as derelict property in 1982, and have done an outstanding job bringing it back from the brink. The main house is furnished with high-quality period antiques; the two rooms on the third floor are a bit cozier than the spacious second floor suites, but guests feel far away from the world when tucked under the slanted eaves. There's now a second, newer building next door with four additional executive-style rooms. Some rooms have Jacuzzis and kitchenettes.

Church Rd., Rustico (mailing address: Rustico, Hunter River RR no. 3, PEI C0A 1N0). ✆ **902/963-2194.** Fax 902/963-2906. www.barachoisinn.com. 8 units (1 with private bathroom down hallway). C$140–C$250 (US$87–US$16) double, including full breakfast. AE, MC, V. Closed Nov–March. **Amenities:** Exercise room; sauna; meeting room; laundry service. *In room:* A/C, TV/VCR, hair dryer, iron.

**Shaw's Hotel** ★ Shaw's is a delightfully old-fashioned compound located down a tree-lined dirt road along a marsh-edged inlet. It's been in the same family since 1860, and even with its regimen of modernization—new in 1999 were a sun deck, a bar, and a dining room addition that accommodates 40 more people—the place still has the feel of a farm-stay vacation in the 19th century. It remains the kind of place where ripply and worn carpeting in the hallways adds to the charm rather than detracts. Fifteen guest rooms are located upstairs; they are "boarding-house style," which is to say, small. The cottages vary in size and vintage. None are lavish, but most have the essentials (some with kitchenettes, some just with cube refrigerators) and some are downright comfy (double Jacuzzis have recently been installed in some of them).

Route 15, Brackley Beach C1E 1Z3. ✆ **902/672-2022.** Fax 902/672-3000. shaws@auracom.com. 10 units, 25 cottages. Inn: C$180–C$230 (US$112–US$143) double, including breakfast and dinner; cottages: C$175–C$320 (US$109–US$198) double. AE, MC, V. Closed Oct–May. Pets allowed in cottages only. **Amenities:** 2 restaurants; canoe, kayak, and bike rental; secretarial services; babysitting; laundry.

## WHERE TO DINE

**Cafe St. Jean** ECLECTIC There's a strong emphasis on local and Celtic music at Cafe St. Jean, with original tunes in the background, live music on the deck some evenings, and even CDs and tapes for sale at the cash register. Don't worry—this isn't a ploy to compensate for the quality of the food. Though meals can be inconsistent, the kitchen often scales culinary heights, producing zesty

## A PEI Tradition: The Lobster Supper

The north shore of Prince Edward Island is home to famous lobster suppers, which are a good bet if you have a craving for one of the succulent local crustaceans. These suppers took root years ago as events held in church basements, in which parishioners would bring a covered hot dish to share and the church would provide a lobster. Everyone would contribute some money, and the church netted a few dollars. Outsiders discovered these good deals, the fame of the dinners spread, and today several establishments offer the bountiful lobster dinners, although few are raising money for charity these days. Figure on C$20 to C$30 (US$12–US$19) per person, depending on the options.

**St. Ann's Church Lobster Suppers** (**© 902/621-0635**) remains a charitable organization, as it was 3 decades ago when it was the first and only lobster supper on PEI. Located in a modern church hall in the small town of St. Ann, just off Route 224 between Routes 6 and 13, St. Ann's has a full liquor license and the home-cooked food is served at your table (no buffet lines). Lobster dinners are served Monday to Saturday from 4 to 9pm, June through late September. (As befits a church, it's closed on Sundays.)

**Fisherman's Wharf Lobster Suppers** (**© 902/963-2669**) in North Rustico boasts a 18m (60-foot) salad bar to go with its lobster; it's open daily noon to 9pm, mid-May to mid-October. And near the PEI Preserve Company in New Glasgow is the barn-like **New Glasgow Lobster Suppers** (**© 902/964-2870**). Meals here include unlimited mussels and chowder; it's on Route 258 (just off Route 13) and is open daily 4 to 8:30pm, June to mid-October.

originals. The menu should appeal to most taste buds: There's Cajun salmon with a creole sauce, shrimp with peppercorns, and chateaubriand.

Route 6, Oyster Bed Bridge. **© 902/963-3133.** Reservations recommended. Lunch C$6–C$11 (US$4–US$7.35), dinner C$12–C$23 (US$7–US$14). Daily 11:30am–9:30pm. Closed Oct to mid-June. Located where Route 6 crosses the Wheatley River, at the southern tip of Rustico Bay.

**Sea Side Fish and Chips** *Value* *Kids* LIGHT FARE This little shack overlooking Rustico Bay is the place to go when you don't have the time for a sit-down dinner. The menu's simple—fried fish and scallops, basically—and not particularly healthy. But portions are huge and tasty, and a bottle of cola washes it down nicely. Take a seat on the back deck, both to be shielded from the persistent winds and to get a nice view of the water.

Route 6, Rusticoville, at bridge over Hunter River. No phone. Meals C$5–C$11 (US$3.10–US$7). Hours vary according to weather, but often open daily 11am–sundown. Closed Sept to mid-June.

## 3 Prince Edward Island National Park ★★

Prince Edward Island National Park encompasses a 40km (24-mile) swath of red-sand beaches, wind-sculpted dunes topped with marram grass, vast salt marshes, and placid inlets. The park is located along the island's sandy north-central coast, which is broached in several spots by broad inlets that connect to harbors. As a result, you can't drive along the entire park's length in one shot. The coastal road is disrupted by inlets, requiring backtracking to drive the entire length. And, actually, there's little point in trying to tour the whole length. It's a better use of your time to pick one spot, then settle in and enjoy your surroundings.

The national park also oversees the Green Gables house and grounds; see "Cavendish: Anne's Hometown," earlier.

## ESSENTIALS

**GETTING THERE** From Charlottetown, Route 15 offers the most direct route to the eastern segments of the park. To head to the Cavendish area, take Route 2 to Hunter River, then head north on Route 13.

**VISITOR INFORMATION** Two visitor centers provide information on park destinations and activities from June to October. The **Cavendish Visitors Centre** (© **902/963-2391** or 902/963-7830) is near the intersection of Routes 6 and 13; it's open daily from 9am to 10pm in the peak summer season (it closes earlier during the shoulder seasons). The **Brackley Visitors Centre** (© **902/672-7474**) is at the intersection of Routes 6 and 15; it's open daily in July and August 9am to 9pm (9am –4:30pm in June, Sept, and Oct). In the off-season, contact the park administration office (© **902/672-6350**) near the Dalvay Hotel.

**FEES** June to September, visitors to the national park must stop at one of the toll houses to pay entry fees. Daily rates in 2001 were C$3.50 (US$2.15) per adult, C$2.50 (US$1.55) per senior, C$1.75 (US$1.10) for children ages 6 to 16, and C$8 (US$5) per family. Ask about multi-day passes if you plan to visit for more than 3 days.

## EXPLORING THE PARK

Hiking is limited here compared to that at Atlantic Canada's other national parks, but you will find a handful of pleasant strolls. And, of course, there's the beach, which is perfect for long walks. The park maintains eight trails for a total of 20km (12 miles). Among the most appealing is the **Homestead Trail,** which departs from the Cavendish campground. The trail offers a 5.5km (3½-mile) loop and an 8km (4¾-mile) loop. The trail skirts wheat fields, woodlands, and estuaries, with frequent views of the distinctively lumpy dunes at the west end of the park.

**Biking** along the shoreline roads in the park is sublime. The traffic is light, and it's easy to make frequent stops to explore beaches, woodlands, or the marshy edges of inlets. The two shoreline drives within the national park—Dalvay to Rustico Island, and Cavendish to North Rustico Harbour—are especially beautiful on a clear evening as sunset edges into twilight. Snack bars are located at Brackley Beach and Covehead Bay.

Your safest bet for bike rentals is in Charlottetown (try **Cycle Smooth,** 172 Prince St., © **800/310-6550** or 902/566-5530), although you can often find rentals closer to the beach. In Brackley Beach, a good option is **Northshore Rentals** (© **902/672-2022**), located at Shaw's Hotel.

## BEACHES

PEI National Park is nearly synonymous with its beaches. The park is home to two kinds of sandy strands: popular and sometimes crowded beaches with changing rooms, lifeguards, snack bars, and other amenities; and other less crowded beaches lacking in amenities. Where you go depends on your temperament. If it's not a day at the beach without the aroma of other people's coconut tanning oil, head to **Brackley Beach** or **Cavendish Beach.** The latter is within walking distance of the Green Gables house and many other amusements (see "Cavendish: Anne's Hometown," earlier) and makes a good destination for families.

If you'd just as soon be left alone with the waves, sun, and sand, you'll need to head a bit farther afield or just keep walking down the beaches until you leave the crowds behind. We won't reveal the best spots here for fear of crowding. But suffice to say, they're out there.

## WHERE TO STAY & DINE

The park offers three **campgrounds.** Reservations are not accepted, so plan to arrive early in the day for the best selection of sites. Campground fees start at C$17 (US$11) per night (slightly less at Rustico Island), with serviced sites C$21 (US$13). For more information, contact the **Cavendish Visitors Centre** (✆ **902/963-2391** or 902/963-7830).

The most popular (and first to fill) is Cavendish, located just off Route 6 west of Green Gables. It has more than 300 sites spread among piney forest and open, sandy bluffs; the sites at the edge of the dunes overlooking the beach are the most popular. The sites aren't especially private or scenic.

The Stanhope campground lies just across the park road from lovely Stanhope Beach, which is on the eastern segment of the park (enter through Brackley Beach). The road isn't heavily traveled, so you don't feel much removed from the water's edge. Most sites are forested, and you're afforded more privacy here than at Cavendish.

Rustico Island is down a dead-end sand-spit, with a number of sites overlooking a placid cove and the rolling countryside beyond. It lacks hookups for RVs, which might explain why sites are usually available here after the other campgrounds fill up.

Also see listings for "Cavendish: Anne's Hometown," earlier and "North & South Rustico to Brackley Beach," above.

**Dalvay-by-the-Sea** ★★ This imposing Tudor mansion was built in 1895 by Alexander MacDonald, a partner of John D. Rockefeller. The place is unusually large for a private home, but it's rather intimate for a luxury inn. There are glimpses of the ocean across the road from the upper floors, even as the landscaping largely focuses on a beautiful freshwater pond out front. Inside, you'll be taken aback by the extraordinary cedar woodwork in the main entryway, and by the grand stone fireplace. The guest rooms are elegantly appointed and wonderfully solid and quiet; in the evening you'll hear mostly the roar of the sea. (The inn is just across the road from one of the park's better beaches; there are also plenty of walking trails nearby.) The well-regarded kitchen features dishes like tea-smoked Atlantic salmon with artichoke salad and crème fraîche; those not on the hotel's meal plan will pay extra for these meals, but they're worth it. The hotel serves afternoon tea each day from 2 to 4pm.

Off Route 6, Grand Tracadie (mailing address: P.O. Box 8, Little York, PEI C0A 1P0). ✆ **902/672-2048**, Fax (summer only) 902/672-2741. www.dalvaybythesea.com. 34 units. June–early Oct: Inn C$170–C$325 (US$105–US$202) double, including breakfast and dinner (C$20/US$12 less in shoulder seasons); cottages C$360–C$420 (US$223–US$260). National park entrance fees also charged. 2-night minimum in summer. AE, DC, MC, V. Closed mid-Oct to early June. **Amenities**: 2-hole fairway; tennis; croquet; lawn bowling; horseshoes; canoeing; bike rental.

## 4 Charlottetown ★

It's not hard to figure out why early settlers put the province's political and cultural capital where they did: It's on a point of land between two rivers and within a large protected harbor. For ship captains plying the seas, this quiet harbor with ample anchorage and wharf space must have been a welcome sight. Of course, travelers rarely arrive by water these days (unless a cruise ship is in port), but the city's harborside location translates into a lovely setting for one of Atlantic Canada's most graceful and relaxed cities.

Named after Queen Charlotte, consort of King George III, Charlottetown is home to some 40,000 people—nearly one of every three islanders. Within Canada, the city is famous for hosting the 1864 conference that 3 years later led to the creation of the independent Dominion of Canada. For this reason, you're never far from the word "confederation," which graces buildings, malls, and bridges. (In a historic twist, PEI itself actually declined to join the new confederation until 1873.) Today, the downtown has a brisk and busy feel to it, with a pleasing mix of modern and Victorian commercial buildings, as well as government and cultural centers. The capital also has the island's best selection of inns and hotels, and a fine assortment of restaurants that ensure you can dine out every night for a week and still be pleasantly surprised. As for scheduling time for exploring the city itself—I'd suggest saving it for a rainy day.

### ESSENTIALS

**GETTING THERE** Both Route 1 (the Trans-Canada Highway) and Route 2 pass through or near Charlottetown. For information on arriving by air, see "Exploring the Island" at the beginning of this chapter. **Square One Shuttle** (✆ **877-675-3830**) runs seven-person vans 4 days a week between Charlottetown and Saint John, NB; Fredericton, NB; and Halifax, NS.

**VISITOR INFORMATION** The city's main **Visitor Information Centre** (✆ **902/368-7795**) is on Water Street (across from 169 Water St. and next to Confederation Landing Park). Look for the brown "?" sign to direct you to a brick building with helpful staffers, an interactive computer kiosk, and an ample supply of brochures. There's also a vacancy board to let you know where rooms are currently available. The center is open daily in July and August 8am to 10pm; in the off-season, 8am to 5pm. There's a second information center at City Hall on Queen Street (✆ **902/566-5548**) that's open daily in summer 8am to 5pm.

### EXPLORING CHARLOTTETOWN

Charlottetown is a compact city that's easy to reconnoiter once you park your car. Three main areas merit exploration: the waterfront, the downtown area near Province House and the Confederation Court Mall, and parks and residential areas near Victoria Park.

You're best off first heading to the main Visitor Information Centre (see above), and then starting your tour from the waterfront. Parking is generally scarce downtown, but it's relatively abundant near the visitor center, both on the street and in free and paid lots. At the visitor center, be sure to ask for a map and one of the free walking tour brochures, "The First Five Hundred: Heritage and History Walks."

The waterfront has been spruced up in recent years with the addition of **Peake's Wharf,** a collection of touristy boutiques and restaurants that attracts hordes in summer. The complex is attractive and offers good people-watching, though it has a somewhat formulaic "festival marketplace" feel to it and is rather

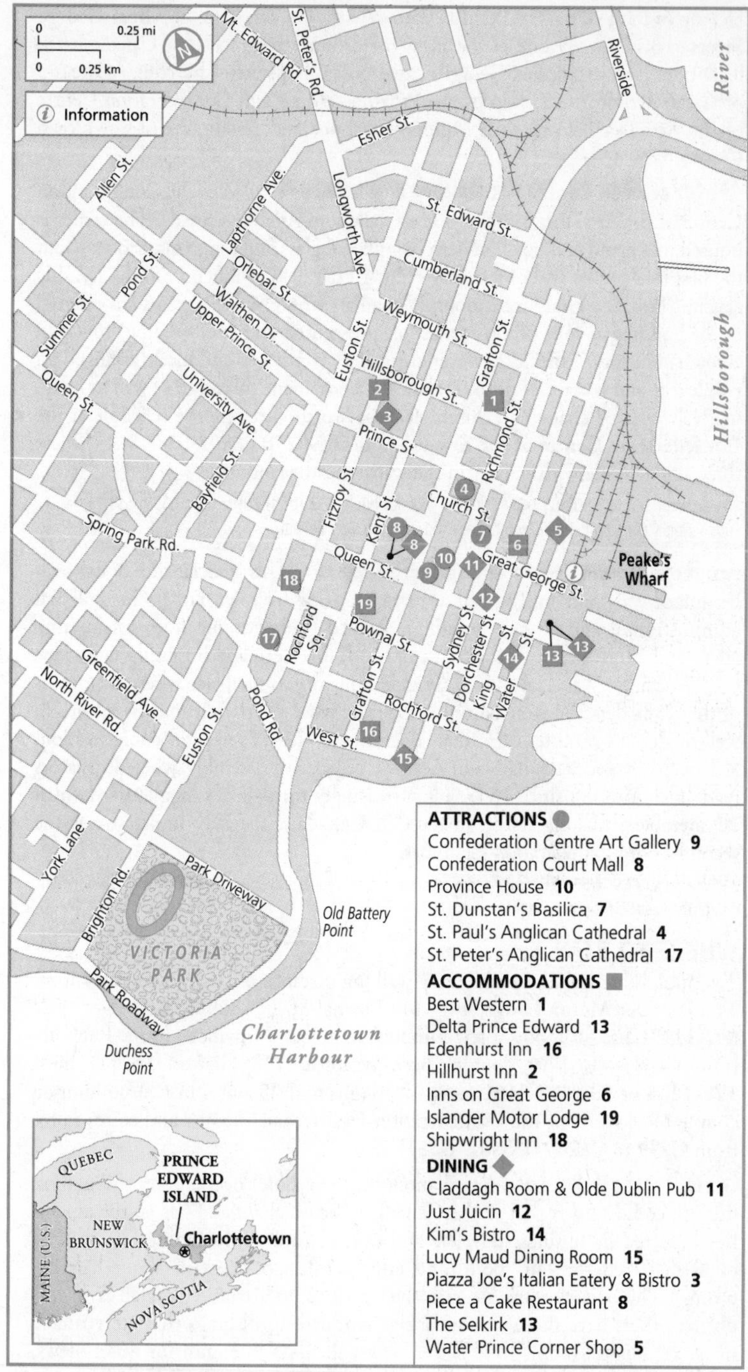
0
0.25 mi
0
0.25 km
Information
Mt. Edward Rd.
St. Peter's Rd.
Riverside
River
Esher St.
Allen St.
Lapthorne Ave.
Longworth Ave.
St. Edward St.
Cumberland St.
Orlebar St.
Pond St.
Walthen Dr.
Summer St.
Upper Prince St.
Weymouth St.
Euston St.
Grafton St.
Hillsborough St.
Hillsborough
Queen St.
University Ave.
Richmond St.
Prince St.
Bayfield St.
Fitzroy St.
Church St.
Kent St.
Spring Park Rd.
Great George St.
Peake's Wharf
Queen St.
Rochford Sq.
Pownal St.
Sydney St.
Dorchester St.
King St.
Water St.
Greenfield Ave.
North River Rd.
Euston St.
Pond Rd.
Grafton St.
Rochford St.
West St.
York Lane
Park Driveway
Brighton Rd.
Old Battery Point
VICTORIA PARK
Park Roadway
Charlottetown Harbour
Duchess Point
QUEBEC
PRINCE EDWARD ISLAND
NEW BRUNSWICK
Charlottetown
MAINE (U.S.)
NOVA SCOTIA
ATTRACTIONS
Confederation Centre Art Gallery 9
Confederation Court Mall 8
Province House 10
St. Dunstan's Basilica 7
St. Paul's Anglican Cathedral 4
St. Peter's Anglican Cathedral 17
ACCOMMODATIONS
Best Western 1
Delta Prince Edward 13
Edenhurst Inn 16
Hillhurst Inn 2
Inns on Great George 6
Islander Motor Lodge 19
Shipwright Inn 18
DINING
Claddagh Room & Olde Dublin Pub 11
Just Juicin 12
Kim's Bistro 14
Lucy Maud Dining Room 15
Piazza Joe's Italian Eatery & Bistro 3
Piece a Cake Restaurant 8
The Selkirk 13
Water Prince Corner Shop 5

lacking in local character. From Peake's Wharf, you can stroll up **Great George Street.** This is surely one of the most handsome streets in all of Canada, with leafy trees, perfectly scaled Georgian rowhouses, and stately churches. At the top of Great George Street, stop by the Province House and Confederation Centre of the Arts (see below), then explore the shops and restaurants of downtown Charlottetown.

**Confederation Centre Art Gallery and Museum** Part of the Confederation Centre of the Arts, this is the largest art gallery in Atlantic Canada. The center is housed in a bland and boxy modern complex of glass and rough sandstone; about the best that can be said of it is that it doesn't detract too much from the stylishly classical Province House next door. (Canadian writer Will Ferguson has referred to the building as "one of the greatest un-prosecuted crimes of urban planning in Canadian history.") Inside, however, the gallery is spacious and nicely arranged on two levels, and it features displays from the permanent collection as well as imaginatively curated changing exhibits. It's also worth checking the schedule at the **Confederation Centre of the Arts** (✆ **800/565-0278** or 902/628-1864), where three stages bustle with activity in the warm-weather months.

145 Richmond St. ✆ **902/628-6142.** C$4 (US$2.50) adult, C$3 (US$1.85) seniors, C$5 (US$3.10) family. Summer daily 9am–6pm, off-season Tues–Sat 11am–5pm, Sun 1–5pm.

**Province House National Historic Site** ★ This neoclassical downtown landmark was built in 1847 in an area set aside by town fathers for colonial administration and church buildings. Ringed by handsome trees, an inviting lawn, and a bustling downtown just beyond, this stern and imposing sandstone edifice occupies a special spot in Canadian history as the place where the details of the Confederation were hammered out in 1864. Start your tour by viewing a well-made, 17-minute film that documents the process of confederation. Afterwards, wander the halls and view the Legislative Assembly, where legislators have been meeting since 1847. It's surprisingly tiny—PEI's legislature has just 27 members, making it the smallest in Canada. Especially impressive is the second-floor Confederation Chamber.

2 Palmer's Ln. ✆ **902/566-7626.** Free admission (donations requested). June to mid-Oct daily 8:30am–5pm, rest of the year 9am–5pm.

## WHERE TO STAY

Two motels are situated within easy walking distance of downtown attractions. The **Islander Motor Lodge,** 146–148 Pownal St. (✆ **800/268-6261** or 902/892-1217), has 50 rooms a few minutes' walk from Province House. Rates are from C$113 (US$70) double. **Best Western,** 238 Grafton St. (✆ **800/528-1234** or 902/892-2461), has 148 rooms and 25 suites in two buildings a couple blocks east of the Confederation Court Mall. Rooms and suites range from C$99 to C$249 (US$61–US$154).

**Delta Prince Edward** ★★ A modern, boxy hotel overlooking the harbor, the Prince Edward is part of the Canadian Pacific chain and has all the amenities expected by business travelers and upscale tourists, including free exercise bikes delivered to your room, and even cordless phones (in about half the rooms). The better rooms are furnished with reproduction Georgian-style furniture; others have those oak and beige-laminate furnishings that are virtually invisible. Higher rooms have better views; there's a premium for water views, but the city views are actually nicer and you can usually still glimpse the water. The in-hotel Selkirk restaurant (see below) might be the city's best, with upscale service and presentation to complement a fine menu. Summers only, a more informal restaurant serves tasty lunches on a patio near the harbor.

18 Queen St., Charlottetown, PEI C1A 8B9. ✆ **800/268-1133** or 902/566-2222. Fax 902/566-2282. 211 units. Peak season C$149–C$199 (US$92–US$123) double; call for off-season rates. AE, DC, DISC, MC, V. Parking C$8 (US$5) per day. Pets allowed. **Amenities:** 2 restaurants; indoor pool; golf simulator; fitness room; sauna; outdoor hot tub; concierge; business center; shopping arcade; salon; room service; babysitting; laundry; dry cleaning. *In room:* A/C, TV, minibar, coffeemaker, hair dryer.

**Edenhurst Inn** ★ James Eden was a prosperous wine merchant on the island, and in 1897 he built this regal Queen Anne Revival mansion in one of the city's better neighborhoods—looking west toward the sunset over the water. It's three floors tall, and the exterior bustles with turrets, gables, and covered porches. The innkeepers have done a fine job restoring this historic property to its former splendor, and the rooms are furnished with the appropriate period antiques. When booking, ask about rooms with deluxe touches, such as fireplaces and Jacuzzis.

12 West St., Charlottetown, PEI C1A 3S4. ✆ **902/368-8323.** Fax 902/894-3707. 7 units. C$115–C$200 (US$71–US$124), including full breakfast. AE, MC, V. Not suitable for children under 8. *In room:* A/C, hair dryer.

**Hillhurst Inn** Another fine mansion built in 1897 in another fine neighborhood, Hillhurst features a raft of nice touches, not the least of which is the extraordinarily detailed woodworking carved by some of the city's shipbuilders. When built, locals called it "the crystal palace" because of its profusion of windows. The rooms are varied in size and style. As is often the case, the third floor rooms require a bit of a hike, and are smaller and cozier than the rooms on the second floor. The drawbacks? Many bathrooms are quite small (often shoehorned into closets), and the furnishings are less historic and creative compared to other comparably priced inns.

181 Fitzroy St., Charlottetown, PEI C1A 1S3. ✆ **877/994-8004** or 902/894-8004. Fax 902/892-1679. www.hillhurst.com. 9 units. High season C$115–C$205 (US$71–US$127). Low season C$85–C$145 (US$53–US$90). Rates include full breakfast. AE, MC, V. *In room:* A/C, hair dryer.

**Inns on Great George** ★★★ The Inns on Great George opened in 1997 and has since established itself as one of Charlottetown's very classiest addresses. The inns encompass a collection of striking buildings on and near historic Great George Street, most of which were renovated from states of former disrepair. (You can learn the story from a series of black-and-white photographs in the attractive lobby.) Twenty-four rooms are located in the old (1846) Pavilion Hotel; others are in smaller, brightly painted town houses and homes nearby. All have been thoroughly updated and refurbished with antiques, down duvets, and early black-and-white prints; all but two rooms are carpeted. The more expensive rooms have fireplaces and Jacuzzis, but many of the others have claw-foot tubs, perfect for soaking in after a day of roaming the city. Families or couples traveling together should ask about Room 662, an attractive three-bedroom suite, or one of a number of other renovated suites. The recent addition of a garden space out back only makes this place more desirable.

589 Great George St., Charlottetown, PEI C1A 4K3. ✆ **800/361-1118** or 902/892-0606. Fax 902/628-2079. www.innsongreatgeorge.com. 46 units (5 share 2 bathrooms). C$165–C$300 (US$102–US$186) doubles and suites, including continental breakfast, C$250 (US$155) apartments. AE, DC, MC, V. Free parking. **Amenities:** Fitness room; limited room service; babysitting; laundry; dry cleaning. *In room:* A/C, TV, hair dryer.

**Shipwright Inn** ★★ This understated Victorian home was built by a shipbuilder, and expertly renovated and refurbished. It's decorated with period furniture and with a deft touch—no over-the-top Victoriana here. All rooms have lovely wood floors (some with original ship-planking floors), and three are in a recent addition, which was built with a number of nice touches. Among the best rooms are those with extras: the Ward Room, a suite with a private deck; the Purser's State Room, which shares a lovely deck with another room; and the newly added Crow's Nest luxury apartment. Full breakfasts have been recently added, and a larger dining room now seats 25. This inn is located right in the city, yet has a settled, pastoral farmhouse feel to it.

51 Fitzroy St., Charlottetown, PEI C1A 1R4. ✆ **888/306-9966** or 902/368-1905. Fax 902/628-1905. www.shipwrightinn.com. 7 units. C$135–C$285 (US$84–US$177) double, including full breakfast; apartment C$165 (US$102). AE, DC, MC, V. **Amenities:** Restaurant; business center; snack trays. *In room:* A/C, TV, minibar, hair dryer.

## WHERE TO DINE

For live Celtic-flavored music and occasional roast beef buffet dinners, head for the fun and popular **Olde Dublin Pub,** below the Claddagh Room (see below) at 131 Sydney St. (✆ **902/892-6992**).

**Claddagh Room** ★ SEAFOOD Despite the Irish name and the Dublin Pub located downstairs, the Claddagh Room isn't the place for corned beef. It's the place for seafood, the house specialty. The seafood chowder is very tasty, as is the bouillabaisse. You can also order lobster from the tank, surf and turf, and a variety of other selections. There's no harbor view, as there is at other seafood places in town, but the preparation and service here are a notch above. Live Irish entertainment is often featured downstairs in the pub during the summer months.

131 Sydney St. ✆ **902/892-9661.** Reservations recommended. Lunch C$6–C$10 (US$3.70–US$6), dinner C$15–C$25 (US$9–US$16). AE, DISC, MC, V. Mon–Fri 11:30am–2pm, Sun–Thurs 5–10pm, Fri and Sat 5–10:30pm.

**Just Juicin'** ★ *Value* *Kids* CAFE This place has been a downtown Charlottetown fixture for four years now, but new ownership is taking it to a new level. Originally a smoothie and juice bar whizzing up incredibly tasty health drinks, it has added pita sandwiches, homemade chocolate cake and other delicious treats. It's a three-generation family operation, too—the owner, her daughter, and her mother have all been spotted working the counter simultaneously during busy summer-vacation times.

62 Queen St. ✆ **902/894-3104.** Reservations not accepted. Juices and sandwiches C$2–C$6 (US$1.20–US$3.70). June–Aug, Mon–Sat 8am–8pm, Sun noon–5pm; rest of the year, Mon–Fri, 8am–5:30pm, Sat 10am–5pm, closed Sun.

**Kim's Bistro** ★ SEAFOOD/BISTRO The small, cheerful restaurant on a side street a short stroll west of downtown opened in 1998, and puts an emphasis on the 18 smoked seafood products made by owner Kim Dormaar (sold elsewhere as Medallion Smoked Salmon). Lunches include smoked salmon on a bagel, or smoked trout on pumpernickel. The dinner menu offers lighter fare (salmon carpaccio or smoked seafood plate), along with more substantial entrees like island lamb served with a ginger honey sauce, and grilled salmon.

45 Water St. ✆ **902/894-5149.** Reservations helpful. Lunch C$4.95–C$10.95 (US$3–US$7), dinner C$7.55–C$21.95 (US$4.70–US$14); entrees mostly C$13–C$15 (US$8–US$9). AE, MC, V. Mon–Fri 11:30am–2pm, 5–10pm, Sat 5–10pm. Closed Oct–May.

**Lucy Maud Dining Room** ★★ REGIONAL The Lucy Maud Dining Room is located within the Culinary Institute of Canada's campus. The building itself is a bit institutional and charmless, but plenty of nice touches offset the lack of personality. Among them: custom china and a beautiful view of the bay and

Victoria Park from oversize windows. Best of all, diners get to sample some of the best of island cuisine, prepared and served by Institute students eager to please. The lunch and dinner menus change each semester, but there's always salmon on the menu and, often, the curried seafood chowder with fresh tarragon, a local favorite.

4 Sydney St. ✆ **902/894-6868.** Reservations recommended for lunch and dinner June–Sept. Lunch C$8–C$13 (US$5–US$8), dinner C$15–C$28 (US$9–US$17). AE, MC, V. Lunch Tues–Fri 11:30am–1:30pm, dinner Tues–Sat 6–8pm. Closed holiday weekends.

**Piazza Joe's Italian Eatery and Bistro** PIZZA/ITALIAN Piazza Joe's, located in a handsome, historic building 1 long block from the Confederation Mall, has gone a bit overboard with the Tuscan-style washed tones and fake ivy climbing fake trellises. But it works in a comic-book kind of way. The wood-fired pizza is consistently quite good. There's also a bistro menu, with items like burgers, chicken wings, and fish and chips.

189 Kent St. ✆ **902/894-4291.** Reservations accepted. Main courses C$9.95–C$14.95 (US$6–US$9), individual pizzas C$7 (US$4.35) and up. AE, DC, MC, V. Mon and Thurs 11am–midnight, Fri–Sat 11am–1am, Sun 10am–midnight.

**Piece a Cake Restaurant** ★★ ECLECTIC This very modern, very handsome restaurant occupies the second floor of a building that's part of the Confederation Court Mall. It's the kind of place where friends who don't see each other very often like to get together and relax over a lively meal. The menu is wonderfully far-ranging, and it's hard to imagine someone not finding something appealing—lunches range from a teriyaki salmon wrap to Thai scallop salad to Tuscan grilled chicken sandwiches. Dinners are similarly eclectic and include a range of adventurous pastas. Also ask about the gourmet brown bag lunches.

119 Grafton St. (upstairs in the Confederation Court Mall). ✆ **902/894-4585.** Reservations recommended. Lunch C$6–C$12 (US$3.70–US$7), dinner C$9–C$18 (US$6–US$11). AE, DC, MC, V. Mon–Sat 11am–11pm, May–Oct Sun 5–9pm. Closed Sun Oct–May.

**The Selkirk** ★★★ NEW CANADIAN Charlottetown's most stylish restaurant is smack in the middle of the lobby of the high-end Prince Edward Hotel. The menu is also more ambitious and creative than you'll find elsewhere in the city. The signature appetizer is lobster and prawns served with a three-melon salsa, or you might opt for pheasant confit. Main courses could include sashimi of salmon, oysters, and scallops with a sauce of lime, ginger, and garlic; or a Maritime jambalaya with lobster, mussels, shrimp, scallops, and salmon. Carnivores aren't ignored, with a selection that includes duck breast with a raspberry and green peppercorn vinaigrette, or beef tenderloin with a shiitake ragout. A downside is that the lobby location can get clamorous at times, especially when conferees are milling about.

In the Delta Prince Edward, 18 Queen St. ✆ **902/894-1208.** Reservations encouraged. Breakfast C$6–C$12 (US$3.70–US$7), lunch C$8–C$15 (US$5–US$9), dinner C$15–C$32 (US$9–US$20). AE, DC, DISC, MC, V. Daily 7:30am–1pm, 5:30–9:30pm.

**Water Prince Corner Shop** ★★ *Finds* SEAFOOD This place is a real find, tucked into an attractive corner building at Water and Prince streets (hence the name) that looks at first glance like a simple newsstand or convenience store. Inside, though, you'll find one of the city's most convivial seafood joints, serving lobster dinners, superb seafood chowder, cooked mussels, and even lobster rolls to an appreciative mixture of tourists and locals. There's a liquor license if you want to tip a few (and you might). If the weather's good, try to get a seat on the street near sundown. You can see the waterfront from some tables.

141 Water St. ✆ **902/368-3212.** Reservations helpful. Lunch C$4.95–C$10.95 (US$3–US$7), dinner C$6.95–C$24.95 (US$4.30–US$15). AE, DISC, DC, MC, V. May to mid-Oct 9am–8pm, Jul–Aug until 10pm.

## 5 Kings County: An Escape from Anne's Land

After a visit to Charlottetown and the island's central towns, Kings County comes as a bit of a surprise. It's far more tranquil and uncluttered than Queens County (Anne's reach is much diminished here), and the landscapes feature woodlots alternating with corn, grain, and potato fields. Although much is made of the county's two great commercial centers on the coast—Souris and Montague—it's good to keep in mind that each of these has a population of around 1,500. In some parts of North America, that wouldn't even rate a dot on the map.

### ESSENTIALS

**GETTING THERE** Several main roads—including Highways 1, 2, 3, and 4—connect eastern PEI with Charlottetown and western points. The ferry to Nova Scotia sails from Woods Island on the south coast. See "Exploring the Island" earlier in this chapter for more information.

**VISITOR INFORMATION** A large provincial **information center** (✆ **902/838-0670**) is located in Pooles Corner at the intersections of Route 3 and Route 4 (north of Montague). The center, which is open June to mid-October, also contains well-presented exhibits about local commerce and history, including how to identify local architectural styles. Another helpful visitor center is located at the old railway depot in Montague on the river. It's open daily in summer.

### MONTAGUE

Montague is the region's main commercial hub, but it's a hub in low gear. It's compact and attractive, with a handsome business district on a pair of flanking hills sloping down to a bridge across the Montague River. (A century and a half ago, the town was called Montague Bridge.) Shipbuilding was the economic mainstay in the 19th century; today, it's dairy and tobacco.

#### EXPLORING THE OUTDOORS

**Cruise Manada** (✆ **800/986-3444** or 902/838-3444) offers seal- and bird-watching tours daily during peak season aboard restored fishing boats; the cost is C$18 (US$11) per adult, C$16 (US$10) per senior or student, and C$9 (US$6) for children under 13. Trips depart from the marina on the Montague River, just below the visitor center in the old railway depot. Reservations are advised.

Southeast of Montague (en route to Murray River) is the **Buffaloland Provincial Park** (✆ **902/652-8950**), where you'll spot a small herd of buffalo. These were a gift to PEI from the province of Alberta, and they now number about 25. Walk down the fenced-in corridor into the paddock and ascend the wooden platform for the best view of the shaggy beasts. Often they're hunkered down at the far end of the meadow, but they sometimes wander near. The park is right off Route 4; watch for signs.

**Brudenell River Provincial Park** (✆ **902/652-8966**) is one of the province's better-bred parks, and a great spot to work up an athletic glow on a sunny afternoon. On its 600ha (1,500-acre) riverfront you'll find two well-regarded golf courses, a golf academy, a full-blown resort (see below), tennis, lawn bowling, a wildflower garden, a playground, a campground, and nature trails. Kids' programs, like Frisbee golf, shoreline scavenger hunts, and crafts workshops, are scheduled daily in summer. You can also rent canoes, kayaks, and jet skis from private operators located within the park. The park is open daily from 9am to 9pm; admission is free. Head north of Montague on Route 4 then east on Route 3 to the park signs. Follow the signs to the park.

## WHERE TO STAY

**Lady Catherine's B&B** ★ Tom Rath has been running this B&B 22km (14 miles) southeast of Montague for more than a decade, and he's a great resource for local attractions and music. The trim 1907 farmhouse has just two guest rooms (each with private bathroom located across the hall), and an idyllic location amid potato fields with views of the bay and the distant shores of Nova Scotia. It's an informal and relaxing spot, popular with couples, and offers good access to Panmure Island and Poverty Beach (bring your bikes!). Breakfasts are more than filling, and often feature "bilingual French toast" (made with English muffins). Rath will prepare a lavish candlelight dinner for two on request.

Route 17, Murray Harbour North (mailing address: RR4, Montague, PEI C0A 1R0). ✆ **800/661-3426.** ladyc@pei.sympatico.ca. 2 units (multi-bedroom suites available), both with private detached bathroom. C$100 (US$62) double, including full breakfast; C$130–C$150 suites (US$81–US$93). AE, MC, V. Pets allowed with advance permission. **Amenities:** Dinner by request. *In room:* Ceiling fans.

**Rodd Brudenell River Resort** ★ *Kids* The attractive Brudenell River Resort was built in 1991, and its sleek, open, and vaguely Frank Lloyd Wright–esque design reflects its recent vintage. It's an especially popular destination with golfers—it's set amid two golf courses that have been garnering plaudits from serious duffers in recent years. The hotel proper has 51 well-appointed guest rooms, each with balcony or terrace. The upmarket and new (1999) Echelon Gold Cottages each have two bedrooms, cathedral ceilings, fireplaces, and large-screen TVs. The more basic Countryside Cabins are the best bet for those traveling on a budget; just beware that the detailing isn't of the highest quality, and the units are clustered together a bit oddly, like pavilions left over from some forgotten world exposition. In addition to the two excellent golf courses (one hosts a Golf Academy offering extensive lessons), the resort has indoor and outdoor pools.

Route 3 (P.O. Box 67), Cardigan, PEI C0A 1G0. ✆ **800/565-7633** or 902/652-2332. Fax 902/652-2886. www.rodd-hotels.ca. 51 units, 82 cabins. C$185 (US$115) double, C$90–C$140 (US$56–US$87) basic cabins; C$160–C$440 (US$99–US$273) deluxe cabins. AE, DC, MC, V. Closed mid-Oct to mid-May. Pets allowed, C$10 (US$6) per pet per night. **Amenities:** Restaurant; 2 pools; 2 night-lit tennis courts; golf course; health club; sauna; Jacuzzi; children's center; babysitting; dry cleaning. *In room:* TV.

**Rodd Marina Inn & Suites** ★ The new Marina Inn was built in 1999, and has the casually modern feel of the sort of mid-size chain hotel you'd expect to find on a strip at the edge of a mid-size town. With this difference: It boasts a great location, tucked off Montague's main street, right along the Montague River (boat tours available), and smack on a spur of the Confederation Trail. The hotel's rooms are mostly standard size and equipped. A dozen "studio-suites" (their term) offer a small sitting area along with microwave, fridge, and Jacuzzi. Request a room on the riverside for the view.

115 Sackville St. (P.O. Box 1540) Montague, PEI C0A 1R0. ✆ **800/565-7633** or 902/838-4075. Fax 902/838-4180. www.rodd-hotels.ca. 52 units. C$69–C$148 (US$43–US$92), including continental breakfast, C$94–C$173 (US$58–US$107) suites. AE, DC, MC, V. **Amenities:** Small exercise room; sun deck. *In room:* A/C, TV, coffeemaker, hair dryer.

### WHERE TO DINE

**Windows on the Water** ★ SEAFOOD If you haven't yet dined on PEI mussels, this is the place to let loose. The blue mussels are steamed in a root mirepoix, with sesame, ginger, and garlic. It's a winner. Main courses include sole stuffed with crab and scallop and topped with hollandaise, and the chef's peppered steak—a filet mignon served with sweet peppers, red onion, and mushrooms in a peppercorn sauce. Lunches are lighter, with choices like grilled chicken and mandarin salad, and homemade fish cakes. The appealing and open dining room features press-back chairs and a lively buzz, but if the weather's agreeable, angle for a seat under the canopy on the deck.

106 Sackville St. (corner of Main St.), Montague. ✆ **902/838-2080.** Reservations recommended. Lunch C$7.50–C$9.95 (US$4.65–US$6), dinner C$14.95–C$20.95 (US$9–US$13). AE, DC, MC, V. Daily 11:30am–9:30pm.

## SOURIS & NORTHEAST PEI

Some 44km (26 miles) northeast of Montague is the town of Souris, an active fishing town attractively set on a gentle hill overlooking the harbor. Souris (pronounced Soo-ree) is French for "mouse"—so named because early settlers were beset by voracious field mice, which destroyed their crops. The town is the launching point for an excursion to the Magdalen Islands, and it makes a good base for exploring northeastern PEI, which is considered by more urban residents as the island's outback—remote and sparsely populated. You'll also find it somewhat less agricultural and more forested, especially away from the coast, than the rest of the island.

### EXPLORING THE AREA

Several good beaches can be found ringing this wedge-shaped peninsula that points like an accusing finger toward Nova Scotia's Cape Breton Island. **Red Point Provincial Park** (✆ **902/357-3075**) is 13km (8 miles) northeast of Souris. It offers a handsome beach and supervised swimming, along with a campground that's popular with families; sites cost C$17 to C$23 (US$11–US$14). Another inviting and often empty beach is a short distance northeast at **Basin Head,** which features a "singing sands" beach that allegedly sings (actually, it's more like a squeak) when you walk on it. The dunes here are especially appealing.

At the island's far eastern tip is the aptly named **East Point Lighthouse** (✆ **902/357-2106** or 902/687-1991). You can simply enjoy the dramatic setting or take a tour of the building. Ask for your East Point ribbon while you're here. If you make it to the **North Cape Lighthouse** on the western shore, you'll receive a Traveller's Award documenting that you've traveled PEI tip-to-tip. Admission to the lighthouse is C$2.50 (US$1.55) per adult and C$1 (US60¢) per child. It is closed September to mid-June.

### WHERE TO STAY

**Inn at Bay Fortune** ★★ This exceptionally attractive, shingled compound on 20ha (46 acres) was built by playwright Elmer Harris in 1910 as a summer home, and it quickly became the nucleus for a colony of artists, actors, and writers. (Most recently the home was owned by Canadian actress Colleen Dewhurst, who sold it to current innkeeper David Wilmer in 1988.) Wilmer pulled out the stops in renovating, bringing it back from the brink of decay. In 1998 he added a wing with six new rooms (two with Jacuzzis); all are quite cozy with a mix of antiques and custom-made furniture. The inn is also home to one of PEI's best restaurants (see below).

Route 310 (off Route 2), Bay Fortune, PEI C0A 2B0. ✆ **902/687-3745,** off-season 860/296-1348. Fax 902/687-3540. www.innatbayfortune.com. 18 units. Summer C$140–C$280 (US$87–US$174) double, fall C$105–C$230 (US$65–US$143). Rates include full breakfast. DC, MC, V. Closed mid-Oct to late May. **Amenities:** Restaurant.

**Inn at Spry Point** ★★ *Finds* All 15 rooms here have comfortable, canopied king-size beds and are tastefully appointed with comfortable sitting areas. Most have their own private balconies, and four have a garden terrace. Outside, the location is top-rate—800m (8,000 feet) of undeveloped shorefront that invites exploration—and you can walk along trails that traverse red-clay cliffs with views of the Northumberland Strait. Later, dine in the outstanding contemporary **dining room** ★ featuring locally grown organic vegetables and island seafood; prix-fixe meals cost C$42 (US$26) per person.

Souris RR no. 4, Little Pond, PEI C0A 2B0. ✆ **800/665-2400** or 902/583-2400. Fax 902/583-2176. www.innatsprypoint.com. 15 units. C$155–C$260 (US$96–US$161) double, including full breakfast. DC, MC, V. Closed early Oct–late May. **Amenities:** Restaurant. *In room:* A/C.

**The Matthew House Inn** ★ Located atop a pleasant lawn overlooking the harbor and ferry to the Magdalen Islands, this stately Victorian dates to 1885 and maintains many of the original flourishes inside and out. Eastlake-style furnishings and William Morris touches give the place an architectural richness without seeming too grandmotherly about it; for big families, a new two-bedroom cottage adjacent to the inn rents by the week, sleeps up to seven, and is equipped with a kitchen and laundry. This place will be appreciated by those passionate about historic architecture.

15 Breakwater St. (P.O. Box 151), Souris, PEI C0A 2B0. ✆ **902/687-3461.** Fax 902-687-3461. www.matthewhouseinn.com. 6 units. C$150–C$200 (US$93–US$124) double, including full breakfast, cottage C$1,050 (US$651) weekly up to 4 people, C$50 (US$31) each additional person. AE, MC, V. Closed early Sept–late June. Children over 10 welcome. **Amenities:** Restaurant; laundry service. *In room:* TV/VCR, hair dryer.

### WHERE TO DINE

**Inn at Bay Fortune** ★★★ CREATIVE CONTEMPORARY To fully appreciate a meal at the Inn at Bay Fortune, arrive early enough to wander the gardens behind the inn. The herbs and edible flowers are a short walk from the kitchen; a little further beyond is the three-acre vegetable garden. This is good introduction to the local products emphasized on the menu. Chef Jeff McCourt worked with founding chef Michael Smith to develop the inn's regional cuisine and its vaunted openness—how many restaurants feature a KITCHEN—WELCOME sign inviting diners to stop in for a visit? The place is wildly successful, with an always-shifting menu that rarely fails to produce a winning meal.

Route 310 (off Route 2), Bay Fortune, PEI C0A 2B0. ✆ **902/687-3745.** Reservations strongly recommended. Main courses C$24–C$32 (US$15–US$20), tasting menu C$110 (US$68), chef's table C$80 (US$50). AE, MC, V. Daily 5–9pm. Closed mid-Oct to late May.

## 6 Prince County: PEI in the Rough

Prince County encompasses the western end of PEI and offers a varied mix of lush agricultural land, rugged coastline, and unpopulated sandy beaches. This is Prince Edward Island with calluses. With a few exceptions, the region is a bit more ragged around the edges in a working-farm, working-waterfront kind of way. It typically lacks the pristine-village charm of Kings County or much of Queens County. Within this unrefined landscape, however, you'll find pockets of considerable charm, such as the village of Victoria on the south coast at the county line, and in Tyne Valley near the north coast, which is reminiscent of a Cotswold hamlet.

## ESSENTIALS

**GETTING THERE** Route 2 is the main highway connecting Prince County with the rest of the island. Feeder roads typically lead from or to Route 2. The Confederation Bridge from the mainland connects to Prince County at Borden Point, southeast of Summerside.

**VISITOR INFORMATION** The best source of travel information for the county is **Gateway Village** (© **800/463-734** or 902/437-8539) at the end of the Confederation Bridge. It's open daily year-round.

## VICTORIA ★★

The town of Victoria—located a short detour off Route 1 between the Confederation Bridge and Charlottetown—is a tiny and unusually scenic village that's attracted a number of artists, boutique owners, and craftspeople. The village is perfect for strolling—parking is near the wharf and off the streets, keeping the narrow lanes free for foot traffic. Wander the short, shady lanes while admiring the architecture, much of which is in elemental farmhouse style, clad in clapboard or shingle and constructed with sharply creased gables. (Some elaborate Victorians break the mold.)

What makes the place so singular is that the village, which was first settled in 1767, has utterly escaped the creeping sprawl that has plagued so many otherwise attractive places. The entire village consists of 4 square blocks, which are surrounded by potato fields and the Northumberland Strait.

### EXPLORING VICTORIA

The **Victoria Seaport Museum** (no phone) is located in a shingled, square lighthouse near the town parking lot. You'll find a rustic local history museum with the usual assortment of artifacts from the past century or so. In summer, it's open daily except Monday from noon to 5pm; admission is by donation.

In the middle of town is the well-regarded **Victoria Playhouse** (© **902/658-2025**). Built in 1913 as a community hall, the building has a raked stage—it drops 18cm over 6.5m (7 inches over 21 feet) to create the illusion of space, four beautiful stained-glass lamps, and a proscenium arch (also unusual for a community hall). Plays staged here in summer attract folks out from Charlottetown for the night. It's hard to say what is more enjoyable: the high quality of the acting or the wonderful big-night-out air of a professional play in a small town where nothing else is going on. There's also a Monday-night concert series, with performers offering up everything from traditional folk to Latin jazz. Tickets are C$18 (US$11) per adult and C$16 (US$10) for seniors and students; matinees cost only C$14 (US$9).

### WHERE TO STAY

**Orient Hotel** You have to book an entire week to stay at the Orient, but it's worth it if you like peace and quiet. Rooms are painted in warm pastel tones and furnished eclectically with flea-market antiques. Although some of the updating has diminished the charm—such as the velour furniture in the lobby and the industrial carpeting—the place has a friendly low-key demeanor, much like the village itself. Mrs. Proffit's Tea Shop, on the first floor, serves lunch and afternoon tea from noon to 5pm daily.

Main St. (mailing address: P.O. Box 162, Charlottetown, PEI C1A 7K4). © **800/565-6743** or 902/658-2503. Fax 902/658-2078. orient@pei.sympatico.ca.6 units. C$80–C$140 (US$50–US$87) double, including full breakfast. AE, MC, V. Closed mid-Oct to mid-May. **Amenities:** Tea room; TV room; games room. *In room:* Ceiling fan.

### WHERE TO DINE

**Landmark Café** CAFE Located across from the Victoria Playhouse, the Landmark Cafe occupies a small, cozy storefront teeming with shelves filled with crockery, pots, jars, and more, some of which is for sale. But the effect is more funky than Ye Olde Quainte, and the limited menu is very inviting. The steamed mussels and vine leaves with feta cheese are a favorite of regulars. Other offerings include salads, lasagna, meat pie, and tarragon-steamed salmon.

Main St. ✆ **902/658-2286.** Reservations recommended. Sandwiches around C$5.50 (US$3.40), main courses C$11–C$16 (US$7–US$10). MC, V. Daily 11am–9:30pm. Closed mid-Sept to mid-June.

## TYNE VALLEY ★

The village of Tyne Valley is just off Malpeque Bay and is one of the most attractive and pastoral areas of western PEI. There's little to do here, but much to admire. Verdant barley and potato fields surround the village of gingerbread homes, and azure inlets encroach here and there; these are the arms of the bay, which is famous for its succulent Malpeque oysters. A former 19th-century shipbuilding center, the village now attracts artisans and others in search of a quiet lifestyle. A handful of good restaurants, inns, and shops cater to visitors.

### EXPLORING TYNE VALLEY

Just north of the village on Route 12 is the lovely **Green Provincial Park** ★ (✆ **902/831-7912**). Once the site of an active shipyard, the 90ha (219-acre) park is now a lush riverside destination with emerald lawns and leafy trees, and it has the feel of a turn-of-the-century estate which, in fact, it was. In the heart of the park is the extravagant gingerbread mansion (1865) once owned by James Yeo, a merchant, shipbuilder, and landowner who in his time was the island's wealthiest and most powerful man.

The historic **Yeo House** and the **Green Park Shipbuilding Museum** (✆ **902/831-7947**) are now the park's centerpieces. Managed by the Prince Edward Island Museum and Heritage Foundation, exhibits in two buildings provide a good view of the prosperous life of a shipbuilder and the golden age of PEI shipbuilding. The museum and house are open daily in summer 10am to 5pm. Admission is C$3.50 (US$2.15) plus tax per adult, and children under 12 go free.

### WHERE TO STAY

**Green Provincial Park** (✆ **902/831-7912**) may be the most gracious and lovely park on the island, and offers camping on grassy sites overlooking an arm of Malpeque Bay.

**Caernarvon in Bayside** *Kids* The sense of quiet and the views over Malpeque Bay across the road are the lure at this attractive, well-maintained cottage compound on 2ha (5 acres) a few minutes' drive from Tyne Valley. Modern (ca. 1990) knotty pine cottages are furnished simply but comfortably. Each has two bedrooms and a sleeping loft, outdoor gas barbecue, cathedral ceiling, and porch with a bay view. This is a good choice if you're looking to get away, but note that it's also popular with families (there's a playground out back) so it may not be the best option for a romantic escape. New in 2001 is a pretty 2.5m (9-ft.-high) gazebo on the lawn, steps from the bay.

Route 12, Bayside, PEI (mailing address: Richmond RR1, C0B 1Y0). ✆ **800/514-9170** or 902/854-3418. www.cottagelink.com/caernarvon. 1 3-bedroom unit, 4 cottages. C$120 (US$74) double for B&B (includes breakfast) or cottage (3-night min); cottages weekly C$740 (US$459) up to 2 people. V. Pets in cottages only. **Amenities:** Playground; grill; laundry. *In room:* Hair dryer, iron.

**Doctor's Inn** ★ *Value* A stay at the Doctor's Inn is a bit like visiting relatives you didn't know you had. Upstairs in this handsome in-town farmhouse are just two guest rooms, which share a bathroom. (Note that you could rent both for less than the cost of a room at some other inns.) There's an upstairs sitting area, and the extensive organic gardens out back to peruse. It's a pleasant retreat, and innkeepers Jean and Paul Offer do a fine job of making guests feel relaxed and at home. The Offers also serve up one of Atlantic Canada's most memorable dining experiences. Look for scallops, arctic char, salmon, veal, or whatever else is fresh. Desserts are fresh-baked and wonderful. Reservations are requested at least 24 hours in advance; dinner is served at 7pm, a four-course meal with wine for about C$40 (US$25) per person.

Route 167 (P.O. Box 92), Tyne Valley, PEI C0B 2C0. ✆ **902/831-3057.** www.peisland.com/doctorsinn. 2 units (both share 1 bathroom). C$60 (US$37) double, including breakfast, additional person C$15/US$10. MC, V. "Well-mannered" pets allowed. **Amenities:** Restaurant.

## WHERE TO DINE

Also see the **Doctor's Inn,** above.

**The Shipwright's Café** REGIONAL This locally popular restaurant moved to the village of Margate in the summer of 2001. It's elegant yet informal, and you'd be comfortable here in either neat jeans or pre-dinner sport clothes. Expect good service, a modest but useful wine list, and salads with greens from the Offer's organic gardens, just down the street. Justly popular dishes include the local oysters broiled with spinach and cheese, and the seafood chowder, which is rich and loaded with plump mussels.

11869 Route 6, Margate, PEI C0B 1M0. ✆ **902/836-3403.** Reservations recommended in summer. Lunch C$9.95–C$16.95 (US$6–US$11), dinner C$14.95–C$19.95 (US$9–US$12), more for lobster. MC, V. Daily June–Sept 11:30am–8:30pm. Closed Oct–June.

6

# Newfoundland & Labrador

*by Wayne Curtis & Paul Karr*

Newfoundland and Labrador might be the Eastern seaboard's last best place. (These two distinct geographic areas are administered as one province, so sometimes the phrase "Newfoundland and Labrador" refers to a single place, sometimes to two places.) Wild, windswept, and isolated, the province often reveals a powerful paradox. Although the landscape is rocky and raw—at times it looks as if the glaciers had receded only a year or two ago—the residents often display a genuine warmth that makes visitors feel right at home. Tourists only recently started arriving here in any number, and long-time residents more often than not like to chat, offer advice, and hear your impressions of their home. Travelers who are usually reluctant to ask questions of locals for fear of embarrassment usually drop their hesitation after an encounter or two.

An excursion to The Rock—as the island of Newfoundland is commonly called—is magical in many ways. Visitors will see this not only in the extraordinary northern landscape and the gracious people, but also in the rich history that catches many first-time visitors off guard. This is where European civilization made landfall in the New World—by both the Vikings and the later fishermen and settlers in the wake of John Cabot's arrival here in 1497—and you'll find traces of that rich legacy at almost every turn. Although other parts of North America might claim an equally historic lineage, there are few places in the New World where one feels as if not a whole lot has transpired since the first settlers sailed into the harbor some centuries ago. History isn't buried here; it's right on the surface.

## 1 Exploring Newfoundland & Labrador

A couple of weeks are enough for a bare-bones tour of the whole island, though you'll be frustrated by all that gets left out. You're better off selecting a few regions and focusing on those.

### VISITOR INFORMATION

Visitor information centers aren't as numerous or well organized in Newfoundland as they are in Nova Scotia or Prince Edward Island, where almost every small community has a place to load up on brochures and ask questions. In Newfoundland, you're better off stocking up on maps and information either in St. John's or just after you disembark from the ferries, where excellent centers are maintained.

The *Newfoundland and Labrador Travel Guide,* published by the province's department of tourism, is hefty and helpful, with listings of all attractions and accommodations. Request a free copy before arriving by contacting the **Department of Tourism, Culture & Recreation,** P.O. Box 8730, St. John's, NF

**Tips** **A Timely Note**

Note that Newfoundland keeps its own clock, and "Newfoundland time" is a half-hour ahead of Atlantic time.

A1B 4K2 (✆ **800/563-6353** or 709/729-2830; fax 709/729-1965; http://public.gov.nf.ca/tourism/).

**GETTING THERE By Plane** Air transportation to Newfoundland is typically through Gander or St. John's, although scheduled flights are also available to Deer Lake and St. Anthony's. Flights originate in Montréal, Toronto, Halifax, and London, England. Airlines serving the island include **Air Canada/Air Nova** (✆ **800/AIR-CANA;** www.aircanada.ca), **Air Labrador** (✆ **800/563-3042** within Newfoundland or 709/896-3387 elsewhere; www.airlabrador.com), and **Provincial Airlines** (✆ **800/563-2800** within Newfoundland or 709/576-1666 elsewhere; www.provair.com). Flight time from Toronto to St. John's is about 3 hours.

**By Ferry** **Marine Atlantic** (✆ **800/341-7981;** www.marine-atlantic.ca) operates a year-round ferry service from North Sydney, Nova Scotia to Port aux Basques, with as many as three sailings each way daily during the peak summer season. The crossing is about 5 hours; one-way fares are C$22 (US$14) adult, plus C$67 (US$42) automobile. A seasonal ferry (summers only) also connects North Sydney with Argentia on the southwest tip of the Avalon Peninsula. This crossing is offered three times weekly in summer and takes 14 to 15 hours. The one-way fare is C$60 (US$37) adult, plus C$135 (US$84) car. On both ferries, children 5 to 12 years old are half-price (children under 5 free). Reserved reclining seats, sleeping berths, and private cabins are available.

Seasonal ferries also connect Lewisporte, Newfoundland with Goose Bay, Labrador. The trip is about 38 hours. On **Coastal Labrador Marine Service** ferries (✆ **709/535-6872**), the fares are C$97 (US$60) per adult, C$48.50 (US$30) for children ages 5 to 12, and C$160 (US$99) per car.

For all ferries, advance reservations are strongly advised during the peak travel season.

## GETTING AROUND

Newfoundland has no rail service, but several bus lines connect the major ports and cities. **DRL Coachlines** (✆ **709/738-8090** or 709/263-2172) has one bus daily from Port aux Basques to St. John's. The trip takes 13 hours, and one-way fare is C$97 (US$60).

To explore the countryside, you'll need a car. Major rental companies with fleets in Newfoundland include **Avis** (✆ 800/879-2847), **Budget** (✆ 800/268-8900), **Hertz** (✆ 800/263-0600), **Thrifty** (✆ 800/367-2277), **National** (✆ 800/227-7368), **Enterprise** (✆ 800/325-8007), and **Rent-A-Wreck** (✆ 800/327-0116).

## THE GREAT OUTDOORS

**BIKING** Bike touring in Newfoundland is for the hearty. It's not that the hills are necessarily brutal (although many are); it's that the weather can be downright demoralizing. Expect more than a handful of blustery days, complete with horizontal rains that seem to swirl around from every direction. The happiest bike tourists seem to be those who allow themselves frequent stays in motels or

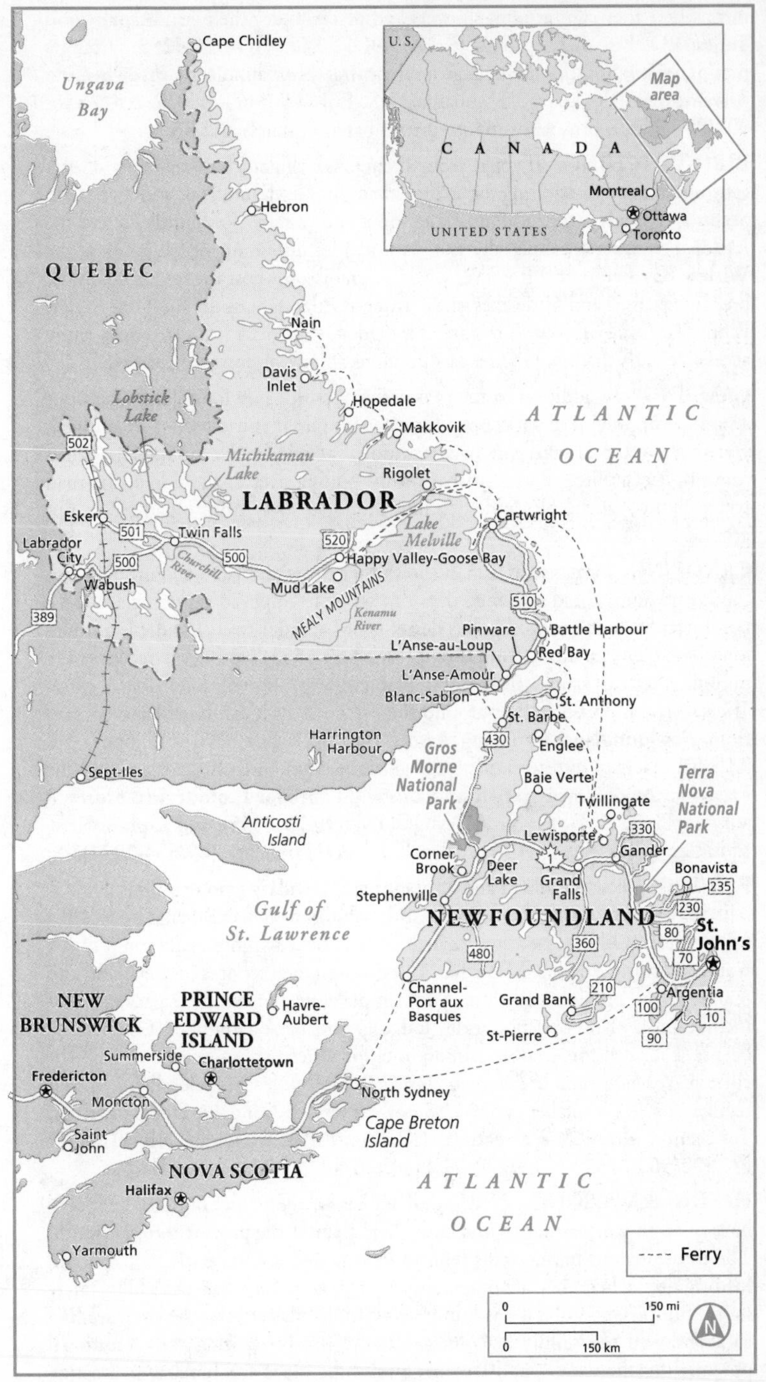

U.S.
Map area
CANADA
Montreal
Ottawa
Toronto
UNITED STATES
Cape Chidley
Ungava Bay
Hebron
QUEBEC
Nain
Davis Inlet
Hopedale
Makkovik
Lobstick Lake
502
Michikamau Lake
Rigolet
LABRADOR
ATLANTIC OCEAN
Esker
501
Twin Falls
Labrador City
500
Wabush
Churchill River
520
Lake Melville
Cartwright
Happy Valley-Goose Bay
Mud Lake
MEALY MOUNTAINS
Kenamu River
389
510
Pinware
Battle Harbour
L'Anse-au-Loup
Red Bay
L'Anse-Amour
Blanc-Sablon
St. Anthony
St. Barbe
430
Englee
Harrington Harbour
Gros Morne National Park
Sept-Iles
Baie Verte
Terra Nova National Park
Twillingate
Anticosti Island
330
Lewisporte
Gander
Corner Brook
Deer Lake
1
Grand Falls
Bonavista
235
230
Stephenville
Gulf of St. Lawrence
NEWFOUNDLAND
St. John's
80
360
70
480
Channel-Port aux Basques
210
Argentia
Grand Bank
100
10
90
St-Pierre
NEW BRUNSWICK
PRINCE EDWARD ISLAND
Havre-Aubert
Summerside
Charlottetown
Fredericton
Moncton
North Sydney
Cape Breton Island
Saint John
NOVA SCOTIA
Halifax
ATLANTIC OCEAN
Yarmouth
Ferry
0
150 mi
0
150 km
N

inns, where they can find hot showers and places to dry their gear. **Aspenwood Tours,** P.O. Box 622, Springdale, NF A0J 1T0 (© **709/673-4255**), arranges mountain biking trips in and around central Newfoundland; **Freewheeling Adventures,** RR no. 1, Hubbards, NS B0J 1T0 (© **800/672-0775** or 902/857-3600), runs van-supported trips based in hotels and B&Bs.

**BIRD-WATCHING** If you're from a temperate climate, bird-watching doesn't get much more interesting or exotic than in Newfoundland and Labrador. Seabirds typically attract the most attention, and eastern Newfoundland and the Avalon Peninsula are especially rich in bird life. Just south of St. John's is the **Witless Bay Ecological Reserve,** where several islands host the largest colony of breeding puffins and kittiwakes in the western Atlantic. On the southern Avalon Peninsula, **Cape St. Mary's** features a remarkable sea stack just yards from easily accessible cliffs that's home to a cacophonous colony of northern gannets.

**CAMPING** In addition to the two national parks, Newfoundland maintains a number of provincial parks open for car camping. If you're properly equipped, you might want to take part in a traditional activity in Newfoundland called "gravel-pit camping." Basically, that means pulling over to the side of the road (typically in a gravel pit) and spending the night away from organized campgrounds.

**CANOEING** A glance at a map shows that rivers and lakes abound in Newfoundland and Labrador. Canoe trips can range from placid puttering around a pond near St. John's to world-class descents of Labrador rivers hundreds of miles long. The **Department of Tourism** (© **800/563-6353**) produces a free brochure outlining several canoe trips. A popular guide—*Canyons, Coves and Coastal Waters*—is sold in bookstores around the province, or it can be ordered by mail from **Newfoundland Canoeing Association,** P.O. Box 5961, St. John's, NF A1C 5X4. Several outfitters offer guided canoe trips, both on the island and the mainland. Among them: **Newfoundland and Labrador Ecotour Adventures,** 8 Virginia Place, St. John's, NF A1A 3G6 (© **709/579-8055**); and **X-plore Newfoundland,** P.O. Box 63, Corner Brook, NF A2H 6C3 (© **709/634-2237**).

**FISHING** Newfoundland and Labrador are legendary among serious anglers, especially those stalking the cagey Atlantic salmon, which can weigh up to 18kg (40 pounds). Other prized species include landlocked salmon, lake trout, brook trout, and northern pike. More than 100 fishing-guide services on the island and mainland can provide everything from simple advice to complete packages that include bush-plane transportation, lodging, and personal guides. One fishing license is needed for Atlantic salmon, one for other fish, so be sure to read the current *Newfoundland & Labrador Hunting and Fishing Guide* closely for current regulations. It's available at most visitor centers or from the **Department of Tourism, Culture & Recreation,** P.O. Box 8730, St. John's, NF A1B 4K2 (© **800/563-6353** or 709/729-2830; http://public.gov.nf.ca/tourism/).

**HIKING & WALKING** Newfoundland has an abundance of trails, but you'll have to work a bit harder to find them here than in the provinces to the south. The most obvious hiking trails tend to be centered around national parks and historic sites, where they are often fairly short—good for a half-day's hike, rarely more. But Newfoundland has hundreds of trails, many along the coast leading to abandoned communities. Some places are finally realizing the recreational potential for these trails, and are now publishing maps and brochures directing you to them.

The best-maintained trails are at **Gros Morne National Park,** which has around 100km (60 miles) of trails. In addition to these, there's also off-track hiking on the dramatic Long Range for backpackers equipped to set out for a couple of days. Ask at the park visitor center for details.

**SEA KAYAKING** Novices should stick to guided tours. **Eastern Edge Outfitters** (© **709/782-5925**) offers a variety of tours, mostly on the Avalon Peninsula. Rates start at C$55 (US$34) for a half-day tour and C$110 (US$68) for a 1-day tour, and go up to C$749 (US$464) for a 6-day South Coast tour with meals and equipment included. Mike Henley of **Sea Kayaking with Whitecap Adventures** (© **709/726-9283**) is based in St. John's and leads paddling tours at Witless Bay, Cape Broyle, and Conception Bay, with prices starting at C$40 (US$25) for a 2-hour sunset paddle. Extended tours and customized trips may be arranged. At Terra Nova National Park, 2-hour sea kayak tours leave from the Marine Interpretation Centre and explore Newman's Cove. (See the "Terra Nova National Park," later.)

## 2 Western Newfoundland: Your Introduction to The Rock

For most travelers arriving by ferry, this region is the first introduction to The Rock. And it's like starting the symphony without a prelude, jumping right to the crescendo. There's instant drama in the brawny, verdant Long Range Mountains that run parallel to the Trans-Canada Highway en route to Corner Brook. There are also the towering seaside cliffs of the Port au Port Peninsula, and intriguing coastal villages that await exploration. You might also be surprised that winds can blow with such intensity hereabouts, yet not attract any comment from the locals.

### ESSENTIALS

**GETTING THERE** **By ferry** Port aux Basques is commonly reached via ferry from Nova Scotia. See "Exploring Newfoundland & Labrador," above, for ferry information. The Trans-Canada Highway (Route 1) links the major communities of southwestern Canada. Port aux Basques is 905km (543 miles) from St. John's via the Trans-Canada Highway.

**By plane** Western Newfoundland is served by two airports, **Deer Lake,** 50km (30 miles) east of Corner Brook, and **Stephenville,** 80km (50 miles) south of Corner Brook. Both offer service to St. John's, and Goose Bay, Labrador. There are car rental agencies at both airports and there is a shuttle available from Deer Lake to Corner Brook.

**VISITOR INFORMATION** In Port aux Basques, the **Provincial Interpretation and Information Centre** (© **709/695-2262**) is located on the Trans-Canada Highway about 3km (2 miles) from the ferry terminal. From mid-May to the middle of October the center is open daily 6am to 11pm.

### PORT AUX BASQUES

Port aux Basques is a major gateway for travelers arriving in Newfoundland, with ferries connecting to Nova Scotia year-round. It's a good way station for those arriving late on a ferry or departing early in the morning. Otherwise, it can easily be viewed in a couple of hours when either coming or going.

The **Gulf Museum,** 118 Main St. (© **709/695-7604**), across from the Town Hall, has a quirky assortment of artifacts related to local history. The museum's centerpiece is a 1628 Portuguese astrolabe recovered from local waters in 1981. Also intriguing is a display about the *Caribou,* a ferry torpedoed by a German

U-boat in 1942 with a loss of 137 lives. The museum is open daily 9am to 7pm; admission is C$2 (US$1.20) for adults, C$1 (US60¢) for children, and C$5 (US$3.10) for families.

On the way out of town you'll pass the **Port aux Basques Railway Heritage Center,** Route 1 (✆ **709/956-2170**), dedicated to the memory of the *Newfie Bullet,* the much-maligned, much-reminisced-about passenger train that ran between Port aux Basques and St. John's from 1898 to 1969. (The highway across the island opened in 1966, dooming the train.) The train required 27 hours to make the trip (at an average speed of 48kmph/30mph), and during a tour of several restored rail cars, you'll learn how the train made the run through deep snows of winter, how the passengers slept at night (very cozily, it turns out), and life aboard the mail car and caboose. The 15-minute tours cost C$2 (US$1.20) for adults, C$1 (US60¢) for children, and C$5 (US$3.10) for families.

Departing from the edge of Railway Heritage Center is the **T'Railway,** a coast-to-coast pathway being converted from the old train line. It's used by pedestrians, bikers, and ATVers, and in this stretch it runs through marsh and along the ocean to **Cheeseman Park** (✆ **709/729-2429**), which boasts a lagoon and a sandy beach that's home to a population of endangered piping plovers. It's a good spot to get your mountain bike limbered up for further adventures.

### WHERE TO STAY

About a half-dozen hotels and B&Bs offer no-frills shelter to travelers at Port aux Basques. The two largest are **Hotel Port aux Basques,** Route 1 (✆ **709/695-2171**), and **St. Christopher's Hotel,** Caribou Road (✆ **800/563-4779**). Both might be described as "budget modern," with clean, basic rooms in architecturally undistinguished buildings. I'd give St. Christopher's the edge since it's located on a high bluff with views of the town and the harbor. Both have around 50 rooms and charge between C$65 and C$90 (US$40–US$56) for a double.

### WHERE TO DINE

Dining opportunities are limited. Both hotels mentioned above have dining rooms, serving basic, filling meals. A 10-minute walk from the ferry terminal on the boardwalk is the **Harbour Restaurant,** 121 Caribou Rd. (✆ **709/695-3238**), a family-style restaurant that serves budget-friendly meals. Expect fried fish, fried chicken, fish cakes, sandwiches, and the like. Most tables have good views of the harbor. Entrees are C$4.95 to C$13.95 (US$3.05–US$9), with most under C$10 (US$6).

## CORNER BROOK

With a population of about 35,000, Corner Brook is Newfoundland's second-largest city. Like St. John's, it's also dramatically sited—in this case, on the banks of the glimmering Humber River, which winds down through verdant mountains from beyond Deer Lake, then turns the corner to flow into Humber Arm. The hills on the south shore of the Humber are nearly as tall as those in Gros Morne National Park, making a great backdrop for the town, which has gradually expanded up the shoulders of the hills.

Corner Brook is a young city with a long history. The area was first explored and charted in 1767 by Captain James Cook, who spent 23 days mapping the islands at the mouth of the bay. But it wasn't until early in this century that the city started to take its present shape. Copper mines and the railroad brought in workers; in the early 1920s the paper mill, which still dominates downtown, was constructed. By 1945 it was the largest paper mill in the world.

The **Corner Brook Museum and Archive,** 2 West St., (✆ **709/634-2518**), is housed in a solid 1920s-era building that once was home to customs offices, the court, and the post and telegraph offices. A visit here offers a quick way to learn just how young the city really is (grainy black and white photos show empty hills surrounding the paper mill as late as the 1920s) and how civilized it has become. An assortment of locally significant artifacts (including a prominent doctor's desk and ship models) rounds out the collection. The museum is open daily from 10am to 8pm; admission is C$3 (US$1.85) per adult and C$2 (US$1.20) per youth.

## WHERE TO STAY

Corner Brook is home to several convenient chain motels. Among others, you'll find the **Best Western Mamateek Inn,** 64 Maple Valley Rd. (✆ **800/563-8600** or 709/639-8901) near the tourist information booth, and the **Holiday Inn,** 47 West St. (✆ **800/399-5381** or 709/634-5381), which is within walking distance of the city's best restaurant (see below). Rooms go for C$80 to C$120 (US$50–US$74) for a double at either place. Camping is offered at **Prince Edward Park** (✆ **709/639-7740**) with 68 sites along a bluff from which you can often spot osprey and bald eagles; sites cost C$12 to C$16 (US$7–US$10).

**Glynmill Inn** ★ *Value* This Tudor inn is set in a quiet, park-like setting and is an easy stroll to the services and shops of West Street. Built in 1924 and extensively renovated in 1994, the hotel has a surfeit of charm and appealing detailing. (The place was designated a Registered Heritage Structure in 2001.) Rooms are tastefully decorated with colonial reproductions; the popular Tudor Suite has a private Jacuzzi. You'll get far more character here than at the chain motels in town, and for about the same price. The inn's two dining rooms are quite popular among local diners; the setting can feel a bit institutional (they do a rousing business with conventions and banquets), but the food is nevertheless pretty good.

1 Cobb Lane (near West St.), Corner Brook, NF A2H 6E6. ✆ **800/563-4400** (in Canada) or 709/634-5181. Fax 709/634-5106. glynmill.inn@nf.sympatico.ca. 81 units (including 24 suites). C$75–C$165 (US$47–US$102) double. AE, DC, MC, V. **Amenities:** 2 dining rooms, bar; exercise center; business center; laundry. *In room:* A/C, TV.

## WHERE TO DINE

**Thirteen West** ★★ GLOBAL Western Newfoundland's best restaurant can easily compete with the better restaurants of St. John's in both the quality of the food and the casual but professional attitude. Tucked along shady West Street in an unobtrusive building (there's a patio fronting the street for the rare balmy night), the kitchen does an outstanding job preparing top-notch meals, and the staff knows how to make good service seem easy. At lunchtime look for offerings like grilled striploin (spiced Montréal-style), salmon salad, and a warm seafood salad of mussels, shrimp, scallops and bacon. In the evening, you'll find a menu with items such as grilled salmon with a dill pesto, roasted rack of lamb, barbecued chicken with Cajun shrimp and black pepper sauce, and a seafood platter.

13 West St. ✆ **709/634-1300.** Reservations recommended. Main courses, lunch C$6–C$13 (US$3.70–US$8), dinner C$16–C$28 (US$10–US$17). AE, DC, MC, V. Mon–Fri 11:30am–2:30pm and 5:30–9:30pm (until 10:30pm Fri); Sat 5:30–10:30pm; Sun 5:30–9:30pm (until 10:30pm in summer).

## DEER LAKE

Deer Lake is an unassuming crossroads town near the head of the Humber River where travelers coming from the south either continue on the Trans-Canada Highway toward St. John's, or veer northwest to Gros Morne National Park, some 71km (43 miles) distant. Deer Lake is the gateway for those coming by air directly to western Newfoundland. There's little to detain a visitor here; it's a good spot to buy gas, peruse the brochures at the provincial information center, and then push on.

Lucky is the traveler who arrives here during the short strawberry season (mid- to late July some years, early August in others). If you're here at the right time, do yourself a favor and stop at one of the several seasonal roadside stands for a pint or two. They're plump, they're cheap, and they're sinfully sweet and flavorful—nothing at all like the tasteless commercial berries that invade grocery stores in the United States and elsewhere.

# 3 Gros Morne National Park: One of Canada's Treasures ★★★

"Gros Morne" translates roughly from the French as "big gloomy," and if you arrive on a day when ghostly bits of fog blow across the road and scud clouds hover in the glacial valleys, you'll get a pretty good idea how this area got its name. Even on brilliantly sunny days there's something about the stark mountains, lonely fjords cut off from the ocean, and miles of tangled spruce forest that can trigger mild melancholia.

Gros Morne National Park is one of Canada's true treasures, and most who visit here leave feeling inspired by what they have seen. The park is divided into two sections, north and south, riven by the multi-armed Bonne Bay (locally pronounced like "Bombay"). Alas, a ferry connecting the two areas has not operated for years, so exploring both sections by car requires backtracking. The park's visitor center and most tourist services are found in the village of Rocky Harbour in the north section. But you'd be shortchanging yourself to miss a detour through the dramatic southern section—a place that looks to have had a rough birth, geologically speaking.

If you'd prefer to let someone else do the planning for you, contact **Gros Morne Adventures** (© **800/685-4624** or 709/458-2722; www.grosmorneadventures.com), which organizes guided sea kayaking and hiking excursions around the park.

## ESSENTIALS

**GETTING THERE** From the Trans-Canada Highway in Deer Lake, turn west on Route 430 (the Viking Trail). This runs through the northern section of the park. For the southern section, turn left (south) on Route 431 in Wiltondale.

**VISITOR INFORMATION** **Tourist offices** The main national park **visitor information center** (© **709/458-2066** or 709/458-2417) is just south of Rocky Harbour on Route 430. It's open daily from 9am to 10pm in summer and from 9am to 4:30pm the rest of the year. The center features exhibits on park geology and wildlife; there's also a short film about the park that's picturesque but not terribly informative. Interactive media kiosks are exceptionally well-done; you can view video clips depicting highlights of all hiking trails and other attractions simply by touching a video screen. The center is also the place to stock up on field guides as well as to request backcountry camping permits.

Across the bay just outside of Woody Point on Route 431 en route to Trout River is the new **Discovery Centre** (© **709/458-2317**). This building is an enlightening stop, with interactive exhibits, a fossil room, and a multimedia theater to help make sense of the Gros Morne landscape. Information on Gros Morne and all of Canada's national parks can be found at **www.parcscanada.gc.ca**.

**FEES** All visitors must obtain a permit for any activity within the park. Daily fees are C$5 (US$3.10) for adults, C$4 (US$2.50) for seniors, C$2.50 (US$1.55) for children ages 6 to 18, and C$10 (US$6) for families. Four-day passes are available for the price of 3 days.

## GROS MORNE'S SOUTHERN SECTION

The road through the southern section dead-ends at Trout River, and, accordingly, it seems to discourage convenience-minded visitors who prefer loops and through-routes. That's too bad because the south contains some of the park's most dramatic terrain. Granted, you can glimpse the rust-colored Tablelands from north of Bonne Bay near Rocky Harbour, thereby saving the 50km (30-mile) detour. But without actually walking through the desolate landscape, you miss much of the impact. The south also contains several lost-in-time fishing villages that predate the park's creation in 1973 and a new Discovery Centre (above) with exhibits about the park's natural history.

The region's scenic centerpiece is **Trout River Pond,** a landlocked fjord some 15km (9 miles) long. You can hike along the north shore to get a great view of the Narrows, where cliffs nearly pinch the pond in two. For a more relaxed view, sign up for a boat tour, which surrounds you with breathtaking views. **Tableland Boat Tours** ★ (✆ **709/451-2101**) offers excursions aboard a 40-passenger tour boat. Two-and-a-half-hour trips are offered daily at 10am, 1pm, and 4pm in July and August (1pm only in June and September). The cost is C$25 (US$16) for adults and C$9.25 (US$6) for children ages 6 to 16. Tickets are sold at a gift shop between the village of Trout River and the pond—watch for signs.

For a hike offering a superb panorama encompassing ocean and mountains, watch for the **Lookout Trail** just outside of Woody Point en route to Trout River. This steep trail is about 5km (3 miles) round-trip. The **Tablelands Trail** departs from barren Trout River gulch and follows an old gravel road up to Winterhouse Brook Canyon. You can bushwhack along the rocky river a bit farther upstream or turn back. It's about 2km (1¼ miles) each way, depending on how adventurous you feel. This is a good trail to get a feel for the unique ecology of the Tablelands. Look for the signboards that explain the geology at the trail head and at the roadside pull-off on your left before reaching the trail head.

Experienced hikers looking for a challenge should seek out the **Green Gardens Trail** ★. There are two trail heads to this loop; I'd recommend the second one (closer to Trout River). You'll start by trekking through a rolling, infertile landscape, and then the plunge begins as you descend down, down, down wooden steps and a steep trail toward the sea. The landscape grows more lush by the moment, and soon you'll be walking through extraordinary coastal meadows on crumbling bluffs high above the surf.

The trail follows the shore northward for about 4km to 5km (6½ miles–8 miles), and it's one of the most picturesque coastal trails I've hiked anywhere in the world. In July, the irises and a whole symphony of other wildflowers are blooming wildly. The entire loop is about 16km (9½ miles) and is rugged and very hilly; allow about 5 or 6 hours. An abbreviated version involves walking clockwise on the loop to the shore's edge, then retracing one's steps back uphill. That's about 9km (5½ miles).

## WHERE TO STAY

The two drive-in **campsites** in the southern section—**Trout River Pond** and **Lomond**—both offer showers and nearby hiking trails. Of the two, Trout River Pond is more dramatic, located on a plateau overlooking the pond; a short stroll brings you to the pond's edge with wonderful views up the fjord. Lomond is near the site of an old lumber town and is popular with anglers. Camping is C$15.25 (US$10) at each site.

**Victorian Manor B&B** This 1920s home is one of the most impressive in the village, but that doesn't mean it's extravagant. It's more solid than flamboyant, set in a residential neighborhood near the town center and a few minutes' walk to the harbor. The attractive guesthouse has its own whirlpool. If that's booked, ask for one of the efficiencies, which cost about the same as the rooms but afford much greater convenience, especially considering the slim dining choices in town.

Main St. (P.O. Box 165), Woody Point, NF A0K 1P0. ✆ **709/453-2485.** www.grosmorne.com/victorianmanor. 6 units, including 3 B&B (2 with shared bathroom), 3 efficiency units, and 1 guesthouse. C$50–C$70 (US$31–US$43) double, C$60–C$80 (US$37–US$50) suites, C$125 (US$78) guesthouse. Rates include continental breakfast. AE, MC, V. **Amenities:** Hot tub; laundry.

## WHERE TO DINE

**Seaside Restaurant** ★ SEAFOOD The Seaside has been a Trout River institution for years, and it's clearly a notch above the tired fare you often find

## Journey to the Center of the Earth

If you see folks walking around the **Tablelands** ★ looking twitchy and excited, they're probably amateur geologists. The Tablelands are one of the world's great geological celebrities, and they're a popular destination among pilgrims who love the study of rock.

To the uninitiated, the Tablelands area—south of Woody Point and the south arm of Bonne Bay—will seem rather bleak and barren. From a distance, the muscular hills rise up all rounded and rust-colored, devoid of trees or even that pale green furze that seems to blanket all other hills. Up close, you discover just how barren they are—little plant life seems to have established a toehold.

There's a reason for that. Some 570 million years ago, this rock was part of the earth's mantle, that part of the earth just under the crust. Riding on continental plates, two land masses collided forcefully hereabouts, and a piece of the mantle was driven up and over the crust, rather than being forced under, as is usually the case. Years of erosion followed, and what's left is a rare glimpse of the earth's skeleton. The rock is so laced with magnesium that few plants can live here, giving it a barrenness that seems more appropriate for a desert landscape in the American Southwest than the rainy mountains of Newfoundland.

in tiny coastal villages. The restaurant is nicely polished without being swank, and it features magnificent harbor views. The pan-fried cod is superb as are a number of other seafood dishes. (Sandwiches and burgers are at hand for those who don't care for seafood.) Desserts are quite good, such as the partridgeberry parfait, but the service can be slow when the place fills up.

Main St., Trout River. ✆ **709/451-3461.** Main courses C$10–C$19 (US$6–US$12). MC, V. Daily noon–9pm. Closed Oct–June.

## GROS MORNE'S NORTHERN SECTION

Gros Morne's northern section flanks Route 430 for some 75km (45 miles) between Wiltondale and St. Paul's. The road winds through the abrupt, forested hills south of Rocky Harbour; beyond these, the road levels out, following a broad coastal plain covered mostly with bog and tuckamore. East of the plain rises the extraordinarily dramatic monoliths of the Long Range. This section contains the park's visitor center as well as the park's one must-see attraction: Western Brook Pond.

The hardscrabble fishing village of Rocky Harbour is your best bet for tourist services that include: motels, B&Bs, Laundromats, and small grocery stores. There is one caveat, however: Rocky Harbour and the surrounding area lack a well-lit, well-stocked grocery store of the sort one might expect near a national park of international importance. What you'll find are modest-size grocery stores—the sorts of places where you'll want to check the dates on bread and milk very carefully.

If you have time for only one activity in Gros Morne—and heaven forbid that's the case—make it the boat trip up **Western Brook Pond** ★. The trip begins with a 20-minute drive north of Rocky Harbour. Park at the Western

Brook Pond trail head, then set off on an easy 45-minute hike across the northern coastal plain, with interpretive signs explaining the wildlife and bog ecology you'll see along the way. (Keep an eye out for moose.) Always ahead, the mighty monoliths of the Long Range rise high above, inviting and mystical, more like a 19th-century scene from the Rockies than the Atlantic seaboard.

You'll soon arrive at the pond's edge, where there's a small collection of outbuildings near a wharf, where the tour boats dock. Once aboard one of the vessels (there are two), you'll set off into the maw of the mountains, winding between the sheer rock faces that define this landlocked fjord. The spiel on the boat is recorded, but even that unfortunate bit of cheese fails to detract from the grandeur of the scene. You'll learn about the glacial geology and the remarkable quality of the water, which is considered among the purest in the world. Bring lots of film and a wide-angle lens. The trip lasts about 2½ hours. The cost is C$30 (US$19) for adults, C$14 (US$9) for students (ages 12–16, must be accompanied by an adult), C$7 (US$4.35) for children ages 7 to 11, and children under 6 are free when with their parents. For reservations, contact the **Ocean View Motel** (✆ **800/563-9887** or 709/458-2730) in Rocky Harbour.

Even if you're not planning on signing up for the Western Brook Pond boat tour (reconsider!), you owe yourself a walk up to the pond's wharf and possibly beyond. The 45-minute one-way trek from the parking lot north of Sally's Cove follows well-trod trail and boardwalk through bog and boreal forest. When you arrive at the wharf, the view to the mouth of the fjord will take your breath away. A very well-executed outdoor exhibit explains how glaciers shaped the landscape in front of you.

Two spur trails continue on either side of the pond for a short distance. The **Snug Harbour Trail,** which follows the northern shore to a primitive campsite (registration required), is especially appealing. After crossing a seasonal bridge at the pond outlet, you'll pass through scrubby woods before emerging on a long and wonderful sand and pebble beach; this is a great destination for a relaxed afternoon picnic and requisite nap. The hike all the way to Snug Harbour is about 8km (4¾ miles) one-way.

### WHERE TO STAY

The northern section has three **campgrounds** open to car campers. The main campground is **Berry Hill,** which is just north of Rocky Harbour. There are 146 drive-in sites, plus 6 walk-in sites on the shores of the pond itself. It's just a 10-minute drive from the visitor center, where evening activities and presentations are held. **Shallow Bay** has 50 campsites and is near the park's northern border and an appealing 4km (2½ miles) sand beach. Both of these campgrounds have showers and flush toilets.

Rocky Harbour has more tourist services than any other village in or around the park, but it still has trouble handling the influx of travelers in July and August. Two or three bus tours can pretty well fill up the town. One B&B owner told me she turned away 20 people seeking a room one night in July. It's an unwise traveler who arrives without a reservation.

The largest motel in town is the **Ocean View Motel** (✆ **709/458-2730**) located on the harbor. It has 44 basic rooms (some have small balconies with bay views), but everything feels a bit chintzy, from the carpeting to the walls to the furnishings. The motel is popular with bus tours, and it often fills up early in the day. Rooms are C$60 to C$85 (US$37–US$53) for a double in season.

**Gros Morne Cabins** What's my favorite thing about the Gros Morne Cabins? It's pulling up and seeing the long lines of freshly laundered sheets billowing in the sea breeze, like a Christo installation. The trim and tidy log cabins are clustered tightly along a grassy rise overlooking Rocky Harbour, and all have outstanding views toward the Lobster Cove Head Lighthouse. Inside they're new and clean, more antiseptically modern than quaintly worn. Gas barbecues are scattered about the property. The complex also includes a store and a Laundromat. There's a pizza place just across the street for relaxed sunset dining at your own picnic table.

P.O. Box 151, Rocky Harbour, NF A0K 4N0. ✆ **888/603-2020,** 709/458-2020, or 709/458-2369. Fax 709/458-2882. 22 units. C$79 (US$49) 1-bedroom; C$129 (US$80) 2-bedroom suite. Price is for 2; C$10 (US$6) per extra person. Open year-round; call for off-season rates. AE, DC, MC, V. Pets allowed. **Amenities:** Laundry; grills. *In room:* Kitchenette, fridge.

**Sugar Hill Inn** ★ This appealing green-shingled inn opened in 1991 on the road between Rocky Harbour and Norris Point. The six rooms are quite comfortable, although some guests have found them a bit condo-like and sterile. Nice touches abound, like hardwood floors in all rooms, plenty of natural wood trim, well-selected furnishings, and a shared sauna and hot tub in a cedar-lined room. The upstairs sitting room is spacious and bright, with a fireplace and modern furnishings; it's a good spot to swap local adventure ideas with other guests. The inn's dining room serves breakfast and dinner daily, although breakfast isn't included in the room rates.

P.O. Box 100, Norris Point, NF A0K 3V0. ✆ **709/458-2147.** Fax 709/458-2166. www.sugarhillinn.nf.ca. 6 units, 1 cottage. C$76–C$172 (US$47–US$109) double. AE, MC, V. Closed mid-Oct to mid-Jan. **Amenities:** Restaurant, bar; sauna; hot tub; laundry. *In room:* TV.

**Wildflower Inn** This 1930s home near the village center was modernized and updated before its opening as a B&B in 1997, giving it a casual country look inside. The rooms are tastefully appointed if a bit small, although two newly added rooms have private baths and are a bit larger. The neighborhood isn't especially scenic (there's an auto repair shop across the way), but the house is very peaceful, the innkeepers are exceptionally friendly, and this is a great choice for those seeking reasonably priced lodging with a comfortable, homey feel.

Main St. North, Rocky Harbour, NF A0K 4N0. ✆ **888/811-7378** or 709/458-3000. wildflowers@nf.aibn.com. 7 units. C$59–C$73 (US$37–US$45) double, including continental breakfast. MC, V. **Amenities:** Restaurant; bar.

### WHERE TO DINE

**Fisherman's Landing** SEAFOOD With its industrial carpeting and generic chain-restaurant chairs and tables, Fisherman's Landing is lacking in homespun character. However, it does offer efficient service and dependable meals, with specialties like fish and chips, cod tongues, and squid rings. For breakfast, there's the traditional Newfie fisherman's breakfast consisting of a mug of tea, served with homemade bread and molasses. Meals are quite reasonably priced, and you can get in and out faster than at most other joints. There's also a glimpse of the harbor from a few tables, provided that not too many RVs park out front.

Main St., Rocky Harbour. ✆ **709/458-2060.** Sandwiches C$3–C$7 (US$1.85–US$4.35), main courses C$7–C$17 (US$4.35–US$11). MC, V. Late June–early Sept, 6am–11pm; limited hours off-season.

## 4 The Great Northern Peninsula: Way Off the Beaten Path

On a map, the Great Northern Peninsula looks like a stout cudgel threatening the shores of Labrador. If Newfoundland can even be said to have a beaten track, rest assured that the peninsula is well off it. It's not as mountainous or starkly dramatic as Gros Morne, but the road unravels for kilometer after kilometer through tuckamore and evergreen forest, along restless coastline and the base of geologically striking hills. There are few services, and even fewer organized diversions. But it has early history in spades, a handful of fishing villages clustering along the rocky coast, and some of the most unspoiled terrain anywhere. The road is in good repair, with the chief hazard being a stray moose or caribou. In the spring the infrequent polar bear might wander through a village, often hungry after a long trip south on ice floes.

## ESSENTIALS

**GETTING THERE** **By car** Route 430, which is also called the Viking Trail, runs from Deer Lake (at the Trans-Canada Highway) to St. Anthony, a 433km (260-mile) jaunt.

**By plane** Scheduled flights on **Air Labrador** (© **800/563-3042** within Newfoundland, 709/896-3387 elsewhere; www.airlabrador.com) and **Provincial Airlines** (© **800/563-2800** within Newfoundland, 709/576-1666 elsewhere; www.provair.com) stop at **St. Anthony,** where rental cars are available. The airport is on Route 430 about 30km (18 miles) west of town.

**VISITOR INFORMATION** For information about the Great Northern Peninsula and the Viking Trail, contact the **Viking Trail Tourism Association,** P.O. Box 430, St. Anthony, NF A0K 4S0 (© **709/454-8888**). Visitor centers are located at **St. Anthony** (© **709/454-4010**) and **Hawkes Bay** (© **709/248-5344**).

## PORT AU CHOIX

A visit to Port au Choix (pronounced *port-a-shwaw*) requires a 13km (8-mile) detour off the Viking Trail, out to a knobby peninsula that's home to a sizeable fishing fleet. The windswept lands overlooking the sea are low, predominantly flat, and lush with grasses. Simple homes speckle the landscape; most are of recent vintage.

**Port au Choix National Historic Site** ★ Kids One of the enduring historical mysteries is the disappearance of the Maritime Archaic Indians from the province about 3,500 years ago; to this day no one can explain their sudden departure. You'll learn about this fascinating historic episode at the modern visitor center here at Port au Choix, a burial site where such artifacts as slate spears and antler harpoon tips have been found. Staffers can direct you to various nearby sites, including the original burial ground, now surrounded by village homes. You can also visit the nearby lighthouse, scenically located on a blustery point thrusting into the Gulf of St. Lawrence.

Point Riche Rd., Port au Choix. © **709/861-3522.** www.parcscanada.gc.ca. Admission C$2.75 (US$1.70) adult, C$2.25 (US$1.40) senior, C$1.50 (US95¢) children (6–16), C$6 (US$3.70) family. Visitor center open daily mid-June to mid-Oct 9am–7pm.

**L'Anse aux Meadows** ★★★ Kids Value Newfoundland's northernmost tip is not only exceptionally remote and dramatic, but is also one of the most historically

---

**Tips The Viking Trail**

This beautiful drive to Newfoundland's northern tip is wild and solitary, with views of curious geology and a wind-raked coast. You'll pass Gros Morne National Park and Port au Choix, and you'll end up at one of the world's great historic sites—L'Anse aux Meadows.

---

significant spots in the world. A Viking encampment dating from A.D. 1,000 was discovered here in 1960, and it has been thoroughly documented by archaeologists in the decades since. An unusually well-conceived and well-managed national historic site (below) probes this earliest chapter in European expansion, and an afternoon spent here piques the imagination.

In the late 1950s a pair of determined archaeologists named Helge Ingstad and Anne Stine Ingstad pored over 13th-century Norse sagas searching for clues about where the Vikings might have landed on the shores of North America. With just a few scraps of description, the Ingstads began cruising the coastlines of Newfoundland and Labrador, asking locals about unusual hummocks and mounds.

They struck gold at L'Anse aux Meadows. In a remote cove noted for its low, grassy hills, they found the remains of an ancient Norse encampment that included three large halls, along with a forge where nails were made from locally mined pig iron. As many as 100 people lived here for a time, including some women. The Vikings abandoned the settlement after a few years to return to Greenland and Denmark, thus ending the first experiment in the colonization of North America by Europeans. It's telling that no graves have ever been discovered here.

Start your visit by viewing the recovered artifacts in the visitor center and watching the half-hour video about the site's discovery. Then I suggest signing up for one of the free, guided tours of the site. The guides offer considerably more information than the simple markers around the grounds. Near the original encampment are several re-created sod-and-timber buildings, depicting how life was lived 1,000 years ago. These are tended by costumed interpreters who have a wonderful knack for staying in character without making you feel like a dork when you ask them questions.

Route 436, L'Anse aux Meadows. ✆ **709/623-2608.** www.parcscanada.gc.ca. Admission C$5 (US$3.10) adult, C$4.25 (US$2.65) senior, C$2.75 (US$1.70) child 6–16, C$10 (US$6) family. Daily 9am–8pm in peak season; 9am–5pm in shoulder season. Closed mid-Oct to early June.

## WHERE TO STAY

**Tickle Inn at Cape Onion** ★ *Finds* If you're seeking that end-of-the-world flavor, you'll be more than a little content here. Set on a remote cove at the end of a road near Newfoundland's northernmost point (you can see Labrador across the straits), the Tickle Inn occupies a solid fisherman's home built around 1890 by the great-grandfather of the current innkeeper, David Adams. After lapsing into decrepitude, the home was expertly restored in 1990, and it has recaptured much of the charm of a Victorian outport home. Guest rooms are small but comfortable, and they share two bathrooms. Before dinner, guests often gather in the parlor and enjoy snacks and complimentary cocktails; afterward, there's often music or some other form of entertainment. One of the highlights of a stay here is exploring the small but superb network of hiking trails maintained by Adams, which ascend open bluffs to painfully beautiful views of the Labrador Straits. The inn is about a 40-minute drive from L'Anse aux Meadows. Meals are served family-style at 7:30pm each evening. (Your only other option for a meal is to drive a considerable distance to the nearest restaurant.) The food here is excellent, featuring local cuisine. You might have Cape Onion soup with a touch of Newman's port, or the "Polaris paella," with squid, scallops, and shrimp. Time your visit for berry season and you can expect such delights as the northern berry flan for dessert.

RR no. 1 (Box 62), Cape Onion, NF A0K 4J0. ✆ **709/452-4321** (June–Sept) or 709/739-5503 (Oct–May). Fax 709/452-4321. adams.tickle@nf.sympatico.ca. 4 units (all share 2 bathrooms). C$55–C$65 (US$34–US$40) double. Rates include deluxe continental breakfast. MC, V. Closed Oct–May. **Amenities:** Meals.

## 5 Terra Nova National Park

Terra Nova National Park is an exceedingly pleasant spot with lots of boreal forest and coastal landscape, along with a surplus of low, rolling hills. Within its boundaries forest and shoreline are preserved for wildlife and recreation, and make for excellent exploration. Activities and facilities at Terra Nova have mostly been designed with families in mind. There's always something going on, from playing with starfish at the interpretation center to games and movies at the main campground. The park has a junior naturalist program, many of the hikes are just the right duration for younger kids, and there's a fine (and relatively warm) swimming area at Sandy Pond.

If your goal is to put some distance between yourself and the noisy masses, plan to head into the backcountry. A number of campsites are accessible by foot, canoe, or ferry. Out here, you'll be able to scout for bald eagles and shooting stars in silence.

### ESSENTIALS

**GETTING THERE** Terra Nova is located on the Trans-Canada Highway. It's about 240km (144 miles) from St. John's, and 630km (378 miles) from Port aux Basques.

**VISITOR INFORMATION** **Tourist offices** Visitor information is available at the **Marine Interpretation Centre** (✆ **709/533-2801**) at the Saltons Day-Use Area, about 5km (3 miles) north of the Newman Sound Campground. It's open daily from June to mid-October 9am to 9pm (limited hours after Labor Day). Information on Terra Nova and all of Canada's national parks can be found at **www.parcscanada.gc.ca.**

**FEES** A park entry fee is required of all visitors, even those just staying overnight at a park campground. Fees are C$3.25 (US$2) per adult per day, C$2.50 (US$1.55) per senior, C$1.75 (US$1.10) for children ages 6 to 16, and C$6.50 (US$4) per family. Four-day passes are available in all categories for the price of 3 days. Fees may be paid at the Marine Interpretation Centre.

### EXPLORING THE PARK

Begin with a visit to the spiffy, modern **Marine Interpretation Centre** (above). It's on a scenic part of the sound, encased in verdant hills, and from here the sound looks suspiciously like a lake. Oceangoing sailboats tied up at the wharf will suggest otherwise, however. The center has a handful of exhibits focusing on local marine life, and many are geared toward kids. There's a touch tank where you can scoop up starfish and other aquatic denizens, and there are informative displays on life underwater. Especially nifty is an underwater video monitor that allows you to check out the action under the adjacent wharf with a joystick and zoom controls. There's also a Wet Lab, where you can conduct your own experiments under the guidance of a park naturalist. The center is free with your paid park admission. You'll also find a snack bar and gift shop.

The park has 80km (48 miles) of maintained **hiking trails.** Many of these are fairly easy treks of an hour or so through undemanding woodlands. The booklet you'll receive when you pay your entrance fee offers descriptions of the various treks. Among the more popular is the 5km (3-mile) **Coastal Trail,** which runs between Newman Sound Campground and the Marine Interpretation Centre. You get great views of the sound, and en route you pass the wonderfully named Pissing Mare Falls.

The park also lends itself quite nicely to **sea kayaking.** If you've brought your own boat, ask for route suggestions at the information center. (Overnight trips to Minchin and South Broad coves are good options, as are day trips to Swale Island.) If you're a paddling novice, sign up with **Terra Nova Adventures** (© **888/533-8687** or 709/533-9797), located at the Marine Interpretation Centre. The crew leads guided tours of the sound three times daily, when you're likely to spot eagles and maybe even a whale. The tours last between 2 and 3 hours and cost C$45 (US$28) per adult and C$35 (US$22) per youth. Reservations are recommended.

For a more passive view from the water, consider a tour with **Ocean Watch Tours** (© **709/533-6024**), which sails in a converted fishing boat four times daily from the wharf at the Marine Interpretation Centre. You're all but certain to see bald eagles and old outports, and, with some luck, whales and icebergs. Tours are C$32 (US$20) for 2 hours, and C$40 (US$25) for 3 hours, half-price for children. Reservations are recommended during peak season.

## WHERE TO STAY & DINE

**Campgrounds** are the only option within the park itself. The main campground is at **Newman Sound.** It has 417 campsites (mostly of the gravel-pad variety) set in and around spruce forest and sheep laurel clearings. The amenities include free showers, limited electrical hookups, a grocery store and snack bar, evening programs, a Laundromat, and hiking trails. Be aware that the campground can be quite noisy and bustling in peak season. Fees are C$12 to C$18 (US$7–US$11).

At the north end of the park, the town of Eastport is 16km (10 miles) from the Trans-Canada Highway on Route 310, and offers several places to stay overnight. Try **Laurel Cottage Bed & Breakfast,** 41 Bank Rd., Eastport, NF A0G 1Z0 (© **888/677-3138** or 709/677-3138), with three bedrooms in a 1926 bungalow tucked off the main road with ocean views. Rooms are C$54 to C$65 (US$33–US$40). Located right on a sandy beach is **Seaview Cottages,** 325 Beach Rd., Eastport, NF A0G 1Z0 (© **709/677-2271**), with 23 basic cottages and a small indoor heated pool. Rates are C$50 to C$60 (US$31–US$37).

**Terra Nova Park Lodge** ★ *Kids* This modern resort is a short drive off Route 1 about 2km (1¼ miles) south of the park's southern entrance, adjacent to the well-regarded, 6,400m (6,500-yd.) Twin River Golf Course, one of Atlantic Canada's more scenic and better regarded links. The hotel isn't lavish and lacks a certain personality. It feels rather inexpensively built (pray that you don't have heavy-footed children staying overhead), and it features bland, cookie-cutter rooms. On the other hand, it's clean, comfortable, and well-located for a golfing holiday or exploring the park. It's a popular spot with families, since kids can roam the grounds, splash around the pool, and congregate at the downstairs video games. The Clode Sound Dining Room is open daily for all three meals. It offers standard resort fare with an emphasis on chicken and beef with some seafood; dinners include fried cod, filet mignon, pork chops and applesauce, and surf and turf. There's also a pub downstairs.

Route 1, Port Blandford, NF A0C 2G0. © **709/543-2525.** Fax 709/543-2201. www.terranovagolf.com. 82 units (including 5 suites). C$99–C$155 (US$61–US$96) double. AE, DC, DISC, MC, V. **Amenities:** Restaurant, bar; heated outdoor pool; driving range; mini-golf; 2 tennis courts; fitness room; sauna; Jacuzzi; free laundry. *In room:* A/C, TV.

## 6 The Bonavista Peninsula: Into Newfoundland's Past ★

The Bonavista Peninsula juts northeast into the sea from just south of Terra Nova National Park. It's a worthy side trip for travelers fascinated by the island's past. You'll find a historic village, a wonderfully curated historic site, and one of the province's most intriguing lighthouses. It's also a good spot to see whales, puffins, and icebergs.

Along the south shore of the peninsula is **Trinity,** an impeccably maintained old village. (It's the only village in Newfoundland where the historic society has say over what can and can't be built.) Some long-time visitors grouse that it's becoming overly popular and a bit dandified with too many B&Bs and traffic restrictions. That might be, but there's still a palpable sense of tradition to this profoundly historic spot. And anyway, it's the region's only destination to find good shelter and a decent meal.

From Trinity it's about 40km (24 miles) out to the tip of the peninsula. Somewhere along the route, which isn't always picturesque, you'll wonder whether it's worth it. Yes, it is. Keep going. Plan to spend at least a couple of hours exploring the dramatic, ocean-carved point and the fine fishing village of **Bonavista** with its three excellent historic properties.

### ESSENTIALS

**GETTING THERE** Depending on the direction you're coming from, the Bonavista Peninsula can be reached from the Trans-Canada Highway via Route 233, Route 230, or Route 230A. Route 230 runs all the way to the tip of the cape; Route 235 forms a partial loop back and offers some splendid water views along the way. The round-trip from Clarenville to the tip is approximately 240km (144 miles).

**VISITOR INFORMATION** The **Southern Bonavista Bay Tourist Chalet** (**© 709/545-2130**) is on Route 230 just west of the intersection with Route 235. It's open daily 8:30am to 8:30pm in summer.

### TRINITY ★

The tiny coastal hamlet of Trinity, with a year-round population of just 200, once had more residents than St. John's. For more than 3 centuries, from its first visit by Portuguese fishermen in the 1500s until well into the 19th century, Trinity benefited from a long and steady tenure as a hub for traders, primarily from England, who supplied the booming fishing economy of Trinity Bay and eastern Newfoundland. Technological advances doomed Trinity's merchant class, but in recent years the provincial government and concerned individuals have taken a keen interest in preserving the town. Several buildings are open to the public as provincial historic sites, two others as local historical museums. Most are open mid-June through early October and are closed the remainder of the year.

Start your adventure into history at the **Trinity Interpretation Center** (**© 709/464-2042**) at the Tibbs House, open 10am to 5:30pm daily. (It's a bit tricky to find, since signs don't seem to be a priority. Follow the one-way road around the village and continue straight past the parish hall. Look on the left for the pale green home with the prominent gable.) Here you can pick up a walking-tour map and get oriented with a handful of history exhibits. Several ticket options exist; if you want to visit just one or two places, individual tickets cost C$2.50 (US$1.55) and up. For a full day, the better bet is the C$6 (US$3.70) ticket, which admits you to six buildings. Most maintain the same hours as the interpretation center.

A minute's walk away is the brick **Lester-Garland Premises** (✆ **709/729-0597**), where you can learn about the traders and their times. This handsome Georgian-style building is a convincing replica (built in 1997) of one of the earlier structures, built in 1819. The original was occupied until 1847, when it was abandoned and began to deteriorate. It was torn down (much to the horror of local historians) in the 1960s, but parts of the building hardware, including some doors and windows, were salvaged and warehoused until the rebuilding. Next door is the **Ryan Building,** where a succession of the town's most prominent merchants kept shop. The grassy lots between these buildings and the water were once filled with warehouses, none of which survived. The new **Rising Tide Theatre,** built in 1999, approximates one of the warehouses; a good imagination is helpful in envisioning the others.

A short walk away, just past the parish house, is the **Hiscock House** (✆ **709/464-2042**), a handsome home where Emma Hiscock raised her children and kept a shop after the untimely death of her husband in a boating accident at age 39. The home has been restored to appear as it might have been in 1910, and helpful guides fill in the details. The **Trinity Historical Society Museum** on Church Road (✆ **709/464-2244** or 709/464-3706) contains a selection of everyday artifacts that one might have seen in Trinity a century or more ago; the nearby **Green Family Forge Blacksmith Museum** will leave you well informed about one of the essential local industries.

An entertaining way to learn about the village's history is through the **Trinity Pageant** (✆ **888/464-1100** or 709/464-3232). On Wednesdays, Saturdays, and Sundays at 2pm, actors lead a peripatetic audience through the streets, acting out episodes from Trinity's past. Tickets are C$10 (US$6) per adult, C$7 (US$4.35) for children ages 13 to 18, and children under 12 go free. In the evenings, the innovative **Rising Tide Theatre** (same phone as the pageant) offers a number of performances throughout the summer, most depicting island episodes or themes. In the past the cast staged their shows at impromptu venues around town (upstairs at the parish hall, in a field at the water's edge, on the front porch of a B&B, and the like). In 2000, they opened a 255-seat theater in a newly constructed building, which is architecturally styled after a historic waterfront warehouse. The performances are top-rate, and well worth the money. Tickets are C$13.50 to C$15 (US$9–US$10).

## WHERE TO STAY

All properties mentioned below are in the heart of Trinity's historic area. Reservations are essential during the peak summer season, especially on Wednesdays, Saturdays, and Sundays when the pageant is scheduled. Those who come unprepared risk a drive to Clarenville to find a room.

**Campbell House** ★ *Finds* This handsome 1840 home and two nearby cottages are set amid lovely gardens on a twisting lane overlooking Fisher Cove. Two rooms are on the second floor of the main house, and these have a nice historic flair, even to the point that they'll require some stooping under beams if you're over 2m (6-ft.) tall. Two rooms are located in a lovely and simple pine-paneled Gover House just beyond the gardens, and they feature an adjacent waterfront deck and a full kitchen on the first floor; the newly renovated Twine Loft also overlooks the water. Innkeeper Tineke Gow recently added a third property on Fisher Cove—the Kelly House, dating from the 1940s. The cottages are rented to just one party at a time, who can use one, two, or three bedrooms (priced accordingly). Gow is a great source of information on local adventures, and maintains a wine cellar on premises. Reserve well in advance for July and August, when the inn only rarely has a free room.

High St., Trinity, Trinity Bay, NF A0C 2S0. ✆ **877/464-7700** or 709/464-3377. www.campbellhouse.nf.ca. 4 units. C$79–C$99 (US$49–US$61) double in main house, C$160–C$190 (US$99–US$118) 2-bedroom suites (up to 4 people), including full breakfast. AE, DC, MC, V. Closed mid-Oct to late May. **Amenities:** Wine cellar; laundry. *In room:* Kitchenette, hair dryer, iron.

**Hangashore Bed & Breakfast** The Hangashore is owned by the same folks who run the always-cordial Monkstown Manor in St. John's, and is a place for travelers happy to trade space for conviviality. The rooms in this historic 1860 home are cozy (read: tiny), just as they would have been in, well, 1860. But they're utterly uncluttered in a modern Scandinavian sort of way, and painted with bold, welcoming colors. There's a parlor with television and telephone downstairs, and relaxed breakfasts are served around a pine picnic-style table in a cheerful ground-floor room; recent renovations have freshened the interior decor, bathrooms and veranda.

1 Ash's Lane, Trinity, Trinity Bay, NF A0C 2S0. ✆ **888/754-7377** or 709/464-3807. Fax 709/722-8557. krussell@pigeoninlet.nfnet.com. 3 units (all share 2 bathrooms). C$55–C$75 (US$34–US$47) double, including full breakfast. AE, MC, V. Closed Nov–May. Pets allowed (C$5/US$3.10 charge). **Amenities:** Shared TV; shared telephone.

**Village Inn** The eight rooms in this handsome old inn, located on what passes for a busy street in Trinity (busy with pedestrians, that is), has a pleasant lived-in feel. It has eclectic (leaning-toward-Victorian) furniture, a newly replaced front porch for relaxing, and a small dining room, which feels as if it hasn't been changed a whit in 75 years. Innkeepers Christine and Peter Beamish do a fine job of making guests feel at home; they also run Ocean Contact, a whale-watch operation that uses a 8m (26-ft.) rigid-hull inflatable. Ask about tour availability when you book your room.

Taverner's Path (P.O. Box 10), Trinity, Trinity Bay, NF A0C 2S0. ✆ **709/464-3269.** Fax 709/464-3700. www.oceancontact.com. 8 units. C$69–C$79 (US$43–US$49) double. MC, V. Open by advance arrangement from Nov–Apr. "Small, well-behaved pets" allowed. **Amenities:** Restaurant (see "Where to Dine," below); shared TV, shared VCR.

## WHERE TO DINE

**Eriksen Premises** ★ TRADITIONAL Despite some inelegant touches (like butter served in those pesky plastic tubs with the peel-off tops), this is Trinity's best restaurant, and it offers good value. The restaurant shares the first floor of a B&B with a gift shop, and has a homey feel with oak floors, bead-board ceiling, and Victorian accents. (There's also dining on an outside deck, which is especially inviting at lunchtime.) The meals are mostly traditional: cod tongue, broiled halibut, scallops, liver and onion, and chicken. The service and food quality are consistently a notch above the expected. Desserts, like the cheesecake with fresh berry toppings, are especially good.

West St. ✆ **877/464-3698** or 709/464-3698. Reservations advisable during peak season. Main courses, lunch C$4.95–C$6.95 (US$3.05–US$4.30), dinner C$9.95–C$18.95 (US$6–US$12). MC, V. Daily 8am–9:30pm. Closed Nov–May.

**Village Inn** ★ *Finds* TRADITIONAL/VEGETARIAN The pleasantly old-fashioned dining room at the Village Inn has a good reputation for its vegetarian meals (something of a rarity in Newfoundland), with options including a lentil shepherd's pie and a rice and nut casserole. But those looking for comfort food are also well-served here, with options like chowder, meat loaf, fried cod, liver and onions, a ham plate, and a seafood platter. This is country cooking at its finest; everything is made from scratch, from soups to dessert.

Taverner's Path. ✆ **709/464-3269.** Main courses: C$8–C$20 (US$5–US$12), lunch items less. MC, V. Daily 8am–9pm.

## BONAVISTA ★

Bonavista is a 45-minute drive from Trinity, and is a strongly recommended day trip for those spending a night or two in the area.

The **Ryan Premises National Historic Site** ★ (✆ **800/213-7275** or 709/468-1600) was opened in 1997 with Queen Elizabeth herself presiding over the ceremonies. Located in downtown Bonavista, the new site is a very photogenic grouping of white clapboard buildings at the harbor's edge. For more than a century, this was the town's most prominent salt-fish complex, where fishermen sold their catch and bought all the sundry goods needed to keep an outport functioning. Michael Ryan opened for business here in 1857; his heirs kept the business going until 1978. (One elderly resident recalled that you could "get everything from a baby's fart to a clap of thunder" from the Ryans.) The spiffy complex today features an art gallery, local history museum, gift shop, handcrafted furniture store, and what may be the most rare and extraordinary of all: a truly fascinating exhibit on the role of the codfish industry in Newfoundland's history. An hour or two here will greatly abet you in making sense of the rest of your visit to the island. The property is open daily from June to October 10am to 6pm. Admission is C$3.50 (US$2.15) per adult, C$3 (US$1.85) per senior, C$1.75 (US$1.10) per youth, and C$7 (US$4.35) per family.

On the far side of the harbor, and across from a field of magnificent irises, is the beautiful **Mockbeggar Property** (✆ **800/563-6363** or 709/468-7300). Named after an English seaport that shared characteristics with Bonavista, the home was occupied by prominent Newfoundland politician F. Gordon Bradley. It's been restored to how it appeared when Bradley moved here in 1940, and it features much of the original furniture. With a few telltale exceptions (note the wonderful 1940s-era carpet in the formal dining room), it shows a strong Victorian influence. The house is managed as a provincial historic site, and admission is C$2.50 (US$1.55) per adult, children under 12 go free (also includes admission to Cape Bonavista Lighthouse, see below). It's open daily from mid-June to early October from 10am to 5:30pm.

A replica of the ***Mathew*** (✆ **709/468-1493**), the ship John Cabot sailed when he first landed in Newfoundland in 1497, opened at Bonavista's harbor in 2000. This compact ship is an exacting replica, based on plans of the original ship. (Don't confuse this ship with the other *Mathew* replica, which crossed the Atlantic and sailed around Newfoundland in 1997.) An interpretive center and occasional performances staged wharfside provide context for your tour aboard the ship, which is designed as a floating museum. Because it's an exact copy, and looks roughly as it did 500 years ago, the ship doesn't have an engine or any modern safety devices, and thus isn't allowed to leave the dock for passenger cruises. It will stay tied up along the dock in summer, and stored in an architecturally striking white clapboard boathouse in the off-season. The ship is open from mid-May to mid-October, daily 10am to 6pm. Tours are C$3 (US$1.85) per adult, C$2.50 (US$1.55) per senior, C$1 (US60¢) for children ages 6 to 16, and C$7 (US$4.35) per family.

The extraordinary **Cape Bonavista Lighthouse Provincial Historic Site** ★ is located 5.5km (3½ miles) north of town on a rugged point. It's open daily in summer 10:30am to 5:30pm; admission is C$2.50 (US$1.55) per adult and is free to those under 12 (also includes admission to Mockbeggar Property, above). Below the lighthouse on a rocky promontory cleft from the mainland is a lively puffin colony, easily seen from just below the lighthouse; bring binoculars for a clearer view.

## 7 St. John's: Bright Lights, Big City ★★

St. John's is a world apart from the rest of Newfoundland. The island's small outports and long roads through spruce and bog are imbued with a deep melancholy. St. John's, on the other hand, is vibrant and bustling. Coming into the city after traveling the hinterlands is like stepping from Kansas into Oz—the landscape suddenly seems to burst with color and life.

This port city of just over 100,000 residents crowds the steep hills around a deep harbor. Like Halifax, Nova Scotia, and Saint John, New Brunswick, St. John's also serves as a magnet for youth culture in the province, and the clubs and restaurants tend to have a more cosmopolitan feel and sharper edge. This is still very much a working harbor; as such, don't expect quaint. Across the way are charmless oil-tank farms, along with off-loading facilities for tankers. Along the water's edge on Harbour Street downtown, you'll usually find hulking ships tied up; pedestrians are welcome to stroll and gawk, but wholesale commerce is the focus here, not boutiques.

### ESSENTIALS

**GETTING THERE** **By plane** **St. John's International Airport** (**© 709/758-8500;** www.stjohns-airport.nf.ca) offers flights to Halifax, Montréal, Ottawa, Toronto, and London, England. The airport is 6.5km (4 miles) from downtown; taxis from the airport to downtown hotels cost approximately C$15 (US$7), C$2 (US$1.20) for each additional traveler.

**By car** St. John's is located 131km (79 miles) from the ferry at Argentia, 905km (543 miles) from Port aux Basques.

**VISITOR INFORMATION** **Tourist office** The city's **Tourist Information office** (**© 709/576-8106**), open all year, is located on the 1st floor of City Hall on New Gower Street. tourism@city.st-johns.nf.ca. The major source of online information is St. John's official website, **www.city.st-johns.nf.ca**.

**GETTING AROUND** **Metro bus** serves much of the city. At press time, fares were C$1.50 (US95¢) for a single trip. Route information is available at the visitor information center or by calling **© 709/722-9400.**

**EVENTS** The annual **Newfoundland and Labrador Folk Festival** ★ (**© 709/576-8508;** www.sjfac.nf.net) celebrates its 27th year in 2003. The 3-day festival is held during the first weekend in early August, and includes performers from all over the province, who gather to play at Bannerman Park in downtown St. John's. (Bring a lawn chair.) Even after all these years tickets are still very affordable (at press time it cost just C$5 (US$3.10) for an afternoon slate of performers, C$7 (US$4.35) for the evening).

### EXPLORING ST. JOHN'S

The city produces a free, informative and helpful 40-page pocket-size brochure, entitled "Exploring the City of Legends: Your Guide to Walking Tours and Auto

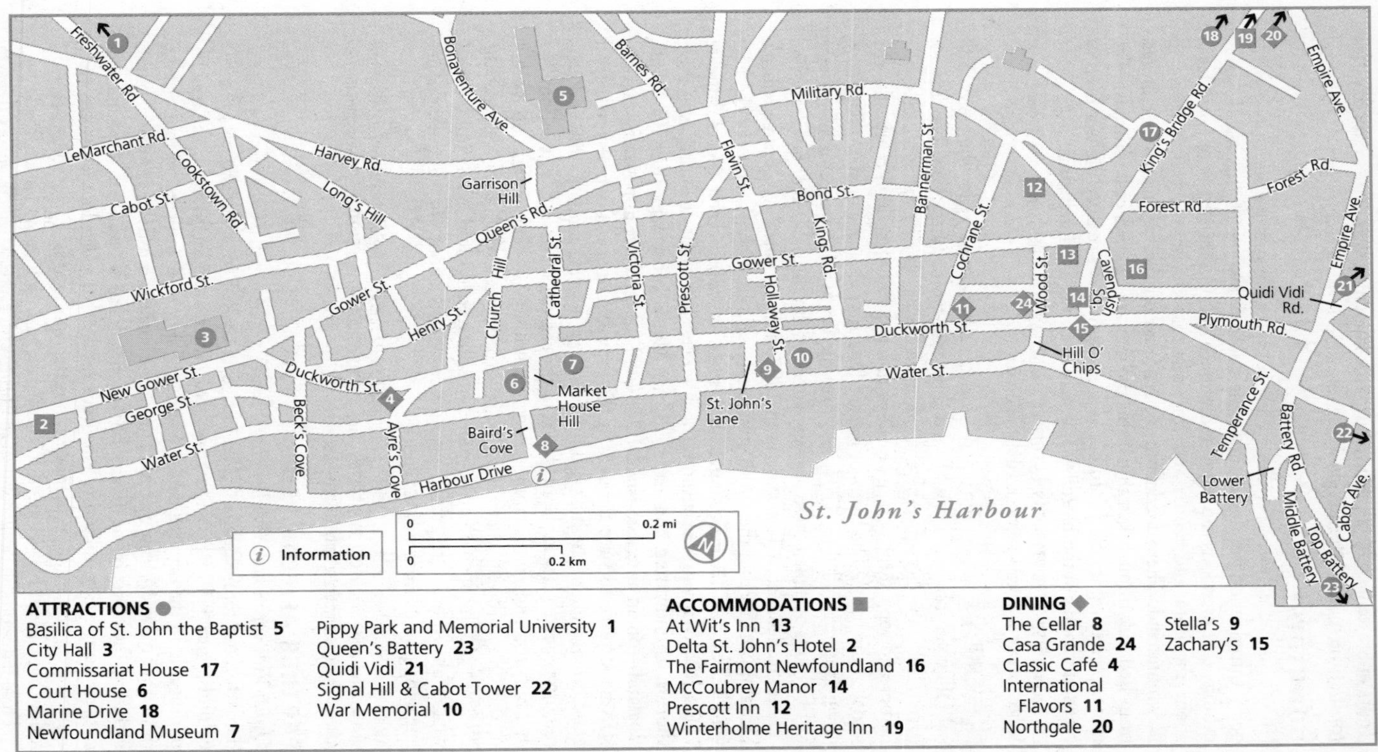
Freshwater Rd.
LeMarchant Rd.
Cookstown Rd.
Cabot St.
Wickford St.
New Gower St.
George St.
Water St.
Harvey Rd.
Long's Hill
Gower St.
Duckworth St.
Beck's Cove
Ayre's Cove
Harbour Drive
Henry St.
Church Hill
Garrison Hill
Queen's Rd.
Bonaventure Ave.
Barnes Rd.
Military Rd.
Cathedral St.
Victoria St.
Prescott St.
Flavin St.
Bond St.
Kings Rd.
Hollaway St.
Bannerman St
Cochrane St.
Wood St.
Cavendish Sq.
Forest Rd.
King's Bridge Rd.
Empire Ave.
Quidi Vidi Rd.
Plymouth Rd.
Hill O' Chips
Temperance St.
Battery Rd.
Lower Battery
Middle Battery
Top Battery
Cabot Ave.
Market House Hill
Baird's Cove
St. John's Lane
St. John's Harbour
Information
0 0.2 mi
0 0.2 km
N
ATTRACTIONS
Basilica of St. John the Baptist 5
City Hall 3
Commissariat House 17
Court House 6
Marine Drive 18
Newfoundland Museum 7
Pippy Park and Memorial University 1
Queen's Battery 23
Quidi Vidi 21
Signal Hill & Cabot Tower 22
War Memorial 10
ACCOMMODATIONS
At Wit's Inn 13
Delta St. John's Hotel 2
The Fairmont Newfoundland 16
McCoubrey Manor 14
Prescott Inn 12
Winterholme Heritage Inn 19
DINING
The Cellar 8
Casa Grande 24
Classic Café 4
International Flavors 11
Northgale 20
Stella's 9
Zachary's 15

Tours of St. John's." It's a good resource for launching your visit to the city. Ask for it at the tourist information office (above).

## DOWNTOWN

**Newfoundland Museum** *Kids* This compact downtown museum offers a good introduction to the natural and cultural history of the island, using exhibits that even kids can enjoy and understand. On the first floor you'll learn about the flora and fauna, and find out that the moose is not native to Newfoundland. The second floor concentrates on the various native cultures, from Beothuk through Inuit (look for the delicate carvings of bear heads). The more sparsely exhibited third floor suggests how 19th-century life was lived in Newfoundland's outports. Allow about an hour for a leisurely tour.

285 Duckworth St. ✆ **709/729-2329.** C$3 (US$1.85) adult, C$2.50 (US$1.55) seniors and students, under 18 free. Summer daily 9am–4:45pm; closed Mon off-season.

**Signal Hill** ★★ *Value* You'll come for the history but stay for the views. Signal Hill is St. John's most visible and most visit-worthy attraction. The rugged, barren hill is the city's preeminent landmark, rising up over the entrance to the harbor and topped by a craggy castle with a flag fluttering high overhead—the signal of the name. The layers of history here are rich and complex—flags have flown atop this hill since 1704, and over the centuries a succession of military fortifications occupied these strategic slopes, as did three different hospitals. The "castle" (called Cabot Tower) dates to 1897, built in honor of Queen Victoria's Diamond Jubilee and the 400th anniversary of John Cabot's arrival in the new world. The hill secured a spot in history in 1901, when Nobel laureate Guglielmo Marconi received the first wireless transatlantic broadcast—three short dots indicating the letter "S" in Morse code, sent from Cornwall, England—on an antennae raised 120m (400 ft.) on a kite in powerful winds.

A good place to start a tour is at the interpretive center, where you'll get a good briefing about the hill's history. Four days a week, military drills and cannon firings take place in the field next to the center (Wed and Thurs at 7pm, Sat and Sun at 3 and 7pm). From here, you can follow serpentine trails up the hill to the Cabot Tower, where you'll be rewarded with breathtaking views of the Narrows and the open ocean beyond. Look for icebergs in the early summer and whales any time. Interpretive placards, scattered about the summit, feature engaging photos from various epochs.

Atop Signal Hill at the entrance to St. John's harbor. ✆ **709/772-5367.** Free admission to grounds; admission to interpretive center C$2.50 (US$1.55) adult, C$2 (US$1.20) senior, C$1.50 (US95¢) children (6–16), C$6 (US$3.70) family. Open daily 8:30am–9pm.

## FARTHER AFIELD

**Quidi Vidi** (pronounced *"kitty vitty"*) is a tiny harbor village that sets new standards for the term "quaint." The village is tucked in a narrow, rocky defile behind Signal Hill, where a narrow ocean inlet provides access to the sea. It's photogenic in the extreme, and a wonderful spot to investigate by foot or bike (it's rather more difficult by car). The village consists mostly of compact homes, including the oldest home in St. John's, with very few shops. Visit here while you can; in recent years, following rancorous local debate, development plans were approved for the addition of modern housing in the area. To get to Quidi Vidi, follow Signal Hill Road to Quidi Vidi Road; turn right onto Forest Road.

From here you can easily connect to **Quidi Vidi Lake,** where **St. John's Regatta** is held the first Wednesday in August, as it has been since 1826. Look for the trail leading to the lake from near the entrance to Quidi Vidi, or ask locally.

**Fluvarium** *Finds* This low, octagonal structure at the edge of Long Pond (near the University) actually descends three stories into the earth. The second level features exhibits on river ecology, including life in the riffles (that's where trout spawn) and in shallow pools, which are rich with nutrients. On the lowest level you'll find yourself looking up into a deep pool that's located alongside the building. Watch for brown trout swimming lazily by.

Pippy Park, off Allandale Rd. ✆ **709/754-3474.** Admission C$5 (US$3.10) adults, C$4 (US$2.50) seniors and students, C$3 (US$1.85) children. Daily Mon–Fri 9am–5pm, Sat–Sun noon–5pm. Guided tours on the half-hour; feeding time 4pm.

**Memorial University Botanical Garden at Oxen Pond** An abundant selection of northern plants makes this garden well worth seeking out (it's tucked over a wooded ridge on the city's western edge, behind Pippy Park). The main plots are arranged in gracious "theme gardens," including a cottage garden, a rock garden, and a peat garden. Among the most interesting is the Newfoundland Heritage Garden, with examples of 70 types of perennials traditionally found in island gardens. The floral displays aren't as ostentatious or exuberant as you'll find in other public gardens in Atlantic Canada (the gardens of Halifax and Annapolis Royal come to mind), but they will be of great interest to amateur horticulturists curious about boreal plants. Behind the gardens are winding hiking trails leading down to marshy Oxen Pond.

Mt. Scio Rd. ✆ **709/737-8590.** Admission C$2 (US$1.20) adult, C$1 (US60¢) seniors and children (5–17). Open May–Nov daily 10am–5pm. Take Thorburn Rd. past Avalon Mall, turn right on Mt. Scio Rd.

## OUTDOOR PURSUITS

**Pippy Park** (✆ **709/737-3655**) is on the city's hilly western side adjacent to the university and contains 1,350ha (3,350 acres) of developed recreation land and quiet trails. The popular park is home to the city campground and Fluvarium (see above), as well as miniature golf, picnic sites, and playgrounds.

One highly recommended hike is the **North Head Trail** ★, which runs from Signal Hill to an improbable cluster of small buildings between rock face and water called The Battery. You should be reasonably fit and unafraid of heights; allow about 2 hours, assuming departure and return from near the Hotel Newfoundland. On foot, follow Duckworth Street between the hotel and Devon House, then bear right on Battery Road. Stay on the main branch (a few smaller branches may confuse you) as it narrows then rises and falls while skirting a rock face to the Outer Battery. The former fishermen's homes at the Battery are literally inches from the road and not much farther from the water, and most have drop-dead views of the Narrows and the city skyline. There's a whimsical, storybook character to the place, and the real estate is now much sought after by city residents.

At the end of the Battery you'll cross right over someone's front porch (it's OK), and then the North Head Trail begins in earnest. It runs along the Narrows, past old gun emplacements, up and down heroic sets of steps, and along some narrow ledges (chains are bolted to rock as handrails for a little extra security in one spot). The trail then ascends an open headland before looping back and starting the final ascent up Signal Hill. After some time exploring here and soaking up the view, you can walk on the paved road back down Signal Hill to Duckworth Street.

## WHERE TO STAY

### EXPENSIVE

**Delta St. John's Hotel** ★★ *Kids* The sleek and modern Delta Newfoundland, built in 1987, is located downtown near City Hall and caters largely to businesspeople. It lacks the views and the ineffable sense of class that you'll find at the Hotel Newfoundland, but it has nice touches like ship models in the lobby and a handsome pool table as the centerpiece of the lounge. It also is well located for prowling the city, and features a number of amenities that choosy travelers will appreciate; management also runs a number of children's programs. The attractive restaurant off the lobby offers a continental menu with a Mediterranean touch, and features dishes like seafood casserole, shrimp brochettes, and beef in various incarnations.

120 New Gower St., St. John's, NF A1C 6K4. ✆ **800/563-3838** or 709/739-6404. Fax 709/570-1622. www.deltahotels.com. 285 units. C$145–C$205 (US$90–US$127) double. AE, DC, DISC, MC, V. Pets allowed with advance permission. **Amenities:** Restaurant; indoor pool; squash courts; fitness room; sauna; Jacuzzi; concierge; limited room service; babysitting; laundry; dry cleaning; children's program. *In room:* A/C, TV, minibar, coffeemaker, hair dryer.

**The Fairmont Newfoundland** ★★ The Hotel Newfoundland was built in 1982 in a starkly modern style, but it boasts a refined sensibility and attention to detail that's reminiscent of a lost era. What I like most about the hotel is how the designers and architects hid their best surprises. The lobby has one of the best views of the Narrows in the city, but you have to wander around to find it. It's a wonderful effect, and one that's used nicely throughout. (This helps compensate for the somewhat generic, conference-hotel feel of much of the decor.) Rooms are standard size and are nothing remarkable. About half have harbor views.

Cavendish Square (P.O. Box 5637), St. John's, NF A1C 5W8. ✆ **800/866-5577** or 709/726-4980. Fax 709/726-2025. www.fairmont.com. 301 units. Weekends C$139–C$232 (US$86–US$144) double, midweek C$129–C$252 (US$80–US$156) double. AE, DC, DISC, MC, V. Pets C$20 (US$12) extra per night. **Amenities:** 3 restaurants; indoor pool; golf simulator; fitness room; Jacuzzi; sauna; concierge; business center; salon; 24-hour room service; babysitting; laundry; dry cleaning. *In room:* A/C, TV, minibar, coffeemaker.

**Winterholme Heritage Inn** ★★ This stout, handsome Victorian mansion was built in 1905 and is as architecturally distinctive a place as you'll find in Newfoundland, with prominent turrets, bowfront windows, bold pediments, elaborate molded plaster ceilings, and woodwork extravagant enough to stop you in your tracks. (The oak woodwork was actually carved in England and shipped here for installation.) Room 7 is one of the most lavish I've seen; the former billiards room features a fireplace and two-person Jacuzzi, along with a plasterwork ceiling and a supple leather wing chair. Room 1 is oval-shaped and occupies one of the turrets; it also has a Jacuzzi. The attic rooms are less extraordinary, but still appealing with their odd angles and nice touches. The mansion is located a 10-minute walk from downtown.

79 Rennies Mill Rd., St. John's, NF A1C 3R1. ✆ **800/599-7829** or 709/739-7979. Fax 709/753-9411. winterholme@nf.sympatico.ca. 12 units. C$109–C$199 (US$68–US$123). AE, DC, MC, V. **Amenities:** Laundry. *In room:* TV, coffeemaker, hair dryer.

## MODERATE

**At Wit's Inn** ★★ *Finds* Forgive the innkeepers of their pun. This lovely century-old home was wonderfully restored and opened as an inn in 1999 by a former Toronto restaurateur. It will appeal to anyone who loathes the "kountry klutter" found in establishments striving too hard for a personality. Decorated with sure eye for bold color and simple style, this is a welcoming urban oasis just around the corner from the Hotel Newfoundland. Rooms are not all that spacious, but neither are they too small. (The largest room is on the top floor, requiring a bit of a hike.) A full breakfast is served in the first floor dining room, wine and cheese are offered in the late afternoon, and there's a butler's pantry for snacking in between times. At Wit's Inn offers luxury touches at a relatively affordable price.

3 Gower St. St. John's, NF A1C 1M9. © **877/739-7420** or 709/739-7420. Fax 709/576-8625. atwitsinn@hotmail.com. 4 units. C$79–C$109 (US$49–US$68) double, includes breakfast. AE, MC, V. *In room:* TV/VCR.

**McCoubrey Manor** ★★ *Kids* McCoubrey Manor offers the convenient location of the Hotel Newfoundland (it's just across the street), but with Victorian charm and a more casual B&B atmosphere. The adjoining 1904 town houses are decorated in what might be called a "contemporary Victorian" style and are quite inviting, especially after a recent renovation job. Upstairs rooms have private double Jacuzzis; Room 1 is brightest, and faces the street. Room 2 has a sunken Jacuzzi, an oak mantled fireplace, and lustrous trim of British Columbia fir. Just around the corner are five spacious one-, two- and three-bedroom apartments with full kitchens. What they lack in elegance they make up for in space; families take note. There's also a washer and dryer on the premises for guests (C$10/US$6 extra to use it). Evening wine and cheese get-togethers and a newly added full breakfast service (except with apartments) only add to the place's charm. Note that kids older than toddler age are welcome.

6–8 Ordnance St., St. John's, NF A1C 3K7. © **888/753-7577** or 709/722-7577. Fax 709/579-7577. www.mccoubrey.com. 9 units. C$89–C$189 (US$55–US$117) double, including full breakfast. AE, DC, MC, V. **Amenities:** Laundry. *In room:* TV/VCR.

**Prescott Inn** *Value* The Prescott Inn is composed of an unusually attractive grouping of wood-frame town houses painted a vibrant lavender-blue. Some of the historical detailing has been restored inside, but mostly the homes have been modernized. Some rooms have carpeting; others have hardwood floors. All are furnished with eclectic antiques that rise above flea-market quality but aren't quite collectibles. The lower-priced rooms have been recently upgraded and increased in price, but are still among the city's better bargains. All guests are welcome to relax on the shared balcony that runs along the back of the building. Room 3 might be the best of the bunch, and it is the only guest room with a private Jacuzzi. If you want a room with one of the best views in the city, ask about the Battery, a scenic village-like neighborhood perched precariously over the harbor a short drive away; the Battery units have private bathrooms and kitchens. Also note that the management owns a small tour company that both puts together self-styled itineraries and arranges car rentals.

19 Military Rd. (P.O. Box 204), St. John's, NF A1C 2C3. © **888/263-3786** or 709/753-7733. Fax 709/753-6036. jpeters@nfld.com. 16 units, plus 2 units at the Battery with kitchen and private bathrooms. C$70–C$105 (US$46.65–US$70) double, including full breakfast. AE, DC, MC, V. Pets allowed. *In room:* TV.

## WHERE TO DINE

Budget travelers should wander up the city's hillside to the intersection of LaMarchant and Freshwater Streets. Within a 2-block radius, you'll find numerous options for cheap eats at both eat-in and take-out establishments.

### EXPENSIVE

**The Cellar** ★★ ECLECTIC The classy interior is a surprise here—the restaurant is located on a nondescript street and through a nondescript entrance. Inside, it's intimate and warm, not unlike an upper-crust gentleman's club. The kitchen has been turning out fine meals for some time now, developing a reputation for creativity and consistency. The menu is constantly in play, but look for reliable standbys like the delicious gravlax, and the homemade bread and pastas. Fish is prepared especially well, and some cuts are paired with innovative flavors like ginger and pear butter. Lunches are the better bargain, featuring tasty offerings like baked brie in phyllo with red currant and pineapple chutney, or scallop crepes with bacon, leeks, and Swiss cheese.

Baird's Cove (near waterfront, just downhill from Supreme Court building). ✆ **709/579-8900.** Reservations encouraged. Main courses: lunch C$8.50–C$20.50 (US$5–US$13), dinner C$7.50–C$33.50 (US$4.65–US$21). AE, DC, DISC, MC, V. Mon–Fri 11:30am–2:30pm and 5:30–9:30pm (until 10:30pm Fri), Sat 5:30–10:30pm, Sun 5:30–9:30pm.

**Stonehouse Restaurant Canadian Northern Catering** ★★ HAUTE NEWFOUNDLAND This restaurant continues to serve up some of the best meals in Newfoundland. The focus is on local fare, with dishes like wild game and seafood prominent on the menu. You might start with cod au gratin or onion soup with cognac and Camembert croutons, but leave room for the generous main courses, such as lamb with garlic sauce, grilled salmon with dill sauce, or Labrador partridge with partridgeberries. Caribou and moose appear as specialties from time to time, when high-quality meat is available. The setting is wonderful, in an 1834 stone house with walls 1m (3 ft.) thick. Quidi Vidi Lake is a short walk away, offering a perfect spot for a postprandial stroll.

8 Kenna's Hill. ✆ **709/753-2425.** Reservations suggested. Main courses: lunch C$12–C$25 (US$7–US$16), dinner C$13–C$33 (US$8–US$20). AE, MC, V. Mon–Fri 11:30am–2:30pm, daily 5:30–11:30pm. Drive north on King's Bridge Rd. to Kenna's Hill.

## MODERATE

**Casa Grande** ★ *Value* MEXICAN If you've developed Mexican-food withdrawal after all those outport meals of fried fish, plan to satisfy your cravings here—you won't find better Mexican food in Newfoundland, and you'd be hard-pressed to find better elsewhere in Atlantic Canada. Seating is on two floors of a narrow storefront just down the hill from the Hotel Newfoundland. Angle for the front room of the upper level, where you'll get views of the harbor. It's often crowded and the service can be irksome; but come prepared for a wait and you'll get excellent value for your money. All the dishes are well prepared; the chile relleno has developed something of a cult following.

108 Duckworth. ✆ **709/753-6108.** Reservations helpful. Main courses: lunch C$7–C$8.95 (US$4.35–US$6), dinner C$10–C$16 (US$6–US$10). AE, DC, MC, V. Mon–Fri 11:30am–2:30pm and 5–10pm (until 11pm Fri), Sat 5–11pm, Sun 5–9pm.

**Classic Café** CANADIAN This come-as-you-are spot is appropriately named—it's truly classic St. John's, and everyone seems to drop in here at one time or another. There's a quiet, more sedate dining room upstairs in this 1894 hillside home. But the real action is in the crowded street-level bistro. Breakfast is served 24 hours a day—but don't expect a limp croissant and tea. Macho breakfasts (for example, a sirloin with eggs, toast, home fries, and baked beans) appeal to a mixed group, from burly longshoremen to hungover musicians. Non-breakfast entrees in the evening are equally generous and often surprisingly good.

364 Duckworth. ✆ **709/579-4444.** Reservations not necessary. Main courses, breakfast, and lunch C$6–C$8 (US$3.70–US$5), dinner C$8–C$17 (US$5–US$11). DC, MC, V. Daily 24 hours.

**Zachary's** TRADITIONAL This informal spot with wood-slat booths offers a slew of Newfoundland favorites, like fish cakes, fried bologna, and toutons—and that's just for breakfast. Dinners emphasize seafood—entrees include grilled salmon, seafood fettuccine, pan-fried cod, and lobster most of the year—but you'll also find steaks and chicken. Desserts are all homemade! Especially tempting are the cheesecake, carrot cake, and date squares. You'll find more inventive spots for dinner, but you probably won't do better for reliable quality if you're on a tight budget. Breakfasts are outstanding and are served all day.

71 Duckworth (across from Hotel Newfoundland). ✆ **709/579-8050.** Reservations encouraged. Main courses: breakfast C$3.29–C$7.49 (US$2.05–US$4.65), lunch C$5.99–C$8.99 (US$3.70–US$6), dinner C$10.99–C$19.99 (US$7–US$12). AE, MC, V. Daily 7am–11pm.

### INEXPENSIVE

**International Flavours** *Value* INDIAN This is my favorite cheap meal in St. John's. This storefront restaurant has just five tables, and all dinners include a decent mound of food. You'll usually have a choice of four or so dishes. Smart money gets the basic curry. Also recommended is the very satisfying mango milk shake.

124 Duckworth St. ✆ 709/738-4636. Reservations not necessary. Dinner plates C$6.95–C$7.95 (US$4.30–US$4.95). V. Mon–Sat 11am–6pm, Wed 11am–7pm (often later). Closed Sun.

## ST. JOHN'S AFTER DARK

The nightlife in St. John's is extraordinarily vibrant, and you'd be doing yourself an injustice if you didn't spend at least one evening on a pub crawl.

**George Street** is packed with energetic pubs and lounges, some fueled by beer, others by testosterone, still more by lively Celtic fiddling. The best strategy for selecting a pub is a slow ramble around 10pm or later, vectoring in to spots with appealing music wafting from the door. At places with live music, cover charges are universally very nominal and rarely top C$5 (US$3.10). **Trapper John's,** 2 George St. (✆ **709/579-9630**), is known for outstanding provincial folk music, but it tries a bit harder for that Ye Olde Newfoundland character. This is a traditional "screeching in" spot for visitors (this involves cheap Newfoundland rum and some embarrassment). For blues and traditional music, there's the lively **Fat Cat,** 5 George St. (✆ **709/722-6409**). For a more upscale spot with lower decibel levels, try **Christian's Bar,** 23 George St. (✆ **709/753-9100**), which offers the nonalcoholic option of specialty coffees.

If George Street's beery atmosphere reminds you of those nights in college you'd just as soon forget, a few blocks away are two pubs tucked down tiny alleys known for their genial public-house atmospheres. The **Duke of Duckworth,** 325 Duckworth St. (✆ **709/739-6344**), specializes in draft beers and pub lunches. **The Ship Inn,** 265 Duckworth St. (✆ 709/753-3870), is a St. John's mainstay, featuring a variety of local musical acts that seem to complement rather than overwhelm the pub's cozy atmosphere.

## 8 The Southern Avalon Peninsula

The Avalon Peninsula—or just "The Avalon," as it's commonly called—is home to some of Newfoundland's most memorable and dramatic scenery, including high coastal cliffs and endless bogs. More good news: It's also relatively compact and manageable, and it can be viewed on long day trips from St. John's, or in a couple of days of scenic poking around. It's a good destination for anyone who's short on time, yet wants to get a taste of the wild. The area is especially notable for its **bird colonies** ★, as well as its herd of wild **caribou** ★. The bad news? It's out in the sea where cold and warm currents collide, resulting in legendary fogs and blustery, moist weather. Bring a rain suit and come prepared for bone-numbing dampness.

## ESSENTIALS

**GETTING THERE** Several well-marked, well-maintained highways follow the coast of the southern Avalon Peninsula; few roads cross the damp and spongy interior. A map is essential.

**VISITOR INFORMATION** Your best bet is to stop in the St. John's tourist bureaus (see above) or at the well-marked tourist bureau just up the hill from the Argentia ferry before you begin your travels. Witless Bay has a tourist information booth at the edge of the cobblestone beach and is stocked with a handful of brochures. It's open irregularly.

## WITLESS BAY ECOLOGICAL RESERVE

The Witless Bay area, about 35km (21 miles) south of St. John's, makes an easy day trip from the city, or can serve as a launching point for an exploration of the Avalon Peninsula. The main attraction here is the **Witless Bay Ecological Reserve** ★ (✆ **709/729-2429**), comprising four islands and the waters around them, and located a short boat ride offshore. Literally millions of seabirds nest and fish here, and it's a spectacle even if you're not a bird watcher.

On the islands you'll find the largest **puffin colony** in the western Atlantic Ocean, with some 60,000 puffins burrowing into the grassy slopes above the cliffs, and awkwardly launching themselves from the high rocks. The tour boats are able to edge right along the shores, about 6m to 8m (20 ft.–25 ft.) away, allowing puffin watching on even foggy days. Also on the islands is North America's second-largest murre colony.

Although the islands are publicly owned and managed, access is via privately operated tour boats, several of which you'll find headquartered along Route 10 in Bay Bulls and Bauline East. It's worth shopping around since prices can vary considerably. Bay Bulls is the closest town to St. John's, and is home to three of the more popular tours: **Mullowney's** (✆ **877/783-3467**), **O'Brien's** (✆ **877/639-4253**), and **Gatherall's** (✆ **800/419-4253**). Two-and-a-half hour tours from here are C$32 to C$39 (US$20–US$24) per adult.

**Captain Murphy's Seabird & Whale Tours** (✆ **888/783-3467** or 709/334-2002) is based in Witless Bay, a bit further south, and offers several trips daily; tours last 2 to 2½ hours and cost C$30 (US$19) per adult, C$20 (US$12) for teens, and C$15 (US$9) for children. Budget travelers would do well to continue further south to Bauline East, where the 9m (30-ft.) ***Molly Bawn*** (✆ **709/334-2621**) offers 1¼-hour tours in search of puffins, whales, and icebergs. Tours depart every hour and a half during peak season; the cost is C$15 (US$9) per adult and C$10 (US$6) for children under 12. A quieter and more intimate way to explore the area is to sign up for a 3-hour tour with **Bay Bulls Sea Kayaking Tours** (✆ **709/334-3394**). You'll kayak along the bay's shores, visit sea caves and small beaches, and possibly spot puffins and whales visiting the bay. The price is C$45 (US$28) per person.

## FERRYLAND

Historic Ferryland is among the most picturesque of the Avalon villages, set at the foot of rocky hills on a harbor protected by a series of abrupt islands at its mouth.

Ferryland was among the first permanent settlements in Newfoundland. In 1621, the Colony of Avalon was established here by Sir George Calvert, First Baron of Baltimore (he was also behind the settlement of Baltimore, Maryland). Calvert sunk the equivalent of C$4 million into the colony, which featured luxe touches like cobblestone roads, slate roofs, and fine ceramics and glassware from

Europe. So up-to-date was the colony that privies featured drains leading to the shore just below the high tide mark, making these the first flush toilets in North America. (Or so the locals insist.) Later the Dutch, and then the French, sacked the colony during ongoing squabbles over territory, and eventually it was abandoned.

Recent excavations have revealed much about life here nearly 4 centuries ago. Visit the **Colony of Avalon Interpretation Centre** (✆ **877/326-5669** or 709/432-3200) with its numerous glass-topped drawers filled with engrossing artifacts, and then ask for a tour of the six archaeological sites currently being excavated (the tour is included in the cost of admission). Other interpretive exhibits include a reproduction of a 17th-century kitchen, and three gardens of the sort you might have overseen had you lived 400 years ago. After your tour, take a walk to the lighthouse at the point (about 1 hr. round-trip), where you can scan for whales and icebergs. Ask for directions at the museum. The site is open daily mid-June to mid-October; admission is C$3 (US$1.85) per adult, C$2.50 (US$1.55) per senior, C$2 (US$1.20) per student, and C$6 (US$3.70) per family.

### WHERE TO STAY

**The Downs Inn** Overlooking the harbor, this building served as a convent between 1914 and 1986, when it was converted to an inn. The furnishings reflect its heritage as an institution rather than a historic building—there's dated carpeting and old linoleum, and the furniture is uninspired. (Much of the religious statuary was left in place—a nice touch.) Ask for one of the two front rooms, where you can watch for whales from your windows. The front parlor has been converted to a tearoom, where you can order a nice pot of tea and a light snack, like carrot cake or a rhubarb tart. Some sandwiches are available. Innkeeper Aidan Costello also operates Southern Shore Eco Adventures and can create custom tour packages for kayaking, hiking, or whale-watching.

Route 10, Ferryland, NF A0A 2H0. ✆ **709/432-2808.** Fax 709/432-2659. acostello@nf.sympatico.ca. 4 units (2 share 1 bathroom). C$50–C$75 (US$31–US$47) double. V. Small pets allowed. **Amenities:** Tearoom; laundry service.

## AVALON WILDERNESS RESERVE

Where there's bog, there's caribou. Or at least that's true in the southern part of the peninsula, which is home to the island's largest caribou herd, numbering some 13,000. You'll see signs warning you to watch for caribou along the roadway; the landscape hereabout is so misty and primeval, though, that you might feel you should also watch for druids in robes with tall walking staffs.

The caribou roam freely throughout the 1,700km$^2$ (650-sq. mile) reserve, so it's largely a matter of happenstance to find them. Your best bet is to scan the high upland barrens along Route 10 between Trepassey and Peter's River (an area that's actually out of the reserve). Check with the **Provincial Parks Division** (✆ **709/729-2421**) in St. John's for more information.

On Route 90 between St. Catherines and Hollyrood is the **Salmonier Nature Park** (✆ **709/229-7189**), where you're certain to see caribou—along with other wildlife—if you can't find the herd on the reserve. This intriguing and well-designed park is fundamentally a 2.5km (1½-mile) nature trail, almost entirely on boardwalk, which tracks through bog and forest, and along streams and ponds. Along the route are more than a dozen unobtrusive pens, in which orphaned or injured wildlife can be observed. (It's the only such facility in the province.) Among the animals represented: arctic fox, snowy owl, moose, bald eagle, mink, otter, beaver, and lynx. It's located 11km (7 miles) south of the Trans-Canada Highway; admission is free. Gates are open in summer daily 10am to 5pm, and all visitors must depart by 6pm. The park is closed mid-October to June 1.

## CAPE ST. MARY'S

Cape St. Mary's Ecological Reserve ranks high on my list of favorite places on Newfoundland. Granted, it's off the beaten track—some 100km (60 miles) from the Trans-Canada Highway—but it's worth it.

**Cape St. Mary's Ecological Reserve** ★★ This natural reserve is home to some 5,500 pairs of northern gannets—big, noisy, beautiful, graceful white birds with cappuccino-colored heads and black wing-tips. While they can be seen wintering off the coast of Florida and elsewhere to the south, they're seldom seen in such cacophonous number as here. Most are nesting literally on top of one another on a compact, 100m (300-ft.) sea stack. At any given moment hundreds are flying above, around and below you, which is all the more impressive given their nearly 2m (6-ft.) wingspan.

You needn't take a boat ride to see this colony. Start your visit at the visitor center, which offers a quick and intriguing introduction to the indigenous bird life. Then walk 15 minutes along a grassy cliff-top pathway—through harebell, iris, and dandelion—until you arrive at an unfenced cliff just a couple dozen yards from the sea stack (it's close enough to be impressive even in a dense fog). Also nesting on and around the island are 10,000 pairs of murre, 10,000 kittiwakes, and 100 razorbills. Note that the viewing area is not fenced, and peering down at the surging surf and hundreds of birds on the wing below is not recommended for acrophobes. Guided tours are offered twice daily (C$5/US$3.10), and are well worthwhile; so is the summer performance series of evening concerts.

Off Route 100 (5km/3 miles east of St. Bride's). ✆ **709/729-2424.** Fax. 709/327-2273. Trail to bird rock is free; admission to interpretive center C$4 (US$2.50) adult, C$2 (US$1.20) child, C$10 (US$6) family. Guided tours C$5 (US$3.10; includes admission to center). Daily 9am–7pm. Closed mid-Oct to April 30.

### WHERE TO STAY

**Atlantica Inn and Restaurant** ★ The Atlantica won't win points for charm—it's a basic, aluminum-sided box among some of the newer houses in the village. But it offers great value at the price, and the five rooms are well-maintained and comfortable, if a bit small. The attached restaurant is by and large the only game in town, offering inexpensive meals.

Route 100, St. Bride's, NF A0B 2Z0. ✆ **888/999-2861** or 709/337-2860. 5 units. C$40 (US$25) double. AE, MC, V. **Amenities:** Restaurant.

**Bird Island Resort** *Value* *Kids* This modern, unaffected motel is located behind Manning's food market, where you'll stop to ask for a room. It's the preferred spot in town, and offers some unexpected amenities, like a mini-golf course (all rooms come with clubs and balls). The rooms vary in size. The double efficiency units feature a separate sitting room, and several of the rooms have kitchenettes, which come in handy given the dearth of restaurants in town; families with kids will especially appreciate them. Indeed, the rooms that get snapped up first are usually 1 through 5, for that reason: all have kitchenettes, some have two bedrooms, and all face the ocean. That means great views—assuming the fog hasn't moved in.

Route 100, St. Bride's, NF A0B 2Z0. ✆ **888/337-2450** or 709/337-2450. Fax 709/337-2903. 20 units. C$49–C$79 (US$30–US$49) double. AE, MC, V. **Amenities:** Mini golf; fitness room; laundry.

## 9 The Labrador Coast: Wilderness Adventure & More

Labrador may be far removed and remote, but it has long played an outsized role in the collective consciousness of the region. For several centuries, this deeply indented coastline was noted for its robust fisheries, and itinerant fleets plied the waters both inshore and offshore, harvesting what the sea had to offer. The empty, melancholy landscape of rolling hills along the coasts and inland serves much the same function that the American West frontier played in the United States—it's both a land of opportunity stemming from the natural resources (primarily mining these days), and a place where lovers of the outdoors have historically tested their mettle in a harsh environment, stalking big game and big salmon.

Only about 30,000 people live in Labrador: 13,000 in western Labrador, 8,000 in Happy Valley-Goose Bay, with the remaining residents spread along the coast. Approximately four-fifths of those born here will remain here, with strong ties to family and neighbors. These close-knit communities typically welcome visitors warmly. Some come here for the sportfishing of brook trout, Atlantic salmon, arctic char, lake trout, white fish, and northern pike. Others come for wilderness adventure, hiking, and camping under the undulating northern lights. Still others are simply curious about a remote part of the world.

### THE LABRADOR STRAITS

The **Labrador Straits** ★ are the easiest part of Labrador to explore from Newfoundland. The southeast corner of Labrador is served by ferries shuttling between St. Barbe, Newfoundland, and Blanc Sablon, Québec. (Blanc Sablon is on the Québec-Labrador border.) From Blanc Sablon, you can travel on the one and only road, which runs 80km (48 miles) northward, dead-ending at Red Bay. (Plans call for extending this road in the future, but it may be another decade.)

Ferries are timed such that you can cross over in the morning, drive to Red Bay, and still be back for the later ferry to Newfoundland. Such a hasty trip isn't recommended, however. Better to spend a night, when you'll have a chance to meet the people, who offer the most compelling reason to visit.

The **M/S *Apollo*** (**© 866/535-2567** or 418/461-2056) runs from May 1 until ice season, usually sometime in early January. The crossing takes about 1 hour and 30 minutes, and reservations are encouraged in summer (half the ferry can be reserved; the other half is first-come, first-served). One-way fares are C$9 (US$6) per adult, C$4.75 (US$2.95) for children ages 5 to 12, and C$18.50 (US$11) per automobile.

The terrain along the Labrador Straits is rugged, and the colors muted except for a vibrant stretch of green along the Pinware River. The few small houses are clustered close together; during the winter it's nice to have neighbors so nearby. Homes are often brightened up with "yard art"—replicas of windmills, wells, and churches. In summer, icebergs float by the coast, and whales breach and spout offshore. The landscape is covered with cotton grass, clover, partridgeberries, bake apples, fireweed, buttercups, and bog laurel. The fog rolls in frequently; it will either stay a while or roll right back out again. The capelin come and go as well. The tiny migrating fish crash-land on the shore by the thousands during a week in late June or early July. Local residents crowd the beach to scoop up the fish and take them home for an easy supper.

The **Visitor Information Centre** (**© 709/931-2360**) in the small, restored St. Andrews Church in L'Anse au Clair, the first town after the ferry, is open from June to September. The tourist association has developed several footpaths and trails in the area, so be sure to ask about them; also ask about the "fairy holes." If you come in mid-August, plan to attend the annual Bake Apple Festival, celebrating the berry that stars in the desserts of Newfoundland and Labrador.

## EXPLORING THE LABRADOR STRAITS

Drive the "slow road" that connects the villages of the Labrador Straits. Traveling southwest to northeast, here is some of what you'll find along the way.

In L'Anse au Clair, **Moore's Handicrafts,** 8 Country Rd., just off Route 510 (✆ **709/931-2022**), sells handmade summer and winter coats, traditional cassocks, moccasins, knitted items, handmade jewelry, and other crafts, as well as homemade jams. They also do traditional embroidery on Labrador cassocks and coats, and if you stop on the way north and choose your design, they'll finish it by the time you return to the ferry—even the same day. Prices are quite reasonable. The shop is open daily in season 8am to 10pm.

The **Point Amour Lighthouse** (1858), at the western entrance to the Strait of Belle Isle, is the tallest lighthouse in the Atlantic provinces and the second tallest in all of Canada. The walls of the slightly tapered, circular tower are 2m (6½ ft.) thick at the base. You'll have to climb 122 steps for the view. The dioptric lens was imported from Europe for the princely sum of C$10,000 (US$6,200). The lighthouse, which kept watch for submarines during World War II, is still in use and was maintained by a resident lightkeeper right up until 1995. It's open to the public June to mid-October 10am to 5:30pm (✆ **709/927-5825**); the fee is C$2.50 (US$1.55), children under 12 free. The lighthouse is a 3.5km (2-mile) drive from the main road.

After you pass the fishing settlements of **L'Anse au Loup** ("Wolf's Cove") and **West St. Modeste,** the road follows the scenic **Pinware River,** where the trees become noticeably taller. Along this stretch of road, you'll see glacial erratics—those odd boulders deposited by the melting ice cap. **Pinware Provincial Park,** 43km (26 miles) from L'Anse au Clair, has a picnic area, hiking trails, and 15 campsites. The 80km (50-mile) long Pinware River is known for salmon fishing.

The highway ends in Red Bay. The **Red Bay National Historic Site Visitor Centre** (✆ **709/920-2051**) showcases artifacts from the late 1500s, when Basque whalers came in number to hunt the right and bowhead whales. Starting in 1977, excavations turned up whaling implements, pottery, glassware, and even partially preserved seamen's clothing. From here you can also arrange tours of Saddle Island, the home of Basque whaling stations in the 16th century. Transportation to archaeological sites on the island is available from mid-June through mid-October, Monday to Saturday from 9am to 4pm. You can also opt to view Saddle Island from the observation level on the third floor. Admission is C$5 (US$3.10) per adult, C$3.75 (US$2.30) per senior, C$2.75 (US$1.70) for ages 6 to 16, and C$10 (US$6) per family. The site is open 9am to 6:30pm daily, sometimes closing earlier in the shoulder season. It is closed mid-October to mid-June.

### WHERE TO STAY

**Beachside Hospitality Home** A stay here offers an excellent opportunity to meet a local family and learn firsthand about life in this region of Labrador. Three bedrooms have a separate entrance, and all share two full baths. There is a whirlpool bath, and guests have access to a telephone. Home-cooked meals are available by arrangement, or you can cook for yourself in the kitchen or outdoors on the grill; the owners also sell homemade breads, jams, and jellies, and sometime arrange accordion-powered Newfoundland jigs at night.

9 Lodge Rd., L'Anse au Clair, Labrador, A0K 3K0. ✆ **877/663-8999** or 709/931-2053. 6 units (all share 2 bathrooms). C$38–C$45 (US$24–US$28) double. MC, V. **Amenities:** Meals; kitchen facilities; grill; whirlpool.

**Grenfell Louie A. Hall** *Value* History buffs love the Grenfell Hall—it was built in 1946 by the International Grenfell Association as a nursing station, and there's plenty of reading material about the coast's early days. Rooms are furnished with basic, contemporary-country furniture, and there's a common room with TV, VCR, and fireplace. The innkeepers can arrange to transport you to and from the ferry. (If you're just curious about the place, you're invited to stop in for C$3/US$1.85 per person or C$5/US$3.10 per couple.) Evening meals are available by advance arrangement, and usually feature seafood (typically cod or salmon) along with homemade bread, preserves, and dessert; the cost is C$15 to C$20 (US$9–US$12) for the three-course meal. Full breakfast costs C$6 (US$3.70) extra.

3 Willow Ave. (P.O. Box 137), Forteau, Labrador, A0K 2P0. ✆ **709/931-2916.** 5 units (all share 2 bathrooms). C$40–C$55 (US$25–US$34) double. V. **Amenities:** Meals; shuttles to ferry; shared TV; shared VCR. *In room:* Iron.

**Northern Light Inn** ★ The largest and most modern hotel in the region (it added 28 rooms in 1998), the Northern Light Inn has long offered comfortable, well-maintained rooms, a friendly staff, and a dining room. Now air-conditioning, new carpets and furniture have been added. The restaurant, open from 8am to 11pm, serves soups, sandwiches, baskets of scallops, fried chicken, and pizza. In the adjacent Basque Dining Room, seafood is the specialty. The coffee shop doubles as a lounge in the evening.

L'Anse au Clair, Labrador, A0K 3K0. ✆ **800/563-3188** (from Atlantic Canada) or 709/931-2332. Fax 709/931-2708. 59 units (includes 5 suites and 5 housekeeping units). C$70–C$120 (US$43–US$74) double. AE, DC, MC, V. **Amenities:** 2 restaurants, lounge; laundry service. *In room:* A/C, TV.

7

# Montréal

*by Herbert Bailey Livesey*

The duality of Canadian life has been called the "Twin Solitudes." One Canada, English and Calvinist in origin, tends to be staid, smug, and work obsessed. The other, French and Catholic, is more creative, lighthearted, and inclined to see pleasure as the end purpose of labor—so go the stereotypes. These two peoples live side by side throughout Québec and in the nine other Canadian provinces, but the blending occurs in particularly intense fashion in Québec's largest city, **Montréal.** French speakers (Francophones) constitute 66% of the city's population, while most of the rest are English speakers (Anglophones). Although both groups are decidedly North American, they are no more alike than Margaret Thatcher and Charles de Gaulle.

Québec's role in the Canadian federation is the most volatile issue in Canadian politics, and the defining dialectic of life here is language, the thorny issue that might yet tear the country apart. Many Québecois believe a separate state is the only way to maintain their culture in the face of the Anglophone ocean enveloping them. When yet another sovereignty referendum was held in 1995, the federalists won, but only by a razor-thin 1%. Fears of the separatist passion for independence have fueled migrations of tens of thousands of Anglophones to English Canada. Secession would be a seismic event, prompting loss of federal subsidies, enormous economic uncertainty—even the possibility of the breakup of the province itself.

Partly as a result, there was an undeniable impression of decline in Montréal in the past decade. A bleak mood prevailed, driven by lingering recession and uncertainty over the future.

But something has happened. Ripples of optimism are spreading through the province and its largest city. Separatist sentiment has faded, for the moment. Unemployment in Québec, long in double digits, shrank to under 7% in 2000, the lowest mark in more than 2 decades and below that of arch-rival Toronto. In a perhaps connected trend, crime in Montréal, already one of the safest cities in North America, hit a 20-year low. Favorable currency exchange and the presence of skilled workers have made the city a favored site for Hollywood film and TV production—recently attracting movies starring Bruce Willis, Robert DeNiro, John Travolta, and Eddie Murphy, among others—that brought in more than $700 million in revenue in a single year. That success inspired the construction of two major film studios, one now complete and another expected to be Canada's largest.

The rash of "For Rent" and "For Sale" signs that disfigured the city in the 1990s has evaporated, replaced by a welcome shortage of store and office space and a billion-dollar building boom that's filling up vacant plots all over downtown. The beloved old Forum hockey arena is undergoing expensive conversion to a dining and entertainment center, and an immense multimedia center for high-tech companies is rising near the St. Lawrence River. To be sure, not every project has enjoyed smooth sailing. A plan to build a downtown stadium for the Expos baseball team was on hold at last look, as was a new $900 million theme park called Technodome to be installed at the Port of Montréal.

Those stumbles won't matter to American visitors, for whom Montréal already might seem an urban near-paradise. Québecois are exceedingly gracious hosts. The subway system, called the Métro, is modern and swift. Streets are clean and safe. Montréal's best restaurants are the equal of their south-of-the-border compatriots in almost every way, yet they are as much as 30% to 40% cheaper. And the government gives visitors back most of the taxes it collects from them. Most Montréalers grow up speaking both French and English, switching from one to the other as the situation dictates. This is especially true for telephone operators, store clerks, waiters, and hotel staff. It's less so in country villages and in Québec City, but there's virtually no problem that can't be solved with a few French words, some expressive gestures, and a little goodwill.

## 1 Essentials

### GETTING THERE

**BY PLANE** **Dorval International Airport** (www.montreal-yul.com), 22km (14 miles) west of the city, is served by most of the world's major airlines, more than 50 in all. (Mirabel Airport, farther from the city, now accepts only air freight and some charter flights.) The major car-rental agencies have desks at the airport.

Most visitors fly into Dorval from other parts of North America on **Air Canada** (✆ 514/393-3333 or 888/247-2262), **American** (✆ 514/397-9635 or 800/433-7300), **Continental** (✆ 800/231-0856), **Delta** (✆ 800/221-1212 or 514/337-5520), or **US Airways** (✆ 800/432-9768). In the United States, Air Canada flies out of New York (Newark and LaGuardia), Miami, Tampa, Chicago, Los Angeles, and San Francisco.

Other carriers that serve Montréal via Dorval include **Air France** (✆ 800/847-1106), **British Airways** (✆ 800/243-6822), and **Swissair** (✆ 800/879-9154). Regional airlines, such as Air Atlantic, American Eagle, and Inter-Canadian, also serve the city.

**BY TRAIN** Montréal is a major terminus on Canada's **VIA Rail** network (✆ **888/VIA-RAIL** or 514/842-7245; www.viarail.ca) and its **Gare Centrale** is at 935 rue de la Gauchetière Ouest (✆ **514/871-1331**). Some of the comfortable trains have dining and sleeping cars, and cell phones. There is scheduled service from Québec City, Ottawa, Toronto, Winnipeg, and points west.

**Amtrak** (✆ **800/USA-RAIL;** www.amtrak.com) has one train a day from Montréal from Washington and New York, with intermediate stops. While it is a no-frills, coach-only affair, its scenic route passes along the eastern shore of the Hudson River and west of Lake Champlain. The Adirondack takes about 10½ hours from New York, if all goes well, but delays aren't unusual. Passengers from Chicago can get to Montréal most directly by taking Amtrak to Toronto, then switching to VIA Rail.

Seniors 62 and older are eligible for a 15% **discount** on some Amtrak trains on the U.S. segment of the trip. VIA Rail has a 10% senior discount. Don't forget to bring along proof of citizenship (a passport or birth certificate) for crossing the border.

## Greater Montréal

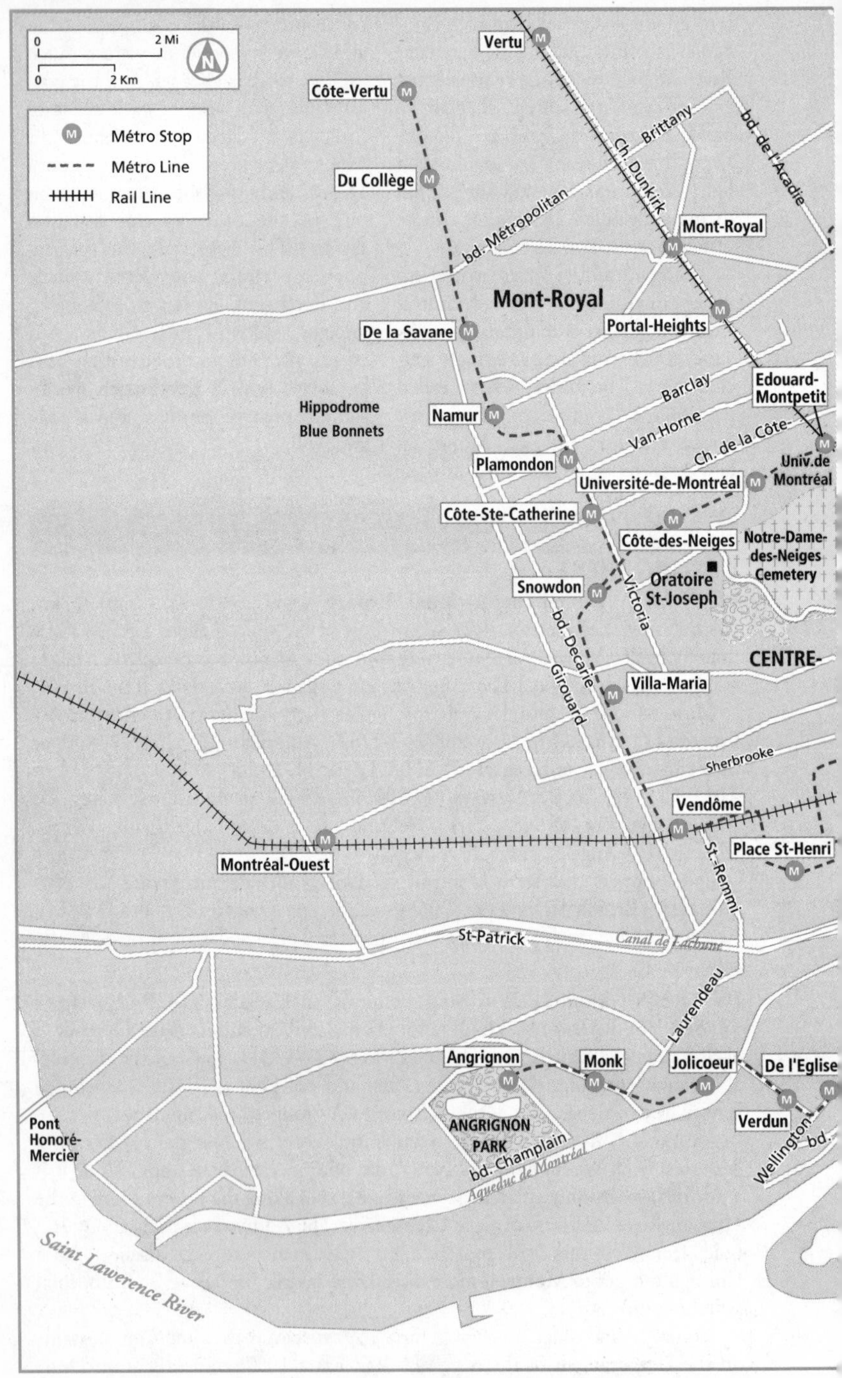
0
2 Mi
0
2 Km
N
Métro Stop
Métro Line
Rail Line
Vertu
Côte-Vertu
Du Collège
Brittany
bd. de l'Acadie
Ch. Dunkirk
bd. Métropolitan
Mont-Royal
Mont-Royal
Portal-Heights
De la Savane
Edouard-Montpetit
Barclay
Hippodrome
Blue Bonnets
Namur
Van Horne
Ch. de la Côte-
Plamondon
Univ. de Montréal
Université-de-Montréal
Côte-Ste-Catherine
Côte-des-Neiges
Notre-Dame-des-Neiges Cemetery
Oratoire St-Joseph
Snowdon
Victoria
bd. Decarie
Girouard
CENTRE-
Villa-Maria
Sherbrooke
Vendôme
Place St-Henri
Montréal-Ouest
St.-Remmi
St-Patrick
Canal de Lachine
Laurendeau
Angrignon
Monk
Jolicoeur
De l'Eglise
Verdun
Pont Honoré-Mercier
ANGRIGNON PARK
bd. Champlain
Aqueduc de Montréal
Wellington
bd.
Saint Lawrence River

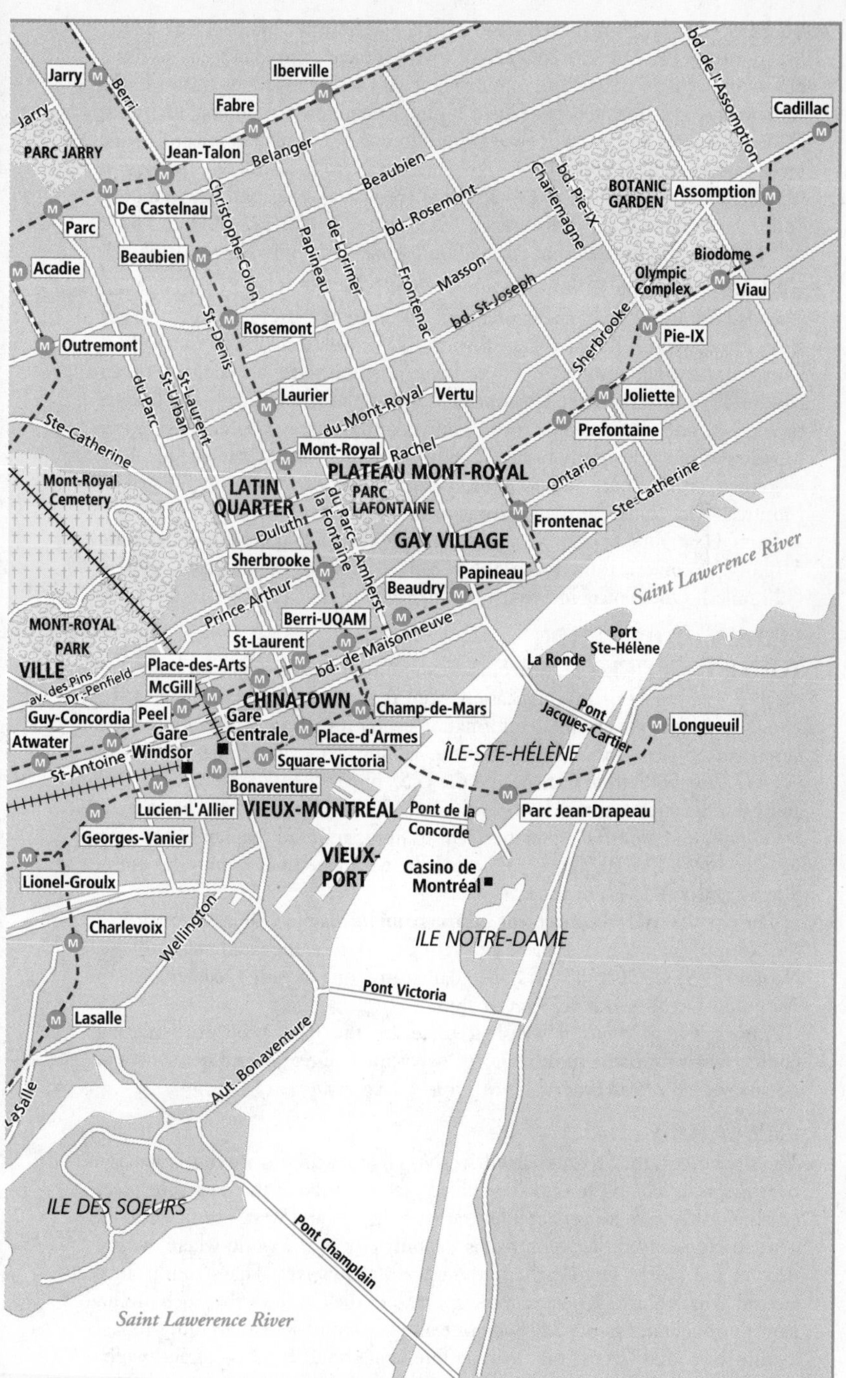
Jarry
Iberville
Fabre
Cadillac
PARC JARRY
Jean-Talon
Belanger
Beaubien
BOTANIC GARDEN
Assomption
De Castelnau
Parc
bd. Rosemont
Beaubien
Acadie
Biodome
Olympic Complex
Viau
Masson
bd. St-Joseph
Rosemont
Pie-IX
Outremont
Sherbrooke
Laurier
du Mont-Royal
Vertu
Joliette
Prefontaine
Ste-Catherine
Mont-Royal
Rachel
PLATEAU MONT-ROYAL
Mont-Royal Cemetery
LATIN QUARTER
PARC LAFONTAINE
Ontario
Frontenac
Ste-Catherine
Duluth
GAY VILLAGE
Sherbrooke
Papineau
Saint Lawerence River
Beaudry
Prince Arthur
Berri-UQAM
MONT-ROYAL PARK
St-Laurent
bd. de Maisonneuve
Port Ste-Hélène
La Ronde
VILLE
Place-des-Arts
av. des Pins
Dr.-Penfield
McGill
CHINATOWN
Champ-de-Mars
Pont Jacques-Cartier
Longueuil
Guy-Concordia
Peel
Gare Centrale
Place-d'Armes
Atwater
Gare Windsor
Square-Victoria
ÎLE-STE-HÉLÈNE
St-Antoine
Bonaventure
Lucien-L'Allier
VIEUX-MONTRÉAL
Pont de la Concorde
Parc Jean-Drapeau
Georges-Vanier
VIEUX-PORT
Casino de Montréal
Lionel-Groulx
Charlevoix
Wellington
ILE NOTRE-DAME
Pont Victoria
Lasalle
Aut. Bonaventure
LaSalle
ILE DES SOEURS
Pont Champlain
Saint Lawerence River
Jarry
Berri
Christophe-Colon
Papineau
de Lorimer
Frontenac
Charlemagne
bd. Pie-IX
bd. de l'Assomption
St-Denis
St-Laurent
St-Urban
du-Parc
du Parc la Fontaine
Amherst

**BY BUS** Montréal's main bus terminal is the **Terminus Voyageur,** 505 bd. de Maisonneuve Est (✆ **514/842-2281;** www.voyageur.com). Voyageur operates buses from all parts of Québec, with frequent runs from the various villages in the Laurentians, and from Québec City. Morning, noon, early afternoon, and midnight buses cover the distance between Toronto and Montréal in less than 7 hours. From Boston or New York, there is daily bus service to Montréal on **Greyhound** (✆ **800/229-9424** or 514/843-8495; www.greyhound.com), and between New York and Montréal on **Adirondack Trailways** (✆ **800/225-6815** or 514/843-8495). A trip from Boston takes 8 hours while a trip from New York takes 9.

**BY CAR** Interstate 87 runs due north from New York City to link up with Canada's Autoroute 15 at the border, and the entire 640km (400-mile) journey is on expressways. Likewise, from Boston, I-93 north joins I-89 just south of Concord, New Hampshire. At White River Junction there is a choice between continuing on I-89 to Lake Champlain, crossing the lake by roads and bridges to join I-87 and Canada Autoroute 15 north, or picking up I-91 at White River Junction to go due north toward Sherbrooke, Québec. At the border, I-91 becomes Canada Route 55 and joins Canada Route 10 west through Estrie to Montréal. The Trans-Canada Highway runs right through the city.

From New York to Montréal is about 644km (400 miles); from Boston, 510km (316 miles); from Toronto, 540km (335 miles); from Ottawa, 190km (120 miles). Once you're in Montréal, Québec City is an easy 3-hour drive.

## VISITOR INFORMATION

**TOURIST OFFICES** Québec tourism authorities produce volumes of detailed and highly useful publications, and they're easy to obtain by mail, by phone, or in person. The main information center for visitors in Montréal is the large and efficient **Infotouriste Centre,** at 1001 rue du Square-Dorchester (✆ **877/266-5687** from Canada and the U.S., or 514/873-2015), between Peel and Metcalfe streets in the downtown hotel and business district. The office is open daily June to early September 7am to 8pm, and mid- September to May 9am to 6pm. The bilingual staff can help with questions about the entire province, as well as Montréal.

The city has its own convenient **information bureau** in Old Montréal at 174 rue Notre-Dame (corner of place Jacques-Cartier), near the monument to Lord Nelson (✆ **514/871-1595**). It's open daily early June to early October, 9am to 7pm; mid-October to June, 9am to 5pm.

Among many Montréal websites, these are the most productive starting points: **www.tourisme-montreal.org**, **www.quebec-region.cuq.qc.ca**, **www.quebecweb.com/tourisme**, and **www.tourisme.gouv.qc.ca**.

## CITY LAYOUT

The city borders the **St. Lawrence River.** As far as its citizens are concerned, the river is south, looking toward the United States, although the river runs more nearly north and south at that point rather than east and west. For that reason, it has been observed that Montréal is the only city in the world where the sun rises in the south. Don't fight it though, face the river. That's south. Turn around. That's north. When examining a map of the city, note that such prominent thoroughfares as rue Ste-Catherine and boulevard René-Lévesque are said to run "east" and "west," the dividing line being boulevard St-Laurent, which runs "north" and "south." To ease the confusion, the directions given below conform to local tradition, since they are the ones that will be given by natives.

### Tips Finding an Address

Boulevard St-Laurent is the dividing point between east and west (*est* and *ouest*) in Montréal. There's no equivalent division for north and south (*nord* and *sud*)—the numbers start at the river and climb from there, just as the topography does. For instance, when you're driving along boulevard St-Laurent and passing number 500, that's Vieux-Montréal, near rue Notre-Dame; number 1100 is near boulevard René-Lévesque; number 1500 is near boulevard de Maisonneuve; and number 3400 is near rue Sherbrooke. Even numbers are on the west side of north-south streets and the south side of east-west streets; odd numbers are on the east and north sides, respectively.

In downtown Montréal, the principal streets running east-west include boulevard René-Lévesque, rue Ste-Catherine, boulevard de Maisonneuve, and rue Sherbrooke. Prominent north-south arteries include rue Crescent, rue McGill, rue St-Denis, and boulevard St-Laurent, the line of demarcation between east and west Montréal (most of the downtown area of interest to tourists and businesspeople lies to the west). In Plateau Mont-Royal, northeast of the downtown area, major streets are avenue du Mont-Royal and avenue Laurier. In Vieux-Montréal (Old Montréal), rue St-Jacques, rue Notre-Dame, and rue St-Paul are the major streets, along with rue de la Commune, which hugs the park that borders the St. Lawrence River.

In earlier days, Montréal was split geographically along ethnic lines: Those who spoke English lived predominantly in the city's western regions, and French speakers were concentrated to the east. Things still do sound more French as you walk east with street names and Métro station names changing from Peel and Atwater to St-Laurent and Beaudry. While boulevard St-Laurent is the east-west dividing line for the city's street-numbering system, the "spiritual split" comes farther west, roughly at avenue de Bleury/avenue de Parc.

Good **street plans** are found inside the free tourist guide supplied by Tourisme Montréal and distributed at the information offices described above throughout the city. The Infotouriste Centre also provides a large foldout city map free.

## NEIGHBORHOODS IN BRIEF

**Downtown** This area contributes the most striking elements of the dramatic Montréal skyline and contains the main railroad station, as well as most of the city's luxury and first-class hotels, principal museums, corporate headquarters, and largest department stores. Loosely bounded by rue Sherbrooke to the north, boulevard René-Lévesque to the south, boulevard St-Laurent to the east, and rue Drummond to the west, downtown Montréal incorporates the neighborhood formerly known as "The Golden Square Mile," an Anglophone district once characterized by dozens of mansions erected by the wealthy Scottish and English merchants and industrialists who dominated the city's politics and social life well into this century. Many of those stately homes were torn down when skyscrapers began to rise here after World War II, but some remain, often converted to institutional use. At the northern edge of the downtown area is the urban campus of prestigious McGill University, which retains its Anglophone identity.

**The Underground City** During Montréal's long winters, life slows on the streets of downtown. The people escape down escalators and stairways into *la ville souterraine,* what amounts to a parallel subterranean universe. Down there, in a controlled climate that's eternally spring, it's possible to arrive at the railroad station, check into a hotel, go out for lunch at any of hundreds of fast-food counters and full-service restaurants, see a movie, attend a concert, conduct business, go shopping, and even take a swim—all without unfurling an umbrella or donning an overcoat. This "city" evolved when such downtown developments as Place Ville-Marie, Place Bonaventure, Complexe Desjardins, and Place des Arts put their below-street-level areas to profitable use, leasing space for shops and other purposes. Over time, in fits and starts and with no master plan in place, these spaces became connected with Métro stations and with each other. It became possible to ride long distances and walk the shorter ones, through mazes of corridors, tunnels, and plazas. There are now more than 1,600 shops, 40 banks, 200 restaurants, 10 Métro stations, and about 30 cinemas down there. Without a logical street grid, the area can be confusing to navigate. There are plenty of signs, but make careful note of landmarks at key corners—and expect to get lost anyway

**Rue Crescent** One of Montréal's major dining and nightlife districts lies in the western shadow of the massed phalanxes of downtown skyscrapers. It holds hundreds of restaurants, bars, and clubs of all styles between Sherbrooke and René-Lévesque, centering on rue Crescent and spilling over onto neighboring streets. From east to west, the Anglophone origins of the quarter are evident in the surviving street names: Stanley, Drummond, Crescent, Bishop, and MacKay. The party atmosphere that pervades after dark here never quite fades, and it builds to crescendos as weekends approach, especially in warm weather, when its largely 20- and 30-something denizens spill out into sidewalk cafes and onto balconies.

**Vieux-Montreal** The city was born here in 1642, down by the river at Pointe-à-Callière, and today, especially in summer, activity centers around place Jacques-Cartier, where cafe tables line narrow terraces and where sun worshipers, flower sellers, artists, street performers, and locals and tourists congregate. The area is larger than it might seem at first—bounded on the north by rue St-Antoine, once the "Wall Street" of Montréal and still home to some banks, and on the south by the Vieux-Port (Old Port), a linear park bordering rue de la Commune that gives access to the river and provides breathing room for cyclists, in-line skaters, and picnickers. To the east, Vieux-Montréal is bordered by rue Berri, and to the west by rue McGill. Several small but intriguing museums are housed in historic buildings, and much of the architectural heritage of the district has been preserved. Its restored 18th- and 19th-century structures have been adapted for use as shops, studios, cafes, bars, offices, and apartments.

**St-Denis** Rue St-Denis, from rue Ste-Catherine Est to avenue du Mont-Royal, is the thumping central artery of Francophone Montréal, running from the Latin Quarter downtown and continuing north into the Plateau Mont-Royal district. Thick with cafes, bistros, offbeat shops, and lively night spots, it is to Montréal what boulevard St-Germain is to Paris, and indeed, once you're here, it isn't difficult to imagine yourself transported to the Left Bank. At the southern end of St-Denis, near the concrete campus of the Université du Québec à Montréal (UQAM), the avenue is decidedly student-oriented, with alternative rock cranked up in the inexpensive bars and clubs, and kids in jeans and leather swapping philosophical insights and telephone numbers. Farther north, above Sherbrooke, a raffish quality persists along the facing rows of three- and four-story row houses, but the average age of residents and visitors nudges past 30. Prices are higher, too, and some of the city's better restaurants are located here.

**Plateau Mont-Rpyal** Northeast of the downtown area, this may be the part of the city where Montréalers feel most at home—away from the chattering pace of downtown and the crowds of touristy Vieux-Montréal. Bounded roughly by boulevard St-Joseph to the north, rue Sherbrooke to the south, avenue Papineau to the east, and rue St-Dominique to the west, it has a vibrant ethnicity that fluctuates in tone and direction with each new surge in immigration. Rue St-Denis (see above) runs the length of the district, but boulevard St-Laurent, running parallel to rue St-Denis, has the more polyglot flavor. Known to all as "The Main," it was once the boulevard first encountered by foreigners tumbling off ships at the waterfront. They simply shouldered their belongings and walked north on St-Laurent, peeling off into adjoining streets when they heard familiar tongues, saw people who looked like them, or smelled the drifting aromas of food they once cooked in the old country. New arrivals still come here to start their lives again, and in the usual pattern, most work hard, save their money, and move to the suburbs. Without its people and their diverse interests, St-Laurent would be just another urban eyesore. But these ground-floor windows are filled with glistening golden chickens, collages of shoes and pastries and aluminum cookware, and even the daringly farfetched garments of those designers on the edge of Montréal's active fashion industry.

**Prince-Arthur & Duluth** These two essentially pedestrian streets connect boulevard St-Laurent with St-Denis, 8 blocks to the east. The livelier rue Prince-Arthur is lined with ethnic restaurants, primarily Greek and Portuguese, but with Asian establishments looking to take their place. Mimes, jugglers, and street musicians try to cajole passersby into parting with their spare change. Four blocks north of rue Prince-Arthur, rue Duluth is fairly quiet in the blocks near St-Laurent, but more engaging near St-Denis. The mix of cuisines is much like that on Prince-Arthur. Tourists are evident in greater numbers on Prince-Arthur, many attracted by menus promising bargain lobster dinners for less than C$12 (US$7) during some times of the year.

**Parc du Mont-Royal** Not many cities have a mountain at their core. Okay, it's really just a tall hill, not a true mountain. Still, Montréal is named for it—the "Royal Mountain"—and it's a notable pleasure to drive, walk, or take a horse-drawn calèche to the top for a view of the city, the island, and the St. Lawrence River, especially at dusk. The park was designed by American landscape architect Frederick Law Olmsted, who created New York City's Central Park. On its far slope are two cemeteries—one Anglophone,

one Francophone—silent reminders of the linguistic and cultural division that persists in the city. With its skating ponds, hiking and running trails, and even a short ski run, the park is well used by Montréalers, who refer to it simply and affectionately as "the mountain."

**Chinatown** Just north of Vieux-Montréal, south of boulevard René-Lévesque, and centered on the intersection of rues Clark and de la Gauchetière (pedestrianized here), Montréal's pocket Chinatown is mostly restaurants and a tiny park, with the occasional grocery, laundry, church, and small business. Most signs are in French or English as well as Chinese. Community spirit is strong—it has had to be to resist the bulldozers of commercial proponents of redevelopment—and Chinatown's inhabitants remain faithful to their traditions despite encroaching modernism. Investors from Hong Kong have poured money into the neighborhood, producing signs that its shrinkage has been halted, even reversed. Signaling that optimism, there are new gates to the area on boulevard St-Laurent, guarded by white stone lions.

**The Gay Village** One of North America's largest gay and lesbian enclaves runs east along rue Ste-Catherine from rue St-Hubert to rue Papineau. It's filled with clothing stores, antique shops, bars, dance clubs, and cafes. A rainbow, symbolic of the gay community, marks the Beaudry métro station, in the heart of the neighborhood. Two major annual celebrations are the Diver/Cité in August and the Black & Blue Party in October.

**Ile Ste-Helene** St. Helen's Island in the St. Lawrence River was altered extensively to become the site of Expo '67, Montréal's very successful world's fair. In the 4 years before Expo opened, construction crews reshaped the island and doubled its surface area with landfill, then went on to create beside it an island that hadn't existed before, Ile Notre-Dame. Much of the earth needed to do this was dredged up from the bottom of the St. Lawrence River, and 15 million tons of rock from the excavations for the Métro and the Décarie Expressway were carried in by truck. The city built bridges and 83 pavilions. When Expo closed, the city government preserved the site and a few of the exhibition buildings. Parts were used for Olympic Games events in 1976, and today the island is home to Montréal's popular casino and an amusement park, La Ronde.

## 2 Getting Around

For a city of more than three million inhabitants, Montréal is easy to negotiate. The Métro is fast and efficient, but, of course, walking is the best way to get to know this vigorous multidimensional city.

### BY METRO OR BUS

For speed and economy, nothing beats Montréal's **Métro** system for getting around. Clean, relatively quiet trains whisk passengers through an expanding network of underground tunnels, with 65 stations at present. Single rides cost C$2 (US$1.25), a strip of 6 tickets is C$8.50 (US$5), a 1-day pass permitting unlimited rides for 24 hours is C$7 (US$4.35); oddly, both the 3-day pass and the 1-week pass are C$14 (US$9). Buy tickets at the booth in any station, and then slip one into the slot in the turnstile to enter the system. Take a transfer (*correspondence*) from the machine just inside the turnstiles of every station,

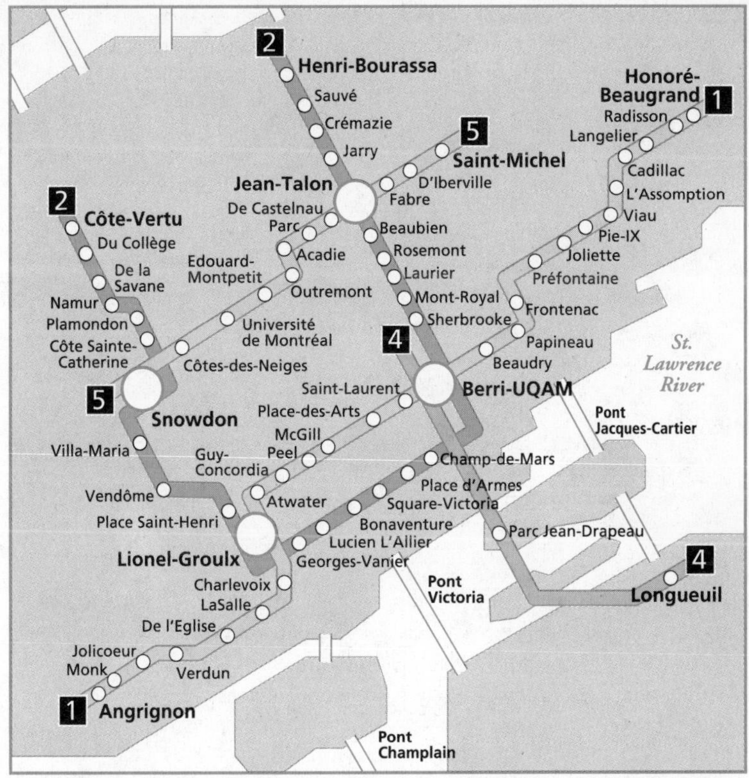


which allows transfers from a train to a bus at any other Métro station for no additional fare. Remember to take the transfer ticket at the station where you first enter the system. (When starting a trip by bus and intending to continue on the Métro, ask the bus driver for a transfer.) Connections from one Métro line to another can be made at the Berri-de Montigny, Jean-Talon, Lionel-Groulx, and Snowdon stations. The orange, green, and yellow Métro lines run from about 5:30am to 1am, and from 5:30am to 11pm on the blue line.

**Buses** cost the same as Métro trains, and Métro tickets are good on buses, too. Exact change is required to pay bus fares in cash. Although they run throughout the city (and give riders the decided advantage of traveling above ground), buses don't run as frequently or as swiftly as the Métro.

For information about the Métro and city buses, contact **STCUM** (**© 514/288-6287;** www.stcum.qc.ca).

## BY TAXI

There are plenty of taxis run by several different companies. Cabs come in a variety of colors and styles, so their principal distinguishing feature is the plastic sign on the roof. At night, the sign is illuminated when the cab is available. Fares aren't too expensive, with an initial charge of C$2.50 (US$1.55) at the flag drop, C$1.20 (US75¢) per kilometer, and C44¢ (US25¢) per minute of waiting. A short ride from one point to another downtown usually costs about C$5 (US$3.10). Tip about 10% to 15%. Members of hotel or restaurant staff can call

# Downtown Montréal

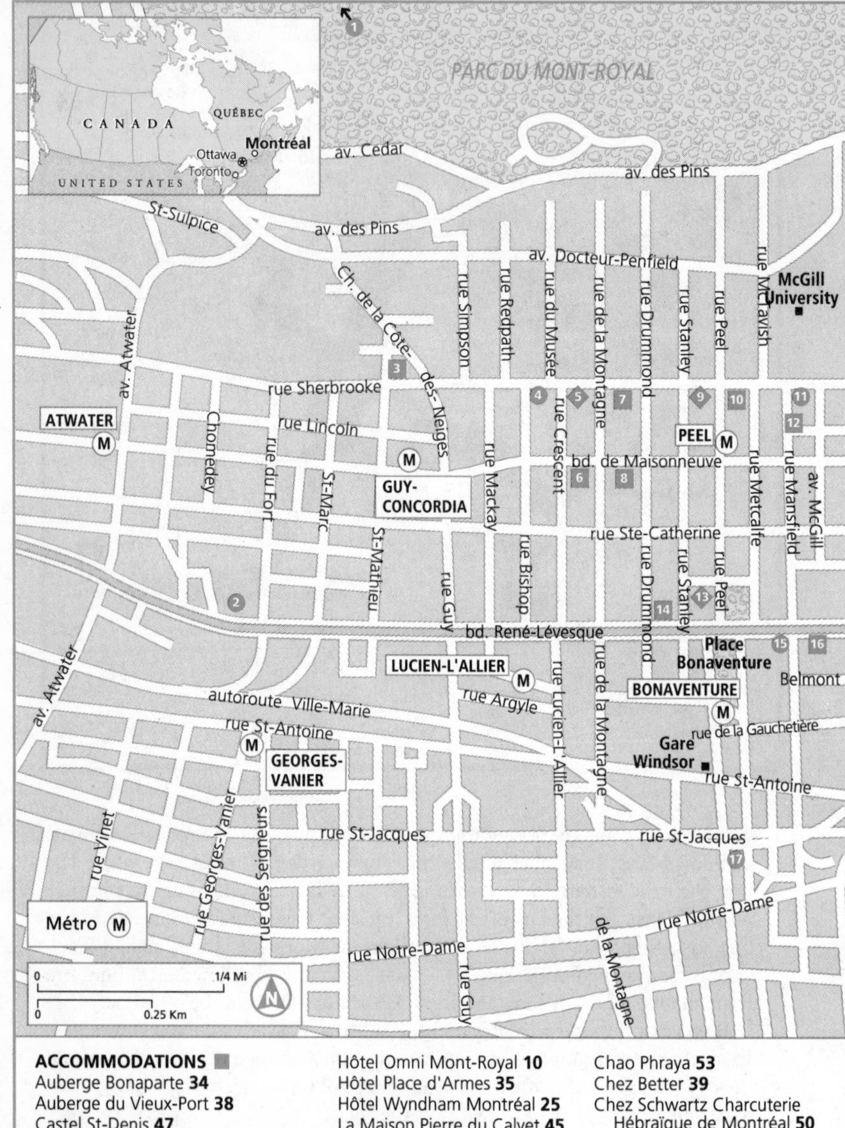


**ACCOMMODATIONS** ■
Auberge Bonaparte **34**
Auberge du Vieux-Port **38**
Castel St-Denis **47**
Château/Hôtel Versailles **3**
Courtyard Marriott Montréal **23**
Delta Centre-Ville **18**
Delta Montréal **22**
Four Points Montréal Centre-Ville **24**
Hilton Montréal Bonaventure **16**
Hôtel de la Montagne **6**
Hôtel Inter-Continental Montréal **26**
Hôtel Le Germain **12**
Hôtel Omni Mont-Royal **10**
Hôtel Place d'Armes **35**
Hôtel Wyndham Montréal **25**
La Maison Pierre du Calvet **45**
La Reine Elisabeth **19**
Le Centre Sheraton **14**
Loews Hôtel Vogue **8**
Ritz-Carlton Montréal **7**

**DINING** ◆
Area **46**
Boris Bistro **28**
Buona Notte **49**
Casa de Matéo **32**
Chao Phraya **53**
Chez Better **39**
Chez Schwartz Charcuterie Hébraïque de Montréal **50**
Katsura **5**
L'Actuel **13**
L'Express **56**
La Chronique **54**
La Maison Kam Fung **27**
Le Beaver Club **19**
Le Taj **9**
Les Ramparts **38**
Maestro S.V.P. **48**

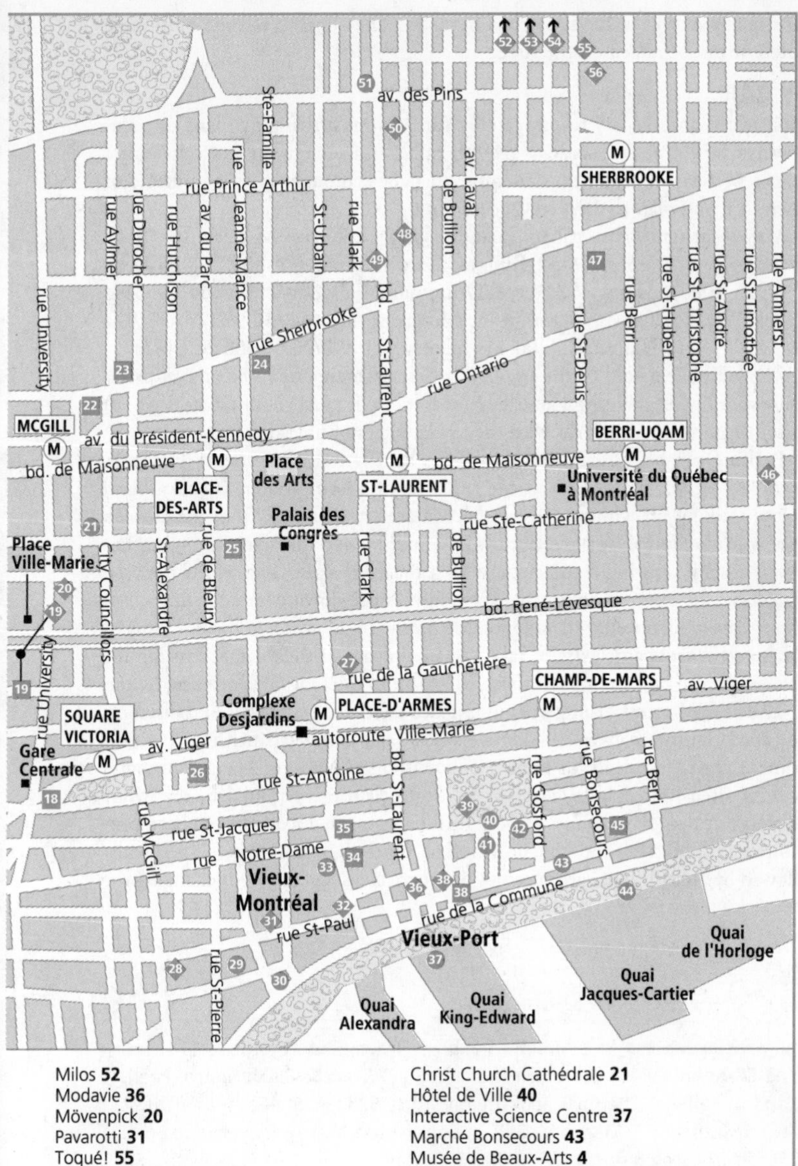


Milos **52**
Modavie **36**
Mövenpick **20**
Pavarotti **31**
Toqué! **55**

**ATTRACTIONS**

Basilique Notre-Dame **33**
Cathédrale-Basilique Maire-Reine-du-Monde **15**
Centre Canadien d'Architecture **2**
Centre d'Histoire de Montréal **29**
Chapelle Notre-Dame-de-Bonsecours/ Musée Marguerite-Bourgeoys **44**
Christ Church Cathédrale **21**
Hôtel de Ville **40**
Interactive Science Centre **37**
Marché Bonsecours **43**
Musée de Beaux-Arts **4**
Musée des Hospitalières de l'Hôtel-Dieu de Montréal **51**
Musée du Château Ramezay **42**
Musée McCord **11**
Oratoire St-Joseph **1**
Place Jacques-Cartier **41**
Planetarium de Montréal **17**
Pointe-à-Callière **30**

cabs, many of which are dispatched by radio. They line up outside most large hotels or can be hailed on the street.

## BY CAR

Montréal is an easy city to navigate by car. Visitors arriving by plane or train, however, will probably want to rely on public transportation and cabs rather than rent-a-car. A rental car can come in handy, though, for trips outside of town or if you plan to drive to Québec City.

Major car-rental companies include **Avis,** 1225 rue Metcalfe (✆ **800/879-2847** or 514/866-7906); **Budget,** Gare Centrale (✆ **800/268-8900** or 514/938-1000); **Hertz,** 1073 rue Drummond (✆ **800/263-0600** or 514/938-1717); **Thrifty,** 1076 rue de la Montagne (✆ **800/367-2277** or 514/845-5954); and **National,** 1200 rue Stanley (✆ **800/227-7368** or 514/878-2771). Gasoline is sold by the Imperial gallon or, more often, the liter, at prices somewhat higher than those in the United States. It costs about C$30 (US$19) to fill the tank of a small car with the lowest grade of unleaded gasoline.

**Parking** can be difficult on downtown's heavily trafficked streets. However, there are plenty of metered spaces, with varying hourly rates. (Look around before walking off without paying. Meters are set well back from the curb so they won't be buried by plowed snow in winter.) Check for signs noting restrictions, usually showing a red circle with a diagonal slash. The words *livraison seulement,* for example, mean delivery only. Most downtown shopping complexes have underground parking lots, as do the big downtown hotels. Some of the hotels don't charge extra to take cars in and out of their garages during the day, which can save money for those who plan to do a lot of sightseeing by car.

The limited-access expressways in Québec are called *autoroutes,* and distances and speed limits are given in kilometers (km) and kilometers per hour (kmph). Some highway signs are in French only, although Montréal's autoroutes and bridges often bear dual-language signs. Seat-belt use is required by law while driving or riding in a car in Québec. Turning right on a red light has been prohibited in Montréal and the province of Québec, except where specifically allowed by an additional green arrow, but there is discussion about changing the law. Ask upon arrival.

## *FAST FACTS:* Montréal

*American Express* The **American Express Travel Service** offices, 1141 bd. de Maisonneuve Ouest near rue Stanley (✆ **514/284-3300;** Métro: Peel), and in La Baie (The Bay) department store, 585 rue Ste-Catherine Ouest (✆ **514/281-4777;** Métro: McGill), are open Monday to Friday 9am to 5pm. For lost or stolen cards, call ✆ **800/268-9824.**

*Area Code* Montréal's telephone area code is **514.** It isn't necessary to dial a country code when calling from the United States.

*Currency Exchange* There are currency-exchange offices near most locations where they're likely to be needed: at the airports, in the train station, in and near Infotouriste on Dorchester Square, and near Notre-Dame Basilica at 86 rue Notre-Dame. The **Bank of America Canada,** 1230 rue Peel (Métro: Peel), also offers foreign-exchange services Monday through Friday 8:30am to 5:30pm and on Saturday 9am to 5pm.

*Doctors & Dentists* The front desks at hotels can contact a doctor quickly. If it's not an emergency, call your country's consulate and ask for a recommendation (see "Embassies & Consulates" below). Consulates don't guarantee or certify local doctors, but they maintain lists of physicians with good reputations. Even if the consulate is closed, a duty officer should be available to help. For dental information, call the hot line at ✆ **514/288-8888** or the 24-hour dental clinic at ✆ **514/342-4444.** In an emergency, dial ✆ **911.**

*Drugstores* Open 24 hours a day, 365 days a year, the branch of **Pharmaprix** at 5122 Côte-des-Neiges, at Chemin Queen Mary (✆ **514/738-8464;** Métro: Côte-des-Neiges), has a fairly convenient location.

*Embassies & Consulates* All embassies are in Ottawa, the national capital. In Montréal, the **American consulate general** is at 1155 rue St-Alexandre (✆ **514/398-9695;** Métro: Square-Victoria). The **United Kingdom consulate general** is at 1000 rue de la Gauchetière Ouest, Suite 4200 (✆ **514/866-5863;** Métro: McGill). Other English-speaking countries (Australia and New Zealand) have their embassies or consulates in Ottawa.

*Emergencies* Dial ✆ **911** for the police, firefighters, or an ambulance.

*Hospitals* Hospitals with emergency rooms are **Hôpital Général de Montréal,** 1650 rue Cedar (✆ **514/937-6011**) and **Hôpital Royal Victoria,** 687 av. des Pins Ouest (✆ **514/842-1231**). **Hôpital de Montréal pour Enfants** (✆ **514/934-4400**) is a children's hospital with a poison center. Other prominent hospitals are **Hôtel-Dieu,** 209 av. des Pins Ouest (✆ **514/843-2611**), and **Hôpital Notre-Dame,** 1560 rue Sherbrooke Est (✆ **514/281-6000**).

*Internet Access* The **CyberGround NetCafé,** 3672 bd. St-Laurent (✆ **514/842-1726;** Métro: Sherbrooke), has 16 computers with big 21-inch monitors for emailing, word processing, or just surfing. Time at the keyboard costs just C$3.50 (US$2.15) per half hour, plus tax. Hours are Monday through Friday 10am to 11pm, Saturday and Sunday 11am to 11pm. Another possibility is **Cybermac Café Internet,** 1425 rue Mackay (✆ **514/287-9100;** Métro: Guy-Concordia).

*Liquor & Wine* All hard liquor and spirits in Québec are sold through official government stores operated by the Société des Alcools du Québec (look for maroon signs with the acronym "SAQ"). Wine and beer can be bought in grocery stores and convenience stores, called *dépanneurs.* The legal drinking age in the province is 18.

*Newspapers & Magazines* Montréal's primary English-language newspaper is the ***Montréal Gazette*** (www.montrealgazette.com). Most large newsstands and those in the larger hotels also carry the ***Wall Street Journal,*** the ***New York Times, USA Today,*** and the ***International Herald Tribune.*** So do the several branches of the **Maison de la Presse Internationale,** two of which are at 550 and 728 rue Ste-Catherine Ouest (Métro: Peel). In Plateau Mont-Royal, a similar operation called **Multimags,** at 3550 av. St-Laurent (Métro: Sherbrooke), sells hundreds of foreign newspapers and magazines. For information about current happenings in Montréal, pick up the Friday or Saturday edition of the ***Montréal Gazette,*** or the free bimonthly booklet called ***Montréal Scope,*** available in some shops and many hotel lobbies.

*Pets* Dogs and cats can be taken into Québec, but the Canadian Customs authorities at the frontier will want to see a rabies vaccination certificate less than 3 years old signed by a licensed veterinarian. If a pet is less than 3 months old and obviously healthy, the certificate isn't likely to be required. Check with U.S. Customs about bringing your pet back into the States. Most hotels in Montréal do not accept pets or require that they be kept in cages, so inquire about their policy before booking a room.

*Police* Dial ✆ **911** for the police. There are three types of officers in Québec: municipal police in Montréal, Québec City, and other towns; Sûreté de Québec officers, comparable to state police or highway patrol in the United States; and RCMP (Royal Canadian Mounted Police), who are similar to the FBI and handle cases involving infraction of federal laws. RCMP officers speak English and French. Other officers are not required to know English, though many do.

*Post Office* The main post office is at 1250 rue University, near Ste-Catherine (✆ **514/395-4909;** Métro: McGill), open Monday to Friday 8am to 6pm. A convenient post office in Old Montréal is at 155 rue St-Jacques, at rue St-François-Xavier (Métro: Square-Victoria). At this writing, it costs C47¢ (US31¢) to send a first-class letter or postcard within Canada, and C60¢ (US40¢) to send a first-class letter or postcard from Canada to the United States. First-class airmail service to other countries costs C$1.05 (US70¢) for the first 20 grams (about ⅔ oz.). These prices are increased by the astonishing imposition of a sales tax, another C8¢ (US5¢) for a first-class stamp!

*Taxes* Most goods and services in Canada are taxed 7% by the federal government. On top of that, the province of Québec has an additional 7.5% tax on goods and services, including those provided by hotels. In Québec, the federal tax appears on the bill as the TPS (elsewhere in Canada, it's called the GST), and the provincial tax is known as the TVQ. Tourists may receive a rebate on both the federal and provincial tax on items they have purchased but not used in Québec, as well as on lodging. To take advantage of this refund, request the necessary forms at duty-free shops and hotels, and submit them, with the original receipts, within a year of the purchase. Contact the Canadian consulate or Québec tourism office for up-to-the-minute information about taxes and rebates.

*Telephones* The telephone system, operated by Bell Canada, closely resembles the American model. All operators speak French and English, and respond in the appropriate language as soon as callers speak to them. Pay phones in Québec require C25¢ (US17¢) for a 3-minute local call. Directory information calls (dial ✆ **411**) are free of charge. Both local and long-distance calls usually cost more from hotels—sometimes a lot more, so check. Directories (*annuaires des téléphones*) come in white pages (residential) and yellow pages (commercial).

*Time* Montréal, Québec City, and the Laurentians are all in the Eastern time zone. Daylight saving time is observed as in the States, moving clocks ahead an hour in the spring and back an hour in the fall.

## 3 Where to Stay

Montréal hoteliers make everyone welcome, at least in part because there are more hotel rooms than can be filled with certainty throughout the year, and still more are opened every year. With the resulting competition for customers and the robust value of the U.S. dollar in relation to its Canadian counterpart, this is the place to splurge.

Québec has a six-level rating system for all establishments offering six or more rooms to travelers. No star is assigned to hotels or inns meeting only basic minimum standards, then one to five stars, the highest rating going to establishments deemed to offer exceptional facilities and services. An ochre-and-brown shield bearing the assigned rating is found near the entrance to most hotels and inns. However, stars in the reviews below are of the zero to three-star Frommer system.

Nearly all hotel staff members, from front-desk personnel to porters, are reassuringly bilingual. The busiest times are July and August, especially during the frequent summer festivals, during annual holiday periods (Canadian or American), and when Montréal and Québec City hold their winter carnivals. At those times, reserve well in advance, especially if special rates or packages are desired. Most other times, expect to find plenty of available rooms.

### DOWNTOWN

#### VERY EXPENSIVE

**Hilton Montréal Bonaventure** ★★ The Hilton's main entrance is at de la Gauchetière and Mansfield, but the lobby is on the 17th floor, for the three stories of the hotel constitute what amounts to a penthouse above the Place Bonaventure Exhibition Hall. It has elevator access to Central Station and the Underground City. From aloft, the hotel looks as if it has a square hole in its top. That's the 3-acre rooftop garden, with strolling pheasants, paddling ducks, and a swimming pool. Many guest rooms have black-and-white sets in the compact bathrooms; views are of the city or the garden. All rooms, public and private, have recently undergone renovation.

1 place Bonaventure (corner of Gauchetière and Mansfield), Montréal, PQ H5A 1E4. ✆ **800/445-8667** or 514/878-2332. Fax 514/878-1442. www.hiltonmontreal.com. 395 units. C$140–C$360 (US$87–US$240) double. Children 18 and under stay free in parents' room. Weekend packages available. AE, DC, MC, V. Self-parking C$15 (US$9); valet C$22 (US$15). Métro: Bonaventure. **Amenities:** 2 restaurants (French, International) with summer dining terraces, 2 bars; year-round heated outdoor pool; health club with sauna; concierge; substantial business center; 24-hour room service; babysitting; laundry service; same-day dry cleaning; nonsmoking room; executive floor. *In room:* A/C, TV w/pay movies, dataport, minibar, coffeemaker, hair dryer, iron.

**Hôtel Omni Mont-Royal** ★★ This used to be the Le Quatre Saisons, and, briefly, the Westin Mont-Royal, but in whatever corporate guise, it's a worthy competitor to the nearby Ritz-Carlton, especially after an ongoing all-floors multi-million-dollar renovation by the new owners. The coolly austere marble

---

**Tips** **Reserving Rooms on the Web**

Useful websites for exploring lodging possibilities and making reservations online are **www.tourism-montreal.org, http://celestia.all-hotels.com,** and **www.destinationquebec.com.**

---

lobby is softened by banks of plants and flowers. Rooms are large, with fresh furnishings, offered in escalating categories of relative luxury, from standard to premium. Buffet breakfasts and lunches are served in the lobby bar, which features piano music in the evenings.

1050 Sherbrooke Ouest (at rue Peel), Montréal, PQ H3A 2R6. ✆ **800/228-3000** or 514/284-1110. Fax 514/845-3025. www.omnihotels.com. 299 units. C$180–C$320 (US$120–US$213) double. Children under 14 stay free in parents' room. Weekend rates and special packages available. AE, DC, MC, V. Self-parking C$14 (US$9); valet C$20 (US$13), plus tax. Métro: Peel. **Amenities:** 2 restaurants (Chinese; International), bar; heated outdoor pool; impressive health club & spa featuring aerobics classes; concierge; children's programs; car and limo rentals; business center; shopping arcade; 24-hour room service; in-room massage; babysitting; laundry service; same-day dry cleaning; nonsmoking rooms; executive floors. *In room:* A/C, TV/VCR w/pay movies, fax, dataport, minibar, coffeemaker, hair dryer, iron, safe.

**Loews Hôtel Vogue** ★★★ The Vogue created quite a stir when it opened in late 1990 after a stunning conversion of an undistinguished office building, when it instantly joined the Ritz-Carlton at the apex of the local luxury-hotel pantheon. Confidence resonates from every member of its staff, and luxury breathes from its lobby to its well-appointed guest rooms. Although some guests find it chilly in look and tone, that's difficult to reconcile with the feather pillows and duvets that dress the oversize beds, the fresh flowers and cherry wood furniture, and the marble bathrooms with Jacuzzis with every unit—double-size in suites. Extra room amenities include bathroom TVs and plush robes. The lobby bar has piano music weekends and an outdoor terrace in summer. All of this suits the international clientele to a tee.

1425 rue de la Montagne (between bd. de Maisonneuve and rue Ste-Catherine), Montréal, PQ H3G 1Z3. ✆ **800/465-6654** or 514/285-5555. Fax 514/849-8903. www.loewshotels.com. 142 units. C$199–C$745 (US$123–US$462) double. Children under 16 stay free in parents' room. Lower weekend rates. AE, DC, MC, V. Valet parking C$15 (US$9). Métro: Peel. **Amenities:** Restaurant (International), bar; small exercise room; concierge; business center; 24-hour room service; babysitting; coin-operated washers and dryers; same-day dry cleaning. *In room:* A/C, TV with pay movies, fax, dataport, minibar, hair dryer, safe.

**The Ritz-Carlton Montréal** ★★★ In 1912, the Ritz-Carlton opened its doors to the carriage trade, and that clientele has remained faithful. Over the years, their Pierce-Arrows gave way to Rolls-Royces, and a few of these (or at least a couple of Mercedes) are always parked in readiness near the front door. A needed $10-million renovation completed in 1999 has restored the gloss the hotel long held, and a skid in service standards has been arrested. Bathrooms are equipped with robes and speakers carrying TV sound. High-speed Internet connections are provided in every room. An umbrella is stashed in the closet. The famed Café de Paris is favored for its high tea, weekend brunches, and weekday power breakfasts, but serves all meals, on the terrace in summer, next to the famous duck pond. There's piano music in the Ritz Bar and Le Grand Prix, with dancing nightly in the latter.

1228 rue Sherbrooke Ouest (at rue Drummond), Montréal, PQ H3G 1H6. ✆ **800/363-0366** or 514/842-4212. Fax 514/842-3383. www.ritzcarlton.com. 229 units. C$225–C$625 (US$140–US$388) double; C$395–C$675 (US$245–US$419) suite. Children under 14 stay free in parents' room. Packages available. AE, DC, MC, V. Self-parking or valet C$24 (US$15), with in/out privileges. Pets accepted (deposit required). Métro: Peel. **Amenities:** 2 restaurants (International), bar; modest fitness room; concierge; business center; 24-hour room service; in-room massage; babysitting; laundry service; same-day dry cleaning; executive floors. *In room:* A/C, TV w/pay movies, fax on request, dataport, minibar, hair dryer, iron, safe.

## EXPENSIVE

**Delta Centre-Ville** ★★ Within walking distance of Gare Centrale, downtown offices, and Vieux-Montréal, this new Delta, formerly a Radisson, serves both businesspeople and families well, with facilities to keep everyone happy. Twenty-eight floors up is the city's only revolving restaurant, fun for a drink at sunset even if you eat elsewhere. One floor down, the once-public bar has become a private lounge to complement the executive Signature Club. There is a direct connection with the Underground City and the Métro.

777 rue University (at rue St-Antoine), Montréal, PQ H3C 3Z7. ✆ **800/268-1133** or 514/879-1370. Fax 514/879-1761. www.deltahotels.com. 711 units. C$195–C$235 (US$121–US$146) double. AE, DC, DISC, MC, V. Indoor parking. Métro: Square Victoria. **Amenities:** 2 restaurants (International), bar; heated indoor pool; well-equipped health club with sauna; children's center; concierge; business center; limited room service; massage; babysitting; laundry service; same-day dry cleaning; executive floors. *In room:* A/C, TV w/pay movies, dataport, minibar, coffeemaker, hair dryer, iron.

**Delta Montréal** ★★ *Kids* This carefully maintained unit of the Canadian chain is targeted to the business traveler, but its supervised children's crafts and games center and outdoor pool make it clear that families are welcome too. Rooms in the 23-story tower have angular dimensions, escaping the boxiness of many contemporary hotels; most have small balconies.

475 avenue du President-Kennedy (at rue City Councillors), Montréal, PQ H3A 1J7. ✆ **877/286-1986** or 514/286-1986. Fax 514/284-4342. www.deltamontreal.com. 453 units. C$119–C$340 (US$74–US$211) double; from C$365 (US$226) suite. Children under 18 stay free in parents' room. Weekend packages available. AE, DC, DISC, MC, V. Parking C$13 (US$8). Métro: Place des Arts or McGill. **Amenities:** 2 restaurants (International and Bistro), bar; outdoor pool (open July and Aug); concierge; superior health club & spa with aerobics instruction, indoor lap pool, 2 squash courts; limited room service; laundry service; same-day dry cleaning; courtesy car; expansive business center with translation service; executive floors. *In room:* A/C, TV w/pay movies, dataport, minibar, coffeemaker, hair dryer.

**Hôtel Le Germain** ★★★ This latest undertaking by the owner of an equally desirable boutique hotel in Québec City brings a shot of panache to the downtown lodging scene. A small office tower was converted, resulting in a magical mix of Asian minimalism with all the Western comforts an international executive might anticipate . . . and not. Discover three polished apples sitting in designated depressions on shelves opposite the elevators. Help yourself. In the capacious rooms, find a vase with an orchid, CD players, big wicker chairs with fat cushions, and beds that cure insomnia. Self-serve breakfasts are set out on the mezzanine, with perfect croissants, a machine that makes excellent cafe au lait, and choices of newspapers in French and English. The bar serves a limited menu from 4:30 to 10pm, featuring Asian soups, salads, sandwiches, and a couple of light main courses.

2050 rue Mansfield (west end of av. President Kennedy), Montréal, PQ H3A 1Y9. ✆ **514/849-2050.** Fax 514/849-1437. www.hotelboutique.com. 101 units. C$210–C$345 (US$130–US$214). Rates include breakfast. AE, DC, MC, V. Parking C$15 (US$9). Métro: Peel. **Amenities:** Bar/cafe; exercise room; limited room service; babysitting; laundry service; same-day dry cleaning. *In room:* A/C, TV, dataport, minibar, coffeemaker, hair dryer, iron.

**Hôtel Wyndham Montréal** ★ *Kids* Its owners and names have changed with some frequency, but not much else has. The hotel is still an integral part of the striking Complexe Desjardins, across the street from the Place des Arts. Ask for one of the rooms that have enjoyed the recent $25 million in renovations. Glass-enclosed elevators (fun for kids) glide up to bedrooms and down to the lower levels of the complex, which contains a shopping plaza and a pool cantilevered over garden terraces. Vieux-Montréal, downtown, and the ethnic neighborhoods along The Main are within easy walking distance. The hotel is often the official headquarters of Montréal's annual jazz festival. Le Bar has piano music nightly. Small pets are accepted.

1255 rue Jeanne-Mance, Montréal, PQ H5B 1E5. ✆ **800/361-8234** or 514/285-1450. Fax 514/285-1243. www.wyndham.com. 600 units. C$126–C$189 (US$78–US$117) double; from C$350 (US$217) suite. Children under 18 stay free in parents' room. Packages available. AE, DC, MC, V. Self-parking C$14 (US$9); valet C$19 (US$12). Métro: Place des Arts and Place d'Arms. **Amenities:** Restaurant (International); bar; heated indoor pool; health club with whirlpool and sauna; concierge; business center; shopping arcade; limited room service; in-room massage; babysitting; laundry service; same-day dry cleaning; executive floors. *In room:* A/C, TV/VCR w/pay movies, fax, dataport, minibar, coffeemaker, hair dryer, iron, safe.

**Le Centre Sheraton** ★★ This Sheraton rep rises near Gare Centrale (Central Station), a few steps off Dorchester Square, and within a short walk of the rue Crescent dining and nightlife district. A high glass wall transforms the lobby atrium into a greenhouse big enough to shelter royal palms. The staff is efficient, and the rooms are comfortably corporate in style. That figures, since earnest people in suits make up most of the clientele. They gravitate to the separate Towers section, which bestows upon its guests complimentary breakfast and a private lounge with great views and free evening hors d'oeuvres. Half of the rooms have minibars, and all provide robes. Jazz is performed evenings in the Impromptu Bar. Pets are accepted at no extra fee, but must be caged in their owner's absence. Unfortunately, previously reasonable room rates have been raised to the levels of U.S. Sheratons.

1201 bd. René-Lévesque Ouest (between rue Drummond and rue Stanley), Montréal, PQ H3B 2L7. ✆ **800/325-3535** or 514/878-2000. Fax 514/878-3958. www.sheraton.com/lecentre. 825 units. C$300–C$390 (US$186–US$242) double; from C$450 (US$279) suite. Children under 17 stay free. Weekend rates available. AE, DC, DISC, MC, V. Self-parking C$12 (US$7) with in/out privileges; valet C$15 (US$9). Métro: Bonaventure or Peel. **Amenities:** Restaurant (International), 2 bars; indoor pool; health club & spa; concierge (in Towers); airport limo; complete business center; shopping arcade; 24-hour room service; babysitting; laundry service; same-day dry cleaning; nonsmoking rooms; executive floors. *In room:* A/C, TV/VCR w/pay movies, coffeemaker, iron, hair dryer.

**Le Reine Elizabeth/The Queen Elizabeth** ★★ Montréal's largest hotel has lent its august presence to the city since 1958. Its 21 floors sit atop VIA Rail's Gare Centrale, with place Ville-Marie, place Bonaventure, and the Métro all accessible by underground arcades. That desirable location makes it a frequent choice for heads of state and touring celebrities, even though other hotels in town offer higher standards of personalized pampering. The Entree Gold 19th floor, has a private concierge and check-in and a lounge serving complimentary breakfasts and cocktail-hour canapés to go with the honor bar. Less exalted rooms on floors 4 through 17 are entirely satisfactory, with most of the expected comforts and gadgets, in price ranges to satisfy most budgets. Le Beaver Club (see "Where to Dine," below) features a combo for dancing on Saturday nights.

900 bd. René-Lévesque Ouest (at rue Mansfield), Montréal, PQ H3B 4A5. ✆ **800/441-1414** or 514/861-3511. Fax 514/954-2258. www.cphotels.ca. 1,050 units. C$199–C$375 (US$123–US$233) double; concierge-level rates about C$80 (US$50) higher; from C$390 (US$242) suite. Children 18 and under stay free in parents' room. Various discounts, weekend, and excursion packages available. AE, DC, DISC, MC, V. Parking C$15 (US$9). Métro: Bonaventure. **Amenities:** 3 restaurants (International), 3 bars; heated indoor pool; large health club & spa with Jacuzzi, steam room, and instructors; concierge; large business center; shopping arcade; salon; 24-hour room service; in-room massage; babysitting; laundry service; same-day dry cleaning; executive floors. *In room:* A/C, TV w/pay movies, dataport, minibar, coffeemaker, hair dryer, iron.

## MODERATE

**Château Versailles/Hôtel Versailles** ★★ This two-part facility underwent a remarkable transformation from popular but dowdy inn to a member in full standing of the growing local ranks of snappy boutique hotels. The Château portion of the property began as a European-style pension in 1958, expanding into adjacent pre-World War I town houses. Those have been given the full decorator treatment, with voluptuous colors, fine modern furnishings with faint Deco tinges and some Second Empire touches. Only one deficiency remains—the lack of an elevator to deal with the three floors. Some years ago, a modern tower was acquired across the street and made into a motel-ish hotel. Guest rooms in both sections are of good size. Breakfast, afternoon tea, and cocktails are served in a small dining room with a fireplace in the Château, and the Tower has a full-service restaurant. Price and location (near Sherbrooke shopping and the Museum of Fine Arts) are competitive, so reserve well in advance.

1659 (north side) and 1808 (south side) rue Sherbrooke Ouest (at St-Mathieu), Montréal, PQ H3H 1E5. ✆ **888/933-8111** or 514/933-8111. Fax 514/933-6967. www.versailleshotels.com. 65 units (town houses), 107 units (hotel). C$129–C$254 (US$80–US$157) double. Children under 17 stay free in parents' room. Special packages Nov–May. AE, DC, MC, V. Valet parking C$15 (US$9). Métro: Guy. **Amenities:** Restaurant (French), lounge; limited room service; laundry service; same-day dry cleaning. *In room:* A/C, TV, dataport, minibar, coffeemaker, hair dryer, safe.

**Courtyard Marriott Montréal** *Kids* Formerly La Citadelle, this fulfills the Marriott chain's promise of providing lodging for business travelers at moderate cost. But with its pool and laundromat, the Courtyard also appeals to families on tight budgets. While the mid-rise slab can hardly be described as grand, needed renovations have perked it up. The restaurant sets out a buffet breakfast (not included in room rate) each morning.

410 rue Sherbrooke Ouest (at av. du Parc), Montréal, PQ H3A 1B3. ✆ **800/449-6654** or 514/844-8855. Fax 514/844-0912. www.courtyard.ca. 181 units. C$109–C$299 (US$68–US$185). AE, DC, MC, V. Valet parking C$14.95 (US$9). Métro: Place des Arts. **Amenities:** Restaurant (International), bar; heated indoor pool; compact health club with sauna and steam room; concierge; limited room service; coin-op washers and dryers; dry cleaning. *In room:* A/C, TV w/pay movies, dataport, coffeemaker, hair dryer, iron.

**Four Points Montréal Centre-Ville** Representing a new brand of the Starwood hotel colossus (which also owns the Westin and Sheraton chains), this mid-price business hotel accomplishes its mission without breathing hard. That is, it provides roomy suites for business-people (and families) on longer stays, with fax machines, copiers, and computers on call—all at reasonable prices. Rooms have Nintendo and the newspaper of your choice is made available.

475 Sherbrooke Ouest (at rue Aylmer), Montréal, PQ H3A 2L9. ✆ **800/842-3961** or 514/842-3961. Fax 514/842-0945. www.fourpoints.com. 195 units. C$155–C$250 (US$96–US$155) double; from C$255 (US$158) suite. Children under 17 stay free in parents' room. Packages available. AE, DC, MC, V. Parking C$12 (US$7). Métro: McGill. **Amenities:** Restaurant (International), bar; modest exercise room; limited room service; laundry service; same-day dry cleaning. *In room:* A/C, TV w/pay movies, dataport, fridge, coffeemaker, hair dryer, iron.

**Hôtel de la Montagne** ★★ *Value* Two white lions stand sentinel at the front door, with a doorman in a pith helmet. The fauna fixation continues in a crowded lobby that incorporates a pair of 6-foot carved elephants, two gold-colored crocodiles, and a nude female figure with stained-glass butterfly wings sitting atop a splashing fountain. Clearly we are not in Kansas. Light meals are available beside the pool on the roof, 20 stories up, with dancing under the stars. Off the lobby, a cabaret lounge featuring a piano player and jazz duos (Mon–Sat) leads into Thursday's, a bar/restaurant with a disco and a terrace on rue Crescent. After all that, the relatively serene bedrooms seem downright bland. With these inducements, a stay here is a genuine bargain, especially in contrast to the expensive Hotel Vogue across the street.

1430 rue de la Montagne (north of Ste-Catherine), Montréal, PQ H3G 1Z5. ✆ **800/361-6262** or 514/288-5656. Fax 514/288-9658. www.intermatch.qc.ca/hoteldelamontagne. 136 units. C$178–C$250 (US$110–US$155) double. Children under 16 stay free in parents' room. AE, MC, V. Parking C$14 (US$9). Métro: Peel. **Amenities:** 3 restaurants, 2 bars; heated outdoor pool; concierge; limited room service; laundry service; same-day dry cleaning. *In room:* A/C, TV/VCR w/pay movies, minibar, dataport, coffeemaker, hair dryer.

### INEXPENSIVE

**Castel St-Denis** *Value* In the bohemian Latin Quarter, the Castel St-Denis is one of the more desirable budget choices. It's a little south of Sherbrooke, among the cafes of the lower reaches of the street, and 2 long blocks from the Terminus Voyageur. Most of the rooms are fairly quiet, and all are tidy and simply decorated, if hardly chic—flowered coverlets and wood dadoes. The bilingual owner is a good source for guidance about nearby restaurants and attractions.

2099 rue St-Denis, Montréal, PQ H2X 3K8. ✆ **514/842-9719.** Fax 514/843-8492. www.castelsaintdenis.qc.ca. 18 units. C$50–$70 (US$31–US$43) double. Extra person C$10 (US$6). MC, V. No parking available. Métro: Berri-155UQAM or Sherbrooke. *In room:* A/C, TV, no phone.

## VIEUX-MONTREAL (OLD MONTREAL)

### VERY EXPENSIVE

**Hôtel Inter-Continental Montréal** ★★★ Only a few minutes' walk from Notre-Dame Basilica and the restaurants and nightspots of Vieux-Montréal, this striking luxury hotel opened in 1991 and was instantly accorded inclusion among the top properties in town. Its tower houses the sleek reception area and guest rooms, while the restored 1888 Nordheimer building contains a bar-bistro. Rooms are quiet and well lit, with photographs and lithographs by local artists on the walls. The turret suites are fun, with their round bedrooms and wraparound windows. All rooms have robes and two or three telephones. The lobby-level piano bar has a light menu and music nightly. Small pets are accepted.

360 rue St-Antoine Ouest (at rue de Bleury), Montréal, PQ H2Y 3X4. ✆ **800/361-3600** or 514/987-9900. Fax 514/847-8550. www.montreal.interconti.com. 357 units. C$159–C$380 (US$99–US$236) double; from C$380 (US$236) suite. Packages available. AE, DC, DISC, MC, V. Valet parking C$23 ($14). Métro: Square Victoria. **Amenities:** 2 restaurants, 2 bars; small enclosed rooftop lap pool; health club with sauna, steam rooms; concierge; substantial business center; 24-hour room service; massage; laundry service; same-day dry cleaning; executive floors. *In room:* A/C, TV w/pay movies, dataport, minibar, coffeemaker, hair dryer, iron, safe.

### EXPENSIVE

**Auberge du Vieux-Port** ★★ Housed in an 1882 building facing the port, this romantic luxury inn has an accomplished cellar restaurant, Les Remparts (see "Where to Dine," below), polished hardwood floors, exposed brick walls, massive beams, and the original windows shape the hideaway bedrooms. Fifteen rooms face the waterfront and 22 have whirlpool baths. CD players are standard (with a selection at the main desk). High-speed Internet access is planned. The three suite-like "lofts" have kitchenettes. Drinks and sandwiches are served on the rooftop terrace, which has unobstructed views of the Old Port, a particular treat when fireworks are scheduled over the river. Pets in cages are accepted.

97 rue de la Commune Est (near rue St-Gabriel), Montréal, PQ H2Y 1J1. ✆ **888/660-7678** or 514/876-0081. Fax 514/876-8923. www.aubergeduvieuxport.com. 27 units. C$140–C$325 (US$87–US$202) double. Extra person C$20 (US$12). Rates include full breakfast. AE, DC, DISC, MC, V. Valet parking C$14 (US$8). Métro: Place d'Armes. **Amenities:** Restaurant (French); concierge; limited room service; in-room massage; babysitting; laundry service; dry cleaning; nonsmoking rooms. *In room:* A/C, TV, dataport, minibar, hair dryer, iron, safe.

**Hôtel Place d'Armes** ★★★ First of a clutch of boutique hotels to open in the last two years in Vieux Montréal, this highly desirable property is housed in a cunningly converted office building dating from the late 19th century. The elaborate architectural details of that era are in abundant evidence, especially in the ground floor lobby. An afternoon wine-and-cheese party is held around the fireplace and bar in back. Room extras include robes, down comforters, high-speed Internet access, and CD players (a collection of disks is available at the front desk). Few wants are left to chance—there's even a rooftop sun deck. Meals can be taken in the basement restaurant, under separate management. There are equal or better choices within a few blocks.

701 Côte de la Place d'Armes, Montréal, PQ H2Y 2X6. ✆ **888/450-1887** or 514/842-1887. Fax 514/842-6469. www.hotelplacedarmes.com. 48 units. C$160–C$295 (US$99–US$183). Extra person C$25 (US$16). Rates include breakfast. AE, DC, DISC, MC, V. Valet parking C$17 (US$11). Métro: Place d'Armes. **Amenities:** Restaurant (French/California), bar; small but efficient exercise room; concierge; secretarial services; limited room service; in-room massage; babysitting; laundry service; same-day dry cleaning. *In room:* A/C, TV, dataport, minibar, hair dryer, iron, safe.

**La Maison Pierre du Calvet** ★ When Ben Franklin was here in 1775 during his attempt to enlist Canada in the revolt against the British, the house was already 50 years old. After a stint as a theme restaurant, the same owners made it into an atmospheric inn that bids to transport guests to an elegant *manoir* beside the Loire. The beamed public areas are furnished with copious antiques, not reproductions, including carpets on the ancient stone floors, leather sofas, gilt-framed portraits, a marquetry-topped reception desk, ship models, and a voluptuously furnished dining room that refers to no specific era but suggests a 19th-century ducal hunting lodge. Bedrooms are no less opulent, some with fireplaces and heavily carved four-poster canopied beds. TV sets would only spoil the ambience. A 50% deposit is required.

405 rue Bonsecours (at rue St-Paul), Montréal, PQ H27 3C3. ✆ **866/544-1725** or 514/282-1725. Fax 514/282-0456. www.pierreducalvet.ca. 9 units. C$195–C$265 (US$121–US$164); C$450 (US$279) suite. Extra person C$35 (US$22). Rates include full breakfast. AE, MC, V. Parking C$10 (US$6). Métro: Place d'Armes or Champ-de-Mars. **Amenities:** Restaurant (French). *In room:* A/C.

### MODERATE

**Auberge Bonaparte** ★★ The restaurant of the same name on the ground floor has long been one of Old Montréal's favorites. Romantic and faded in a Left Bank way, it has now undergone massive renovation. While they were at it, the owners undertook to transform the overhead floors into this modish urban inn. Even the smallest rooms are surprisingly spacious, and they have a variety of combinations of furniture—queen, king, and double beds—that are useful for families. Of the eight units on each floor, four have whirlpool baths with separate showers. Spring for the handsome suite on the top floor and get superb views of Notre-Dame, cloistered gardens, and cobblestone streets.

447 rue St-François-Xavier (north of St-Paul), Montréal, PQ H2Y 2T1. ✆ **514/844-1448.** Fax 514/844-0272. www.bonaparte.com. 31 units. C$145–C$195 (US$90–US$121) double; C$325 (US$202) suite. Extra person C$15 (US$10). Rates include full breakfast. AE, DC, MC, V. Parking C$12.75 (US$8). Métro: Place d'Armes or Square Victoria. **Amenities:** Restaurant (French); concierge; children's programs; 24-hour room service; in-room massage; babysitting; laundry service; same-day dry cleaning. *In room:* A/C, TV/VCR, dataport, hair dryer, iron.

## 4 Where to Dine

Montréal brims with more than 4,000 eating places. Until only a decade ago, they were overwhelmingly French. A few *temples d'cuisine* delivered haute standards of gastronomy, numerous accomplished bistros served up humbler ingredients in less grand settings, and folksy places featured the hearty fare of the colonial era, which employed the ingredients available in New France—game, maple syrup, and root vegetables. Yes, some places offered Asian and Mediterranean cooking, but they didn't enjoy the same favor they did in other cities of North America. Québec was French, and that was that.

While waves of food crazes washed over the continent in the 1980s, introducing their citizens to re-discovered ethnic, regional, and fusion cuisines,

**Tips** **Take Advantage of the Table d'Hôte**

The city's *table d'hôte* (fixed-price) meals are eye-openers. Entire two- to four-course meals, often with a beverage, can be had for little more than the price of an a la carte main course alone. Even the best restaurants offer them; so, *table d'hôte* represent a considerable savings and the chance to sample some excellent restaurants without breaking the bank.

Montréalers were resolute. Now that's changed, dramatically. The recession of the 1990s forced many restaurateurs to reexamine their operations. Immigration continued to grow, and along with it, the introduction of still more foreign cooking styles. Montréalers began sampling the exotic edibles emerging in new storefront eateries all around them—Thai, Moroccan, Vietnamese, Portuguese, Turkish, Mexican, Indian, Creole, Szechuan, and Japanese. Innovation and intermingling of styles, ingredients, and techniques were inevitable.

Deciding where to dine among the many resulting and tempting choices can be bewildering. The establishments recommended below include some of the most popular and honored restaurants in town, but getting to any of them involves passing many other worthy possibilities, for numbers of good restaurants often cluster in concentrated neighborhoods or along particular streets, such as **rues Crescent, St-Denis,** or **St-Laurent.** Nearly all have menus posted outside, prompting the local tradition of stopping every few yards for a little mouthwatering reading and comparison shopping before deciding on a place for dinner.

It's a good idea to make reservations for any of the city's top restaurants. Unlike larger American and European cities, however, a few hours or a day in advance is usually sufficient. Dress codes are all but nonexistent, except in a handful of luxury restaurants, but Montréalers are a fashionable lot, and manage to look smart even in casual clothes.

Québecers are no longer the heaviest smokers in Canada, the distinction having shifted to Nova Scotia's puffers. Even in still-addicted Montréal, nonsmoking areas in restaurants are multiplying at a rate that couldn't have been predicted a couple of years ago, in anticipation of a governmental decree that all restaurants must soon provide smoke-free sections.

## DOWNTOWN

### VERY EXPENSIVE

**Le Beaver Club** ★ FRENCH The restaurant takes its name from an organization of socially prominent explorers and trappers established in 1785. Their wilderness adventures are depicted in a stained-glass mural and carved wood panels that reveal the L-shaped room's 1950s origins. They are scheduled for updating, but still undergird the clubby ambience of the room. With widely spaced tables allowing a measure of privacy, it has long been a magnet for the city's power brokers (although, with about 120 seats to fill, it's hardly exclusive). Lunch is the time for the gentlest prices. The menu changes twice a year, always including the trademark roast beef, but expanding from the former meat-and-potatoes regimen to lighter, more fetchingly presented fish and fowl. The lobster carpaccio and morel soup with foie gras and truffles are typical. On Saturday evenings, a trio plays for dancing.

In Fairmont Le Reine Elizabeth Hotel, 900 René-Lévesque Ouest. ✆ **514/954-2214.** Reservations recommended. Jacket required for men. Main courses C$29–C$36 (US$18–US$22); table d'hôte lunch (Mon–Fri) C$18.50–C$23 (US$11–US$14). AE, DISC, MC, V. Mon noon–3pm; Tues–Fri noon–3pm and 6–10:30pm; Sat 6–11pm (late June–Aug, Tues–Sat 6–11pm only). Métro: Bonaventure.

## EXPENSIVE

**Katsura** JAPANESE A tuxedoed maître d' greets patrons at the door and leads them to one of the large convivial tables in the front room, to the smaller areas in back, or to the three-sided marble sushi bar in the middle (which serves as a refuge for those who arrive without a reservation). Whatever you choose, waitresses in kimonos move quickly and quietly to serve and, if asked, to explain the extensive menu. Katsura has been around long enough to claim credit for introducing sushi to Montréal. Although no longer a novelty, sushi and sashimi are still prepared with close attention to craft by the three chefs working behind the bar; part of the pleasure of dining here is watching those practitioners at work. It's a common gesture, by the way, to give them a small gratuity separate from that added to the bill. A meal here can be relatively economical, but sample a lot of their creations and the bill shoots into a much costlier category.

2170 rue de la Montagne (between bd. de Maisonneuve and rue Sherbrooke). ✆ **514/849-1172.** Reservations recommended. Main courses C$11–C$27 (US$7–US$17); table d'hôte lunch C$8.75–C$15 (US$5–US$9), dinner C$27–C$31 (US$17–US$19). AE, DC, MC, V. Mon–Fri 11:30am–2:30pm and 5:30–10pm (Fri until 11pm); Sat 5:30–11pm; Sun 5:30–9:30pm. Métro: Peel or Guy-Concordia.

## MODERATE

**L'Actuel** BELGIAN Dine one flight up, where the most desirable of a sea of tables overlook the square. Mussels are the house specialty, in more than a dozen variations, curried to Provençal, for C$17 to C$24 (US$11–US$16), and in uniformly big portions. They are brought to the table in the cast-iron pot in which they were cooked. Double-fried potatoes are the delectable accompaniment, and complimentary second helpings are customary. A sturdy muscadet goes well with mussels. If mollusks aren't to your liking, other options include veal cutlets and tournedos in 18 different sauces and preparations; there's also a spicy steak tartare. Although the establishment is very popular, there's almost always an available table, even on a Saturday night.

1194 rue Peel (on Square Dorchester). ✆ **514/866-1537.** Main courses C$14.50–C$35.50 (US$9–US$22); table d'hôte lunch and dinner C$13.50–$18 (US$8–US$11). AE, MC, V. Mon–Tue 11:45am–10pm; Wed 11:45am–10:30pm; Thurs–Fri 11:45am–11pm; Sat 5–11pm. Métro: Bonaventure or Peel.

**Le Taj** ★ NORTHERN INDIAN A large temple sculpture occupies pride of place in this dramatic setting of cream and apricot. In the glassed cubicle in the corner, a chef works diligently over a pair of tandoor ovens. Seasonings of the dishes he sends forth tend more toward the tangy than the incendiary, but say you want your food spicy and you'll get it. (And watch out for the innocent-looking green coriander sauce.) Whatever the degree of heat, dishes are perfumed with selections of turmeric, saffron, ginger, sumin, mango powder, and garam masala. For a rare treat, order the marinated lamb chops roasted in the tandoor; they arrive at the table sizzling and nested on braised vegetables. Vegetarians have a choice of eight dishes, the chickpea-based channa masala among the most complex. Main courses are huge, arriving in a boggling array of bowls, saucers, cups, and dishes, all with naan, the pillowy flat bread, and basmati rice. Evenings are quiet, and lunchtimes are busy but not hectic.

2077 rue Stanley (near rue Sherbrooke). ✆ **514/845-9015.** Main courses C$9.95–C$19.95 (US$6–US$12); luncheon buffet C$9 (US$6). AE, DC, MC, V. Sun–Fri 11:30am–2:30pm; daily 5–10:30pm. Métro: Peel.

## INEXPENSIVE

**La Maison Kam Fung** SZECHUAN/CANTONESE Weekends are the big days, when suburban Chinese families return to indulge in their comfort food. Although regular meals are served in the evening, the morning to mid-afternoon hours are reserved for dim sum. That's the time. Go to the second floor, obtain a ticket from the young woman at the podium, and wait. Once summoned to a table, be alert to the carts being trundled out of the kitchen. They are stacked with covered baskets and pots, most of which contain dumplings of one kind or another, such as balls of curried shrimp or glistening envelopes of pork nubbins or scallops, and, for the adventuresome, steamed chicken feet and squid. Order until sated. Resist the desire to gather up the first five items that appear. Much more is on the way.

1008 rue Clark (near Gauchetièrie Est). ✆ **514/878-2888.** Main courses C$7.25–C$14 (US$4.50–US$9). AE, DC, MC, V. Daily 7am–3pm and 5–10:30pm. Métro: Place d'Armes.

**Mövenpick** *Kids* INTERNATIONAL The central gimmick of this outpost of the Swiss chain is its theme-park simulation of a European market. Placed around the 9,000m² (30,000 sq. ft.) space are more than a dozen food stations where diners line up for pizzas, crepes, sushi, coffee, pastas, omelettes, waffles, salads, rôtisserie birds, grilled meats, baked goods, and seafood, including freshly opened oysters. Faux grapevines, fake flowers, and an ersatz tree are meant to evoke a Mediterranean setting, for this is a playland cafeteria, and the food, much of it prepared to order, ranges from satisfactory to pretty good. Upon entrance, you are handed a "passport," which the servers stamp with the prices of the items ordered. Pay up when you leave. Eat a course at a time or load a tray with a complete meal and take it to the nearby tables. Children are welcome in the designated romper room. The bistro has table service, and two bars serve wine, beer, and spirits. Almost everything is available for take-out.

Rue University at rue Cathcart. ✆ **514/861-8181.** Most items under C$15 (US$9). MC, V. Daily 7:30am–2am. Métro: McGill or Bonaventure

## VIEUX-MONTREAL

### EXPENSIVE

**Les Remparts** ★★ CONTEMPORARY FRENCH A cellar seems an unlikely setting for what has recently emerged as one of the city's most accomplished kitchens. The under-30 chef started here as an assistant and took over a few months later. He works whenever possible with products of the region, re-drawing his menu with the seasons to take full advantage of what's available. One of Canada's most desirable fish, halibut, is slow-roasted and presented with tapenade on an artichoke purée, while fork-tender venison comes with a scatter of wild mushrooms, gooseberry sauce and braised salsify. Lunch is a particular bargain, with a top price of C$18.30 (US$11.35), but the chef's true showmanship blossoms at dinnertime, not in tortured presentations, but with greater sophistication.

93 rue de la Commune Est (near rue St-Gabriel). ✆ **514/392-1649.** Reservations recommended on weekends. Table d'hôte lunch C$14–C$17 (US$9–US$11), main courses, lunch C$9.75–C$16.50 (US$6–US$10); dinner C$29.95–C$36.95 (US$19–US$23). Mon–Fri noon–2:30 and 6–10pm, Sat–Sun 6–10pm. Métro: Place d'Armes.

**Modavie** ★ MEDITERRANEAN A highly visible location no doubt helps keep this wine bar/resto filled, but the management leaves little to chance. Arrayed around the handsome center bar are walls of shelves stacked with bottles of wine, single-malt scotches, and fine cigars. There are free bar snacks during the 4 to 7pm happy hours from Monday to Friday. Live jazz takes over Friday and Saturday nights. Candle flames flicker in river breezes welcomed by front and side windows flung wide on summer nights. Nor does the food disappoint, either in preparation or portion. Lamb is their proclaimed specialty, in one version propping four double chops over a composition of sweet peppers, cauliflower and broccoli rabe. This is one ingratiating place.

1 rue St-Paul Ouest (cor rue St-Laurent). ✆ **514/287-9582.** Reservations recommended on weekends. Table d'hôte lunch C$14 (US$9), dinner C$20–C$31 (US$12–US$19). Main courses, dinner C$19–C$29 (US$12–US$18). Daily 11:30am–3pm and 6–11pm. Métro: Place d'Armes.

## MODERATE

**Boris Bistro** ★ FRENCH BISTRO "Boris" is the owner's dog, depicted in the restaurant logo as a canine sophisticate in a turtleneck. Putting aside questions of Gallic relationships with their pets, this popular eatery takes full advantage of the excitement evident in the far western end of Vieux-Montréal, opposite the new Cité Multimédia. Despite the minimalist surroundings of concrete floors and beams, the staff and patrons transform it into a lighthearted space, aided in great part by very reasonable prices and such bistro classics as bouillabaise, beef tartar, and mussels du jour. Don't pass up the super frites with mayo. If it's good weather, head straight for the courtyard and tables that seat 160 under market umbrellas.

465 av. McGill (near rue des Récollets). ✆ **514/848-9575.** Reservations suggested weekend nights. Main courses at lunch and dinner C$12–C$14 (US$7–US$9). AE, MC, V. Daily 11:30am–11:30pm (may close Sun and Mon nights in winter). Closed three weeks at Christmas. Metro: Square Victoria.

**Casa de Matéo** MEXICAN Stepping into Casa de Matéo feels like wandering into a party in progress, especially on Friday and Saturday evenings, when mariachis come to kick the fiesta up a notch. Get in the mood with a birdbath-sized frozen margarita. The cheerful staff from Mexico and other Latin American countries lends authenticity. With these generous servings, appetizers can be skipped—but that would mean missing the plato Mexicano, a sampler of all the starters. Because the plato Mexicano is a meal in itself, some diners may want to stop there—but that would mean missing the pescado Veracruzano, whole red snapper quickly marinated and fried and served with a nest of crisp vegetables. The usual burritos and enchiladas are easy to forget.

440 rue St-François-Xavier (near rue St-Paul). ✆ **514/844-7448.** Reservations suggested weekend nights. Main courses C$12.95–C$17.50 (US$8–US$11). AE, DC, MC, V. Mon–Fri 11:30am–10pm; Sat–Sun 11am–11pm. Métro: Place d'Armes.

**Pavarotti** CONTEMPORARY ITALIAN Dean Martin sings about a moon hitting your eye like a big pizza pie and basso profundos commit arias. This 125-year-old stone house has a thrown-together quality, with brick walls, old photos of the port, ship models, hanging bundles of herbs, and a candle chandelier that would do justice to the lair of the Phantom of the Opera—all of which is so dimly lit that the menu is hard to make out. That's okay. Take a blind poke; you probably won't be disappointed. There isn't anything too odd, and servings are ample. The bruschetta is typical, not one or two pieces of toast, but a ring of six, with a do-it-yourself heap of chopped tomato, onion, garlic, and olives in the middle. After that, plates of feathery pasta, made right there, become evening specials, like the one that came with a tumble of clams, mussels, and shrimp. The soupy house risotto supports your choice of seafood or vegetables. By mid-evening, the place is a friendly babble, orchestrated by the always-present owner.

408 rue St-François-Xavier (north of rue St-Paul). ✆ **514/844-9656.** Reservations recommended on weekends. Main courses C$11.50–C$16.25 (US$7–US$10), table d'hôte C$16.95–C$17.95 (US$11–US$11). AE, DC, MC, V. Mon 11am–3pm; Tues–Thurs 11am–9pm; Fri 11am–10pm; Sat 5–10pm. Métro: Square Victoria.

### INEXPENSIVE

**Chez Better** *Value* GERMAN They aren't making a half-hearted boast with the name of this place. This and the other five outposts of this local chain are named for the founder, a Canadian born in Germany. Presumably he grew homesick for tastes of his native land and opened his first restaurant in this 1811 building near the top of Place Jacques Cartier. Think multiple variations of chipolata, kasseler, sauerkraut, and 100 brands of beer—that gives the general outline of the menu. Forget grease and oozing globules of fat, though, for these are lighthearted sausages, brightly seasoned with herbs, curry, hot pepper, and even truffle shavings. A special lunchtime sampler of bratwurst, cevapcici, and diable comes with fries and kraut and costs just C$7.50 (US$5)—a terrific deal. While sausage plates are the stars, there are also mixed grills, chicken schnitzels, fondues, salads, and mussels nine ways. Two other branches tourists are likely to encounter are at 4382 bd. St-Laurent (© **514/845-4554**) and 1430 rue Stanley (© **514/848-9859**).

160 rue Notre-Dame (near place Jacques-Cartier). © **514/861-2617.** Main courses C$8.50–C$14.50 (US$5–US$9); table d'hôte lunch C$7.95–C$11.95 (US$5–US$7), dinner C$13.75–C$15.75 (US$9–US$10). AE, DC, MC, V. Daily 11am–10pm. Métro: Champ-de-Mars.

## PLATEAU MONT-ROYAL

### VERY EXPENSIVE

**Milos** ★★★ GREEK/SEAFOOD Avenue du Parc used to be lined with Hellenic fish houses. That culinary population has thinned out, but the top dog remains and still holds to a standard higher than its rivals are ever likely to achieve. Inside, it is what a taverna at a picturesque Aegean fishing port would look like if it had the necessary drachmas—white plaster walls, bleached wooden floors, Greek vases, blue tiles, and refrigerated cases for the finny main events. The freshest available fish, flown in from wherever they are at peak, are the reason Milos prevails. Show the slightest interest and you'll be taken on a tour of the iced and clear-eyed denizens offered for your pleasure—Icelandic char, Nova Scotia lobsters, Florida pompano, Mediterranean loup-de-mer. Pick your very own meal or leave it to the chefs. They'll even cook a veal chop if you absolutely insist. With drinks comes grilled bread, the waiter pouring a dish of fragrant olive oil and snipping fresh oregano into it. The excellent Greek salad is the usual first course, but oh-so-lightly battered soft-shelled crabs are terrific, if in season. Expect to part with about C$150 (US$93) for two plus tax, wine, and tip—it's worth it.

5357 av. du Parc (between rue St-Viateur and av. Fairmont). © **514/272-3522.** Reservations essential on weekends. Main courses C$28.95–C$38 (US$18–US$24). AE, MC, V. Mon–Fri noon–3pm and 5–11pm; Sat 5–11pm; Sun 5–10pm. Métro: Outremont, then a 12-block walk.

**Toqué!** ★★★ FRENCH CONTEMPORARY A meal here is virtually obligatory for anyone who admires superb food dazzlingly presented. Post-nouvelle might be an apt description of the edibles, for while presentations are eye-openers, the portions are quite sufficient and the singular combinations of ingredients are intensely flavorful. Asian influences are evident, but they are still working within the dictates of the contemporary French kitchen. Duck, veal, quail, and venison are unfailingly memorable, while salmon and Arctic char are often the most desirable fish. If you choose one of the tasting menus, each of the four or five courses is accompanied by wines selected to complement specific course preparations. The restaurant fills up later than most, with prosperous-looking suits and women who sparkle at throat and wrist, so while there is no stated dress code, you'll want to look your best. Service is efficient, helpful, and not a whit self-important. Allow 2 hours for dinner and call at least a day ahead for reservations. They are open for lunch from Monday to Friday the two weeks before Christmas.

3842 rue St-Denis (at rue Roy). ✆ **514/499-2084.** Reservations essential. Menu dégustation C$70 or C$80 (US$43 or US$50), C$97 or C$107 (US$60 or US$66) with wine. Main courses C$28–C$34 (US$17–US$21). AE, DC, MC, V. Daily 5:30–11pm. Closed Dec 24–Jan 6. Métro: Sherbrooke.

## EXPENSIVE

**Area** ★ FUSION The chef seems far too young to know as much as he so obviously does about the world's cuisines. But he deftly manipulates techniques and ingredients found around the Pacific and Mediterranean rims, in precociously assured concoctions that challenge taste assumptions. In none of this does he neglect such Canadian staples as duck and venison. Convention is disregarded, though, as with the "brick" of salmon brushed with saffron oil and accompanied by Israeli couscous, and raviolis filled with ricotta and married with duck confit, mushrooms, asparagus, and oh, yes, white truffle oil. Servings are attractively put together, and, it must be said, wastefully large. The cheese list is commendable for its focus on Québec products; choose Pied-de-vent and Ciel de Charlevoix to get an idea of the possibilities.

1429 rue Amherst (north of rue Ste-Catherine). ✆ **514/890-6691.** Reservations recommended. Main courses C$18–C$24 (US$11–US$15). Table d'hôte C$35 or C$45 (US$22 or US$28). AE, MC, V. Tues–Fri 11:30am–2 and 6–11pm, Sat–Sun 6–11pm. Métro: Beaudry.

**La Chronique** ★★ *Finds* CREATIVE FRENCH Montréal's top chefs are recommending this modest-looking storefront resto near Outremont, and the word is spreading. Conceding that the resulting buzz might spoil the place, this is too good to skip. For one thing, smoking is entirely excluded. For another, the chef allows you to discover how remarkable traditional dishes can be when in the hands of a master. Presentations are so impeccable you hate to disturb them, tastes so eye-rolling you want to scrape up every last smear of food. The menu isn't hidebound, with Mediterranean and Southwestern touches appearing. Ingredients like foie gras and caviar elevate the place from its once humbler level. That relates to prices, too, with one tasting menu reaching C$112 (US$69) per person, with wine. Tantalizing desserts look as if they might take flight. Menus are only in French, but the cordial waiters speak English.

99 rue Laurier Ouest (at rue St-Urbain). ✆ **514/271-4770.** Reservations recommended. Main courses C$23–C$29 (US$14–US$18); table d'hôte lunch C$17–C$25 (US$11–US$16), dinner C$52 or C$72 (US$32 or US$45). AE, DC, MC, V. Tues–Fri 11:30am–2:30pm and 6–10pm; Sat 6–10pm. Closed first 2 weeks in July. Metro: Laurier.

## MODERATE

**Buona Notte** ★ ITALIAN CONTEMPORARY This could be in Robert DeNiro's SoHo. A principal component of the decor is a collection of plates painted by celebrity diners, among them Ben Kingsley, Danny DeVito, and Nicolas Cage. Funk and hip-hop thump over the stereo, and the dishy waitresses look ready to depart on the next fashion shoot. They are in black, as are most of their customers, all with cellphones at the ready. Although the food takes second place to preening, it's surprisingly worthwhile. Pastas prevail, while the kitchen exhibits less reliance on meat than most. Service is stretched thin at dinner, and the noise level cranks up after 7pm. The active bar in back stays open until 2am Sunday to Wednesday and until 3am Thursday to Saturday.

If the velvet rope is up at Buona Notte, there are several other similar ventures on the half block from there to Sherbrooke, including **Mediterraneo** (3500 bd. St-Laurent, ✆ **514/844-0027**), **Primadonna** (3479 bd. St-Laurent, ✆ **514/282-6644**), and **Globe** (3455 bd. St-Laurent, ✆ **514/284-3823**).

3518 bd. St-Laurent (near rue Sherbrooke). ✆ **514/848-0644.** Reservations recommended. Pizzas and risottos C$7.50–C$17.25 (US$4.65–US$11), main courses C$21–C$28 (US$13–US$17); table d'hôte C$31 (US$19). AE, DC, MC, V. Mon–Wed 11:30am–midnight; Thurs–Sat 11:30am–1am; Sun 5pm–midnight. Métro: St-Laurent.

**Chao Phraya** ★ THAI As the current contender for best Thai in town, this ups the panache ante a few notches above most of its rivals. It brightens its corner on increasingly fashionable Laurier Avenue with white table linen and sprays of orchids on each table. Dumplings in peanut sauce were a deservedly popular appetizer, as was the main event of mixed seafood, composed of squid, scallops, shrimp, crab claws, mussels, and chunks of red snapper. This food is tangy, at the least, and menu items are given one to three hot pepper symbols grading hotness. Two printed peppers are about right for most people. A cooling cucumber salad helps, and you'll want a side of sticky rice, too. There are several wines by the glass—try the semi-dry Alsatians.

50 av. Laurier Ouest (1 block west of boul. St-Laurent). ✆ **514/272-5339.** Reservations recommended. Main courses C$12.95–C$16.95 (US$8–US$11). AE, DC, MC, V. Tues–Sun 5:30–10pm. Métro: Laurier.

**L'Express** ★★ FRENCH BISTRO No obvious sign announces the presence of this restaurant, only its name discreetly spelled out in white tiles in the sidewalk. There's no need to call attention to itself, since tout Montréal knows exactly where it is. While there are no table d'hôte menus, the food is fairly priced for such an eternally busy place and costs the same at midnight as at noon. Substantial starters that include bone marrow with coarse salt and a potted chicken paté may suggest one of the lighter main courses, such as the ravioli maison, round pasta pockets flavored, more than stuffed, with a mixture of beef, pork, and veal. Larger appetites might step up to full-flavored duck breast with chewy chanterelles in a sauce with the scent of deep woods. Or simply stop by for a croque monsieur or a bagel with smoked salmon and cream cheese. Although reservations are usually necessary for tables, single diners can often find a seat at the zinc-topped bar, where meals are also served. Breakfast is served from 8 to 11:30am.

3927 rue St-Denis (at rue Roy). ✆ **514/845-5333.** Reservations recommended. Main courses C$10.95–C$18.25 (US$7–US$11). AE, DC, MC, V. Mon–Fri 8am–3pm, Sat 10am–3am, Sun 10am–2am. Métro: Sherbrooke.

**Maestro S.V.P.** SEAFOOD You could eat well for a week on the 2 blocks of The Main north of Sherbrooke. Make this storefront bistro one of those stops. The name of the place and the musical instruments mounted on the walls have no particular relevance to the menu, unless you count the jazz trio the owner brings in Sundays at 6:30pm. Those are only a few of the attractions likely to get your attention; others include the several types of oysters always on hand and all-you-can-eat mussels offered every Monday. Blackboards list the recommended wines of the day, in glasses costing C$6.50 to C$11.50 (US$4.35–US$8). The $55 meal mentioned below is an extravagant medley of lobster stuffed with clams and mussels, shrimps in a mirin orange sauce, scallops, and king crab. Service is casual, but alert, and there is valet parking Thursday to Saturday.

3615 St-Laurent (near rue Sherbrooke). ✆ **514/842-6447.** Reservations recommended. Main courses C$16–C$55 (US$10–US$34). Table d'hôte lunch C$9–C$19 (US$6–US$12), dinner C$23 (US$14). AE, DC, MC, V. Mon–Wed 11am–11pm; Thurs–Fri 11am–midnight; Sat 4pm–midnight; Sun 4–11pm. Métro: Sherbrooke.

### INEXPENSIVE

**Chez Schwartz Charcuterie Hébraïque de Montréal** ★ DELI French-first laws turned this old-line delicatessen into this linguistic mouthful, but it's still known simply as Schwartz's to its many ardent fans. They are convinced it is the only place on the continent to indulge in the guilty treat of smoked meat. Housed in a long, narrow space, it has a lunch counter and a collection of simple tables and chairs crammed impossibly close to each other. Any empty seat is up for grabs. Few mind the inconvenience or proximity to strangers, for they are soon delivered plates described either as small (meaning large) or large (meaning humongous) heaped with slices of the trademark delicacy, along with piles of rye bread. Most people also order sides of french fries and one or two mammoth garlicky pickles. There is a handful of alternative edibles, but tofu and leafy green vegetables aren't included. Expect a wait. Schwartz's has no liquor license, but it does have a nonsmoking section.

3895 bd. St-Laurent (north of rue Prince-Arthur). ✆ **514/842-4813.** Most items C$4–C$12 (US$2.50–US$7). No credit cards. Mon–Thurs 9am–12:30am; Fri 9am–1:30am; Sat 9am–2:30am; Sun 9am–12:30am. Métro: St-Laurent.

### PICKNICKING

When planning a picnic or a meal to eat back in your hotel room, consider a stop at the revitalized **Faubourg Ste-Catherine,** on rue Ste-Catherine Ouest between Guy and St-Mathieu. It's a market and fast-food complex that sells takeout foods like sushi, enchiladas, and sandwiches, as well as breads and fresh fruits. You'll find similar bounty at **Les Halles de la Gare,** an accumulation of food stalls, delis, and cafes beneath the Queen Elizabeth hotel and adjacent to the main concourse of the railroad station. Among them is a SAQ wine store. Downtown, the **Marché Mövenpick,** at the corners of Cathcart and University and Mansfield and René Lévésque, sells just about everything for takeout, including sushi, panini, fruits, baked goods, cheeses, pizzas, and grills.

Better still, make the short excursion by Métro (the Lionel-Grouix stop) to **Marché Atwater,** the public market at 3025 St-Ambroise. The long shed is bordered by stalls of gleaming produce and flowers, the two-story center section given to wine purveyors, food counters, bakeries, and cheese stores. The best representatives of the last two are **La Fromagerie** (✆ **514/932-4653**), whose highly knowledgeable attendants know every detail of production of the 450 to 550 different North American and European cheeses on offer, and the **Boulangerie Première Moison** (✆ **514/932-0328**), which fills its space with the tantalizing aromas of baskets of breads and cases of pastries. From either location, it isn't far by taxi to Parc du Mont-Royal, a wonderful place to enjoy a picnic.

In Vieux-Montréal, pick up supplies at the new food market in the historic **Marché Bonsecours** (✆ **514/872-4560**) on rue de la Commune and take them to the linear park of the Vieux-Port, only steps away.

## 5 Seeing the Sights

A superb Métro system, a fairly logical street grid, wide boulevards, and the vehicle-free Underground City all aid in the swift, largely uncomplicated movement of people from place to place. The difficulty lies in making choices. After all, the possibilities include hiking up Mont-Royal, cycling beside the Lachine Canal, taking in the artworks and ephemera of over 20 museums and as many historic buildings, attending a Canadiens hockey match or an Expos baseball game. With riverboat rides, the fascinating Biodôme, a sprawling amusement park, Montréal also assures kids of a good time.

### *Value* The Montréal Museums Pass

The Montréal Museums Pass allows entry to 25 of the city's museums and attractions and is available year-round. Good for 2 out of 3 consecutive days, the pass costs C$20 (US$12). It is sold at all participating museums, the Infotouriste Centre on Square Dorchester, and at many Montréal hotels. For further information, call ✆ **877/266-5687** from outside Montréal or 514/873-2015 within the metropolitan area. When planning visits, you might want to note in the listings below which museums have restaurants, a few of which are pretty good. Most museums are closed Monday.

## DOWNTOWN

**Cathédrale-Basilique Marie-Reine-du-Monde** No one who has seen both will confuse Montréal's Mary Queen of the World Cathedral with St. Peter's Basilica in Rome, but a scaled-down homage was the intention. Bishop Ignace Bourget was moved to act in the middle of the last century, after the first Catholic cathedral burned to the ground in 1852. Construction lasted from 1875 to 1894, its start delayed by the Bishop's desire to place it not in Francophone east Montréal but in the heart of the Protestant Anglophone west. The resulting structure covers less than a quarter of the area of its Roman inspiration. Most impressive is the 77m (252-ft.) high dome, about half the size of the original. A local touch is provided by the statues standing on the roofline, representing patron saints of the region. The interior is less rewarding visually than the outside.

Bd. René-Lévesque (at rue Mansfield). ✆ **514/866-1661.** Free admission; donations accepted. Mon–Fri 7am–7:30pm; Sat 7:30am–8:30pm; Sun 8:30am–7:30pm. Métro: Bonaventure.

**Centre Canadien d'Architecture** The handsome home of the C.C.A. occupies a city block. Doubling as both a study center and a museum, it mounts changing exhibits devoted to the art of architecture and its history, including architects' sketchbooks, elevation drawings, and photography. The collection is international in scope and encompasses architecture, urban planning, and landscape design. Texts are in French and English. Opened in 1989, the museum has received rave notices from scholars, critics, and serious architecture buffs. It is only fair to note that the average visitor is likely to find it less enthralling. The sculpture garden across the Ville-Marie autoroute is part of the CCA, designed by artist/architect Melvin Charney.

1920 rue Baile (at rue du Fort). ✆ **514/939-7026.** www.cca.qc.ca. Admission C$6 (US$3.75) adults, C$4 (US$2.50) seniors, C$3 (US$1.85) students, free for children under 12. June–Sept Tues–Sun 11am–6pm (until 9pm Thurs); rest of year Wed–Fri 11am–6pm (until 8pm Thurs), Sat–Sun 11am–5pm. Guided tours available on request. Métro: Atwater or Guy-Concordia.

**Christ Church Cathedral** This Anglican cathedral, reflected in the post-modernist Maison des Coopérants office tower, stands in glorious Gothic contrast to the city's glassy downtown skyscrapers. Sometimes called the "floating cathedral" because of the many tiers of malls and corridors beneath it, the building was completed in 1859. It is host to concerts throughout the year, notably from mid-January through August on Wednesdays at 12:30pm.

635 rue Ste-Catherine (at rue University). ✆ **514/843-6577** (office) or 514/288-6421 (recorded information). Free admission; donations accepted. Daily 8am–6pm; services Sun 8am, 10am, and 4pm. Métro: McGill.

**Musée d'Art Contemporain de Montréal** ★ The only repository in Canada devoted exclusively to contemporary art, the museum moved into this new facility at the Place des Arts in 1992. "Contemporary" is defined here as art produced since 1939. About 60% of the permanent collection of some 6,000 works is composed of the work of Québecois artists, but it also includes examples of such international artists as Jean Dubuffet, Max Ernst, Jean Arp, Larry Poons, and Antoni Tàpies, as well as photographers Robert Mapplethorpe, Ansel Adams, and Montréaler Michel Campeau. A few larger pieces are seen on the ground floor, but most are one flight up, with temporary exhibitions to the left and the permanent collection on the right. Expect to see installations both small and room-filling; video displays; evocations of Pop, Op, and abstract expressionism; and accumulations of objects simply piled on the floor. The works often arouse strong opinions signifying a museum that is doing something right. The restaurant, La Rotonde, has a summer dining terrace.

185 rue Ste-Catherine Ouest. ✆ **514/847-6226.** www.macm.org. Admission C$6 (US$3.75) adults, C$4 (US$2. 50) seniors, C$3 (US$1.85) students, free for children under 12, C$12 (US$7) families; free to all Wed 6–9pm. Tues–Sun 11am–6pm (until 9pm Wed). Métro: Place des Arts.

**Musée des Beaux-Arts** ★★★ The Museum of Fine Arts, Montréal's most prominent museum, was opened in 1912 in Canada's first building designed specifically for the visual arts. The original Neo-Classical pavilion is on the north side of Sherbrooke. Years ago, museum administrators recognized that the collection, now totaling more than 30,000 works, had outgrown the building. That problem was solved in late 1991 with the completion of the stunning new annex, the Jean-Noël Desmarais Pavilion, directly across the street. Designed by Montréal architect Moshe Safdie, the new pavilion tripled exhibition space, adding two sub-street-level floors and underground galleries that connect the new building with the old.

For the best look at the results, enter the new annex, take the elevator to the top, and work your way down. The permanent collection is largely devoted to international contemporary art and Canadian art since 1960, and to European paintings, sculpture, and decorative arts from the Middle Ages to the 19th century. On the upper floors are many of the gems of the collection. The fourth floor is introduced by a chess set by Dalí in which the pawns are thumbs. More seriously are paintings by 16th to 19th Century artists Hogarth, Tintoretto, Reynolds, Brueghel, El Greco, Ribera, and the portraitist George Romney. (For a bonus, be sure to walk to the sculpture court for a splendid panoramic view of the city.) On subsequent levels, view examples—representative, if not world-class—of more recent artists, including Renoir, Monet, Picasso, Matisse, Cézanne, Léger, and Rodin. On the subterranean floors are works by 20th-century modernists, primarily those who rose to prominence after World War II, including the abstract expressionists and those who followed.

From the lowest level of the new pavilion, follow the under-street corridor past primitive artworks from Oceana and Africa into the old building, with its pre-Columbian ceramics, Inuit carvings, and Amerindian crafts. Across the street are a street-level store—with an impressive selection of quality books, games, and folk art—and a cafe that has received good reviews.

1379–1380 rue Sherbrooke Ouest (at rue Crescent). ✆ **514/285-2000.** www.mmfa.qc.ca. Permanent collection free (but donations are welcome); temporary exhibitions C$12 (US$7) adults, C$6 (US$3.75) seniors and students, C$3 (US$1.85) children 12 and under. AE, MC, V. Half-price Wed 5:30–9pm. Tues and Thurs–Sun 11am–6pm; Wed 11am–9pm. Métro: Peel or Guy-Corcordia.

**Musée McCord d'Histoire Canadienne** Associated with McGill University, the McCord Museum of Canadian History showcases the eclectic—and not infrequently eccentric—collections of scores of 19th- and 20th-century benefactors. Expect to view furniture, clothing, china, silver, paintings, photographs, and folk art that reveal rural and urban life as it was lived by English-speaking immigrants of the past three centuries. The original 1905 building was rebuilt and a new wing added in 1992. The First Nations room displays portions of the museum's extensive collection of ethnology and archaeology, including jewelry and meticulous beadwork. Exhibits are intelligently mounted, with texts in English and French, although the upstairs rooms are of narrower interest. There's a popular cafe near the front entrance.

690 rue Sherbrooke Ouest (at rue Victoria). ✆ **514/398-7100.** www.mccord-museum.qc.ca. Admission C$7 (US$4.35) adults, C$5 (US$3.10) seniors, C$4 (US$2.50) students, C$1.50 (US95¢) ages 7–11, free for children under 7, C$14 (US$9) families. Free admission Sat 10am–noon. Tues–Fri 10am–6pm; Sat–Sun 10am–5pm (summer daily from 9am). Métro: McGill. Bus: 24.

## VIEUX-MONTREAL (OLD MONTREAL) ★★

For further information about this quarter, log on to **www.vieux.montreal.qc.ca.**

**Basilique Notre-Dame** ★★★ Big enough to hold 4,000 worshipers, and breathtaking in the richness of its interior furnishings, this magnificent structure was designed in 1824 by an Irish-American Protestant architect, James O'Donnell. So profoundly was he moved by the experience, he converted to Catholicism after the basilica was completed. The impact is understandable. None of the hundreds of churches on the island of Montréal approaches this interior in its wealth of exquisite detail, most of it carved from rare woods delicately gilded and painted. O'Donnell, one of the proponents of the Gothic Revival style in the early decades of the 19th century, is the only person honored by burial in the crypt.

The main altar was carved from linden wood, the work of Victor Bourgeau. Behind it is the Chapelle Sacré-Coeur (Sacred Heart Chapel), much of it destroyed by a deranged arsonist in 1978 but rebuilt in 1982. It is such a popular place for weddings that couples have to book it 18 months in advance. The altar was cast in bronze by Charles Daudelin of Montréal, with 32 panels representing birth, life, and death. A 10-bell carillon resides in the east tower, while the west tower contains a single massive bell. Nicknamed "Le Gros Bourdon," it weighs more than 12 tons and has a low, resonant rumble that vibrates right up through the feet. It is tolled only on special occasions.

Although you can go through on your own, there are guided tours in English starting at 8am and leaving at various times through the day, but usually on the hour and half hour during tourist season.

110 rue Notre-Dame Ouest (on place d'Armes). ✆ **514/842-2925.** Basilica C$2 (US$1.25) adults, C$1 (US65¢) students, free for praying. MC, V. June 24–Labour Day daily 7am–8pm; rest of the year daily 7am–6pm; tours all year. Métro: Place d'Armes.

**Centre d'Histoire de Montréal** Built in 1903 as Montréal's Central Fire Station, the brick and sandstone building is now the Montréal History Center, which traces the development of the city from the Amerindians to the European settlers who arrived in 1642 to the present day. Throughout its 14 rooms, carefully conceived presentations chart the contributions of the city fathers and mothers and subsequent generations. The development of the railroad, Métro, and related infrastructure are recalled, as is that of domestic and public architecture, in imaginative exhibits, videos, and slide shows. On the second floor is memorabilia from the early 20th century.

335 place d'Youville (at St-Pierre). ✆ 514/872-3207. www.ville.montreal.qc.ca/jard_mus/chm. Admission C$4.50 (US$2.80) adults; C$3 (US$1.85) seniors, students, and children 6–17; free for children under 6. May–Sept daily 10am–5pm; Sept–Dec 30 and Jan 15–Apr 30 Tues–Sun 10am–5pm. Métro: Square-Victoria.

**Chapelle Notre-Dame-de-Bon-Secours/Musée Marguerite-Bourgeoys** Just east of Marché Bonsecours, Notre Dame de Bonsecours Chapel is called the Sailors' Church because of the special attachment to it felt by fishermen and other mariners. That devotion is manifest in the several ship models hanging inside. A revered 16th-century 15cm-high (6-inch-high) carving of the Madonna is once again on display. The first church building, the project of an energetic teacher named Marguerite Bourgeoys, was built in 1678. She arrived with de Maisonneuve to undertake the education of the children of Montréal in the latter half of the 17th century. Later, she and several sister teachers founded a nuns' order called the Congregation of Notre-Dame, Canada's first. Bourgeoys was recognized as a saint in 1982. There's an excellent view of the harbor and the old quarter from the church's tower. The present church, which dates from 1773, incorporates a new museum and a restored 18th-century crypt, an archaeological site that has unearthed ruins and materials from the earliest days of the colony.

400 rue St-Paul Est (at the foot of rue Bonsecours). ✆ **514/282-8670.** Chapel free; museum C$5 (US$3.10) adults, C$3 (US$1.85) seniors and students, C$2 (US$1.25) ages 6–12, free for children under 6. May–Oct Tues–Sun 10am–5pm; Nov–Jan 15 and Mar 15–Apr 30 Tues–Sun 11am–3:30pm. Closed Jan 15–Mar 15. Métro: Champ-de-Mars.

**Hôtel de Ville** City Hall, finished in 1878, is of French Second Empire design, which makes it look as though it was imported stone by stone from the mother country. Balconies, turrets, and mansard roofs detail the exterior, seen to particular advantage when illuminated at night. It was from the balcony above the awning that an ill-mannered Charles de Gaulle proclaimed, "Vive le Québec Libre!" in 1967, thereby pleasing his immediate audience but straining relations with the Canadian government for years. Fifteen-minute guided tours are given throughout the day on weekdays May to October. The Hall of Honour is made of green Italian marble, and houses Art Deco lamps from Paris.

275 rue Notre-Dame (at the corner of rue Gosford). ✆ **514/872-3355.** Free admission. Daily 8:30am–4:30pm. Métro: Champ-de-Mars.

**Interactive Science Centre (iSci)** *Kids* Occupying a new steel-and-glass building running the length of King Edward Pier, this ambitious $49-million complex was inaugurated in May 2000. Focusing on science and technology, it employs a variety of interactive displays and a cinema as well as a pre-existing IMAX theater (see "Especially for Kids," later) to enlighten visitors about the life sciences, energy conservation, and 21st-century communications. With its extensive use of computers, monitors, and electronic visual displays, it's no surprise that youngsters take to the exhibits more readily than their elders. The most popular component is the IMAX.

King Edward Pier, Vieux-Port. ✆ **514/496-4724.** www.isci.ca. C$9.95–C$21.95 (US$6–US$14) adults, C$8.95–C$18.95 (US$6–US$13) ages 13–17 and 60 and over, C$7.95–C$16.95 (US$5–US$11) ages 4–12. Summer Sun–Wed 10am–6pm, Thurs–Sat 10am–9pm; rest of year Sun–Thurs 10am–6pm, Fri–Sat 10am–9pm (hours subject to change). Metro: Square Victoria, Place d'Armes, or Champ-de-Mars.

**Marché Bonsecours** Bonsecours Market, an imposing Neo-Classical building with a long facade, a colonnaded portico, and a silvery dome, was built in the mid-1800s and was first used as Montréal's City Hall, then for many years after 1878 as the central market. It has never been decided with finality what it will be since then. Essentially abandoned for much of the 20th century, it was restored in 1964 to house city government offices, and in 1992 became the information and exhibition center for the celebration of the city's 350th birthday. It continues to be used as an exhibition space, and room was made for shopping stalls and three restos with terraces. Currently, it has a fairly large food market, too, to serve the growing resident population of Vieux-Montréal. The architecture alone makes a brief visit worthwhile.

350 rue St-Paul Est (at the foot of rue St-Claude). ✆ **514/872-7730.** www.marchebonsecours.qc.ca. Free admission. Sat–Thurs 10am–6pm, Thurs–Fri 10am–9pm. Métro: Champ-de-Mars.

**Musée du Château Ramezay** ★ Claude de Ramezay, the 11th governor of the colony, built his residence at this site in 1705. The château was the home of the city's royal French governors for almost 4 decades, but in 1745, his heirs sold it to a trading company. They apparently rebuilt it, using portions of the original structure. Fifteen years later, it was taken over by the British conquerors. In 1775 an army of American revolutionaries invaded and held Montréal, using the château as their headquarters. Benjamin Franklin, sent to persuade Québecois to rise with the American colonists against British rule, stayed in the château for a time, but failed to persuade the city's people to join his cause. After the American interlude, the house was used as a courthouse, a government office building, a teachers' college, and headquarters for Laval University before being converted into a museum in 1895. Old coins and prints, portraits, furnishings, tools, a loom, Amerindian artifacts, and other memorabilia related to the economic and social activities of the 18th century and first half of the 19th century blanket the main floor. Descriptive placards are in both French and English.

280 rue Notre-Dame (east of Place Jacques-Cartier). ✆ **514/861-3708.** www.chateauramezay.qc.ca. Admission C$6 (US$3.75) adults, C$5 (US$3.10) seniors, C$4 (US$2.50) students, free for children under 6, C$12 (US$7) families. MC, V. June–Sept daily 10am–6pm; Oct–May Tues–Sun 10am–4:30pm. Métro: Champ-de-Mars.

**Place Jacques-Cartier** Across the street from the Hôtel de Ville (City Hall) is the focus of summer activity in Vieux-Montréal. The most active of the old city's plazas has two recently repaved streets bracketing a center promenade that slopes down to the port past venerable stone buildings surviving from the 1700s. Its outdoor cafes, street performers, flower sellers, and the horse-drawn carriages that gather at its base recall the Montréal of a century ago. Montréalers insist they would never go to a place so thronged by tourists—which begs the question of why so many of them in fact congregate here. They take the sun and sip sangria on the bordering terraces on warm days, enjoying the unfolding pageant just as much as visitors do.

Between rue Notre-Dame and rue de la Commune. Métro: Place d'Armes.

**Pointe-à-Callière (Montréal Museum of Archaeology and History)** ★★★ A first visit to Montréal might best begin here. Built on the very site where the original colony was established in 1642 (Pointe-à-Callière), the Museum of Archaeology and History engages visitors in beguiling ways. The striking new building echoes the triangular Royal Insurance building (1861) that stood here for many years. Go first to the 16-minute multimedia show in an auditorium that actually stands above exposed ruins of the earlier city. Images pop up, drop down, and slide out on rolling screens accompanied by music and a playful bilingual narration that keeps the history slick and painless (if a little too chamber-of-commerce upbeat), with enough quick cuts and changes to keep even the youngest viewers from fidgeting.

Pointe-à-Callière was the point where the St-Pierre River merged with the St. Lawrence. Evidences of the many layers of occupation at this spot—from Amerindians to French trappers to Scottish merchants—were unearthed during archaeological digs that persisted here for more than a decade. They are on view in display cases set among the ancient building foundations and burial grounds below street level. The bottom shelves of the cabinets are for items dating from before 1600, and there are other shelves for consecutive centuries. Wind your way on the self-guided tour through the subterranean complex until you find yourself in the former Custom House, where there are more exhibits and a well-stocked gift shop. Allow at least an hour for a visit.

New expansion has incorporated the Youville Pumping Station, across from the main building, as an interpretation center. The main building contains L'Arrivage cafe and affords a fine view of Old Montréal and the Old Port.

350 place Royale (at rue de la Commune). ✆ **514/872-9150.** www.musee-pointe-a-calliere.qc.ca. Admission C$9.50 (US$6) adults, C$7 (US$4.35) seniors, C$5.50 (US$3.40) students, C$3 (US$1.85) children 6–12, free for children under 6, C$19 (US$12) families. AE, MC, V. July–Aug, Tues–Fri 10am–6pm, Sat–Sun 11am–6pm; rest of year Tues–Fri 10am–5pm, Sat–Sun 11am–5pm. Métro: Place d'Armes.

**Vieux-Port** ★★ Montréal's Old Port, a once-dreary commercial wharf area, was transformed in 1992 into an appealing 2km-long (1¼-mile), 54ha (133-acre) promenade and park with public spaces, bicycle paths, tram rides, exhibition halls, and a variety of family activities. Cyclists, in-line skaters, joggers, strollers, lovers, and sunbathers all make use of the park in good weather. A variety of harbor cruises leave from here. To get an idea of all there is to see and do, hop aboard the small Balade tram that travels throughout the port. At the far eastern end of the port is a 1922 clock tower, La Tour de l'Horloge, with 192 steps leading past the exposed clockworks to observation decks at three different levels (admission is free). Most cruises, entertainment, and special events take place from mid-May to October. Information booths with bilingual attendants assist visitors during that period. The Old Port stretches along the waterfront from rue McGill to rue Berri. Quadricycles, bicycles, and in-line skates are available for rent.

333 rue de la Commune Ouest (at rue McGill). ✆ **514/496-7678.** www.oldportofmontreal.com. Port and interpretation center, free. Interpretation Center mid-May to early Sept daily 10am–9pm; hours for specific attractions vary. Métro: Champ-de-Mars, Place d'Armes, or Square-Victoria.

## ELSEWHERE IN THE CITY

**Biodôme de Montréal** ★★★ *Kids* Near Montréal's Botanical Garden and next to the Olympic Stadium is the engrossing Biodôme, possibly the only institution of its kind. Originally built as the velodrome for the 1976 Olympics, it has been refitted to house replications of four distinct ecosystems—a Laurentian forest, the St. Lawrence marine system, a tropical rain forest, and a polar environment—complete with appropriate temperatures, flora, fauna, and changing seasons. All four re-creations are allowed a measure of freedom to grow and shift, so the exhibits are never static. With more than 6,000 creatures of 210 species and 4,000 trees and plants, the Biodôme incorporates exhibits gathered from an old aquarium and the modest zoos at the Angrignon and LaFontaine parks. Among these are specimens of certain threatened and endangered species, including macaws, marmosets, and tamarins, while the Polar World has puffins and four kinds of penguins. Biodôme also has a game room for kids called Naturalia, a shop, a restaurant, and a cafeteria.

4777 av. Pierre-de-Coubertin (next to Olympic Stadium). ✆ **514/868-3000.** www.biodome.qc.ca. Admission C$10 (US$6) adults, C$7.50 (US$4.65) seniors and students over 17, C$5 (US$3.10) children 5–17, free for children under 5. AE, MC, V. Daily 9am–5pm (until 7pm in summer). Métro: Viau.

**La Biosphère** Not to be confused with the Biodôme at Olympic Park, this facility is located in the geodesic dome designed by Buckminster Fuller to serve as the American Pavilion for Expo '67. A fire destroyed the acrylic skin of the sphere in 1976, and it served no purpose other than as a harbor landmark until 1995. The motivation behind the Biosphère is unabashedly environmental, with four exhibition areas, a water theater, and an amphitheater, all devoted to promoting awareness of the St. Lawrence-Great Lakes ecosystem. Multimedia shows and hands-on displays invite the active participation of visitors, and there is an exhibition related to the activities of the ocean explorer Jacques-Yves Cousteau. In the highest point of the so-called Visions Hall is an observation level with an unobstructed view of the river. Connections Hall offers a "Call to Action" presentation employing six giant screens and three stages. There is a preaching-to-the-choir quality to all this that slips over the edge into zealous philosophizing. But the various displays and exhibits are put together thoughtfully and will divert and enlighten most visitors, at least for a while. Just don't make a special trip.

160 Chemin Tour-de-l'Isle (Ile Ste-Hélène). ✆ **514/283-5000.** http://biosphere.ec.qc.ca. Admission C$8.50 adults (US$5.25), C$6.50 (US$4) seniors and students, C$5 (US$3.10) children 7–17, free for children under 7, C$19 (US$13) families. June 24–Labour Day daily 10am–6pm; Sept–May Tues–Sun 10am–5pm. Métro: Parc Jean-Drapeau, then a short walk.

**Musée David M. Stewart** ★ After the War of 1812, the British prepared for a possible future American invasion by building this moated fortress, which now houses the David M. Stewart Museum. The Duke of Wellington ordered its construction as a link in the chain of defenses along the St. Lawrence. Completed in 1824, it was never involved in armed conflict, and the British garrison left in 1870. Today the low stone barracks and blockhouses contain the museum, which displays maps and scientific instruments that helped Europeans explore the New World, as well as military and naval artifacts, weaponry, uniforms, housewares, and related paraphernalia from the time of Jacques Cartier (1535) through to the end of the colonial period. Useful labels are in both French and English.

Late June to late August, the fort comes to life with reenactments of military parades and retreats by La Compagnie Franche de la Marine and the 78th Fraser Highlanders, at 11am, 3pm, and 4:30pm. The presence of the French unit is an unhistorical sop to Francophone sensibilities, since New France had become English Canada almost 65 years before the fort was erected. If you absolutely must be photographed in stocks, they're provided on the parade grounds.

Vieux Fort, Ile Ste-Hélène. ✆ **514/861-6701.** www.stewart-museum.org. Admission C$7 (US$4.35) adults, C$5 (US$3.10) seniors and students, C$14 (US$10) families, free for children under 7. May–Sept daily 10am–6pm; Sept–May Wed–Mon 10am–5pm. Métro: Parc Jean-Drapeau, then a 15-minute walk. By car: Take the Jacques-Cartier Bridge to the Parc Jean-Drapeau exit, then follow signs to Vieux Fort.

**Stade Olympique** Centerpiece of the 1976 Olympic Games, Montréal's controversial Olympic Stadium and its associated facilities provide considerable opportunities for both active and passive diversion. It incorporates a natatorium with six different pools, including one of competition dimensions with an adjustable bottom and a 15m (50-ft.) version for scuba diving. The stadium seats 60,000 to 80,000 spectators, who come here to see the Expos, rock concerts, and trade shows.

A 65-ton retractable Kevlar roof is winched into place by 125 tons of steel cables, which are attached to a 190m (626-ft.) inclined tower that looms over the arena like an egret bobbing for fish in a bowl. When everything functions as was intended, it takes about 45 minutes to raise or lower the roof. In reality, the roof malfunctions frequently, and high winds have torn large rents in the fabric. That is only one reason that what was first known as "The Big O" was scorned as "The Big Owe" after cost overruns led to heavy increases in taxes. Plans for its future have run from total demolition to adding thousands of seats.

The tower, leaning at a 45° angle, also does duty as an observation deck, with a funicular that whisks 90 passengers to the top in 95 seconds. On a clear day, you get a 55km (35-mile) view over Montréal and into the neighboring Laurentides. A free shuttle bus links the Olympic Park and the Botanical Garden.

4141 av. Pierre-de-Coubertin (bd. Pie IX). ✆ **514/252-8687.** www.rio.gouv.qc.ca. Funicular ride, C$9 (US$6) adults, C$5.50 (US$3.40) students and children. Guided tours of the stadium are available. Public swim periods are scheduled daily, with low admission rates. Cable car mid-June to early Sept, Mon noon–6pm, Tues–Thurs 10am–9pm, Fri–Sat 10am–11pm; early Sept to mid-Jan and mid-Feb to mid-June, Mon–Sun noon–6pm. Closed mid-Jan to mid-Feb. Métro: Pie-IX or Viau (choose the Viau station for the guided tour).

## PLATEAU MONT-ROYAL

For further information about this area, log on to **www.tpmr.qc.ca**.

**Musée des Hospitalières de l'Hôtel-Dieu de Montréal** Opened in 1992, this unusual museum, in the former chaplain's residence of Hôtel-Dieu Hospital, traces the history of Montréal from 1659 to the present and focuses on the evolution of health care spanning 3 centuries in the history of the hospital, including an exhibit of medical instruments. It bows to the missionary nurse Jeanne Mance, who arrived in 1642 and founded the first hospital in Montréal. The museum's three floors are filled with memorabilia, including paintings, books, reliquaries, furnishings, and a reconstruction of a nun's cell. Its architectural high point is a marvelous "floating" oak staircase brought to the New World in 1634 from the Maison-Dieu hospital in La Flèche, France. The original Hôtel-Dieu was built in 1645 near the site of the present Notre-Dame Basilica. This building was erected in 1861. Guided tours are on Sundays at 2pm.

201 av. des Pins Ouest. ✆ **514/849-2919.** www.museedeshospitalieres.qc.ca. Admission C$5 (US$3.10) adults, C$3 (US$1.85) seniors and students 12 and over, free for children 11 and under. Mid-June to mid-Oct Tues–Fri 10am–5pm, Sat–Sun 1–5pm; mid-Oct to mid-June Wed–Sun 1–5pm. Métro: Sherbrooke. Bus: 144.

**Oratoire St-Joseph** ★ This huge basilica with a giant copper dome was built by Québec's Catholics to honor St. Joseph, patron saint of Canada. Dominating the north slope of Mont-Royal, its imposing dimensions are seen by some as inspiring, by others as forbidding. It came into being through the efforts of Brother André, a lay brother in the Holy Cross order who enjoyed a reputation as a healer. By the time he had built a small wooden chapel in 1904 near the site of the basilica, he was said to have affected hundreds of cures. Those celebrated powers attracted supplicants from great distances, and Brother André performed his work until his death in 1937. His dream of building this shrine to his patron saint became a reality only years after his death, in 1967. He is buried in the basilica and was beatified in 1982, a status one step below sainthood. The basilica is largely Italian Renaissance in style, its dome recalling the shape of the Duomo in Florence, but of much greater size and less grace. Inside is a museum where a central exhibit is the heart of Brother André. Outside, a Way of the Cross lined with sculptures was the setting of scenes for the Canadian film *Jesus of Montréal.* Brother André's wooden chapel, with his tiny bedroom, is on the grounds and open to the public. Pilgrims, some ill, come to seek intercession from St. Joseph and Brother André and often climb the middle set of 100 steps on their knees. At 263m (862 ft.), the shrine is the highest point in Montréal. A cafeteria and snack bar are on the premises. Ninety-minute guided tours are offered in several languages at 10am and 2pm daily in summer and on weekends in September and October (donation only).

3800 Chemin Queen Mary (on the north slope of Mont-Royal). © **514/733-8211.** www.saint-joseph.org. Free admission, but donations are requested. Daily 6am–9:30pm; museum daily 9am–5pm. The 56-bell carillon plays Wed–Fri noon–3pm; Sat–Sun noon–2:30pm. Métro: Côtes-des-Neiges, bus 165.

## PARKS & GARDENS

**Jardin Botanique** ★★ *Kids* Across the street from the former Olympic sports complex, the Botanical Garden spreads across 74ha (180 acres). Begun in 1931, it has grown to include 21,000 varieties of plants, ensuring something beautiful and fragrant year-round. Ten large conservatory greenhouses shelter tropical and desert plants, and bonsai and penjings, from the Canadian winter. One greenhouse, called the Wizard of Oz, is especially fun for kids. Roses bloom here from mid-June to the first frost, May is the month for lilacs, and June for the flowering hawthorn trees. The 2.5ha (6-acre) Chinese Garden, a joint project of Montréal and Shanghai, is the largest of its kind ever built outside Asia. Meant to evoke the 14th to 17th Century era of the Ming Dynasty, it incorporates pavilions, inner courtyards, ponds, and myriad plants indigenous to China. The serene Japanese Garden fills 6ha (15 acres) and contains a cultural pavilion with an art gallery, a tearoom where the ancient tea ceremony is performed, a stunning bonsai collection, and a Zen garden. The grounds are also home to the Insectarium, displaying some of the world's most beautiful insects, not to mention some of its sinister ones (see "Especially for Kids," below). Birders should bring along binoculars on summer visits to spot some of the more than 130 species of birds that spend at least part of the year in the garden. In summer, an outdoor aviary is filled with butterflies. Year-round, a free shuttle bus links the Botanical Garden and nearby Olympic Park; a small train runs regularly through the gardens and is worth the small fee charged to ride it.

4101 rue Sherbrooke Est (opposite Olympic Stadium). © **514/872-1400.** www.jardin-botanique@ville.montreal.qc.ca. For the outside gardens, greenhouses, and insectarium, May–Oct C$10 (US$6) adults, C$7.50 (US$4.65) seniors and students, C$4.75 (US$2.95) children 5–17; Nov–Apr C$7.25 (US$4.50) adults, C$5.75 (US$3.55) seniors and students, C$3.75 (US$2.30) children. A ticket for the Botanical Garden, Insectarium, and Biodôme, good for 30 days, C$16 (US$10) adults, C$12 (US$7) seniors, C$8 (US$5) children. MC, V. Daily 9am–5pm (until 7pm in summer). Métro: Pie-IX; then walk up the hill to the gardens, or take the shuttle bus from Olympic Park (Métro: Viau).

**Parc du Mont-Royal** Montréal is named for the 232m (761-ft.) hill that rises at its heart—the "Royal Mountain." Joggers, cyclists, dog walkers, skaters, and others use it throughout the year. On Sundays, hundreds congregate around the statue of George-Etienne Cartier to listen and sometimes dance to improvised music. In summer, Lac des Castors (Beaver Lake) is surrounded by sunbathers and picnickers (no swimming allowed, however). In wintertime, cross-country skiers follow the miles of paths, snowshoers tramp along other trails laid out for their use, and there's a tow for the short downhill skiing run above the lake. In the cold months, the lake fills with whirling ice skaters of various levels of aptitude. The large, refurbished Chalet Lookout near the crest of the hill provides both a sweeping view of the city from its terrace and an opportunity for a snack. Up the hill behind the chalet is the spot where, tradition has it, de Maisonneuve erected his wooden cross in 1642. Today the cross is a 30m (100-ft.) high steel structure visible from all over the city, illuminated at night. Park security is provided by mounted police. There are three cemeteries on the northern slope of the mountain—Catholic, Protestant, and Jewish.

✆ **514/844-4928** (general information) or 514/872-6559 (special events). Daily 6am–midnight. Métro: Mont-Royal. Bus: 11; hop off at Lac des Castors.

**Parc Lafontaine** The European-style park in Plateau Mont-Royal is one of the city's oldest. Illustrating the dual identities of the city's populace, half the park is landscaped in the formal French manner, the other in the more casual English style. Among its several bodies of water is a lake used for paddleboating in summer and ice skating in winter. Snowshoeing and cross-country trails curl through the trees. An open amphitheater, the Théâtre de Verdure, is the setting for free outdoor theater and movies in summer. Joggers, bikers, picnickers, and tennis buffs (there are 14 outdoor courts) share the space.

Rue Sherbrooke and av. Parc Lafontaine. ✆ **514/872-2644.** Free admission; small fee for use of tennis courts. Always open. Tennis courts summer daily 9am–10pm. Métro: Sherbrooke.

## ESPECIALLY FOR KIDS

**IMAX Theatre** The images and special effects are larger than life, always visually dazzling, thrown on a five-story screen in the renovated theater of the Interactive Science Centre (iSci). Recent films made the most of charging elephants, underwater scenes in Yucatán cenotes once used for Mayan sacrifices, and cameras swooping low over glaciers and through the Grand Canyon. Running time is usually under an hour. Arrive for shows at least 10 minutes before starting time, earlier on weekends and evenings. Tickets can be ordered online.

Vieux-Port, Quai King Edward (end of bd. St-Laurent). ✆ **800/349-4629** or 514/496-4629 (information and tickets). www.isci.ca/en/imax/mixte.htm. Admission C$9.95 (US$6) adults, C$8.95 (US$6) seniors and students 13–17, C$7.95 (US$5) children 4–11. MC, V. Daily. Call for current schedule of shows in English. Métro: Place d'Armes.

**Insectarium de Montréal** ★ A recent addition to the Botanical Garden, this two-level structure near the Sherbrooke gate exhibits the collections of two avid entomologists: Georges Brossard (whose brainchild this place is) and Father Firmia Liberté. More than 3,000 mounted butterflies, scarabs, maggots, locusts, beetles, tarantulas, and giraffe weevils are displayed, and live exhibits feature scorpions, tarantulas, crickets, cockroaches, and praying mantises. Needless to say, kids are delighted by the creepy critters. Their guardians are apt to be less enthusiastic, except in summer in the Butterfly House, when beautiful live specimens flutter among the nectar-bearing plants.

Botanical Garden, 4581 rue Sherbrooke Est. ✆ **514/872-1400.** www.ville.montreal.qc.ca/insectarium. May–Oct C$10 (US$6) adults, C$7.50 (US$4.65) seniors, C$5 (US$3.10) children 6–17; Nov–Apr C$7.25 (US$4.50) adults, C$5.75 (US$3.55) seniors, C$3.75 (US$2.30) children. MC, V. Summer daily 9am–7pm; rest of year daily 9am–5pm. Métro: Pie-IX or Viau.

**La Ronde** Montréal's amusement park was run for most of its 35 years by the city. Lately, that arrangement clearly wasn't working, with the facility sliding into massive disrepair. Now, though, it has been sold to the American-owned Six Flags theme park empire, which plans to invest in a $90 million renovation. Those changes should start showing up soon. The park fills the northern reaches of the Ile Ste-Hélène with a sailing lagoon, an "Enchanted Forest" with costumed storytellers, and a Western town with saloon, as well as ferris wheels, carousels, roller coasters, carnival booths, and plenty of places to eat and drink. Thrill-seekers like the rides called Le Boomerang, Le Monstre, and Le Cobra, a stand-up roller coaster that incorporates a 360° loop and reaches speeds in excess of 40kmph (60 mph). While many of the 35 rides test adult nerves and stomachs, there are ample attractions for youngsters, such as the Tchou Tchou Train and the Super Volcanozor, which manages to combine 3-D images of dinosaurs with swooping, twirling transport among them. A big attraction every year is the **International Fireworks Competition** (see "Special Events & Festivals," below).

Parc des Iles, Ile Ste-Hélène. © **800/797-4537** or 514/872-4537. www.laronde.com. Unlimited all-day pass C$29.99 (US$19) for those 12 and over, C$15.99 (US$10) under 12, C$15.99 (US$10) grounds admission only. Seniors are free Mon–Thur, but pay adult rates on weekends. Last week in May, Sat–Sun only; June–Aug and Labour Day weekend daily 10am–9pm. Parking C$8 (US$5). Métro: Papineau and bus no. 169, or Parc Jean-Drapeau and bus no. 167.

**Planétarium de Montréal** A window on the night sky with mythical monsters and magical heroes, Montréal's planetarium is right downtown, 3 blocks south of Centre Molsen. Changing shows under the 20m (65-ft.) dome dazzle and inform kids at the same time. Shows change with the seasons, exploring time and space travel and collisions of celestial bodies. The special Christmas show, "Star of the Magi," seen in December and early January, is based on recent investigations of historians and astronomers into the mysterious light that guided the Magi. Shows in English alternate with those in French.

The future location of the Planetarium is in doubt, with some talk of moving it to the Biodôme area. It stands on desirable downtown acreage that is being eyed by developers.

1000 rue St-Jacques (at Peel). © **514/872-4530.** www.planetarium.montreal.qc.ca. Admission C$6 (US$3.75) adults, $4.50 (US$2.80) seniors and students, C$3 (US$1.85) children 6–17. MC, V. Schedule of shows changes frequently, call ahead. Métro: Bonaventure (Cathédrale exit).

## 6 Special Events & Festivals

In summer, the city becomes even livelier than usual with several enticing events. The **Festival de Théâtre des Amériques** (© **514/842-0704;** www.fta.qc.ca), held in odd-numbered years from late May to early June, presents innovative dramatic and musical stage productions that are international in scope, not simply North American, as the name suggests. There have been works from Vietnam and China as well as from Canada, the United States, and Mexico. The plays are performed in the original languages, as a rule, with simultaneous translations in French and/or English, when appropriate.

The popular **Montréal International Fireworks Competition** (© **514/872-7044;** www.montrealfeux.com) is held at the La Ronde amusement park once a week in June and July (postponed in bad weather). The pyromusical displays are launched at 10pm and last at least 30 minutes. (Many Montréalers choose to watch them from the Jacques Cartier Bridge, which is closed to traffic during the display. Take along a Walkman to listen to the accompanying music.)

The respected and heavily attended **Festival International de Jazz** ★ (© **888/515-0515** or 514/871-1881; www.montrealjazzfest.com), held in early July, sustains interest in the most original American art form. During the nine days of the event, more than 2,000 musicians perform on 16 stages for an average total audience of one million. Scores of events are scheduled, indoors and out, many of them free. *Jazz* is broadly interpreted, including everything from Dixieland to reggae, world beat, and the unclassifiable experimental. In 2001, for example, Prince was featured. Performers more closely associated with jazz have included George Benson, Pat Metheny, Gil Evans, Dave Brubeck, and B.B. King. Piano legend Oscar Peterson grew up here and sometimes returns to perform.

The **Juste pour Rire/Just for Laughs Festival** is held in late July (✆ **514/845-2322**; www.justforlaughs.com). Performances are in French or English (about 50/50, it seems) or both. In late September to early October, the **Festival International de Nouvelle Danse** (✆ **514-287-1423**; www.festivalnouvelledanse.ca) attracts modern-dance troupes and choreographers from around the world. To this bursting roster has been added the **Montréal Highlights Festival/Festival Montréal en Lumière,** mid-February to early March (✆ **888/477-9955**; www.montrealenlumiere.com), dedicated to the arts, which, by this gastronomic city's measure, includes chefs the caliber of Paul Bocuse.

## 7 Outdoor Activities & Spectator Sports

### OUTDOOR ACTIVITIES

**BICYCLING** Cycling is hugely popular in Montréal, and the city enjoys an expanding network of 350km (217 miles) of cycling paths. Heavily used routes include the nearly flat 11km (7-mile) **Old Port Route** ★ along the Lachine Canal that leads to Lac St-Louis, the 16km (10-mile) path west from the St-Lambert Lock to the city of Côte Ste-Catherine, and Angrignon Park with its 6.5km (4-mile) biking path and inviting picnic areas (Métro: Angrignon; the Métro accepts bikes in the last two doors of the last car). Bikes can be rented at the Vieux-Port (at the end of boulevard St-Laurent) for C$6.50 to C$7 (US$4–US$4.35) an hour or C$20 to C$22 (US$12–US$14) a day. **Velo Montréal** at 3870 rue Rachel (✆ 514/236-8356, www.velomontreal.com) is a principal source. Bikes, along with the popular four-wheel "Q Cycles," may also be rented at the Place Jacques-Cartier entrance to the Old Port. The Q Cycles, for use in the Old Port only, cost C$4.25 (US$2.65) per half hour for adults and C$3.50 (US$2.20) per half hour for children. Another source is Caroule, which also rents in-line skates (see below).

A useful booklet, Pédaler Montréal, is available at the Infotourist office on Square Dominion. For additional information, log on to **www.velo.qc.ca**.

**CROSS-COUNTRY SKIING** Parc Mont-Royal has a 2km (1¼-mile) cross-country course called the *parcours de la croix*. The Botanical Garden has an ecology trail used by cross-country skiers. The problem for either is that skiers have to supply their own equipment. Just an hour from the city, in the Laurentides, are almost 20 ski centers, all offering cross-country as well as downhill skiing.

**HIKING** The most popular—and obvious—hike is up to the top of Mont-Royal. Start downtown on rue Peel, which leads north to a stairway, which in turn leads to a 1km (½ mile) path of switchbacks called Le Serpent. Alternatively, opt for the 200 steps that lead up to the Chalet Lookout, with the reward of a panoramic view of the city. Figure about 2km (1¼ miles) one-way.

**IN-LINE SKATING** More than 230 pairs of in-line skates and all the requisite protective gear can be rented from **Caroule** (✆ **514/866-0633**) at 27 rue de la Commune Est bordering the Vieux-Port. The cost is C$7.50 (US$4.65) weekdays or C$9 (US$6) weekends for the first hour up to a maximum of C$20 (US$12) for a full day. Protective gear is included. A deposit is required. Lessons on skates are available for C$25 (US$16) for 2 hours.

**RUNNING** There are many possibilities for running. One is to follow rue Peel north to Le Serpent switchback path on Mont-Royal, continuing uphill on it for 1km (½ mile) until it peters out. Turn right and continue 2km (1 mile) to the monument of George-Etienne Cartier, one of Canada's fathers of confederation. From here, either take a bus back downtown or run back down the same route or along avenue du Parc and avenue des Pins (turn right when you get to it). It's also fun to jog along the Lachine Canal.

**ICE SKATING** One of the most agreeable venues for ice skating is the atrium in the downtown skyscraper named after its address, **1000 de la Gauchertière** (© **514/395-0555;** www.le1000.com). For one thing, it's indoors and warm. For another, it's surrounded by cafes and places to relax after a twirl around the big rink. It's open Sunday and Tuesday to Friday 11:30am to 6pm, Saturday 10 to 11am for children and their families, 11:30am to 7pm for all, and 7pm to 10pm for "DJ Nights". Admission is C$5 (US$3.10) for adults 16 and up and C$3 (US$1.85) for seniors and children.

## SPECTATOR SPORTS

Montréalers are as devoted to ice hockey as are other Canadians, with plenty of enthusiasm left over for baseball, football, and soccer. There are several prominent annual sporting events of other kinds, such as the **Grand Prix Air Canada** (© **514/350-0000** for information) in June, The Player's Ltd. International men's tennis championship in late July, and the Montréal Marathon in September.

**BASEBALL** Now that plans for a new $200 million downtown stadium have been scrapped, the National League **Montréal Expos** presumably will continue to play at Stade Olympique (Olympic Stadium), 4549 av. Pierre-de-Coubertin (© **514/790-1245;** www.montrealexpos.com; Métro: Pie-IX). However, after a number of low-attendance seasons due to losing records, there are rumors that the team might be moved to another city or dropped altogether. Subject to anticipated increases, tickets are C$8 (US$5) for general admission to C$25 (US$16) for box seats.

**FOOTBALL** Canadian professional football returned to Montréal after an experimental 3-year league with U.S. teams. The team that was briefly the ersatz Baltimore Colts is now in its second incarnation as the **Montréal Alouettes** (© **514/790-1245;** www.alouettes.net for information, www.admission.com for tickets). The team has enjoyed considerable success since its return, frequently appearing in the Grey Cup, the CFL's Super Bowl. The Alouettes (French for "larks") play at McGill University's Molson Stadium on a schedule that runs from June into October. Tickets start at C$10 (US$6.20).

**HARNESS RACING** Popularly known as Blue Bonnets Racetrack, the **Hippodrome de Montréal,** 7440 bd. Décarie, in Jean-Talon (© **514/739-2741;** www.hippodrome-montreal.ca; Métro: Namur, and then a shuttle bus), is the host facility for international harness-racing events, including the Coupe des Elevers (Breeders Cup). Restaurants, bars, a snack bar, and pari-mutuel betting can make for a satisfying evening or Sunday-afternoon outing. There are no races on Tuesday and Thursday. General admission is free, C$5 (US$3.10) for the VIP section. Races begin at 7:30pm on Monday, Wednesday, Friday, and Saturday; on Sunday at 1:30pm.

**HOCKEY** The NHL's **Montréal Canadiens** play at the Centre Molson, 1260 rue de la Gauchetière (© **514/932-2582;** Métro: Bonaventure). The team has won 24 Stanley Cup championships since 1929. The season runs from October into April, with playoffs continuing to mid-June. Tickets range from about C$16 to C$95 (US$10–US$59).

## 8 Shopping

Whether you view shopping as a focus of your travels or just a diversion, you won't be disappointed. You can shop in Montréal until your eyes cross and your feet swell. It ranks right up there with dining out as a prime activity among the natives. Most Montréalers are of French ancestry, after all, and seem to believe that impeccable taste bubbles through the Gallic gene pool. The city has produced a thriving fashion industry, from couture to ready-to-wear, with a history that reaches back to the earliest trade in furs and leather. In any event, it is unlikely that any reasonable consumer need—and even outlandish fantasies—cannot be met here. There are more than 1,500 shops in the Underground City alone, and many more than that at street level and above.

Try **Rue Sherbrooke** for fashion, art, and luxury items, including furs and jewelry. **Rue Crescent** has a number of upscale boutiques, while funkier **boulevard St-Laurent** covers everything from budget practicalities to off-the-wall handmade fashions. Look along **avenue Laurier** between St-Laurent and de l'Epée for French boutiques, home accessories shops, and young Québécois designers. **Rue St-Paul** in Vieux-Montréal has a growing number of art galleries. More than 50 tempting shops can be found along the lengthening "Antiques Alley" of **rue Notre-Dame,** especially between Guy and Atwater. **Rue St-Denis** north of Sherbrooke has strings of shops filled with fun items. Some of the best shops are found in city museums; the best among them are those in Pointe-è-Callière in Vieux-Montréal, and the Musée des Beaux-Arts and the Musée McCord, both on rue Sherbrooke in the center city.

**Rue Ste-Catherine** is home to the city's four top department stores and myriad satellite shops, while **rue Peel** is known for its men's fashions and some crafts. Montréal's long history as a center for the fur trade is reflected in the "fur row" of **rue Mayor,** between rue de Bleury and rue City Councillors.

---

### *Tips* Taxes & Refunds

Although taxes are high, visitors can obtain refunds of those incurred for lodgings and shop purchases (but not for food or drink, auto rentals, or other transportation). Save your sales receipts from any store in Montréal or the rest of Québec, and ask shopkeepers for tax-refund forms. A new step in the procedure requires that receipts be "validated" by either (1) enclosing your original airline boarding pass, or (2) having receipts for goods validated by Canadian customs officials or by staff members at border duty-free shops.

After returning home, mail the originals (not copies) to the specified address with the completed form. Refunds usually take a few months but are in the currency of the applicant's home country. A small service fee is charged. For faster refunds, follow the same procedure, but hand in the receipts and form at a duty-free shop designated in the government pamphlet *Tax Refund for Visitors to Canada,* available at tourist offices and in many stores and hotels.

---

## ANTIQUES

The best places to find antiques and collectibles are the more than 50 storefronts along **Rue Notre-Dame** between rues Guy and Atwater.

**Antiques Puces-Libres** Three fascinatingly cluttered floors are packed with pine and oak furniture, lamps, clocks, vases, and more, most of it 19th- and early 20th-century French-Canadian Art Nouveau. 4240 rue St-Denis (near rue Rachel). ✆ **514/842-5931.** Metro: Mont-Royal.

## ARTS & CRAFTS

**Boutique Canadiana Worn Doorstep** The ongoing development of the Bonsecours Market has altered focus from temporary exhibitions to shops and food stalls. This one concentrates on crafts, children's storybooks, maps, small furniture, and packaged foods, all with a Canadian connection. 350 St-Paul Est, Vieux-Montréal. ✆ **514/397-0666.** Métro: Champ-de-Mars.

**Guilde Canadienne des Métier d'Art Québec** A small but choice collection of craft items is displayed in a meticulously arranged gallery setting. Among the objects are blown glass, paintings on silk, pewter, tapestries, and ceramics. The stock is particularly strong in avant-garde jewelry and Inuit sculpture. A small carving might be had for C$100 to C$200 (US$62–US$124), but the larger, more important pieces go for hundreds, even thousands, more. 2025 rue Peel (at bd. de Maisonneuve). ✆ **514/849-6091.** Métro: Peel.

**L'Empreinte** This is a craftsperson's collective, 1 block off place Jacques-Cartier at the corner of rue du Marché Bonsecours. The ceramics, textiles, glassware, and other items on sale often occupy that vaguely defined territory between art and craft. Quality is uneven but usually tips toward the high end. 272 rue St-Paul Est, Vieux-Montréal. ✆ **514/861-4427.** Métro: Champ de Mars.

## BOOKS

**Chapters** This is the flagship store of a chain with many branches, the result of a merger between the Smithbooks and Coles booksellers. (The Indigo bookstores also merged with Chapters recently, but retain their own identity.) Thousands of titles are available in French and English on both general and specialized subjects. 1171 rue Ste-Catherine Ouest (at rue Stanley). ✆ **514/849-8825.** Métro: Peel.

**Paragraphe** Prowl the rows of shelves in this long storefront, then take your purchases to the adjoining Second Cup cafe, popular with students from the McGill campus, a block away. The store hosts frequent autograph parties, author readings, and occasional musical performances. 2220 av. McGill College (south of rue Sherbrooke). ✆ **514/845-5811.** Métro: McGill.

## DEPARTMENT STORES

Montréal's major shopping emporia stretch along **rue Ste-Catherine** (except for Holt Renfrew), from rue Guy eastward to Carré Phillips at Aylmer. An excursion along this 12-block stretch can keep a diligent shopper busy for hours, even days. Most of the stores mentioned below have branches elsewhere.

**Henry Birks et Fils** Across from Christ Church Cathedral stands this jeweler, highly regarded since 1879. The beautiful old store, with its dark-wood display cases, stone pillars, and marble floors, is a living part of Montréal's Victorian heritage. Valuable products on display go well beyond jewelry to encompass pens and desk accessories, watches, leather goods, glassware, and china. 1240 Carré Phillips (at av. Union). ✆ **514/397-2511.** Métro: McGill.

**Holt Renfrew** This showcase for international style focuses on fashion for men and women. Such prestigious names as Giorgio Armani, Prada, Gucci, and Chanel are displayed with a tastefulness bordering on solemnity. The marquee outside reads only HOLTS. 1300 rue Sherbrooke Ouest (at rue de la Montagne). © **514/842-5111.** Métro: Guy or Peel.

**La Baie** No retailer has an older or more celebrated name than that of the Hudson's Bay Company, a name shortened in recent years to "The Bay," then transformed into "La Baie" by the language laws. The company has done business in Canada for the better part of 300 years. Its main store emphasizes clothing, but also offers crystal, china, and their famous Hudson's Bay blankets. 585 rue Ste-Catherine Ouest (near rue Aylmer). © **514/281-4422.** Métro: McGill.

**La Maison Simons** This is the first foray out of its home area for Québec City's long-established family owned department store. Most Montréalers had never heard of it, but that changed fast. One guidebook describes it as "swanky," but it is actually closer to "softer side of Sears", with good prices. 977 rue Ste-Cathrine Ouest (at rue Mansfield). © **514/282-1840.** Métro: McGill.

**Ogilvy** Established in 1866, Ogilvy has been at this location since 1912. Besides having a reputation for quality merchandise, the store is known for its eagerly awaited Christmas windows. A bagpiper still announces the noon hour, but the store now contains over 50 boutiques highlighting such high-profile purveyors as Guy Laroche, Escada, Anne Klein, Aquascutum, and Rodier Paris. 1307 rue Ste-Catherine Ouest (at rue de la Montagne). © **514/842-7711.** Métro: Guy or Peel.

## FASHION FOR MEN

**America** One of the many links in a popular Canadian chain, it carries casual and dressy clothes, including suits, jackets, and slacks. There's a women's section upstairs. 1101 Ste-Catherine Ouest (at rue Peel). © **514/289-9609.** Métro: Peel.

**Brisson & Brisson** Apparel of the nipped-and-trim British and European cut fills three floors, from makers as diverse as Burberry, Brioni, and Valentino. 1472 rue Sherbrooke Ouest (near rue Mackay). © **514/937-7456.** Métro: Guy.

**Club Monsieur** Hugo and Boss styles prevail, for those with the fit frames to carry them and the required discretionary income. 1407 rue Crescent (near bd. de Maisonneuve). © **514/843-5476.** Métro: Guy.

**L'Uomo** Largely Italian menswear by such forward-thinking designers as Cerruti, Missoni, Ungaro, Versace, Armani, and Dolce & Gabbana. 1452 rue Peel (near rue Ste-Catherine). © **514/844-1008.** Métro: Peel.

## FASHION FOR WOMEN

**Ambre** Sonia Kozma is the star designer here, of fashionable suits, cocktail dresses, and casual wear made of linen, rayon, and cotton. There are bold but complementary accessories, as well. 201 rue St-Paul Ouest (at place Jacques-Cartier). © **514/982-0325.** Métro: Square-Victoria.

**Artefact Montréal** Browse here among articles of clothing and paintings by up-and-coming Québecois designers and artists. 4117 rue St-Denis (near rue Rachel). © **514/842-2780.** Métro: Mont-Royal.

**Kyoze** The eye-catching creations of Québecois and other Canadian designers are featured, including jewelry and accessories. Centre Mondial du Commerce, 393 rue St-Jacques Ouest, second floor. © **514/847-7572.** Métro: Square-Victoria.

### FASHION FOR MEN & WOMEN

**Aritmetik** This fun shop features sportswear by young, forward-looking Toronto and California designers of a sort you don't see everywhere. 3688 bd. St-Laurent (north of Sherbrooke). ✆ **514/985-4130.** Métro: St-Laurent.

**Club Monaco** This Canadian-owned international chain is growing, as is appreciation of its minimalist, monochromatic garments for men and women, along with silver jewelry and cosmetics. Think Prada but affordable, with a helpful young staff. 1455 rue Peel (north of rue Ste-Catherine). ✆ **514/499-0959.** Métro: Peel.

**EnrgXchange** If you're young and sleek, male or female, the stretchy garments purveyed here shouldn't put you off, nor will the substantial discounts on items from terminated lines by Dolce & Gabbana, Moschino, Helmut Lang, and others of their acknowledged loftiness. 1455 rue Peel (in Les Cours Mont-Royal). ✆ **514/282-0912.** Métro: Peel.

**Felix Brown** A diverse selection of designers and manufacturers, mostly Italian, makes choices difficult. Among them are Bruno Magli, Moschino, Karl Langerfeld, Casadel, Armani, and Vicini. 1233 rue Ste-Catherine Ouest (at rue Drummond). ✆ **514/287-5523.** Métro: Peel.

**Les Cuirs Danier** This coast-to-coast national chain got that way with quality leather garments, belts, bags, and such—mostly for women, but men aren't ignored. 730 rue Ste-Catherine Ouest (near av. McGill College). ✆ **514/392-0936.** Métro: McGill.

**Terra Nostra** An exclusively Québec chain, this spiffy new store features mostly casual ware for men and women in deceptively simple shapes—sort of an upscale Gap. 900 rue Ste-Catherine. ✆ **514/861-6315.** Métro: McGill.

**Terra Firma** The sign reads T. FIRMA, but everyone knows it by the full name, which is the only way you'll get directions in Le Centre Eaton (it's toward the back on the ground floor). Shoes are the products, with labels that include Ecco, Stonefly, Rockport, Cole Haan, and pricey Mephisto. 705 rue Ste-Catherine Ouest. ✆ **514/288-3708.** Métro: McGill.

## 9 Montréal After Dark

Montréal's reputation for effervescent nightlife goes back to the Roaring Twenties and the 13-year U.S. experiment with Prohibition. Canadian distillers and brewers made fortunes—usually without much regard for legalities—and Americans streamed into Montréal for temporary relief from alcohol deprivation. That the city already enjoyed a both sophisticated and slightly naughty reputation as the Paris of North America added to the allure. Nightclubbing and barhopping remain popular, with much later hours than those of archrival Toronto, still in thrall to Calvinist notions of propriety and early bedtimes.

Montréalers' nocturnal pursuits are often as cultural as they are social. The city has its own outstanding symphony orchestra and ballet troupes, French- and English-speaking theater companies, and it's on the concert circuit that includes Chicago, Boston, and New York, so rock bands, internationally known entertainers, classical virtuosos, and dance companies pass through frequently.

For details of current performances or special events, pick up a free copy of ***Montréal Scope,*** a weekly ads-and-events booklet, at any large hotel reception desk, or the free weekly newspapers ***Mirror*** and ***Hour*** (in English) or ***Voir*** (in French). Place des Arts puts out a monthly calendar of events ***(Calendrier des Spectacles)*** describing concerts and performances to be held in the various halls of the performing-arts complex. Pick one up in most large hotels, or near the box offices in Place des Arts. Montréal's newspapers, the French-language ***La Presse*** and the English ***Gazette*** (www.montrealgazette.com), carry listings of films, clubs, and performances in their Friday and Saturday editions. The self-described "bilingual queer newspaper" ***Village*** provides news and views of gay and lesbian events, clubs, restaurants, and activities. For extensive listings of largely mainstream cultural and entertainment events, log on to **www.montreal online.com**. A similar service is provided by the alternative newspaper, ***Hour*** (www.afterhour.com). Also try the **Place des Arts** (www.infoarts.net), and **Tourisme Montréal** (www.tourism-montreal.org).

Concentrations of pubs and discos underscore the city's linguistic dichotomy, too. While there's a great deal of crossover mingling, the parallel blocks of **rue Crescent, rue Bishop,** and **rue de la Montagne** north of rue Ste-Catherine have a pronounced Anglophone character, while Francophones dominate the **Latin Quarter,** with college-age patrons most evident along the lower reaches of **rue St-Denis** and their yuppie elders gravitating to the nightspots of the slightly more uptown blocks of the same street. **Vieux-Montréal,** especially along **rue St-Paul,** has a more universal quality, where many of the bars and clubs feature live jazz, blues, and folk music. In the **Plateau Mont-Royal** area, **boulevard St-Laurent,** parallel to St-Denis and known locally as "The Main," has become a miles-long haven of hip restaurants and clubs, roughly from rue Laurier to rue Sherbrooke. Boulevard St-Laurent is a good place to wind up in the wee hours, as there's always some place with the welcome mat still out.

## THE PERFORMING ARTS

### THEATER

**Centaur Theatre** A former stock-exchange building (1903) is home to Montréal's principal English-language theater. A mix of classics, foreign adaptations, and works by Canadian playwrights is presented, including such past productions as *Driving Miss Daisy, Oliver!, The Gin Game, Waiting for Godot, Dancing at Lughnasa,* and *Cabaret,* as well as such new works as *Venus of Dublin.* Off-season, the recently refurbished theater is rented out to other groups, both French- and English-speaking. Performances are held October to June, Tuesday through Saturday at 8pm and Sunday at 7pm, with 2pm matinees on Saturday and most Sundays. Box office hours are Sunday and Monday noon to 5pm, and Tuesday through Saturday noon to 8pm. 453 rue St-François-Xavier (near rue Notre-Dame). ✆ **514/288-3161.** www.centaurtheatre.com. Tickets C$20–C$36 (US$12–US$22). Métro: Place d'Armes.

**Saidye Bronfman Centre for the Arts** Montréal's Yiddish Theatre, founded in 1937, is housed here, not far from St. Joseph's Oratory. It stages plays in both Yiddish and English, usually running 3 to 4 weeks in June and October. At other times during the year, the 300-seat theater hosts dance and music recitals, a bilingual puppet festival, occasional lectures, and three English-language plays. There's also an art gallery on the premises, with exhibits that change almost monthly. Across the street, in the Edifice Cummings House, is a small Holocaust museum and the Jewish Public Library. The center takes its name from philanthropist Saidye Bronfman, widow of Samuel Bronfman, founder of the Seagram CompanyShe died in 1995 at the age of 98. The box office is usually open Monday through Thursday 11am to 8pm and Sunday noon to 7pm—call ahead. Performances are held Tuesday through Thursday at 8pm and Sunday at 1:30 and 7pm. 5170 Côte-Ste-Catherine (near bd. Décarie). ✆ **514/739-2301** for information, or 514/739-4816 for tickets. Tickets C$15–C$35 (US$9–US$22). Métro: Côte-Ste-Catherine. Bus: 129 Ouest.

## DANCE

Frequent appearances by notable dancers and troupes from other parts of Canada and the world—among them Paul Taylor, the Feld Ballet, and Le Ballet National du Canada—augment the accomplished resident company. During the summer, Les Grands Ballets Canadiens often perform at the outdoor Théâtre de Verdure in Parc Lafontaine.

**Les Grands Ballets Canadiens** This prestigious company has developed a following far beyond national borders for more than 35 years, performing a both classical and modern repertoire. In the process, it has brought prominence to many gifted Canadian choreographers and composers. It tours internationally and was the first Canadian ballet company to be invited to the People's Republic of China. The troupe's production of *The Nutcracker* the last couple of weeks in December is always a big event in Montréal. The box office is open Monday to Saturday noon to 8pm. Performances are held late October to early May at 8pm. The fall season is kicked off by the always-provocative **Festival International de Nouvelle Danse,** (see "Special Events & Festivals," earlier). Salle Wilfrid-Pelletier, Place des Arts, 200 bd. de Maisonneuve Ouest. ✆ **514/849-8681.** www.grandsballets.qc.ca. Tickets C$12–C$40 (US$7–US$25). Métro: Place des Arts.

**Tangente** A September-to-June season of contemporary dance and often out-there performance art is laid out by this nonprofit organization. Housed in a new building devoted exclusively to the dance, its approximately 90 performances per year give priority to Quebéc artists, but leavened by appearances by other Canadian and international artists and troupes. Agora de la Danse, 840 rue Cherrier. ✆ **514/525-5584.** Tickets C$5–C$15 (US$3.10–US$9). Metro: Sherbrooke.

## CLASSICAL MUSIC & OPERA

**L'Opéra de Montréal** Founded in 1980, this outstanding opera company mounts six productions a year in Montréal, with artists from Québec and abroad participating in such shows as *La Traviata, Don Carlo, Carmen, Salome, La Bohème, Otello,* and *Mefistofele.* Video translations are provided from the original languages into French and English. The box office is open Monday to Friday 9am to 5pm. Performances are held from September to June, usually at 8pm, in three theaters at Place des Arts and occasional other venues. Salle Wilfrid-Pelletier, Place des Arts, 260 bd. de Maisonneuve Ouest. ✆ **514/985-2222** for information, or 514/985-2258 for tickets. www.operademontreal.qc.ca. Tickets C$32–C$99 (US$20–US$61). Métro: Place des Arts.

**Orchestre Métropolitain de Montréal** This orchestra has a regular season at Place des Arts but also performs in the St-Jean-Baptiste Church and tours regionally. Most musicians are in their mid-30s or younger. The box office is open Monday to Saturday noon to 8pm. Performances are held mid-October to early April, usually at 8pm. Outdoor concerts are given in Parc Lafontaine in August. Maisonneuve Theatre, Place des Arts, 260 bd. de Maisonneuve Ouest. ✆ **514/598-0870.** Tickets C$13–C$40 (US$8–US$25). Métro: Place des Arts.

**L'Orchestre Symphonique de Montréal (OSM)** This world-famous orchestra, under the baton of Swiss conductor Charles Dutoit, performs at Place des Arts and the Notre-Dame Basilica, as well as around the world, and may be heard on numerous recordings. In the balanced repertoire are works from Elgar to Rabaud to Saint-Saëns, in addition to Beethoven and Mozart. The box office is open Monday to Saturday noon to 8pm. Performances are usually at 8pm, during a full season that runs September to May, supplemented by Mozart concerts in Notre-Dame Basilica on six evenings in June and July, interspersed with free performances at three parks in the metropolitan region. People under

25 can purchase tickets for only C$10 (US$6) on the day of the concert. Salle Wilfrid-Pelletier, Place des Arts, 260 bd. de Maisonneuve Ouest. ✆ **514/842-9951** (for tickets, Mon–Fri 9am–5pm). www.osm.ca. Tickets C$16–C$42 (US$10–US$26). Métro: Place des Arts.

## CONCERT HALLS & AUDITORIUMS

Montréal has a score of music venues, so check the papers upon arrival to see who's playing where during your stay. When concerts are scheduled, printed flyers, posters, and radio and TV ads make certain everyone knows.

**Centre Molson** Big-name rock bands and pop stars that used to play at the Forum now show up at this sparkling downtown arena. The home of the Montréal Canadiens also hosts international pop stars on the order of Ricky Martin, the Backstreet Boys, Rod Stewart, and Alanis Morissette, as well as such dissimilar attractions as Disney's World On Ice. The box office is open Monday to Friday 10am to 6pm (to 9pm on days of events). Performances are at 7:30pm or 8pm. Ticket prices vary greatly, depending on the attraction. 1260 rue de la Gauchetière Ouest. ✆ **514/932-2582.** www.centre-molson.com. Métro: Bonaventure.

**Place des Arts** Founded in 1963 and in its striking present home in the heart of Montréal since 1992, Place des Arts mounts performances of musical concerts, opera, dance, and theater in five halls: **Salle Wilfrid-Pelletier** (2,982 seats), where the Orchestre Symphonique de Montréal often performs; the **Théâtre Maisonneuve** 1,460 seats), where the Orchestre Métropolitan de Montréal and the McGill Chamber Orchestra perform; the **Théâtre Jean-Duceppe** 755 seats); the **Cinquième Salle** 350 seats); and the small **Studio-Théâtre du Maurier Ltée** 138 seats). Traveling productions of Broadway classics on the order of *Smokey Joe's Café* and *Showboat* have limited runs at the center. Noontime performances are often scheduled. The box office is open Monday through Saturday noon to 8pm, and performances are usually at 8pm. Ticket prices vary according to hall and the group performing. 175 rue Ste-Catherine Ouest. ✆ **514/285-4200** for information, 514/842-2112 for tickets. www.pdarts.com. AE, DC, MC, V. Métro: Place des Arts.

**Pollack Concert Hall** In a landmark building dating from 1899 that's fronted by a statue of Queen Victoria, this hall is in nearly constant use, especially during the university year. Among the attractions are concerts and recitals by professionals, students, or soloists from McGill's music faculty. Recordings of some of the more memorable concerts are available on the university's own label, McGill Records. Box office hours are Monday to Friday noon to 6pm. Concerts are also given in the campus's smaller **Redpath Hall,** 3461 rue McTavish (✆ **514/398-4547**). Performances are at 8pm; they are often free, but tickets for some events can cost up to C$22 (US$14). On the McGill University campus, 555 rue Sherbrooke Ouest. ✆ **514/398-4547.** www.music.mcgill.ca. Métro: McGill.

**Spectrum de Montréal** A broad range of Canadian and international performers, usually of a modest celebrity unlikely to fill the larger Centre Molson, use this converted movie theater. Rock acts on the order of Musical Box and Phish are among the higher-profile acts, comedians are sometimes booked, and the space also hosts segments of the city's annual jazz festival. Seats are available on a first-come, first-served basis, and all ages are admitted. The box office is open Monday to Friday noon to 9pm and Saturday and Sunday noon to 5pm. Performances are at 8:30 or 9pm. 318 rue Ste-Catherine Ouest (at rue de Bleury). ✆ **800/361-4595** or 514/861-5851. www.admission.com (for tickets). Métro: Place des Arts; then take the Bleury exit.

**Théâtre de Verdure** Nestled in a popular park in Plateau Mont-Royal, this open-air theater presents free music and dance concerts and theater, often with well-known artists and performers. Sometimes they show outdoor movies. Many in the audience pack picnics. Performances are held from June to August; call for days and times. In Lafontaine Park. © **514/872-2644.** Métro: Sherbrooke.

**Théâtre St-Denis** Recently refurbished, this theater in the heart of the Latin Quarter hosts a variety of shows, including pop singers and groups and comedians, as well as segments of the Juste pour Rire (Just for Laughs) Festival in summer. It's actually two theaters, one seating more than 2,000, the other almost 1,000. The box office is open daily noon to 9pm. Performances are usually at 8pm. 1594 rue St-Denis (at Emery). © **514/790-1111.** Métro: Berri–UQAM.

## COMEDY & MUSIC CLUBS

### COMEDY

The once enthusiastic market for comedy clubs across North America has cooled, but Montréal still has a couple of laugh spots, mostly because it's the home to the **Juste pour Rire/Just for Laughs Festival** (see "Special Events & Festivals," above). Those who have so far eluded the comedy-club experience should know that profanity, bathroom humor, and assorted ethnic slurs are common fodder for performers.

**Comedy Nest** Mostly local talent is showcased at this club in the Nouvel Hotel, but among the comics who stopped off here on their way up were Howie Mandel, Norm MacDonald, and superstar Jim Carrey. Shows are held Wednesday through Sunday at 8:30pm, with added shows on Friday and Saturday at 11:30pm. Drinks cost C$5 to C$8 (US$3.10–US$5). 1740 bd. René-Lévesque (at rue Guy). © **514/932-6378.** www.comedynest.com. Cover C$10 (US$7). Métro: Guy-Concordia.

**Comedyworks** There's a full card of comedy at this long-running club, up the stairs from Jimbo's Pub on a jumping block of rue Bishop south of rue Ste-Catherine. Monday is usually open-mike night, while on Tuesday and Wednesday, improvisational groups work off the audience. Headliners of greater or lesser magnitude—usually from Montréal, Toronto, New York, or Boston—take the stage Thursday through Sunday. No food is served, just drinks. Reservations are recommended, especially on Friday, when early arrival may be necessary to secure a seat. Shows are nightly at 9pm, and also at 11:15pm on Fridays and Saturdays. Most drinks cost C$5 to C$8 (US$3.10–US$5). 1238 rue Bishop (at rue Ste-Catherine). © **514/398-9661.** Cover up to C$15 (US$9), C$5 (US$3.10) for students Thursday nights. Métro: Guy-Concordia.

### FOLK, ROCK & POP

Scores of bars, cafes, theaters, clubs, and even churches present live music on at least an occasional basis, even if only at Sunday brunch. The performers, local or touring, traffic in every idiom, from metal to funk and reggae to grunge and unvarnished Vegas. Here are a few places that focus their energies on the music.

**Café Campus** When anyone over 25 shows up inside this bleak club on touristy Prince-Arthur, he or she is probably a parent of one of the musicians. Alternative rock prevails, but metal and retro-rock bands also make appearances. Followers of the scene may be familiar with such groups as Liquid Soul, Come, and Carapace, all of whom have hit the stage here. Disco parties are often scheduled Wednesday nights, and a smaller room, Petit Café Campus, usually has hip-hop—no cover. 57 rue Prince-Arthur Est (near bd. St-Laurent). © **514/844-1010.** Cover usually C$5–C$12 (US$3.10–US$7). Métro: Sherbrooke.

**Club Soda** These new quarters for the long-established club are even larger than the old location on avenue du Parc. It remains one of the prime destinations for attractions below the megastar level and is a principal venue for the "Just for Laughs" festival. Performers are given a stage in a hall that seats several hundred fans. Five bars pump audience enthusiasm. Musical choices hop all over the charts—folk, rock, blues, country, Afro-Cuban, heavy metal—you name it. Acts for the annual jazz and comedy festivals are booked here, too. 1225 bd. St-Laurent (at Ste-Catherine). ✆ **514/790-1111**, ext. 200 (box office). www.clubsoda.ca. Cover C$5 (US$3.10) and up. AE, MC, V. Métro: St-Laurent.

**Hard Rock Café** No surprises here, not with clones around the world. Guitars, costumes, and other rock memorabilia decorate the walls, and the usual Hard Rock souvenirs are available. The formula still works, and it gets crowded at lunch and on weekend evenings. Open Sunday to Thursday 11:30am to midnight, Friday to Saturday 11:30am to 3am; the disco is up and going 11:30pm to 1am. Drinks cost C$4 to C$8 (US$2.50–US$5). 1458 rue Crescent (near bd. de Maisonneuve). ✆ **514/987-1420.** No cover. Métro: Guy-Concordia.

**Hurley's Irish Pub** The Irish have been one of the largest immigrant groups in Montréal since the famine of the 1840s, and their musical tradition thrives here. Celtic instrumentalists and dancers perform every night of the week, often both on the ground floor and upstairs, usually starting around 9:30pm. Guinness and other drinks go for C$3 to C$8 (US$1.85–US$5). 1225 rue Crescent (south of rue Ste-Catherine). ✆ **514/861-4111.** No cover. Métro: Peel or Guy-Concordia.

**Le Pierrot/Aux Deaux Pierrots** Perhaps the best known of Montréal's *boîtes-à-chansons*—song clubs—Le Pierrot is an intimate French-style cabaret. The singers interact animatedly with the crowd, often bilingually. Le Pierrot is open daily from early June to late September, Thursday to Sunday the other months, with music into the wee hours. Its sister club next door, the larger Les Deux Pierrots, features live bands playing rock Friday and Saturday nights, with vocals half in French and half in English. The terrace joining the two clubs is open on Friday and Saturday nights in summer. Shooters cost C$3 (US$1.85), other drinks to C$8 (US$5). 114 and 104 rue St-Paul Est (west of place Jacques-Cartier). ✆ **514/861-1270.** www.lespierrots.com. Cover: Le Pierrot, C$3 (US$1.85) Fri–Sat, free other nights; Aux Deux Pierrots, C$5 (US$3.10). Métro: Place d'Armes.

**Le P'tit Bar** One of many cramped, packed, smoky, and entertaining *boîtes-à-chansons* featuring the kinds of French pop and folk songs made known by Charles Azvanour and Jacques Brel, you'll find this near the east end of Square St-Louis. In between sets of the singers occupying the postage-stamp stand near the front door, express your views of Sartre and Camus. 3451 rue St-Denis. ✆ **514/281-9124.** No cover. Métro: Sherbrooke.

**Le Swimming** A nondescript entry and a stairway that smells of stale beer lead to a trendy pool hall that attracts many men and women who come to drink, socialize, and play pool (*le swimming,* get it?). Many Montréal bars have a pool table, but this one has 13, along with nine TVs and a terrace. On Wednesdays, there's a DJ. Thursday to Saturday nights they usually have bands embracing ska, funk, reggae, or jazz. It's open daily from 1pm to 3am, and pool is free until 5pm. 3643 bd. St-Laurent (north of rue Sherbrooke). ✆ **514/282-7665.** Cover C$5 (US$3.10) Thurs–Sat (when live bands are booked). Métro: Sherbrooke.

**O'Donnell's** Replacing a rock/blues club called Déjà Vu, this casual family-owned room feeds a local enthusiasm for Gaelic music and libations. It's a fun, friendly place, relatively inexpensive, with a couple of dance floors and live Irish music every weekend. 1224 rue Bishop (near rue Ste-Catherine). ✆ **514/877-3128.** www.bar-resto.com/odonnell. No cover. Métro: Guy-Concordia.

## JAZZ & BLUES

There are many more clubs featuring jazz and related forms than the sampling that follows. Pick up a copy of *Mirror* or *Hour,* distributed free everywhere, or buy the Friday or Saturday editions of the *Gazette* for the entertainment section. These publications have full listings of the bands and stars appearing during the week.

**Biddle's** Right downtown, where there's little after-dark action, this stalwart is a club-restaurant with hanging plants and faux Art Nouveau glass. It fills up early with lovers of barbecued ribs and jazz. The live music starts around 5:30pm (at 7pm on Sunday and Monday) and continues until closing time. Charlie Biddle plays bass when he doesn't have a gig elsewhere. He and his stand-ins favor jazz of the swinging mainstream variety, with occasional digressions into more esoteric forms. It's open Sunday 4pm to 12:30am, Monday to Thursday 11:30am to 1:30am, and Friday and Saturday 11:30am to 2:30am. Drinks cost C$5 to C$8 (US$3.10–US$5), and there's a mandatory paid coat check. 2060 rue Aylmer (south of rue Sherbrooke). ✆ **514/842-8656.** No cover, but a drink minimum Fri–Sat. Métro: McGill.

**L'Air du Temps** A Montréal tradition since 1976, L'Air du Temps is an ardent jazz emporium of the old school— seedy and beat up, and no gimmicks or frippery to distract from the music. The main room and an upper floor in back can hold more than 135, and the bar stools and tables fill up quickly. Get there by 9:30pm or so to secure a seat. The bands go on at 10:30pm or thereabouts. L'Air du Temps doesn't serve food, just a wide variety of drinks, but there are several good mid-priced restaurants nearby. The most likely of Montréal's jazz clubs to get semi-name acts, it doesn't take reservations. It's open Thursday to Monday from 9pm to 3am. Drinks cost C$4 to C$8 (US$2.50–US5). 191 rue St-Paul Ouest (at rue St-François-Xavier). ✆ **514/842-2003.** Cover C$5–C$25 (US$3.10–US$16), depending on the attraction. Métro: Place d'Armes.

**Maestro S.V.P.** Good eats and live music aren't strangers in Montréal. Although this bistro is best known for seafood, especially its oyster bar (see "Where to Dine," earlier), the owner brings in a trio Sunday nights at 6:30. That justifies the name and the musical instruments that constitute most of the decor. 3615 bd. St-Laurent (north of Sherbrooke). ✆ **514/842-6447.** No cover. Metro: Sherbrooke.

## DANCE CLUBS

Montréal's dance clubs change in tenor and popularity in mere eyeblinks, and new ones sprout like toadstools after heavy rain and wither as quickly. For the latest fever spots, quiz concierges, guides, and waiters—all those who look as if they might follow the scene. Here are a few that appear more likely to survive the whims of night owls and landlords. At some, you'll encounter steroid abusers with funny haircuts guarding the doors. Usually, they'll let you inside; the admittance game is not as strict nor as arbitrary as the "hipper than thou" criteria encountered at some New York and Los Angeles clubs.

**Club Balattou** An infectious, sensual tropical beat issues from this club-with-a-difference on The Main, a hot, happy variation from the prevailing grunge and murk of what might be described as mainstream clubs. Although most of the patrons revel in their ancestral origins in the Caribbean and Africa, the sources of the live and recorded music, everyone is welcome. Admittedly, the hip-waggling expertise of the dancers might be intimidating to the rhythmically challenged. Things get going about 10pm every night but Monday. The cover charge includes one beer or glass of wine; additional drinks are C$4 to C$8 (US$2.50–US$5). 4372 bd. St-Laurent (at rue Marie-Anne). ✆ **514/845-5447.** Cover C$8 (US$5). Métro: Mont-Royal.

**FunkyTown** For most of the vivacious crowd that swirls through this downtown disco, the Seventies were the old days and they were still in rompers. Much of the music is of that era, with a supportive decor. Think mirrored balls, floors lit from below, and a setting resembling that in which John Travolta committed The Hustle in his ice cream suit. Go too late and you'll most likely encounter a line and a wait. Most drinks are in the C$4 to C$9 range (US$2.50–US$6). It opens at 10pm, Thursday to Saturday. 1454 rue Peel. ✆ **514/282-8387.** Metro: Peel.

**Les Foufounes Electriques** On the scene for more than a decade, this multilevel disco-rock club has mellowed somewhat from its outlaw days, although it stills features hardcore rock and industrial bands. An occasional one-hit wonder puts in an appearance—Vanilla Ice, anyone? With three dance floors and a couple of beer gardens in back, there's plenty to keep you busy, starting with the C$1.50 (US95¢) beers during the 4 to 6pm happy hour, shooters for C$1.25 to C$2.50 (US80¢–US$1.55), and pitchers for C$6 to C$9.50 (US$3.75–US$6), the higher prices applied at the weekend. Look for the rocket ship over the door. 87 Ste-Catherine Est (near St-Denis). ✆ **514/844-5539.** www.foufounes.qc.ca. Cover C$10 (US$6) and up. Métro: Berri–UQAM.

**Newtown** Huge fanfare, both orchestrated and word-of-mouth, trumpeted the Summer 2001 opening of this tri-level club in the white-hot center of the Rue Crescent night scene. One of the owners is Formula One race-car driver and local hero Jacques Villenueve, whose last name can be translated as "New Town". Adjoining town houses were scooped out to make one big trendy nightspot at a reported cost of C$7.5 million (US$4.7 million), with a disco in the basement, a big barroom on the main floor, and restaurant up top. Reservations are usually required for the resto, but admission to the bar and dance floor shouldn't be a problem. At this writing, there's no cover and no minimum. 1476 rue Crescent (at de Maisonneuve). ✆ **514/284-6555.** Métro: Peel.

**Salsathèque** It's been on the scene for years, so they're obviously doing something right. The big upstairs room is all glittery, bouncing, mirrored light, the better to get the dancers moving to mambo, merengue, and other tropical beats. Open Wednesday to Sunday from 9pm to 3am, it rarely kicks into high gear before midnight. The house band comes on at 11pm or thereabouts, and they bring in other acts. The main source of entertainment, though, is the patrons themselves, a highly proficient lot on the dance floor. Drinks run about C$4 to C$8 (US$2.50–US$5). 1220 rue Peel (at Ste-Catherine). ✆ **514/875-0016.** Cover C$5 (US$3.10) Fri–Sat. Métro: Peel.

**Wax Lounge** A jovial, thoroughly mixed crowd ankles over to this second-floor club after dinner at one of the half-dozen scene restaurants clustered around this busy south end of The Main. The velvet-rope policy is more in the interest of crowd control than exclusivity. When the live band (usually soul/rock with rap undertones) takes a break, the DJ pumps the house music right up through the soles of your shoes. Good brands of booze are poured, most from C$4 to C$8 (US$2.50–US$5) per drink. 3481 bd. St-Laurent (north of rue Sherbrooke). ✆ **514/282-0919.** Cover C$5 (US$3.10) Mon–Thurs, C$7 (US$4.35) Fri–Sat. Metro: Sherbrooke.

## BARS & CAFES

An abundance of restaurants, bars, and cafes masses along the streets near the **downtown commercial district,** from rue Stanley to rue Guy between rue Ste-Catherine and boulevard de Maisonneuve. **Rue Crescent,** in particular, hums with activity from late afternoon until far into the evening, especially after 10pm on a summer weekend night, when the street swarms with people careening from bar to restaurant to club. **Boulevard St-Laurent,** another nightlife hub, abounds in bars and clubs, most with a distinctive European—particularly French—personality, as opposed to the Anglo flavor of the rue Crescent area. Increasingly active **rue St-Paul,** west of place Jacques-Cartier in Vieux Montréal, falls somewhere in the middle on the Anglophone-Francophone spectrum. It's also a little more likely to get rowdy on late weekend nights.

In all cases, bars tend to open around 11:30am and go late. Many of them have *heures joyeuses* (happy hours) from as early as 3pm to as late as 9pm, but usually for a shorter period within those hours. At those times, two-for-one rather than discount drinks are the rule. Last call for orders is 3am, but patrons are often allowed to dawdle over those drinks until 4am.

### DOWNTOWN/RUE CRESCENT

**Lutetia Bar** Within sight of the trademark lobby fountain with its nude bronze sprite sporting stained-glass wings, this appealing bar draws a standing-room-only crowd of youngish to middle-aged professionals after 5:30pm. Later on, there's often music by jazz duos. In summer the hotel opens the terrace bar on the roof by the pool. In L'Hôtel de la Montagne, 1430 rue de la Montagne (north of rue Ste-Catherine). ✆ **514/288-5656.** Métro: Guy-Concordia.

**Ritz Bar** A mature, prosperous crowd seeks out the quiet Ritz Bar in the Ritz-Carlton, adjacent to its semi-legendary Café de Paris restaurant. Anyone can take advantage of the tranquil room and the professionalism of its staff, but because the atmosphere is rather formal, most men will be more at ease with a jacket. Piano music flutters softly around conversation during cocktail hour Monday to Friday 5 to 8pm and at dinnertime (5–11pm) September to mid-May. The bar is just off the hotel lobby, to the right. In the Ritz-Carlton Hôtel, 1228 rue Sherbrooke Ouest (at rue Drummond). ✆ **514/842-4212.** Métro: Peel.

**Sir Winston Churchill Pub** The three levels of bars and cafes incorporated here are rue Crescent landmarks. One reason is the sidewalk terrace, open in summer, enclosed in winter, and a vantage for checking out the pedestrian traffic all the time. Inside and down the stairs, the pub, with English ales on tap, attempts to imitate a British public house. Dishy waitresses in miniskirts bring food, but the burgers and such have to look up to reach mediocrity. A mixed crowd of questing young professionals mills around a total of 17 bars and two dance floors. Winnie, on the second floor, is a restaurant with a terrace of its own and a new cigar lounge. Open daily noon to 2am. During the 5 to 8pm happy hour, drinks are two-for-one. 1459 rue Crescent (near rue Ste-Catherine). ✆ **514/288-0623.** Métro: Guy-Concordia.

**Thursday's** A prime watering hole of Montréal's young professional set—those who are ever alert to the possibilities of companionship. The pubby bar spills out onto the terrace that hangs over the street, and there's a glittery disco in back, both in the Hôtel de la Montagne. Thursday's presumably takes its name from the Montréal custom of prowling nightspots on Thursday evening in search of the perfect date for Friday. 1441–1449 rue Crescent (near rue Ste-Catherine). ✆ **514/288-5656.** Métro: Guy-Concordia.

**Moments** **Sunset over the City**

Memorable. Breathtaking. The view, that is, from Montréal's only revolving bar/restaurant, **Le Tour de Ville,** in the Delta Centre-Ville Hôtel, 777 rue University (✆ **514/879-1370;** Métro: Square-Victoria). The bar doesn't revolve, but you still get a great view. The best time to go is when the sun is setting and the city lights are beginning to blink on. In the bar, one floor down from the restaurant, the same wonderful vistas are augmented by a dance floor, with a band Thursday to Saturday 9pm to 1 or 2am. There's no cover, but drinks range from C$6 to C$9 (US$3.75–US$6).

### PLATEAU MONT-ROYAL

**Bleu Est Noir** Wear anything better than a tank top and jeans or the January equivalent and you'll feel conspicuously overdressed. Grungy and beery it is, with a battered sheet-metal bar, a pool table, and a beat-up fireplace—all the better to receive neighborhood regulars from 3pm to dinnertime, and clogs of students from then until the third wee hour. A DJ works the turntables most nights, with live bands many Sundays. When there's a cover charge, it's usually C$5 to C$7 (US$3.10–US$4.35). 812 rue Rachel Est (near St-Hubert). ✆ **514/524-4809.** Metro: Mont-Royal.

**Blizzarts** Remnants of mismatched fifties modern decor fill the space around the small dance floor. Most nights, heavy-beat dance music is designed to get the 20ish crowd up and moving. Next to the DJ booth is a full bar with an espresso machine. On weekends, there's usually a band. Last we saw, the bartender on duty poured with a generous tilt of the bottle. His efforts go for about C$3 to C$7 (US$1.85–US$4.35). 3956a bd. St-Laurent (near rue Duluth). ✆ **514/843-4860.** Cover up to C$5 (US$3.45). Metro: Mont-Royal.

**Champs** Montréalers are no less enthusiastic about sports, especially hockey, than other Canadians, and fans both avid and casual drop by this three-story sports emporium to catch up with their teams and hoist a few. Games from around the world are fed to 35 TV monitors through 20 satellites, so they don't miss a goal, run, or touchdown. Food is what you expect—burgers, steaks, and such. 3956 bd. St-Laurent (near rue Duluth). ✆ **514/987-6444.** Metro: Mont-Royal.

**Laïka** Newer than most of the St-Laurent watering stops, this bright little boîte has an open front in summer and fresh flowers on the bar and some of the tables. Tasty sandwiches and tapas are served, and the Sunday brunch is popular. The DJ spins house, funk, and the mirrored ball from 8pm to 3am for the mostly 18- to 35-year-old crowd. Drinks range from C$3 to C$7 (US$1.85–US$4.35). 4040 bd. St-Laurent, near rue Duluth. ✆ **514/842-8088.** Metro: Mont-Royal.

**Shed Café** This place used to look as if the ceiling was caving in. Now, transformed into a Gothic dungeon, it's not a whit less frenetically popular. There are local beers on tap, as well as good fries and oversize portions of cake. The crowd skews young, but with enough diversity to make an hour or two interesting. 3515 bd. St-Laurent, north of rue Sherbrooke. ✆ **514/842-0220.** Métro: Sherbrooke.

**Whisky Café** Those who enjoy scotch, particularly single-malts like Laphraoig and Glenfiddich, find 30 different labels to sample here. Trouble is, the Québec government applies stiff taxes for the privilege, so most of the patrons (suits to students) seem to stick to beer. The decor is sophisticated, with exposed beams and vents, handmade tiled tables, and large wood-enclosed columns, but the real decorative triumph is the men's urinal, with a waterfall for a *pissoir.* Women are welcome to have a look. 5800 bd. St-Laurent (at rue Bernard). ✆ **514/278-2646.** www.whiskycafe.ca. Métro: Outremont.

### QUARTIER LATIN/LATIN QUARTER

**Jello Bar** Lava lamps and other fixtures make it look like the rumpus room of a suburban ranch house of the Sixties, but central to the rep of this goofy throwback is the card of more than 30 kinds of martinis. Most are flavored excuses for people who don't really like liquor, but the classic gin and vodka versions are stalwarts to be savored. Live music helps fuel the rollicking good mood (Bruce Willis stopped by once with his band), usually Tuesday, Wednesday, Friday, and Saturday. Other times, there's DJ and a dance floor. Martinis are only C$5 (US$3.10). 151 rue Ontario Est (near bd. St-Laurent). ✆ **514/285-2621.** www.jello-bar.com. Metro: St-Laurent or Berri–UQAM.

**Le Sainte-Elisabeth** Aided by Guinness "on draught," this place comes closer to resembling an Irish pub than most of the many efforts in town. Past the Queen Anne Victorian facade is a copper-topped bar near the fireplace with a smattering of heavily used sofas, and beyond all that is a boxy, tree-shaded, vine-covered open courtyard, known as a *terrasse* in these parts. University and grad students predominate but don't overwhelm. Blues and jazz are on the stereo and live (usually Tuesdays). 1412 rue Ste-Elizabeth (north of rue Ste-Catherine). ✆ **514/286-4302.** Metro: Berri–UQAM.

**Le Saint-Sulpice** Adjoining four-story buildings still can't absorb the youthful crowds, both straight and gay, longing to be a part of the scene here. Expect lines up to six people deep and a block long on any night of even slightly tolerable weather. The club has a crowded terrace, a DJ most nights and live music on some, and dance floors and bars always. Beer is the favored quaff, with drinks going for C$3 to C$8 (US$1.85–US$5). 1680 rue St-Denis (near rue St-Catherine). ✆ **514/844-9458.** Metro: Berri–UQUAM.

### QUARTIER GAI/GAY VILLAGE

One of the largest gay and lesbian enclaves in North America, it is action central for both natives and visitors, especially during such annual events as the ten days celebrating sexual diversity known as **Divers/Cité** (✆ **514/286-4011;** www.diverscite.org) in early August.

**Complexe Bourbon** Stop first in this block-long, block-wide compound billed as "the largest gay complex in the world" and you might never get to the Village's other attractions. Open 24 hours, it incorporates a 37-room hotel, a sauna, the 3-floor La Track disco, a theater, an ice cream parlor, several bars and restaurants. One of the latter is **Le Club Sandwich,** a take on a Fifties diner with lots of neon and glass block. The signature edibles are huge, with slabs of bread as thick as a couple of fingers and ingredients to match. The large terrace is a prominent Village gathering place. Rooms in the Hôtel Bourbon cost C$75 to C$230 (US$47–US$143), depending on the season. 1574 rue Ste-Catherine Est (at Plessis).✆ **514/523-4679.** Metro: Papineau.

**L'Entre-Peau** This drag-queen cabaret has prospered for more than 10 years, drawing an increasingly straight audience. As many as 20 female impersonators, done up as the usual suspects, plus some unexpected figures, take to the stage every night, year-round. The name of the club, we're told, means "between the skins," which couldn't be more apt. The owner and star boasts a personal wardrobe of more than 200 dresses, 100 wigs, and more shoes than notorious Imelda. Drinks cost about C$3 to C$7 (US$1.85–US$4.35). 1115 rue Ste-Catherine (near rue Amherst). ✆ **514/525-7566.** Cover C$5 (US$3.10) and up. Métro: Beaudry.

**Sisters** It comes and goes, so to speak, but this dance club above the Saloon restaurant is thriving once again. Lesbians and bi women constitute most of the celebrants and contribute to the high energy level. Men, straight or gay, will almost certainly find more congenial surroundings elsewhere, but they are allowed entrance Sunday afternoons. 1313 rue Ste-Catherine Est (near rue St-Hubert). ✆ **514/523-0292.** No cover. Métro: Berri–UQAM.

**Sky Pub** Thought by many to be the city's best gay club, Sky continues to thrive after its recent closing for renovations. Spiffy decor and thumping (usually house) music in the upstairs disco contribute to the popularity. Up to six transvestite performers constitute a cabaret show 2 or 3 nights a week. There's an outdoor terrace in summer, and frequent two-for-one beer hours. 1474 rue Ste-Catherine Est (near rue Amherst). ✆ **514/529-6969.** No cover. Métro: Beaudry.

**Stéréo** One of a growing number of after-hours clubs, this hyper-hip entry doesn't crank up the jaw-dropping sound system until 2am. If you remember Richard Nixon, you'll feel like grandpa in this crowd, which stays on until dawn and beyond. 858 rue Ste-Catherine Est (near rue Berri). No phone. Métro: Berri–UQAM.

**Unity** Easily the Village's biggest nightclub, with several rooms, dance floors, a top-floor terrasse (popular for viewing the fireworks from La Ronde in summer), and five bars on different levels. There's plenty of room for dancing to house and techno music and a modest light show. Upstairs, the Diva Lounge has drag shows every Sunday at 9pm, and there's a cabaret show Tuesdays. On the ground floor, with three pool tables, happy hour drinks are two-for-one Friday and Saturday from 4 to 10pm. Unity is open from Thursday to Sunday 10pm to 3am throughout the year, while the terrace is open every evening in summer. 1171 rue Ste-Catherine Est (at rue Montcalm). ✆ **514/523-4429.** Métro: Beaudry.

## GAMBLING

Québec's first gambling emporium, the **Casino de Montréal** (✆ **800/665-2274** or 514/392-2746; www.casinos-quebec.com; Métro: Ile Ste-Hélène, then walk or take shuttle bus), is on Ile Notre-Dame in the former French Pavilion, which was left over from the 1967 Expo world's fair. Its several floors contain 118 game tables, including roulette, craps, blackjack, and baccarat, and more than 3,000 slot machines. It can accommodate 8,000 people, most of whom come to try their luck, of course; but the four restaurants get good notices, especially Nuances. There are four bars, live shows, and two shops selling gifts and souvenirs. No alcoholic beverages are served in the gambling areas.

Patrons must be 18 or over. The casino is open around the clock. Tickets to the cabaret can be purchased at the casino or on the Internet, at www.admission.com. They are priced from C$37 (US$23) for the show alone, from C$61 (US$38) for the show and dinner. The originally strict dress code has been relaxed somewhat, but the following items of clothing are still prohibited: "cut-off sweaters and shirts, tank tops, jogging outfits, cut-off shorts and bike shorts, beachwear, work or motorcycle boots, and clothing associated with violence or with an organization known to be violent." Admission and parking are free.

# 8

# Québec City & the Gaspé Peninsula

*by Herbert Bailey Livesey*

**Québec City** is the soul of New France. It was Canada's first significant settlement and today it is the capital of politically prickly Québec, a province larger than Alaska. The St. Lawrence makes a majestic sweep beneath the palisades on which the old city stands, a tumble of slate-roofed granite houses clustered around the dominating Château Frontenac as romantic as any on the continent. Because of its history, beauty, and stature as the only walled city north of Mexico, the historic district of Québec was named a UNESCO World Heritage site in 1985.

Québec City is almost entirely French in feeling, in spirit, and in language; 95% of the population is Francophone. Perhaps because of that homogeneity and its status as the putative capital of a future independent nation, its citizens seem to suffer less over what might happen down the road. They're also aware that a critical part of their economy is based on tourism and are less likely to show the hostility Americans can encounter in English Canada. There are far fewer bilingual residents here than in Montréal, but many of Québec City's 648,000 citizens speak some English, especially those who work in hotels, restaurants, and shops. This is also a college town, and thousands of young people study English as a second language.

Almost an entire visit can be spent in Vieux-Québec, the old walled city, since many hotels, restaurants, and visitor services are there. The original colony was built down by the St. Lawrence at the foot of Cap Diamant (Cape Diamond), and it was there that merchants, traders, and boatmen earned their livelihoods. But due to unfriendly fire in the 1700s, this Basse-Ville (Lower Town) became primarily a wharf/warehouse area, and residents moved to safer houses atop the steep cliffs. That trend is being reversed today, with several new auberges and many attractive bistros and shops revitalizing the area.

Haute-Ville (the Upper Town), the Québecois discovered, wasn't immune from cannon fire either, as British general James Wolfe was to prove. Nevertheless, the division into Upper and Lower Towns persisted for obvious topographical reasons. The Upper Town remains enclosed by fortification walls, and several ramp-like streets and a cliff-side funicular (*funiculaire*) connect it to the Lower Town.

A stroll through old Québec is comparable to exploring similar *quartiers* in northern Europe. Carriage wheels creak behind muscular horses, sunlight filters through leafy canopies to fall on drinkers and diners in sidewalk cafes, stone houses huddle close, and shrieks of childish laughter echo down cobblestoned streets. And, a bewitching vista of river and mountains is bestowed by the Dufferin promenade, at the edge of the upper town. In winter, the city takes on a Dickensian quality, with lamp glow behind curtains of falling snow.

After exploring the city, you may want to consider a trip to the Ile d'Orléans, a getaway island within sight of the Château Frontenac; a drive along the northern coast to the provincial park and ski center at Mont Ste-Anne, with the option of continuing along the coast to the resort villages of Charlevoix, where there is the possibility of a whale-watching cruise.

## 1 Essentials

### GETTING THERE

**BY PLANE** **Jean-Lesage International Airport** is small, despite the grand name. Buses into town are operated by **Autobus La Québécoise** (**✆ 418/872-5525**). The 20km (12-mile) trip costs C$9 (US$6). Buses leave at variable times depending on the season, but roughly speaking, they leave every 1½ hours from 8:45am to 8:45pm Monday to Friday and every 2 hours from 9am to 8:30pm Saturday and Sunday. A taxi into town costs about C$28 (US$17).

**BY TRAIN** Canada's **VIA Rail** (**✆ 888/VIA-RAIL** or 418/692-3940; www.viarail.ca) provides service from Montréal (trip time: 3 hours) to the **Gare du Palais,** 450 rue de la Gare-du-Palais (**✆ 418/692-3940**), designed by Bruce Price, who was also responsible for the fabled Château Frontenac. Handsome though it is, the Lower Town location isn't central. Plan on a moderately strenuous uphill hike or a C$6 to C$8 (US$3.70–US$5) cab ride to the Upper Town. That's per trip, incidentally, not per passenger, as an occasional cabbie may pretend.

**BY BUS** The bus station, **Gare d'Autobus de la Vieille Capitale,** at 320 rue Abraham-Martin (**✆ 418/525-3000**), is near the train station. As from the train station, it is an uphill climb or quick cab ride to Château Frontenac and the Upper Town. A taxi should cost about the same as from the train station.

**BY CAR** From New York City and points south, follow I-87 to Autoroute 15 to Montréal, picking up route 20 to Québec City. Take 73 Nord across Pont Pierre-Laporte and exit onto boulevard Champlain immediately after crossing the bridge. This skirts the city at river level. Turn left up the hill and through the Parc des Champs-de-Bataille (Battlefields Park), then right onto the Grande Allée. Alternatively, take Autoroute 40 from Montréal, which follows the north shore of the St. Lawrence. The trip takes about 2½ hours.

From Boston, take I-89 to I-93 to I-91 in Montpelier, Vermont, which connects with Autoroute 55 in Québec to link up with Autoroute 20. Or follow I-90 up the Atlantic coast, through Portland, Maine, to route 201 west of Bangor, then Autoroute 173 to Lévis, where there's a car-ferry to Québec City, a 10-minute ride across the St. Lawrence. The ferry between Lévis and Québec City runs daily, every 30 minutes from 6am to 3:45pm and every 60 minutes from 3:45pm to 3:45am. It costs C$5.60 (US$3.50) for the car, C$2.50 (US$1.55) for passengers ages 12 to 64, C$1.75 (US$1.10) for passengers 5 to 11, and C$2.25 (US$1.40) for passengers over 64; children under 5 are free. Fares are lower in winter.

### VISITOR INFORMATION

**TOURIST OFFICES** The **Greater Québec Area Tourism and Convention Bureau** (www.quebecregion.com) operates two useful information centers in

# Québec City

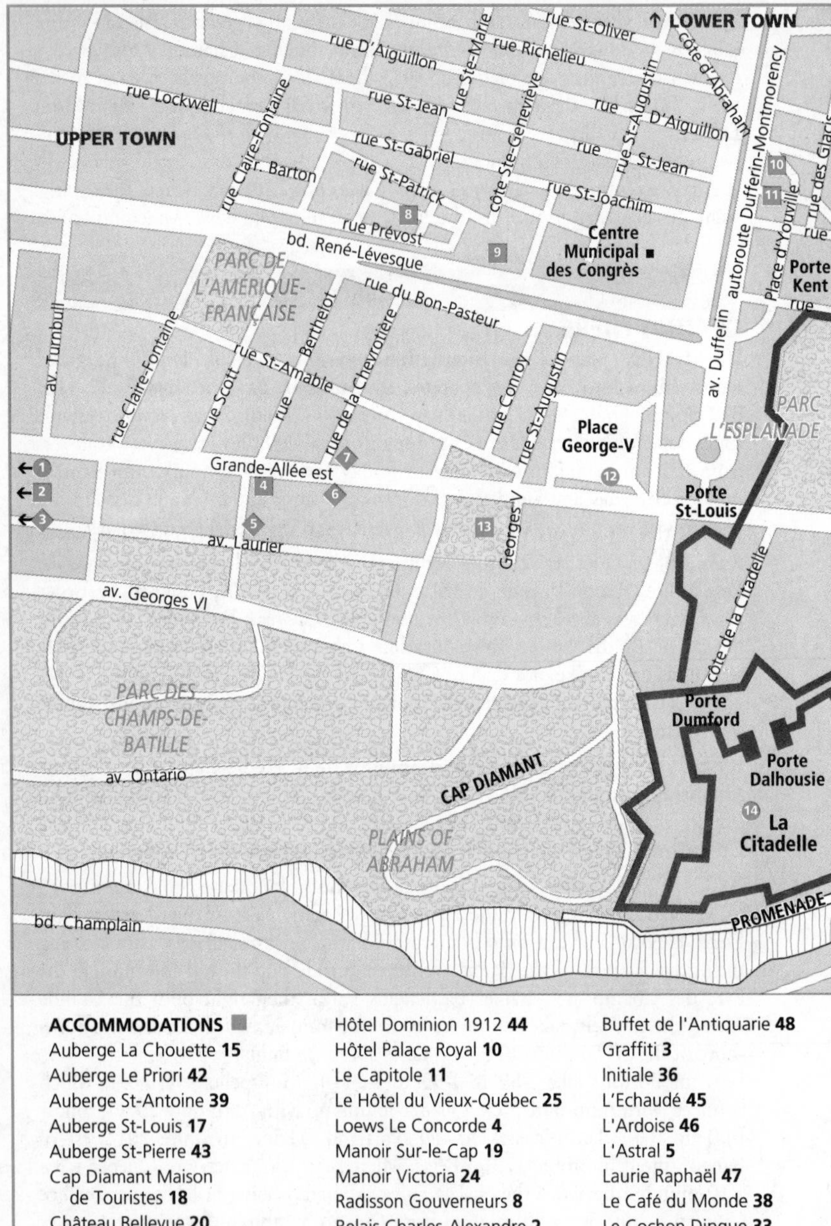


**ACCOMMODATIONS ■**
Auberge La Chouette **15**
Auberge Le Priori **42**
Auberge St-Antoine **39**
Auberge St-Louis **17**
Auberge St-Pierre **43**
Cap Diamant Maison de Touristes **18**
Château Bellevue **20**
Château Lauier **13**
Fairmont Château Frontenac **31**
Hilton Québec **9**
Hôtel Dominion 1912 **44**
Hôtel Palace Royal **10**
Le Capitole **11**
Le Hôtel du Vieux-Québec **25**
Loews Le Concorde **4**
Manoir Sur-le-Cap **19**
Manoir Victoria **24**
Radisson Gouverneurs **8**
Relais Charles-Alexandre **2**

**DINING ◆**
Aux Anciens Canadiens **22**
Buffet de l'Antiquarie **48**
Graffiti **3**
Initiale **36**
L'Echaudé **45**
L'Ardoise **46**
L'Astral **5**
Laurie Raphaël **47**
Le Café du Monde **38**
Le Cochon Dingue **33**
Le Marie-Clarisse **34**
Le Paris-Brest **7**
Le St-Amour **14**

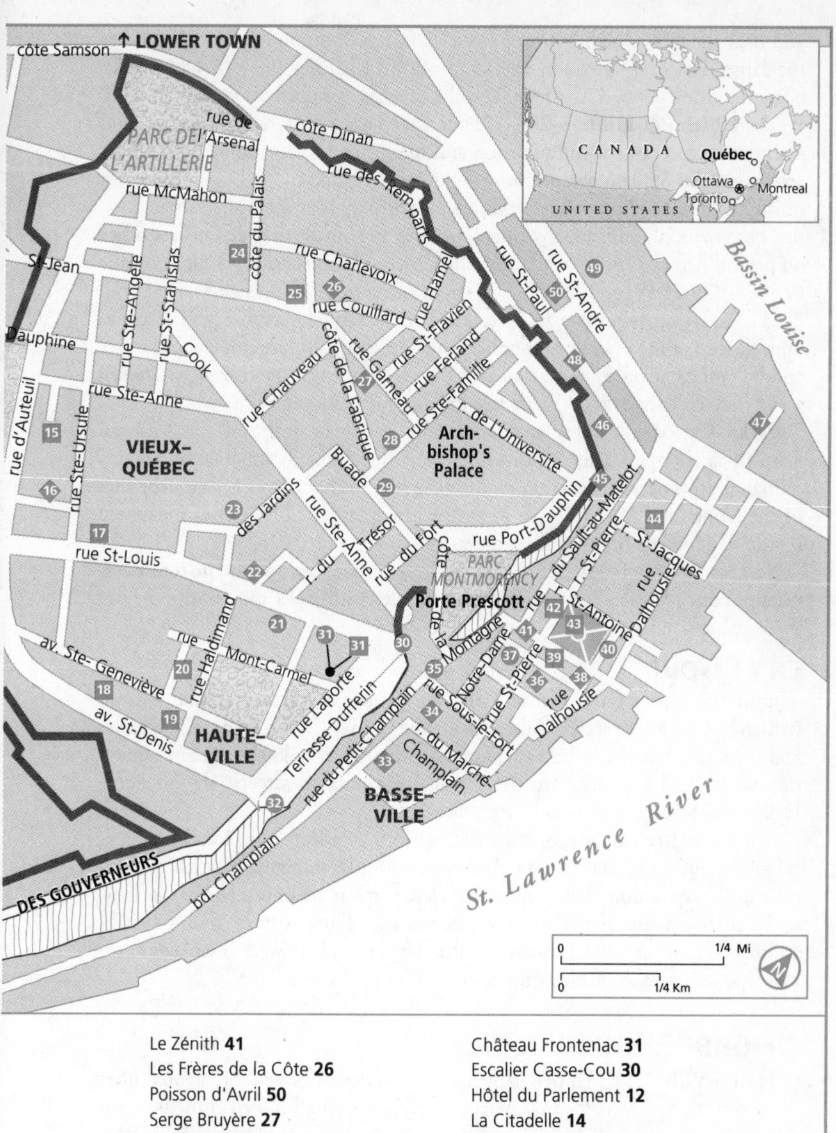


Le Zénith **41**
Les Frères de la Côte **26**
Poisson d'Avril **50**
Serge Bruyère **27**
Voodoo Grill **6**

**ATTRACTIONS** ●

Basilique-Cathédrale Notre-Dame **29**
Centre d'Interprétation du Vieux-Port **49**
Chapelle/Musée des Ursulines **23**
Château Frontenac **31**
Escalier Casse-Cou **30**
Hôtel du Parlement **12**
La Citadelle **14**
Maison Chevalier **35**
Musée d'Art Inuit Brousseau **21**
Musée de l'Amérique Française **28**
Musée de la Civiliization **40**
Musée du Québec **1**
Place Royale/Eglise Notre-Dame-des-Victoires **37**
Terrasse Duyfferin **32**

and near the city. One has moved from its former location on rue d'Auteuil to the larger Discovery Pavilion at 835 av. Wilfrid-Laurier (© **418/649-2608**), bordering the Plaines d'Abraham, and the other is in suburban Ste-Foy, at 3300 av. des Hôtels (© **418/651-2882**). They have rack after rack of brochures and attendants who can answer questions and make hotel reservations. Both offices are open daily 8:30am to 7pm from June 24 to Thanksgiving Day and the rest of the year 9am to 5pm Monday through Saturday, 10am to 4pm Sunday.

The provincial tourism department operates an **Infotouriste de Québec** office on place d'Armes, down the hill from the Château Frontenac, at 12 rue Ste-Anne (© **514/873-2015,** or 800/363-7777 from other parts of Québec, Canada, and the U.S.). It's open 9:30am to 5pm late June to early September, and 10am to 5pm the rest of the year. The office has many brochures, information about cruise and bus tour operators, a souvenir shop, a 24-hour ATM (*guichet automatique*), a currency-exchange office, and a free lodging reservation service.

**Parks Canada** operates an information kiosk in front of the Château Frontenac; it's open daily 9am to noon and 1 to 5pm. From June to August, bilingual university students on motorbikes station themselves near tourist sites in the Upper and Lower Towns to answer the questions of visitors. Spot them by the flags on the backs of their bikes.

Besides **www.quebecregion.com** noted above, go to **http://connect-quebec.com** for their Québec-Vacation Guide, with links to sites throughout the province.

## CITY LAYOUT

Within the walls of the **Haute-Ville,** the principal streets are rues St-Louis (which becomes the Grande-Allée outside the city walls), Ste-Anne, and St-Jean, and the pedestrians-only Terrasse Dufferin, which overlooks the river in front of the Château Frontenac. In the **Basse-Ville,** major streets are St-Pierre, Dalhousie, St-Paul, and parallel to it, St-André.

If it were larger, the historic district, with its winding and plunging streets, might be confusing to negotiate. As compact as it is, though, most visitors have little difficulty finding their way around. Most streets are only a few blocks long, so when the name of the street is known, it is fairly easy to find a specific address. There are good maps of the Upper and Lower Towns and the metropolitan area available at the tourist offices.

## NEIGHBORHOODS IN BRIEF

**Haute-Ville** The Upper Town, surrounded by thick ramparts, occupies the crest of Cap Diamant and overlooks the Fleuve Saint-Laurent (St. Lawrence River). It includes many of the sites for which the city is famous, among them the Château Frontenac, Place d'Armes, Basilica of Notre-Dame, Québec Seminary and Museum, and the Terrasse Dufferin. At a higher elevation, to the south of the Château, is the Citadel, a partially star-shaped fortress begun by the French in the 18th century and augmented often by the English well into the 19th. Since most buildings are at least 100 years old, made of granite in similar styles, the Haute-Ville is visually harmonious, with few jarring modern intrusions. The overall grayness is offset by the tin roofs and trim, coated with a silvery metallic paint that covers the churches and many institutional buildings. When they added a new wing to the château a few years ago, they modeled it with considerable care after the original—standing policy here. The Terrasse Dufferin is a pedestrian promenade that attracts crowds in all seasons for its magnificent views of the river and the land to the south. Ferries glide back and forth, while cruise ships and Great Lakes freighters put in at the harbor below.

**Basse-Ville** The Lower Town encompasses the restored Quartier du Petit-Champlain, including pedestrian-only rue du Petit-Champlain; Place Royale and the small Notre-Dame-des-Victoires church, and, nearby, the impressive Museum of Civilization, a highlight of any visit. Basse is linked to Haute by a funicular and several streets and stairways, including one near the entrance to the funicular. Petit-Champlain is undeniably touristy, but not to the point where it's unpleasant: T-shirt vendors have been held in check, though hardly banned. It contains several agreeable cafes and shops. Restored Place Royale is perhaps the most attractive of the city's many squares, upper or lower.

**Grande-Allee** This boulevard is the western extension of rue St-Louis, from the St-Louis Gate in the fortified walls to avenue Taché. It passes the stately Parliament building, in front of which Winter Carnival takes place every year, as well as the numerous terraced bars and restaurants that line both sides from rue de la Chevrotière to rue de Claire-Fontaine. Later, it skirts the Musée des Beaux-Arts and the Plains of Abraham, where one of the most important battles in the history of North America took place.

## 2 Getting Around

Once you're within or near the walls of the Haute Ville, virtually no place of interest nor hotel or restaurant is beyond walking distance. In bad weather, or when you're traversing between opposite ends of Lower and Upper Towns, a taxi might be necessary, but in general, walking is the best way to explore the city.

### BY BUS

Local buses run often and charge C$2.25 (US$1.40) in exact change; tickets purchased in a *dépanneur* (convenience store) cost C$1.70 (US$1.05). A 1-day pass is C$4.50 (US$2.80). Discounts are available for seniors and students. Bus no. 7 travels up and down rue St-Jean; no. 11 shuttles along Grande-Allée/rue St-Louis and, along with nos. 7 and 8, also goes well into suburban Ste-Foy, for those who want to visit the shopping centers there.

### BY FUNICULAR

Although there are streets and stairs between the Château Frontenac on the top of the cliff and Place Royale in the Lower Town, there is also a funicular, which runs along an inclined 64m (210-ft.) track between the Terrasse Dufferin and the Quartier du Petit-Champlain. It was closed for a couple of years due to a fatal accident in 1996. Repaired now—although subject to occasional stoppages—the **upper station** is near the front of the Château Frontenac and Place d'Armes, while the **lower station** is actually inside the Maison Louis-Jolliet, on rue du Petit-Champlain. It runs all year, daily from early morning until 11:30pm. Wheelchairs are accommodated. The one-way fare is C$1.25 (US80¢).

### BY TAXI

They're everywhere, cruising and parked in front of the big hotels and in some of the larger squares of the Upper Town. In theory, they can be hailed, but they are best obtained by locating one of their stands, as in the Place d'Armes or in front of the Hôtel-de-Ville (City Hall). Restaurant managers and hotel bell captains will also summon them. Fares are the same as in Montréal, meaning they're somewhat expensive here, given the short distances of most rides. The starting rate is C$2.50 (US$1.55), each 1km (½ mile) costs C$1.20 (US75¢), and each minute when stopped costs another C40¢ (US25¢). A taxi from the train station to one of the big hotels is about C$6 to C$7 (US$3.70–US$4.35) plus tip. To call a cab, try **Taxi Coop** (✆ **418/525-5191**) or **Taxi Québec** (✆ **418/525-8123**).

## BY CAR

On-street parking is very difficult in the cramped quarters of old Québec City. When you find a rare space on the street, be sure to check the signs for the hours when parking is permissible. When meters are in place, the charge is C25¢ (US16¢) per 15 minutes up to 120 minutes. Metered spots are free on Sundays, before 9am and after 6pm Monday through Wednesday and on Saturday, and before 9am and after 9pm Thursday and Friday.

Many of the smaller hotels have arrangements with local garages, resulting in discounts for their guests of 30% or more per day than the usual C$10 (US$6) a day. Check at the hotel first before parking in a lot or garage. If a particular hotel or auberge doesn't have access to a garage or lot, plenty are available, clearly marked on the foldout city map available at tourist offices.

To rent a car to explore the environs or travel elsewhere in Canada, try **Avis,** at the airport (✆ **800/879-2847** or 418/872-2861) and in the city (✆ **418/523-1075**); **Budget,** at the airport (✆ **800/268-8900** or 418/872-9885) and in the city (✆ **418/687-4220**); **Hertz Canada,** at the airport (✆ **800/654-3131** or 418/871-1571) and in the city (✆ **418/697-4949**); **Thrifty,** at the airport (✆ **800/367-2277** or 418/877-2870) and in the city (✆ **418/648-7766**); and **National,** at the airport (✆ **418/ 871-1224**) and in the city (✆ **418/692-1727**). A firm specializing in economical rates is **Discount,** in Vieux-Québec (✆ **418/692-1244**).

## *FAST FACTS:* Québec City

*American Express* There's no office right in town, but for lost traveler's checks or credit cards, call ✆ **418/692-0997.** American Express keeps a customer-service desk in Ste-Foy, a bus or taxi ride away: **Place Laurier,** 2700 bd. Laurier (✆ **418/658-8820**), open Monday to Friday 9am to 5pm.

*Area Code* Québec City's area code is **418.**

*Consulate* The **U.S. Consulate** is near the Château Frontenac, facing Jardin des Gouverneurs at 2 place Terrasse-Dufferin (✆ **418/692-2095**).

*Currency Exchange* Conveniently located near the Château Frontenac, the **Bureau de Change** at 19 rue Ste-Anne and rue des Jardins is open Monday, Tuesday, and Friday from 10am to 3pm, and Wednesday and Thursday from 10am to 6pm. On weekends, it's possible to change money in hotels and shops, but you'll get an equal or better rate at an ATM, such as the one at the corner of rues Ste-Anne and des Jardins.

*Dentists* Call ✆ **418/653-5412** any day or ✆ **418/524-2444** Monday through Saturday. Both numbers are hot lines that refer callers to available dentists.

*Doctors* For emergency treatment, call **Info-Santé** (✆ **418/648-2626**) 24 hours a day, or the **Hôtel-Dieu de Québec** hospital emergency room (✆ **418/ 691-5042**).

*Drugstores* **Caron & Bernier,** in the Upper Town, 38 Côte du Palais, at rue Charlevoix (✆ **418/692-4252**), is open 8:15am to 8pm Monday to Friday, and 9am to 3pm on Saturday. In an emergency, it's necessary to travel to the suburbs to **Pharmacie Brunet,** in Les Galeries Charlesbourg, 4250 Première Ave. (1ère or First Avenue), in Charlesbourg (✆ **418/623-1571**), open 24 hours, 7 days.

*Emergencies* For police or ambulance, call ✆ **911. Marine Search and Rescue** (Canadian Coast Guard), 24 hours a day, ✆ **418/648-3599** (Greater Québec area) or ✆ **800/463-4393** (St. Lawrence River). **Poison Control Center,** ✆ **800/ 463-5060** or 418/656-8090.

*Laundromat* Handy to the Château Frontenac, the **Buanderie du Vieux-Québec** 41½ rue St-Louis is open daily 7am to 10pm.

*Liquor & Wine* A supermarket-sized **Société des Alcools** store is located at 1059 av. Cartier. Wine and beer can be bought in grocery stores and supermarkets. The legal drinking age in the province is 18.

*Newspapers & Magazines* English-language newspapers and magazines are available in the newsstands of the large hotels and at **Maison de la Presse Internationale,** at 1050 rue St-Jean.

*Pets* For emergency pet illnesses or injuries, call ✆ **418/872-5355** 24 hours a day. Pet owners must by law pick up after their animals, which have to be kept on leashes.

*Police* For the Québec City police, call ✆ **911.** For the **Sûreté du Québec,** comparable to the state police or highway patrol, call ✆ **800/461-2131.**

*Post Office* The main post office (*bureau de poste*) is in the Lower Town, at 300 rue St-Paul near rue Abraham-Martin, not far from Carré Parent (Parent Square) by the port (✆ **418/694-6175**). Hours are 8am to 5:45pm Monday to Friday. A convenient branch in the Upper Town, half a block down the hill from the Château Frontenac at 3 rue Buade (✆ **418/ 694-6102**), keeps the same hours.

*Taxes* Most goods and services in Canada are taxed 7% by the federal government. On top of that, the province of Québec has an additional 7.5% tax on goods and services, including those provided by hotels. In Québec, the federal tax appears on the bill as the TPS (elsewhere in Canada, it's called the GST), and the provincial tax is known as the TVQ. Tourists may receive a rebate on both the federal and provincial tax on items they have purchased but not used in Québec, as well as on lodging. To take advantage of this refund, request the necessary forms at duty-free shops and hotels, and submit them, with the original receipts, within a year of the purchase. Contact the Canadian consulate or Québec tourism office for up-to-the-minute information about taxes and rebates.

*Telephones* The telephone system closely resembles the American model. All operators (dial ✆ **00** to get one) speak French and English, and respond in the appropriate language as soon as callers speak to them. Pay phones in Québec require C25¢ (US17¢) for a 3-minute local call. Directory information calls (dial ✆ **411**) are free of charge. Both local and long-distance calls usually cost more from hotels—sometimes a lot more, so check. Directories (*annuaires des téléphones*) come in white pages (residential) and yellow pages (commercial).

*Time* Québec City is on Eastern Time, the same as New York, Boston, Montréal, and Toronto. It's an hour behind Halifax.

## 3 Where to Stay

Staying in one of the small hotels or inns within the walls of the Upper Town can be one of Québec City's memorable experiences. That isn't to say it necessarily will be enjoyable. Standards of comfort, amenities, and prices fluctuate so wildly from one place to another—even within a single establishment—that it's wise to shop around and examine rooms before registering. From rooms with private bathrooms, minibars, and cable TVs to walk-up budget accommodations with linoleum floors and toilets down the hall, Québec City has a wide enough variety of lodgings to suit most tastes and wallets.

If cost is a prime consideration, note that prices drop significantly from November to April, except for such events as the Winter Festival. Or if you prefer the conveniences of large chain hotels and the Château Frontenac is fully booked, you'll need to go outside the ancient walls to the younger part of town. The handful of high-rise hotels out there are within walking distance of the attractions in the Old City, or are only a quick bus or taxi ride away. Although Québec City has far fewer first-class hotels than Montréal, there are still a sufficient number to provide for the crowds of businesspeople and well-heeled tourists who flock to the city year-round. And in recent years, a clutch of new boutique hotels and small inns has greatly enhanced the lodging stock.

The cheapest rooms are usually found in smaller establishments, typically converted residences or carved out of several row houses. They offer fewer of the usual electronic gadgets—air-conditioning and TV are far from standard at this level—and may have four or five floors, without elevators. Even with an advance reservation, always ask to see two or three rooms before making a choice in this price category. Unless otherwise noted, all rooms in the lodgings listed below have private bathrooms—*en suite,* as they say in Canada.

### HAUTE-VILLE (UPPER TOWN)

#### VERY EXPENSIVE

**Fairmont Château Frontenac** ★★★ *Kids* Québec City's magical "castle" turned 100 years old in 1993. The hotel has hosted Queen Elizabeth and Prince Philip, and during World War II, Winston Churchill and Franklin D. Roosevelt had the entire place to themselves for a conference. It was built in phases, following the landline, so the wide halls take crooked paths. The highly variable room prices depend on size, location, view or lack of one, and on how recently it was renovated. As a result, the rates given below should be treated as a very rough guide because day of the week, time of year, and even the weather can determine what rates may be offered. The casual Café de la Terrasse has dancing on Saturday nights. Two bars overlook the Terrasse Dufferin.

1 rue des Carrières (at rue St-Louis), Québec City, PQ G1R 4P5. ✆ **800/828-7447** or 418/692-3861. Fax 418/692-1751. www.cphotels.ca. 626 units. Mid-May to mid-Oct C$429–C$629 (US$266–US$390) double, Mid-Oct to mid-May C$199–C$512 (US$123–US$317) double, C$559–C$975 (US$347–US$605) suite. AE, DC, DISC, MC, V. Parking C$18 (US$11) per day. **Amenities:** 2 restaurants (International), 2 bars; new indoor pool

and kiddie pool; large health club with weight machines and Jacuzzi; children's programs; video arcade; concierge; car-rental desk; courtesy limo; business center; shopping arcade; limited room service; in-room massage; babysitting; laundry service; same-day dry cleaning; executive floors. *In room:* A/C, TV w/pay movies, dataport, minibar, coffeemaker, hair dryer, iron.

## EXPENSIVE

**Manoir Victoria** ★ The sprawling lobby isn't especially beguiling, but there are two serviceable restaurants on the premises, and the location beside the St-Jean resto and bar scene is a plus for many. An added extra is the indoor pool, rare in the city. The hotel sprawls all the way from the main entrance on Côte de Palais to adjacent St-Jean, zigzagging around a couple of stores. A long staircase reaches the lobby, but elevators make the trip to most of the rooms. All rooms were redecorated in recent years.

44 Côte du Palais (rue St-Jean), Québec City, PQ G1R 4H8. ✆ **800/463-6283 or** 418/692-1030. Fax 418/692-3822. www.manoir-victoria.com. 145 units. Mid-May to mid-Oct C$135–C$255 (US$84–US$158) double, C$250–C$425 (US$155–US$264) suite; late Oct–early May C$95–C$215 (US$59–US$133) double, C$175–C$325 (US$109–US$202) suite. Extra person C$30 (US$19). AE, DC, DISC, MC, V. Children under 18 share parents' room free. Valet parking C$15 (US$9). **Amenities:** 2 restaurants (French), 2 bars; heated indoor pool; health club with sauna; concierge; car-rental; limited room service; babysitting; laundry service; dry cleaning. *In room:* A/C, TV w/pay movies, minibar, hair dryer, iron.

## MODERATE

**Cap Diamont Maison de Touristes** Every room is different in this amiable guesthouse, its assortment of furniture including brass beds, Victorian memorabilia, and nonspecific retro pieces retrieved from attics. In the back of the 1826 house are an enclosed porch and a garden. The Cap Diamant is only 2½ blocks from the Jardin des Gouverneurs. Rooms overlook the rooftops of the Old City. Stairs are very steep throughout, including the entrance, and there is no elevator. When reserving, ask about the just-renovated rooms next door that are totally nonsmoking.

39 av. Ste-Geneviève (near de Brébeuf), Québec City, PQ G1R 4B3. ✆ **418/694-0313.** www.hcapdiamant.qc.ca. 12 units. Summer C$100–C$150 (US$62–US$93) double. Winter C$75–C$125 (US$47–US$78) double. Rates include breakfast. Extra person C$15 (US$9). MC, V. Parking C$10 (US$6) in nearby lot. **Amenities:** Concierge; laundry service; dry cleaning; nonsmoking rooms. *In room:* A/C, TV, fridge, coffeemaker.

**Château Bellevue** Occupying several row houses at the top of the Parc des Gouverneurs, this mini-hotel has a pleasant lobby with leather couches and chairs and a helpful staff, as well as some of the creature comforts that smaller inns in the neighborhood lack. Although the rooms are small, they are quiet for the most part; a few higher-priced units overlook the park. The hotel's private parking is directly behind the building, although there are only a few spaces. A first-night deposit by check or credit card is required. If you're searching for a room on the spot and this is full, there are 10 other lodgings within a block in any direction.

16 rue Laporte, Québec City, PQ G1R 4M9. ✆ **800/463-2617** or 418/692-2573. Fax 418/692-4876. www.vieux-quebec.com/bellevue. 57 units. Late Oct–Apr 30 C$89–C$119 (US$55–US$74) double; Winter Carnival and May–late Oct C$119–C$149 (US$74–US$92). Extra person C$10 (US$6). Rates include breakfast (except May to mid-Oct). Packages available Oct–May. AE, DC, MC, V. Free valet parking. *In room:* A/C, TV.

**L'Hôtel du Vieux Québec** *Kids* This century-old brick hotel has been renovated with care. Guest rooms are equipped with sofas, two double beds, and modern bathrooms. Most have kitchenettes. Ask for one recently redone with new carpeting and furniture; two of these are junior suites with Jacuzzis. It's understandably popular with families and the groups of visiting high-school students who descend upon the city in late spring. In addition to Les Frères de la Côte on the ground floor there are many moderately priced restaurants and nightspots nearby.

1190 rue St-Jean (at rue de l'Hôtel Dieu), Québec City, PQ G1R 1S6. ✆ **800/361-7787** or 418/692-1850. Fax 418/692-5637. www.hvq.com. 41 units. July to mid-Oct, Christmas week, and Winter Carnival C$135–C$235 (US$84–US$146) double; late Oct–June C$89–C$109 (US$55–US$68) double. Extra person C$15 (US$9). DC, MC, V. Parking C$9 (US$6). *In room:* A/C, TV, fridge, hair dryer.

**Manoir Sur-le-Cap** All is fresh, painted, and shellacked at this inn on the south side of the Parc des Gouverneurs, opposite the Château Frontenac. Overhauled from top to bottom, all its bedroom floors gleam, and many have exposed stone or brick walls. Obviously the price is right, unless you require air-conditioning or a phone, and understand that these four floors have no elevator. Upgrade to what they call their "condo"—an apartment in a separate building in back—and get an apartment with a working fireplace, a phone, a VCR, and a kitchenette with microwave oven, coffeemaker, and basic crockery. When booking, request parking at one of the nearby lots. This is a nonsmoking facility.

9 av. Ste-Geneviève (near rue Laporte), Québec City, PQ G1R 4A7. ✆ **418/694-1987.** Fax 418/627-7405. www.manoir-sur-le-cap.com. 14 units. May–Oct C$105–C$175 (US$65–US$109) double, C$225 (US$140) suite; Nov–Apr C$75–C$125 (US$47–US$78) double, C$150 (US$93) suite. Additional person C$15 (US$9) AE, MC, V. **Amenities:** Nonsmoking rooms. *In room:* TV, coffeemaker, hair dryer, iron, no phone.

### INEXPENSIVE

**Auberge La Chouette** Near the Porte St-Louis, this inn has a capable Asian restaurant, Apsara, on the main floor. Despite its presence, the rooms on three floors reached by the spiral stairway (no elevator) are quiet. All of them have full bathrooms but are without frills. Examine your room first. The Citadelle, and Winter Carnival and Québec Summer Festival activities, are only minutes away.

71 rue d'Auteuil (near rue St-Louis), Québec City, PQ G1R 4C3. ✆ **418/694-0232.** 10 units. May–Sept C$85–C$120 (US$58–US$74) double; Oct–Apr C$65–C$90 (US$40–US$56) double. AE, MC, V. Parking C$9 (US$6) a day. *In room:* A/C, TV.

## ON OR NEAR THE GRANDE-ALLEE

### EXPENSIVE

**Hilton Québec** ★★ This Hilton is entirely true to the breed, the clear choice for executives and those leisure travelers who can't bear to live without their gadgets. And, it was renovated top to bottom as of 2000. The location—across the street from the city walls and near the Parliament—is excellent. It's also connected to the Place Québec shopping complex, which has 75 shops, two cinemas, and the convention center. The public rooms are big and brassy, Hilton-style. Upper-floor views of the St. Lawrence River and old Québec are grand.

1100 bd. Rene-Levesque Est, Québec City, PQ G1K 7K7. ✆ **800/445-8667** or 418/647-2411. Fax 418/647-2986. www.hilton.quebec.com. 571 units. C$149–C$300 (US$92–US$186) double; from C$375 (US$233) suite. Extra person C$20 (US$12). Children of any age stay free in parents' room. Children 7–12 eat for half price. Packages available. AE, DC, DISC, MC, V. Parking C$16 (US$10). Head east along Grande-Allée, and just before the St-Louis Gate in the city wall, turn left on rue Dufferin, then left again as you pass the Parliament building; the hotel is 1 block ahead. **Amenities:** Restaurant (International), bar; heated outdoor pool (all-year); well-equipped health club with whirlpool and sauna; children's programs; concierge; activities desk; car rental; courtesy limo; substantial business center; limited room service; in-room massage; babysitting; laundry service; same-day dry cleaning; executive floors. *In room:* A/C, TV w/pay movies, dataport, minibar, coffeemaker, hair dryer.

**Hôtel Palace Royal** ★★ The newest and most luxurious in a small, family-owned Québec hotel group, it elevates standards of the business hotels outside the walls. Admittedly, it lacks a distinctive personality, perhaps because it's still young. Shooting for a Parisian ambiance, lots of bronze statuary and marble are lavished on the lobby areas, while the kidney-shaped pool is at the heart of a virtual tropical garden. Over two-thirds of the units are suites, with unstocked fridges, extra TV sets, and, in many cases, whirlpool baths meant for two. Secure underground garage parking is provided.

775 ave. Dufferin-Montmorency (at place d'Youville), Québec City, PQ G1R 6A5. ✆ **418/694-2000.** Fax 418/380-2553. www.jaro.qc.ca. 234 units. C$209–C$375 (US$130–US$233). AE, DC, MC, V. Valet parking C$25 (US$16). **Amenities:** Restaurant (Steakhouse), bar; kidney-shaped indoor pool; decently-equipped health club; whirlpool; concierge; limited room service; laundry service; same-day dry cleaning. *In room:* A/C, TV w/pay movies, dataport, coffeemaker, hair dryer.

**Le Capitole** ★★ As gleefully eccentric as the three business hotels described elsewhere in this section are conventional, the entrance to this hotel is squeezed almost to anonymity between a restaurant and two theaters on Place d'Youville. Rooms, which are all curves and obtuse angles, borrow from Art Deco and incorporate stars in the carpets and clouds on the ceiling. Most bathtubs have whirlpools, and beds have down comforters. All rooms are equipped with VCRs and CD players, with 120 videos available free of charge.

972 rue Saint-Jean (1 block west of Porte Saint-Jean), Québec City, PQ G1R 1R5. ✆ **800/363-4040** or 418/694-4040. Fax 418/694-1916. www.lecapitole.com. 40 units. Late May–Sept C$152–C$212 (US$94–US$131) double, C$260 (US$161) suite; Oct–early May C$99–C$185 (US$61–US$115) double, C$189–C$215 (US$117–US$133) suite. Packages available. AE, MC, V. **Amenities:** Restaurant (Italian, International), bar; concierge; limited room service; laundry service; dry cleaning. *In room:* A/C, TV/VCR, dataport, minibar, coffeemaker, hair dryer.

**Loews le Concorde** ★★ From outside, the building that houses this hotel is a visual insult to the skyline, rising from a neighborhood of late-Victorian town houses. Enter, and the affront might be forgotten, at least by those with business to do who can't be bothered with architectural aesthetics. Standard rooms have marble bathrooms and three telephones. They bestow spectacular views of the river and the old city, even from the lower floors. A nice touch is the executive floor reserved for women only. L'Astral is a revolving rooftop restaurant, with a bar and live piano music most nights. Of all the hotels listed here, this is the farthest from the old town, about a 20-minute walk to the center of the Haute-Ville.

1225 cours du Géneral de Montcalm (at Grande-Allée), Québec City, PQ G1R 4W6. ✆ **800/463-5256** or 418/647-2222. Fax 418/647-4710. www.loewshotels.com. 404 units. May–Oct C$169–C$245 (US$105–US$152), Nov–Apr C$99–C$149 (US$61–US$92) double; from C$225 (US$140) suite. Extra person over 17, C$25 (US$16). Children under 17 share parents' room free. Ski and weekend packages available. AE, DC, MC, V. Self-parking C$15 (US$9), valet parking C$18 (US$11). **Amenities:** Restaurant (International), 2 bars; heated outdoor pool (Apr–Nov); well-equipped health club with sauna; concierge; car-rental desk; business center; shopping arcade; limited room service; in-room massage; babysitting; laundry service; same-day dry cleaning; executive floors. *In room:* A/C, TV w/pay movies, fax, dataport, minibar, coffeemaker, hair dryer, iron.

**Radisson Gouverneurs** ★ *Kids* Part of Place Québec, a multi-use complex, the hotel is also connected to the city's convention center. It is 2 blocks from Porte (Gate) Kent in the city wall, and not far from the Québec Parliament, a location likely to fit almost any businessperson's needs. It is, however, an uphill climb from the old city (like all the hotels and inns along or near the Grande-Allée). Some rooms have minibars. Every inch has benefited from a $5.2-million renovation completed in 2000. The reception is two levels up.

690 bd. René-Lévesque Est, Québec City, PQ G1R 5A8. ✆ **888/910-1111** from eastern Canada, 800/333-3333 from elsewhere, or 418/647-1717. Fax 418/647-2146. www.radisson.com. 377 units. C$235–C$295 (US$146–US$183) double; from C$305 (US$189) suite. Extra adult C$20 (US$12). Children under 16 stay free in parents' room. AE, DC, DISC, MC, V. Parking C$15 (US$9). Turn left off Grande-Allée, and then left again onto Dufferin, just before the St-Louis Gate in the city wall. Once past the Parliament building,

take the first left. The hotel is 2 blocks ahead. **Amenities:** Restaurant (International); bar; outdoor pool (summer only); fully equipped health club with sauna and whirlpool; concierge; business center; limited room service; babysitting; laundry service; same-day dry cleaning; executive floors. *In room:* A/C, TV w/pay movies, dataport, coffeemaker, hair dryer.

## MODERATE

**Château Laurier** ★★ Anchoring the east end of the Grande-Allée action strip, this old-timer has lifted its formerly dowdy countenance by taking over an adjoining building and adding 65 newer, larger, jazzier units. Some have working fireplaces and Jacuzzis; all enjoy the comforts and doodads of a first-class hotel, a giant step up from its previous incarnation. The new rooms are clearly more desirable than those in the plainer and more cramped original wing. A bar and bistro remain in front, while the expansive new lobby is located on the Georges V side. The hotel is only 2 blocks west of the St-Louis Gate and across the way from Parliament Hill.

1220 place Georges V Ouest (near corner of Grande-Allée), Québec City, PQ G1R 5B8. ✆ **800/463-4453** or 418/522-8108. Fax 418/524-8768. www.vieux-quebec.com/laurier. 113 units. May–mid-Oct C$109–C$179 (US$68–US$111) double; late Oct–Apr C$79–C$149 (US$49–US$92) double. AE, DC, MC, V. Parking C$10 (US$6). **Amenities:** Restaurant (Bistro), bar; concierge; limited room service; laundry service; dry cleaning. *In room:* A/C, TV w/pay movies, dataport, coffeemaker, hair dryer.

## INEXPENSIVE

**Relais Charles-Alexander** *Value* On the ground floor of this brick-faced B&B is an art gallery, which also serves as the breakfast room. This stylish use of space extends to the bedrooms as well, which are crisply maintained and decorated with eclectic antique and wicker pieces and reproductions. Rooms in front are larger, most have showers, not tubs, some have phones. They are pretty quiet, since the inn is just outside the orbit of the sometimes-raucous Grande-Allée terrace bars. Yet the St-Louis Gate is less than a 10-minute walk away. This place is totally nonsmoking.

91 Grande-Allée Est (avenue Galipeault), Québec City, PQ G1R 2H5. ✆ **418/523-1220.** Fax 418/523-9556. www.quebecweb.com/rca. 23 units (19 with bathroom). C$95–C$115 (US$59–US$71) double. Rates include breakfast. MC, V. Parking nearby C$8 (US$5). **Amenities:** Same-day dry cleaning; nonsmoking rooms. *In room:* A/C, TV, hair dryer.

# BASSE-VILLE (LOWER TOWN)

## VERY EXPENSIVE

**Auberge Saint-Antoine** ★★ The centerpiece of this uncommonly attractive boutique hotel is the 1830 maritime warehouse that contains the lobby and meeting rooms, with the original dark beams and stone floor still intact. Buffet breakfasts and afternoon wine and cheese are set out in the lobby, where guests relax in wing chairs next to the hooded fireplace. Canny mixes of antique and reproduction furniture are found in both public and private areas. The bedrooms, in an adjoining modern wing and a separate, newly remodeled 1727 house, are spacious, with such extra touches as custom-made bedsteads and tables. The big bathrooms have robes. Several rooms have private terraces, one of which has a three-hole putting green. Prices are highest for the 13 rooms with river views, but since a large parking lot intervenes, those without the view are a better deal. The eight new suites have kitchenettes and fax machines.

10 rue St-Antoine (Dalhousie), Québec City, PQ G1K 4C9. ✆ **888/692-2211** or 418/692-2211. Fax 418/692-1177. www.saint-antoine.com/info.html. 31 units. C$219–C$299 (US$136–US$185) double; C$299–C$479 (US$185–US$297) suite. Rates include breakfast. Extra person C$20 (US$12). Children under 12 stay free in parents' room. AE, DC, DISC, MC, V. Parking C$10 (US$6). Follow rue Dalhousie around the

Lower Town to rue St-Antoine. The hotel is next to the Musée de la Civilisation. **Amenities:** Concierge; limited room service; in-room massage; babysitting; laundry service; same-day dry cleaning. *In room:* A/C, TV, fax, dataport, hair dryer, iron.

## EXPENSIVE

**Auberge Saint-Pierre** ★ The doors only opened in 1997, but the paint was barely dry before they expanded into the adjacent building to add another 13 rooms. Included full breakfasts are special, cooked to order by the chef in the open kitchen. Most rooms are surprisingly spacious, and the even more commodious suites are a possible luxury on a longer visit, especially since they have modest kitchen facilities. The made-to-order furnishings are meant to suggest, rather than replicate, traditional Québec styles. Bare floors with area rugs contribute to the minimalist feel. Robes are provided.

79 Saint-Pierre (behind the Musée de la Civilisation), Québec City, PQ G1K 4A3. ✆ **888/268-1017** or 418/694-7981. Fax 418/694-0406. www.auberge.qc.ca. 45 units. May–Oct C$125–C$199 (US$78–US$200) double, C$260–C$350 (US$161–US$217) suite; Oct 15–May 16 C$119–C$179 (US$74–US$111) double, C$189–C$209 (US$117–US$130) suite. Rates include full breakfast. AE, DC, MC, V. Parking nearby C$11.50 (US$7). **Amenities:** Bar; concierge; breakfast room service; in-room massage; babysitting; laundry service; same-day dry cleaning; nonsmoking rooms. *In room:* A/C, TV, dataport, coffeemaker, hair dryer.

**Hôtel Dominion 1912** ★★★ If there were space enough to recommend only one hotel in the city, this would be it. The owners stripped the inside of the 1912 Dominion Fish & Fruit building down to the studs and started over. Even the least expensive rooms are large with the queen- or king-size beds heaped with linen-covered pillows and covered with feather duvets. Custom-made bedside tables swing into place or out of the way. Neutral colors extend to the spacious bathrooms and the robes hanging there. A fruit basket awaits. Chairs embrace sitters for work or leisure. Continental breakfast is set out in the handsome lobby along with morning newspapers. They can be taken out to the terrace in back. After buying the building next door, 20 new units have been added, including two suites and the spiffy new bistro. Prices have risen, but even so, this remains one of the most desirable hotels in town.

126 rue Saint-Pierre (at rue Saint-Paul), Québec City, PQ G1K 4A8. ✆ **888/833-5253** or 418/692-2224. Fax 418/692-4403. www.hoteldominion.com. 60 units. Oct 15–Apr 30 C$149–C$199 (US$92–US$123) double; May 1–Oct 14 C$205–C$275 (US$127–US$171) double. Rates include breakfast. AE, DC, MC, V. Parking C$6–C$10 (US$3.70–US$6). **Amenities:** Restaurant (Light Fare); access to nearby health club; concierge; limited room service; in-room massage; babysitting; laundry service; same-day dry cleaning. *In room:* A/C, TV/VCR, dataport, minibar, coffeemaker, hair dryer, iron.

## MODERATE

**Le Priori** A forerunner of the burgeoning Lower Town hotel scene, Le Priori provides a playful postmodern ambience behind the somber facade of a 1766 house. French designer Phillipe Starck inspired the original owners, who deployed versions of his conical stainless-steel sinks in the bedrooms and sensual multinozzle showers in the small bathrooms. In some rooms, a claw-foot tub sits beside the queen-size beds, which are covered with duvets. New table lamps help dispel the former dim lighting. Suites have sitting rooms with wood-burning fireplaces, kitchens, and bathrooms with Jacuzzi. There's a casual restaurant off the lobby.

15 rue Sault-au-Matelot (at rue St-Antoine), Québec City, PQ G1K 3Y7. ✆ **800/351-3992** or 418/692-3992. Fax 418/692-0883. www.hotellepriori.com. 26 units. May–Oct C$109–C$179 (US$68–US$111) double, C$219–C$309 (US$136–US$192) suite; Nov–Apr C$89–C$129 (C$55–C$80) double, C$179–C$239 (US$111–US$148) suite. Rates include breakfast. Packages available. AE, DC, MC, V. Self parking C$10 (US$6) a day. **Amenities:** Restaurant (French), bar; concierge; limited room service; laundry service; same-day dry cleaning. *In room:* A/C, TV, dataport, coffeemaker, hair dryer, iron.

## 4 Where to Dine

Once you're within these ancient walls, walking along streets that look to have been transplanted intact from Brittany or Provence, it's understandable if you imagine that you have in store one supernal dining experience after another. Expectations aside, the truth is that this gloriously scenic city has no *temples de cuisine* comparable to those of Montréal. Although it is easy to eat well in the capital—even, in a few isolated cases, *quite* well—the greater pleasures of a stay here will likely lie in other areas.

But that's not to imply that you're in for barely edible meals served by sullen waiters. By sticking to any of the many competent bistros, you'll be content. Another step up, two or three ambitious enterprises tease the palate with hints of higher achievement. Even the blatantly touristy restaurants along rue St-Louis and around the Place d'Armes can produce decent meals.

Curiously, for a city beside a great waterway and but a day's sail from some of the world's best fishing grounds, seafood isn't given much attention. Mussels and salmon are on most menus, but look for places that go beyond those staples. Game is popular, and everything from venison, rabbit, and duck to more exotic quail, goose, caribou, and wapiti is available.

Reservations are all but essential during traditional holidays and the festivals that pepper the social calendar. Other times, it's usually necessary to book ahead only for weekend evenings. Dress codes are rare, but "dressy casual" works almost everywhere. Remember that for the Québecois, *dîner* (dinner) is lunch, and *souper* (supper) is dinner, though for the sake of consistency, the word *dinner* is used below in the common American sense. The evening meal tends to be served earlier in Québec City than in Montréal, at 6 or 7 rather than 8pm.

### HAUTE-VILLE (UPPER TOWN)

#### EXPENSIVE

**Aux Anciens Canadiens** ★ QUEBECOIS Smack in the middle of the tourist swarms, this venerable restaurant is in what is probably the oldest (1677) house in the city. Surprisingly, the food at this famous attraction is both well prepared and fairly priced (at least at lunch). It's also one of the best places in La Belle Province to sample the cooking that has its roots in the earliest years of New France. Don't count on the ancient Québecois recipes tasting this good anywhere else. Caribou and maple syrup figure in many dishes, including the meat pie, duck, and a definitive rendering of luscious sugar pie.

34 rue St-Louis (at rue Haldimand). ✆ **418/692-1627.** Reservations recommended. Main courses C$18.50–C$45 (US$11–US$28), table d'hôte lunch C$13.75 (US$9), dinner C$27.50–C$54 (US$17–US$33). AE, DC, MC, V. Daily noon–midnight

**Le Saint Amour** ★ CONTEMPORARY FRENCH This is a restaurant for the coolly attractive and the amorously inclined. Patrons pass through a front room with lace curtains into a covered terrace lit by flickering candles. Easily the most romantic setting for dining in a city that knows about seductive atmosphere, the courtyard has been re-created with mirrors and polished wood paneling. In recent years there had been a perceptible slip in both food and service, but that slide has been reversed. They're proud of the caribou filet with its wild mushroom crust, the lobster out of its shell looks as good as it tastes, and desserts are dazzlers. A final enhancement would be to move the pace of the meal along.

48 rue Ste-Ursule (near rue St-Louis). ✆ **418/694-0667.** Reservations recommended for dinner. Main courses C$24–C$33.50 (US$15–US$21); table d'hôte lunch C$11–C$15.50 (US$7–US$10), dinner

C$28.50–C$32.50 (US$18–US$20), tasting dinner C$72 (USD$45). AE, DC, MC, V. Mon–Fri 11:30am–2:30pm and 5:30–11pm, Sat–Sun 5:30–11pm.

**Serge Bruyère** ★★ ECLECTIC No moss grows on this place. The eponymous owner bought the building in 1979 and set about creating a multilevel dining emporium that had something for everyone. Serge Bruyère, however, died young. His executive chef carries on, serving all meals from informal breakfasts to lavish late dinners.

At ground level in front is the casual Café Bruyère. Up a long staircase at the back is the Bistro Livernois, with windows looking down on the street. It is especially good for lunches, concentrating on grills and pastas. Foods are adroitly seasoned. Another flight up is the formal La Grand Table, offering a pricey menu that is both highly imaginative and immaculately presented. Gaps between the eight courses of the gastronomic extravaganza stretch on for an entire evening. Whether the unquestionably showy creations justify the raves and the sedate pace of the meal is up to you.

1200 rue Saint-Jean (Côte de la Fabrique). ✆ **418/694-0618.** Reservations recommended for dinner. Café Bruyère, table d'hôte,C$14.95–C$34.95 (US$9–US$22), Bistro Livernois table d'hôte C$18–C$27.95 (US$11–US$17); Café Bruyère mains C$13.95–C$27.95 (US$9–US$17), Bistro Livernois mains C$15–C$34.75 (US$9–US$22); La Grand Table mains C$24–C$35 (US$15–US$22), gastronomic dinners C$85 and C$145 (US$53 and US$90). AE, DC, MC, V. Daily 8am–10:30pm.

### MODERATE

**Les Frères de la Côte** *Kids* MEDITERRANEAN At the east end of the old town's liveliest nightlife strip, this supremely casual cafe-pizzeria is as loud as any dance club, all hard surfaces, with patrons shouting over the booming stereo music. None of this discourages a single soul—even on a Monday night. Chefs in straw hats in the open kitchen in back crank out a dozen different kinds of pizza—thin-crusted, with unusual toppings that work—and about as many pasta versions, which are less interesting. Bountiful platters of fish and meats, often in the form of brochettes, make appetizers unnecessary. Keep this spot in mind when kids are in tow; there's no way they could make enough noise to bother other customers. Outside tables are available in warm weather. Brunch is served Sundays, 10:30am to 3pm.

1190 rue St-Jean (near Côte de la Fabrique). ✆ **418/692-5445.** Reservations recommended. Main courses C$10.75–C$14.75 (US$7–US$9); table d'hôte dinner C$18.95–C$22.95 (US$12–US$14). AE, DC, MC, V. Daily 11:30am–11pm.

## ON OR NEAR THE GRANDE-ALLEE

### EXPENSIVE

**Le Paris Brest** ★ CONTEMPORARY FRENCH Named for a French dessert, this is easily one of the best eating places outside the walls, with a polished performance from greeting to reckoning. Within minutes after the doors are opened at lunchtime, a happy noise ensues, drowning out the cell phone

---

*Tips* **Take Advantage of the Table d'Hôte**

As throughout the province, the best dining deals are the table d'hôte (fixed-price) meals. Most full-service restaurants offer them, if only at lunch. As a rule, they include at least soup or salad, a main course, and dessert. Some places add in an extra appetizer and/or a beverage, for the approximate a la carte price of the main course alone.

---

users. (Dinner is quieter.) A fashionable crowd comes in everything from bespoke suits to designer jeans—tacky T-shirts and children are out of place. They are attended by a comely waitstaff dressed in black who convey as much warmth as the rushed process permits. The menu shuns hyperbole—the mere listing of component ingredients is sufficiently intriguing. One sparkling appetizer is the scallop tartare with mango and dill on salmon caviar. Game and seafood are featured and what they do with pasta is impressive, as with the linguine tossed in a curry pepper sauce with tiny clams and mussels. Find the entrance on rue de la Chevrotière. Free valet parking is available after 5:30pm.

590 Grande-Allée Est (at rue de la Chevrotière). ✆ **418/529-2243.** Reservations recommended. Main courses C$26–C$30 (US$16–US$19); table d'hôte lunch C$9.95–C$15.75 (US$6–US$10), dinner C$21–C$34 (US$13–US$21). AE, DC, MC, V. Mon–Fri 11:30am–2:30pm; Mon–Sat 6–11:30pm; Sun 5:30–11:30pm.

## MODERATE

**Graffiti** ★ *Finds* CONTEMPORARY FRENCH/ITALIAN These 2 or 3 blocks of rue Cartier off Grande-Allée are just outside the perimeter of tourist Québec, but close enough to remain convenient. Enthusiasm for this ebullient establishment hasn't flagged a bit, stoked by an attractive staff that hustles about leaving droplets of good feelings in their wake. The kitchen blends bistro with trattoria, often on the same plate. Emblematic are the pike with leeks and grilled almonds and the sautéed rabbit with angel-hair pasta powerfully scented with tarragon. Choice seats are in the glassed-in terrace, all the better to scope out the street scene.

1191 av. Cartier (near Grande-Allée). ✆ **418/529-4949.** Reservations recommended. Main courses C$7.25–C$28.25 (US$4.50–US$18), table d'hôte lunch C$10.25–C$14.25 (US$6–US$9), dinner C$21.50–C$30.25 (US$13–US$19). AE, DC, MC, V. Mon–Sat 5–11pm; Sun noon–10pm.

**L'Astral** *Value* INTERNATIONAL If you share the common conviction that cuisine diminishes and prices rise in direct proportion to the height at which the food is served, you have a legitimate case—especially if your table also moves in a circle. Here's an exception, an undramatic one, but still . . . It sits atop the Hôtel Loews le Concorde, and it turns, 360° in about an hour. The panorama thus revealed is truly splendid, enough to excuse most deficiencies on the plate. But here's the double surprise—the food is above average and the cost entirely reasonable. You have the choice of an all-you-can-eat buffet at lunch or dinner or a la carte selections, and the buffet is as good a deal as you're likely to find. Appearances are made by monkfish, lamb, breast of pheasant as well as more familiar chicken and beef.

1225 cours du Général-de Montcalm (cor Grande-Allée). ✆ **418/647-2222.** Reservations recommended. Main courses C$19.50–C$43.95 (US$12–US$27), lunch buffet C$18.95 (US$12), dinner buffet C$40.95 (US$25) adults, C$20.50 (US$13) children under 12. AE, DC, DISC, MC, V. Daily 11:45am–1am.

**Voodoo Grill** ★ ECLECTIC Of all the unlikely places to find food that surpasses what can be found at more conventional local restaurants, this takes the laurels. African carvings adorn the walls, and a trio of drummers circulate, beating out insistent rhythms on bongos. It's loud, young, extremely casual, and most of the customers couldn't seem less interested in what is on the plates set before them. Their loss. The menu swings around the Pacific Rim, with stops in Hawaii, Thailand, and Indonesia. Authenticity isn't the point, taste is. Tuna, for only one example, is barely touched by the flame, then set upon a pad of shredded vegetables tossed with linguine and soy sauce.

575 Grande-Allée Est (cor. rue de la Chevro tiére). ✆ **418/647-2000.** Reservations recommended. Main courses C$15.50–C$29.95 (US$10–US$19). AE, DC, MC, V. Daily 6–11pm.

## BASSE-VILLE (LOWER TOWN)

### EXPENSIVE

**Initiale** ★★ CONTEMPORARY FRENCH This location hasn't been kind to restaurateurs, with two ambitious failures in the last 5 years. This latest effort, however, may have what it takes to turn a profit, despite the empty tables witnessed many nights. Certainly the palatial setting of tall windows, columns, and deeply recessed ceiling aids in setting the gracious tone. Subdued lighting and the muffled noise level help, too, but the result may be too sedate for diners who prefer a little more aural combustion with their food. Choose from prix fixe menus of three to six courses, changed often, because the chef values freshness over novelty. One headliner was roast guinea hen joined by the intact meat of a lobster claw and a sweet fleshy shrimp over a spoonful of spätzle. A particular treat is the selection of impressive Québec cheeses.

54 rue St-Pierre (corner Côte de la Montagne). ✆ **418/694-1818.** Reservations recommended on weekends. Main courses C$21–C$28 (US$13–US$17), table d'hôte C$43–C$49 (US$27–US$30). AE, DC, MC, V. Daily 6–10pm.

**Laurie Raphaël** ★★ CONTEMPORARY QUEBECOIS Here is a restaurant all but alone at the pinnacle of the local dining pantheon. The owners, who named the place after their two children, moved to these larger, more glamorous quarters in 1996, a suitable arena for the city's most accomplished kitchen. Servers happily explain dishes in as much detail as their customers care to absorb. Appetizers aren't really necessary, since the main course comes with soup or salad, but they're so good that a couple might wish to share one—the little stack of lightly fried calamari rings, perhaps. Main courses run to caribou and salmon in unconventional guises, often with Asian touches. Coupled with an evident concern for "healthy" saucing and exotic combinations, the food closely resembles that associated with serious California restaurants. That includes something of an edifice complex in the towering presentations, held together with skewers and panache.

117 rue Dalhousie (at rue St-André). ✆ **418/692-4555.** Reservations recommended. Main courses C$19–C$40 (US$12–US$25), table d'hôte lunch C$10.50–C$20.50 (US$7–US$13), gourmet menu C$79 (US$49). AE, DC, MC, V. Mon–Fri 11:30–2pm and 5:30–10pm; Sat 5:30–10pm.

### MODERATE

**L'Ardoise** BISTRO FRENCH This is one of several bistros that wrap around the intersection of rues St-Paul and Sault-au-Matelot. Most are inexpensive and cater more to locals than to tourists. Mussels are staples at Québec restaurants, prepared in the Belgian manner, with bowls of *frites* on the side. Here, they come with 14 different sauces and, with soup or salad, cost only C$16.95 (US$11)—with free seconds. The rest of the food is vibrant and flavorful, served at banquettes along the walls and at tables inside and out on the sidewalk. This is a place to leaf through a book, sip a double espresso, meet neighbors.

71 rue St-Paul (near Navigateurs). ✆ **418/694-0213.** Reservations recommended at dinner. Main courses C$8–C$17 (US$5–US$11); table d'hôte lunch C$9.95–C$12.95 (US$6–US$8), dinner C$22.95–C$30.95 (US$14–US$19). AE, DC, MC, V. Mon–Fri 11am–10pm, Sat–Sun 9am–10pm.

**Le Café du Monde** ★ FRENCH/INTERNATIONAL A relentlessly convivial spot near the Musée de la Civilisation, the Café du Monde enjoys a constant popularity. The international flavor to which it once aspired has been distilled down to that of a Lyonnaise brasserie. This is seen in its most-ordered items—patés, quiches, roasted lamb knuckle, duck confit with garlic sautéed potatoes, and several versions of mussels with frites—from a kitchen overseen by a chef from Brittany. Imported beers and favored beverages, along with wines by the glass. Service is friendly, but easily distracted. Waiters and customers sit down at the upright piano for impromptu performances.

57 rue Dalhousie (at rue de la Montagne). ✆ **418/692-4455.** Reservations recommended. Main courses C$10.95–C$17.95 (US$7–US$11); table d'hôte (after 3pm) the price of your main course plus C$6.95 or C$10.95 (US$4.30 or US$7). AE, DC, MC, V. Mon–Fri 11:30am–11pm; Sat–Sun brunch 9:30am–11pm.

**L'Echaudé** ★ *Value* BISTRO FRENCH One of the necklace of restaurants rounding this Basse-Ville corner, and the most polished, it has sidewalk tables with butcher paper on top and a zinc-topped bar inside the door. The grilled meats and fishes and seafood stews blaze no new trails, but they are very satisfying and an excellent value. Good-deal lunch mains go from cheese omelette to steak tartar, wrapped around with appetizer, dessert, and coffee. Among many classics on the card are steak frites, ravioli with blue cheese, and salmon tartare. They keep 24 brands of beer on ice and cellar 125 varieties of wine, a generous 10 of which are available by the glass. They're not so traditional that they're unaware of fads—a Cosmopolitan is C$7 (US$4.35).

73 rue Sault-au-Matelot (near rue St-Paul). ✆ **418/692-1299.** Main courses C$12–C$26.50 (US$8–US$18); table d'hôte lunch C$9.95–C$15.95 (US$7–US$11), dinner C$23–C$36 (US$16–US$25). AE, DC, MC, V. Mon–Wed 11:30am–2:30pm and 5:30–10pm; Thurs–Fri 11:30am–2:30pm and 5:30–11pm; Sat 5:30–11pm; Sun 10am–2:30pm and 5:30–10pm. Closed 2 weeks in Jan.

**Le Cochon Dingue** *Value* *Kids* FRENCH/INTERNATIONAL This "Crazy Pig" faces the river and has sidewalk tables and several indoor dining rooms sprawling through three buildings. It is heavily used and shows it, as a result of its highly successful efforts to be a one-stop eating center with long hours to cover every possibility from breakfast to late snack. Choose from mussels, spring rolls, smoked salmon, half a dozen salads, onion soup, pastas, quiches, sandwiches, grilled meats, and more than 20 desserts. Good shoestring frites accompany most dishes. There is an offering for kids 10 and under for only C$4.95 (US$3.05). Maybe they are the target audience for the mistakenly cutesy menu urging that you eat parts of the trademark anthropomorphic pig.

46 bd. Champlain (near rue du Marché-Champlain). ✆ **418/692-2013.** Main courses C$12.95–C$19.75 (US$8–US$12); table d'hôte C$17.95–C$20.95 (US$11–US$13). AE, MC, V. Mon–Thurs 7am–midnight, Fri 7–1am, Sat 8am–1am, Sun 8am–midnight (closes an hour earlier in winter).

**Le Marie-Clarisse** ★ BISTRO FRENCH/SEAFOOD Nothing much beyond sustenance is expected of restaurants at the intersections of galloping tourism. That's why this ambitious cafe is such a happy surprise. There it sits, at the bottom of Breakneck Stairs, the streets awash with day-packers and shutterbugs. Yet it serves what many consider to be the best seafood in town, and a more pleasant hour cannot be passed anywhere in Québec City than here, over a platter of shrimp or patés, out on the terrace on an August afternoon. In January, cocoon by the stone fireplace inside, indulging in bouillabaisse with a boat of saffron mayo to slather on croutons. Try a Québec wine to wash them down, maybe the l'Orpailleur from Dunham.

12 rue du Petit-Champlain (at rue Sous-le-Fort). ✆ **418/692-0857.** Main courses C$9.75–C$29.75 (US$6–US$18); table d'hôte lunch C$14.75 (US$9), dinner C$16.75–C$23.75 (US$10–US$15). AE, DC, MC, V. Mon–Sat 11:30am–2:30pm and 6–10pm; terrace open daily Apr 15–Oct 31 11:30am–10pm.

**Poisson d'Avril** SEAFOOD Whoever christened this place was having a little joke: its name means both "April Fool" and "April Fish." Nautical trappings include model ships, marine prints, and mounted sailfish make the real intent clear. The dinner menu, changed daily, is replete with seafood, including some costly crustaceans responsible for the stiffer prices noted below. One of this is the "Commodore Platter," laden with snow crabs, giant shrimp, glossy sea scallops, piled mussels, and a half-lobster. Lunch is a more modest event, with more land-based dishes, pastas, and individual pizzas. In good weather, there's a covered dining terrace.

115 quai Saint-André (in Vieux-Port, near rue St-Thomas). © **418/692-1010.** Table d'hôte lunch C$8.95–C$21.95 (US$6–US$14), dinner C$14.95–C$39.95 (US$9–US$25). Sun–Fri noon–3pm and 5–10pm, Sat 5–10pm, dinner only Oct–May.

### INEXPENSIVE

**Buffet de l'Antiquaire** *Value* QUEBECOIS Another inhabitant of the rue St-Paul antique row, this is the humblest eating place of the lot. It is the place to go when every other Lower Town cafe is closed, as for Sunday breakfast. And, since it caters mostly to homefolks rather than tourists, reliable versions of native Québecois cooking are always available, including pea soup, *poutine,* and *fèves au lard.* Essentially a upgraded luncheonette, it serves sandwiches, salads, and pastries at all hours, backed by full bar service.

95 rue St-Paul (near rue du Sault-au-Matelot). © **418/692-2661.** Most menu items under C$12 (US$7), including table d'hôte. AE, MC, V. Daily 7am–11pm.

## 5 Seeing the Sights

Wandering at random through the streets of Vieux-Québec is a singular pleasure. On the way, happen on an ancient convent, blocks of gabled houses with steep tin roofs, a battery of 18th-century cannons in a leafy park, or a bistro with a blazing fireplace on a chilly day. This is such a compact city it's hardly necessary to plan precise itineraries. Start at the **Terrasse Dufferin** ★★ and go off on a whim, down the Breakneck Stairs to the Quartier Petit-Champlain and place Royale, or up to the Citadelle and onto the Plains of Abraham, where Wolfe and Montcalm fought to the death in a 20-minute battle that changed the destiny of the continent.

Most of what there is to see is within the city walls, or below, in the Lower Town. It's fairly easy walking. While the Upper Town is hilly, with sloping streets, it's nothing like San Francisco, and only people with physical limitations will experience difficulty. If rain or ice discourages exploration on foot, tour buses and horse-drawn calèches are options. Most attractions have discounted admission fees for families.

### BASSE-VILLE (LOWER TOWN)

The **Escalier Casse-Cou (Breakneck Stairs)** connects the **Terrasse Dufferin** at the top of the cliff with rue Sous-le-Fort at the base. The name will be self-explanatory as soon as you see the stairs. They lead from Haute-Ville to the **Quartier Petit-Champlain** in Basse-Ville.

A short walk from the bottom of the Breakneck Stairs, via rue Sous-le-Fort, is picturesque **place Royale,** Lower Town's literal and spiritual heart. In the 17th and 18th centuries, it was the town marketplace and the center of business and industry. Dominating the square is the **Eglise Notre-Dame-des-Victoires,** Québec's oldest stone church, built in 1688 and restored in 1763 and 1969. The paintings, altar, and large model boat suspended from the ceiling were votive offerings brought by early settlers to ensure safe voyages. The church is usually open during the day, unless a wedding is in progress.

An empty storefront on the square was refurbished in 1997 to become an **information center,** 215 rue du Marché-Finlay (© **418/643-6631**); June 5 to

**Fun Fact** **No Animals on the Stairs**

A stairway has existed on the site of the Escalier Casse-Cou (Breakneck Stairs) since the settlement began, but human beings weren't the only ones to use it. In 1698, the town council forbade citizens to take their animals up or down the stairway or face a fine.

October 1, it's open daily 10am to 6pm. Note the ladders on some of the other roofs, a common Québec device for removing snow and fighting fires. Folk dances, impromptu concerts, and other festive gatherings are often held near the bust of Louis XIV in the square.

**Centre d'Interprétation du Vieux-Port** A unit of Parks Canada, the four floors of Old Port Interpretation Center depict the Port of Québec as it was during its maritime zenith in the 19th century. Exhibits illustrate the shipbuilding and lumbering enterprises, employing animated figures and docents in costumes appropriate to the era. The modern port and city can be viewed from the top level, where reference maps identify landmarks. Guided tours of the harbor are available. Texts are in French and English, and most exhibits invite interaction.

100 rue St-Andre (at rue Rioux). ✆ **418/648-3300.** Admission C$3 (US$1.85) adults, C$2.25 (US$1.40) seniors and students over 17, C$2 (US$1.25). May–Labour Day daily 10am–5pm; schedule varies the rest of the year (call for hours).

**Maison Chevalier** Built in 1752 for ship owner Jean-Baptiste Chevalier, the existing structure incorporated two older buildings, dating from 1675 and 1695. It was run as an inn throughout the 19th century. The Québec government restored the house in 1960, and it became a museum 5 years later. Inside, with its exposed wood beams, wide-board floors, and stone fireplaces are changing exhibits on Québec history and civilization, especially in the 17th and 18th centuries. While exhibit texts are in French, guidebooks in English are available at the sometimes-unattended front desk.

60 rue du Marché-Champlain (near rue Notre-Dame). ✆ **418/643-2158.** Free admission. May–June Tues–Sun 10am–5:30pm, June 24–Oct 31 daily 10am–5:30pm, Nov–Apr Sat–Sun 10am–5pm.

**Musée de la Civilisation** ★★★ Try to set aside at least 2 hours for a visit to this special museum, one of the most engrossing in Canada. Designed by McGill University-trained Moshe Safdie and opened in 1988, it is an innovative presence in the historic Basse-Ville, near Place Royale. A dramatic atrium-lobby sets the tone with a massive sculpture rising like jagged icebergs from the watery floor, a representation of the mighty St. Lawrence at spring breakup. Through the glass wall in back can be seen the 1752 Maison Estèbe, now restored to contain the museum shop.

In the galleries upstairs are five permanent exhibitions, supplemented by up to six temporary shows on a variety of themes, many of them interactive. The mission of the museum has never been entirely clear, leading to some opaque metaphysical meanderings in its early years. However, through highly imaginative display techniques, hands-on devices, computers, holograms, videos, and even an ant farm, the curators have ensured that visitors will be so enthralled by the experience they won't pause to question its intent. Notice, as an example of the museum's thoroughness, how a squeaky floorboard has been installed at the entrance to a dollhouse-size display of old Québec houses.

If time is short, definitely use it to take in "Memoires" ("Memories"), a sprawling examination of Québec history, moving from the province's roots as a fur-trading colony to the present. Furnishings from frontier homes, tools of the trappers' trade, worn farm implements, religious garments from the 19th century, old campaign posters, and a re-created classroom from the past envelop visitors with a rich sense of Québec's daily life from generation to generation. A new permanent exhibition, "Encounter with the First Nations," examines the products and visions of aboriginal tribes that inhabit Québec. Exhibit texts are in French and English. There's a cafe on the ground floor.

85 rue Dalhousie (at rue St-Antoine). ✆ **418/643-2158.** www.mcq.org. Admission C$7 (US$4.35) adults, C$6 (US$3.70) seniors, C$4 (US$2.50) students over 16, C$2 (US$1.25) children 12–16, free for children under 12. Tues free to all (except in summer). June 23–Labour Day daily 10am–7pm; Sept–June 22 Tues–Sun 10am–5pm.

## HAUTE-VILLE (UPPER TOWN)

**Basilique-Cathédrale Notre-Dame** ★ Notre-Dame Basilica, representing the oldest Christian parish north of Mexico, has weathered a tumultuous history of bombardment, reconstruction, and restoration. Parts of the existing basilica date from the original 1647 structure, including the bell tower and portions of the walls, but most of today's exterior is from the reconstruction completed in 1771. The interior, a re-creation undertaken after a fire in 1922, is flamboyantly neo-Baroque, with shadows wavering by the fluttering light of votive candles. Paintings and ecclesiastical treasures still remain from the time of the French regime, including a chancel lamp given by Louis XIV. In summer, the basilica is the backdrop for a 30-minute multimedia sound-and-light show called "Feux Sacrés" (Act of Faith), which dramatically recalls 5 centuries of Québec's history, and that of this building itself. The basilica is connected to the group of old buildings that makes up Québec Seminary. To enter that complex, go to 7 rue de l'Université (about a block away).

20 rue Buade (at Côte de la Fabrique). ✆ **418/694-0665.** Free admission to basilica and guided tours. "Feux Sacrés" sound-and-light show C$7.50 (US$4.65) adults, C$5 (US$3.10) seniors, students with ID, and children over 6; free for children under 6. Cathedral daily 7:30am–4:30pm. Guided tours May 1–Nov 1 Mon–Fri 9am–2:30pm, Sat 9am–4:30pm, Sun 12:30pm–4:30pm. "Feux Scarés" sound-and-light show May 1–Oct 15 daily 1pm, 2, 3, 5, 6, 7, 8 and 9pm; Oct 16–Apr 30, group reservations only.

**Chapelle/Musée des Ursulines** The chapel, open only May to October, is notable for the sculptures that inform its pulpit and two retables. They were created by Pierre-Noël Levasseur between 1726 and 1736. Although the present building dates only from 1902, much of the interior decoration is nearly 2 centuries older. The tomb of the founder of this teaching order, Marie de l'Incarnation, is to the right of the entry. She arrived here in 1639 at the age of 40 and was declared blessed by Pope John Paul II in 1980. The museum displays accoutrements of the daily and spiritual life of the Ursulines. A cape made of drapes from the bedroom of Anne of Austria and given to Marie de l'Incarnation when she left for New France in 1639 is on display. There are also musical instruments and Amerindian crafts, including the flèche, or arrow sash, still worn during Winter Carnival. Some of the docents are nuns of the still-active order. The Ursuline convent, built originally as a girls' school in 1642, is the oldest one in North America.

12 rue Donnacona (des Jardins). ✆ **418/694-0694.** Chapel free. Museum C$4 (US$2.65) adults, C$3.50 (US$2.20) seniors, C$2.50 (US$1.55) students 17 and over, C$2 (US$1.20) ages 12–16, free under age 11. Museum Oct–Apr Tues–Sun 1–4:30pm; May–Sept Tues–Sat 10am–noon and 1–5pm, Sun 1–5pm. Chapel May–Oct same days and hours as museum.

**La Citadelle** ★★ The Duke of Wellington had this partially star-shaped fortress built at the east end of the city walls in anticipation of renewed American attacks after the War of 1812. Some remnants of earlier French military structures were incorporated into the Citadel, including a 1750 magazine. Dug into the Plains of Abraham, the fort has a low profile that keeps it all but invisible until walkers are actually upon it. Never having exchanged fire with an invader, it continues its vigil from the tip of Cap Diamant. British construction of the fortress, now a national historic site, was begun in 1820 and took 30 years to complete. As events unfolded, it proved to be an exercise in obsolescence. Since 1920, it has been home to Québec's Royal 22e Régiment, the only fully Francophone unit in Canada's armed forces. That makes it the largest fortified group of buildings still occupied by troops in North America. As part of a guided tour only, the public may visit the Citadel and its 25 buildings, including the small regimental museums in the former powder house and prison. Despite a couple of spectacular overlooks, the length of the tour and the dry narration are likely to test the patience of younger visitors and the legs of many older people. In those cases, it might be better to attend the ceremonies of the changing of the guard or beating the retreat (see below). Walk or drive up the Côte de la Citadelle (entrance near the St-Louis Gate); there are many parking spaces inside the walls.

1 Côte de la Citadelle (enter off rue St-Louis). ✆ **418/694-2815.** www.lacitadelle.qc.ca. Admission C$6 (US$3.70) adults, C$5 (US$3.10) seniors, C$3 (US$1.85) children 7–17, free for persons with disabilities and children under 7. Guided 55-minute tours daily, Apr–mid-May 10am–4pm; mid-May to June 9am–5pm; July–Labour Day 9am–6pm; Sept 9am–4pm; Oct 10am–3pm. Nov–Mar, group reservations only. Changing of the Guard (30 mins.) June 24–Labour Day daily at 10am, Beating the Retreat (20 mins.) July and Aug Wed–Sat at 6pm. May be cancelled in the event of rain. Walk up the Côte de la Citadelle from the St-Louis Gate.

**Le Château Frontenac** ★ Opened in 1893 to house railroad passengers and encourage tourism, the monster version of a Loire Valley palace is the city's emblem, its Eiffel Tower. The hotel can be seen from almost every quarter, commanding its majestic position atop Cap Diamant. Franklin D. Roosevelt and Winston Churchill held two important summit conferences here in 1943 and 1944. Visitors curious about the interior may wish to take one of the 50-minute guided tours offered daily 10am to 6pm, May 1 to October 15; Saturday and Sunday 1 to 5pm, October 16 to April 30 (departures on the hour). They cost C$6.50 (US$4.) for adults, C$5.50 (US$3.40) for seniors, and C$3.75 (US$2.30) for children ages 6 to 16. To make reservations, which are required, call ✆ **418/691-2166.**

1 rue des Carrières, Place d'Armes. ✆ **418/692-3861.**

**Musée d'Art Inuit Brousseau** A creation of the people who operate the three most reputable galleries of Inuit art in the city, this private museum is an extension of the lifelong interest of collector Raymond Brousseau. The permanent collection is supplemented by occasional thematic exhibitions. In addition to carvings in stone and tusk, there are examples of fishing and hunting gear and clothing.

39 rue St-Louis. ✆ **418/694-1828.** Admission C$6 (US$3.70) adults, C$4 (US$2.50) seniors and students 13 and older, free for children 12 and under with parent. Summer, daily 9am–5:30pm; winter, 9:30am–5:30pm.

**Musée de l'Amerique Française** Housed at the site of the Québec Seminary, which dates from 1663, the Museum of French America focuses on the beginnings and the evolution of French culture and civilization in North America. Its extensive collections include paintings by European and Canadian artists, engravings and parchments from the early French regime, old and rare books, coins, early scientific instruments, and even mounted animals and an Egyptian mummy.

The museum is located in three parts of the large seminary complex, the Guillaume-Couillard and Jérôme-Demers wings, and the beautiful François-Ranvoyze section, with its trompe l'oeil ornamentation, which served as a chapel for the seminary priests and students. Recent construction has added an annex to the chapel, an underground passage, and a new entrance lobby. Concerts are held in the chapel.

2 Côte de la Fabrique. ✆ **418/692-2843.** Admission C$4 (US$2.50) adults, C$3 (US$1.85) seniors and students over 16, C$1 (US60¢) children 12–16, free for children under 12. June 24–Labour Day daily 10am–5:30pm; Sept 8–June 23 Tues–Sun 10am–5pm. Guided tours of exhibitions and some buildings daily in summer, Sat and Sun rest of the year. Reservations ✆ **418/692-2843.**

**Parc de l'Artillerie** Fortifications erected by the French in the 17th and 18th centuries enclose the Artillery Park. In addition to protecting the garrison, the defensive works contained an ammunition factory that was functional until 1964. On view are the old officers' mess and quarters, an iron foundry, and a scale model of the city created in 1806. Costumed docents give tours.

It may be a blow to romantics and history buffs to learn that the nearby St-Jean Gate in the city wall was built in 1940, the fourth in a series that began with the original 1693 entrance, replaced in 1747 and again in 1867.

2 rue d'Auteuil (near Porte St-Jean). ✆ **418/648-4205.** Admission C$3.25 (US$2) adults, C$2.75 (US$1.70) seniors ans students 17 and over, C$2 (US$1.20 ages 6–16, free under 6. July–Labour Day Wed–Sun 10am–5pm; rest of year, call for hours.

## NEAR THE GRANDE-ALLEE

**Musée du Québec** ★★ Toward the western end of the Parc de Champs de Bataille (Battlefields Park), just off the Grande-Allée and a half-hour walk or a short bus ride from the Haute-Ville, the Museum of Québec is an art museum that now occupies two buildings, one a former prison, linked together by a soaring glass-roofed "Grand Hall" housing the reception area, a stylish cafe, and a shop.

The original 1933 building houses the permanent collection, the largest aggregation of Québec art in North America, filling eight galleries with works from the beginning of the colony to the present. On the top floor are regional landscapes and canvases of other Québec themes, with some additional examples of North American and British painters. On the ground floor is a splendid assortment of African masks, carvings, musical instruments, and ceremonial staffs. Unfortunately, most descriptive plaques are only in French. Traveling exhibitions and musical events are often arranged. An addition to the museum is the 1867 Baillairgé Prison, which in the 1970s became a youth hostel nicknamed the "Petite Bastille." One cellblock has been left intact as an exhibit. Four of its galleries house temporary shows, and the tower contains a provocative sculpture called *Le Plongeur* (The Diver) by Irish artist David Moore. Also incorporated in the building is the Parc des Champs-de-Bataille Interpretation Centre (see below). An accomplished cafe-restaurant serves table d'hôte lunches from Monday to Saturday, brunch on Sunday, and dinner on Wednesday and Saturday nights.

1 av. Wolfe-Montcalm (near av. George VI). ✆ **418/643-2150.** www.mdq.org. Admission (excluding special exhibitions) C$7 (US$4.35) adults, C$6 (US$3.70) seniors, C$2.75 (US$1.70) students, C$2 (US$1.20) ages 12 to 16, free for children under 12; Wed free for everyone. June 1–Labour Day daily 10am–5:45pm (Wed until 9:45pm); Sept –May 31 Tues–Sun 11am–5:45pm (Wed until 8:45pm). Bus no. 11.

**Hôtel du Parlement** Since 1968, what the Québecois choose to call their "National Assembly" has occupied this imposing Second Empire château constructed in 1886. Twenty-two bronze statues of some of the most prominent figures in Québec's tumultuous history gaze out from the facade. Highlights are the Assembly Chamber, and the Room of the Old Legislative Council, where parliamentary committees meet. Throughout the building, representations of the fleur-de-lis and the initials VR (for Victoria Regina) remind visitors of Québec's dual heritage. The sumptuous chambers can be toured unaccompanied, but there are 30-minute guided tours in both French and English. *Note:* Tour times change without warning.

The Restaurant Le Parlementaire (© **418/643-6640**) is open to the public. Featuring Québec products and cuisine, it serves breakfast and lunch Monday to Friday most of the year, and dinner Tuesday to Friday in June and December.

Entrance at corner of Grande-Allée Est and av. Honoré-Mercier. © **418/643-7239.** Free admission. Guided tours, early Sept–June Mon–Fri 9am–4:30pm; June 24–Labour Day Mon–Fri 9am–4:30pm, Sat and Sun 10am–4:30pm.

**Parc des Champs-de-Bataille** ★★ Covering 109ha (270 acres) of grassy knolls, sunken gardens, monuments, fountains, and trees, Québec's Battlefields Park stretches over the Plains of Abraham, where Wolfe and Montcalm engaged in their swift but crucial battle in 1759. It is a favorite place for Québecois when they want some sunshine or a bit of exercise. They jog here, glide along on rollerblades, ride bikes, ski, skate, picnic, play soccer. Free concerts are given at the bandstand in the park, the Kiosque Edwin-Bélanger, during the summer. Be sure to see the Jardin Jeanne d'Arc (Joan of Arc Garden), just off avenue Laurier between Loews le Concorde Hôtel and the Ministry of Justice. The statue was a gift from anonymous Americans, and it was here that "O Canada," the country's national anthem, was sung for the first time. Within the park are two Martello towers, cylindrical stone defensive structures built between 1808 and 1812, when Québec feared an invasion from the United States.

Today Battlefields Park contains almost 5,000 trees representing more than 80 species. Prominent among these are sugar maple, silver maple, Norway maple, American elm, and American ash. There are frequent special activities, including theatrical and musical events, presented in the park during the summer.

Year-round, the park's **Maison de la Découverte** (Discovery Pavilion), at 835 av. Wilfrid Laurier (© **418/648-4071**) provides insights into the significance of the Plains of Abraham to Québec over the years, employing effective multimedia techniques. For C$3.50 (US$2.15), visitors are provided with wireless headsets and directed through several chambers—actually corridors and cells in what was once a prison—to witness dramatic presentations in sound and pictures of episodes in Quebec's long history. The narration doesn't fail to describe some of the racier components of that tenure, including a number of elaborate executions, tales of the prostitutes who serviced the garrison at the Citadelle, and the landing of Charles Lindburgh on the Plains in 1928.

The Maison de la Découverte also serves as starting point for bus and walking tours of the park. In summer, a shuttle bus tours the park in 45 minutes with narration in French and English.

Discovery Pavilion of the Plains of Abraham, 835 av. Wilfrid Laurier © **418/648-4071.** www.ccbn-nbc.qc.ca. Free admission to park. Bus tour in summer C$3.50 (US$2.15) for visitors ages 18–64, C$2.75 (US$1.70) ages 13–17 and 65 and over, free for ages 12 and under. Daily 9am–5pm.

## ESPECIALLY FOR KIDS

Children who have responded to Arthurian tales of fortresses and castles or to the adventures of Harry Potter often delight in simply walking around this storybook city. As soon as possible, head for **Terrasse Dufferin,** which has those coin-operated telescopes kids like. In decent weather, there are always street entertainers, whether a Peruvian musical group or men who play saws or wine glasses. A few steps away at Place d'Armes are **horse-drawn carriages,** and not far in the same direction is the **Musée de Cire (Wax Museum),** on Place d'Armes at 22 rue Ste-Anne.

Also at Place d'Armes is the top of **Breakneck Stairs.** Halfway down, across the road, are giant **cannons** ranged along the battlements on rue des Ramparts. The gun carriages are impervious to the assaults of small humans, so kids can scramble over them at will.

At the bottom of the Stairs, on the left, is a **glass-blowing workshop,** the Verrerie la Mailloche. In the front room, craftsmen give informative glass-blowing demonstrations. The glass is melted at 1,396°C (2,545°F) and is worked at 1,093°C (2,000°F). Also in the Lower Town, at 86 rue Dalhousie, the playful **Musée de la Civilisation** keeps kids occupied for hours in its exhibits, shop, and cafe.

Military sites are usually a hit, at least with boys. The **Citadel** has tours of the grounds and buildings and colorful **changing of the guard** and **beating retreat** ceremonies.

The **ferry** to Lévis across the St. Lawrence is inexpensive, convenient from the Lower Town, pleasant, and exciting for kids. The crossing, over and back, takes less than an hour. To run off the kids' excess energy, head for the **Plains of Abraham,** which is also Battlefields Park. To get there, take rue St-Louis, just inside the St-Louis Gate, or, more vigorously, the walkway along Terrasse Dufferin and the Promenade des Gouverneurs, with a long set of stairs. Acres of grassy lawn give children room to roam and provide the perfect spot for a family picnic.

Even better is the **Village Vacances Valcartier** (© **418/844-2200**) at 1860 bd. Valcartier in St-Gabriel-de-Valcartier, about 20 minutes' drive north of downtown. In summer, it's a water park, with slides, a huge wave pool, and diving shows. In winter, those same facilities are put to use for snow rafting on inner tubes, ice slides, and skating.

## 6 Special Events & Festivals

Usually, Québec is courtly and dignified, but all that's cast aside when the symbolic snowman called Bonhomme (Good Fellow) presides over 10 days of merriment in early February during the annual **Carnaval d'Hiver/Winter Carnival** ★★ (www.carnaval.qc.ca) More than a million revelers descend, eddying around the monumental ice palace and ice sculptures and attending a full schedule of concerts, dances, and parades. The mood is heightened by the availability of plastic trumpets and canes filled with a concoction called Caribou, the principal ingredients of which are cheap whisky and sweet red wine. Perhaps its presence explains the eagerness with which certain Québecers participate in the canoe race across the treacherous ice floes of the St. Lawrence. You must make hotel reservations far in advance. Scheduled events are free.

On June 24, **St-Jean Baptiste Day** honors St. John the Baptist, the patron saint of French Canadians. It's marked by more festivities and far more enthusiasm throughout Québec Province than national Dominion Day on July 1. It's their "national" holiday.

Claimed to be the largest cultural event in the French-speaking world, the **Festival d'Eté de Québec/Québec City Summer Festival** (✆ **418/651-2882;** www.infofestival.com) has attracted artists from Africa, Asia, Europe, and North America since it began in 1967. The more than 250 events showcase theater, music, and dance, with 600 performers from 20 countries. One million people come to watch and listen. Jazz and folk combos perform free in an open-air theater next to City Hall; visiting dance and folklore troupes put on shows; and concerts, theatrical productions, and related events fill the days and evenings. It's held for about 10 days in mid-July.

During the 5-day **Medievales de Québec/Québec Medieval Festival** (✆ **418/692-1993**), hundreds of actors, artists, entertainers, and other participants from Europe, Canada, and the United States converge on Québec City in period dress to re-create scenes from 5 centuries ago, playing knights, troubadours, and ladies-in-waiting. The highlights are parades, jousting tournaments, recitals of ancient music, and La Grande Chevauchée (Grand Cavalcade) featuring hundreds of costumed horseback riders. Fireworks are the one modern touch. It's held only in odd-numbered years for about a week in early to mid-August.

## 7 Outdoor Activities & Spectator Sports

### OUTDOOR ACTIVITIES

The waters and hills around Québec City provide countless opportunities for outdoor recreation, from swimming, rafting, and fishing to skiing, snowmobiling, and sleigh rides. There are two centers in particular to keep in mind for most winter and summer activities, both within easy drives from the capital. Thirty minutes from Québec City, off Route 175 north, is the provincial **Parc de la Jacques-Cartier** (✆ **418/848-3169**). Closer by 10 minutes or so is **Parc Mont-Ste-Anne** (✆ **418/ 827-1871**), only 40km (24 miles) northeast of the city. Both are mentioned repeatedly in the listings below. From mid-November to late March, taxis participate in a **winter shuttle** program, **HiverExpress,** picking up passengers at 16 hotels at 8:30am, taking them to Mont-Sainte-Anne and Station Stoneham, and returning them to Québec City at about 4:30pm. Round-trip fare is C$18 (US$11). Call ✆ **418/525-5191** to make a reservation or ask if your hotel participates when booking a room.

**BIKING** Given the hilly topography of the Upper Town, biking isn't a particularly attractive option. But rented bicycles are available at a shop on a hill that descends to the flatter Lower Town. Bikes are about C$8 (US$5) an hour or C$30 (US$19) a day. The shop, **Vélo Passe-Sport Plein Air,** 22 Côte du Palais (✆ **418/692-3643**), also rents in-line skates. It's open daily from 9am to 11pm. Bikes can also be rented at **Cyclo Services,** 84 rue Dalhousie in the Old Port (✆ **418/692-4052**), open all year. For more vigorous mountain biking, the **Mont-Ste-Anne recreational center** (✆ **418/827-4561**) has 200km (124 miles) of trails.

**CAMPING** There are almost 30 campgrounds in the greater Québec area, with as few as 20 individual campsites and as many as 368. All of them have showers and toilets available. One of the largest is in the **Parc de Mont-Ste-Anne,** and they accept credit cards. One of the smallest, but with a convenience store and snack bar, is **Camping La Loutre** (✆ **418/846-2201**) on Lac Jacques-Cartier in the park of the same name. It's north of the city, off Route 175. The booklet available at the tourist offices provides details about all the sites.

**CANOEING** The several lakes and rivers of **Parc de la Jacques-Cartier** are fairly easy to reach, yet in the midst of virtual wilderness. Canoes are available to rent in the park itself.

**CROSS-COUNTRY SKIING** Greater Québec has 22 cross-country ski centers with 278 trails. In town, the **Parc des Champs-de-Bataille** (Battlefields Park) has 11km (6 miles) of groomed cross-country trails, a convenience for those who don't have cars or the time to get out of town. Those who do have transportation should consider **Station Mont-Ste-Anne,** which has more than 225km (140 miles) of cross-country trails at all levels of difficulty; equipment is available for rent.

**DOG-SLEDDING** **Aventures Nord-Bec,** 665 rue Ste-Aimé in Saint-Lambert-de-Lauzon (© **418/889-8001**), about 20 minutes south of the city, offers dog-sledding expeditions. While they aren't the equivalent of a 2-week mush across Alaska, there are choices of half-day to 5-day expeditions, and participants obtain a sense of what that experience is like. They get a four-dog sled meant for two and take turns standing on the runners and sitting on the sled. (Shout "Yo" to go left, "Gee" to go right.) Out on the trail it's a hushed world of snow and evergreens. With the half-day trip costing C$69 (US$43) per adult, C$59 (US$37) for students, and C$20 (US$12) for children 12 and under, it's expensive for families, but the memory stays with you. Another firm providing similar experiences is **Aventure Québec,** 3987 av. Royale at Mont Ste-Anne (© **418/827-2227**).

**DOWNHILL SKIING** Foremost among the five area downhill centers is the one at **Parc Mont-Ste-Anne** (© **418/525-5191**), containing the largest total skiing surface in eastern Canada, with 51 trails (many of them lit for night skiing) and 11 lifts. From November 15 to March 30, a daily shuttle service called "HiverExpress" operates between downtown hotels and alpine and cross-country ski centers. The cars or minivans are equipped to carry ski gear and cost about C$18 (US$11) round-trip per person.

**FISHING** From May to early September, anglers can wet their lines in the river that flows through the **Parc de la Jacques-Cartier** and at the national wildlife reserve at **Cap-Tourmente** (© **418/827-3776**), on the St. Lawrence, not far from Mont-Ste-Anne. Permits are available at many sporting-goods stores.

**GOLF** **Parc Mont-Ste-Anne** has two 18-hole courses, plus practice ranges and putting greens. Reservations are required, and fees are C$60 to C$70 (US$37–US$43), including golf cart. In all, there are 24 courses in the area, most of them in the suburbs of Ste-Foy, Beauport, and Charlesbourg. All but three of the courses in the nearby suburbs are open to the public.

**ICE SKATING** Outdoor rinks are located at Place d'Youville, Terrasse Dufferin, and Parc de l'Esplanade inside the walls, and at Parc de Champs-de-Bataille (Battlefields Park), where rock climbing, camping, canoeing, and mountain biking are also possible. Skates can be rented at **Vélo Passe-Sport Plein Air,** 22 Côte du Palais in the old town (© **418/692-3643**).

**SWIMMING** Those who want to swim during their visit should plan to stay at one of the handful of hotels with pools. **Château Frontenac** has a new one, and the **Radisson** has a heated outdoor pool that can be entered from inside. Other possibilities are the **Hilton, Manoir Victoria,** and **Loews le Concorde.**

A two-season recreational center in St-Gabriel-de-Valcartier, **Village Vacances Valcartier,** 1860 bd. Valcartier (✆ **418/844-2200**), has an immense wave pool and water slides, as well as 38 trails for snow rafting. It's about 20 minutes west of the city.

**TOBOGGANING** A toboggan run is created every winter down the stairs at the south end of the Terrasse Dufferin and all the way to the Château Frontenac. Tickets (only C$1/US60¢per person) are sold at a temporary booth near the end of the run.

### SPECTATOR SPORTS

The city is without a team in any of the professional major leagues, even hockey, but harness races take place at the **Hippodrome de Québec,** 250 boul. Wilfrid-Hamel ExpoCité (✆ **418/524-5283**). General admission is only C$1 (US60¢), free with presentation of your parking ticket. Races take place year-round Thursday to Tuesday at 1:30 or 7:30pm (times vary from season to season; call ahead). Fans have been coming to the Hippodrome for afternoons or evenings of harness racing since 1916. Le Cavallo clubhouse is open year-round.

## 8 Shopping

The compact size of the Old Town, with its upper and lower sections, makes it especially convenient for browsing and shopping. Though similar from one place to the next, the merchandise is generally of high quality. There are several art galleries deserving of attention, including an outdoor version in the Upper Town. Antique shops proliferate along rue St-Paul in the Lower Town.

In the Upper Town, wander along **rue St-Jean** and on **rue Garneau** and **Côte de la Fabrique.**

The **Quartier du Petit-Champlain,** just off place Royale and encompassing rue du Petit-Champlain, boulevard Champlain, and rue Sous-le-Fort (opposite the funicular entrance), offers many possibilities—clothing, souvenirs, gifts, household items, collectibles.

### ARTS & CRAFTS

Handmade sweaters, Inuit art, and other crafts are among the desirable items not seen everywhere else. An official igloo trademark identifies authentic Inuit (Eskimo) art, although the differences between the real thing and the manufactured variety become apparent with a little careful study. Inuit artwork, usually carvings in stone or bone, are best buys not because of low prices, but because of their high quality. Expect to pay hundreds of dollars for even a relatively small piece.

**Abaca** The owners conduct their own buying trips abroad for masks, jewelry, musical instruments, sculpture, and related pieces from Africa, India, Afghanistan, Japan, Korea, China, and a score of other countries. Some jewelry and handcrafts by Québec artists are also sold here. 38 rue Garneau (near rue St-Jean). ✆ **418/694-9761.**

**Aux Multiples Collections** Inuit, vernacular, and modern Canadian art are on offer in this gallery. The most appealing items, and those given prominence in display, are the Native Canadian carvings in stone, bone, and tusk. Prices are high, but competitive for merchandise of similar quality. Open 7 days. 69 rue Ste-Anne. ✆ **418/692-1230.**

**Boutique Métiers d'Art** Just off place Royale, this large new store showcases exclusively the arts and crafts of Quebecois artisans, including bird carvings,

### Tips Outdoor Gallery

Sooner or later, everyone passes rue du Trésor, a short alley near the Place d'Armes between rue Ste-Anne and rue Buade. Artists gather along here much of the year to exhibit and sell their work, much like the artists on St-Amable Lane in Vieux-Montréal. Although none of them are likely ever to find their etchings and serigraphs collected by major art museums, neither do they produce the equivalent of tiger and Elvis paintings on black velvet. Most of the prints on view are of Québec scenes, and one or two might make attractive souvenirs. The artists seem to enjoy chatting with interested passersby.

leather bags, jewelry, glassware, Inuit soapstones, prints, and puppets. The ceramics of Dominique Didier are especially good buys. 29 rue Notre-Dame. ✆ **418/694-0267.**

**Galerie d'Art du Petit-Champlain** This shop features the superbly detailed carvings of Roger Desjardins, who applies his skills to meticulous renderings of waterfowl. The inventory has been expanded to show lithographs, paintings, and some Inuit art. Open daily. 88 rue de Petit-Champlain (near bd. Champlain). ✆ **418/692-5647.**

**Galerie d'Art Trois Colombes** Québecois and other Canadian artisans, including Inuits and Amerindians, produce the weavings, carvings, snowshoes, duck decoys, and soapstone sculptures (some by non-Inuits). Upstairs are handmade hats, coats, sweaters, high-top boots, moccasins, and rag dolls. They ship worldwide. 46 rue St-Louis. ✆ **418/694-1114.**

**Les Artisans Bas-Canada** Crafts and kicky hand-knits predominate, all a little on the expensive side. Duck decoys and burly sweaters for adults and kids are among the most engaging items, supplemented by lots of hats, gloves, mittens, headbands, moccasins, lumberjack coats, soapstone carvings, and Canada-themed books. The inventory has been expanded under the new third-generation owners. 30 Côte de la Fabrique. ✆ **418/692-2109.**

## BOOKS & RECORDS

**Archambault** The shop has two large floors of recorded music, mostly CDs with some cassettes, and the helpful staff goes to some lengths to find what you want. 1095 rue St-Jean. ✆ **418/694-2088.**

**Librairie du Nouveau Monde** In the Lower Town, this store has a wide variety of books, many in English. Ask if the *Historical Guide to Québec* is still available; it's a good read about the city's past, filled with illustrations and photographs. Otherwise, there are two rooms of books concerned with cooking, architecture, boating, and travel. 103 rue St-Pierre (behind the Musée de la Civilisation). ✆ **418/694-9475.**

**Maison de la Presse Internationale** As the name says, this large store in the midst of the St-Jean shopping and nightlife bustle stocks magazines, newspapers, and paperbacks from around the world, in many languages. It stays open daily 7am to 11pm or midnight, and it carries *The New York Times, The Wall Street Journal,* the *International Herald Tribune,* and many U.S. periodicals. There's another branch in the Place Québec, the mall between the Hilton and Radisson hotels. 1050 rue St-Jean (at the corner of rue Ste-Angèle). ✆ **418/694-1511.**

### WINES

**Société des Alcools de Québec (SAQ)** A virtual supermarket of wines and spirits, with thousands of bottles in stock. They recently expanded the selling area to incorporate a section of more than 120 kinds of imported beers. There's another SAQ outlet at 888 rue St-Jean (✆ **418/643-4337**). 1059 av. Cartier (near rue Fraser). ✆ **418/643-4334.**

## 9 Québec City After Dark

While Québec City can't pretend to match the volume of nighttime diversions in exuberant Montréal, there's more than enough to do. And apart from theatrical productions, almost always in French, a knowledge of the language is rarely necessary. Drop in at the tourism information office for a list of events.

Check the "Night Life" section of the ***Greater Québec Area Tourist Guide*** for suggestions. A weekly information leaflet called ***L'Info-Spectacles,*** listing headline attractions and the venues in which they're appearing, is found at concierge desks and in many bars and restaurants, as is the free tabloid-size ***Voir,*** which provides greater detail. Both are in French, but salient points aren't difficult to decipher.

### THE PERFORMING ARTS

Many of the city's churches host **sacred and secular music concerts,** as well as special Christmas festivities. Among them are the Cathedral of the Holy Trinity, the Eglise St-Jean-Baptiste, and the Chapelle Bon-Pasteur. **Outdoor performances** in summer are staged beside the City Hall in the Jardins de l'Hôtel-de-Ville, in the Pigeonnier at Parliament Hill, on the Grande-Allée, and at place d'Youville.

**L'Orchestre Symphonique de Québec,** Canada's oldest, performs at the Grand Théâtre de Québec from September to May. The **Québec Opéra** mounts performances there in the spring and fall, as does, more occasionally, the **Danse-Partout** ballet company.

**Agora** The 6,000-seat amphitheater, in the Vieux-Port, is the scene of rock and occasional classical concerts and a variety of other shows in the summer. Iron Maiden, Jethro Tull, Joe Cocker, and Johnny Winter have all appeared. The city makes a dramatic backdrop. The box office, at 84 rue Dalhousie, is open daily 10am to 6pm. 120 rue Dalhousie (Vieux-Port). ✆ **418/692-4672.**

**Colisée Pepsi** Rock concerts by name acts on the order of perennials Phil Collins and Led Zeppelin and new bands like New Radicals and Fun Loving Criminals are often held in this arena, located in a park on the north side of the St-Charles River. The box office is open in summer Monday to Friday 9am to 4pm, in winter 10am to 5pm. 250 bd. Wilfrid-Hamel (ExpoCité). ✆ **418/691-7110.**

**Grand Théâtre de Québec** Classical music concerts, opera, dance, and theatrical productions are performed in two halls, one of them containing the largest stage in Canada. Visiting conductors, orchestras, and dance companies often perform here when resident organizations are away. The Trident Theatre troupe performs in French in the Salle Octave-Crémazie. Québec's Conservatory of Music lies underneath the theater. The box office is open Monday to Saturday 10am to 6pm. 269 bd. René-Lévesque Est (near av. Turnbull). ✆ **418/643-8131.** www.grandtheatre.qc.ca.

**Kiosque Edwin-Bélanger** The bandstand at the edge of the Battlefields Park is the site of a 10-week summer music season, from mid-June to late August. Performances are Wednesday through Sunday and range from operas and classical recitals to jazz, pop, and blues. All are free. 390 av. de Bernières (near the Musée de Québec). ✆ **418/648-4050.**

**Le Capitole** Mixtures of live shows and other attractions are offered on an irregular schedule in the historic 1,312-seat theater. Dramatic productions and comedic performances are in French, but they also host rock groups and occasional classical recitals. 972 rue St-Jean (near Porte St-Jean). ✆ **800/261-9903** for tickets, or 418/694-9903 for information.

**Palais Montcalm** The main performance space is the 1,100-seat Raoul-Jobin theater, with a mix of dance programs, classical music concerts, and plays. More intimate recitals and jazz groups are found in the much smaller Café-Spectacle. 995 place d'Youville (near Porte Saint-Jean). ✆ **418/670-9011** for tickets.

## MUSIC CLUBS

Most bars and clubs stay open until 2 or 3am, closing earlier if business doesn't warrant the extra hour or two. Cover charges and drink minimums are all but unknown in the bars and clubs that provide live entertainment. There are three principal streets to choose among for nightlife: the **Grande-Allée, rue St-Jean,** and the emerging **avenue Cartier.**

**Café des Arts** Recently moved from above a store on rue St-Jean, this unusual enterprise still puts on a variety of offbeat theatrical pieces, mime, poetry readings, dance, jazz, and *chanson.* Admission charges are as low as C$3 (US$1.85), as high as C$16 (US$10). Shows usually start around 8:30pm. 870 ave. de Salaberry (near rue St-Jean). ✆ **418/694-1499.**

**Chez Son Père** A musical institution in Québec since 1960, this is the place where French-Canadian folksingers often get their start. The stage is on the second floor, with the usual brick walls and sparse decor. A young, friendly crowd can be found here. The club is a few steps uphill from bustling rue St-Jean. 24 rue St-Stanislas (near rue St-Jean). ✆ **418/692-5308.** No cover.

**D'Orsay** Visitors who are well into their mortgages will want to keep this chummy pub-bistro in mind. Most of the clientele is on the far side of 35, and they start up conversations easily—two active bars help. There's a small dance floor with a DJ, and in summer, entertainers perch on a stool on the terrace out back. Full meals are served. 65 rue de Buade (opposite Hôtel-de-Ville). ✆ **418/694-1582.**

**Kashmir** Upstairs, over the Pizzeria d'Youville, this show bar puts on an eclectic variety of musical and artistic presentations, including rock, blues, and art exhibitions, with the added attraction of dancing to a deejay 3 or 4 nights a week. Scheduling is erratic. Pass the time before the evening's performances at the pool tables or poker machines. 1018 rue St-Jean (near rue St-Stanislas). ✆ **418/694-1648.** Cover depends upon performer, usually about C$3 (US$1.85).

**L'Emprise** Live jazz, usually of the mainstream or fusion variety, is a long-standing tradition in this mellow room. Seating is at tables and around the bar off the lobby of the Hôtel Clarendon. Music is nightly, from about 10pm. 57 rue Ste-Anne (at des Jardins). ✆ **418/692-2480.** No cover.

**Les Yeux Bleus** At the end of an alleyway off rue St-Jean, it looks tumbledown from the outside but isn't intimidating inside. The music is mostly Québecois *chanson,* partly international pop. 1117½ rue St-Jean. ✆ **418/694-9118.** No cover.

**Théâtre du Petit-Champlain** Québecois and French singers alternate with jazz groups in this roomy cafe-theater in the Lower Town. Have a drink on the patio before the show. The box office is open Monday to Friday 1 to 5pm, to

7pm the night of a show. Ticket prices range from C$15 to C$30 (US$9–US$19) depending on the artist. Performances are usually Tuesday to Saturday. 68 rue du Petit-Champlain (near the funicular). ✆ **418/692-2631.**

## BARS & CAFES

The strip of the **Grande-Allée** between place Montcalm and place George V, near the St-Louis Gate, has been compared to the Boulevard St-Germain in Paris. That's a real stretch, but it is lined on both sides with cafes, giving it a passing resemblance. Many have terraces abutting the sidewalks, so cafe-hopping is an active pursuit. Eating is definitely not the main event. Meeting and greeting and partying are aided in some cases by glasses of beer so tall they require stands to support them. This leads, not unexpectedly, to a beery frat-house atmosphere that can get sloppy and dumb as the evening wears on. But early in the evening, it's fun to sit and sip and watch. The following bars are removed from the Grande-Allée melée.

**Aviatic Club** A favorite for after-work drinks since 1945 is located in the front of the city's train station. Food is served, ranging from sushi to Tex-Mex in loose inspiration, along with local and imported beers. 450 de la Gare-du-Palais (near rue St-Paul, Lower Town). ✆ **418/522-3555.**

**Le Pape-Georges** This cozy stone-and-beamed wine bar features blues and *chansonniers*, from Thursday to Sunday at 10pm. Light fare—plates of assorted cheeses, cold meats, smoked salmon—is served. Most of the patrons appear to be locals. 8 rue Cul-de-Sac (near bd. Champlain, Lower Town). ✆ **418/692-1320.**

**Saint Alexandre Pub** Roomy and sophisticated, this is one of the best-looking bars in town. It's done in British pub mode, with polished mahogany, exposed brick, and a working fireplace that's a particular comfort 8 months of the year. It claims to serve 40 single-malt scotches and more than 200 beers, 24 of them on tap, along with hearty victuals that complement the brews. Sometimes it presents jazz duos and trios, usually on Monday nights from 7:30 to 11:30pm. Large front windows provide easy observation of the busy St-Jean street life; open daily 5pm to 2am. 1087 rue St-Jean (near St-Stanislas). ✆ **418/694-0015.**

## DANCE CLUBS

**Le Dagobert** Long the top disco in Québec City, this three-story club has an arena arrangement on the ground floor for live bands, with raised seating around the sides. Upstairs are more bars, a large dance floor, TV screens to keep track of sports events, and video games. The sound system, whether emitting live (mostly homage or alternative bands) or recorded music, is a decibel short of bedlam; more than a few habitués are seen donning earplugs. Things don't start jamming until well after 11pm. The crowd divides into students and their more fashionably attired older brothers and sisters. A whole lot of eyeballing and approaching goes on. 600 Grande-Allée (near av. Turnbull). ✆ **418/522-2645.** No cover.

**Le Bistro Plus** A bistro by day, things change at night when the dance floor in back fills with writhing young bodies—very young, in many cases. During

***Moments*** **A Room with a View**

Spinning slowly above a city that twinkles below like tangled necklaces, **L'Astral,** atop the Hôtel Loews le Concorde, 1225 place Montcalm, at the Grande-Allée (✆ **418/647-2222**), unveils a breathtaking 360° panorama. You can make it for dinner or just drinks and the view.

the week, the music is recorded, with live Latino groups on weekends on the ground floor, a disco on the second floor. It gets frat-house raucous and messy, especially after the 4 to 7pm happy hour, but congenial, too, with darts, a pool table, and TVs tuned to sports. 1063 rue St-Jean (near rue St-Stanislas). ✆ **418/694-9252.** No cover.

**Liquid Bar** With a Grande Allée address but an entrance a few steps down rue de la Chevrotière, its doors are clogged every weekend with under-25 celebrants eager to gain entrance. Lights rotate and flash across the dance floor underscoring rap and house music. 580 Grande Allée. ✆ **418/524-1367.**

**Living Lounge** The newest club on Grand Allée has two grungy floors—pool tables, fussball, and a bar downstairs, a dance space upstairs with a couple more bars and house and hip-hop played at the sound levels of jets taking off. 690 Grande Allée Est. No phone. Sometimes a cover of up to C$5 (US$3.10).

**Maurice** Successfully challenging Chez Dagobert (across the street) at the top rung of the nightlife ladder, this triple-tiered enterprise occupies a converted mansion at the thumping heart of the Grande-Allée scene. It includes a surprisingly good restaurant, a couple of bars, and a dance room that alternates live Latin and blues bands with DJ music. Downstairs, the Charlotte Bar has live music most nights. Theme nights are frequent, and the balconies and bars overflow with up to 1,000 post-boomers. Happy hour has two-for-one drinks. 575 Grande Allée Est. ✆ **418/647-2000.** No cover.

**Vogue/Sherlock Holmes** This pair of double-decked bars is less frenetic than the Monkey Bar, next door, with a small disco upstairs in Vogue, and the "pubby" eatery Sherlock below, with a pool table and dart board. Grad students and Gen-Xers spending the disposable income of first jobs make up most of the clientele. 1170 d'Artgny (off Grande-Allée). ✆ **418/529-9973.** No cover.

### GAY BARS

The gay scene in Québec City is a small one, centered in the Upper Town just outside the city walls, on **rue St-Jean** between **avenue Dufferin** and **rue St-Augustin,** and also along rue St-Augustin and nearby **rue d'Aiguillon,** which runs parallel to rue St-Jean. One popular bar and disco, frequented by both men and women (and by men who appear to be women), is **Le Ballon Rouge,** at 811 rue St-Jean (✆ **418/647-9227**). Upstairs is the **Lazyboy** lounge, with a bathroom you have to see. Nearby is a club called **Le Drague** ("The Drag"), at 815 rue St-Augustin (✆ **418/649-7212**), which has a dance room, pool tables, and (you guessed it) drag shows on Sunday. There are live performances of other kinds Thursdays through Saturdays.

### EVENING CRUISES

Dancing and dining await passengers on the MV ***Louis Jolliet*** (✆ **418/692-1159**), which offers a 2½-hour "Love Boat" evening cruise 8 to 10:30pm. Full dinners are available for C$18 to C$27 (US$11–US$17) and a complete bar lubricates the evening. The fare is C$22 (US$14). Cruises depart from quai Chouinard at the port.

## 10 Day Trips from Québec City: Ile d'Orléans & More

The first four excursions described below can be combined and completed in a day. It will be a breakfast-to-dark undertaking, to be sure, but the farthest of the four destinations is only 40km (25 miles) from Québec City.

Bucolic Ile d'Orléans, with its maple groves, orchards, farms, and 18th- and 19th-century houses, is a mere 15 minutes away. The famous shrine of Ste-Anne-de-Beaupré and the Mont Ste-Anne ski area are only about half an hour from the city by car. With 2 or more days available, you can continue along the northern shore to Charlevoix, where inns and a gambling casino invite an overnight.

While it's preferable to drive through this region, tour buses go to Montmorency Falls and the shrine of Ste-Anne-de-Beaupré, and circle the Ile d'Orléans. For organized bus tours, contact **La Tournée du Québec Métro** (✆ **418/836-8687**), **Old Québec Tours** (✆ **418/624-0460**), or **Gray Line** (✆ **418/523-9722**). If you'd like a guide, **Maple Leaf Guide Services** (✆ **418/622-3677**) can provide one, your car or theirs.

For more information, log on to **www.quebec-region.cuq.qc.ca**.

## ILE D'ORLEANS ★★

It's a short drive from Québec City to the island. Follow avenue Dufferin (in front of the Parliament building) to connect with Autoroute 440 east, in the direction of Ste-Anne-de-Beaupré. In about 15 minutes, the Ile d'Orléans bridge is seen on the right.

After arriving on the island, turn right on Route 368 East toward Ste-Pétronille. The **Bureau d'Information Touristique** (✆ **418/828-9411**) is in the house on the right, and it has a useful guidebook (C$1/US60¢) for the island. It's open daily 9am to 7pm June to August; the rest of the year, Monday to Friday only, 9am to 5pm. A good substitute for the Ile d'Orléans guide is the *Greater Québec* guide, which includes a short tour of Ile d'Orléans. A driving-tour cassette can be rented or purchased at the tourist office, and cycling maps are available there.

Until 1935, the only way to get to Ile d'Orléans was by boat (in summer) or over the ice (in winter). The highway bridge since built has allowed the fertile fields of Ile d'Orléans to become Québec City's primary market-garden. During harvest periods, fruits and vegetables are picked fresh on the farms and trucked into the city daily. In mid-July, hand-painted signs posted by the main road announce FRAISES: CUEILLIR VOUS-MEME (Strawberries: Pick 'em yourself). The same invitation is made during apple season, September and October. Farmers hand out baskets and quote the price, paid when the basket's full.

The island was long isolated from the mainland, evident in three **stone churches** that survive from the days of the French regime. There are only seven such churches left in all of Québec, so this is a point of pride for Ile d'Orléans. A firm resistance to development has kept many of its old houses intact as well. This could easily have become just another sprawling bedroom community, but it has remained a rural farming area—and island residents work to keep it that way. They even hope to bury their telephone lines and to put in a bicycle lane to cut down on car traffic.

A coast-hugging road circles the island, 34km (21 miles) long and 8km (5 miles) wide, and another couple of roads bisect it. Farms and picturesque houses dot the east side of the island, and abundant apple orchards enliven the west side. There are six tiny villages on Ile d'Orléans, each with a church as its focal point. It's possible to do a quick circuit of the island in half a day, but a full day may be justified if you eat in a couple of restaurants, visit a sugar shack, skip stones from the beach, and stay the night in one of several waterside inns. If you're strapped for time, drive as far as St-Jean, then take Route du Mitan across the island, and return to the bridge, and Québec City, via Route 368 West.

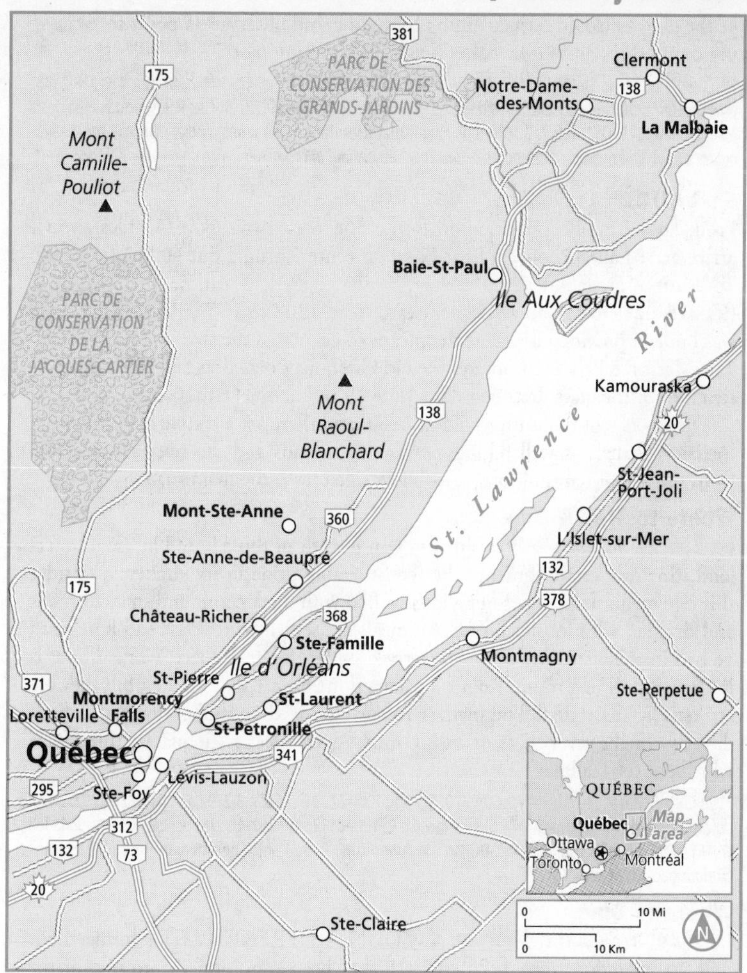


## STE-PETRONILLE

The first village reached on the recommended counterclockwise tour is Ste-Pétronille, only 3km (2 miles) from the bridge. With 1,050 inhabitants, it is best known for its Victorian inn, La Goéliche (below), and also claims the northernmost stand of red oaks in North America, dazzling in autumn. The houses were once the summer homes of wealthy English in the 1800s; the church dates from 1871. Even if you don't stay at the inn, drive down to the water's edge, where a small public area with benches is located. Strolling down the picturesque rue Laflamme is another pleasant way to while away an hour or two.

### Where to Stay & Dine

**La Goéliche** On a rocky point of land at the southern tip of the island stands this country house with a wraparound porch. Actually, this is a replica of the 1880 Victorian that stood here until it burned to the ground in 1996. This one manages to retain the period flavor with tufted chairs, Tiffany-style lamps, and a few antiques. Only the two suites have TV. The river slaps at the foundation of the glass-enclosed terrace dining room, a grand observation point for watching cruise ships and Great Lakes freighters steaming past.

22 Chemin du Quai, Ste-Pétronille, PQ G0A 4C0. ✆ **888/511-2248** or 418/828-2248. Fax 418/828-2745. www.oricom.ca/aubergelagoeliche. 18 units. C$157–C$197 (US$97–US$122) double. Rates include breakfast. MAP available. AE, DC, DISC, MC, V. Free parking. **Amenities:** Restaurant (Contemporary French), bar; heated outdoor pool; golf nearby; tennis nearby; massage; babysitting. *In room:* Minibar, coffeemaker, hair dryer.

## ST-LAURENT

From Ste-Pétronille, continue on Route 368 East. After 6km (4 miles), you'll arrive at St-Laurent, once a boat-building center turning out 400 crafts a year. To learn more about that heritage, visit Le Parc Maritime de St-Laurent (✆ **418/828-9672**), an active boat yard from 1908 to 1967. Before the bridge was built, it provided islanders the means to get across the river to Québec City. The Maritime Park incorporates the old Godbout Boatworks and offers demonstrations of the craft. It's open daily June 19 to Labour Day, 10am to 5pm.

The town's church was erected in 1860, and there are a couple of picturesque roadside chapels as well. Good views of farmlands and the river are available from the St-Laurent golf course—follow signs from the main road.

### Where to Stay & Dine

**Le Canard Huppé** A roadside inn reminiscent of those found in the motherland, this tidy establishment takes considerable pride in its kitchen. Consider this one menu item: crimson raviolis stuffed with duck confit and smoked snails and drizzled with lobster butter. All meals are served—breakfast and lunch can be had in the bistro/bar or on the terrace under the linden tree, while dinner is in the main dining room. Rooms upstairs don't have TV or phones, but they are attractively decorated. The owners recently opened an annex down the road, directly on the river. Five of its six rooms have electric fireplaces, three have whirlpool tubs, all have TVs.

2198 Chemin Royal, St-Laurent, PQ G0A 3Z0. ✆ **800/838-2292** or 418/828-2292. Fax 418/828-2292. www.canard-huppe.qc.ca. 10 units in inn, 6 units in villa. C$100–C$125 (US$62–US$78) double. Rates include full breakfast. Meal plans available. AE, DC, MC, V. **Amenities:** Restaurant (Contemporary French), bar; small outdoor pool. *In room:* A/C.

### Where to Dine

**Le Moulin de Saint-Laurent** ★ COUNTRY FRENCH This former flour mill, in operation from 1720 to 1928, has been transformed into one of the island's most romantic restaurants. Rubble-stone walls and hand-wrought beams form the interior, with candlelight glinting off hanging copper and brass pots. On a warm day, sit on the shaded terrace beside the waterfall, and be sure to wander upstairs to see the Québecois antiques. Lunch can be light—an omelette or a plate of assorted patés or cheeses, perhaps. The light, dry cider made on the island is a refreshing alternative to wine. On weekends, a small combo plays in the evenings.

The owners also have cottages for rent at the shore. Two-night/3-day packages are C$225 to C$249 (US$140–US$154) per person, including breakfast, dinner, and either a 1½-hour cruise or 1-day bike rental.

754 Chemin Royal. ✆ **888/629-3888** or 418/829-3888. Fax 418/829-3716. www.moulinstlaurent.qc.ca. Reservations recommended at dinner. Main courses, C$9.95–C$18.95 (US$6–US$12), dinner C$12.95–C$23.95 (US$8–US$15); table d'hôte, add C$12.95 (US$8) to the price of the main course. AE, DC, MC, V. Daily 10:30am–2pm and 6–9pm. Closed mid-Oct to May 1.

## ST-JEAN

St-Jean, 6km (4 miles) from St-Laurent, was home to sea captains. That might be why the houses in the village appear more prosperous than others on the island. The yellow bricks in the facades of several of the homes were ballast in boats that came over from Europe. The village church was built in 1732, and the walled cemetery is the final resting place of many fishermen and seafarers.

On the left as you enter the village is one of the largest and best-preserved houses on the island: **Manoir Mauvide-Genest,** 1451 av. Royale (© **418/829-2630**). Completed in 1752, it is filled with period furnishings. A small chapel was added in 1930, and Huron Indians made the altar. Next door, there's an active summer theater.

If you're pressed for time, pick up **Route du Mitan,** which crosses Ile d'Orléans from here to St-Famille on the west side of the island. Route du Mitan, not easy to spot, is on the left just past the church in St-Jean. A brief detour down that road is a diverting drive through farmland and forest. Return to St-Jean and proceed east on Route 368 to St-François.

## ST-FRANÇOIS

The 9km (5½-mile) drive from St-Jean to St-François exposes vistas of the Laurentian Mountains off to the left on the western shore of the river. Just past the village center of St-Jean, Mont Ste-Anne can be seen, its slopes scored by ski trails. At St-François, home to about 500 people, the St. Lawrence, a constant and mighty presence, is 10 times wider than when it flows past Québec City. Regrettably, the town's original church (1734) burned in 1988. At St-François, 24km (15 miles) from the bridge, the road becomes Route 368 West.

### Where to Dine

**Chaumonot** QUEBECOIS At this riverside inn, the food reflects what farmers have eaten on this island for generations—pork chops, lamb, salmon, meatball stew, pheasant paté, tomato-and-onion relish, and plenty of warm bread. The kitchen mixes in a few relatively modern touches, such as quiche Lorraine and shrimp and duck paté. Picture windows look out on the river. There's a pool.

The inn has eight ordinary but orderly rooms available; doubles with breakfast go for C$89 to C$149 (US$55–US$92). The inn does not have a phone.

425 av. Royale, St-François. © **418/829-2735.** Reservations recommended. Main courses C$18–C$27 (US$11–US$17); table d'hôte, lunch C$9.95–C$18.95 (US$6–US$12), dinner C$27–C$32 (US$17–US$20). AE, MC, V. Daily 11am–3pm and 5–9pm (until 10pm July–Aug). Closed Nov–Apr.

## STE-FAMILLE

Founded in 1661 at the northern tip of the island, Ste-Famille is the oldest parish on the island. With 1,660 inhabitants, it is 8km (5 miles) from St-François and 19km (12 miles) from the bridge. Across the road from the triple-spired church (1743) is the convent of Notre-Dame Congregation, founded in 1685 by Marguerite Bourgeoys, one of Montréal's prominent early citizens. This area supports dairy and cattle farms and apple orchards.

Anglers might wish to swing by **Etang Richard Boily,** 4739 Chemin Royal (© **418/829-2874**), where they can cast their lures for speckled or rainbow trout in a stocked pond, daily 9am to sunset. It isn't *entirely* like fishing in a rain barrel. Poles and bait are supplied—no permit is required—and customers pay only for what they catch, about C45¢ (US30¢) per inch; the fish run 9 to 12 inches. They'll clean, cut, and pack what you catch. Some island restaurants can even be persuaded to cook the fish for you. For more passive activity, buy a handful of fish pellets, toss them in the water, and watch the ravenous trout jump.

On the same property is a *cabane à sucre,* the traditional "sugar shack" where maple syrup is made. See demonstrations of the equipment and get briefed on the process that turns the sap of a tree into syrup. Free tastes are offered and several types of products are for sale in a shop on the premises.

Farther along, near the village church, you might wish to visit the **Boulangerie G.H. Blouin,** 3967 Chemin Royal (© **418/829-2590**), run by a family of bakers who have lived on the island for 300 years. You'll also find a little shop called **Le Mitan** (© **418/829-3206**) that stocks local crafts and books about the island.

## ST-PIERRE

By Ile d'Orléans standards, St-Pierre is a big town, with a population of about 2,000. Its central attraction is the island's oldest church (1717). Services are no longer held there; it now contains a large handicraft shop in the back, behind the altar, which is even older than the church (1695). The pottery, beeswax candles, dolls, scarves, woven rugs, and blankets aren't to every taste but are worth a look.

Thousands of migrating snow geese, ducks, and Canada geese stop by in the spring, a spectacular sight when they launch themselves into the air in flapping hordes so thick they almost blot out the sun.

### Where to Stay & Dine

**Le Vieux Presbytère** Down the street running past the front of the church, the former 1790 rectory has been converted to a homey inn. Filled with antiques and other old pieces, its sitting and dining rooms and glassed sun porch coax strangers into conversation. For privacy, choose one of the cottages behind the main house; for more space and enough beds for a family of five, ask for room number one. A fireplace warms the dining room much of the year. Main courses run from about C$15 to C$27 (US$9–US$17), with a table d'hôte of C$29.50 (US$20). They have ostriches, elk, and bison in the adjoining lot, an unexpected sight and a hint about the menu.

1247 av. Mgr. d'Esgly, St-Pierre, PQ G0A 4E0. © **888/828-9723** or 418/828-9723. Fax 418/828-2189. www.presbytere.com. 8 units (2 share a bathroom). C$65–C$115 (US$40–US$71) double. Rates include breakfast. Meal plan available. AE, DC, MC, V. **Amenities:** Restaurant (Regional); bike rental; limited room service; laundry service. *In room:* No phone.

## MONTMORENCY FALLS & STE-ANNE-DE-BEAUPRE ★

Take Autoroute 40, north of Québec City, going east. At the end of the autoroute, where it intersects with Route 360, the falls come into view (they are also seen from the bridge when returning from Ile d'Orléans). A **tourist booth** (© **418/663-2877;** www.chutemontmorency.qc.ca) is located beside the parking area at the falls, just after the turnoff from the highway. It's open early June to early September 9am to 7pm, and early September to mid-October 11am to 5pm. Admission to the falls is free.

At 83m (274 ft.), the falls, named by Samuel de Champlain for his patron, the duke of Montmorency, are 30m (100 ft.) higher than Niagara—a boast no visitor is spared. They are, however, far narrower. The waterfall is surrounded by the provincial Parc de la Chute-Montmorency, where, from early May to late October, visitors can stop to take in the view or have a picnic. In winter, the plunging waters contribute to a particularly impressive sight: The freezing spray sent up by the falls builds a mountain of white ice at the base called the "Sugarloaf," which sometimes grows as high as 30m (100 ft.). On summer nights the falls are illuminated, and toward the end of July and into August, there is an international fireworks competition overhead. The yellow cast of the waterfall results from the high iron content of the riverbed. **Manoir Montmorency,** above the falls, was opened in 1994, replacing an earlier structure that burned down. Lunches and dinners of notably improved quality are served there daily, all year, except Monday and Tuesday dinners January to March. The dining room and porch have a sideways vista of the falls.

From Montmorency Falls, it's a 24km (15-mile) drive along Route 138 to the town of **Ste-Anne-de-Beaupré.** The highway goes right past the basilica, with an easy entrance into the large parking lot. An **information booth** at the southwestern side of the basilica, 10018 av. Royale (✆ **418/827-3781**), is open year-round, daily 8:30am to 4:30pm. The basilica itself is open year-round. Admission is free. Masses are held daily but hours vary.

Legend has it that French mariners were sailing up the St. Lawrence River in the 1650s when they ran into a terrifying storm. They prayed to their patroness, St. Anne, to save them, and when they survived they dedicated a wooden chapel to her on the north shore of the St. Lawrence, near the site of their perils. Not long afterward, a laborer on the chapel was said to have been cured of lumbago, the first of many documented miracles. Since that time, pilgrims have made their way here—over a million a year—to pay their respects to St. Anne, the mother of the Virgin Mary and grandmother of Jesus.

Reactions to the **religious complex** inevitably vary. To the faithful, this is a place of wonder, perhaps the most important pilgrimage site in North America. Others see it as a building that lacks the grandeur its great size is intended to impart, a raw and ponderous structure without the ennobling patina of age. The former group will want to schedule at least a couple of hours to absorb it all; the latter won't need more than 15 minutes to satisfy their curiosity.

The towering **basilica** is the most recent building raised on this spot in St. Anne's honor. After the sailors' first modest wooden chapel was swept away by a flood in the 1600s, another chapel was built on higher ground. Floods, fires, and the ravages of time dispatched later buildings, until a larger, presumably sturdier structure was erected in 1887. In 1926, it, too, lay in ruins, gutted by fire.

As a result of a lesson finally learned, the present basilica is constructed in stone, following an essentially neo-Romanesque scheme. Marble, granite, mosaics, stained glass, and hand-carved wood are employed with a generous hand throughout. The pews, for instance, are of wood with hand-carved medallions at the ends, each portraying a different animal. Behind the main altar are eight side chapels and altars, each different. The hundreds of crutches, canes, braces, and artificial limbs strapped to columns and stacked on the floor of the vestibule, left behind by those who no longer needed them, attest to the conviction that miracles routinely occur here.

Other attractions in Ste-Anne-de-Beaupré include the **Way of the Cross,** with life-size bronze figures, on the hillside opposite the basilica; the **Scala Santa Chapel** (1891); and the **Memorial Chapel** (1878), with a bell tower and altar from the late 17th and early 18th centuries, respectively. More commercial than devotional are the **Historial,** a **wax museum,** and the **Cyclorama,** a 360° painting of Jerusalem. My recommendation is not to bother with them.

## WHERE TO STAY & DINE

**Auberge La Camarine** ★★ Why they named it after a bitter berry is uncertain, but this inn has a kitchen that is equaled by only handful of restaurants in the entire province. The cuisine bears a resemblance to that variety of fusion cookery that joins French, Italian, and Asian techniques and ingredients.

Salmon tartar married with leaves of smoked sturgeon and crisply sautéed lettuce is illustrative. Presentation is of the edifice variety, but contrasting colors, flavors, and textures are made to work magically together. The owners are justly proud of their wine cellar. Only dinner is served (overnight guests can get breakfast and light lunch), daily from 6 to 8:30pm. Table d'hôte are C$45 to C$55 (US$28–US$34). Reservations are required. The restaurant is open nightly for ten months a year, closed Sunday and Monday in November and May.

Guest rooms blend antique and contemporary notions, and some have fireplaces and/or Exercycles. Two have Jacuzzis. The ski slopes of Mount Ste-Anne are a short drive away by car or regular shuttle.

10947 bd. Ste-Anne, Beaupré, PQ G0A 1E0. ✆ **800/567-3939** or 418/827-1958. Fax 418/827-5430. www.camarine.com. 31 units. C$105–C$149. (US$65–C$92) double. Many packages available. AE, DC, MC, V. Go past the Promenades Ste-Anne outlet center, turning left off Route 138. **Amenities:** Restaurant (Fusion), bar; golf nearby; access to nearby health club; babysitting; coin-op laundry. *In room:* A/C, TV, coffeemakers.

## MONT STE-ANNE: SKIING & SUMMER SPORTS

Continue along Route 138 toward the Mont Ste-Anne recreational area, about 10km (6 miles) NE of Ste-Anne-de-Beaupre. The park entrance is easy to spot.

Like Montréal, Québec City has its Laurentian hideaways. But there are differences: The Laurentians sweep down quite close to the St. Lawrence at this point, so Québecois need drive only about 30 minutes to be in the woods. And since Québec City is much smaller than Montréal, the Québec resorts are more modest in size and fewer in number, but their facilities and amenities are equal to those of resorts elsewhere in the Laurentian range.

Mont-Ste-Anne Park, 49km$^2$ (30 sq. miles) surrounding an 800m (2,625-ft.) high peak, is an outdoor enthusiast's bonanza. In summer, there are camping, golfing, in-line skating, cycling, hiking, jogging, paragliding, and a 241m (150-mile) network of mountain biking trails (bikes can be rented at the park). An eight-passenger gondola to the top of the mountain operates every day for the benefit of cyclists between late June and early September, weather permitting. In winter, the park is Québec's largest and busiest single ski area. Twelve lifts, including the gondola and three quad chair lifts, transport downhill skiers to the starting points of 50 trails and slopes. Paragliding instruction is available in winter as well as summer.

### WHERE TO STAY & DINE

**Château Mont Sainte-Anne** ★ Settled in at the base of its namesake mountain, the resort, opened in 1979, continues to grow, and will have added more rooms by the time these words are in ink. Much as the management would like to increase its summer business, citing its two golf courses, kid's day camp, and horseback and cycling trails, its identity is as ski center. (As a result, summer rates are about 45% cheaper than in winter.) It is well-suited in that role, with comprehensive facilities that include cable car lifts, two summit chalets, downhill trails on both the north and south faces of the mountain, a fleet of 15 snowmobiles, ample snowmaking equipment and related diversions—ice skating and dog-sledding among them. They boast skiing many years into mid-May. What's more, the menu in the main dining room is unusually inventive for a mass feeding operation, and the two bars provide satisfying pub grub. A free shuttle van carries guests to and from Québec City.

500 boul. Beau-Pré, Beaupré, PQ G0A 1E0. ✆ **800/463-4467** or 418/827-1862. Fax 418/827-5072. www.chateaumontsaintanne.com. 240 units plus 185 condos. C$109–C$196 (US$68–US$122). Children under 17 stay free in parents' room. Many packages available. AE, DC, MC, V. **Amenities:** 2 restaurants (Eclectic,

International), 2 bars; indoor and outdoor pools; golf on premises; health club & spa; children's programs; game room; activities desk; courtesy van; massage; babysitting; laundry service; dry cleaning. *In room:* A/C, TV, dataport, kitchenettes, fridge, coffeemaker, hair dryer.

## CHARLEVOIX ★

Take Route 138 as far as Baie-St-Paul, the gateway to Charlevoix, 98km (61 miles) from Québec City. After a look around or an overnight stay, pick up Route 362 to La Malbaie, merging once again with Route 138 to reach the ferry at St-Siméon. Baie-St-Paul has a **tourist office** at 444 bd. boul. Mgr-de Laval (✆ **418/435-4160**), open daily mid-June to Labour Day 9am to 7pm, from September to early June daily 9am to 5pm.

The Laurentians move closer to the shore of the St. Lawrence as they approach what used to be called Murray Bay at the mouth of the Malbaie River. While the entire length of Route 138 from Beaupré isn't necessarily fascinating, the Route 362 detour from Baie-St-Paul is scenic, with wooded hills slashed by narrow riverbeds and billowing meadows ending in harsh cliffs plunging down to the river. The air is scented by sea salt and rent by the shrieks of gulls.

In 1988, Charlevoix was named a UNESCO World Biosphere Reserve. Though only one of 325 such regions throughout the world, it was the first one to include human settlement. In addition to the country inns dotting the region from Baie-St-Paul to Cap à l'Aigle to La Malbaie and beyond, Pointe-au-Pic has a casino, a newer, smaller offshoot of the one in Montréal. The northern end of the region is marked by the confluence of the Saguenay River and the St. Lawrence. These waters attract six species of whales, many of which can be seen from shore mid-June to late October; whale-watching cruises are increasingly popular.

### BAIE-ST-PAUL

The first town of any size reached in Charlevoix via Route 138, this attractive community of 6,000 has borne a reputation as an artist's retreat since the start of the 20th century. More than a dozen boutiques and galleries and a couple of small museums show the work of local painters and artisans. Given the setting, it isn't surprising that many of the artists are landscapists, but other styles and subjects are represented. Some of their production is merely of the kitchen-hobbyist level, but much of it is highly professional. A small local museum, **Le Centre d'Exposition,** 23 rue Ambroise-Fafard (✆ **418/435-3681;** www.centre-bsp.qc.ca) opened in 1992 with three floors of work primarily by regional artists, both past and present. Inuit sculptures are included, and temporary one-person and group shows are mounted throughout the year. Admission is C$3 (US$1.85) for adults, C$2 (US$1.20) for seniors and students, and children under 12 go free. It's open from September to May daily 9am to 5pm; from June to August daily 9am to 7pm.

#### Where to Stay & Dine

**La Maison Otis** Prices look steep at first, but that's because big breakfasts and dinners are included (and required). The meals are no sacrifice, served in a room with a stone fireplace and shaded candlesticks on pink tablecloths. Excellent clam chowder, salmon tartare, and pheasant have been notable in the past. A wide range of facilities and amenities allow guests who reserve far enough in advance to customize their lodgings. Combinations of fireplaces, whirlpools, stereo systems, VCRs, four-poster beds, and suites that sleep four are all available, distributed among three buildings. Housekeeping is meticulous. A long porch fronts the colorful main street, and a kidney-shaped indoor pool is on the premises, as is a jovial piano bar.

23 rue St-Jean-Baptiste, Baie-St-Paul, PQ G0A 1B0. © **800-267-2254** or 418/435-2255. Fax 418/435-2464. www.quebecweb.com/maisonotis. 30 units. Late June–late Oct, Christmas–mid-Apr C$213–C$273 (US$132–US$169) double; late Oct–Dec 23, Apr 15–late June C$185–C$265 (US$115–US$164) double. Rates include breakfast and dinner. AE, DC, MC, V. Pets accepted. **Amenities:** Restaurant (Regional), bar; indoor pool; golf nearby; exercise room; whirlpool; sauna; massage; babysitting. *In room:* A/C, TV, hair dryer.

## ST-IRENEE

From Baie-St-Paul, take Route 362 toward La Malbaie. It roller-coasters over bluffs above the river, and in about 32km (20 miles) is this cliff-top hamlet of fewer than 800 year-round residents. Apart from the setting, the best reason for dawdling here is the lengthy music and dance festival held every summer. **Domaine Forget,** 398 Chemin les Bains (© **888/336-7438** or 418/452-3535 for reservations; www.domaineforget.com), offers concerts from mid-June to late August on Wednesday, Saturday, and some Friday evenings, and Sunday from 11am to 2pm. Ten more weekend concerts are spaced through autumn from September to late November. This performing arts festival was initiated in 1977, with the purchase of a large hillside property overlooking the river. Stables and barns were converted to use as studios and rehearsal halls, and the surrounding lawns were used to stage the concerts and recitals. Their success prompted the construction of a new 600-seat hall, which opened for the 1996 season. While the program emphasizes classical music with solo instrumentalists and chamber groups, it is peppered with appearances by jazz combos. During the summer season, tickets are C$20 to C$30 (US$12–US$19); children under 12 are free. The fall concerts cost C$12 to C$24 (US$7–US$15).

## POINTE-AU-PIC

From St-Irénée, the road starts to bend west after 10km (6 miles), as the mouth of the Malbaie River starts to form. Pointe-au-Pic is one of the trio of villages collectively known as La Malbaie, or Murray Bay, as it was known to the wealthy Anglophones who made this their resort of choice from the Gilded Age through the 1950s. Although inhabitants of the region wax poetic about their hills and trees "where the sea meets the sky," they have something quite different to preen about now: their new casino.

**Casino de Charlevoix** This is the second of Québec's gambling casinos (the first in Montréal, the third in the Ottawa/Hull area). Tasteful cherry-wood paneling and granite floors enclose the ranks of 780 slot machines, a Keno lounge, and 22 tables, including blackjack, roulette, stud poker, and mini-baccarat. Only soft drinks are allowed at the machines and tables, so players have to go to an adjacent bar to mourn their losses. And there is a dress code, forbidding, among other items, tank tops, bustiers, and "clothing associated with organizations known to be violent." Running shoes and "neat" blue jeans are allowed. There may be a wait for entrance on weekends.

183 av. Richelieu (Route 362). © **800/665-2274** or 418/665-5300; www.casinos-quebec.com. Free admission (persons 18 and over only). Daily 10am–3am. Signs are frequent on Route 362 coming from the south, and on Route 138 from the north.

**Musée de Charlevoix** In existence since 1975, the museum moved to its present quarters in 1990. Folk art, sculptures, and paintings of variable quality by regional artists figure prominently in the permanent collection, supplemented by frequent temporary exhibitions with diverse themes.

1 Chemin du Havre (at the intersection of Route 362/bd. Bellevue). ✆ **418/665-4411.** Admission C$4 (US$2.50) adults, C$3 (US$1.85) seniors and students, free for children under 12. June 24–Sept 2 daily 10am–6pm; Sept 3–June 23 Tues–Fri 10am–5pm, Sat–Sun 1–5pm.

### Where to Stay & Dine

**Fairmont Le Manoir Richelieu** ★★ Since 1899, there has been a resort hotel here, long the aristocratic haven of swells summering in Murray Bay. The opening of the new casino just across the drive-up circle changed the makeup of visitors. To the mix of families seeking all-ages diversions and elderly people who have been coming here since they were youngsters have been added those willing to go anywhere for the thrill of losing money. When it became clear that facilities had become worn and service was falling short, the hotel was closed for a massive C$140-million renovation. It reopened in June 1999, bright and shiny as a new loonie, with marked improvements in every category. Rooms now brush up against deluxe standards, with all conveniences, including robes, two or three phones, and easy modem connection. The executive floor has 21 rooms with a lounge serving complimentary breakfasts and evening hors d'oeuvres. Buffet-lovers are pleased with the dozens of platters and trays of food set out for all three meals of the day. The house band plays on past midnight for dancing.

181 rue Richelieu, La Malbaie, PQ G5A 1X7. ✆ **800/441-1414** or 418/665-3703. Fax 418/665-4566. www.fairmont.com. 405 units. C$199–C$299 (US$123–US$185) double, from C$459 (US$285) suite. MAP and other packages available. AE, DC, MC, V. Valet parking C$17 (US$11). **Amenities:** 2 restaurants (International), bar; indoor and outdoor pools; golf on premises; 3 tennis courts; health club & spa; watersports equipment rentals; children's center; concierge; car-rental desk; business center; shopping arcade; limited room service; massage; babysitting; laundry service; same-day dry cleaning; executive rooms. *In room:* A/C, TV w/pay movies, fax, dataport, minibar, coffeemaker, hair dryer, iron, safe.

## CAP-A-L'AIGLE

Route 362 rejoins Route 138 in La Malbaie, the largest town in the area, with almost 4,000 inhabitants. It serves as a provisioning center, with supermarkets, hardware stores, and gas stations. There is a **tourist information office** at 630 bd. de Comporté, open mid-June to Labour Day daily 9am to 9pm, the rest of the year daily 9am to 5pm. Continue through the town center and cross the bridge on the right, making a sharp right again on the other side. This is Route 138, with signs pointing to Cap-à-l'Aigle.

William Howard Taft spent many summers in what used to be known as Murray Bay, starting in 1892 and extending well past his presidency. Given his legendary girth, it may be assumed that Taft knew something about the good life. For much of his time, the only way to get here was by boat—the railroad didn't arrive until 1919. Some of the other folks who made this their summer home, namely the Cabots of Boston, the Duke of Windsor, and Charlie Chaplin, could confirm that Taft loved the region. And if any of them could return today, they would probably choose what is arguably the premier inn in Murray Bay.

### Where to Stay & Dine

**La Pinsonnière** ★★★ This is one of only eight small hotels in the prestigious Relais & Châteaux organization in all of Canada. Associated properties offer limited size, bedrooms that often border on princely luxury, but most of all, an obsessive emphasis on food and wine. Bedrooms come in several categories, the priciest of which are equipped with Jacuzzis and gas fireplaces. A major renovation of the entire facility has just been completed. Packages include whale-watching cruises, dogsled runs, and skiing at Mont Grand-Fonds. There's access to the river, but that water is *very* cold.

You'll know where the owners focus their attention when you're seated in the serene dining room beside the picture window, anticipating a dinner that will become the evening's entertainment. With drinks and menus comes the *amuse-guele*—say, quail leg on a bed of slivered asparagus—immediately followed by soup. The main event might be a succulent veal chop with a nest of shaved carrots, fiddleheads, and purple potatoes. Wines are a particular point of pride here, and the owner needs no urging to conduct tours of his impressive cellar.

124 rue St-Raphaël, La Malbaie (secteur Cap-à-l'Aigle), PQ G5A 1X9. ✆ **800/387-4431** or 418/665-4431. Fax 418/665-7156. www.lapinsonniere.com. 25 units. May–Oct 7 and Christmas–New Year C$160–C$500 (US$99–US$310) double; Nov–Apr C$140–C$475 (US$87–US$295) double. MAP available but not required. Packages available, minimum 2-night stay on weekends. AE, DISC, MC, V. **Amenities:** Restaurant (Creative French), bar; heated indoor pool; golf nearby; tennis; access to nearby health club; spa; sauna; concierge; limited room service; massage; babysitting; dry cleaning. *In room:* A/C, TV, hair dryer.

## ST-SIMEON

Rejoin Route 138 and continue 32km (20 miles) to St-Siméon. If you've decided to cross to Rivère-du-Loup on the other side of the St. Lawrence, returning to Québec City along the south shore, the ferry departs from here. St-Siméon has **seasonal tourist offices** at 494 rue St-Laurent and at the ferry landing, open mid-June to Labour Day daily 9am to 7pm. Also check **www.tourisme-charlevoix.com**. With discretionary time left, I recommend continuing on to Baie-Ste-Catherine and Tadoussac, but if that isn't an option, it's only 150km (93 miles) back to the city the way you came on the north shore.

In St-Siméon, signs direct cars and trucks down to the ferry terminal. Boarding is on a first-come, first-served basis, and ferries leave on a carefully observed schedule, weather permitting, from April to early January. Departure times of the two to five daily sailings vary substantially from month to month, however, so get in touch with the company, **Clarke Transport Canada** (✆ **418/638-2856**), to obtain a copy of the schedule. For current fares, call ✆ **418/862-5094** or check the website, **www.travrdlstsim.com**. Always subject to change, fares for passengers remaining on board for the round-trip are C$13.50 (US$8) for ages 12 to 64 years, C$12.10 (US$8) for seniors, and C$9.10 (US$6) for children ages 5 to 11. For cars, the one-way fare is C$28.80 (US$18). MasterCard and Visa accepted. Arrive at least 30 minutes before departure, one hour ahead in summer. Voyages take 65 to 75 minutes.

From late June to September, passengers may enjoy a bonus. Those are the months the whales are most active. They are estimated at more than 500 in number when migratory species join the resident minke and beluga whales. They prefer the northern side of the estuary, roughly from La Malbaie to Baie-Ste-Catherine, at the mouth of the Saguenay River. Since that is the area the ferry steams through, sightings are an ever-present possibility, especially in summer.

## BAIE STE-CATHERINE

To enhance your chances of seeing **whales** ★, continue northeast from St-Siméon on Route 138, arriving 32km (20 miles) later in Baie-Ste-Catherine, near the estuary of the Saguenay River. A half dozen companies offer cruises to see whales or the majestic Saguenay Fjord from here or from Tadoussac, on the opposite shore. The cruise companies use different types of watercraft, from powered inflatables called zodiacs that carry 10 to 25 passengers up to stately catamarans and cruisers that carry up to 500. The zodiacs don't provide food, drink, or narration, while the larger boats have snack bars and naturalists on board to describe the action. The small boats, though, are more maneuverable, darting about at each sighting to get closer to the rolling and breaching behemoths.

Zodiac passengers are issued life jackets and waterproof overalls but should expect to get wet anyway. It's cold out there, too, so layers and even gloves are a good idea. People on the large boats sit at tables inside or ride the observation bowsprit, high above the waves. Big boats are the wimp's choice for whale-watching. Mine, too.

Most cruises last 2 to 3 hours. One of the most active companies offering trips is **Croisières AML,** with offices in Québec City (© **800/563-4643** all year, 418/237-4274 in season). From June to mid-October, they have up to four departures daily. Fares on the larger boats are C$45 (US$28) for adults, C$20 (US$12) for children ages 6 to 12, while zodiac fares are an extra C$10 each (US$6). Excursions of comparable duration and with similar fares are provided on the catamaran maintained by **Famille Dufour Croisières** (© **800/463-5250** or 418/692-0222). Yet another company is **Croisières 2001** (© **800/694-5489** or 418/235-3333), which uses a 175-passenger catamaran. Fares are C$45 (US$28) for adults, C$41 (US$25) for seniors, C$20 (US$12) for children ages 6 to 13, and free for children 5 and under. Departures are from the Tadoussac and Baie-Ste-Catherine wharves.

From Baie Ste-Catherine, it's less than a half-hour drive back to St-Siméon and the ferry across to the opposite shore. Alternatively, continue north to the ferry, **Traverse Tadoussac** (© **418/235-4395**), at the mouth of the dramatic Saguenay River. Palisades rise sharply from both shores, the reason it is often referred to as a fjord. The ferry can board up to 400 passengers and 75 vehicles for the trip across to Tadoussac, which takes only 10 minutes. Departure times vary according to season and demand, of course, but in summer figure every hour from midnight to 6am, every 40 minutes from 6:20 to 8am, every 20 minutes from 8am to 8pm, and every 40 minutes from 8:20pm to midnight.

## 11 The Gaspé Peninsula ★★

The southern bank of the St. Lawrence sweeps north and then eastward toward the Atlantic. At the river's mouth, the thumb of land called the Gaspé Peninsula—Gaspésie in French—pokes into the Gulf of St. Lawrence. The Gaspé is a primordial region heaped with aged, blunt hills covered with hundreds of square miles of woodlands. Over much of its northern perimeter, their slopes fall directly into the sea. Winter here is long and harsh, making the crystal days of summer all the more precious.

The fishing villages huddled around the coves cut from the coast are as sparsely populated as they've always been, with many of the young residents moving inland toward brighter lights (unemployment in the region is close to 30%). Left behind are the crash of the surf, eagles and elk in the high grounds, and timber to be harvested gingerly by lumber companies.

All that makes it the perfect place for camping, hiking, biking, hunting, and fishing in near-legendary salmon streams. Almost every little town has a modest but clean motel and a restaurant to match. The purpose of a trip is a complete escape from the cities, and your destination is the tip of the thumb, the village of Percé and the famous rock for which it's named.

From Québec City, driving around the peninsula and back to the city takes at least 4 days, assuming only an overnight stay when you get to Percé. The first half of the trip is the most scenic, while the underside of the peninsula is largely a flat coastal plain beside a regular shoreline. That southern shore is the route of Via Rail trains, a thrice-weekly service between Montréal, Québec, and intermediate stops on the way to the town of Gaspé. The train, called the *Chaleur,* makes a stop at Lévis, opposite Québec City. It leaves Lévis at 10:35pm on Monday, Thursday, and Saturday and arrives at Percé at 10:34am the next morning. Passengers in sleeping cars have the use of showers and a domed lounge car.

For more information about the Gaspé, log on to **www.gaspesie.qc.ca**.

## FROM RIVIERE-DU-LOUP TO RIMOUSKI

Past **Riviére-du-Loup** along Route 132, the country slowly grows more typically Gaspésien. Bogs on the river side of the road yield bales of peat moss, shipped to gardeners throughout the continent. Past the town of Trois Pistoles (the name derives from a French coin, the *pistole,* not from firearms) are low rolling hills and fenced fields for dairy cattle. Along the roadside, hand-painted signs advertise ***pain de ménage*** (homemade bread) and other baked goods for sale.

**Rimouski** (pop. 40,000) is the region's largest city. Much of it has the look of a boomtown, with many new buildings, but travelers not there on business are likely to pass on through. Rimouski marks the start of the true Gaspé, free of the gravitational pull of Greater Québec. The number of the two-lane highway is 132, running all the way around the peninsula to join itself again at Mont Joli. Thus the confusing signs: 132 EST (east) and 132 OUEST (west).

## THE JARDINS DE METIS ★

Near Grand Métis is the former Reford estate, now the **Jardins de Métis** (**© 418/775-2221**)—easily the north shore's stellar attraction. The gardens were last owned by a woman with such a passion for gardening that even in Gaspé's relatively severe climate she was able to cultivate a horticultural wonderland of some 100,000 plants in 2,500 varieties. Full of fragrances and birdsong and tumbling water, the six sections are laid out in the informal English manner. Butterflies float and hummingbirds zip among the blossoms, all but oblivious to humans. The provincial government took over the gardens in 1962, and they can be visited June to August daily 8:30am to 6:30pm (Sept–Oct to 5pm). Admission is C$12 (US$7) for adults, C$11 (US$7) for seniors and students, and C$3 (US$1.85) for children ages 6 to 13; children under 6 are free. Elsie Reford's mansion now houses a museum of limited interest and a busy restaurant, open daily 9am to 5pm.

## MATANE

The highway enters commercial **Matane,** whose traffic rivals the bustle in Rimouski. But the focal point is the Matane River, a thoroughfare for the annual migration of up to 3,000 spawning salmon. They begin their swim up the Matane in June through a specially designed dam that facilitates their passage, continuing to September. Near the lighthouse the town maintains a seasonal **information bureau** (**© 418/562-1065**), open mid-June to early September daily 8am to 8pm.

It takes 5 nonstop driving hours to get to Percé from Matane, so plan to spend a full day getting there. There are frequent picnic grounds (look for signs announcing *Halte Municipale*), a couple of large nature preserves, and ample opportunities to sit by the water and collect driftwood. While towns along the way are smaller and more spread out, there are many small motels and modest

B&Bs called *gîtes.* Simple sustenance isn't a problem either, for there are many *casse-croûtes,* the roadside snack stands also known as *cantines.*

### WHERE TO STAY

**Riôtel Matane** Directly on the beach, the former Hôtel des Gouverneurs is now part of a small Gaspé chain. The best guest rooms are on the third floor, which have ocean views, minibars, Internet access, and other big city conveniences. A piano bar helps pass an evening, and the licensed dining room serves all meals. The exceedingly modest exercise room is scheduled for upgrade, as are the standard rooms on the second floor. You may be encouraged to eat at the beach restaurant next door. Don't.

250 av. du Phare Est, Matane, PQ G4W 3N4. ✆ **888/427-7374** or 418/566-2651. Fax 418/562-7365. www.riotel.com. 96 units. C$69–C$119 (US$43–US$74) double. Packages and Sept–May discounts available. AE, DC, MC, V. Free parking. **Amenities:** 2 restaurants (Continental), bar; heated outdoor pool; small exercise room. *In room:* A/C, TV w/pay movies.

### WHERE TO DINE

**Le Rafiot** SEAFOOD/CANADIAN Surely Matane's busiest restaurant, it routinely fills its two floors, at least on summer weekends. While there are extra-cost appetizers on the table d'hôte menu, the soup or salad included with the main courses should be sufficient unless you're really hungry. Shellfish and fish are featured, and most are worth it just for the sides of good frites (fries). Large parties are common, but the solicitous waitresses make sure that lone diners and couples aren't made to feel like orphans. Desserts are of the prettily constructed spun sugar school. The upstairs rooms are open only in summer. A piano player helps while winter evenings away.

1415 av. du PhareOouest (route 132). ✆ **418/562-8080.** Reservations suggested on weekends. Table d'hôte C$14.95–C$20.95 (US$9–US$13), main courses C$14.75–C$23.50 (US$9–US$15). AE, MC, V. Mon–Fri 11am–9pm, Sat–Sun 5–10pm (shorter hours Oct–May).

## STE-ANNE-DES-MONTS & THE PARC DE LA GASPESIE

Still another small fishing town, **Ste-Anne-des-Monts** has a seasonal **tourist booth** (✆ **418/763-5832**) on Route 132, half a mile past the bridge, and also stores, gas stations, and other necessary services.

Rising higher inland are the Chic-Choc mountains, the northernmost end of the Appalachian range. Most of them are contained by the **Parc de la Gaspésie** and adjoining preserves. For a scenic detour of about 100km (60 miles) round-trip, turn south onto route 299 in Ste-Anne-des-Monts. The road climbs into the mountains, some of which are naked rock at the summits. After about 24km (15 miles), a welcome station provides information about the wilderness park. Back there, the rivers brim with baby salmon and speckled trout, and the forests and meadows sustain herds of moose, caribou, and deer.

## MONT ST-PIERRE: PERFECT FOR HANG GLIDING

Back on Route 132, turning right from Ste-Anne, the highway becomes a narrow band crowded up to water's edge by sheer rock walls. Offshore, seabirds perch on rocks, pecking at tidbits. High above the shore are many waterfalls that spill from the cliffs beside the highway.

Around a rocky point and down a slope, **Mont St-Pierre** is much like other Gaspésian villages except for the eye-catching striations in the rock of the mountain east of town. Such geological phenomena are quickly forgotten at the startling sight of hang gliders suddenly appearing overhead. Due to its favorable updrafts, the site is regarded as nearly perfect for the sport. In late July and early

August, the town holds a 2-week **Fête du Vol-Libre** (Hang-Gliding Festival), when the sky is filled with birdmen and women in flight hundreds of feet above the town, looping and curving on the air currents until landing in the sports grounds behind city hall. For more information about the event, contact the **Corporation Vol Libre,** C.P. 82, Mont St-Pierre, Gaspésie (✆ **418/797-2222;** fax 418/797-5101).

## PARC NATIONAL FORILLON ★

Soon the road winds up into the mountains, over a rise, down into the valley, and again up to the next. The settlements get smaller, but still there are roadside stands advertising fresh-baked homemade bread and fresh and smoked fish. At Petite-Rivière-au-Renard, route 197 heads southwest toward Gaspé while route 132 continues east to the tip of the peninsula. Shortly after that intersection is the reception center for the **Parc National Forillon** (✆ **418/368-5505**). Bilingual attendants on duty there can advise on park facilities, regulations, and activities. Route 132 continues along the edge of the park until it turns south at a lighthouse.

Chosen because of its representative terrain, the park's 238km$^2$ (92 sq. miles) of headlands capture a surprising number of the features characteristic of eastern Canada. A rugged coastline, dense forests, and an abundance of wildlife attract hikers and campers from all over North America. On the northern shore are sheer rock cliffs carved from the mountains by the sea, and on the south is the broad Bay of Gaspé. The park has a full program of nature walks, trails for hiking and cycling, beaches, sea kayaking, picnic spots, and campgrounds. A daily pass to enter the park from early June to early October is C$3.75 (US$2.30) for adults, C$3 (US$1.85) for seniors, C$2 (US$1.20) for students and children ages 6 to 16, and C$8.75 (US$5) for families. Camping fees are C$16.50 to C$20 (US$10–US$12). Of the 371 campsites at four designated campgrounds, 77 have electricity. Only four are open all year; most of the others are closed mid-October to late May.

**Croisière Forillon** (✆ **418/892-5629** in summer or 418/368-2448 in winter) operates "discovery" cruises from Cap des Rosiers harbor daily in the warm months. Its 95-passenger *Félix-Leclerc* steams around the rim of the headlands past colonies of seals and seabirds. Fares are C$16 (US$10) for adults and C$10 (US$6) for children. Whales are sometimes encountered, but cruises specifically intended to get close to those magnificent creatures are provided by **Croisières Baie de Gaspé** (✆ **418/892-5500;** www.baleines-forillon.com). The *Narval III,* a powered inflatable, is the means of transport, with a capacity of 46 passengers. Its 2½-hour cruises leave from Grande-Grave Harbor, on the south shore of the park. Fares are C$33 (US$20) for adults, C$27 (US$17) for seniors and students, and C$10 (US$6) for children. Reserve in advance, if possible.

## GASPE

In 1534, Jacques Cartier stepped ashore in Gaspé to claim the land for the king of France, erecting a wooden cross to mark the spot. Today Gaspé is important economically because of its deep-water port and the three salmon rivers emptying into it. The principal attraction is the **Gaspésie Museum,** at Jacques Cartier Point on Route 132 (✆ **418/368-5710**), which endeavors to tell the story of Cartier's landing (hours vary), and the carved granite dolmens out front are meant to be reminiscent of the explorer's native Brittany.

**Moments A Sun-pierced Rock**

A famous Québec landmark, Percé Rock is a narrow butte rising straight out of the water, resembling a beached supertanker from some angles. Pierced by a sea-level hole at its far end, it's especially striking in the slanting sun of late afternoon.

## PERCE ★

As you wind around the hills and along the water toward Percé, the Pic de l'Aurore (Peak of the Dawn) dominating the town's northern reaches, comes into view. From the Pic, you'll see Percé Rock—*Rocher Percé*—and Bonaventure Island, further out.

The town of Percé isn't large, and except for a few quiet inland residential streets, it's confined to the main road running along the shore. A mile of closely spaced souvenir shops, snack bars, restaurants, and motels, some of it leans toward garish, but the tone is well short of honky-tonk. People in swimsuits or shorts and T-shirts give it a family-oriented beach-party ambiance.

A yellow building at the north end of town houses the **Percé Information Touristique** office, at 142 Route 132 Est (✆ **418/782-5448**). It's open daily 8am to 8pm in summer, with shorter hours off-season.

### EXPLORING THE AREA

After checking into a motel, most people take a boat trip out to the **Rock** ★ and to the humpbacked island bird sanctuary, now the provincial **Parc de l'Ile-Bonaventure-et-du-Rocher-Percé** ★ (✆ **418/782-2240**). The island's lure is the quantity, rather than the diversity, of its tens of thousands of nesting birds. Among them are gannets, cormorants, puffins, black guillemots, kittiwakes, and razorbills. Naturalists are available to answer questions and there are hiking trails, observation decks, a modest cafe. A 10-minute film of the bird colonies is shown in the interpretation center, and there are saltwater aquariums. June to mid-October, it's open daily 9am to 5pm, with shorter hours the rest of the year. Birders and hikers can get off at the dock, later picking up one of the ferries arriving two or three times an hour 8am to 5pm. Fares are C$13 (US$8) for adults and C$5 (US$3.10) for children under 12.

Several operators hawk a variety of excursions, including island tours, fishing trips, and whale-watching cruises. There isn't a great deal to distinguish among their offerings, but **Les Bateliers de Percé** 162 route 132 Est (✆ **418/782-2974**) has glass-bottomed **catamarans** that sail from the town wharf on tours to the Rock, Bonaventure Island, and Forillon National Park. The cats have lounges, large windows, bar service, rest rooms, and bilingual crews. Fares for most tours are C$20 (US$12) for adults and C$10 (US$6) for children, amounts consistent with those charged by the other outfits. Many of these have booths in the large orange building labeled simply "Billeterie", near the main jetty. Two-hour whale-watching cruises typically cost C$35 (US$22) for adults and C$15 (US$9) for children.

For underwater explorations, contact the **Club Nautique de Percé,** 199 route 132 Est (✆ **418/782-5403** in summer or 418/782-5222 in winter; fax 418/782-5624), which can lead you on SCUBA outings to over a dozen dive sites. The water is about 10°C to 18°C (50°F–64°F) June to August and about

14°C (57°F) until mid-October. The Club has a lifeguarded pool and rents kayaks for two hours at C$30 (US$19) for one, and C$39 (US$24) for two.

At low tide walk out to the fossil-encrusted Rock, a temptation few visitors resist. Almost all the shops along route 132 carry variations of the same stock - film, model boats, waterfowl woodcarvings, and the usual coffee mugs and sweatshirts. One of the largest and marginally more tasteful is **Au Bon Secours,** 150 route 132 Ouest (✆ **418/782-2011**).

## WHERE TO STAY & DINE

Business starts to tail off in mid-August, when it should be easier to find the lodgings you desire.

**La Normandie** ★ This small hotel is the class act of the town, in style, service, dining, and facilities. All the guest rooms have small sitting areas, and those facing the water have decks (rooms numbered in the 60s and 70s are tops). The kitchen is fairly ambitious, sending five-course table d'hôte dinners (C$25–C$46/US$16–US$29) into a dining room with unobstructed views of the Rock from every chair. Lobster, salmon, scallops, and halibut are always on the card. Reserve ahead.

221 route 132 Ouest, C.P. 129, Percé, PQ G0C 2L0. ✆ **800/463-0820** or 418/782-2112. Fax 418/782-2337. www.normandieperce.com. 45 units. C$110–C$150 (US$68–US$93) double. Packages available. AE, DC, MC, V. Closed mid-Oct to Apr. **Amenities:** Restaurant, bar. *In room:* A/C, TV, hair dryer, iron.

## WHERE TO DINE

**La Maison du Pêcheur** ★ *Kids* SEAFOOD It's close to sacrilegious to eat anything but fish here, within sight of the most important fishing grounds in the North Atlantic. So order up a bowl of the splendid seafood chowder, the lavish platter of various smoked fish, the giant scallops in an unusual whisky, raisin, and nut sauce—all specialties of the house. They are preceded by a bread basket with cod butter, so maybe you'll be psyched to try the delectable cod tongues in a citrusy sea urchin cream. You won't regret it. The pizza's pretty good, too, if you absolutely must. This is an accommodating place for families, where kids are given crayons and accorded their own *menu des petits.* A cafe below the main room serves breakfast and lunch from 8am to 1pm.

End of quai de Percé. ✆ **418/782-5331.** Table d'hôte C$21.50–C$39.50 (US$13–US$24). AE, MC, V. June to mid-Oct daily 11:30am–2:30pm and 5–10pm.

**L'Auberge du Gargantua** COUNTRY FRENCH On the wall are photos of the owner feeding a bear and François Mitterand (separately). He often sits at your table to take your order, even if all those ups and downs are a chore when you're well past 80. Dining at his log-cabin mountaintop restaurant is as fun as ever, starting with great views of both ocean and mountains. Check this procession of courses: A plate of hors d'oeuvres with bits of paté and salami and spoonfuls of pasta, rice, and cucumber salads. A tureen of soup from which you serve yourself, plus a choice of several fish and game main courses with vegetables from the garden out back. Sweets are chosen from the array on the dessert buffet. All are served by the busy, but infectiously cheerful staff. When you pay the boss at the bar, he'll probably pour you a complimentary cordial.

Chemin des Falls. ✆ **418/782-2852.** Reservations recommended. Table d'hôte C$25–C$39 (US$16–US$24). V. Mid-May to mid-Oct daily 4–10pm. Drive south on Rte. 132 from town, watching for the sign L'AUBERGE DU GARGANTUA on the right.

9

# Ottawa & Eastern Ontario

*by Herbert Bailey Livesey*

**Ottawa** may be the most underappreciated national capital east of Ulan Bator, even though on most counts it's an urban standard against which many North American cities might well gauge themselves. Ottawa's downtown is striking, with more renovations to its 19th- and early 20th-century buildings happening every year. The miles of tidy late-Victorian brick houses serving as shops, restaurants, and homes are real characteristics of the city. The Gothic spires and towers of Parliament Hill look like the grand estate of an overachieving Scottish laird, with the voluptuous Gatineau Hills as a backdrop. In spring, carpets of tulips and daffodils embrace residences and ministries and cast visual fire against the deep greens of the city's scores of parks. Cutting a swath through Ottawa is the Rideau Canal, a magnet for houseboats and cabin cruisers and a scene out of a Dutch painting in winter, when the citizenry takes to the ice on sleighs and skates.

The reality of Ottawa is far from the dour Calvinist sobriety often depicted. It's clean—men with pans and brooms let not a wad of paper linger in downtown gutters—and the city's streets are not yet choked. It possesses, in fact, a certain romance in its lanes and parks and cul-de-sacs. See for yourself with a walk down to Victoria Island. Looking east, as the Ottawa River rushes by the bluffs where Parliament stands, it doesn't take much imagination to summon a picture of those early days when waterborne fur traders and explorers sped westward and great logs rolled down these rivers to what was then a clamorous lumber town. Developers and builders have yet to obscure the treasured vistas of hills and water. And, in this most British of Canadian cities, observe troops of sentries in scarlet tunics and black shakos marching to drum and bagpipe to the morning changing of the guard, just as they do at Buckingham Palace.

Admittedly, Ottawa was an unlikely candidate for Canada's capital when it was chosen in the mid-19th century. The two provinces of Upper Canada (Ontario) and Lower Canada (Québec) were fused into the United Provinces of Canada, but their rivalry was so bitter the legislature had to meet alternately in Toronto and Montréal. Queen Victoria selected the village of Ottawa in 1858, no doubt in the hope that its location on the Ontario-Québec border would smooth the differences between the French and English Canadas. Her choice wasn't met with much praise: Essayist Goldwin Smith called it "a sub-Arctic village, converted by royal mandate into a political cockpit." Other assessments weren't as kind.

For nearly a century the city languished in an undeniable provincialism and worked on its reputation for propriety. In its early days, though, it managed to nurture some colorful characters, not the least of whom was Canada's longest-serving prime minister, William Lyon Mackenzie King, who conducted World War II with the guidance of his dog, his deceased mother, and frequent consultations with his predecessor, Sir Wilfrid Laurier, who was by then two decades dead.

In the 1960s, perhaps because of Canada's burgeoning nationalism or because the government wished to create a real capital, Ottawa began to change. The National Arts Centre was built, ethnic restaurants multiplied, the Byward Market area and other historic buildings were renovated, and public parks and recreation areas were created. This process has continued into the present with the building of the National Gallery of Canada. Hull, the Québecois city across the river, has been undergoing a similar transformation, highlighted by the opening of the superb Museum of Civilization and the Casino de Hull. Those twin cities are now full of unexpected pleasures—you can watch the debates and pomp of parliamentary proceedings, take in the street scene from a sidewalk terrace, ski or camp or hike in wilderness only 15 minutes away, and then put your feet up before the fireplace of a rustic inn.

After visiting Ottawa, you may wish to explore **eastern Ontario** for a few days. The high points are covered here: **Kingston,** an appealing lakefront town, is the principal gateway to the **Thousand Islands** of the St. Lawrence River. East from **Port Hope**—a worthy stop for antiques hounds—stretches the **Bay of Quinte** and **Quinte's Isle,** a tranquil region of farms, orchards, quaint villages, and riverside parks. Still outside the usual tourist circuits, it was settled by colonials, loyal to the Crown, who fled the American Revolution.

## 1 Essentials

### GETTING THERE

**BY PLANE** **Ottawa International Airport** (www.ottawa-airport.ca) is about 20 minutes south of the city. **Air Canada** (✆ **888/247-2262**) is the main airline serving Ottawa. Other choices are **US Air** (✆ **800/428-4322**), **Northwest** (✆ **800/225-2525**), and **Delta** (✆ **800/221-1212**). A shuttle bus (✆ **613/736-9993**) operates between the airport and downtown for C$9 (US$6) one-way or C$14 (US$9) for adults and C$4 (US$2.65) for seniors/students round-trip. A taxi from the airport to the city costs about C$20 (US$13).

**BY TRAIN** **VIA Rail** (✆ **888/VIA-RAIL** or 613/244-8289; www.viarail.ca) trains arrive at the station at 200 Tremblay Rd., at boulevard St-Laurent, in the southeastern area of the city. From here buses connect to downtown.

**BY BUS** Buses arrive at the **Central Bus Station,** 265 Catherine St., between Kent and Lyon. **Voyageur** (✆ **613/238-5900**; www.voyageur.com) provides service to Montréal and Kingston, Ontario, while **Greyhound Canada** (✆ **800/661-TRIP** or 613/238-6668; www.greyhound.ca) provides service to Toronto and western Canada.

**BY CAR** Driving from New York, take Interstate 81 to Canada's Route 401 east to Route 16 north. From the west, come via Toronto, taking Route 401 east to Route 16 north. From Montréal, take Route 17 to Route 417.

### VISITOR INFORMATION

**TOURIST OFFICES** The **Ottawa Tourism and Convention Authority,** 130 Albert St., on the 18th floor (✆ **613/237-5158;** www.ottawa-conventions.com), is open Monday to Friday 9am to 5pm, but the most convenient place to gather info is the **Capital Infocentre,** 90 Wellington St., across from Parliament Hill

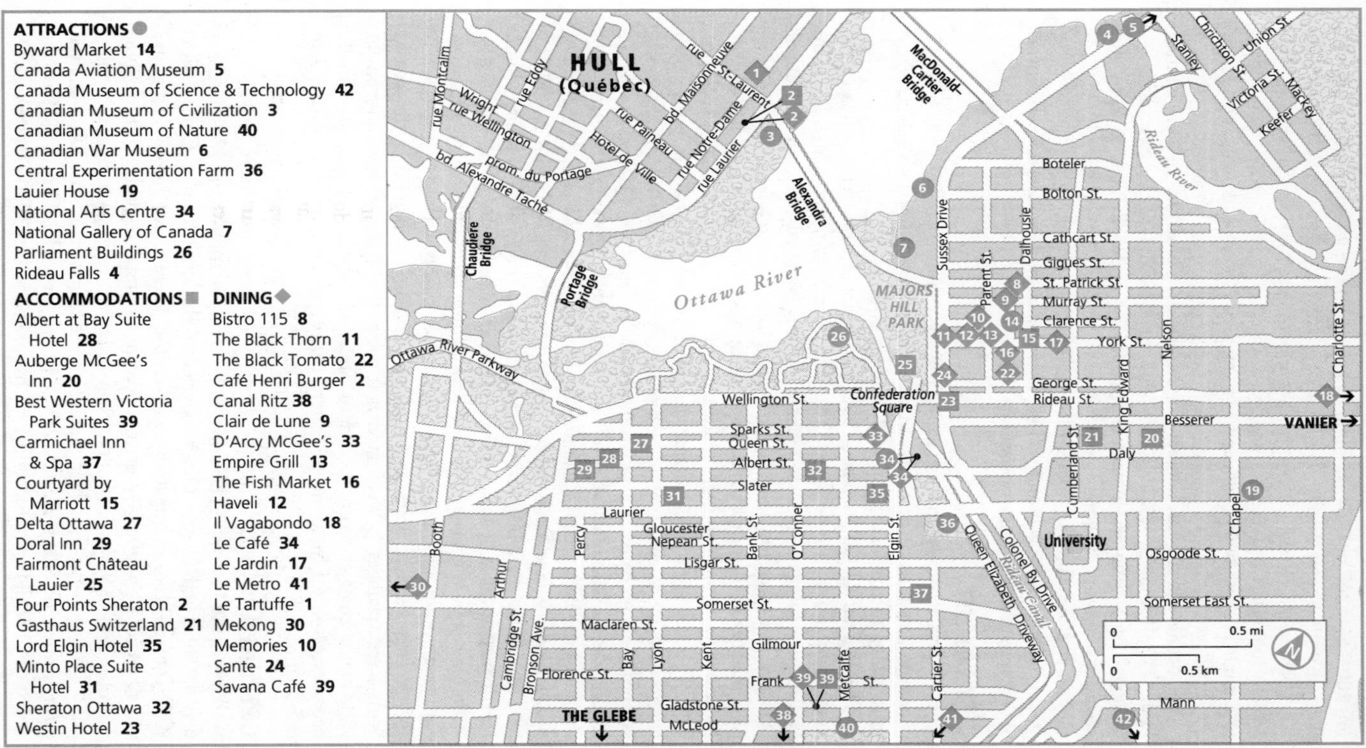
ATTRACTIONS
Byward Market 14
Canada Aviation Museum 5
Canada Museum of Science & Technology 42
Canadian Museum of Civilization 3
Canadian Museum of Nature 40
Canadian War Museum 6
Central Experimentation Farm 36
Lauier House 19
National Arts Centre 34
National Gallery of Canada 7
Parliament Buildings 26
Rideau Falls 4
ACCOMMODATIONS
Albert at Bay Suite Hotel 28
Auberge McGee's Inn 20
Best Western Victoria Park Suites 39
Carmichael Inn & Spa 37
Courtyard by Marriott 15
Delta Ottawa 27
Doral Inn 29
Fairmont Château Lauier 25
Four Points Sheraton 2
Gasthaus Switzerland 21
Lord Elgin Hotel 35
Minto Place Suite Hotel 31
Sheraton Ottawa 32
Westin Hotel 23
DINING
Bistro 115 8
The Black Thorn 11
The Black Tomato 22
Café Henri Burger 2
Canal Ritz 38
Clair de Lune 9
D'Arcy McGee's 33
Empire Grill 13
The Fish Market 16
Haveli 12
Il Vagabondo 18
Le Café 34
Le Jardin 17
Le Metro 41
Le Tartuffe 1
Mekong 30
Memories 10
Sante 24
Savana Café 39
HULL (Québec)
rue Montcalm
Wright
rue Wellington
rue Eddy
prom. du Portage
bd. Alexandre Taché
rue St-Laurent
bd. Maisonneuve
rue Notre-Dame
rue Laurier
rue Paineau
Hotel de Ville
Chaudiere Bridge
Portage Bridge
Alexandra Bridge
MacDonald-Cartier Bridge
Ottawa River
Ottawa River Parkway
MAJORS HILL PARK
Confederation Square
Rideau River
Rideau Canal
Stanley
Chrichton St.
Union St.
Victoria St.
Mackey
Keefer
Boteler
Bolton St.
Cathcart St.
Gigues St.
St. Patrick St.
Murray St.
Clarence St.
York St.
George St.
Rideau St.
Sussex Drive
Parent St.
Dalhousie
Nelson
King Edward
Charlotte St.
Besserer
Daly
Cumberland St.
Chapel
University
Osgoode St.
Somerset East St.
Mann
VANIER
Wellington St.
Sparks St.
Queen St.
Albert St.
Slater
Laurier
Gloucester
Nepean St.
Lisgar St.
Somerset St.
Maclaren St.
Gilmour
Florence St.
Frank
Gladstone St.
McLeod
Booth
Arthur
Cambridge St.
Bronson Ave.
Percy
Bay
Lyon
Kent
Bank St.
O'Conner
Metcalfe St.
Elgin St.
Cartier St.
Queen Elizabeth Driveway
Colonel By Drive
THE GLEBE
0 0.5 mi
0 0.5 km

(✆ **800/465-1867** or 613/239-5000; www.capcan.ca); it's open daily 8:30am to 9pm in summer and 9am to 5pm in winter. An "Info-tent" on Parliament Hill lawn behind the West Block is where you book free tours of Parliament. Mid-May to about the third week in June, hours are daily 9am to 5pm; the rest of June to Labour Day, it's open Monday to Friday 9am to 8pm and Saturday, Sunday, and holidays 9am to 5pm.

For details about Hull, contact the **Bureau du Tourisme,** 101 rue Laurier, Hull, PQ J8X 3V8 (✆ **800/265-7822** or 819/778-2222; www.tourisme-outaouais.org). Summer hours are Monday to Friday 8:30am to 8pm and Saturday and Sunday 9am to 6pm; winter hours are Monday to Friday 8:30am to 5pm and Saturday and Sunday 9am to 4pm.

On the Net, you may want to check out **www.ottawakiosk.com**, **www.festivalseeker.com**, and **www.tourottawa.org**.

## CITY LAYOUT

The **Ottawa River**—Canada's second longest at over 1,125km (700 miles)—curves around the northern edge of city. The compact downtown area, where most major attractions are clustered, is south of the river.

The **Rideau Canal,** sweeping past the National Arts Centre, divides the downtown area in two—Centre Town and Lower Town. In **Centre Town** are Parliament Hill, the Supreme Court, and the National Museum of Natural Sciences. In **Lower Town,** on the east side of the canal, are the National Gallery of Canada, the Byward Market, and, along Sussex Drive, the Canadian War Museum, the Prime Minister's residence, diplomats' row, and finally Rockcliffe Park. The area south of the Queensway, west to Bronson and east to the canal, is known as the **Glebe,** containing a number of popular restaurants and clubs, especially along Bank Street. North across the river, in Québec, lies **Hull,** reached by the Macdonald-Cartier and Alexandra bridges from the east end of town and the Portage and Chaudière bridges from the west end. At the end of the Alexandra Bridge stands the curvaceous Museum of Civilization, and nearby are some of the city's best French restaurants and the liveliest nightlife action. North and east of Hull stretch the Gatineau Hills and ski country.

Finding your way around can be bewildering, since streets have a habit of halting abruptly and then reappearing a few blocks farther on, and others change names several times. For example, the main street starts in the west as Scott Street, changes to Wellington as it passes through downtown in front of Parliament, changes again to Rideau Street in downtown east, and finally becomes Montréal Road on the eastern fringes of town. So carry a map. The information office provides a serviceable one.

## GETTING AROUND

Walking is the best way. The only public transportation is the 130-route bus network operated by the **Ottawa-Carleton Regional Transit Commission (OC Transpo).** For information about routes, where to buy tickets, and more, call ✆ **613/741-4390** (www.octtranspo.com) Monday to Friday 7am to 9pm, Saturday 8am to 9pm, and Sunday 9am and 6pm. To inquire about schedules, call ✆ **560** plus the four-digit number of the nearest bus stop. **Exact-change fares** or **one-ride tickets** are C$2.25 (US$1.50) for adults, C$1.25 (US85¢) for ages 6 to 11; children 5 and under are free. A C$5 (US$3.35) **DayPass** allows unlimited travel on all routes. Exact change, tickets, or the pass is required. You can buy tickets at 300 retail outlets, such as at newsstands and at Pharma Plus.

### *Tips* Getting Oriented

The main streets running east-west through center city are **Wellington, Laurier,** and **Somerset;** the **Rideau Canal** separates east from west and Centre Town from Lower Town; and the main north-south streets are **Bronson, Bank,** and **Elgin.**

All routes converge downtown at the Rideau Centre; they begin to close down at midnight, and there's no service 1 to 6am.

In Hull, buses are operated by the **Société de Transport l'Outaouais** (✆ **819/770-3242**). Transfers between the two systems are obtainable when you pay your fare on the bus.

Taxis can be hailed on the street but can be found more readily in front of major hotels and important buildings. Or, summon one by phone, something restaurant headwaiters are happy to do. One 24-hour company is **Blue Line** (✆ **613/238-1111**), with more than 600 cabs. Fares are C$2 (US$1.35) at the drop and C10¢ (US7¢) for each extra 85m (½ mile). Most drivers accept credit cards, usually MasterCard or Visa.

In summer, athletic young men, mostly university students, pull one to two passengers around the tourist districts in **rickshaws.** Negotiate the fare before setting out.

You may not want to drive in Ottawa, although traffic isn't too bad except during rush hours, but a car is essential to explore the environs or continue elsewhere in Canada. Rental agencies based in Ottawa include **Avis** (✆ **613/739-3334** or **613/230-2847**), **Budget** (✆ **613/729-6666**), **National** (✆ **613/737-7023** or **613/232-3536**), and **Thrifty** (✆ **613/737-4510** or **613/238-8000**), all with offices at the airport and various downtown locations. However, you can save money by arranging for the rental before leaving home.

Parking will cost about C$1.50 to C$3 (US$1–US$2) for an hour or less, with about a C$15 (US$10) maximum at most local garages. The best parking bets are the municipal parking lots, marked with a large green "P" in a circle.

When driving, remember that Ontario has a compulsory seat-belt requirement, and pay careful attention to the city's system of one-way streets, which often have three or four streets in a row going in the same direction, rather than alternating. The Queensway (Route 417) cuts right across the city, adding to the confusion. The downtown entrance to the highway is at O'Connor Street. Exit the highway at Kent Street for downtown. Know, too, that cars can turn right after stopping at a red light in Ottawa, but that hasn't been the case across the river in Hull. Over there, they are now experimenting with that policy, preliminary to passage of such a law throughout the province of Québec. Inquire when you arrive, but when in doubt, don't turn right on red in Hull.

## *FAST FACTS:* Ottawa

*American Express* The **American Express Travel Service** office, 220 Laurier Ave. West (✆ **613/563-0231**), is open Monday to Friday 9 am to 5pm.

*Area Code* The telephone area code for Ottawa is **613;** for Hull, **819.** When calling from Ottawa to Hull, you don't need to use the area code.

*Doctors/Dentists* There's a walk-in clinic, the **Family Medical Centre,** 244 Slater St. (**©613/235-4140**). Or, check with the hotel front desk or with your consulate for the nearest doctor or dentist.

*Embassies/High Commissions* The **U.S. Embassy** has moved to a large new building on Sussex Drive, north of Rideau Street (**© 613/238-5335**). It's open Monday to Friday 8:30am to 5pm. The **U.K. Embassy** is at 80 Elgin (**© 613/237-1530**). The **Australian High Commission** is at 50 O'Connor (**© 613/236-4376**), the **New Zealand High Commission** is at 99 Bank, Suite 727 (**©613/238-5991**), and the **Irish Embassy** is at 130 Albert St., (**©613/233-6281**). Consulates are primarily in Toronto, Montréal, and Vancouver.

*Emergencies* Call **© 911** for police, fire, or ambulance.

*Hospital* Your best bet is the **Ottawa Hospital General Campus,** 501 Smythe Rd. (**© 613/737-6111**).

*Internet Access* Check your e-mail and send messages at **The Internet Cafe,** 200 Bank St., at Somerset (**© 613/230-9000**). It's open Monday to Friday 9:30am to 11pm, Saturday 11am to 11pm, and Sunday 11am to 8pm.

*Laundromat* **Market Cleaners,** 286 Dalhousie St (**© 613/241-6222**) provides clean machines and surroundings, a TV, and an attendant to hand out change and soap.

*Liquor & Wine* The government controls liquor distribution, selling liquor and wine at certain LCBO stores and beer at others. Liquor stores are generally open Monday to Saturday 10am to 6pm (to 9pm Thurs and Fri). Beer outlets are open Monday to Saturday noon to 8pm (to 9pm on Thurs and Fri). The legal drinking age is 19 in Ottawa but 18 in Hull. Two convenient liquor stores are in the **Rideau Centre** (just inside the Rideau St. entrance) and in the **Byward Market** area at 140 George St., between Dalhousie and Cumberland, and there's a beer store at 1546 Scott St.

*Newspapers/Magazines* A great variety of international publications, including the *New York Times,* the *Wall Street Journal,* and the *International Herald Tribune,* are sold at **Planet News,** 143 Sparks St. (**© 613/232-5500**).

*Police* Call **© 911.**

*Post Office* The most convenient post office is at 59 Sparks St., at Elgin Street (**© 613/844-1545**), open Monday to Friday 8am to 6pm.

*Taxes* In Ontario there's an 8% provincial sales tax (PST), a lodging tax of 5%, and a 16% tax on liquor, as well as the national 7% goods-and-services tax (GST). In Québec there's a 7½% tax on food, liquor, merchandise, and accommodations.

*Telephones* The telephone system, operated by Bell Canada, closely resembles the American model. All operators speak French and English.

*Time* Ontario and Québec are in the Eastern time zone. Daylight saving time is observed as in the States.

## 2 Where to Stay

While reasonably priced doubles are available at a few B&B inns, you'll have to look to the outer districts for truly inexpensive lodgings, primarily in motels. There are ample choices for mid-priced to first-class rooms, however. For more information and possibilities, try **www.all-hotels.com/canada**. Rates quoted here do not include the 5% hotel tax and 7% GST unless otherwise stated.

### DOWNTOWN

#### VERY EXPENSIVE

**Fairmont Château Laurier** ★★★ Built at the same time (1912) and in the same French Renaissance style as Québec City's Château Frontenac, the Laurier has always attracted royalty and celebrities to its ideal location beside the Rideau Canal at the east end of Parliament Hill. There was no stinting on materials or dimensions, as seen in its wide halls and acres of public lounges and lobbies. The spacious guest rooms are decorated with many Louis XV reproductions, and the upper floors offer impressive views over the Ottawa River to the Gatineau Hills.

1 Rideau St. (at MacKenzie Ave.), Ottawa, ON K1N 8S7. ✆ **800/441-1414** or 613/241-1414. Fax 613/562-7030. www.chateaulaurier.com. 429 units. C$209–C$369 (US$139–US$246) double. Packages available. AE, DC, DISC, MC, V. Parking C$20 (US$13). **Amenities:** 2 restaurants (International), lounge; large indoor pool; health club with sauna; concierge; business center; shopping arcade; 24-hour room service; in-room massage; babysitting; same-day dry cleaning/laundry; executive floors. *In room:* A/C, TV w/pay movies, dataport, minibar, coffeemaker, hair dryer, iron, safe.

**Westin Hotel** ★★ The atrium lobby and many guest rooms offer views over the canal, and the hotel connects directly to both the Rideau Centre shopping complex and the Ottawa Congress Centre. Carefully furnished rooms contain oak furniture, brass lamps, and half-poster beds. Adult fitness swimmers have the pool to themselves daily 6:30 to 8am. Hartwells, a bar and dance club just off the lobby, is a popular gathering spot Tuesday to Saturday for locals as well as guests.

11 Colonel By Dr. (a block south of Rideau St.), Ottawa, ON K1N 9H4. ✆ **800/228-3000** or 613/560-7000. Fax 613/234-5396. www.westin.com. 515 units. C$335–C$435 (US$223–US$290) double. AE, DC, MC, V. Parking C$19 (US$13). Pets allowed. **Amenities:** 2 restaurants (International), lounge; large indoor pool; health club with whirlpool and saunas; concierge; business center; 24-hour room service; massage; babysitting; same-day dry cleaning/laundry. *In room:* A/C, TV w/pay movies, dataport, minibar, coffeemaker, hair dryer.

#### EXPENSIVE

**The Albert at Bay Suite Hotel** ★★ This downtown hotel is a converted apartment house and one of Ottawa's best buys for longer stays. It's just as desirable for a night or two, since all the customary conveniences of a conventional hotel are in place. All the units are suites, the smallest having one bedroom with a sofa bed, a living room with terrace, two bathrooms, two TVs, and a kitchen with appliances, dishes, and flatware. High-speed Internet access is also provided. Parking is in a secured garage beneath the hotel.

435 Albert St. (at Bay St.), Ottawa, ON K1R 7X4. ✆ **800/267-6644** or 613/238-8858. Fax 613/238-1433. www.albertatbay.com. 197 units. C$119–C$289 (US$79–US$193) Rates include continental breakfast. Weekend packages available. AE, DC, DISC, MC, V. Parking C$10 (US$7). **Amenities:** Restaurant (International), bar; exercise room with weight and cardio machines; whirlpool; sauna; children's program; secretarial services; limited room service; babysitting; coin-op washers and dryers; dry cleaning. *In room:* A/C, TV w/pay movies, dataport, kitchen, fridge, coffeemaker, hair dryer, iron.

**Carmichael Inn and Spa** ★ Three blocks west of the Rideau Canal, this fetching 1901 retreat served as a Supreme Court judge's residence and a convent, before being converted to an inn. It's named after a Group of Seven painter, and the decor recalls their art as well as their early 20th-century life and times. All guest rooms are furnished uniquely with a mix of antiques and reproductions. A variety of spa treatments and packages are available, including herbal and mud wraps, hydrotherapy, aromatherapy, and reflexology. Before or after, guests relax on the couches in front of the marble fireplace or laze in chairs on the veranda. The inn is full nearly all the time, so reserve for both room and spa treatments at least a month in advance.

46 Cartier St. (at Somerset St.), Ottawa, ON K2P 1J3. © **877/416-2417** or 613/236-4667. Fax 613/563-7529. www.carmichaelinn.com. 11 units. C$149–C$189 (US$99–US$126) double. Rates include continental breakfast and parking. Weekend and spa packages available. AE, DC, MC, V. **Amenities:** Spa; secretarial services; in-room massage; dry cleaning/laundry service. *In room:* A/C, TV, dataport

**Delta Ottawa** ★ *Kids* A 1973 member structure of the admirable Canadian chain has a sky-lit marble lobby with a fireplace in winter and island-style reception desks for a more personal welcome. The recently renovated guest rooms are in 14 configurations, spacious and refreshingly decorated; a substantial number are one- or two-bedroom suites with kitchenettes, and more than half have balconies. All have Nintendo and robes. While businesspeople rule during the week, every effort is made to make families welcome Friday to Sunday. At check-in, kids receive bags of diverting goodies, and parents can leave them to supervised play in the "creative center" (parents are issued beepers).

361 Queen St. (at Bay St.), Ottawa, ON K1R 7S9. © **800/268-1133** or 613/238-6000. Fax 613/238-2290. www.deltahotels.com. 328 units. C$400 (US$267) double. Weekend packages available. AE, DC, MC, V. Parking C$12 (US$8). **Amenities:** 2 restaurants (International), 2 bars; indoor pool with waterslide; exercise room; sauna; children's programs; game room; business center; concierge; limited room service; babysitting; coin-op washers and dryers; same-day dry cleaning; executive rooms. *In room:* A/C, TV w/pay movies, dataport, minibar, coffeemaker, hair dryer, iron, safe.

**Lord Elgin Hotel** ★ Only 3 blocks south of Parliament Hill and opposite the National Arts Centre, the Lord Elgin offers good value. Built in 1941, the dignified stone edifice with its green copper roof was named after the eighth earl of Elgin, once Canada's governor-general. In recent years, the guest rooms were enlarged, the decor lightened, and indoor pool added. The Connaught dining room is an airy galleria popular with Ottawans. Many of the tile and faux-granite bathrooms have windows that open—a benefit bestowed by the building's age. About half the rooms have unstocked fridges.

100 Elgin St. (at Queen St.), Ottawa, ON K1P 5K8. © **800/267-4298** or 613/235-3333. Fax 613/235-3223. www.lordelginhotel.ca.com. 300 units. C$109–C$185 (US$73–US$123) double. Children under 19 stay free in parents' room. DC, DISC, MC. Parking C$13.80 (US$9). **Amenities:** Restaurant (International), bar; heated indoor pool; exercise room; concierge; limited room service; same-day dry cleaning/laundry. *In room:* A/C, TV w/pay movies, dataport, coffeemaker, hair dryer.

**Minto Place Suite Hotel** ★★ Reminding many guests of a luxury cruise ship, the high-rise Minto Place stacks over 400 studio and one- and two-bedroom suites above a ground-floor shopping arcade. Upper-floor units have sweeping views, and all have sofa beds and either kitchenettes or full kitchens, some with washers and dryers. The spacious living rooms are fully furnished, with desks, multi-line phones, and dining tables. All this, and more, at no greater cost than a conventional hotel.

433 Laurier Ave. W. (at Lyon St.), Ottawa, ON K1R 7Y1. © **613/232-2200.** Fax 613/232-6962. www.mintohotel.com. 417 units. C$171–C$278 (US$114–US$185) suite. Children under 18 stay free in parents' room. Weekend rates available. AE, DC, MC, V. Parking C$16 (US$9). **Amenities:** 2 restaurants (International), 2 bars; sky lit indoor pool; substantial health club; whirlpool; sauna; summer children's program; secretarial

services; shopping arcade; limited room service. *In room:* A/C, TV w/pay movies, dataport, equipped kitchen or kitchenette, fridge, coffeemaker, hair dryer, iron.

**Sheraton Ottawa** ★ Frequent travelers know what to expect of a downtown Sheraton—a middle-of-everything location, fitness facilities, executive floors, conference rooms, and spacious guest rooms with the usual electronics, including two phone lines, voice mail, and video games. This one meets the expectations of businesspeople, most of whom probably prefer not to deal with the eccentricities of many inns and boutique hotels, but leisure travelers will be satisfied, too. Almost half the rooms are nonsmoking.

150 Albert St. (at O'Connor St.), Ottawa, ON K1P 5G2. ✆ **800/489-8333** or 613/238-1500. Fax 613/238-8497. www.sheratonottawa.com. 236 units. C$179–C$314 (US$89–US$209) double. Packages available. Children under 18 stay free in parents' room; under 6 eat free. AE, DC, DISC, MC, V. Valet parking C$18 (US$12). Pets accepted. **Amenities:** Restaurant (International), lounge; indoor pool; extensive health club with sauna; children's programs; business center; 24-hour room service; babysitting; same-day dry cleaning/laundry; executive rooms. *In room:* A/C, TV w/pay movies, dataport, coffeemaker, hair dryer, iron.

## MODERATE

**Auberge McGee's Inn** On a quiet street only blocks from the University of Ottawa, this no-smoking inn occupies a handsome Victorian with a steep dormer roof and an awning-protected entrance. Each guest room is distinctively decorated, often with touches reflective of the owner's Anglo-Peruvian upbringing. All the rooms with queen-size beds have minibars, and two have Jacuzzis and fireplaces. Breakfast is served in a room with a carved cherry-wood fireplace and Oriental rugs. The inn has no elevator.

185 Daly Ave. (at Nelson St.), Ottawa, ON K1N 6E8. ✆ **800/262-4337** or 613/237-6089. Fax 613/237-6201. www.mcgeesinn.com. 14 units. C$98–C$198 (US$65–US$132) double. Rates include full breakfast. AE, MC, V. Free parking. From downtown, take Laurier Ave. E. and turn left at Nelson St. **Amenities:** Nonsmoking rooms. *In room:* A/C, TV, coffeemaker, hair dryer.

**Best Western Victoria Park Suites** *Value* It isn't glamorous and it's a bit too far south of the center city for easy walking, so this member of the well-known chain piles on several other incentives. All units have kitchenettes, the larger ones have pullout sofas and two TVs, and 24 have whirlpools. There is also free indoor parking, making this is an economical choice for families arriving by car. Some floors have high-speed Internet access. A new restaurant is planned. The Canadian Museum of Nature is a couple of blocks away.

377 O'Connor St. (at Gladstone St.), Ottawa, ON K2P 2M2. ✆ **800/465-7275** or 613/567-7275. Fax 613/567-1161. www.victoriapark.com. 124 units. C$109–C$179 (US$73–US$119) suite. Rates include continental breakfast. Packages available. AE, DC, MC, V. Free parking. **Amenities:** Exercise room; sauna; coin-op washers and dryers; same-day dry cleaning/laundry; executive rooms. *In room:* A/C, TV w/pay movies, dataport, kitchenette, fridge, coffeemaker, hair dryer, iron.

**Courtyard by Marriott** Though this structure once housed another hotel, this is really a new facility, opened in 1999. The formula for this expanding chain sets it roughly midway between a roadside motel and a first-class hotel, with limited personal service but fairly complete facilities. Guest rooms are intentionally businesslike, with thoughtfully designed work areas and voice mail. A large parking lot adjoins, and all of Byward Market lies just beyond.

350 Dalhousie St. (at York St.), Ottawa, ON K1N 7E9. ✆ **800/341-2210** or 613/241-1000. Fax 613/241-4804. 183 units. C$139–C$169 (US$93–US$113) double. AE, DC, MC, V. **Amenities:** Restaurant (International), lounge; heated indoor pool; exercise room; whirlpool; secretarial services; 24-hour room service; coin-op washers and dryers; same-day dry cleaning/laundry. *In room:* A/C, TV w/pay movies, dataport, coffeemaker, hair dryer, iron.

## INEXPENSIVE

**Doral Inn** *Value* A good choice on the price-value scale, this amiable inn occupies an expanded brick town house characteristic of many residential blocks in Ottawa. Guest rooms have brass bedsteads, floral wallpaper, desks, and armchairs. On the ground floor, two bay-windowed rooms serve as a lounge/sitting room and a breakfast area. Guests have use of a nearby pool.

486 Albert St. (at Bay St.), Ottawa, ON K1R 5B5. ✆ **800/263-6725** or 613/230-8055. Fax 613/237-9660. www.doralinn.com. 40 units. C$89–C$129 (US$59–US$86) double. Extra person C$10 (US$7). Children under 12 stay free in parents' room. Rates include continental breakfast. Packages available. AE, DC, DISC, MC, V. Free parking. **Amenities:** Cafe (International); access to nearby health club. *In room:* A/C, TV, dataport, fridge, coffeemaker, hair dryer.

**Gasthaus Switzerland** In an old stone building, this B&B possesses the familiar hallmarks of red gingham and country pine associated with rural Swiss hospitality. There's a common sitting room, and guests have use of the garden and its barbecue in summer. Puffy duvets cover the beds of the guest rooms; four have gas fireplaces. There's no elevator, and stairs are steep. A Swiss-style breakfast buffet of breads, eggs, french toast, cheese, and cereal is served. The Gasthaus is east of Rideau Centre and 2 blocks south of the Byward Market area.

89 Daly Ave. (at Cumberland St.), Ottawa, ON K1N 6E6. ✆ **888/663-0000** or 613/237-0335. Fax 613/594-3327. www.gasthausswitzerland.com. 22 units. C$88–C$158 (US$59–US$105) double; C$208–C$228 (US$139–US$152) suite. Rates include full breakfast. AE, DC, MC, V. Free parking. *In room:* A/C, TV, dataport.

## IN HULL

### MODERATE

**Four Points Sheraton** ★ Directly opposite the Canadian Museum of Civilization, this shiny new entry in the growing mid-priced chain equals pricier competitors in most regards. While intended primarily to serve business travelers, families should be content enough here, if not thrilled. Give management a gold star for restoring the rectory of the adjacent 19th Century Notre-Dame Church, now serving as an annex to the hotel. Ample indoor and outdoor parking are provided.

35 rue Laurier, Hull, QC J8X 4E9 ✆ **800/567-9607** or 819/778-6111. Fax 819/778-8548. www.fourpoints.com. 201 units. C$179–C$224 (US$119–US$149) double. AE, DC, MC, V. Parking $12 (US$8). **Amenities:** Restaurant (International), bar; heated indoor pool; exercise room; children's programs; business center; limited room service; babysitting; same-day dry cleaning/laundry; executive rooms. *In room:* A/C, TV w/pay movies, dataport, coffeemaker, hair dryer, iron.

## A RESORT IN NEARBY MONTEBELLO

**Fairmont Le Château Montebello** ★★ A log palace constructed in the grand manner of the sprawling hideaways of the Alps and Rockies, this was an exclusive private resort until 1970, when it was converted to a hotel. Its most striking feature is the six-sided granite fireplace that occupies the center of the three-story lobby. But what really stuns is the roster of activities available. To those listed below add clay shooting, guided nature walks and hikes, ice skating,

---

*Tips* **An Outing on the Ottawa River**

For a break from city stress and traffic, drive east into Québec on route 148 to Montebello. It takes only an hour, and you'll have access to golf, boating on the river, a wildlife park, and hiking, fishing, and canoeing in an unspoiled wilderness.

---

cross-country ski trails, and curling. Much of this is undertaken on the adjacent Kenauk preserve, a protected natural environment of over 2,630ha (6,500 acres). After a day of that, hunger is addressed in several restaurants, where the food and service are better than can usually be expected of resorts of this size.

392 rue Notre-Dame, Montebello, PQ J0V 1L0. ✆ **819/423-6341.** Fax 819/423-5283. www.fairmont.com. 210 units. C$139–C$289 (US$93–US$193) double. Packages available. AE, DC, MC, V. Free parking. **Amenities:** 4 restaurants (International, 2 in summer), 3 bars; very large indoor pool; expansive health club; 2 indoor and 6 outdoor tennis courts; 18-hole golf course; bike and kayak rental; business center; salon; limited room service; massage; children's programs; babysitting; same-day dry cleaning/laundry. *In room:* A/C, TV w/pay movies, dataport, minibar, coffeemaker, hair dryer, iron.

## 3 Where to Dine

To experience a true Ottawa tradition, stop at the **Hooker's** stand (closed weekdays in Jan and Feb) at the corner of George and William streets in the center of the Byward Market and purchase a **beaver tail.** No, really. Furry rodents aren't involved. This beaver tail is actually a deep-fried pastry about the size of a Ping-Pong paddle, served either sweet, with cinnamon and sugar or raspberry jam, or savory, with garlic butter, cheese (or cream cheese), and scallions. It is tasty and cheap.

Nearby, and in commercial districts around town, step up to one of the rolling grill carts and order a **hot Polish** or **German sausage.** Cooked to your request, it's cradled in a bun for you to slather with mustard and heap with sauerkraut, pickles, peppers, and onions. Another inexpensive solution for the munchies are the **chip wagons** found in parking lots and vacant spaces around the city and out in the Ontario countryside. Similar to the *casse-croutes* of Québec, they serve limited menus of sandwiches, soft drinks, and the namesake french fries. And you'll find units of the national coffeehouse chain, **Second Cup,** at strategic locations around town (often in competition with a nearby Starbucks).

### CENTRE TOWN

#### MODERATE

**D'Arcy McGee's** IRISH If this avowed Irish pub looks like an unadulterated replica of the real thing (albeit not plagued with smoke and chill drafts), that's because the whole thing was shipped over from the Emerald Isle. The etched and stained-glass panels, dark wood partitions, and mosaic tiled floor were installed in a Dublinesque building near the Arts Center. Some feel that the result is a little formulaic, and that isn't unfair. But the menu has "Dublin Coddle" (sausage, smoked bacon, and roasted root vegetables atop mashed potatoes), fish-and-chips, and chicken cottage pie for tastes of the Auld Sod, along with daily specials less slavishly evocative of the homeland. No one leaves hungry with these man-size portions, including the burgers and other sandwiches. Imported and domestic brews are on tap, as are single-malt scotches and Irish whiskeys. Live music fills the place Wednesday to Saturday nights, most of it Celtic, of course, but with a little New World folk and rock squeezed in. In warm weather, tables wrap around the exterior.

44 Sparks St. (at Elgin St.). ✆ **613/230-4433.** Main courses C$7–C$19 (US$4.65–US$13). AE. MC, V. Daily 11am–1am.

**Le Café** CONTEMPORARY CANADIAN Finding it is a bit of a challenge (in back, at canal level), but the National Arts Centre's Le Café commands an enticing view from its long summer terrace and offers imaginatively executed food year-round in its glass-enclosed main dining room. Featured are dishes employing such prime Canadian ingredients as Petrie Island mussels, Nova Scotia scallops, Brome Lake duck, and Alberta beef and lamb. Atlantic salmon usually figure in both appetizers and main dishes. The lunch and dinner menus are similar, but with lower prices at midday. The interesting wine list is decently priced, most in the C$28 to C$32 (US$19–US$21) range. To keep with the Canadian theme, try the Mission Hill chardonnay from the Niagara Frontier.

In the National Arts Centre, 53 Elgin St. (at Confederation Sq.). ✆ **613/594-5127.** Reservations recommended. Table d'hôte dinner (after 8pm) C$19.95 (US$13). Main courses C$12.95–C$29.95 (US$9–US$20). AE, DC, MC, V. Mon–Fri 12noon–2pm and 5–11pm Sat 5–11pm.

**Le Métro** CLASSIC FRENCH The owner-chef's warm welcome is signaled in every detail of this south center-city town house. On the walls are gold-framed prints of Modigliani, with burgundy linen on the tables, baroque bronze and silver candelabra, lavish flower arrangements, and tufted leather chairs as embracing as might be asked. If you'd like a more intimate location, ask for a table in the less populated back section. The menu changes daily, the better to highlight market-fresh ingredients and to remind us what French cooking was before it became the trampoline that launched pan-oceanic fusion cuisine. For proof, try the nicely balanced lobster bisque. And for evidence that the kitchen doesn't resist outside influences, note the platter of mussels flavored with lemongrass and hoisin sauce. Fish, fowl, and meats are cooked to the very edge of moist perfection. Carafes of the house wines are shaped as Eiffel Towers, which comes off as witty, not kitsch.

315 Somerset St. W. (between Bank and O'Connor sts.). ✆ **613/230-8123.** Reservations recommended. Main courses C$17.50–C$25.50 (US$12–US$17); table d'hôte dinner C$35 (US$23). AE, MC, V. Mon–Fri 11:30am–2:30pm and 6–10:30pm, Sat 6–10:30pm.

**Mekong** ASIAN This modest restaurant started as a Vietnamese eatery in what passes for Ottawa's Chinatown. That cuisine didn't attract patrons, so they started phasing in Chinese dishes. That worked, and only a few Thai and Vietnamese options remain on the substantial menu. Enter up a few stairs past a goldfish aquarium to the greetings of the outgoing staff. You write your own order on a scratch pad—tiger prawns with lemongrass, perhaps, or five spices squid—but whatever your choice, the price is right. Spring rolls, a main course, tea, and beer should be under C$20 (US$13).

637 Somerset St. W. (near Bronson Ave.). ✆ **613/237-7717.** Reservations recommended on weekends. Main courses C$7–C$14 (US$4.85–US$9). AE, DC, MC, V. Daily 11am–midnight.

**Savana Café** ★ CARIBBEAN FUSION Its tropical flavor, splashy Caribbean art, and peppery cuisine have kept this place super-heated for over 15 years. Start with the fabulous kalaloo soup—the real thing, with okra, spinach, thyme, Congo peppers, and lime. Among main-course favorites are fresh grilled marlin with wasabi mousseline, cubana chicken stuffed with bananas and cream cheese, lamb glazed with guava, and (just to show they won't be hemmed in by arbitrary geographical borders) spicy Thai noodles and chicken satays. They have daily fish specials. The bar and front terrace fill early each night, usually with young to 40-ish professional types intent on unwinding as fast as easy companionship and rum drinks will allow. You can order most dishes mild, medium, or hot (and they mean *hot!*). In winter, the fire on the hearth adds a welcome touch.

431 Gilmour (between Bank and Kent sts.). ✆ **613/233-9159.** Reservations recommended. Main courses C$11–C$17 (US$7–US$11). AE, DC, MC, V. Tues–Fri 11:30am–3pm, Mon–Sat 5–10pm.

### Pubbing it Outside Ottawa

For both of these pubs, take Route 417 west to Route 5, and then drive north toward Carp.

This side of the Big Briney, English country pubs don't get more authentic than the **Cheshire Cat,** 2193 Richardson Side Rd. (© **613/831-2183**). In an 1883 stone cottage with a wood-burning stove and horse brasses, it offers cool (not icy) draft bitter in dimpled mugs and snatches of Cockney rhyming slang among the regulars at the bar. A variety of adequate sandwiches is available, as well as such traditional main courses as liver and bacon, mixed grill, steak-and-kidney pie, and shepherd's pie. The beers are mostly British, along with a few Canadian microbrews. On summer days the garden is a happy spot to idle. The kitchen is open Tuesday to Saturday 11:30am to 9pm and Sunday noon to 9pm; the bar is open to 11pm Sunday to Wednesday and to 1am Thursday to Saturday.

Another corner of Blighty waits at the **Swan at Carp,** Falldown Lane, Carp (© **613/839-7926**), in a brick pile that was a Presbyterian rectory built in 1902. It was converted to a pub in 1987, complete with separate public and lounge bars, and named after a pub the owners had managed back in Stoke, England. There are no videos or TVs, so conversation flows, real ale is drawn at cellar temperature, and British events and special days are celebrated. The pub fare includes bangers and mash, Guinness stew, and fish-and-chips with mushy peas, but go for the atmosphere and companionability. It's open Tuesday to Saturday 11am to midnight and Sun 11am to 11pm. Bear left at the fork when you enter the town from the south, then take the first right to the pub.

While you're in the vicinity, you might want to stop by for a look at one of Ontario's odder sights, the **Diefenbunker,** north of Carp at 3911 Carp Road (© **613/839-0007;** www.diefenbunker.ca). Designated Canada's Cold War Museum, it is a four-story underground H-bomb shelter built during the earliest, scariest days of confrontation between the Democratic West and the Communist East. Prime Minister John Diefenbaker ordered it built in secret between 1959 and 1961. The eerie, echoing labyrinth was to provide haven to key Canadian political and military figures as well as to the nation's gold reserves in the event of attack. It's open June 30 to Labour Day 10pm to 4pm, 11am to 3pm the rest of the year. Admission is C$12 (US$8) for adults, C$10 (US$7) for seniors and students, and C$5 (US$3.35) for ages 6 to 17. Access is limited, and reservations are recommended.

## LOWER TOWN & BYWARD MARKET AREA

### EXPENSIVE

**Le Jardin** ★ FRENCH In a 19th-century brick house with gingerbread trim outside the Byward Market area, Le Jardin impresses with rooms of gilt-framed mirrors and paintings, and lush sprays of fresh flowers; there's a fireplace in one room. (No garden, despite the name.) The two dining rooms are upstairs, subdued and seductively lit (ask for the one in front). The waiters are professionally attired in tuxedos, in a city where amateur status is more often the rule. They dole out chewy warm balls of bread, bring perfect cocktails, and remain attentive but unobtrusive. A carefully considered wine library includes *grand vins* running into hundreds of dollars, but no half bottles. Most dishes are intensely flavored and aromatic, although less often as wonderful as in the past. Conceding the possibility that the kitchen is coasting, the overall experience is so agreeable you might feel impelled to thank each of the staff personally.

127 York St. (east of Dalhousie St.). ✆ **613/241-1424.** Reservations recommended. Main courses C$18.95–C$31 (US$13–US$21); table d'hôte dinner C$45 (US$30). AE, DC, MC, V. Daily 5:30–11pm (lunch Mon–Fri Dec 1–23 only).

## MODERATE

**Bistro 115** FRENCH This casual bistro is out of the clutch of the more frenetic streets of the Byward Market area. Lace tablecloths and a fireplace make the dining room inviting in winter, while the patio with its fountain and roof of trellised grapevines is an echo of sun-splashed Provence. The seasonal menu changes weekly, but starters have included shrimp Provençal with aioli toast triangles followed by duck confit with baked goat cheese. On warmer days, watch for the vegetable-scallop and phyllo-wrapped spring rolls ringed with honeyed curry sauce. Weekend brunch (10:30am–2pm) is a treat, but the best deal is the weekday table d'hôte lunch. More than a dozen wines are available by the glass and half-bottle.

110 Murray St. (east of Dalhousie St.). ✆ **613/562-7244.** Reservations recommended. Main courses C$15–C$26 (US$10–US$17); weekday table d'hôte lunch C$18 (US$12); 3-course prix-fixe dinner C$27–C$38 (US$18–US$25). AE, MC, V. Mon–Fri 11:30am–10pm, Sat–Sun 10:30am–10pm.

**The Black Tomato** *Overrated* ECLECTIC "Trendy" isn't a synonym for "excellent," but one can hope—in vain, in this case. Local enthusiasm to the contrary, the food here aspires to greater heights but is rarely better than satisfactory. Further, when the kitchen backs up, the gaps between courses can average 30 minutes, which makes for a long meal. Those crotchets might not matter, given amiable companions and the good-time atmosphere. The CDs on the stereo are also for sale, if you like what you hear. The front room is furnished with thickly painted tables and chairs that might have first seen use in a 1930s school cafeteria, and there's a large dining patio in back. And one can say this for the food; it hasn't been pulled and pushed into place by the line cooks. Try it with one of the two dozen beers in draft—Creemore Springs Lager is a good choice.

11 George St. (east of Sussex St.) ✆ **613/789-8123.** Reservations suggested. Main courses C$15.95–C$24 (US$11–US$16). AE, DC, MC, V. Daily 11:30am–11pm.

**Clair de Lune** CONTEMPORARY FRENCH This long-running bistro is a favorite of many regulars to the market area. Main courses at lunch, such as the duck and lentil salad with endive and pears and seared tuna with Niçoise salad, often show up as appetizers at dinner. That meal might be salmon tartare with sourbread toast or grilled pork medallions with Port-Roquefort sauce. The fish of the day and pasta du jour are often worthwhile. The restaurant has a glass-block bar and dividers, mahogany tabletops, and stamped tin ceiling and ducts overhead. Live jazz is on offer Saturday nights, and in summer, the sidewalk and rooftop terraces fill with diners watching the stars and passersby. On a sour note, complaints about inept and sometimes rude service do persist.

81B Clarence St. (west of Dalhousie St.). ✆ **613/241-2200.** Reservations recommended. Main courses, lunch C$9.50–C$15 (US$6–US$10), dinner C$16.50–C$27.50 (US$11–US$18). AE, DC, MC, V. Mon–Sat 11:30am–11pm, Sun 10:30am–10pm (slightly later in summer).

**Empire Grill** ★ ECLECTIC It says something that area chefs and waiters make this booming New York–ish bistro/bar/club a stop on their after-work circuit. The martinis are the driest, the company is congenial, and the food is piquant and mildly venturesome. Attractive young servers bring duck quesadillas and fried calamari starters that segue to the likes of Thai chicken curry, duck breast dusted with cocoa, and Southwestern chicken and chipotle pasta with roasted vegetables and caramelized pearl onions sprinkled with toasted pine nuts. The bar, in a question-mark shape that encourages conversation, is ringed with tables, augmented with a warm weather dining deck. Customers range from those barely over drinking age to well past retirement with no apparent social unease. A DJ works the turntables after late dinner, and they have live jazz Sunday 6 to 10pm. All this and fair prices, too.

47 Clarence St. (at Parent St.). ✆ **613/241-1343.** Reservations recommended in evening. Main courses C$14–C$32 (US$9–US$21). AE, DC, MC, V. Mon–Sat 11:30am–1pm, Sun 11:00am–1am.

**The Fish Market** ★ SEAFOOD In an 1875 heritage building on a prominent Market corner are this sprawling fish restaurant; the casual, less expensive upstairs cafe, **Coasters,** which stays open through the afternoon and offers pastas, pizzas, and fish-and-chips; and the basement tavern, **Vineyards,** which features boutique wines and microbrews. The main room is enclosed by rough wood and brick, with nautical trappings and old advertising signs. Fish cooked without artifice or complications is often the most satisfying, not to mention fast out of the kitchen, and waits between courses aren't long. The dauntingly large menu includes just about any marine creature available at the docks that day, cooked to your preference. One Brobdingnagian repast called the "Marine Platter" incorporates a whole lobster, Alaskan crab legs, two jumbo tiger shrimp, a smoked salmon filet, sea scallops, crabmeat-stuffed mushroom caps, two thick onion rings, and rice pilaf—for C$40 (US$27). They're proud of their wine list—the Alsatian Rieslings go well with most of these dishes.

54 York St. (at Byward St.). ✆ **613/241-3474.** Reservations not accepted. Main courses C$12–C$24 (US$8–US$16); fixed-price dinner C$21 (US$14). AE, DC, MC, V. Mon–Fri 11:30am–2pm and 4:30–10pm, Sat 11:30am–2:30pm and 4:30–11pm, Sun 11:30am–3pm and 4:30–11pm.

**Haveli** INDIAN Admirers of exemplary Indian food find that everything here is characterized by bold, simple, clean, intense flavors. A good sampler (and no appetizer will be needed if you order it) is *thal-e-Haveli,* a tray of tandoori chicken, lamb curry, vegetables, raita, chutney, and rice, with pillowy Nan bread on the side. Other possibilities are chicken tika masala and *bhaingan bharta* (roasted pureed eggplant, tomatoes, and onions). The most expensive item is marinated lobster tails broiled in the tandoor oven, while the best deals are the lunch and Sunday buffets. The cheerful owner and his staff are happy to advise on selections and solicitous about your reactions. But when they ask how you like your food spiced, don't say "hot" if you don't really mean it.

39 Clarence St. (at Sussex St.). ✆ **613/241-1700.** Reservations recommended. Main courses C$9.75–C$13.50 (US$7–US$9). AE, MC, V. Mon–Fri 11:45am–2:15pm and 5:30–9:30pm, Sat 5:30–10:30pm, Sun noon–2:30pm and 5–9pm.

**Sante** FUSION This second-floor restaurant overlooking a busy downtown corner promotes a multicultural approach to cooking, skipping from Thailand to California to the Caribbean and to the Mediterranean. The tables are set with flowers, the walls are hung with works by local artists, and you may be seated at a table with armchairs. Start with the delicious callaloo soup, following with a sizzling-hot plate like the Thai spicy shrimp stir-fried in tamarind, lemongrass, and chiles. The menu also lists specialties like chicken escabeche steeped in raspberry vinegar with bell peppers and red onion.

45 Rideau St. (at Sussex St.). ✆ **613/241-7113.** Reservations recommended. Main courses C$15–C$22 (US$10–US$15). AE, DC, MC, V. Mon–Sat 11:30am–3pm and 5–10pm. In summer, Sante often closes for Sat lunch.

### INEXPENSIVE

**The Black Thorn** MEDITERRANEAN The converted 19th-century brick house draws substantial crowds to its fenced sidewalk terrace, to the covered terrace in back beside a courtyard fountain, and to the small dining room centered around an impressive mahogany bar. The kitchen turns out moderately creative food that includes a dozen pizzas from the wood-burning oven, one version of which has toppings of smoked salmon, red onion, capers, and dill. Belgian beer stew and Cajun chicken pasta are winners, and there are a number of vegetarian dishes. Always available are a market catch of the day, wraps, specials, and desserts baked on the premises.

15 Clarence St. (west of Parent St.). ✆ **613/562-0705.** Reservations not accepted. Pizzas and other dishes C$12–C$20 (US$8–US$13). AE, MC, V. Sun–Thurs 11:30am–11pm, Fri–Sat 11:30am–midnight.

**Memories** BISTRO Next door to The Black Thorn (above), this popular cafe with sidewalk tables under an awning offers a menu of snacks and mostly light meals. The fixed-price lunch is composed of soup or salad and a main course, maybe Malaysian lamb curry. Options are sandwiches like ham and cheese with marinated mushrooms and Dijon mustard on a croissant, plus salads, pita pizzas, soups, patés, and pastas. Weekend brunch brings the usual croissants, quiches, and eggs, as well as waffles with a choice of fruit toppings. Smoking is allowed only on the patio out front, which fills up quickly.

7 Clarence St. (east of Sussex St.). ✆ **613/232-1882.** Reservations not accepted. Main courses C$9–C$11.95 (US$6–US$8); fixed-price lunch C$7 (US$4.65). AE, MC, V. Mon 11:30am–11pm, Tues–Fri 11:30am–midnight, Sat 10:30am–1am, Sun 11am–11pm.

## VANIER

### MODERATE

**Il Vagabondo** ITALIAN A short hop across the bridge in Vanier, this neighborhood trattoria in an 1890 corner house has a lot going for it. The modest bi-level dining room has an oak bar, colorful tablecloths, and a tiled floor. Chalkboard daily specials include the likes of *pollo a basilico* (basil chicken) or *fettuccine con erbe*—but they disappear early. The a la carte menu features top-drawer veal and a variety of pastas made on premises. Preparation is good to excellent, with judicious applications of fresh herbs, although I'm not talking culinary innovation here. Everything comes in somewhat daunting portions, but delivery is often slow and some of the waiters are prone to sullenness.

186 Barrette St. (off Beechwood Ave.). ✆ **613/749-4877.** Reservations recommended. Main courses C$10–C$28 (US$7–US$19). AE, DC, MC, V. Tues–Fri noon–11pm; Sat 5–11pm, Sun 5–10pm.

## THE GLEBE

### INEXPENSIVE

**Canal Ritz** ITALIAN/INTERNATIONAL This outpost of a small local chain occupies a converted boat house with an airy two-story interior and a dining terrace a foot or two above the water. Houseboats and powerboats glide by. There are a few non-Italian selections, but the specialty is pizza baked in the wood-burning oven. Some versions reach for the designer edges: pears and Brie on braised onions? Forgive them that detour and look to the less bizarre choices:

the shrimp, cappicola ham, figs, and mozzarella, or the mozzarella and plum tomato dressed with pesto. They're thin-crusted and uncut, requiring the use of the provided fork and serrated knife. Grilled chicken, shrimp, and sausage on penne highlight the pasta selections, most available in small or full versions for C$10 to C$13 (US$7–US$9). Charcoal-grilled fish and brochettes are other options. Among the desserts are caramel pecan cheesecake and numerous chocolate fancies. The waitstaff is always pleasant, if occasionally a little ditzy.

375 Queen Elizabeth Dr. (on the Rideau Canal). ✆ **613/238-8998.** Reservations recommended. Pizzas, pastas, and main courses C$9–C$17 (US$6–US$11). AE, MC, V. Daily 11:30am–11:30pm. Shorter hours in winter.

## HULL

### EXPENSIVE

**Café Henri Burger** ★ FRENCH/QUEBECOIS Henri Burger founded his eponymous restaurant across the river from the capital in the 1920s. He died in 1936, but his dining landmark continues to attract long-loyal patrons as well as visitors to the Museum of Civilization, across the street. Its reputation holds up. The seasonally altered menu might offer chilled berry soup and lobster salad out on the covered terrace in July or bouillabaisse and juniper-scented elk osso bucco with wild mushroom risotto in January. Meat and game prevail, including venison, wapiti, and partridge, but salmon, Dover sole, and shrimp are regulars. Vegetarians have options, too, with ratatouille-stuffed eggplant appearing often. There's a fat book of judiciously chosen wines, those from the Loire Valley among the best values. For dessert, the tarte au citron (lemon tart) is a must.

69 rue Laurier. ✆ **819/777-5646.** Reservations recommended. Main courses C$18–C$34 (US$9–US$23); table d'hôte menu C$14–C$18 (US$9–US$12) at lunch, C$42 (US$28) at dinner. AE, DC, MC, V. Mon–Fri noon–3pm; daily 6–11pm. Terrace May–Sept daily noon–11pm.

**Le Tartuffe** ★★ FRENCH What a delight this almost-hidden town house restaurant and its inspired kitchen are. (To find it, walk 2 blocks west on rue Laurier from the Museum of Civilization and turn right on rue Papineau.) The 42 seats in the two dining rooms are matched by another 40 on the shaded terrace. Choices on the table d'hôte cards are unusually generous in number and composition. Of the seven dinner mains, for example, you can have roasted Barbarie duck breast with raspsberry sauce or saddle of rabbit stuffed with apples. Starters (of seven) might be vegetable terrine with lovage oil and radish sprouts or lamb capaccio marinated in peppered white truffle oil. The service is genial and attentive.

133 rue Notre-Dame (at rue Papineau). ✆ **819/776-6424.** Reservations recommended. Table d'hôte lunch C$13–C$18 (US$9–US$12), dinner C$25–C$36 (US$17–US$24) at dinner. AE, DC, MC, V. Mon–Wed 11:30am–9:30pm, Thurs–Fri 11:30am–10:30pm, Sat 5:30–10:30pm. Closed Mon Oct–May.

## 4 Seeing the Sights

Most of Ottawa's major sights are clustered downtown, so it's not difficult to walk from one to another.

**Paul's Boat Lines Ltd.,** 219 Colonnade Rd., Nepean (✆ **613/225-6781** or 613/235-8409 in summer), offers two cruises. One departs from the Conference Centre in Hull and proceeds along the Ottawa River, picking up additional passengers at the Ottawa Locks 30 minutes later. The other cruises along the Rideau Canal, leaving from the docks opposite the Arts Centre and down to the Experimental Farm and Carleton University. The 1¼-hour canal cruises leave the Locks at 10am, 11:30am, 1:30pm, 3pm, and 4:30pm, plus summer-only at 7pm and 8:30pm. River trips take 1½ hours, leaving at 11am, 2pm, and 4pm, with an extra 7:30pm departure in summer. Each trip is C$14 (US$9) for adults, C$12 (US$8) for seniors, C$10 (US$7) for students, and C$7 (US$4.65) for children.

The *Sea Prince II* cruises daily along the Ottawa River as well, from both the Ottawa and the Hull docks. The adult fare is C$15 (US$10), students and seniors are C$13 (US$9), and children ages 6 to 12 pay C$7.50 (US$5). The boat also hosts Sunday brunch cruises, theme events, and day trips to Château Montebello. For details, contact the **Ottawa Riverboat Company,** 30 Murray St., Suite 100 (✆ **613/562-4888**). An intriguing variation kids love is offered by the "amphi-bus" of **Lady Dive,** 90 Wellington St. (✆ **613/223-6211** or 613/524-2221). The boat-shaped wheeled red vehicle lumbers around the land-based sights, then eases into the river and cruises past the waterside attractions. Find it beside the Info-Centre or in front of the Museum of Civilization in Hull. It leaves daily: May, June, September, and October 9am to 5pm and July and August 9am to 9pm. Fares are C$24 (US$16) for adults, C$22 (US$15) for students, and C$20 (US$13) for children ages 14 and under.

## THE TOP ATTRACTIONS

**Discover the Hill Walking Tours,** exploring the events and personalities that shaped Parliament Hill and the nation, are given daily late June to September 1. Make reservations at the Info-tent (see below).

**Parliament Hill ★★** With their steeply pitched copper roofs, dormers, and towers, the several buildings of Parliament are quite impressive, especially on first sighting from river or road. In 1860, Prince Edward (later Edward VII) laid the cornerstone for the structures, which were finished in time to host the inaugural session of the first Parliament of the new Dominion of Canada in 1867. Entering through the south gate off Wellington Street, pass the **Centennial Flame,** lit by Lester Pearson on New Year's Eve 1966 to mark the passing of 100 years since that historic event.

On September 14, 2001, over 100,000 people gathered on this broad lawn in a day of remembrance after the terrorist attacks against the United States three days earlier.

**THE BUILDINGS** Parliament is composed of three expansive structures—the **Centre Block,** straight ahead, and the flanking **West Block** and **East Block.** They're at the heart of Canadian political life, containing the House of Commons and the Senate. Sessions of the **House of Commons** can be observed, the 295 elected members debating in their handsome green chamber with tall stained-glass windows. Parliament is usually in recess from late June to early September and occasionally between September and June, including the Easter and Christmas holidays. Otherwise, the House usually sits on Monday from 11am to 6:30pm, Tuesday and Thursday 10am to 6:30pm, Wednesday 2 to 8pm, and Friday 10am to 4pm. The 104 appointed members of the **Senate** sit in an opulent red chamber with murals depicting Canadians fighting in World War I.

The imposing 92m (302-ft.) campanile dominating the Centre Block's facade is the **Peace Tower.** It houses a 53-bell carillon, a huge clock, an observation deck, and the Memorial Chamber, commemorating Canada's war dead, most notably the 66,650 who lost their lives in World War I. Stones from the deadliest battlefields are lodged in the chamber's walls and floors. Atop the tower is a 11m (35-ft.) bronze mast flying a Canadian flag. When Parliament is in session, the tower is lit. Going up the tower, most visitors notice something strange about the elevator. For the first 30m (98 ft.) of the journey it travels at a 10° angle.

A 1916 fire destroyed the original Centre Block; only the Library at the rear was saved. A glorious 16-sided dome, supported outside by flying buttresses and paneled inside with Canadian white pine, features a marble statue of the young Queen Victoria and splendid carvings—gorgons, crests, masks, and hundreds of rosettes. The West Block, containing parliamentary offices, is closed to the public, but the East Block can be visited, housing offices of prime ministers, governors-general, and the Privy Council. Four historic rooms are on view: the original governor-general's office, restored to the period of Lord Dufferin (1872–78); the offices of Sir John A. Macdonald and Sir Georges-Etienne Cartier (the principal Fathers of Confederation); and the Privy Council Chamber, with anteroom.

Stroll the grounds clockwise around the Centre Block—they're dotted with statues honoring such prominent figures as Queen Victoria, Sir Georges-Etienne Cartier, William Lyon Mackenzie King, and Sir Wilfrid Laurier. Behind the building is a promenade with sweeping views of the river. Here, too, is the old Centre Block's bell, which crashed to the ground shortly after tolling midnight on the eve of the 1916 fire. At the bottom of the cliff behind Parliament (accessible from the entrance locks on the Rideau Canal), a pleasant path leads along the Ottawa River.

**CHANGING OF THE GUARD** *Kids* From late June to late August, a colorful half-hour ceremony is held daily on the Parliament Hill lawn, weather permitting. Two historic regiments—the Governor-General's Foot Guards and the Canadian Grenadier Guards—compose the Ceremonial Guard. The parade of 125 soldiers in busbies and scarlet jackets (guard, color party, and band) assembles at Cartier Square Drill Hall (by the canal at Laurier Avenue) at 9:30am and marches up Elgin Street to reach the hill at 10am. On arrival on the hill, the Ceremonial Guard splits, one division of the old guard positioned on the west side of the Parliament Hill lawn and two divisions of the new guard, or "duties," on the east side. Inspection of dress and weapons follows. The colors are then marched before the troops and saluted, the guards presenting arms. Throughout, sergeant-majors bellow unintelligible commands that prompt the synchronized stomp and clatter of boots and weapons. Finally, the outgoing guard commander gives the key to the guard room to the incoming commander, signifying the end of the process. The relieved unit marches back down Wellington Street to the beat of their drums and to the skirl of bagpipes.

**SOUND & LIGHT SHOW** For years Canada's history has unfolded in a dazzling half-hour display of sound and light against the dramatic backdrop of the Parliament buildings. From May to August, weather permitting, two performances are given per night, one in English, the other in French. There's bleacher seating for the free show. The shows were cancelled in 1999 to permit technical upgrading but are expected to be renewed in May 2002. For details, contact the **National Capital Commission** at ✆ **800/465-1867** or 613/239-5000.

**Canadian Museum of Civilization** ★★ Kids Canadian Indian architect Douglas Cardinal designed this spectacular museum rising from the banks of the Ottawa River as though its curvilinear forms had been sculpted by wind, water, and glacier. The exhibits within tell the history of Canada, starting with the **Grand Hall,** the high windows of which provide fine views of the skyline. It's devoted to the "First Nations"—in this case, Native-Canadian bands of the west coast—featuring a ranked collection of huge totem poles and facades representing lodges. Behind these are small galleries of utensils, tools, weavings, and other artifacts. From there, take escalators to the third floor and its **Canada Hall.** Laid out in chronological order is the history of the country, starting with the arrival of the Vikings. There are effective tableaux of shipboard life through the whaling period, with human-size models, moving images, and recorded shrieks of gulls and creaks of hawsers.

Replications of fortified settlements of 18th-century New France follow, on through the military past to the rise of cities, including a walk along an early-1900s street. On the second floor are a **Children's Museum** and a **Postal Museum,** but the principal attraction is the **CINEPLUS** theater, containing an IMAX screen and an OMNIMAX (dome-shaped) screen that propel the viewer giddily into the film's action. There are also a cafeteria and a restaurant, **Les Muses** (**© 819/776-7009**).

100 Laurier St., Hull. **© 819/776-7000.** www.civilization.ca/cmc/cmce.asp. Admission C$8 (US$5.35) adults, C$7 (US$4.65) seniors, C$4 (US$2.65) students and children, C$20 (US$13) families. Free to all Thurs 4pm–9pm, half-price Sun. Tickets to CINEPLUS extra, combination museum and CINEPLUS tickets available. May–June Fri–Wed 9am–6pm; July–Aug Sat–Wed 9am–6pm, Thurs–Fri 9am–9pm; Sept to mid-Oct Fri–Wed 9am–6pm, Thurs 9am–9pm; rest of year Fri–Sun and Tues–Wed 9am–5pm, Thurs–9pm.

**Canadian War Museum** ★★ Kids Kids love to clamber over the tanks outside this museum, and they enjoy (almost as much) imagining themselves in firefights in the life-size replica of a World War I trench. They seem unaffected by the innate solemnity of the collection, which traces Canada's long and often tragic military history. The country has lost more than 115,000 men and women in 20th-century wars, more than 60,000 killed in World War I alone, and its population is one-tenth that of the United States. On display are intact airplanes, military equipment, antique and modern weaponry, a Mercedes used by Adolf Hitler, ephemera like General Wolfe's chess set, and uniforms (among them that of Canadian air ace Billy Bishop, credited with shooting down the Red Baron). There are several large mock-ups of famous battle scenes, including the D-Day landings at Normandy, with martial music and other sound effects. Exhibits begin at the beginning, taking note of skirmishes between Vikings and Canadian Natives (ca. 1000), and proceed chronologically through the War of 1812, the disaster at Dieppe in World War II, and Korea. It ends with an outline of the military's more recent role in peacekeeping missions, of which Canadians are especially proud.

330 Sussex Dr. (at Bruyere St.). **© 819/776-8600.** www.civilization.ca/cwm/cwme.asp. Admission C$4 (US$2.65) adults, C$3 (US$2) seniors/ages 13–17, C$2 (US$1.35) children 2–12; free for everyone Thurs 4–8pm, half-price Sunday. May to mid-Oct daily 9:30am–5pm (to 10pm Thurs), mid-Oct to Apr Tues–Sun 9:30am–5pm (to 8pm Thurs). Closed Christmas Day.

**Canada Aviation Museum** ★★★ Kids This collection of more than 115 aircraft is one of the best of its kind in the world. In the main exhibit hall, a "Walkway of Time" traces aviation history from the start of the 20th century through the two world wars to the present. All the planes are either the real thing or full-size replicas, starting with the Silver Dart, a biplane built by a consortium headed by Alexander Graham Bell. It took off from the ice of Baddeck Bay, Nova Scotia, in February 1909, Canada's first powered flight. It flew for 9 minutes—not bad, considering it looks as though it were built out of bicycle parts and kites. The other sections are concerned with specific uses, including the often-amphibious craft of bush pilots so critical in servicing the road-less outer reaches of monster Canada, and the development of the airlines and of military and naval aircraft from World War I through to the jet age. Examples are partially stripped of their outer skins to reveal their construction, and there are cockpit mock-ups with videos simulating takeoffs, a hit with kids.

At Rockcliffe Airport. ✆ **613/993-2010.** www.aviation.nmstc.ca Admission C$10 (US$6.65) adults, C$4 (US$2.65) seniors/students, C$2 (US$1.35) children 7–15; children 6 and under free. Free to all Thurs 5–9pm. May–Labour Day daily 9am–5pm (to 9pm Thurs), rest of the year Tues–Sun 10am–5pm (to 9pm Thurs). From Sussex Dr., take Rockcliffe Pkwy. and exit at the National Aviation Museum.

**National Gallery of Canada** ★★★ Architect Moshe Safdie, famed for his Habitat apartment block and Musée des Beaux-Arts in Montréal, designed this rose-granite crystal palace that gleams from a promontory overlooking the Ottawa River. A dramatic long glass concourse leads to the Grand Hall, commanding glorious views of Parliament Hill. Natural light also fills the galleries, thanks to ingeniously designed shafts with reflective panels.

The museum displays about 800 examples of Canadian art, part of the 10,000 works in the permanent collection. A good way to take it all in is to go to the second floor and proceed down counterclockwise. Among the highlights are Benjamin West's famous 1770 history painting of General Wolfe's death at Québec; the fabulous Rideau Convent Chapel (1888), a rhapsody of wooden fan vaulting, cast-iron columns, and intricate carving created by architect/priest Georges Bouillon; the works of early Québecois artists like Antoine Plamondon, Abbé Jean Guyon, and Frère Luc; Tom Thomson and the Group of Seven landscapists; and the Montréal Automatistes Paul-Emile Borduas and Jean-Paul Riopelle. The European masters are also represented, from Corot and Turner to Chagall and Picasso, and contemporary galleries feature pop art and minimalism, plus later abstract works, both Canadian and American.

Pause for a contemplative moment on the balcony of the central atrium looking down on a garden of triangular flower beds and a grove of trees that repeat the lines of the pyramidal glass roof. Each year, three or four major traveling exhibits are displayed, including recent ones on Monet and van Gogh. Facilities include two restaurants, a gift shop/bookstore, and an auditorium.

380 Sussex Dr. (at St. Patrick St.). ✆ **613/990-1985.** http://national.gallery.ca. Permanent collection free; admission to special exhibitions varies, but approximately C$15 (US$10) adults, C$12 (US$8) seniors/students; age 12–19 free. Advance purchase recommended, since tickets are for specific times and dates. Special exhibits are extra. Wed–Sun 10am–6pm (to 8pm Thurs). Guided tours daily at 11am and 2pm; register at the information desk. Closed major holidays.

## MORE ATTRACTIONS

**Billings Estate Museum** This imposing manse allows you to peer into the social life of the period from 1829, when Braddish Billings, head of one of Ottawa's founding families, oversaw its construction, to the 1970s, when the home was turned into a museum. Visitors can use the picnic area and stroll the 3ha (8-acre) grounds, an experience heightened when tea and scones are served on the lawn June 1 to September 1, 2 or 3 days a week (call ahead for current details).

2100 Cabot St. ✆ **613/247-4830.** Admission C$2.50 (US$1.65) adults, C$2 (US$1.35) seniors, C$1.50 (US$1) ages 5–17; children under 5 free. May–Oct Tues–Sun noon–5pm. Go south on Bank St., cross the Rideau River at Billings Bridge and take Riverside East; turn right on Pleasant Park and right on Cabot.

**Byward Market** ★ A traditional farmers' market still sells all manner of foods, flowers, plants, and produce around a central building that houses two floors of boutiques displaying a wide variety of wares and crafts. During market season, enjoy a snack at more than 70 indoor and outdoor stand-up counters and cafes and watch life surging by over a cold beer or glass of wine.

The surrounding neighborhood is a mix of rehabilitated 19th-century brick buildings and contemporary commercial structures. Street performers and balloon manipulators provide brief diversion (though someone seems to have rounded up the mimes).

If planning a picnic, pick up some cheese or cold cuts at **International Cheese & Deli,** 40 Byward Market St.; bread from **The French Baker** (Le Boulanger Français), 119 Murray St.; and wine at **Vintages Wines & Spirits,** 299 Dalhousie St.

Area bounded by Sussex, Rideau, St. Patrick, and King Edward sts. May–Nov Mon–Sat 9am–6pm, Sun 10am–6pm; Dec–Apr daily 10am–6pm.

**Bytown Museum** Housed in Ottawa's oldest stone building (1827), which served as the Commissariat for food and material during construction of the Rideau Canal, this museum displays possessions of Lieutenant-Colonel By, the Canal's builder and one of young Ottawa's most influential citizens. Additional artifacts reflect the social history of the pioneer era of Bytown/Ottawa in three period rooms and a number of changing exhibits. The museum is beside the Ottawa Locks, between Parliament Hill and Château Laurier.

540 Wellington St. (at Commissioner St.). ✆ **613/234-4570.** Admission C$5 (US$3.35) adults, C$2.50 (US$1.65) seniors/students, C$1.50 (US$1) children, C$12 (US$8) families. Apr to mid-May and mid-Oct to Nov Mon–Fri 10am–4pm; mid-May to mid-Oct Mon–Sat 10am–5pm, Sun 1–5pm. Closed Dec–Mar.

**Canadian Museum of Nature** *Kids* Seven permanent exhibit halls trace the history of life on Earth from its beginnings 4,200 million years ago. A huge tree of life traces the evolutionary threads of life from 500 million years ago to the present. The third-floor dinosaur hall is a popular highlight, with fossils, skulls, and the intact skeleton of a mastadon. In an opposite gallery is a variety of snails, bugs, spiders, and other "creepy critters," some of them live. Down one floor are mineral galleries and exhibits of Canadian birds and large mammals preserved by taxidermy and placed in natural settings. Kids enjoy the Discovery Den activity area.

240 McLeod St. (at Metcalfe). ✆ **613/566-4700.** www.nature.ca. Admission C$6 (US$4) adults, C$5 (US$3.35) seniors/children ages 13 and up, C$2.50 (US$1.65) ages 3–12, C$13 (US$8.65) families; children under 3 free. Half price on Thurs 9:30am–5pm, free 5–8pm. May–Labour Day daily 9:30am–5pm (to 8pm Thurs); rest of the year daily 10am–5pm (to 8pm Thurs).

**Canada Science & Technology Museum** *Kids* Interactive displays encourage visitor participation in demonstrations of such physical principles as viscosity, climb aboard a steam locomotive, launch a rocket from a mini–control room, observe the heavens in the evening through Canada's largest refracting telescope (appointments necessary), see chicks hatching, and walk through the Crazy Kitchen, where everything looks normal but the floor is tilted at a sharp angle. The permanent exhibits deal with Canada in space, land and marine transportation, communications, and all kinds of modern industrial and household technology. The adjacent outdoor technology park features machines and devices from the windmill and lighthouse to radar and rocket.

## A Scenic Drive

For a picturesque outing, drive east on Wellington Street past Parliament Hill, through Confederation Square. After Château Laurier, on the left, turn left (north) on Sussex Drive. After passing the new **American Embassy,** glorious views open up to the left over the islands.

Proceed along Sussex Drive to St. Patrick Street, turning left into **Nepean Point Park.** Here share a fine river view with the statue of Samuel de Champlain. Across the road is **Major's Hill Park,** between Château Laurier and the National Gallery, where the noonday gun is fired (at 10am on Sun to avoid disturbing church services). Return to Sussex Drive, continuing in the same direction. Just beyond the Macdonald-Cartier Bridge stands **Earnscliffe,** once the home of Sir John A. Macdonald, first Prime Minister of the Dominion of Canada, and now the residence of the British High Commissioner.

Farther along, Sussex Drive crosses the Rideau River, passing the contemporary **Ottawa City Hall,** in the middle of Green Island near Rideau Falls, to the left. The parkway proceeds past the Prime Minister's house, shielded by trees at 24 Sussex Dr., and on to **Rideau Hall,** at no. 1, also known as Government House, the Governor-General's residence. On the 35ha (88-acre) grounds are scores of ceremonial trees planted by visiting dignitaries and heads of state, from Queen Victoria to John F. Kennedy, Richard Nixon, and Princess Diana. They're identified by nameplates at the base of the trees. In summer, a brief changing-of-the-guard ceremony is held at noon at the main gate. Tours of the grounds and the interior public rooms are conducted daily in July and August and on weekends the rest of the year. For information, stop in at the **Visitor Centre** (open daily 9:30am to 5:30pm) or call ✆ **613/991-4422.**

Continuing, the drive becomes **Rockliffe Driveway,** a beautiful route along the Ottawa River and through **Rockcliffe Park.** Where the road splits in the park, follow the right fork to Acacia Avenue to reach the **Rockeries,** where April blossoms herald spring. If you wish, continue on Rockliffe Driveway to reach the **Aviation Museum.** Or proceed on Acacia, which doubles back and connects once again with the Driveway back to the city.

1867 St. Laurent Blvd. (at Lancaster Rd.). ✆ **613/991-3044.** www.science-tech.nmstc.ca. Admission C$6 (US$4) adults, C$5 (US$3.35) seniors/students, C$2 (US$1.35) ages 6–14; C$12 (US$8) family. May 1–Labour Day daily 9am–5pm (to 9pm Fri); rest of the year Tues–Sun 9am–5pm. Closed Dec 25. Appointments needed to enter the observatory (call ✆ **613/991-3053** 8am–4pm).

**Laurier House** This comfortable 1878 brick home is filled with mementos of the two Canadian prime ministers who lived here over a span of 50 years. From 1897 to 1919, it was occupied by Sir Wilfrid Laurier, Canada's seventh Prime Minister and the first French-Canadian elected to that office. He was followed by William Lyon Mackenzie King, who held the same post for 21 years and lived

**Tips Man of Stone**

In city parks and before country mansions, visitors come upon arrangements in rough-cut stone stacked to suggest standing men. These are "Inuksuk", originally created by the Inuit peoples.

here from 1923 to 1950. King is said to have held séances in the library; on display is the crystal ball he supposedly had coveted in London but said he couldn't afford—an American bought it for him when he overheard King's remarks. A portrait of the PM's mother is here, in front of which King used to place a red rose daily. You'll also find a copy of the program Abraham Lincoln held on the night of his assassination, plus copies of his death mask and hands. Lester B. Pearson's library has also been re-created and contains the Nobel Peace Prize medal he won for his role in the 1956 Arab-Israeli dispute.

335 Laurier Ave. E. (at Chapel St.). © **613/992-8142.** Admission C$2.50 (US$1.65) adults, C$2 (US$1.35) seniors, C$1.50 (US$1) ages 6–16. Apr–Sept Tues–Sat 9am–5pm, Sun 2–5pm; Oct–Mar call ahead for hours.

**Royal Canadian Mounted Police Musical Ride** *Kids* The famous Musical Ride mounted drill team first performed in Regina in 1878. Horses and riders practice at the Canadian Police College, and the public is welcome to attend. Check before you go, though, because the Ride is often on tour, especially during the warmer months, and schedules are extremely tentative.

8900 St. Laurent Blvd. N. © **613/993-3751.** At St. Laurent Blvd. N., take Sussex Dr. east past Rideau Hall and pick up Rockville Driveway; turn left at Sandridge Rd. and continue to the corner of St. Laurent.

## PARKS & GARDENS

The **Central Experimental Farm,** at Experimental Farm Drive and Prince of Wales Drive (© **613/991-3044**), isn't a traditional park, as is obvious by the name—but with its 480 ha (1,200 acres), it qualifies as the largest green space of all. Though now surrounded by suburban Ottawa, the farm has livestock barns housing various breeds of cattle, pigs, chickens, sheep, and horses. Milking time is 4pm. The greenhouses shelter a noted chrysanthemum show every November, and there are also an ornamental flower garden and an arboretum with 2,000 varieties of trees and shrubs. May to early October, you can ride in wagons drawn by brawny Clydesdales, weather permitting, Monday to Friday 10 to 11:30am and 2 to 3:30pm. In winter there are sleigh rides. Admission is C$3 (US$2) for adults and C$2 (US$1.35) for students, seniors, and children ages 3 to 15. March to October, the agricultural museum, barns, and tropical greenhouse are open daily 9am to 5pm; November to February, except Christmas and New Year's Day, the barns and tropical greenhouse are open daily 9am to 4pm, but the museum's exhibits are closed.

Another star attraction in the Ottawa area is **Gatineau Park,** across the river in Québec, north of Hull. Only 3km (2 miles) from Parliament lie 35,600ha (88,000 acres) of woodland and lakes named after notary-turned-explorer Nicolas Gatineau of Trois-Rivières. The park was inaugurated in 1938, when the federal government bought land in the Gatineau Hills to stop forest destruction. Black bear, timber wolf, otter, marten, and raccoon are joined by white-tailed deer, beaver, and more than 100 species of birds. Also resident, but rarely glimpsed, are lynx and wolverines.

Park facilities include 145km (90 miles) of **hiking trails** and supervised **swimming beaches** at Meech Lake, Lac Philippe, and Lac la Pêche. Vehicle access fees to beach areas are C$7 to C$9 (US$4.65–US$6). Canoes, kayaks, and rowboats can be rented at Lac Philippe and Lac la Pêche. Call © **819/456-3555** to make reservations. Motorboats are only permitted on Lac la Pêche, where motors up to 10 horsepower may be used for fishing. Most lakes can be fished (if it's not allowed, it's posted). A Québec license is required and can be obtained at many convenience stores around the park.

**Camping facilities** are at or near Lac Philippe, accessible by highways 5, 105, and 366; there are also 35 canoe camping sites at Lac la Pêche. For details on this and other camping facilities, contact the **Gatineau Park Visitor Centre,** 318 Meech Lake Rd., Old Chelsea, PQ J0X 1N0 (© **819/827-2020**), or write the **National Capital Commission,** 40 Elgin St., Suite 202, Ottawa, ON K1P 1C7. Reservations are vital. Call © **819/456-3016** mid-May to September 9am to 4pm.

In winter, hiking trails become **cross-country ski trails,** marked by numbers on blue plaques, with chalets along the way. Winter camping is available at Lac Philippe.

In the middle of the park is the summer retreat of Mackenzie King at **Kingsmere.** Serving as Prime Minister for a record 22 years, King collected the architectural fragments on view at the estate, transported here from the Centre Block Parliament building after the 1916 fire and from London's House of Commons after the 1941 Blitz. Linger over a beverage and snack in a cottage called the Moorside Tearoom; May 1 to Oct 31 it's open daily 11am to 6pm. For reservations, call © **819/827-3405.**

There are several routes to the park: Cross over to Hull and take boulevard Taché (Route 148) to the Gatineau Parkway, which leads to Kingsmere, Ski Fortune, and eventually Meech Lake. Or take Route 5 (Autoroute de la Gatineau) north, take Exit 12 for Old Chelsea, turn left, and proceed 1km (½ mile) on Meech Lake Road to the Gatineau Park Visitor Centre. To reach Lac Philippe, take Route 5 north out of Hull and then Route 105 to the intersection of Route 366 west. Just before reaching Ste-Cecile-de-Masham, turn off to Lac Philippe; to reach Lac la Pêche, keep going along the Masham road to St-Louis-de-Masham and enter the park just beyond.

Open all year, **Parc Oméga,** Route 323 nord, Montebello (© **818/423-5487;** www.parc-omega.com), a nearby wildlife park, is distinctive in each of the seasons, barely recognizable in both fauna and vegetation in summer as compared to winter. From the entrance gate, visitors see the first of the elk waiting for one of the carrots purchased with your tickets. They are only a foreshadowing of the animals to be spotted on the drive, most of which stroll right up to your car to take their snacks from your hand. Among the most visible are whitetail deer, wapiti, bison, fallow deer, raccoons, and wild boar, all of which roam free. Kept in large enclosures are black bears, timber wolves, and raptors, including bald eagles. With luck, the reclusive moose might be spotted. A restaurant and picnic grounds are positioned above a pretty lake. Tune your radio to 88.1 FM for a continuous commentary. From June to September, admission is C$13 (US$9) for adults, October to May it costs C$10 (US$7) for adults; year-round admission is C$7 (US$4.65) for children ages 6 to 15 and C$3 (US$2) for ages 2 to 5.

## ESPECIALLY FOR KIDS

Kids love the bands, rifles, and uniforms of the **Changing of the Guard** on Parliament Hill. The **Canada Aviation Museum** is a fantasyland for many, especially the mock-ups of cockpits where they can pretend to be pilots. The perennial favorites at the **Canadian Museum of Nature** are the dinosaurs, the animals, and the Discovery Den, especially created for children. Extra-special attractions at the **Canadian Museum of Civilization** are the Children's Museum and CINEPLUS for action movies. Kids enjoy picnicking or taking a hayride at the **Central Experimental Farm.** At the **Canada Science and Technology Museum,** the hands-on exhibits entertain while learning. Kids also love the tanks and weaponry on display at the **Canadian War Museum** and the **Royal Canadian Mounted Police Musical Ride** practices at the Canadian Police College. All these attractions are described in detail earlier in this chapter.

When it's time to let off some steam, there's **canoeing** or **boating** at Dow's Lake, **biking** along the canal or **ice-skating** on it, plus activities outside the city in Gatineau Park.

Outside Ottawa is the **Storyland Family Park,** Storyland Road (RR #5), off Route 17 about 9.5km (6 miles) northwest of Renfrew (✆ **613/432-2222**), with a puppet theater, paddleboats, mini-golf, a petting zoo, and more. Admission is C$9 (US$6) for adults, C$8 (US$5) for children ages 5 and over, and C$6 (US$4) for seniors and children ages 2 to 4. Early June to mid-September, it's open daily 9:30am to 6pm. And the **Logos Land Resort,** Route 17 (RR #1), Cobden (✆ **613/646-9765**), has five water slides, mini-golf, paddleboats, and sleigh rides and cross-country skiing in winter. Admission is C$13 (US$8.65). June to August, it's open daily 9am to 8pm (to 5pm the rest of the year).

## 5 Special Events & Festivals

On weekends in February, it's **Winterlude** (✆ **613/239-5000;** www.capcan.ca), with parades, an ice-sculpture competition, fireworks, speed skating, snowshoe races, ice boating, curling, and more. One offbeat contest is the bed race on the frozen canal, while the most exciting event may be the harness racing on ice.

Ottawa's biggest event is the **Canadian Tulip Festival** (✆ **888/465-1867;** www.capcan.ca) for about 2 weeks in mid-May, when the city is ablaze with 200 varieties of tulips enlivening public buildings, monuments, embassies, homes, and driveways. (Among the best viewing points is Dow's Lake.) The festival began in 1945, when the Netherlands sent 100,000 tulip bulbs to Canada in appreciation of the role Canadian troops played in liberating Holland. Festival events include fireworks, concerts, parades, and a flotilla on the canal.

At the end of May the **R.C.M.P. Musical Ride Sunset Ceremony** (✆ **613/993-3751;** www.rcmp-grc.gc.ca) takes place, with outdoor evening performances of music and horsemanship, including jumping and dressage, as well the ride itself. In early June, the Canadian Museum of Nature holds a **Children's Festival** (✆ **613/728-5863;** www.childfest.ca), an extravaganza of dance, mime, puppetry, and music. Late June brings the **Festival Franco-Ontarien** (✆ **613/741-1225;** www.leroux.ca), a 5-day celebration of Francophone Canada,

### *Fun Fact* Born on Dutch Soil—In Ottawa

Queen Juliana of the Netherlands, who'd spent the war years in Canada, arranged for an annual bulb presentation to celebrate the birth of her daughter, Princess Margriet, in Ottawa in 1943. To ensure that the princess was born a Dutch citizen, the Canadian government proclaimed her room in the Ottawa Civic Hospital part of the Netherlands.

featuring classical and other musical concerts, fashion shows, street performers, games and competitions, crafts, and French cuisine.

On July 1, Canadians flock to the city to celebrate **Canada Day** (© **800/465-1867;** www.capcan.ca), a huge birthday party with many kinds of entertainment, including fireworks. For 10 days in mid-July, the city is filled with the sounds of the **Ottawa International Jazz Festival** (© **613/241-2633;** www.jazz.ottawa.com). Local, national, and international artists give more than 125 performances at more than 20 venues. That event is followed by the 2-week **Ottawa Chamber Music Festival** (© **613/234-8008;** www.chamberfest.com), North America's largest, with 74 concerts in the city's churches.

On Labour Day weekend, scores of brilliantly colored balloons fill the skies over Ottawa, while on the ground, people flock to musical events and midway rides during the **Gatineau Hot Air Balloon Festival** (© **819/243-2330;** www.ville.gatineau.qc.ca/). Other major events include the **National Capital Air Show** in late May (© **613/526-1030;** www.ncas.ottawa.com), the **National Capital Dragon Boat Race Festival** in late June (© **613/238-7711;** www.dragonboat.net), and the 10-day **Central Canada Exhibition** (© **613/237-7222;** www.the-ex.com) in mid- to late August.

## 6 Outdoor Activities & Spectator Sports

### OUTDOOR ACTIVITIES

**BIKING** Ottawans are enthusiastic cyclists, fully utilizing the more than 160km (99 miles) of bike paths running along the Ottawa and Rideau rivers, along the Rideau Canal, and in Gatineau Park—and more miles are being added. A blue, black, and white cyclist logo marks all bikeways. April to Canadian Thanksgiving in October, bicycles are available at **RentABike,** 1 Rideau St., in the parking lot behind Château Laurier (© **613/241-4140**). Town bikes, sport bikes, mountain bikes, and in-line skates are available, with standard bikes from C$8 (US$5) per hour to C$28 (US$19) for 24 hours, and performance bikes from C$38 (US$25) per day. Take the kids along in a bike trailer with two seats and a harness for another C$6 (US$4) per hour. The company will also provide maps of self-guided pathway tours around the city, as well as guided tours. Bikes and in-line skates can also be rented at **Dow's Lake Marina** (© **613/232-5278**). The public transportation company, **OC Transpo,** has what it chooses to call a "Rack & Roll" program. Bicycle racks are installed on the outside of over 150 buses for the use of passengers, first-come, first-served. For details about specific routes, call © **613/741-4390.**

**BOATING/CANOEING** Rent paddleboats and canoes at the marina (© **613/232-1001**) at **Dow's Lake Pavilion,** 1001 Queen Elizabeth Dr., for C$12 (US$8) per hour. The C$3 million (US$2 million) glass-and-steel complex, which looks like a flotilla of sails from a distance, has several restaurants and provides a welcome haven after a winter skate or a summer running or biking jaunt. Boats can also be rented in Gatineau Park at Lac la Pêche and Lac Philippe (© **819/827-2020**) for C$8 (US$5) per hour or C$28 (US$19) per day.

**GOLF** The Ottawa metro region has over 60 courses, including the one on the premises of the **Château Montebello** (© **819/423-6341**) in Québec (see page 316). Other desirable courses in the area are the **Emerald Links Golf & Country Club** (© **613/822-4653**); **Canadian Golf and Country Club** (© **613/253-3290**); **Le Dome Golf Club** (© **819/770-5557**); and **Manderley**

## Ottawa's Pride: The Rideau Canal

Built in the early 19th century under the leadership of Lt. Colonel John By, a civil and military engineer, the **Rideau Canal** was meant to bypass the Thousand Islands section of the St. Lawrence River, thought to be vulnerable to American attack in the hostile atmosphere following the War of 1812. It connected Kingston with the Ottawa River, allowing the transporting of troops and supplies to Canada's capital and from there on to Montréal. The fear of invasion never came to fruition, railroads soon became the desired mode of transportation, and the quickly outmoded canal was left to evolve over time from neglected historical artifact into one of eastern Ontario's most impressive visual and recreational assets. In summer, walk or cycle along the canal paths or row a canoe or boat on a gentle journey before stopping at the canal-side cafe at the National Arts Centre. You can rent houseboats to navigate its entire length. In winter, it's turned into a 8km (5-mile-long) skating course worthy of Hans Brinker, as people glide to and from work, briefcases in hand, and families take to the ice with children perched atop their backs or drawn on sleighs.

Construction of the 198km (123 mile) canal began in 1826 and ended in 1832. Starting in Ottawa, it follows the course of the Rideau River to its summit on Upper Rideau Lake, which is connected to Newboro Lake, where the canal descends the Cataraqui River through a series of lakes controlled by dams to Kingston. In Ottawa, a flight of eight locks allows boats to negotiate the 24m (80 ft.) difference between the artificially constructed portion of the canal and the Ottawa River—a sight not to be missed. You can observe this fascinating maneuver between Parliament Hill and Château Laurier.

**on the Green** (✆ **613/489-2066.** Greens fees for these run C$25 to C$40 (US$17–US$27).

**HIKING & NATURE WALKS** A band of protected wetlands and woodlands surrounds the capital on the Ontario side of the Ottawa River, and here you can find ideal hiking areas. At **Stony Swamp Conservation Area** (✆ **613/239-5000**) in the region's west end are 39km (24 miles) of trails, including the Old Quarry Trail, the Jack Pine Nature Trail, and the Sasparilla Trail. It's also good for cross-country skiing and snowshoeing. Regional maps are available from the Capital InfoCentre downtown at 14 Metcalfe St. **Gatineau Park** (✆ **819/827-2020**) has a network of hiking trails through its 35,000ha (86,500-acre) preserve. West of the city in Kanata, **Riverfront Park** (✆ **613/592-4281**) has nature trails along the Ottawa River. On the Québec side in Luskville, a trail leads to Luskville Falls from the Chemin de Hôtel de Ville. **The Rideau Trail,** running from Ottawa to Kingston, is the area's major serious hiking trail.

**SKATING** Usually late December to late February, the **Rideau Canal** becomes the world's longest and most romantic skating rink, stretching from the National Arts Centre to Dow's Lake and Carleton University; every morning the radio news reports ice conditions. Rent skates at several locations for C$12 to C$15 (US$8–US$10) for 2 hours. The canal is serviced with heated huts, sleigh rentals, boot-check and skate-sharpening services, food concessions, and rest rooms. In-line skates are available at the Rent-A-Bike facility behind Château Laurier and from Dow's Lake Marina.

**SKIING** Few visitors ski the areas around Ottawa, to tell the truth, heading instead for Québec's more sophisticated Laurentian resorts, only a hour or so east. In many ways, the following ski resorts are more compelling summer attractions with their water parks and other fun facilities. (See "Mont Ste-Anne: Skiing & Summer Sports," in chapter 8, "Québec City & the Gaspé Peninsula," for two of Québec's most popular ski resorts.)

**Mont Cascades,** just 30 minutes north of Ottawa across the Gatineau River, outside of Cantley on Highway 307 (© **819/827-0301**), has 13 trails, one triple- and three double-chair lifts, and two T-bars. The longest run is 670m (2,200 ft.). There are two day lodges with a cafeteria and a restaurant/bar at the hill. Night skiing is available. During summer, there are six water slides in the state-of-the-art water park. **Mont Ste-Marie,** 89km (55 miles) north of Ottawa at Lac Ste-Marie (© **819/467-5200**), offers skiing on twin hills, with a 380m (1,250-ft.) drop, and a 3km (2-mile) ski run. There are two quads and a Poma. Mont Ste-Marie also offers cross-country skiing. **Gatineau Park,** with 185km (115 miles) of groomed trails, offers the best cross-country skiing. In town, you can also ski along the bike paths paralleling the Eastern or Western parkways.

**SWIMMING** Pools open to the public include those at **Carleton University** (© **613/520-5631**) on Colonel By Drive, the University of Ottawa (© **613/562-5789**) at 125 University Dr., and the YMCA-YWCA (© **613/788-5000**) at 180 Argyle Dr. Lake swimming is available in **Gatineau Park, Meech Lake, Lac la Pêche,** and at **Lac Philippe.**

**WHITE-WATER RAFTING** Enjoy the exhilaration of a day of white-water rafting and be back in your hotel bed that night. Outings are available from mid-May to September, depending on the river. **Owl Rafting,** Box 29, Foresters Falls, ON K0J 1V0 (© **613/646-2263** in summer or 613/238-7238 in winter), offers 1- and 2-day white-water rafting trips within 90 minutes of the city, pounding over extensive rapids for the fit and adventurous and floating on gentler stretches for families. Prices start at C$75 (US$50) per person per day during the week, meals included. Companies operating similar trips and facilities are **Esprit Rafting Adventures,** Box 463, Pembroke, ON K8A 6X7 (© **800/596-7238** or 819/683-3241); **Ottawa Adventures Rafting,** Box 212, Bryson, QC J0X 1H0 (© **800/690-7238** or 819/647-3625); **Riverrun,** P.O. Box 179, Beachburg, ON K0J 1C0 (© **800/267-8504** or 613/646-2501); and **Wilderness Tours,** Foresters Falls, ON K0J 1V0 (© **800/267-9166** or 613/646-2291).

## SPECTATOR SPORTS

The **Ottawa Senators** (© **613/599-0300**) are one of the youngest teams in the National Hockey League (a previous incarnation won a string of Stanley Cups earlier in this century) and currently play at the Corel Centre in Kanata. Tickets cost C$28 to C$80 (US$19–US$53); call **Ticketmaster** at © **613/755-1166.** The **Ottawa Lynx** (© **613/747-5969**), the Triple A affiliate of the Montréal Expos, play baseball at Jetform Park, 300 Coventry Rd. Tickets, which are generally available, cost C$4.25 to C$8 (US$2.85–US$6); call © **613/749-9947.**

At this writing, plans were afoot to return professional football to the capital with a new team in the Canadian Football League (CFL).

## 7 Ottawa After Dark

Ottawa's culture and nightlife offerings aren't up to those of Toronto or Montréal, extending largely to the National Arts Centre, several bars, the Byward Market area, and a few dance clubs, the raciest of which are concentrated across the river in Hull. Still, there's certainly enough to occupy the evenings of a long weekend.

The biggest recent news in this regard was the opening of the **Casino de Hull,** 1 bd. du Casino (✆ **800/665-2274** or 819/772-2100), under 5km (3 miles) from Parliament Hill and open daily 11am to 3am. It imposes a dress code forbidding tank tops, jogging outfits, motorcycle boots, cutoffs, shorts, and beachwear. Both the exterior and the interior are dramatically landscaped with tropical plants, pools, and waterfalls. There are over 1,300 slot machines and more than 50 gambling tables, including blackjack, roulette, baccarat, and stud poker (no craps, though, and alcoholic drinks aren't allowed in gambling areas). A dance-and-music revue provides respite from losing for C$28 to C$38 (US$19–US$25) per show. The complex also has two lounges and three restaurants—fine dining in Le Baccara, a buffet in Banco, and a snack bar. A new 23-floor hotel opened for business in late 2001. Shuttles operate from Ottawa hotels to the casino for C$9 (US$6) per round-trip.

For Ottawa entertainment information, pick up a copy of ***Where,*** a free guide usually provided by hotels; ***Ottawa*** magazine; the free ***X-Press*** weekly newspaper; or the Friday edition of the ***Ottawa Citizen.***

### THE PERFORMING ARTS

Canadian and international musical, dance, and theater artists—including the resident National Arts Centre (NAC) Orchestra—perform at the elaborate **National Arts Centre,** 53 Elgin St., at Confederation Square (✆ **613/947-7000**). The building, created by architect Fred Lebensold, is made of three interlocking hexagons beside the Rideau Canal, its terraces tendering views of Parliament Hill and the Ottawa River. There are three auditoriums: the European-style **Opera,** seating 2,300; the 950-seat **Theatre,** with its innovative apron stage; and the 350-seat **Studio,** used for experimental works. The **National Arts Centre Orchestra** (✆ **613/996-5051**) performs in seven or eight main concert series per year. The center also offers classic and modern drama in English and French. For reservations, call Ticketmaster at ✆ **613/755-1111** or visit the NAC box office Monday to Saturday noon to 9pm and Sunday and holidays when performances are scheduled noon to curtain time. Guided tours are available. A free monthly *Calendar of NAC Events* is available from the **NAC Marketing and Communications Department,** Box 1534, Station B, Ottawa, ON K1P 5W1 (✆ **613/996-5051;** www.nac-cna.ca). See "Where to Dine," earlier, for a review of the Centre's canal-side restaurant, Le Café.

Augmenting the main events at the National Arts Centre, the ensemble at the **Great Canadian Theatre Company,** 910 Gladstone Ave. (✆ **613/236-5196;** www.gctc.ca), presents contemporary drama and comedy with Canadian themes September to May. Tickets start at C$22 (US$15).

### LIVE-MUSIC CLUBS

**Barrymore's Music Hall** This suitably disreputable-looking rock palace in a former cinema showcases bands bearing names like Buskerbash, Good

Riddance, and Little Bones. Open nightly, it presents a good mix of tribute bands, alternative groups, disco and DJs, switching on Sundays to "retro" 1980s sounds. 323 Bank St. (✆ **613/233-0307**) Covers vary, but up to C$30 (US$20) for more important attractions.

**Café Quo Vadis** Fridays and Saturdays, jazz by duos and trios comes with the gelati, coffee, and snacks. 521 Sussex Dr. (✆ **613/789-1819**).

**Molly McGuire's** A rollicking scene in Byward Market is hosted by this cavernous pub, where a variety of musical tastes—rock, folk, jazz—carry into the small hours Friday and Saturday nights. 130 George St. (✆ **613/241-1972**).

**Rasputin's** Check this out for acoustic folk leavened with New Age melodies and unpredictable open-mike nights, all in a thoroughly relaxed atmosphere. 696 Bronson Ave. (✆ **613/230-5102**).

**The Rainbow** Blues action energizes the upstairs lounge here with live music every single night. It has hosted such artists as K.D. Lang and Buckwheat Zydeco, and though acts aren't often that noteworthy, there's always someone worth hearing. Cover charges run C$3 to C$10 (US$2–US$7) as the week rolls on, but there are free matinees from Monday to Friday, at 3 and 7pm. 76 Murray St. (✆ **613/241-5123**).

**Vineyards** Beneath The Fish Market restaurant in Byward Market is one of the city's cozier hangouts, in a rusticated cellar setting with stone floors and checked tablecloths. Several house wines are featured every night, from among more than 60 varieties, and there's an ample roster of imported beers. Sunday and Wednesday bring live jazz. Light meals and snacks are available. 54 York St. (✆ **613/241-4270**).

**Zaphod Beeblebrox 2** Smaller and even more ragged than Barrymore's, this club used to be a shadow next door, but moved. Usually, it's open Thursday to Saturday for live underground and alternative rock, with DJs the other nights. 27 York St. (✆ **613/562-1010**).

**Zoe's** Piano soloists and jazz combos enhance the sedate surroundings in this popular lounge of the Hôtel Château Laurier. 1 Rideau St. (✆ **613/241-1414**, ext. 3213).

## BARS & PUBS

Ottawa has an abundance of English and Irish pubs of varying degrees of authenticity (for the two best choices nearby, see the "Pubbing It Outside Ottawa" box earlier in this chapter). In addition to those places listed below, check out the **Brig,** 23 York St. (✆ **613/562-6666**), in the Byward Market area, and the **Elephant and Castle,** 50 Rideau St. (✆ **613/234-5544**).

**Big Daddy's** Elgin Street, from Gladstone to about Somerset, blooms with bars and eating places. Dominating them all is this muscular tavern, which enjoys a reputation for attracting large numbers of striking young women, accounting for the striking numbers of young men. Frozen margaritas don't come any bigger, and other drinks are generously poured for the heavy traffic in the bar and out on the terrace. It's a good place to start an evening, and with inertia or a bit of luck connecting, you can stay on for the Creole-Cajun crawfish boil, gumbo, catfish, or oysters from the raw bar. 339 Somerset St. (✆ **613/569-5200**).

**Maxwell's** Close by Big Daddy's, this open-fronted destination has a shellfish bar, too, with karaoke Tuesday and (often) live bands Wednesday to Saturday; call ahead to be sure. 340 Elgin St. (✆ **613/232-5771**).

**Bravo Bravo** A fun place to drop in for a drink and some pool, this bar-*ristorante* has decent Italian food and Sunday brunch, as well. 292 Elgin St. (✆ **613/233-0057**).

**Delta Ottawa Hotel** For an even more relaxing atmosphere, sink into plush upholstery and enjoy the lilting piano strains of the lobby bar at this downtown hotel. 361 Queen St. (✆ **613/238-6000**).

**The Earl of Sussex** Similar to the above, but with a more pronounced English flavor, this pub is diagonally across from the new U.S. Embassy. Wingbacks huddle around the fireplace and are arranged by the front windows. They have darts, of course, with live jazz on Friday and Saturday. In addition to daily chalkboard specials, menu standards include steak-and-kidney pie, liver and onions, bangers and mash, and Cornish pasties. There are 30 ales, stouts, and lagers on draft. 431 Sussex Dr. (✆ **613/562-5544**).

**Friday's Victorian Music Parlour** For quiet drinking, this homey retreat, with its clubby atmosphere and wingback chairs, plus an inviting fire in winter, is a good choice, especially for single women who just want to have a quiet drink. A pianist entertains nightly. 150 Elgin St. (✆ **613/237-5353**).

**Full House** A similar upstairs parlor here provides piano entertainment and a playful atmosphere Wednesday to Saturday. 337 Somerset St. W. (✆ **613/238-6734**).

**Heart & Crown** Crammed almost every night from the bar to the wrap-around deck, a principal attraction here is live music Wednesday to Saturday, usually composed of rousing Celtic tunes joined in with infectious enthusiasm by patrons who know every word. Many English, Irish, and Canadian brews are on tap, with Harp and Guinness prominent. 67 Clarence St. (✆ **613/562-0674**).

**Patty's Pub** Sooner or later, every Ottawan of drinking age squeezes into this rollicking tavern, to raise a pint or two, tuck into fish-and-chips or Irish stew, and listen to the stirring Irish ballads rendered by a folk singer (resident Thurs–Sat). It's the kind of place where a brave leap into the fray will have you playing darts, chatting, and singing with the regulars in no time. 1186 Bank St. (✆ **613/730-2434**).

## GAY & LESBIAN BARS

***Capital XTRA!*** is Ottawa's gay/lesbian news-and-events magazine, a source for up-to-date info on the local scene.

**Club Polo Pub** This is the hot spot for dancing, with underwear parties and go-go dancers to spur you on, and it also features free pool and Internet access, with no cover and a full gamut of age ranges. A rooftop patio adds another element in summer. 65 Bank St., second floor (✆ **613/235-5995**).

**Coral Reef Club** Ottawa's oldest gay bar is underneath a parking garage (no flashy entrance here). Theme parties are frequent. A cover of about C$3 (US$2) is customary. Lesbians welcome. 30 Nicholas St. (✆ **613/234-5118**).

**Icon** Start with a bar and dance floor with pounding techno and industrial sounds and add female impersonators some nights and live music on the first Thursday of each month. The cover is usually modest, around C$2 (US$1.35). 366 Lisgar St. (✆ **613/235-4005**).

## DANCE CLUBS

Nightlife used to close down at 1am (11pm on Sun) in Ottawa but thumped on until 3am across the river in Hull. In recent years, though, the strip where most of the popular bars and clubs were located developed a reputation for late-night fights, muggings, even near riots. The authorities on both sides of the river acted, agreeing to synchronize closing times at 2am. That's taken the heat off, and the area is both calmer and less exciting.

**Au Zone** Farther along the same street is this popular destination, where the decor evokes an off-kilter Camelot and a hip-hop emphasis ensures crowds of decidedly younger revelers. 117 promenade du Portage (© **819/771-6677**).

**Hartwells** The disco in the lower level of the Westin Hotel fills with a 25-plus crowd for dancing to DJ selections Tuesday to Saturday. 11 Colonel By Dr. (© **613/560-7000**).

**Le Bop** In Hull, tucked away off promenade du Portage, this disco/bar/restaurant has a fairly new Italian menu to enhance its appeal to its mainly over-30 patrons. 9 Aubry St. (© **819/777-3700**).

**Zoe's** On Saturdays, there's dancing to live entertainment in this cushy lounge of the Hôtel Château Laurier. 1 Rideau St. (© **613/241-1414**).

## 8 Exploring Eastern Ontario: Kingston & More

From Port Hope, about 105km (65 miles) east of Toronto, the coast of Lake Ontario incorporates the Bay of Quinte and Quinte's Isle. Once off the main highway, Route 401, you'll discover a tranquil region of farms and orchards largely settled by United Empire Loyalists, who fled the new republic to the south during and after the American Revolution. It's still off the beaten track—except to those in the know, who come to explore the attractive villages, go antiquing, or enjoy the beaches, dunes, and waterfront activities of its provincial parks. Kingston, a most appealing lakefront town with a thrice-weekly flea-and-farmers' market, is intriguing both architecturally and historically. It's also the gateway to the mighty St. Lawrence River, the Thousand Islands, and the St. Lawrence National Park.

To get from Ottawa to this region, take Route 16/416 south to 401 west, which connects the towns, parks, and townships from Brockville to Port Hope. From Toronto, take Route 401 east. An especially beguiling detour is the Thousand Islands Parkway, running between Brockville and Kingston parallel to Route 401. That expressway, while swift, is heavily trafficked and often stressful—if you're looking for relaxation, avoid it when possible. The more scenic Route 2, while slower, is a desirable alternative, where available.

### KINGSTON ★

A 2-hour drive from Ottawa and about 3 hours from Toronto (172km/107 miles southwest of Ottawa, 255km/158 miles northeast of Toronto), Kingston cherishes its more than 300 years of history, which includes a brief tenure as capital of Canada. That rich heritage lingers in the grand old limestone public buildings and private residences lining the downtown streets and giving the city a gracious air, in the four martello towers that once formed a string of defense works guarding the waterways along the U.S.–Canadian border, and the Christopher Wren–style St. Georges Church, which contains a Tiffany window.

The city stands at the confluence of Lake Ontario, the Rideau Canal, and the St. Lawrence Seaway. This makes for remarkable scenery, best viewed by taking the **free ferry trip to Wolfe Island.** Ferries leave at frequent intervals for the sparsely populated island that doubles as a quiet offshore retreat of pronounced rural character. (See the box "Along the St. Lawrence: The Thousand Islands," below, for details about other seagoing sightseeing voyages.) A stroll along Kingston's waterfront, site of many hotels and restaurants as well as marinas, pocket parks, gardens, and a maritime museum, is also a must.

During summer, **Confederation Park** at the harbor is the site for band concerts, an August blues festival, and other performances, while in winter you might catch a local hockey contest. On Tuesdays, Thursdays, and Saturdays, a farmers' market is assembled behind the City Hall in **Market Square.** On Sundays, it's transformed into a flea market, with a few lingering produce stalls.

## ESSENTIALS

**GETTING THERE** If you're driving from Ottawa, take Route 16 south to 401 and drive west to the Kingston exits. Or, with a little more time, take the more scenic Route 2 instead of 401. From Toronto, take 401E to the Kingston exits. Several daily **VIA Rail** (✆ **888/VIA-RAIL;** www.viarail.ca) trains come from Ottawa, Toronto, and Montréal. **Voyageur** (✆ **613/238-5900;** www.voyageur.com) provides bus service from Montréal and Ottawa.

**VISITOR INFORMATION** Stop by the **Kingston Tourist Information Office,** 209 Ontario St., Kingston, ON K7L 2Z1 (✆ **613/548-4415**), on the waterfront across from the City Hall. Its attendants can help you find lodging and sell tickets for the bus tours that start out front. Check out **http://tourism.kingstoncanada.com** or **www.kingston-ontario.com** for more information.

## EXPLORING THE TOWN

A good way to get acquainted with the town is aboard the **Confederation Tour Trolley** (✆ **613/546-4453**), a bus made to look like a streetcar. It leaves from in front of the Kingston Tourist Information Office (above), every hour on the hour from mid-May to Labour day 10am to 5pm (to 7pm in July and Aug). The tour lasts 50 minutes and costs C$9.95 (US$7) for adults and C$7.95 (US$5) for seniors and youths. If you want to explore **Wolfe Island,** there's a free 25-minute trip aboard the **car ferry** from downtown Kingston; it departs frequently from the dock near the intersection of Queen and Ontario streets. For serious hiking, the Rideau Trail runs 388km (241 miles) along the canal from Kingston to Ottawa. For details, contact the **Rideau Trail Association** at ✆ **613/545-0823.**

Kingston spent decades of its early years anticipating an attack that never came, the reason for its still-evident defenses. You can view some of these along the waterfront, where **Confederation Park** stretches from the front of the old 19th-century town hall down to the yacht basin. Several blocks west of the park is one of the finest Martello towers, built during the Oregon Crisis of 1846 to withstand the severest of naval bombardments. The **Murney Tower** (✆ **613/544-9925**) is now a museum where you can see the basement storage rooms, the barrack room, and the gun platform. Mid-May to Labour Day, it's open daily 10am to 5pm, charging C$2 (US$1.35); children under 6 are free.

When exploring downtown and ambling along the waterfront, visit the **City Hall,** 2162 Ontario St. (✆ **613/546-4291**), where free guided tours are offered Monday to Friday 10am to 4pm and Saturday and Sunday 11am to 3pm. If there isn't enough time, at least take a look at the stained-glass windows upstairs in Memorial Hall, each one commemorating a World War I battle. It's open weekdays 8:30am to 4:30pm.

## Eastern Ontario

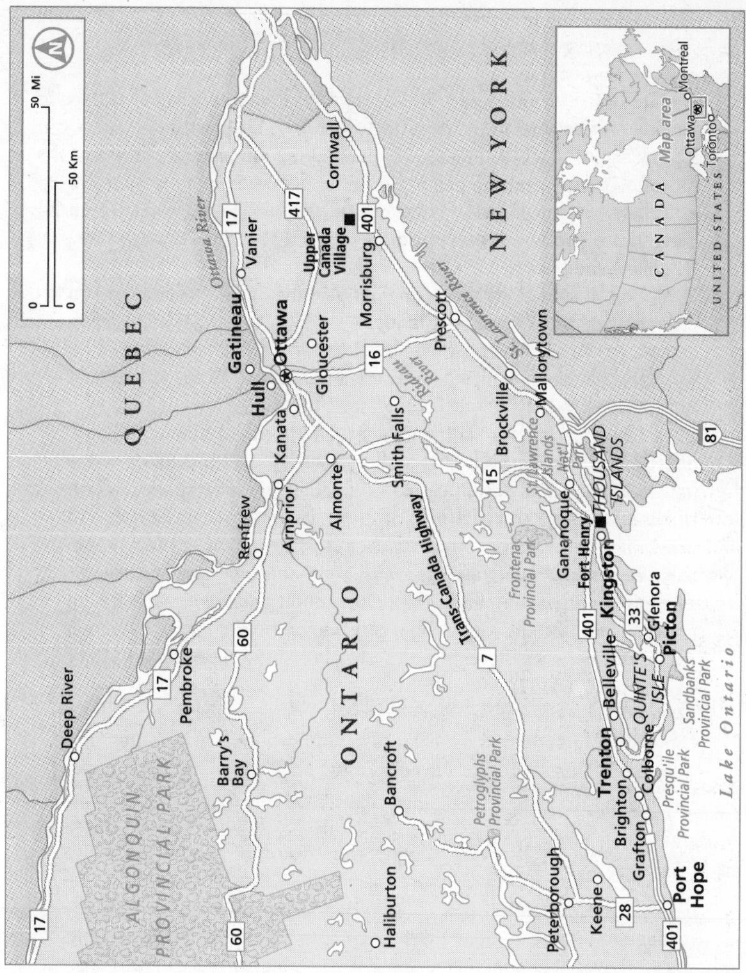


**Agnes Etherington Art Centre** On the campus of Queen's University, the Centre displays a fairly extensive, if somewhat disjointed, collection in seven galleries. The emphasis is Canadian, though also contained are gatherings of African sculpture and 16th- to 19th-century European masters. The center's heart is the original 19th-century home of benefactor Agnes Richardson Etherington (1880–1954) and features three rooms furnished in period style.

University Ave. at Queen's Crescent. ✆ **613/533-2190.** Admission C$4 (US$2.65) adults, C$2.50 (US$1.65) seniors, free for students and children. Free for all Thursday. Tues–Fri 10am–4:30pm, Sat–Sun 1–5pm.

**Bellevue House** On July 1, 1867, the Canadian Confederation was proclaimed in Kingston's Market Square. A chief architect of that momentous political construction was Canada's first Prime Minister, Sir John A. Macdonald. Kingston was his home for most of his life, and Macdonald lived at Bellevue House as a young lawyer and rising member of Parliament. The building is a

### *Tips* Along the St. Lawrence: The Thousand Islands

The St. Lawrence River was the main route into the heart of Upper Canada and beyond from the 17th to the mid–19th century, traveled first by explorers, fur traders, and missionaries and later by settlers en route to Ontario and the plains west. The river is a magnificent sight, especially where it flows around the outcroppings and pine-covered islets of the Thousand Islands region; in some stretches it's over 19km (12 miles) wide.

Along this part of its substantial length, the St. Lawrence is known primarily for the **Thousand Islands.** According to a Native-Canadian legend, petals of heavenly flowers fell to earth and were scattered on the river, creating Manitouana, the Garden of the Great Spirit. That isn't difficult to believe once you've seen them.

**St. Lawrence Islands National Park (The Thousand Islands)** is headquartered at 2 County Rd. 5, Mallorytown (✆ **613/923-5261;** www.parkscanada.pch.gc.ca/sli). Canada's smallest national park encompasses an 80km (50-mile) stretch of the St. Lawrence, from Kingston to Brockville. Along that length are a sufficiency of motels, cabin colonies, campgrounds, RV sites, and boat-launching sites, but development has been contained. The visitor center and headquarters is on the mainland, where you'll find a picnic area, beach, and nature trail. Access to the park's island facilities is via boat only; mooring is C$15 to C$26 (US$10–US$17) overnight, depending on boat size. Most of the islands have docking and picnicking facilities, available on a first-come, first-served basis. The largest campground has 18 sites; the smallest, 2. Three consecutive nights is the docking limit at each island. Parking is C$5 (US$3.35) per car at the Mallorytown Landing.

**Kingston** is a good jumping-off point for touring the Thousand Islands, especially if you're coming from Toronto. In summer, **cruise boats** circulate through the more than 1,800 islands, past such extraordinary sights as **Boldt Castle,** built on Heart Island in the early 1900s by millionaire George Boldt as a gift for his wife. (When she died suddenly, the work was abandoned, and it stands as a poignant relic of lost love.)

From Kingston Harbour at City Hall in May to mid-October, you can take a 3-hour cruise (C$17/US$11 for adults and C$9/US$6 for children ages 4–12) on the ***Island Queen,*** a triple-deck paddle wheeler. The 90-minute cruises (C$16/US$11 for adults and C$8/US$5 for children ages

stucco-faced, vaguely Italianate villa with green trim and a red roof, jokingly referred to as the "Pekoe Pagoda" and "Tea Caddy Castle" by many locals. Apple trees and hollyhocks fill the front yard, and costumed docents greet visitors. It has been restored to the period of 1848 to 1849.

35 Centre St. ✆ **613/545-8666.** Admission C$3 (US$2) adults, C$2.50 (US$1.65) seniors/students over 16, C$1.50 (US$1) children 6–15. June–Labour Day daily 9am–6pm; Apr–May and Labour Day–Oct daily 10am–5pm.

**Fort Henry** Fort Henry, erected in 1812 and largely unchanged since its reconstruction in the 1830s, commands a high promontory overlooking the

4–12) aboard its sister boat, the ***Island Belle,*** take in the Kingston Harbour and waterfront. Both boats are used for 2-hour sunset cruises. For details, call ✆ **613/549-5544** or check out **www.1000islandscruises.ca**. In season, the nimble catamaran ***Sea Fox II*** also cruises the islands and the harbor from the bottom of Brock Street in Kingston. The 2-hour islands tour is C$16 (US$11) for adults and C$8 (US$5) for children ages 6 to 12. For details, call ✆ **613/542-4271** or check out **www.travelinx.com**.

From Kingston, you can also cruise the Rideau Canal or explore the Thousand Islands aboard a houseboat. Contact any of the following: **Aquaventures,** P.O. Box 70, Brockville, ON K6V 5T7 (✆ **888/498-2727**); **Houseboat Holidays,** RR #3, Gananoque, ON K7G 2V5 (✆ **613/382-2842**); or **St. Lawrence River Houseboat and Cruiser Rentals,** c/o Halliday Point, Wolfe Island, ON K0H 2Y0 (✆ **613/385-2290**). Most houseboats sleep up to six and have fully equipped kitchens, hot and cold running water, and propane systems for heat and light. Weekly summer rentals on the canal system average C$1,000 to C$1,200 (US$667–US$800). On the St. Lawrence, in August, the cost starts at about C$600 (US$400) for a weekend and costs C$900 to C$1,250 (US$600–US$834) for a week. Prices are higher in July but lower in May, June, and September, as well as during the week. You need to bring only sleeping bags and towels.

From the waterfront in **Gananoque** in May to mid-October, the **Thousand Islands Gananoque Boat Line** (✆ **613/382-2144** or 613/382-2146; www.ganboatline.com) offers 3-hour and 1-hour cruises at C$16 and C$12 (US$11 and US$8), respectively; children ages 7 to 12 on both are C$6 (US$4). The longer cruise stops at the fantastical Boldt Castle. Note, though, that to visit the castle, which is in U.S. territory, you'll need the same ID you showed when crossing the Canada/U.S. border. Call ahead for the schedule. The same company operates 1-hour trips from **Ivy Lea,** leaving from west of the International Bridge on the Thousand Islands Parkway. The cost is C$12 (US$8) for adults and C$6 (US$4) for children ages 7 to 12. For a dramatic view from above, climb the Skydeck on Hill Island near Ivy Lea, which reaches 120m (400 ft.) above the river. On clear days, the reward is a sweeping 65km (40-mile) panoramic vista.

harbor and town. May 23 to Labour Day, the Fort Henry Guard and their goat mascot, David, perform 19th-century drills, musters, and parades. Regular programming includes music and marching displays by the fife-and-drum band, exhibitions of infantry drill, and mock battles of tall ships, many of them brought to a close with the firing of the garrison artillery and the lowering of the Union Jack. Parts of the fort—the officers' quarters, men's barracks, kitchens, and artisans' shops—have been restored to show the military way of life as it was around the year 1867. The most imposing events are the "Sunset Ceremonies," elaborate military tattoos with martial music performed Wednesdays at 7:30pm in July and August. Wednesdays in July and August, an extra treat is a three-course dinner served in the officers' dining room followed by seatings in bleachers or in the balcony to view the sunset ceremonies. This package costs C$48.95 (US$33) for adults, C$45.95 (US$31) for students, C$37.95 (US$25) for children ages 5 to 12, and C$6.50 (US$4.35) for children under 5.

On Rte. 2, just east of Kingston. ✆ **613/542-9127.** www.parks.on.ca/fort. Admission C$10.75 (US$7) adults, C$8.50 (US$6) ages 13-18, C$5.25 (US$3.50) children 5–12, C$1.50 (US$1) children 2–4. Sunset Ceremonies, C$14 (US$9) adults, C$8 (US$5) children 5–16, C$1.50 (US$1) children 2–4. Late May to early Oct daily 10am–5pm.

**Marine Museum of the Great Lakes** Stop by the Maritime Museum to get a handle on the importance of shipping on the Great Lakes, critical in the development of central Canada. With model boats, memorabilia, vintage photos, and salvaged engines, it outlines the evolution from sail in the 17th century to steam in the 19th century and from the great schooners in the 1870s to today's bulk carriers that still ply these waters. Moored at the far end of the museum is the 64m (210-ft.) **Alexander Henry Museum Ship** (✆ **613/542-2261**). It can be toured, and it also functions as a bed & breakfast with 25 compact cabins available from mid-May to September 30th; rates per cabin are C$50 to C$70 (US$33 to US$47).

55 Ontario St. ✆ **613/542-2261.** www.marmus.ca. Admission C$4.25 (US$2.85) adults, C$3.75 (US$2.50) seniors/students; children under 6 free. May–Oct daily 10am–5pm, Nov–Apr Mon–Fri 10am–4pm.

**Royal Military College Museum** The Royal Military College, Canada's West Point, is across Navy Bay from Fort Henry. The campus occupies the site of a Royal Navy Dockyard, which played a key role in the War of 1812. Though you can tour the grounds year-round, the museum, in a large martello tower, is open only in summer. It houses displays about the college's history and Kingston's Royal Dockyard, plus the Douglas collection of small arms and weapons.

On Point Frederick. ✆ **613/541-6000,** ext. 6664. Free admission. Museum July–Labour Day daily 10am–5pm.

## SIDE TRIPS TO FRONTENAC PROVINCIAL PARK & UPPER CANADA VILLAGE

**Frontenac Provincial Park** (✆ **613/376-3489**), near Sydenham about 143km (89 miles) from Kingston and 72km (45 miles) from Ottawa, is a wilderness park with more than 182km (113 miles) of hiking trails that explore such intriguing areas as Moulton Gorge, the Arkon Lake bogs, and the Connor-Daly mine.

There are also terrific opportunities here to combine camping with self-propelled water journeys. The adventure might include sea-kayaking among the Thousand Islands. Local outfitters can provide all the equipment—canoes, kayaks, paddles, life jackets, car-top carriers, tents, sleeping bags, stoves, and utensils—for relatively modest fees, ranging from C$22 to C$29 (US$15–US$19) per person per day. Trips run April to November. For details, contact **Frontenac Outfitters** at ✆ **613/376-6220** (in season) or 613/382-1039 (off-season).

About 50km (31 miles) east of Brockville along Route 2, **Upper Canada Village,** just east of Morrisburg (✆ **613/543-3704**), is Ontario's effort to preserve its pre-Dominion past, a riverfront museum village representing frontier life in the 1860s. Some 40 brick-and-stone structures and interiors have been accurately restored using hand-forged nails and wooden pegs. They appear as if still inhabited, especially because they're occupied by costumed bilingual docents who perform the chores and crafts of the time (sew quilts, mill lumber, fashion tinware, conduct church services) and answer questions. In the woolen mill, the waterwheel turns the old machinery weaving wool into blankets, the bellows wheeze and hammers clang on anvils in the blacksmith's shop, and the heady aroma of fresh bread drifts from the bake shop near Willard's Hotel (early Apr to late Oct, stop at the hotel for lunch or high tea). "True Canadian" draft horses draw both tour wagons and the barge on the carp-filled canal cutting through from the river to a small lake behind the village. Admission is C$13 (US$9) for adults, C$12 (US$8) for seniors, C$9 (US$6) for students, and C$6 (US$4) for children ages 6 to 12; children under 6 are free, and families get a 10% discount. From May to Canadian Thanksgiving, it's open daily 9:30am to 5pm.

## WHERE TO STAY

Three chains commandeer prime positions beside the harbor—the **Holiday Inn,** 1 Princess St. (✆ **800/549-8400** or 613/549-8400), charging C$110 to C$190 (US$73–US$127) double; the **Howard Johnson Kingston,** 237 Ontario St. (✆ **800/446-4656** or 613/549-6300), charging C$69 to C$179 (US$46–US$119); and the **Ramada Plaza Harbourfront,** 1 Johnson St. (✆ **800/272-6232** or 613/549-8100), charging C$130 to C$170 (US$87–US$113). And there's a **Comfort Inn** at 1454 Princess St. (✆ **800/228-5150** or 613/549-5550), charging C$69 to C$115 (US$46–US$77) double.

**Best Western Fireside Inn** ★ Put aside preconceptions about motels with the Best Western logo. The lounge off the lobby looks like a Yukon cabin, with log siding, a moose head, and wing chairs. *Every* room has a gas fireplace, Canadian pine furnishings, and an unstocked fridge. Spring for a fantasy suite and your bed might be in a real Rolls-Royce, in the basket of a 2½-story-high hot air balloon, or in a simulated "Tranquility Moon Base." Lesser suites have whirlpools next to the fireplaces. Even the most ordinary rooms trump most big-city hotels for comfort (not counting the thin towels), equipped with puffy quilts, sofas, and shelves of old books. The Bistro Stefan is unexpectedly capable.

1217 Princess St., Kingston, ON K7M 3E1. ✆ **800/567-8800** in Ontario and Québec, 800/528-1234 elsewhere, or 613/549-2211. Fax 613/549-4523. www.bestwestern.kingston.on.ca. 77 units. C$126 (US$84) double; C$209–C$269 (US$139–US$179) suite. Suites and corporate rates include full breakfast Mon–Fri. AE, DC, MC, V. **Amenities:** Restaurant (International), lounge; heated outdoor pool; limited room service; same-day dry cleaning/laundry. *In room:* A/C, TV w/pay movies, dataport, unstocked fridge, coffeemaker, hair dryer, iron, safe.

**Four Points Hotel & Suites** ★★ The newest hotel in town has the sterile whiff of a furniture showroom, not yet dented and scraped by human use. That is hardly a bad thing. All is whisker-clean, unstained, sturdy, and ready to deal with messy humanity. The location is excellent, views of town and lake from the upper floors unobstructed, the staff ever-ready to help (if not always precise in their directions). There are six rooms for disabled guests. The 47 suites have unstocked fridges and microwaves, and all have Playstations and high-speed Internet access. Parking in the underground garage is complimentary.

285 King St. East, Kingston, ON K7L 3B1. ✆ **888/478-4333** or 613/544-4434. Fax 613/548-1782. www.fourpoints.com. 171 units. C$99–C$144 (US$66–US$96) double, from C$154 (US$103) suite. **Amenities:** Restaurant (International), bar; heated indoor pool with whirlpool; decently equipped exercise room with access to sun deck; business center; limited room service; coin-op washers and dryers; same-day dry cleaning; nonsmoking rooms. *In room:* A/C, TV w/pay movies, dataport, coffeemaker, hair dryer, iron.

**Hochelaga Inn** All the guest rooms are distinctively furnished in this 1880s Victorian. A favorite is no. 301, an oddly shaped space with love seat and a bed set on a diagonal, a large armoire, while steps lead to an 11-sided tower with windows, and a stepladder reaches a tiny sitting area. Other rooms are furnished with oak pieces and wing chairs. Enjoy the common sitting room with its carved ebony fireplace, or take a seat on the veranda viewing the garden.

24 Sydenham St., Kingston, ON K7L 3G9. ✆ **877/933-9433** or ✆ and fax 613/549-5534. www.someplacesdifferent.com. 23 units. C$145–C$190 (US$97–US$127) double. Extra person C$15 (US$10). Rates include buffet breakfast. AE, MC, V. *In room:* A/C, TV, dataport, hair dryer.

**Hotel Belvedere** ★ Many regulars list this as their first choice in Kingston. The mansard-roofed brick mansion is in a residential district several blocks west of the downtown hubbub. All the rooms have large beds and sitting areas, and some have whirlpool baths. Typical of the diversity of the decor is no. 204, with a tile-faced fireplace, tasseled curtains, and a bed with a lace-embroidered coverlet. Relax in the elegant sitting room with a coal-burning fireplace and French windows opening onto a porch with tables and chairs and plants in classical urns.

141 King St. E., Kingston, ON K7L 2Z9. ✆ **800/559-0584** or 613/548-1565. Fax 613/546-4692. www.hotelbelvedere.com. 20 units. C$110–C$195 (US$73–US$130) double. Special weekend rates. Rates include continental breakfast. AE, DC, MC, V. **Amenities:** Bike rental; limited room service; babysitting; same-day dry cleaning/laundry. *In room:* A/C, TV, dataport.

**Prince George Hotel** Often overlooked due to its modest entrance between cafe terrace tables, this most satisfactory hotel (no elevator) has origins dating all the way to 1809. There have been many face-lifts since then, and it has taken in guests since the mid-19th century. Guest rooms are easily large enough to contain king or queen beds, armoire closets, and spacious sitting areas, most with pull-out sofas. It's right in the middle of things, downtown next to City Hall, and there are entrances from the lobby into a martini lounge and a sprawling pub/restaurant, Tir na n'Og.

200 Ontario St., Kingston, ON K7L 2Y9. ✆ **613/547-9037.** Fax 613/542-5297. 28 units. C$90–C$175 (US$60–US$117) double. AE, DC, MC, V. **Amenities:** Restaurant (Pub), 2 bars. *In room:* A/C, TV, coffeemaker, hair dryer

## WHERE TO DINE

**Casa Dominico** ★ ITALIAN The front windows open in summer, a fireplace blazes in winter, and this upscale downtown rendezvous chatters blissfully away almost every night of the year. New patrons know what they're getting into when the server brings a basket of bread and pours a saucer of spiced extra-virgin olive oil for dipping. Clearly, this isn't a red-sauce-and-spag joint, and even the *vitello modeira*—veal scallopine in a shallot, wild mushroom, Madeira demiglaz—is cuts above the norm. Popular with large celebratory parties as well as amatory couples, and with brick-and-stone walls and bare floors doing little to baffle the uproar, a quiet hour or two is not to be expected. The food is worth it, and the waitstaff is fleetingly attentive.

35 Brock St. ✆ **613/542-0870.** Reservations recommended. Main courses C$18–C$26 (US$12–US$17). AE, MC, V. Mon–Sat 11:30am–2:30pm and 5–10pm (until 11pm Fri–Sat), Sun 5–10pm.

**Chez Piggy** ★ ECLECTIC Kingston's most popular restaurant is just off Princess Street in a complex of renovated 19th Century buildings. Out front is a paved dining courtyard, and inside are a long bar with director's chairs and an upstairs dining room enhanced by two striking Tunisian rugs. Along with daily specials, fixed menu possibilities include duck leg confit with braised red cabbage, monkfish with spicy cilantro sauce, and any one of the half-dozen pastas. To begin, there are several salads and such dishes as mussels *piri piri* (steamed, with perky Portuguese chili oil). Representative of the high quality and fair prices is Sunday brunch, at only C$7.95 (US$5). Those dishes deviate from the usual, too, like the teriyaki salmon with wasabi mayo or fried chorizo with black-bean cakes and eggs.

68R Princess St. ✆ **613/549-7673.** Reservations recommended on weekends. Main courses C$17.50–C$23 (US$12–US$15). AE, DC, MC, V. Mon–Sat 11:30am–midnight, Sun 11am–10pm.

**Hoppin' Eddie's** CREOLE/CAJUN This funky-as-all-get-out interior looks as if it had been airlifted intact from the lip of Louisiana bayou a quick hop from the Big Easy. Since the food wears that cloak too, this isn't a place for you if you don't like your eats spicy-hot. What issues from the open kitchen are jambalaya, blackened catfish, and several po' boy sandwiches. Oysters (when available) are opened to order and served on ice. They're prepared at the big bar, where more eating than boozing goes on, at least until late. Fans of hot sauce will want to stop by the kitchen, where a dozen shelves display more bottled brands than they knew existed, with names like Global Warming, Endorphin Rush, After Death, and Scorned Woman.

393 Princess St. ✆ **613/531-9770.** Main courses C$14.95–C$21.95 (US$10–US$15). AE, MC, V. Daily 11:30am–10pm (to 11pm Fri–Sat).

**Kingston Brewing Company** PUB FARE Peer through the window behind the bar at the huge brewing tanks in this, one of Ontario's earliest microbrew pubs. Beer, several ales, and a pleasant lager are produced there, the best-known of which is Dragon's Breath ale, so rich as to be almost syrupy. Locals come here for substantial victuals of the brewhouse kind—monster burgers, fat onion rings, pizzas, smoked beef and ribs, and charbroiled chicken wings with fiery barbecue sauce, as well as curries and pastas. All is served inside at polished wood tables, in the rear courtyard, or on the covered sidewalk terrace.

34 Clarence St. ✆ **613/542-4978.** Most items under C$10 (US$7). AE, DC, MC, V. Mon–Sat 11am–1am, Sun 11:30am–1am.

# 10

# Toronto & the Golden Horseshoe

*By Hilary Davidson*

Chances are that even if you've never set foot in Toronto, you've seen the city a hundred times over. Known for the past decade as Hollywood North, Toronto has stood in for international centers from European capitals to New York. Rarely does it play itself. Self-deprecating Torontonians embody a paradox: Proud of their city's architectural, cultural, and culinary charms, they are unsure whether it's all up to international snuff.

After spending a single afternoon wandering around Toronto, you might wonder why this is a question at all. The sprawling city boasts lush parks, renowned architecture, and excellent galleries. There's no shortage of skyscrapers, particularly in the downtown core. Still, many visitors marvel at the number of Torontonians who live in houses on tree-lined boulevards that are a walk or a bike ride away from work.

Out-of-towners can see the fun side of the place, but Torontonians aren't so sure. They recall the stuffiness of the city's past. Often called "Toronto the Good," it was a town where you could walk down any street in safety, but you couldn't get a drink on Sunday.

Then a funny thing happened on the way through the 1970s. Canada loosened its immigration policies and welcomed waves of Italians, Greeks, Chinese, Vietnamese, Jamaicans, Indians, Somalis, and others, many of whom settled in Toronto. Political unrest in Quebec drove out Anglophones, many into the waiting arms of Toronto. The city's economy flourished, which in turn gave its cultural side a boost.

Natives and visitors alike feel the benefits of this rich cultural mosaic. More than 5,000 restaurants are scattered across the city, serving everything from simple Greek souvlaki to five-star, Asian-accented fusion cuisine. Festivals such as Caribana and Caravan draw tremendous crowds to celebrate heritage through music and dance. Its newfound cosmopolitanism has made Toronto a key player on the arts scene, too. The Toronto International Film Festival in September and the International Festival of Authors in October draw top stars of the film and publishing worlds. The theater scene rivals London's and New York's.

Toronto now ranks at or near the top of any international urban quality-of-life study. The city has accomplished something rare, expanding and developing its daring side while holding on to its traditional strengths. It's a great place to visit, but watch out: You might just end up wanting to live here.

At the end of this chapter, we cover our favorite parts of the stretch of the Ontario lakefront that is often called the Golden Horseshoe. *Golden* because the communities along the lake are wealthy, *horseshoe* because of its shape, this stretch of the Ontario lakefront from Niagara-on-the-Lake to Toronto offers the visitor some golden opportunities: **Niagara Falls** itself; **Niagara-on-the-Lake,** home of the famous Shaw Festival; the **Welland Canal,** an engineering wonder; Niagara **wineries;** and Dundurn Castle and Royal Botanical Gardens in Canada's steel town of **Hamilton.** Niagara Falls, Niagara-on-the-Lake, St. Catharines to Port Colborne, and Hamilton can be visited together. The best way to see them is to take the Niagara Parkway from Niagara-on-the-Lake to Niagara Falls and then drive to Port Colborne on Lake Erie and follow the Welland Canal north to Port Dalhousie on Lake Ontario. Although this is, for the most part, a densely populated area with a tangled network of roads, there are several scenic routes: the parkway and the Wine Route, which takes you from Stoney Creek to Niagara Falls.

## 1 Essentials

### GETTING THERE

**BY PLANE** Most flights arrive at **Pearson International Airport** (© **905/676-3506** for terminals 1 and 2 information, 905/612-5100 for terminal 3; www.gtaa.com), in the northwest corner of Metro Toronto, approximately 30 minutes from downtown. The trip will invariably take 10 to 15 minutes longer during the weekday morning rush (7–9am). A few (mostly commuter) flights land at the **Toronto City Centre Airport** (© **416/203-6942;** www.torontoport.com/TCCA.htm), a short ferry ride from downtown.

Pearson has three terminals, and is served by more than 50 airlines. The most impressive terminal is the **Trillium Terminal 3.** This airy, modern facility has moving walkways, a huge food court, and many retail stores. There is a new, equally grand terminal currently under construction, which will one day replace the existing terminals 1 and 2.

To get from the airport to downtown, take Highway 427 south to the Gardiner Expressway East. A **taxi** costs about C$36 (US$23). A slightly sleeker way to go is by flat-rate **limousine,** which costs around C$40 (US$25). Two limo services are **Aaroport** (© **416/745-1555**) and **AirLine** (© **905/676-3210**). You don't need a reservation. Most first-class hotels run their own **hotel limousine** services; check when you make your reservation.

The convenient **Airport Express bus** (© **905/564-6333**) travels between the airport, the bus terminal, and all major downtown hotels—Harbour Castle Westin, the Royal York, Crowne Plaza Toronto Centre, the Sheraton Centre, and the Delta

Chelsea Inn—every 20 minutes all day. The adult fare is C$12.50 (US$8) one-way, C$21.50 (US$13) round-trip; children under 11 accompanied by an adult ride free.

The cheapest way to go is by **bus and subway,** which takes about an hour. From Terminal 2, take bus 58 to Lawrence West station, bus 192 "Airport Rocket" to Kipling station, or bus 307 to Eglinton West station. From Terminal 3 you can catch only bus 192; there are no TTC buses from Terminal 1 (though there is a shuttle that will drop you off at Terminal 2 or 3). The fare of C$2.25 (US$1.40) includes free transfer to the subway. For more information, call © **416/393-4636.**

**BY CAR** From the United States you are most likely to enter Toronto via Highway 401, or via Highway 2 and the Queen Elizabeth Way if you come from the west. If you come from the east via Montréal, you'll also use highways 401 and 2.

## Metropolitan Toronto

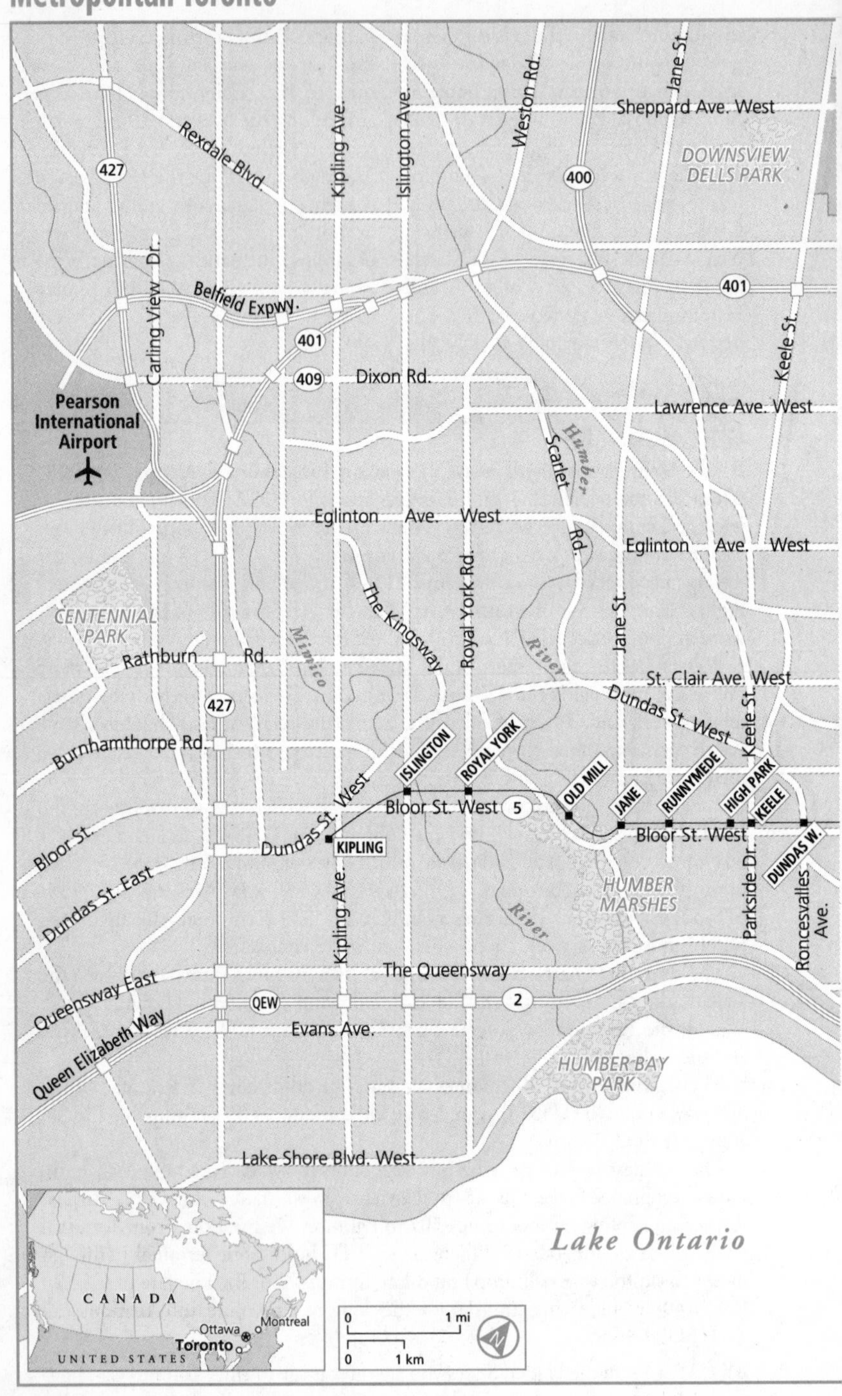

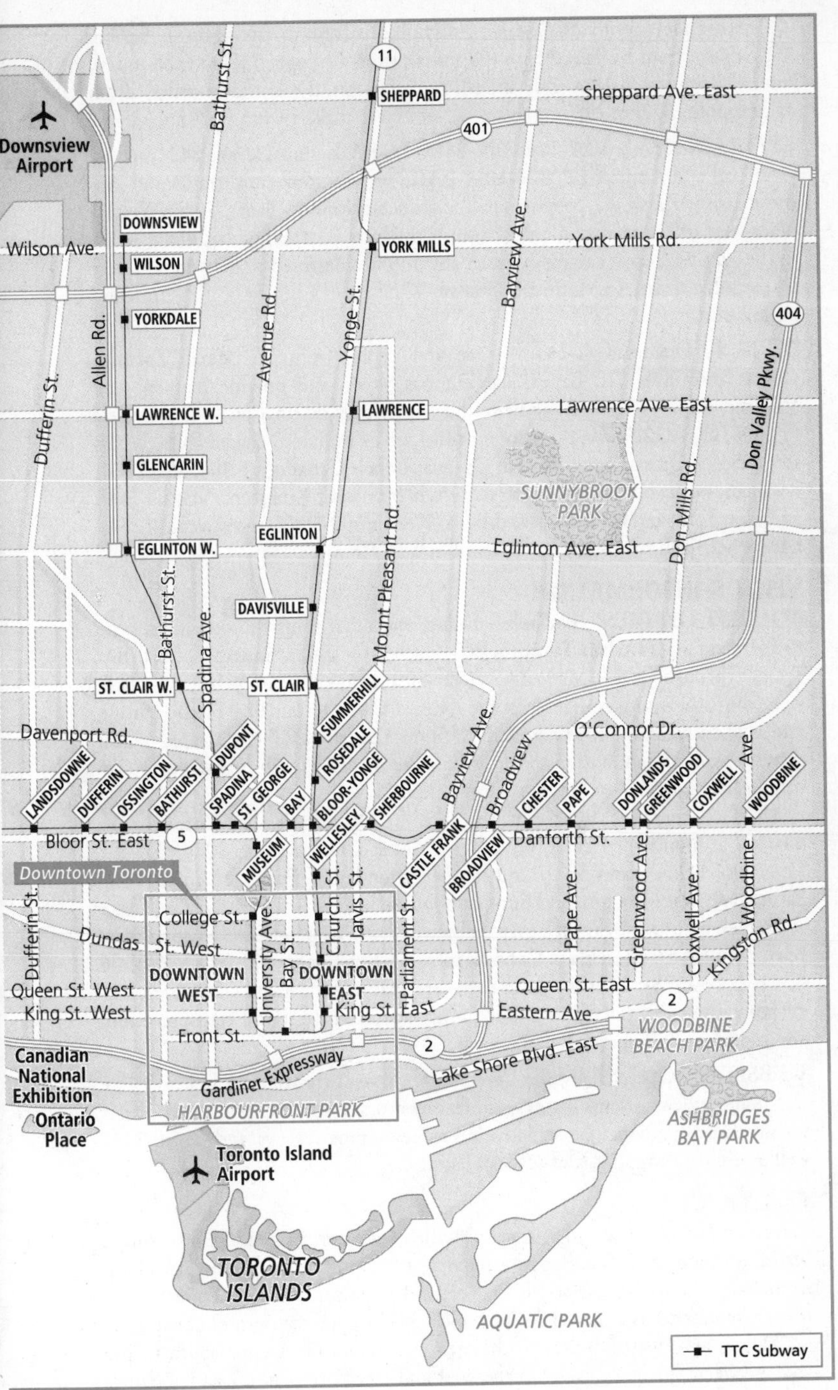
Downsview Airport
Sheppard Ave. East
York Mills Rd.
Wilson Ave.
Lawrence Ave. East
Eglinton Ave. East
Davenport Rd.
O'Connor Dr.
Bloor St. East
Danforth St.
College St.
Dundas St. West
Queen St. West
King St. West
Front St.
Queen St. East
King St. East
Eastern Ave.
Kingston Rd.
Lake Shore Blvd. East
Gardiner Expressway
Bathurst St.
Avenue Rd.
Yonge St.
Bayview Ave.
Allen Rd.
Dufferin St.
Don Valley Pkwy.
Don Mills Rd.
Mount Pleasant Rd.
Spadina Ave.
Broadview
Woodbine Ave.
University Ave.
Bay St.
Church St.
Jarvis St.
Parliament St.
Pape Ave.
Greenwood Ave.
Coxwell Ave.
11
401
404
5
2
SHEPPARD
YORK MILLS
LAWRENCE
EGLINTON
DAVISVILLE
ST. CLAIR
SUMMERHILL
ROSEDALE
BLOOR-YONGE
WELLESLEY
DOWNSVIEW
WILSON
YORKDALE
LAWRENCE W.
GLENCARIN
EGLINTON W.
ST. CLAIR W.
DUPONT
SPADINA
ST. GEORGE
BAY
MUSEUM
LANDSDOWNE
DUFFERIN
OSSINGTON
BATHURST
SHERBOURNE
CASTLE FRANK
BROADVIEW
CHESTER
PAPE
DONLANDS
GREENWOOD
COXWELL
WOODBINE
SUNNYBROOK PARK
Downtown Toronto
DOWNTOWN WEST
DOWNTOWN EAST
WOODBINE BEACH PARK
Canadian National Exhibition
Ontario Place
HARBOURFRONT PARK
ASHBRIDGES BAY PARK
Toronto Island Airport
TORONTO ISLANDS
AQUATIC PARK
TTC Subway

Here are a few approximate driving distances to Toronto: from Boston, 566km (340 miles); from Buffalo, 96km (58 miles); from Chicago, 534km (320 miles); from Cincinnati, 501km (301 miles); from Detroit, 236km (142 miles); from Minneapolis, 972km (583 miles); and from New York, 495km (297 miles).

**BY TRAIN** Both **VIA Rail** (© **888/VIA-RAIL** or 416/366-8411; www.viarail.ca) and **Amtrak** (© **800/USA-RAIL;** www.amtrak.com) trains pull into the massive, classically proportioned **Union Station,** 65 Front Street West, 1 block west of Yonge opposite the Royal York Hotel. The station has direct access to the subway so you can easily reach any Toronto destination from here. There is scheduled service to Montréal, Ottawa, Windsor, Niagara Falls, New York and points west.

**BY BUS** Out-of-town buses arrive and depart from the **Metro Toronto Coach Terminal,** 610 Bay St., at Dundas Street, and provide frequent and efficient service from Canadian and American destinations. **Greyhound** (© **800/231-2222;** www.greyhound.com) serves Buffalo, Niagara Falls, Windsor, Detroit, Ottawa, and Western Canada; **Coach Canada** (© **800/461-7661;** www.coachcanada.com) offers service from Montréal, Kingston, Niagara Falls, and New York; and **Ontario Northland** (© **416/393-7911;** www.webusit.com) has service from towns such as North Bay and Timmins.

## VISITOR INFORMATION

**TOURIST OFFICES** For hotel, dining, and other tourist information, head to (or write to) **Tourism Toronto,** 207 Queens Quay W., Suite 590 (P.O. Box 126), Toronto, ON M5J 1A7 (© **800/363-1990** or 416/203-2600; www.tourismtoronto.com). It's in the Queens Quay Terminal at Harbourfront, and is open Monday to Friday 9am to 5pm. Take the LRT (light rapid transit system) from Union Station to the York Street stop. The website has up-to-the-minute city calendar and events information.

More conveniently located is the drop-in **Ontario Visitor Information Centre,** in the Eaton Centre, on Yonge Street at Dundas Street. It's on Level 1 (one floor below street level) and is open Monday to Friday 10am to 9pm, Saturday 9:30am to 6pm, and Sunday noon to 5pm.

To pick up brochures and a map before you leave **Pearson International Airport,** stop by the **Transport Canada Information Centre** (© **905/676-3506** or 416/247-7678). There's one in each terminal. A staff fluent in a dozen languages can answer questions about tourist attractions, ground transportation, and more.

**WEBSITES** Operated by the *Toronto Star,* **www.toronto.com** has extensive restaurant reviews, events listings and feature articles. Another popular choice is **www.torontolife.com**, particularly for its restaurant reviews and contests, as well as events, shopping, and services listings.

## CITY LAYOUT

Toronto is laid out in a grid system . . . with a few interesting exceptions. **Yonge Street** (pronounced *Young*) is the main north-south thoroughfare, stretching from Lake Ontario in the south well beyond Highway 401 in the north. The main east-west artery is **Bloor Street,** which cuts through the heart of downtown.

"Downtown" usually refers to the area from Eglinton Avenue south to the lake, between Spadina Avenue in the west and Jarvis Street in the east. Because this is such a large area, I have divided it into **Downtown West** (from the lake north to College Street; the eastern boundary is Yonge Street), **Downtown East** (from the lake north to Carlton Street, east of Yonge Street); **Midtown West** (College Street north to Davenport Road, west of Yonge Street); **Midtown East/The East End** (Carlton Street north to Davenport Road and further east along Danforth Avenue, east of Yonge Street); and **Uptown** (north of Davenport Road). In Downtown West, you'll find many of the lakeshore attractions—Harbourfront, Ontario Place, Fort York, Exhibition Place, and the Toronto Islands. It also boasts the CN Tower, City Hall, the SkyDome, Chinatown, the Art Gallery, and the Eaton Centre. Downtown East includes the St. Lawrence Market, the Hummingbird Centre, the St. Lawrence Centre for the Arts, and St. James Cathedral. Midtown West includes the Royal Ontario Museum, the Gardiner Museum, the University of Toronto, Markham Village, and chic Yorkville, a prime area for browsing and dining alfresco. Midtown East/The East End features Riverdale Farm, the historic Necropolis cemetery, and Greektown. Uptown has traditionally been a residential area, but it's now a fast-growing entertainment area, too. Its attractions include the Sunnybrook park system and the Ontario Science Centre.

Toronto sprawls so widely that quite a few of its primary attractions lie outside the downtown core. They include the Toronto Zoo, Paramount Canada's Wonderland, and the McMichael Canadian Art Collection. Be prepared to journey somewhat.

There's also underground Toronto. You can walk from the Dundas subway station south through the Eaton Centre until you hit Queen Street, turn west to the Sheraton Centre, then head south. You'll pass through the Richmond-Adelaide Centre, First Canadian Place, and Toronto Dominion Centre, and go all the way (through the dramatic Royal Bank Plaza) to Union Station. En route, branches lead off to the stock exchange, Sun Life Centre, and Metro Hall. Additional walkways link Simcoe Plaza to 200 Wellington West and to the CBC Broadcast Centre. Other walkways run around Bloor Street and Yonge Street and elsewhere in the city. While its wide-ranging network makes this an excellent way to get around the downtown core when the weather is grim, the underground city has its own attractions, too. First Canadian Place in particular is known for hosting free lunch-hour lectures, opera and dance performances, and art exhibits.

## 2 Getting Around

The **Toronto Transit Commission,** or TTC (© **416/393-4636** for 24-hour information; www.city.toronto.on.ca/ttc), operates the subway, bus, streetcar, and light rapid transit (LRT) system. **Fares** (including transfers to buses or streetcars) are C$2.25 (US$1.40) or 10 tickets for C$18 (US$11) for adults. Students under 20 and seniors pay C$1.50 (US95¢), 10 tickets for C$12 (US$7) Children under 12 pay C50¢ (US30¢), 10 tickets for C$4 (US$2.50). You can buy a special day pass C$7.50 (US$4.65) that's good for unlimited travel for one person after 9:30am on weekdays, and good for up to six people (a maximum of two adults) anytime on Sunday and holidays. There's no Saturday pass, and no multiple-day deals.

For surface transportation, you need a ticket, a token, or exact change. You can buy tickets and tokens at subway entrances and at authorized stores that display the sign TTC TICKETS MAY BE PURCHASED HERE. Bus drivers do not sell tickets, nor will they make change. Always obtain a free transfer *where you board the train or bus,* in case you need it. In the subways, use the push-button machine just inside the entrance. On streetcars and buses, ask the driver for a transfer.

**THE SUBWAY** It's fast (especially when you compare it to snarly surface traffic), clean, and very simple to use. There are two lines—Bloor-Danforth and Yonge-University-Spadina—that basically form a cross. The Bloor Street east-west line runs from Kipling Avenue in the west to Kennedy Road in the east (where it connects with Scarborough Rapid Transit to Scarborough Centre and McCowan Rd.). The Yonge Street north-south line runs from Finch Avenue in the north to Union Station (Front St.) in the south. From there, it loops north along University Avenue and connects with the Bloor line at the St. George station. A Spadina extension runs north from St. George to Downsview station at Sheppard Avenue.

The light rapid transit (LRT) system connects downtown to Harbourfront. The fare is one ticket or token. It runs from Union Station along Queen's Quay to Spadina, with stops at Queen's Quay ferry docks, York Street, Simcoe Street, and Rees Street, then continues up Spadina to the Spadina subway station. The transfer from the subway to the LRT (and vice versa) at Union Station is free.

The subway operates Monday to Saturday 6am to 1:30am and Sunday 9am to 1:30am. From 1am to 5:30am, the Blue Night Network operates on basic surface routes. It runs about every 30 minutes. For route information, pick up a "Ride Guide" at subway entrances or call ✆ **416/393-4636.** You can also use the automated information service at ✆ **416/393-8663.**

Smart commuters park their cars at subway terminal stations at Kipling, Islington, Finch, Wilson, Warden, Kennedy, York Mills, Victoria Park, and Keele. Certain conditions apply. Call ✆ **416/393-8663** for details. You'll have to get there very early.

**BUSES & STREETCARS** Where the subway leaves off, buses and streetcars take over. They run east-west and north-south along the city's arteries. When you pay your fare (on bus, streetcar, or subway), always pick up a transfer, so that if you want to transfer to another mode of transportation, you won't have to pay another fare.

## BY TAXI

As usual, this is an expensive mode of transportation. It's C$2.50 (US$1.55) the minute you step in, and C25¢ (US15¢) for each additional quarter of a kilometer (fifteenth of a mile). Cab fares can quickly mount up, especially during rush hours. You can hail a cab on the street, find one in line in front of a big hotel, or call one of the major companies—**Diamond** (✆ **416/366-6868**), **Royal** (✆ **416/777-9222**), or **Metro** (✆ **416/504-8294**). If you experience problems with cab service, call the Metro Licensing Commission (✆ **416/392-3082**).

## BY CAR

**The Canadian Automobile Association** (CAA), 60 Commerce Valley Dr. E., Thornhill (✆ **905/771-3111**), provides aid to any driver who is a member of AAA.

**RENTALS** You can rent cars from any of the major companies at the airport. In addition, **Budget** has a convenient location at 141 Bay St. (✆ **416/364-7104**), and **Tilden** is at 930 Yonge St. (✆ **416/925-4551**).

**PARKING** Parking lots downtown run about C$4 to $6 (US$2.50–US$3.70) per half hour, with a C$16 to $20 (US$10–$12) maximum between 7am and 6pm. After 6pm and on Sunday, rates drop to around C$8 (US$5). Generally the city-owned lots, marked with a big green "P," are slightly cheaper than private

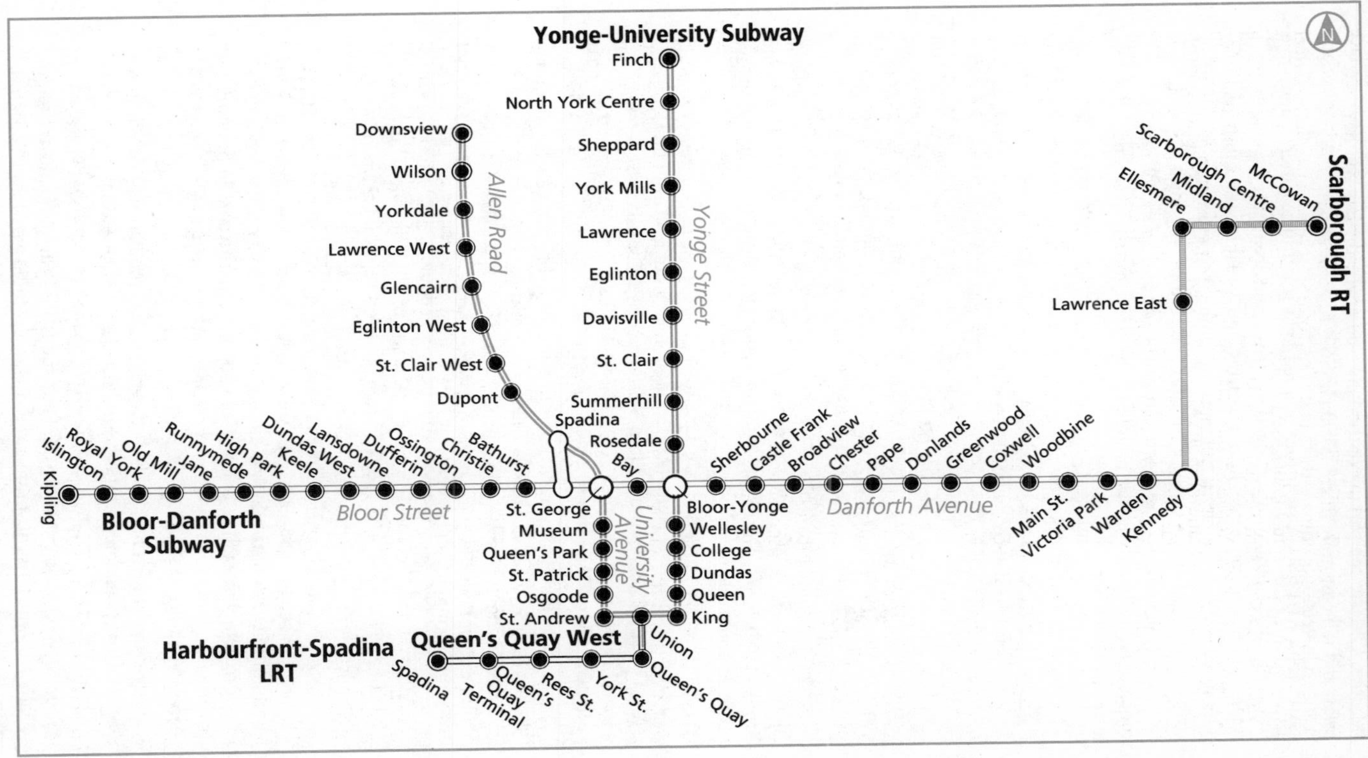
Yonge-University Subway
Finch
North York Centre
Sheppard
York Mills
Lawrence
Eglinton
Davisville
St. Clair
Summerhill
Rosedale
Yonge Street
Downsview
Wilson
Yorkdale
Lawrence West
Glencairn
Eglinton West
St. Clair West
Dupont
Allen Road
Spadina
Scarborough RT
McCowan
Scarborough Centre
Midland
Ellesmere
Lawrence East
Kipling
Islington
Royal York
Old Mill
Jane
Runnymede
High Park
Keele
Dundas West
Lansdowne
Dufferin
Ossington
Christie
Bathurst
Bay
Sherbourne
Castle Frank
Broadview
Chester
Pape
Donlands
Greenwood
Coxwell
Woodbine
Main St.
Victoria Park
Warden
Kennedy
Bloor-Danforth Subway
Bloor Street
Danforth Avenue
St. George
Museum
Queen's Park
St. Patrick
Osgoode
St. Andrew
University Avenue
Bloor-Yonge
Wellesley
College
Dundas
Queen
King
Union
Harbourfront-Spadina LRT
Queen's Quay West
Spadina
Queen's Quay Terminal
Rees St.
York St.
Queen's Quay

facilities. Observe the parking restrictions—otherwise the city will tow your car away, and it'll cost more than C$100 (US$62) to get it back.

**DRIVING RULES** A right turn at a red light is permitted after coming to a full stop, unless posted otherwise. The driver and front-seat passengers must wear seat belts; if you're caught not wearing one, you'll incur a substantial fine. The speed limit in the city is 50kmph (30 mph). You must stop at pedestrian crosswalks. If you are following a streetcar and it stops, you must stop well back from the rear doors so passengers can exit easily and safely. (Where there are concrete safety islands in the middle of the street for streetcar stops, this rule does not apply, but exercise care nonetheless.) Radar detectors are illegal.

## *FAST FACTS:* Toronto

*American Express* The **American Express Travel Service** offices are located at the Holt Renfrew Building, 50 Bloor St. W. (✆ **416/967-3411;** subway: Yonge/Bloor), open Monday to Friday 9am to 5pm, and the Royal York Hotel, 100 Front St. W. (✆ **416/363-3883;** subway: Union), open Monday to Friday 8:30am to 5pm and Saturday 9am to 4pm. For lost or stolen cards, call ✆ **800/268-9824.**

*Area Code* Toronto's area codes are **416** and **647;** outside the city, the code is **905** or **289.** Ten-digit dialing is required for all local phone numbers (see box above).

*Consulates* All embassies are in Ottawa, but local consulates include: **Australian Consulate-General,** 175 Bloor St. E., Suite 314, at Church Street (✆ **416/323-1155;** subway: Bloor-Yonge); **British Consulate-General,** 777 Bay St., Suite 2800, at College (✆ **416/593-1290;** subway: College); and the **U.S. Consulate,** 360 University Ave. (✆ **416/595-1700;** subway: St. Patrick).

*Dentist* For emergency services from 8am till midnight, call the **Dental Emergency Service** (✆ **416/485-7121**). After midnight, your best bet is the **Toronto General Hospital,** 200 Elizabeth St. (✆ **416/340-3948**). Otherwise, ask the front-desk staff or concierge at your hotel.

*Doctor* The staff or concierge at your hotel should be able to help you locate a doctor. You can also call the **College of Physicians and Surgeons,** 80 College St. (✆ **416/967-2600,** ext. 626), for a referral between 9am to 5pm. See also "Emergencies," below.

*Drugstores* One big chain, **Pharma Plus,** has a store at 68 Wellesley St., at Church Street (✆ **416/924-7760;** subway: Wellesley), open daily 8am to midnight. Other Pharma Plus branches are in College Park, Manulife Centre, Commerce Court, and First Canadian Place. The only 24-hour drugstore near downtown is **Shopper's Drug Mart,** 700 Bay St., at Gerrard Street West (✆ **416/979-2424**).

*Emergencies* Call ✆ **911** for fire, police, or ambulance. The **Toronto General Hospital,** 200 Elizabeth St., provides 24-hour emergency service (✆ **416/340-3946** for emergency or 416/340-4611 for information).

*Liquor & Wine* The minimum drinking age is 19. Drinking hours are daily 11am to 2am. The government is the only retail vendor. The **Liquor Control Board of Ontario** (LCBO) stores sell liquor, wine, and some beers.

Most are open Monday to Saturday 10am to 6pm; some stay open evenings, and a few are open Sunday noon to 5pm.

Wine lovers will want to check out **Vintages** stores (operated by the LCBO), which carry a more extensive, specialized selection of wines. The most convenient downtown locations are in the lower-level concourse of **Hazelton Lanes** (✆ **416/924-9463**) and at **Queen's Quay** (✆ **416/864-6777**). The **Wine Rack,** 560 Queen St. W. (✆ **416/504-3647**), and 77 Wellesley St. E., at Church (✆ **416/923-9393**), sells only Ontario wines.

Most branches of the **Beer Store** (also part of the LCBO) are open Monday to Friday 10am to 10pm and Saturday 10am to 8pm. There's a downtown location at 614 Queen St. W. (✆ **416/504-4665**).

*Newspapers/Magazines* The four daily newspapers are the *Globe and Mail,* the *National Post,* the *Toronto Star,* and the *Toronto Sun. Eye* and *Now* are free arts-and-entertainment weeklies. *Xtra!* is a free weekly targeted at the gay and lesbian community. *Toronto Life* is the major monthly city magazine; its sister publication is *Toronto Life Fashion. Where Toronto* is usually free at hotels and in some Theater District restaurants.

*Police* In a life-threatening emergency, call ✆ **911.** For all other matters, contact the Metro police, 40 College St. (✆ **416/808-2222**).

*Post Office* Postal services are available at convenience and drug stores. Almost all sell stamps, and many have a separate counter where you can ship packages from 8:30am to 5pm. Look for the sign in the window indicating such services. There are also post-office windows in **Atrium on Bay** (✆ **416/506-0911**), in **Commerce Court** (✆ **416/956-7452**), and at the **TD Centre** (✆ **416/360-7105**).

*Safety* As large cities go, Toronto is generally safe, but be alert and use common sense, particularly at night. The Yonge/Bloor, Dundas, and Union subway stations are favorites for pickpockets. In the downtown area, Moss Park is considered one of the toughest areas to police. Avoid Allan Gardens and other parks at night.

*Taxes* The provincial retail sales tax is 8%; on accommodations it's 5%. There is an additional 7% national goods-and-services tax (GST). These taxes are invariably added to the price of an item when you pay for it—they're not included on the price tag.

*Time* Toronto is on Eastern Time, the same as New York, Boston, and Montréal. It's an hour ahead of Chicago.

## 3 Where to Stay

Toronto has no shortage of hotels. Whether you're seeking old-world elegance in a historic building or looking for all the conveniences of the office in your home away from home, you'll find it here. But there is one catch: Bargains are hard to come by, particularly in the downtown core.

The city has become increasingly popular with both business and leisure travelers, and demand has driven prices skyward. In exchange for proximity to top attractions like the Harbourfront Centre, SkyDome, and the Eaton Centre, even budget hotels charge more than C$100 (US$62) a night in the high season, which runs April to October. Factor in the 5% accommodations tax and the 7%

# Downtown Toronto

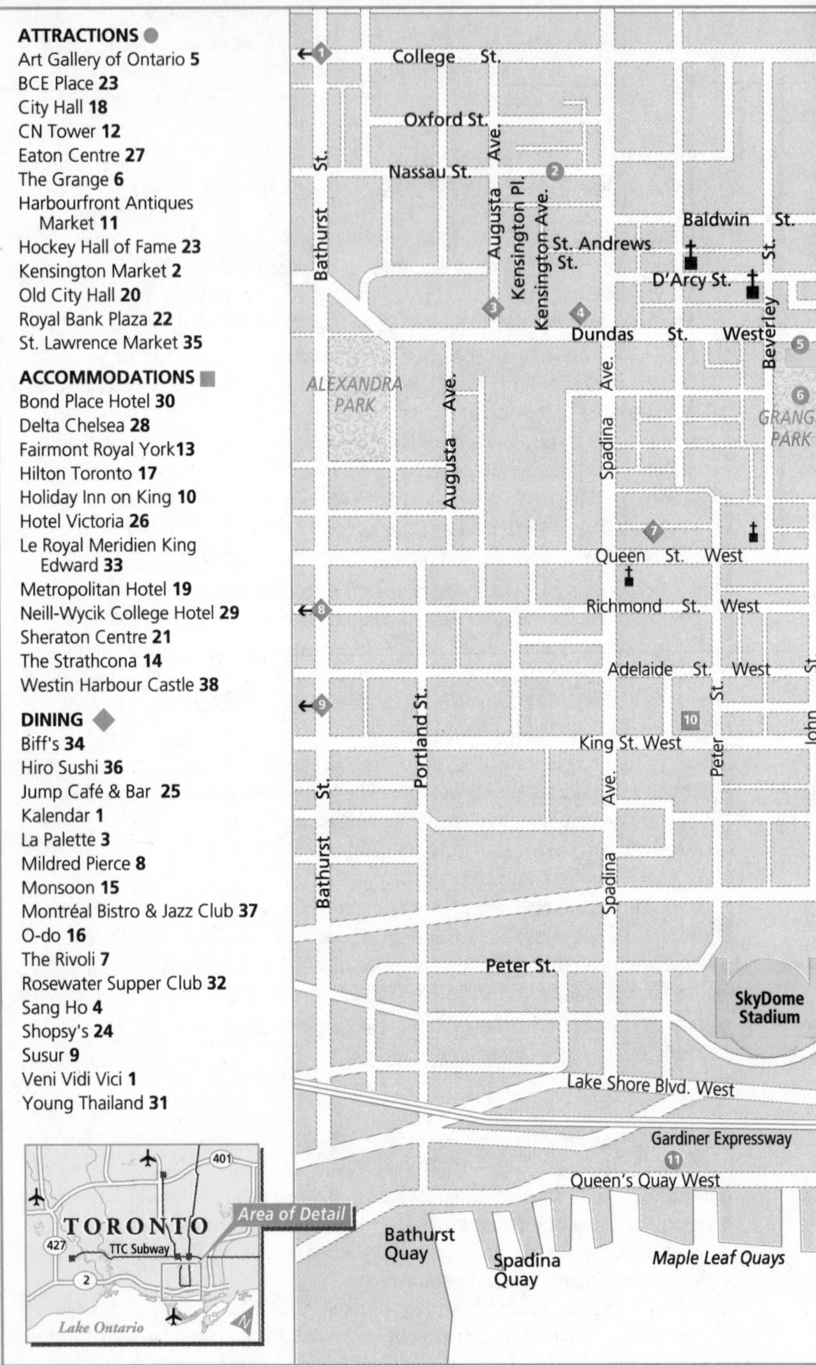

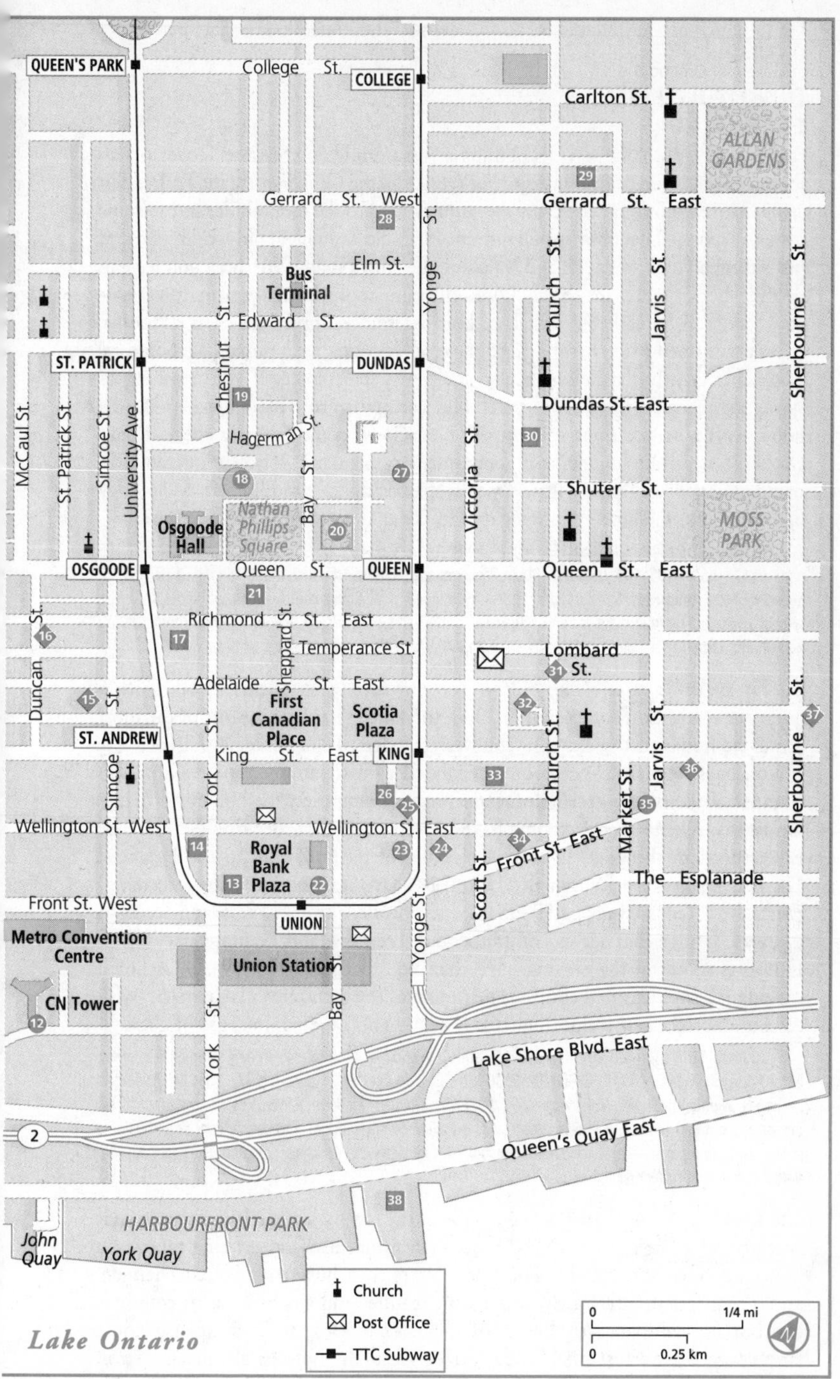

QUEEN'S PARK
College St.
COLLEGE
Carlton St.
ALLAN GARDENS
Gerrard St. West
Gerrard St. East
Elm St.
Bus Terminal
Edward St.
Yonge St.
Church St.
Jarvis St.
Sherbourne St.
ST. PATRICK
DUNDAS
Chestnut St.
Dundas St. East
Hagerman St.
McCaul St.
St. Patrick St.
Simcoe St.
University Ave.
Bay St.
Victoria St.
Shuter St.
Nathan Phillips Square
Osgoode Hall
MOSS PARK
OSGOODE
Queen St.
QUEEN
Queen St. East
Richmond St. East
Sheppard St.
Temperance St.
Lombard St.
Duncan St.
Adelaide St. East
First Canadian Place
Scotia Plaza
ST. ANDREW
King St. East
KING
York St.
Market St.
Wellington St. West
Wellington St. East
Royal Bank Plaza
Front St. East
Scott St.
The Esplanade
Front St. West
UNION
Metro Convention Centre
Union Station
CN Tower
Lake Shore Blvd. East
Queen's Quay East
HARBOURFRONT PARK
John Quay
York Quay
Lake Ontario
Church
Post Office
TTC Subway
0
1/4 mi
0.25 km

GST (which are refundable to nonresidents), and you're looking at spending a sizable sum of money.

## DOWNTOWN WEST

### EXPENSIVE

**Fairmont Royal York** ★★ Looming across from Union Station, Toronto's hub for rail travel, is the Fairmont Royal York, built by the Canadian-Pacific Railroad in 1929. The Fairmont hotels across the country tend to the monolithic, and this one is no exception. The lobby is magnificent in an old-fashioned, old-world way, and just sitting on a plush couch and watching the crowd is an event. Still, you have to decide whether you want to stay under the same roof with more than 1,000 others. Service is remarkably efficient, but necessarily impersonal. Guest rooms, though furnished with charming antique reproductions, are a mixed bag. Some are reasonably airy, but there's generally not much spare space. If you're willing to spring for an Entrée Gold room, you'll find a setup that runs like a hotel within the hotel, with a private floor with superior, spacious rooms, separate check-in and concierge, a private lounge, and complimentary breakfast. If you're interested in pampering yourself, ask about the special spa packages—the Elizabeth Milan Day Spa, located in the hotel's shopping arcade, is one of the best in the city.

100 Front St. W., Toronto, ON M5J 1E3. ✆ **800/441-1414.** Fax 416/368-9040. www.fairmont.com. 1,365 units. C$175–C$270 (US$109–US$167) double. Packages available. AE, DC, DISC, MC, V. Parking C$26 (US$16). Subway: Union. **Amenities:** 6 restaurants, 3 bars; sky lit indoor pool; fitness center; sauna; whirlpool; spa (with special packages for guests); concierge; business center; shopping arcade; salon; 24-hour room service; babysitting; same-day dry cleaning/laundry. *In room:* A/C, TV, minibar, coffeemaker, hair dryer, iron.

**Hilton Toronto** ★★ The Hilton Toronto isn't what it used to be. With a gorgeous renovation completed in 2000, the Hilton has become one of the most attractive hotels in the city. On the western edge of the Financial District, the Hilton boasts generous-size rooms decorated with streamlined luxury in mind. Because of the hotel's excellent location overlooking the wide boulevard that is University Avenue, many rooms have superb vistas (another fine view can be experienced in the glass elevators). Because of its proximity to the Financial District, it's no surprise that the Hilton is a favorite among business travelers. Executive rooms include perks such as a terry robe, a trouser press, and access to a private lounge that serves complimentary breakfast and evening snacks. The Hilton is more on the cutting edge than you'd expect from a business hotel, making it a sophisticated choice. The design of the grand foyer is dramatic, with an illuminated canopy, floor lights and back-lights, and copious use of glass.

145 Richmond St. W., Toronto, ON M5H 2L2. ✆ **800/445-8667** or 416/869-3456. Fax 416/869-1478. www.hilton.com. 601 units. C$210–C$300 (US$130–US$186) double. Extra person C$22 (US$14). Weekend packages available. AE, MC, V. Parking C$22 (US$15). Subway: Osgoode. **Amenities:** 3 restaurants, bar; indoor and outdoor lap pools; fitness center with exercise room, whirlpool, and sauna; concierge; business center; 24-hour room service; in-room massage; babysitting; same-day dry cleaning/laundry. *In room:* A/C, TV, dataport, minibar, coffeemaker, hair dryer, iron.

**The Metropolitan Hotel** ★★★ One of the few major hotels in Toronto that isn't part of a large chain, the Metropolitan prides itself on offering more of a boutique-hotel atmosphere. The hotel caters to a business-oriented clientele, and it manages to offer many of the same features and amenities as its competitors but at a comparatively lower cost (which is not to say it's inexpensive, just very competitive). Just off Dundas Street West, the hotel is a 5-minute stroll north of the business district and about 2 minutes west of the Eaton Centre. But why walk when you can take advantage of the complimentary limo service to any downtown core address? That perk is just one of the ways in which the

Metropolitan attempts to compete with its pricier competitors. Rooms are well-sized and furnished with comfort in mind. The luxury and executive suites boast Jacuzzis, Dolby Surround Sound televisions, CD players, and cordless phones. Also, the Metropolitan has a partnership with the Toronto Symphony Orchestra, which offers guests special packages.

108 Chestnut St., Toronto, ON M5G 1R3. ✆ **416/977-5000.** Fax 416/977-9513. www.metropolitan.com. 426 units. C$280–C$310 (US$174–US$192) double. Children under 18 stay free in parents' room. AE, DC, DISC, V. Parking C$19 (US$12). Subway: St. Patrick. **Amenities:** 2 restaurants, bar; indoor pool; fitness center with sauna, whirlpool, and massage treatments; courtesy limo; 24-hour business center (with PCs and Macs); concierge; limited room service; babysitting; same-day dry cleaning/laundry. *In room:* A/C, TV, dataport, minibar, hair dryer, safe.

**The Sheraton Centre Toronto** ★★ *Kids* A convention favorite, the Sheraton is across the street from New City Hall, a block from the Eaton Centre, and a short stroll from the trendy restaurant and boutique area of Queen Street West. It's entirely possible to stay here and never venture outside—the Sheraton complex includes restaurants, bars and a cinema, and the building connects to Toronto's fabled underground city. If you long for a patch of green, you'll find a manicured garden with a waterfall on the south side of the lobby. Am I making the place sound like a giant monolith? Well, it is. But it's an excellent home base for families because of its location and extensive list of child-friendly features. Most of the guest rooms lack a serious view, since this part of town is heavy on competing skyscrapers, though as you near the top of the 46-story complex the sights are inspiring indeed. Designed for business travelers, the Club Level rooms, renovated in 2001, boast mini business centers that include a fax/printer/copier and two-line speakerphone.

123 Queen St. W., Toronto, ON M5H 2M9. ✆ 800/325-3535 or 416/361-1000. Fax 416/947-4854. www.sheratoncentretoronto.com. 1,377 units. C$260–C$295 (US$161–US$183) double. Extra person C$20 (US$12). 2 children under 18 stay free in parents' room. Packages available. AE, DC, V. Parking C$28 (US$17). Subway: Osgoode. **Amenities:** 2 restaurants, 2 bars; gigantic heated indoor/outdoor pool; fitness center with sauna, and whirlpool; spa; children's center; concierge; activities desk; business center; shopping arcade; 24-hour room service; babysitting; dry cleaning/laundry. *In room:* A/C, TV, dataport, coffeemaker, hair dryer, iron.

## MODERATE

**Delta Chelsea** ★★ *Value* *Kids* While not a budget hotel, the Delta Chelsea offers bang for the buck. Its downtown location draws heaps of tour groups and a smattering of business travelers, its family-friendly facilities lure those with tykes, and its weekend packages capture the cost-conscious. It's impossible for a hotel to be all things to all people, but the Delta Chelsea comes pretty close. The guest rooms are bright and cheery as ever; a few have kitchenettes. On the special Signature Club floor for business travelers, rooms have cordless speakerphones, faxes, well-stocked desks, and ergonomic chairs. One special feature of the Delta Chelsea is its entertainment department. The hotel has ongoing partnerships with CanStage, Soupepper Theatre, the CN Tower and the Canadian National Exhibition, to mention a few. They have excellent access to tickets for everything from blockbuster shows to special events.

33 Gerrard St. W., Toronto, ON M5G 1Z4. ✆ **800/243-5732** or 416/595-1975. Fax 416/585-4362. www.deltahotels.com. 1,590 units. C$129–C$340 (US$80–US$211) double with signature service; C$149–C$360 (US$92–$US223)deluxe double; C$195–C$380 (US$121–US$236) Signature Club double (on business floor); from C$475 (US$295) suite. Extra person C$20 (US$12). Children under 18 stay free in parents' room. Weekend packages available. AE, DC, DISC, MC, V. Valet parking C$26 (US$16); self-parking C$21 (US$13; parking available only to 575 cars). Subway: College. **Amenities:** 3 restaurants, 3 bars; 2 pools (1 for adults only); fitness center with whirlpool, sauna; children's center; concierge; business center; activities desk; billiards room; salon; babysitting; dry cleaning/laundry. *In room:* A/C, TV, coffeemaker, hair dryer, iron.

**Holiday Inn on King** The blinding-white facade of this building suggests that some architect mistook Toronto for the tropics. No matter, its location is hot, with the Theater District, Gourmet Ghetto, Chinatown, and SkyDome nearby. The pastel-colored rooms are vintage Holiday Inn.

370 King St. W. (at Peter St.), Toronto, ON M5V 1J9. © **800/263-6364** or 416/599-4000. Fax 416/599-7394. www.hiok.com. 431 units. C$179–C$319 (US$111–US$198) double. Extra person C$15 (US$9). AE, DISC, MC, V. Parking C$22 (US$14). Subway: St. Andrew. **Amenities:** 2 restaurants, bar; small outdoor pool; fitness center with exercise room, whirlpool, and sauna. *In room:* A/C, TV, coffeemaker, hair dryer.

### INEXPENSIVE

**The Strathcona** ★ *Value* *Kids* The Strathcona has a unique status. It's pretty much the only budget hotel in the Financial District, and for years it's been one of the best buys in the city. It sits in the shadow of the Fairmont Royal York, making this hotel a short walk from all major downtown attractions. If you want to be in this neighborhood but don't want to pay a bundle, this is your best option. The tradeoffs that you make aren't as extensive as you might think. The Strathcona's rooms may be on the small side, but they're designed with efficiency in mind. In-hotel dining options are limited, but the Strathcona offers notable amenities, like a children's center, that you don't see in many budget hotels.

60 York St., Toronto, ON M5J 1S8. © **416/363-3321.** Fax 416/363-4679. 193 units. May–Oct C$90–C$159 (US$56–US$99) double; Nov–Apr C$75–C$129 (US$47–US$80) double. AE, DC, MC, V. Parking nearby C$20 (US$12). Subway: Union. **Amenities:** Cafe, bar; access to nearby health club; bike rental; children's center; car-rental desk; tour desk; concierge; babysitting; limited room service; dry cleaning/laundry. *In room:* A/C, TV, hair dryer, iron.

## DOWNTOWN EAST

### VERY EXPENSIVE

**Le Royal Meridien King Edward** ★★ With its rosy marble columns and a glass-domed rotunda dominating the lobby, the King Eddy was at one time the only place in Toronto that Hollywood royalty like Liz Taylor and Richard Burton would consider staying. The sense of grandeur carries into the guest rooms and suites. Not every room is spacious, but they're all charmingly appointed; unlike those at many uptown competitors, the King Eddy's rooms feel personally designed. Bathrooms are particularly nice, with generously proportioned marble tubs. Top-of-the-line features include plush robes, fluffy towels and makeup mirrors.

37 King St. E., Toronto, ON M5C 2E9. © **416/863-3131.** Fax 416/367-5515. www.lemeridien-hotels.com. 294 units. C$239–C$383 (US$148–US$237) double; from C$445 (US$276) suite. AE, DC, MC, V. Parking C$25 (US$16). Pets accepted. Subway: King. **Amenities:** 2 restaurants, bar; fitness center with Jacuzzi and sauna; concierge; 24-hour room service, dry cleaning/laundry. *In room:* A/C, TV, minibar, hair dryer, iron.

### EXPENSIVE

**Westin Harbour Castle** ★ A popular spot for conventions, the Westin is on the lakefront, just across from the Toronto Islands ferry docks and down the road from the Harbourfront Centre and Queen's Quay. Not surprisingly, the views are among the best in the city. The trade-off is that this hotel is somewhat out of the way. Physically, it's a 5-minute walk to Union Station, but to get there you have to cross under the Gardiner Expressway, one of the ugliest and most desolate patches of the city. The hotel tries to get around this difficulty with a shuttle bus service; there's also a public-transit stop and a queue of cabs at the hotel. Perhaps recognizing the lack of things to do in the vicinity, the Westin has populated the hotel itself with attractions. Dining options are extremely fine: the excellent new restaurant, Toula, is attracting Toronto residents in droves, never mind hotel guests. There are also terrific sports facilities, giving this monolithic hotel the feel of a resort. Who needs to go outside anyway?

1 Harbour Sq., Toronto, ON M5J 1A6. ✆ **800/228-3000** or 416/ 869-1600. Fax 416/361-7448. www.westin.com. 980 units. C$180–C$300 (US$112[ndUS186) double; from C$335 (US$208) suite. Extra person C$20 (US$12). Children stay free in parents' room. Weekend packages and long-term rates available. AE, DC, MC, V. Parking C$25 (US$16). Subway: Union, then LRT to Queen's Quay. **Amenities:** 2 restaurants, bar; indoor pool; excellent health club with whirlpool, sauna, and steam room; 2 squash courts; 2 outdoor tennis courts; massage clinic; concierge; business center; children's center; salon; 24-hour room service; babysitting; dry cleaning/laundry. *In room:* A/C, TV, dataport, minibar, coffeemaker, hair dryer, iron.

### MODERATE

**Bond Place Hotel** The location is right—a block from Eaton Centre, around the corner from the Pantages and Elgin theaters—and so is the price. Perhaps that's why it tends to be popular with tour groups. (The fact that the staff speaks several European and Asian languages doesn't hurt, either). Rooms are on the small side, and can best be described as quaint.

65 Dundas St. E., Toronto, ON M5B 2G8. ✆ **416/362-6061.** Fax 416/360-6406. www.bondplacehoteltoronto.com. 287 units. High season C$160 (US$99) single or double; low season C$109 (US$68) single or double. Extra person C$15 (US$9). Weekend packages available. AE, DC, DISC, MC, V. Parking C$12 (US$7). Subway: Dundas. **Amenities:** Restaurant, bar; concierge; tour desk; car-rental desk; limited room service; dry cleaning/laundry. *In room:* A/C, TV.

### INEXPENSIVE

**Hotel Victoria** In a landmark downtown building near the Hummingbird Centre and the Hockey Hall of Fame, the Victoria boasts the glamorous touches of an earlier age, such as crown moldings and marble columns in the lobby. Guest rooms underwent a complete renovation in 2000. The Victoria has as its claim to fame the fact that built in 1909, it's Toronto's second-oldest hotel. Because of its small size, the hotel offers an unusually high level of personal service and attention, which you normally wouldn't expect in a budget accommodation. Standard rooms are small and simply decorated; select rooms are larger.

56 Yonge St. (at Wellington St.), Toronto, ON M5E 1G5. ✆ **416/363-1666.** Fax 416/363-7327. www.toronto.com/hotelvictoria. 48 units (30 with tub-shower combination, 18 with shower only). C$125–C$169 (US$78–US$71) double. Extra person C$15 (US$9). AE, DC, MC, V. Parking C$20 (US$12). Subway: King. **Amenities:** Restaurant; access to nearby health club; dry cleaning/laundry. *In room:* A/C, TV, dataport, coffeemaker, hair dryer.

**Neill-Wycik College Hotel** During the school year, this is a residence for nearby Ryerson Polytechnic University. Some students work here in the summer, when the Neill-Wycik morphs into a guesthouse. Travelers on tight budgets won't mind the minimalist approach—rooms have beds, chairs, desks, and phones, but no air-conditioning or TVs. It's less than a 5-minute walk from here to the Eaton Center, in case you're interested. The neighborhood is not as appealing as that around Victoria University, which offers a similar service (see below).

96 Gerrard St. E. (between Church and Jarvis sts.), Toronto, ON M5B 1G7. ✆ **800/268-4358** or 416/ 977-2320. Fax 416/977-2809. www.neill-wycik.com. 300 units (none with private bathroom). C$41–C$51 (US$28–US$35) double; C$45–C$58 (US$28–US$36) family (2 adults plus children). MC, V. Closed Sept–early May. Limited parking nearby C$10 (US$6). Subway: College. **Amenities:** Cafe; groups of 5 bedrooms share 2 bathrooms and kitchen with fridge and stove; 2 roof decks (5th and 23rd floors); TV lounge; sauna; 24-hour laundry room. *In room:* No phone.

## MIDTOWN WEST

### VERY EXPENSIVE

**Four Seasons Hotel Toronto** ★★ The Four Seasons is famous as the favored haunt of visiting celebrities. During the Toronto International Film

# Midtown Toronto

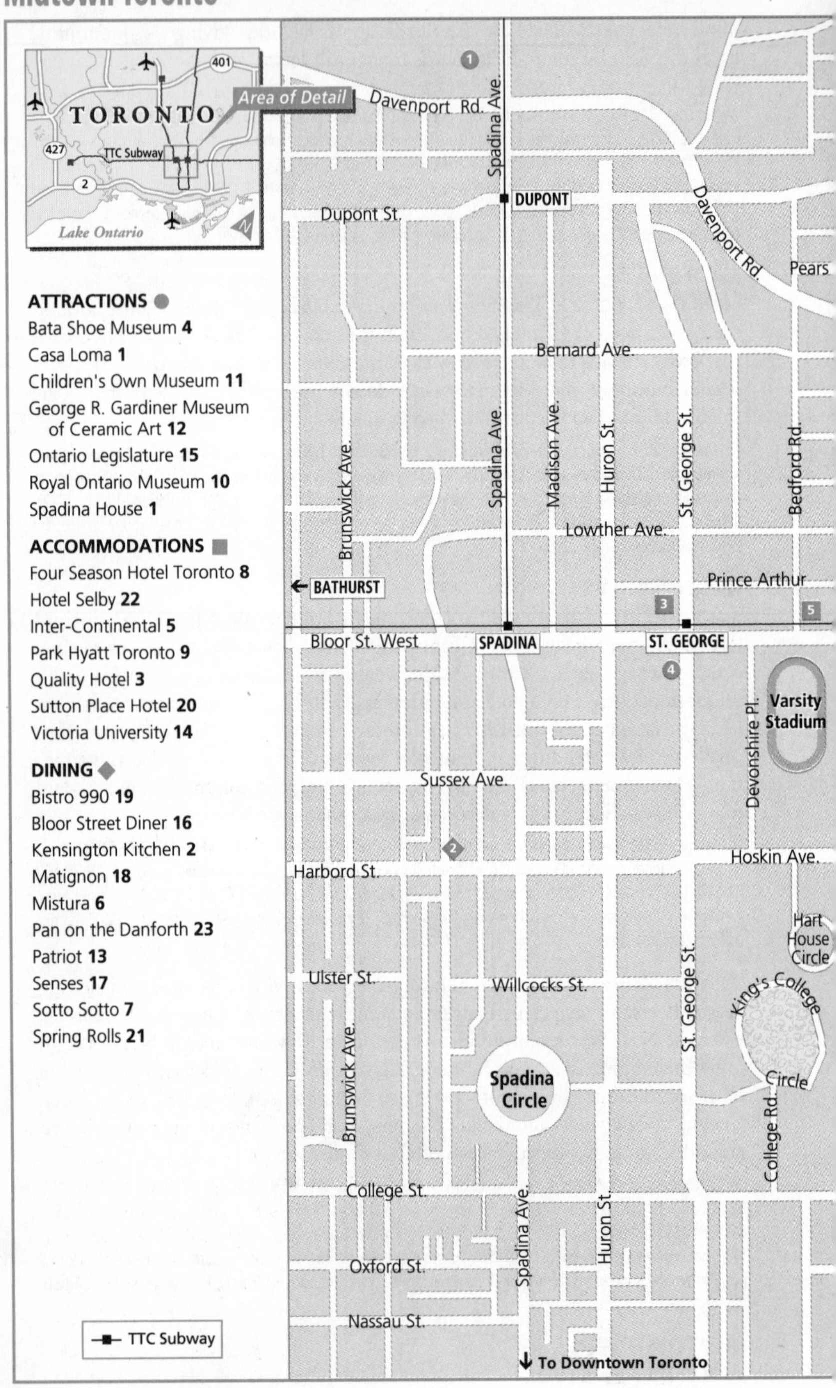

401
TORONTO
Area of Detail
427
TTC Subway
2
Lake Ontario
ATTRACTIONS
Bata Shoe Museum 4
Casa Loma 1
Children's Own Museum 11
George R. Gardiner Museum of Ceramic Art 12
Ontario Legislature 15
Royal Ontario Museum 10
Spadina House 1
ACCOMMODATIONS
Four Season Hotel Toronto 8
Hotel Selby 22
Inter-Continental 5
Park Hyatt Toronto 9
Quality Hotel 3
Sutton Place Hotel 20
Victoria University 14
DINING
Bistro 990 19
Bloor Street Diner 16
Kensington Kitchen 2
Matignon 18
Mistura 6
Pan on the Danforth 23
Patriot 13
Senses 17
Sotto Sotto 7
Spring Rolls 21
TTC Subway
Davenport Rd.
Spadina Ave.
DUPONT
Dupont St.
Davenport Rd.
Pears
Bernard Ave.
Brunswick Ave.
Madison Ave.
Huron St.
St. George St.
Bedford Rd.
Lowther Ave.
Prince Arthur
BATHURST
Bloor St. West
SPADINA
ST. GEORGE
Varsity Stadium
Devonshire Pl.
Sussex Ave.
Hoskin Ave.
Harbord St.
Hart House Circle
Ulster St.
Willcocks St.
King's College Circle
Spadina Circle
College Rd.
College St.
Oxford St.
Nassau St.
To Downtown Toronto

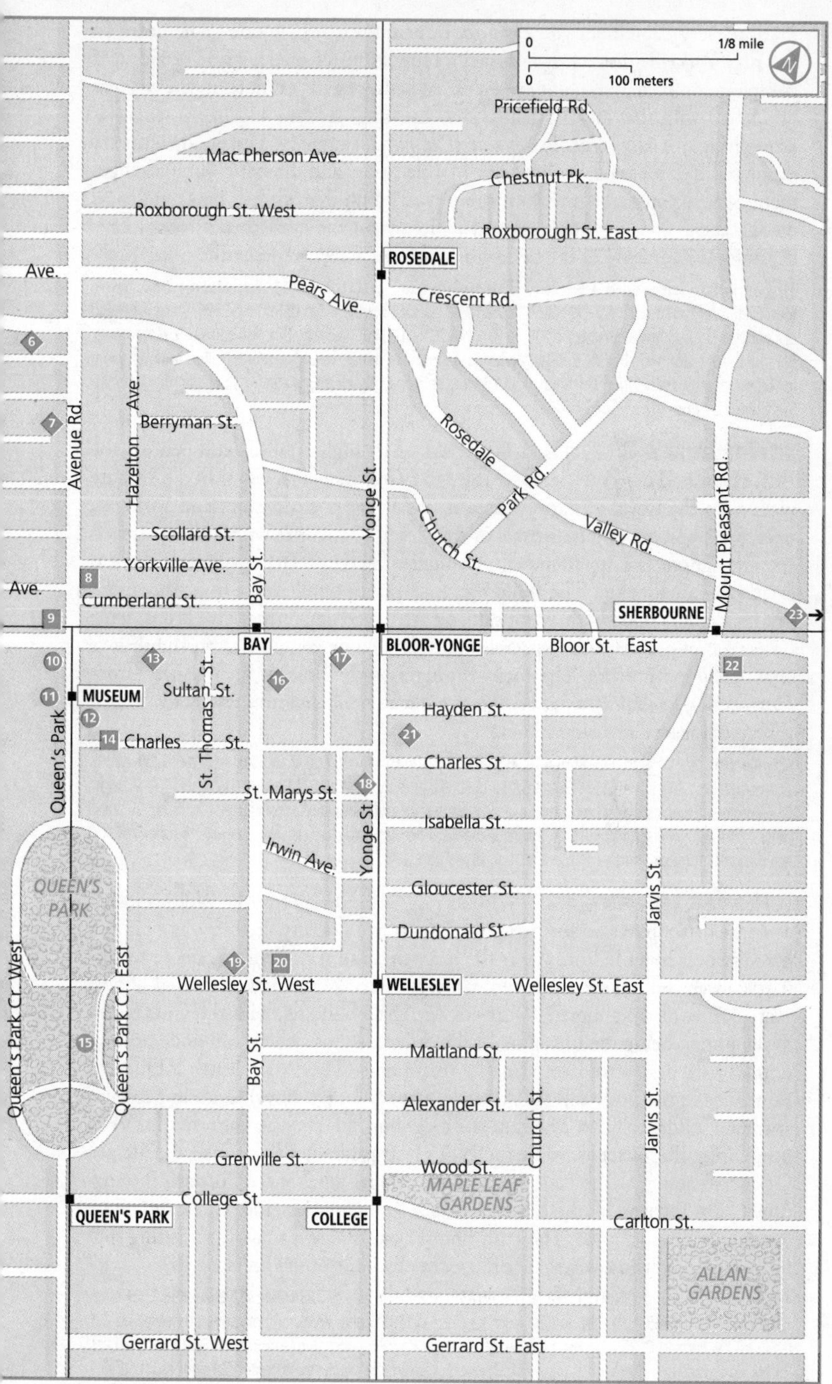

0
1/8 mile
0
100 meters
Pricefield Rd.
Mac Pherson Ave.
Chestnut Pk.
Roxborough St. West
Roxborough St. East
ROSEDALE
Ave.
Pears Ave.
Crescent Rd.
Avenue Rd.
Hazelton Ave.
Berryman St.
Rosedale
Park Rd.
Valley Rd.
Mount Pleasant Rd.
Yonge St.
Church St.
Scollard St.
Yorkville Ave.
Bay St.
Ave.
Cumberland St.
SHERBOURNE
BAY
BLOOR-YONGE
Bloor St. East
MUSEUM
Sultan St.
St. Thomas St.
Hayden St.
Charles St.
Charles St.
Queen's Park
St. Marys St.
Isabella St.
Irwin Ave.
Yonge St.
QUEEN'S PARK
Gloucester St.
Jarvis St.
Dundonald St.
Wellesley St. West
WELLESLEY
Wellesley St. East
Queen's Park Cr. West
Queen's Park Cr. East
Bay St.
Maitland St.
Alexander St.
Church St.
Jarvis St.
Grenville St.
Wood St.
MAPLE LEAF GARDENS
College St.
QUEEN'S PARK
COLLEGE
Carlton St.
ALLAN GARDENS
Gerrard St. West
Gerrard St. East

Festival every September you can't get in here for love or money. The hotel, in the ritzy Yorkville district, has earned a reputation for offering fine service and complete comfort. While not even close to being the largest hotel in the city, the building—with its myriad ballrooms, meeting rooms, and restaurants—is monolithic. It's easy to get lost inside (I've done it myself). The public areas are decorated like a French parlor, with marble floors and dramatic floral arrangements. Once you make it to your room, you'll find that while it may tend to be on the small side, it's well designed and easy on the eye. Corner rooms have charming balconies—all the better to appreciate street scenes with.

21 Avenue Rd., Toronto, ON M5R 2G1. ✆ **800/268-6282** or 416/964-0411. Fax 416/964-2301. www.fourseasons.com. 380 units. C$295–C$545 (US$183–US$338) double; from C$590 (US$366) suite. Weekend discounts and packages available. AE, DC, V. Parking C$25 (US$16). Subway: Bay. **Amenities:** 2 restaurants, bar; indoor/outdoor pool; health club with whirlpool; business center; weekday courtesy limo to downtown; in-room massage; babysitting; 24-hour room service, same-day dry cleaning/laundry. *In room:* A/C, TV, minibar, hair dryer, iron.

**Inter-Continental** ★ Just a little west of its higher profile competitors the Park Hyatt and the Four Seasons, the Inter-Continental is less than a 5-minute walk from the Royal Ontario Museum, the Bata Shoe Museum, and Yorkville, one of the best shopping districts in the city. It's a favorite with business travelers, who appreciate its attentive, personalized service. The atmosphere here is exclusive, but low-key. The building looks rather nondescript from the street, but inside, it is filled with European and Art Deco details that give it character. Guest rooms are definitely spacious, and they come equipped with stylish love seats and roomy desks. The focus throughout the hotel is on business, from room design to the extensive business center to the Signatures restaurant, which is perfect for business entertaining.

220 Bloor St. W., Toronto, ON M5S 1T8. ✆ **800/267-0010** or 416/960-5200. Fax 416/960-8269. www.interconti.com. 220 units. C$365–C$445 (US$226–US$276) double. AE, DC, V. Parking C$25 (US$16). Subway: St. George. **Amenities:** Restaurant, bar; indoor pool; health club with sauna; concierge; tour desk; business center; 24-hour room service; in-room massage; babysitting; same-day dry cleaning/laundry. *In room:* A/C, TV, fax, dataport, minibar, fridge, coffeemaker, hair dryer, iron, safe.

**Park Hyatt Toronto** ★★★ With its ongoing renovations, the Park Hyatt has cemented its reputation for being the last word in luxury. It is, in my opinion, the very best hotel in Toronto at the moment, and it's where I'd choose to stay if price were no object. Its owner, Chicago-based Hyatt, has renovated almost every corner of the almost 70-year-old Art Deco building, with the most recent development being the unveiling of the Stillwater Spa, which is unique both in terms of its design and some of its treatments. The Park Hyatt's location is prime: it's in the posh Yorkville district, steps from the Royal Ontario Museum and the Children's Own Museum. Its neighbor, the Four Seasons, has for years been luring the glitterati, while the Park Hyatt prides itself on luring the literati. Of course now that the Park Hyatt is the official hotel of the Toronto International Film Festival, it's the venue of choice for many stars, too. Guest rooms are generously proportioned. The 18th-floor Roof Lounge is a favorite meeting spot for journalists, who congregate on couches in front of the fireplace.

4 Avenue Rd., Toronto, ON M5R 2E8. ✆ **800/233-1234** or 416/925-1234. Fax 416/924-6693. 346 units. C$225–C$499 (US$95–US$309) double; from C$299 (US$185) suite. Weekend packages available. AE, DC, DISC, MC, V. Parking C$25 (US$16). Subway: Museum or Bay. Pets accepted. **Amenities:** Restaurant, 2 bars; indoor pool; fitness center with sauna and whirlpool; spa; concierge; business center; 24-hour room service; babysitting; dry cleaning/laundry. *In room:* A/C, TV, fax, dataport, minibar, coffeemaker, hair dryer, iron, safe.

## EXPENSIVE

**The Sutton Place Hotel** ★★ Although it towers over the intersection of Bay and Wellesley, the Sutton Place boasts the advantages of a small hotel—most particularly in terms of detail-oriented, personalized service. In addition to hosting a galaxy of stars and celebrities, the hotel draws sophisticated business and leisure travelers in search of some serious pampering. The emphasis here is on sophisticated—famous guests expect to be left alone, and the Sutton is devoted to protecting their privacy. The Sutton aims for European panache, littering the public spaces with antiques and tapestries. The spacious guest rooms are decorated in a similar, though scaled-down, style. A few suites have full kitchens. Not that you'd want to cook while here—the lovely Accents restaurant serves up Continental fare on the ground-floor level, and across the street Bistro 990 produces perfect French cuisine. One downside is that the Sutton stands close to alone in its neighborhood. It's about a 10- to 15-minute walk to attractions such as the Royal Ontario Museum and the Yorkville shopping district. In the immediate neighborhood, there's virtually nothing to see.

955 Bay St., Toronto, ON M5S 2A2. ✆ **800/268-3790** or 416/924-9221. Fax 416/924-1778. www.suttonplace.com. 292 units. C$235–C$325 (US$146–US$202) double; from C$400 (US$248) suite. Extra person C$20 (US$12). Children under 18 stay free in parents' room. Weekend discounts available. AE, DC, V. Valet parking C$25 (US$16); self-parking C$20 (US$12). Subway: Museum or Wellesley. Pets accepted. **Amenities:** Restaurant, bar; indoor pool; fitness center with sauna; concierge; business center; 24-hour room service; in-room massage; babysitting; dry cleaning/laundry. *In room:* A/C, TV, data port, minibar, coffeemaker, hair dryer, iron, safe.

## MODERATE

**Quality Hotel** *Value* Considering this hotel's tony location—steps from Yorkville and several museums, including the Royal Ontario Museum—the price is hard to beat. Rooms are small but comfortable, and outfitted with well-lit worktables. Choice Club members have access to in-house secretarial services; executive rooms have fax-modem hookups. However, there aren't many other amenities or services. This is a good home base for a leisure traveler who prioritizes location over other considerations. If you're not planning on hanging out a lot in your hotel room, it's a small tradeoff to make for the price.

280 Bloor St. W. (at St. George St.), Toronto, ON M5S 1V8. ✆ **416/968-0010.** www.choicehotels.ca. 210 units. C$139–C$209 (US$86–US$130) double. Weekend and other packages available. AE, DC, DISC, MC, V. Parking C$12 (US$7). Subway: St. George. **Amenities:** Restaurant, coffee shop; access to nearby health club; limited room service; dry cleaning/laundry. *In room:* A/C, TV, coffeemaker, hair dryer, iron.

## INEXPENSIVE

**Hotel Selby** ★ *Finds* This hotel is one of Toronto's better-kept secrets. Ornate chandeliers, stucco moldings, and high ceilings make the 1890s Victorian building an absolute stunner. In a predominantly gay neighborhood, the Selby attracts gay and straight couples, as well as students and seniors. Most rooms with private bath have a good-size claw-footed tub. The staff is very friendly, and while there's no concierge as such, there's no shortage of advice and recommendations for what to see and do.

592 Sherbourne St., Toronto, ON M4X 1L4. ✆ **800/387-4788** or 416/921-3142. Fax 416/923-3177. 67 units (8 with shared bathroom). C$95–C$110 (US$59–US$68) double; C$120–C$145 (US$74–US$90) suite. Rates include continental breakfast. Senior and student discounts available. AE, MC, V. Limited free parking; otherwise C$12 (US$7). Subway: Sherbourne. **Amenities:** Access to nearby fitness center; laundry room. *In room:* A/C, TV.

**Victoria University** ★ *Value* This is a summer steal: you could not find a better deal in this part of town. From early May to late August, Victoria

University (which is federated with the University of Toronto) makes its student accommodations available to travelers. Furnishings are simple—a bed, desk, and chair are standard—but the surroundings are splendid. Many of the rooms are in Burwash Hall, a 19th-century building that overlooks a peaceful, leafy quad. All rooms are down the street from the Royal Ontario Museum, and up the street from Queen's Park. Guests are provided with linens, towels, and soap.

140 Charles St. W., Toronto, ON M5S 1K9. © **416/585-4524.** Fax 416/585-4530. Accom.victoria@utoronto.ca. 700 units (none with bathroom). C$65 (US$40) double. Rates include breakfast. Senior and student discounts available. MC, V. Closed Sept–April. Nearby parking C$12 (US$7). Subway: Museum. **Amenities:** Tennis courts; access to fitness center with Olympic-size pool; laundry room. *In room:* No phone.

## 4 Where to Dine

The city is a restaurant-goer's nirvana for a wealth of reasons. For starters, there are more than 5,000 eateries, which represent cooking styles from any country or nationality you can name, making Toronto's culinary scene both eclectic and palate-teasing. However, there is trouble brewing in paradise, in the shape of the new anti-smoking bylaw which came into effect on June 1, 2001. Effectively, all restaurants are entirely nonsmoking now, with the possible exceptions of patios and separately ventilated dining rooms. Many restaurateurs are vowing to fight the bylaw, which subjects both patrons and establishments with fines between C$200 and C$5,000 (US$124–US$3,100) for infractions.

Dining out in Toronto does not have to be an expensive venture, but the tax level is high. Meals are subject to the 8% provincial sales tax and to the 7% GST. In other words, tax and tip together can add 30% to your bill. Tips are normally left to the diners' discretion, unless there are six or more people at the table; 15% is the usual amount for good service, though at the pricier establishments, tipping hovers around 15% to 20%. The price of a bottle of wine is generally quite high because of the tax on imports; get around it by ordering an Ontario vintage—local wines enjoy a rising international reputation. Remember that there is a 10% tax on alcohol, whatever you're sipping. Checked items warrant C$1 (US60¢) per piece for the attendant.

### DOWNTOWN WEST

This is where you will find Toronto's greatest concentration of great restaurants. **Little Italy,** which runs along **College Street,** and **Chinatown,** which radiates from **Spadina Avenue,** have more restaurants than any other parts of the city.

#### VERY EXPENSIVE

**Susur** ★★★ FUSION If you visited Toronto a few years ago you might have had the good fortune to dine at an exquisite restaurant called Lotus. The city's foodies had their hearts broken when the eatery's chef and owner, Susur Lee, decided to close it and travel abroad. But after some stints in foreign kitchens Lee is back and better than ever. The eponymous Susur is a delight. For such a high-end establishment, its décor is refreshingly low-key, with stark white walls and oyster-pale upholstery warmed up with colored lights. But of course the biggest draw is what's on the plate. Lee serves up stellar cuisine in the true fusion spirit, blending Asian and Western ingredients, cooking methods, and presentation. The menu changes frequently, with bold, savory offerings like rare venison loin with a gorgonzola-hawberry red wine sauce. The cooking here is complex, and fortunately the wine list, while pricey, has been put together with extreme care to complement it.

601 King St. W. ✆ **416-603-2205.** Reservations required. Main courses C$29–C$43 (US$18–US$27). AE, MC, V. Mon–Sat 6pm–10pm. Subway: St. Andrew, then streetcar west to Bathurst Ave. and walk 1 block west to Portland St.

## EXPENSIVE

**Jump Café and Bar** ★★ AMERICAN Jump is, appropriately enough, always hopping; a sprawling space in Commerce Court, one of the Financial District's towering monoliths, it can be tricky to find. Just follow the buzz—as the decibel level rises, you'll know you're on the right track. The restaurant is such a see-and-be-seen spot that you might suspect it's all show and no substance. Actually, the food is anything but an afterthought. The menus feature "suit-able" dishes like grilled 10-ounce New York black Angus steak with Yukon Gold fries, salsa, and mushroom gravy. The more gastronomically adventurous have other choices, such as roasted sea bass with fragrant coconut basmati rice and green curry, or osso bucco with spinach-and-lemon risotto. To start, consider steamed mussels in ginger-and-coconut-milk broth, or grilled tiger shrimps on top of Thai mango-peanut salad. Luxe desserts will put your diet back by about a month.

1 Wellington St. W. ✆ **416/363-3400.** Reservations required. Main courses C$19–C$32 (US$18–US$27). AE, DC, V. Mon–Fri 11:30am–11pm, Sat 4:30–11pm. Subway: King.

**O-do** ★ FRENCH/JAPANESE The setting sounds like an *Iron Chef* competition: at O-do, there are two in-house chefs, one specializing in French cooking and the other in Japanese. But the atmosphere is entirely harmonious. There are few a la carte choices, since the drawing cards here are the prix fixe menus, which change frequently. On the eight-course French tasting menu, you may find the likes of pan-fried turbot served atop slivered oyster and chanterelle mushrooms. The Japanese set menu boasts 21 small dishes, such as sea eel wrapped around crisp burdock root and treated with sweet soy sauce. While the food is delightful, be warned that there are a few bumps on the path to get here, such as the lack of a street entrance (you need to enter through Wow Sushi, a separate restaurant).

205 Richmond St. W. ✆ **416-979-2882.** Reservations strongly recommended. Fixed price menus from C$50–C$90 (US$31–US$56). AE, MC, V. Subway: Osgoode.

## MODERATE

**La Palette** ★ BISTRO This is a terrific, albeit offbeat, addition to the Kensington Market neighborhood. It's so good, in fact, that you almost wonder why no one ever before thought of setting down roots for a classic French bistro here, on the edge of Chinatown. A quartet of Gallic flags announce its presence on the street; inside the 30-seat dining room is cozy and informal—tables are set elbow-to-elbow. The menu is classic hearty bistro fare, from the ballantine of chicken stuffed with peppers and rice, to lamb chops with a de rigeur crusty coating of mustard and rosemary. If you're as much as a dessert fiend as I am, don't forget to save some room, because the citron tart and the dark chocolate cake are irresistible. But the real icing on the cake is that the low-key but considerate service here is just right.

256 Augusta Ave. ✆ **416-929-4900.** Reservations recommended. Main courses C$10–C$18 (US$6–US$11). AE, MC, V. Sun–Thurs 5:30pm–11pm, Fri–Sat noon–midnight. Subway: St. Patrick, then streetcar west to Augusta Ave.

**Mildred Pierce** ★ ECLECTIC Named after a Joan Crawford film, this restaurant is appropriately theatrical, with organza drapes tumbling down from the high ceiling. Murals of a Roman feast cover the walls (a local in-joke, they depict characters including the restaurant's owner and a few food critics). The menu fits right in, rich in inspiration and dramatic flourishes borrowed from different countries. Grilled salmon accompanies saffron risotto and a ragout of fennel, baby beets, and bok choy, while a Thai hot pot boasts tiger shrimp, scallops, mussels, and clams brewing in a coconut-lime-cilantro sauce. The wine list is short but includes options from Italy, Spain, South Africa, and California. Lush desserts include maple crème brûlée, and a rustic cranberry and walnut tart.

99 Sudbury St. ✆ **416/588-5695.** Reservations recommended for lunch and dinner; reservations not accepted for Sunday brunch. Main courses C$17–C$26 (US$11–US$16). AE, DC, MC, V. Mon–Fri noon–2pm, Sun 10am–3pm; Sun–Thurs 6–10pm, Fri–Sat 6–11pm. Subway: Osgoode, then any streetcar west to Dovercourt; walk south on Dovercourt and turn right at Sudbury.

**Sang Ho** CHINESE There's no end of eateries in the eastern end of Chinatown, but Sang Ho will be the one with the longest queue out front. This restaurant boasts not only a top-notch kitchen, but also a lovely dining room filled with several teeming aquariums. The regular menu of 100-plus dishes never changes, but many specials of the day are listed on wall-mounted boards. Seafood—shrimp, clams, or red snapper—is the obvious choice. Service is speedy and responsive. Try to go on a weeknight, when there's no more than a short wait for a table.

536 Dundas St. W. ✆ **416/596-1685.** Reservations not accepted. Main courses C$8–$18 (US$5–US$11). MC, V. Sun–Thurs noon–10pm, Fri–Sat noon–11pm. Subway: St. Patrick.

**Veni Vidi Vici** ★ ITALIAN/FUSION This is Little Italy's brightest new addition, a little gem of a restaurant that serves up delicious food in a swanky setting—but, unlike many of its neighborhood cousins, it does so without attitude. On the Italian side, there are pasta dishes such as linguine with mixed seafood, or risotto with portobello, cremini, and porcini mushrooms. But the Asian-inspired Fusion plates are the showstoppers: Think cashew-studded sea bass with fennel, or phyllo-wrapped salmon with basmati rice. Desserts return to the classics, like crème brûlée with fresh berries. The wine list is particularly strong in Italian reds.

650 College St. (at Grace St.). ✆ **416/536-8550.** Reservations recommended. Main courses C$13–C$25 (US$8–US$16). AE, MC, V. Tues–Sun 11am–3pm and 5pm–midnight.

## INEXPENSIVE

**Kalendar** LIGHT FARE I can't go to this restaurant without snickering at the menu—pizzas are called *nannettes,* for example—but the food inspires satisfied sighs. There are sandwiches stuffed with portobello mushrooms, havarti, and roasted red peppers, and five *scrolls*—phyllo pastries filled with delights like artichoke hearts, eggplant, and hummus. The nannettes are baked naan breads topped with ingredients like smoked salmon, capers, and red onions. The restaurant consists of two mirrored rooms. The ambiance is very like that of a French bistro. In summer the sidewalk patio is just the place to sit and watch the world go by.

546 College St. (just west of Bathurst St.). ✆ **416/923-4138.** Main courses C$10–C$13 (US$6–US$8). MC, V. Mon–Fri 11am–4pm. Subway: Queen's Park, then any streetcar west to Bathurst St.

**The Rivoli** ★ FUSION The Riv is better known as a club than as a restaurant—the 125-seat back room plays host to live music, stand-up comics, and poetry readings. What most people don't know is that the kitchen is just as creative. Chicken marinated in jerk spices comes with sautéed spinach and a slaw of Asian veggies; mussels are steamed in red curry jazzed up with tarragon pesto, and served on a bed of glass noodles. The less adventurous can partake of the heaping Caesar salad or the house burger (beef on a challah bun with caramelized onions). The low prices draw a mixed crowd of starving artists, budget-conscious boomers, and Gen-Xers. In summer the sidewalk patio is in high demand. One caveat: If you're planning to talk over dinner, get there before the back room starts filling up.

332 Queen St. W. ✆ **416/597-0794.** Reservations not accepted. Main courses C$9–C$15 (US$6–US$9). AE, MC, V. Daily 11:30am–2am. Subway: Osgoode.

## DOWNTOWN EAST

### EXPENSIVE

**Biff's** ★ BISTRO The same team that created Jump has been hard at work again. The setting hits all the right notes, with wood paneling and potted palms among the cozy-but-chic touches. The menu is equally fine, with the likes of pan-fried halibut covered with a second skin of thinly sliced potatoes, and traditional roast leg of lamb. The prime downtown location at Yonge and Front streets is a boon for Financial District types at lunch and theatergoers in the evening (the St. Lawrence and the Hummingbird centers are a stone's throw away).

4 Front St. E. ✆ **416-860-0086.** Reservations strongly recommended. Main courses C$18–C$28 (US$11–US$17). AE, DC, MC, V. Mon–Fri 11:30am–2:30pm and 5:30–11pm, Sat 5:30–11pm. Subway: Union or King.

**Hiro Sushi** ★ JAPANESE Widely regarded as the best sushi chef in the city, Hiro Yoshida draws a horde of Financial District types at lunch, though dinner patrons are mainly couples. The monochromatic setting is comfortably minimalist, and diners are encouraged to relax and leave their meal in Hiro's capable hands. The sushi varieties range from the expected to the inventive, and you can also choose sashimi, tempura, and bento box combinations. Service can be rather slow. Forget the few wines listed in favor of sake or beer.

171 King St. E. ✆ **416/304-0550.** Reservations recommended. Main courses C$20–C$30 (US$12–US$19). AE, DC, MC, V. Mon–Fri noon–2:30pm; Mon–Sat 6–10:30pm. Subway: King.

### MODERATE

**Montreal Bistro and Jazz Club** QUEBECOIS Ontario and Quebec share a border, but it's no mean feat to find top-notch *tourtière* (traditional beef, veal, and pork pie) in Toronto. Anyone who craves Quebecois staples like pea soup and smoked-meat sandwiches can return their train ticket and stop at this bistro. Besides being a restaurant, this is one of the city's premier jazz clubs, so you can *écoutes* while you *manges.*

65 Sherbourne St. (at Adelaide). ✆ **416/363-0179.** Reservations recommended. Main courses C$10–C$18 (US$6–US$11). AE, MC, V. Mon–Fri 11:30am–3pm; Mon–Thurs 6–11pm, Fri–Sat 6pm–midnight. Subway: King, then any streetcar east to Sherbourne St.

### INEXPENSIVE

**Shopsy's** *Kids* DELI This Toronto institution has been in business for more than three-quarters of a century. Its large patio, festooned with giant yellow umbrellas, draws crowds for breakfast, lunch, and dinner and in between. This is where you go for heaping corned beef or smoked-meat sandwiches served on fresh rye. There's also a slew of comfort foods, like macaroni and cheese and chicken pot pie. Shopsy's also boasts one of the largest walk-in humidors in the city.

33 Yonge St. ✆ **416/365-3333.** Sandwiches and main courses C$7–C$14 (US$4.35–US$9). AE, DC, MC, V. Mon–Wed 6:30am–11pm, Thurs–Fri 6:30am–midnight, Sat–Sun 8am–midnight. Subway: Union.

**Young Thailand** ★ THAI Wandee Young was one of the first chefs to awake Toronto's taste buds to the joys of Thai cuisine. That was more than 2 decades ago, and Young Thailand is still going strong, with several locations around the city. The large dining room contains a few Southeast Asian decorative elements, but it's the low-priced, high-quality cuisine that attracts the hip-but-broke and boomers alike. The bargain buffet at lunch is always a mob scene. The dinner menu is a la carte, with popular picks like spiced chicken and bamboo shoots in coconut milk, satays with fiery peanut sauce, and the ever-present pad Thai. Soups tend to be sinus-clearing, though mango salads offer a sweet antidote.

81 Church St. (south of Lombard St.). ✆ **416/368-1368.** Reservations recommended. Lunch buffet C$9.95 (US$6); main courses C$8–C$16 (US$5–US$10). AE, DC, MC, V. Mon–Fri 11:30am–2pm; daily 4:30–11pm. Subway: Queen or King.

## MIDTOWN WEST

### VERY EXPENSIVE

**Bistro 990** ★★★ FRENCH Because Hollywood types frequent Toronto, it's no surprise to see the stars out for a night on the town. Bistro 990 is just across the street from the tony Sutton Place hotel, so it drags in more than its fair share of big names. (One friend has had a couple of Whoopi Goldberg sightings here. Why do these things never happen when I'm around?) In any case, the Gallic dining room is charming, and the service is all-around attentive. The menu offers updated hors d'oeuvres, such as octopus and veggies in citrus marinade. Main dishes stick to grand-mère's recipes, like the satisfying roasted half chicken with garlicky mashed potatoes, and calf's liver in white-wine sauce. Sweets, fruit tarts, and sorbets are made daily.

990 Bay St. (at St. Joseph). ✆ **416/921-9990.** Reservations required. Main courses C$19–C$40 (US$12–US$25). AE, DC, MC, V. Mon–Fri noon–3pm; Mon–Sat 5–11pm. Subway: Museum or Wellesley.

### EXPENSIVE

**Mistura** ITALIAN While the curvy bar up front is still the place to meet, the modern Italian menu is the real draw at Mistura. The food is satisfying without being overly heavy—think spinach and ricotta gnocchi with light but creamy Gorgonzola sauce and toasted walnuts. The meaty entrees might include a tender veal chop with rosemary roasted potatoes and portobello mushrooms, or sweetbreads with chickpea polenta and caramelized root veggies. The well-organized wine list is heavy with Italian and California vintages.

265 Davenport Rd. ✆ **416/515-0009.** Reservations recommended. Main courses C$20–C$28 (US$12–$17). AE, DC, MC, V. Mon–Sat 5–11pm. Subway: Bay.

**Patriot** ★★ CANADIAN Canadians are often accused of having a lack of patriotism; perhaps this elegant eatery was designed to arouse some national pride? The ingredients are certainly all there: most of the menu staples, from veal to lobster and from cheeses to mushrooms, are proudly sourced in Canada. But what really counts in the end is what the kitchen makes of its bounty, and the results here are compelling, like the pairing of artichoke and oka cheese atop a rich carrot soup, or a slightly seared lam carpaccio served with beet juice, basil oil and balsamic vinegar. Since Canadians themselves hail from all parts of the globe, it's only fair to throw in a few foreign elements, as the excellent pineapple *tarte tatin* demonstrates. The wine list is dominated by Canadian vintages, so diners have a chance to learn first-hand why so many of them are winning international wine competitions.

131 Bloor St. W. ✆ 416-922-0025. Reservations recommended. Main courses C$17–C$27 (US$11–US$17). AE, MC, V. Mon-Sat 11am–11pm. Subway: Museum or Bay.

**Senses** ★★ INTERNATIONAL Senses is a combination bakery, gourmet food emporium (see "Shopping," later), and restaurant, all in one sophisticated, romance-minded space. Dining here is an experience for all the senses. The serene sandy tones are serious eye candy, the background music soothes, and velvety banquettes rub you the right way. Smell and taste get revved up for starters like venison salad with snow peas, cashews and caramelized wedges of Asian pear. Main-course roasted chicken breast is enlivened by the addition of green curry. As always, the service here is extremely well-informed and professional.

15 Bloor St. W. ✆ **416/935-0400.** Reservations required. Main C$18–C$36 (US$11–US$22). AE, DC, MC, V. Mon–Fri 11:30am–2:30pm, Sat 11:30am–3pm; Mon–Sat 5–10pm. Subway: Yonge/Bloor.

## MODERATE

**Matignon** *Finds* FRENCH A little bit off the beaten track, this small restaurant offers the thrill of discovery. Spread over two floors, the intimate rooms are festooned with all things French. The crowd includes many regulars, and the ambiance is that of a low-key bistro. The short menu is filled with classics from the old county, including Angus steak rolled in crushed pepper and flambéed with cognac, and rack of lamb with mustard and herbs of Provence. Desserts stay on the same track, like vanilla ice cream under hot chocolate sauce. Bon appétit!

51 St. Nicholas St. ✆ **416/921-9226.** Reservations recommended. Main courses C$14–C$18 (US$9–US$11). AE, MC, V. Mon–Fri 11:30am–2:30pm; Mon–Thurs 5–10pm, Fri–Sat 5–11pm. Subway: Wellesley.

**Sotto Sotto** ITALIAN Imagine the Bat Cave decorated by a Florentine, with aged frescoes, wall-mounted stonework, and wax-dripping gilt candelabra. A few steps down from street level, this restaurant transports diners a world away. Tables are cheek-by-jowl, but the jovial suits and couples who make the scene don't seem to mind. Efficient service lacks warmth, though the kitchen makes up for it. The Northern Italian menu leans to the lightweight, with a few irresistible creamy-sauced pastas. Main courses of meat or fish, like Cornish hen and swordfish, are nicely grilled. The risotto is fine—though, annoyingly, at least two people at the table must order it. There's a nice wine list, with many selections available by the glass.

116A Avenue Rd. (north of Bloor St.). ✆ **416/962-0011.** Reservations required. Main courses C$14–C$24 (US$9–US$15). AE, MC, V. Mon–Sat 5:30–11:30pm. Subway: Bay or Museum.

## INEXPENSIVE

**Bloor Street Diner** LIGHT FARE If you've shopped until you've dropped along Bloor Street West, this is just the place to grab a bite to eat and let your feet and your Visa card recover. It's two restaurants in one. Le Café/Terrasse is an informal bistro that serves decent soups, salads, and sandwiches all day long, and La Rotisserie is a slightly more upscale dining room with heartier Provençal-style fare. The basics are what they do best. Try to snag a seat on the umbrella-covered patio overlooking Bay Street (all the better for people watching).

In the Manulife Centre, 55 Bloor St. W. ✆ **416/928-3105.** Main courses C$10–C$18 (US$6–US$11). AE, DC, MC, V. Sun–Thurs 8am–1am, Fri–Sat 8am–2am. Subway: Bay or Yonge/Bloor.

**Kensington Kitchen** ★ *Kids* MEDITERRANEAN Drawing a crowd of regulars—students and professors—from the nearby University of Toronto, Kensington Kitchen is a perennial gem. The decor hasn't changed in years, with the same Oriental carpets covering the walls, painted wood floor, and decorative objects scattered about. The tradition of big portions at small cost stays constant, too. The menu ventures between the ports of the Mediterranean.

There's angel-hair pasta with heaps of shrimp, scallops, and mussels in tomato-coriander sauce; saffron paella with chicken and sausage; and Turkish-style braised lamb stuffed with raisins, eggplant, apricots, and figs. Nice weather? Head up to the rooftop patio, shaded by a mighty Manitoba maple.

124 Harbord St. ✆ **416/961-3404.** Reservations recommended. Main courses C$10–C$14 (US$6–US$9). AE, DC, MC, V. Mon–Sat 11:30am–11pm, Sun 11:30am–10pm. Subway: Spadina, then LRT south to Harbord St.

**SpringRolls** ASIAN What to have for dinner tonight: Chinese, Vietnamese, Thai, Singaporean? If you can't decide, your best bet is SpringRolls. The name may make you think its offerings are meager, but the multi-page menu will set you straight. There is no end in sight of barbecued pork or fried shrimp dishes, which are tenderly executed. Vegetarians don't have as many choices as you might expect, though there are a few top-notch vermicelli-and-veggie plates.

687 Yonge St. ✆ **416/972-7655.** Reservations recommended. Main courses C$5–C$11 (US$3.10–US$7). Mon–Sat 5:30–10:30pm. Subway: Yonge/Bloor.

## MIDTOWN EAST/THE EAST END

Just about everything *will* be Greek to you in the East End along Danforth Avenue. Known appropriately enough as Greektown, this is where to come for low-cost, delicious dining, or for a midnight meal—the tavernas along this strip generally stay open until the wee hours, even on weeknights.

### MODERATE

**Pan on the Danforth** ★ GREEK To the best of my knowledge, Pan was a god of music, not of food. I must have mixed it up because if he's the inspiration for this restaurant, he certainly knows his way around a kitchen. This long-established eatery takes classic Greek dishes and updates them with panache. Grilled swordfish is wrapped in vine leaf and served with spinach orzo, and a smoked and baked pork chop comes with scalloped feta potatoes and zucchini relish. The well-chosen wine list favors the New World. The crowd is fairly sophisticated, which may explain the cryptic message over the bar: "You've done it already."

516 Danforth Ave. ✆ **416/466-8158.** Reservations accepted only for parties of 3 or more. Main courses C$13–C$19 (US$8–US$12). AE, MC, V. Sun–Thurs 5pm–11pm, Fri–Sat 5pm–midnight. Subway: Chester or Pape.

## UPTOWN

This area is too large to be considered a neighborhood, stretching as it does from north of Davenport Road to Steeles Avenue. While it doesn't have the concentration of restaurants that the downtown area enjoys, it has a number of stellar options that make the trip north worthwhile.

### VERY EXPENSIVE

**Centro** ★★ CONTINENTAL The palace-grand main room, with its oxblood walls, is always bustling. French-born executive chef Marc Thuet, a motorcycle-riding local celebrity, takes his food seriously. The seasonal menu pays tribute to the restaurant's Northern Italian origins, with pasta dishes like pennette with Parma prosciutto and roasted sage. Many choices lean to contemporary Canadiana, like lean caribou chops with cloudberries and crabapple compote, or French modern, like rack of lamb in a Provençal honey mustard crust served with ratatouille. Delicious desserts run the gamut from traditional tiramisu to chocolate-vanilla baked Alaska. The stellar wine list is sure to thrill oenophiles.

2472 Yonge St. ✆ **416/483-2211.** Reservations required. Main courses C$28–C$42 (US$17–US$26). AE, DC, MC, V. Mon–Sat 5–11:30pm. Subway: Eglinton.

**North 44** ★★★ INTERNATIONAL This is the one restaurant that even people who've never set foot in Toronto have heard about. The Art Deco–inspired setting is sleek, with soft lighting and strategically situated mirrors wrap the dining room—and its occupants—in a gorgeous glow. The menu, which changes with the seasons, borrows from Mediterranean, American, and Asian sources. On the list of main courses you might find grilled veal tenderloin with orange peppercorns, toasted barley, and root veggies, or roasted Muscovy duck breast with orange-soy marinade and foie gras. There are always a few pasta and pizza choices, such as caramelized squash ravioli with black truffle essence. It's impossible to come here without being seduced into a three-course meal. The desserts, like lemon meringue mille-feuille, are among the best in the city, and there's a wide selection of accompanying ice wines. The wine list is comprehensive, though most of the prices veer off into the stratosphere. What really sets North 44 apart is its seamless service. Those who don't like to be pampered should stay away.

2537 Yonge St. ✆ **416/487-4897.** Reservations required. Main courses C$27–C$45 (US$17–US$28). AE, DC, MC, V. Mon–Sat 5–11pm. Subway: Eglinton.

### EXPENSIVE

**Lakes** BISTRO Plush banquettes and close-set tables heighten the sense of intimacy in the narrow dining room. A casually well-dressed crowd drops by during the week; on Saturday night, work-obsessed couples spend candlelit quality time. The menu changes every few months, but jazzed-up bistro classics such as duck confit with cranberry-shallot glaze and garlic mashed potatoes, grilled provimi veal liver, and Gruyère-and-Emmenthal fondue for two make frequent appearances. The banana crème brûlée on the short dessert menu is a perennial favorite.

1112 Yonge St. ✆ **416/966-0185.** Reservations strongly recommended. Main courses C$14–C$26 (US$9–US$16). AE, DC, MC, V. Mon–Fri noon–3pm and 5:30–11pm, Sat 6–11pm. Subway: Rosedale.

## 5 Seeing the Sights

First the good news: Toronto has amazing sights to see and places to be that appeal to travelers of all stripes. The bad news? No matter how long your stay, you won't be able to fit everything in. Toronto is a sprawling city, and while downtown and midtown boast a sizable collection of attractions, some truly wonderful sights are in less accessible areas.

Another difficulty is that many attractions could take up a day of your visit. Ontario Place, Harbourfront, the Ontario Science Centre, and Paramount Canada's Wonderland all come to mind. That's not even mentioning the expansive parks, the arts scene, or the shopping possibilities. My best advice is to relax and bring a good pair of walking shoes. There's no better way to appreciate the kaleidoscopic metropolis that is Toronto than on foot.

### THE TOP ATTRACTIONS

#### ON THE LAKEFRONT

**Ontario Place** ★ *Kids* When this 39ha (96 acre) recreation complex on Lake Ontario opened in 1971, it seemed futuristic—and 29 years later, it still does. (The 1989 face-lift no doubt helped.) From a distance, you'll see five steel-and-glass pods suspended on columns 32m (105 ft.) above the lake, three artificial islands, and a huge geodesic dome. The five pods contain a multimedia theater, a children's theater, a high-technology exhibit, and displays that tell the story of

Ontario in vivid kaleidoscopic detail. The dome houses Cinesphere, where IMAX movies are shown year-round.

Under an enormous orange canopy, the Children's Village is the most creative playground you'll find anywhere. In a well-supervised area, children under 13 can scramble over rope bridges, bounce on an enormous trampoline, explore the foam forest, or slide down a twisting chute. The most popular activity allows them to squirt water pistols and garden hoses, swim, and generally drench one another in the water-play section. Afterward, parents can pop them into the convenient dryers before moving on to other amusements.

A stroll around the complex reveals two marinas full of yachts and other craft, the HMCS *Haida* (a destroyer, open for tours, that served in World War II and the Korean War), an 18-hole miniature golf course, and plenty of grassland for picnicking and romping. The restaurants and snack bars serve everything from Chinese, Irish, and German food to hot dogs and hamburgers. And don't miss the wildest rides in town—the Hydrofuge, a tube slide that allows you to reach speeds over 50kmph (30 mph); the Rush River Raft Ride, which carries you along a lengthy flume in an inflatable raft; the pink twister and purple pipeline (water slides); plus bumper boats and go-karts. For something more peaceful, you can navigate pedal boats or remote-control boats between the artificial islands.

At night, the **Molson Amphitheatre** accommodates 16,000 under a copper canopy and outside on the grass. It features top-line entertainers such as Kenny G, James Taylor, the Who, and Hank Williams. For information, call ✆ **416/260-5600.** For tickets, call **Ticketmaster** (✆ **416/870-8000**).

955 Lakeshore Blvd. W. ✆ **416/314-9811**, or 416/314-9900 for recorded info. www.ontarioplace.com. Free admission to grounds. Separate fee for some events. Admission to attractions C$12 (US$7); Play All Day pass C$22 (US$14) adults, C$11 (US$7) children 4–5, free for children 3 and under. IMAX movies after Labour Day (included in Play All Day pass) C$10 (US$6) adults, C$6 (US$3.70) seniors and children 13 and under. Mid-May to Labour Day, daily 10am–dusk; evening events end and dining spots close later. Parking C$9 (US$6). Subway: Bathurst or Dufferin, then Bathurst streetcar south.

**Harbourfront Centre** ★★ *Kids* In 1972, the federal government took over a 39ha (96-acre) strip of prime waterfront land to preserve the vista—and since then Torontonians have rediscovered their lakeshore. Abandoned warehouses, shabby depots, and crumbling factories have been refurbished, and a tremendous urban park now stretches on and around the old piers. Today it's one of the most popular hangouts for Torontonians and visitors—a great place to spend a day sunbathing, picnicking, biking, shopping, and sailing.

**Queen's Quay,** at the foot of York Street, is the closest quay to town, the first one you'll encounter as you approach from the Westin Harbour Castle. From here, boats depart for harbor tours, and ferries leave for the Toronto Islands. In this renovated warehouse you'll find the Premiere Dance Theatre (which was specially designed for dance performances), and two floors of shops, restaurants, and waterfront cafes.

After exploring Queen's Quay, walk west along the glorious waterfront promenade to **York Quay.** You'll pass the **Power Plant,** a contemporary art gallery, and behind it, the **Du Maurier Theatre Centre.** At York Quay Centre, you can pick up information on Harbourfront programming. Galleries here include the **Craft Studio,** where you can watch artisans blow glass, throw pots, and make silk-screen prints. On the other side of the center, you can attend a free outdoor concert, held all summer long at Molson Place. Also on the quay is the Water's

Edge Cafe, overlooking a small pond for electric model boats (there's skating here in the winter) and a children's play area.

Take the footbridge to John Quay, crossing over the sailboats moored below, to the stores and restaurants on **Pier 4**—Wallymagoo's Marine Bar and the Pier 4 Storehouse. Beyond, on Maple Leaf Quay, lies the Nautical Centre. At the **Harbourside Boating Centre** (part of the Nautical Centre), 283 Queen's Quay W. (✆ **416/203-3000**), you can rent sailboats and powerboats or sign up for sailing lessons (see "Boating/Canoeing," later).

The **Harbourfront Antiques Market,** 390 Queen's Quay W., at the foot of Spadina Avenue (✆ **416/260-2626**), will keep antique-lovers busy browsing for hours. More than 100 antiques dealers spread out their wares—jewelry, china, furniture, toys, and books. Indoor parking is adjacent to the market, and a cafeteria serves fresh salads, sandwiches, and desserts. It's open Tuesday through Sunday from 10am to 6pm.

At the west end of the park stands **Bathurst Pier,** with a large sports field plus two adventure playgrounds, one for older kids and the other (supervised) for 3 to 7 year olds.

More than 4,000 events take place annually at Harbourfront, including the **Harbourfront Reading Series** in June, and the **International Festival of Authors** in October. Other happenings include films, dance, theater, music, children's events, multicultural festivals, and marine events.

235 Queen's Quay W. ✆ **416/973-3000** for information on special events, or 416/973-4000 (box office). www.harbourfront.on.ca. Subway: Union, then LRT to York Quay.

**The Toronto Islands** ★ *Kids* In only 7 minutes, an 800-passenger ferry takes you across to 250ha (612 acres) of island parkland crisscrossed by shaded paths and quiet waterways—a glorious spot to walk, play tennis, bike, feed the ducks, putter around in boats, picnic, or lap up the sun. There are 14 islands, but the three major ones are **Centre, Ward's,** and **Algonquin.** The first is the busiest; the other two are home to about 600 people who live in modest cottages. Originally, the land was a peninsula, but in the mid-1800s a series of storms shattered the finger of land into islands.

On Centre Island, families enjoy **Centreville** (✆ **416/203-0405**), an old-fashioned amusement park. You won't see the usual neon signs, shrill hawkers, and greasy hot-dog stands. Instead you'll find a turn-of-the-last-century village complete with a Main Street, tiny shops, a firehouse, and even a small working farm where the kids can pet lambs and chicks and enjoy pony rides. They'll also love trying out the antique cars, fire engines, old-fashioned train, authentic 1890s carousel, flume ride, and aerial cars. Individual rides (19 of them) cost C$1.50 to $3.50 (US95¢–US$2.15). An all-day ride pass costs C$12 (US$7) for those under 125cm (49 inches) tall, C$17.50 (US$11) for taller folk. Centreville is open 10:30am to 6pm, daily from mid-May to Labour Day, and weekends in early May and September.

✆ **416/392-8193** for ferry schedules. Round-trip fare C$4 (US$2.50) adults, C$2 (US$1.25) seniors and youths 15–19, C$1 (US62¢) children under 15. Ferries leave from docks at the bottom of Bay St. Subway: Union Station, then LRT to Queen's Quay.

## DOWNTOWN

**CN Tower** *Kids* As you approach the city, whether by plane, train, or automobile, the first thing you notice is this slender structure. Glass-walled elevators glide up the 553m (1,815-ft.) tower, the tallest freestanding structure in the world. The elevators stop first at the 346m (1,136-ft.) high, 7-level sky pod (it takes just under a minute, so prepare for popping ears). From here, on a clear day you can't quite see forever, but the sweeping vista stretches to Niagara Falls, 150km (100 miles) south, and to Lake Simcoe, 200km (120 miles) north. The tower attractions are often revamped. Some perennial draws are the IMAX theater and the two airplane simulators (one gentle and calm, the other a rugged ride through caves and over mountains). A series of interactive displays showcases the CN Tower along with such forerunners as the Eiffel Tower and the Empire State Building. The pod also contains broadcasting facilities, a nightclub, and the underwhelming **360 Revolving Restaurant** (✆ **416/362-5411**).

Atop the tower sits a 102m (335-ft.) antenna mast erected over 31 weeks with the aid of a giant Sikorsky helicopter. It took 55 lifts to complete the operation. Above the sky pod is the world's highest public observation gallery, the Space Deck, 447m (1,465 ft.) above the ground (C$4/US$2.50 additional charge); unless you're really taken with the tower, I wouldn't recommend it—the view from the sky pod is majestic enough for me. The pod also boasts my favorite spot in the vicinity: a glass floor that will let you see all the way down to street level (even as your heart drops into your shoes). As an added bonus, if you wait long enough, you'll undoubtedly see some alpha males daring each other to jump on the glass (they do, and no, it doesn't break). The tower is built of sturdy stuff to resist the elements—contoured reinforced concrete covered with thick glass-reinforced plastic designed to keep ice accumulation to a minimum. The structure can withstand high winds, snow, ice, lightning, and earth tremors.

301 Front St. W. ✆ **416/868-6937.** www.cntower.ca. Admission C$16 (US$10) adults, C$14 (US$9) seniors, C$11 (US$7) children 5–12. Motion simulator rides C$7.50 (US$4.65). Combination tickets C$23 (US$14) and up. May–Sept daily 8am–11pm; Oct–Apr 9am–10pm. Subway: Union, then walk west on Front St.

**Art Gallery of Ontario** ★ Kids The exterior gives no hint of the light and openness inside this beautifully designed gallery. The space is dramatic, and the paintings imaginatively displayed. Throughout, audiovisual presentations and interactive computer presentations provide information on particular paintings or schools of painters. The European collections are fine, but the Canadian galleries are the real treat. The paintings by the Group of Seven—which includes Tom Thomson, F. H. Varley, and Lawren Harris—are extraordinary. In addition, other galleries show the genesis of Canadian art from earlier to more modern artists. And don't miss the extensive collection of Inuit art. The **Henry Moore Sculpture Centre,** with more than 800 pieces (original plasters, bronzes, maquettes, woodcuts, lithographs, etchings, and drawings), is the largest public collection of his works. The artist gave them to Toronto because he was so moved by the citizens' enthusiasm for his work—public donations bought his sculpture *The Archer* to decorate Nathan Phillips Square at City Hall after politicians refused to free up money for it. In one room, under a glass ceiling, 20 or so of his large works stand like silent prehistoric rock formations. Along the walls flanking a ramp are color photographs showing Moore's major sculptures in their natural locations, which reveal their magnificent dimensions.

The European collection ranges from the 14th century to the French impressionists and beyond. Works by Pissarro, Monet, Boudin, Sisley, and Renoir fill an octagonal room. De Kooning's *Two Women on a Wharf* and Karel Appel's *Black Landscape* are just two of the modern examples. There are several works of particular interest to admirers of the pre-Raphaelite painters, including one by Waterhouse. Among the sculptures, you'll find two beauties—Picasso's *Poupée* and Brancusi's *First Cry.* Behind the gallery, connected by an arcade, stands the **Grange** (1817), Toronto's oldest surviving brick house, which was the gallery's first permanent space. Originally the home of the Boulton family, it was a gathering place for many of the city's social and political leaders and for such eminent guests as Matthew Arnold, Prince Kropotkin, and Winston Churchill. It has been meticulously restored and furnished to reflect the 1830s, and is a living museum of mid-19th-century Toronto life. Entrance is free with admission to the art gallery. The gallery has an attractive restaurant, Agora, which is open for lunch, as well as a cafeteria and a gallery shop; there's also a full program of films, concerts, and lectures.

317 Dundas St. W. (between McCaul and Beverley sts.). © **416/977-0414.** www.ago.net. Pay what you can; suggested adult admission C$8 (US$5). Extra fee for special exhibits. Tues and Thurs–Fri 11am-6pm, Wed 11am–8:30pm, Sat–Sun 10am–5:30pm. Grange House Tues–Sun noon–4pm, Wed noon–9pm. Closed Jan 1, Dec 25. Subway: St. Patrick.

## MIDTOWN

**Royal Ontario Museum** ★★★ *Kids* This is one of my favorite museums anywhere. The ROM (rhymes with "tom"), as it's affectionately called, is Canada's largest museum, with more than 6 million objects in its collections. Among the many highlights are the world-renowned **T. T. Tsui Galleries of Chinese Art,** which contain priceless Ming and Qing porcelains, embroidered silk robes, and objects made of jade and ivory. One of the collection's treasures is the procession of 100 earthenware figures, including ox-drawn carts, soldiers, musicians, officials, and attendants dating from the early 6th to the late 7th century. Another is the collection of 14 monumental Buddhist sculptures from the 12th to the 16th century. Visitors can also see outstanding examples of early weapons and tools, oracle bones, bronzes, ceramic vessels, human and animal figures, and jewelry.

The **Sigmund Samuel Canadiana galleries** display a premier collection of early Canadian decorative arts and historical paintings. More than 1,200 objects in elaborate period room settings reveal in a concrete way the French and English contributions to Canadian culture. Other highlights include the **Ancient Egypt Gallery,** which features several mummies, the **Roman Gallery** (the most extensive collection in Canada), the excellent textile collection, and nine life-science galleries (devoted to evolution, mammals, reptiles, and botany). The **Gallery of Indigenous Peoples** features changing exhibitions that explore the past and present cultures of Canada's indigenous peoples. A recent addition is the **Gallery of Korean Art,** the largest exhibit of its kind in North America. It holds more than 200 works from the Bronze Age through modern times.

A favorite with kids is the **Bat Cave Gallery,** a miniature replica of the St. Clair bat cave in Jamaica. It's complete with more than 3,000 very lifelike bats roosting and flying through the air amid realistic spiders, crabs, a wildcat, and snakes. Kids also enjoy the spectacular **Dinosaur Gallery,** with 13 realistically displayed dinosaur skeletons, and the **Discovery Gallery,** a mini-museum where youngsters (and adults) can touch authentic artifacts from Egyptian scarabs to English military helmets.

The ROM's light, airy dining lounge, **Jamie Kennedy at the Museum** (© **416/586-5578**), has a small terrace for outdoor dining. It's under the expert supervision of Jamie Kennedy, one of Canada's top chefs. It's well worth stopping in for lunch.

100 Queen's Park Crescent. © **416/586-8000.** www.rom.on.ca. Admission C$12 (US$7) adults; C$7 (US$4.35) seniors and students (with valid ID), C$6 (US$3.70) children 5–14; C$30 (US$19) families (2 adults and 2 children); free for children 4 and under. Pay what you can Fri 4:30–9:30pm. Mon–Thurs 10am–6pm, Fri 10am–9:30pm, Sat 10am–6pm, Sun 11am–6pm. Closed Jan 1, Dec 25. Subway: Museum.

### Finds A Place of Peace

While the permanent collections and special exhibitions at the Royal Ontario Museum are impressive, the best room in the entire gallery is barely known—and usually empty. It's called the **Bishop White Gallery,** and it houses a group of serene Southeast Asian Buddhas. They stand together in the center of the room, facing outwards; the walls are covered with murals taken from the region, too. Some of the Buddhas are in better shape than others (you'll see wounds and scars where jewels were plucked out), but all of them radiate peace. This is one place I go to recharge.

**George R. Gardiner Museum of Ceramic Art** Across the street from the ROM, North America's only specialized ceramics museum houses a great collection of 15th- to 18th-century European pieces. The pre-Columbian gallery contains fantastic Olmec and Mayan figures, and objects from Ecuador, Colombia, and Peru. The majolica gallery displays spectacular 16th- and 17th-century salvers and other pieces from Florence, Faenza, and Venice, and a Delftware collection that includes fine 17th-century chargers. Upstairs, the galleries are given over to 18th-century continental and English porcelain—Meissen, Sèvres, Worcester, Chelsea, Derby, and other great names. All are spectacular. Among the highlights are objects from the Swan Service—a 2,200-piece set that took 4 years (1737–41) to make—and an extraordinary collection of commedia dell'arte figures.

111 Queen's Park. ✆ **416/586-8080.** Suggested donation C$5 (US$3.10). Mon and Wed–Sat 10am–5pm, Tues 10am–8pm, Sun 11am–5pm. Closed Jan 1, Dec 25. Subway: Museum.

## ON THE OUTSKIRTS

**Ontario Science Centre** ★ *Kids* Described as everything from the world's most technical fun fair to a hands-on museum for the 21st century, the Science Centre holds a series of wonders for children—800 interactive exhibits in 10 cavernous exhibit halls. More than a million people visit every year, so it's best to arrive promptly at 10am—that way, you'll be able to get around with less hassle. Wherever you look, there are things to touch, push, pull, or crank. Test your reflexes, balance, heart rate, and grip strength; surf the Internet; watch frozen-solid liquid nitrogen shatter into thousands of icy shards; study slides of butterfly wings, bedbugs, fish scales, or feathers under a microscope; tease your brain with a variety of optical illusions; land a spaceship on the moon; watch bees making honey; see how many lights you can light or how high you can elevate a balloon with your own pedal power. The fun goes on and on in 10 exhibit halls. Throughout, small theaters show film and slide shows, and you can see regular 20-minute demonstrations of lasers, metal casting, and high-voltage electricity (watch your friend's hair stand on end). Another draw is the Omnimax Theatre, with a 24m (79-ft.) domed screen that creates spectacular effects. The center has a restaurant and lounge (which serves alcohol), cafeteria, and science shop.

While most of what the Science Centre has to offer is fun for the small fry, one area that adults will appreciate is the re-creation of a rain-forest environment. Located on the bottom level of the building, it's large enough that you can wander a bit and forget the noise and blinking lights of the science arcade just beyond. One caveat: roam in here for long and you'll feel like you've hit a sauna.

770 Don Mills Rd. (at Eglinton Ave. E.). ✆ **416/696-3127,** or 416/696-1000 for Omnimax tickets. www.osc.on.ca. Admission C$12 (US$7) adults, C$7 (US$4.35) seniors and youths 13–17, C$6 (US$3.70) children 5–12, free for children under 5. Omnimax admission C$10 (US$6) adults, C$6 (US$3.70) seniors and youths 13–17, C$5.50 (US$3.40) children 5–12. Combination discounts available. Daily 10am–5pm. Closed Dec 25. Parking C$7 (US$4.35). Yonge St. subway to Eglinton, then no. 34 Eglinton bus east to Don Mills Rd. By car from downtown, take Don Valley Pkwy. to Don Mills Rd. exit and follow signs.

**The Toronto Zoo** *Kids* Covering 285ha (710 acres) of parkland, this unique zoological garden contains some 5,000 animals, plus an extensive botanical collection. The plants and animals are housed in pavilions—including Africa, Indo-Malaya, Australasia, and the Americas—or in outdoor paddocks. It's a photographer's dream.

One popular zoo attraction is at the **African Savannah** project. It re-creates a market bazaar and safari through Kesho (Swahili for "tomorrow") National Park, past such special features as a bush camp, rhino midden, elephant highway, and several watering holes.

Six miles of walkways offer access to all areas of the zoo. During the warmer months, the Zoomobile takes visitors around the major walkways to view the animals in the outdoor paddocks. The zoo has restaurants, a gift shop, first aid, and a family center. Visitors can rent strollers and wagons, and borrow wheelchairs. The zoo is equipped with ramps and washrooms for those with disabilities. The African pavilion has an elevator for strollers and wheelchairs. There's ample parking and plenty of picnic areas with tables.

Meadowvale Rd. (north of Hwy. 401 and Sheppard Ave.), Scarborough. ✆ **416/392-5900.** www.torontozoo.com. Admission C$13 (US$8) adults, C$10 (US$6) seniors, C$8 (US$5) children 4–14, free for children 3 and under. Summer daily 9am–7:30pm; spring and fall 9am–5pm; winter 9:30am–4:30pm. Last admission 1 hour before closing. Closed Dec 25. Parking C$6 (US$3.70). Subway: Bloor–Danforth line to Kennedy, then bus no. 86A north. By car: From downtown, take Don Valley Pkwy. to Hwy. 401 east, exit on Meadowvale Rd., and follow signs.

**The McMichael Canadian Art Collection** In Kleinburg, 40km (25 miles) north of the city, the McMichael is worth a visit for the setting as well as the art. The collection is in a log-and-stone gallery that sits amid quiet stands of trees on 40ha (100 acres) of conservation land. Specially designed for the landscape paintings it houses, the gallery is a work of art. The lobby has a pitched roof that soars 8m (27 ft.) on massive rafters of Douglas fir; throughout the gallery, panoramic windows look south over white pine, cedar, ash, and birch.

The collection includes the work of Canada's famous group of landscape painters, the Group of Seven, as well as David Milne, Emily Carr, and their contemporaries. These artists—inspired by the turn-of-the-century Canadian wilderness, particularly in Algonquin Park and northern Ontario—recorded the rugged landscape in highly individualistic styles. An impressive collection of Inuit and contemporary Native Canadian art and sculpture is also on display. In addition, four galleries contain changing exhibitions of works by contemporary artists.

Founded by Robert and Signe McMichael, the gallery began in 1965 when they donated their property, home, and collection to the Province of Ontario. The collection has expanded to include more than 6,000 works. The museum has a good book and gift store, and a fine restaurant that features Canadian cuisine.

10365 Islington Ave., Kleinburg. ✆ **905/893-1121.** www.mcmichael.com. Admission C$9 (US$6) adults, C$7 (US$4.35) seniors and students, free for children 5 and under. May–Oct weekdays 10am–4pm, Sat 11am–4pm, Sun 11am–5pm; Nov–Apr Tues–Sat 11am–4pm, Sun 11am–5pm. Parking C$5 (US$3.10). Buses run from the Bay and Dundas and the Yorkdale GO train stations. By car from downtown, take the Gardiner Expwy. to Hwy. 427 north, follow it to Hwy. 7, and turn east. Turn left (north) at the first light onto Hwy. 27.

Turn right (east) at Major Mackenzie Dr. and left (north) at the first set of traffic lights to Islington Ave. and the village of Kleinburg. Or take Hwy. 401 to Hwy. 400 north. At Major Mackenzie Dr., go west to Islington Ave. and turn right.

**Paramount Canada's Wonderland** ★ *Kids* Thirty minutes north of Toronto lies Canada's answer to Disney World. The 120ha (300-acre) park features more than 140 attractions, including 50 rides, a 8ha (20-acre) water park, a participatory play area (Kid's Kingdom), and live shows.

Adults and kids alike come for the thriller rides. Because the park relies on the local audience, it introduces new rides every year. One of the top attractions is the Fly, a roller coaster designed to make every seat feel as if it's in the front car—the faint of heart can't hide at the back of this one! Other stomach-churners include the Drop Zone, in which riders free-fall 70m (230 ft.) in an open cockpit, Cliffhanger, a "super swing" that makes 360° turns and makers riders feel immune to gravity, and the Xtreme Skyflyer, a hang-gliding and skydiving hybrid that plunges riders 45m (150 ft.) in a free fall. The most popular rides are the nine roller coasters, which range from a nostalgic, relatively tame wooden version to the looping, inverted Top Gun, the stand-up looping Sky Rider, and the suspended Vortex. The Splash Works water park offers a huge wave pool and 16 water rides, from speed slides and tube rides to special scaled-down slides and a kids' play area. To add to the thrills for Star Trek fans, Klingons, Vulcans, Romulans, and Bajorans (along with Hanna-Barbera characters) stroll around the park. Additional attractions include Speedcity Raceway, featuring two-seat go-karts, miniature golf, batting cages, restaurants, and shops. The Kingswood Theatre books top-name entertainers.

You'll probably need a full day to see everything. If you picnic on the grounds and forgo souvenirs, a family of four can "do" the park for about C$150 (US$93), depending on the age of the kids. Watch out, though, for the extra attractions not included in the admission pass, particularly the many carnival-type "games of skill," which the kids love, but your purse may not.

With the extensive fanfare given to the new rides that are introduced each summer, many park-goers overlook the older attractions. The Wilde Beaste is one of the original roller coasters, and it's still one of the best. The first few times you hurtle along the track you'll be convinced that the whole rickety structure is about to fall down at any moment. Guess what—it was designed to feel that way! (Wonderland's safety standards are top-notch, so have no worries on that front.) Other tried-but-true favorites include the Minebuster and the Dragon Flyer. An added bonus: shorter queues!

9580 Jane St., Vaughan. ✆ **905/832-7000** or 905/832-8131. www.canadaswonderland.com. Pay-One-Price Passport (includes unlimited rides and shows but not parking, special attractions, or Kingswood Music Theater) C$43 (US$27) adults and children age 4 and up, C$21.50 (US$13) seniors and children 3–6, free for children 2 and under. Admission only (no rides) C$25 (US$16). June 1–25 Mon–Fri 10am–8pm, Fri–Sat 10am–10pm; June 26–Labour Day daily 10am–10pm; late May and early Sept–early Oct Sat–Sun 10am–8pm. Closed mid-Oct to mid-May. Parking C$6.50 (US$4). Subway: Yorkdale or York Mills, then GO Express Bus to Wonderland. By car: Take Yonge St. north to Hwy. 401 and go west to Hwy. 400. Go north on Hwy. 400 to Rutherford Rd. exit and follow signs. By car from the north, exit at Major Mackenzie.

## MORE ATTRACTIONS

### ARCHITECTURAL HIGHLIGHTS

**Casa Loma** ★ *Kids* Every city has its folly, and Toronto has an unusually charming one. It's complete with Elizabethan-style chimneys, Rhineland turrets, secret passageways, an underground tunnel, and a mellifluous name: Casa Loma.

Sir Henry Pellatt, who built it between 1911 and 1914, is credited with having a lifelong fascination with castles. He studied medieval palaces and gathered materials and furnishings from around the world, bringing marble, glass, and paneling from Europe, teak from Asia, and oak and walnut from North America. He imported Scottish stonemasons to build the massive walls that surround the 2ha (6 acre) site.

It's a fascinating place to explore. Wander through the majestic Great Hall, with its 18m (60-ft.) high hammer-beam ceiling; the Oak Room, where three artisans took 3 years to fashion the paneling; and the Conservatory, with its elegant bronze doors, stained-glass dome, and pink-and-green marble. The castle has battlements and a tower; Peacock Alley, designed after Windsor Castle; and a 1,700-bottle wine cellar. A 245m (800-ft.) tunnel runs to the stables, where horses were quartered amid the luxury of Spanish tile and mahogany.

The tour is self-guided; you'll be given an audiocassette, available in eight languages, upon arrival. From May to October, the gardens are open, too. There are special events every March, July, and December.

Several doors on the first storey open to a grand terrace that overlooks the gardens; most visitors step out, look at the gorgeous fountain and flowers below, then proceed with the castle tour. However there is one mistake. From the terrace it's almost impossible to see the entrances to several winding paths that lead you around the extensive grounds and command amazing views. Follow the grand staircase down and enjoy a leisurely ramble.

1 Austin Terrace. ✆ **416/923-1171.** www.casaloma.org. Admission C$10 (US$6) adults, C$6.50 (US$4) seniors and youths 14–17, C$6 (US$3.70) children 4–13, free for children 3 and under. Daily 9:30am–5pm (last entry at 4pm). Closed Jan 1, Dec 25. Subway: Dupont, then walk 2 blocks north.

**City Hall** ★ An architectural spectacle, City Hall houses the mayor's office and the city's administrative offices. Daringly designed in the late 1950s by Finnish architect Viljo Revell, it consists of a low podium topped by the flying-saucer-shaped Council Chamber, enfolded between two curved towers. Its interior is as dramatic as its exterior. A cafeteria and dining room are in the basement.

In front stretches **Nathan Phillips Square** (named after the mayor who initiated the project). In summer you can sit and contemplate the flower gardens, fountains, and reflecting pool (which doubles as a skating rink in winter), as well as listen to concerts. Here you'll find Henry Moore's *The Archer* (formally, *Three-Way Piece No. 2*), purchased through a public subscription fund, and the Peace Garden, which commemorates Toronto's sesquicentennial in 1984. In contrast, to the east stands the **Old City Hall,** a green-copper-roofed Victorian Romanesque-style building.

100 Queen St. W. ✆ **416/338-0338.** www.city.toronto.on.ca. Free admission. Self-guided tours Mon–Fri 8:30am–4:30pm. Subway: Queen, then walk west to Bay.

**Fort York** *Kids* Established by Lieutenant Governor Simcoe in 1793 to defend "little muddy York," as Toronto was then known, Fort York was sacked by Americans in 1813. You can tour the soldiers' and officers' quarters, clamber over the ramparts, and view demonstrations. The fort really comes to life in summer, with daily demonstrations of drill, music, and cooking. The fort is a few blocks west of the CN Tower and 2 blocks east of Exhibition Place.

Garrison Rd., off Fleet St., between Bathurst St. and Strachan Ave. ✆ **416/392-6907.** Admission C$5 (US$3.10) adults, C$3.25 (US$2) seniors and youths 13–18, C$3 (US$1.85) children 6–12, children 5 and under free. June–Oct Mon–Wed and Fri 10am–5pm, Thurs 10am–7pm, Sat–Sun noon–5pm; Nov–May Tues–Fri 10am–5pm, Sat–Sun noon–5pm. Subway: Bathurst, then streetcar no. 511 south.

**Ontario Legislature** ★ At the northern end of University Avenue, with University of Toronto buildings to the east and west, lies Queen's Park. Embedded in its center is the rose-tinted sandstone-and-granite Ontario Legislature, with stately domes, arches, and porte cocheres. At any time of year other than summer, drop in around 2pm—when the legislature is in session—for some pithy comments during the question period, or take one of the regular tours. It's best to call ahead to check times.

111 Wellesley St. W. (at University Ave.). ✆ **416/325-7500.** www.ontla.on.ca. Free admission. Mon–Fri and weekends Victoria Day–Labour Day. Weekend tours every ½ hour 9–11:30am and 1–4pm; call ahead at other times. Subway: Queen's Park.

**Spadina House** ★ Here's a trick locals play on unsuspecting visitors: get them to pronounce "Spadina." In the case of the avenue, it's "spa-DYE-na"; for this lovely landmark, it's "spa-DEE-na". Why? Who knows! But if you want to see how the leading lights of the city lived in days gone by, visit the historic home of financier James Austin. The exterior is beautiful, but indoors it's even more impressive. Spadina House contains a remarkable collection of art, furniture, and decorative objects. Best of all, it's not a standard period piece: the Austin family occupied the house from 1866 to 1980 and successive generations modified and added to the house and its decor.

Tours (the only way to see the house) start on the quarter hour. Be warned that while the guides are excellent, the video that they force you to watch before the tour is laughable (the narrator is the "spirit of the house," and his rambling comments - paired with a stagy Irish brogue - will make you wonder if the video is some kind of in-joke). In summer, you can also tour the gorgeous gardens.

285 Spadina Rd. ✆ **416/392-6910.** Guided tour C$5 (US$3.10) adults, C$3.25 (US$2) seniors and youths, C$3 (US$1.85) children under 13. Tues–Fri noon–4pm, Sat–Sun noon–5pm. Subway: Dupont.

## MUSEUMS

**The Bata Shoe Museum** Imelda Marcos—or anyone else obsessed with shoes—will love this museum, which houses the Bata family's 10,000-item collection. The building, designed by Raymond Moriyama, is spectacular. The main gallery, "All About Shoes," traces the history of footwear. It begins with a plaster cast of some of the earliest known human footprints (discovered in Africa by anthropologist Mary Leakey), which date to 4 million B.C., then wanders through the fads and fashions of every era.

You'll come across such specialty shoes as spiked clogs used to crush chestnuts in 17th-century France, Elton John's 12-inch-plus platforms, and Prime Minister Pierre Trudeau's well-worn sandals. One display focuses on Canadian footwear fashioned by the Inuit, while another highlights 19th-century ladies' footwear. The second-storey galleries house changing exhibits.

327 Bloor St. W. (at St. George St.). ✆ **416/979-7799.** www.batashoemuseum.ca. Admission C$6 (US$3.70) adults, C$4 (US$2.50) seniors and students, C$2 (US$1.25) children 5–14; C$12 (US$7) family admission (2 adults, 2 children). Free to all first Tues of the month. Tues–Wed and Fri–Sat 10am–5pm, Thurs 10am–8pm, Sun noon–5pm. Subway: St. George.

**Black Creek Pioneer Village** *Kids* Life here moves at the gentle pace of rural Ontario as it was 100 years ago. You can watch the authentically dressed villagers going about their chores, spinning, sewing, rail splitting, sheep shearing, and threshing. Enjoy the villagers' cooking, wander through the cozily furnished homesteads, visit the working mill, shop at the general store, or rumble past the farm animals in a horse-drawn wagon. The beautifully landscaped village has more than 30 restored buildings to explore. Special events take place throughout the year, from a great Easter egg hunt to Christmas by lamplight. The dining room (open May to Thanksgiving and December) serves lunch and afternoon tea.

1000 Murray Ross Pkwy. (at Steeles Ave. and Jane St.), Downsview. ✆ **416/736-1733.** Admission C$9 (US$6) adults, C$7 (US$4.35) seniors, C$5 (US$3.10) children 5–14, free for children 4 and under. May–June weekdays 9:30am–4:30pm, weekends and holidays 10am–5pm; July–Sept daily 10am–5pm; Oct–Dec weekdays 9:30am–4pm, weekends and holidays 10am–4:30pm. Closed Jan–Apr, Dec 25. Parking C$5 (US$3.10). Subway: Finch, then bus no. 60 to Jane St.

**Design Exchange** In the old Stock Exchange Building, this has become Toronto's design center. It showcases professionals' work, but the main purpose of the institution is to nurture designers of all types—graphic, industrial, interior, landscape, and urban. It also serves as a clearinghouse and resource center for the design community. Small free exhibitions on the first floor are open daily, while those in the upstairs Exhibition Hall are generally on view for 3 to 6 months and require admission. There's also a good bookstore and Cafe Deco, a relaxed eatery open Monday to Friday 7:30am to 5pm.

234 Bay St. ✆ **416/363-6121.** Admission C$6 (US$3.70) adults, C$4.50 (US$2.80) students and seniors, free for children 13 and under. Mon–Fri 10am–6pm, Sat–Sun noon–5pm. Subway: King.

## SPORTS HIGHLIGHTS

**Air Canada Centre** Toronto's newest sports and entertainment complex is home to the Maple Leafs (hockey) and the Raptors (basketball). While longtime fans were crushed when the Leafs moved here in 1999 from Maple Leaf Gardens—the arena that had housed the team since 1931—the Air Canada Centre has quickly become a fan favorite. Seating 18,700 for hockey games, 19,500 for basketball, and 20,000 for concerts, the center was designed with comfort in mind. Seating is on a steeper-than-usual grade so that even the "nosebleed" sections have decent sightlines, and the seats are wider . . . and upholstered.

40 Bay St. (at Lakeshore Blvd.). ✆ **416/815-5500.** Tours C$9.50 (US$6) adults, C$7.50 (US$4.65) students and seniors, C$6.50 (US$4) children 12 and under. Tours on the hour Mon-Sat 10–3, Sun 11–3. Call ahead; no tours during events. Subway: Union, then LRT to Queen's Quay.

**Hockey Hall of Fame** ★ *Kids* Ice hockey fans will be thrilled by the artifacts collected here. They include the original Stanley Cup (donated in 1893 by Lord Stanley of Preston), a replica of the Montreal Canadiens' locker room, Terry Sawchuck's goalie gear, Newsy Lalonde's skates, and the stick Max Bentley used. You'll also see photographs of the personalities and great moments in hockey history. Most fun are the shooting and goalkeeping interactive displays, where you can take a whack at targets with a puck or don goalie gear and face down flying video pucks or sponge pucks.

In BCE Place, 30 Yonge St. (at Front St.). ✆ **416/360-7765.** www.hhof.com. Admission C$12 (US$7) adults, C$7 (US$4.35) seniors and children/youths 4–18, free for children 3 and under; family rate (2 adults and 2 children/youths) C$32 (US$20). Late June through Labour Day Mon–Sat 9:30am–6pm, Sun 10am–6pm; Sept through mid-June Mon–Fri 10am–5pm, Sat 9:30am–6pm, Sun 10:30am–5pm. Closed Jan 1, Dec 25. Subway: Union.

**SkyDome** In 1989, the opening of the 53,000-seat SkyDome, home to the Toronto Blue Jays baseball team and the Toronto Argonauts football team, was a gala event. In 1992, SkyDome became the first Canadian stadium to play host to the World Series, and the Blue Jays won the championship for the first of 2 consecutive years. The stadium represents an engineering feat, featuring the world's first fully retractable roof, which spans more than 3ha (8 acres), and a gigantic video scoreboard. It is so large that a 31-story building would fit inside the complex when the roof is closed. The 11-story hotel has 70 rooms that face directly onto the field.

1 Blue Jays Way. ✆ **416/341-2770.** www.skydome.com. Tours C$12.50 (US$8) adults, C$8 (US$5) students 12–17 and seniors, C$7 (US$4.35) children 4–11, free for children 4 and under. Call ahead; tours usually begin on the hour daily 10am–4pm but are not given during events. Subway: Union.

## PARKS & GARDENS

**Allan Gardens** George William Allan gave the city these gardens. He was born in 1822 to wealthy merchant and banker William Allan, who gave him a vast estate (it stretched from Carlton St. to Bloor St. between Jarvis and Sherbourne). George married into the ruling Family Compact when he wed John Beverley Robinson's daughter. A lawyer by training, he became a city councilor, mayor, senator, and philanthropist. The lovely old concert pavilion was demolished, but the glass-domed Palm House still stands in all its radiant Victorian glory. Today the park is rather seedy and certainly should be avoided at night.

Between Jarvis, Sherbourne, Dundas, and Gerrard sts. ✆ **416/392-7259.** Free admission. Daily dawn–dusk. Subway: Dundas.

**Edwards Gardens** This quiet, formal 14ha (35 acre) garden is part of a series of parks that stretch over 250ha (600 acres) along the Don Valley. Gracious bridges arch over a creek, rock gardens abound, and rose and other seasonal flowerbeds add color and scent. The garden is famous for its rhododendrons. The Civic Garden Centre operates a gift shop and offers free walking tours on Tuesday and Thursday at 11am and 2pm. The Centre also boasts a fine horticultural library.

Lawrence Ave. E. and Leslie St. ✆ **416/397-1340.** Free admission. Daily dawn–dusk. Subway: Eglinton, then no. 51 (Leslie) or no. 54 (Lawrence) bus.

**High Park** This 160ha (400 acre) park was surveyor and architect John G. Howard's gift to the city. He lived in Colborne Lodge, which still stands in the park. The grounds contain a large lake called Grenadier Pond (great for ice-skating), a small zoo, a swimming pool, tennis courts, sports fields, bowling greens, and vast expanses of green for baseball, jogging, picnicking, bicycling, and more.

South of Bloor St. to the Gardiner Expwy., West End. Free admission. Daily dawn–dusk. Subway: High Park.

## ESPECIALLY FOR KIDS

The city puts on a fabulous array of special events for children at **Harbourfront.** In March, the **Children's Film Festival** screens 40 entries from 15 countries. In April, **Spring Fever** celebrates the season with egg decorating, puppet shows, and more; on Saturday mornings in April, **cushion concerts** are given for the 5 to 12 set. In May, the **Milk International Children's Festival** brings 100 international performers to the city for a week of great entertainment. For additional information, call ✆ **416/973-3000.** For the last 30 years, the **Young Peoples Theatre,** 165 Front St. E., at Sherbourne Street (✆ **416/862-2222** for box office or 416/363-5131 for administration), has been entertaining youngsters. Its season runs from August to May. ***Help! We've Got Kids*** is an all-in-one directory for attractions, events, shops and services appropriate for kids ages 12 and under in the Greater Toronto Area. Many of the listings are online at **www.helpwevegotkids.com**.

Here are Toronto's best venues, at least from a kid's point of view. Kids race to be the first at **Ontario Science Centre,** a paradise of hands-on games, experiments, and push-button demonstrations—800 of them. The kids can't wait to get on **Paramount Canada's Wonderland** roller coasters and daredevil rides. And don't forget to budget for video games. At **Harbourfront,** Kaleidoscope is an ongoing program of creative crafts, active games, and special events on weekends and holidays. There's also a pond, winter ice-skating, and a crafts studio. At **Ontario Place,** the Children's Village, water slides, a huge Cinesphere, a futuristic pod, and other entertainment are the big hits at this recreational and cultural park. In the Children's Village, kids under 13 can scramble over rope bridges, bounce on an enormous trampoline, or drench one another in the water-play section. **Toronto Zoo** is one of the best in the world, modeled after San Diego's—the animals in this 284ha (710-acre) park really do live in a natural environment.

Other venues address more specialized interests. Riding a ferry to the turn-of-the-century amusement park **Centreville** on the **Toronto Islands** is part of the fun. Visit the **CN Tower** especially for the interactive simulator games and the terror of the glass floor. The top hits of the **Royal Ontario Museum** are the dinosaurs and the spooky bat cave. At **Fort York,** see reenactments of battle drills, musket and cannon firing, and musical marches with fife and drum. At the **Hockey Hall of Fame,** who wouldn't want the chance to tend goal against Mark Messier and Wayne Gretzky (with a sponge puck), and to practice with the fun and challenging video pucks? Go to **Black Creek Pioneer Village** for craft and other demonstrations. **Casa Loma**'s stables, secret passageway, and fantasy rooms really capture children's imaginations. Go to the **Art Gallery of Ontario** for its hands-on kids' exhibit.

**Children's Own Museum** The ROM's next-door neighbor is another favorite with tykes. At the Children's Own Museum, everything is designed with kids aged 1 to 8 in mind. This interactive learn-while-you-play center includes a sensory tunnel, a construction site, a garden, an animal clinic, and a theater. Well-trained staff members are on hand to answer the inevitable endless questions.

In the McLaughlin Planetarium Building, 90 Queen's Park. ✆ **416/542-1492.** Admission C$4.50 (US$2.80). Tues 10am–8pm, Wed–Sat 10am–5pm, Sun noon–5pm. Subway: Museum.

**Playdium** The Playdium is an up-to-the-minute interactive pleasure palace, filled with more than 260 games and simulators like Speedzone (an IndyCar race). It also has rock-climbing walls, a go-kart track, an IMAX theater, batting cages, and mini golf. When you need a break, there's a lounge and restaurant. Beyond the sliding steel door activated by an infrared sensor, you'll discover a surreal scene of huge TV screens, circuit boards, and neon and strobe-lit "alien squid mushrooms."

126 John St. ✆ **416/260-1400.** www.playdium.com. C$2–$23 (US$1.25–US$14) per game or attraction. Sun–Wed 11am–11pm, Thurs 11am–midnight, Fri 11am–2:30am, Sat 10am–2:30am. Subway: St. Andrew.

**Riverdale Farm** ★ Idyllically situated on the edge of the Don Valley Ravine, this working farm right in the city is a favorite with small tots. They enjoy watching the cows and pigs, and petting the other animals. There are farming demonstrations daily at 10:30am and 1:30pm.

201 Winchester St., off Parliament, 1 block north of Carlton. ✆ **416/392-6794.** Free admission. Daily 9am–5pm.

**Wild Water Kingdom** A huge water theme park, Wild Water Kingdom is complete with a 1,880m² (20,000-sq. ft.) wave pool, tube slides, speed slides, giant hot tubs, and the super-thrilling Cyclone water ride. There are bumper boats, pedal boats, canoes, batting cages, and mini-golf, too. Note that the park may not be open in inclement weather, so call ahead if in doubt.

Finch Ave., 1 mile west of Hwy. 427, Brampton. ✆ **416/369-0123** or 905/794-0565. www.wildwaterkingdom.com. Admission C$21.50 (US$13) adults, C$16.50 (US$10) children 4–9, children 3 and under free. June 1–15 weekends only 10am–6pm; July–Labour Day daily 10am–8pm. Take Hwy. 401 to Hwy. 427 north; exit at Finch Ave. and drive 1 mile west. Or from downtown, take Queen Elizabeth Way (QEW) to Hwy. 427 north; exit at Finch Ave. and drive 1 mile west.

## 6 Special Events & Festivals

February is a busy month. The **Chinese New Year** is ushered in with traditional and contemporary performances of Chinese opera, dancing, music, and more (for Harbourfront events, call ✆ **416/973-3000;** for SkyDome, call 877/666-3838). **Winterfest** (✆ **416/338-0338**) is a 3-day celebration spread over various neighborhoods, and features ice-skating shows, snow play, midway rides, performances, and ice sculpting. During the last weekend of the month there is the **Toronto Festival of Storytelling** at Harbourfront (✆ **416/973-3000;** www.storytellingtoronto.org), which features 60 storytellers imparting legends and fables from around the world.

In late April, there is **Santé-The Bloor-Yorkville Wine Festival** (✆ **416/504-3977;** www.santewinefestival.net). It's a 4-day gourmet extravaganza that brings together the award-winning Ontario vintages, food from the city's top-rated chefs, and live jazz.

May brings the **Milk International Children's Festival** at Harbourfront. This is a 9-day celebration of the arts for kids—from theater and music to dance, comedy, and storytelling.

June boasts the **Harbourfront Reading Series** (✆ **416/973-3000**), a festival celebrates the best of Canadian literature. Top writers such as Timothy Findley, Anne Michaels and Barbara Gowdy flock here to read from their latest works. Alternative music fans flock to the **North by Northeast Music Festival** (✆ **416/469-0986;** www.nxne.com), a 3-day event that features rock and indie bands at 28 venues around Toronto. Toronto's multicultural diversity is celebrated at the **Toronto International Festival Caravan** (✆ **416/977-0466**), a 9-day event that features more than 40 themed pavilions, craft demonstrations, opportunities to sample authentic dishes, and traditional dance performances by 100 different cultural groups. The last week in June is **Gay and Lesbian Pride Celebration** (✆ **416/92PRIDE** or 416/927-7433; www.torontopride.com), and the week of events, performances, symposiums, and parties culminates in an extravagant Sunday parade. For sports lovers, there is the **Queen's Plate** at the Woodbine Race Track (✆ **416/675-7223**), in which the world's best thoroughbreds compete in the second leg of the Triple Crown.

July's most important event is the 2-week **Caribana** celebration (✆ **416/465-4884**). Toronto's version of Carnival features traditional foods from the Caribbean and Latin America, ferry cruises, island picnics, children's events, concerts, and arts-and-crafts exhibits. It draws more than a million people from across North America and Britain. On the third weekend of July there's the **Molson Indy** at the Exhibition Place Street circuit (✆ **416/922-7477;** www.molsonindy.com). This is one of Canada's major races on the IndyCar circuit.

August brings the **Canadian National Exhibition** at Exhibition Place (✆ **416/393-6000;** www.theex.com), locally known as "The Ex." One of the world's largest fairs, this 18-day extravaganza features midway rides, display buildings, free shows, and grandstand performers.

In September, Toronto is lit up by stars at the **Toronto International Film Festival** ★★★ (✆ **416/967-FILM;** www.e.bell.ca/filmfest). Second only to Cannes, the 10-day festival features more than 250 films from 70 countries.

October boasts the **International Festival of Authors** at Harbourfront (✆ **416/973-3000**). This renowned 11-day literary festival draws more than 100 authors from 25 countries to perform readings and on-stage interviews. Among the literary luminaries who have appeared are Salman Rushdie, Margaret Drabble, Thomas Kenneally, Joyce Carol Oates, A.S. Byatt, and Margaret Atwood.

In November there's fun for the whole family at the **Royal Agricultural Winter Fair and Royal Horse Show** at Exhibition Place (✆ **416/393-6400;** www.royalfair.org). This 12-day show is the largest indoor agricultural and equestrian competition in the world; the horse show is traditionally attended by a member of the British royal family. There's also the **Santa Claus Parade** (✆ **416/249-7833;** www.thesantaclausparade.org), which has been a favorite with kids since 1905, with its marching bands, magical floats, and clowns. It's usually the third Sunday of November so that jolly St. Nick can avoid driving his reindeer through slushy snow.

In December there's the **Canadian Aboriginal Festival** at SkyDome (✆ **519/751-0040;** www.canab.com). More than 1,500 Native American dancers, drummers, and singers attend this weekend celebration. There are also literary readings, an arts-and-crafts marketplace and traditional foods to savor.

Contact **Tourism Toronto** (✆ **800/363-1990** or 416/203-2600; www.torontotourism.com) for additional information on festivals and events.

## 7 Outdoor Activities & Spectator Sports

Toronto residents love the great outdoors, whatever the time of year. In summer, you'll see people cycling, boating, and hiking; in winter, there's skating, skiing, and snowboarding. So make like a native and enjoy the city's vast expanse of parkland.

For additional information on facilities in the parks, golf courses, tennis courts, swimming pools, beaches, and picnic areas, call **Metro Parks** (✆ **416/392-8186**) or **City Parks** (✆ **416/392-1111**). Also see "Parks & Gardens," above.

### OUTDOOR ACTIVITIES

**BEACHES** **The Beaches** is the neighborhood running along Queen Street East from Coxwell Avenue to Victoria Park. It has a charming boardwalk that connects the beaches, starting at **Ashbridge's Bay Park,** which has a sizable marina. There's also **Woodbine Beach,** which connects to **Kew Gardens Park** and is a favorite with sunbathers and volleyball players. Woodbine also boasts the **Donald D. Summerville Olympic Pool.** Snack bars and trinket sellers line the length of the boardwalk.

The **Toronto Islands** are where you'll find the city's favorite beaches. The ones on **Centre Island,** always the busiest, are favored by families because of nearby attractions like **Centreville.** The beaches on **Wards Island** are much more secluded. They're connected by the loveliest boardwalk in the city, which is bordered by masses of fragrant flowers and raspberry bushes. **Hanlan's Point,** also in the Islands, is Toronto's only nude beach.

**BOATING/CANOEING** At the **Harbourside Boating Centre,** 283 Queen's Quay W. (✆ **416/203-3000**), you can rent sailboats or powerboats and take sailing lessons. Depending on the boat's size, a 3-hour sailboat rental costs at least C$60 (US$37). Powerboats cost C$95 (US$59) and up. Weeklong and weekend sailing courses are also offered. The **Harbourfront Canoe and Kayak School,** 283A Queens Quay W. (© **416/203-2277**), rents kayaks for C$40 to $50 (US$25–US$31) a day (the higher rates apply on weekends). Canoes go for C$35 to C$45 (US$22–US$28). It is open daily mid-June to Labour Day, weekdays only spring and fall, weather permitting.

You can also rent canoes, rowboats, and pedal boats on the **Toronto Islands** just south of Centreville.

**CROSS-COUNTRY SKIING** Just about every park in Toronto becomes potential cross-country skiing territory as soon as snow falls. Best bets are Sunnybrook Park and Ross Lord Park, both in North York. For more information, call **Metro Parks** (© **416/392-8186**). Serious skiers interested in day trips to excellent out-of-town sites like Horseshoe Valley can call **Trakkers Cross Country Ski Club** (© **416/763-0173**), which also rents equipment.

**CYCLING** With biking trails through most of the city's parks and more than 29km (18 miles) of street bike routes, it's not surprising that Toronto has been acclaimed as one of the best cycling cities in North America. Favorite pathways include the **Martin Goodman Trail** (from the Beaches to the Humber River along the waterfront); the **Lower Don Valley** bike trail (from the east end of the city north to Riverdale Park); **High Park,** with winding trails over 160ha (400 acres); and the **Toronto Islands,** where bikers roam free without fear of cars. For advice, call **Ontario Cycling** (© **416/426-7242**) or **Toronto Parks and Recreation** (© **416/392-8186**).

Official bike lanes are marked on College/Carlton streets, the Bloor Street Viaduct leading to the Danforth, Beverly/St. George streets, and Davenport Road. Tourism Toronto can supply more detailed information.

There's no shortage of bike-rental options. Renting a bike usually runs about C$12 to C$24 (US$7–US$15) a day. On Centre Island, try **Toronto Island Bicycle Rental** (© **416/203-0009**). In the city, head for **Wheel Excitement,** 5 Rees St., near Harbourfront (© **416/260-9000**); **McBride Cycle,** 180 Queens Quay W., at York Street, on the Harbourfront (© **416/203-5651**); or **High Park Cycle and Sports,** 24 Ronson Dr. (© **416/614-6689**). If you're interested in cycling with a group, call the **Toronto Bicycling Network** (© **416/766-1985**) for information about daily excursions and weekend trips.

**GOLF** Toronto is obsessed with golf, as evidenced by its more than 75 public courses within an hour's drive of the downtown core. Here's information on some of the best. **Don Valley,** Yonge Street south of Highway 401 (© **416/392-2465**); designed by Howard Watson, this is a scenic par-71 scenic course with some challenging elevated tees. The par-3 13th hole is nicknamed the Hallelujah Corner (because it takes a miracle to make par). It's a good place to start your kids. Greens fees are C$35 (US$22) on weekdays and C$45 (US$28) on weekends. **Humber Valley** (© **416/392-2488**), Albion Road at Beattie Avenue; the relatively flat par-70 course is easy to walk, and gets lots of shade from towering trees. The three final holes require major concentration (the 16th and 17th are both par-5s). Greens fees are C$27 to C$39 (US$17–US$24). The **Tam O'Shanter,** at Birchmount Avenue, north of Sheppard (© **416/392-2547**); another par-70 course, it features links holes and water hazards among its challenges. Greens fees are C$29 to C$39 (US$18–US$24). The

**Glen Abbey Golf Club,** Oakville (✆ **905/844-1800;** www.glenabbey.com); the championship course is one of the most famous in Canada. Designed by Jack Nicklaus, the par-73 layout often plays host to the Canadian Open. Greens fees are C$125 (US$78) in early spring and fall and C$230 (US$143) in summer.

**ICE SKATING** **Nathan Phillips Square** in front of City Hall becomes a free ice rink in winter, as does an area at Harbourfront Centre. Rentals are available on-site. Artificial rinks (also free) are in more than 25 parks, including Grenadier Pond in High Park—a romantic spot, with a bonfire and vendors selling roasted chestnuts. They're open from November to March.

**IN-LINE SKATING** In summer, in-line skaters pack Toronto's streets (and sidewalks). Go with the flow and rent some blades from **Planet Skate,** 2144 Queen St. E. (✆ **416/690-7588**) or **Wheel Excitement** (see "Cycling," above). A 1-day rental runs C$18 to C$22 (US$11–US$14). Popular sites include the Beaches, Harbourfront, and the Toronto Islands.

**JOGGING** Downtown routes might include **Harbourfront** and along the lakefront, or through **Queen's Park** and the University. The **Martin Goodman Trail** runs 20km (13 miles) along the waterfront from the Beaches in the east to the Humber River in the west. It's ideal for jogging, walking, or cycling. It links to the **Tommy Thompson Trail,** which travels the parks from the lakefront along the Humber River. Near the Ontario Science Centre in the Central Don Valley, **Ernest Thompson Seton Park** is also good for jogging. Parking is available at the Thorncliffe Drive and Wilket Creek entrances.

**ROCK CLIMBING** The dilemma: indoors or outdoors? Toronto has several climbing gyms, including **Joe Rockhead's,** 29 Fraser Ave. (✆ **416/538-7670**), and the **Toronto Climbing Academy,** 100 Broadview Ave. (✆ **416/406-5900**). You can pick up the finer points of knot-tying and belaying. Both gyms also rent equipment.

For the real thing, you need to head out of town. Weekend excursions to the Elora Gorge are organized through **Humber College** (✆ **416/675-5097**).

**SNOWBOARDING** The snowboard craze shows no sign of abating. Popular sites include Earl Bales Park and Centennial Park. Call **Metro Parks** (✆ **416/392-8186**) or **City Parks** (✆ **416/392-1111**) for more information. Rentals are available on-site at both Earl Bales and Centennial.

**SWIMMING** There are a dozen or so outdoor pools (open June–Sept) in the municipal parks, including High and Rosedale parks. Several community recreation centers have indoor pools. For **pool information,** call ✆ **416/392-1111.**

The pools at the **YMCA,** 20 Grosvenor St. (✆ **416/975-9622**), and the **University of Toronto Athletic Centre,** 55 Harbord St., at Spadina Avenue (✆ **416/978-4680**), can be used on a day-pass basis; each costs C$15 (US$9).

**TENNIS** More than 30 municipal parks have free tennis facilities. The most convenient are the courts in High, Rosedale, and Jonathan Ashridge parks. They are open in summer only. At Eglinton Flats Park, west of Keele Street at Eglinton Avenue, six of the courts can be used in winter. Call the city (✆ **416/392-1111**) or Metro Parks (✆ **416/392-8186**) for additional information.

## SPECTATOR SPORTS

**AUTO RACING** **The Molson Indy** (✆ **416/872-4639;** www.molsonindy.com) runs at the Exhibition Place Street circuit, usually on the third weekend in July.

**BASEBALL** **SkyDome,** 1 Blue Jays Way, on Front Street beside the CN Tower, is the home of the **Toronto Blue Jays.** The team won the World Series in 1992 and 1993. For information, contact the Toronto Blue Jays, P.O. Box 7777, Adelaide St., Toronto, ON M5C 2K7 (✆ **416/341-1000**; www.bluejays.ca). For tickets, which cost C$15 to C$60 (US$9–US$37), call ✆ **888/654-6529** or 416/341-1234.

**BASKETBALL** Toronto's basketball team, the **Raptors,** has generated urban fever. The team's home ground is the **Air Canada Centre,** 40 Bay St., at Lakeshore Boulevard. The NBA schedule runs from October to April. The arena seats 19,500 for basketball. For information, contact the **Raptors Basketball Club,** 40 Bay St. (✆ **416/815-5600;** www.nba.com/raptors). For tickets, which cost C$25 to C$125 (US$16–US$78), call **Ticketmaster** (✆ **416/870-8000**).

**FOOTBALL** Remember Kramer on *Seinfeld*? He would only watch Canadian football. Here's your chance to catch a game. **SkyDome,** 1 Blue Jays Way, is home to the **Argonauts** of the Canadian Football League. They play between June and November. For information, contact the club at SkyDome, Gate 3, Suite 1300, Toronto, ON M5V 1J3 (✆ **416/341-5151;** www.argonauts.on.ca). Argos tickets cost C$10 to C$40 (US$6–US$25); call ✆ **888/654-6529** or 416/341-1234.

**GOLF TOURNAMENTS** Canada's national golf tournament, the **Bell Canadian Open,** is usually held at the **Glen Abbey Golf Club** in Oakville, about 40 minutes from the city (✆ **905/844-1800**). Most years, it's played over the Labour Day weekend.

**HOCKEY** While basketball is still in its honeymoon phase in Toronto, hockey is a longtime love. The **Air Canada Centre,** 40 Bay St., at Lakeshore Boulevard, is the home of the **Toronto Maple Leafs** (www.torontomapleleafs.com). Though the arena seats 18,700 for hockey, tickets are not easy to come by, because many are sold by subscription. The rest are available through **Ticketmaster** (✆ **416/870-8000**); prices are C$25 to C$100 (US$16–US$62).

**HORSERACING** Thoroughbred racing takes place at **Woodbine Racetrack,** Rexdale Boulevard and Highway 427, Etobicoke (✆ **416/675-6110** or 416/675-7223). It's famous for the Queen's Plate (usually contested on the third Sunday in June); the Canadian International, a classic turf race (September or October); and the North America Cup (mid-June). Woodbine also hosts harness racing in spring and fall.

Harness racing takes place at **Mohawk Raceway,** 48km (30 miles) west of the city at Highway 410, and **Guelph Line** (✆ **416/675-7223**) plays host to the Breeder's Crown in October.

**TENNIS TOURNAMENTS** Canada's international tennis championship, the **Du Maurier Ltd. Open** (✆ **416/665-9777;** www.tenniscanada.com), is an important stop on the pro tennis tour. It attracts stars like Pete Sampras, Andre Agassi, and Arantxa Sanchez-Vicario to the National Tennis Centre at York University in late August. The men's and women's championships alternate cities. In 2002, the women play in Montreal and the men in Toronto.

## 8 Shopping

Toronto's major shopping districts are the **Bloor/Yorkville** area for designer boutiques and top-name galleries; **Queen Street West** for a funkier mix of fashion, antiques and bookstores, and the **Eaton Centre,** which stands at 220 Yonge Street.

Stores usually open at around 10am Monday to Saturday. From Monday to Wednesday, most stores close at 6pm; on Thursday and Friday, hours run to 8pm or 9pm; on Saturdays, closings are quite early, usually around 6pm. Most stores are open on Sunday, though the hours may be restricted—11am or noon to 5pm is not unusual.

## ANTIQUES

Toronto's antiques scene has exploded. Throw a stone in any direction and you're bound to hit an Edwardian console, or at least a classic Eames chair. For fine antiques, head north from Bloor Street along Avenue Road until you reach Davenport Avenue, or walk north on Yonge Street from the Rosedale subway station to St. Clair Avenue. Another top area is Mount Pleasant Road from St. Clair Avenue to Eglinton Avenue. For less pricey finds, head west on Queen Street to the Bathurst Street area.

**Harbourfront Antique Market** Merchandise here varies widely in quality and price. 390 Queen's Quay W. ✆ **416/260-2626.** www.hfam.com. Subway: Union, then LRT to Rees St.

## ART

**Bau-Xi** After viewing the masterworks at the Art Gallery of Ontario, you can head across the street and buy your own contemporary Canadian works. 340 Dundas St. W. ✆ **416/977-0600.** Subway: St. Patrick.

**Sandra Ainsley Gallery** This renowned gallery represents more than 50 artists from across North America, including Dale Chihuly, Jon Kuhn, Peter Powning, Tom Scoon, Susan Edgerley, and David Bennett. The Exchange Tower, 130 King St. W. ✆ **416/362-4480.** Subway: St. Andrew

## BOOKS

**The Children's Book Store** This place is stocked with every book, cassette, and video a kid could possibly want. 2532 Yonge St. ✆ **416/480-0233.** Subway: Eglinton.

**Indigo Books Music & More** The chain dominates Toronto's bookstore scene. Indigo offers a wide selection of merchandise, tables and chairs to encourage browsing, special events, and a cafe. There are also locations at the Eaton Centre (✆ **416/591-3622**) and at 2300 Yonge St., at Eglinton Avenue (✆ **416/544-0049**). 55 Bloor St. W. ✆ **416/925-3536.** Subway: Yonge/Bloor or Bay.

**Nicholas Hoare** This delightful old-fashioned bookshop has the cozy feel of an English library, with hardwood floors, plush couches, and a fireplace. 45 Front St. E. ✆ **416/777-2665.** Subway: Union.

## DEPARTMENT STORES

**The Bay** It started as a fur-trading business when the first French-speaking settlers came to Canada; now it boasts good selections of clothing and housewares. 176 Yonge St. (at Queen St.). ✆ **416/861-9111.** Subway: Queen

**Eatons** It's back—after closing its doors in 1999, Sears bought the name and reopened the shop just in time for the 2000 holiday season. Eaton Centre. ✆ **416/343-2111.** Subway: Dundas.

## FASHION

**Harry Rosen** This men's store carries the crème de la crème of menswear designers, including Hugo Boss, Brioni, and Versace. 82 Bloor St. W. ✆ **416/972-0556.** Subway: Bay.

**Linda Lundstrom** For women's fashion, this is the name to remember. The designer is famous for her sportswear, which incorporates native Canadian art and themes. 136 Cumberland St. ✆ **416/927-9009.** Subway: Bay.

**Price Roman** The husband-and-wife team of Derek Price and Tess Roman produces sleek, tailored clothes with a sultry edge. 267 Queen St. W. ✆ **416/979-7363.** Subway: Osgoode.

**Roots** Come here for casual fashions for the whole family. This is one Canadian retailer that Hollywood types love. The clothes are designed with comfort in mind, from hooded sweats to fleece jackets, and there's a good selection of leather footwear. 95A Bloor St. W. ✆ **416/323-3289.** Subway: Bay.

**Wenches & Rogues** This upscale store carries the latest and greatest in Canadian design for men and women. Featured labels include Misura by Joeffer Caoc, as well as up-and-coming talent from around the country. 110 Yorkville Ave. ✆ **416/920-8959.** Subway: Bay.

## FOOD

**House of Tea** Visitors can drink in the heady scent of more than 150 loose teas. 1017 Yonge St ✆ **416/922-1226.** Subway: Rosedale.

**Kensington Market** It's a very different scene at this market, bordered by Baldwin, Kensington, and Augusta avenues, and by Dundas St to the south. This neighborhood has changed dramatically in the past 40 years. Originally a Jewish community, it now borders on Chinatown. There are several Asian herbalists and grocers, as well as many West Indian and Middle Eastern shops. No phone. Subway: Spadina, then LRT to Baldwin St. or Dundas St. W.

**St. Lawrence Market** A local favorite for fresh produce, it even draws people who live a good distance away. Hours are Tuesday to Thursday 9am to 7pm, Friday 8am to 8pm, Saturday 5am (when the farmers arrive) to 5pm. 92 Front St. E. ✆ 416/392-7219. Subway: Union.

**Senses** The food here is delicate, exquisite, and priced accordingly: there are counters of terrines and patés, caviar, pastries and chocolates, as well as grocery shelves filled with bottled Hong Kong sauces and boxed Dean & Deluca spices. 15 Bloor St. W. ✆ **416/961-0055.** Subway: Yonge/Bloor.

**Simone Marie** All of the rich truffles, colorful almond dragèes, and fruit jellies are flown in from Belgium. 126A Cumberland St. ✆ **416/968-7777.** Subway: Bay.

## JEWELRY

**Birks** Among the silver, crystal, and china is an extensive selection of top-quality jewelry, including exquisite pearls and knockout diamond engagement rings. There are Birks branches at the Eaton Centre (✆ **416/979-9311**) and at First Canadian Place (✆ **416/363-5663**). At the Manulife Centre, 55 Bloor St. W. ✆ 416/922-2266. Subway: Bay.

## TOYS

**Kidding Awound** Wind-up gadgets are the specialty, and there are hundreds to choose from. There are also some antique toys (which you won't let the kids near) and gag gifts. 91 Cumberland St. ✆ **416/926-8996.** Subway: Bay.

**Science City** Kids and adults alike love this store filled with games, puzzles, models, kits, and books—all related to science. Whether your interest is in astronomy, biology, chemistry, archaeology, or physics, you'll find something here. 50 Bloor St. W. ✆ **416/968-2627.** Subway: Yonge/Bloor.

## WINE

In Ontario, Liquor Control Board of Ontario (LCBO) outlets and small boutiques at upscale grocery stores sell wine; no alcohol is sold at convenience stores. There are LCBO outlets all over the city, and prices are the same at all of them. The loveliest shop is at the **Manulife Centre,** 55 Bloor St. W. (✆ **416/925-5266**). Other locations are at 20 Bloor St. E. ✆ **416/368-0521**); the **Eaton Centre** (✆ **416/979-9978**); and **Union Station** (✆ **416/925-9644**). **Vintages** stores have a different name, but they're still LCBO outlets. Check out the one at **Hazelton Lanes** (✆ **416/924-9463**) and at **Queen's Quay** (✆ **416/864-6777**).

## 9 Toronto After Dark

The major companies to see in Toronto are the National Ballet of Canada, the Canadian Opera Company, the Toronto Symphony Orchestra, the Toronto Dance Theatre, and Tafelmusik. You can catch major Broadway shows or a performance by one of the many small theater companies that make Toronto one of the leading theater centers in North America. For additional entertainment, there are enough bars, clubs, cabarets, comedy clubs and other entertainment to keep anyone spinning.

For local happenings, check ***Where Toronto*** and ***Toronto Life*** (www.torontolife.com), as well as the ***Globe and Mail*** (www.globeandmail.ca), the ***Toronto Star*** (www.thestar.com), the ***Toronto Sun*** (www.fyitoronto.com), and the two free weekly papers, ***Now*** and ***Eye.*** Events of particular interest to the gay and lesbian community are listed in ***Xtra!,*** another free weekly.

For **Ticketmaster's** telecharge service, call ✆ **416/872-1111.** Ticketmaster (✆ **416/870-8000**) also runs the **T.O. Tix** booth, which sells half-price day-of-performance tickets. Cash and credit cards are accepted; all sales are final. T.O. Tix is open Tuesday to Friday from noon to 7:30pm and on Saturday from noon to 6pm; the booth is closed Sunday and Monday. T.O. Tix is located at the Eaton Centre Dundas Mall on Level 2 (that's actually one level below street level); the easiest access to the booth is from Dundas Street. Discount tickets for a limited number of shows are also available from the **Toronto Theatre Alliance,** 720 Bathurst St. (✆ **416/536-6468**).

## THE PERFORMING ARTS

The major performing-arts venues include **Massey Hall,** 178 Victoria St. (✆ **416/593-4828;** subway: Queen), which is a Canadian musical landmark, hosting a variety of musical programming from classical to rock. The **Hummingbird Centre,** 1 Front St. E. (✆ **416/872-2262;** subway: King or Union), is home to the Canadian Opera Company and the National Ballet; it also presents Broadway musicals, headline entertainers, and other national and international theater, music, and dance companies. **Roy Thomson Hall,** 60 Simcoe St. (✆ **416/593-4828;** subway: St. Andrew), is the premier concert hall and home to the Toronto Symphony Orchestra, which performs here September to June. The **St. Lawrence Centre,** 27 Front St. E. (✆ **416/366-7723;** subway: King or Union), hosts musical and theatrical events and is home to the CanStage Theatre Company in the Bluma Appel Theatre and to Music Toronto and public debates in the Jane Mallett Theatre. And then there's the **Premiere Dance Theatre,** 207 Queen's Quay W. (✆ **416/973-4000;** subway: Union, then LRT to York Quay), home to a leading contemporary dance season featuring local companies—the Toronto Dance Theatre, the Danny Grossman Dance

Company, and other Canadian and international companies including the Desrosiers Dance Theatre.

## OPERA

The **Canadian Opera Company** (✆ **416/872-2262** for tickets, 416/363-6671 for information; www.coc.ca) began life in 1950 with 10 performances of three operas. It now stages eight different operas a season at the Hummingbird Centre and the Elgin Theatre from September to April.

## CLASSICAL MUSIC

The **Toronto Symphony Orchestra** performs at Roy Thomson Hall, 60 Simcoe St. (✆ **416/593-4828** for tickets, 416/593-7769 for information; www.tso.on.ca), from September to June. In June and July, concerts are also given at outdoor venues throughout the city. The world-renowned **Toronto Mendelssohn Choir** also performs at Roy Thomson Hall (✆ **416/598-0422**). This choir, which was founded in 1895, performs the great choral works not only of Mendelssohn, but also of Bach, Handel, Elgar, and others. Its most famous recording, though, is undoubtedly the soundtrack from Spielberg's film *Schindler's List.*

For 19 seasons the **Tafelmusik Baroque Orchestra** (✆ **416/964-6337** for tickets, 416/964-9562 for information; www.tafelmusik.org), celebrated in England as "the world's finest period band," has been playing baroque music on authentic period instruments. Concerts featuring Bach, Handel, Telemann, Mozart, and Vivaldi are given at **Trinity-St. Paul's United Church,** 427 Bloor St. W., and also at **Massey Hall,** 178 Victoria St.

## DANCE

**Toronto Dance Theatre** (✆ **416/973-4000** for tickets, 416/967-1365 for information; www.tdt.org), the city's leading contemporary dance company, burst onto the scene 27 years ago, bringing an inventive spirit and original Canadian dance to the stage. Today, Christopher House directs the company; he joined in 1979 and has contributed 30 new works to the repertoire. Exhilarating, powerful, and energetic—don't miss their Handel Variations, Artemis Madrigals, Sacra Conversazione, and the Cactus Rosary.

One of the most beloved and famous of all Toronto's cultural icons is the **National Ballet of Canada** ★★★, 157 King St. E. (✆ **416/872-2262** for tickets, 416/366-4846 for information; www.national.ballet.ca; subway: King). It was launched at Eaton Auditorium in Toronto on November 12, 1951, by English ballerina Celia Franca, who served initially as director, dancer, choreographer, and teacher. Among the highlights of its history have been its 1973 New York debut (which featured Nureyev's full-length *Sleeping Beauty*), Baryshnikov's appearance with the company soon after his defection in 1974, and the emergence of such stars as Karen Kain and Kimberly Glasco. The company performs its regular seasons in Toronto at the Hummingbird Centre in the fall, winter, and spring, as well as giving summer appearances before enormous crowds at the open-air theater at Ontario Place. The repertory includes works by Glen Tetley, Sir Frederick Ashton, William Forsythe, and Jerome Robbins. James Kudelka was appointed artist in residence in 1991 and has created *The Miraculous Mandarin, The Actress,* and *Spring Awakening.* Tickets are C$14 to C$90 (US$6–US$56).

## THEATER

With theaters and theater companies galore, Toronto has a very active theater scene, with a reputation second only to that of Broadway's in all of North

## Landmark Theaters

The following major theaters all offer guided tours, usually for a charge of C$5 (US$3.10) or less; call ahead for schedules.

*The Elgin and Winter Garden Theatres* These two historic landmark theaters first opened their doors in 1913, and they have been restored to their original gilded glory. The downstairs Elgin is the larger of the pair, seating 1,500 and featuring a lavish domed ceiling and gilded decoration on the boxes and proscenium. The 1,000-seat Winter Garden possesses a striking interior adorned with hand-painted frescoes. Suspended from its ceiling and lit with lanterns are more than 5,000 branches of beech leaves, which were harvested, preserved, painted, and fireproofed. Both theaters offer everything from Broadway musicals and dramas to concerts and opera performances. 189 Yonge St. ✆ **416/872-5555** for tickets, 416/314-2871 for tour info. Tickets are C$20 to C$85 (US$12–US$53). Subway: Queen.

*Ford Centre for the Performing Arts* This gigantic complex is home to the North York Symphony and the Amadeus Choir. It is really several performance venues in one: the 1,850-seat Apotex theater, which has featured award-winning musicals such as *Sunset Boulevard* and *Ragtime*; the 1,025-seat George Weston Recital Hall, for music events; a 250-seat studio theater; and an art gallery that covers 459m² (5,000 sq. ft.). 5040 Yonge St. (✆ **416/872-2222**). Tickets are C$40 to C$110 (US$25–US$68). Subway: North York Centre.

*Pantages Theatre* This glamorous building, which first opened in 1920, has been restored to the tune of C$18 million (US$11 million); it was originally a silent film house and vaudeville theater. 244 Victoria St. ✆ **416/872-2222.** Tickets are C$51 to C$92 (US$32–US$57); discount seats are available 2 hours before the performance. Subway: Dundas.

*Princess of Wales Theatre* This spectacular 2,000-seat state-of-the-art theater was built for the production of *Miss Saigon* and has a stage that was large enough to accommodate the landing of the helicopter in that production. The exterior and interior walls have been spectacularly decorated by Frank Stella. 300 King St. W. ✆ **416/872-1212.** www.mirvish.com. Tickets are C$25 to C$115 (US$16–US$71). Subway: St. Andrew.

*Royal Alexandra Theatre* When shows from Broadway migrate north, they usually head for the Royal Alex. Tickets are often snapped up by subscription buyers, so your best bet is to call or write ahead of time to the theater at the above address. Recent favorites have included *Masterclass, Oliver,* and *Fame*. The Royal Alex itself is a magnificent spectacle. Constructed in 1907, it's a riot of plush reds, gold brocade, and baroque ornamentation. 260 King St. W., Toronto, ON, M5V 1H9. ✆ **416/872-1212.** www.mirvish.com. Tickets are C$27 to C$91 (US$17–US$56). Subway: St. Andrew.

America. Many small theater groups are producing exciting offbeat drama—a burgeoning Toronto equivalent of Off Broadway. I have picked out only the few whose reputations have been established rather than bombarding you with a complete list of all the offerings. Your choice will no doubt be made by what's scheduled while you're in town, so to do your own talent-scouting, check the local newspaper or magazine for listings of the myriad productions offered.

The **CanStage Company** (✆ **416/368-3110**) performs comedy, drama, and musicals in the St. Lawrence Centre, and also presents free summer Shakespeare performances in High Park. Since 1970, the experimental **Factory Theatre,** 125 Bathurst St. (✆ **416/504-9971;** www.factorytheatre.ca), has been a home to Canadian playwriting, showcasing the best new authors, as well as established playwrights.

The **Tarragon Theatre,** 30 Bridgman Ave., near Dupont and Bathurst (✆ **416/536-5018**), opened in 1971 and continues to produce original works by such famous Canadian literary figures as Michael Ondaatje, Michel Tremblay, and Judith Thompson. It's a small, intimate theater. **Theatre Passe Muraille,** 16 Ryerson Ave. (✆ **416/504-7529;** www.passemuraille.on.ca), started in the late 1960s when a pool of actors began experimenting and improvising original Canadian material. Set in another warehouse, there's a main space seating 220, and a back space for 70. Take the Queen Street streetcar to Bathurst.

**Buddies in Bad Times,** 12 Alexander St. (✆ **416/975-8555;** www.buddiesinbadtimestheatre.com), is Canada's premier gay theater. Its cutting-edge reputation has been built by American Sky Gilbert. In addition to plays that push out social boundaries, the theater also operates a popular bar and cabaret called Tallulah's (see below).

### DINNER THEATER, CABARET & COMEDY

For the art of campy impersonation, there's **La Cage Dinner Theatre,** 278 Yonge St. (✆ **416/364-5200;** subway: Dundas), which hosts a concert given by the shades of Buddy Holly, Roy Orbison, and Elvis among others. For a unique show that can only be likened to Disney's Fantasia performed live on stage, go to **Famous Players Dinner Theatre,** 110 Sudbury St. (✆ **416/532-1137;** subway: Osgoode, then any streetcar west to Dovercourt; walk south on Dovercourt and turn right at Sudbury).

Top comedy clubs include **Yuk-Yuk's,** 2335 Yonge St. (✆ **416/967-6425**), which has nurtured comedians like Jim Carrey, Harland Williams, Howie Mandel, and Norm MacDonald, and has also hosted such major American stars as Jerry Seinfeld and Robin Williams.

Another popular spot is **Second City** ★, 56 Blue Jays Way (✆ **416/343-0011**), which has been and still is the cauldron of Canadian comedy. If you enjoy *Saturday Night Live* or *SCTV,* you'll love the improvisational comedy of Second City. Dan Aykroyd, John Candy, Bill Murray, Martin Short, Mike Myers, Andrea Martin, and Catherine O'Hara all got their start here.

## COUNTRY, FOLK, ROCK & REGGAE

**The BamBoo** Colorful confusion reigns here. The granddaddy of Toronto's reggae scene, the 'Boo also books calypso, salsa, jazz, soul, and R&B. Tables set for dinner surround the teensy dance floor, and the menu is as diverse as the music. Pad Thai, barbecued burgers, and jerk chicken are top choices. Forget quiet conversation, even if you score a seat on the rooftop patio—you're here for the music. 312 Queen St. W. ✆ **416/593-5771** (staffed 10am–5pm). Cover C$5–C$10 (US$3.10–US$6). Subway: Osgoode.

**El Mocambo** This rock-and-roll institution has played peekaboo in recent years—it regularly closes and reopens. But the El Mo can never really die. It's where the Rolling Stones rocked in the '70s and Elvis Costello jammed in the '80s. Today it books artists such as alternative diva Liz Phair. Its rough-and-tumble atmosphere won't suit all comers; the genteel should steer clear of the washrooms. 464 Spadina Ave. ✆ **416/968-2001.** Cover C$4–C$12 (US$2.50–US$7). Subway: Spadina, then LRT to College St.

**The Horseshoe Tavern** This old, traditional venue has showcased the sounds of the decades: blues in the '60s, punk in the '70s, New Wave in the '80s, and everything from ska to rockabilly to Celtic to alternative rock in the '90s. It's the place that launched Blue Rodeo, the Tragically Hip, the Band, and Prairie Oyster, and staged the Toronto debuts of the Police and Hootie & the Blowfish. It attracts a cross section of 20- to 40-year-olds. 368 Queen St. W. ✆ **416/598-4753.** No cover; cover from C$10 (US$6) for special concerts. Subway: Osgoode.

**Lee's Palace** Versailles this isn't. Still, that fact hasn't deterred the crème de la crème of the alternative music scene. Nirvana, Red Hot Chili Peppers, the Tragically Hip, and Alanis have performed here. Despite the graffiti grunge, Lee's does boast the best sight lines in town. The audience is young and rarely tires of slam-dancing in the mosh pit in front of the stage. 529 Bloor St. W. ✆ **416/532-1598.** Cover C$10 (US$6) or less. Subway: Bathurst.

**The Rivoli** ★ Currently this is the club for an eclectic mix of performances, including grunge, blues, rock, jazz, comedy, and poetry reading. Holly Cole launched her career here, Tori Amos made her Toronto debut in the back room, and the Kids in the Hall still consider it home (see "Comedy Clubs," above). Shows begin at 8pm and continue until 2am. People dance if they're inspired. Upstairs, there's a billiards room and espresso bar. 332 Queen St. W. ✆ **416/597-0794.** Cover C$5–C$15 (US$3.10–US$9). Subway: Osgoode.

## JAZZ, RHYTHM & BLUES

In addition to the clubs listed below, **Bamboo,** listed under "Country, Folk, Rock & Reggae," above, also offers some of the hottest jazz in town.

**Montreal Bistro and Jazz Club** ★ Here's a great two-for-one deal. Top performers like Oscar Peterson (still performing after his stroke 1993), Molly Johnson, Ray McShann, and George Shearling perform in a small room lit by rose-tinted lamps; the neighboring room (see "Where to Dine," above) is a Quebecois eatery that features tourtiere and smoked-meat sandwiches. 65 Sherbourne St. ✆ **416/363-0179.** www.montrealbistro.com. Cover C$8–C$20 (US$5–US$12). Subway: King, then any streetcar east to Sherbourne St.

**Reservoir Lounge** ★ This perennial favorite is a modern-day speakeasy. The cramped space—it only seats 100—is below street level, and feels intimate rather than claustrophobic. Live jazz, whether Dixieland, New Orleans, or swing, belts out 6 nights a week. The epicenter for the swing dance craze in Toronto, this is still the place to watch glam hepcats groove. 52 Wellington St. E. ✆ **416/955-0887.** www.thereservoirlounge.com. Cover C$5–C$7 (US$3.10–US$4.35). Subway: King.

**Southern Po Boys** This new restaurant and club bills itself as the "Mardi Gras of the North." The menu is strictly rich Southern fare, and the sounds are bluesy and soulful. 159 Augusta St. ✆ **416/993-6768.** Cover C$2–C$5 (US$1.20–US$3.10). Subway: Spadina, then LRT south to Dundas.

**Top O' the Senator** ★ Upstairs from the Torch Bistro and the Senator Diner, this is one of the classiest jazz joints in town. The long, narrow space has been graced by top performers, such as vocalist Molly Johnson and sax goddess

Jane Bunnett. Leathery couches and banquettes add to the lounge-lizard ambiance. For those who still care, the third-floor humidor has a premium collection of Cuban smokes. 249 Victoria St. ✆ **416/364-7517.** Cover C$10–C$20 (US$6.20–US$12). Subway: Dundas.

## DANCE CLUBS

**The Docks** Another vast waterfront party—this one a complex that hosts live entertainers like James Brown, Blue Rodeo, and the Pointer Sisters. The dance club boasts more than a dozen bars, the latest in lighting, and other party effects. Thursday night is foam fun. There's a restaurant and full raft of sports facilities, too. Open Tuesday to Sunday. 11 Polson St. ✆ **416/461-DOCKS.** Subway: Union, then take a taxi to Lakeshore Blvd. East and Cherry St.; Polson runs off Cherry St.

**Garage Paradise** If the thought of getting all gussied up to spend the night *waiting* to get into a trendy club leaves you cold, drop by Garage Paradise. The low-key jeans-clad crowd here just wants to have fun, and they fill the dance floor for contemporary and classic rock. In case you're wondering, this club was a garage in another lifetime; now license plates decorate its walls. 175 Richmond St. W. ✆ **416/351-8101.** www.garageparadise.com. No cover. Subway: Osgoode.

## THE BAR SCENE

### HOTEL BARS

Some of the best bars are located in hotels. **Accents,** at the Sutton Place, 955 Bay St. (✆ **416/924-9221**), boasts a pianist and a great selection of wines by the glass. The **Consort Bar,** at the King Edward Hotel, 37 King St. E. (✆ **416/863-9700**), is a wonderfully clubby, old-fashioned bar. **La Serre,** at the Four Seasons, 21 Avenue Rd. (✆ **416/964-0411**), is a charming piano bar that welcomes cigar aficionados. The **Library Bar,** at the Royal York, 100 Front St. W. (✆ **416/863-6333**), specializes in "fishbowl" martinis. **The Roof,** at the Park Hyatt, 4 Avenue Rd. (✆ **416/924-5471**), is an old literary haunt, with comfortable couches in front of a fireplace and excellent drinks; the view from the outdoor terrace is splendid—it's one of the best in the city.

### OTHER BARS & PUBS

The **Amsterdam,** 600 King St. W. at Portland St. (✆ **416/504-6882;** subway: St. Andrew, then streetcar west) is a beer-drinker's heaven, serving more than 200 different labels as well as 30 different types on draft. At **Bar Italia & Billiards,** 582 College St. (✆ **416/535-3621;** subway: Queen's Park, then streetcar west), a young, trendy, and good-looking crowd quaffs drinks or coffee and snacks on Italian sandwiches. The **Brunswick House,** 481 Bloor St. W. (✆ **416/964-2242;** subway: Spadina or Bathurst)—affectionately known as the Brunny House—has been described as a cross between a German beer hall and an English north-country workingmen's club. Impromptu dancing to background music and pool- and shuffleboard playing drowns out the sound of at least two of the large-screen TVs, if not the other 18.

Despite the ominous-sounding name, the **Devil's Martini,** 136 Simcoe St. (✆ **416/591-7541;** subway: St. Andrew) is a great spot to slurp up a generous martini. The scene aims for hip, but is actually fairly relaxed. **The Pilot,** 22 Cumberland St. (✆ **416/923-5716;** subway: Yonge/Bloor) dates back to the early years of World War II. It's an unpretentious place with pool tables and a wonderful rooftop patio. At **Wayne Gretzky's,** 99 Blue Jays Way (✆ **416/979-7825;** subway: Union), forget the food; instead, enjoy a drink at the long bar or head upstairs to the rooftop **Oasis,** which is scented with hibiscus and affords a fine view of the CN Tower.

### WINE BARS

The name **Sottovoce,** 537 College St. (✆ **416/536-4564;** subway: Queen's Park, then streetcar west) must be some kind of in-joke, because the decibel level here is outrageous. This wine bar is still a great find, not least because it serves up some truly inspired foccacia sandwiches and salads. **Vines,** 38 Wellington St. E. (✆ **416/955-9833;** subway: King) provides a pleasant atmosphere in which to sample a glass of champagne or any one of 30 wines, priced from C$6 to C$10 (US$3.70–US$6) for a 4-ounce glass. Salads, cheeses, and light meals, served with fresh French sticks, are available.

### GAY & LESBIAN BARS

A popular spot for cruising, **Crews,** 508 Church St. (✆ **416/972-1662;** subway: Wellesley), is a complex with two patios. Friday and Saturday nights are for drag shows, too. The adjoining **Tango** bar draws a lesbian crowd; it hosts Tuesday and Sunday night karaoke. A friendly and very popular local bar, **Woody's,** 467 Church St., south of Wellesley (✆ **416/972-0887;** subway: Wellesley), is frequented mainly by men, but welcomes women. Next door is **Sailor,** 465 Church St. (✆ **416/972-0887;** subway: Wellesley), a bar and restaurant that boasts a Sunday night drag show.

**Pope Joan,** 547 Parliament St. at Winchester. (✆ **416/925-6662;** subway: Wellesley, then streetcar east) is the city's most popular lesbian bar, with a pool table and game room downstairs that's furnished with old, cozy couches, and a restaurant and dance area upstairs. In summer, the fenced-in patio is the place to cool off. The incredibly popular **Slack Alice,** 562 Church St. (✆ **416/969-8742;** subway: Wellesley) bar draws a gay and lesbian crowd. The menu features home-style comfort food; on weekend evenings, a DJ gets the crowd on its feet.

## 10 Niagara-on-the-Lake & the Shaw Festival ★★

Only 1½ hours from Toronto, Niagara-on-the-Lake is one of the best-preserved and prettiest 19th-century villages in North America. Handsome clapboard and brick period houses border the tree-lined streets. It's the setting for one of Canada's most famous events, the **Shaw Festival.** The town is the jewel of the **Ontario wine region.**

### ESSENTIALS

**VISITOR INFORMATION** The **Niagara-on-the-Lake Chamber of Commerce,** 153 King St. (P.O. Box 1043), Niagara-on-the-Lake, ON L0S 1J0 (✆ **905/468-4263;** www.niagara-on-the-lake.com), provides information and can help you find accommodations at one of the 120 local bed-and-breakfasts. It's open Monday to Friday 9am to 5pm and Saturday and Sunday 10am to 5pm.

**GETTING THERE** Niagara-on-the-Lake is best seen by **car.** From Toronto, take the Queen Elizabeth Way (signs read QEW), Niagara via Hamilton and St. Catharines, and exit at Highway 55. The trip takes about 1½ hours.

**Amtrak** (✆ **800/USA-RAIL**) and **VIA Rail** (✆ ✆ **800/361-1235** or 416/366-8411) operate **trains** between Toronto and New York, but they go only as far as St. Catharines and Niagara Falls. From either place, you'll need to rent a car. Rental outlets in St. Catharines include **National Tilden,** 162 Church St.

### The Shaw Festival

The Shaw is devoted to the dramatic and comedic works of George Bernard Shaw and his contemporaries. From April to October, the festival offers a dozen plays in the historic Court House, the exquisite Festival Theatre, and the Royal George Theatre. Some recent performances have included *Six Characters in Search of an Author, Peter Pan, The Mystery of Edwin Drood,* and Shaw's own *The Millionairess.*

Free chamber concerts take place Sunday at 11am. Chats introduce performances on Friday evenings in July and August, and question-and-answer sessions follow Tuesday evening performances.

The Shaw announces its festival program in mid-January. Tickets are difficult to obtain on short notice, so book in advance. Prices range from C$35 to C$70 (US$22–US$43). For more information, contact the **Shaw Festival,** P.O. Box 774, Niagara-on-the-Lake, ON L0S 1J0 (✆ **800/511-7429** or 905/468-2172; www.shawfest.com).

(✆ **905/682-8611**), and **Hertz,** 404 Ontario St. (✆ **905/682-8695**). In Niagara Falls, **National Tilden** is at 4523 Drummond Rd. (✆ **905/374-6700**).

## EXPLORING THE TOWN

A stroll along the town's main artery, Queen Street, will take you by some entertaining, albeit touristy, shops. The **Niagara Apothecary Shop,** at no. 5 (✆ **905/468-3845**), dates to 1866. Its original black-walnut counters and the contents of the drawers are marked in gold-leaf script. **Loyalist Village,** no. 12 (✆ **905/468-7331**), stocks Canadian clothes and crafts, including Inuit art, native Canadian decoys, and sheepskins. **Maple Leaf Fudge,** no. 14 (✆ **905/468-2211**), offers more than 20 varieties that you can watch being made on marble slabs. At no. 16 is a charming toy store, the **Owl and the Pussycat** (✆ **905/468-3081**).

**Niagara Historical Society Museum** The Niagara Historical Society Museum houses more than 20,000 artifacts pertaining to local history. They include many possessions of United Empire Loyalists who first settled the area at the end of the American Revolution.

43 Castlereagh St. (at Davy). ✆ **905/468-3912.** Admission C$6 (US$3.70) adults, C$4 (US$2.50) seniors, C$3 (US$1.85) students, C$1 (US62¢) children 5–12. Jan–Feb weekends 1–5pm; Mar–Apr and Nov–Dec daily 1–5pm; May–Oct daily 10am–5pm.

**Fort George National Historic Park** ★ This fort played a key role in the War of 1812, until the Americans invaded and destroyed it in May 1813. Although rebuilt by 1815, it was abandoned in 1828 and not reconstructed until the 1930s. You can view the guard room (with its hard plank beds), the officers' quarters, the enlisted men's quarters, and the sentry posts. The self-guided tour includes interpretive films and, occasionally, performances by the Fort George Fife and Drum Corps. Those who believe in ghosts, take note: The fort is one of Ontario's favorite "haunted" sites.

Niagara Pkwy. ✆ **905/468-6614.** Admission C$6 (US$3.70) adults, C$5 (US$3.10) seniors, C$4 (US$2.50) children 6–16, C$20 (US$12) family, free for children under 6. Apr–June and Sept–Oct daily 10am–5pm; July–Aug Sun–Fri 10am–5pm, Sat 10am–8pm.

## JET-BOATING THRILLS

**Jet boat** excursions leave from the dock across from 61 Melville St. at the King George III Inn. Don a rain suit, poncho, and life jacket, and climb aboard. The boat takes you out onto the Niagara River for a trip along the stone-walled canyon to the whirlpool downriver. The ride starts slow but gets into turbulent water. Trips, which operate from May to October, last an hour and cost C$50 (US$31) for adults and C$40 (US$25) for children ages 6 to 16. Reservations are required. Call the **Whirlpool Jet Boat Company** (✆ **905/468-4800**).

## TOURING LOCAL WINERIES

Visiting a local winery is one of the loveliest (and tastiest) ways to pass an hour or two in this region. For maps of the area and information about all the region's vintners, contact the **Wine Council of Ontario,** 110 Hanover Dr., Suite B-205, St. Catharines, ON L2W 1A4 (✆ **888/5-WINERY** or 905/684-8070; www.wineroute.com). The wineries listed below are close to the town of Niagara-on-the-Lake. Tours are free. Prices for tastings vary with the winery and the wine you're sampling, and usually run C$3 to C$10 (US$1.85–US$6.20).

Take Highway 55 (Niagara Stone Rd.) out of Niagara-on-the-Lake, and you'll come to **Hillebrand Estates Winery** (✆ **905/468-7123;** www.hillebrand.com), just outside Virgil. It's open year-round, plays host to a variety of special events (including a weekend concert series that features jazz and blues), and even offers bicycle tours. Hillebrand's Vineyard Café, with views of both the barrel-filled cellar and the Niagara Escarpment, is a delightful spot for lunch or dinner. Winery tours start on the hour daily from 10am to 6pm.

If you turn off Highway 55 and go down York Road, you'll reach **Château des Charmes,** west of St. Davids (✆ **905/262-5202;** www.chateaudes charmes.com). The winery was built to resemble a French manor house, and its architecture is unique in the region. One-hour tours are given daily. It is open 10am to 6pm year-round.

To reach the **Konzelmann Winery,** 1096 Lakeshore Road (✆ **905/935-2866;** www.konzelmannwines.com), take Mary Street out of Niagara-on-the-Lake. This vintner is famous for its award-winning ice wines. Tours are given from May to late September, Monday to Saturday.

## WHERE TO STAY

In summer, hotel space is in high demand, but don't despair if you're having trouble nailing down a room. Contact the Chamber of Commerce, which provides an accommodations-reservations service. Your best bets are generally bed-and-breakfasts.

### IN TOWN

#### Expensive

**Gate House Hotel** ★ Unlike many of the Canadiana-influenced lodgings in town, the Gate House Hotel is decorated in cool, clean-lined Milanese style. Guest rooms have a marbleized look, accented with ultramodern black lamps, block marble tables, leatherette couches, and bathrooms with sleek Italian fixtures. The effect is quite glamorous. The **Ristorante Giardino** (see "Where to Dine," below) is one of the best places to dine in town.

142 Queen St. (P.O. Box 1364), Niagara-on-the-Lake, ON L0S 1J0. ✆ **905/468-3263.** www.gatehouse-niagara.com. 10 units. C$170–C$185 (US$105–US$115) double. AE, MC, V. **Amenities:** Restaurant. *In room:* A/C, TV.

**Oban Inn** ★★ With a prime location overlooking the lake, the Oban Inn is the place to stay. It's in a charming white Victorian house with a green dormer-style roof and windows, plus a large verandah. (The house is a re-creation of the original 1824 structure, which burned down in 1992.) The gorgeous gardens are the source of the bouquets throughout the house. Each of the comfortable rooms is unique. They are furnished with antique reproductions—corn-husk four-poster beds with candlewick spreads, ginger-jar lamps, and club-style sofas. It's all very homey and old-fashioned. One recent change to take note of: the Oban Inn, which used to welcome pets, no longer allows them in the rooms. Bar snacks and light lunches and dinners are available downstairs in the piano bar, which has leather Windsor-style chairs and a fireplace. Dinner main courses run C$21 to C$27 (US$13–US$17).

160 Front St. (at Gate St.), Niagara-on-the-Lake, ON L0S 1J0. ✆ **888/669-5566** or 905/468-2165. www.vintageinns.com. 25 units. C$160 (US$99) standard double, C$220 (US$136) double with lake view. Winter packages available. AE, DC, MC, V. **Amenities:** Restaurant, piano bar. *In room:* A/C, TV.

**Pillar & Post Inn** ★ The discreetly elegant Pillar & Post is a couple of blocks from the madding crowds on Queen Street. In recent years it has been transformed into one of the most sophisticated accommodations in town, complete with a spa that offers the latest in deluxe treatments. The light, airy lobby boasts a fireplace, lush plantings, and comfortable seating. The style is classic Canadiana: The spacious rooms all contain old-fashioned furniture, Windsor-style chairs, a pine cabinet (albeit with color TV tucked inside), and historical engravings. Warmed by fires on cool evenings, the two dining rooms occupy a former tomato and peach canning factory and basket manufacturing plant. Entrees run C$17 to C$30 (US$11–US$19). The adjoining wine bar features a large selection of local and international wines. The spa offers a full range of body treatments and massage therapies (prices start at C$45/US$28), plus a Japanese-style warm mineral-spring pool, complete with cascading waterfall.

48 John St. (at King St.), Niagara-on-the-Lake, ON L0S 1J0. ✆ **888/669-5566** or 905/468-2123. Fax 905/468-1472. www.vintageinns.com. 123 units. C$235–C$250 (US$146–US$155) double; C$280–C$335 (US$174–US$208) suite. Extra person C$20 (US$12). AE, DC, MC, V. **Amenities:** Restaurant, wine bar; indoor and outdoor pools; spa; sauna; whirlpool; bike rental. *In room:* A/C, TV, minibar.

**Prince of Wales Hotel** ★ The Prince of Wales has it all: a central location across from the lovely gardens of Simcoe Park; full recreational facilities; lounges, bars, and restaurants; and attractive rooms, all beautifully decorated with antiques or reproductions. It has a lively atmosphere yet retains the elegance and charm of a Victorian inn. Bathrooms have bidets, and most rooms have minibars. The hotel's original section was built in 1864; in 1999 the hotel was renovated and restored to its original glory, and it is now the most luxurious hotel in the district. **Royals,** the elegant main dining room, offers a dozen classic entrees, priced from C$18 to C$28 (US$11–US$17).

6 Picton St., Niagara-on-the-Lake, ON L0S 1J0. ✆ **888/669-5566** or 905/468-3246. Fax 905/468-5521. www.vintageinns.com. 108 units. From C$220 (US$136) double. Extra person C$20 (US$12). Packages available. AE, MC, V. **Amenities:** 2 restaurants, 2 bars; indoor pool; fitness center; aerobics classes; spa; whirlpool; bike rental; massage. *In room:* A/C, TV.

**Queen's Landing Inn** ★ Overlooking the river and within walking distance of the theaters, the Queen's Landing Inn is a modern, Georgian-style mansion. It has 71 rooms with fireplaces, and 32 with fireplaces and Jacuzzis. The spacious rooms are comfortably furnished with half-canopy or brass beds, wingback chairs, and large desks. This hotel attracts a business-oriented crowd, in part because of its excellent conference facilities, which include 20 meeting rooms. The circular **Tiara** dining room looks out over the yacht-filled (in summer) harbor. Dinner main courses run C$24 to C$36 (US$15–US$22).

155 Byron St., at Melville St., (P.O. Box 1180), Niagara-on-the Lake, ON L0S 1J0. ✆ **888/669-5566** or 905/468-2195. www.vintageinns.com. 142 units. C$145 (US$90) double; C$275–C$310 (US$171–US$192) double with fireplace; from C$420 (US$260) double with fireplace and Jacuzzi. AE, DC, MC, V. **Amenities:** Restaurant, bar; indoor and lap pools; exercise room; sauna; whirlpool; bike rental; room service 7am–11pm. *In room:* A/C, TV, minibar.

**White Oaks Conference Resort & Spa** ★ Not far from Niagara-on-the-Lake, the White Oaks is a sports enthusiast's paradise. It's entirely possible to arrive here, be caught in a flurry of athletic activity all weekend, and not set foot outside the resort. The rooms are as good as the facilities, with oak furniture, vanity sinks, and niceties like a phone in the bathroom. Suites have brick fireplaces, marble-top desks, Jacuzzis (some heart-shaped), and bidets. Deluxe suites have sitting rooms. In 2000, White Oaks added a full-service luxury spa, which has become one of its main attractions. The long list of treatments for men and women includes facials, massage, body wraps, and manicures. Some of the less orthodox therapies include *reiki* (a Japanese massage to "align your energy field"), and *Danse de la Mains*, a massage choreographed to music and performed by two therapists working in tandem.

Taylor Rd., Niagara-on-the-Lake, ON L0S 1J0. ✆ **800/263-5766** or 905/688-2550. Fax 905/688-2220. www.whiteoaksresort.com. 90 units. July–Aug C$160–C$190 (US$99–US$118) double; C$185–C$260 (US$115–US$161) suite. Off-season discounts available. AE, DC, MC, V. From QEW, exit at Glendale Ave. **Amenities:** 4 restaurants, wine bar; 4 outdoor and 8 indoor tennis courts; 6 squash and 2 racketball courts; spa; exercise room; tanning beds; bike rental; day-care center. *In room:* A/C, TV, hair dryer.

### Moderate

**Moffat Inn** This is a fine choice in a convenient location. Most rooms are outfitted with brass-framed beds and furnishings in traditional-style wood, wicker, and bamboo. They come with a tea kettle. Seven rooms have fireplaces. Free coffee is available in the lobby.

60 Picton St. (at Queen St.), Niagara-on-the-Lake, ON L0S 1J0. ✆ **905/468-4116.** www.moffatinn.com. 22 units. Apr 15–Oct and late Dec C$89–C$159 (US$55–US$99) double; Nov to mid-Dec and Jan–Apr C$69–C$139 (US$43–US$86) double. AE, MC, V. **Amenities:** Restaurant; bar. *In room:* A/C, TV, hair dryer.

**The Old Bank House** ★ Beautifully situated down by the river, this two-story Georgian was built in 1817 as the first branch of the Bank of Canada. Several tastefully decorated units have private entrances, like the charming Garden Room, which also has a private trellised deck. All but one have a refrigerator and coffee or tea supplies. The most expensive suite accommodates four in two bedrooms. The extraordinarily comfortable sitting room has a fireplace and eclectic antique pieces. All of the bedrooms and baths were refurbished and redecorated in 2001.

10 Front St. (P.O. Box 1708), Niagara-on-the-Lake, ON L0S 1J0. ✆ **877/468-7136** or 905/468-7136. www.oldbankhouse.com. 9 units. C$125–C$195 (US$78–US$121) double; C$230 (US$143) 2-bedroom suite. Rates include breakfast. AE, MC, V. *In room:* A/C.

## ALONG THE WINE ROAD

**The Vintner's Inn** In the village of Jordan, about 30km (18 miles) from Niagara-on-the-Lake, this modern accommodation consists entirely of handsome suites. Each has an elegantly furnished living room with a fireplace, and a whirlpool tub in the bathroom. Seven are duplexes—one of them, the deluxe loft, has two double beds on its second level—and three are single-level suites with high ceilings. The inn's restaurant, On the Twenty, is across the street (see "Where to Dine," below).

3845 Main St., Jordan, ON L0R 1S0. ✆ **905/562-5336.** 9 units. C$225–C$325 (US$95–US$202) double. AE, DC, MC, V. From QEW, take Jordan Rd. exit; at first intersection, turn right onto 4th Ave., then right onto Main St. Amenities: Restaurant. *In room:* A/C.

## WHERE TO DINE

### IN TOWN

In addition to the listings below, don't forget the dining rooms at the **Pillar & Post, Queen's Landing,** and the **Prince of Wales,** all listed above.

The stylish **Shaw Cafe and Wine Bar,** 92 Queen St. (✆ **905/468-4772**), serves lunch and light meals, and has a patio. The **Epicurean,** 84 Queen St. (✆ **905/468-3408**), offers hearty soups, quiches, sandwiches, and other fine dishes in a sunny Provence-inspired dining room. Service is cafeteria style. Half a block off Queen, the **Angel Inn,** 224 Regent St. (✆ **905/468-3411**), is a delightfully authentic English pub. For an inexpensive down-home breakfast, go to the **Stagecoach Family Restaurant,** 45 Queen St. (✆ **905/468-3133**). It also serves basic family fare, such as burgers, fries, and meat loaf. No credit cards are accepted. **Niagara Home Bakery,** 66 Queen St. (✆ **905/468-3431**), is the place to stop for chocolate-date squares, cherry squares, croissants, cookies, and individual quiches.

**The Buttery** CANADIAN/ENGLISH/CONTINENTAL The Buttery has been a dining landmark for years. It's known for its weekend Henry VIII feasts, when "serving wenches" bring food and wine while "jongleurs" and "musickers" entertain. You'll be served "four removes"—courses involving broth, chicken, roast lamb, roast pig, sherry trifle, syllabub, and cheese, all washed down with a goodly amount of wine, ale, and mead. The tavern menu features spareribs, 8-ounce New York strip, shrimp in garlic sauce, and such English pub fare as lamb curry and steak, kidney, and mushroom pie. On the dinner menu, I highly recommend rack of lamb served with pan juices, or shrimp curry. Finish with mud pie or Grand Marnier chocolate cheesecake. You can take home fresh baked goods—pies, strudels, dumplings, cream puffs, or scones.

19 Queen St. ✆ **905/468-2564.** Reservations strongly recommended; reservations required for Henry VIII feast. Henry VIII feast C$49 (US$30); tavern main courses (available Tues–Sun 11am–5pm, all day Mon) C$8–C$15 (US$5–US$9); dinner main courses C$14–C$22 (US$9–US$14). MC, V. April–Nov daily 11am–11pm; Nov–Mar Sun–Thurs 11am–7:30pm. Afternoon tea year-round daily 2–5pm.

**Fans Court** CHINESE Some of the best food in town can be found in this comfortable spot, decorated with fans, cushioned bamboo chairs, and round tables spread with golden tablecloths. In summer, there's outdoor dining in the courtyard. The cuisine is primarily Cantonese and Szechwan. Singapore beef, moo shu pork, Szechwan scallops, and lemon chicken are just a few of the dishes available.

135 Queen St. ✆ **905/468-4511.** Reservations recommended. Main courses C$13–C$20 (US$8–US$12). AE, DC, MC, V. Tues–Sun noon–9pm.

**Ristorante Giardino** ITALIAN On the ground floor of the Gate House Hotel is this sleek, ultramodern Italian restaurant with a gleaming marble-top bar and brass accents throughout. The food is Northern Italian with fresh American accents. Main courses might include baked salmon seasoned with olive paste and tomato concasse, veal tenderloin marinated with garlic and rosemary, and braised pheasant in juniper-berry-and-vegetable sauce. There are several pasta dishes, plus such appealing appetizers as medallions of langostine garnished with orange and fennel salad. Desserts include a fine tiramisu, and panna cotta with seasonal berries.

In the Gate House Hotel, 142 Queen St. ✆ **905/468-3263.** www.gatehouse-niagara.com. Main courses C$25–C$40 (US$16–US$25). AE, MC, V. May–Sept daily 11:30am–2:30pm and 5–10pm; Oct–Apr daily 5:30–9pm.

### ALONG THE WINE ROAD

**Hillebrand's Vineyard Café** ★ CONTINENTAL This dining room is light and airy, and its floor-to-ceiling windows offer views over the vineyards to the distant Niagara Escarpment, or of wine cellars bulging with oak barrels. The food is excellent. The seasonal menu might feature such dishes as poached Arctic char with shellfish ragout, or prosciutto-wrapped pheasant breast atop linguine tossed with mushrooms, roasted eggplant, and shallot. The starters are equally luxurious. Try roasted three-peppercorn pear served warm with salad greens, pine nuts, and Parmesan slivers, or maybe spiced goat cheese and grilled portobello "sandwich" with walnuts and endive. My favorite among the irresistible desserts is chocolate tortellini with ice-wine ganache and stewed berries.

Hwy. 55, near Niagara-on-the-Lake. ✆ **905/468-7123.** Fax 905/468-4789. www.hillebrand.com. Main courses C$24–C$35 (US$15–US$22). Open daily 11:30am–11pm (closes earlier in winter).

**Inn On the Twenty Restaurant & Wine Bar** CANADIAN This restaurant is a favorite among foodies. The gold-painted dining rooms cast a warm glow. The cuisine features ingredients from many producers, giving On the Twenty a small-town feel. For example, the quail is from Joe Speck, and the guinea fowl originates at Keyhole Ranch. Naturally, there's an extensive selection of Ontario wines, including some wonderful ice wines to accompany such desserts as lemon tart and fruit cobbler. Inn on the Twenty Restaurant is associated with the Vintner's Inn, across the street (see "Where to Stay: Along the Wine Road," above).

At Cave Spring Cellars, 3836 Main St., Jordan. ✆ **905/562-7313;** www.innonthetwenty.on.ca. Main courses C$28–C$35 (US$17–US$22). AE, DC, MC, V. Daily 11:30am–3pm and 5–10pm.

**Vineland Estates** ★ CONTINENTAL This inspired eatery serves some of the most innovative food along the wine trail. On warm days you can dine on a deck under a spreading tree, or you can stay in the airy dining room. The kitchen uses local ingredients wherever possible. Start with a goat cheese soufflé on local Cookstown greens, caramelized onion, and sweet pepper coulis. Follow with one of four pastas, including radiatore with sautéed sweetbreads and marinated artichokes in mustard jus. Those craving something meatier could go for venison with wild rice and mashed veggies in a juniper-thyme reduction. For dessert, there's a wonderful tasting plate of Canadian farm cheeses, including Abbey St. Benoit blue Ermite. Those with sweet tooths will probably prefer one of the decadent chocolate delights.

3620 Moyer Rd., Vineland. ✆ **888/846-3526** or 905/562-7088. Fax 905/562-3071. www.vineland.com. Reservations recommended. Main courses C$19–C$35 (US$12–US$22). AE, DC, MC, V. Daily 11am–3pm and 5pm–9pm year-round.

## 11 Niagara Falls: A Honeymoon Haven ★★★

Niagara Falls was for decades the region's honeymoon capital. I say this in an attempt to explain its endless motels—each with at least one suite that has a heart-shaped pink bed. Today, it is better known for its casino, amusement parks, and wax museums. Nonetheless, nothing can steal the thunder of the falls. (Well, almost nothing—longtime locals fondly reminisce about Marilyn Monroe's coming here to film *Niagara* in 1953.) If the tacky commercial side starts to grate on your nerves, get out of town by driving along the Niagara Parkway. With its endless parks and gardens, it's an oasis for nature-lovers. (See "Along the Niagara Parkway," below.)

## ESSENTIALS

**VISITOR INFORMATION** Contact the **Niagara Falls Canada Visitor and Convention Bureau,** 5433 Victoria Ave., Niagara Falls, ON L2G 3L1 (✆ **905/356-6061;** www.nfcvb.com), or the **Niagara Parks Commission,** Box 150, 7400 Portage Rd. S., Niagara Falls, ON L2E 6T2 (✆ **905/356-2241;** www.niagaraparks.com).

**Summer information centers** are open daily 9am to 6pm at Table Rock House, Maid of the Mist Plaza, Rapids View parking lot, and Niagara-on-the-Lake.

**GETTING THERE** If you're driving from Toronto, take the Queen Elizabeth Way (signs read QEW) Niagara. The trip takes 1½ to 1¾ hours.

**Amtrak** (✆ **800/USA-RAIL**) and **VIA Rail** (✆ **800/361-1235** or 416/366-8411) operate trains between Toronto and New York, stopping in St. Catharines and Niagara Falls.

**GETTING AROUND** The best way to get around is aboard the **Niagara Parks People Movers** (✆ **905/357-9340**), which costs C$5.50 (US$3.40) for adults and C$2.75 (US$1.70) for children ages 6 to 12. Parking at Rapid View, several kilometers from the falls, is free. Preferred Parking (overlooking the falls) costs C$9.75 (US$6) with no in-out privileges. The People Mover, which serves both parking areas, is an attraction in itself. It travels in a loop, making nine stops from Rapid View to the Spanish Aero Car, from 8am to 10pm.

**Shuttles** to the falls also operate from downtown and Lundy's Lane; an all-day pass costs C$7 (US$4.35) for adults and C$4 (US$2.50) for children ages 6 to 12.

## SEEING THE FALLS ★★★

You simply can't do anything else before you've seen the falls, the seventh natural wonder of the world. The most exciting way to do that is from the decks of the **Maid of the Mist** ★, 5920 River Rd. (✆ **905/358-5781;** www.maidofthemist.com). The sturdy boat takes you right in—through the turbulent waters around the American Falls, past the Rock of Ages, and to the foot of the Horseshoe Falls, where 34.5 million Imperial gallons of water tumble over the 54m (176-ft.) high cataract each minute. You'll get wet, and your glasses will mist, but that won't detract from the thrill.

Boats leave from the dock on the parkway just down from the Rainbow Bridge. Trips operate daily mid-May to mid-October. Fares are C$12.25 (US$8)

---

**Tips** **A Money-saving Pass**

The **Explorer's Passport Plus** includes admission to Journey Behind the Falls, Great Gorge Adventure, and the Butterfly Conservatory, plus all-day transportation aboard the People Movers. It's available at information booths and costs C$24 (US$15) for adults and C$12 (US$7) for children ages 6 to 12.

---

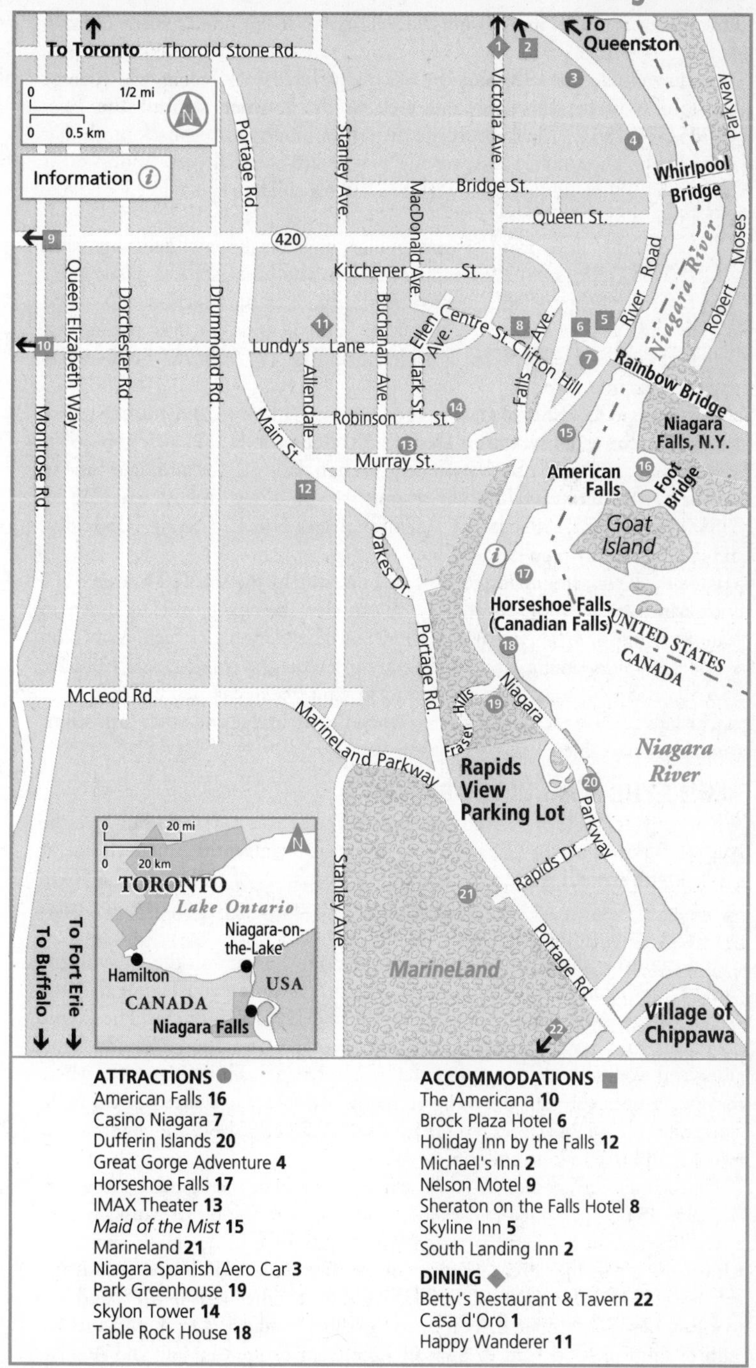


**ATTRACTIONS**
American Falls **16**
Casino Niagara **7**
Dufferin Islands **20**
Great Gorge Adventure **4**
Horseshoe Falls **17**
IMAX Theater **13**
*Maid of the Mist* **15**
Marineland **21**
Niagara Spanish Aero Car **3**
Park Greenhouse **19**
Skylon Tower **14**
Table Rock House **18**

**ACCOMMODATIONS**
The Americana **10**
Brock Plaza Hotel **6**
Holiday Inn by the Falls **12**
Michael's Inn **2**
Nelson Motel **9**
Sheraton on the Falls Hotel **8**
Skyline Inn **5**
South Landing Inn **2**

**DINING**
Betty's Restaurant & Tavern **22**
Casa d'Oro **1**
Happy Wanderer **11**

for adults, C$7.50 (US$4.65) for children ages 6 to 12, and children under 6 are free.

Go down under the falls using the elevator at Table Rock House, which drops you 45m (150 ft.) through solid rock to the **Journey Behind the Falls** (✆ **905/354-1551**). You'll appreciate the yellow biodegradable mackintosh that you're given. The tunnels and viewing portals are open all year. Admission is C$7 (US$4.35) for adults, C$3.50 (US$2.10) for children ages 6 to 12, and free to children under 6.

To view the falls from a spectacular angle, take a 12-minute spin (C$195/US$121 for two) in a chopper over the whole Niagara area. Helicopters leave from the heliport, adjacent to the whirlpool at the junction of Victoria Avenue and Niagara Parkway, daily from 9am to dusk, weather permitting. Contact **Niagara Helicopters,** 3731 Victoria Ave. (✆ **905/357-5672;** www.niagarahelicopters.com).

You can ride the external glass-fronted elevators 158m (520 ft.) to the top of the **Skylon Tower Observation Deck,** 5200 Robinson St. (✆ **905/356-2651;** www.skylon.com). The observation deck is open daily 8am to midnight June to Labour Day; hours vary in other seasons, so call ahead. Adults pay C$8.50 (US$5), seniors C$7.50 (US$4.65), children ages 6 to 12 C$4.50 (US$2.80), and children under 6 go free.

For a thrilling introduction to Niagara Falls, stop by the **IMAX Theater,** 6170 Buchanan Ave. (✆ **905/358-3611**). You can view the raging, swirling waters in *Niagara: Miracles, Myths, and Magic,* shown on a six-story-high screen. Admission is C$8 (US$5) for adults, C$7 (US$4.35) for seniors and children ages 12 to 18, C$5.50 (US$3.40) for children ages 5 to 11, and free to children under 5.

The falls are also exciting in winter, when the ice bridge and other formations are quite remarkable.

## ALONG THE NIAGARA PARKWAY ★

Whatever you think of the tourist-oriented town, you can't help but love the Niagara Parkway, on the Canadian side of the falls. Unlike the American side, it is filled with natural wonders, including vast expanses of parkland. The 56km (35-mile) parkway, with **bike path** ★, makes a refreshing respite from the neon glow that envelops the town both day and night.

You can drive all the way from Niagara Falls to Niagara-on-the-Lake on the parkway, taking in attractions en route. The first diversion you'll come to is the **Great Gorge Adventure,** 4330 River Rd. (✆ **905/374-1221**). The scenic boardwalk runs beside the raging white waters of the Great Gorge Rapids. Stroll along and wonder how it must have felt to challenge this mighty torrent, where the river rushes through the narrow channel at an average speed of 22 mph. Admission is C$5.75 (US$3.55) for adults, C$2.90 (US$1.80) for children ages 6 to 12, and free to kids under 6.

Half a mile farther north, you'll arrive at the **Niagara Spanish Aero Car** (✆ **905/ 354-5711**), a red-and-yellow cable-car contraption that whisks you on a 1,100m (3,600-ft.) jaunt between two points in Canada. High above the whirlpool, you'll enjoy excellent views of the surrounding landscape. Admission is C$6 (US$3.70) for adults, C$3 (US$1.85) for children ages 6 to 12, and free to kids under 6. It is open daily May to the third Sunday in October. Hours are 9am to 6pm in May, 9am to 8pm in June, 9am to 9pm in July and August, 10am to 7:30pm in September, and 9am to 5pm in October.

At **Ride Niagara,** 5755 River Rd. (✆ **905/374-7433;** www.rideniagara.com), you can experience what going over the falls must be like—without

### Tips The Falls by Night

Don't miss seeing the falls after dark. They're lit by 22 xenon gas spotlights, in shades of rose pink, red magenta, amber, blue, and green. Call © **800/563-2557** (in the U.S.) or 905/356-6061 for schedules. The show starts around 5pm in winter, 8:30pm in spring and fall, and 9pm in summer. In addition, from July to early September, free fireworks start at 11pm every Friday.

risking your life. Before going "over" the falls in the computerized motion simulator, you'll see a short video showing some of the weirder contraptions folks have devised for the journey. Then you take an elevator down to the simulator. Admission is C$9 (US$6) for adults, C$4.50 (US$2.80) for children ages 5 to 13, and free to children ages 3 to 4; children under 3 years old aren't admitted. Open daily year-round; summer hours are 9:15am to 10:30pm.

After passing the **Whirlpool Golf Club,** stop at the **School of Horticulture** (© **905/356-8119**) for a free view of the vast gardens and a look at the Floral Clock, which contains 25,000 plants in its 40-foot-diameter face. The new **Butterfly Conservatory** is also in the gardens. In this lush tropical setting, more than 2,000 butterflies (50 international species) float and flutter among such nectar-producing flowers as lantanas and pentas. The large bright blue luminescent Morpho butterflies from Central and South America are particularly gorgeous. Interpretive programs and other presentations take place in the auditorium and two smaller theaters. The native butterfly garden outside attracts the more familiar swallowtails, fritillaries, and painted ladies. The school opens at 9am daily. It closes at 8pm in May and June; 9pm in July and August; 6pm in March, April, September, and October; and 5pm from November through February. It's closed December 25. Admission is C$8.50 (US$5) for adults, C$4 (US$2.50) for children ages 6 to 12, and free to children under 6.

From here you can drive to **Queenston Heights Park,** site of a famous War of 1812 battle. You can take a walking tour of the battlefield. Picnic or play tennis (for C$6/US$3.70 per hour) in this shaded arbor before moving to the **Laura Secord Homestead,** Partition Street, Queenston (© **905/262-4851**). This heroic woman threaded enemy lines to alert British authorities to a surprise attack by American soldiers during the War of 1812. Her home contains a fine collection of Upper Canada furniture from the period, plus artifacts recovered from an archaeological dig. Stop at the candy shop and ice-cream parlor. Tours are given every half hour. Admission is C$2 (US$1.20). Open from late May to Labour Day, daily 10am to 6pm.

Also worth viewing just off the parkway in Queenston is the **Samuel Weir Collection and Library of Art,** R.R. #1, Niagara-on-the-Lake (© **905/262-4510**). The small personal collection is displayed as it was originally, when Samuel Weir occupied the house. Weir (1898–1981), a lawyer from London, Ontario, was an enthusiastic collector of Canadian, American, and European art as well as rare books. It is open from Victoria Day to Canadian Thanksgiving (U.S. Columbus Day) Wednesday to Saturday 11am to 5pm, Sunday 1 to 5pm. Admission is free.

From here, the parkway continues into Niagara-on-the-Lake. It's lined with fruit farms, like **Kurtz Orchards** (© **905/468-2937**), and wineries such as the **Inniskillin Winery,** Line 3, Service Road 66 (© **905/468-3554** or

905/468-2187). Inniskillin is open daily 10am to 6pm from June to October, Monday to Saturday and 10am to 5pm November to May. The self-guided free tour has 20 stops that explain the wine-making process. A free guided tour is also given at 2:30pm, daily in summer and Saturday only in winter.

The next stop between Niagara Falls and Niagara-on-the-Lake is the Georgian-style **McFarland House,** 15927 Niagara River Pkwy. (© **905/468-3322**). Built in 1800, it was home to John McFarland, "His Majesty's Boat Builder" to George III. It's open daily late May through June noon to 5pm, July to Labour Day 11am to 6pm. Admission is C$4 (US$2.50) for adults and C$2 (US$1.20) for children. The last tour starts 30 minutes before closing.

A trip south from Niagara Falls along the parkway will take you by the Table Rock complex to the old-fashioned **Park Greenhouse,** a free attraction. It's open daily 9:30am to 7pm in July and August and 9:30am to 4:15pm September to June.

Farther along are the **Dufferin Islands.** The children can swim, rent a paddleboat, and explore the surrounding woodland areas while you play a round of golf on the illuminated 9-hole par-3 course. Open from the second Sunday in April to the last Sunday in October.

A little farther on, stop for a picnic in **King's Bridge Park** and stroll along the beaches. Continue to **Historic Fort Erie,** 350 Lakeshore Rd., Fort Erie (© **905/871-0540**). It's a reconstruction of the fort that was seized by the Americans in July 1814, besieged later by the British, and finally blown up as the Americans retreated across the river to Buffalo. Guards in period costume stand sentry duty, fire the cannons, and demonstrate drill and musket practice. It is open 10am to 6pm, daily from the first Saturday in May to mid-September, and weekends only to Canadian Thanksgiving (U.S. Columbus Day). Admission is C$6.50 (US$4) for adults, C$4 (US$2.50) for children ages 6 to 16, and free to kids under 6.

Another Fort Erie attraction, in the summer only, is the scenic, historic **Fort Erie horseracing track,** 320 Catherine St. (© **905/871-3200**). Take the Bertie Street exit from the QEW to get to the track.

## MORE NIAGARA FALLS ATTRACTIONS

The biggest crowds aren't here for the falls; they head to **Casino Niagara,** 5705 Falls Ave. (© **905/374-3598**). The monolithic complex features 123 gambling tables that offer blackjack, roulette, baccarat, several different pokers, plus 3,000 slot and video poker machines. The casino contains five restaurants, including the Hard Rock Cafe, seven lounges, and several shops. It's open 24 hours a day, 365 days a year.

A don't-miss spot for families is **Marineland,** 7657 Portage Rd. (© **905/356-9565;** www.marinelandcanada.com). At the aquarium-theater, King Waldorf, Marineland's mascot, presides over performances by killer whales, talented dolphins, and sea lions. Friendship Cove, a 17-million-liter (4½-million-gallon) breeding and observation tank, lets the little ones see killer whales up close. Another aquarium features displays of freshwater fish. At the small wildlife display, kids enjoy petting and feeding the deer and seeing bears and Canadian elk.

Marineland also has theme-park rides, including a roller coaster, Tivoli wheel, and Dragon Boat rides, and a fully equipped playground. The big thriller is Dragon Mountain, a roller coaster that loops, double-loops, and spirals through 300m (1,000 ft.) of tunnels. There are three restaurants, or you can picnic.

In summer, admission is C$30 (US$19) for adults, C$26 (US$16) for children ages 5 to 9/seniors, and free to children under 5. Off-season discounts are available. Marineland is open daily July and August 9am to 6pm; mid-April to mid-May and September to mid-October 10am to 4pm; mid-May to June 10am to 5pm. It is closed November to April. Rides open in late May and close the first Monday in October. In town, drive south on Stanley Street and follow the signs; from the QEW, take the McCleod Rd. exit.

## WHERE TO STAY

Every other sign in Niagara Falls advertises a motel. In summer, rates go up and down according to the traffic, and some proprietors will not even quote rates ahead of time. You can secure a reasonably priced room if you're lucky enough to arrive on a "down night," but with the casino in town that's becoming rare. Still, always request a lower rate and see what happens.

### EXPENSIVE

**Brock Plaza Hotel** ★ For an unmarred view of the falls, try the Brock Plaza, which has entertained honeymooners and sightseers since 1929. It has a certain air of splendor, with a huge chandelier and marble walls in the lobby. About 150 of the rooms face the falls. City-view rooms are slightly smaller and less expensive. For **dining,** the 10th-floor Rainbow Room offers a lovely view.

5685 Falls Ave., Niagara Falls, ON L2E 6W7. ✆ **800/263-7135** or 905/374-4444; www.niagarafallshotels.com. 233 units. Mid-June to Sept C$159–C$519 (US$99–US$322) double; Oct–Dec and Apr to mid-June C$99–C$369 (US$61–US$229) double; winter C$80–C$369 (US$50–US$229) double. Children under 18 stay free in parents' room. Extra person C$10 (US$6). Packages available. AE, DC, DISC, MC, V. Parking C$6 (US$3.70) Sun–Thurs, C$8 (US$5) Fri–Sat. **Amenities:** 2 restaurants, bar. *In room:* A/C, TV.

**Sheraton on the Falls Hotel** ★ A hotel to consider if you're looking for a room with a view—many of the rooms have balconies. There are also several Jacuzzi suites, and a few bi-level suites. Each unit has in-room movies and individual climate control. The hotel is adjacent to Casino Niagara. There are 1- and 2-night packages that include meals. The 14th-floor penthouse dining room takes fair advantage of the view, with large glass windows. There's nightly dancing to a live band (in season).

5875 Falls Ave., Niagara Falls, ON L2E 6W7. ✆ **888/229-9961** or 905/374-4445. Fax 905/371-8349. www.niagarafallshotels.com. 670 units. June–early Oct C$199–C$999 (US$123–US$619) double; mid-Oct to Apr C$119–C$999 (US$74–US$619) double; May C$159–C$999 (US$144–US$619) double. Extra person C$10 (US$6). Children under 18 stay free in parents' room. Packages available. AE, DC, DISC, JMC, V. Valet parking C$16 (US$10), self-parking C$8 (US$). **Amenities:** 2 restaurants, bar; outdoor rooftop pool. *In room:* A/C, TV.

### MODERATE

**The Americana** The Americana is one of the nicer moderately priced motels on this strip. It sits on 10ha (25 acres), with a pleasant picnic area. The large rooms are fully equipped and have vanity sinks. Some suites have whirlpool tubs and fireplaces.

8444 Lundy's Lane, Niagara Falls, ON L2H 1H4. ✆ **800/263-3508** or **905/356-8444**. Fax 905/356-8576. www.americananiagara.com. 120 units. Late June–Aug C$99–C$229 (US$61–US$142) double; Sept to mid-June C$59–C$129 (US$37–$80) double. Extra person C$10 (US$6). AE, DISC, MC, V. Free parking. **Amenities:** 2 restaurants, bar; indoor and outdoor pools; tennis and squash courts; sauna; whirlpool. *In room:* A/C, TV.

**Holiday Inn by the Falls** The Holiday Inn by the Falls has a prime location right behind the Skylon Tower, only minutes from the falls. It's *not* part of the international hotel chain—the owner had the name first and refuses to sell it. Rooms are large and have ample closet space, an additional vanity sink, and modern furnishings. Most units have balconies. The restaurant, Mr. Coco's, is a steak house, pizzeria, and bar all in one.

5339 Murray St. (at Buchanan), Niagara Falls, ON L2G 2J3. ✆ **905/356-1333.** 122 units. Late June–Labour Day C$125–C$195 (US$78–US$121) double; spring and fall C$75–C$155 (US$47–US$96) double; winter C$64–C$109 (US$40–$68) double. Extra person C$10 (US$6); rollaway bed C$10 (US$6); crib C$5 (US$3.10). AE, DC, DISC, MC, V. Free parking. **Amenities:** Restaurant, bar; indoor pool, outdoor heated pool. *In room:* A/C, TV.

**Michael's Inn** At this four-story white building overlooking the Niagara River Gorge, the large rooms are nicely decorated and have modern conveniences. Many are whirlpool-theme rooms, like the Garden of Paradise or Scarlett O'Hara room. There's a solarium pool out back. The Ember's Open Hearth Dining Room boasts a glass-enclosed charcoal pit so that you can see all the cooking action.

\599 River Rd., Niagara Falls, ON L2E 3H3. ✆ **800/263-9390** or 905/354-2727. Fax 905/374-7706. www.michaelsinn.com. 130 units. June–Sept 15 C$98–C$208 (US$42–US$129) double; Sept 16–May C$59–C$178 (US$37–$110) double. AE, DC, MC, V. Free parking. **Amenities:** Restaurant, bar; indoor and solarium pool; fitness center; sauna. *In room:* A/C, TV.

### INEXPENSIVE

**Nelson Motel** *Kids* For budget accommodations, try the Nelson Motel, run by John and Dawn Pavlakovich, who live in the large house adjacent to the motel. The lodgings have character, especially the family units—each has a double bedroom and an adjoining twin-bedded room for the kids. Regular units have modern furniture. Singles have a shower only. The Nelson Motel is a short drive from the falls, overlooking the Niagara River.

10655 Niagara River Pkwy. Niagara Falls, ON L2E 6S6. ✆ **905/295-4754.** 25 units. June 16–Sept 12 C$60–C$100 (US$37–US$62) double; mid-Mar to June 15 and Sept 13 to mid-Nov C$45–C$55 (US$28–US$34) double. Closed mid-Nov to mid-Mar. Rollaways and cribs extra. MC, V. Free parking. **Amenities:** Outdoor pool. *In room:* A/C, TV, no phone.

**The Skyline Inn** Right by Casino Niagara, behind the Skyline and the Sheraton hotels, the Village Inn has unusually large rooms. Some suites measure 65m$^2$ (700 sq. ft.) and include a bedroom with two double beds and a living room. Because of its proximity to the casino, it's a popular choice with people who want to spend some time gambling.

5685 Falls Ave., Niagara Falls, ON L2E 6W7. ✆ **800/263-7135** or **905/374-4444;** www.niagarafallshotels.com. 205 units. Nov to mid-June C$59–C$179 (US$37–US$111) double; mid-June to Oct from C$79–C$249 (US$49–US$154) double. Packages available. AE, DC, DISC, MC, V. Parking C$4 (US$2.50). *In room:* A/C, TV.

### A PLACE TO STAY IN NEARBY QUEENSTON

**South Landing Inn** ★ The original section of Queenston's South Landing Inn was built in the 1800s. Today it has five attractive rooms with early Canadian furnishings, including four-poster beds. Other rooms are across the street in the modern annex. There's a distant view of the river from the inn's balcony. In the original inn, you'll also find a cozy dining room with red-gingham-covered tables, where breakfast is served for C$5 (US$3.10) per person.

Corner of Kent and Front sts. (P.O. Box 269), Queenston, ON L0S 1L0. ✆ **905/262-4634.** Fax 905/262-4639. 23 units. Mid-Apr to Oct C$95–C$125 (US$59–$78) double; Nov to mid-Apr C$65–C$75 (US$40–$47) double. AE, MC, V. Free parking. Follow Niagara Pkwy. to Queenston; turn right at Kent St. *In room:* A/C, TV, no phone.

## WHERE TO DINE

Niagara Falls has never been a culinary hotbed, though you can find standard fare at decent prices. If you want to dine well, reserve a table at one of the dining rooms in the wine-country towns of Jordan, Virgil, or Vineland (see above).

Alternatives in Niagara Falls include the **Pinnacle,** 6732 Oakes Dr. (✆ **905/356-1501**), which offers a Canadian and continental menu and a remarkable view from the top of the Minolta Tower. There's also a vista from atop the 158m (520-ft.) tower at the **Skylon Tower Restaurants,** 5200 Robinson St. (✆ **905/356-2651,** ext. 259). Reasonably priced breakfast, lunch, and dinner buffets are served in the Summit Suite dining room, and pricier continental fare for lunch and dinner in the Revolving Restaurant.

### EXPENSIVE

**Casa d'Oro** ITALIAN Don't be intimidated by the wealth of kitsch. For Italian dining amid gilt busts of Caesar, Venetian-style lamps, statues of Roman gladiators, and murals of Roman and Venetian scenes, go to Casa d'Oro. Start with clams casino or *brodetto Antonio* (a giant crouton topped with poached eggs, floating on a savory broth garnished with parsley, and accompanied by grated cheese). Follow with specialties like saltimbocca alla romana or sole basilica (flavored with lime juice, paprika, and basil). Finish with a selection from the dessert wagon, or really spoil yourself with cherries jubilee or bananas flambé.

5875 Victoria Ave. ✆ **877/296-1178** or 905/356-5646. www.thecasadoro.com. Reservations recommended. Main courses C$16–C$40 (US$99–US$25). AE, DC, DISC, MC, V. Mon–Fri noon–3pm and 4–11pm, Sat 4pm–1am, Sun noon–10pm.

**Happy Wanderer** GERMAN Warm hospitality reigns at the chalet-style Happy Wanderer, which offers a full selection of schnitzels, wursts, and other German specialties. Beer steins and game trophies adorn the walls. You might dine in the Black Forest Room, with a huge, intricately carved sideboard and cuckoo clock, or the Jage Stube, with solid wood benches and woven tablecloths. At lunch there are omelettes, cold platters, sandwiches, and burgers. Dinner might start with goulash soup and proceed with bratwurst, knockwurst, rauchwurst (served with sauerkraut and potato salad), or a Wiener schnitzel, Holstein, or jaeger. All entrees include potatoes, salad, and rye bread. Desserts include, naturally, Black Forest cake and apple strudel.

6405 Stanley Ave. ✆ **905/354-9825.** Reservations not accepted. Main courses C$10–C$26 (US$6–US$16). AE, MC, V. Daily 9am–11pm.

### MODERATE

**Betty's Restaurant & Tavern** *Value* *Kids* CANADIAN Betty's is a local favorite for hearty food at fair prices. It's a family dining room where the staff will attempt to stuff you to the gills with massive platters of fish-and-chips, roast beef, and seafood. All include soup or juice, vegetable, and potato. There are burgers and sandwiches, too. It's all but impossible to save room for the enormous portions of home-baked pies. Breakfast and lunch also offer good budget eating.

8921 Sodom Rd. ✆ **905/295-4436.** www.bettysrestaurant.com. Main courses C$8–C$16 (US$5–US$10). AE, MC, V. Daily 8am–9pm.

### NIAGARA PARKWAY COMMISSION RESTAURANTS

The Niagara Parkway Commission has commandeered the most spectacular scenic spots, where it operates reasonably priced dining outlets. **Table Rock Restaurant** (✆ **905/354-3631**) and **Victoria Park Restaurant** (✆ **905/356-2217**) are both on the parkway right by the falls and are pleasant, if crowded. **Diner on the Green** (✆ **905/356-7221**) is also on the parkway, at the Whirlpool Golf Course near Queenston. It's very plain. Queenston Heights offers the best dining experience.

**Queenston Heights** CANADIAN The star of the Niagara Parkway Commission's eateries stands dramatically atop Queenston Heights. Set in the park among firs, cypresses, silver birches, and maples, the open-air balcony affords a magnificent view of the lower Niagara River and the rich fruit-growing land through which it flows. Alternatively you can sit under the cathedral ceiling in a room where the flue of the stone fireplace reaches to the roof. Dinner options might include filet of Atlantic salmon with Riesling-chive hollandaise, prime rib, or grilled pork with apples and cider-Dijon mustard sauce. Afternoon tea is served from 3 to 5pm in the summer. If nothing else, go for a drink on the deck and the terrific view.

14276 Niagara Pkwy. ✆ **905/262-4274.** Reservations recommended. Main courses C$21–C$30 (US$13–US$19). AE, MC, V. Daily 11:30am–3pm; Sun–Fri 5–9pm, Sat 5–10pm. Closed Jan to mid-Mar.

## 12 St. Catharines to Port Colborne & Hamilton

In the heart of wine country and the Niagara fruit belt, the historic city of **St. Catharines** is home to two major events: the **Royal Canadian Henley Regatta** in early August and the 10-day **Niagara Grape and Wine Festival,** held in late September.

Year-round you can also observe the operations of the **Welland Canal,** which runs through the town of Port Colborne, south of St. Catharines. Built to circumvent Niagara Falls, the Welland Canal connects Lake Ontario to Lake Erie, which is 100m (327 ft.) higher than Lake Ontario. Some 8m (27 ft.) deep, the canal enables large ocean vessels to navigate the Great Lakes. The 42km (26-mile-long) canal has seven locks, each with an average lift of 14m (47 ft.). The average transit time for any vessel is 12 hours. More than a thousand oceangoing vessels travel through in a year, the most common cargoes being wheat and iron ore.

The best places to observe the canal are at the **Welland Canal Viewing and Information Centres,** at Lock 3 in St. Catharines (on Government Road, north of Glendale Avenue off the QEW) and at Lock 8 in Port Colborne. At the first, from a raised platform you can watch ships from over 50 countries passing between Lake Ontario and Lake Erie. The Canal Parkway allows visitors to walk beside the canal and follow the vessels. From the road below the canal you can observe the funnels only moving along above the top of the bank. It's also fun to bike along the canal between Locks 1 and 3.

Also at Lock 3, the **St. Catharines Museum** (✆ **905/984-8880**) houses displays illustrating the construction and working of the Welland Canal, as well as pioneer and War of 1812 memorabilia. Kids enjoy the Discovery Room where they can operate a telephone switchboard or dress up in pioneer clothing and enjoy other hands-on fun. Admission is C$3 (US$1.85) for adults, C$2 (US$1.20) for students/seniors, C$1 (US60¢) for children ages 5 to 13, and C$7 (US$4.35) for families. It is open Labour Day to Victoria Day daily from 9am to 5pm; Victoria Day to Labour Day daily from 9am to 9pm. It is closed December 25 and 26, and New Year's Day.

If you drive to St. Catharines from Niagara-on-the-Lake, on the right just before you enter St. Catharines, you'll find **Happy Rolph Bird Sanctuary and Children's Petting Farm** (✆ **905/935-1484**), which the kids will love. It's free and open daily from late May to mid-October from 10am to dusk.

At Port Colborne, the southern end of the canal opens into Lake Erie. A good sense of the area's history and development can be gained at the **Port Colborne**

**Historical and Marine Museum,** 280 King St. (✆ **905/834-7604**). The six-building complex downtown has a fully operational blacksmith shop and a tearoom. It's free and open daily May to December from noon to 5pm.

In Vineland, **Prudhomme's Landing-Wet 'n' Wild,** off Victoria Avenue (✆ **905/562-7304**), features water slides, a wave pool, go-carts, kids' rides, and miniature golf. An all-day pass costs C$10.65 (US$7) for adults and for children ages 5 or over. It is open mid-June to Labour Day daily from 10am to 8pm (the water park closes at 7pm).

## ATTRACTIONS NEAR HAMILTON

Situated on a landlocked harbor spanned at its entrance by the Burlington Skyway's dramatic sweep, Hamilton has long been known as "Steeltown." Although it has steel mills and smoke-belching chimneys, the town has received an extensive face-lift in the last decade, but, more important, it is home to a couple of worthwhile attractions.

On the northern approaches to the city, the **Royal Botanical Gardens** ★, Highway 6 (✆ **905/527-1158**), spreads over 1,200ha (3,000 acres). The Rock Garden features spring bulbs in May, summer flowers from June to September, and chrysanthemums in October. The Laking Garden blazes during June and July with iris, peonies, and lilies. The arboretum fills with the heady scent of lilac from the end of May to early June, and the exquisite color bursts of rhododendrons and azaleas thereafter. The Centennial Rose Garden is at its best from late June to mid-September. Admission is C$8 (US$5) for adults, C$6.50 (US$4) for seniors/students, C$2.50 (US$1.55) for children ages 5 to 12, and free to children under 5. The outdoor garden areas are open daily 9:30am to 6pm; the Mediterranean Garden is open daily 9:30am to dusk.

Crisscrossing the area are 40km (25 miles) of nature trails, while nearby, and still part of the gardens, is **Cootes Paradise,** a natural wildlife sanctuary with trails leading through some 7,300ha (18,000 acres) of water, marsh, and wooded ravines. For a trail-guide map, stop in at either the Nature Centre (open daily 10am–4pm) or at headquarters at 680 Plains Rd. W. (Highway 2), Burlington. Two tea houses—one overlooking the Rock Garden, the other the Rose Garden—serve refreshments.

**Dundurn Castle,** Dundurn Park, York Boulevard (✆ **905/546-2872**), affords a glimpse of the opulent life as it was lived in this part of southern Ontario in the mid-19th century. It was built between 1832 and 1835 by Sir Allan Napier MacNab, prime minister of the United Provinces of Canada in the mid-1850s and a founder of the Great Western Railway, who was knighted by Queen Victoria for the part he played in the Rebellion of 1837. The mansion has over 35 rooms and has been restored and furnished in the style of 1855. The gray stucco exterior, with its classical Greek portico, is impressive enough, but inside from the grand and formal dining rooms to Lady MacNab's boudoir, the furnishings are equally rich. The museum contains a fascinating collection of Victoriana. In December the castle is decorated quite splendidly for a Victorian Christmas. From downtown Hamilton, take King Street West to Dundurn Street, turn right, and Dundurn will run into York Boulevard. Admission is C$7 (US$4.35) for adults, C$6 (US$3.70) for seniors, C$5.50 (US$3.40) for students, C$2.50 (US$1.55) for children ages 6 to 14, and free to children under 6. It's open daily June to Labour Day 10am to 4pm. The rest of the year, it's open Tuesday to Sunday noon to 4pm. It is closed Christmas and New Year's days.

Just a half-hour drive northwest of Hamilton, off Highway 8 between Hamilton and Cambridge, is the **African Lion Safari** (✆ **519/623-2620**). You can drive your own car or take the guided safari bus through this 300ha (750-acre) wildlife park containing rhinos, cheetahs, lions, tigers, giraffes, zebras, vultures, and many other species. There are scenic railroad and boat rides, plus special kids' jungle and water (bring bathing suits) play areas. Admission, including a tour of the large game reserves plus the rides and shows, costs C$19.95 (US$12) for adults, C$15.95 (US$10) for seniors/youths ages 13 to 17, and C$13.95 (US$9) for children ages 3 to 12. It is open daily April to October. Opening hours from July to Labour Day are 9am to 4pm; at other times it closes earlier.

## WHERE TO DINE

**Café Garibaldi** ★ *Finds* ITALIAN This relaxed spot is a favorite among locals. It serves Italian staples such as zuppa di pesce and veal scalloppine; homemade lasagna is the most-requested dish. The wine list features the local vintners' goods and some fine bottles from Italy.

375 St. Paul St., St. Catharines. ✆ **905/988-9033.** Reservations recommended for dinner. Main courses C$13–C$27 (US$8–$17). AE, DC, MC, V. Tues-Sat 11:30am-2:30pm and 5pm-10pm.From QEW, exit at Ontario St., follow DOWNTOWN sign to St. Paul St. and turn left.

**Hennepin's** CONTEMPORARY The region's first tapas bar, Hennepin's still stands out. The dining rooms display the works of local artists. The specialty of the house is Mediterranean- and Asian-inspired tapas—coconut shrimp, olive-stuffed meatballs, chicken satay, samosas—which are served all day. At dinner, there are always such temptations as escargots in Pernod, or pan-seared game paté with blueberry kirsch sauce to start. Of the main courses, game and serious meats dominate—venison bordelaise, liver in chausseur sauce, steak, and pork tenderloin with portobello calvados sauce. The desserts are seriously rich—try the death by chocolate cake. The wine list is extensive; 28 selections are available by the glass.

1486 Niagara Stone Rd. (Hwy. 55), at Creek Rd., Virgil. ✆ **905/468-1555.** Tapas C$4–C$8 (US$2.50–US$5); main courses C$15–$28 (US$9–US$17). AE, MC, V. Sun–Wed 11:30am–9pm, Fri–Sat 11:30am–11pm. From QEW, exit at York Rd., turn left, follow to Niagara Stone Rd., turn right.

**Iseya** JAPANESE Chef Yasutoshi Hachoitori has had a virtual monopoly since he opened this eatery because Iseya is one of the region's few traditional Japanese restaurants. It serves fresh sushi and sashimi as well as teriyaki, tempura, and sukiyaki dishes.

22 James St. (between St. Paul and King sts.), St. Catharines. ✆ **905/688-1141.** Reservations recommended for dinner. Main courses C$12–C$27 (US$7–$17). AE, MC, V. Mon–Fri 11:30am–2:30pm; Mon–Sat 5–11pm. From QEW, exit at St. Paul St., turn right, follow to St. James St., turn right.

**Rinderlin's** CONTINENTAL An intimate town-house restaurant, Rinderlin's has evolved from a traditional French restaurant to one with a continental flair. As a result, the dishes tend to be lighter; there are several vegetarian options. On the dinner menu, you might find sautéed shrimps and scallops in medium-hot curry sauce on a bed of basmati rice, roast pork tenderloin with honey-mustard-bacon sauce, herb polenta with grilled bell pepper, eggplant and zucchini, and local venison with wild mushrooms and game sauce. Desserts are seasonal—one favorite is the white chocolate torte flavored with brandy and served with raspberry sauce.

24 Burgar St., Welland. ✆ **905/735-4411.** Reservations recommended. Main courses C$21–C$30 (US$13–US$19). AE, DC, MC, V. Mon–Fri 11:30am–1:30pm; daily 6–8pm. From QEW, take Hwy. 406 to Burgar St. exit, turn left.

**Wellington Court Restaurant** CONTINENTAL In an Edwardian town house with a flower trellis, the dining rooms here sport contemporary decor with modern lithographs and photographs. The menu features daily specials—fish and pasta of the day, for example—along with such items as a beef tenderloin in shallot-and-red-wine reduction, roasted breast of chicken served on gingered plum preserves, and grilled sea bass with cranberry vinaigrette.

11 Wellington St., St. Catharines. ✆ **905/682-5518.** Reservations recommended. Main courses C$20–C$28 (US$12–US$17). MC, V. Tues–Sat 11:30am–2:30pm and 5pm–9:30pm. From QEW, exit at St. Paul St., turn right, follow to Wellington Ave., turn left.

11

# Southwestern Ontario

*by Hilary Davidson*

This lush, temperate region brushes up against three Great Lakes, making for some of the best farmland in Canada. A mix of Carolinian forests, rolling hills and fertile plains, the southwestern corner of the province can claim more rare flora and fauna than anywhere else in the country. This region attracted Canada's early pioneers. Different ethnic groups built their own towns, and these early influences are still felt today in local traditions and celebrations. Scots built towns such as Elora, Fergus, and St. Marys; the Germans, Kitchener-Waterloo; the Mennonites, Elmira and St. Jacobs; and the English Loyalists, Stratford and London. This cultural heritage feeds festivals such as Oktoberfest, the Highland Games, and the Mennonite quilt sale, but the biggest draw is the world-famous theater festival at Stratford.

## 1 Exploring the Region

Windsor sits across from Detroit on the Canadian side of the border. From here visitors can travel along either Highway 401 east or the more scenic Highway 3 (called the Talbot Trail, which runs from Windsor to Fort Erie), stopping along the way to visit some major attractions on the Lake Erie shore.

East of Windsor lies London, and from London it's an easy drive to Stratford. From Stratford visitors can turn west to Goderich and Bayfield on the shores of Lake Huron or east to Kitchener-Waterloo and then north to Elmira, Elora, and Fergus.

### VISITOR INFORMATION

Contact **Ontario Tourism,** P.O. Box 104, Toronto ON M5B 2H1 (✆ **800/ONTARIO** or 416/314-0944; www.ontariotravel.net), or visit the travel center in the Eaton Centre on Level 1 at Yonge and Dundas. It's open Monday to Friday 10am to 9pm, Saturday 9:30am to 6pm, and Sunday noon to 5pm. Another good resource is the **Southern Ontario Tourism Organization** (✆ **800/267-3399;** www.soto.on.ca).

### THE GREAT OUTDOORS

Ontario's 260 provincial parks offer a staggering array of opportunities for outdoor recreation. There are two classifications: operating parks, which charge fees, offer facilities and services, and have staff; and non-operating parks, which have no fees or staff and only limited facilities. The daily in-season entry fee for a vehicle at an operating park is C$6 to C$10 (US$3.70–US$6) depending on the park; campsite costs start at C$15 (US$9), though many are higher. For more information, contact the **Ontario Ministry of Natural Resources** (✆ **416/314-2000;** www.ontarioparks.com).Their website has information about every park in the system, and identifies which ones are operating parks.

# Southern Ontario

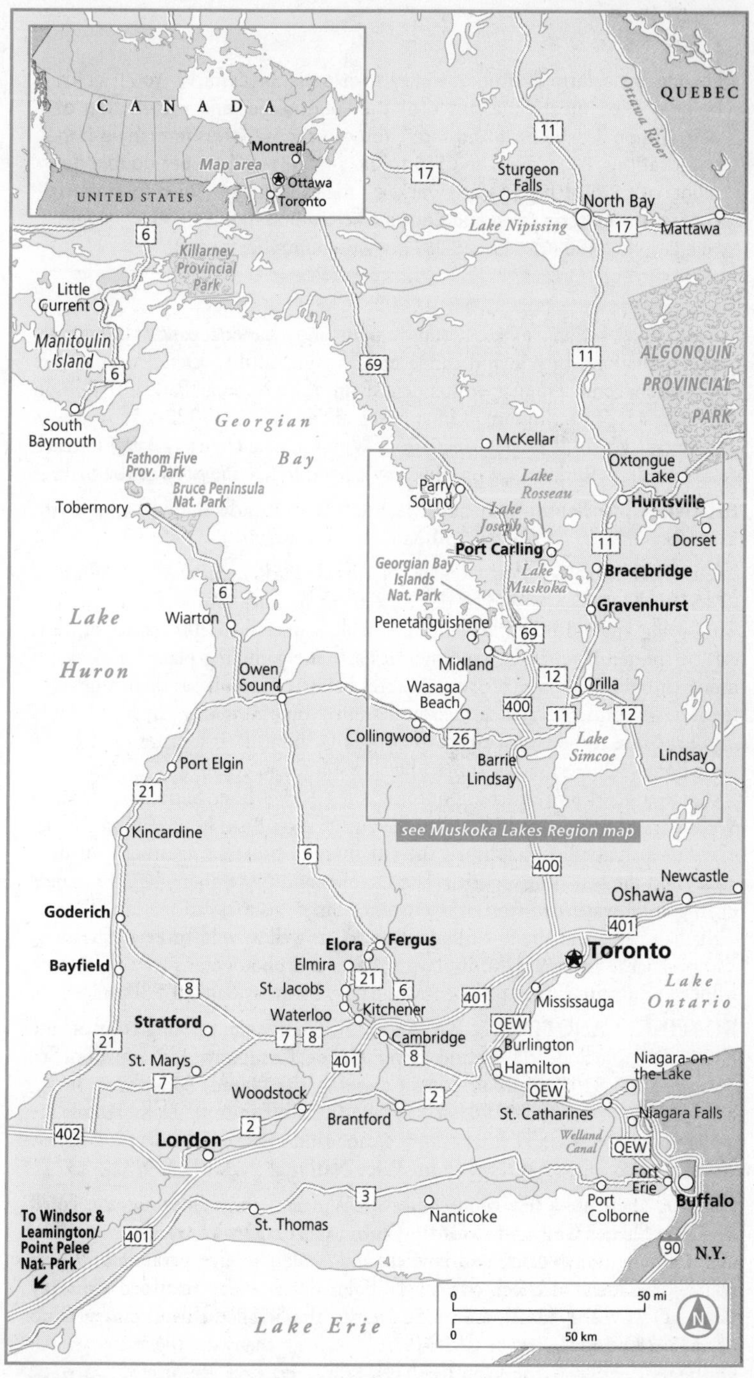

**Tips** **Farm Stays**

Staying on a farm is a unique way to experience Ontario. You'll enjoy home-cooked meals, the peace of the countryside, and the rhythm of daily life on a dairy or mixed farm. You can choose farms in many different locations. Rates average C$50 to C$75 (US$31–US$47) per double per night, or C$250 (US$155) per week, all meals included. For information, contact the **Ontario Farm and Country Accommodations,** RR #2, Vankleek Hill, ON, K0B 1R0 (✆ **613/678-2873;** www.countryhosts.com).

**Point Pelee** is Canada's southernmost point and a national park. It offers year-round hiking and bicycle and canoe rentals from April to October. For more information, contact the Superintendent, Point Pelee National Park, 407 Robson St., RR #1, Leamington, ON, N8H 3V4 (✆ **519/322-2365;** www.parcscanada.gc.ca). If you're driving from Windsor, take Highway 3 east to reach Pelee Island. At Ruthven get on Highway 18 and follow the signs to the park.

**BIKING** The South Point and Marsh trails in **Rondeau Provincial Park,** near Blenheim (✆ **519/674-1750**), are great for cycling.

**BIRD-WATCHING** **Point Pelee National Park,** southeast of Windsor (✆ **519/322-2371**), is one of the continent's premier bird-watching centers. The spring and fall migrations are spectacular; more than 300 species of birds can be spotted here. In late summer, it's also the gathering place for flocks of monarch butterflies, which cover the trees before taking off for their migratory flight down south. Located at the southernmost tip of Canada, which juts down into Lake Erie at the same latitude as northern California, it features some of the same flora—white sassafras, sumac, black walnut, and cedar.

Another good bird-watching outpost is the **Jack Miner Sanctuary,** Road 3 West, 3km (2 miles) north of Kingsville off Division Road (✆ **519/733-4034**). The famed naturalist established the sanctuary to protect migrating Canadian geese, and the best time to visit is late October and November when thousands of migrating waterfowl stop over. At other times, visitors can see the 50 or so Canadian geese and the few hundred ducks, as well as wild turkeys, pheasant, and peacocks. The museum displays artifacts and photographs relating to Jack Miner. Admission is free; it's open Monday to Saturday 8am to 5:30pm.

**BOATING, CANOEING & KAYAKING** Companies offering trips on the Grand River include the **Grand River Canoe Company,** 132 Rawdon St., Brantford (✆ **519/759-0040**), and **Canoeing the Grand,** 3734 King St. E., Kitchener (✆ **519/896-0290,** or 519/893-0022 off-season). Daily rentals are available for about C$35 (US$22) for a canoe, and C$32 (US$20) for a kayak. There are also canoe rentals in **Point Pelee National Park** (✆ **519/322-2371**).

**GOLF** There are a few good courses in Windsor, and in Leamington you'll find **Erie Shores Golf and Country Club,** (✆ **519/326-4231**). London offers half a dozen good courses; and Bayfield and Goderich have a couple of 9-hole courses. In Stratford check out the 18-hole course at the **Stratford Country Club** (✆ **519/271-4212**), and in St. Mary's, the **Science Hill Country Club** (✆ **519/284-3621**).

**HIKING** The 60km (37-mile) **Thames Valley Trail** follows the Thames River through London, past the University of Western Ontario and into farmlands all the way to St. Mary's. For information, contact **Thames Valley Trail Association,**

Grosvenor House, 1017 Western Rd., London, ON, N6G 1G5 (© **519/645-2845**).

The 100km (62-mile) **Avon Trail** follows the Avon River through Stratford, cuts through the Wildwood Conservation Area, and spans farmlands around Kitchener. It links up with the Thames Valley Trail at St. Marys and the Grand Valley Trail at Conestoga. For information, contact Avon Trail, Box 20018, Stratford, ON, N5A 7V3 (no phone; www.avontrail.ca).

The 124km (77-mile) **Grand Valley Trail** follows the Grand River from Dunnville, north through Brantford, Paris, and farmlands around Kitchener-Waterloo to the Elora Gorge (see "Elora & Fergus: The Elora Gorge & More," later), connecting with the Bruce Trail at Alton. For information, contact Grand Valley Trails Association, 75 King St. S., P.O. Box 40068, RPO Waterloo Square, Waterloo, ON, N2J 4V1 (no phone; www.gvta.on.ca).

**HORSEBACK RIDING** The **Cinch Stables,** 309 Gideon Dr., London (© **519/471-7071**), offers hour-long trail rides for C$25 (US$16) per person. West of London, in Delaware, the **Circle R Ranch,** 3017 Carriage Rd., RR #1 (© **519/471-3799**), leads 1-hour trail rides in the Dingman Creek Valley for C$25 (US$16) per person. Reservations are necessary for both.

**ROCK CLIMBING** The Elora Gorge is the climber's destination of choice in this region. Weekend excursions are organized through the **Humber College** School of Continuing Education (© **416/675-5005**).

**SWIMMING** The Elora Gorge is also a favorite swimming spot. So is **Rondeau Provincial Park** (© **519/674-1750**), which is located on Lake Erie (off Highway 21 near Blenheim); lots of other watersports are available here as well.

### *Finds* The Real Uncle Tom's Cabin

One of the most interesting visitor sites in Southwestern Ontario is **Uncle Tom's Cabin Historic Centre,** 29251 Uncle Tom's Road, RR#5, Dresden (© **519/683-2978;** www.uncletomscabin.org). The center focuses on the life of Josiah Henson, who was born in slavery in Maryland in 1789, and escaped via the Underground Railroad into Canada in 1830. Henson and a group of ex-slaves, Quakers and other abolitionists purchased 200 acres of land in 1841, where they established a vocational school, the British American Institute for Fugitive Slaves. In 1849, Henson narrated his life story to Harriet Beecher Stowe, who went on to publish *Uncle Tom's Cabin* in 1852. The center includes an interpretive center, a theater, and a gallery, as well as the sawmill and the smokehouse built by Henson and his colleagues. One of the gallery's most fascinating exhibits is the collection of quilts used by the Underground Railroad; these carried elaborate, coded designs that helped lead many slaves to freedom. Admission is C$6 (US$3.70) for adults, C$5 (US$3.10) for seniors and students, C$4 (US$2.50) for children ages 6 to 12, and free for kids 5 and under. The Centre is open mid-May to mid-October Tuesday to Saturday 10am to 4pm, Sunday noon to 4pm; Mondays in July and August 10am to 4pm.

## 2 London: A Great Stop for Families

If you're driving into Canada from the U.S. Midwest, you certainly should plan on stopping in this pretty university town that sits on the Thames River—particularly if you have kids in tow.

### ESSENTIALS

**VISITOR INFORMATION** Contact **Tourism London,** 300 Dufferin Ave. (P.O. Box 5035), London, ON, N6A 4L9 (✆ **519/661-5000;** www.city.london.on.ca).

**GETTING THERE By plane** Direct flights from Toronto, Ottawa, and Detroit arrive at **London International Airport** (✆ **519/452-4015;** www.londonairport.on.ca). A taxi from the airport into town will cost about C$25 (US$16).

**By rail VIA Rail** (✆ **888/VIA-RAIL** or 416/366-8411; www.viarail.ca) operates a Toronto-Brantford-London-Windsor route and also, in conjunction with **Amtrak** (✆ **800/USA-RAIL,** www.amtrak.com), a Toronto-Kitchener-Stratford-London-Sarnia-Chicago route. Both offer several trains a day. The VIA Rail station in London is at 197 York St. (✆ **519/434-2149**).

**By bus Greyhound** (✆ **800/231-2222;** www.greyhound.ca) provides service to Toronto, Detroit, Buffalo, and other Canadian and American destinations.

**By car** If you're driving, London is about 192km (120 miles) from Detroit via Highway 401, 110km (68 miles) from Kitchener via Highway 401, 195km (121 miles) from Niagara Falls via QEW, highways 403 and 401, and 65km (40 miles) from Stratford via 7 and 4.

**GETTING AROUND** For bus schedules, contact the **London Transit Commission** (✆ **519/451-1347**). Exact fare of C$2.25 (US$1.40) is required, C$1.10 (US70¢) for children ages 5 to 12. Or you can purchase five tickets at C$7.75 (US$4.80) for adults and C$4.50 (US$2.80) for children.

Taxis charge an initial C$2.40 (US$1.50) plus C10¢ (US5¢) per 1km (½ mile) thereafter. There's an additional charge from 11pm to 6am. Taxi companies include **Aboutown Taxi** (✆ **519/663-2222**) and **U-Need-A-Cab** (✆ **519/438-2121**).

**SPECIAL EVENTS** The **London Air Show & Balloon Festival** (✆ **800/INFLIGHT** or 519/473-6444; www.londonairshow.com) ushers in the summer season each June. It's followed by the **Royal Canadian Big Band Festival** (✆ **800/461-2263**), a tribute to hometown boy Guy Lombardo, held in late June and early July. The **London Balloon Festival** (✆ **519/696-2088**) takes place in early August. The 10-day **Western Fair** (www.westernfair.com), held in September, is the seventh largest in Canada.

### EXPLORING THE TOWN

**Banting House Museum** Sir Frederick G. Banting won the Nobel Prize for his discovery of insulin, and this museum is dedicated to his life and work as a doctor and as an artist. There are displays about his medical research at the University of Toronto, his years as a soldier, and his drawings. The museum is operated by the Canadian Diabetes Association.

442 Adelaide St. N. ✆ **519/673-1752.** Admission C$3 (US$1.85) adults, C$2 (US$1.20) seniors and students, kids under 6 free. Tues–Sat noon–4pm; open year round except Dec. 21–Jan 5 and on public holidays.

**Eldon House/Museum London** The city's oldest remaining house, built in 1843, now contains Museum London, which features ever-changing exhibits about the city's early life. There's information about the daily life of the first settlers as well as about London's "dark side" of fire, flood, and pestilence. Also in the building is the London Regional Art Museum, where you'll find works by local artists and students.

401 Ridout N. ✆ **519-661-5169.** www.londonmuseum.on.ca. Admission C$3 (US$1.85) adults, C$2 (US$1.20) seniors, C$1 (US60¢) children 5 to 16; admission free to all Wed and Sun. Tues–Sun noon–5pm.

**Fanshawe Pioneer Village** The Pioneer Village is a complex comprised of 25-plus buildings where you can see craft demonstrations (broom making, candle dipping, for example), enjoy wagon rides, and imagine what life was like during the 18th century. In **Fanshawe Park** (**✆ 519/451-2800**) there's a large pool and beach at the 6km (4-mile-long) lake.

In Fanshawe Park (entrance off Fanshawe Park Rd., east of Clarke Rd.). ✆ **519/457-1296.** www.pioneer.wwdc.com. Admission to park C$5.50 (US$3.40) per vehicle; Pioneer Village C$5 (US$3.10) adults, C$4 (US$2.50) seniors and students, C$3 (US$1.85) children 3–12; children under 3 free. Village May 1–Nov 30 Wed–Sun 10am–4:30pm. Dec 1–Dec 20 daily 10am–4:30pm.

**Guy Lombardo Music Centre** Stroll back through memory lane in this outdoor band shell where bandleader Guy Lombardo began playing in the 1930s. This local kid made good—once he hit the big time he became famous for ringing in the New Year at the Waldorf-Astoria in New York. There's also a Guy Lombardo Music Centre filled with memorabilia. June 19, 2002, marks the 100th anniversary of the bandleader's birth, and the Music Centre is gearing up to celebrate it in swinging style.

205 Wonderland Rd. S. ✆ **519/473-9003.** Admission C$2 (US$1.20) adults, C$1.75 (US$1.10) seniors; children under 12 free. Mid-May to Labour Day Thurs–Mon 11am–5pm. Limited winter hours; call ahead.

**London Museum of Archaeology** The museum contains artifacts from various periods of native-Canadian history—projectiles, pottery shards, effigies, turtle rattles, and more. The most evocative exhibit is the on-site reconstruction of a 500-year-old Attawandaron village. Behind the elm palisades, longhouses built according to original specifications and techniques have been erected on the 2ha (5 acres) where archaeological excavations are taking place. About 1,600 to 1,800 people once lived in the community, about 70 sharing one longhouse. The houses have been constructed of elm, sealed with the pitch from pine trees, and bound together with the sinew of deer hide.

1600 Attawandaron Rd. (off Wonderland Rd. N., just south of Hwy. 22). ✆ **519/473-1360.** Admission C$3.50 (US$2.15) adults, C$2.75 (US$1.70) seniors and students, C$1.50 (US95¢) children under 12, C$8 (US$5) families; children under 5 free. Daily May 1 to–Labour Day 10am–5pm; Sept–Dec Tues–Sun 10am–5pm; Jan–Apr Wed–Sun only 1–4pm.

**London Regional Children's Museum** ★ This interactive museum for kids occupies several floors of an old school building. A family can easily spend a whole day here—there's more than enough to do. In every room children can explore, experiment, and engage their imaginations. For example, on "The Street Where You Live," kids can dress up in firefighters' uniforms, don the overalls of those who work under the streets, and assume the role of a dentist, doctor, or construction worker. Some rooms contrast how people lived long ago with how they live today. A child can stand in a train station, send a Morse-code message, shop in a general store, and sit in a schoolhouse—all experiences that they can share with their grandparents. More up-to-the-minute experiences can be enjoyed at the photosensitive wall, the zoetrobe, or in the kitchen where children can see exactly how the appliances work. In the garden out back, there's also a fun tree house with a spiral slide. It's fun for children and for adults.

21 Wharncliffe Rd. S. ✆ **519/434-5726.** Admission C$5 (US$3.10) all ages, children under 2 free. Tues–Sun 10am–5pm; also open Mon Jun–Aug and on holiday Mon; closed Dec 25–26 and Jan 1.

**Springbank Park Storybook Gardens** The Springbank Park Storybook Gardens is a children's zoo with a storybook theme. Special daily events include the seal feeding at 3:30pm, and a variety of live entertainment. There's also a maze and Playworld, with many activities for children.

Off Commissioners Rd. W. ✆ **519/661-5770.** Admission C$5.25 (US$3.25) adults, C$4 (US$2.50) seniors, C$3.25 (US$2) children 3–14; children 2 and under $1. May–Labour Day daily 10am–8pm; Labour Day–early Oct Mon–Fri 10am–5pm, Sat–Sun 10am–6pm. Closed Oct–Apr.

## WHERE TO STAY

For B&B accommodations priced from C$35 to C$90 (US$22–US$56) per night, contact the **London and Area Bed and Breakfast Association** (✆ **519/673-6797;** www.londonbb.com).

London also has several modest hotel chains: **Best Western Lamplighter Inn & Conference Centre,** 591 Wellington Rd. S. (✆ **888-232-6747** or 519/681-7151); **Ramada Inn London,** 817 Exeter Rd. (✆ **800-303-3733** or 519/681-4900); **Travelodge London South,** 800 Exeter Rd. (✆ **800-578-7878** or 519-681-1200); and **Comfort Inn,** 1156 Wellington Rd. S. (✆ **800-228-5150** or 519/685-9300).

**Delta London Armouries Hotel** Built into the facade of a castle-like armory, this hotel is an impressive example of architectural conservation and conversion. The armory's 3.5m (12-ft.) thick walls, built in 1905, form the building's main floor and base, and above the crenellated turrets and ramparts soars a modern glass tower. Inside, the well-equipped rooms are furnished with Federal reproductions. Some rooms (for an additional C$15/US$9) have been specially outfitted for the business traveler with fax, laser printer, cordless speakerphone, halogen-lit desk, and ergonomically designed chair, plus a computer on request. Guests and locals alike are drawn to the Sunday jazz brunch.

325 Dundas St., London, ON, N6B 1T9. ✆ **519/679-6111.** Fax 519/679-3957. www.deltahotels.com. 250 rms. C$125–C$200 (US$78–US$124) double; from C$235 (US$146) suite. Extra person C$10 (US$6). Children under 18 stay free in parents' rm. Special weekend rates available. AE, DC, DISC, MC, V. Parking C$7 (US$4.35). **Amenities:** Restaurant, lounge; pool; squash court; exercise room; children's activity center. *In room:* A/C, TV, minibar.

**Idlewyld Inn** Located in a house that a wealthy leather industrialist built in 1878, the inn is filled with fine details—2.5m (8-ft.) tall windows, oak and cherry carved fireplaces, casement windows, oak-beamed ceilings, and wallpaper crafted to look like tooled leather in the dining room. All the rooms are furnished in a unique way. Room 302 has a tiny Romeo and Juliet balcony, while room 202 has a marvelous fireplace of green cabbage-leaf tiles and a scallop-shell marble sink stand. Room 101 is the largest—huge carved cherry columns separate the sitting area from the bedroom, which has a comfortable chaise lounge and a glazed tile fireplace. At breakfast guests help themselves in the large, comfortable kitchen equipped with toasters, coffeemakers, and refrigerators, and can sit on the porch to eat.

36 Grand Ave., London, ON, N6C 1K8. ✆ and fax **519/433-2891.** 17 rms; 10 suites and Jacuzzi rms. C$99 (US$61) double; from $125 (US$78) suite; from $155 (US$96) Jacuzzi rms. Rates include continental breakfast. AE, DC, MC, V. Free parking. *In room:* A/C, TV.

## WHERE TO DINE

**Caribou Creek** LIGHT FARE This cottage-themed restaurant is a favorite with kids. The rambling main room is paneled with rough-hewn wood and decorated with everything from canoe paddles to fisherman's nets; up front there's a sunny patio that fills up fast in clement weather. The menu is packed with old-faithful standbys such as sandwiches, burgers, and salads, but there's also a choice of chicken and steak main courses.

557 Wellington Rd. © **519/686-1113.** Main courses C$7–C$12 (US$4.35–US$7). AE, MC, V. Daily 11am–3pm, 5pm–10:30pm.

**Michael's on the Thames** ★ CONTINENTAL The restaurant boasts a lovely location overlooking the river. In winter a blazing fire makes the dining room cozy. Among the main dishes you might find pan-seared chicken breast with sun-dried tomato, basil and cashew pesto and cream sauce, rack of lamb roasted with mint finished with demiglace and port wine, or salmon with hollandaise. Desserts include a flamboyant cherries jubilee. The wine list is impressive.

1 York St. © **519/672-0111.** Reservations recommended. Main courses C$12–C$22 (US$7–US$14). AE, DC, MC, V. Mon–Fri 11:30am–2:30pm; daily 5–11pm.

**Mongolian Grill** ASIAN This is cooking as performance art. Diners assemble their own meal-in-a-bowl with raw ingredients ranging from chicken to shrimp, broccoli to bok choy, and ginger to coriander. The bowl is presented to the cooks, who labor at a huge wheel-shaped grill that sizzles and steams. The young cooks know how to put on a good show, though I couldn't get past wondering how they could stand the intense heat.

645 Richmond St. © **519/645-6400.** All-you-can-eat C$9.95 (US$6). AE, DC, MC, V. Daily noon–2:30pm and 5pm–10:30pm.

**Riverview Dining Room** Kids CONTINENTAL Still a favorite venue for special family occasions, the Wonderland Riverview Dining Room offers such dishes as rack of lamb with a Dijon mustard sauce, charbroiled beef tenderloin, prime rib, and surf and turf. Around the walls are framed clips of events that took place here in the thirties and forties—dancing to Ozzie Williams, Shep Fields, and Mart Kenney. There's a lovely outdoor dining terrace under the trees and an outdoor dancing area overlooking the river.

285 Wonderland Rd. S. © **519/471-4662.** Reservations recommended. Main courses C$13–C$28 (US$8–US$17). AE, MC, V. Daily 11:30am–2:30pm and 5–9pm. Closed Mon–Tues Jan–Mar.

## LONDON AFTER DARK

The **Grand Theatre,** 471 Richmond St. (© **519/672-9030**), features drama, comedy, and musicals from September to June. There are also performances by visiting troupes, including the National Ballet of Canada. The theater itself, built in 1901, has been described as one of the country's most beautiful.

**Harness racing** takes place from October to June at the **Western Fairgrounds** (© **519/438-7203**) track; races usually start at 7:45pm. The other big attractions at the Fairgrounds are the **Slots Lounge**—with its 300 one-armed bandits—and the **IMAX theater.**

London also has a few bars and clubs: **Barneys,** 671 Richmond St. (© **519/432-1232**), attracts a young professional crowd and has a very popular summer patio; **Joe Kool's,** 595 Richmond at Central (© **519/663-5665**), is a popular site for students.

## 3 Goderich & Bayfield

Goderich is best explored on foot. The town's most striking feature is the central octagonal space with the Huron County Courthouse at its hub. Another highlight is the **Historic Huron Gaol,** with walls 5.5m (18 ft.) high and .5m (2 ft.) thick. This also houses the **Huron County Museum,** 110 North St. (**© 519/524-2686**). Admission is C$4 (US$2.50) for adults, C$3 (US$1.85) for seniors, and C$2.25 (US$1.40) for children ages 6 to 13, and it's open daily 10am to 4:30pm. **Goderich Tourism** (**© 519/524-6600;** www.town.goderich.on.ca) operates a visitor center at 91 Hamilton St., which is open daily in summer.

**Bayfield** is a pretty, well-preserved 19th-century town about 20km (13 miles) from Goderich and 65km (40 miles) from Stratford. Once a major grain-shipping port, it became a quiet backwater when the railroad passed it by. Today the main square, High Street, and Elgin Place are part of a Heritage Conservation District. Walk around and browse in the appealing stores—the **information center** (**© 519/565-2021**) has a helpful walking-tour pamphlet.

### WHERE TO STAY

**Benmiller Inn** ★ The heart of the inn is the original wool mill, which dates from 1877, and now contains the dining room, bar, reception, and 12 guest rooms. When it became an inn in 1974, many mechanical parts were refashioned into decorative objects—mirrors made from pulley wheels, lamps from gears. Rooms feature barn-board siding, desks, floor lamps, heated ceramic tile in the bathrooms, and handmade quilts. The 17 rooms in Gledhill House, the original mill-owner's home, are generously proportioned, while the four suites have fireplaces, bidets, and Jacuzzis. Ground-floor rooms have pressed-tin ceilings. There are more rooms in the River Mill, which is attached to a silo-style building containing the swimming pool, whirlpool, and running track. The brick patio overlooking the gardens is a pleasant place to sit and look at the totem pole, brought from British Columbia. Spa day packages start at C$164 (US$102).

RR #4, Goderich, ON, N7A 3Y1. **© 519/524-2191.** www.benmiller.on.ca. 47 rms. C$112–C$205 (US$69–US$127) double; C$305 (US$189) deluxe suite. Rates include breakfast buffet; some plans include dinner. AE, DC, MC, V. **Amenities:** Restaurant (continental); indoor pool; billiards room; table tennis, cross-country ski trails; spa; sauna. *In room:* A/C, TV.

**Clifton Manor Inn** ★ This elegant house was built in 1895 for the reve (bailiff or governor) of Bayfield. The interior features ash wood, etched glass panels in the doors, and other attractive period details. Today owner Elizabeth Marquis has added many touches—Oriental rugs, comfortable sofas and love seats in the living room, and elegant silver and sideboards in the dining room. There are four rooms, each named after an artist or composer. The bathroom in the charming Renoir room has a deep, 2m (6-ft.) long tub. The Mozart boasts a canopied bed. All rooms have cozy touches like mohair throws, sheepskin rugs, wingback chairs, fresh flowers, and so on. Lilac bushes and fruit trees fill the yard. Breakfast consists of egg dishes like omelettes or crêpes, plus fresh fruit often plucked from the trees in the garden. The Clifton is a romantic hideaway for adults—no children are allowed.

19 The Square, P.O. Box 454, Bayfield, ON, N0M 1G0. **© 519/565-2282.** www.cliftonmanor.com. 4 rms. C$110–C$150 (US$68–US$93). No credit cards. **Amenities:** Breakfast, garden. *In room:* No phone.

**The Little Inn at Bayfield** The inn, originally built in 1832, has been thoroughly modernized. The older rooms in the main building are small and have only showers, but they are comfortably furnished with oak or sleigh beds. Rooms in the newer section are larger and feature platform beds and modern furnishings. The suites across the street in the carriage house have platform beds, pine hutches, and feature whirlpool bathrooms, propane-gas fireplaces, and verandas. The popular restaurant is open for lunch and dinner 7 days a week.

Main St., P.O. Box 100, Bayfield, ON, N0M 1G0. ✆ **519/565-2611.** Fax 519/565-5474. www.littleinn.com. 20 rms, 10 suites across the street. C$115–C$155(US$71–US$96) double, from C$235 (US$146) suite. Special packages available. AE, DC, MC, V. **Amenities:** Restaurant. *In room:* A/C, TV.

## WHERE TO DINE

The **Benmiller Inn** (see above) has an impressive formal dining room. For casual dining, Bayfield offers several choices. The **Albion Hotel** on Main Street (✆ **519/565-2641**) features a fun, wall-length bar decorated with hundreds of baseball hats and other sports paraphernalia. The fare consists of English specialties plus ribs, pizza, and sandwiches. It also has seven rooms available starting at C$60 (US$37) double, sharing a bath. **Admiral Belfield's,** 5 Main St., is fun, too. A converted general store, it serves diner, deli, and pub fare, and occasionally there's jazz and other entertainment.

**Red Pump. Main St., Bayfield** ★ INTERNATIONAL This charming restaurant boasts an inviting patio and some of the area's most innovative cooking. Typical main dishes might include lamb chops with grilled vegetables and potatoes mashed with truffle oil, or sautéed jumbo scallops with rice noodles and hoisin jus. The decor is plush and comfortable.

✆ **519/565-2576.** www.theredpump.com. Reservations recommended. Main courses C$20–C$30 (US$12–US$19). AE, MC, V. Daily noon–3pm and 5–9pm. Closed Jan–Mar and Mon–Tues in late fall and winter.

# 4 Stratford & the Stratford Festival ★★

The Stratford Festival was born in 1953 when director Tyrone Guthrie lured Alec Guinness to perform. The festival has become one of the most famous in North America, and it has put this scenic town on the map. While visitors will notice the Avon River and other sights named in honor of the Bard, they may not realize that Stratford has another claim to fame. It's home to one of the best cooking schools in the country, making it a delight to dine at many of the spots in town.

## ESSENTIALS

**VISITOR INFORMATION** For first-rate visitor information, go to the **Information Centre** (✆ **519/273-3352**) by the river on York Street at Erie. From May to early November, it's open Sunday to Wednesday 9am to 5pm, and Thursday to Saturday 9am to 8pm. At other times, contact **Tourism Stratford,** 88 Wellington St., P.O. Box 818, Stratford, ON N5A 6W1 (✆ **800/561-SWAN** or 519/271-5140; www.city.stratford.on.ca).

**GETTING THERE By plane Stratford Airporter** (✆ **519/273-0057** or 519/273-5968) provides airbus service from Pearson International Airport in Toronto (see chapter 10). Ground transportation is also available from London International Airport (see above).

**By rail VIA Rail** (✆ **888/VIA-RAIL** or 416/366-8411; www.viarail.ca) and **Amtrak** (✆ **800/USA-RAIL,** www.amtrak.com) operate several trains daily along the Toronto–Kitchener–Stratford route.

**By car** Driving from Toronto, take Highway 401 west to Interchange 278 at Kitchener. Follow Highway 8 west onto Highway 7/8 to Stratford.

## EXPLORING THE TOWN

Stratford has a wealth of attractions that complement the theater offerings. It's a compact town, easily negotiable on foot. Within sight of the Festival Theatre, **Queen's Park** has picnic spots beneath tall shade trees and by the Avon River. There are also some superb dining and good shopping prospects.

Past the Orr Dam and the 90-year-old stone bridge, through a rustic gate, lies a very special park, the **Shakespearean Garden.** In the formal English garden, where a sundial measures the hours, you can relax and contemplate the herb and flowerbeds and the tranquil river lagoon, and muse on a bust of Shakespeare by Toronto sculptor Cleeve Horne.

If you turn right onto Romeo Street North from highways 7 and 8 as you come into Stratford, you'll find the **Gallery/Stratford,** 54 Romeo St. (✆ **519/271-5271;** www.gallerystratford.on.ca). It's in a historic building on the fringes of Confederation Park. Since it opened in 1967, it has mounted fine Canadian-focused shows, often oriented to the theater arts. If you're an art lover, do drop in—you're sure to find an unusual show in one of the four galleries. It is open daily in summer 9am to 6pm; Tuesday to Sunday 10am to 4pm off-season. Admission is C$10 (US$6) for adults, C$8 (US$5) for seniors and students ages 12 and up.

Stratford is a historic town, dating to 1832. Free 1-hour **guided tours of early Stratford** take place Monday to Saturday from July to Labour Day. They leave at 9:30am from the visitors' booth by the river. Many fine shops lie along Ontario and Downie streets and are tucked down along York Street. Antiques lovers will want to visit the nearby town of Shakespeare (11km/7 miles out of town on Highway 7/8), which has several stores.

Paddleboat and canoe rentals are available at the **Boathouse,** behind and below the information booth. It's open daily 9am until dark in summer. Contact **Avon Boat Rentals,** 40 York St. (✆ **519/271-7739**).

## A COUPLE OF EXCURSIONS FROM STRATFORD

Only half an hour or so away, the twin cities of **Kitchener** and **Waterloo** have two drawing cards: the **Farmer's Market** and the famous 9-day **Oktoberfest.** The cities still have a German-majority population (of German descent, and often German speaking), and many citizens are Mennonites. On Saturdays starting at 6am, you can sample shoofly pie, apple butter, kochcase, and other Mennonite specialties at the market in the Market Square complex, at Duke and Frederick streets in Kitchener. For additional information, contact the **Kitchener–Waterloo Area Visitors and Convention Bureau,** 2848 King St. E., Kitchener, ON N2A 1A5 (✆ **519/748-0800;** www.kw-visitor.on.ca). It's open 9am to 5pm weekdays only in winter, daily in summer. For Oktoberfest information, contact **K-W Oktoberfest,** P.O. Box 1053, 17 Benton St., Kitchener, ON N2G 4G1 (✆ **519/570-4267;** www.oktoberfest.ca).

The town of **St. Jacobs** lies 8km (5 miles) north of Kitchener. It has close to 100 shops in venues such as a converted mill, silo, and other factory buildings. For those interested in learning more about the Amish-Mennonite way of life, the **Meetingplace,** 33 King St. (✆ **519/664-3518**), shows a short film about it (daily in summer, weekends only in winter).

## WHERE TO STAY

When you book your theater tickets, you can book your accommodations at no extra charge. The festival will reserve the type of accommodation and price

**ATTRACTIONS** ●
- Avon Boat Rentals **18**
- Avon Theatre **16**
- Confederation Park **2**
- Festival Theatre **3**
- Gallery/Stratford **1**
- Shakespearean Garden **19**
- Tom Patterson Theatre **8**

**ACCOMMODATIONS** ■
- Acrylic Dreams **12**
- Ambercroft **11**
- Avonview Manor **21**
- Bentley's **7**
- Deacon House **13**
- Festival Inn **5**
- The Queen's Inn **4**
- 23 Albert Place **10**
- Woods Villa **22**

**DINING** ◆
- Bentley's **7**
- The Church **14**
- Keystone Alley Café **15**
- Let Them East Cake **17**
- The Old Prune **6**
- Rundles **9**
- York Street Kitchen **20**

### Tips The Play's the Thing

On July 13, 1953, *Richard III,* starring Alec Guinness, was staged in a huge tent. From that modest start, Stratford's artistic directors have built on the radical, but faithfully classic, base established by Tyrone Guthrie to create a repertory theater with a glowing international reputation.

Stratford has three theaters. The **Festival Theatre,** 55 Queen St., in Queen's Park, has a dynamic thrust stage. The **Avon Theatre,** 99 Downie St., has a classic proscenium. The **Tom Patterson Theatre,** Lakeside Drive, is an intimate 500-seat theater.

World famous for its Shakespearean productions, the festival also offers classic and modern theatrical masterpieces. Recent productions have included *The Sound of Music, Private Lives,* and *Who's Afraid of Virginia Woolf?* Offerings from the Bard have included *The Merchant of Venice, Twelfth Night,* and *Macbeth.* Among the company's famous alumni are Dame Maggie Smith, Sir Alec Guinness, Sir Peter Ustinov, Alan Bates, Christopher Plummer, Irene Worth, and Julie Harris. Present company members include Brian Bedford, Cynthia Dale, Martha Henry, and Barbara Byrne.

In addition to attending plays, visitors may enjoy "Meet the Festival," a series of informal discussions with members of the acting company, production, or administrative staff. "Post Performance Discussions" follow Thursday evening performances. Backstage or warehouse tours are offered every Wednesday, Saturday, and Sunday morning from early June to mid-October. The tours cost C$5 (US$3.10) for adults and C$3 (US$1.85) for seniors and students; make tour reservations when you purchase tickets.

The season usually begins in May and continues through October, with performances Tuesday to Sunday nights and matinees on Wednesday, Saturday, and Sunday. Ticket prices range from C$39 to C$70 (US$24–US$43), with special prices for students and seniors. For tickets, contact the **Stratford Festival,** P.O. Box 520, Stratford, ON N5A 6V2 (✆ **800/567-1600** or 519/273-1600; www.stratford-festival.on.ca). Tickets are also available in the United States and Canada at Ticketmaster outlets. The box office opens for mail and fax orders only in late January; telephone and in-person sales begin in late February.

category you prefer, from guest homes for as little as C$40 (US$25) to first-class hotels charging more than C$125 (US$78). Call or write the **Festival Theatre Box Office,** P.O. Box 520, Stratford, ON N5A 6V2 (✆ **800/567-1600** or 519/273-1600).

## HOTELS & MOTELS

**Bentley's** The soundproof rooms here are luxurious duplex suites with efficiency kitchens. Period English furnishings and attractive drawings, paintings, and costume designs on the walls make for a pleasant ambiance. Five units have skylights. The adjoining British-style pub, also called Bentley's, is popular with festival actors (see "Where to Dine," below).

107 Ontario St., Stratford, ON N5A 3H1. ✆ **519/271-1121.** 13 units. Apr–Nov C$150 (US$) double; Nov–June C$90 (US$56) double. Extra person C$20 (US$12). AE, DC, MC, V. **Amenities:** Bar. *In room:* A/C, TV.

**Festival Inn** The Festival Inn is set back off Highway 7/8, on 8ha (20 acres) of landscaped grounds. The place has an Old English air, with stucco walls, Tudor-style beams, and high-backed red settees in the lobby. Tudor style prevails throughout the large, motel-style rooms. All have wall-to-wall carpeting, matching bedspreads, and floor-to-ceiling drapes, and reproductions of old masters on the walls. Some units have charming bay windows with sheer curtains, and all rooms in the main building, north wing, and annex have refrigerators.

1144 Ontario St. (P.O. Box 811), Stratford, ON N5A 6W1. ✆ **519/273-1150.** Fax 519/273-2111. www.festivalinnstratford.com. 182 units. C$140–C$200 (US$87–US$124) double. Extra person C$10 (US$6). Winter discounts (about 30%) available. AE, DC, MC, V. Free parking. **Amenities:** 2 restaurants; indoor pool. *In room:* A/C, TV, fridge.

**The Queen's Inn** The Queen's Inn has the best location in Stratford—it's located right in the town center. The historic building is about a century-and-a-half old, but the guest rooms are given a fresh look every year as the inn's owners use the winter months for refurbishing. The Boar's Head Pub is on the premises.

161 Ontario St., Stratford, ON N5A 3H3. ✆ **800/461-6450** or 519/271-1400. Fax 519/271-7373. www.queensinnstratford.ca. 31 units. May–Nov 15 C$105–C$130 (US$65–US$81) double, C$165–C$190 (US$102–US$118) suite; Nov 16–April C$65 (US$40) double, from C$85 (US$53) suite. AE, DC, MC, V. Free parking. **Amenities:** Bar. *In room:* A/C, TV.

**23 Albert Place** Around the corner from the Avon Theatre, the Albert Place has large rooms with high ceilings. Furnishings are simple and modern. Some units have separate sitting rooms. Complimentary coffee, tea, and doughnuts are available in the lobby for guests in the early morning.

23 Albert St., Stratford, ON N5A 3K2. ✆ **519/273-5800.** Fax 519/273-5008. 34 units. C$95–C$105 (US$59–US$65) double; C$115 (US$71) mini-suite; from C$140 (US$87) suite. MC, V. *In room:* A/C, TV.

## A PICK OF THE BED & BREAKFASTS

For more information on the bed-and-breakfast scene, write to **Tourism Stratford,** P.O. Box 818, 88 Wellington St., Stratford, ON N5A 6W1 (✆ **519/271-5140**). It's open 9am to 5pm Monday to Friday.

**Acrylic Dreams** As its name suggests, Acrylic Dreams has a fun, modern atmosphere, thanks to its artist owners. Most of the house is furnished with cottage-style antiques, but the living room is done in new wave style, with transparent acrylic furniture. Upstairs, there's a suite decorated in Provençal colors that has a separate sitting room with a TV and refrigerator. On the ground floor, there are two doubles that share a refrigerator. The full breakfast varies from day to day, but might include peaches and peach yogurt, and homemade scones and preserves using ingredients from the garden (but no meat—the owners are vegetarians). There's a phone for guests' use. Co-owner Karen Zamara offers in-room reflexology treatments; guests are also welcome to attend yoga classes at her downtown studio (C$12/US$7 per class).

66 Bay St., Stratford, ON N5A 4K6. ✆ **519/271-7874;** fax number the same. www.bbcanada.com/3718.html. 4 units. C$95–C$100 (US$59–US$62) double; C$115–C$130 (US$71–US$81) suite. C$25 (US$16) extra for 3rd person in suite. Rates include breakfast. 2-night minimum on weekends. No credit cards. *In room:* A/C.

**Ambercroft** This inviting 1878 home in a quiet downtown area is convenient to the theaters and restaurants. The quirky, angular rooms are country cozy. There's a comfy front parlor, a small TV room, and front and rear porches. Guests have the use of a refrigerator. An extended continental breakfast is served—seasonal fruits, cereals, homemade baked goods, and more. No smoking, and no pets accepted.

129 Brunswick St., Stratford, ON N5A 3L9. ✆ **519/271-5644.** Fax 519/272-0156. www.bbcanada.com/2482.html. 4 units. C$95–C$130 (US$59–US$81) double. Rates include full breakfast. MC, V. *In room:* A/C.

**Avonview Manor** In an Edwardian house on a quiet street, Avonview Manor has attractively and individually furnished rooms. Three have queen-size beds; the suite contains four singles, a sitting room, and a private bath. Breakfast is served in a bright dining room that overlooks the garden. A kitchen equipped with an ironing board is available on the first floor. The living room is very comfortable, particularly in winter, when guests can cozy up in front of the stone fireplace. Smoking is allowed only on the porch.

63 Avon St., Stratford, ON N5A 5N5. ✆ **519/273-4603.** www.bbcanada.com/avonview. 4 units (2 with bathroom). C$85–C$110 (US$53–US$68) double; C$110–C$160 (US$68–US$99) suite. Rates include full breakfast. No credit cards, though personal checks are accepted. **Amenities:** Pool; hot tub.

**Deacon House** ★ Deacon House, a shingle-style structure built in 1907, has been restored by Dianna Hrysko and Mary Allen. Rooms are decorated in country style, with iron-and-brass beds, quilts, pine hutches, oak rockers, and rope-style rugs. The living room, with a fireplace, TV, wingback chairs, and a sofa, is comfortable. The main-floor guest kitchen is a welcome convenience, as is the second-floor sitting and reading room. The entire house is nonsmoking. This is a great location, within walking distance of everything.

101 Brunswick St., Stratford, ON N5A 3L9. ✆ 877-825-6374 or **519/273-2052.** Fax 519/273-3784. www.bbcanada.com/1152.html. 6 units. C$117–C$127 (US$73–US$79) double. Extra person C$25 (US$16). Rates include full breakfast. Off-season packages available. MC, V. *In room:* A/C.

**Woods Villa** This handsome 1870 house is home to Ken Vinen, who collects and restores the Wurlitzers, Victrolas, and player pianos found throughout the house. In the large drawing room there are six—and they all work. Ken will happily demonstrate, drawing upon his vast library of early paper rolls and records. Five rooms have fireplaces, and the handsome suite boasts a canopy bed. Rooms are large and offer excellent value. Morning coffee is delivered to your room, followed by breakfast prepared to order and served in the dining room. There's an attractively landscaped outdoor pool and terrace.

62 John St. N., Stratford, ON N5A 6K7. ✆ **519/271-4576.** www.woodsvilla.orc.ca. 6 units. C$145–C$250 (US$90–US$155) double. Rates include full breakfast. MC, V. *In room:* A/C, TV.

## WHERE TO DINE

### EXPENSIVE

**The Church** ★★ CONTINENTAL The Church is simply stunning. The organ pipes and the altar of the 1873 structure are intact, along with the vaulted roof, carved woodwork, and stained-glass windows. You can sit in the nave or the side aisles and dine to appropriate sounds—usually Bach. Fresh flowers and elegant table settings further enhance the experience. In summer, there's a special four-course fixed-price dinner menu and an after-theater menu. Appetizers might include asparagus served hot with black morels in their juices, white wine, and cream; or sauté of duck foie gras with leeks and citron, mango, and ginger sauce. Among the selection of eight or so entrees you might find Canadian caribou with port and blackberry sauce, cabbage braised in cream with shallots and glazed chestnuts, or lobster salad with green beans, new potatoes, and truffles scented with caraway. Desserts are equally exciting—try charlotte of white chocolate mousse with summer fruit and dark chocolate sauce, or nougat glace with kiwi sauce.

To dine here during the festival, make reservations in March or April when you buy your tickets. The upstairs Belfry Bar is a popular pre- and post-theater gathering place.

70 Brunswick St. (at Waterloo St.). ✆ **519/273-3424.** www.churchrestaurant.com. Reservations strongly recommended. Fixed-price dinner (summer only) C$59–C$73 (US$37–US$45); main courses C$33–$46 (US$20–US$29). AE, DC, MC, V. Tues–Sat 11:30am–1am, Sun 11:30am–11pm (hours vary and are generally shorter in the off-season). Call for Mon hours during special events.

**The Old Prune** ★ CONTINENTAL Two charming, whimsical women—Marion Isherwood and Eleanor Kane—run the Prune. In a lovely Edwardian home, it has three dining rooms and an enclosed garden patio. Former Montrealers, the proprietors demonstrate Quebec flair in both decor and menu. Marion's inspired paintings grace the walls.

Chef Bryan Steele selects the freshest local ingredients, many from the region's dedicated community of organic farmers, and prepares them simply to reveal their abundant flavor. Among the main courses, you might find Perth County pork loin grilled with tamari and honey glaze and served with shiitake mushrooms, pickled cucumbers, and sunflower sprouts; steamed bass in Napa cabbage with curry broth and lime leaves; or rack of Ontario lamb with smoky tomatillo–chipotle pepper sauce. Among the appetizers might be outstanding house-smoked salmon with lobster potato salad topped with Sevruga caviar, or refreshing tomato consommé with saffron and sea scallops. Desserts, such as rhubarb strawberry Napoleon with vanilla mousse, are always inspired. The Old Prune is also lovely for lunch or a late supper, when it offers such light specialties as sautéed quail with grilled polenta, Italian greens, mushrooms, roasted tomatoes, balsamic jus, and smoked trout terrine.

151 Albert St. ✆ **519/271-5052.** Reservations required. 3-course fixed-price dinner C$53 (US$33); main courses C$7–C$12 (US$4.35–$7) at lunch, C$7–C$14 (US$4.35–$9) at dinner. AE, MC, V. Wed–Sun 11:30am–1:30pm; Tues–Sat 5–9pm, Sun 5–7pm. After-theater menu Fri–Sat from 9pm. Call for winter hours.

**Rundles** ★ INTERNATIONAL Rundles provides a premier dining experience in a serene dining room overlooking the river. Proprietor Jim Morris eats, sleeps, thinks, and dreams food, and chef Neil Baxter delivers the exciting, exquisite cuisine to the table. The fixed-price dinner offers palate-pleasing flavor combinations. Among the five main dishes might be poached Atlantic salmon garnished with Jerusalem artichokes, wilted arugula, and yellow peppers in a light carrot sauce, or pink roast rib-eye of lamb with ratatouille and rosemary aioli. Appetizers might include shaved fennel, arugula, artichoke, and Parmesan salad or warm seared Quebec foie grass with caramelized endive, garlic-flavored fried potatoes, and tomato and basil oil. My dessert choice is glazed lemon tart and orange sorbet, but hot mango tart with pineapple sorbet is also a dream.

9 Cobourg St. ✆ **519/271-6442.** Reservations required. 3-course fixed-price dinner C$59 (US$37). AE, DC, MC, V. Apr–Oct Wed and Sat–Sun 11:30am–1:30pm; Tues 5–7pm, Wed–Sat 5–8:30pm, Sun 5–7pm. Closed Mondays and throughout Nov–Mar.

## MODERATE

**Bentley's** ★ CANADIAN/ENGLISH Bentley's is *the* local watering hole, and a favorite theater company gathering spot. The popular pastime is darts, but you can also watch TV. In summer you can sit on the garden terrace and enjoy the light fare—grilled shrimp, burgers, gourmet pizza, fish-and-chips, shepherd's pie, and pasta dishes. More substantial fare—including lamb curry, sirloin steak, and salmon baked in white wine with peppercorn-dill butter—is offered at dinner. The bar has 16 drafts on tap.

107 Ontario St. ✆ **519/271-1121.** Reservations not accepted. Main courses C$8–C$14 (US$5–$9). AE, DC, MC, V. Daily 11:30am–1am.

**Keystone Alley Café** ★ CONTINENTAL Theater actors often stop here for lunch—perhaps a sandwich, like the maple-grilled chicken and avocado club, or a main dish like cornmeal-crusted Mediterranean tart. At dinner, entrees range from breast of Muscovy duck with stir-fried Asian vegetables and egg noodles in honey-ginger sauce, to escalopes of calf's liver accompanied by garlic potato puree and creamed Savoy cabbage with bacon. The short wine list is reasonably priced, and the food is better than the fare at some pricier competitors.

34 Brunswick St. ✆ **519/271-5645;** www.keystonealley.com. Reservations recommended. Main courses C$17–C$26.50 (US$11–US$16). AE, DC, MC, V. Mon–Sat 11:30am–2:30pm; Tues–Sat 5pm–9pm.

### INEXPENSIVE

**Let Them Eat Cake** LIGHT FARE Let Them Eat Cake is great for breakfast (bagels and scones) and lunch (soups, salads, sandwiches, quiche, and chicken pot pie), but best of all for dessert. There are 15 to 20, including pecan pie, orange Bavarian cream, lemon bars, carrot cake, Black Forest cake, and chocolate cheesecake.

82 Wellington St. ✆ **519/273-4774.** www.letthemeatcake.on.ca. Reservations not accepted. Lunch items less than C$10 (US$6); desserts C$1–C$4 (US60¢–$2.50). V. Apr–Oct Mon 7:30am–4pm, Tues–Sat 7:30am–12:30am, Sun 9am–6pm; Nov–Mar until 4pm daily.

**York Street Kitchen** ECLECTIC This small, narrow restaurant is a fun, funky spot loved for its reasonably priced but high-quality food. You can come here for breakfast burritos and other morning fare, and for lunch sandwiches, which you build yourself by choosing from a list of fillings. In the evenings, expect to find comfort foods like meat loaf and mashed potatoes or barbecued chicken and ribs.

41 York St. ✆ **519/273-7041.** Reservations not accepted. Main courses C$8–C$13 (US$5–US$8). AE, V. Daily 8am–8pm from April to early Oct; daily 8am–3pm from mid-Oct to March; closed Dec 24–Jan 5.

### PICNICKING IN STRATFORD

Stratford is a picnicking place. Take a hamper down to the banks of the river or into the parks. Plenty of places cater to this business. **Rundles** (see above) will make you a super-sophisticated hamper. **Café Mediterranean,** 10 Downie St. in the Festival Square Building (no phone), has salads, quiches, crepes, and flaky meat pies and pastries. It's open Tuesday to Sunday, May to September from 10am to 6pm, and October to April from noon to 4pm.

## WHERE TO STAY & DINE NEARBY

**Langdon Hall** ★ This elegant house stands at the head of a curving, tree-lined drive. It was completed in 1902 by Eugene Langdon Wilks, a great-grandson of John Jacob Astor. It remained in the family until 1987, when its transformation into a small country-house hotel began. Today its 80ha (200 acres) of lawns, gardens, and woodlands make for an ideal retreat. The main house, of red brick with classical pediment and Palladian-style windows, has a beautiful symmetry. Throughout, the emphasis is on comfort rather than grandiosity. Most rooms are around the cloister garden. Each is individually decorated; most have fireplaces. The furnishings consist of handsome antique reproductions, mahogany wardrobes, ginger-jar porcelain lamps, and armchairs upholstered with luxurious fabrics. Rooms boast such nice touches as live plants and terry robes. The light, airy dining room serves fine regional cuisine. Main courses run C$22 to C$30 (US$14–US$19). Tea is served on the veranda. Spa packages start at C$180 (US$112).

RR #3, Cambridge, ON N3H 4R8. ✆ **800/268-1898** or 519/740-2100. Fax 519/740-8161. 49 units. C$259–$699 (US$161–$433) double. Rates include continental breakfast. Pets C$50 (US$31) extra. AE, DC, MC, V. From Hwy. 401, take Exit 275 south, turn right onto Blair Rd., follow signs. **Amenities:** Restaurant (regional), bar; pool; tennis court; cross-country ski trails; croquet; billiard room; exercise room; spa; sauna; whirlpool. *In room:* A/C, TV.

**Westover Inn** This Victorian manor house, built in 1867, features carved gingerbread decoration and leaded-glass windows. The house is set on 7.5ha (19 acres), making for a secluded retreat. Inside the limestone house, rooms have been furnished in modern antique style with reproductions. Some rooms have balconies. Six rooms are located in the manor itself, including a luxury suite with a whirlpool bathroom. The least expensive and smallest rooms (12 of them) are found in the Terrace, built in the 1930s as a dorm for the priests who attended what was then a seminary. The Thames Cottage, a modern building, also contains two two-bedroom suites. Downstairs in the manor, guests may use the comfortable lounge.

300 Thomas St., St. Mary's, ON, N4X 1B1. ✆ **519/284-2977.** Fax 519/284-4043. www.westoverinn.com. 22 rms and suites. C$95–C$175 (US$59–US$109) double; C$180–C$225 (US$112–US$140) suite. AE, MC, V. **Amenities:** Outdoor pool. *In room:* A/C, TV.

## 5 Elora & Fergus: The Elora Gorge & More

If you're driving from Toronto, take Highway 401 west to Highway 6, drive north to Highway 7 east, then get back on Highway 6 north and take it into Fergus. From Fergus take Highway 18 west to Elora.

**Elora** has always been a special place. To the natives, the gorge was a sacred site, home of spirits who dwelt within the great cliffs. Early explorers and Jesuit missionaries also wondered at the natural spectacle, but it was Scotsman William Gilkinson who put the town on the map in 1832 when he purchased 5,700ha (14,000 acres) on both sides of the Grand River and built a mill and a general store, and named it Elora, after the Ellora Caves in India.

Most of the houses that the settlers built in the 1850s stand today. You'll want to browse the stores along picturesque Mill Street. For real insight into the town's history, pick up a walking-tour brochure from the tourist booth on Mill Street.

The **Elora Gorge** is a 140ha (350-acre) park on both sides of the 20m (70-ft.) limestone gorge. Nature trails wind through it. Overhanging rock ledges, small caves, a waterfall, and the evergreen forest on its rim are some of the gorge's scenic delights. The park (✆ **519/846-9742**) has camping and swimming facilities, plus picnic areas and playing fields. It's a favorite with rock-climbers. Located just west of Elora at the junction of the Grand and Irvine rivers, it is open from May 1 to October 15 from 10am to sunset. For information, write or call the **Grand River Conservation Authority,** 400 Clyde Rd. (P.O. Box 729), Cambridge, ON, N1R 5W6 (✆ **519/621-2761;** www.grandriver.ca).

An additional summer attraction is the **Elora Festival,** a 3-week music celebration held from mid-July to early August. For more information, contact the **Elora Festival,** P.O. Box 990, Elora, ON, N0B 1S0 (✆ **519/846-0331;** www.elora.org).

**Fergus** (pop. 7,500) was founded by Scottish immigrant Adam Ferguson. There are more than 250 fine old 1850s buildings to see—examples of Scottish limestone architecture—including the Foundry, which now houses the Fergus market.

The most noteworthy Fergus event is the **Fergus Scottish Festival,** which includes Highland Games, featuring pipe-band competitions, caber tossing, tug-of-war contests, Highland dancing, and the North American Scottish Heavy Events, held usually on the second weekend in August. For more information on the games, contact **Fergus Scottish Festival and Highland Games,** P.O. Box 25, Fergus, ON, N1M 2W7 (✆ **519/787-0099;** www.fergusscottishfestival.com).

## WHERE TO STAY & DINE

**Breadalbane Inn** ★ Located in the heart of Fergus, the inn is an excellent example of 1860s architecture. The stone imported from Scotland is complemented by intricate ironwork, walnut bannisters and newel posts. It was built by the Honorable Admiral Ferguson as a residence, but also served as a nursing home and rooming house before it was converted 23 years ago. Guest rooms are all extremely comfortable and elegantly furnished with early Canadian-style furniture. In the back, the Coach House contains a suite with fireplace, Jacuzzi tub, and private patio.

The Breadalbane dining room is divided into two rooms, with French doors leading into the garden. Here you can dine to the strains of classical music, at darkly polished tables set with Royal Doulton china. At dinner, start with the smooth chicken-liver pate with brandy and peppercorns or the baked escargots with garlic and herb butter and follow with such dishes as oven-roasted salmon with a ginger-cucumber sauce or grilled venison medallions in a black-currant-and-juniper sauce. Prices range from C$18 to C$27 (US$11–US$17). It's open Tuesday to Sunday from 11:30am to 10pm.

487 St. Andrew St. W., Fergus, ON, N1M 1P2. ✆ **519/843-4770.** 6 rms. Doubles C$75–C$175 (US$47–US$109) double. Rates include continental breakfast. AE, MC, V. **Amenities:** Restaurant, bar.

**Elora Mill Inn** This inn is located in a five-story gristmill built in 1870 and operated until 1974. Downstairs, a lounge with the original exposed beams and a huge stone fireplace overlooks the falls. Upstairs are similarly rustic dining areas. Each guest room is furnished individually, some with four-posters, others with cannonball pine beds. Most beds are covered with quilts, and each room has a comfy rocker or hoop-back chair. Some rooms in adjacent buildings are duplexes and have decks and river views. Many inn rooms have gorge views, and some units have fireplaces.

The dining room's eight or so appetizers might include Bermuda chowder, a spicy broth of fish, vegetables, spiced sausage, dark rum, and sherry pepper. The main dishes are priced from C$18 to C$32 (US$11–US$20); the most popular option is the prime-rib cart, followed by a dessert—chocolate decadence or shoofly pie are popular choices. It's open daily for lunch and dinner.

77 Mill St. W., Elora, ON, N0B 1S0. ✆ **519/846-5356.** Fax 519/846-9180. 32 rms. C$160–C$175 (US$99–US$109) double; from C$190 (US$118) suite. Extra person C$25 (US$16). Rates include breakfast. AE, DC, MC, V. **Amenities:** Restaurant. *In room:* A/C, TV.

12

# North to Ontario's Lakelands & Beyond

*by Hilary Davidson*

If southern Ontario is marked by its sprawling cities and picturesque towns, the northern part of the province is remarkable for its vast wilderness. You'll be struck by the rugged beauty of the landscape, the forests of old-growth pine, and the thousands of lakes in the region. The most popular destinations are **Georgian Bay, Algonquin Provincial Park,** and the cottage country of **Huronia** and the **Muskoka Lakes.**

## 1 Exploring the Region

On weekends, many Torontonians head north to the cottage or to a resort to unwind. But if you want to explore the whole region, drive out from Toronto via Highway 400 north to Barrie. Here you can either turn west to explore Georgian Bay, the Bruce Peninsula, and Manitoulin Island or continue due north to the Muskoka Lakes, Algonquin Provincial Park, and points farther north.

### VISITOR INFORMATION

Contact **Ontario Tourism,** P.O. Box 104, Toronto ON M5B 2H1 (© **800/ONTARIO** or 416/314-0944; www.ontariotravel.net), or visit the travel center in the Eaton Centre on Level 1 at Yonge and Dundas. It's open Monday to Friday 10am to 9pm, Saturday 9:30am to 6pm, Sunday noon to 5pm. There's a **Travel Information Centre** in Barrie at 21 Molson Park Dr. at Highway 400. Those who are interested in exploring Northern Ontario's rich native culture should contact the **Northern Ontario Native Tourism Association,** 100 Back St., RR #4, Thunder Bay, ON P7C 4Z2 (© **807-623-0497;** www.nonta.net).

### THE GREAT OUTDOORS

In the parts of northern Ontario covered by this chapter, you'll find plenty of terrific places to canoe, hike, bike, or fish. Some 260 provincial parks in Ontario offer ample opportunities for outdoor recreation. They fall into one of two classifications: operating parks, which charge fees, offer facilities and services, and have staff; and non-operating parks, which have no fees or staff and only limited facilities. The daily in-season entry fee for a vehicle at an operating park is about C$6 to $10 (US$3.70–US$6); campsite costs start at C$15 (US$9), though many are higher. For more information, contact the **Ontario Ministry of Natural Resources** (© **416/314-2000;** www.ontarioparks.com); the ministry has information about every park in the system, and identifies which ones are operating parks.

Topographic maps are vital on extended canoeing/hiking trips and can be purchased from **Federal Maps Inc.,** 52 Antares Dr., Unit 1, Nepean, ON, K2E 7Z1 (© **888-545-8111** or 613/723-6366; http://maps.nrcan.gc.ca).

**BIKING** You'll find networks of biking and hiking trails in the national and provincial parks. Contact the individual parks directly for more information. One good route is the **Georgian Cycle and Ski Trail,** running 32km (20 miles) along the southern shore of Georgian Bay from Collingwood via Thornbury to Meaford. The **Bruce Peninsula** and **Manitoulin Island** also offer good cycling opportunities. In the Burk's Falls–Magnetawan area, the **Forgotten Trail** has been organized along old logging roads and railroad tracks. For details, contact the **Georgian Triangle Tourist Association,** 19 Mountain Rd., Unit 3B, Collingwood, ON L9Y 4M2 (✆ **705-445-7722;** www.georgiantriangle.org).

**CANOEING & KAYAKING** Northern Ontario is a canoeist's paradise. You can enjoy exceptional canoeing in **Algonquin, Killarney,** and **Quetico Provincial Parks;** along the rivers in the **Temagami** (Lady Evelyn Smoothwater Provincial Park) and **Wabakimi** regions; along the **Route of the Voyageurs** in Algoma Country (Lake Superior Provincial Park); and along the rivers leading into James Bay, like the **Missinaibi. Killbear Provincial Park, Georgian Bay,** and **Pukaskwa National Park** also are good places to paddle.

Alas, many places are getting overcrowded. One of the quietest, least-trafficked areas is the **Missinaibi River** in the Chapleau Game Reserve. Another truly remote canoeing area, accessible by plane only, is in **Winisk River Provincial Park,** where you're likely to see polar bears who establish their dens in the park. These areas are for advanced canoeists who can handle white water and orient themselves in the wilderness. For details on all these areas and detailed maps, contact the **Ministry of Natural Resources** (✆ **416/314-2000;** www.ontarioparks.com). Also see the individual park entries in this chapter.

Around Parry Sound and Georgian Bay, canoeing and kayaking trips are arranged by the **White Squall Paddling Centre,** RR #1, Nobel, ON, P0G 1G0 (✆ **705/342-5324;** www.whitesquall.com). Half-day paddling clinics are C$72 ($45), day trips are C$100 (US$62); 4-day trips start at C$510 (US$316); trips include instruction, meals, and equipment. In Algonquin Provincial Park, several outfitters serve park visitors, including **Algonquin Outfitters,** Oxtongue Lake (RR #1), Dwight, ON, P0A 1H0 (✆ **705/635-2243;** www.algonquinoutfitters.com), and **Opeongo Algonquin Outfitting Store,** Box 123, Whitney, ON, K0J 2M0 (✆ **613/637-2075**). Complete canoe outfitting runs C$45 to C$65 (US$28–US$40) per day, depending on the length of trip and extent of equipment. Canoe rentals are C$15 to C$35 (US$9–US$22) per day and C$98 to C$225 (US$61–US$140) per week.

**Killarney Outfitters,** on Highway 637, 5km (3 miles) east of Killarney (✆ **705/287-2828;** www.killarneyoutfitters.com), offers complete outfitting for C$65 (US$40) per day or C$410 (US$254) per week. Canoe and kayak rentals range from C$20 to C$30 (US$12–US$19) and C$23 to C$40 (US$14–US$25), respectively. In the Quetico area, contact **Canoe Canada Outfitters,** Box 1810, 300 O'Brien St., Atikokan, ON, P0T 1C0 (✆ **807/597-6418;** www.canoecanada.com).

North of Thunder Bay is excellent wilderness for camping, fishing, hunting, and canoeing in the Wabakimi (accessed from Armstrong), with plenty of scope for beginners, intermediates, and advanced paddlers. Contact **Mattice Lake Outfitters** (✆ **807/583-2483;** www.matticelake.com) for multi-day trips: 3-day excursions run about $650 (US$403), 5-day $750 (US$465), and 7-day $850 (US$527). For other outfitters, call the **Northern Ontario Tourist Outfitters Association** (✆ **705/472-5552;** www.noto.net).

*Note:* In most provincial parks you must register with park authorities and provide them with your route.

**FISHING** Ontario is one of the world's largest freshwater fishing grounds, with more than 250,000 lakes and 96,000km (60,000 miles) of rivers supporting more than 140 species. The northern area covered in this chapter is the province's best fishing region. Before you go, check out the **Fish Ontario!** website (www.fishontario.com) for the latest information. In summer, on **Manitoulin Island,** fishing for Chinook, coho, rainbow, lake trout, perch, and bass is excellent in Georgian Bay or any of the island lakes—**Mindenmoya, Manitou, Kagawong,** and **Tobacco,** to name a few. Trips can be arranged through **Timberlane Lodge** (✆ **800/890-4177** or 705/377-4078; www.timberlane.ca).

Around **Nipissing** and **North Bay** there's great fishing for walleye, northern pike, smallmouth bass, muskie, whitefish, and perch. In addition to these, the **Temagami** region offers brook, lake, and rainbow trout. You can find more remote fishing in the **Chapleau** and **Algoma** regions, the **James Bay Frontier,** and north of **Lake Superior.**

Some outfitters will rent lakeside log cabins equipped with a propane stove and refrigerator and motorboat to go along with it. The cost varies from C$900 to C$1,150 (US$558–US$713) per person for 3 to 7 days. One outfitter to contact is **Mattice Lake Outfitters** (see above). **Polar Bear Camp,** P.O. Box 2436, Cochrane, ON, P0L 1C0 (✆ **705/272-5680**), offers similar packages. For additional suggestions, contact **Ontario Tourism** or the **Northern Ontario Tourist Outfitters Association** (see above).

*Note:* You must follow fishing limits and regulations. Licenses are required, costing about C$15 (US$9). These licenses are usually available at boat shops and sporting goods stores; or contact the **Ministry of Natural Resources** (✆ **416/314-2000**).

**GOLF** Barrie has two exceptional courses—the **National Pines Golf and Country Club** (✆ **800/663-1549** or 705/431-7000; www.golfnationalpines.com) and the **Horseshoe Resort** golf course (✆ **800/461-5627** or 705/835-2790; www.horeshoeresort.com). Collingwood offers the scenic **Cranberry Resort** course (✆ **800/465-9077;** www.cranberry-resort.on.ca). In the Huronia region, there's the **Bonaire Golf and Country Club** (✆ **705/835-3125;** www.bonairegolf.on.ca), in the town of Coldwater. In Bracebridge, you'll find the **Muskoka Highlands Golf Course** (✆ **705/646-1060;** www.muskokahighlands.com) and, farther north near North Bay, the **Mattawa Golf Resort** (✆ **800/762-2339** or 705/744-5818). Thunder Bay has five par-71 or -72 courses, while Timmins and Kenora have one each.

**HIKING & BACKPACKING** The region is a hiker's paradise. The **Bruce Trail,** starting at Queenston, runs for 782km (469 miles), crossing the Niagara escarpment and Bruce Peninsula and ending up in Tobermory. The Bruce Trail Association publishes a map you can get from sporting-goods stores specializing in outdoor activities. In the Bruce Peninsula National Park are four trails, three linked to the Bruce Trail. There's also a hiking trail around Flowerpot Island in Fathom Five National Park.

Manitoulin Island is popular with hikers, particularly the **Cup and Saucer Trail.** South of Parry Sound, hikers can follow the 66km (41-mile) **Seguin Trail,** which meanders around several lakes. In the Muskoka region, trails abound in **Arrowhead Provincial Park** at Huntsville and the Resource Management Area on Highway 11, north of Bracebridge, and in **Algonquin Park.** Algonquin is a great choice for an extended backpacking trip, along the Highland Trail or the Western Uplands Hiking Trail, which combines three loops for a total of 170km (105 miles).

You can do a memorable 7- to 10-day backpacking trip in **Killarney Provincial Park** on the 97km (60-mile) La Cloche Silhouette Trail, which takes in some stunning scenery. **Sleeping Giant Provincial Park** has more than 81km (50 miles) of trails. The Kabeyun Trail provides great views of Lake Superior and the 245m (800-ft.) high cliffs of the Sleeping Giant. And the **Pukaskwa National Park** offers a coastal hiking trail between the Pic and Pukaskwa rivers along the northern shore of Lake Superior.

For additional hiking information, see the park entries later in this chapter.

**HORSEBACK RIDING** **Harmony Acres,** RR #1, Tobermory (✆ **519/596-2735**), offers overnight trail rides to the shores of Georgian Bay, as well as 1-hour and day rides. On Manitoulin Island, **Honora Bay Riding Stables,** RR #1, Little Current, ON, P0P 1K0 (✆ **705/368-2669**), operates an overnight trail ride May to October.

In Collingwood, there's **Braeburn Farms Limited,** RR #1 (✆ **705/446-2262**), which has 1-hour guided trail rides as well as day rides. Near Sault Ste. Marie, **Cedar Rail Ranch,** RR #3, Thessalon (✆ **705/842-2021**), offers both hourly and overnight trail rides with stops for swimming breaks along the route. Riding fees run the gamut from C$20 to C$25 (US$12–US$16) for an hour's guided trail ride to C$75 to C$100 (US$47–US$62) for a day on horseback.

**SKIING & SNOWMOBILING** Ontario's largest downhill-skiing area is the **Blue Mountain Resorts** in Collingwood. In the Muskoka region there's downhill skiing at **Hidden Valley Highlands** (✆ **705/789-1773** or 705/789-5942; www.skihiddenvalley.on.ca). Up north around Thunder Bay try **Loch Lomond** (✆ **807/475-7787;** www.loch.on.ca), **Big Thunder** (✆ **807/475-4402**), and **Mount Baldy** (✆ **807/683-8441**).

You can cross-country ski at Big Thunder and in several provincial parks, such as **Sleeping Giant** and **Kakabeka Falls.**

One of the top destinations is the **Parry Sound** area, which has an extensive network of cross-country ski trails and more than 1,047km (650 miles) of well-groomed snowmobiling trails. There are nine snowmobiling clubs in the area, and the **Chamber of Commerce** (✆ **705/746-4213**) can put you in touch with them. For details on cross-country skiing, contact the **Georgian Nordic Ski and Canoe Club,** Box 42, Parry Sound, ON, P2A 2X2 (✆ **705/746-5067;** www.georgiannordic.com), which permits day use of its ski trails.

You'll also find groomed cross-country trails at **Sauble Beach** on the Bruce Peninsula and in many of the provincial parks farther north. Along the mining frontier, contact the **Porcupine Ski Runners** at ✆ **705/360-1444** in Timmins.

## 2 From Collingwood/Blue Mountain to Tobermory/Bruce Peninsula National Park

Nestled at the base of Blue Mountain, **Collingwood** is the town closest to Ontario's largest skiing area. Collingwood first achieved prosperity as a Great Lakes port and shipbuilding town that turned out large lake carriers. Many mansions and the Victorian main street are reminders of those days. And just east of Blue Mountain sweep 14km (9 miles) of golden sands at **Wasaga Beach.**

North beyond Collingwood stretches the **Bruce Peninsula National Park,** known for its limestone cliffs, wetlands, and forest. From Tobermory, you can visit an underwater national park.

## ESSENTIALS

**GETTING THERE** If you head west from Barrie, northwest from Toronto, you'll go along the west Georgian Bay coast from Collingwood up to the Bruce Peninsula. Driving from Toronto, take Highway 400 to Highway 26 west.

**VISITOR INFORMATION** For information, contact the **Georgian Triangle Tourist Association** (✆ **705/445-7722;** www.georgiantriangle.org).

## BLUE MOUNTAIN SKI TRAILS, SLIDES, RIDES & MORE

In winter, skiers flock to **Blue Mountain Resort,** at RR #3, Collingwood (✆ **705/445-0231;** www.bluemountain.ca). Ontario's largest resort has 16 lifts, 98% snowmaking coverage on 35 trails, and three base lodges. In addition, there are three repair, rental, and ski shops, a ski school, and day care. Lift rates are C$45 (US$28) daily.

In summer, you can take advantage of the "Green Season" attractions, as they're known. These include tennis, golfing, and mountain biking; there's also a private beach on the shores of Georgian Bay that's a 10-minute ride by shuttle from the resort. Blue Mountain offers many programs for kids, ranging from tennis camp to weekend scavenger hunts on the beach.

The area is also famous for its dark-hued **Blue Mountain pottery,** and you can take a free factory tour and perhaps buy a few pieces. A pottery outlet is at 2 Old Mountain Rd., on Highway 26 in Collingwood (✆ **705/445-3000**). On Highway 26, 5km (3 miles) east of Collingwood, at Nottawa Sideroad, kids can enjoy testing their mettle and skills at **Blue Mountain Go-Kart Rides** (✆ **705/445-2419**).

My own favorite spot in Collingwood is the **Scenic Caves Nature Preserve,** P.O. Box 215, Collingwood, ON L9Y 3Z5 (✆ **705/446-0256;** www.scenic caves.com). The area was carved out by glaciers during the Ice Age and today is one of Canada's UNESCO biosphere reserves. The caves are set into limestone cliffs, and offer unique sights—including the "chilling" Ice Cave, a natural refrigerator that boasts icicles even on the hottest days of summer. The lush Fern Cavern is another don't-miss spot. The caves were once home to the Huron village of Ekarenniondi, and you can still see the famous worshiping rock that souls were said to pass on their way to the afterlife.

## BRUCE PENINSULA NATIONAL PARK

**Bruce Peninsula National Park,** Box 189, Tobermory, ON, N0H 2R0 (✆ **519/596-2233** or 519-596-2263; www.parcscanada.gc.ca), features limestone cliffs, abundant wetlands, quiet beaches, and forest sheltering more than 40 species of orchids, 20 species of ferns, and several insectivorous plants. About 100 species of bird also inhabit the park. Three campgrounds (one trailer, two tent) offer 242 campsites (no electricity).

The **Bruce Trail** winds along the Georgian Bay Coastline, while Route 6 cuts across the peninsula; both end in Tobermory. It's one of Ontario's best-known trails, stretching 700km (434 miles) from Queenston in Niagara Falls to Tobermory. The most rugged part of the trail passes through the park along the Georgian Bay shoreline. **Cypress Lake Trails,** from the north end of the Cyprus Lake campground, provide access to the Bruce Trail and lead to cliffs overlooking the bay. You can use canoes and manpowered craft on Cyprus Lake. The best swimming is at **Singing Sands Beach** and **Dorcas Bay,** both on Lake Huron on the west side of the peninsula. Winter activities include cross-country skiing, snowshoeing, and snowmobiling.

## AN UNDERWATER NATIONAL PARK

From Tobermory you can visit an underwater national park, the **Fathom Five National Marine Park,** P.O. Box 189, Tobermory, ON, N0H 2R0 (✆ **519/596-2233;** www.parcscanada.gc.ca), where at least 21 known shipwrecks lie waiting for diving exploration around the 19 or so islands in the park. The most accessible is **Flowerpot Island,** which you can visit by tour boat to view its weird and wonderful rock pillar formations. Go for a few hours to hike and picnic. Six campsites are available on the island on a first-come, first-served basis. Boats leave from Tobermory harbor.

## WHERE TO STAY

**Beaconglow Motel** The Beaconglow has nicely furnished efficiency units ranging from a compact one-bedroom with a kitchenette to a two-bedroom/two-bathroom suite with a fully equipped kitchen (including coffeemaker, microwave, and dishwasher), a living room with a wood-burning fireplace and VCR, and a bath with a Jacuzzi. For fun, there's a game room with a pool table and a library of 375 movies. Reserve at least 3 months ahead for weekend or holiday stays.

RR #3, Collingwood, ON, L9Y 3Z2. ✆ **800/461-2673** or 705/445-1674. Fax 705/445-7176. 33 units. Motel and efficiency units from C$59 (US$37) double; C$109 (US$69) standard suite weekends; C$119 (US$74) luxury 2-bedroom suite. Midweek and other packages available. Special weekly rates available. AE, MC, V. **Amenities:** Indoor pool; sauna; whirlpool. *In room:* A/C, TV/VCR.

**Beild House** ★ Bill Barclay and his wife, Stephanie, are the enthusiastic owners of this handsome 1909 Edwardian house. Bill prepares the breakfasts and gourmet dinners, while Stephanie is responsible for the inviting decor. The downstairs public areas are personalized by their collections of folk art, quill boxes from Manitoulin, and sculptures by Stephanie's mother. Two fireplaces make the place cozy in winter. Guest rooms are individually furnished with elegant pieces. Room 4 contains a bed once owned by the duke and duchess of Windsor, royal portraits, and a souvenir program of Prince Edward's 1860 trip to Canada. The five third-floor rooms have canopied beds and fireplaces. The hotel offers a sumptuous breakfast and a five-course dinner that's even more so, with such dishes as Georgian Bay trout on spinach with herbed buerre blanc, and pork tenderloin with rhubarb sauce and apple-prune stuffing. Beild (the Scottish word for "shelter") House has been selected as one of the best country inns by *Canadian Country Inns* magazine.

64 Third St., Collingwood, ON, L9Y 1K5. ✆ **888/322-3453** or 705/444-1522. Fax 705/444-2394. www.beildhouse.com. 12 units. C$400–C$500 (US$248–US$310) for 2 on weekends, meals included; C$200–C$239 (US$124–US$148) midweek for same 2-night package for 2; extra nights starts at C$95 (US$59). Rates include breakfast. AE, MC, V. **Amenities:** Restaurant; spa. *In room:* A/C.

**Blue Mountain Resort** ★ *Kids* Stay here right at the mountain base and you can beat the winter lift lines. In summer, the resort boasts access to a private beach, which is 10 minutes away by shuttle. The real reason to stay at Blue Mountain is its unbeatable selection of activities—it's impossible to be bored here. Guest rooms are on the smallish side and are simply furnished in a country style. You can also rent one- to three-bedroom condos, either slope-side or overlooking the fairway. This is an excellent choice for families—Blue Mountain has a great deal to offer kids.

RR #3, Collingwood, ON, L9Y 3Z2. ✆ **705/445-0231.** www.bluemountain.ca. 98 units. Ski season from C$109 (US$68) per person midweek, C$139 (US$86) per person weekends; off-season from C$99 (US$61). Condos from C$179 (US$111). Special packages available. AE, MC, V. **Amenities:** Dining room, 3 lounges; outdoor and indoor pools; 18-hole golf course; 12 tennis courts; squash courts; fitness center; spa; mountain-bike and kayak rental; children's programs. *In room:* A/C, TV.

## WHERE TO DINE

**Alphorn Restaurant** SWISS Bratwurst, Wiener schnitzel, chicken Ticino, and cheese fondue are just some of the favorites served at this chalet-style restaurant, which is loaded with Swiss atmosphere. It's a very popular place; crowded winter and summer. Save room for the Swiss crepes with chocolate and almonds.

Hwy. 26 W., Collingwood. ✆ **705/445-8882.** Reservations not accepted. Main courses C$14–C$20 (US$9–US$12). AE, MC, V. Mon–Fri 4–10pm, Sat–Sun 3–11pm; summer only, daily 11:30–3pm.

**Chez Michel** ★ FRENCH Small and charming, Chez Michel possesses a very French air created by chef/proprietor Michel Masselin, who hails from Normandy. The food is excellent and carefully prepared. Among the specials you may find venison tenderloin with a red wine game sauce, along with more traditional favorites like coquilles St-Jacques. From 5 to 6:30pm, there's a special three-course menu for C$20 (US$12). There's a good wine list too, and the desserts are worth waiting for, like the strawberries romanoff.

Hwy. 26 W., Craigleith. ✆ **705/445-9441.** Reservations recommended. Main courses C$17–C$21 (US$11–US$13). AE, MC, V. Tues-Sat 11:30am–2pm and 5–9pm.

**Christopher's** ★ INTERNATIONAL Dinner in this handsome Edwardian mansion—probably the grandest in Collingwood when it was built in 1902—might find you sampling such dishes as New York steak with sun-dried tomatoes and Dijon cream, or a classic paella with shrimp and mussels. This is also the place to stop for High Tea in the late afternoon, with a classic platter including scones, cucumber sandwiches, quiche, cake, shortbread and fruit for C$8.95 (US$6) per person. In summer, you can dine al fresco on the mansion's wraparound veranda.

167 Pine St. ✆ **705/445-7117.** Reservations recommended. Main courses C$15–C$20 (US$9–US$12). AE, MC, V. Daily 11:30am–10pm.

**Spike & Spoon** CONTINENTAL In an elegant mid-19th-century redbrick house that once belonged to a Chicago millionaire, this restaurant offers food prepared with fresh ingredients and herbs grown out back. There are three dining rooms, each with a different atmosphere, plus a closed-in porch for pleasant summer dining. The bread and the desserts are all freshly made on the premises. The menu changes with the seasons, and mains may include charbroiled beef tenderloin medallions with a cognac-mushroom sauce; there's always at least one vegetarian dish.

637 Hurontario St. ✆ **705/446-1629.** Reservations recommended. Main courses C$13–C$23 (US$8–US$14). MC, V. Tues–Sat noon–2:30pm; Tues–Sun 6–9:30pm.

# 3 Manitoulin Island: A Spiritual Escape

**Manitoulin Island,** named after the Great Indian Spirit Gitchi Manitou, is for those who seek a quiet, remote, and spiritual place, where life is slow.

## ESSENTIALS

**VISITOR INFORMATION** Contact the **Manitoulin Tourism Association,** P.O. Box 119, Little Current, ON, P0P 1K0 (✆ **705/368-3021;** www.manitoulin-tourist.com), open daily late April to late October 10am to 4pm, or stop by the **information center** just past the swing bridge in Little Current open daily from May through September 10am to 4pm.

**GETTING THERE** By road, you can cross over the swing bridge connecting Little Current to Great Cloche Island and via Highway 6 to Espanola. You can also reach the island via the **Chi-Cheemaun ferry,** which transports people and cars from Tobermory to South Baymouth on a 1¾- to 2-hour trip. Ferries operate early May to mid-October, with four departures a day in summer. Reservations are strongly recommended (though in summer you cannot make reservations on two of the four daily departures). One-way fare is C$11.50 (US$7) for adults and C$5.75 (US$3.55) for children ages 5 to 11; an average-size car costs C$25 (US$16) one-way, and bicycles cost C$5 (US$3.10). For information, call **Ontario Northland Transportation** (✆ **800/265-3163** or 519/376-6601) or the **Tobermory terminal** (✆ **519/596-2510**).

## EXPLORING THE ISLAND

Native peoples have lived on this land for centuries, and you can visit the **Ojibwa Indian Reserve,** occupying the large peninsula on the island's eastern end. It's home to about 2,500 people of Odawa, Ojibwa, and Potawotami descent; the area was never ceded to the government. The reserve isn't a tourist attraction but might appeal to anyone genuinely interested in modern life on a reservation. Summer weekends are filled with powwows, with the **Wikwemikong Annual Competition Powwow** in early August being one of the biggest draws. It's worth seeking out the few native art galleries, like the **Kasheese Studios,** outside West Bay at highways 540 and 551 (✆ **705/377-4141**), operated by artists in residence Blake Debassige and Shirley Cheechoo, and the **Ojibwa Cultural Foundation,** also outside West Bay (✆ **705/377-4902**), open erratically and then only to 4pm. You can also visit individual artists' studios.

Although there are several communities on the island, the highlights are scenic and mostly outside their perimeters, like the **Mississagi Lighthouse,** at the western end outside Meldrun Bay. Follow the signs that'll take you about 6km (4 miles) down a dirt road past the limestone/dolomite quarry entrance (from which materials are still shipped across the Great Lakes) to the lighthouse. There you can see how the light keeper lived in this isolated area before the advent of electricity. The dining room is open in summer. From the lighthouse, several short trails lead along the shoreline.

One gallery worth a visit is the **Perivale Gallery,** RR #2, Spring Bay (✆ **705/377-4847**), open the May holiday to mid-September, daily 10am to 6pm. Owners Sheila and Bob McMullan scour the country searching for the remarkable artists and craftspeople whose work they display in their log-cabin gallery overlooking Lake Kagawong. Glass, sculpture, paintings, engravings, fabrics, and ceramics fill the space. From Spring Bay, follow Perivale Road east for about 3km (2 miles); turn right at the lake and keep following the road until you see the gallery on the right.

The island is great for hiking, biking, bird-watching, boating, cross-country skiing, and just plain relaxing. Charters also operate from Meldrun Bay. You'll find golf courses in Mindemoya and Gore Bay. Fishing is excellent either in

Georgian Bay or in the island's lakes and streams. You can arrange trips through **Timberlane Lodge** (© **800/890-4177** or 705/377-4078; www.timberlane.ca). May to October, **Honora Bay Riding Stables,** RR #1, Little Current, ON, P0P 1K0 (© **705/368-2669**), 27km (17 miles) west of Little Current on Highway 540, offers trail rides, including an overnight program. A 3-hour ride is about C$35 (US$22).

There are several nature trails on the island. Among the more spectacular is the **Cup and Saucer Trail,** starting 18km (11 miles) west of Little Current at the junction of Highway 540 and Bidwell Road. Also off Highway 540 lies the trail to **Bridal Veil Falls** as you enter the village of Kagawong. Halfway between Little Current and Manitowaning, stop at **Ten Mile Point** for the view over the North Channel, dotted with 20,000 islands. The best beach with facilities is at **Providence Bay** on the island's south side.

## WHERE TO STAY

Your best bet is to seek out one of several B&Bs, which will most likely be plain and simple but clean. Contact **Manitowaning Tourism Association,** Box 119 Little Current, ON, P0P 1K0 (© **705/368-3021**).

**Manitowaning Lodge & Tennis Resort** ★ This idyllic place, a lodge and cottages on 4.5ha (11 acres) of spectacularly landscaped gardens, lacks the pretension of so many resorts. Artists were employed to create a whimsical decor with trompe-l'oeil painting and furniture sporting hand-painted scenes and designs. The buildings themselves have a delightful rustic air created by their beamed ceilings; in the lodge is a large fieldstone fireplace with a carved mask of the Indian Spirit of Manitowaning looming above. The cottages are comfortably furnished with wicker or painted log furniture, beds with duvets and pillows, dhurries, log tables, and hand-painted furnishings; all have fireplaces. None has a TV or phone—it's a real retreat. The dining room is airy, serving food that features fine local meats like lamb and fish. You might find Manitowaning poached trout, smoked pork loin with plum sauce, or tiger shrimp with coconut couscous. Lunch is served on the terrace overlooking the water.

Box 160, Manitowaning, ON, P0P 1N0. © **866/644-4403** or 705/859-3136. Fax 705/859-3270. 9 units, 13 cottages. C$125 (US$78) per person in standard room; C$165 (US$102) per person in 1-bedroom cabin with fireplace. Rates include breakfast and dinner. Special tennis packages available. AE, MC, V. Closed Canadian Thanksgiving (U.S. Columbus Day) to 2nd Fri in May. **Amenities:** Restaurant, bar; outdoor pool; nearby golf course; 4 tennis courts; exercise room; Jacuzzi; canoes, kayaks, and bikes (all free of charge); concierge; activities desk; business center. *In room:* No phone.

**Rock Garden Terrace Resort** This family resort, on the rocks above Lake Mindemoya, has a Bavarian flair. Most accommodations are in motel-style units furnished in contemporary style, but there are also four log-cabin-style suites. The dining room seems like an Austrian hunting lodge, with trophies displayed on the oak-paneled walls and a cuisine featuring German-Austrian specialties like Wiener schnitzel, sauerbraten, goulash, and beef rolladen.

RR #1, Spring Bay, ON, P0P 2B0. © **705/377-4652.** www.rockgardenresort.on.ca. 18 motel units, 4 chalet suites. Summer and winter C$86–C$105 (US$53–US$65) per person, including breakfast and dinner. Spring and fall rates slightly lower. Weekend and weekly packages available. MC, V. **Amenities:** Restaurant, lounge; outdoor pool; nearby golf course; Jacuzzi; sauna; bike rental; fishing pier. *In room:* TV.

## WHERE TO DINE

The food on the island is simple and homey. For more sophisticated palate-pleasers, go to the **Manitowaning Lodge Golf & Tennis Resort** (© **705/859-3136**) or the **Rock Garden Terrace Resort** (© **705/377-4642**), both near

Spring Bay. In Little Current, one of the nicest casual spots on the island for breakfast, lunch, or dinner is **The Old English Pantry,** 13 Water St. (© **705/368-3341**). At dinner you'll find a pasta and fish dish of the day as well as English specialties like roast beef and Yorkshire pudding and baked pot pies, at C$10 to C$18 (US$6–US$11)). Afternoon cream teas and takeout are also available. Only a smaller selection of dishes like quiche, stuffed baked potato, and steak pie is offered after Labour Day. In summer, it's open Sunday to Thursday 9am to 9pm and Friday and Saturday to 11pm; winter hours are Monday to Wednesday 9am to 5pm and Thursday to Saturday 9am to 8pm.

## 4 Along Georgian Bay: Midland & Parry Sound

### MIDLAND

Midland is the center for cruising through the thousands of beautifully scenic Georgian Islands, and **30,000 Island Cruises** (© **705/549-3388;** www.georgianbaycruises.com) offers 3-hour cruises following the route of Brele, Champlain, and La Salle up through the inside passage to Georgian Bay. May to Canadian Thanksgiving (U.S. Columbus Day), boats usually leave the town dock twice a day. Fares are C$16 (US$10) for adults, C$14 (US$9) for seniors, and C$7 (US$4.35) for children ages 2 to 12.

Midland lies 53km (33 miles) east of Barrie and 145km (90 miles) north of Toronto. If you're driving from Barrie, take Highway 400 to Highway 12W to Midland.

#### EXPLORING THE AREA

See the box below for details on **Sainte Marie Among the Hurons.** Across from the Martyrs' Shrine, the **Wye Marsh Wildlife Centre** (© **705/526-7809;** www.wyemarsh.com) is a 60ha (150-acre) wetland/woodland site offering wildlife viewing, guided and self-guided walks, and canoe excursions in the marsh. A floating boardwalk cuts through the marsh, fields, and woods, where trumpeter swans have been reintroduced into the environment and now number 40 strong. Reservations are needed for the canoe trips (call the number above) offered in July and August and occasionally September. In winter, cross-country skiing and snowshoeing are available. For information, write Highway 12 (P.O. Box 100), Midland, ON, L4R 4K6. Admission is C$6.50 (US$4) for adults, C$5.50 (US$3.40) for students and seniors, and free to children 3 and under. Victoria Day (late May) to Labour Day (first Monday in September), the center is open daily 10am to 6pm; other months, hours are daily 10am to 4pm.

In town, **Freda's,** in an elegant home at 342 King St. (© **705/526-4851**), serves traditional continental cuisine, with main courses at C$12 to C$28

*Fun Fact* **Bright Lights in the Wilderness**

While most visitors to northern Ontario are drawn by the peaceful expanses of wilderness, increasing numbers are gravitating to the **Casino Rama,** RR #6, Rama, L0K 1T0 (© **888/817-7262** or 705/329-3325), the 18,000m² (195,000-sq. ft.) state-of-the-art casino just east of Orillia. Open 24 hours, the casino boasts more than 2,100 slot machines and 109 gaming tables. There are also three full-service restaurants, a food arcade, and a smoky lounge with live entertainment. So when all that peace and quiet starts getting to you, you know where to turn.

## The Tragic Tale of Sainte Marie Among the Hurons

Midland's history dates from 1639, when Jesuits established here a fortified mission, **Sainte Marie Among the Hurons,** to bring Christianity to the Huron tribe. However, the mission retreat lasted only a decade, for the Iroquois, jealous of the Huron-French trading relationship, stepped up their attacks in the area. By the late 1640s, the Iroquois had killed thousands of Hurons and several priests and had destroyed two villages within 10km (6 miles) of Sainte Marie. Ultimately the Jesuits burned down their own mission and fled with the Hurons to Christian Island, about 32km (20 miles) away. But the winter of 1649 was harsh, and thousands of Hurons died. In the end, only a few Jesuits and 300 Hurons were able to make the journey back to the relative safety of Quebec. The Jesuits' mission had ended in martyrdom. It was 100 years before the native Canadians in the region saw Europeans again, and those newcomers spoke a different language.

Today local history is recaptured at the **mission** (**© 705/526-7838**), 8km (5 miles) east of Midland on Highway 12 (follow the HURONIA HERITAGE signs). The blacksmith stokes his forge, the carpenter squares a beam with a broadaxe, and the ringing church bell calls the missionaries to prayer, while a canoe enters the fortified water gate. A film depicts the life of the missionaries. Special programs given in July and August include candlelight tours and a 1½-hour canoeing trip (at extra cost). Admission is C$7.25 (US$4.50) for adults, C$4.50 (US$2.80) for students, and free to children under 6. Mid-May to mid-October, it's open daily 10am to 5pm.

Just east of Midland on Highway 12 rise the twin spires of the **Martyrs' Shrine** (**© 705/526-3788**), a memorial to the eight North American martyr saints. As six were missionaries at Sainte Marie, this imposing church was built on the hill overlooking the mission, and thousands make pilgrimages here each year. The bronzed outdoor stations of the cross were imported from France. Admission is C$2 (US$1.20) for adults and free to children under 16. Mid-May to mid-October, it's open daily 8:30am to 9pm.

(US$7–US$17). You can choose from a variety of meat and seafood dishes—steaks, beef Stroganoff, chicken Kiev, coquilles St-Jacques, and more.

### EN ROUTE TO THE MUSKOKA LAKES: ORILLIA

Traveling to the Muskoka Lakeland region, you'll probably pass through **Orillia** (from Barrie, take Highway 11). Here you can visit Canadian author/humorist **Stephen Leacock**'s summer home (**© 705/329-1908**), a green-and-white mansard-roofed and turreted structure with a central balcony overlooking the beautiful lawns and garden sweeping down to the lake. The interior is filled with heavy Victorian furniture and mementos of this Canadian Mark Twain, author of 35 volumes of humor, including *Sunshine Sketches of a Little Town,* which caricatured many of the residents of Mariposaa barely fictionalized version of Orillia. Admission is C$7 (US$4.35) for adults, C$6.50 (US$4) for seniors, C$2 (US$1.20) for students, and C$1 (US60¢) for children ages 5 to 13. The end of June to Labour Day, it's open daily 10am to 7pm; in other months, you need to make an appointment.

### GEORGIAN BAY ISLANDS NATIONAL PARK

The park consists of 59 islands in Georgian Bay and can be reached via water taxi from Honey Harbour, a town north of Midland right on the shore. (As you're taking Highway 400 north, branch off to the west at Port Severn to reach Honey Harbour.) Hiking, swimming, fishing, and boating are the name of the game in the park. In summer and on weekends and holidays, the boaters really do take over—but it's a quiet retreat weekdays, late August, and off-season. The park's center is on the largest island, **Beausoleil,** with camping and other facilities. For more information, contact the Superintendent, **Georgian Bay Islands National Park,** Box 28, Honey Harbour, ON, P0E 1E0 (© **705/756-241;** www.parcscanada.gc.ca).

## THE PARRY SOUND AREA

Only 225km (140 miles) north of Toronto and 161km (100 miles) south of Sudbury, the Parry Sound area is the place for active vacations. For details, contact the **Parry Sound Area Chamber of Commerce,** 70 Church St. (© **705/746-4213**), which is open Monday to Friday 10am to 4pm, or the **information center,** 1 Church St. (© **705/378-5105**), open daily 10am to 4pm.

There's excellent canoeing and kayaking; if you need an outfitter, contact **White Squall,** RR #1, Nobel, ON, P0G 1G0 (© **705/342-5324;** www.whitesquall.com), which offers both day trips and multi-day excursions. Run by **30,000 Island Cruise Lines,** 9 Bay St., Parry Sound, ON, P2A 1S4 (© **705/549-3388;** www.georgianbaycruises.com), the *Island Queen* cruises through the 30,000 islands for 3 hours. It leaves the town dock once or twice a day and charges C$16 (US$10) for adults, C$14 (US$9) for seniors, and C$7 (US$4.35) for children.

And there are many winter diversions as well—loads of cross-country ski trails and more than 1,000km (650 miles) of well-groomed snowmobiling trails. For details on cross-country skiing, contact the **Georgian Nordic Ski and Canoe Club,** Box 42, Parry Sound, ON, P2A 2X2 (© **705/746-5067;** www.georgiannordic.com), which permits day use of their ski trails.

Nature lovers will head for **Killbear Provincial Park,** P.O. Box 71, Nobel, ON, P0G 1G0 (© **705/342-5492,** or 705/342-5227 for reservations), farther north up Highway 69; it offers 1,600ha (4,000 acres) set in the middle of 30,000 islands. There are plenty of watersports—swimming at a 3km (2-mile) beach on Georgian Bay, snorkeling or diving off Harold Point, and fishing for lake trout, walleye, perch, pike, and bass. The climate is moderated by the bay, which explains why trillium, wild leek, and hepatica bloom. Among the more unusual fauna are the Blandings and Map turtles that inhabit the bogs, swamps, and marshes.

There are three **hiking trails,** including 3.5km (2¼-mile) Lookout Point, leading to a commanding view over Blind Bay to Parry Sound; and the Lighthouse Point Trail, crossing rocks and pebble beaches to the lighthouse at the peninsula's southern tip. There's also **camping** at 883 sites in seven campgrounds.

### WHERE TO STAY

The inn below is exquisite and expensive, but there are other places to stay in the area. Contact the **Parry Sound and District Bed and Breakfast Association,** P.O. Box 71, Parry Sound, ON, P2A 2X2 (© **705/746-5399**), for its listings at

C$50 (US$31) and up for a double. There's also a **Comfort Inn,** 112 Bowes St. (✆ **705/746-6221**); Rates are C$80 to C$100 (US$50–US$62). And at the edge of Otter Lake, the modest, family-oriented **Tapatoo Resort,** Box 384, Parry Sound, ON, P2A 2X5 (✆ **705/378-2208**), rents cottages, rooms, and suites and offers boating, windsurfing, waterskiing, canoeing, fishing, and swimming in an indoor pool. Rates are C$98 to C$150 (US$61–US$93), with C$21.75 (US$13) per person extra for meals.

**Inn at Manitou** ★★ The Inn at Manitou is a stunner. Everything about the foyer glows; the space is opulently furnished in French style with elegant touches of chinoiserie. Beyond the foyer and a sitting area, a veranda stretches around the building's rear, with wicker and bamboo chairs overlooking the tennis courts. To the foyer's left is the very inviting Tea Room with a view of the lake. A steep staircase leads down to the swimming and boating dock. The accommodations are up the hill in several cedar lodges overlooking the lake. The standard rooms are small and simple; the deluxe units contain fireplaces, small sitting areas, and private sundecks, while the luxury rooms feature sizable living rooms with fireplaces, whirlpool baths, saunas, and private decks.

Downstairs in the main building is the Club Lounge nightclub, a billiard room, and an open-to-view wine cellar, filled with fine vintages, where twice-weekly wine tastings are held. The resort's cuisine is renowned and is part of the reason the Relais and Chateaux organization awarded the property the distinguished Gold Shield. At dinner, a casual three-course bistro menu and a more elaborate four-course gourmet menu are offered along with a special spa menu. Afterward, you can retire to the Tea Room for coffee, petit fours, and truffles.

McKellar, ON, P0G 1C0. ✆ **800/571-8818** or 705/389-2171. Fax 705/389-3818. 34 units, one 3-bedroom country house, one 4-bedroom country house. July–Aug C$261–C$418 (US$162–US$259) per person double; May–June and Sept–early Oct C$250–C$352 (US$155–US$218) per person double. Rates for country houses start at C$1,200 (US$744). Rates include breakfast, lunch, afternoon tea, and dinner. Special packages available; special musical, cooking, and other events scheduled. AE, MC, V. Closed late Oct–early May. **Amenities:** Restaurant, bar; outdoor heated pool; nearby golf course; instructional golfing range; 20 tennis courts; spa; bikes, sailboats, canoes; concierge; room service (7am–11pm); babysitting; dry cleaning. *In room:* A/C, TV, minibar, hair dryer, iron, safe.

## 5 The Muskoka Lakes: A Land of Resorts ★

To settlers coming north in the 1850s, this region, with its 1,600-plus lakes north of the Severn River, was impossible to farm and difficult to traverse. But even then the wilderness attracted sports people and adventurers like John Campbell and James Bain, who explored the three major lakes—Rosseau, Joseph, and Muskoka. They later started the Muskoka Club, purchased an island in Lake Joseph, and began annual excursions here. Roads were difficult to cut, and waterways became the main transportation routes. It wasn't until the late 1800s that a fleet of steamers was running on the lakes and the railway arrived. Muskoka was then finally effectively linked by water and rail to the urban centers in the south.

The Muskoka Lakes area was wired for tourism. Some folks gambled that people would pay to travel to the wilderness if they were wined and dined once they got there. The idea caught on, and grand hotels like Clevelands House, Windermere House, and Deerhurst opened. The lakes became the enclave of the well-to-do from Ontario and the United States. By 1903, there were eight big lake steamers, countless steam launches, and supply boats (floating grocery stores) serving a flourishing resort area.

*Tips* **Finding a B&B**

If you don't want to pay resort rates or restrict yourself to staying at an American Plan resort, contact the **Muskoka Bed and Breakfast Association,** 175 Clairmont Rd., Gravenhurst, ON, P1P 1H9 (✆ **705/687-4511;** www.bbmuskoka.com), which represents 28 or so B&Bs throughout the area. Prices range from C$45 to C$100 (US$28–US$62) for a double.

And though the advent of the car ended the era of the steamboats and grand hotels, the area still flourishes. The rich have been joined by families in their summer cottages and sophisticated young professionals from Toronto. You'll note that many resorts don't look impressive from the road—but just take a look at the other side and remember they were built to be approached by steamship.

## ESSENTIALS

**VISITOR INFORMATION** For information on the region, contact **Muskoka Tourism,** on Highway 11 at Severn Bridge, RR #2, Kilworthy, ON, P0E 1G0 (✆ **800-267-9700** or 705/689-0660; www.muskoka-tourism.on.ca).

**GETTING THERE** You can drive from the south via Highway 400 to Highway 11, from the east via highways 12 and 169 to Highway 11, and from the north via Highway 11. It's about 160km (100 miles) from Toronto to Gravenhurst, 15km (9 miles) from Gravenhurst to Bracebridge, 25km (16 miles) from Bracebridge to Port Carling, and 34km (21 miles) from Bracebridge to Huntsville. **VIA Rail** (✆ **416/366-8411;** www.viarail.ca) services Gravenhurst, Bracebridge, and Huntsville from Toronto's Union Station.

## GRAVENHURST

Gravenhurst is Muskoka's first town—the first you reach if you're driving from Toronto and the first to achieve town status (in 1887 at the height of the logging boom).

The **Norman Bethune Memorial House** is the restored 1890 birthplace of Dr. Norman Bethune, 235 John St. N. (✆ **705/687-4261**). In 1939, this surgeon, inventor, and humanitarian died tending the sick in China during the Chinese Revolution. Tours of the historic house include a modern exhibit on Bethune's life. A visitor center displays gifts from Chinese visitors and an orientation video is shown. In summer, the house is open daily 10am to noon and 1 to 5pm (weekdays only in winter). Admission is C$2.25 (US$1.40) for adults, C$1.75 (US$1.10) for seniors, and C$1.25 (US80¢) for children ages 6 to 16.

Mid-June to mid-October, you can also cruise aboard the old steamship **RMS *Segwun*** (1887), leaving from Gravenhurst and Port Carling. Aboard you'll find two lounges and a dining salon. The cruises on the lake vary from 1 hour at a cost of C$9.75 (US$6) to a full day's outing for C$50 (US$31). For details, call ✆ **705/687-6667.**

Year-round theater performances are given in the **Gravenhurst Opera House** (✆ **705/687-5550**), which celebrated its 100th anniversary in 2001; in summer only, there are shows at the **Port Carling Community Hall** (✆ **705/765-5221**). Tickets are C$20 to C$30 (US$12–US$19) for adults.

### WHERE TO STAY

**Severn River Inn** The Severn River Inn, 19km (12 miles) north of Orillia and 14km (9 miles) south of Gravenhurst, occupies a 1906 building that has

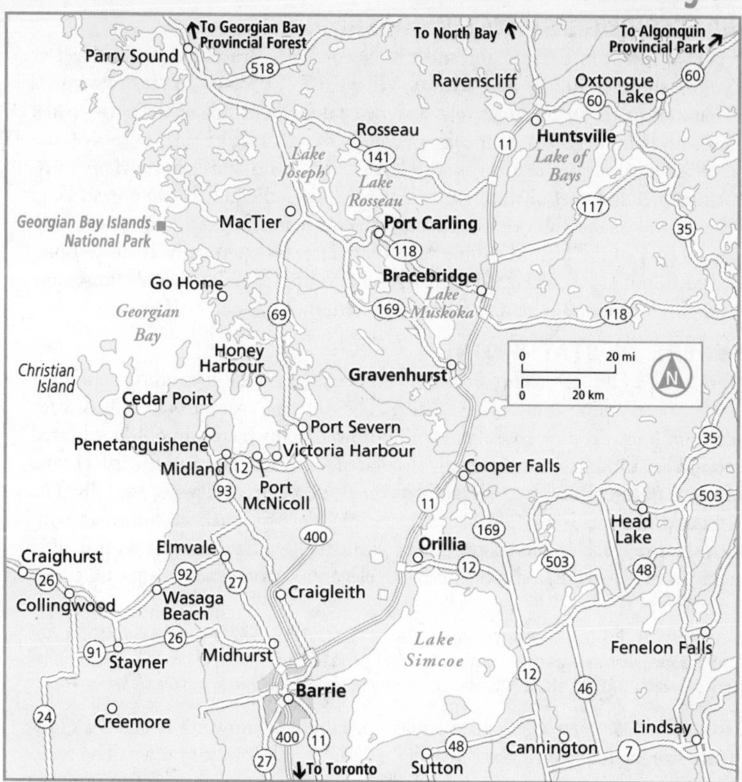


served as a general store, post office, telephone exchange, and boardinghouse. Guest rooms, which were refurbished in 2001, are individually furnished with pine and oak pieces, brass beds, flounce pillows, lace curtains, and quilts; the suite contains a sitting room and the original old bathtub and pedestal sink (this is the only room with a bathtub—the others all have showers only). The intimate restaurant, with a Victorian ambiance, is candlelit at night. In summer, the screened-in porch and outdoor patio overlooking the river are favored dining spots. The menu features contemporary continental cuisine, with dishes at C$14 to C$19 (US$9–US$12).

Cowbell Lane off Hwy. 11 (P.O. Box 100), Severn Bridge, ON, P0E 1N0. ✆ **705/689-6333.** Fax 705/689-2691. www.severnriverinn.com. 10 units. A/C. C$70–C$90 (US$43–US$56) double; C$120–C$200 (US$74–US$124) suite. Rates include breakfast. V. **Amenities:** Dining room, lounge; nearby golf course. *In room:* A/C.

## WHERE TO DINE

**Three Guys and a Stove** ★ *Kids* INTERNATIONAL The name might sound casual—and the atmosphere is indeed unpretentious—but the cooking is very fine. This is a family restaurant (with a special menu for kids), but the gourmet quotient is high. The curried pumpkin and sweet potato soup is an absolute must-have when it's on the menu; the spicy chicken stew is another surefire winner.

Hwy 60, Huntsville. ✆ **705/789-1815.** Main courses C$15–C$25 (US$9–US$16). AE, MC, V. Daily 11am–9:30pm.

## BRACEBRIDGE: SANTA'S WORKSHOP

Halfway between the equator and the North Pole, **Bracebridge** bills itself as Santa's summer home, and **Santa's Village** (✆ **705/645-2512;** www.santasvillage.on.ca) is an imaginatively designed fantasyland full of delights—pedal boats and bumper boats on the lagoon, a roller-coaster sleigh ride, a Candy Cane Express, a carousel, and a Ferris wheel. At Elves' Island, kids can crawl on a suspended net and over or through various modules—the Lunch Bag Forest, Cave Crawl, and Snake Tube Crawl. Rides, water attractions, and roving entertainers are all part of the fun. Mid-June to Labour Day, it's open daily 10am to 6pm. Admission is C$16.95 (US$11) for ages 5 and up, C$11.95 (US$7) for seniors and children ages 2 to 4, and free to children under 2.

### WHERE TO STAY & DINE

**Inn at the Falls** ★ This attractive inn occupies a Victorian house on a quiet street overlooking Bracebridge Falls. The inviting gardens are filled with delphiniums, peonies, roses, and spring flowers, plus there's an outdoor heated pool. Guest rooms are individually decorated, with antiques and English chintz. Some have fireplaces, Jacuzzis, and balconies; others have views of the falls. The Fox and Hounds is a popular local gathering place at lunch or dinner. In winter, the fire crackles and snaps, but in summer the terrace is filled with flowers and umbrella-shaded tables. The more elegant Victoria's serves upscale continental fare.

1 Dominion St., P.O. Box 1139, Bracebridge, ON, P1L 1V3. ✆ **877-645-9212** or 705/645-2245. Fax 705/645-5093. www.innatthefalls.net. 42 units. C$82–C$150 (US$51–US$93) double; C$195 (US$121) suite. Rates include breakfast. AE, DC, MC, V. **Amenities:** 2 restaurants; outdoor pool; nearby golf course. *In room:* TV.

**Tamwood Resort** ★ A great choice for families, Tamwood Lodge is a moderate-size log lodge on Lake Muskoka, 10km (6 miles) west of town. The main lodge has 35 units, all simply but nicely decorated, and there are a few cottages. The four deluxe loft accommodations are stunningly appointed in pine, and each features two bedrooms with skylights, plus a loft area, two baths, an efficiency kitchen, and a living room with a Franklin stove and a balcony from which you can dive into Lake Muskoka. Three new waterfront units come with fireplaces. Knotty-pine furnishings and large granite fireplaces imbue the lounge and main dining room with character. The resort offers a wealth of activities, including fishing, tennis, volleyball, badminton, and shuffleboard, plus free waterskiing and boating, and all the winter sports imaginable. There's also lots of organized family fun—such as baseball games, marshmallow roasts, and bingo.

Hwy 118, RR #1, Bracebridge, ON, P1L 1W8. ✆ **800/465-9166** or 705/645-5172. www.tamwoodresort.com. 35 units. C$80–C$130 (US$50–US$81) per person double. Special discount weekly rates available. MC, V. **Amenities:** Indoor pool; nearby golf course; 3 tennis courts; spa; watersports equipment rentals; children's programs; game room. *In room:* A/C, TV, fridge.

### A NEARBY PLACE TO STAY

**Sir Sam's Inn** ★ Sir Sam's takes some finding, but that's the way politician/militarist Sir Sam Hughes probably wanted it when he built his stone-and-timber mansion in 1917 in the woods above Eagle Lake. The atmosphere is friendly yet sophisticated. A comfy sitting room with a large stone fireplace serves as its focal point. Accommodations are in the inn or in a series of new chalets or in two lakefront suites. The chalets have fetching bed-sitting rooms with light-pine furnishings, and wood-burning fireplaces; some have whirlpool baths. Inn rooms are a little more old-fashioned, except in the Hughes Wing, where they're similar to the chalets with whirlpool baths and fireplaces. The suites come with full kitchens and whirlpools.

Eagle Lake P.O., ON, K0M 1M0. ✆ **705/754-2188.** Fax 705/754-4262. www.sirsamsinn.com. 25 units. Summer C$165–C$185 (US$102–US$115) per person. Rates include breakfast and dinner. Weekly rates and room-only rates available. Off-season rates drop about 10%. AE, MC, V. Follow the signs to Sir Sam's ski area. From Hwy. 118, take Rte. 6 to Sir Sam's Rd. **Amenities:** Restaurant, bar; exercise room with rowing machine and stationary bicycle; 2 tennis courts; spa; outdoor pool; beach; sailing; windsurfing; waterskiing; canoeing; paddleboats; mountain bikes; massage; Sir Sam's ski area and cross-country skiing close by. *In room:* TV, fridge, coffeemaker, hair dryer.

## PORT CARLING

As waterways became the main means of transportation in the region, **Port Carling** grew into the hub of the lakes. It became a boatbuilding center when a lock was installed connecting Lakes Muskoka and Rosseau, and a canal between Lakes Rosseau and Joseph opened all three to navigation. The **Muskoka Lakes Museum** on Joseph Street (✆ **705/765-5367**) captures the flavor of this era. July and August, it's open Monday to Saturday 10am to 5pm and Sunday noon to 4pm; June, September, and October, hours are Tuesday to Saturday 10am to 4pm and Sunday noon to 4pm. Admission is C$2.25 (US$1.40) for adults and C$1.25 (US80¢) for seniors and students.

### WHERE TO STAY

**Sherwood Inn** Accommodations here are either in the lodge or in beachside cottages. The latter are very appealing, with fieldstone fireplaces, comfortable armchairs, TVs, phones, and screened porches overlooking the lake. Some are more luxurious than others and have additional features like VCRs or private docks. The older rooms in the lodge feature painted wood paneling, while the newer wing has air-conditioning and wicker furnishings.

P.O. Box 400, Lake Joseph, Port Carling, ON, P0B 1J0. ✆ **705/765-3131.** Fax 705/765-6668. 40 units. C$75–C$180 (US$47–US$112) per person in inn; C$159–C$242 (US$99–US$150) per person in cottages. Rates include breakfast and dinner. B&B rates and special packages available. AE, MC, V. From Hwy. 400, take Hwy. 69 north to Foot's Bay. Turn right and take 169 south to Sherwood Rd. Turn left just before the junction of Hwy. 118. Or you can arrive via Gravenhurst and Bala or Bracebridge and Port Carling.

**Windermere House** ★ The appearance is a little bit deceiving: the Windermere looks like a striking 1870s stone-and-clapboard turreted mansion. In fact, the building was destroyed by fire in 1996 and rebuilt, according to its original design, in 1997. It overlooks well-manicured lawns that sweep down to Lake Rosseau. Out front stretches a broad veranda furnished with Adirondack chairs and geranium-filled window boxes. Rebuilding allowed the guest rooms to enjoy modern conveniences (including air-conditioning), while retaining a traditional, homey look. Most of the rooms have gorgeous views (the best look over the lake), and a few have balconies or walk-out decks.

Off Muskoka Rte. 4 (P.O. Box 68), Windermere, ON, P0B 1P0. ✆ **800/461-4283** or 705/769-3611. Fax 705/769-2168. www.windermerehouse.com. 78 units. C$130–C$185 (US$81–US$115) per person. Rates include breakfast and dinner. Weekly rates and European Plan (no meals) also available. AE, MC, V. **Amenities:** Restaurant, lounge; outdoor pool; tennis courts; golf; watersports (fishing; windsurfing; sailing); children's program; room service (7am–10pm); laundry/dry cleaning. *In room:* A/C, TV, minibar.

## HUNTSVILLE

Since the late 1800s, lumber has been the name of the game in Huntsville, and today it's Muskoka's biggest town, with major manufacturing companies.

You can see some of the region's early history at the **Muskoka Heritage Place,** which includes **Muskoka Pioneer Village,** 88 Brunel Rd., Huntsville (✆ **705/789-7576;** www.muskokaheritage.com). June to Canadian Thanksgiving (U.S. Columbus Day), it's open daily 11am to 4pm; October hours are Saturday and Sunday 11am to 4pm. Admission is C$6 (US$3.70) for adults, C$4 (US$2.50) for children ages 6 to 12, and free to children under 6. You can also visit the **Brunel Locks** in nearby Brunel. The locks consist of a system of gates and sluices that can raise or lower the water level, and they are a key link in the Mary-Fairy-Vernon lake chain.

**Robinson's General Store** on Main Street in Dorset (✆ **705/766-2415**) is so popular it was voted Canada's best country store. Woodstoves, dry goods, hardware, pine goods, and moccasins—you name it, it's here.

## WHERE TO STAY

**Deerhurst Resort** ★ *Kids* The Deerhurst opened in 1896 but has expanded over the last 2 decades, scattering building units all over the property. It's on 365ha (900 acres) of rolling landscape fronting on Peninsula Lake, and it attracts a crowd of urban dwellers—including many young families. The accommodations range from hotel rooms in the Terrace and Bayshore buildings to fully appointed one-, two-, or three-bedroom suites, many with fireplaces and/or whirlpools. The suites come with all the comforts, including stereos, TVs, and VCRs; some have full kitchens with microwaves, dishwashers, and washer/dryers. The most expensive suites are the three-bedroom units on the lake. One major draw is the top-of-the-line spa. It's also popular with conference groups. The dining room offers romantic dining overlooking the lake. Live entertainment includes a musical show in the theater as well as in the lounge.

1235 Deerhurst Dr., Huntsville, ON, P1H 2E8. ✆ **800/461-4393** or 705/789-6411. Fax 705/789-2431. www.deerhurstresort.com. 425 units. C$109–C$279 (US$68–US$173) double; C$209–C$750 (US$130–US$465) suite. AE, DC, DISC, MC, V. Take Canal Rd. off Hwy. 60 to Deerhurst Rd. **Amenities:** 2 restaurants, 3 bars; pool; 2 18-hole golf courses; 8 tennis courts; indoor sports complex with 3 tennis courts, 3 squash courts, racquetball court, indoor pool, whirlpool, sauna, full-service spa; beach; canoes, kayaks, sailboats, paddleboats; waterskiing; windsurfing; horseback riding; full winter program with on-site cross-country skiing, snowmobiling, dog-sledding, downhill skiing at nearby Hidden Valley Highlands; children's activity program summer and weekends year-round. *In room:* A/C, TV, dataport, minibar, hair dryer.

**Grandview Inn & Resort** ★ If the Deerhurst is for the folks on the fast track, the Grandview is for those looking for a more measured pace. This smaller resort retains the natural beauty and contours of the original farmstead even while providing the latest resort facilities. Eighty accommodations are traditional hotel-style rooms, but most units are suites in a series of buildings, some down beside the lake and others up on the hill with a lake view. All are spectacularly furnished. Each executive suite contains a kitchen, a dining area, a living room with a fireplace and access to an outside deck, a large bedroom, and a large bathroom with a whirlpool bath. The main dining room, in the old farmhouse, is decorated in paisleys and English chintz and has an awninged patio overlooking the gardens.

RR #4, Huntsville, ON, P0A 1K0. ✆ **705/789-4417.** Fax 705/789-6882. 200 units. Late July–Aug C$164–C$258 (US$102–US$160) double; C$100 (US$62) and up in low season. Outdoors and other packages, plus meal plans available. Children under 19 stay free in parents' room. AE, MC, V. **Amenities:** 2 restaurants, lounge; outdoor and indoor pools; 9-hole golf course; 2 outdoor and one indoor tennis court; exercise room; waterskiing; windsurfing; sailing; canoeing; cross-country skiing; mountain bikes; boat cruises offered aboard a yacht; nature trails, resident naturalist. *In room:* A/C, TV.

## 6 Algonquin Provincial Park: Canoeing, Fishing & More

Immediately east of Muskoka lie **Algonquin Provincial Park**'s 7,770km$^2$ (3,000 sq. miles) of wilderness—a haven for the naturalist, camper, and fishing and sports enthusiast. It's an especially memorable destination for the canoeist, with more than 1,610km (1,000 miles) of canoe routes for paddling. One of Canada's largest provincial parks, it served as a source of inspiration for the famous Group of Seven artists. Algonquin Park is a sanctuary for moose, beaver, bear, and deer and offers camping, canoeing, backpacking trails, and plenty of fishing for speckled, rainbow, and lake trout and smallmouth black bass (more than 230 lakes have native brook trout and 149 have lake trout).

There are eight **campgrounds** along Highway 60. The most secluded sites are at **Canisbay** (248 sites) and **Pog Lake** (281 sites). **Two Rivers** and **Rock Lake** have the least secluded sites; the rest are average. Four remote wilderness campgrounds are set back in the interior: **Rain Lake** with only 10 sites; **Kiosk** (17 sites) on Lake Kioshkokwi; **Brent** (28 sites) on Cedar Lake, great for pickerel fishing; and **Achray** (39 sites), the most remote site on Grand Lake, where Tom Thomson painted many of his great landscapes (the scene that inspired his Jack Pine is a short walk south of the campground). Call the **Visitor Centre** (**© 705/633-5572**) for details.

Among the **hiking trails** is the 2.4km (1½-mile) self-guided trail to the 100m (325-ft.) deep Barron Canyon on the park's east side. In addition, there are 16 day trails. The shortest is the 1km (½-mile) **Hardwood Lookout Trail,** which goes through the forest to a fine view of Smoke Lake and the surrounding hills. Other short walks are the 1.5km (1 mile) **Spruce Bog Boardwalk** and the **Beaver Pond Trail,** a 2km (1¼-mile) walk with good views of two beaver ponds.

For longer backpacking trips, the **Highland Trail** extends from Pewee Lake to Head, Harness, and Mosquito lakes for a round trip of 35km (22 miles). The **Western Uplands Hiking Trail** combines three loops for a total of 169km (105 miles), beginning at the Oxtongue River Picnic Grounds on Highway 60. The first 32km (20-mile) loop will take 3 days; the second and third loops take longer. There's also a **mountain bike trail.** Call the visitors center below for more details on all trails.

Fall is a great time to visit—the maples usually peak in the last week of September. Winter is wonderful too; you can **cross-country ski** on 80km (50 miles) of trails. Three trails lie along the Highway 60 corridor with loops ranging from 5km (3 miles) to 24km (15 miles). Mew Lake Campground is open in winter, and you can rent skis at the west gate. Spring offers the best **trout fishing** and great **moose-viewing** in May and June. During summer, the park is most crowded, but it's also when park staff lead expeditions to hear the timber wolves howling in response to naturalists' imitations. More than 250 **bird species** have been recorded in the park, including the rare gray jay, spruce grouse, and many varieties of warbler. The most famous bird is the common loon, found nesting on nearly every lake.

For additional **information,** contact the park at P.O. Box 219, Whitney, ON, K0J 2M0 (**© 705/633-5572**).

### WHERE TO STAY

**Arowhon Pines** ★ Located 8km (5 miles) off Highway 60 down a dirt road, Arowhon guarantees you total seclusion and serenity. The cabins are dotted around the pine forests surrounding the lake, and each is furnished uniquely with assorted Canadian pine antiques; they vary in layout but all have bedrooms with private baths and sitting rooms with fireplaces. You can opt for a private cottage or one containing anywhere from 2 to 12 bedrooms and sharing a communal sitting room with a stone fireplace. Sliding doors lead onto a deck. There are no TVs or phones—just the sound of the loons, the gentle lap of the water, the croaking of the frogs, and the sound of oar paddles cutting the smooth surface of the lake. You can swim in the lake or canoe, sail, row, or windsurf. At the heart of the resort is a hexagonal dining room beside the lake with a spacious veranda. A huge fireplace is at the room's center. The food is good, with fresh ingredients, and there's plenty of it. No alcohol is sold in the park, so if you wish to have wine with dinner you'll need to bring your own (the staff will uncork it free of charge).

Algonquin Park, ON, P1H 2G5. © **705/633-5661** in summer or 416/483-4393 in winter. Fax 705/633-5795 in summer or 416/483-4429 in winter. www.arowhonpines.ca. 50 units. From C$149–C$192 (US$92–US$119) per person, double occupancy, in standard accommodations; from C$200 (US$124) per person in cabins. 20% discount in spring and 5% in fall, except on weekends. Rates include all meals. V. Closed mid-Oct to mid-May. **Amenities:** Dining room; 2 tennis courts; sauna; free use of canoes, sailboats, kayaks; hiking trails. *In room:* hair dryer

**Killarney Lodge** The Killarney isn't as secluded as Arowhon (the highway is still visible and audible), but it too has charm. The pine-log cabins, with decks, stand on a peninsula jutting out into the Lake of Two Rivers. Furnishings include old rockers, country-house-style beds, desks, chests, and braided rugs. A canoe comes with every cabin. Home-style meals are served in an attractive rustic log dining room. You can relax in the log cabin lounge warmed by a woodstove.

Algonquin Park, ON, P1H 2G9. © **705/633-5551.** Fax 705/633-5667 (summer only). www.killarneylodge.com. 26 cabins. High season C$170–C$250 (US$105–US$155) per person double. Off-season rates about 30% less. Rates include all meals. MC, V. Closed mid-Oct to mid-May. Enter the park on Hwy. 60 from either Dwight or Whitney. **Amenities:** Dining room, lounge; watersports equipment rentals.

## 7 Some Northern Ontario Highlights: Driving Along Highways 11 & 17

From the Muskoka region, **Highway 11** winds up toward the province's northernmost frontier via North Bay, Kirkland Lake, Timmins (using Route 101), and Cochrane before sweeping west to Nipigon. There it links up briefly with **Highway 17,** the route traveling the northern perimeters of the Great Lakes from North Bay via Sudbury, Sault Ste. Marie, and Wawa, to Nipigon. At Nipigon, highways 11 and 17 combine and lead into Thunder Bay. They split again west of Thunder Bay, with Highway 17 taking a more northerly route to Dryden and Kenora and Highway 11 proceeding via Atikokan to Fort Frances and Rainy River.

### TRAVELING HIGHWAY 11 FROM HUNTSVILLE TO NORTH BAY, COBALT & TIMMINS

From Huntsville, Highway 11 travels north past **Arrowhead Provincial Park** (© **705/789-5105**), with close to 400 campsites. The road heads through the town of Burk's Falls, at the head of the Magnetawan River, and the town of South River, the access point for **Mikisew Provincial Park** (© **705/386-7762**), with sandy beaches on the shore of Eagle Lake.

From South River, the road continues to **Powassan,** famous for its excellent cedar-strip boats. Stop in at B. Giesler and Sons to check out these reliable specimens. The next stop is **North Bay,** on the northeast shore of Lake Nipissing. The town originated on the northern Voyageurs route traveled by fur traders, explorers, and missionaries. Noted for its nearby hunting and fishing, North Bay became world famous in 1934, when the Dionne quintuplets were born in nearby Corbeil; their original home is now a local museum.

From North Bay, Highway 11 continues north toward New Liskeard. Along the route you'll pass **Temagami,** at the center of a superb canoeing region. Its name is Ojibwa for "deep waters by the shore." The region is also associated with the legendary figure Grey Owl, who first came to the area in 1906 as a 17-year-old named Archie Belaney. Archie had always dreamed of living in the wilderness among the Indians; eventually he learned to speak Ojibwa and became an expert in forest and wilderness living. He abandoned his original identity and name, renamed himself Grey Owl, married an Indian woman, and became accepted as a native trapper. He subsequently published a series of books that quickly made him a celebrity.

**Finlayson Point Provincial Park** (**© 705/569-3205**) is on Lake Temagami. The small park—only 94ha (232 acres)—is a great base for exploring the lake and its connecting waterways. Steep rugged cliffs, deep clear waters dotted with 1,300 islands, and magnificent stands of tall pines along its shore make for an awesome natural display. The park offers 113 secluded campsites (many on the lakeshore), plus canoeing, boating, swimming, fishing, hiking, and biking.

**Lady Evelyn Smoothwater Provincial Park** is 45km (28 miles) northwest of Temagami and encompasses the highest point of land in Ontario Maple Mountain and Ishpatina Ridge. Waterfalls are common along the Lady Evelyn River, with Helen Falls cascading more than 24m (80 ft.). White-water skills are required for river travel. There are no facilities. For details, contact District Manager, **Temagami District,** Ministry of Natural Resources, P.O. Box 38, Temagami, ON, P0H 2H0 (**© 705/569-3205**).

The next stop is **Cobalt,** which owes its existence to the discovery of silver here in 1903. Legend has it that blacksmith Fred LaRose threw his hammer at what he thought were fox's eyes, but he hit one of the world's richest silver veins. Cobalt was also in the ore; hence the name of the town. By 1905 a mining stampede extended to Gowganda, Kirkland Lake, and Porcupine. A little farther north, **New Liskeard** is at the northern end of Lake Timikaming at the mouth of the Wabi River. Strangely, this is a dairy center, thanks to the "Little Clay Belt," a glacial lake bed that explains the acres of farmland among the rock and forest.

Even farther north, **Kap-kig-iwan Provincial Park** (**© 705/544-2050**) lies just outside **Englehart,** also the name of the river rushing through the park, and is famous for its "high falls," which give the park its name. Recreational facilities are limited to 64 campsites and self-guided trails. Farther along Highway 11, **Kirkland Lake** is the source for more than 20% of Canada's gold. One original mine is still in production after more than half a century.

At **Iroquois Falls,** a town on the Abitibi River, it's said some Iroquois once raided the Ojibwa community near the falls. After defeating the Ojibwa, the Iroquois curled up to sleep in their canoes tied along the riverbank. But when the Ojibwa cut the canoes loose, the Iroquois were swept over the falls to their deaths. From Iroquois Falls, you can take Route 101 southwest to **Timmins.** Along the way you'll pass the access road to **Kettle Lakes Provincial Park,** 896 Riverside Dr. (**© 705/363-3511**). The park's name refers to the depressions that

**Northern Ontario**

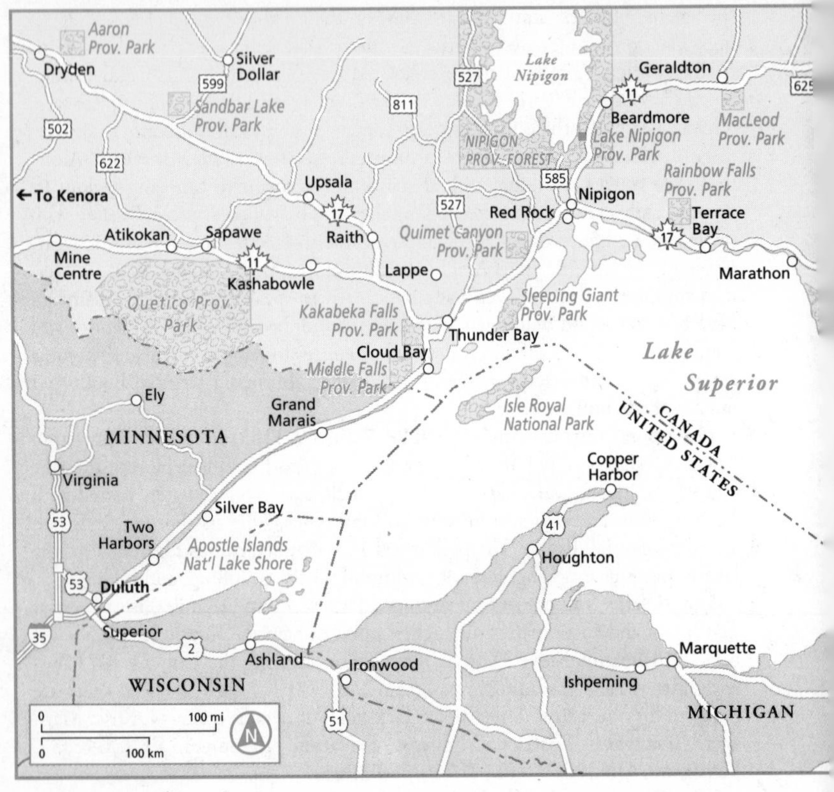


are formed as a glacier retreats. It has 137 camping sites, 5 trails, 3 small beaches, and 22 lakes to fish and enjoy.

In Timmins, you can tour the **Hollinger Gold Mine,** James Reid Road (✆ **705/267-6222**). Discovered by Benny Hollinger in 1909, it produced more than C$400-million (US$248-million) worth of gold in its day. You don helmets, overalls, and boots and grab a torch before walking down into the mine to observe a scaling bar, slusher, mucking machine, and furnace at work and to view the safety room to which the miners rushed in the event of a rockfall. At the surface is a panoramic view from the Jupiter Headframe and ore samples to be inspected along the Prospector's Trail. Admission is C$17 (US$11) for adults, C$15 (US$9) for students, and C$6 (US$3.70) for surface tours only. July to August, it's open daily from 10am to 4pm; May to June and September to October, hours are Wednesday to Sunday from noon to 4pm (call ahead at other times).

Adjacent to the Gold Mine is a center dedicated to a more recent—but just as valuable—Timmins export: Shania Twain. The country-pop singer's hometown has dedicated a **Shania Twain Centre** (✆ **800-387-8466** or 705-360-8510; www.shaniatwaincentre.com), which opened in June 2001. Filled with memorabilia detailing the star's climb, this is really just for devoted fans—particularly those willing to shell out good money to see sights like Shania's suede parka. Admission is C$8 (US$5) for adults and C$6 (US$3.70) for

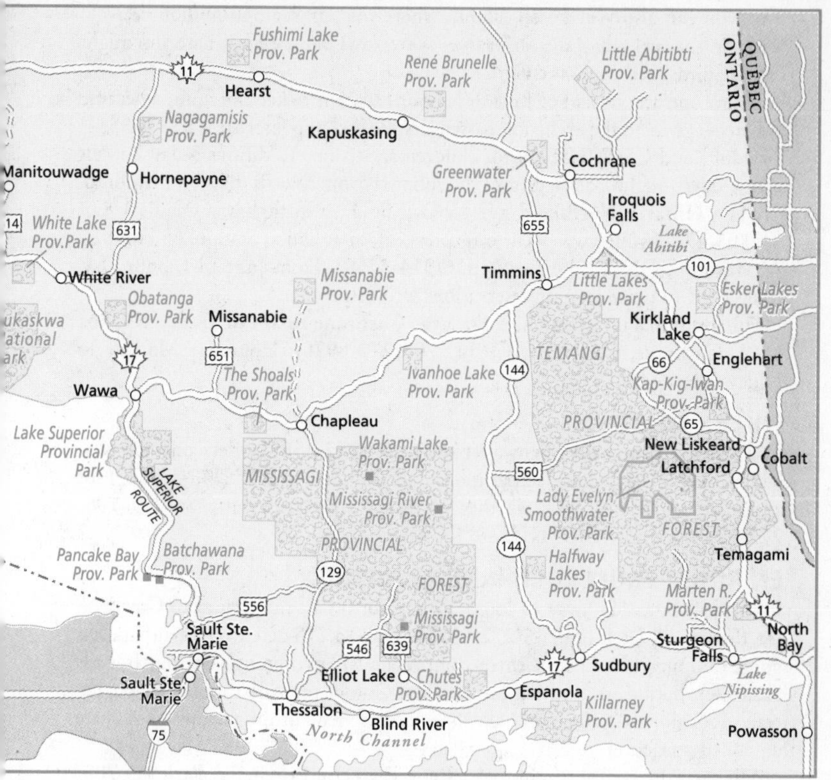


students and seniors. A combined ticket with gold mine is C$21 (US$13) for adults and C$18 (US$11) for students and seniors. It is open Wednesday to Saturday from 10am to 6pm and Sunday noon to 5pm.

For additional city information, contact the **Timmins Convention and Visitors Bureau,** 54 Spruce St. S. (✆ **705/264-0811;** www.city.timmins.on.ca). Hours are daily from 10am to 4pm from June through August, and noon to 3pm during the rest of the year.

## COCHRANE: STARTING POINT OF THE *POLAR BEAR EXPRESS*

Back on Highway 11, the next stop is **Cochrane,** at the junction of the Canadian National Railway and the Ontario Northland Railway. From here, the famous ***Polar Bear Express*** ★ departs to Moosonee and Moose Factory, making one of the world's great railroad/nature excursions. The train travels 4½ hours, 299km (186 miles) from Cochrane along the Abitibi and Moose rivers (the latter, by the way, rises and falls 2m (6 ft.) twice a day with the tides) to Moosonee on James Bay, gateway to the Arctic.

Your destination, **Moosonee** and **Moose Factory,** on an island in the river, will introduce you to frontier life—still challenging, though it's easier today than when native Cree and fur traders traveled the rivers and wrenched a living from the land 300 years ago. You can take the cruiser ***Polar Princess*** or a freighter-canoe across to Moose Factory (site of the Hudson's Bay Company, founded in 1673) and see the 17th-century Anglican church and other sights. If you stay over, you can also visit **Fossil Island,** where you can see 350-million-year-old fossils in the rocks, and the **Shipsands Waterfowl Sanctuary,** where you might see rare birds, including the Gyrfalcon.

Trains operate the end of June to Labour Day, but tickets are limited because priority is given to the excursion passengers. Round-trip fares are C$55 (US$34) for adults and C$47 (US$29) for children ages 5 to 11. Various 3-day/2-night and 4-day/3-night packages are also offered from North Bay and Toronto. Contact **Ontario Northland** at 555 Oak St. E., North Bay, ON, P1B 8L3 (✆ **705/472-4500;** www.polarbearexpress.ca), or at Union Station, 65 Front St. W., Toronto, ON, M5J 1E6 (✆ **416/314-3750**). From June to Labour Day, you'll need to make lodging reservations well in advance.

For additional information, contact the **Cochrane Board of Trade,** P.O. Box 1468, Cochrane, ON, P0L 1C0 (✆ **705/272-4926**). Hours are Monday to Friday 9am to 4pm.

### WHERE TO STAY

The **Chimo Motel** on Highway 11 (✆ **705/272-6555**) offers one- or two-bedroom efficiencies and Jacuzzi rooms at C$65 to C$75 (US$40–US$47) for a double. Another option is the **Westway Motel,** 21 First St. (✆ **705/272-4285**), at only C$65 (US$40) for a double.

## EN ROUTE FROM COCHRANE TO NIPIGON

From Cochrane, Highway 11 loops further north past the turnoff to **Greenwater Provincial Park** (✆ **705/272-6335**). This 13,215-acre (5,350ha) park has good camping (90 sites in three campgrounds), swimming, boating (rentals available), hiking, and fishing on 26 lakes. One of the park's more challenging trails goes along Commando Lake. Spectacular views of the northern lights are an added attraction.

Highway 11 continues west past **Rene Brunelle Provincial Park** (✆ **705/367-2692**) and **Kapuskasing,** where General Motors has its cold-weather testing facility, to **Hearst,** Canada's "moose capital," at the northern terminus of the Algoma Central railway. It continues all the way to **Lake Nipigon Provincial Park** (✆ **807/887-5000**) on the shores of Lake Nipigon. The lake is famous for its black-sand beaches. Facilities include 60 camping sites, boat rentals, and self-guided trails.

The nearby town of **Nipigon** stands on Lake Superior at the mouth of the Nipigon River. It's where the world-record brook trout, weighing 6.5kg (14½ pounds), was caught. At this point highways 17 and 11 join and run all the way into Thunder Bay.

## TRAVELING HIGHWAY 17 ALONG THE PERIMETER OF THE GREAT LAKES

Instead of traveling north from North Bay up Highway 11 to explore the northern mining frontier, you could choose to take Highway 17 along the perimeter of the Great Lakes. I consider this the more scenic and interesting route.

### SUDBURY

The road travels past Lake Nipissing through Sturgeon Falls to **Sudbury,** a nickel-mining center. With a population of 160,000, this is northern Ontario's largest metro area, a rough-and-ready mining town with a landscape so barren that U.S. astronauts were trained here for lunar landings.

Sudbury's two major attractions are **Science North,** 100 Ramsey Lake Rd. (✆ **705/522-3701,** or 705/522-3700 for recorded info; www.scincenorth. on.ca) and the **Big Nickel Mine** (see below). The first occupies two giant stainless-steel snowflake-shaped buildings dramatically cut into a rock outcrop overlooking Lake Ramsey. You can conduct experiments like simulating a hurricane, monitoring earthquakes on a seismograph, or observing the sun through a solar telescope. In addition to the exhibits, a 3-D film/laser experience, *Shooting Star,* takes you on a journey 5 billion years into the past, charting the formation of the Sudbury Basin. A performance in another theater tells the story of naturalist Grey Owl. There's also a water playground (kids can play and adults can build a sailboat), space-exploration and weather command centers, and a fossil-identification workshop. It's open daily: May and June 9am to 5pm and July to Canadian Thanksgiving (U.S. Columbus Day) 9am to 6pm; call ahead for winter hours (usually 10am–4pm). Admission is C$13 (US$58) for adults, C$10 (US$6) for students and seniors, and is free to children under 5.

The **Big Nickel Mine,** 100 Ramsey Lake Rd. (© **705/522-3701**), will be closed until 2003, when it will unveil the dramatic new **Dynamic Earth** exhibit; there is information about Dynamic Earth on the Science North website at www.sciencenorth.on.ca.

The **Path of Discovery** is a 2-hour bus tour providing the only public access to INCO Ltd., the biggest nickel producer in the Western world. On the tour, given July to Labour Day daily at 10am and 2pm, you observe the surface processing facilities and one of the world's tallest smokestacks. Contact **Science North** (© **705/522-3701**).

For further information on Sudbury, contact the **Sudbury Welcome Centre** on Whippoorwill Rd (© **877/304-8222** or 705/523-5587; www.sudburytourism.ca), open Monday to Friday 9am to 4:30pm.

### Where to Stay

Your best bets for lodgings are the chains—**Comfort Inn,** 2171 Regent St. S. (© **705/522-1101**), and 440 2nd Ave. N. (© **705/560-4502**); **Ramada Inn,** 85 St. Anne Rd. (© **705/675-1123**); or **Venture Inn,** 1956 Regent St. S. (© **705/522-7600**). There's also the **Sheraton Four Points,** 1696 Regent St. S. (© **705/522-3000**). Rates are about C$60 to C$95 (US$37–US$59) for a double.

## A CROWN JEWEL: KILLARNEY PROVINCIAL PARK

Less than an hour's drive southwest of Sudbury is **Killarney Provincial Park** (© **705/287-2900**), called the "crown jewel" of the province's park system. This 48,479ha (119,795-acre) park on the north shore of Georgian Bay, accessible only on foot or by canoe, features numerous lakes and a fabulous range of quartzite ridges. More than 100 species of birds breed here, including kingfishers and loons on the lakes in summer. Four members of the Group of Seven painted in the region: Frank Carmichael, Arthur Lismer, A. Y. Jackson, and A. J. Casson. The park has 122 campsites at the George Lake campground near the entrance.

Killarney is a paradise for the canoeist (rentals are available in the park). Compared to Algonquin Park, it's much quieter—you have to cross only one lake to find total privacy at Killarney, while at Algonquin you may have to canoe across three lakes. Three hiking trails loop from the campground and can be completed in 3 hours.

For a more ambitious backpacking tour, the park's **La Cloche Silhouette Trail** winds for more than 97km (60 miles) through forest and beaver meadows past crystal-clear lakes. The trail's main attraction is Silver Peak, towering 370m

(1,214 ft.) above Georgian Bay and offering views of 81km (50 miles) on a clear day. This is a serious undertaking; it'll take 7 to 10 days to complete the whole trail.

The best fishing is in Georgian Bay; sadly, acid rain has killed off most of the fish in the lakes.

## DRIVING WEST FROM SUDBURY

From Sudbury it's 305km (189 miles) west along Highway 17 to Sault Street. Marie, or the Soo, as it's affectionately called. At Serpent River you can turn off north to the town of Elliot Lake, which is near **Mississagi Provincial Park** (**© 705/848-2806**) and the river of the same name. The park has 90 campsites and swimming and offers some fine canoeing. Hikers will find short self-guided trails as well as trails from 6km to 16km (3¾ miles–10 miles) long.

Continuing along Highway 17, bordering the North Channel, will bring you past the access point to **Fort St. Joseph National Park** (**© 705/941-6203**) on St. Joseph Island (between Michigan and Ontario) and into the Soo, 305km (189 miles) west of Sudbury.

## SAULT STE. MARIE

The highlights of any visit to **Sault Ste. Marie** are the **Soo locks,** the **Agawa Canyon Train,** and the **Bon Soo,** one of North America's biggest winter carnivals, celebrated in late January and early February. There's a **Tourism Information Centre** at 261 Queen St. W., at the International Bridge.

The **Soo,** at the junction of Lakes Superior and Huron, actually straddles the border. The twin cities, one in Ontario and the other in Michigan, are separated by the St. Marys River rapids and now are joined by an international bridge. The Northwest Fur Trading Company founded a post here in 1783, building a canal to bypass the rapids from 1797 to 1799. That canal was replaced later by the famous **Soo locks**—four on the American side and one on the Canadian. The locks are part of the St. Lawrence Seaway system, enabling large international cargo ships to navigate from the Atlantic along the St. Lawrence to the Great Lakes. Lake Superior is about 7m (23 ft.) higher than Lake Huron, and the locks raise and lower the ships. You'll find a viewing station at both sets of locks. June to about October 10, you can take a 2-hour cruise through the lock system daily at a cost of C$20 (US$12) for adults, C$15 (US$9) for youths, and C$10 (US$6) for children. For information, contact **Lock Tours Canada,** Roberta Bondar Park Dock off Foster Drive, Box 325, Sault Ste. Marie, ON, P6A 5L8 (**© 705/253-9850;** www.locktours.com).

The Algoma Central Railway, which operates the **Agawa Canyon Train Tours** ★, was established in 1899. The Canadian artists known as the Group of Seven used to shunt up and down the track in a converted boxcar they used as a base camp for canoe excursions into the wilderness. Today the tour train takes you on a 184km (114-mile) trip from the Soo to the Agawa Canyon, where you can enjoy a 2-hour stop to view the waterfalls, walk the nature trails, or enjoy a picnic. The train snakes through a vista of deep ravines and lakes, hugging the hillsides and crossing gorges on skeletal trestle bridges. The most spectacular time to take the trip is mid-September to mid-October. The train operates daily early June to mid-October; on weekends only January to March. June to August, fares are C$58 (US$36) for adults, C$19 (US$12) for youths ages 5 to 18, and C$14 (US$9) for children under 5. September to October, the fares are C$77 (US$48) for adults, C$46 (US$29) for youths, and C$21 (US$13) for children under 5. You can, of course, ride the passenger train from the Soo to Hearst,

**Fun Fact** **Where Winnie-the-Pooh Was Born**

On Highway 17, 98km (61 miles) from Wawa, is **White River,** birthplace of Winnie-the-Pooh. In 1916, Winnipeg soldier Harry Colebourne, on his way to Europe from his hometown, bought a mascot for his regiment here and named it Winnie. When he shipped out from London he couldn't take the bear cub, so it went to the London Zoo, where it became the inspiration for A. A. Milne's classic character. Just outside White River are the spectacular **Magpie High Falls.**

though there are no stops en route. Round-trip fares are C$130 (US$81). For information, contact the **Algoma Central Railway,** Passenger Sales, P.O. Box 130, 129 Bay St., Sault Ste. Marie, ON, P6A 6Y2 (✆ **800/242-9287** or **705/946-7300;** www.agawacanyontourtrain.com).

The surrounding area offers great fishing, snowmobiling, cross-country skiing, and other sports opportunities. For cross-country skiing info, call the **Stokely Creek Ski Touring Centre,** at **Stokely Creek Lodge,** Karalash Corners, Goulais River (✆ **705/649-3421**). Contact the **Sault Ste. Marie Economic Development Corporation,** 360 Great Northern Rd. (✆ **800/242-9287** or 705/949-7152; www.sault-canada.com), for more sports information.

### Where to Stay

Whatever you do, make your reservations in advance. If you're taking the Algoma Train, the most convenient hotel is the **Quality Inn,** 180 Bay St. (✆ **705/945-9264**), across from the train station. It offers 128 units (6 with Jacuzzi tubs), as well as an indoor pool, an exercise room, and an Italian restaurant. Rates are C$98 to C$150 (US$61–US$93) for a double and C$180 (US$112) for a suite.

You can also try the other chains: the **Holiday Inn,** 208 St. Marys River Dr., on the downtown waterfront (✆ **705/949-0611**), or **Comfort Inn,** 333 Great Northern Rd. (✆ **705/759-8000**). The **Ramada Inn,** 229 Great Northern Rd. (✆ **705/942-2500**), has great facilities for families—a water slide, bowling, indoor golf, and more. Rates run about C$60 to $120 (US$37–US$74).

## LAKE SUPERIOR PROVINCIAL PARK

Alona and Agawa bays are in **Lake Superior Provincial Park** ★ (✆ **705/856-2284**). The 1,540km$^2$ (955-sq. mile) park, one of Ontario's largest, offers the haunting shoreline and open waters of Longfellow's "Shining Big-Sea Water," cobble beaches, rugged rocks, and limitless forests. Dramatic highlights include rock formations such as Lac Mijinemungsing, the Devil's Chair, and Old Woman Bay. At the park's east end the Algoma Central Railway provides access to the park along the Agawa River. At Agawa Rock, you can still see traces of the early Ojibway people—there are centuries-old paintings depicting animals and scenes from their legends.

The magnificent scenery has attracted artists for years, including the Group of Seven. Among the most famous paintings of the park are Frank Johnston's *Canyon and Agawa,* Lawren Harris's *Montreal River,* A. Y. Jackson's *First Snows,* and J. E. H. MacDonald's *Algoma Waterfall and Agawa Canyon.* As for wildlife, you may see moose as well as caribou, which once were common here and have been reintroduced along the coast areas and offshore islands. More than 250 bird species have been identified here; about 120 types nest in the area.

Some 269 camping sites are available at three **campgrounds.** The largest, at Agawa Bay, has a 3km (2-mile) beach. Crescent Lake, at the southern boundary, is the most basic, while Rabbit Blanket Lake is well located for exploring the park's interior.

The park has eight canoe routes, ranging in length from 3km to 56km (2 miles–35 miles) and range in difficulty from easy to challenging, with steep portages and white water. Rentals are available at the campgrounds, but outfitter services are limited. Contact the **Wawa Chamber of Commerce,** P. O. Box 858, Wawa, ON, P0S 1K0 (© **705/856-4538**).

The 11 **hiking trails** range from short interpretive trails to rugged overnight trails up to 55km (34 miles) long. The most accessible is the **Trapper's Trail,** featuring a wetlands boardwalk from which you can watch beaver, moose, and great blue heron. The 16km (10-mile) **Peat Mountain Trail** leads to a panoramic view close to 150m (500 ft.) above the surrounding lakes and forests. The 26km (16-mile) **Toawab Trail** takes you through the Agawa Valley to the 25m (81-ft.) Agawa Falls. The **Orphan Lake Trail** is popular due to its moderate length and difficulty, plus its panoramic views over the Orphan and Superior lakes, a pebble beach, and Baldhead Falls. The **Coastal Trail,** along the shoreline, is the longest at 55km (34 miles), stretching from Sinclair Cove to Chalfant Cove, and will take 5 to 7 days to complete. The fall is the best time to hike, when the colors are amazing and the insects are few.

In winter, though there are no formal facilities or services provided, you can cross-country ski, snowshoe, and ice-fish at your own risk.

### WAWA & THE CHAPLEAU GAME RESERVE

From the park, it's a short trip into **Wawa,** 230km (142 miles) north of the Soo, the site of the famous salmon derby. Wawa serves as a supply center for canoeists, fishermen, and other sports folks.

East of Wawa is the **Chapleau Game Reserve,** where there's some of Ontario's best canoeing and wildlife viewing in **Chapleau Nemegosenda River Provincial Park**—200km (124 miles) northeast of the Soo and 100km (62 miles) west of Timmins. It's accessible from Chapleau or by Emerald Lake on Highway 101 to Nemegosenda Lake. There are no facilities. Nonresidents need a permit to camp, costing C$10 (US$6) per person per night. For additional info, contact the **Ministry of Natural Resources Northeast Zone,** 190 Cherry St., Chapleau, ON, P0M 1K0 (© **705/864-1710,** ext. 214).

### PUKASKWA NATIONAL PARK

Southwest of White River on the shores of Lake Superior is Ontario's only national park in the wilderness, **Pukaskwa National Park,** Hattie Cove, Heron Bay, ON, P0T 1R0 (© **807/229-0801;** www.parcscanada.gc.ca), reached via Highway 627 from Highway 17. The interior is accessible only on foot or by boat.

In this 1,878km² (388-sq. mile) park survives the most southerly herd of **woodland caribou**—only 40 of them. Lake Superior is extremely cold, and for this reason rare Arctic plants are also found here. **Hattie Cove** is the center of most park activities and services, including a 67-site campground, a series of short walking trails, access to three sand beaches, parking facilities and a visitor center.

The 60km (37-mile) **Coastal Hiking Trail** winds from Hattie Cove south to the North Swallow River and requires proper planning and equipment (camping areas are every half- to a full-day's hike apart). A 15km (9-mile) day hike along this trail can be taken to the White River Suspension Bridge. There are also backcountry trails. In winter, cross-country skiers can use 6km (3¾ miles) of groomed trails or hazard the fast slopes and sharp turns created by the topography. Snowshoers are welcome, too.

## CANOEING THE WHITE & PUKASKWA RIVERS

The White and Pukaskwa rivers offer white-water adventure. You can paddle the easily accessed **White River** any time during the open-water season. Many wilderness adventurers start from nearby **White Lake Provincial Park** and travel 4 to 6 days to the mouth of the White River and then paddle about an hour north on Lake Superior to Hattie Cove.

The **Pukaskwa River** is more remote, more difficult (with rugged and long portages and an 260m (850-ft.) drop between the headwaters at Gibson Lake and the river mouth at Lake Superior), and navigable only during the spring runoff. The best place to start is where the river crosses Highway 17 near Sagina Lake and paddle to Gibson Lake via Pokei Lake, Pokei Creek, and Soulier Lake. Otherwise, you'll have to fly in from White River or Wawa.

Outfitters include **Pukaskwa Country Outfitters,** P.O. Box 603, Marathon, ON, P0T 2E0 (✆ **807/229-0265;** www.pcoutfitters.on.ca); **Naturally Superior Adventures,** RR #1 Lake Superior, Wawa ON, P0S 1K0 (✆ **800/203-9092** or 705/856-2939; www.naturallysuperior.com); and **U-Paddle-It,** P.O. Box 374, Pinewood Drive, Wawa, ON, P0S 1K0 (✆ **705/856-1493**).

## MORE PROVINCIAL PARKS

From White River it's 270km (167 miles) to **Nipigon** and **Nipigon Bay,** offering fine rock, pine, and lake vistas. It's another 12km (7½ miles) to **Ouimet Canyon Provincial Park** (✆ **807/977-2526**), at the location of a spectacular canyon 100m (330 ft.) deep, 150m (500 ft.) wide, and a 1.5km (1 mile) long. When you stand on the edge of the canyon and gaze out over the expanse of rock and forest below, you can sense the power of the forces that shaped, built, and split the earth's crust and then gouged and chiseled this crevasse—one of Eastern Canada's most striking canyons. The park is for day use only.

About 25km (15½ miles) on, the next stop is **Sleeping Giant Provincial Park** (✆ **807/977-2526**), named after the rock formation the Ojibwa Indians say is Nanabosho (the Giant), turned to stone after disobeying the Great Spirit. The story goes that Nanabosho, who had led the Ojibwa to the north shore of Lake Superior to save them from the Sioux, discovered silver one day, but fearing for his people, he told them to bury it on an islet at the tip of the peninsula and keep it a secret. But vanity got the better of one of the chieftains, who made silver weapons for himself. Subsequently, he was killed in battle against the Sioux. Shortly afterward, Nanabosho spied a Sioux warrior leading two white men in a canoe across Lake Superior to the source of the silver. To keep the secret, he disobeyed the Great Spirit and raised a storm that sank and drowned the white men. For this, he was turned into stone.

Take Route 587 south along the Sibley Peninsula, which juts into the lake. Among the park's natural splendors are bald eagles, wild orchids, moose, and more than 190 species of birds. Facilities include 168 campsites at Marie Louise Campground plus about 40 interior sites. There's a beach at the campground.

The trail system consists of three self-guided nature trails, three walking trails, and a network of about 70km (44 miles) of hiking trails, including the 2-day Kabeyun Trail, which originates at the Thunder Bay lookout and follows the shoreline south to Sawyer Bay. The park has great cross-country skiing with 30km (19 miles) of trails.

### THUNDER BAY

Just before you enter Thunder Bay, stop and honor Terry Fox at the **Monument and Scenic Lookout.** Not far from this spot he was forced to abandon his heroic cross-Canada journey to raise money for cancer research. To access the remote **Wabakimi region,** take Route 527 north just east of Thunder Bay. It'll take you to Armstrong, the supply center for this wilderness region.

From the port city of **Thunder Bay**—an amalgam of Fort William and Port Arthur—wheat and other commodities are shipped out via the Great Lakes all over the world. Fifteen grain elevators still dominate the skyline. You can't really grasp the city's role and its geography unless you take the **Harbor Cruise.** Other highlights include **Old Fort William** (✆ **807/473-2344;** www.oldfortwilliam.on.ca), about 16km (10 miles) outside the city on the Kaministiquia River. From 1803 to 1821, this reconstructed fort was the headquarters of the North West Fur-Trading Company, which was later absorbed by the Hudson's Bay Company.

#### Where to Stay

For B&B accommodations, contact the **North of Superior B&B Association** at ✆ **807/475-5630** or e-mail nosbba@norlink.net. Your best bets are the chains: **The Best Western NorWester,** 2080 Highway 61, RR #4, ON, P7C 4Z2 (✆ **807/473-9123**), which has rooms for C$74 to C$95 (US$46–US$59) for a double, plus an indoor pool and lounge/restaurant; **Comfort Inn by Journey's End,** 660 W. Arthur St. (✆ **807/475-3155**), where rooms are C$75 to C$120 (US$47–US$74) for a double; and the **Venture Inn,** 450 Memorial Ave. (✆ **807/345-2343**), which also has a lounge/restaurant and indoor pool and rents rooms for C$78 to C$100 (US$48–US$62) for a double.

There are a couple of independents that are worth considering, too. The **Airlane Hotel,** 698 W. Arthur St., Thunder Bay, ON, P7E 5R8 (✆ **807/473-1600**), has modern guest rooms with amenities like coffeemakers. Facilities include an indoor pool and fitness center, as well as a lounge/restaurant and dance club. Suites with whirlpools are available, too. Rates are C$100 to C$108 (US$62–US$67) for a double and C$160 (US$99) for a suite. The **White Fox Inn,** RR #4, 1345 Mountain Rd., Thunder Bay, ON, P7C 4Z2 (✆ **807/577-3699**), is set on 6ha (15 acres) with a view of the Norwester Mountain range, and was once a lumber magnate's home. The individually decorated guest rooms have fireplaces and VCRs, while the three largest rooms have in-room Jacuzzis. There's also a fine dining room serving Mediterranean cuisine. Rates are C$110 to C$220 (US$68–US$136) for a double.

### FROM THUNDER BAY TO FORT FRANCES/RAINY RIVER VIA HIGHWAY 11

From Thunder Bay it's 480km (298 miles) along the Trans-Canada Highway to **Kenora.** Several provincial parks line the route.

**Kakabeka Falls Provincial Park,** 435 James St. S., Suite 221, Thunder Bay (✆ **807/473-9231**), with its fantastic 40m (130-ft.) high waterfall, is 29km (18 miles) along the Trans-Canada Highway. The gorge was carved out of the Precambrian Shield when the last glaciers melted, and fossils dating back 1.6 billion years have been found here. The park has several nature trails, plus safe swimming at a roped-off area above the falls. Two campgrounds provide 166 sites

(C$10 to C$17/US$6 to US$11, depending on season and site). In winter, there are 13km (8 miles) of groomed cross-country ski trails.

Atikokan is the gateway to **Quetico Provincial Park** ★ (✆ **807/597-2737**), primarily a wilderness canoeing park. The 4,662km² (1,800-sq.-mile) park has absolutely no roads and only two of the six entrance stations are accessible by car (those at French Lake and Nym Lake, both west of Thunder Bay). Instead, there are miles of interconnecting lakes, streams, and rivers with roaring white water dashing against granite cliffs. It's one of North America's finest canoeing areas. **Dawson Trail Campgrounds,** with 133 sites at French Lake, is the only accessible site for car camping. Extended hikes are limited to the 13km (8-mile) trip to Pickerel Lake; there are also six short trails in the French Lake area (three interpretive). The park can be skied, but there are no groomed trails. Also in the park on some rocks near Lac la Croix you can see 30 ancient pictographs representing moose, caribou, and other animals, as well as hunters in canoes.

**Fort Frances** is an important border crossing to the United States and the site of a paper mill. Here you'll find a **Travel Information Centre** at 400 Central Ave. at the Minnesota border. Another 90km (56 miles) will bring you to **Rainy River** at the extreme western point of Ontario across from Minnesota. There's a **Travel Information Centre** at 301 Atwood Ave. off the International Bridge exit. The district abounds in lake land scenery, much of it in **Lake of the Woods Provincial Park,** RR #1, Sleeman (✆ **807/488-5531**), 43km (26 miles) north of Rainy River. This shallow lake has a 169m (185-yd.) long beach and is good for swimming and waterskiing. In spring you can fish for walleye, northern pike, and large- and smallmouth bass. You can rent canoes and boats in nearby Morson. The park has 100 campsites as well as a couple of easy nature trails to hike.

Almost due north of Thunder Bay via Route 527 lies **Wabakimi Provincial Park,** which has some fine canoeing and fishing. It's accessible from Armstrong.

## FROM THUNDER BAY TO KENORA VIA HIGHWAY 17

Instead of taking Highway 11 west from Thunder Bay as described above, you can take Highway 17, which follows a more northerly route. Just follow 17 where it branches off at Shabaqua Corners, about 56km (34 miles) from Thunder Bay. Continue northwest to **Ignace,** the access point for two provincial parks.

At Ignace, turn off onto Highway 599 to **Sandbar Lake** (✆ **807/934-2995,** or 807/934-2233 for local Natural Resources office), which offers more than 5,000ha (12,350 acres) of forest with nine smaller lakes plus the large one from which it takes its name. The park's most notable inhabitants are the painted turtle, whose tracks you can often see in the sand, the spotted sandpiper, the loon, the common merganser, and several species of woodpecker. The campground has 75 sites; the beach has safe swimming; and there are several short and long canoe routes plus several hiking trails, including the 2km (1¼-mile) **Lookout Trail,** which begins on the beach.

**Turtle River Provincial Park** is a 120km (74-mile-long) waterway from Ignace to Mine Centre. The canoe route begins on Agimak Lake at Ignace and follows a series of lakes into the Turtle River, ending on Turtle Lake just north of Mine Centre. The park also includes the famous log castle built by Jimmy McQuat in the early 1900s on White Otter Lake. Follow Highway 599 farther north to the remote Albany and Apawapiskat rivers, which drain into James Bay.

Back on Highway 17 from Ignace, it's another 40km (24 miles) to the turnoff on Highway 72 to **Ojibway Provincial Park** (✆ **807/737-2033**), which has only 45 campsites but offers swimming, boating, and self-guided trails. Back on Highway 17, it's only a short way beyond Highway 72 to **Aaron Provincial Park** (✆ **807/938-6534,** or 807/223-3341 for Natural Resources office), where you'll find close to 100 campsites, facilities for boating and swimming, plus some short nature trails. Nearby Dryden is the supply center for Aaron.

From Dryden it's about 43km (26 miles) to Vermilion Bay, where Route 105 branches off north to Red Lake, the closest point to one of the province's most remote provincial parks, **Woodland Caribou** (✆ **807/727-2253**). Offering superb fishing, the 450,000ha (1,111,500-acre) park has no facilities except picnic tables and boat rentals nearby. It's home to one of the largest herds of woodland caribou south of the Hudson Bay lowlands. It's also inhabited by black bear, great blue heron, osprey, and bald eagles. There are 1,600km (992 miles) of canoe routes. Contact the **Northern Ontario Tourist Outfitters Association** (✆ **705/472-5552;** www.noto.net) for details on fly-in camps. Back on Highway 17 from Vermilion Bay, it's only 72km (43 miles) until the road links up with Highway 71 outside Kenora, just shy of the Manitoba border. West of Kenora there's a **Visitors Information Centre** on Highway 17 at the Manitoba border

## Where to Stay & Dine Near Kenora

**Totem Lodge** At the end of Long Bay on Lake of the Woods, this lodge caters to outdoor enthusiasts and families who come for the fishing and hunting. The main lodge is an *A*-frame featuring a dining room, a lounge, and decks with umbrella-shaded tables overlooking the water. The timber-and-stone decor is appropriately rustic. The cabins have full modern baths, beds with Hudson's Bay blankets, fireplaces, and screened-in porches or outdoor decks, plus cooking facilities. Rooms above the boathouse lack cooking facilities but do have refrigerators. Management will arrange fly-out fishing trips for guests. Fish-cleaning facilities and freezer service are available on-site.

Box 180, Sioux Narrows, ON, P0X 1N0. ✆ **800-668-6836** or 807/226-5275. Fax 807/226-5187. www.totemresorts.com. 27 cabins, 3 units. C$200 (US$124) per person per night. Weekly and special packages available. MC, V. Access is off Hwy. 71, 1 mile north of Sioux Narrows. **Amenities:** Dining room; 5m (16-ft.) fishing boats; canoes; windsurfing. *In room:* A/C, TV.

**Wiley Point Lodge** This lodge is accessible only by boat and therefore offers more of a wilderness experience. Renovated and expanded in 2000, Wiley Point boasts new guest rooms as well as new amenities such as a games room. The main lodge has eight suites, plus there are seven cabins (two- or three-bedroom), all with full bath, refrigerator, and screened-in porch. The lodge contains a dining room, lounge, and deck overlooking the lake. Spring and fall bear hunts are offered, as well as more traditional hunting.

Box 180, Sioux Narrows, ON, P0X 1N0. ✆ **800-668-6836** or 807/543-4090. 8 units, 7 cabins. Fishing packages C$200 (US$124) per person per night based on 2 per boat (this includes boat, gas, and bait). Hunting packages also available. MC, V. **Amenities:** Dining room, lounge; beach with a diving raft; paddleboats; windsurfing; hot tub; sauna; exercise room; games room.

13

# Manitoba & Saskatchewan

*by Bill McRae*

Visitors don't exactly flock to central Manitoba and Saskatchewan, but that can be a plus if you like unpopulated, wide-open spaces. Part of the great prairies, these two provinces boast some beautiful wilderness and parkland and an almost infinite chain of lakes, making them terrific choices for fishing, canoeing, wildlife-watching, and more.

**Manitoba** is famous for its friendly people, who not only brave long, harsh winters but also till the southern prairie lands in summer, making the region a breadbasket for the nation and the world. Along the southern border outside Winnipeg, wheat, barley, oats, and flax wave at the roadside, the horizon is limitless, and grain elevators pierce the skyline. Beyond the province's southern section, punctuated by Lake Winnipeg and Lake Manitoba, stretches one of the last wilderness frontiers, a paradise for anglers and outdoors enthusiasts of all sorts. Here you'll find many of the province's thousands of lakes, which cover about 20% of Manitoba (the province is sometimes claimed to have 100,000 lakes). You'll also see polar bears and beluga whales and hear the timber wolves cry on the lonesome tundra surrounding the Hudson Bay port of Churchill.

Five times the size of New York State, with a population of a little over a million, **Saskatchewan** produces about 55% of Canada's wheat. Here you'll find a hunting and fishing paradise in the northern lakes and forests; several summer playgrounds (including Prince Albert National Park and 31 provincial parks); and the cities of Regina, the capital, and Saskatoon.

## 1 Exploring the Provinces

The **Trans-Canada Highway** (Highway 1) cuts across the southern part of both provinces. In Manitoba, you can stop along Highway 1 at Whiteshell Provincial Park in the east. You can return to the highway or visit the shores of Lake Winnipeg at Grand Beach Provincial Park and then head south via Selkirk and Lower Fort Garry to Winnipeg, the provincial capital. From Winnipeg, you can take the train north to Churchill to explore the Northern tundra around Hudson Bay. On your return trip to Winnipeg, you can pick up Highway 1 again and drive west across the province, stopping for a detour to Riding Mountain National Park or to Spruce Woods Provincial Park before exiting into Saskatchewan.

Highway 1 leads from Manitoba to Regina, with a stop perhaps at Moose Mountain Provincial Park along the way. From Regina it's a 2½-hour or so drive to Saskatoon, and about another 2½-hour drive to Prince Albert National Park (you can stop at Batoche en route). From Prince Albert you can return via Fort Battleford National Historic Park to Saskatoon and then to Highway 1 at Swift Current, or you can take Route 4 directly from Battleford to Swift Current. From here, the Trans-Canada Highway heads west to the Alberta border.

## VISITOR INFORMATION

Contact **Travel Manitoba,** 7-155 Carlton St., Dept. SV2, Winnipeg, MB R3C 3H8 (✆ **800/665-0040, ext. SV2;** www.travelmanitoba.com). Or you can visit the **Explore Manitoba Centre** at 21 Forks Market Rd., open daily 10am to 6pm, year round. For taped info on the latest happenings, call ✆ **204/942-2535.**

In Saskatchewan, contact **Tourism Saskatchewan,** 1922 Park St., Regina, SK S4P 3V7 (✆ **877/237-2273** or 306/787-2300; www.sasktourism.com); it's open year-round Monday to Friday from 7:30am to 7pm, and from March to mid-October on Saturday and Sunday from 9am to 4pm (but hours may vary).

## THE GREAT OUTDOORS

Manitoba's major playgrounds are **Riding Mountain National Park** and the provincial parks of **Whiteshell, Atikaki, Spruce Woods, Duck Mountain,** and **Grass River.** For information on Manitoba parks contact **Manitoba Conservation,** 200 Salteaux Crescent, Winnipeg, MB R3J 3W3 (✆ **800/214-6497** or 204/945-6784; www.manitobaparks.com).

Saskatchewan boasts 80,290km$^2$ (30,889 sq. miles) of water, and 1.2 million hectares (3 million acres) are given over to parks—nearly 900,000ha (1 million acres) alone constitute Prince Albert National Park. In addition, there are 34 provincial parks. The major ones are **Cypress Hills** (✆ **306/662-5411**), **Moose Mountain** (✆ **306/577-2600**), **Lac La Ronge** (✆ **800/772-4064** or 306/425-4234), and **Meadow Lake** (✆ **306/236-7680**). For information about all provincial parks, contact **Saskatchewan Environment and Resource Management** (✆ **306/787-2700** or 800/667-2757 in Saskatchewan; www.serm.gov.sk.ca/parks).

At the parks you can camp for C$11 to C$24 (US$7–US$15), plus a C$7 to C$20 (US$4.35–US$12) daily entry fee for vehicles. Some parks, such as Cypress Hills and Moose Mountain, also have cabins which rent for anywhere from C$55 to C$100 (US$34–US$62) a night.

Summers in both provinces can be simply magnificent, with warm sunny days and cool refreshing evenings and nights. Average winter temperatures are pretty harsh at 18°C to 12°C (0°F–10°F), but that doesn't stop winter-sports enthusiasts.

**BIRD-WATCHING** In Manitoba, you'll find a goose sanctuary at **Whiteshell Provincial Park.** Gull Harbour's **Hecla/Grindstone Provincial Park,** on Lake Winnipeg, has a wildlife-viewing tower; the Grassy Narrows Marsh there is home to a wide variety of waterfowl. **Riding Mountain National Park** boasts more than 200 species of birds. And many varieties stop near **Churchill** on their annual migrations.

In Saskatchewan, **Moose Mountain Provincial Park** is home to many waterfowl and songbirds, including the magnificent blue heron and the red-tailed hawk. As you might expect, **Prince Albert National Park** has a wide variety of bird life, with the highlight being an enormous colony of white pelicans at Lavallee Lake. And there's even a waterfowl park right in the middle of downtown **Regina,** where you can see more than 60 species. A naturalist is on duty weekdays.

**CANOEING** In Manitoba, the best places to canoe are Riding Mountain National Park, Whiteshell Provincial Park, Woodland Caribou Provincial Park, Atikaki Provincial Park (on the Bloodvein River), and the chain of lakes around Flin Flon, which is right on the border between the two provinces.

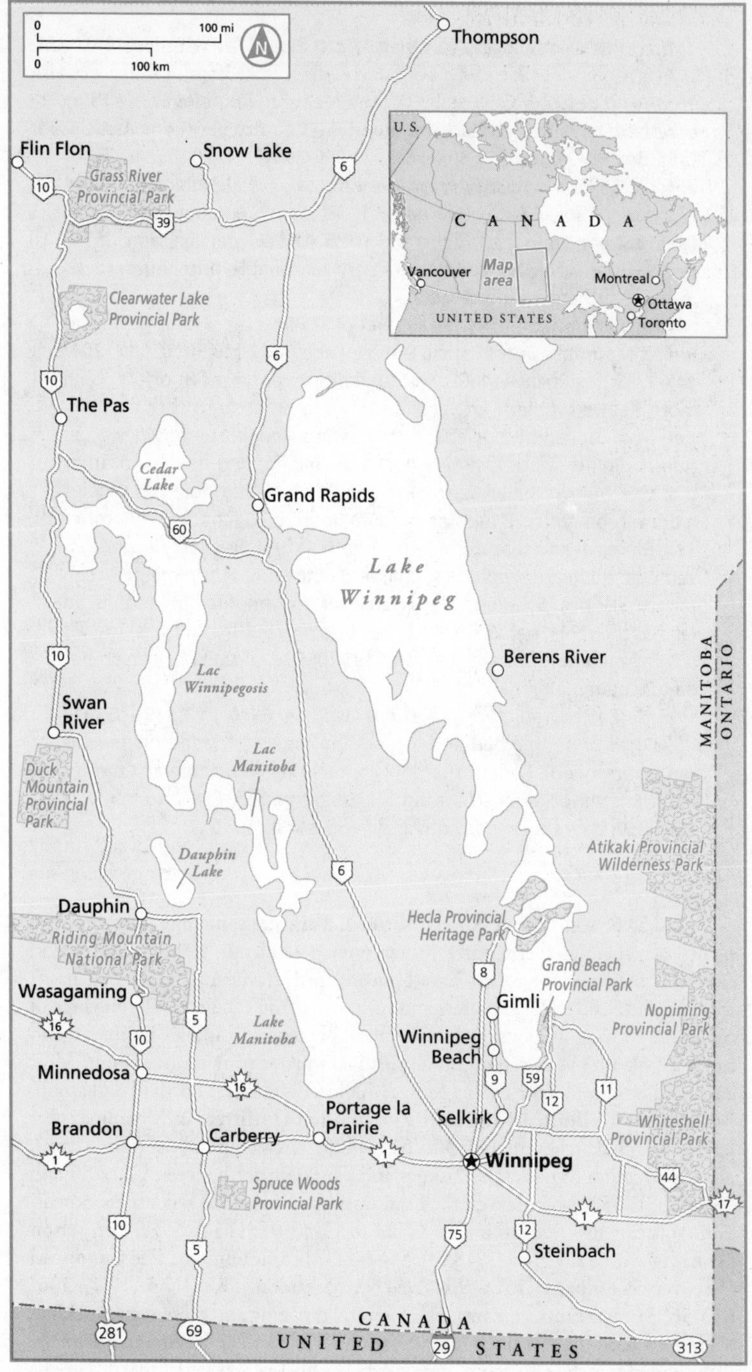

0
100 mi
0
100 km
N
Thompson
U.S.
CANADA
Vancouver
Map area
Montreal
Ottawa
Toronto
UNITED STATES
Flin Flon
Snow Lake
Grass River Provincial Park
Clearwater Lake Provincial Park
The Pas
Cedar Lake
Grand Rapids
Lake Winnipeg
Berens River
MANITOBA
ONTARIO
Lac Winnipegosis
Swan River
Duck Mountain Provincial Park
Lac Manitoba
Dauphin Lake
Atikaki Provincial Wilderness Park
Dauphin
Riding Mountain National Park
Hecla Provincial Heritage Park
Grand Beach Provincial Park
Wasagaming
Gimli
Nopiming Provincial Park
Lake Manitoba
Winnipeg Beach
Minnedosa
Selkirk
Portage la Prairie
Brandon
Carberry
Whiteshell Provincial Park
Winnipeg
Spruce Woods Provincial Park
Steinbach
CANADA
UNITED STATES
10
39
6
60
16
5
8
9
59
12
11
1
44
17
75
281
69
29
313

### Tips Farm & Ranch Vacations on the Prairies

There's no better way to really get the feel of the prairies than to stay on a farm or ranch. Contact the **Manitoba Country Vacations Association,** Box 93, Minto, MB R0K 1M0 (© **866/284-9014,** 204/776-2176, or 204/322-5525; www.countryvacations.mb.ca), for details about farm accommodations. Rates average C$75 (US$47) per day and C$450 (US$186) per week for adults and C$25 (US$16) per day and C$150 (US$93) per week for children—a very reasonable price for such an exciting authentic experience.

Just outside Riding Mountain National Park, the 290ha (720-acre) **Riding Mountain Guest Ranch,** Box 11, Lake Audy, MB R0J 0Z0 (© **204/848-2265;** fax 204/848-4658; www.wildlifeadventures.ca), offers much more than a simple farm vacation. Among numerous other possibilities, you can enjoy horseback trail riding and horse-drawn wagon rides, wildlife safaris, cowboy cookouts, hiking, and loon- and other bird-watching at the lake. Accommodations consist of four rooms, plus a dorm room with 12 beds and a bunkhouse accommodating another 12. The ranch also features a lounge with a stone fireplace, a sunroom veranda, a billiards room, a sauna, and a hot tub. In summer, you can take trail rides. Evenings are given over to campfire sing-alongs. In winter, the ranch has 20km (12 miles) of cross-country ski trails. There's a 2-day minimum stay, at C$85 to C$95 (US$53–US$59) per person per day, including all meals.

In Saskatchewan, farm vacations average C$50 to C$75 (US$31–US$47) for a double bed and a real farm breakfast (additional meals can be arranged). For information, contact the **Saskatchewan Country Vacations Association,** 709 King St., Saskatoon, SK S7K 0N6 (© **306/664-4350;** www.bbcanada.com/associations/saskcountry).

In Saskatchewan, **Prince Albert National Park** has some fine canoeing, and plenty of other northern water routes offer a challenge to both novice and expert. Some 55 canoe routes have been mapped, traversing terrain that hasn't changed since the era of explorers and fur traders. You can get to all but three of the routes by road. Various outfitters will supply tents, camping equipment, and canoes; look after your car; and transport you to your trip's starting point. Most are in either Flin Flon or Lac La Ronge, 400km (248 miles) north of Saskatoon.

**Horizons Unlimited Churchill River Canoe Outfitters** in Missinipe, near La Ronge, Saskatchewan (© **306/635-4420;** www.churchillrivercanoe.com), offers a selection of packages. Canoes and kayaks go for between C$27.50 and $34 (US$17–$21) per day, or they can outfit you for a real wilderness expedition. You can also rent cabins for C$23 to C$30 (US$14–US$19) per person per night, with a C$75 to C$185 (US$47–US$115) minimum. The **Canoe Ski Discovery Company,** 1618–9th Ave. N., Saskatoon, SK S7K 3A1 (© **306/653-5693;** www.canoeski.com), offers several canoeing and cross-country skiing wilderness ecotours in Prince Albert National Park, in Lac La Ronge Provincial Park, and along the Churchill and Saskatchewan rivers. The trips last 2 to 12 days, cost C$145 to C$1,795 (US$90–US$1,113), and are led by qualified eco-interpreters. For additional information, contact **Tourism Saskatchewan,** 1922

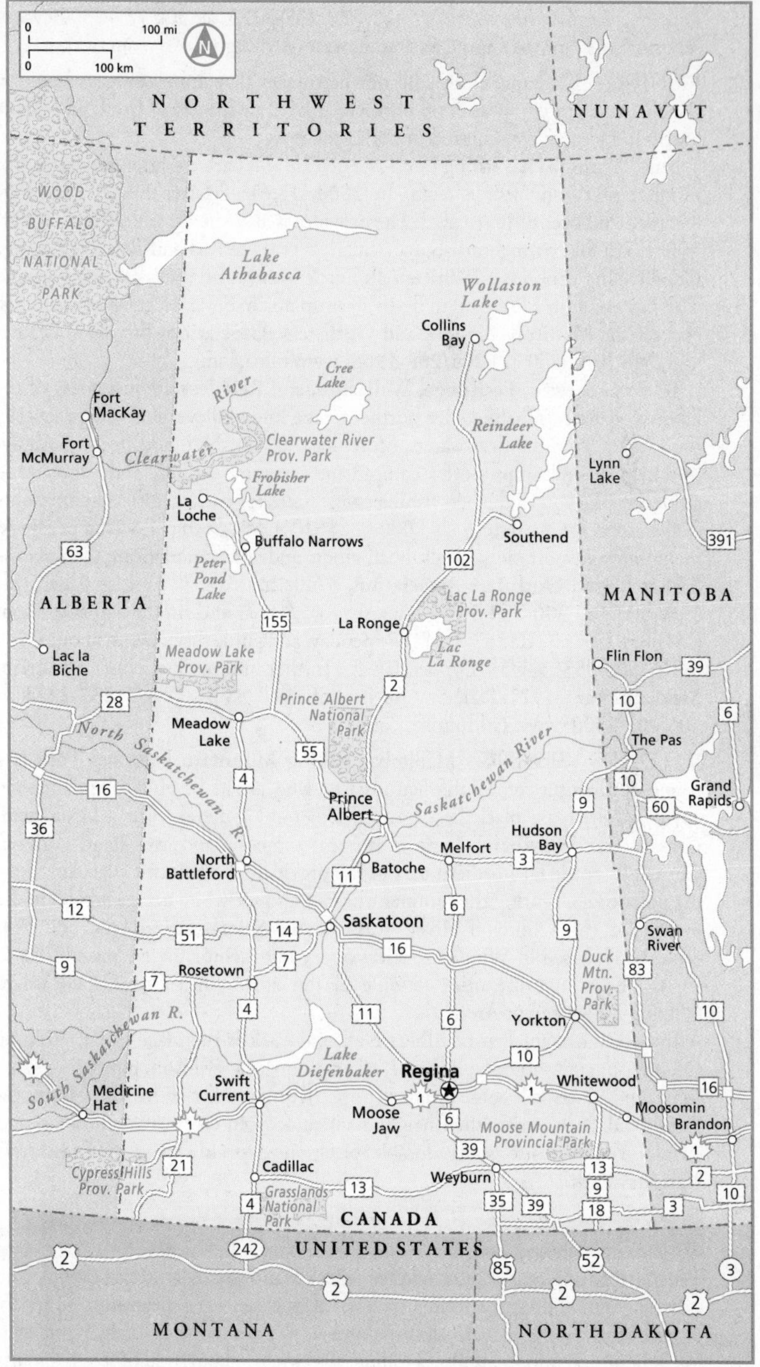

0
100 mi
0
100 km
N
NORTHWEST TERRITORIES
NUNAVUT
WOOD BUFFALO NATIONAL PARK
Lake Athabasca
Wollaston Lake
Collins Bay
Cree Lake
River
Fort MacKay
Fort McMurray
Clearwater
Clearwater River Prov. Park
Frobisher Lake
Reindeer Lake
Lynn Lake
La Loche
Buffalo Narrows
Southend
63
102
391
Peter Pond Lake
ALBERTA
MANITOBA
155
La Ronge
Lac La Ronge Prov. Park
Lac La Ronge
Lac la Biche
Meadow Lake Prov. Park
Flin Flon
39
2
28
Prince Albert National Park
10
6
North Saskatchewan R.
Meadow Lake
The Pas
55
Saskatchewan River
4
10
Grand Rapids
16
Prince Albert
9
60
36
Hudson Bay
Melfort
North Battleford
Batoche
3
11
12
6
Saskatoon
Swan River
51
14
16
9
9
7
Duck Mtn. Prov. Park
83
Rosetown
7
South Saskatchewan R.
4
11
6
Yorkton
10
Lake Diefenbaker
10
Regina
Medicine Hat
Swift Current
1
1
Whitewood
16
Moose Jaw
Moosomin
Brandon
6
Moose Mountain Provincial Park
1
1
39
21
Cadillac
13
Cypress Hills Prov. Park
Weyburn
2
13
Grasslands National Park
9
10
4
35
39
18
3
CANADA
242
UNITED STATES
2
85
52
3
2
2
2
MONTANA
NORTH DAKOTA

Park St., Regina, SK S4P 3V7 (✆ **877/237-2273** or 306/787-2300; www.sasktourism.com), or **Canoe Saskatchewan** (www.lights.com/waterways).

**FISHING** The same clear, cold northern lakes that draw canoeists hold out the chance of catching walleye, northern pike, four species of trout, and Arctic grayling. Licenses are required in both provinces.

Since Manitoba has strong catch-and-release and barbless-hook programs, the number of trophy fish is high. In 2000, 11,610 Master Angler Fish were recorded and over 85% released. The province is also known as the North American mecca for channel catfish, particularly along the Red and Bloodvein rivers. Good fishing abounds in **Whiteshell, Duck Mountain,** the lake chains around **The Pas** and **Flin Flon,** and in fly-in areas up north. For a selection of outfitters, contact the **Manitoba Lodges and Outfitters Association,** Box 399, Beausejour, MB R0E 0C0 (✆ **204/268-1968;** www.mloa.com).

In Saskatchewan, **La Ronge, Wollaston,** and **Reindeer** are just a few of the lakes so densely inhabited by northern pike and walleye you can practically pluck them from the clear waters. More than 300 northern outfitters—both fly-in and drive-in camps—offer equipment, accommodations, and experienced guides to take you to the best fishing spots. Rates for packages vary—commonly in the range of C$1,000 to C$3,000 (US$620–US$1,860) per person per week, including transportation, meals, boat, guide, and accommodations. Contact the **Saskatchewan Outfitters Association,** 3700–2nd Ave. W., Prince Albert, SK S6W 1A2 (✆ **306/763-5434;** www.soa.ca). A boat and motor will cost about C$100 to C$250 (US$67–US$167) per day, and guide services run about C$80 to C$150 (US$53–US$100) per day. For further information, contact **Tourism Saskatchewan,** 1922 Park St., Regina, SK S4P 3V7 (✆ **877/237-2273** or 306/787-2300; www.sasktourism.com).

**WILDLIFE VIEWING** Manitoba's **Riding Mountain National Park** is a prime destination for wildlife enthusiasts, who might be able to spot moose, coyote, wolf, lynx, black bear, beaver, and more—there's even a bison herd. **Grass River Provincial Park** is home to moose and woodland caribou. Churchill, in the far northern part of the province, is a fantastic place for viewing polar bears. During the summer, you can also see white beluga whales in the mouth of the Churchill River. **Kaskattama Safari Adventures** (✆ **204/667-1611**), based in Winnipeg, offers pricey but memorable organized trips to see the bears and the other wildlife in the north, including Cape Tatnam Wildlife Management Area.

In Saskatchewan, **Prince Albert National Park** is the place to be; you'll be able to spot and photograph moose, elk, caribou, shaggy bison, lumbering black bears, and more. It'll come as no surprise that moose live in **Moose Mountain Provincial Park,** where their neighbors include deer, elk, beaver, muskrat, and coyote. You can also spot adorable black-tailed prairie dogs in **Grasslands National Park.**

## 2 Winnipeg: Capital of Manitoba ★★

Tough, sturdy, muscular, midwestern—that's Winnipeg, Manitoba's capital. The cast-iron warehouses, stockyards, railroad depots, and grain elevators all testify to its historical role as a distribution-and-supply center, first for furs and then for agricultural products. It's a toiling city where about 680,000 inhabitants sizzle in summer and shovel in winter.

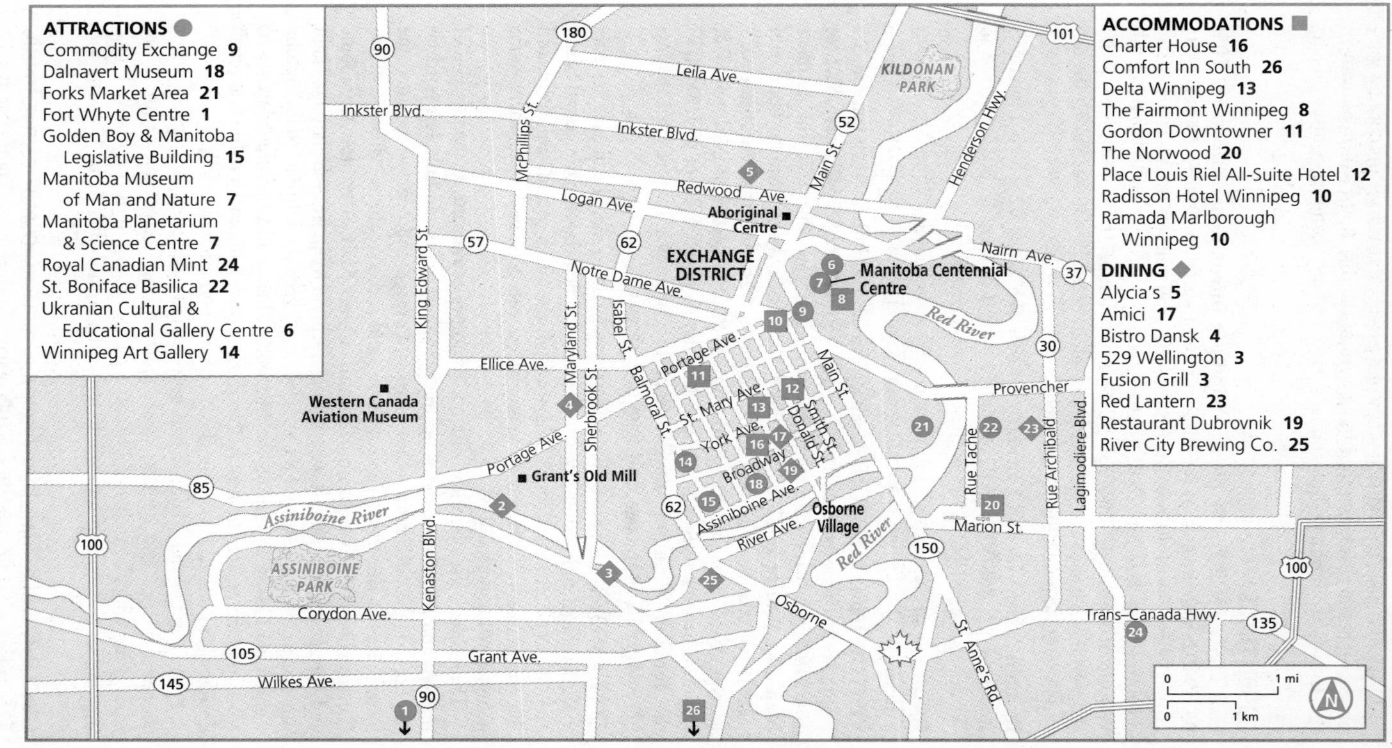
ATTRACTIONS
Commodity Exchange 9
Dalnavert Museum 18
Forks Market Area 21
Fort Whyte Centre 1
Golden Boy & Manitoba Legislative Building 15
Manitoba Museum of Man and Nature 7
Manitoba Planetarium & Science Centre 7
Royal Canadian Mint 24
St. Boniface Basilica 22
Ukranian Cultural & Educational Gallery Centre 6
Winnipeg Art Gallery 14
ACCOMMODATIONS
Charter House 16
Comfort Inn South 26
Delta Winnipeg 13
The Fairmont Winnipeg 8
Gordon Downtowner 11
The Norwood 20
Place Louis Riel All-Suite Hotel 12
Radisson Hotel Winnipeg 10
Ramada Marlborough Winnipeg 10
DINING
Alycia's 5
Amici 17
Bistro Dansk 4
529 Wellington 3
Fusion Grill 3
Red Lantern 23
Restaurant Dubrovnik 19
River City Brewing Co. 25
Leila Ave.
KILDONAN PARK
Inkster Blvd.
Inkster Blvd.
McPhillips St.
Henderson Hwy.
Main St.
Redwood Ave.
Logan Ave.
Aboriginal Centre
EXCHANGE DISTRICT
Nairn Ave.
Manitoba Centennial Centre
Notre Dame Ave.
King Edward St.
Red River
Isabel St.
Maryland St.
Portage Ave.
Ellice Ave.
Sherbrook St.
Balmoral St.
St. Mary Ave.
Main St.
Provencher
Smith St.
Donald St.
York Ave.
Western Canada Aviation Museum
Portage Ave.
Broadway
Grant's Old Mill
Rue Tache
Rue Archibald
Lagimodiere Blvd.
Assiniboine Ave.
Osborne Village
Assiniboine River
Kenaston Blvd.
River Ave.
Red River
Marion St.
ASSINIBOINE PARK
Osborne
Corydon Ave.
Trans–Canada Hwy.
Grant Ave.
St. Anne's Rd.
Wilkes Ave.
0 1 mi
0 1 km

That's one side. The other is a city and populace that have produced a symphony orchestra that triumphed in New York, the first Royal ballet company in the British Commonwealth, and a theater-and-arts complex worthy of any national capital.

## ESSENTIALS

**GETTING THERE** **By plane** **Winnipeg International Airport** (✆ **204/987-9402;** www.ywg.com) is only about 20 minutes west-northwest of the city center (allow 30 to 40 min. in rush hours). You can get from the airport to downtown by taxi for C$12 to C$15 (US$7–US$9), or by city bus on **Winnipeg Transit** (✆ **204/986-5700;** www.winnipegtransit.com) for C$1.65 (US$1). Buses run to Portage and Garry about every 15 minutes during the day and every 22 minutes during the night.

**By train** The **VIA Rail** Canada depot is at 123 Main St., where it intersects Broadway (✆ **888/VIA-RAIL** or 800/561-8630 in Canada, 204/943-3578 in Winnipeg, or 800/561-3949 in the U.S.; www.viarail.ca).

**By car** If you're driving, Winnipeg is 697km (432 miles) from Minneapolis, Minnesota, and 235km (146 miles) from Grand Forks, North Dakota.

**VISITOR INFORMATION** Contact **Travel Manitoba,** 7-155 Carlton St., Dept. SV2, Winnipeg, MB R3C 3H8 (✆ **800/665-0040, ext. SV2** or 204/945-3777; www.travelmanitoba.com). You can also visit the **Explore Manitoba Centre** at 21 Forks Market Rd., open daily 10am to 6pm, year round. For specific Winnipeg information, contact **Tourism Winnipeg,** 279 Portage Ave., Winnipeg, MB R3B 2B4 (✆ **800/665-0204** or 204/943-1970; www.tourism.winnipeg.mb.ca), open Monday to Friday 8:30am to 4:30pm, or the **Tourism Winnipeg InfoCentre** at the Winnipeg International Airport (✆ **204/982-7543**), open daily 8am to 9:45pm.

**CITY LAYOUT** A native Winnipegger once said to me, "I still can't get used to the confined and narrow streets in the east." When you see Portage and Main, each 40m (132 ft.) wide (that's 9m/10 yd. off the width of a football field), and the eerie flatness that means no matter where you go, you can see where you're going, you'll understand why.

**The Forks**—the site of the original Winnipeg settlement, at the junction of the Red and Assiniboine rivers—is the city's focal point and hub. Just north of the Forks is the city's most famous corner, **Portage and Main**—known as the historic site of the 1919 General Strike, and today as the windiest corner in Canada. The Red River runs north-south, as does Main Street; the Assiniboine and Portage Avenue run east-west. Going north on Main from the Portage-Main junction will bring you to the City Hall, the Exchange District, the Manitoba Centennial Centre (including the Manitoba Theatre Centre), the Museum of Man and Nature, and on into the North End, once a mosaic of cultures and still dotted with bulbous Ukrainian church domes and authentic delis.

From Portage and Main, if you go 6 blocks west along Portage (a major shopping district) and 2 blocks south, you'll hit the Convention Centre. From here, going 1 block south and 2 blocks west brings you to the Legislative Building, the art gallery, and south, just across the Assiniboine River, Osborne Village.

**GETTING AROUND** For information, contact **City of Winnipeg Transit,** 421 Osborne St. (✆ **204/986-5700;** www.winnipegtransit.com). For regular buses, you need C$1.65 (US$1) in exact change (C$1.25/US85¢ for seniors/children) to board. Call for route and schedule info, or visit the information booth in the Portage and Main concourse, open Monday to Friday 8:30am to 4:30pm.

Car-rental companies in Winnipeg include **Avis,** at the airport, 234 York Ave., or 1350 King Edward St. (© 204/956-2847, 204/989-7521, or 204/956-2847); **Budget,** at the airport, 593 Ellice Ave., or 1355 Regent Ave. (© **800/268-8900** or 800/472-3355 in Canada); **Hertz,** at the airport, 276 Colony St., or 1577 Erin St. (© **204/925-6625,** 204/925-6600, or 204/925-6600; www.hertz.com); **National,** at the airport or at 5 in-town locations (© **204/925-3531** at the airport); and **Thrifty,** at the airport, 420 Kensington St., or 112 Garry St. (© **204/949-7608,** 204/949-7622, or 204/949-7620).

You can find taxis at the downtown hotels. They charge C$2.95 (US$1.80) when the meter drops and C10¢ (US5¢) every 8 seconds thereafter. Try **Duffy's Taxi** (© **204/772-2451** or 204/775-0101) or **Unicity Taxi** (© **204/925-3131**).

**SPECIAL EVENTS** The **Red River Exhibition,** 3977 Portage Ave., Winnipeg, MB R3K 2ES (© **204/888-6990;** www.redriverex.com), usually starting the third week of June, celebrates the city's history, showcasing agricultural, horticultural, commercial, and industrial achievements. There are also a midway, a photography show, and other themed features like a lumberjack show.

The **Winnipeg Folk Festival,** 264 Taché Ave., Winnipeg, MB R2H 1Z9 (© **204/231-0096;** www.wpgfolkfest.com), held over the first weekend of July, is the oldest and one of the largest folk music festivals in the world. Over 85 acts perform on five daytime stages and one main stage each evening.

**Folklorama,** a Festival of Nations, is a 2-week cultural festival in August featuring more than 35 pavilions celebrating ethnic culture, with traditional food, dancing, music, costumes, entertainment, and crafts. It attracts more than 400,000 guests yearly. For more information, contact the Folk Arts Council of Winnipeg, 2nd Fl., 183 Kennedy St., Winnipeg, MB R3C 1S6 (© **800/665-0234** or 204/982-6210; www.folklorama.ca).

The 10-day **Festival du Voyageur,** Le Rendez-Vous at 768 Taché Ave., Winnipeg, MB R2H 2C4 (© **204/237-7692;** www.festivalvoyageur.mb.ca), held in mid-February in St. Boniface, celebrates the adventures of the original French *voyageurs,* or fur traders, the first Europeans to settle in Canada; as well as French Métis culture.

Film buffs may want to check out the National Screen Institute of Canada's **FilmExchange** film festival, running for over a week from late February into early March. Screening only Canadian films, this festival is striving to become what the Sundance festival is for the U.S. For more information, contact the **National Screen Institute—Canada,** 206–70 Arthur St., Winnipeg, Manitoba R3B 1G7 (© **204/956-7800;** www.nsi-canada.com).

Between late November and early January, you might be drawn to see the spectacle of **Canad Inns' Winter Wonderland** (© **204/888-6990**), a drive-through Christmas- and winter-themed light show at Red River Exhibition Park; on Portage Avenue west of the Perimeter Highway, next to the Assiniboia Downs Race Track.

## EXPLORING THE CITY

### THE TOP ATTRACTIONS

At the junction of the Red and Assiniboine rivers, the **Forks Market Area** (© **204/957-7618;** www.theforks.com), is a major attraction created in the late

1980s when the old rail yard was redeveloped. A major draw is the market—a wonderful display of fresh produce and specialty foods. There are also restaurants and specialty stores, with programs, exhibits, and events scheduled throughout the year. Other attractions include the **Forks National Historic Site,** which hosts interpretive walking tours; **Oodena Celebration Circle,** a shallow, bowl-like platform surrounded by a set of astronomically arranged monoliths, commemorating the region's First Nations people; and **Festival Park Stage,** the site of summer concerts. In summer, you can stroll on the river walks along the Red and Assiniboine rivers; in winter, there's free public skating on outdoor artificial ice or along groomed river trails. From the Forks National Historic site you get a view across to St. Boniface, where all kinds of special events and interpretive programs are held. It's also a great place for a picnic. The **Manitoba Children's Museum** (✆ **204/924-4000**) and the new **Manitoba Theatre for Young People** (✆ **204/947-0394**) are both here at the Forks as well. Fun **Splash Dash Water Buses** (✆ **204/783-6633**) link the forks to The Exchange District, St. Boniface, and Osborne Village.

The **Exchange District,** close to the famous corner of Portage and Main, is the best-preserved turn-of-the-20th-century district in North America. Now a national historic site, the area encompasses over 30 city blocks, featuring unparalleled examples of terra-cotta and cut-stone architecture. In recent years, the area has been in great demand as a backdrop for movie production by filmmakers from across the continent. The Exchange District is also home to two of Winnipeg's best art galleries: the **Plug In Gallery,** 286 McDermott Ave. (✆ **204/942-1043;** www.plugin.org), and the **<SITE> Gallery,** 2nd Fl., 55 Arthur St. (✆ **204/942-1618;** www.mts.net/~site). For more information on things to do and places to go in the Exchange District, see the **Exchange District Business Improvement Zone** (BIZ) website at www.exchangebiz.winnipeg.mb.ca.

The BIZ also offers guided walking tours of historic sites in the Exchange District—including the interiors of some buildings—from the end of the Victoria Day weekend through Labour Day, weather permitting. Tours begin at the Exchange District Info Centre in Old Market Square (King St. and Bannatyne Ave.), Tuesday to Sunday at 11am and 2pm, lasting roughly 1½ to 2 hours each. The cost is C$5 (US$3.10) for adults, C$4 (US$2.50) for seniors, C$3 (US$1.85) for youths up to 17, or C$10 (US$6) for families. For more information contact the Exchange District BIZ at ✆ **204/942-6716.** In addition, for C$2 (US$1.20) you can obtain a self-guided walking tour brochure, the "Illustrated Guide to Winnipeg's Exchange District," from **Heritage Winnipeg,** Suite 509 63 Albert St. Winnipeg, MB R3B 1G4 (✆ **204/942-2663;** www.escape.ca/heritage).

**Manitoba Museum of Man and Nature** ★ *Kids* This museum is a fascinating place, with galleries depicting local history, culture, and geology through life-size exhibits like a buffalo hunt, prehistoric creatures, pioneer life, pronghorn antelope, teepees, sod huts, and log cabins. In the Urban Gallery, you can walk down a 1920s Winnipeg street past typical homes and businesses of the era. The Boreal Forest Gallery depicts Manitoba's most northerly forested region. You can climb aboard the Nonsuch, a full-size replica of the 17th-century ketch that returned to England in 1669 with the first cargo of furs out of Hudson Bay. A new wing housing the collection of the Hudson's Bay Company Gallery—over 10,000 artifacts and artworks from a private archive the company began amassing in 1920—has also recently opened to the public.

In the Manitoba Centennial Centre, 190 Rupert Ave. ✆ **204/956-2830** or 204/943-3139 for recorded info. www.manitobamuseum.mb.ca. Admission C$6.50 (US$4) adults; C$4 (US$2.50) seniors, students, and youths 3–17; C$20 (US$12) families. AE, MC, V. Victoria Day–Labour Day daily 10am–6pm; the rest of the year Tues–Fri 10am–4pm, Sat–Sun and holidays 10am–5pm.

**Manitoba Planetarium & Science Gallery** *Kids* The planetarium, part of the Manitoba Museum of Man and Nature (above), offers shows in its 280-seat Star Theatre exploring everything from cosmic catastrophes to the reality of UFOs. The Science Gallery is a hands-on science gallery containing close to 100 interactive exhibits explaining a gamut of phenomena in all realms of science.

In the Manitoba Centennial Centre, 190 Rupert Ave. ✆ **204/943-2830** or 204/956-3139 for recorded info. www.manitobamuseum.mb.ca. Planetarium or Science Gallery C$5 (US$3.10) adults; C$4 (US$2.50) seniors, students, and youths 3–17; C$15 (US$9) families; free for children under 3. AE, MC, V. Planetarium shows daily mid-May to Labour Day; Sat–Sun and holidays the rest of the year; call for show times. Science Gallery, Victoria Day–Labour Day daily 10am–6pm; rest of the year Tues–Fri 10am–4pm, Sat–Sun and holidays 10am–5pm.

**Royal Canadian Mint** A producer of currency for countries worldwide, one in four people in the world carry coins made in Winnipeg's mint. The process of making money is mind-boggling, and the tour offered here will prove it to you. Dies are produced; a roof crane lifts 1818kg (4,000-pound) strips of bronze and nickel; three 150-ton presses stamp out up to 8,800 coin blanks per minute; and coining presses turn out up to 18,000 coins per hour to the telling machines that count the number for bagging. The whole process from start to finish represents an extraordinary engineering feat streamlined by conveyor belts and an overhead monorail.

520 Lagimodière Blvd. ✆ **204/983-6429.** www.rcmint.ca. Admission C$2 (US$1.20) adults, C$8 (US$5) families, free for children under 6. Tours given regularly during listed hours, or by appointment. Spring and summer Mon–Fri 9am–5pm plus June–Aug Sat 10am–2pm; Fall and winter Mon–Fri 10am–2pm. Take Main St. south over the Assiniboine/Red rivers, turn left onto Marion St., and then right onto Lagimodière. You'll see the mint rise up just beyond the Trans-Canada Hwy. (Rte. 135).

**Ukrainian Cultural & Educational Centre (Oseredok)** The Oseredok, or Ukrainian Centre, one of the largest such institutions in North America, conserves the artifacts and heritage of the Ukrainian people. The art gallery and museum feature changing exhibits on such subjects as 18th-century icons, embroidery, weaving, painted eggs, wood carving, ceramics, clothing, and other folk arts. The gift shop stocks traditional and contemporary folk Arts and Crafts. There's also an extensive library, and guided tours of the museum are available on request.

184 Alexander Ave. E. (at the corner of Main and the Disraeli Freeway). ✆ **204/942-0218.** www.oseredok.org. Donations requested. Mon–Sun 10am–4pm.

**Winnipeg Art Gallery** ★★ A distinctive triangular building of local Tyndall stone, the Winnipeg Art Gallery houses one of the world's largest collections of contemporary Inuit art—a treasure house that includes wry works like Leah Qumaluk Povungnituk's Birds Stealing Kayak from Man. Other collections focus on historic and contemporary Canadian art, as well as British and European artists. The decorative art collections feature works by Canadian silversmiths and studio potters, while the photography collection contains more than 200 works by Andre Kertesz and represents other 20th-century photographers, like Diane Arbus and Irving Penn. You'll always find a number of interesting rotating exhibits on display, as well. The penthouse restaurant overlooks the fountain and flowers in the sculpture court.

## A Taste of France Across the River: The Historic District of St. Boniface

Across the river in **St. Boniface,** a street becomes a *rue* and a hello becomes *bonjour.* Here you'll find the largest French-speaking community in western Canada, dating from 1783, when Pierre Gaultier de Varennes established Fort Rouge at the junction of the Red and Assiniboine rivers. The junction became the center of a thriving fur trade for the North West Company, which rivaled and challenged the Hudson's Bay Company. A basilica built in 1819 was dedicated to Boniface, and in 1846, four Grey Nuns arrived and began their ministry.

The original basilica was replaced in 1908 by a beautiful church that was subsequently destroyed by a fire in 1968. The massive Gothic arches remain, and cradled within the shell of the old building is the new basilica, built in 1972. In front of the cathedral, the cemetery is the resting place of Louis Riel, whose grave is marked by a replica of a Red River cart. Riel, leader of the Métis uprising and president of the provincial government formed from 1869 to 1870, tried to prevent the transfer of the Red River settlement to Canada. For walking tours of St. Boniface—including the summer-only "In Riel's Footsteps," a 45-minute theatrical tour of the cemetery, with actors playing the roles of some of Manitoba's most interesting and noteworthy historical characters—contact the Economic Development Council for Manitoba Bilingual Municipalities' **Riel Tourism Bureau** (✆ **866/808-8338;** www.cdem.com/tourisme/en).

300 Memorial Blvd. ✆ **204/786-6641.** www.wag.mb.ca. Admission C$6 (US$3.70) adults, C$4 (US$2.50) students and seniors, C$3 (US$1.85) youths 6–12, C$15 (US$9) families; free or by donation Wed 5–9pm, all day Sat, and always free for children under 6. Late June–Labour Day Thurs–Tues 10am–5pm, Wed 10am–9pm. After Labour Day–late June Tues and Thurs–Sun 11am–5pm, Wed 11am–9pm.

## MORE ATTRACTIONS

**Commodity Exchange** Organized in 1887 as a grain exchange, the Commodity Exchange is the only exchange in Canada that trades in agricultural commodities. Once this was the heart and soul of Winnipeg: the world's premier grain market until World War II. Today it has about 240 members and 77 companies registered for trading privileges. It's best to come around 9:30am or right near closing at 12:55pm, when you're more likely to see some feverish action on the floor.

On the 4th floor of the Commodity Exchange Tower, 400–360 Main St. ✆ **204/925-5000.** www.wce.mb.ca. Viewing gallery open Mon–Fri 9:30am–1:15pm. Tours for groups at 9:10am and 12:50pm daily, but call ahead to arrange.

**Dalnavert Museum** Just 2 blocks east of the Legislative Building (see below) stands the Victorian home built in 1895 for Hugh John Macdonald, the only son of Canada's first prime minister. It's a fine example of a late-Victorian gingerbread house with a wraparound veranda and the latest innovations of the time—electric lighting, indoor plumbing, central hot-water heating, and walk-in closets—opulently decorated and full of heirloom objects.

61 Carlton St. (between Broadway and Assiniboine Ave.). ✆ **204/943-2835.** www.mhs.mb.ca. Admission C$4 (US$2.50) adults, C$3 (US$1.80) seniors, C$2 (US$1.20) ages 6–18, C$8 (US$5) families; children under 6 free. V. June–Aug Tues–Thurs and Sat–Sun 10am–5pm; Sept–Dec and Mar–May Tues–Thurs and Sat–Sun noon–4pm; Jan–Feb Sat–Sun noon–4pm.

**Fort Whyte Centre** About 15 minutes from downtown, some old cement quarries have been converted into lakes at Fort Whyte Centre and now serve as a feature-packed environmental educational facility. A large interpretive center houses Manitoba's largest indoor aquarium, which displays local freshwater species such as the northern pike and walleye. Outside you can view a herd of 25 bison on a 28ha (70-acre) prairie field, and as of 2002 a prairie dog town will be on view. There are also self-guided nature trails, bike paths, waterfowl gardens, a new restaurant, and a gift shop.

1961 McCreary Rd., Fort Whyte. ✆ **204/989-8355.** or 204/989-8350 for recorded info. www.fortwhyte.org. Admission C$5 (US$3.10) adults, C$4 (US$2.50) seniors, C$3 (US$1.85) students and children over 3. MC, V. Mon–Fri 9am–5pm, Sat–Sun 10am–5pm. Extended evening hours June–Oct.

**The Golden Boy & Manitoba Legislative Building** There he stands, 73m (240 ft.) above ground atop the Legislative Building's dome, clutching a sheaf of wheat under his left arm and holding aloft in his right an eternally lit torch symbolizing the spirit of progress. French sculptor Charles Gardet created his 5-ton, 4m (13½-ft.) bronze statue during World War I. The building, a magnificent classical Greek structure, was designed in 1919 by British architect Frank Worthington Simon. The building's focal point is, of course, the Legislative Chamber, where the 57 members of Manitoba's legislative assembly meet.

450 Broadway. ✆ **204/945-5813.** July–Labour Day free tours given hourly Mon–Sun 9am–6pm; by reservation at other times for groups of 10 or more. Self-guided tours year round, daily 8am–8pm. Two-hour visitor parking on grounds; on bus line.

**Western Canada Aviation Museum** *Kids* Among the numerous historic flying treasures at the Western Canada Aviation Museum is Canada's first helicopter, designed and test-flown between 1935 and 1939. There's also a plane flight simulator, and portions of a new Spaceways exhibit, including a space flight simulator, are currently being opened to the public. The children's Skyways interactive area—where kids can learn about the physics of aeronautics—is also popular.

958 Ferry Rd. ✆ **204/786-5503.** www.wcam.mb.ca. Admission C$3 (US$1.85) adults, C$2 (US$1.20) students 3–17. Mon–Sat 10am–4pm, Sun 1–4pm. Closed Dec 25–26, Jan 1, and Good Friday.

## PARKS & GARDENS

Comprising 160ha (393 acres) for playing, picnicking, or biking, **Assiniboine Park,** at 2355 Corydon Ave., contains a miniature railway, a duck pond, an English garden (which opens in June), and a conservatory. In winter you can go skating on the pond or tobogganing. The park also contains a 40ha (98-acre) zoological park (see "Especially for Kids," below). Art lovers will also want to visit the **Leo Mol Sculpture Garden** (✆ **204/986-6531**) to see his works and visit the **Leo Mol Schoolhouse Studio.** The park is open daily dawn to dusk. The elegant new **Tavern in the Park** (✆ **204/896-7275**) offers lunch 11:30am to 2:30pm (C$8–C$14/US$5–US$9) and dinner 5 to 9:30pm (C$16–C$37/US$10–US$23), Tuesday to Sunday. Reservations suggested. The free **Pavilion Gallery** (✆ **204/888-5466**) houses a permanent collection of works by three Manitoba artists. And the new outdoor **Lyric Theatre** (✆ **204/888-5466 ext.5**) provides free entertainment in summer with performances by the Winnipeg Symphony, The Royal Winnipeg Ballet, local jazz combos, and so on. In late August, this theater hosts the **Winnie the Pooh Festival**—the famous A.A. Milne character was inspired by a local bear named Winnipeg, brought to London during World War I as a military mascot.

**Kildonan Park** is quite delightful, with landscaped gardens, picnic spots, biking paths, outdoor swimming, and wading pools, as well as a restaurant and dining room overlooking a small artificial lake. Also look for the Witch's House from *Hansel and Gretel* in the park. Rainbow Stages musicals are performed here in July and August.

## CRUISES & A STEAM-TRAIN EXCURSION

During summer, the cruise ships **MS *River Rouge*** and **MS *Paddlewheel Queen*** depart from their dock at Water and Gilroy at the foot of the Provencher Bridge on a variety of cruises, including a sunset dinner-dance cruise beginning at 7pm and a moonlight version on weekends leaving at 10pm. Both cost C$13.75 (US$9) for adults. The sunset cruise costs C$12.15 (US$8) for seniors and C$7.50 (US$4.65) for children under 12. Two-hour sightseeing trips costing C$12.75 (US$8) for adults, C$11.20 (US$7) for seniors, and C$7 (US$4.35) for children under 12, depart at 1pm and provide fine views of the city from the Red and Assiniboine rivers. Fares cover the cruises only; drinks and meals are extra. The company also offers day-long tours to Lower Fort Garry. For details, contact **Paddlewheel River Rouge Tours,** P.O. Box 3930, Postal Station B, Winnipeg, MB R2W 5H9 (**© 204/942-4500;** www.paddlewheelcruises.com).

A 1900 steam-era train, the ***Prairie Dog Central,*** takes you on a 2½-hour, 58km (36-mile) round-trip from Winnipeg north on the Oak Point line. En route you really get a feel for the prairie and what the late 19th-century immigrants might've seen when they arrived. The train operates Saturdays—plus Sundays in July and August—and holiday Mondays, late May to September. A newer engine is used on Saturday runs during July and August. Admission is C$18 (US$11) for adults, C$15 (US$9) for seniors and youths ages 12 to 17, and C$10 (US$6) for children ages 2 to 11. For details, contact the **Vintage Locomotive Society** (**© 204/832-5259;** www.vintagelocomotivesociety.mb.ca). You can also call **© 204/780-SEAT** to purchase tickets in advance.

## ESPECIALLY FOR KIDS

At the Forks, there's a **Children's Museum** (**© 204/956-1888;** www.childrensmuseum.com), specially designed with participatory exhibits for 2- to 13-year-olds. There are several themed galleries, including Under the Big Top, where kids can run away to the circus and devise a show of their very own; and the TV studio, where they can create their own television shows, as performers or as technicians. Admission is C$4.50 (US$2.80) for adults, C$4 (US$2.50) for seniors, C$4.95 (US$3.05) for children ages 2 to 17, and free for children under 2. September to June the museum is open Monday to Wednesday from 9am to 4:30pm; Thursday and Friday 9am to 8pm; Saturday 10am to 8pm; and Sunday 10am to 5pm. In July and August, it's open Monday to Saturday from 10am to 8pm and Sunday or holidays from 10am to 6pm. Call for other holiday hours. The museum's closed for four days following Labour Day, Christmas and the following two days, and Easter Sunday.

**Assiniboine Park,** 2355 Corydon Ave., is a great place to picnic or play. Its top attraction, however, is the 40ha (98-acre) **zoo** (**© 204/986-2327;** www.zoosociety.com) where the animals—including bears, tigers, zebras, flamingos, bison, elk, and deer—are kept in as natural an environment as possible. Some exotic species on display are snow leopards, ruffed lemurs, and Irkutsk lynx.

Many spectacular birds live and breed in the Tropical House. A special Discovery Centre with a barnful of young farm animals is fun. March to October, admission is C$3 (US$1.85) for adults, C$2.75 (US$1.70) for seniors, C$1.50 (US95¢) for youths ages 13 to 17, and C$1 (US60¢) for children ages 2 to 12; November to February, it's C$1 (US60¢) for everyone. The park is open daily dawn to dusk with the zoo open daily 10am to dusk. To get there, take Portage Avenue west, exit onto Route 90 south, and then turn right onto Corydon.

**Darkzone,** 230 Osborne St. (✆ **204/287-8710;** www.darkzonewinnipeg.ca), is the hippest game at the moment for kids and adults—an advanced laser game in which as many as 30 players and three teams compete against one another in trying to deactivate the opposing players and their bases using a phaser and computerized vest. It's open Monday to Thursday from 4 to 11pm, Friday from 4pm to midnight, Saturday from 10am to midnight, and Sunday from noon to 10pm. Admission is C$6 (US$3.90) for one game or C$15 (US$10) for three games.

Kids love the thrills at **Fun Mountain Water Slide Park,** 6km (3¾ miles) east of the mint on Highway 1 East at Murdock Rd. (✆ **204/255-3910**). There are 10 slides, as well as rides, including bumper boats, a giant hot tub, and a kids' playground with a wading pool. All-day admission is C$12 (US$7) for adults, C$6 (US$3.70) for seniors, and C$9.50 (US$6) for children ages 3 to 12, and free for children under 3. It's open in June daily from 10am to 6pm, and July to August daily from 10am to 8pm, weather permitting.

The **Manitoba Theatre for Young People,** in the CanWest Global Performing Arts Centre at Forks Market (✆ **204/947-0394** or 204/942-8898 for the box office; www.mtyp.ca), presents plays for children and teens. The season runs October to May, and tickets are C$10 to $12 (US$6–US$7).

### SHOPPING AND ROAMING

Several areas in Winnipeg are known for their shops, galleries, and cafes; and make good destinations for those spending a few days in town, to get a better feel for the city and its diversity. Broken down by interest to specific demographic groups, these areas are: **Academy Road,** trending toward upscale shops and appealing to a middle-age and older crowd; **Corydon Avenue,** or Little Italy, known for its restaurants as well as plenty of boutiques, second-hand and curio shops, and galleries; **Osborne Village,** on Osborne Street, the city's most densely populated area, catering to the young and fashion-minded; the **Exchange District,** as described above, the most historic part of town, with many shops, galleries, restaurants, and clubs; the **Wolseley** area (a.k.a., the "Granola Belt"), particularly along Westminster Avenue, with shops catering to ecological and spiritual interests, plus bakeries and cafes; and **Chinatown,** between James and Logan avenues west of Main St., where you can find excellent restaurants, visit herbalists and import shops, and view some beautiful architecture.

## WHERE TO STAY

### EXPENSIVE

**Delta Winnipeg** ★ The massive 17-story Delta Winnipeg, right downtown, is connected by a skywalk to the Convention Centre and is right next to the Portage Place shopping center. The pleasantly decorated guest rooms feature the usual amenities. Poolside rooms are a couple of dollars more than standard rooms, while club-floor rooms include such extras as breakfast and evening hors d'oeuvres, overnight shoeshine, in-room trouser presses, and heated tiles in the bathrooms. The Elephant and Castle pub is for all-day dining, as well as billiards, and the Blaze Bistro and Lounge offers fine contemporary cuisine.

Winnipeg Downtown. 350 St. Mary's Ave., Winnipeg, MB R3C 3J2. ✆ **800/268-1133** or 204/942-0551. Fax 204/943-8702. www.deltahotels.com. 393 units. C$89–$229 (US$55–$142) double. Children under 18 stay free in parents' room. AE, DC, DISC, MC, V. Heated self-parking C$9 (US$6), valet parking C$14 (US$9). **Amenities:** Restaurant, bar, lounge; indoor, outdoor, children's pools; fitness center; Jacuzzi; sauna; concierge, tour and activities desk, business center; 24-hour room service; in-room massage; children's center; babysitting; laundry service; same-day dry cleaning; nonsmoking rooms; executive-level rooms. *In room:* A/C, TV, dataport, minibar, coffeemaker, hair dryer, iron, safe.

**The Fairmont Winnipeg** ★ At the corner of Portage and Main rises the white concrete Fairmont, a few minutes' walk from the Manitoba Centennial Centre. Its rooms are furnished with white colonial-style pieces and the usual amenities. Extras such as complimentary robes, mini fridges, and dataports are available in some rooms by request; and more expensive rooms add such niceties as a Jacuzzi, gas fireplace, and even a baby grand piano. The hotel has recently undertaken a major renovation to upscale all rooms on select floors and to add private access and club privileges. Wheelchair accessible rooms are also available. The Velvet Glove features luxurious dining amid gilt-framed portraits, wood paneling, and brass torchières. You might choose an entree such as pepper-roasted wild boar with apple-turnip compote or roast cedar-plank salmon and onion marmalade. Prices are C$16 to C$25 (US$10–US$16). If you want that C$100-plus (US$62-plus) bottle of wine, it's available. The self-serve Cafe Express offers deli sandwiches and hot specials.

Two Lombard Pl., Winnipeg, MB R3B 0Y3. ✆ **800/441-1414** or 204/957-1350. Fax 204/949-1486. www.cphotels.ca. 340 units. C$$139–159 (US$86–$99) double. Weekend packages available. AE, DC, DISC, MC, V. Self-parking C$12.50 (US$8), valet parking C$18 (US$11). Small pets allowed, add C$25 (US$16). **Amenities:** Restaurant, lounge; indoor pool; fitness center; Jacuzzi; sauna; concierge; business center; shopping arcade; 24-hour room service; babysitting; laundry service; same-day dry cleaning; executive-level rooms. *In room:* A/C, TV w/pay movies, minibar, coffeemaker, hair dryer, iron.

**Place Louis Riel All-Suite Hotel** ★ *Kids* In the heart of downtown is a friendly, all-suite hotel with excellent, personalized service. Here you can stay in a studio (with a sleeping/living area partitioned from the kitchen) or a beautifully furnished one- or two-bedroom suite. Units on the hotel's premier floor add extra amenities, including free local calls and cordless phones, CD stereos, and pillowtop mattresses and down comforters on the beds. For convenience, a laundromat, grocery store, and restaurant and lounge are on the ground floor. Wheelchair accessible suites are available, and this is a pet- and kid-friendly hotel.

190 Smith St. (at St. Mary's Ave.), Winnipeg, MB R3C 1J8. ✆ **800/665-0569** or 204/947-6961. Fax 204/947-3029. www.placelouisriel.com. 287 units. C$146–C$176 (US$91–US$109) double; $220–$240 (US$136–$149) for premier floor double. Extra person C$10 (US$6). Children under 17 stay free in parents' room. Weekend rates, senior and AAA discounts available. AE, DC, MC, V. Pets allowed with waiver. Parking C$6 (US$3.70). **Amenities:** Restaurant, bar; exercise room; tour and activities desk; room service (6:30am–10:30pm); coin-op laundry; laundry service; same-day dry cleaning; nonsmoking rooms; executive-level rooms. *In room:* A/C, TV w/pay movies, dataport; kitchen, fridge, coffeemaker, hair dryer, iron.

**Radisson Hotel Winnipeg** Guest rooms occupy floors 15 to 29. All offer good views of the city and are well equipped. The hotel is right next door to a promenade accessing the shops in Portage Place mall. A business lounge is on the P-level. The oak-paneled candlelit Peak Bistro offers fine dining and piano entertainment, and in the lounge you can watch sports events on a big-screen TV. There's also a newsstand and coffee bar.

288 Portage Ave. (at Smith St.), Winnipeg, MB R3C 0B8. ✆ **800/333-3333** or 204/956-0410. Fax 204/947-1129. www.radisson.com/winnipegca. 272 units. Weekdays C$129–$244 (US$80–$151) double. Weekend packages available. AE, DC, DISC, MC, V. Self- or valet-parking, maximum C$9.75 (US$6) per day. **Amenities:** Restaurant, lounge; indoor pool; golf course nearby; exercise room; Jacuzzi; sauna; concierge; tour and activities desk; business center; 24-hour room service; children's center; babysitting; laundry service; same-day dry cleaning; nonsmoking rooms; executive-level rooms. *In room:* A/C, TV, dataport, coffeemaker, hair dryer, iron.

## MODERATE

In addition to the following choices, you may want to look at any of 7 newer **Canad Inns** (✆ **888/33-CANAD;** www.canadinns.com) hotels, locally owned and operated by the Canad Corporation, which also operates many clubs, casinos, and even a record label in town. Many of these places tend toward a Las Vegas-like atmosphere, with casinos in the lobbies and theme rooms and common areas. If that's your style, the hotels are reasonably affordable, very new, and offer plenty of amenities.

**Charter House** A block from the Convention Centre, the Charter House offers attractively decorated guest rooms. The top-floor rooms are designed for business travelers, featuring ergonomically designed furniture. The other rooms have modern amenities like voice mail, and about half have balconies. The Rib Room is well-known locally for good prime rib, steaks, and seafood, with main courses at C$13 to C$24 (US$8–US$15). Wheelchair accessible rooms are available.

York Ave. and Hargrave St., Winnipeg, MB R3C 0N9. ✆ **800/782-0175** or 204/942-0101. Fax 204/956-0665. 91 units. C$89–C$109 (US$55–US$68) double. Extra person C$10 (US$6). Children under 16 stay free in parents' room. Weekend rates, senior and AAA discounts available. AE, DC, DISC, MC, V. Free parking. Pets allowed. **Amenities:** 2 restaurants; outdoor pool; exercise room; tour and activities desk; room service (7am–11pm); laundry service; same-day dry cleaning; nonsmoking rooms; executive-level rooms. *In room:* A/C, TV, dataport, coffeemaker, hair dryer, iron.

**Ramada Marlborough Winnipeg** This isn't your average Ramada. Built in 1914, the Marlborough retains its vaulted ceilings, stained-glass windows, and Victorian Gothic exterior but now offers all the modern amenities, including a fine-dining room, Victor's. There is also a club with live entertainment on weekends. The recently renovated rooms feature tasteful decor that maintain the period charm of the building while offering every modern comfort. If you're looking for extra space, ask for one of the Club Rooms, which are somewhat larger. The Marlborough offers a free shuttle to and from the airport, and wheelchair accessible rooms are available.

331 Smith St. (at Portage), Winnipeg, MB R3B 2G9. ✆ **800/272-6232** or 204/942-6411. Fax 204/942-2017. www.ramada.ca/winnmarl. 148 units. C$135–$150 (US$84–$93) double. Children under 18 stay free in parents' room. Special weekend rates, and senior and AAA discounts available. AE, DC, DISC, MC, V. Pets allowed. Free parking. **Amenities:** 2 restaurants, lounge; exercise room; courtesy limo; room service (7am–11pm); coin-op laundry; laundry service; dry cleaning; nonsmoking rooms; executive-level rooms. *In room:* A/C, TV, dataport, coffeemaker.

## INEXPENSIVE

For reliable, clean, and attractively decorated rooms, the **Comfort Inn South,** 3109 Pembina Highway (✆ **204/269-7390**), is hard to beat. Doubles are C$83 to C$96 (US$51–US$60). Local phone calls are free. Probably the best budget hotel downtown is the **Gordon Downtowner** at 330 Kennedy St. (✆ **204/943-5581;** www.curtis.mb.ca/downtown.html), right by the Portage Place shopping center. It's a basic motor inn, but the guest rooms (C$80–$83/

US$50–$51 for a double) are recently renovated and boast touches like extra phones in the bathrooms. Amenities include a pub and a comfortable restaurant (open 7am–8pm).

**The Norwood** Although you can't tell by looking this large, modern building near the Forks district and St. Boniface, the Norwood is Manitoba's oldest family-owned and -operated hotel, dating back to 1885. Bearing no resemblance to its original wooden structure, this is a comfortable and clean hotel with plenty of standard amenities in even its basic rooms. Executive suites add full living rooms and refrigerators. For dining, you can choose between the Jolly Friar restaurant and the Wood Tavern & Grill pub. Another historical distinction for the Norwood: It opened the first self-serve beer store in Canada in 1982, setting a national standard by using the deceptively simple name "Beer Store." Wheelchair accessible rooms are available.

112 Marion St. (at Ave. Taché), Winnipeg MB R2H 0T1. ✆ **888/888-1878** or 204/233-4475. Fax 204/231-1910. www.norwood-hotel.com. 52 units. C$88–$115 (US$55–$71) double. Senior and AAA discounts available. AE, DC, MC, V. **Amenities:** Restaurant, bar; room service (7am–9pm); same-day dry cleaning; nonsmoking rooms; executive-level rooms. *In room:* A/C, TV, dataport, coffeemaker, hair dryer, iron.

## WHERE TO DINE

An excellent place to go looking for a good Mediterranean restaurant (or a funky bar or eclectic shopping) is along **Corydon Avenue,** south of downtown across the Assiniboine River. Known as **Little Italy,** the area was settled by Italian immigrants and still has a strong continental feel, with lots of cafes and streetside restaurants.

### EXPENSIVE

**Amici** ★★ CONTINENTAL/ITALIAN The atmosphere is plush and comfortable and the northern Italian cuisine is tops in the city. You have your choice of 12 or more pastas, with selections like fettuccini alla boscaiola (with wild mushrooms, veal, and lingonberries) and spaghetti alla carbonara. Or you can have such richly flavored meat and fish dishes as venison with wild mushrooms and potato gnocchi, lamb loin with spinach and mushrooms wrapped in puff pastry, medallions of beef with Barolo wine sauce, and sea bass in saffron broth with Mediterranean vegetables. The menu changes regularly, but the ingredients are always fresh and the preparations top notch. For a casual drink and light meal, Amici is also home to Bombolini's wine bar, downstairs.

326 Broadway Ave. ✆ **204/943-4997.** www.amiciwpg.com. Reservations recommended. Main courses C$16–C$38 (US$10–US$24). AE, DC, MC, V. Mon–Fri 11:30am–2pm; Mon–Sat 5–11pm.

**529 Wellington** ★ STEAKS/SEAFOOD Situated in a lushly renovated, grand old stone-faced mansion—once home to the family of Winnipeg businessman and mayor, J.H. Ashdown—the 529 serves up a wide array of excellently prepared meat and seafood dishes in an elegant setting. Worthy starters include maple-smoked Steelhead salmon; seared marinated tuna with olive vinaigrette; and a salad of fire-roasted peppers with shaved garlic, herbs, and chèvre. You can choose among many cuts and preparations of choice-graded Canadian beef. Or you might go for any of a number of fresh seafood choices, ranging from Atlantic salmon or lobster to sushi-grade Ahi tuna. Half of the extensive list of vegetable sides consists of potatoes, and though all must be ordered a la carte, the portions are ample—consider sharing. After your meat and potatoes, you might as well finish off boldly, maybe choosing a warm blueberry bread pudding with caramel cream or a dark chocolate raspberry cheesecake. To top things off, the wine list features about 400 selections.

529 Wellington Crescent. ✆ **204/487-8325.** Reservations recommended. Main courses C$28–$44 (US$17–$27). Thurs–Fri 11:30am–2pm and daily starting at 5pm. Take Broadway/Hwy. 1 west, then go left/south on Maryland St., cross the Assiniboine, and turn left on Wellington Crescent.

**Restaurant Dubrovnik** ★ CONTINENTAL Dubrovnik offers a romantic setting for fine continental cuisine and Eastern European specialties. It occupies a beautiful Victorian brick town house with working fireplaces, leaded-glass windows, and an enclosed veranda. Each dining area is decorated tastefully with a few plants and colorful gusle (beautifully carved musical instruments, often inlaid with mother-of-pearl). Start with the traditional Russian borscht, wild-game paté, or fois gras sautéed and served in port wine. Then follow with the chicken breast stuffed with wild rice and shrimp in a beurre blanc sauce, muscovy duck with wild honey sauce, or Atlantic salmon baked in a cashew nut crust. Game lovers can also choose preparations of caribou, venison, and wild boar. Finish with a coffee Dubrovnik (sljivovica, kruskovac bitters, coffee, whipped cream, and chopped walnuts).

390 Assiniboine Ave. ✆ **204/944-0594.** Reservations recommended. Main courses C$19–C$40 (US$12–US$25). AE, MC, V. Mon–Fri 11am–2pm; Mon–Sat 5–11pm.

### MODERATE

**Bistro Dansk** ★ DANISH In this warm chalet-style bistro, bright-red gate-back chairs complement the wooden tables and raffia place mats. Main courses include seven superlative Danish specialties, such as *frikadeller* (Danish meat patties, made from ground veal and pork, served with red cabbage and potato salad), and *aeggekage* (a Danish omelette with bacon, garnished with tomatoes and green onions, served with home-baked Danish bread). At lunch, specialties include nine or so open-face sandwiches, served on homemade rye or white bread, most at C$3 to C$7 (US$1.85–US$4.35).

63 Sherbrook St. (near Wolseley Ave.). ✆ **204/775-5662.** Reservations recommended. Main courses C$8–C$14 (US$5–US$9). AE, V. Mon–Sat 11am–3pm; Tues–Sat 5–9:30pm.

**Fusion Grill** ★ INTERNATIONAL/CANADIAN A hip and fun place serving up some of Winnipeg's best non-traditional cuisine. Begin by getting into a different mindset with the "Soup of Tomorrow," featured daily. Then the fusion experience begins. The menu changes daily, but some sample items follow. Tantalizing starters might include a barley risotto with Danish blue cheese and duck jus lie; Québec quail stuffed with ostrich, apricot, and filberts on a blueberry Cumberland sauce; or grilled jumbo prawns with jalapeno lime butter and white bean humous. Entrees continue the trend with such possible choices as grilled Manitoba beef tenderloin with wild-rice risotto cake and a wild mushroom mussel ragout; potato crusted pickerel filets with cumin, tomatillo salsa, and roasted red pepper coulis; or a grilled, grain-fed veal chop with fresh porcini mushrooms and pinot noir reduction. The Fusion has an award-winning wine list.

550 Academy Rd. (near Lanark St.). ✆ **204/489-6963.** www.fusiongrill.mb.ca. Main courses C$15–$25 (US$9–$16). AE, DC, V, MC. Tues–Sat 11:30am–2pm and 5:30–10pm. From Portage Ave./Rte. 85/Hwy. 1 west, left on Maryland St., cross the Assiniboine where it becomes Academy Rd.

**Red Lantern** CONTINENTAL A red lantern stands outside the small house occupied by this restaurant, which offers a cozy dining room. The food is excellent, nicely presented, graciously served, and very reasonably priced. French background music adds to the atmosphere. Among the specialties are veal

St. Jacques; sole papillote; filet mignon en croute; rack of lamb with a black current sauce; and chicken breast stuffed with brie, spinach, and carrots served with thyme cream sauce. A fine selection of wines is also available.

302 Hamel Ave. (at St. John Baptiste), St. Boniface. ✆ **204/233-4841.** Reservations recommended. Main courses C$13–C$28 (US$8–US$17). AE, DC, MC, V. Mon–Fri 11:30am–2pm; Mon–Thurs 5–9pm, Fri–Sat 5–10pm.

**River City Brewing Co.** PUB FARE Winnipeg's first brewpub, the River City serves up good handcrafted beers plus excellent food. The usual pub grub suspects are here—burgers, ribs, and fish-and-chips—plus steaks, grilled chicken and fish, and vegetarian dishes that verge on fine dining.

437 Stradbrook Ave. ✆ **204/452-2739.** Reservations recommended. Main courses C$12–C$20 (US$7–$12). DC, MC, V. Mon–Wed 11:30am–midnight, Thurs–Sat 11:30am–2am, Sun 4pm–midnight.

### INEXPENSIVE

**Alycia's** ★ *Value* UKRAINIAN Famed as one of the late comedian John Candy's favorite restaurants, Alycia's is the ultimate place for comfort food, and lets you sample Winnipeg's Ukrainian culture gastronomically. The atmosphere is homey and warm, bedecked with Ukrainian knick-knacks and art, and the place is often full of Ukrainian diners. The menu prominently features three types of dishes—pirogies, potato-and-cheese stuffed dumplings, pan fried or boiled; holubtsi, cabbage rolls stuffed with bacon and rice or buckwheat and draped in a tomato sauce; and homemade kolbassa sausages. Soups include an excellent borscht and kapusnyak (zesty sauerkraut). Alycia's menu also features many North American standards, including plenty of sandwiches on the lunch menu. The restaurant also serves breakfasts. Prices are extremely reasonable, and the service is quick and friendly.

559 Cathedral Ave. (at McGregor). ✆ **204/582-8789.** Main courses C$4.50–$8 (US$2.80–$5). AE, DC, MC, V. Mon–Fri 8am–8pm, Sat 9am–8pm. Go north on Hwy. 52 to Cathedral Ave., and turn left.

## WINNIPEG AFTER DARK

**THE PERFORMING ARTS** The **Manitoba Centennial Centre,** 555 Main St. (✆ **204/956-1360**), is a complex that includes the Centennial Concert Hall (home to the Royal Winnipeg Ballet, the Winnipeg Symphony, and the Manitoba Opera). Nearby are the Manitoba Theatre Centre, the Warehouse Theatre, and Pantages Playhouse Theatre.

Other spaces offering frequent concerts and performances include the **Winnipeg Art Gallery** (✆ **204/786-6641;** www.wag.mb.ca), with blues/jazz, chamber music, and contemporary music groups; and the **Pantages Playhouse Theatre,** 180 Market Ave. E. (✆ **204/989-2889;** www.pantagesplayhouse.com).

The world-renowned **Royal Winnipeg Ballet** ★, 380 Graham Ave., at Edmonton Street (✆ **204/956-2792** for the box office; www.rwb.org), was founded in 1939 by two British immigrant ballet teachers, making it North America's second-oldest ballet company (after San Francisco's). By 1949, it was a professional troupe and in 1953 it was granted a royal charter. Today its repertoire includes both contemporary and classical works, such as Ashton's *Thais, Giselle,* and *Sleeping Beauty.* The company performs at the Centennial Concert Hall, usually for a week in October, November, December, March, and May. Tickets are C$11 to C$50 (US$7–US$31), with discounts for students, seniors, and children.

The **Winnipeg Symphony Orchestra,** 555 Main St. (✆ **204/949-3950,** or 204/949-3999 for the box office; www.wso.mb.ca), was established in 1947.

The orchestra's prestige has attracted guest artists like Itzhak Perlman, Isaac Stern, Tracey Dahl, and Maureen Forrester. The season usually runs September to mid-May, and tickets are C$11 to C$41 (US$7–US$25). In late January, the **New Music Festival** hosts 9 nights of cutting-edge classical music—one of Winnipeg's best-kept musical secrets. Contact the WSO for details.

The **Manitoba Opera,** 380 Graham Ave., (© **204/942-7479,** or 204/957-7842 for the box office; www.manitobaopera.mb.ca), features a season of two or three operas each year at the Centennial Concert Hall, with performances in February and April, and possibly November. English subtitles are used. Tickets range from C$15.50 to $66 (US$10–$41).

**THEATER** You can enjoy theater in the park at the **Rainbow Stage,** in Kildonan Park at 2021 Main St. (© **204/989-5261;** www.rainbowstage.net), Canada's largest and oldest continuously operating outdoor theater. The theater group actually presents two musical classics, running about 3 weeks each, one in the summer at Kildonan and one in mid-winter at the Pantages Playhouse Theatre (see above). On the banks of the Red River, the outdoor Rainbow Stage is easily accessible by bus or car. For tickets, which vary in price from show to show, call © **888/780-SEAT** or 204/780-SEAT, or visit www.selectaseat.mb.ca.

The **MTC Warehouse,** at 140 Rupert Ave. at Lily (© **204/943-4849** or 204/942-6537 for the box office; www.mtc.mb.ca), presents more cutting-edge, controversial plays in an intimate 300-seat theater. Its four-play season runs generally runs mid-October to mid-May, and tickets are C$12 to C$41 (US$7–US$25). Since its founding by Tom Hendry and John Hirsch, the **Manitoba Theatre Centre,** 174 Market Ave. (© **877/446-4500** or 204/942-6537; www.mtc.mb.ca), has been dedicated to producing good serious theater, and this is indeed one of Canada's best regional companies. A recent season's offerings included *Hamlet* starring Keanu Reeves. The season usually features six productions and runs October to April, with tickets at C$11 to C$59 (US$7–US$37).

The **Prairie Theatre Exchange,** 3rd level, Portage Place, 393 Portage Ave. (© **204/942-7291** or 204/942-5483 for the box office; www.pte.mb.ca), also offers about six productions from October to April, and provides the most serious alternative to MTC shows. A recent season featured *The Glass Menagerie* and Virginia Woolf's *A Room of One's Own.* Standard ticket prices are about C$30 to $32 (US$19–US$20) for adults, C$21.50 to C$24 (US$13–US$15) for seniors, and C$19.50 (US$12) for students. Some less expensive shows run at the end of the season.

**CASINOS** The tropical-themed **Club Regent,** 1425 Regent Ave. (© **888/957-4652** or 204/957-2700; www.clubregent.com), offers slots, electronic blackjack, bingo, poker, keno, and breakopen games, plus traditional bingo and the Fountain of Fortune, a series of progressive slot machines. Huge, walk-through aquariums and two live music stages add to the diversions. The club is open Monday to Saturday 10am to 3am and Sunday noon to 3am.

The Grand Railway Hotel-themed **McPhillips Station,** 484 McPhillips St. (© **204/957-3900;** www.clubregent.com) is your other major casino option in town, featuring many of the same gaming choices as at the Club Regent (both are operated and regulated by the Manitoba Lotteries Corporation). The side show here is the Millennium Express multimedia theater presentation, a quasi-time-travel ride and show taking you back into Manitoba's past. McPhillips Station operates during the same hours as its sister casino, and both have restaurants and gift shops.

**DANCE CLUBS** Country-western dance bars used to be a large part of the nightlife in Winnipeg, but the scene is rapidly changing. If you're looking for a hoe-down, though, the best place to sample cowboy boot and line dancing is the **Palomino Club,** 1133 Portage Ave. (© **204/722-0454**). **Silverado's,** 2100 McPhillips St., in the Canad Inn Garden City (© **204/633-0024;** www.canadinns.com/silverados), has three floors of dancing to country bands and rock acts, plus DJ-spun dancefloor hits.

The dance club scene has really exploded in Winnipeg with the opening of several new upscale clubs in the past few years; a small sampling follows. **The Empire,** at 436 Main St., near Portage Ave. (© **204/943-3979**), features a Roman-themed dance floor in a historic bank building. **Mezzo,** in the Exchange District at 291 Bannatyne Ave. (© **204/987-3399**), is a high-tech, contemporary club with catwalks and a private, members-only lounge. **The Beach,** in the Canad Inns Fort Garry Express at 1792 Pembina Highway (© **204/269-6955;** www.canadinns.com/thebeach), attracts young revelers (and many college students) to its tropical-themed beach dance parties. **Kokonuts,** in the Exchange District at 114 Market Ave. (© **204/944-1117**), features live cover bands and a huge aquarium (aquariums are evidently popular in this town). As dance clubs can be ephemeral, you might want to check out the latest news when you visit town; see the Winnipeg Sun's website at www.fyiwinnipeg.com to search the latest club information and listings.

## SIDE TRIPS FROM WINNIPEG

**LOWER FORT GARRY NATIONAL HISTORIC SITE** The oldest intact stone fur-trading post in North America is **Lower Fort Garry** (© **877/534-3678** or 204/785-6050; www.parkscanada.gc.ca), only 32km (20 miles) north of Winnipeg on Highway 9. Built in the 1830s, Lower Fort Garry was an important Hudson's Bay Company trans-shipment and provisioning post. Within the walls of the compound are the governor's residence; several warehouses, including the fur loft; and the Men's House, where male employees lived. Outside the compound are company buildings—a blacksmith's shop, the farm manager's home, and so on. The fort is staffed by costumed volunteers who make candles and soap; forge horseshoes, locks, and bolts; and generally demonstrate the ways of life of the 1850s. In a lean-to beside the fur-loft building stands an original York boat; hundreds of these once traveled the waterways from Hudson Bay to the Rockies and from the Red River to the Arctic carrying furs and trading goods.

Mid-May through Labour Day, the site is open daily from 9am to 5pm. Admission is C$5.50 (US$3.40) for adults, C$4 (US$2.50) for seniors, C$2.75 (US$1.70) for youths ages 6 to 16, C$15 (US$9) for families, and free for children under 6. Call **Beaver Bus Lines** (© **204/989-7007**), to get a charter bus from downtown Winnipeg to Lower Fort Garry. Also **Paddlewheel River Rouge Tours** (© **204/942-4500;** www.paddlewheelcruises.com) offers a day-long cruise to Lower Fort Garry for C$22 (US$14) for adults, C$18 (US$11) for seniors, and C$12 (US$7) for children under 12. Fort admission, meals, and drinks aren't included in these fares.

**STEINBACH MENNONITE HERITAGE VILLAGE** ★ About 48km (30 miles) outside Winnipeg is the **Steinbach Mennonite Heritage Village** (© **204/326-9661**), 2.5km (1½ miles) north of Steinbach on Highway 12, south off Highway 1, east from town. This 16ha (40-acre) museum complex is worth a detour. Between 1874 and 1880, about 7,000 Mennonites migrated here from the Ukraine, establishing settlements like Kleefeld, Steinbach, Blumenort, and others. After World War I, many moved to Mexico and Uruguay when Manitoba closed all unregistered schools between 1922 and 1926, but they were replaced by another surge of emigrants fleeing the Russian Revolution. Their community life is portrayed here in a complex of about 20 buildings. In the museum building, dioramas display daily life and community artifacts, like woodworking and sewing tools, sausage makers, clothes, medicines, and furnishings. Elsewhere in the complex, you can view the windmill grinding grain, ride in an ox-drawn wagon, watch the blacksmith at work, or view any number of homes, agricultural machines, and more. In summer, the restaurant serves Mennonite food—a full meal of borscht, thick-sliced homemade brown bread, coleslaw, pirogies, and sausage, plus rhubarb crumble, at very reasonable prices.

The village is open Monday to Saturday: May and September 10am to 5pm; June, July, and August 10am to 6pm. On Sunday the gates don't open until noon. October to April, the museum is open Monday to Friday 10am to 4pm. Admission is C$5 (US$3.10) for adults, C$4 (US$2.50) for seniors, C$3 (US$1.85) for students grades 1 to 12, and C$15 (US$9) for families.

## 3 Whiteshell Provincial Park & Lake Winnipeg

### WHITESHELL PROVINCIAL PARK ★

Less than a 2-hour drive east of Winnipeg (144km/89 miles) lies a network of a dozen rivers and more than 200 lakes in the 2,590km2 (1,000-sq.-mile) **Whiteshell Provincial Park** (✆ **204/369-5246**). Among the park's natural features are Rainbow and Whitemouth falls; a lovely lily pond west of Caddy Lake; West Hawk Lake, Manitoba's deepest lake, created by a meteorite; and a goose sanctuary (best seen mid-May to July, when the goslings are about). You can also view petroforms, stone arrangements fashioned by an Algonquin-speaking people to communicate with the spirits. In fall, you can witness an ancient ritual—First Nations Canadians harvesting wild rice. One person poles a canoe through the rice field while another bends the stalks into the canoe and knocks the ripe grains off with a picking stick.

In July and August, the **Manitoba Naturalist's Society,** headquartered at 401-63 Albert St. in Winnipeg (✆ **204/943-9029;** www.manitobanature.ca), operates wilderness programs and other workshops at their cabin on Lake Mantario. There are six self-guided trails, plus several short trails you can complete in less than 2 hours. For serious backpackers, the **Mantario Trail** is a 3- to 6-day hike over 60km (37 miles) of rugged terrain. There are also all-terrain biking trails. You can choose among one of several canoe routes, including the Frances Lake route, which covers 18km (11 miles) of pleasant paddling with 12 beaver-dam hauls and three portages, and takes about 6 hours. There is swimming at Falcon Beach; scuba diving in West Hawk Lake; and sailing, windsurfing, waterskiing, and fishing in other places.

Horseback riding is offered at **Falcon Beach Riding Stables** (✆ **877/949-2410** or 204/349-2410; www.granite.mb.ca/~imriemm). In winter, there is downhill skiing, cross-country skiing, snowmobiling, snowshoeing, and skating. Most recreational equipment, including skis, canoes, snowshoes, and fishing gear, is available from the **Falcon Trail Resort** (✆ **204/349-8273**).

Within the park, Falcon Lake is the center of one of Canada's most modern recreational developments, including various resorts with tennis courts, an 18-hole par-72 golf course, hiking trails, horseback riding, fishing, canoeing, and skiing. Most park resorts and lodges charge C$70 to C$110 (US$43–US$68) for a double or C$450 to C$750 (US$279–US$465) per week for a cabin. Most resorts offer recreational equipment rentals. Camping facilities abound. For more info, call the park at ✆ **204/369-5246** or contact **Travel Manitoba,** Dept. SV2, 7-155 Carlton St., Winnipeg, MB R3C 3H8 (✆ **800/665-0040,** ext. SV2, or 204/945-3777, ext. SV2; www.travelmanitoba.com).

## LAKE WINNIPEG

The continent's seventh largest, **Lake Winnipeg** is 425km (264 miles) long, and its shores shelter some interesting communities and attractive natural areas. At its southern end, **Grand Beach Provincial Park** (✆ **204/754-2212**) has white-sand beaches backed by 10m (30-ft.) high dunes in some places. This is a good place to swim, windsurf, and sail. There are three self-guided nature trails. Campsites are available in summer only.

About 97km (60 miles) north of Winnipeg, on the western shore, the farming-and-fishing community of **Gimli** (www.townofgimli.com) is the hub of Icelandic culture in Manitoba. Established over a century ago as the capital of New Iceland, it had its own government, school, and newspapers for many years. It still celebrates an Icelandic festival known as Islendingadagurinn, on the first long weekend in August.

**Hecla Island,** 165km (103 miles) northeast of Winnipeg, was once a part of the Republic of New Iceland and was home to a small Icelandic-Canadian farming-and-fishing community. Today it's the site of **Hecla/Grindstone Provincial Park** (✆ **204/378-2945**). Open year-round, it's an excellent place to hike (with five short trails), golf, fish, camp, bird-watch, canoe, swim, windsurf, play tennis (two courts), cross-country ski, snowshoe, or snowmobile and toboggan. (Gull Harbour Resort has bicycle, tennis, ski, toboggan, and other sports equipment rental.) Camping is available in summer. Photographers and wildlife enthusiasts appreciate the park's wildlife-viewing tower and the **Grassy Narrow Marsh,** which shelters many species of waterfowl. There are a campground and 17 cabins available. For campground and cabin reservations at all provincial parks call ✆ **888/482-2267** or see www.gov.mb.ca/natres/parks/reservations. Another option is the Gull Harbour Resort (see below).

### WHERE TO STAY IN GULL HARBOUR

**Gull Harbour Resort and Conference Centre** This is an ideal place to take the family. Though it boasts first-class resort facilities, it also reflects a concern for the environment. The beaches and woods have been left intact. Facilities include an indoor pool, a whirlpool, and a sauna; activities include badminton, volleyball, a game room with a pool table, an 18-hole golf course, a putting green, mini-golf, two tennis courts, a skating rink, shuffleboard, and more. The resort also has a full line of rental equipment, from bicycles, skis, toboggans, and snowmobiles. The lodge buildings all reflect an Icelandic style, with carved doors, shuttered windows, and steeply sloped rooflines. The Icelandic touches end at the guest rooms, which are comfortably furnished and fully modern, but lack some of the flair applied to the rest of this marvelous resort.

Box 1000, Riverton, MB R0C 2R0. ✆ **800/267-6700** or 204/279-2041. Fax 204/279-2000. www.gullharbourresort.com. 93 units. May to mid-Oct C$107–$283 (US$66–$175) double, mid-Oct to Apr C$72–$242 (US$45–$150). Extra person C$10 (US$6). Children under 18 stay free in parents' room. Specials available year-round. AAA/CAA discounts available. AE, DC, MC, V. **Amenities:** Restaurant; indoor pool; golf course; tennis courts; fitness center; Jacuzzi; sauna; equipment rental; bike rental; children's playground; nonsmoking rooms; executive-level rooms. *In room:* A/C, TV, dataport, fridge.

## 4 West Along the Trans-Canada Highway to Spruce Woods Provincial Park & Brandon

About 67km (42 miles) west of Portage la Prairie, before reaching Carberry, turn south on Highway 5 to **Spruce Woods Provincial Park,** Box 900, Carberry, MB R0K 0H0 (✆ **204/827-8850** in summer, or 204/834-8800). The park's unique and most fragile feature is **Spirit Sands,** a 5km$^2$ (2-sq.-mile) tract of open, blowing sand dunes that are the remains of the once-wide Assiniboine Delta. Only a few hardy creatures—including the prairie skink (Manitoba's only lizard), hognose snake, Bembix wasp, one type of wolf spider, and 2 species of cactus—live here. The rest of the park is forest and prairie grasslands inhabited by herds of wapiti (elk).

There's camping at **Kiche Manitou** as well as at hike-in locations. The park is on the Assiniboine River canoe route, which starts in Brandon and ends north of Holland. You can rent canoes at Pine Fort IV in the park. The park's longest trail is the 40km (25-mile) **Epinette Trail,** but its most fascinating is the **Spirit Sands/Devil's Punch Bowl,** accessible from Highway 5. It loops through the Dunes and leads to the Devil's Punch Bowl, which was carved by underground streams. There are also bike and mountain-bike trails; swimming at the campground beach; and in winter, cross-country skiing, skating, tobogganing, and snowmobiling.

**Brandon** is Manitoba's second-largest city, with a population of about 45,000. This university town features the **Art Gallery of Southwestern Manitoba** at 638 Princess Ave. (✆ **204/727-1036**); the **B. J. Hales Museum of Natural History** on the university campus (✆ **204/727-7307;** http://flinflon.brandonu.ca/bjhales), with mounted specimens of birds and mammals; plus interesting tours, by request, of the **Agriculture and Agri-Food Canada Research Centre** (✆ **204/726-7650;** http://res2.agr.ca/brandon). Another interesting attraction is the **Commonwealth Air Training Plan Museum** at the airport (✆ **204/727-2444;** www.airmuseum.ca), which features historical aircraft and artifacts from Royal Canadian Air Force training schools of World War II.

## 5 Riding Mountain National Park & Duck Mountain Provincial Park

### RIDING MOUNTAIN NATIONAL PARK ★★

About 248km (154 miles) northwest of Winnipeg, **Riding Mountain National Park,** Wasagaming, MB R0J 2H0 (✆ **800/707-8480** or 204/848-7275), is set in the highlands atop a giant wooded escarpment sheltering more than 260 species of birds, plus moose, wolf, coyote, lynx, beaver, black bear, and a bison herd at Lake Audy.

The park has more than 400km (248 miles) of **hiking trails.** Twenty are easily accessible, short, and easy to moderate in difficulty; another 20 are long backcountry trails. Call the number above for more info. You can ride many trails on mountain bike and horseback and can rent bikes in Wasagaming. The **Triangle Ranch Ltd.,** P.O. Box 275, Onanole, MB R0J 1N0 (✆ **204/848-4583**), offers 1-hour, 2-hour, and day rides for C$18, $30, and C$65 (US$11, US$19, and US$40), respectively; available May to November.

You can rent canoes and other boats at **Clear Lake Marina** (✆ **204/867-7298**). As for **fishing,** northern pike is the main game fish and specimens up to 14kg (30 pounds) have been taken from Clear Lake. Rainbow and brook trout populate Lake Katherine and Deep Lake. The park also has one of the province's best **golf courses;** greens fees are between C$30 and $40 (US$19–$25). In winter, there's **ice fishing** and **cross-country skiing** (call the park for permits and information).

The **visitor center** is open daily in summer 9am to 9pm. For information, contact the park at the address or numbers above. The park is easily accessed from Brandon, about 95km (59 miles) north along Highway 10. Entry is C$3.25 (US$2) for adults and C$7.50 (US$4.65) for families; multi-day passes are also available.

## WHERE TO STAY

At the **Shawenequanape Kipi-Che-Win** (Southquill Camp; ✆ **204/947-3147**), you can stay in a traditional teepee for C$50 (US$31) double and learn about the traditional ceremonies, arts, crafts, and culture of the Anishinabe (Ojibwe) First Nation. Each interpretive program is C$5 (US$3.10). For information, contact **Anishinabe Village,** P.O. Box 644, Erickson, MB R0J 0P0 (✆ **204/848-2815** or 204/636-2571), or **Anishinabe Camp & Cultural Tours,** 36 Roslyn Rd., 2nd Fl., Winnipeg, MB R3L 0G6 (✆ **204/925-2030**).

In Wasagaming, you can stay at five park **campgrounds** or in motel and cabin accommodations for anywhere from about C$50 to C$180 (US$31–US$112) for a double. Wasagaming also has six tennis courts, lawn-bowling greens, a children's playground, and a log-cabin movie theater in the **Wasagaming Visitor Centre** beside Clear Lake. There is also a dance hall, picnic areas with stoves, and a band shell down by the lake for Sunday-afternoon concerts. At the lake itself you can rent boats and swim at the main beach.

**Wasagaming Campground** has more than 500 sites, most unserviced. Facilities include showers and toilets, kitchen shelters, and a sewage-disposal station nearby. Rates range from C$9 (US$6) unserviced in the off-season to C$19.50 (US$12) for full service in the summer. Other outlying campgrounds (93 sites) are at **Moon Lake, Lake Audy, Whirlpool,** and **Deep Lake.** None of these is serviced. For reservations, call ✆ **800/707-8480.** Outlying campgrounds are C$9 or $10.50 (US$6 or $7), site only. Backcountry camping is also available with a permit. Advance reservations (✆ **800/707-8480**) are strongly recommended.

**Elkhorn Resort & Conference Centre** This year-round lodge is on the edge of Wasagaming with easy access to Riding Mountain, overlooking quiet fields and forest. The newly renovated guest rooms are large, comfortable, and nicely appointed with modern pine furnishings; some have fireplaces and private balconies. At the ranch's common room, you can join a game of bridge or cribbage in the evening. In summer, facilities include a riding stable, and there's a lake nearby for water activities; winter pleasures include sleigh rides, cross-country skiing, outdoor skating, and tobogganing. Also on the property are several fully equipped two- and three-bedroom chalets (with fireplaces, fire extinguishers, toasters, dishwashers, microwaves, and balconies with barbecues) designed after Quonsets.

Mooswa Dr. E., Clear Lake, MB R0J 1N0. ✆ **866/ELKHORN** or 204/848-2802. Fax 204/848-2109. www.elkhornresort.mb.ca. 57 units. Mid-May to Sept and late Dec–Jan 1 C$109–$189 (US$71–$123) lodge room double, C$250–$500 (US$163–$325) chalet; Oct–late Dec and Jan 2 to mid-May C$89–$179 (US$58–$116) lodge room double, C$225–$400 (US$146–$260) chalet. Weekly chalet rates available. Extra person in lodge C$15 (US$10). Children under 17 stay free in parents' room. AE, DC, DISC, MC, V. **Amenities:**

Restaurant; indoor pool; golf course; tennis courts; exercise room; Jacuzzi; sauna; bike rental; activities desk; room service; massage; children's center; babysitting; coin-op laundry; nonsmoking rooms; executive-level rooms. *In room:* TV/DVD, fridge, coffeemaker, hair dryer.

### DUCK MOUNTAIN PROVINCIAL PARK

Northwest of Riding Mountain via Highway 10, off Route 367, **Duck Mountain Provincial Park** (no phone) is popular for fishing, camping, boating, hiking, horseback riding, and biking. **Baldy Mountain,** near the park's southeast entrance, is the province's highest point at 831m (2,727 ft.). **East Blue Lake** is so clear the bottom is visible at 9m to 12m (30 ft.–40 ft.).

For accommodations in Duck Mountain, the place to stay is **Wellman Lake Lodge,** Box 249, Minitonas, MB R0L 1G0 (✆ **204/525-4422**), which has 7 cabins starting at C$65 (US$40) for two. All are modern and winterized, with full bathrooms and well-equipped kitchenettes, plus a covered deck with picnic table. Two have fireplaces or pellet stoves. Full services for anglers and hunters are offered. There's also a beach for swimming. There are three campgrounds in Duck Mountain that offer various levels of service. For reservations, call ✆ **888/482-2267.**

## 6 On to the Far North & Churchill, the World's Polar Bear Capital ★★

The best way to explore the north is aboard **VIA Rail's *Hudson Bay*** on a 2-night, 1-day trip from Winnipeg to Churchill, via **The Pas,** a mecca for fishing enthusiasts, and the mining community of Thompson. You can also drive to Thompson and take the train from there. No other land route has yet penetrated this remote region, which is covered with lakes, forests, and frozen tundra. The train leaves Winnipeg at about 8:45pm and arrives about 36 hours later in Churchill. A round-trip ticket for two including a double bedroom costs C$2,200 (US$1,364) June to October or C$1,320 (US$818), 7-day advance purchase, at other times. If you're okay sleeping in reclining seats, two can travel round-trip for C$876 (US$543) or C$552 (US$342), 7-day advance purchase, in economy class any time of year. For more information, contact your travel agent or **VIA Rail** (✆ **888/VIA-RAIL,** 800/561-8630 in western Canada, or 800/561-3949 in the U.S.; www.viarail.ca). You can also fly into Churchill on **Calm Air,** booked through **Air Canada** (✆ **888/247-2262;** www.aircanada.com).

If you're up this way in February, The Pas hosts the annual **Northern Manitoba Trappers' Festival** ★ (✆ **204/623-2912;** www.trappersfestival.com), with world-championship dogsled races, ice fishing, beer fests, moose calling, and more. It's usually held the third week in February.

**Churchill** is the polar-bear capital of the world. To the south and east of the city lies one of the largest polar bear maternity denning sites. The area was placed under government protection in 1996 when the **Wapusk National Park** was established. Visit October to early November to see these awesome creatures. The area is also a vital habitat for hundreds of thousands of waterfowl and shorebirds. More than 200 species, including the rare Ross Gull, nest or pass through on their annual migration. In summer, white beluga whales frolic in the mouth of the Churchill River, and you can sight seals and caribou along the coast. You can also see the aurora borealis from here. For additional info, contact **Parks Canada,** Box 127, Churchill, MB R0B 0E0 (✆ **888/748-2928** or 204/675-8863; www.parcscanada.gc.ca).

Churchill, population around 1,100, is a grain-exporting terminal, and grain elevators dominate its skyline. You can watch the grain being unloaded from grain cars onto ships—25 million bushels of wheat and barley clear the port in only 12 to 14 weeks of frantic nonstop operation. You can also take a boat ride to **Prince of Wales Fort** (**© 204/675-8863;** www.parcscanada.gc.ca). Construction of this partially restored, large stone fort was started in 1730 by the Hudson's Bay Company and took 40 years. Yet after all that effort, Gov. Samuel Hearne and 39 clerks and tradesmen surrendered the fort to the French without resistance in 1782, when faced with a possible attack by three French ships. From here you can observe beluga whales. June 1 to November 10, the park is open daily 1 to 5pm and 6 to 9pm. Admission to the grounds is free, though there are C$3 or $5 (US$1.85 or $3.10) fees for special interpretive programs that may be scheduled or guided tours.

**Cape Merry,** at the mouth of the Churchill River, is also an excellent vantage point for observing beluga whales and is a must for birders (it's open continuously June–Aug). The town's **Visitor Centre** is open daily mid-May to mid-November, weekdays only otherwise. For Churchill information, contact the **Churchill Chamber of Commerce,** Box 176, Churchill, MB R0B 0E0 (**© 888/389-2327** or 204/675-2022; www.cancom.net/~cccomm). In town, the **Eskimo Museum,** 242 Laverendrye St. (**© 204/675-2030**), has a collection of fine Inuit carvings and artifacts. In the summer (June to mid-November), it's open Monday from 1 to 5pm and Tuesday to Saturday from 9am to noon and 1 to 5pm, and in winter (mid-November to May), the hours are Monday to Saturday from 1 to 4:30pm; the museum is closed Sundays and statutory holidays. Admission is free, but donations are welcome.

Some 240km (149 miles) southeast of Churchill, the very remote **York Factory National Historic Site** was established by the Hudson's Bay Company in 1682 as a fur-trading post. It operated for nearly 2 centuries until it was abandoned in 1957. Several generations of structures have been built near or on the site. The current site referred to as York Factory III was developed after 1788. The depot building is the oldest wood structure still standing on permafrost; its unattached walls and floors allow for the buckling of the earth due to frost heaves. Across Sloop Creek are the remains of a powder magazine and a cemetery with headstones dating from the 1700s. Guided tours are C$5 (US$3.10) for adults. The site is staffed from June to September only. Access is limited to charter planes or by canoe down the Hayes River. For more info on these sites, contact **Parks Canada,** Box 127, Churchill, MB R0B 0E0 (**© 888/748-2928** or 204/675-8863; www.parcscanada.gc.ca).

North of The Pas are two provincial parks. The first is **Clearwater Lake Provincial Park** (no phone), at the junction of highways 10 and 287; the lake lives up to its name because the bottom is visible at 11m (35 ft.). It offers great fishing, plus swimming, boating, hiking, and camping. The second is **Grass River Provincial Park** (grass river), on Highway 39, a wilderness home to woodland caribou, moose, and plenty of waterfowl. The Grass River is good for fishing and canoeing.

**Kaskattama Safari Adventures,** 170 Harbison Avenue W., Winnipeg, MB R2L 0A4 (**© 204/667-1611**), offers a comfortable way to view the polar bears. Their 5- or 6-day trips start in Winnipeg, where you stay at the Radisson or other hotels before flying to Kaskattama Lodge, built as a fur-trading post in 1923 by the Hudson's Bay Company. Today, the storeroom and warehouse serve as the main visitor lodge and dining room. Two four-bedroom/four-bathroom cabins, each with a screened porch, accommodate a total maximum of 16. A naturalist introduces you to the **Cape Tatnam Wildlife Management Area,** home to more than 200 species of birds, caribou, moose, black bear, Arctic wolves, fox, and the great white bears who head to land in July and can be seen foraging along the grasslands, with cubs in tow. Three or four days are spent at the lodge. The trips cost US$2,195 or $2,395 per person for a double. In August, for an extra US$500 per person, you can take a helicopter trip to York Factory.

**Churchill Nature Tours,** P.O. Box 429, Erickson, MB R0J 0P0 (✆ **204/636-2968;** www.churchillnaturetours.com) offers several polar bear- and other wildlife-viewing safari packages that include lodging in the rustic White Whale Lodge, a former trading post and brothel; the new Great White Bear Lodge; or Churchill's Aurora Inn. The lodges afford excellent viewing of wildlife and the northern sky. All packages include a helicopter nature-viewing tour, plus plenty of trips out for bear-viewing in tundra vehicles. Naturalists lead the tours, and you'll be sure to see plenty of other tundra wildlife. Trips last a total of 6 or 8 days, and include return airfare from Winnipeg and two nights in the Radisson there; prices range from C$2,695 to C$3,195 (US$1,671–US$1,981), and pre-safari wildlife tours of southern parks are available for an additional charge.

### WHERE TO STAY

In Churchill, the 26-room **Churchill Motel,** at Kelsey and Franklin (✆ **204/675-8853**), charges C$75 to C$90 (US$47–US$56) per double, offers a free airport or train shuttle, and has a restaurant. Additional amenities, like room service and a bar, are offered at the **Seaport Hotel,** 299 Kelsey Blvd. (✆ **204/675-8807**), with 21 rooms at C$95 to C$105 (US$59–US$169) for a double. The **Tundra Inn,** 34 Franklin St. (✆ **800/265-8563** or 204/675-8831), has 31 comfortable rooms with fridges and coffeemakers for C$80 to C$105 (US$50–US$65) for a double. The **Aurora Inn,** 24 Bernier St. (✆ **888/840-1344** or 204/675-2071; www.cancom.net/~aurora) is one of Churchill's newest hotels, and features 19 spacious, split-level loft suites with fully equipped kitchens, plus 3 smaller standard rooms. Suite doubles go for C$169 (US$105) during peak polar bear viewing season (Oct and Nov), and C$139 (US$86) or C$105 (US$65) in shoulder- or off-seasons, respectively. The **Polar Inn & Suites,** 153 Kelsey Blvd. (✆ **877/POLAR33** or 204/675-8878; www.cancom.net/~polarinn) offers standard rooms plus one bedroom apartments and kitchenette suites with fridges coffeemakers for C$90 to C$140 (US$56–US$87). The **Lazy Bear Lodge** (✆ **204/675-2969**) is a newer, log-cabin-type hotel with 32 spacious rooms, a restaurant, and free shuttle; rates range from C$80 to C$150 (US$50–US$93).

For accommodations near Grass River Provincial Park, try Reed Lake's **Grass River Lodge,** P.O. Box 1680, The Pas, MB R9A 1L5 in summer; or Box 4615, Steinbach, MB R0A 2A0 in winter (✆ **204/358-7171** in summer; 888/244-7453, 204/326-3977, or 918/455-2324 in winter; www.grassriverlodge.com). This is a full-package fishing cabin and lodge resort, and rates reflect the services and minimum stay of 4 days; lodge, full-meal or outpost-cabin options are available. There's also the drive-in **Peterson's Reed Lake Lodge,** Box 1648, The Pas, MB R9A 1L4 (✆ **204/955-3078**), with much lower rates.

## 7 Regina: Capital of Saskatchewan

Originally named "Pile O' Bones" after the heap of buffalo skeletons the first settlers found (Native Canadians had amassed the bones in the belief they would lure the vanished buffalo back again), the city of **Regina** (pronounced Re-*jeye*-na) has Princess Louise, daughter of Queen Victoria, to thank for its more regal name. She named the city in her mother's honor in 1882 when it became the capital of the Northwest Territories. Despite the barren prairie landscape and the infamous Regina mud, the town grew.

Today the provincial capital of Saskatchewan, with a population of about 200,000, Regina still has a certain prairie feel, though it's becoming more sophisticated, with some good hotels and some rather interesting attractions.

## ESSENTIALS

**GETTING THERE** **By plane** **Regina Airport** (www.yqr.ca) is west of the city, only 15 minutes from downtown. It is served largely by **Air Canada** (© 888/247-2262), **Northwest** (© 800/447-4747), and **WestJet** (© 877/952-4638).

**By car** If you're driving, Regina is right on the Trans-Canada Highway.

**VISITOR INFORMATION** Contact **Tourism Saskatchewan,** 1922 Park St., Regina, SK S4P 3V7 (© **877/237-2273** or 306/787-2300; www.sasktourism.com), open Monday to Friday 8am to 5pm. For on-the-spot Regina info, contact **Tourism Regina,** P.O. Box 3355, Regina, SK S4P 3H1 (© **800/661-5099** or 306/789-5099; www.tourismregina.com), or visit the **Visitor Information Centre,** Highway 1 East, just east of the city and west of CKCK-TV; it's open summer (mid-May to Labour Day) weekdays 8am to 7pm and weekends or holidays 10am to 6pm, and winter weekdays only 8am to 5pm.

**CITY LAYOUT** The two main streets are **Victoria Avenue,** which runs east-west, and **Albert Street,** which runs north-south. South of the intersection lies the **Wascana Centre.** Most of the downtown hotels stretch along Victoria Avenue between Albert Street on the west and Broad Street on the east. The RCMP barracks are to the north and west of the downtown area. **Lewvan Drive** and **Ring Road** together encircle the city.

**GETTING AROUND** **Regina Transit,** 333 Winnipeg St. (© **306/777-7433;** www.reginatransit.com), operates nine bus routes that make it easy to get around. For schedules and maps, go to the **Transit Information Centre** at 2124 11th Ave., at the Cornwall Centre, next to Eaton's; open weekdays 7am to 9pm and Saturday 9am to 4pm. Fares are C$1.60 (US$1) for adults, C$1.15 (US70¢) for high-school students, and C$1.05 (US65¢) for elementary-school students. Exact fare is required.

For car rentals, try **Avis,** at 4950 Buffalo Tr. (the airport) or 655 Broad St. (© **306/757-5460** or 306/757-1653); **Budget,** at the airport or 505 McIntyre St. (© **800/527-0700** in the U.S. or 800/267-6810 in Saskatchewan); **Hertz,** at the airport or 601 Albert St. (© **306/791-9131** or 306/791-9136); **National,** 2627 Airport Rd. (© **306/757-5757**); and **Thrifty,** at the airport or 1975 Broad St. (© **306/352-1000** or 306/525-1000). You can most easily find **taxis** at downtown hotels. They charge C$2.55 (US$1.60) when you get in and C10¢ (US5¢) per 89m (292 ft.) thereafter. From downtown to the airport the cost is about C$10 (US$6). **Regina Cab** (© **306/543-3333**) is the most used service.

**SPECIAL EVENTS** During the first week of June, **Mosaic** (© **306/757-9550**) celebrates the city's multiethnic population. Special passports entitle you to enter pavilions and experience the food, crafts, customs, and culture of each group. Regina's **Buffalo Days,** P.O. Box 167, Exhibition Park, Regina, SK S4P 2Z6 (© **888/734-3975** or 306/781-9200; www.reginaexhibition.com), usually held the end of July into the first week in August, recalls the time when this noble beast roamed the west. Throughout the city, businesses and individuals dress in Old West style, while the fair itself sparkles with a midway, grandstand shows, big-name entertainers, livestock competitions, beard-growing contests, and much more.

## EXPLORING THE WASCANA CENTRE

This 930ha (2,300-acre) park in the city center—one of the largest urban parks in North America—contains its own **waterfowl park,** frequented by 60 or more species of marsh and water birds. There's a naturalist on duty Monday to Friday 9am to 4pm. Another delightful spot is **Willow Island,** a picnic island reached by a small ferry from the overlook west of Broad Street on Wascana Drive.

**Wascana Place,** the headquarters building for the **Wascana Centre Authority** (© **306/522-3661;** www.wascana.sk.ca), provides public information. You can get a fine view from its fourth-level observation deck. Victoria Day to Labour Day, it's open daily 9am to 6pm; winter hours are Monday to Saturday 9:30am to 5:30pm.

The center also contains the **Legislative Building,** the **University of Regina,** the **Royal Saskatchewan Museum,** the **MacKenzie Art Gallery,** and the **Saskatchewan Centre of the Arts.** Also in the park stands the **Diefenbaker Homestead,** the unassuming one-story log home of John Diefenbaker, prime minister from 1957 to 1963, which was moved here from Borden, Saskatchewan. John Diefenbaker helped his father build the three-room house, which is furnished in pioneer style and contains some original family articles. It's open daily 9am to 6pm. Admission is free, Victoria Day to Labour Day.

**Legislative Building** This splendid, stately edifice built from 1908 to 1912 boasts 30 kinds of marble in the interior. Check out the mural Before the White Man Came, depicting aboriginal people in the Qu'Appelle Valley preparing to attack a herd of buffalo on the opposite shore. See also the Legislative Assembly Chamber, the 400,000-volume library, and the art galleries in the basement and on the first floor.

2405 Legislative Dr., Wascana Centre. © **306/787-5358.** Tours daily every half hour 8am–5pm in winter (Sept–May), 8am–9pm in summer (Victoria Day–Labour Day). Tours can be arranged through the visitor services office. On sessional nights, tours available 6–9pm. Groups please call ahead. Free admission.

**MacKenzie Art Gallery** The art gallery's approximately 1,600 works concentrate on Canadian artists, particularly such Saskatchewan painters as James Henderson and Inglis Sheldon-Williams; contemporary American artists; and 15th- to 19th-century Europeans who are represented with paintings, drawings, and prints.

3475 Albert St., T.C. Douglas Bldg. © **306/584-4250.** www.mackenzieartgallery.sk.ca. Free admission. Daily 11am–6pm (Wed–Thurs to 10pm).

**Royal Saskatchewan Museum** *Kids* This museum focuses on the province's anthropological and natural history, displaying a life-size mastodon and a robotic dinosaur that comes roaring to life, plus other specimens. A video cave, a rock table, and a laboratory with a resident paleontologist are all found in the interactive Paleo Pit. A new life-sciences gallery, with large dioramas of Saskatchewan flora and fauna, and an environmental wing are currently being added to the museum. The Apperley Place gift shop offers, among other things, traditional Native art and Saskatchewan crafts.

## The Trial of Louis Riel

**Louis Riel** was tried and hanged in Regina in 1885. Bitter arguments have been fought between those who regard Riel as a patriot and martyr and those who regard him as a rebel. Whatever the opinion, Riel certainly raises some extremely deep and discomforting questions. As G. F. Stanley, professor of history at the Royal Military College, Kingston, has written, "The mere mention of his name bares those latent religious and racial animosities which seem to lie so close to the surface of Canadian politics." Riel has gained some official respect from the Anglo-European community in recent years; in his honor, the Saskatchewan government has renamed Highway 11 from Prince Albert to Regina the **Louis Riel Trail.**

Even though he took up the cause of the mixed-blood population of the west, French-speaking Canadians often regarded Riel as a martyr and English-speaking Canadians damned him as a madman. Written by John Coulter, *The Trial of Louis Riel* is a play based on the actual court records of the historical trial. It's presented Wednesday to Friday at the MacKenzie Art Gallery over a month between July and August. Nothing if not provocative, the play raises such issues as language rights, prejudice, and justice. Tickets are C$12 (US$7) for adults, C$10 (US$6) for seniors and students, and C$9 (US$6) for children ages 12 and under. For information or reservations, call ✆ **306/584-8890** or 306/525-1185.

Wascana Centre, College Ave. and Albert St. ✆ **306/787-2815.** www.royalsaskmuseum.ca. Free admission, with suggested donations. May–Labour Day daily 9am–5:30pm; day after Labour Day–Apr daily 9am–4:30pm. Closed Christmas.

## MORE ATTRACTIONS

**RCMP Training Academy & Museum** ★ This fascinating museum traces the history of the Royal Canadian Mounted Police since 1874, when they began the Great March West to stop liquor traffic and enforce the law in the Northwest Territories, using replicas, newspaper articles, artifacts, uniforms, weaponry, and mementos to document the lives of the early Mounties and the pioneers. It traces the Mounties' role in the 1885 Riel Rebellion, the Klondike Gold Rush (when the simple requirements they laid down probably saved the lives of many foolhardy gold diggers who came pitifully ill-equipped), the Prohibition era (when they sought out stills), World Wars I and II, the 1935 Regina labor riot, and the capture of the mad trapper (who was chased in Arctic temperatures for 54 days from 1931 to 1932). Kids and even adults will love to role-play in the cockpit of the de Havilland single-engine Otter from the Air Services Division and see an audiovisual presentation of training.

A tour also goes to the **chapel**—the oldest building in Regina—and, when possible, allows you to see cadets in training. The highlight is the **Sergeant Majors Parade,** which normally takes place around 12:45pm Monday to Friday. The schedule is tentative, so call before you go. In July and early August, the **Sunset Retreat Ceremony**—an event that dates back to the RCMP's roots—

takes place on Tuesdays just after 6:30pm; it's an exciting 45-minute display of horsemanship by the Mounties accompanied by pipe and bugle bands and choir.

Off Dewdney Ave. W. ✆ **306/780-5838.** www.rcmpmuseum.com. Free admission. Victoria Day weekend–Labour Day weekend daily 8am–6:45pm; the rest of the year daily 10am–4:45pm. Tours weekdays at 1:30pm. Closed Christmas and New Year's Day. Regina Transit Rte. 8.

**Saskatchewan Science Centre** *Kids* The Saskatchewan Science Centre is home to the Powerhouse of Discovery and the Kramer IMAX Theatre. The first houses more than 80 thought-provoking and fun hands-on exhibits demonstrating basic scientific principles, ranging from a hot-air balloon that rises three stories in the central mezzanine to exhibits where you can test your strength, reaction time, and balance. The Kramer IMAX Theatre shows films on a five-story screen accompanied by thrilling six-channel surround-sound. Call for show times (most are in the afternoon).

Winnipeg St. and Wascana Dr. ✆ **800/667-6300** or 306/522-4629. www.sciencecentre.sk.ca. Admission to Powerhouse of Discovery C$6.50 (US$4) adults, C$4.75 (US$2.95) seniors and youth 4–13; free for children 3 and under. IMAX theater C$7 (US$4.35) adults, C$5 (US$3.10) seniors and youth 4–13, C$3.75 (US$2.35) children 3 and under. Combination tickets C$12 (US$7) adults, C$9 (US$6) seniors and youths 4–13, C$3.75 (US$2.35) children 3 and under. MC, V. Summer Mon–Fri 9am–6pm, Sat–Sun 11am–6pm; winter Tues–Fri 9am–5pm, Sat–Sun noon–6pm, holiday Mondays 9am–5pm.

## WHERE TO STAY

### EXPENSIVE

**Delta Regina Hotel** ★ Conveniently located downtown in the Saskatchewan Trade and Convention Centre, the Delta Regina is adjacent to a large retail mall, the Cornwall Centre, and connected by a walkway to the Casino Regina. The modern guest rooms are elegantly appointed with marble vanities, sitting areas, and desks. Business traveler rooms have other amenities, such as printer/fax/copiers and ergonomic work chairs. The hotel also has a waterworks recreation complex with a three-story indoor water slide and whirlpool. Also on site you'll find the casual Summerfield's Dining Room.

1919 Saskatchewan Dr., Regina, SK S4P 4H2. ✆ **800/268-1133** or 306/525-5255. Fax 306/781-7188. www.deltaregina.com. 255 units. C$99–$140 (US$61–$87) double. Extra person C$15 (US$9). Children under 18 stay free in parents' room. Weekend, senior, and package rates available. AE, DC, DISC, MC, V. Adjacent parking C$5 (US$3.10). **Amenities:** Restaurant; lounge; indoor pool; golf course nearby; fitness center; Jacuzzi; business center; room service (6:30am–11pm); same-day dry cleaning; nonsmoking rooms. *In room:* A/C, TV, dataports, hair dryer, iron.

**Hotel Saskatchewan Radisson Plaza** ★★ The hotel's ivy-covered limestone exterior has a rather solid old-world air about it, a satisfying prelude to the modern comfort within. The large, almost heart-shaped clock in the lobby is original to the 1927 Georgian-style building. Guest rooms have elegant high ceilings and decorative moldings. There are also deluxe living-room suites, luxury suites with dining rooms, and Jacuzzi suites. If you really want to splurge, spend C$999 (US$619) for a night in the 240m$^2$ (2,000 sq. ft.) Royal Suite, with a luxurious dining room, a whirlpool tub, and warmed towel bars in the bathroom. The **Cortlandt Hall** restaurant—boasting terraced seating, stately windows, and a coffered oak ceiling with brass chandeliers—specializes in grills, seafood, veal, and chicken dishes. The Monarch Lounge is a full service pub with small menu, and you can take high in the Victoria Tea Room. Wheelchair accessible rooms are available.

2125 Victoria Ave. (at Scarth St.), Regina, SK S4P 0S3. ✆ **800/333-3333** or 306/522-7691. Fax 306/522-8988. www.hotelsask.com. 217 units. C$144–C$199 and up (US$89–US$123 and up) double. Extra person C$15 (US$9). Children under 12 stay free in parents' room. Group, senior, and package rates offered. AE, DC, DISC, MC, V. **Amenities:** Restaurant; fitness center; Jacuzzi; sauna; room service; nonsmoking rooms; executive-level rooms. *In room:* A/C, TV, dataport, fridge, coffeemaker, hair dryer, iron.

**Ramada Hotel & Convention Centre** ★ You notice the Ramada's organic natural quality in the lobby with its earth-color stone walls and plant-filled coffee plaza. The attractive guest rooms have modern furnishings and the usual amenities. Rooms accessible for those with disabilities are available.

1818 Victoria Ave., Regina, SK S4P 0R1. ✆ **800/272-6232** or 306/569-1666. Fax 306/352-6339. www.ramada.ca. 233 units. C$130–C$175 (US$81–US$109) double. Children under 18 stay free in parents' room. Weekend packages, senior and AAA discounts available. AE, DC, MC, V. Parking C$3.50 (US$2.15). Some pets allowed. **Amenities:** Restaurant, lounge, bar; indoor pool; exercise room; Jacuzzi; sauna; room service, children's center; coin-op laundry, same-day dry cleaning, nonsmoking rooms; executive-level rooms. *In room:* A/C, TV w/pay movies, coffeemaker.

**Regina Inn** ★ This recently renovated inn occupies an entire block and offers numerous facilities. Guest rooms, most with balconies, have a contemporary decor and louvered closets. Various types of suites are available, the top-level including Jacuzzi tubs. The hotel offers the Botanica all-day cafe, dining and drinks at Vic's Steakhouse and Lounge, and the Applause Feast & Folly live dinner theater.

1975 Broad St., Regina, SK S4P 1Y2. ✆ **800/667-8162** in Canada, or 306/525-6767. Fax 306/352-1858. 235 units. www.reginainn.com. C$119–C$189 (US$74–US$117) double. Extra person C$10 (US$6). Children under 18 stay free in parents' room. Weekend and other packages, and group and senior rates available. AE, DC, DISC, MC, V. **Amenities:** 2 restaurants, lounge, nightclub; fitness center; car rental desk; room service; nonsmoking rooms; executive-level rooms. *In room:* TV w/video games and pay movies, dataport, coffeemaker, iron.

## MODERATE

**Chelton Suites Hotel** Located downtown, the Chelton is small enough to provide friendly personal service. The large guest rooms sport modern furnishings. A bedroom/sitting room will contain a table, chairs, drawers, and a couch. Even the smallest rooms are bright and spacious compared to most other accommodations. Suites have separate bedrooms and living areas. An exercise room is available to all guests.

1907 11th Ave., Regina, SK S4P 0J2. ✆ **800/667-9922** in Canada, or 306/569-4600. Fax 306/569-3531. 78 units. C$99–C$175 (US$61–US$109) suites. Rates include continental breakfast. Weekend rates and seniors and AAA discounts available. Free parking and local phone calls. AE, DC, MC, V. **Amenities:** Exercise room; nonsmoking rooms; executive-level rooms. *In room:* A/C, TV, dataport, fridge, coffeemaker, hair dryer, iron.

## INEXPENSIVE

**Turgeon International Hostel** ★ Regina is fortunate to have one of Canada's best youth hostels, located in a handsome 1907 town house adjacent to the Wascana Centre. Accommodations are in dorms with three or four bunks; the top floor has two larger dorms, and each dorm has access to a deck. Downstairs is a comfortable sitting room worthy of any inn, with couches in front of the oak fireplace and plenty of magazines and books. The basement contains an impeccably clean dining and cooking area with electric stoves. Picnic tables are available in the backyard.

2310 McIntyre St., Regina, SK S4P 2S2. ✆ **306/791-8165.** Fax 306/721-2667. hihostels.sask@sk.sympatico.ca. 29 beds. C$17 (US$11) members, C$22 (US$14) nonmembers. Group rates available. MC, V. Limited street parking. Closed Dec 25–Jan 31. Lights out at 11:30pm. **Amenities:** Tour and activities desk; coin-op laundry. *In room:* A/C, no phone.

## WHERE TO DINE

In addition to the places below, try **Neo Japonica,** 2167 Hamilton St., at 14th Avenue (© **306/359-7669**), for good Japanese cuisine; it's open Monday to Friday 11am to 1:30pm, Sunday to Thursday 5 to 9:30pm, Friday and Saturday 5 to 10:30pm. Although this is beef country, the **Heliotrope Whole Food Vegetarian Restaurant,** 2204 McIntyre St. (© **306/569-3373;** www.heliotrope.sk.ca), serves good ethnic vegan cooking prepared from organic produce. It's open Monday to Friday 11am to 3pm and 5 to 9pm, and Saturday from 5 to 9pm (closed Jan 1–Mar 1).

**The Diplomat Steak House** ★ CANADIAN This old-style steak house boasts semicircular banquettes and tables set with pink cloths, burgundy napkins, and tiny lanterns. Around the room hang portraits of eminent-looking prime ministers; there is a fireplace and lounge up front. The sizeable menu's main attractions are the steaks—20-ounce porterhouse, 18-ounce T-bone—along with chicken en croute, rack of lamb, grilled salmon, and other traditional favorites. In addition, you'll find such specialties as quail stuffed with wild rice in a rosemary game sauce and a Steak Neptune, butterflied filet mignon topped with crabmeat, asparagus, and a hollandaise sauce. Elk and buffalo steaks can also be had here. The Diplomat has over 135 wines to compliment your meal.

2032 Broad St. © **306/359-3366.** Reservations recommended. Main courses C$13–C$43 (US$8–US$27). AE, DC, MC, V. Mon–Fri 11am–2pm; Mon–Sat 4pm–midnight.

**Golf's Steak House** CANADIAN In this venerable Regina institution, the atmosphere is decidedly plush (note the large fireplace, the piano and antique organ, the heavy gilt-framed paintings, and the high-backed carved-oak Charles II-style chairs). The menu offers traditional steak house fare.

1945 Victoria Ave. (at Hamilton St.). © **306/525-5808.** Reservations recommended. Main courses C$16–C$40 (US$10–US$25). AE, DC, MC, V. Mon–Fri 11am–midnight; Sat 4pm–midnight, Sun and holidays 4–10pm.

**Saje Gourmet Cafe** NEW CANADIAN Saje is a low-key, almost nonchalant little cafe with quite good food and a pleasantly unfocused atmosphere. There are two menus: The small fine-dining menu offers innovative preparations of beef, chicken, seafood, and wild game; the other menu is almost more inviting, featuring several pages of salads, sandwiches, and bagel creations. Both are available at dinner, making this a good place to go if there are different levels of appetite in your group. The desserts and breads are homemade and very good. The wine list is small but thoughtful.

2330 Albert St. © **306/569-9726.** Reservations recommended. Main courses C$18–C$25 (US$11–US$16). AE, DC, MC, V. Mon–Fri 11:30am–2pm and 6–10pm (Fri until 11pm), Sat 6–11pm.

## REGINA AFTER DARK

The focus of the city's cultural life is the **Saskatchewan Centre of the Arts,** on the southern shore of Wascana Lake (© **800/667-8497** or 306/525-9999 for the box office; www.centreofthearts.sk.ca). With two theaters and a large concert hall, the Centre is home to the **Regina Symphony Orchestra** and features many other performance companies. Ticket prices vary depending on the show. The box office at 200 Lakeshore Dr. (© **306/525-9999**) is open Monday to Saturday 10am to 6pm.

Late September to early May, the **Globe Theatre,** Old City Hall, 1801 Scarth St. (© **306/525-6400;** www.globetheatrelive.com), a theater-in-the-round, presents six plays. Productions run the gamut from classics (Shakespeare,

Molière, Shaw, and others) to modern dramas, musicals, and comedies. Tickets are C$12 to C$22 (US$7–US$14). Box Office hours are Monday to Saturday 10am to 5pm.

The **Casino Regina,** 1880 Saskatchewan Dr., at Broad St. (✆ **800/555-3189** or 306/565-3000; www.casinoregina.com), is the latest year-round amusement. It has over 35 gaming tables plus over 600 slots, as well as a restaurant and live show theater, and is open daily 9am to 4am (closed Christmas). The college crowd favors **Checkers,** at the Landmark Inn, 4150 Albert St. (✆ **306/586-5363**), a comfortable, rustic, and relaxed dance spot. In summer, the outdoor area called **Scotland Yard** is also crowded.

A slightly older crowd (25–35) frequents the **Manhattan Club and Island Pub** at 2300 Dewdney St. (✆ **306/359-7771**). The upstairs dance club here is open Thursday to Saturday. For more relaxed entertainment, there's the **Applause Feast and Folly Dinner Theatre** at the Regina Inn, 1975 Broad St. (✆ **306/525-6767**), or the **Ramada's Mulligan Lounge,** 1818 Victoria Ave. (✆ **306/569-1666**). A couple of other pubs with an Irish flavor, popular in Regina, are **McNally's,** at 2226 Dewdney Ave. (✆ **306/522-4774;** www.mcnallys-tavern.com), which also features live music; and the **Blarney Stone,** at 4177 Alberta Street S., in the Travelodge Hotel (✆ **306/586-3443**).

## 8 Saskatchewan Highlights Along the Trans-Canada Highway

### MOOSE MOUNTAIN PROVINCIAL PARK & WEST TO REGINA

Just across the Manitoba/Saskatchewan border at Whitewood, you can turn south down Highway 9 to **Moose Mountain Provincial Park** (✆ **306/577-2600**); it's also accessible from highways 16 and 13. About 106km (66 miles) southeast of Regina, this 388km$^2$ (150-sq. mile) park is dotted with lakes and marshes. The park harbors a variety of waterfowl and songbirds—blue-winged teal, red-necked ducks, blue heron, red-tailed hawk, ovenbird, rose-breasted grosbeak, and Baltimore oriole—and animals, including deer, elk, moose, beaver, muskrat, and coyote.

In summer, park rangers lead guided hikes. The Beaver Youell Lake and the Wuche Sakaw trails are also easy to follow. You can hike or bike along the **nature trails;** swim at the **beach** south of the main parking lot and at several of the lakes; cool off at the super-fun **giant water slides** on Kenosee Lake, which include an eight-story free-fall slide (open mid-May to Labour Day); **golf** at the 18-hole course; go **horseback riding;** or play **tennis.** In winter, the park has more than 56km (35 miles) of **cross-country ski trails** and more than 120km (74 miles) of **snowmobiling trails.**

The modern, no-nonsense **Kenosee Inn,** Box 1300, Carlyle, SK S0C 0R0 (✆ **306/577-2099;** fax 306/577-2465; www.kenoseeinn.com), offers 30 rooms and 23 cabin accommodations (with air-conditioning, TV, and phone) overlooking Kenosee Lake in the park. Facilities include a restaurant, a bar, an indoor pool, and a hot tub. Rates are C$82 to C$89 (US$51–US$55) for a double room, C$69 to C$89 (US$43–US$55) for a one-bedroom cabin, and C$89 to C$110 (US$55–US$68) for a two-bedroom cabin, depending on its age and size. Off-season rates are available. The park also has two **campgrounds.**

### MOOSE JAW

**Moose Jaw** gained notoriety as Canada's rum-running capital; it was known as "Little Chicago" in the 1920s. Today some restored buildings still retain the underground tunnels used for the illicit trade. You can take two guided tours of the tunnels, one detailing the "Chicago Connection"—including stories of Al Capone beating the heat up north—and the other, "Passage to Fortune," telling the story of Chinese immigrants who came to Moose Jaw looking for economic opportunity through work in the tunnels. Another tour devoted to bootlegging and an amphitheater show are slated to open, as well. There's also a small museum archive of documents and pictures from Moose Jaw's heyday, located at Tunnels Central, 18 Main Street North. Tours cost C$12 (US$7) for adults, C$9 (US$6) for seniors and students, and C$6 (US$3.70) for children. For more information, contact **Tunnels of Moose Jaw** (© **306/693-5261** or 306/693-7273; www.tunnelsofmoosejaw.com).

The **Moose Jaw Art Museum, Gallery & Historical Museum,** 461 Langdon Crescent, in Crescent Park (© **306/692-4471;** www.mjmag.ca) has a fine collection of Cree and Sioux beadwork and clothing, plus plenty of contemporary art and history exhibits. It's open Tuesday to Sunday noon to 5pm and Tuesday through Thursday 7 to 9pm; admission is by donation. Moose Jaw is also known for its 26 outdoor murals depicting aspects of the city's heritage. For information, call **Murals of Moose Jaw** at © **306/693-4262,** or visit www.citymoosejaw.com for a detailed list of the murals.

The **Western Development Museum**'s **History of Transportation** branch, at 50 Diefenbaker Dr., by the intersection of highways 1 and 2 (© **306/693-5989**), showcases the roles that air, rail, land, and water transportation played in opening up the West. One gallery pays tribute to the Snowbirds, Canada's famous air demonstration squadron. You can see a large-screen film about the squadron and experience the thrills for yourself on the flight simulator. Museum admission is C$6 (US$3.70) for adults, C$5 (US$3.10) for seniors, C$4 (US$2.50) for students, C$2 (US$1.20) for children under 12, and C$14 (US$9) for families; preschoolers enter free. **Wakamow Valley** (© **306/692-2717**), which follows the course of the river through town, includes six parks with walking and biking trails, canoeing, and skating facilities. Free guided walking tours are available to groups on request.

If you stop in Moose Jaw, the place to stay is the **Temple Gardens Mineral Spa Hotel and Resort,** 24 Fairford Street East (© **800/718-7727** or 306/694-5055; www.templegardens.sk.ca), offering 96 rooms and 24 spa suites with private mineral-water Jacuzzis. It's a full-facility resort with special mineral pools where you can take the waters. The spa offers a full range of body treatments. Rates are C$102 to C$170 (US$63–US$105) for a double and C$170 to C$245 (US$105–US$152) for spa Jacuzzi suites.

For more information, contact **Tourism Moose Jaw,** 99 Diefenbaker Dr., Moose Jaw, SK S6H 4P2 (© **866/693-8097;** www.citymoosejaw.com/tourism).

## SWIFT CURRENT, CYPRESS HILLS INTERPROVINCIAL PARK & FORT WALSH

**Swift Current** (www.city.swift-current.sk.ca), Saskatchewan's base for western oil exploration and a regional trading center for livestock and grain, is 167km (104 miles) along the Trans-Canada Highway from Moose Jaw. It's known for its **Frontier Days** in June and **Old Tyme Fiddling Contest** in September. From Swift Current it's about another 201km (125 miles) to the Alberta border.

Straddling the border is **Cypress Hills Interprovincial Park,** P.O. Box 850, Maple Creek, SK S0N 1N0 (© **306/662-5411**), and the **Fort Walsh National Historic Site.** En route to Cypress Hills, off the Trans-Canada Highway, is **Maple Creek,** a thoroughly Western cow town with many heritage storefronts on the main street. On the Saskatchewan side, the provincial park is divided into a Centre Block, off Route 21, and a West Block, off Route 271. Both blocks are joined by Gap Road, which is impassable when wet. The park's core is in the Centre Block, where there are six campgrounds; an outdoor pool; canoe, row/paddleboat, and bike rentals; a nine-hole golf course; tennis courts; a riding stable; and swimming at the beach on Loch Leven. In winter there are 24km (15 miles) of **cross-country skiing trails.** Entry to the park costs C$7 (US$4.35); camping in the summer costs C$11 to C$24 (US$7–US$15).

The **Cypress Park Resort Inn** (✆ **306/662-4477;** www.cypressresortinn.com) offers nice hotel-style rooms for C$75 (US$47), as well as cabins starting at C$65 (US$40) and condominium accommodations from C$99 (US$61) in high season; off-season rates are also available. The resort features amenities like an indoor pool and full-service dining room.

**Fort Walsh National Historic Site,** Box 278, Maple Creek, SK S0N 1N0 (✆ **306/298-2257;** www.parcscanada.gc.ca) can be accessed from Route 271 or directly from the park's West Block by gravel and clay roads. Built in 1875, the fort's soldiers tried to contain the local Native tribes and the many Sioux who sought refuge here after the Battle of Little Bighorn in 1876, as well as keep out American criminals seeking sanctuary. It was dismantled in 1883. Today the reconstruction consists of five buildings and a trading post staffed with folks in period costume. Victoria Day weekend to Labour Day, it's open daily 9:30am to 5:30pm. Admission is C$6 (US$3.70) for adults, C$4.50 (US$2.80) for seniors, C$3 (US$1.85) for youths ages 6 to 16, C$15 (US$9) for families, and free for children under 6. There are additional fees for various presentations or scheduled events.

### GRASSLANDS NATIONAL PARK

About 121km (75 miles) south of Swift Current along the U.S. border stretches **Grasslands National Park,** P.O. Box 150, Val Marie, SK S0N 2T0 (✆ **360/298-2257:** www.parcscanada.gc.ca)—2 blocks of protected land separated by about 27km (17 miles). On this mixed prairie- and grassland there's no escape from the sun and the wind. The **Frenchman River** cuts deep into the West Block, where you can spot pronghorn antelope. Black-tailed **prairie dogs,** which bark warnings at intruders and reassure each other with kisses and hugs, also make their home here. In the East Block, the open prairie is broken with coulees and the adobe hills of the Killdeer Badlands, so called because of their poor soil.

Although the park doesn't have facilities, there are two self-guided **nature trails,** and you can also climb to the summit of **70 Mile Butte** and no-trace camp. The **information center** (✆ **306/298-2257**) is in Val Marie at the junction of Highway 4 and Centre Street (closed weekends in winter).

## 9 Saskatoon: The Progressive City on the Plains

**Saskatoon** (pop. about 230,000) is the progressive city on the plains. The town still retains a distinctly Western air. The downtown streets are broad and dusty and dotted in summer with many a pickup truck. Those same downtown streets just seem to disappear on the edge of town into the prairie, where grain elevators and telegraph poles become the only reference points and the sky your only company.

Scenically, Saskatoon possesses some distinct natural advantages. The South Saskatchewan River cuts a swath through the city. Spanned by several graceful bridges, its banks are great for strolling, biking, and jogging. Much of the city's recent wealth has come from the surrounding mining region that yields potash, uranium, petroleum, gas, and gold; Key Lake is the world's most productive uranium mine.

## ESSENTIALS

**GETTING THERE** **By plane** **Saskatoon John G. Diefenbaker Airport** (© **306/975-8900;** www.yxe.ca) is served largely by **Air Canada** (© 888/247-2262), **Northwest** (© 800/447-4747), and **WestJet** (© 877/952-4638).

**By train** **VIA Rail** (© **888/VIA-RAIL,** 800/561-8630 in western Canada, or 800/561-3949 in the U.S.; www.viarail.ca), trains arrive in the west end of the city on Chappel Drive.

**By car** If you're driving, Highway 16 (the Yellowhead Highway) leads to Saskatoon from the east or west. From Regina, Route 11 leads northwest to Saskatoon, 257km (159 miles) away.

**VISITOR INFORMATION** From mid-May to the end of August, a booth is open at Avenue C North at 47th Street. Otherwise, contact **Tourism Saskatoon,** 6-305 Idylwyld Dr. N., Saskatoon, SK S7L 0Z1 (© **800/567-2444** or 306/242-1206; www.tourismsaskatoon.com). Summer hours—also for the information booth—are Monday to Friday 8:30am to 7pm and Saturday and Sunday 10am to 7pm; winter hours for the Tourism Saskatoon office, in the old CP Railway Station at Idylwyld and 24th St., are Monday to Friday 8:30am to 5pm.

**CITY LAYOUT** The South Saskatchewan River cuts a diagonal north-south swath through the city. The main downtown area lies on the west bank; the **University of Saskatchewan** and the long neon-sign-crazed **8th Street** dominate the east bank. Streets are laid out in a numbered grid system—22nd Street divides north- and south-designated streets; **Idylwyld Drive** divides, in a similar fashion, east from west. **First Street** through **18th Street** lie on the river's east side; **19th Street** and up, are situated on the west bank in the downtown area. **Spadina Crescent** runs along the river's west bank, where you'll find such landmarks as the Bessborough Hotel, the Ukrainian Museum, and the art gallery.

**GETTING AROUND** You may need to use transportation only when you visit the University of Saskatchewan and the Western Development Museum. **Saskatoon Transit System**, 301–226 23rd St. E. (© **306/975-3100;** www.city.saskatoon.sk.ca/org/transit), operates buses to all city areas Monday to Saturday 6am to 12:30am and Sunday 9:15am to 9pm for an exact-change fare of C$1.60 (US$1.05) for adults, C$1.10 (US70¢) for high-school students, and C85¢ (US55¢) for grade-school students.

Car-rental companies include **Avis,** 2625 Airport Dr. or 114–2301 Avenue C N. (© **306/652-3434**); **Budget,** at the airport or 3 in-town locations in Saskatoon (© **800/844-7888**); **Hertz,** at the airport (© **306/373-1161**); **National,** at the airport or Avenue C N. (© **306/665-7703** or 306/664-8771); and **Thrifty,** at the airport or 143 Robin Crescent (© **306/244-8000** or 306/244-8000). Taxis cost C$2.90 (US$1.80) when you step inside and C10¢ (US5¢) every 90m (246 ft.). Try **Saskatoon Radio Cab Ltd.** (© **306/242-1221**), which runs taxis and 6-passenger minivans; or **United/Blueline Taxi** (© **306/652-2222**), which also operates the limousine to the airport or VIA Rail for C$8 (US$5) from downtown hotels.

**SPECIAL EVENTS** The 8-day **Saskatoon Prairieland Exhibition** (P.O. Box 6010, Saskatoon, SK S7K 4E4; ✆ **888/931-9333** or 306/931-7149; www.saskatoonex.com), usually held the second week of July, provides some grand agricultural spectacles, like the threshing competition in which steam power is pitted against gas—sometimes with unexpected results—and the tractor-pulling competition, when standard farm tractors are used to pull a steel sled weighted down with a water tank. The pay-one-price admission of C$8 (US$5) for adults and C$5 (US$3.10) for youths ages 10 to 15 (children under 10 are free with an adult) lets you in all the entertainments—a craft show, talent competitions, thoroughbred racing, midway, and Kidsville, which features clowns, games, and a petting zoo. Parking is C$2.00 (US$1.20).

In mid-August, a **Folkfest** (✆ **306/931-0100;** www.folkfest.sk.ca) celebrates the city's many ethnic groups through food, displays, and performances; admission is C$12 (US$7) for adults, and children under 12 are free if accompanied by an adult. The **Canadian Cowboys Association Rodeo Finals** are held at the **Saskatchewan Place** exhibition center (✆ **306/975-3155,** 306/975-2907, or 800/970-7328 for tickets; www.saskatchewanplace.com) in late October.

## EXPLORING THE CITY

Housed in a striking modern building overlooking the South Saskatchewan River, a short walk from downtown, the **Mendel Art Gallery,** 950 Spadina Crescent E. (✆ **306/975-7610;** www.mendel.ca), has a good permanent collection of Canadian paintings, sculpture, watercolors, and graphics. Admission is free. The gallery is open daily 9am to 9pm (closed Christmas).

Nearby is the **Ukrainian Museum of Canada,** 910 Spadina Crescent E. (✆ **306/244-3800;** www.umc.sk.ca). Reminiscent of an early-1900s Ukrainian home in western Canada, this museum preserves the Ukrainian heritage in clothing, linens, tools, books, photographs, documents, wooden folk art, ceramics, pysanky (Easter eggs), and other treasures and art forms brought from the homeland by Ukrainian immigrants to Canada. Admission is C$2 (US$1.20) for adults, C$1 (US60¢) for seniors, and C50¢ (US30¢) for children ages 6 to 12. It's open Victoria Day to Labour Day, Monday to Saturday 10am to 5pm and Sunday 1 to 5pm; closed Monday but with the same hours other days during the rest of the year.

At the **Saskatoon Zoo,** 1903 Forest Dr. (✆ **306/975-3395;** www.city.saskatoon.sk.ca), 300 species of Canadian and Saskatchewan wildlife are on view—wolves, coyotes, foxes, bears, eagles, owls, hawks, deer, caribou, elks, and bison. There's a children's zoo too. During winter you can cross-country ski the 4km (2½-mile) trail. Admission is C$4.50 (US$2.80) for adults, C$2.75 (US$1.70) for seniors and children ages 6 to 18, and C$9 (US$6) for families. May 1 to Labour Day there's a C$2 (US$1.20) vehicle charge. The zoo is open daily May 1 to Labour Day 9am to 9pm and the rest of the year 10am to 4pm. It's in northeast Saskatoon; follow the signs on Attridge Drive from Circle Drive.

The **University of Saskatchewan** (✆ **306/966-4343;** www.usask.ca) occupies a dramatic 1,030ha (2,550-acre) site overlooking the South Saskatchewan River and is attended by some 20,000 students. The actual campus buildings are set on 145ha (360 acres) while the rest of the area is largely given over to the university farm and experimental plots. The **Diefenbaker Canada Centre** (✆ **306/966-8384;** www.usask.ca/diefenbaker) contains the papers and memorabilia of one of Canada's best-known prime ministers and is open Monday and Friday

9:30am to 4:30pm; and Saturday, Sunday, and holidays noon to 4:30pm. The archives are open Monday to Friday 9:30am to 12:30 pm. Admission is C$2 (US$1.20) for adults, C$1 (US60¢) for children, and C$5 (US$3.10) for families. The **University Observatory** (✆ **306/966-6429;** open Saturday evenings after dusk) houses the Duncan telescope. The **Little Stone Schoolhouse** (✆ **306/966-8384**), built in 1887, served as the city's first school and community center. It's open May 1st to Labour Day, Monday to Friday 9:30am to 4:30pm, and Saturday and Sunday noon to 4:30pm; admission is by donation. You can arrange special tours of the research farm and many of the colleges. Contact the Office of Communications, University of Saskatchewan (✆ **306/966-6607;** www.usask.ca/communications). To get there, take bus no. 7 or 19 from downtown at 23rd Street and 2nd Avenue.

**Wanuskewin Heritage Park** ★ This park is built around the archaeological discovery of 19-plus Northern Plains Indian, pre-contact sites. Walking along the trails, you'll see archaeological digs in progress, habitation sites, stone cairns, teepee rings, bison jumps, and other trace features of this ancient culture. At the amphitheater, First Nations performers present dance, theater, song, and storytelling, while at the outdoor activity area you can learn how to build a teepee, bake bannock, tan a hide, or use a travois (a transportation device). The main exhibit halls feature computer-activated displays and artifacts, multimedia shows exploring the archaeology and culture of the Plains peoples, contemporary art, and a Living Culture exhibit that tells the stories behind the daily headlines.

RR #4, 5km (3 miles) north of Saskatoon off Hwy. 11 and Warman Rd. ✆ **306/931-6767.** www.wanuskewin.com. Admission C$6.50 (US$4) adults, C$5.50 (US$3.40) seniors, C$4.50 (US$2.80) students 6–18, C$25 (US$16) families, children under 6 free. Victoria Day–Labour Day daily 9am–9pm, Labour Day–Thanksgiving and Apr–Victoria Day daily 9am–5pm, Thanksgiving–Mar Wed–Sun 9am–5pm. Follow Bison signs as you near the park.

**Western Development Museum** The energetic years of Saskatchewan settlement are vividly portrayed by Boomtown 1910, an authentic replica of prairie community life in that year. When you step onto the main street of Boomtown, the memories of an earlier age flood your senses. Browse through the shops, crammed with the unfamiliar goods of days gone by; savor the past through the mysterious aromas that permeate the drugstore; step aside as you hear the clip-clop of a passing horse and buggy; or wander down to Boomtown Station drawn by the low wail of an approaching steam locomotive. The museum truly comes to life during Pion-Era in July, when volunteers in authentic costume staff Boomtown and many pieces of vintage equipment are pressed into service once again.

2610 Lorne Ave. S. ✆ **306/931-1910.** www.wdmuseum.sk.ca. Admission C$6 (US$3.70) adults, C$5 (US$3.10) seniors, C$4 (US$2.50) students, C$2 (US$1.20) children 6–12, C$14 (US$9) families, children under 5 free. Daily 9am–5pm; closed Monday Jan–Mar. Take Idylwyld Dr. south to the Lorne Ave., exit and follow Lorne Ave. south until you see the museum on the right. Bus 1 from the 23rd St. Bus Mall between 2nd and 3rd aves.

## SHOPPING

For Canadian merchandise, stop in at **The Trading Post,** 226–2nd Ave. S. (✆ **800/653-1769** or 306/653-1769), which carries Inuit soapstone carvings, native-Canadian art, Cowichan sweaters, mukluks, beadwork, and more. Some galleries showing local artists that are worth browsing include the **AKA Gallery,** 3rd Floor, 12–23rd St. E. (✆ **306/652-0044;** www.quadrant.net/aka); the **Photographers Gallery,** also at 12–23rd St. E. (✆ **306/244-8018**); the **Arlington**

**Frame Gallery,** 265–2nd Ave. S. (✆ **306/244-5922**); the **Collector's Choice Art Gallery,** 625D 1st Ave. N. (✆ **306/665-8300**); and the **Handmade House Handcraft Store,** 710 Broadway Ave. (✆ **306/665-5542**), which specializes in crafts.

## WHERE TO STAY

**Delta Bessborough** ★★ A gracious hostelry built in 1930 and finished in 1935, the Bessborough looks like a French château, with a copper roof and turrets. Each guest room is unique, though all have venerable oak entrance doors and antique or traditional furniture. Front rooms are large and most have bay windows. Riverside rooms are smaller but have lovely views across the Saskatchewan River. For food there is the river-view coffee shop and the Samurai Japanese Steakhouse.

601 Spadina Crescent E., Saskatoon, SK S7K 3G8. ✆ **800/268-1133** or 306/244-5521. Fax 306/665-7262. www.deltahotels.com. 225 units. C$119–$179 (US$74–111) double. Extra person C$10 (US$6). Children under 18 stay free in parents' room. Weekend packages available. AE, DC, MC, V. Self- or valet-parking C$6 (US$3.70) per day. **Amenities:** 2 restaurants, lounge; indoor pool; fitness center; Jacuzzi; sauna; business center; executive-level rooms. *In room:* A/C, TV w/video games, dataport, coffeemaker, hair dryer, iron.

**Quality Hotel Downtown** This modern hotel has a very convenient location, right downtown opposite the Eaton's complex and Centennial Auditorium. Standard family rooms come with either two double or one queen bed, while larger business rooms have a king bed plus a work desk. This is a very affordable and comfortable option for downtown lodging.

90–22nd Street E., at 1st Ave. ✆ **800/228-5151** or 306/244-2311. www.choicehotels.ca. 298 units. C$76 to C$99 (US$47–US$61) double. AE, MC, V. Free parking. **Amenities:** Restaurant, lounge; indoor heated pool; Jacuzzi; room service; babysitting. *In room:* A/C, TV w/pay movies, dataport, coffeemaker, iron.

**Radisson Hotel Saskatoon** Offering a riverside location in the heart of downtown, the Radisson is a luxury property, with well-decorated guest rooms. About a third of the units offer river views; the corner rooms are particularly attractive. Summerfield's Café and Loft serves three meals daily, Capers Lounge offers drinks and hors d'oeuvres, and guests enjoy a three-story recreation complex. Jogging and cross-country ski trails adjoin the property. Wheelchair accessible rooms are available.

405 20th St. E., Saskatoon, SK S7K 6X6. ✆ **800/333-3333** or 306/665-3322. Fax 306/665-5531. www.radisson.com/saskatoonca. 291 units. From C$174–C$255 (US$108–US$158) double. Extra person C$10 (US$6). Children under 16 stay free in parents' room. Weekend packages, senior citizen and AAA discounts available. AE, DC, MC, V. Parking C$6 (US$3.70). **Amenities:** Restaurant, lounge; indoor pool; fitness center; Jacuzzi; sauna; bike rental; room service (6:30am–11pm); same-day dry cleaning; nonsmoking rooms; executive-level rooms. *In room:* A/C, TV, dataport, coffeemaker, hair dryer, iron.

**Sheraton Cavalier** This handsome hotel offers a lot of luxury and facilities in an excellent downtown location overlooking the Saskatchewan River. All rooms were refurbished in 2001, with all new beds and furnishings. Traveling families will love the extensive indoor water park, with two large waterslides, swimming pool, children's wading pool, and hot tubs. There is also a special executive floor for businesspeople with a work desk and fax printer in each room. The Majestic Grille, with New Canadian cuisine, and Carver's Steakhouse are among the best in Saskatoon.

612 Spadina Crescent E. ✆ **800/325-3535** or 306/652-6770. www.sheratonsaskatoon.com. 249 units. C$169 (US$105) double, C$249 (US$154) one-bedroom suite. AE, MC, V. Heated parking C$5 (US$3.10). **Amenities:** 3 restaurants, 2 bars; pool complex; fitness center; room service; laundry service. *In room:* A/C, TV/VCR w/pay movies, dataport, minibar, coffeemaker, hair dryer, iron.

## WHERE TO DINE

**Black Duck Freehouse** PUB FARE The Black Duck is Saskatoon's great meeting place, where students, office workers, and travelers come together for a drink (there's a hefty selection of regional ales, as well as 30-odd brands of Scotch), as well as for good bar meals, which range from burgers to fish-and-chips to daily specials. The Duck has a friendly publike atmosphere where you'll find it easy to find someone local to talk to—exactly what you may be looking for after a few days on the road.

154 2nd Ave. S. ✆ **306/244-8850.** www.link.ca/blackduck. Reservations accepted. Main courses C$7–C$12 (US$4.35–US$7). AE, DC, MC, V. Daily 11am–2am.

**Prime's Steakhouse and Bar** STEAK/SEAFOOD This new steakhouse offers quality fare in a formal, but comfortable interior of fine woodwork and stained glass, complete with 3 fireplaces. The menu features a wide range of cuts of AAA western Canadian beef—including prime rib, T-bone, and filet mignon—as well as lamb, chicken, and seafood entrees. The wine list is one of the most extensive in town. Prime's also features live entertainment several nights a week.

1110 Grosvenor Ave. (between 7th and 8th sts.). ✆ **306/374-2020.** Reservations recommended. Main courses C$16–C$35 (US$10–US$22). AE, DC, MC, V. Daily 4–11pm.

**St. Tropez Bistro** CONTINENTAL This is one of my favorite downtown restaurants, where the background music is classical or French and the tables are covered in Laura Ashley-style floral-design prints. For dinner, you can choose from a variety of pastas and stir-fries or such dishes as a peppercorn filet mignon or blackened chicken. For dessert, you might try the triple-chocolate mousse pie or daily cheesecake. This is one place where you can find out what's happening culturally in Saskatoon.

238 2nd Ave. S. ✆ **306/652-1250.** Reservations recommended. Main courses C$14–C$24 (US$9–US$15). AE, MC, V. Sun–Thurs 5–10pm and Fri–Sat 5–11pm.

**Saskatoon Station Place** GREEK/STEAK HOUSE This is a restaurant with a lot of thematic convergence going on. The dining room faces into a real vintage rail dining car, and the decor reflects Golden Age of Rail nostalgia. However, about half the menu (the better half?) is Greek, with excellent souvlaki and grilled ribs. Otherwise, there's a good selection of steaks and seafood available if the Greek and rail themes don't charm. This is a nice place to come for a drink and nibbles.

221 Idylwyld Dr. N. ✆ **306/244-7777.** www.saskatoonstation.com. Reservations recommended. Main courses C$15–C$25 (US$9–US$16). AE, DC, MC, V. Mon–Thurs 10:30am–midnight, Fri–Sat 10:30am–12:30am, Sun 10am–11pm.

## SASKATOON AFTER DARK

There's not an awful lot of nightlife, but the **Saskatoon Centennial Auditorium,** 35 22nd St. E. (✆ **306/975-7777,** or 800/970-7328 or 306/938-7800 for tickets; www.saskcent.com), provides a superb 2,003-seat theater, with a range of shows. The **Saskatoon Symphony** (✆ **306/665-6414;** www.saskatoonsymphony.org) regularly performs in a September-to-April season. Tickets for adults are C$15 to C$33 (US$9–US$20); with discounts for seniors, students, and children.

Among local theater companies, the **Persephone Theatre,** 2802 Rusholme Rd. (✆ **306/384-2126** or 306/384-7727 for the box office; www.persephonetheatre.org), offers six shows per fall-to-spring season (dramas, comedies, and musicals); tickets are C$14 to C$25 (US$9–US$16). **Shakespeare on the Saskatchewan,** 602–245 3rd Avenue S., Saskatoon, SK S7K 1M4 (✆ **306/653-2300** or 306/652-9100 for the box office; www.shakespeareonthe saskatchewan.com), produces the Bard in two tents overlooking the river from July to mid-August. Three Shakespeare plays are performed, plus a special Festival Frolics during the season. Tickets are C$22 (US$14) for adults, C$18 (US$11) for seniors and students, and C$13 (US$8) for matinees or children ages 6 to 12; children under 6 are free. Summer stock matinees are C$12 (US$7) and late-night shows are C$7.50 (US$4.65).

For quiet drinking and conversation, you can't beat **Stovin's Lounge** in the **Bessborough Hotel,** 601 Spadina Crescent E. (✆ **306/244-5521**). For a more pub-like atmosphere, try the **Black Duck Freehouse,** 154 2nd Ave. S. (✆ **306/244-8850**).

The **Marquis Downs** racetrack, in the Prairieland Park Exhibition Centre at the corner of Ruth Street and St. Henry Avenue (✆ **306/242-6100**), is open for live and simulcast racing. The live season goes mid-May to mid-October. The racetrack has a lounge, a cafeteria, and terrace dining overlooking the paddock and home stretch. Admission is free. The other place to wager is the **Emerald Casino,** also at Prairieland Park (✆ **306/683-8840**), where you can play five or so table games. It opens at 5:30pm weekdays and at 2pm weekends. Take the Ruth Street exit off Idylwyld Freeway.

## SIDE TRIPS FROM SASKATOON

In addition to the national historic parks listed below, visitors looking for a little healthful rejuvenation may want to consider a trip to the resort town of **Manitou Beach** near Watrous, about an hour's drive southeast of Saskatoon on the transcontinental Yellowhead Highway 16 and Saskatchewan Highway 2. On the shores of **Little Manitou Lake,** the **Manitou Springs Resort and Mineral Spa,** Box 610, Watrous, SK S0K 4T0 (✆ **800/667-7672** or 306/946-2233), offers guests an opportunity to soak in heated pools of the lake's mineral-rich waters; of a composition found only here, in eastern Europe, and in Israel's Dead Sea. The water contains magnesium, carbonate, sulphate, potassium, mineral salts, sodium, calcium, iron, silica, and sulphur; all combining to give it a high specific gravity. This property offers increased buoyancy to bathers, so that they float in it effortlessly. In addition to its mineral spring pools, the resort complex offers guests a variety of therapeutic services, including massages, reflexology, and body wraps; as well as an exercise facility. Guests can visit for the day or stay in a 60-room lodge with an upscale dining room.

**FORT BATTLEFORD NATIONAL HISTORIC PARK** About 138km (86 miles), a 1½-hour drive, northwest of Saskatoon on Highway 16, **Fort Battleford** (✆ **306/937-2621;** www.parcscanada.gc.ca) served as the headquarters for the Northwest Mounted Police from 1876 to 1924. Outside the interpretative gallery, a display relates the role of the mounted police from the fur-trading era to the events that led to the rebellion of 1885. You'll see a Red River cart, the type used to transport police supplies into the West; excerpts from the local Saskatchewan Herald; a typical settler's log-cabin home, which is amazingly tiny; articles of the fur trade; and an 1876 Gatling gun.

Inside the palisade, the Visitor Reception Centre shows two videos about the 1885 Uprising and the Cree People. From there, proceed to the guardhouse (1887), containing a cell block and the sick horse stable (1898), and the Officers Quarters (1886), with police documents, maps, and telegraph equipment.

Perhaps the most interesting building is the Commanding Officer's Residence (1877), which, even though it looks terribly comfortable today, was certainly not so in 1885 when nearly 100 women took shelter in it during the siege of Battleford. Admission is C$4 (US$2.50) for adults, C$3 (US$1.85) for seniors, C$2 (US$1.20) for students, and C$10 (US$6) for families. It's open daily Victoria Day to Labour Day, 9am to 5pm.

**BATOCHE NATIONAL HISTORIC SITE** In spring 1885, the Northwest Territories exploded in an armed uprising led by the Métis Louis Riel and Gabriel Dumont. Trouble had been brewing along the frontier for several years. The Indians were demanding food, equipment, and farming assistance that had been promised to them in treaties. The settlers were angry about railway development and protective tariffs that meant higher prices for the equipment and services they needed.

The Métis were the offspring of the original French fur traders, who had intermarried with the Cree and Saulteaux women. Initially they'd worked for the Hudson's Bay and North West companies, but when the two companies merged, many were left without work and returned to buffalo hunting or became independent traders with the Indians in the west. When Riel was unable to obtain guarantees for the Métis in Manitoba from 1869 to 1870, even when he established a provisional government, it became clear the Métis would have to adopt the agricultural ways of the whites to survive. In 1872, they established the settlement at **Batoche** along the South Saskatchewan River; but they had a hard time acquiring legal titles and securing scrip, a certificate that could be exchanged for a land grant or money. The Métis complained to the government but received no satisfactory response. So they called on Riel to lead them in what became known as the Northwest Rebellion.

Of the rebellion's five significant engagements, the Battle of Batoche was the only one government forces decisively won. From May 9 to May 12, 1885, fewer than 300 Métis and Indians led by Riel and Dumont defended the village against the Northwest Field Force commanded by Gen. Frederick Middleton and numbering 800. On the third day, Middleton succeeded in breaking through the Métis lines and occupying the village. Dumont fled to the United States but returned and is buried at the site; Riel surrendered, stood trial, and was executed (see the box, "The Trial of Louis Riel" earlier).

At the park you can view four battlefield areas and see a film at the visitor center. It'll take 4 to 6 hours to walk to all four areas or 2½ hours to complete areas 1 and 2. For more information, contact **Batoche National Historic Park,** P.O. Box 999, Rosthern, SK S0K 3R0 (© **306/423-6227;** www.parcscanada.gc.ca). Admission is C$4 (US$2.50) for adults, C$3 (US$1.85) for seniors, C$2 (US$1.20) for children ages 6 to 16, and C$10 (US$6) for families; special events and presentations may cost an additional fee. Early May through the end of September, Batoche is open daily 9am to 5pm. The site is about an hour from Saskatoon via Highway 11 to 312 to 225.

## 10 Prince Albert National Park: A Jewel of the National Park System ★

The 400,000ha (1 million-acre) wilderness area of Prince Albert National Park, 240km (149 miles) north of Saskatoon and 91km (56 miles) north of the town of Prince Albert, is one of the jewels of Canada's national park system. Its terrain is astoundingly varied, since it lies at the point where the great Canadian prairie grasslands give way to the pristine evergreen forests of the north. Here you'll find clear, cold lakes, ponds, and streams created thousands of years ago as glaciers receded. It's a hilly landscape, forested with spruce, poplar, and birch.

The park offers outdoor activities from canoeing and backpacking to nature hikes, picnicking, swimming, and great wildlife viewing. You can see and photograph moose, caribou, elk, black bear, bison, and loons. (The moose and caribou tend to wander through the forested northern part of the park, while the elk and deer graze on the southern grasslands.) Lavallee Lake is home to Canada's second-largest white-pelican colony.

In the 1930s, this park's woods and wildlife inspired famed naturalist Grey Owl, an Englishman adopted by the Ojibwe who became one of Canada's pioneering conservationists and most noted naturalists. For 7 years, he lived in a simple one-room cabin called Beaver Lodge on Ajawaan Lake; many hikers and canoeists make a pilgrimage to see his cabin and nearby grave site.

Entry fees are C$4 (US$2.50) for adults, C$3 (US$1.85) for seniors, and C$2 (US$1.20) for youth ages 6 to 16. The park is open year-round, but many campgrounds, motels, and facilities are closed after October. There are a handful of winter campsites, though, if you've come to ice fish or to cross-country ski on the more than 150km (93 miles) of trails.

The town of **Waskesiu,** which lies on the shores of the lake of the same name, is the supply center and also has accommodations. At the **Visitor Service Centre** at park headquarters in Waskesiu, you'll find an 18-hole golf course, tennis courts, bowling greens, and a paddle wheeler that cruises Waskesiu Lake. The staff can tell you about the weather and the condition of the trails; check in with them before undertaking any serious canoe or backcountry trip. The park's **Nature Centre** (✆ **306/663-4512**) presents an audiovisual program called "Up North" daily in July and August.

The park has 10 short **hiking trails,** plus 4 or so longer trails for backpackers, ranging from 10km to 41km (6¼ miles–25 miles). Several easier ones begin in or near Waskesiu, though the best begin farther north. From the northwest shore of Lake Kingsmere, you can pick up the 20km (12-mile) trail leading to Grey Owl's cabin. **Canoeing** routes wind through much of the park through a system of interconnected lakes and rivers. Canoes can be rented at three lakes, including Lake Waskesiu, and paddled along several routes, including the Bagwa and Bladebone routes. There's terrific fishing in the park, but anglers must have a national-park fishing license you can buy at the information center.

The park offers six **campgrounds,** two with more than 100 sites and two with fewer than 30. They fill up fast on summer weekends; rates are C$10 to C$20 (US$6–US$12). The information office in Waskesiu can issue backcountry camping permits to backpackers and canoeists. Other accommodations are available in Waskesiu, including hotels, motels, and cabins, with rates starting at C$45 (US$28) for a double and rising to C$180 (US$112) for a suite sleeping six to eight. Most cabins and lodges are rustic in style and often contain stone fireplaces. You could also base yourself in the town of Prince Albert and come into the park on a long day trip.

For additional info, contact **Prince Albert National Park,** P.O. Box 100, Waskesiu Lake, SK S0J 2Y0 (✆ **306/663-4522;** www.parcscanada.gc.ca).

14

# Alberta & the Rockies

*by Bill McRae*

Stretching from the Northwest Territories to the U.S. border of Montana in the south, flanked by the Rocky Mountains in the west and Saskatchewan in the east, Alberta is a big, beautiful, empty chunk of North America. At 661,188km$^2$ (255,291 sq. miles), the province has just 2 million inhabitants.

Culturally, Alberta is a beguiling mix of big-city swagger and affluence and rural Canadian sincerity. Its cities, Calgary and Edmonton, are models of modern civic pride and hospitality; in fact, an anonymous behavioral survey recently named Edmonton Canada's friendliest city.

Early settlers came to Alberta for its wealth of furs; the Hudson's Bay Company established Edmonton House on the North Saskatchewan River in 1795. The Blackfoot, one of the West's most formidable Indian nations, maintained control of the prairies until the 1870s, when the Royal Canadian Mounted Police arrived to enforce the white man's version of law and order. Open-range cattle ranching prospered on the rich grasslands, and agriculture is still the basis of the rural Alberta economy. Vast oil reserves were discovered in the 1960s, introducing a tremendous 30-year boom.

More than half the population lives in Edmonton and Calgary, leaving the rest of the province a tremendous amount of breathing room and unspoiled scenery. The Canadian Rockies rise to the west of the prairies and contain some of the finest mountain scenery on earth. Between them, Banff and Jasper national parks preserve much of this mountain beauty, but vast and equally spectacular regions of the Rockies, as well as portions of the nearby Columbia and Selkirk mountain ranges, are protected by other national and provincial parks.

All this wilderness makes outdoor activity Alberta's greatest draw. Hiking, biking, and pack trips on horseback have long pedigrees in the parks, as does superlative skiing—the winter Olympics were held in Calgary in 1988. Outfitters throughout the region offer white-water and float trips on mighty rivers; and calmer pursuits like fishing and canoeing are also popular.

In addition, some of Canada's finest and most famous hotels are in Alberta. The incredible mountain lodges and châteaux built by early rail entrepreneurs are still in operation, offering unforgettable experiences in luxury and stunning scenery. These grand hotels established a standard of hospitality that's observed by hoteliers across the province. If you're looking for a more rural experience, head to one of Alberta's many guest ranches, where you can saddle up, poke some doggies, and end the evening at a steak barbecue.

## 1 Exploring the Province

It's no secret that Alberta contains some of Canada's most compelling scenery and outdoor recreation. Mid-June to August, this is a very busy place; Banff is generally acknowledged to be Canada's single-most-popular destination for foreign travelers. A little planning is essential, especially if you're traveling in summer or have specific destinations or lodgings in mind.

Skiers should know that heavy snowfall closes some mountain roads in winter. However, major passes are maintained and usually remain open. Highways 3, 1, and 16 are open year-round, though it's a good idea to call to check road conditions. You can inquire locally or call **Travel Alberta** (✆ **800/661-8888**) or the **Alberta Motor Association** (✆ **403/474-8601;** www.ama.ab.ca). If you're a member of AAA or CAA, call their information line (✆ **800/642-3810**). Always carry traction devices like tire chains in your vehicle, plus plenty of warm clothes and a sleeping bag if you're planning winter car travel.

### VISITOR INFORMATION

For information about the entire province, contact **Travel Alberta,** Box 2500, Edmonton, AB T5J 2Z1 (✆ **800/661-8888;** www.travelalberta.com). Be sure to ask for a copy of the accommodations and visitors guide (**www.explorealberta.com** has many listings), as well as the excellent *Traveler's Guide* and a road map. There's a separate guide for campers, which you should ask for if you're considering camping at any point during your trip.

Alberta has no provincial sales tax. There's only the national 7% goods-and-services tax (GST), plus a 5% accommodations tax.

### THE GREAT OUTDOORS

Banff and Jasper national parks have long been Alberta's center of mountain recreation. If you're staying in Banff, Jasper, or Lake Louise, you'll find that outfitters and recreational rental operations in these centers are pretty sophisticated and professional: They make it easy to get outdoors and have an adventure. Most hotels offer a concierge service that can arrange activities; for many, you need little or no advance registration. Shuttle buses to more distant activities are usually available as well.

You don't even have to break a sweat to enjoy the magnificent scenery—hire a horse and ride to the backcountry or take an afternoon trail ride. Jasper, Banff, and Lake Louise have gondolas to lift you from the valley floor to the mountaintops. Bring a picnic or plan a ridge-top hike. If you're not ready for whitewater, the scenic cruises on Lake Minnewanka and Maligne Lake offer a more relaxed waterborne adventure.

**BACKPACKING** Backcountry trips through high mountain meadows and remote lakes provide an unforgettable experience; Banff Park alone has 3,059km (1,897 miles) of hiking trails.

---

*Tips* **A Warning**

Accommodations are very tight throughout the province, especially so in the Rockies. Make room reservations for Banff and Jasper as early as possible; likewise, Calgary is solidly booked for the Stampede, as is Edmonton for Klondike Days. Advance reservations are mandatory for these events, so call ✆ **888/800-PARK** or 780/471-7210.

---

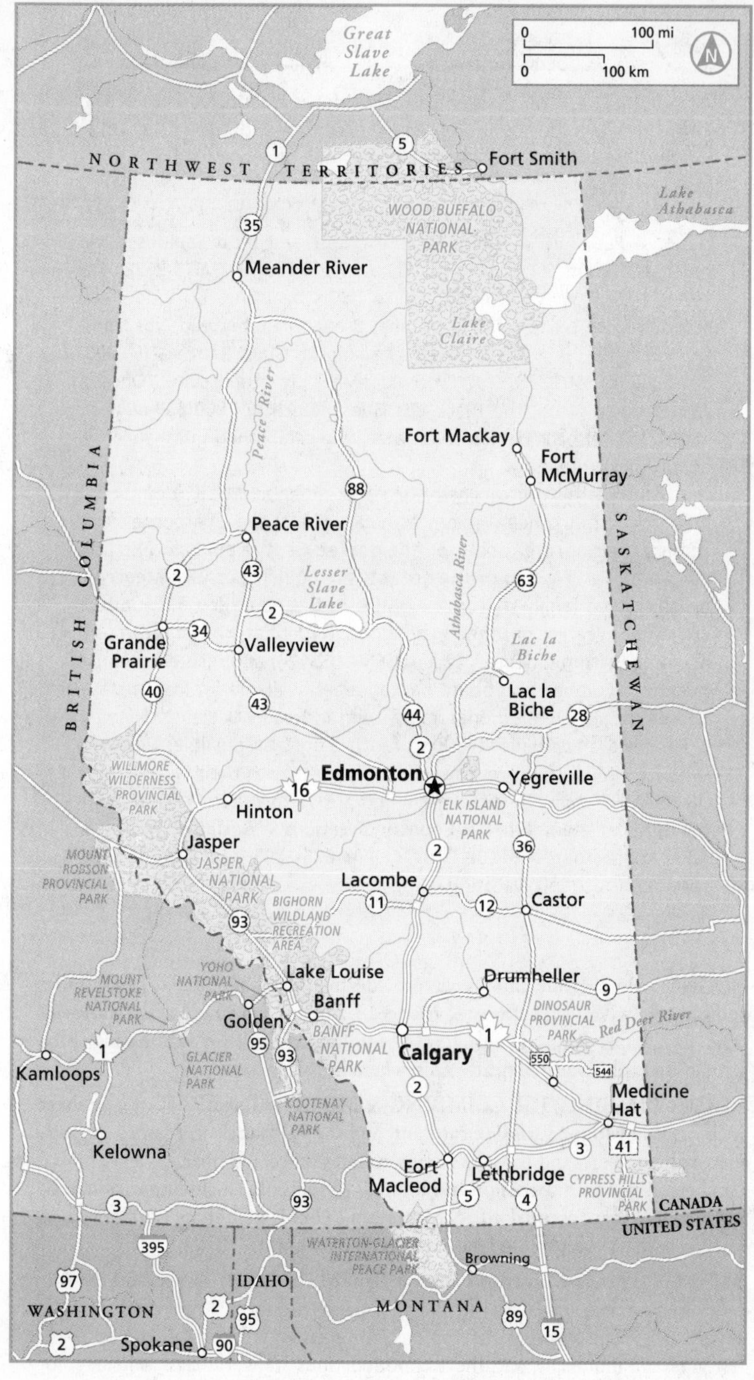
Great Slave Lake
0 100 mi
0 100 km
N
NORTHWEST TERRITORIES
Fort Smith
Lake Athabasca
WOOD BUFFALO NATIONAL PARK
Meander River
Lake Claire
Peace River
Fort Mackay
Fort McMurray
BRITISH COLUMBIA
SASKATCHEWAN
Peace River
Lesser Slave Lake
Athabasca River
Grande Prairie
Valleyview
Lac la Biche
Lac la Biche
WILLMORE WILDERNESS PROVINCIAL PARK
Edmonton
Yegreville
Hinton
ELK ISLAND NATIONAL PARK
Jasper
MOUNT ROBSON PROVINCIAL PARK
JASPER NATIONAL PARK
Lacombe
BIGHORN WILDLAND RECREATION AREA
Castor
YOHO NATIONAL PARK
MOUNT REVELSTOKE NATIONAL PARK
Lake Louise
Drumheller
Banff
Golden
DINOSAUR PROVINCIAL PARK
Red Deer River
BANFF NATIONAL PARK
Calgary
Kamloops
GLACIER NATIONAL PARK
KOOTENAY NATIONAL PARK
Medicine Hat
Kelowna
Fort Macleod
Lethbridge
CYPRESS HILLS PROVINCIAL PARK
CANADA
UNITED STATES
WATERTON-GLACIER INTERNATIONAL PEACE PARK
Browning
IDAHO
WASHINGTON
MONTANA
Spokane

## Getting a Taste of the Old West at a Guest Ranch

Alberta has been ranch country for well over a century, and the Old West lifestyle is deeply ingrained in its culture. Indulge in a cowboy fantasy and spend a few days at one of the province's many historic guest ranches.

At Seebe, in the Kananaskis Country near the entrance to Banff National Park, are a couple of the oldest and most famous guest ranches. **Rafter Six Ranch** (✆ **888/267-2624** or 403/673-3622; fax 403-673-3961; www.raftersix.com), with its beautiful log lodge, can accommodate up to 60. The original Brewster homestead was transformed in 1923 into the **Brewster's Kananaskis Guest Ranch** ★ (✆ **800/691-5085** or 403/673-3737; www.brewsteradventures.com). Once a winter horse camp, the **Black Cat Guest Ranch** (✆ **800/859-6840** or 780/865-3084) near Hinton is another long-established guest ranch in beautiful surroundings.

At all these historic ranches, horseback riding and trail rides are the main focus, but other Western activities, like rodeos, barbecues, and country dancing, are usually on the docket. Gentler pursuits, like fishing, hiking, and lolling by the hot tub, are equally possible. Meals are usually served family-style in the central lodge, while accommodations are either in cabins or in the main lodge. A night at a guest ranch usually ranges from C$90 to C$200 (US$56–US$124) and includes a ranch breakfast. Full bed-and-board packages are available for longer stays. There's usually an additional hourly fee for horseback riding.

Homestays at smaller working ranches are also possible. Here you can pitch in and help your ranch-family hosts with their work or simply relax. For a stay on a real mom-and-pop farm, obtain a list of member ranches from **Alberta Country Vacations Association,** P.O. Box 1206, Claresholm, AB T0L 0T0 (✆ **403/625-2295;** fax 403/625-3126, www.albertacountryvacation.com).

**BIKING** Both Banff and Jasper provide free maps of local mountain-bike trails; the **Bow Valley Parkway** ★ between Banff and Lake Louise and **Parkway 93A** ★ in Jasper Park are both good less-trafficked roads for road biking. Bike rentals are easily available nearly everywhere in the parks.

**ROCK CLIMBING, ICE CLIMBING & MOUNTAINEERING** The sheer rock faces on **Mount Rundle** near Banff and the **Pallisades** near Jasper are popular with climbers, and the area's many waterfalls become frozen ascents for ice climbers in winter. Instruction in mountaineering skills, including rock climbing, is offered by **Yamnuska Inc. Mountain School,** a climbing outfitter based in Canmore (✆ **403/678-4164;** www.yamnuska.com).

**SKIING** There are **downhill** areas at Banff, Lake Louise, Jasper, and the former Olympic site at Nakiska in the Kananaskis Country. At its best, skiing is superb here: The snowpack is copious, the scenery is beautiful, the après-ski festivities are indulgent, and the accommodations are world-class. There's a lot of value in an Alberta ski holiday—lift tickets here are generally cheaper than those at comparable ski areas in the United States.

*Tips* **Bed & Breakfast Networks**

B&Bs are abundant in Alberta and are cheaper than most hotels. If you're looking for a B&B, try the **Alberta Bed and Breakfast Association** (www.bbalberta.com), which provides listings of member inspected and approved B&Bs throughout the province.

Alberta is rich with hostels as well, especially in the Rocky Mountain national parks, where they're often the only affordable lodging option. Hostels run by **All Hostelling International** (www.hostellingintl.ca/alberta) in Alberta welcome guests of all ages.

**Heli-skiing** isn't allowed in the national parks but is popular in the adjacent mountain ranges near Golden in British Columbia. **CMH Heli-Skiing,** 217 Bear St., Banff (✆ **800/661-0252** or 402/762-7100; fax 403/762-5879; www.cmhski.com), is the leader in this increasingly popular sport, which uses helicopters to deposit skiers on virgin slopes far from the lift lines and runs of ski resorts. CMH offers 7- and 10-day trips to eight locations; prices begin at C$4,400 (US$2,728), including lodging, food, and transport from Calgary.

**Cross-country** skiers will also find a lot to like in the Canadian Rockies. A number of snowbound mountain lodges remain open throughout winter and serve as bases for adventurous Nordic skiers.

**WHITE-WATER RAFTING & CANOEING** The Rockies' many glaciers and snowfields are the source of mighty rivers. Outfitters throughout the region offer white-water rafting and canoe trips of varying lengths and difficulty—you can spend a single morning on the river or plan a 5-day expedition. Jasper is central to a number of good white-water rivers; **Maligne Rafting Adventures Ltd.** (✆ **780/852-3370;** www.mra.ab.ca) has packages for rafters of all experience levels.

**WILDLIFE VIEWING** If you're thrilled by seeing animals in the wild, you've turned to the right chapter. No matter which one you choose, the Rocky Mountain national parks are all teeming with wildlife—bighorn sheep, grizzly and black bears, deer, mountain goats, moose, coyotes, lynxes, wolves, and more. See "Introducing the Canadian Rockies," later in this chapter, for important warnings about how to handle wildlife encounters in the parks responsibly and safely. Aside from the Rockies, there's also **Elk Island National Park** ★ just outside Edmonton, which harbors the tiny pygmy shrew and the immense wood buffalo.

## 2 Calgary: Home to the Annual Stampede ★★

Historically, Calgary dates back just over a century, to the summer of 1875, when a detachment of the Northwest Mounted Police reached the confluence of the Bow and Elbow rivers. The solid log fort they built had attracted 600 settlers by the end of the year. Gradually the lush prairie lands around the settlement drew tremendous beef herds, many of them from overgrazed U.S. ranches in the south. Calgary grew into a cattle metropolis and a large meatpacking center. When World War II ended, the placid city numbered barely 100,000.

The oil boom erupted in the late 1960s, and in one decade the pace and complexion of the city changed utterly. The population shot up at a pace that made statisticians dizzy. In 1978 alone, C$1 billion (US$620 million) worth of construction was added to the skyline, creating office high rises, hotel blocks, walkways, and shopping centers so fast even locals weren't sure what was around the next corner. In the mid-1990s, the oil market heated up again, and Alberta's pro-business political climate tempted national companies to build their headquarters here.

In February 1988, Calgary was the site of the Winter Olympics, giving it the opportunity to roll out the welcome mat on a truly international scale. The city outdid itself in hospitality, erecting a whole network of facilities, including the Canada Olympic Park, by the Trans-Canada Highway, some 15 minutes west of downtown.

Calgary (pop. 850,000) has an imposing skyline boasting dozens of business towers topping 40 stories. Despite this, the city doesn't seem urban. With its many parks and convivial populace, Calgary retains the atmosphere of a much smaller, friendlier town.

## ESSENTIALS

**GETTING THERE** **By Plane** **Calgary International Airport** (www.calgaryairport.com) lies 16km (10 miles) northeast of the city. You can go through U.S. Customs right here if you're flying home via Calgary. The airport is served by **Air Canada** (© 800/372-9500), **Delta** (© 800/221-1212), **American Airlines** (© 800/433-7300), **United** (© 800/241-6522), **Continental** (© 800/525-0280), and **Northwest** (© 800/447-4747), among others.

A shuttle service to and from Edmonton is run almost hourly by Air Canada and Canadian Airlines. Cab fare to downtown hotels comes to around C$25 (US$16). The **Airporter bus** (© **403/531-3909**) takes you downtown for C$9 (US$6).

**By Train** The nearest **VIA Rail** station is in Edmonton (see below). You can, however, take a scenic train ride to/from Vancouver/Calgary on the **Rocky Mountaineer,** operated by the **Great Rocky Mountaineer Railtours** (© **800/665-7245** or 604/606-7245; www.rockymountaineer.com). The lowest-priced tickets begin at C$1,176 (US$729) for 2 days of daylight travel, which includes meals and overnight accommodation in Kamloops.

**By Bus** **Greyhound** buses (© **800/661-8747** or 403/260-0877; www.greyhound.ca) link Calgary with most other points in Canada, including Banff and Edmonton, as well as towns in the United States. The depot is at 877 Greyhound Way SW.

**By Car** From the U.S. border in the south, Highway 2 runs to Calgary. The same excellent road continues north to Edmonton (via Red Deer). From Vancouver in the west to Regina in the east, take the Trans-Canada Highway.

**VISITOR INFORMATION** **Tourist offices** The **Visitor Service Centres** at Tower Centre, Ninth Avenue SW and Centre Street, and at the airport, provide free literature, maps, and information. These are run by the **Calgary Convention and Visitors Bureau,** 200, 238 11th Ave. SE, Calgary, AB, T2G 0X8, which also operates a useful, no-charge **accommodations bureau** (© **800/661-1678** or 403/263-8510; www.tourismcalgary.com). For more information visit **www.calgaryview.com** and **www.calgary.net**. Find out what's happening around town at **www.downtowncalgary.com** and **www.greatwest.ca/ffwd**.

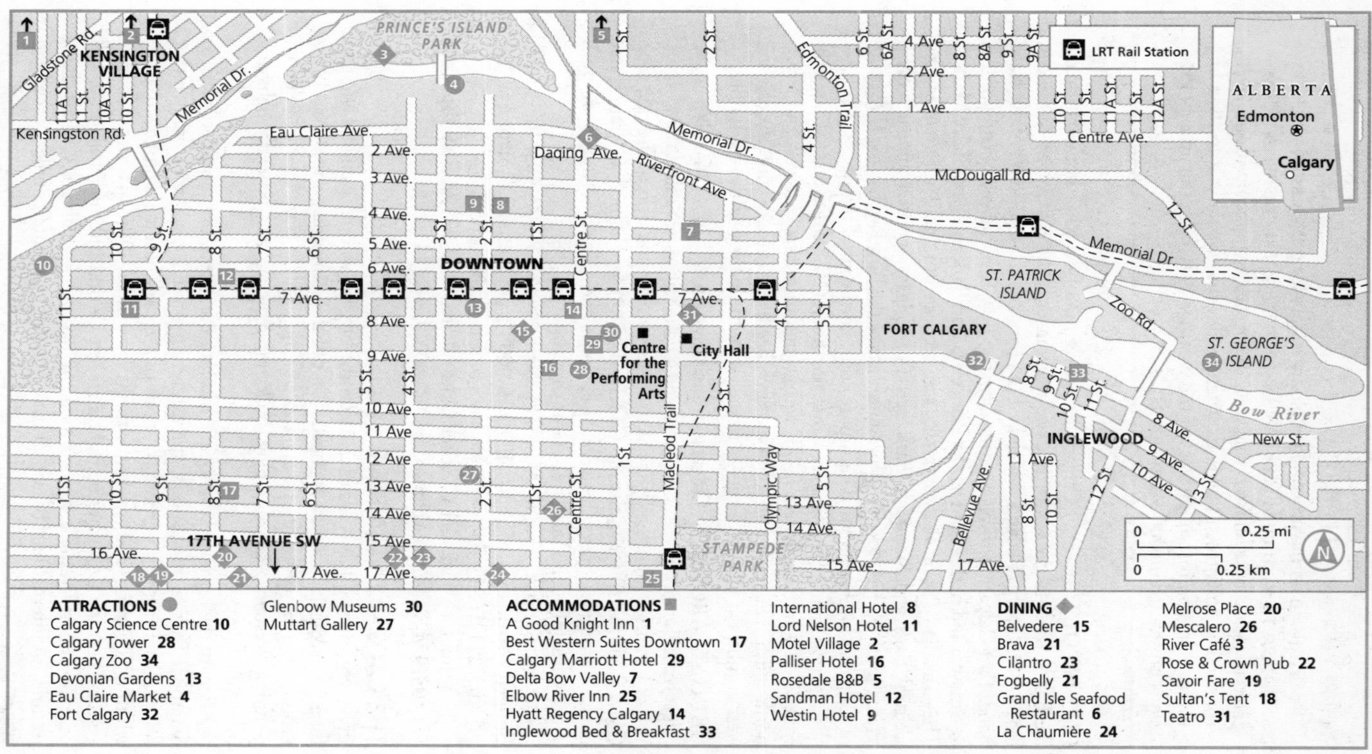
PRINCE'S ISLAND PARK
KENSINGTON VILLAGE
Gladstone Rd.
Kensington Rd.
Memorial Dr.
Eau Claire Ave.
Daqing Ave.
Riverfront Ave.
Edmonton Trail
McDougall Rd.
Centre Ave.
LRT Rail Station
ALBERTA
Edmonton
Calgary
DOWNTOWN
Centre for the Performing Arts
City Hall
Macleod Trail
Olympic Way
STAMPEDE PARK
17TH AVENUE SW
FORT CALGARY
ST. PATRICK ISLAND
ST. GEORGE'S ISLAND
Zoo Rd.
Bow River
INGLEWOOD
Bellevue Ave.
New St.
0.25 mi
0.25 km
ATTRACTIONS
Calgary Science Centre 10
Calgary Tower 28
Calgary Zoo 34
Devonian Gardens 13
Eau Claire Market 4
Fort Calgary 32
Glenbow Museums 30
Muttart Gallery 27
ACCOMMODATIONS
A Good Knight Inn 1
Best Western Suites Downtown 17
Calgary Marriott Hotel 29
Delta Bow Valley 7
Elbow River Inn 25
Hyatt Regency Calgary 14
Inglewood Bed & Breakfast 33
International Hotel 8
Lord Nelson Hotel 11
Motel Village 2
Palliser Hotel 16
Rosedale B&B 5
Sandman Hotel 12
Westin Hotel 9
DINING
Belvedere 15
Brava 21
Cilantro 23
Fogbelly 21
Grand Isle Seafood Restaurant 6
La Chaumière 24
Melrose Place 20
Mescalero 26
River Café 3
Rose & Crown Pub 22
Savoir Fare 19
Sultan's Tent 18
Teatro 31

**Tips A Walking Warning**

The first thing you'll note about Calgary is how long the east-west blocks are. Allow 15 minutes to walk 5 blocks. You'll also like the "Plus-15" system, a series of enclosed walkways 4.5m (15 ft.) above street level connecting downtown buildings. These walkways enable you to shop in living-room comfort, regardless of the weather. Watch for the little "+15" signs on the streets for access points.

**CITY LAYOUT** Central Calgary lies between the Bow River in the north and the Elbow River to the south. The two rivers meet at the eastern end of the city, forming **St. George's Island,** which houses a park and the zoo. South of the island stands Fort Calgary, birthplace of the city. The Bow River makes a bend north of downtown, and in this bend nestles **Prince's Island Park** and **Eau Claire Market.** The Canadian Pacific Railway tracks run between 9th and 10th avenues, and **Central Park** and **Stampede Park,** scene of Calgary's greatest annual festival, stretch south of the tracks. Northwest, just across the Bow River, is the **University of Calgary**'s lovely campus. The airport is just northwest of the city.

Calgary is divided into four segments: **northeast** (NE), **southeast** (SE), **northwest** (NW), and **southwest** (SW), with avenues running east-west and streets north-south. The north and south numbers begin at Centre Avenue, the east and west numbers at Centre Street—a recipe for confusion if ever there was one.

**GETTING AROUND** **Calgary Transit System** (✆ **403/276-1000;** www.calgarytransit.com) operates the buses and a light-rail system called the C-Train. You can transfer from the light rail to buses on the same ticket. The ride costs C$1.75 (US$1.10) for adults and C$1.10 (US70¢) for children; C-Train is free in the downtown stretch between 10th Street and City Hall (buses are not). Tickets are only good for travel in one direction.

Car-rental firms include **Avis,** 211 Sixth Ave. SW (✆ **403/269-6166**); **Budget,** 140 Sixth Ave. SE (✆ **403/226-0000**); and **Hertz,** 227 Sixth Ave. SW (✆ **403/221-1681**). Each of these has a bureau at the airport.

To summon a taxi, call **Checker Cabs** (✆ **403/299-9999**), **Red Top Cabs** (✆ **403/974-4444**), or **Yellow Cabs** (✆ **403/974-1111**).

## THE CALGARY STAMPEDE ★★★

Every year during July, Calgary puts on the biggest, wildest, woolliest Western fling on earth: the Calgary Stampede. To call the stampede a show would be a misnomer. The whole city participates by going mildly crazy for the occasion, donning Western gear, whooping, hollering, dancing, and generally behaving uproariously.

Many of the organized events spill out into the streets, but most take place in Stampede Park, a show, sports, and exhibition ground south of downtown that was built for just this purpose. Portions of the park become amusement areas, whirling, spinning, and rotating with the latest rides. Other parts are set aside especially for the kids, who romp through Kids' World and the Petting Zoo. Still other areas host livestock shows, a food fair, handicraft exhibitions, an art show, lectures, an international bazaar, a casino, lotteries, and entertainment on several stages.

The top attractions, though, are the **rodeo events,** the largest and most prestigious of their kind in North America. Cowboys from all over the world take part in such competitions as riding bucking broncos and bulls, roping calves, and wrestling steers for prize money totaling C$1.1 million (US$682,000). At the world-famous **Chuckwagon Race** you'll see old-time Western cook wagons thundering around the track in a fury of dust and pounding hooves. At night the arena becomes a blaze of lights when the Stampede Grandstand—the largest outdoor extravaganza in the world—takes over with precision-kicking dancers, clowns, bands, and spectacles. On top of that, the Stampede offers a food fair, an art show, dancing exhibitions, an international bazaar, a gambling casino, lotteries, and free entertainment on several stages.

The whole city is absolutely packed for the occasion, not just to the rafters but way out into the surrounding countryside. Reserving accommodations well ahead is essential—as many months ahead of your arrival as you can possibly foresee. (For help with lodging, call Calgary's **Convention and Visitors Bureau** © **800/661-1678;** www.tourismcalgary.com) Some downtown watering holes even take reservations for space at their bar; that should give you an idea of how busy Calgary gets.

The same advice applies to reserving tickets for all of the park events. Tickets cost between C$20 and C$54 (US$12–US$33), depending on the event, the seats, and whether it takes place in the afternoon or evening. For mail order bookings, contact the **Calgary Exhibition and Stampede,** P.O. Box 1060, Station M, Calgary, AB, T2P 2K8 (© **800/661-1767;** fax 403/223-9736; www.calgarystampede.com).

## FAST FACTS: Calgary

*American Express* The office at 421 7th Ave. SW (© **403/261-5982**) is open Monday to Friday 9am to 5pm.

*Area Code* Calgary's area code is **403.**

*Doctors* If you need nonemergency medical attention, check the phone number for the closest branch of **Medicentre,** a group of walk-in clinics open daily 7am to midnight.

*Drugstores* Check the phone book for **Shoppers Drug Mart,** which has more than a dozen stores in Calgary, most open till midnight. The branch at the Chinook Centre, 6455 Macleod Trail S. (© **403/253-2424**), is open 24 hours.

*Emergency* For medical, fire, or crime emergencies, dial © **911.**

*Hospitals* If you need medical care, try **Foothills Hospital,** 1403 29th St. NW (© **403/670-1110**).

*Newspapers* Calgary's two dailies, the *Calgary Herald* (www.calgary herald.com) and the *Calgary Sun* (www.calgarysun.com), are both morning papers. The local arts and events newspapers are *Avenue* and *Cityscope. Ffwd* (www.greatwest.ca/ffwd) is more youth-oriented and a good place to look for information on the local music scene.

*Police* The 24-hour number is © **403/266-1234.** Dial © **911** in emergencies.

*Post Office* The main post office is at 207 9th Ave. (© **403/974-2078**). Call © **403/292-5434** to find other branches.

*Time* Calgary is on Mountain Time, the same as Edmonton and Denver.

## WHERE TO STAY

If you enjoy B&Bs, try the **Alberta B&B Association** (www.bbalberta.com), which has several dozen listings for Calgary. The visitors bureau (✆ **800/661-1678;** www.tourismcalgary.com) can also book a B&B for you.

### DOWNTOWN

#### Very Expensive

**Delta Bow Valley** ★ *Kids* The Delta is one of Calgary's finest hotels, with excellent restaurants and an airy, attractive lobby. The focus of the hotel is upscale business travel: Each corner business suite contains a desk furnished with printer, fax, cordless phone, and ergonomic chair. The standard rooms are spacious, equipped with all the niceties you'd expect in this class of hotel. The Delta also goes the distance to make families welcome. In summer and on weekends, you can leave the kids at the children's activity center while you head out to dinner. Ask about weekend specials, which more than halve the weekday rate.

209 Fourth Ave. SE, Calgary, AB, T2G 0C6. ✆ **403/266-1980.** Fax 403/266-0007. 398 units. C$225 (US$140) double, C$245–C$299 (US$152–US$185) suite. Children under 18 stay free in parents' room; children under 6 eat free from children's menu. AE, DC, DISC, MC, V. Parking C$15 (US$9) weekdays; free on weekends. **Amenities:** 2 restaurants, lounge; marvelous rooftop pool and deck; exercise room; Jacuzzi; sauna; concierge; business center; room service; laundry service; same-day dry cleaning; executive level rooms. *In room:* A/C, TV, dataport, minibar, fridge, coffeemaker, hair dryer, iron.

**The Fairmont Palliser** ★★ This is the classiest address in all of Calgary. Opened in 1914 as one of the Canadian Pacific Railroad hotels, the Palliser is Calgary's landmark historic hotel. The vast marble-floored lobby, surrounded by columns and lit by gleaming chandeliers, is the very picture of Edwardian sumptuousness. You'll feel like an Alberta Cattle King in the Rimrock Dining Room, with vaulted ceilings, period murals, a massive stone fireplace, and hand-tooled leather panels on teak beams. The lounge bar looks like a gentlemen's West End club. Guest rooms are large for a hotel of this vintage—the Pacific Premier rooms would be suites at most other properties—and they preserve the period charm while incorporating modern luxuries. Entree Gold-class rooms come with their own concierge and a private lounge with complimentary breakfast, drinks, and hors d'oeuvres. A recent C$30-million (US$18.6-million) renovation delivered new carpets, upholstery, and furniture throughout.

133 Ninth Ave. SW, Calgary, AB, T2P 2M3. ✆ **800/441-1414** or 403/262-1234. Fax 403/260-1260. www.fairmont.com. 421 units. C$178–C$299 (US$110–US$185) double, from C$299 (US$185) suite. AE, DC, DISC, MC, V. Valet parking C$18 (US$11) per day; self-parking C$15 (US$9). **Amenities:** Restaurant, bar; indoor pool; health club and spa; concierge; business center; salon; 24-hour room service; babysitting; laundry service; same-day dry cleaning; concierge-level rooms. *In room:* A/C, TV, dataport, minibar, hair dryer, iron.

#### Expensive

**Calgary Marriott Hotel** ★ The recently renovated Marriott is about as central as things get in Calgary: Linked to the convention center and convenient to the goings-on at the Centre for the Performing Arts and the Glenbow Museum, the Marriott is also connected via skywalk with Palliser Square, Calgary Tower, and loads of downtown shopping. Its large guest rooms are subtly decorated and outfitted with niceties like windows that open, lots of mirrors, and desks set up for business travelers. The even larger, tasteful suites are worth the extra money—especially the French Parlour suites, with lots of room to decompress. Yes, it's a convention hotel—but a lot nicer than the stereotype.

110 Ninth Ave. SE (at Centre St.), Calgary, AB, T2G 5A6. ✆ **800/228-9290** or 403/266-7331. Fax 403/262-8442. www.marriotthotels.com. 384 units. From C$185–C$285 (US$115–US$177) double. Suites

C$189–C$259 (US$117–US$161). Extra person C$20 (US$12). Weekend packages available. AE, DC, DISC, MC, V. Valet parking C$19 (US$12) per day; self-parking C$15 (US$9). **Amenities:** Restaurant, lounge; indoor pool; exercise room; Jacuzzi; sauna; concierge; business center; room service; same-day dry cleaning; executive-level rooms. *In room:* A/C, TV, dataport, fridge, microwave, coffeemaker, hair dryer, iron.

**International Hotel** ★ A soaring tower with a breathtaking view from the upper balconies, the International is an all-suite hotel. Just out the back door are Chinatown and the Eau Claire Market area. Originally built as an apartment building, the International's guest rooms are some of the largest in Calgary. The suites contain private balconies and large bathrooms; some units have full kitchens. The downside? The three elevators date from the days when this was an apartment building; in summer, when tour buses hit, it can be exasperating to wait for them to serve guests on all 35 floors. Otherwise, this is a delightful lodging choice if you're looking for spacious accommodations.

220 Fourth Ave. SW, Calgary, AB, T2P 0H5. ✆ **800/637-7200** or 403/265-9600. Fax 403/265-6949. www.internationalhotel.ca. 247 units. C$220–C$245 (US$136–US$152) 1-bedroom suite; C$230–C$265 (US$143–US$164) 2-bedroom suite. Children under 16 stay free in parents' room. AE, DC, MC, V. Parking C$8 (US$5) per day. **Amenities:** Restaurant, bar; indoor pool; exercise room; Jacuzzi; sauna; concierge; limited room service; babysitting; same-day dry cleaning. *In room:* A/C, TV w/pay movies, dataport, minibar, coffeemaker, hair dryer, iron.

**Westin Hotel** ★★ *Kids* The Westin is a massive modern luxury block in the heart of the financial district, and probably the single nicest hotel in Calgary. Despite its anonymous business-hotel exterior, the interior has a subtle western feel that's reflected in comfortable Mission-style furniture, Navajo-look upholstery, feather duvets, and in-room period photos that commemorate Calgary's bronco-busting and oil-boom past. Beautiful barn-wood breakfronts and lowboys dispel the feeling that you're in one of the city's most modern hotels. The hotel rolls out the welcome mat for kids, with a full array of children's furniture, babysitting, and a children's menu. Special needs are anticipated, from strollers, potty chairs, and playpens to room-service delivery of fresh diapers!

320 Fourth Ave. SW, Calgary, AB, T2P 2S6. ✆ **800/937-8461** or 403/266-1611. www.westin.com. 525 units. C$99–C$299 (US$62–US$185) double, from C$349 (US$216) suite. Extra person C$20 (US$12). Family and senior rates also available. AE, DC, DISC, MC, V. Parking C$14 (US$9) per day. **Amenities:** 7 restaurants including the exquisite Owl's Nest (see "Where to Dine," below), lounge; panoramic 17th-floor indoor pool; sauna and whirlpool; health club and spa; concierge; business center; 24-hour room service; laundry service; same-day dry cleaning. *In room:* A/C, TV, dataport, minibar, coffeemaker, hair dryer, iron.

## Moderate

Travelers on a budget have excellent though limited choices downtown. Luckily, Calgary's light-rail system makes it easy to stay outside the city center yet have easy access to the restaurants and sites of downtown.

**Best Western Suites Downtown** This all-suites hotel is an excellent value. You get a choice of standard, one-, or two-bedroom units; some come with efficiency kitchens (microwave and fridge). The rooms are quite large, almost apartment-size, and fitted with quality furniture and fixtures. This Best Western is a few blocks from downtown, but it's near the trendy street life of 17th Avenue.

1330 Eighth St. SW, Calgary, AB, T2R 1B3. ✆ **800/981-2555** or 403/228-6900. Fax 403/228-5535. www.bestwesternsuites.com. 123 units. C$125–C$145 (US$78–US$90) junior suite, C$165 (US$102) 1-bedroom suite, C$185 (US$115) 2-bedroom suite. Extra person C$5 (US$3.10). Senior, weekly, and monthly rates available. AE, DISC, MC, V. Free parking. **Amenities:** Restaurant; Jacuzzi; guest laundry. *In room:* A/C, TV, dataport, kitchenette, coffeemaker, hair dryer.

**Sandman Hotel** ★ *Value* This hotel on the west end of downtown is one of Calgary's best deals. The Sandman is conveniently located on the free rapid-transit mall, just west of the main downtown core. The standard rooms are a good size, but the real winners are the very large corner units, which feature small kitchens and great views. The Sandman is a popular place with corporate clients, due to its central location and good value. It also boasts the most complete fitness facility of any hotel in Calgary. Its private health club, available free to guests, has a lap pool, three squash courts, aerobics, and weight-training facilities.

888 Seventh Ave. SW, Calgary, AB, T2P 3J3. ✆ **800/726-3626** or 403/237-8626. Fax 403/290-1238. www.sandmanhotels.com. 301 units. C$111–C$159 (US$69–US$99) double. Children under 16 stay free in parents' room. AE, DC, DISC, MC, V. Parking C$6 parking (US$3.70). **Amenities:** Restaurant; bar; indoor pool; health club & spa; concierge; business center; limited room service; laundry service; same-day dry cleaning. *In room:* A/C, TV, dataport, fridge, microwave, coffeemaker, hair dryer, iron.

### Inexpensive

**Lord Nelson Inn** *Value* One of the best deals in the city, the Lord Nelson is a modern nine-story structure with recently renovated rooms and suites. Although on the edge of downtown, it's just a block from downtown's free *C*-Train, which will put you in very center of downtown in 5 minutes (or you can walk there in 10). Although it's not the last word in luxury, the Lord Nelson offers clean, well-equipped and perfectly pleasant motel rooms- and you don't have to pay extortionate rates for parking, even though you're right downtown.

1020 Eighth Ave. SW, Calgary, AB, T2P 1J3. ✆ **800/661-6017** or 403/269-8262. Fax 403/269-4868. 57 units. C$95 (US$59) double, C$105–C$195 (US$65–US$121) suite. Extra person C$10 (US$6). Children under 18 stay free in parents' room. AE, ER, MC, V. Free parking. **Amenities:** Restaurant, pub; Jacuzzi; laundry service. *In room:* A/C, TV, dataport, fridge.

## IN INGLEWOOD

### Inexpensive

**Inglewood Bed & Breakfast** ★ *Finds* It's a great location: minutes from downtown, on a quiet residential street backed up to a park and the swift waters of the Bow River. The Inglewood is a rambling modern structure in Queen Anne style built as a B&B. The three guest rooms are simply but stylishly furnished with handmade pine furniture and antiques; all have private bathrooms. Two of the turret rooms have great views over the river. If you're in Calgary with a family or on an extended stay, ask about the suite, with full kitchen facilities, a fireplace, and TV. Both of the owners are professional chefs, so expect an excellent breakfast.

1006 8th Ave. SE, Calgary, AB T2G 0M4. ✆ **403/262-6570.** www.inglewoodbedandbreakfast.com. 3 units. C$90 (US$56) double. Rates include breakfast. MC, V.

## ALONG THE MACLEOD TRAIL

Once this was a cattle track, but now it's the main expressway heading south toward the U.S. border. The northern portions of the Macleod Trail are lined with inns and motels—from upper-middle range to economy. Here's an example of what you'll find.

### Inexpensive

**Elbow River Inn** The Elbow River Inn is the Macleod Trail establishment closest to downtown, and directly opposite the Stampede grounds. The only hotel on the banks of the little Elbow River, the inn has a pleasant dining room with a view of the water, and—if you're feeling lucky—a casino. The bedrooms are simply furnished; it's a completely adequate, comfortable hostelry with near-budget rates.

1919 Macleod Trail S., Calgary, AB, T2G 4S1. ✆ **800/661-1463** or 403/269-6771. Fax 403/237-5181. www.sil-org.com. 73 units. C$79–C$129 (US$49–US$80) double. AE, DC, MC, V. Free parking. **Amenities:** Restaurant, bar; limited room service. *In room:* A/C, TV, dataports, fridge, microwave.

## NORTH OF DOWNTOWN

### Moderate

**A Good Knight B&B** North of the trendy Kensington district in a quiet tree-lined neighborhood, the Good Knight is a modern home built to resemble the Victorian homes surrounding it. The guest rooms, decorated according to whimsical themes, all have private bathrooms. The nicest room is the large Buttons and Bows Suite, with a private balcony, arched ceilings, a jetted tub, and a two-person shower. The owners are avid collectors, and you'll smile at their large collection of teapots.

1728 7th Ave. NW, Calgary, AB T2N 0Z4. ✆ **800/261-4954** or 403/270-7628. www.agoodknight.com. 3 units. C$90–C$150 (US$56–US$93). Lower off-season rates. V. *In room:* TV, coffeemaker, no phone.

**Rosedale House B&B** This rambling modern place has a pleasingly ersatz quality. Built as a trophy home by a recent central European immigrant, it included such oddities as a huge two-story foyer with wraparound mezzanines and a pool in the basement. That was then. Now the Rosedale is a friendly B&B—sans indoor pool—with three large comfortable guest rooms and two very spacious guest lounges, one with a pool table, a fireplace, a fridge and microwave, couches and chairs, and a hot tub.

1633 7A St. NW, Calgary, AB T2M 3K2. ✆ **403/284-0010** or 403/284-9568. 3 units. C$90–C$130 (US$56–US$81). AE, MC, V.

## MOTEL VILLAGE

Northwest of downtown, Motel Village is a triangle of more than twenty large motels, plus restaurants, stores, and gas stations, forming a self-contained hamlet near the University of Calgary. Enclosed by Crowchild Trail, the Trans-Canada Highway, and Highway 1A, the village is arranged so that most of the costlier establishments flank the highway; the cheaper ones lie off Crowchild Trail, offering a wide choice of accommodations in a small area with good transportation connections. If you're driving and don't want to deal with downtown traffic, just head here to find a room.

Except during the Stampede, you'll be able to find a vacancy without reservations; on C-Train, use either Lions Park or Banff Park stops. Your favorite chain hotels are located here, including **Days Inn,** 1818 16th Ave. NW (✆ **800/661-9564** or 403/289-3901), **Best Western Village Park Inn,** 1804 Crowchild Trail NW (✆ **888/774-7716** or 403/289-4645), **Travelodge North,** 2304 16th Ave. NW (✆ **800/578-7878** or 403/289-0211), and the **Quality Inn Motel Village,** 2359 Banff Trail NW (✆ **800/661-4667** or 403/289-1973).

## BUDGET OPTIONS

**Calgary International Hostel** The 120 beds at the Calgary hostel are the city's most affordable lodgings—but there are reasons beyond economy to stay here. The hostel is near downtown, convenient to bars and restaurants along Stephen Avenue and theaters near the performing-arts center. Facilities include two family rooms, a common area, and a small convenience store.

520 Seventh Ave. SE, Calgary, AB, T2G 0J6. ✆ **403/269-8239.** Fax 403/266-6227. www.hihostels.ca. Members C$16 (US$10), nonmembers C$20 (US$12). MC, V. Free parking. **Amenities:** Coin-op laundry.

## CAMPING

The **Calgary West KOA,** on the Trans-Canada Highway West (Box 10, Site 12, SS no. 1), Calgary, AB, T2M 4N3 (© **403/288-0411**), allows tents and pets. Facilities include washrooms, toilets, laundry, a dumping station, hot showers, groceries, and a pool. The price for two people is C$28 (US$17) per night; tent sites are C$25 (US$16) per night.

# WHERE TO DINE

Calgary has very stylish and exciting restaurants. The city is going through an unparalleled period of prosperity, and the citizenry's average age is 30. Put these two factors together and you've got the ingredients for a vibrant bar-and-restaurant scene. In general, you'll find fine dining downtown, with more casual bistros and restaurants along 17th Avenue.

## DOWNTOWN

### Expensive

**Belvedere** ★★ NEW CANADIAN Very stylish and very up-to-date, Belvedere is one of the most impressive of Calgary's many new restaurants. The shadowy dining room exudes a darkly elegant, 1930s atmosphere, while the exposed ductwork, brick walls, and dozens of mirrors give the restaurant a faint Lady from Shanghai look. The menu blends traditional North American favorites with stand-up-and-take-notice preparations. An outstanding appetizer is trio of fois gras, which presents local pan-seared duck liver in three completely different, completely fabulous ways. For an entree, choose from osso buco with fig and vanilla glaze or braised beef ribs and rib eye with Stilton and rosemary. The front bar is a coolly sophisticated spot for a drink and a predinner snack.

107 Eighth Ave. SW. © **403/265-9595.** Reservations recommended. Main courses C$21–C$38 (US$13–US$24). AE, DC, MC, V. Mon–Fri 11:30am–10pm, Sat 5:30–10pm.

**Owl's Nest** ★ FRENCH/CONTINENTAL One of Calgary's most wide-ranging upscale menus is found in this atmospheric dining room. Entree choices range from fine hand-cut Alberta steaks and fresh lobster to continental delicacies like Dover sole with caviar. Each week, there's also a specialty menu—usually under C$30 (US$19) for four courses—often featuring an ethnic cuisine. Service is excellent and the wine list is noteworthy.

In the Westin Hotel, Fourth Ave. and Third St. SW. © **403/266-1611.** Reservations required. Main courses C$20–C$30 (US$12–US$19). AE, DC, DISC, MC, V. Mon–Fri 11:30am–2pm; Mon–Sat 5:30–10:30pm.

**River Café** ★★ NEW CANADIAN If you have one meal in Calgary, it should be here. It takes a short walk through the Eau Claire Market area, then over the footbridge to lovely Prince's Island Park in the Bow River, to reach the aptly named River Café. On a lovely summer evening, the walk is a plus, as are the restaurant's lovely park-side decks (no vehicles hurtling by) and excellent food. Wood-fired, free-range, and wild-gathered foods teamed with organic whole breads and fresh-baked desserts form the backbone of the menu. There's a wide range of appetizers and light dishes—many vegetarian—as well as pizza-like flat breads topped with zippy cheese, vegetables, and fruit. Specialties from the grill braised pheasant breast with mustard spaetzle, black cherry oil and roasted apple. Menus change seasonally and read like a very tasty adventure novel.

Prince's Island Park. © **403/261-7670.** www.river-cafe.com. Reservations recommended. Main courses C$12–C$37 (US$7–US$23). AE, MC, V. Mon–Fri 11am–11pm, Sat–Sun 10am–11pm. Closed Jan.

**Téatro** ★★ ITALIAN Located in the historic Dominion Bank building just across from the Centre for the Performing Arts, Teatro delivers the best New Italian cooking in Calgary. The high-ceilinged dining room is dominated by columns and huge panel windows, bespeaking class and elegance. The extensive menu is based on "Italian Market Cuisine," featuring what's seasonally best and freshest, which is then cooked skillfully and simply to preserve natural flavors; some of the best dishes come from the wood-fired oven that dominates one wall. For lighter appetites, there's a large selection of antipasti, boutique pizzas, and salads; the entrees, featuring Alberta beef, veal, pasta, and seafood, are prepared with flair and innovation. Service is excellent.

200 Eighth Ave. SE. ✆ **403/290-1012.** www.teatro-rest.com. Reservations recommended. Main courses C$12–C$40 (US$7–US$25). AE, DC, MC, V. Mon–Fri 11:30am–11pm, Sat 5pm–midnight, Sun 5–10pm.

## Moderate

**Divino** ★ CALIFORNIA/ITALIAN Divino is housed in a landmark building (the Grain Exchange) and is both a wine bar and an intimate, bistro-style restaurant. The fare is unusual and tasty—steamed mussels in ginger-and-garlic broth, broccoli salad with toasted almonds and ginger dressing, and lamb pistachio burger with cambrozolo cheese. There are also full-fledged entrees, like steak, stuffed chicken breast, and pasta dishes. Divino is a great downtown option for tasty yet casual dining.

817 First St. SW. ✆ **403/263-5869.** Reservations recommended on weekends. Main courses C$10–C$15 (US$6–US$9). AE, MC, V. Mon–Sat 11:30am–10:30pm.

**Grand Isle Seafood Restaurant** CANTONESE/SEAFOOD One of Chinatown's best restaurants, the Grand Isle's beautiful dining room overlooks the Bow River. Pick your entree from the saltwater tanks, then enjoy the view. Dim sum is served daily; there's a huge lunch buffet on weekdays and brunch service on weekends.

128 Second Ave. SE. ✆ **403/269-7783.** Reservations recommended on weekends. Most dishes under C$12 (US$7). AE, MC, V. Daily 10am–midnight.

**Joey Tomato's** ITALIAN Located in the popular Eau Claire Market complex (see "Exploring Calgary," earlier), the very lively Joey Tomato's serves great pizza and other Italian food to throngs of appreciative Calgarians. And no wonder it's often packed: The food is really good, the prices moderate (by the city's standards), and there's a lively bar scene. What more could you want? Thin-crust pizzas come with traditional toppings or with zippy, more cosmopolitan choices. Pasta dishes are just as unorthodox, with dishes like linguini and smoked chicken, jalapeño, cilantro, and lime cream sauce. It's a fun, high-energy place to eat, and the food is always worth trying.

208 Barclay Parade SW. ✆ **403/263-6336.** Reservations not accepted. Pizza and pasta C$9–C$15 (US$6–US$9). AE, MC, V. Sun–Thurs 11am–midnight, Fri–Sat 11am–1am.

**The King & I** THAI This restaurant was the first to introduce Thai cuisine to Calgary, and it still ranks high. Chicken, seafood and vegetables predominate—one of the outstanding dishes is chicken fillet sautéed with eggplant and peanuts in chili-bean sauce. For more seasoned palates, there are eight regional curry courses, ranging from mild to downright devilish.

820 11th Ave. SW. ✆ **403/264-7241.** Main courses C$7–C$20 (US$4.35–US$12). AE, DC, MC, V. Mon–Thurs 11:30am–10:30pm, Fri 11:30am–11:30pm, Sat 4:30–11:30pm, Sun 4:30–9:30pm.

### Inexpensive

Budget diners have two strongholds in downtown Calgary: Chinatown and the Eau Claire Market. There are dozens of inexpensive restaurants in **Chinatown,** not all Chinese: check out Vietnamese and Thai options. Dim sum is widely available and inexpensive. **Eau Claire Market,** just north of downtown along the river, is a food grazer's dream. Two floors of food stalls and tiny restaurants in the market itself only begin to paint the picture. Put together a picnic with fresh bread, cheese, and wine or grab an ethnic takeout, and mosey on over to the park like everyone else in Calgary.

## ON 17TH AVENUE

Seventeenth Avenue, roughly between 4th Street SW and 10th Street SW, is home to many of Calgary's best casual restaurants and bistros. Take a cab or drive over and walk the busy cafe-lined streets, perusing the menus; the restaurants listed below are just the beginning.

A good place to go and get a feel for the avenue is **Melrose Place,** 730 17th Ave. SW (✆ **403/228-3566**), a bar/restaurant that has the best deck seating in the area (sit by the street or by a waterfall). Also check out **Fogbelly,** 719 17th Ave. SW (✆ **403/228-7898**), an amazing deli and gourmet takeout joint run by the same folks who operate Brava (below).

### Expensive

**La Chaumière** ★ FRENCH Winner of half a dozen awards, La Chaumière is a discreetly luxurious temple of fine dining. A meal here is an occasion to dress up, and this is one of the few spots in town that enforces a dress code. In addition to the coolly elegant dining room, La Chaumière offers plenty of patio seating in summer. The impressively broad menu is based on classic French preparations, but features local Alberta meats and produce.

139 17th Ave. SW. ✆ **403/228-5690.** Reservations recommended. Jacket and tie required for men. Main courses C$18–C$35 (US$11–US$22). AE, DC, MC, V. Mon–Fri noon–2pm; Mon–Sat 6pm–midnight.

### Moderate

**Bistro Jo Jo** PROVENÇAL Jo Jo's is a classic French bistro, right down to the tiled floor, mirrors, banquettes, fanback chairs, and tiny tables. The food is moderately priced for the quality and atmosphere. All your French favorites are here: duck breast, escargot, lamb, and even seafood marmite (saffron-infused sea bass, tuna, and mussels in fennel-and-carrot broth). The desserts are worth a trip in themselves.

917 17th Ave. SW. ✆ **403/245-2382.** Reservations recommended on weekends. Main courses C$15–C$20 (US$9–US$12). AE, DC, MC, V. Mon–Fri 11:30am–2pm (except summer) and 5:30–10:30pm, Sat 5:30–10:30pm.

**Brava** ★★ NEW CANADIAN One of Calgary's most exciting new restaurants, Brava is an offshoot of a successful catering company. In the relaxed, beautifully lit dining room, you can try a variety of dishes, from elegant appetizers and boutique pizzas to traditional main courses with contemporary zest. For an appetizer, try the beef carpaccio with Gorgonzola nuggets and chokecherry vinaigrette. Among the entrees, the venison schnitzel comes with lemon oregano cream, while grilled salmon is served with guava barbecue sauce. Eighty varieties of wine are available by the glass.

723 17th Ave. SW. ✆ **403/228-1854.** Reservations recommended. Main courses C$15–C$21 (US$9–US$13). AE, DC, MC, V. Mon–Tues 11am–11pm, Wed–Sat 11am–midnight.

**Cilantro** INTERNATIONAL Cilantro has an attractive stucco storefront, plus a tucked-away garden patio with a veranda bar. The food here is eclectic (some would call it California cuisine). You can snack on sandwiches, pasta or burgers (in this case, an elk burger) or have a full meal of grilled buffalo rib-eye or grilled sea bass. The wood-fired pizzas—with mostly Mediterranean ingredients—are great for lunch. The food is always excellent, and the setting casual and friendly.

338 17th Ave. SW. © **403/229-1177.** Reservations recommended on weekends. Main courses C$9–C$30 (US$6–US$19). AE, DC, MC, V. Mon–Thurs 11am–11pm, Fri 11am–midnight, Sat–Sun 5pm–11pm.

**Rose and Crown Pub** PUB FARE This traditional English pub has lots of quiet outdoor seating, good ales, and a menu featuring sandwiches, fish and chips, and other light entrees. This is a good place to gather if you find the scene on 17th Avenue a little too precious.

1503 4th St. SW. (just off 17th Ave. SW). © **403/244-7757.** Reservations not accepted. Main courses C$7–C$13 (US$4.35–US$8). MC, V. Mon–Sat 11am–2am, Sun 10am–2pm.

**Savoir Fare** ★★ NEW CANADIAN One of 17th Avenue's most coolly elegant eateries, Savoir Fare offers a tempting selection of seasonally changing and inventive menus. Preparations tend to mix classic technique and nouveau ingredients, with very tasty results. You don't have to overindulge to enjoy yourself—there's a good selection of interesting salads and sandwiches—but entrees are hard to resist: A vegetable Napoleon or a beef tenderloin crusted with pepper and ground coffee beans are sure to please.

907 17th Ave. SW. © **403/245-6040.** Reservations recommended. Main courses C$13–$26 (US$8–US$16). AE, DC, MC, V. Mon–Thurs 11am–11pm, Fri–Sat 11am–midnight, Sun 11am–10pm (May–end of Aug open 5–10pm only).

**Sultan's Tent** ★ MOROCCAN Although the Sultan's Tent is located in a modern western building, the restaurant's interior has been transformed by carpets and tapestries into a pretty good imitation of a Saharan tent. If you like great couscous, you should definitely make this a stop. Go all out and order the C$30 (US$19) Sultan's Feast, which includes all the trimmings and provides an evening's worth of eating and entertainment.

909 17th Ave. SW. © **403/244-2333.** Reservations recommended on weekends. Main courses C$11–C$19 (US$7–US$12). AE, DC, MC, V. Mon–Sat 5:30–11pm.

### Inexpensive

**Pongo Noodle and Beer House** FUSION One of the hottest cocktail scenes is at Pongo, and with its late hours, this is a place that just gets more popular as the evening wears on. The dining room is sleek and moderne. The menu stresses "Asian comfort food": appetizers like pot stickers and sake salmon sashimi, noodle dishes, noodle soups, and rice bowls. The food is very flavorful and inexpensive, and the cocktails shaken not stirred.

524 17th Ave. SW. © **403/209-1073.** Reservations not needed. Main courses C$7–C$9 (US$4.35–US$6). AE, MC, V. Sun–Wed 11am–2am, Thurs–Sat 11am–5am.

## INGLEWOOD

**The Cross House Garden Cafe** ★ FRENCH Located in a historic home, the Cross House serves upscale French cuisine in a quiet, almost rural setting. In summer, the dining room extends into the shaded yard, where the bustle of Calgary feels far away. The menu emphasizes French classic cuisine, artfully updated for zest and interest. For appetizers, choose caramelized scallops with Cambozola port soufflé. A grilled duck breast is served with orange and star anise sauce, and lobster is served with vanilla-perfumed curry sauce. The kitchen does a great job with grilled meats like rack of lamb and Alberta steaks.

1240 8th Ave. SE. ✆ **403/531-2767.** Reservations recommended. Main courses C$15–C$36 (US$9–US$22). MC, V. Mon–Sat 11:30am–2pm and 5:30–9pm, Sat 5–9pm.

**Hose and Hound Pub** ★ PUB After long day of shopping in Inglewood, Calgary's premier antique district, you will understandably think longingly of a pint and a nice casual bite to eat. This friendly pub is just the place. Located in one of the city's original fire halls, the Hose and Hound offers good local brews and excellent pub food. Besides favorites like burgers and fish and chips, the pub also offers pasta, home-made soups and sausage specialties from local sausage-makers extraordinaire, Spolumbo's.

1030 9th Ave. SE. ✆ **402/234-0508.** Reservations not needed. Main courses C$7–C$14 (US$4.35–US$9). MC, V. Mon–Thurs 11:30am–midnight, Fri–Sat 11:30–2am, Sun noon–midnight.

## EXPLORING CALGARY

### THE TOP ATTRACTIONS

**Glenbow Museum** ★★ One of the country's finest museums, the Glenbow is a must for anyone with an interest in the history and culture of western Canada. What sets it apart from other museums chronicling the continent's native cultures and pioneer settlement is the excellence of its interpretation. Especially notable is the third floor, with its vivid evocation of native cultures and compelling description of western Canada's exploration and settlement. You'll enjoy the brief asides into whimsy, like the display of early washing machines. Other floors contain displays of West African carvings, gems and minerals, and a cross-cultural look at arms and warfare.

130 Ninth Ave. SE (at First St.). ✆ **403/268-4100.** www.glenbow.org. Admission C$10 (US$6) adults, C$7.50 (US$4.65) seniors, C$6 (US$3.70) students and children, C$30 (US$19) families, free for children under 3. Discounted admission Thurs & Fri 5–9pm. Daily 9am–5pm, Thurs & Fri to 9pm. LRT: First St. E.

**Fort Calgary Historic Park** ★★ *Kids* On the occasion of the city's centennial in 1975, Fort Calgary became a public park of 16ha (40 acres), spread around the ruins of the original Mounted Police stronghold. At the moment, volunteers are reconstructing an exact replica of the original fort, using traditional methods and building materials. The replica of the 1888 barracks was completed in 2001. The Interpretive Centre captures the history of Calgary, from its genesis as a military fort to the beginnings of 20th-century hegemony as an agricultural and oil boomtown. Kids can do time in the 1875-era jail, or dress up as a Mountie. There are a number of interesting videos and docent-led displays; always in focus are the adventures and hardships of the Mounties a century ago. The rigors of their westward march and the almost unbelievable isolation these pioneer troopers endured, now seems incredible.

If all this history whets your appetite, cross the Elbow River on 9th Avenue and head to the Deane House. This historic home was built by a Fort Calgary superintendent nearly 100 years ago and is now the **Deane House Restaurant** operated by Fort Calgary (✆ **403/269-7747**), open Monday to Saturday from 11am to 2pm and Sunday from 10am to 2pm.

750 Ninth Ave. SE. ✆ **403/290-1875.** www.fortcalgary.com. Admission C$6.50 (US$4) adults, C$5.50 (US$3.40) seniors & students, C3.50 (US$2.15) youths 7–17, children under 7 free. May to mid-Oct daily 9am–5pm. LRT: Bridgeland.

**Eau Claire Market & Prince's Island Park** ★★ Calgary's most dynamic shopping, social, and dining center is Eau Claire Market, a car-free pedestrian zone north of downtown on the banks of the Bow River. This is where much of downtown Calgary comes to eat, drink, shop, sunbathe, jog, and hang out—it's easy to spend hours here just watching people and exploring. The market itself is a huge two-story warehouse containing boutiques; fresh fish, meat, vegetable, and fruit stalls; innumerable casual restaurants and bars; and a four-screen cinema. Also accessed from the market is the **IMAX Theatre** (✆ **403/974-4629**), with its five-story domed screen. Surrounding the market are lawns, fountains, and pathways leading to Prince's Island Park, a bucolic island in the Bow River lined with paths, shaded by cottonwood trees, and populated by hordes of Canada geese.

Near Second Ave. SW and Third St. SW. ✆ **403/264-6450.** Free admission. Market building open 9am–9pm, shops and restaurants have varying hours. LRT: Third St. W.

**Calgary Zoo, Botanical Garden & Prehistoric Park** ★ *Kids* Calgary's large and thoughtfully designed zoo lies on St. George's Island in the Bow River. The Calgary Zoo comes as close to providing natural habitats for its denizens as is technically possible. You'll particularly want to see the troop of majestic lowland gorillas and the African warthogs. The flora and fauna of western and northern Canada are on display in the Botanical Garden, and there's an amazing year-round tropical butterfly enclosure as well. Adjoining the zoo is the Prehistoric Park, a three-dimensional textbook of ancient dinosaur habitats populated by 22 amazingly realistic replicas—these imposing reproductions will give Barney-loving children something to think about. Call to inquire about special summer events, like Thursday Jazz Nights and free interpretive talks called "Nature Tales."

1300 Zoo Rd. NE. ✆ **403/232-9300.** www.calgaryzoo.ab.ca. Admission C$11 (US$7) adults, seniors half-price Tues–Thurs; C$5.50 (US$3.40) children 2–17; off-season discounts. Mid-May to Sept daily 9am–6pm; Oct to mid-May daily 9am–4pm. LRT: Zoo station.

**Calgary Tower** Reaching 762 steps or 190m (626 ft.) into the sky, this Calgary landmark is topped by an observation terrace offering unparalleled views of the city and mountains and prairies beyond. The high-speed elevator whisks you to the top in just 63 seconds. A stairway from the terrace leads to the cocktail lounge, where you can enjoy drinks and a panoramic vista. Photography from up here is fantastic. The **Panorama Restaurant** ✆ **403/266-7171**) is the near-mandatory revolving restaurant.

Ninth Ave. and Centre St. SW. ✆ **403/266-7171.** www.calgarytower.com. Elevator ride C$7.95 (US$4.90) adults, C$3 (US$1.85) children. June 15–Sept 15 daily 7:30am–11pm; Sept 16–June 14 daily 8am–10pm. LRT: First St. E.

**Calgary Science Centre** *Kids* The Calgary Science Centre features a fascinating kid-oriented combination of exhibitions, a planetarium, films, laser shows, and live theater, all under one roof. The hands-on, science-oriented exhibits change, but always invite visitors to push, pull, talk, listen, and play. The 360° Star Theatre opens windows to the universe.

701 11th St. SW. ✆ **403/221-3700.** www.calgaryscience.ca. Admission (exhibits and star shows) C$9 (US$6) adults, C$7 (US$4.35) youths and seniors, C$6 (US$3.70) children 3–12, free for children under 3. Summer daily 9:3am–5:30pm; off-season Tues–Fri 10am–4pm, Sat, Sun & holidays 10am–5pm. LRT: 10th St. W.

**Canada Olympic Park** *Kids* This lasting memento of Calgary's role as host of the 1988 Winter Olympics stands in the Olympic Park. Exhibits include the world's largest collection of Olympic souvenirs, such as the torch used to bring the flame from Greece, costumes and equipment used by the athletes, superb photographs, and a gallery of all medal winners. Activities include summer luge rides for C$13 (US$8) that will get the adrenaline pumping for road-trip weary teenagers, a new mountain-bike course, and chairlift rides up to the ski-jump tower.

88 Canada Olympic Park Rd. SW. ✆ **403/247-5452.** www.coda.ab.ca. Admission C$7 (US$4.35) per person, C$24 (US$15) per family. Summer daily 8am–9pm; off-season daily 8am–5pm. Take Hwy. 1 west.

## MORE ATTRACTIONS

**Devonian Gardens** These indoor gardens are a patch of paradise in downtown, a 1ha (2½-acre) park 46 feet above street level. Laid out in natural contours with 1.5km (1 mile) of pathways and a central stage for musical performances, they contain 20,000 plants (a mix of native Alberta and tropical plants), a reflecting pool, a sun garden, a children's playground, a sculpture court, and a water garden.

8th Ave. and 3rd St. SW, 4th floor. ✆ **403/268-3830.** Free admission. Daily 9am–9pm. LRT: 3rd St. W.

**Fish Creek Provincial Park** On the outskirts of town but easily accessible, Fish Creek Park is one of the largest urban parks in the world—actually, a kind of metropolitan wildlife reserve. Spreading over 1,175ha (2,900 acres), it provides a sheltered habitat for a vast variety of animals and birds. You can learn about them by joining in the walks and slide presentations given by park interpreters. For information on their schedules and planned activities, visit the administration office or call.

Canyon Meadows Dr. and Macleod Trail SE. ✆ **403/297-5293.** Bus: 78, 83.

**Museum of the Regiments** The largest military museum in western Canada tells the story of four famous Canadian regiments from the early 1900s to today. A series of lifelike miniature and full-size displays re-create scenes from the Boer War in 1900 to World War II; contemporary peacekeeping operations are also depicted. You also see videos, weapons, uniforms, medals, and photographs relating the history of the regiments and hear the actual voices of the combatants describing their experiences.

4520 Crowchild Trail SW (at Flanders Ave.). ✆ **403/974-2850.** www.nucleus.com/~regiments. Admission C$5 (US$3.10) adults, C$3 (US$1.85) seniors, C$2 (US$1.20) students and children, military personnel and veterans free. Daily 10am–4pm. Bus: 20 to Flanders Ave., then 1 block south.

**Art Gallery of Calgary** This contemporary art gallery, housed in two recently renovated downtown buildings, places a special emphasis on the contribution of local and regional talent and is a good place to see Calgary's contribution to the modern-art scene. National and regional shows also travel to the Art Gallery.

117 8th Ave. SW. ✆ **403/770-1350.** www.artgallerycalgary.com. Admission by donation. Tues–Sat 10am–5pm, Sun noon–4pm. LRT: 1st St E.

## TOURS & EXCURSIONS

For tours of the city, contact **White Stetson Tours** (✆ **403/274-2281**), whose 4-hour narrated van tour is C$35 (US$22). The company also offers day trips to Banff and Lake Louise for C$79 (US$49). **Exclusive Mountain Transportation and Tours** (✆ **403/246-9586**) offers tours of Calgary for C$35 (US$22) and trips to Lake Louise and the Drumheller badlands. **Hammer Head Scenic Tours** (✆ **403/260-0940;** www.hammerheadtours.com) has 9-hour tours to the

Drumheller badlands and the Royal Tyrell Museum for C$60 (US$37). Once weekly, the company runs its van to Head-Smashed-In Buffalo Jump for C$55 (US$34).

**Brewster Transportation** (© **877/791-5500**), in conjunction with Gray Line Bus Lines, offers a wide variety of bus tours. In addition to a 4-hour Calgary tour for C$40 (US$25), destinations include Banff, Lake Louise, Jasper, the Columbia Icefield, and Waterton Lakes.

## SHOPPING

### SHOPPING DISTRICTS OF NOTE

The main shopping district is downtown along **Eighth Avenue SW,** between Fifth and First streets SW. The lower part of Eighth Avenue has been turned into a pedestrian zone called the **Stephen Avenue Mall.** Major centers lining Eighth Avenue between First and Fourth streets include the Hudson's Bay Company and Holt Renfrew. A hip hangout for the young at heart, **Kensington Village** is just northwest of downtown across the Bow River, centered at 10th Street NW and Kensington Road. Crowded between the ubiquitous coffeehouses are bike shops and trendy boutiques. The stretch of **17th Avenue SW** between 4th and 10th streets SW has developed a mix of specialty shops, boutiques, cafes, and bars that makes browsing a real pleasure. Many of Calgary's galleries and interior-decor shops are also located here.

**Eau Claire Market,** near Second Ave. SW and Third St. SW. (© **403/264-6450**), is the best place to find edible gifts from Alberta's natural bounty. In addition, there are a jumble of import shops, music stores and enough odd little boutiques to make this a good place to while away an hour.

**Mountain Equipment Co-op,** 830 10th Ave. SW. (© 403/269-2420), is the largest outdoor store in Calgary, with everything from kayaks to ice axes. Come here before you head to the backcountry. If you like the look of pearl-snap shirts and the cut of Wranglers jeans, head to **Riley & McCormick,** 209 Eighth Ave. SW. (© **403/262-1556**), one of Calgary's original western-apparel stores. If you're looking for cowboy boots, **Alberta Boot Company,** 614 10th Ave. SW. (© **403/263-4605**), is the place. ABC is Alberta's only remaining boot manufacturer.

The Inglewood neighborhood is filled with antique stores, but if you love fine old furniture, **Juntiques,** 1226 Ninth Ave. SE. (© **403/263-0619**), is the place to shop. Juntiques has a fantastic selection of handmade Québecois furniture.

## CALGARY AFTER DARK

**THE PERFORMING ARTS** The sprawling **Calgary Centre for the Performing Arts,** 205 Eighth Ave. SE (© **403/294-7455;** www.theartscentre.org), provides the kind of cultural hub that many cities twice as big still lack. The center houses the Jack Singer Concert Hall, home of the **Calgary Philharmonic Orchestra** (© **403/571-0849;** www.cpo-live.com); the Max Bell Theatre, home of **Theatre Calgary** (© **403/294-7440;** www.theatrecalgary.com); and the Martha Cohen Theatre, home of **Alberta Theatre Projects** (© **403/294-7402;** www.atplive.com).

An acoustic marvel, **Jubilee Auditorium,** 14th Avenue and 14th Street NW, on the Southern Alberta Institute of Technology campus (© **403/297-8000;** www.jubileeauditorium.com), is located high on a hill with a panoramic view of downtown Calgary. The **Calgary Opera** (© **403/262-7286;** www.calgary opera.com) and the **Alberta Ballet** (© **403-254-4222;** www.albertaballet.com) both stage performances here.

### Tips Summer Jazz & Shakespeare

Every Thursday evening late June to August, the Calgary Zoo sponsors **Jazzoo (✆ 403/232-9300)**, with live bands. The concerts start at 6pm, and tickets are usually C$5 (US$3.10). You can buy dinner from concessionaires or bring your own.

Early July to mid-August, **Shakespeare in the Park (✆ 403/240-6374)** presents the Bard's works Thursday to Saturday at 7pm at Prince's Island Park in the Bow River. Admission is free (donations are appreciated, though).

---

Calgary loves dinner theater, and **Stage West,** 727 42nd Ave. SE (✆ **403/243-6642;** www.stagewestcalgary.com), puts on polished performances as well as delectable buffet fare. Tickets are C$32 to C$72 (US$20–US$45). Performances are Tuesday to Sunday.

**THE CLUB & BAR SCENE** Cover charges at most clubs are C$5 to C$10 (US$3.10–US$6) for live music. Pick up a copy of *Ffwd* (www.greatwest.ca/ffwd) or *Calgary Straight* for up-to-date listings.

Eau Claire Market is the home of the **Garage** (✆ **403/262-67620**), a hip warehouse-of-a-bar to play billiards and listen to loud alternative rock.

If you're just looking for a convivial drink, Bottlescrew **Bill's Old English Pub,** First Street and 10th Avenue SW (✆ **403/263-7900**), is a great choice. This friendly neighborhood pub is just on the edge of downtown, has lots of outdoor seating, and pours Alberta's widest selection of micro-brewed beers.

**Barleymill Neighbourhood Pub,** 201 Barclay Parade SW (✆ **403/290-1500**), is an Oldsy Worldsy pub plunked down in the plaza across from the Eau Claire Market. This popular watering hole is a cross between a collegiate hangout and a brewpub.

If you're looking for dance clubs, head to the corner of First Street SW and 12th Avenue. **Crazy Horse,** 1315 First St. SW (✆ **403/266-3339**), long one of the city's hottest dance and club scenes, is a popular, slightly precious place with lines out the door. It's just one of a half-dozen night clubs and dancehalls in a very small, very rocking area.

Put on your cowboy boots and swing your partner out to **Ranchman's,** 9615 Macleod Trail S. (✆ **403/253-1100**), the best country-western dance bar in the city. Free swing and line dance lessons are usually offered on Sunday afternoons; call to confirm.

**Kaos Jazz and Blues Bistro,** 718 17th Ave. SW (✆ **403/228-9997**), is one of western Canada's most storied jazz clubs. You'll see both international stars and local legends at this venerated bar and concert venue.

With three dance floors, **Boyztown,** 213 10th Ave. SW (✆ **403/265-2028**), is Calgary's best gay dance club. It's at the center of the city's small gay bar area.

**CASINO** Calgary has several legitimate casinos whose proceeds go wholly to charities. None impose a cover. Located across from the Stampede grounds, the **Elbow River Inn Casino,** 1919 Macleod Trail S. (✆ **403/266-4355**), offers Las Vegas-style gaming plus a poker variation called Red Dog. It is open 22 hours a day.

## THE TRAIL OF DINOSAURS IN THE ALBERTA BADLANDS ★★

The Red Deer River slices through Alberta's rolling prairies east of Calgary, revealing underlying sedimentary deposits that have eroded into badlands. These expanses of desert-like hills, strange rock turrets, and banded cliffs were laid down about 75 million years ago, when this area was a low coastal plain in the heyday of the dinosaurs. Erosion has incised through these deposits spectacularly, revealing a vast cemetery of Cretaceous life. Paleontologists have excavated here since the 1880s, and the Alberta badlands have proved to be one of the most important dinosaur-fossil sites in the world.

Two separate areas have been preserved and developed for research and viewing.

**Royal Tyrrell Museum of Palaeontology** ★ North of Drumheller, and about 145km (90 miles) northeast of Calgary, this is one of the world's best paleontology museums and educational facilities. It offers far more than just impressive skeletons and life-size models, though it has dozens of them. The entire fossil record of the earth is explained, era by era, with an impressive variety of media and educational tools. You walk through a prehistoric garden, watch numerous videos, use computers to "design" dinosaurs for specific habitats, watch plate tectonics at work, and see museum technicians preparing fossils. The museum is also a renowned research facility where scientists study all forms of ancient life.

Radiating out from Drumheller and the museum are a number of interesting side trips. Pick up a map from the museum and follow an hour's loop drive into the badlands along North Dinosaur Trail. The paved road passes two viewpoints over the badlands and crosses a free car-ferry on the Red Deer River before returning to Drumheller along the South Dinosaur Trail. A second loop passes through Rosedale to the south, past a ghost town, hoodoo formations, and a historic coal mine.

P.O. Box 7500, Drumheller, AB T0J 0Y0. ✆ **888/440-4240** or 403/823-7707. Fax 403/823-7131. www.tyrrellmuseum.com. Admission C$8.50 (US$5) adults, C$6.50 (US$4) seniors, C$4.50 (US$2.80) children, C$20 (US$12) families. Mid-May to Sept daily 9am–9pm; Oct to mid-May Tues–Sun 10am–5pm.

**Dinosaur Provincial Park** ★★ In Red Deer River Valley near Brooks, about 225km (140 miles) east of Calgary and 193km (120 miles) southeast of Drumheller, this park contains the world's greatest concentration of fossils from the late Cretaceous period. More than 300 complete dinosaur skeletons have been found in the area, which has been named a World Heritage Site. Park excavations continue from early June to late August, based out of the Field Station of the Royal Tyrrell Museum. Much of the park is a natural preserve, with access restricted to guided interpretive bus tours and hikes. Space on these tours is limited, so be prepared to be flexible with your choices. "Rush" tickets are sold at 8:30am for that day's events. Reservations are strongly encouraged in July and August. May to August, lab tours run so you can view fossil preparation.

Five self-guiding trails and two outdoor fossil displays are also available. Facilities at the park include a campground, a picnic area, and a service center.

P.O. Box 60, Patricia, AB T0J 2K0. ✆ **403/378-4342** or 403/378-4344 for tour reservations. Fax 403/378-4247. www.gov.ab.ca/env/parks/prov_parks/dinosaur/. Fees for bus tours and hikes C$4.50 (US$2.80) adults and C$2.25 (US$1.40) youths 6–15; children under 6 are free. Lab tours C$2 (US$1.20) adults, C$1 (US$.60) youths. Tours daily mid-May to Labour Day, weekends Labour Day to mid-October.

## Digging for Dinosaurs

If you're really keen on dinosaurs, you can participate in one of the digs. Day programs only are offered at the Royal Tyrrell Museum and include a half-day kids' event, a dig watch at C$12 (US$6) for adults, or a day spent helping with the dig at C$85 (US$53) for adults. Weeklong programs only are offered at Dinosaur Provincial Park. On the Field Experience Program, you get to be part of the dig crew for 7 days for C$800 (US$496), including bed and board. For all programs, contact the Bookings Officer at the **Royal Tyrrell Museum,** P.O. Box 7500, Drumheller, AB T0J 0Y0 (© **403/823-7707**; fax 403/823-7131).

## DAY TRIPS FROM CALGARY: THE OLD WEST

The Old West isn't very old in Alberta. If you're interested in the life and culture of the cowboy and rancher, stop at one of the following sights. Both are short and very scenic detours on the way from Calgary to the Rocky Mountains.

**Western Heritage Centre** ★ Fifteen minutes west of Calgary in the little ranching town of Cochrane, this museum and interpretive center is located at the Cochrane Ranche Provincial Historic Site, which preserves Alberta's first large-scale cattle ranch, established in 1881. The center commemorates traditional farm and ranch life, contains a rodeo hall of fame, and offers insights into this most western of sporting events. Special events—often rodeo-related—are scheduled throughout the summer; call for a schedule.

To reach Cochrane, follow Crowchild Trail (which becomes Hwy. 1A) out of Calgary; or from Hwy. 1 to Banff, take Hwy. 22 north to Cochrane. © **403/932-3514.** www.westernheritage.net. Admission C$8 (US$5) adults, C$6 (US$3.70) students and seniors, C$3.50 (US$2.15) children, and C$20 (US$12) family. Open late May–early September.

**Bar U Ranch National Historic Site** ★★ An hour southwest of Calgary is this a well-preserved and still-operating cattle ranch that celebrates both past and present traditions of the Old West. Tours of the ranch's 35 original buildings (some date from the 1880s) are available; a video of the area's ranching history is shown in the interpretive center. Special events include displays of ranching activities and techniques; since this is a real ranch, you might get to watch a branding or roundup.

Follow Hwy. 22 south from Calgary to the little community of Longview. © **403/395-2212.** www.parkscanada.gc.ca. Admission C$6 (US$3.70) adults, C$4.60 (US$2.85) seniors, C$2.90 (US$1.80) for children. Open 10am–6pm from late May–early October.

# 3 Southern Alberta Highlights

South of Calgary, running through the grain fields and prairies between Medicine Hat and Crowsnest Pass in the Canadian Rockies, Highway 3 roughly parallels the U.S.–Canadian border. This rural connector links several smaller Alberta centers and remote but interesting natural and historic sites.

## MEDICINE HAT & CYPRESS HILLS PROVINCIAL PARK

Medicine Hat, 291km (180 miles) southeast of Calgary, is at the center of Alberta's vast natural-gas fields. To be near this inexpensive source of energy, a lot of modern industry has moved to Medicine Hat, making this an unlikely factory town surrounded by grain fields. In the early 1900s, the primary industry was fashioning brick and china from the local clay deposits. Consequently, the town's old downtown is a showcase of handsome frontier-era brick buildings; take an hour and explore the historic city center, flanked by the South Saskatchewan River.

Cypress Hills Provincial Park, 81km (50 miles) south of Medicine Hat, is 316km$^2$ (122 sq. miles) of highlands—outliers of the Rockies—that rise 450m (1,500 ft.) above the flat prairie grasslands. In this preserve live many species of plants and animals, including elk and moose, which are usually found in the Rockies.

## LETHBRIDGE ★

East of Fort Macleod, 105km (65 miles) north of the U.S. border and 216km (134 miles) southeast of Calgary, lies Lethbridge, a delightful garden city and popular convention site (it gets more annual hours of sunshine than most places in Canada). Lethbridge started out as Fort Whoop-up, a notorious trading post that traded whiskey to the Plains Indians in return for buffalo hides and horses. The post boomed during the 1870s, until the Mounties arrived to bring order. Today Lethbridge is a pleasant prairie city and Alberta's third largest, with a population of 66,000. For details, contact the **Lethbridge Visitor Centre,** 2805 Scenic Dr., Lethbridge, AB T1K 5B7 (✆ **800/661-1222** or 403/320-1222), open daily from 9am to 5pm.

Lethbridge has two good art centers that display regional and touring art. The **Southern Alberta Art Gallery,** 601 3rd Ave. S. (✆ **403/327-8770**), has a number of changing art shows throughout the year; the gift shop is a good place to go for local crafts. It's open Tuesday to Saturday from 10am to 5pm and Sunday from 1 to 5pm. The **Bowman Arts Centre,** 811 5th Ave. (✆ **403/327-2813**), is housed in an old school and is the fine-arts hub of Lethbridge, with studios, classes, offices for arts organizations, and two galleries featuring the works of area artists; it's open Monday to Friday from 9am to 9pm and Saturday from 10am to 4pm.

The **Sir Alexander Galt Museum and Archives,** at the west end of 5th Avenue S. (✆ **403/320/3898**), is an excellent regional museum located in a historic former hospital. Exhibit galleries focus on the local Native culture, the city's coal-mining past, and the role of immigrants in the region's growth. Two of the galleries are devoted to the works of regional artists. The back windows of the museum overlook the impressive Oldman River Valley with its natural park systems. It's open daily from 10am to 4:30pm, with free admission.

The city's heritage as a frontier whiskey-trading center is commemorated at the **Fort Whoop-Up Interpretive Center** (✆ **403/329-0444**) in Indian Battle Park (follow 3rd Avenue South toward the river). A replica of the fort—built by Montana-based traders of buffalo skins and whiskey in the 1870s—stands in the park, with costumed docents providing horse-drawn carriage tours, interpretive programs, and historic reenactments. Mid-May to September, it's open Monday to Saturday from 10am to 6pm and Sunday from noon to 6pm; the rest of the year, it's open Tuesday to Friday from 10am to 4pm and Sunday from 1 to 4pm. Admission is C$5 (US$3.10) for adults, C$3 (US$1.85) for seniors and students, and free for children under 6.

The pride of Lethbridge is the **Nikka Yuko Japanese Garden** (✆ **403/328-3511**) in Henderson Lake Park on Mayor Mangrath Drive, east of downtown. Its pavilion and dainty bell tower were built by Japanese artisans without nails or bolts. The garden is one of the largest Japanese gardens in North America; Japanese-Canadian women in kimonos give tours and explain the philosophical concepts involved in Japanese garden design. From late June to Labour Day, the gardens are open daily 9am to 9pm; mid-May to late June and Labour Day to early October, it's open daily 10am to 4pm. Admission is C$5 (US$3.10) for adults, C$4 (US$2.50) for seniors, C$3 (US$1.85) for youths ages 6 to 17, and free for children under 6.

## WHERE TO STAY & DINE

**Heritage House B&B** This wonderful B&B will come as an architectural surprise: In an otherwise early-1900s neighborhood, this Art Deco jewel really stands out. Considered one of the finest examples of International Art Moderne in the province, the house is a designated provincial historic site. The interior retains the look of the 1930s, including some original wall murals. The comfortable guest rooms are spacious and share a bathroom and a half.

1115-8 Ave. S., Lethbridge, AB T1J 1P7. ✆ **403/328-3824.** Fax 403/328-9011. www.ourheritage.net/bb.html. 2 units, neither with bathroom. C$65 (US$40) double. Rates include breakfast. No credit cards. *In room:* TV, no phone.

**Ramada Hotel & Suites** *Kids* New in 1999, the Ramada is the nicest lodging in Lethbridge. Though many of its amenities are designed to attract business travelers, vacationers will also find it a very comfortable place to stay. If the kids are along, it may be hard to convince them to leave the indoor water park with its two waterslides and a wave pool.

2375 Mayor Magrath Dr. S., Lethbridge, AB T1K 7M1. ✆ **800/272-6232** or 403/380-5050. Fax 403/380-5051. www.ramada.ca/leth.html. 119 units. C$119–C$159 (US$74–US$99) double. AE, DC, DISC, MC, V. **Amenities:** Pool; Jacuzzi; exercise room; business center; convenience store. *In room:* A/C, TV, dataport, fridge, microwave, coffeemaker, hair dryer, iron.

## WHERE TO DINE

For breakfast pastries or lunchtime sandwiches, the **Penny Coffee House,** 331 5th St. S. (✆ **403/320-5282**), is a friendly hangout open Monday to Saturday 7am to 10pm and Sunday 9am to 5pm. **Dionysios,** 635 13th St. N. (✆ **403/320-6554**), has slow service but tasty Greek food and is open daily from 5 to 11pm. With good food and a lively atmosphere, **Coco Pazzo,** 1264 3rd Ave. S. (✆ **403/329-8979**), is probably one of the best places to eat in town, with a menu focusing on pizza and specialties from the wood-fired oven; it's open daily from 11am to midnight.

# FORT MACLEOD

**Fort Museum** Forty-four kilometers (27 miles) west of Lethbridge stands what was in 1873 the western headquarters of the Northwest Mounted Police. Named after Colonel MacLeod, the redcoat commander who brought peace to Canada's west, the reconstructed Fort Macleod is now a provincial park and is still patrolled by Mounties in their traditional uniforms.

The fort is filled with fascinating material on the frontier period. Among its treasured documents is the rule sheet of the old Macleod Hotel, written in 1882: "All guests are requested to rise at 6am. This is imperative as the sheets are needed for tablecloths. Assaults on the cook are prohibited. Boarders who get killed will not be allowed to remain in the house." The fort grounds also contain the Centennial Building, a museum devoted to the history of the local

Plains Indians. A highlight of visiting the fort in summer is the **Mounted Patrol Musical Ride** at 10am, 11:30am, 2pm, and 3:30pm, with eight horseback Mounties performing a choreographed equestrian program to music.

219 25th St, Fort Macleod, AB T0L 0Z0. © **403/553-4703.** www.nwmpmuseum.com. Admission C$7.50 (US$4.65) adults, C$7 (US$4.35) seniors, C$5.50 (US$3.40) children 12–17, and C$4.50 (US$2.80) kids 6–11; children under 6 are free. March–Dec 24, daily 9am–5pm (to 8pm July and Aug).

**Head-Smashed-In Buffalo Jump** ★ One of the most interesting sights in southern Alberta, and a World Heritage Site, is the curiously named Head-Smashed-In Buffalo Jump. This excellent interpretive center/museum is built into the edge of a steep cliff over which the native Canadians used to stampede herds of bison, the carcasses then providing them with meat, hides, and horns. The multimillion-dollar facility tells the story of these ancient harvests by means of films and native-Canadian guide-lecturers. Other displays illustrate and explain the traditional life of the prairie-dwelling natives in precontact times and the ecology and natural history of the northern Great Plains. Hiking trails lead to undeveloped jump sites.

Fort Macleod, AB T0L 0Z0. © **403/553-2731.** www.head-smashed-in.com. Admission C$6.50 (US$4) adults, C$5.50 (US$3.40) seniors, and C$3 (US$1.85) children 17 and under. Daily 9am–6pm in summer, 10am–5pm in winter. Spring Point Road, 19km (12 miles) west of Fort Macleod on Hwy. 2.

## 4 Waterton Lakes National Park ★

In the southwestern corner of the province, Waterton Lakes National Park is linked with Glacier National Park in neighboring Montana; together these two beautiful tracts of wilderness compose Waterton-Glacier International Peace Park. Once the hunting ground of the Blackfoot, 526km$^2$ (203-sq. mile) Waterton Park contains superb mountain, prairie, and lake scenery and is home to abundant wildlife.

During the last Ice Age, the park was filled with glaciers, which deepened and straightened river valleys; those peaks that remained above the ice were carved into distinctive thin, finlike ridges. The park's famous lakes also date from the Ice Ages; all three of the Waterton Lakes nestle in glacial basins.

The park's main entrance road leads to **Waterton Townsite,** the only commercial center, with a number of hotels, restaurants, and tourist facilities. Other roads lead to more remote lakes and trail heads. Akamina Parkway leads from the townsite to Cameron Lake, glimmering beneath the crags of the Continental Divide. At the small visitors center, you can rent canoes; this is a great spot for a picnic. Red Rock Parkway follows Blackiston Creek past the park's highest peaks to Red Rock Canyon. From here, three trails lead up deep canyons to waterfalls.

The most popular activity in the park is the **International Shoreline Cruise** (© **403/859-2362**) which leaves from the townsite and sails Upper Waterton Lake past looming peaks to the ranger station at Goat Haunt, Montana, in Glacier Park. These tour boats leave five times daily; the cruise usually takes 2 hours, including the stop in Montana. The price is C$22 (US$14) for adults, C$12 (US$7) for youths ages 13 to 17, and C$8 (US$5) for children ages 4 to 12.

For more information, contact the **Waterton Park Chamber of Commerce and Visitors Association,** P.O. Box 5599, Waterton Lakes National Park, AB T0K 2M0 (© **403/859-5133** summer or 403/859-2224 winter; www.parkscanada.gc.ca and www.discoverwaterton.com). The per-day park entry fee is C$4 (US$2.50) for adults, C$3 (US$1.85) for seniors, and C$2 (US$1.20) for children.

## WHERE TO STAY

**Kilmorey Lodge** Beloved by oft-returning guests, the Kilmorey is a rambling old lodge from the park's heyday. One of the few lodgings that has direct lake views, it offers small but elegantly appointed rooms. Expect down comforters, antiques, squeaky floors, and loads of character and charm. The Lamp Post is one of Waterton's most acclaimed restaurants; also on site are the Gazebo Café and the Ram's Head Lounge.

P.O. Box 100, Waterton Park, AB, T0K 2M0. ✆ **888/859-8669** or 403/859-2334. Fax 403/859-2342. www.kilmoreylodge.com. 23 units. C$98–C$194 (US$61–US$120) double. Extra person C$20 (US$12). Children under 16 stay free in parents' room. AE, DC, DISC, MC, V. **Amenities:** Fine dining restaurant, outdoor café, bar. *In room:* Hair dryer, no phone.

**Prince of Wales Hotel** *Overrated* Built in 1927 by the Great Northern Railway, this beautiful mountain lodge, perched on a bluff above Upper Waterton Lake, is reminiscent of the historic resorts in Banff. Rooms have been renovated, though many are historically authentic in that they're rather small. Operated by the same dilatory Greyhound/Dial Soap consortium that manages the historic lodges in Glacier National Park in Montana, the Prince of Wales is in need of some serious reinvestment (at these prices, you don't expect water-stained acoustic ceiling tile in the lobby bar). You'll want to at least visit this landmark for the view and perhaps for a meal at the Garden Court restaurant. Historic-monument status aside, however, there are better places to stay than this handsome doyen—until someone who actually values these grand lodges pries them away from Greyhound.

P.O. Box 33, Waterton Lakes National Park, AB, T0K 2M0. ✆ **403/859-2231.** Fax 403/859-2630. www.princeofwaleswaterton.com. In off-season, contact 1225 N. Central Ave., Phoenix, AZ 85077 ✆ **602/207-6000.** 86 units. C$289–C$329 (US$179–US$204) double. Extra person C$15 (US$9). Children under 12 stay free in parents' room. MC, V. Closed Sept 27–May 13. **Amenities:** 2 restaurants, 2 bars; nonsmoking rooms.

**Waterton Lakes Lodge** ★ This new and classy complex sits on 1.5ha (4 acres) in the heart of Waterton Townsite. The 80 rooms are in nine separate lodge-like buildings that flank a central courtyard. There are three types of accommodations: large standard rooms with queen beds; deluxe rooms with two queen beds and a sofa bed, a gas fireplace, a two-person shower, and a jetted tub; and kitchenette units with all the features of deluxe rooms plus a dining area and kitchen. All are decorated with an environmental theme and appointed with handsome pine furniture. The Wildflower Dining Room, the Good Earth Deli, and the Wolf's Den Lounge are part of the resort complex. Also on the property are a guest and community sports facility, with a large pool, fitness center, and spa. Winter sports and cross-country ski rentals are available.

P.O. Box 4, Waterton Park, AB, T0K 2M0. ✆ **888/98-LODGE** or 403/859-2150. Fax 403/859-2229. www.watertonlakeslodge.com. 80 units. C$160–C$265 (US$99–US$164) double. Extra person C$15 (US$9). Off-season rates available. AE, MC, V. **Amenities:** 2 restaurants, bar; health club with pool; fitness center and spa; coin-op laundry; nonsmoking rooms. *In room:* A/C, TV, dataport, fridge, coffeemaker, hair dryer.

## 5 Introducing the Canadian Rockies

Few places in the world are more dramatically beautiful than the Canadian Rockies. Banff and Jasper national parks are famous for their mountain lakes, flower-spangled meadows, spire-like peaks choked by glaciers, and abundant wildlife. Nearly the entire spine of the Rockies—from the U.S. border north for 1,127km (699 miles)—is preserved as parkland or wilderness.

That's the good news. The bad news is that this Canadian wilderness, the flora and fauna that live in it, and the lovers of solitude who come here, are going to need all this space as the Rockies become more popular. More than 5 million people annually make their way through Banff National Park. But it seems that Draconian measures like limiting visitors are, as of yet, brought up only in order to be dismissed. Advance planning for a trip to the Canadian Rockies is absolutely necessary if you're going to stay or eat where you want or if you want to evade the swarms of visitors that throng the parks in summer.

## ESSENTIALS

Canada's Rocky Mountain parks include Jasper and Banff, which together comprise 17,519km$^2$ (6,764 sq. miles); the provincial parklands of the Kananaskis Country and Mount Robson; and Yoho and Kootenay national parks to the west in British Columbia.

The parks are traversed by one of the finest highway systems in Canada, plus innumerable nature trails leading to more remote valleys and peaks. The two "capitals," Banff and Jasper, lie 287km (177 miles) apart, connected by Highway 93, one of the most scenic routes you'll ever drive. Banff is 128km (80 miles) from Calgary via Highway 1; Jasper, 375km (225 miles) from Edmonton on Route 16, the famous Yellowhead Highway.

Admission to Banff, Jasper, Yoho, and Kootenay parks costs C$5 (US$3.10) per person per day, or C$10 (US$6) per group or family per day.

## TOURS & EXCURSIONS

You'll get used to the name Brewster, associated with many things in these parts. In particular, these folks operate the park system's principal tour-bus operation. **Brewster Transportation and Tours,** 100 Gopher St., Banff, AB, T0L 0C0 (© **403/762-6767,** www.brewster.ca), covers most of the outstanding scenic spots in both parks. Call for a full brochure, or ask the concierge at your hotel to arrange a trip. A few sample packages:

**Banff to Jasper** (or vice versa): Some 9½ hours through unrivaled scenery, this tour takes in Lake Louise and a view of the ice field along the parkway. (The return trip requires an overnight stay, not included in the price.) In summer, the adult fare costs C$95 (US$59) one-way and C$47.50 (US$29) for children. If you don't want the tour, there's also a daily express bus between Banff and Jasper for C$59 (US$37) one-way; children pay half price.

**Columbia Icefields:** On this 9½-hour tour from Banff, you stop at the Icefields Centre and get time off for lunch and a Snocoach ride up the glacier. Adults pay C$95 (US$59) in summer and children pay C$47.50 (US$29). The Snocoach Tour costs an extra C$28 (US$17) for adults and C$14 (US$9) for children; tickets must be purchased in advance.

---

*Tips* **Warning: Reserve Far Ahead**

If you're reading this on the day you plan to arrive in Banff, Jasper, or Lake Louise and haven't yet booked your room, start worrying. Most hotels are totally booked for the season by July 1. To avoid disappointment, reserve your room as far in advance as you know your travel dates.

---

# The Canadian Rockies

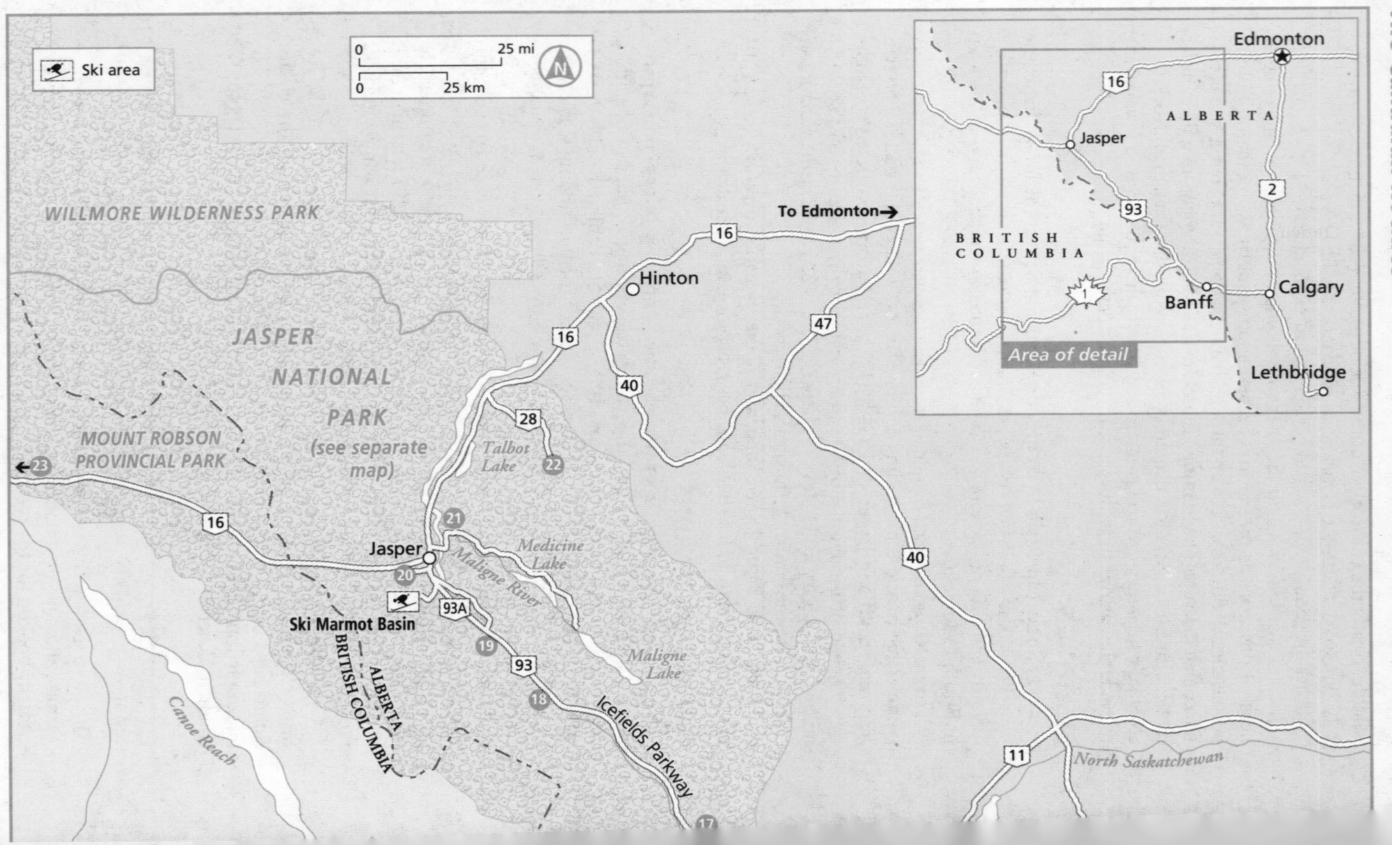

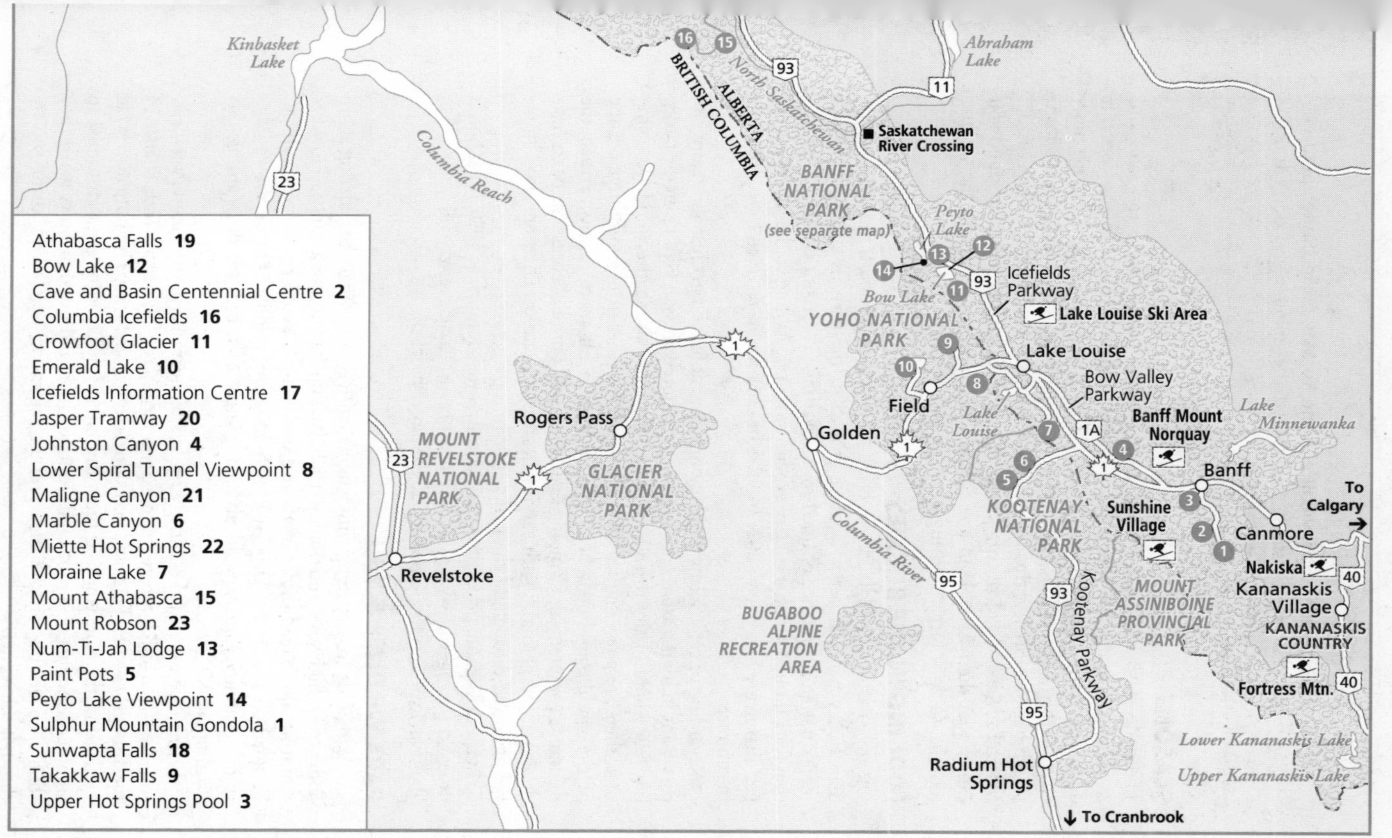
Athabasca Falls 19
Bow Lake 12
Cave and Basin Centennial Centre 2
Columbia Icefields 16
Crowfoot Glacier 11
Emerald Lake 10
Icefields Information Centre 17
Jasper Tramway 20
Johnston Canyon 4
Lower Spiral Tunnel Viewpoint 8
Maligne Canyon 21
Marble Canyon 6
Miette Hot Springs 22
Moraine Lake 7
Mount Athabasca 15
Mount Robson 23
Num-Ti-Jah Lodge 13
Paint Pots 5
Peyto Lake Viewpoint 14
Sulphur Mountain Gondola 1
Sunwapta Falls 18
Takakkaw Falls 9
Upper Hot Springs Pool 3
Kinbasket Lake
Columbia Reach
ALBERTA
BRITISH COLUMBIA
North Saskatchewan
Abraham Lake
Saskatchewan River Crossing
BANFF NATIONAL PARK
(see separate map)
Peyto Lake
Bow Lake
Icefields Parkway
Lake Louise Ski Area
YOHO NATIONAL PARK
Lake Louise
Bow Valley Parkway
Field
Lake Louise
Banff Mount Norquay
Lake Minnewanka
Rogers Pass
Golden
MOUNT REVELSTOKE NATIONAL PARK
GLACIER NATIONAL PARK
Revelstoke
Banff
To Calgary
KOOTENAY NATIONAL PARK
Sunshine Village
Canmore
Nakiska
Kananaskis Village
KANANASKIS COUNTRY
Fortress Mtn.
Columbia River
MOUNT ASSINIBOINE PROVINCIAL PARK
Kootenay Parkway
BUGABOO ALPINE RECREATION AREA
Lower Kananaskis Lake
Upper Kananaskis Lake
Radium Hot Springs
To Cranbrook

**Tips A Wildlife Warning**

Whenever you come across wildlife in the Rockies, avoid the temptation to get up-close and personal. Don't feed the animals and don't touch them! You can get fined—or worse.

## SEASONS

The parks have two peak seasons during which hotels charge top rates and restaurants are jammed. The first is summer, mid-June to late August, when it doesn't get terribly hot, rarely above 25°C (80°F), though the sun's rays are powerful at this altitude. The other peak time is winter, the skiing season from December to February; this is probably the finest skiing terrain in all Canada. March to May is decidedly off-season: Hotels offer bargain room rates, and you can choose the best table in any eatery. There's plenty of rain in the warmer months, so don't forget to bring some suitable rainwear.

## LODGING IN THE ROCKIES

On any given day in high season, up to 50,000 people wind through the Canadian Rocky national parks. Because growth in the parks is strictly regulated, there's not an abundance of hotel rooms waiting. The result is strong competition for a limited number of very expensive rooms. Adding to the squeeze is the fact that many hotels have 80% to 90% of their rooms reserved for coach tours in summer.

Regarding price, it seems that lodgings can ask for and get just about any rate they want in high season. For the most part, hotels are well kept up in the parks, but few would justify these high prices anywhere else in the world. Knowing that, there are a few choices. You can decide whether or not to splurge on one of the world-class hotels here, actually only a bit more expensive than the midrange competition. Camping is another good option, because the parks have dozens of campgrounds with varying degrees of facilities. There are also a number of hostels throughout the parks.

In the off-season, prices drop dramatically, often as much as 50%. Most hotels offer ski packages in winter, as well as other attractive getaway incentives. Ask about any special rates, especially at the larger hotels.

## PARK WILDLIFE & YOU

The parklands are swarming with wildlife, with some animals meandering along and across highways and hiking trails, within easy camera range. However tempting, **don't feed the animals and don't touch them!** For starters, you can be fined up to C$500 (US$310) for feeding any wildlife. There's also the distinct possibility you may end up paying more than cash for disregarding this warning.

It isn't easy to resist the blithely fearless bighorn sheep, mountain goats, elk, soft-eyed deer, and lumbering moose you meet. (You'll have very little chance of meeting the coyotes, lynx, and occasional wolves, since they give humans a wide berth.) But the stuff you feed them can kill them. Bighorns get accustomed to summer handouts of bread, candy, potato chips, and marshmallows when they should be grazing on the high-protein vegetation that'll help them survive through the winter.

Moose involve additional dangers. They've been known to take over entire picnics after being given an initial snack, chase off the picnickers, and eat up everything in sight—including cutlery, dishes, and the tablecloth.

Portions of the parks may sometimes be closed to hikers and bikers during elk calving season. A mother elk can mistake your recreation for an imminent attack on her newborn; or an unsuspecting hiker could frighten a mother from her calf, separating the two for good. Pay attention to—and obey—postings at trail heads.

Bears pose the worst problems. The parks contain two breeds: the big grizzly, standing up to 2m (7 ft.) on its hind legs, and the smaller black bear, about 1.5m (5 ft.) long. The grizzly spends most of the summer in high alpine ranges, well away from tourist haunts. As one of North America's largest carnivores, its appearance and reputation are awesome enough to make you beat a retreat on sight. But the less formidable black bear is a born clown with tremendous audience appeal and takes to human company like a squirrel. The black bear's cuddly looks and circus antics, plus its knack for begging and rummaging through garbage cans, tend to obscure the fact that these are wild animals: powerful, faster than a horse, and completely unpredictable.

Hiking in bear country (and virtually all parkland is bear country) necessitates certain precautions—ignore them at your peril. Never hike alone and never take a dog along. Dogs often yap at bears, then when the animal charges, they run toward their owners for protection, bringing the pursuer with them. Use a telephoto lens when taking pictures. Bears in the wild have a set tolerance range that, when encroached upon, may bring on an attack. Above all, never go near a cub. The mother is usually close by, and a female defending her young is the most ferocious creature you'll ever face—and possibly the last.

## 6 Kananaskis Country & Canmore

Kananaskis Country is the name given to three Alberta provincial parks on the Rocky Mountains' eastern slope, southeast of Banff National Park. Once considered only a gateway region to more glamorous Banff, the Kananaskis has developed into a recreation destination on a par with more famous brand-name resorts in the Canadian Rockies.

Located just west of the Kananaskis and just outside the eastern boundary of Banff National Park, **Canmore** is a sprawl of condominium and resort developments in a dramatic location beneath the soaring peaks of Three Sisters Mountain. Only 20 minutes from Banff, Canmore hasn't yet topped the list of Canadian resort destinations, but the scenery is magnificent and the accommodations generally much less expensive and considerably less overbooked than those in Banff.

Weather is generally warmer and sunnier here, which is conducive to great golf: The championship course at **Kananaskis** is considered one of the best in North America.

When the 1988 Olympics were held in Calgary, the national park service wouldn't allow the alpine ski events to be held in the parks. Nakiska, in the Kananaskis, became the venue instead, vaulting this ski area to international prominence.

The main road through the Kananaskis Country is Highway 40, which cuts south from Highway 1 at the gateway to the Rockies and follows the Kananaskis River. Kananaskis Village, a collection of resort hotels and shops, is the center of activities in the Kananaskis and is convenient to most recreation areas. Highway

40 eventually climbs up to 2,206m (7,239-ft.) Highwood Pass, the highest pass in Alberta, before looping around to meet Highway 22 south of Calgary.

For information on Kananaskis and Canmore, contact **Kananaskis Country** (✆ **866/432-4322;** www.kananaskisvalley.com) or the **Barrier Lake Visitor Information Centre,** Box 32, Exshaw, AB, G0L 2C0 (✆ **403/673-3985**). The province-wide **Travel Alberta Visitor Information Centre,** at the Bow Valley Trail exit off Highway 1 at Canmore (✆ **403/678-5277**) also has lots of information.

## ADVENTURE SPORTS

It's the excellent access to outdoor recreation that makes Canmore and the Kananaskis such a prime destination. Recreation here is highly organized and easy to indulge in. From its offices in Kananaskis Village and in Canmore at 999 Bow Valley Trail, #3, **Mirage Adventure Tours** (✆ **888/312-7238** or 403/678-4919; fax 403/609-3210; www.miragetours.com) represents most local outfitters and most activities available in the area. You'll find bicycle trips, horseback trail rides, rafting, hiking, sightseeing tours, and other recreational opportunities on offer. Mirage also rents cross-country skis and equipment.

**DOWNHILL SKIING** Kananaskis gained worldwide attention when it hosted the alpine ski events for the Winter Olympics in 1988, and skiing remains a primary attraction in the area. At **Nakiska,** skiers can follow in the tracks of past Winter Olympians. A second ski area, **Fortress Mountain,** is 19km (12 miles) south of Kananaskis Village. Although overshadowed by Nakiska's Olympic reputation, Fortress Mountain offers an escape from the resort crowd and features overnight accommodations in an on-site dormitory. Both areas offer terrain for every age and ability, and are open from early December to mid-April. Adult lift tickets cost C$46 (US$29) at Nakiska, C$34 (US$21) at Fortress; tickets are completely transferable between the two areas. For more information, contact **Ski Nakiska,** P.O. Box 1988, Kananaskis Village, AB, T0L 2H0 (✆ **800/258-7669** or 403/591-7777, www.skinakiska.com).

**CROSS-COUNTRY SKIING & MORE** The **Canmore Nordic Centre** ★, south of town off Spray Lakes Road (1988 Olympic Way, Canmore, AB, T1W 2T6; ✆ **403/678-2400**), was developed for the Olympics's cross-country skiing competition, though the facility is now open year-round. In winter, the center offers 70km (44 miles) of scenic cross-country trails, plus the on-site **Trail Sports** shop (✆ **403/678-6764**) for rentals, repairs, and sales. In summer, hikers and mountain bikers take over the trails, and Trail Sports offers bike rentals, skill-building courses, and guided rides.

**GOLF** Kananaskis features three championship golf courses and one of Canada's premier golf resorts. **Kananaskis Country Golf Course** ★ boasts two 18-hole, par-72 courses set among alpine forests and streams, and featuring water hazards on 20 holes, 140 sand traps, and four tee positions. Kananaskis is rated among the top courses in Canada. For information, contact **Golf Kananaskis,** Kananaskis Country Golf Course, P.O. Box 1710, Kananaskis Village, AB, T0L 2H0 (✆ **403/591-7154;** www.kananaskisgolf.com). Greens fees are C$65 (US$40).

Near Canmore, the 18-hole **Canmore Golf Course** is right along the Bow River at 2000 Eighth Ave. (✆ **403/678-4785**). Greens fees are C$48 (US$30).

The Les Furber–designed **Golf Course at Silvertip** ★ (✆ **403/678-1600;** www.silvertipresort.com) is an 18-hole, par-72 course high above Canmore, off Silvertip Drive. You'll look eye-to-eye with the Canadian Rockies here. Boasting a length of 6,675m (7,300 yd.), the course has sand bunkers on all holes, and water on eight. Greens fees range from C$89 to C$129 (US$55–US$80).

**HORSEBACK TRIPS** The Kananaskis is noted for its dude ranches (see "Guest Ranches," below), which offer a variety of horseback adventures from short trail rides to multi-day pack trips. Mirage Adventure Tours (see above) is also a good clearinghouse for information.

**RAFTING** The Kananaskis and Bow rivers are the main draw here. In addition to half-day (C$55/US$34), full-day (C$85/US$53), and 2-day (C$229/US$142) white-water trips, there are excursions that combine a half-day of horseback riding or mountain biking with an afternoon of rafting (C$119–C$129/US$74–US$80). Contact Mirage Adventure Tours, above, for information.

## WHERE TO STAY

Kananaskis is a major camping destination for families in Calgary, and the choice of **campgrounds** is wide. There's a concentration of campgrounds at Upper and Lower Kananaskis Lakes, some 32km (20 miles) south of Kananaskis Village. A few campgrounds are scattered nearer to Kananaskis Village, around Barrier Lake and Ribbon Creek. For a full-service campground with RV hookups, go to **Mount Kidd RV Park** (✆ **403/591-7700**) just south of the Kananaskis golf course.

### KANANASKIS VILLAGE

The lodgings in Kananaskis Village were built for the Olympics, so all are new and well maintained. There's no more than a stone's throw between them, and to a high degree, public facilities are shared among all the hotels.

**Delta Lodge at Kananaskis** ★ This resort hotel consists of two separate buildings that face each other across a pond at the center of Kananaskis Village. The Lodge is the larger building, with a more rustic facade, a shopping arcade, and a number of drinking and dining choices. Its guest rooms are large and well furnished; many have balconies and some have fireplaces. The Signature Club service rooms are in the smaller—and quieter—of the two lodge buildings. Rooms here are generally more spacious than those in the Lodge, and even more sumptuously furnished. Additionally, the Signature Club rooms include deluxe continental breakfast, afternoon hors d'oeuvres, honor bar and full concierge service.

Kananaskis Village, AB, T0L 2H0. ✆ **800/268-1133** or 403/591-7711. Fax 403/591-7770. www.deltalodgeatkananaskis.ca. 321 units. High season C$225–C$330 (US$140–US$205). Ski/golf package rates and discounts available. AE, DC, MC, V. Parking C$8 (US$5); valet parking C$11 (US$7). **Amenities:** 4 restaurants, bar; indoor pool; golf courses nearby; tennis courts; health club; complete spa with salt water pool, whirlpool, and beauty treatments; bike rental; concierge; tour desk; car-rental desk; business center; shopping arcade; room service (7am–1am); babysitting; laundry service; dry cleaning; concierge-level rooms. *In room:* A/C (Signature Club), TV/VCR w/pay movies, dataport (Signature Club), minibar, coffeemaker, hair dryer, iron.

**Kananaskis Mountain Lodge** This handsome, wood-fronted hotel is the most affordable place to stay in Kananaskis—although that doesn't mean it's inexpensive. The hotel offers a wide variety of room types—all renovated in

2001 with new comfortable furnishings—including many loft units with kitchenettes that can sleep up to six. There are mountain views from practically every room.

P.O. Box 10, Kananaskis Village, AB, T0L 2H0. ✆ **888/591-7501** or 403/591-7500. Fax 403/591-7633. www.kananaskismountainlodge.com. 90 units. C$110–C$230 (US$68–US$143) double, C$170–C$290 (US$105–US$180) suite. AE, DC, DISC, MC, V. Free parking. **Amenities:** Wildflower Bistro, Woody's Pub; golf courses nearby; tennis courts; health club and spa; exercise room; concierge; tour desk; business center; room service (7am–1am); babysitting; laundry service; dry cleaning. *In room:* TV w/pay movies, dataport, fridge, coffeemaker, hair dryer, iron.

**Ribbon Creek Hostel** This is a great place for a recreation-loving traveler on a budget. The hostel is located right at the Nakiska ski area, within walking distance of Kananaskis Village, and is close to 60 mountain biking, hiking and cross-country trails. Area outfitters offer special discounts to hostel guests. The hostel has a common room with a fireplace and four private family rooms.

At Nakiska Ski Area. ✆ **403/762-3441** for reservations, or 403/591-7333 for the hostel itself. 44 beds. C$15 (US$9) members, C$19 (US$12) nonmembers. MC, V. **Amenities:** Laundry facilities.

### CANMORE

Much of the hotel development in Canmore dates from the Calgary Olympics in 1988, though the town is presently going through an intense period of growth. To a large degree, this is due to the restrictions on development within the national parks to the west: Hoteliers, outfitters, and other businesses designed to serve the needs of park visitors find Canmore, right on the park boundary, a much easier place to locate than Banff. As a result, Canmore is booming, and is now a destination in its own right.

The main reason to stay in Canmore is the price of hotel rooms. Rates here are between a half and a third lower than in Banff, and the small downtown area is beginning to blossom with interesting shops and good restaurants.

For a complete list of B&Bs, contact the **Canmore–Bow Valley B&B Association,** P.O. Box 8005, Canmore, AB, T1W 2T8 (www.bbcanmore.com).

**Best Western Green Gables Inn** Located along Canmore's hotel strip, this pleasant Best Western has queen beds throughout, with many units boasting whirlpool baths and fireplaces. All rooms have private patios or balconies.

1602 Second Ave., Canmore, AB, T1W 1M8. ✆ **800/661-2133** or 403/678-5488. Fax 403/678-2670. www.pocaterrainn.com/GreenGables/index.html. 61 units. C$159–C$199 (US$99–US$123) double. Children under 18 stay free in parents' room. AE, DISC, MC, V. **Amenities:** Restaurant, bar; exercise room; Jacuzzi. *In room:* A/C, TV, fridge, hair dryer.

**Best Western Pocaterra Inn** ★ One of the nicest of the hotels along the Bow Valley Trail strip is the Pocaterra Inn. All rooms are spacious and come with gas fireplaces, balconies, queen beds, and lots of thoughtful niceties.

1725 Mountain Ave., Canmore, AB, T1W 2W1. ✆ **888/678-6786** or 403/678-4334. Fax 403/678-3999. www.pocaterrainn.com. 83 units. C$169–C$249 (US$105–US$154) double. Children under 18 stay free in parents' room. Rates include continental breakfast. AE, DISC, MC, V. **Amenities:** Indoor pool with water slide; whirlpool; exercise room; sauna; coin-op laundry. *In room:* A/C, TV, dataport, fridge, microwave, coffeemaker, hair dryer.

**An Eagle's View B&B** New and well designed, An Eagle's View is located in one of the recent developments high above Canmore. Views of the Three Sisters and the Bow Valley are eye-popping. The two bedrooms take up the entire main floor of the house. Each is large and nicely furnished, with a private bathroom and an individual thermostat. Guests share a lounge (with TV, VCR, and tea and coffee makings), a garden patio, and a sunny second-floor deck overlooking the mountains.

6 Eagle Landing, Canmore, AB, T1W 2Y1. ✆ **877/609-3887** or 403/678-3264. www.aneaglesview.com. 2 units. C$100–$130 (US$62–$81) double. Rates include breakfast. AE, MC, V. *In room:* TV.

**McNeill Heritage Inn ★★** Built in 1907 as a trophy home for the manager of the local coal mine, the McNeill Heritage Inn is a marvelous bit of historic architecture combined with modern comforts. The inn is just west of downtown Canmore, literally at the end of the road on the south banks of the Bow River, perched on an outcrop of rock above the waters. The seclusion and privacy of the inn are a treat after a day out in bustling Banff or Canmore. The rambling old home's bedrooms are decorated with uncluttered, handsome simplicity; all rooms have private bathrooms. The ceilings are 3m (10 ft.) high throughout, which gives the already large rooms an even more spacious feel. Guests share a living room with fireplace, a library stocked with outdoor guides, and a veranda that runs the length of the house. You'll find a friendly welcome and professional service, plus an excellent breakfast. This is a good choice for cross-country skiers, as it's adjacent to the Canmore Nordic Centre.

500 Three Sisters Dr., Canmore, AB, T1W 2P3. ✆ **877/MCNEILL** or 403/678-4884. Fax 403/609-3450. www.mcneillinn.ab.ca. 5 units. C$125–C$185 (US$78–US$115) double. Extra person C$25 (US$16). Rates include breakfast. MC, V. **Amenities:** Laundry service. *In room:* TV/VCR, dataport, fridge, coffeemaker, hair dryer, iron.

**Quality Inn Chateau Canmore ★** You can't miss this enormous complex along the hotel strip. Like a series of 10 four-story conjoined chalets, the all-suite Chateau Canmore offers some of the largest rooms in the area. The accommodations are very nicely decorated in a comfortable rustic style, while the lobby and common rooms look like they belong in a log lodge. Each standard suite has a fireplace and separate bedroom, while the deluxe one- or two-bedroom suites add a living room, dining room, and washer/dryer. Just like home, but with a better view.

1720 Bow Valley Trail, Canmore, AB, T1W 2X3. ✆ **800/261-8551** or 403/678-6699. Fax 403/678-6954. www.chateaucanmore.com. 120 suites. C$169 (US$105) standard suite, from C$189 (US$117) deluxe suite. AE, DISC, MC, V. **Amenities:** Restaurant, lounge; indoor pool; health club with spa; room service. *In room:* AC, TV, dataport, fridge, microwave, hair dryer.

**Radisson Hotel and Conference Centre Canmore** This vast complex is Canmore's largest hotel and also serves as the town's convention center. With all of the functions and services offered here, it's almost a self-contained community. There are two styles of accommodations: standard guest rooms in the main building, all with balconies and quality furnishings, or luxury lodge rooms, most with kitchenettes. A few two-bedroom lodge units with full kitchens are available as well (call for rates).

511 Bow Valley Trail, Canmore, AB, T1W 1N7. ✆ **800/333-3333** or 403/678-3625. Fax 403/678-3765. www.radisson.com/canmoreca. 224 units. C$139–C$179 (US$86–US$111) double. AE, MC, V. **Amenities:** Restaurant, bar; indoor pool; exercise room; Jacuzzi; sauna; car rental desk; room service (6:30–10pm); babysitting; laundry service; same-day dry cleaning; meeting facilities; gift shop and gallery. *In room:* A/C, TV w/pay movies, dataport, coffeemaker, hair dryer, iron.

## GUEST RANCHES

**Brewster's Kananaskis Guest Ranch ★** The Brewsters were movers and shakers in the region's early days, playing a decisive role in the formation of Banff and Jasper national parks. They were also the first outfitters (and transport providers) in the parks. The original family homestead from the 1880s was transformed into a guest ranch in 1923. Located right on the Bow River near the mouth of the Kananaskis River, the original lodge buildings now serve as common areas. The 33 guest rooms, in chalets and cabins, are fully modern, each with full bathroom facilities. Activities include horseback riding, river rafting, canoeing, hiking, and more. Long-distance backcountry horseback rides are a specialty—a 2-day trip costs under C$300 (US$186)—and backcountry campsites have newly constructed cabins for sleeping accommodations.

30 minutes east of Banff on Hwy. 1. P.O. Box 964, Banff, AB, T0L 0C0. ✆ **800/691-5085** or 403/673-3737. Fax 403/673-2100. www.brewsteradventures.com. C$79–C$94 (US$49–US$58) double, dinner and breakfast included. AE, MC, V. **Amenities:** Restaurant, bar with the ranch's only TV; 15-person Jacuzzi.

**Rafter Six Ranch Resort** Another old-time guest ranch with a long pedigree, this full-service resort is located in a meadow right on the banks of the Kananaskis River and accommodates visitors in an especially inviting old log lodge (with restaurant, barbecue deck, and lounge). Comfortable lodging is provided in the historic lodge, in various sizes of log cabins, and in large chalets that sleep up to six and have full kitchens. All rooms have private bathrooms. Casual horseback and longer pack trips are offered, as well as raft and canoe trips. Seasonal special events might include rodeos, country dances, and hay or sleigh rides. It is open year round.

P.O. Box 6, Seebe, AB, T0L 1X0. ✆ **888/26-RANCH** or 403/673-3622. Fax 403/673-3961. www.raftersix.com. 60 rooms. C$110–C$250 (US$68–US$155) double in the lodge, C$125–C$250 (US$78–US$155) double in the cabins and chalets. 3- and 4-day recreation packages available. AE, MC, V. **Amenities:** Restaurant, bar; outdoor pool; Jacuzzi; playground.

## WHERE TO DINE

The dining rooms at both Rafter Six and Kananaskis guest ranches are open to nonguests with reservations. For Creole and Cajun food, go to the **French Quarter,** 102 Boulder Crescent, Canmore (✆ **403/678-3612**), open Monday to Saturday from 6:30am to 10pm and Sunday from 4 to 10pm. A popular pub with good food is the **Rose and Crown,** 749 Railway Ave., Canmore (✆ **403/678-5168**).

**Sherwood House** CANADIAN This handsome log restaurant on the busiest corner of downtown Canmore (which isn't that busy) is a longtime favorite. The wide-ranging and well-executed menu, which offers everything from pizza and pasta to prime Angus steaks, has something for everyone, but what makes this one of Canmore's favorite gathering spots is the wonderful landscaped deck. In summer, there's no better place to spend the afternoon. In winter, you'll enjoy the traditional lodge building with its cozy fireplace.

At Main St. and Eighth Ave. ✆ **403/678-5211.** Reservations recommended. Main courses C$13–C$29 (US$8–US$18). AE, MC, V. Daily 7am–10pm.

**Sinclair's** ★★ NEW CANADIAN Right downtown in a converted heritage home, Sinclair's is the most ambitious of the new restaurants in Canmore. The menu is very broad, offering an excellent selection of appetizers and small plates—perfect if you'd prefer to snack around a number of dishes rather than stick to a traditional dinner. There are also a number of individual pizzas and pasta dishes for lighter appetites. The entrees, however, are hard to resist. Seared pancetta-wrapped salmon is served with a warm horseradish lemon lentil salad, while broiled marinated lamb chops come with chili-glazed applesauce and wild-mushroom polenta tortilla. Jasmine-tea-steamed halibut with pomegranate juice, beef tenderloin, and squid with goat-cheese crème fraîche—there's nothing ordinary about the food at Sinclairs. Good wine list and excellent service.

637 Main St., Canmore. ✆ **403/678-5370.** Reservations recommended. Main courses C$12–C$20 (US$8–US$12). AE, MC, V. Daily 11am–10pm.

**Zona's Late Night Bistro** *Value* INTERNATIONAL Zona's is where you should go if you don't want to spend a fortune, but still seek sophisticated food with some zip. This friendly little hangout looks like a coffeehouse, but the warm and casual atmosphere only makes the spicy and unusual foods that much more beguiling. The menu trots the globe: Moroccan pomegranate-molasses lamb curry, coconut lime chicken lasagna, and salmonkepita (phyllo-wrapped salmon, spinach, and cheese) are a few of the main dishes. You can also choose from a number of smaller tapas dishes and wraps, plus ample vegetarian choices.

710 Ninth St. ✆ **403/609-2000.** Reservations not accepted. Main courses C$10–C$14 (US$6–US$9). MC, V. Daily 11:30am–midnight.

## 7 Banff National Park: Canada's Top Tourist Draw ★★★

Banff is Canada's oldest national park, founded in 1885 as a modest 26km² (10-sq.-mile) reserve by the country's first prime minister, Sir John A. Macdonald. The park is now 6,641km² (2,564 sq. miles) of incredibly dramatic mountain landscape, glaciers, high morainal lakes, and rushing rivers. Its two towns, Lake Louise and Banff, are both splendid counterpoints to the wilderness, with beautiful historic hotels, fine restaurants, and lively nightlife.

If there's a downside to all this sophisticated beauty, it's that Banff is incredibly popular—it's generally considered Canada's number-one tourist destination. About 4 million people visit Banff yearly, with the vast majority squeezing in during June, July, and August.

Happily, the wilderness invites visitors to get away from the crowds and from the congestion of the developed sites. Banff Park is blessed with a great many outfitters who make it easy to get on a raft, bike, or horse and find a little mountain solitude. Alternatively, consider visiting the park off-season, when prices are lower, the locals are friendlier, and the scenery is just as stunning.

### SPORTS & OUTDOOR ACTIVITIES IN THE PARK

Lots of great recreational activities are available in Banff National Park, so don't just spend your vacation shopping the boutiques on Banff Avenue. Most day trips require little advance booking—a day in advance is usually plenty—and the easiest way to find a quick adventure is just to ask your hotel's concierge to set one up. Multi-day rafting and horseback trips do require advance booking, because places are limited and keenly sought after. There are many more outfitters in Banff than the ones I list, but the offerings and prices below are typical of what's available.

**BIKING** The most popular cycling adventure in the Canadian Rockies is the 287km (178-mile) trip between Banff and Jasper along the Icefields Parkway, one of the world's most magnificent mountain roads. If you're fit and ready for a high elevation ride, but don't want to bother with the logistics yourself, consider signing on with a bike-touring outfitter. An Internet search will reveal dozens of tour operators; **The Great Canadian Adventure Company** (✆ **888/285-1676** or 780/414-1676; www.adventures.com), offers six-day supported trips starting at C$725 (US$450).

If you'd prefer a self-guided tour, simply rent a bike in Banff or Lake Louise and peddle along the Bow Valley Parkway—Highway 1A—between Banff and Lake Louise, which makes an easy day trip for the average cyclist. Hardier types may want to challenge themselves with the longer Icefields Parkway between Lake Louise and Jasper. Most cyclists will need 3 days to make the trip, spending the nights at the numerous and charming hostels found along this amazing mountain road.

**FISHING** **Banff Fishing Unlimited** (✆ **403/762-4936;** www.banff-fishing.com) offers a number of fly-fishing expeditions on the Bow River as well as lake fishing at Lake Minnewanka. All levels of anglers are accommodated, and packages include part- or whole-day trips.

**GOLF** The **Banff Springs Golf Course** ★ (✆ **403/762-6801**) rolls out along the Bow River beneath towering mountain peaks. One of the most venerable courses in Canada, and one of the most expensive, it offers 27 holes of excellent golf. Although associated with the resort hotel, the course is open to the public.

**HELICOPTER TOURS** If you'd like to see the beautiful scenery of the Canadian Rockies from the air, contact **Alpine Helicopters** (✆ **403/678-4802;** www.alpinehelicopter.com), which operates out of Canmore. This company's flights over the Rockies start at C$130 (US$81). **Alpenglow Aviation** (✆ **888/244-7117** or 250/344-7117; www.rockiesairtours.com) operates out of Golden, B.C., and offers a variety of flight-seeing trips.

**HIKING** One of the great virtues of Banff is that many of its most scenic areas are easily accessible by day hikes. The park has more than 80 maintained trails, ranging from interpretive nature strolls to long-distance expeditions (you'll need a permit if you're planning on camping in the backcountry). For a good listing of popular hikes, pick up the free *Banff/Lake Louise Drives and Walks* brochure.

One of the best day hikes in the area is up **Johnston Canyon** ★, 24km (15 miles) north of Banff on Highway 1A. This relatively easy hike up a limestone canyon passes seven waterfalls before reaching a series of jade-green springs known as the Inkpots. Part of the fun of this trail is the narrowness of the canyon—the walls are more than 30m (100 ft.) high, but only 5.5m (18 ft.) across; the path skirts the cliff face, tunnels through walls, and winds across wooden footbridges for more than 1.5km (1 mile). The waterfalls plunge down through the canyon, soaking hikers with spray; watch for black swifts diving in the mist. The hike through the canyon to Upper Falls takes 1½ hours; all the way to the Inkpots will take at least 4 hours.

It's easy to strike out from **Banff Townsite** and find any number of satisfying short hikes. Setting off on foot can be as simple as following the paths along both sides of the Bow River. From the west end of the Bow River Bridge, trails lead east to Bow Falls, past the Banff Springs Hotel to the Upper Hot Springs. Another popular hike just beyond town is the **Fenlands Trail,** which begins past the train station and makes a loop through marshland wildlife habitat near the Vermillion Lakes.

Two longer trails leave from the Cave and Basin Centennial Centre. The **Sundance Trail** follows the Bow River for nearly 5km (3 miles) past beaver dams and wetlands, ending at the entrance to Sundance Canyon. Keen hikers can continue up the canyon another 2.5km (1½ miles) to make a loop past Sundance Falls. The Marsh Loop winds 2.5km (1½ miles) past the Bow River and marshy lakes.

## Banff Town & Banff National Park

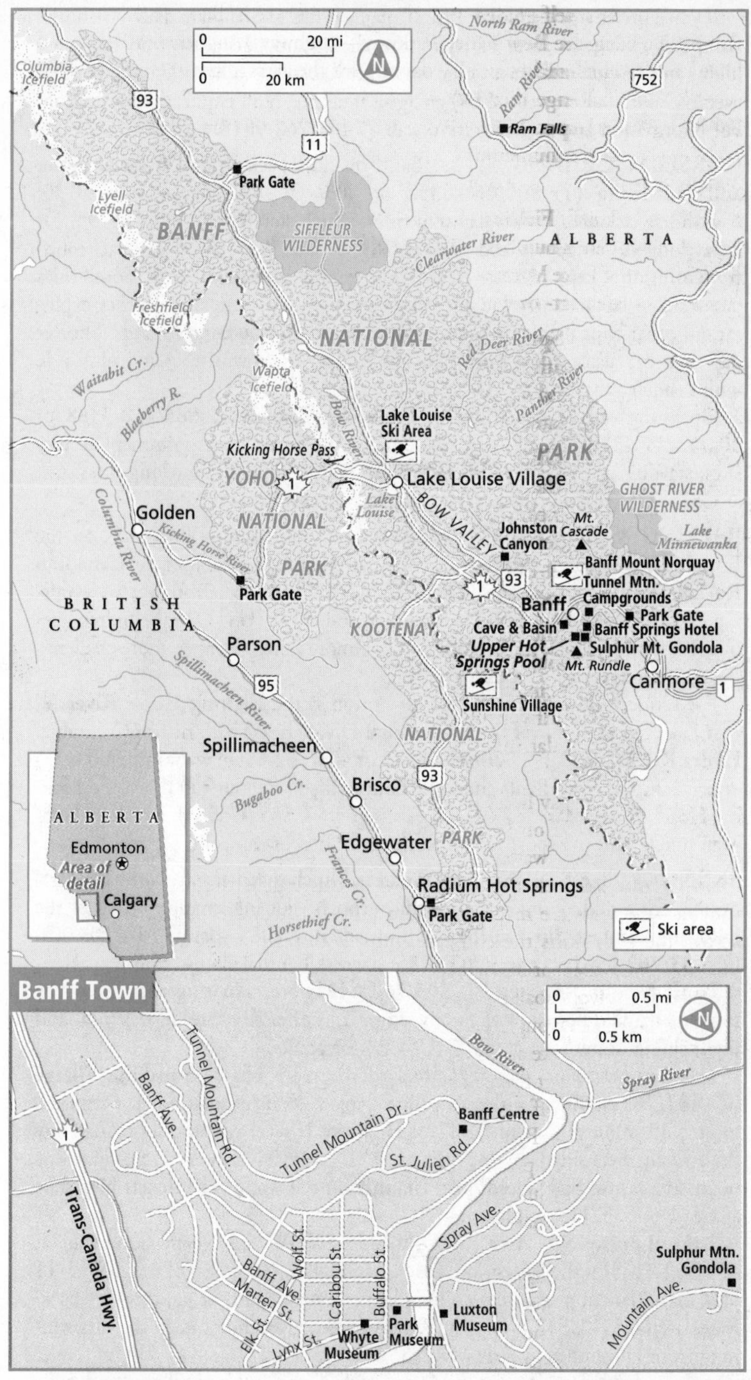

If you'd prefer a guided hike, Parks Canada offers several hikes daily. Ask at the Banff Information Centre or check the chalkboard outside to find out what hiking options are available. Some walks are free, while others (like the popular evening Wildlife Research Walks) charge a small fee; both require preregistration. For information and preregistration, call © **403/762-9818.**

**HORSEBACK RIDING** ★ See Banff on horseback with **Warner Guiding and Outfitting** (© **800/661-8352** or 403/762-4551; fax 403/762-8130; www.horseback.com) multi-day trail rides, which start at C$475 (US$295) for 3 day lodge-to-lodge trip and peak at C$958 (US$594) for a 6-day backcountry tenting trip, explore some of the most remote areas of the park. Some rides climb up to backcountry lodges, which serve as base camps for further exploration; other trips involve a backcountry circuit, with lodging in tents. Shorter day rides are also offered from two stables near the townsite. A morning ride with brunch goes for C$67 (US$42).

Operating out of Lake Louise, **Timberline Tours** (© **888/858-3388** or 403/522-3743) offers day trips to some of the area's more prominent beauty sites, starting at C$45 (US$28) for 90 minutes of riding. Hour-long rides start at C$25 (US$16). Three- to 10-day pack trips are also offered.

**RAFTING & CANOEING** One and a half hour family float trips on the Bow River just below Banff are popular diversions, available from **Canadian Rockies Rafting Company** (© **877/226-7625** or 403/678-6535; www.rafting.ca). Trips are C$40 (US$25) for adults and C$28 (US$17) for children ages 6 to 16, with free pick up at Banff and Canmore hotels. Longer, more challenging trips on area rivers are also available.

For serious white-water, the closest option is the **Kicking Horse River** ★, past Lake Louise just over the Continental Divide near Field, British Columbia. **Hydra River Guides** (© **800/644-8888** or 403/762-4554; www.raftbanff.com) offers transport from Banff and Lake Louise, then a 3-hour run down the Kicking Horse through Grade IV rapids. Trips go for C$85 (US$53), which includes gear, lunch, and transport to and from your hotel or campsite.

**SKIING** ★ Banff Park has three ski areas, which together have formed a partnership for booking and promotional purposes. For information on all of the following, contact **Ski Banff/Lake Louise,** Box 1085, Banff, AB, T0l 0C0 (© **403/762-4561;** fax 403/762-8185; www.skibanfflakelouise.com).

**Banff Mount Norquay** (© **403/762-4421**) are twin runs just above the town of Banff. They cater to family skiing and offer day care, instruction, and night skiing. Rates start at C$47 (US$29) for adults.

Skiers must ski or take a gondola to the main lifts at **Sunshine Village** (© **403/762-6500**) and the Sunshine Inn, a ski-in/ski-out hotel. Sunshine, located 15 minutes west of Banff off Highway 1, receives more snow than any ski area in the Canadian Rockies (more than 9m/30 ft. per year!). Sunshine boasts the fastest high-speed quad chairlifts in the world. Lift tickets here start at C$60 (US$37) for adults.

**Lake Louise Ski Area** (© **800/258-SNOW** in North America, or 403/552-3555) is the largest in Canada, with 64km (40 miles) of trails. With 11 lifts, management guarantees no long lines on major lifts, or your money back! Rates are C$59 (US$37) for adults. Snowmaking machines keep the lifts running from November to early May.

A special lift pass for Banff Mount Norquay, Sunshine Village, and Lake Louise Ski Area allows skiers unlimited access to all three resorts (and free rides on shuttle buses between the ski areas). Passes for 3 days (minimum) cost C$175 (US$109) for adults and C$64 (US$40) for children.

## BANFF TOWNSITE ★★★

Few towns in the world boast as beautiful a setting as Banff. The mighty Bow River courses right through town, while massive mountain blocks rear up on Banff's outskirts. Mount Rundle, a finlike mountain that somehow got tipped over on its side, parades off to the south. Mount Cascade rises up immediately north of downtown. In every direction, still more craggy peaks fill the sky.

This is a stunning, totally unlikely place for a town, and Banff has been trading on its beauty for more than a century. The Banff Springs Hotel was built in 1888 as a destination resort by the Canadian Pacific Railroad. As outdoor-recreation enthusiasts began to frequent the area for its scenery, hot springs, and access to fishing, hunting, climbing, and other activities, the little town of Banff grew up to service their needs.

While the setting hasn't changed since the early days of the park, the town certainly has. Today, the streets of Banff are lined with exclusive boutiques; trendy cafes spill out onto the sidewalks; and bus after bus filled with tourists choke the streets. Japanese, English, French, and German visitors are very much in evidence. There's a vital and cosmopolitan feel to the town; just don't come here expecting a bucolic Alpine village—Banff in summer is a very busy place.

### ESSENTIALS

**GETTING THERE** **By plane** If you're flying into Calgary and heading straight to Banff, call and reserve a seat on the **Banff Airporter** (**© 403/762-3330;** www.banffairporter.com). Vans depart from Calgary Airport roughly every 2 hours; a one-way ticket costs C$22 (US$14).

**By rail** The closest VIA Rail train service is at Jasper, 178 miles (287km) north. **Brewster Transport** (**© 403/762-6767**) offers an express bus between the two park centers five times weekly for C$59 (US$37) one-way.

**By bus** **Greyhound** (**© 800/661-8747** or 403/260-0877 www.greyhound.ca) operates buses that pass through Banff on the way from Calgary to Vancouver. One-way fare between Banff and Calgary is C$20 (US$12). The depot is at 100 Gopher St. (**© 403/762-6767**).

**By car** If you're driving, the Trans-Canada Highway takes you right to Banff's main street; the town is 129km (80 miles) west of Calgary.

**VISITOR INFORMATION** The **Banff Information Centre,** at 224 Banff Ave., houses both the Banff Tourism Bureau and a national-park information center. Contact the office at P.O. Box 1298, Banff, AB, T0L 0C0 (**© 403/762-0270;** fax 403/762-8545, www.banfflakelouise.com). The center is open daily June 15 to October 15 from 9am to 9pm and the rest of the year from 9am to 5pm. Be sure to ask for the *Official Visitors Guide,* which is packed with information about local businesses and recreation. For information on the park, go to **www.parkscanada.gc.ca**.

**TOWN LAYOUT** Getting your bearings is easy. The **Greyhound and Brewster Bus Depot** is located at the corner of Gopher and Lynx streets (**© 403/762-2286**). The main street—Banff Avenue—starts at the southern end of town at the Bow River and runs north until it's swallowed by the Trans-Canada Highway. Along this broad, bright, and bustling thoroughfare, you'll find most of Banff's hotels, restaurants, stores, office buildings, and nightspots.

Just beyond the river stands the park administration building amid a beautifully landscaped garden. Here the road splits: **Banff Springs Hotel** and the **Banff Gondola** are to the left; to the right are the **Cave and Basin Hot Springs,** Banff National Park's original site. At the northwestern edge of town is the old railroad station, and a little farther northwest the road branches off to Lake Louise and Jasper. In the opposite direction, northeast, is the highway going to Calgary.

**GETTING AROUND** Banff offers local bus service along two routes designed to pass through downtown and by most hotels. Service on the **Banff Bus** (✆ **403/760-8294**) is pretty informal, but there's generally a bus every half hour. One route runs from the Banff Springs Hotel down Banff Avenue to the northern end of town; the other runs between the train station and the Banff Hostel on Tunnel Mountain; the fare is C$1 (US60¢). The bus operates in summer only.

For a taxi, call **Banff Taxi and Limousine** (✆ **403/762-4444**).

For a rental car, contact **National,** at Caribou and Lynx streets (✆ **403/762-2688**), or **Banff Rent A Car,** 204 Lynx St. (✆ **403/762-3352**) for a less expensive but reliable vehicle. Avis, Budget, and Hertz also have offices in Banff.

**SPECIAL EVENTS** The **Banff Centre,** St. Julien Road (✆ **800/413-8368** or 403/762-6300; www.banffcentre.ab.ca), is a remarkable year-round institution devoted to the arts and entertainment in the widest sense. From June to August, the center hosts the **Banff Arts Festival** ★, offering a stimulating mixture of drama, opera, jazz, ballet, classical and pop music, and the visual arts. Highlights include the International String Quartet Competition, with 10 world-class quartets vying for a cash prize and a national tour, and the Digital Playgrounds series, which brings performance artists to the stage. Tickets for some of the events cost from pay-what-you-can to C$25 (US$16); a great many are absolutely free. In November, the center is home to the **Festival of Mountain Films.** Find out what's currently on by getting the program at the Banff Tourism Bureau or by checking out the Banff Centre's website.

## EXPLORING BANFF

**Banff Goldola** ★ Apart from helicopter excursions (see above), the best way to get an overall view of Banff's landscape is this high wire act (formerly the Sulphur Mountain Gondola). In 8 minutes, the enclosed gondolas lift you 698m (2,292 ft.) from the valley floor up to the top of Sulphur Mountain, at 2,281m (7,486 ft.). Up here, at the crest of the mountains behind Banff, the panoramas are stunning. Trails lead out along the mountain ridges; hike back to the bottom of the mountain, or spend the day exploring the subarctic zone along the mountaintop. Also at the upper terminal are two restaurants, a snack bar and gift shop. Lines to get on the gondola can be very long in summer; if you are set on riding up to the high country, try to go as early as possible.

The lower terminal is 4 miles (6km) southeast of town on Mountain Avenue. ✆ **403/762-5438.** www.banffgondola.com. Admission C$19 (US$12) adults, C$9.50 (US$6) children. Open May 1–Labour Day 7:30am–9pm, check website for off-season schedule.

**Lake Minnewanka Boat Tours** These very popular scenic and wildlife-viewing trips in glassed-in motor cruisers take place on Lake Minnewanka, a glacial lake wedged between two mountain ranges. These trips—usually 1½ hours long, are amongst those excursions that nearly every visitor to Banff ends up taking, so unless you want to be part of a huge shuffling throng, try to go early in the day. Reservations are suggested. In high season, there are five sailings a day and buses depart daily from Banff to meet these departures, both from the bus station and from most hotels.

24km (15 miles) north of Banff. ✆ **403/762-3473.** Fax 403/762-2800. www.lakemineenwankaboattours.com. Tickets C$28 (US$17) adult, C$12 (US$7) children. Mid-May to early October.

**Luxton Museum of the Plains Indian** Housed in a log fort south of the Bow River, just across the bridge from downtown Banff, this museum is devoted to the native history of the Canadian Rockies and Northern Plains. It offers realistic dioramas, a sun-dance exhibit, artifacts, and ornaments.

1 Birch Ave. ✆ **403/762-2388.** Admission C$8 (US$5) adult, C$4 (US$2.50) seniors and students, C$2.50 (US$1.55) for children. Daily 9am–7pm.

**Whyte Museum of the Canadian Rockies** Part art gallery, part local-history museum, this is the only museum in North America that collects, exhibits, and interprets the history and culture of the Canadian Rockies. Two furnished heritage homes on the grounds are open in summer and stand as a memorial to the pioneers of the Rockies. Interpretive programs and tours are offered year-round. The Elizabeth Rummel Tea Room is open from mid-May to mid-October and serves light lunches, desserts, and coffee.

111 Bear St. ✆ **403/762-2291.** Admission C$6 (US$3.70) adults, C$3.50 (US$2.15) seniors and students, free for children under 5; C$15 (US$9) family. Daily 10am–5pm.

**Banff Park Museum** Housed in a lovely wood-lined building dating from the 1910s, this, museum beside the Bow River Bridge is largely a paean to taxidermy, but there's a lot to learn here about the wildlife of the park and how the various ecosystems interrelate. The real pleasure, though, is the rustic, lodge-style building, now preserved as a National Historic Site.

Banff Ave. and Buffalo St. ✆ **403/762-1558.** Admission C$3 (US$1.85) adults C$2 (US$1.20) seniors, C$1.50 (US95–) youths 6–16. Daily 1–5pm, summer 10am–6pm.

**Cave and Basin National Historic Site** ★ Although most people now associate Banff with skiing or hiking, in the early days of the park, travelers streamed in to visit the curative hot springs. In fact, it was the discovery of the hot springs now preserved at this historic site that spurred the creation of the national park in 1888. During the 1910s, these hot mineral waters, which rise in a limestone cave, were piped into a rather grand natatorium. Although the Cave and Basin springs are no longer open for swimming or soaking, the old pool area and the original cave have been preserved; interpretive displays and films round out the experience.

1.5km (1 mile) west of Banff; turn right at the west end of the Bow River Bridge. ✆ **403/762-1566.** Admission C$2.50 (US$1.55) adults, C$2 (US$1.20) seniors, C$1.50 (US95¢) youths 6–18. Daily 9am–6pm.

**Upper Hot Springs Pool** If visiting the Cave and Basin makes you long for a soak in mountain hot springs, then drive up Mountain Avenue to this spa. In addition to the redesigned swimming pool filled with hot, sulfurous waters, you'll find a restaurant, snack bar, and home spa boutique. If you're looking more for a cure than a splash, try the adjacent **Upper Hot Springs Spa** (✆ **403/760-2500**) with a steam room, massage, plunge pools, and aromatherapy treatments.

At the top of Mountain Avenue, 5km (3 miles) west of Banff. ✆ **403/762-1515.** Pool admission C$7.50 (US$4.65) adult, C$6.50 (US$4) seniors and children, C$21.50 (US$13) per family. Spa treatments begin at C$32 (US$20) and are open to adults only.

*Tips* **Off-season Rates**

All accommodation prices listed are for high season, which normally runs from mid-May to mid-October; nearly all hotels have a complex rate schedule with discounts for late fall, holidays, winter, late winter and spring accommodation. Call for information on these reduced off-season rates, as well as for ski and other packages. If you're having trouble finding affordable lodgings in Banff, try properties in Canmore, located 20 minutes away (earlier).

## SHOPPING

The degree to which you like the town of Banff will depend largely upon your taste for shopping. **Banff Avenue** is increasingly an open-air boutique mall, with throngs of shoppers milling around. Of course, you would expect to find excellent outdoor-gear and sporting-goods stores here, as well as the usual T-shirt and gift emporiums. What's more surprising are the boutiques devoted to Paris and New York designers, the upscale jewelry stores, and the high-end galleries. What's most surprising of all is that many visitors seem to actually prefer to while away their time in this masterpiece of nature called Banff by shopping for English soaps or Italian shoes. There are no secrets to shopping here: Arcade after arcade opens onto Banff Avenue, where you'll find everything you need. Quality and prices are both quite high.

## WHERE TO STAY

Banff National Park offers hundreds of campsites within easy commuting distance of Banff. The closest are the three **Tunnel Mountain campgrounds** ★, just past the youth hostel west of town. Two of the campgrounds are for RVs only and have both partial and full hookups (C$22/US$14); the third has showers and is usually reserved for tenters (C$16/US$10). For more information, call the park's visitor center (✆ **403/762-1500**). Campsites within the park cannot be reserved in advance.

### Very Expensive

**Banff Park Lodge Resort Hotel and Conference Centre** ★ A handsome cedar-and-oak structure with a cosmopolitan air, the Banff Park Lodge is a quiet block-and-a-half off the town's main street, near the Bow River. Calm and sophisticated are the key words here: All of the rooms are soundproofed, and wild, après-ski cavorting isn't the norm, or even much encouraged. The lodge will feel like a tranquil retreat after a day in frantic Banff. The standard rooms are spacious and exceptionally well furnished; all with balconies. Most suites have a whirlpool, jetted tub and fireplace. With its abundant ground-floor rooms and wide hallways, this lodging is popular with travelers with disabilities or mobility concerns.

222 Lynx St., Banff, AB, T0L 0C0. ✆ **800/661-9266** or 403/762-4433. Fax 403/762-3553. www.banffparklodge.com. 211 units. C$259 (US$161) double. Suites from C$379 (US$235). Extra person C$10–C$15 (US$6–US$9). Children 16 and under stay free in parents' room. Off-season and ski packages available. AE, DC, MC, V. **Amenities:** Formal and family restaurants, bar; indoor pool; access to nearby health club; exercise room; spa; Jacuzzi; concierge; tour and activities desk; business center; shopping arcade; salon; room service (7am–midnight); babysitting; laundry service; same-day dry cleaning. *In room:* A/C, TV, dataport, fridge, coffeemaker, hair dryer.

**Buffalo Mountain Lodge** ★★ The most handsome of the hotel developments on Tunnel Mountain, 1.5km (1 mile) northeast of Banff, this is the perfect place to stay if you'd rather avoid the frenetic pace of downtown and yet remain central to restaurants and activities. Its quiet location, beautiful lodge, and choice of room types make this a good alternative to equally priced lodgings in the heart of town. The lodge building itself is an enormous log cabin, right out of your fantasies. The three-story lobby is supported by massive rafters and filled with Navajo-style carpets. A fieldstone fireplace dominates the interior, separating the dining room from the lounge.

Guest rooms are located in units scattered around the forested 3ha (8-acre) property. There are three room types, ranging from one-bedroom apartments with full kitchens to exceptionally handsome rooms in brand-new buildings. The nicest are the Premier units, which feature slate-floored bathrooms with both claw-foot tubs and slate-walled showers. The quality pine-and-twig furniture lends a rustic look to the otherwise sophisticated decor. All units have fireplaces (wood is free and stacked near your door), balconies or patios, and beds made up with feather duvets and pillows. These are some of the most attractive rooms in Banff.

One mile northeast of Banff on Tunnel Mountain Rd. P.O. Box 1326, Banff, AB, T0L 0C0. ✆ **800/661-1367** or 403/762-2400. Fax 403/760-4492. www.crmr.com. 108 units. C$255 (US$158) double, C$325 (US$202) 1-bedroom apt. AE, ER, MC, V. **Amenities:** 2 restaurants, including the superlative Buffalo Mountain Lodge Dining Room (see "Where to Dine" below); lounge; exercise room; outdoor Jacuzzi; steam room; laundry service; same-day dry cleaning. *In room:* TV, dataport, iron, coffeemaker, hair dryer.

**The Fairmont Banff Springs** ★ Standing north of Bow River Falls like an amazing Scottish baronial fortress, the Banff Springs Hotel is one of the most beautiful and famous hotels in North America. Founded in 1888 as an opulent destination resort by the Canadian Pacific Railroad, this stone castle of a hotel is still the best address in Banff—especially so after the renovation of all guest rooms. Expect sumptuous linens, fancy soaps and lotions, real art, and quality furniture. This venerable hotel doesn't offer the largest rooms in Banff, but the amenities are superlative. With the views, the spa, and the near pageantry of service, this is still the most amazing resort in an area blessed with beautiful accommodations. The Springs maintains a staff of 1,200 and stages such events as medieval banquets for convention groups.

405 Spray Ave. (P.O. Box 960), Banff, AB, T0L 0C0. ✆ **800/441-1414** or 403/762-2211. Fax 403/762-5755. www.fairmont.com. 770 units. C$255–C$627 (US$158–US$389) double, C$457–C$1,007 (US$283–US$624) suite. Rates include full breakfast, service charges and valet parking. AE, DC, DISC, MC, V. Valet parking C$20 (US$12); self-parking C$7 (US$4.35). **Amenities:** 15 restaurants, 3 lounges; Olympic-size pool; the famed Banff Springs golf course (considered one of the most scenic in the world); 4 tennis courts; the European-style Solace Spa; with mineral baths; a full range of beauty and health treatments; plus fitness training; nutritional consultation and lifestyle programs; Jacuzzi; bike rental; concierge; tour and activities desk; business center; shopping arcade; 24-hour room service; babysitting; laundry service same-day dry cleaning. *In room:* A/C, TV/VCR w/pay movies and video games, dataport, coffeemaker, hair dryer, iron.

**Rimrock Resort Hotel** ★ If you seek modern luxury and great views, this is your hotel. The enormous, stunningly beautiful Rimrock drops nine floors from its roadside lobby entrance down a steep mountain slope, affording tremendous views from nearly all of its rooms. Aiming for the same quality of architecture and majesty of scale as venerable older lodges, the Rimrock offers a massive glass-fronted lobby that's lined with cherry wood, tiled with unpolished marble floors, and filled with inviting chairs and Oriental rugs. The limestone fireplace, open on two sides, is so large that staff members step inside it to ready the kindling.

Guest rooms are large and well appointed with handsome furnishings; some have balconies. All were refurbished in 2000. Standard rooms are all the same size; their prices vary only depending on the view. The suites are truly large, with balconies, wet bars, and loads of cozy couches.

Mountain Ave. (5km /3 miles south of Banff), P.O. Box 1110, Banff, AB, T0L 0C0. ✆ **800/661-1587** or 403/762-3356. Fax 403/762-1842. www.rimrockresort.com. 366 units. C$255–C$355 (US$158–US$220) double, C$375–C$1,200 (US$233–US$744) suite. AE, DC, DISC, MC, V. Valet parking C$10 (US$6); free self-parking in heated garage. **Amenities:** 2 restaurants, including the four-star Ristorante Classico (see "Where to Dine," later), 2 bars; health club with pool; squash court; hot tub; aerobics; beauty treatments; massage; wraps and more weight training and fitness devices than many professional gyms; concierge; tour and activities desk; business center; shopping arcade; 24 hour room service; babysitting; laundry service; same-day dry cleaning. *In room:* A/C, TV w/pay movies and video games, dataport, minibar, coffeemaker, hair dryer, iron.

## Expensive

**Banff Caribou Lodge** ★ The Caribou, with its gabled green roof, outdoor patio, bay windows, and wooden balconies, has a western-lodge look that blends well with the alpine landscape. The interior is equally impressive, especially the vast lobby with slate-tile floor, peeled-log woodwork, and huge stone fireplace. The finely furnished bedrooms continue the western theme with rustic pine chairs and beds decked out with snug down comforters. The bathrooms are spacious; some of the rooms have balconies. The lodge is long on service and friendliness. The Keg is a local favorite for steaks. Although it's not in the absolute center of town (about 10 min. on foot), a free shuttle bus ferries guests to destinations throughout Banff.

521 Banff Ave., Banff, AB, T0L 0C0. ✆ **800/563-8764** or 403/762-5887. Fax 403/762-5918. 207 units. www.bestofbanff.com. C$220–C$235 (US$136–US$146) double, C$300–C$350 (US$186–US$217) suite. Up to 2 children under 16 stay free in parents' room. AE, DC, DISC, MC, V. Free heated parking. **Amenities:** Restaurant, bar; exercise room; Jacuzzi; sauna; concierge; room service (7:30am–10pm). *In room:* TV w/pay movies, dataport, coffeemaker, hair dryer, iron.

**Brewster's Mountain Lodge** ★ *Value* All in all, for the comfort, convenience and moderate (by Banff standards) priced rooms, this is one of the top picks in central Banff. This handsome lodge-like hotel, right in the heart of Banff, is operated by the Brewster family, who dominate much of the local recreation, guest ranching, and transportation scene. The modern hotel does its best to look rustic: peeled log posts and beams fill the lobby and foyer, while quality pine furniture and paneling grace the spacious guest rooms. Wheelchair-accessible rooms are available. Although there's no fine dining in the hotel, you'll find plenty adjacent in central Banff. The Brewster affiliation makes it simple to take advantage of lodging and adventure packages involving horseback riding and hiking.

208 Caribou St., Banff, AB, T0L 0C0. ✆ **888/762-2900** or 403/762-2900. Fax 403/762-2970. www.brewsteradventures.com. 73 units. C$179–C$199 (US$111–US$123) double. AE, MC, V. Self parking C$4 (US$2.50). **Amenities:** Restaurant; Jacuzzi; sauna; car-rental desk; same-day dry cleaning. *In room:* TV/VCR, dataport, iron, hair dryer.

**Ptarmigan Inn** ★ This pine-green hotel on the edge of downtown Banff has a few advantages over most of the other hotels along busy Banff Avenue. For one, the rooms are set well back from the street, minimizing road noise. It's also a good choice for families: Some of the double rooms have sleeping areas divided by the bathroom, which offers a little privacy for everyone. Half of the rooms have balconies; 16 rooms (the least expensive) look into the lodge-like, three-story central atrium. Accommodations are outfitted with rustic looking pine furnishings and down comforters.

337 Banff Ave., Banff, AB, T0L 0C0. ✆ **800/661-8310** or 403/762-2207. Fax 403/762-3577. www.bestofbanff.com. 166 units. C$220–C$235 (US$136–US$146) double, C$250 (US$155) suite. Children under 16 stay free in parents' room. AE, DC, DISC, MC, V. Free heated parking. **Amenities:** Restaurant, bar; exercise room; Jacuzzi; sauna; concierge; room service (7:30am–10pm), nonsmoking rooms. *In room:* TV w/pay movies, dataport, coffeemaker, hair dryer, iron.

**Thea's House** ★ The most upscale and elegant bed-and-breakfast in Banff, Thea's is a modern home that was designed as a B&B. Just a couple minutes walk from downtown, this striking log-and-stone structure boasts 8m (25-ft.) ceilings, antiques and exquisite artwork, and discreet and friendly service. Guest rooms are all very large and beautifully outfitted, with vaulted pine ceilings, fir floors, rustic pine and antique furniture, fireplaces, sitting areas, cassette and CD players, and private balconies. All guests have access to a lounge area with a stocked minibar and refrigerator and a coffee and tea service; a full breakfast is included in the rates. "Elegant Alpine" is how Thea's describes itself, and you'll have no trouble imagining yourself in a fairy-tale mountain lodge. It is the perfect spot for a romantic getaway.

138 Otter St. (Box 1237), Banff, T0L 0C0. ✆ **403/762-2499.** Fax 403/762-2496. www.theashouse.com. 3 units. C$225–C$245 (US$140–US$152) double. MC, V. **Amenities:** Complimentary health club pass available; bike rental. *In room:* TV, hair dryer, iron.

**Traveller's Inn** ★ *Value* Located a 5 minute-walk from downtown, the Traveller's Inn is a very well maintained motel that offers reasonably good value for the dollar—remember, this is Banff. Rooms are quite large and pleasantly decorated, all with twin vanities and king or queen beds. Some are divided into two sleeping areas by the bathroom, a great configuration for families or groups. All units have balconies or patio access.

401 Banff Ave., Banff, AB, T0L 0C0. ✆ **800/661-0227** or 403/762-4401. Fax 403/762-5905. www.banfftravellersinn.com. 89 units. C$200 (US$124) double. AE MC, V. **Amenities:** Outdoor Jacuzzi; sauna; coin op laundry and laundry service. *In room:* TV, coffeemaker.

## Moderate

**Bed & Breakfast on Mountain Lane** Reserve early if you want a shot at this very pleasant ground-floor suite in a quiet neighborhood between park headquarters and the Banff Springs Hotel. Essentially a self-contained apartment, it has a full kitchen, fireplace, TV/VCR, queen bed, and sofa bed by the fireplace. The suite can sleep up to four comfortably. The room opens onto the backyard with a patio, swing, and slides; kids are welcome. Your hostess will bring down a basket of fresh-baked muffins and rolls in the morning.

104 Mountain Lane (Box 12), Banff, AB, T0L 0C0. ✆ **403/762-2009.** Fax 403/762-8043. www.standishbanff.com. 1 suite. C$140 (US$87). No credit cards. *In room:* TV/VCR, dataport, kitchen, coffeemaker, hair dryer, iron.

**Blue Mountain Lodge** This rambling place east of downtown began its life in 1908 as a boardinghouse. As you might expect in an older building constructed at the edge of the wilderness, the bedrooms were never exactly palatial to begin with—and when the rooms were redesigned to include private bathrooms, they got even smaller. That's the bad news. The good news is that the lodge is full of charm and funny nooks and crannies. Those small rooms just mean that you'll be spending time with new friends in the lounge and common kitchen. Sound familiar? The owner admits that guests refer to the Blue Mountain Lodge as an upscale hostel, and it's an accurate characterization. Whatever you call it, it's one of the least expensive and friendliest places to stay in central Banff. Breakfast is served buffet-style, or you can cook up some eggs on your own. Many guests here are avid outdoorsy types, making this a great place to stay if you're on your own and would appreciate meeting other people to hike with. The staff is young, friendly, and eager to help you get out on the trails.

137 Muskrat St. (Box 2763), Banff, AB, T0L 0C0. © **403/762-5134.** Fax 403/762-8081. www.bluemtnlodge.com. 10 units. From C$85–C$110 (US$53–C$68) double. Extra person C$10 (US$6). Rates include continental breakfast and afternoon hot beverages and homemade cookies. Extended-stay discounts available. MC, V. *In room:* TV.

**Dynasty Inn** One of the newest accommodations in Banff, the Dynasty is a very handsome, mountain-lodge-like structure. Like most of the other hotels along Banff Ave. strip, the illusion of the lodge ends at the lobby—the rooms are comfortable, nicely furnished and identical to corporate hotel rooms across North America, except that some units have private balconies and fireplaces. Facilities include a breakfast-only coffee shop and heated underground parking. The Dynasty is located about a mile from downtown. The inexpensive Banff Bus has a stop right outside the hotel, with frequent transport to the city center.

P.O. Box 1018, 501 Banff Ave., Banff, AB, T0L 0C0. © **800/667-1464** or 403/762-8844. Fax 403/762-4418. www.banffdynastyinn.com. 99 units. C$189 (US$117) double. Extra person C$15 (US$9). Children under 12 stay free in parents' room. Early-bird specials available. AE, MC, V. **Amenities:** Breakfast room; Jacuzzi; sauna. *In room:* A/C, TV, hair dryer.

**Eleanor's House** One of the most spacious and comfortable B&Bs in Banff, Eleanor's is a large home on the south side of the Bow River, an easy walk from downtown. The lounge has a western feel to it, complete with stuffed game heads, while each bedroom reflects the lives of the owners: a childhood on the prairies and a career as a park ranger. The rooms are quite large, have nice mountain views, and have full en suite bathrooms and sitting areas. There's a separate entrance for guests. The welcome is gracious and the service very professional.

125 Kootenay Ave., Box 1553, Banff, AB, T0L 0C0. © **403/760-2457.** Fax 403/762-3852. www.bbeleanor.com. 2 units. C$160 (US$99) double. Rates include full breakfast and evening drinks. MC, V. Closed mid-Oct to mid-April. Children must be 16 or older. Free off-street parking. *In room:* Hair dryer.

**Homestead Inn** *Value* One of the best lodging deals in Banff is the Homestead Inn, only a block from all the action on Banff Avenue. Though the amenities are modest compared to upscale alternatives, the rooms are tastefully furnished and equipped with armchairs and stylish bathrooms. Factor in the free downtown parking and this well-maintained older motel seems all the more enticing.

217 Lynx St., Banff, AB, T0L 0C0. © **800/661-1021** or 403/762-4471. Fax 403/762-8877. www.homesteadinnbanff.com. 27 units. C$149 (US$92) double. Extra person C$10 (US$6). Children under 12 stay free in parents' room. AE, MC, V. **Amenities:** Family restaurant. *In room:* TV, hair dryer.

**King Edward Hotel** *Value* Youthful travelers—and others who don't mind the bustle—will like the newly remodeled King Edward, one of Banff's originals, dating from 1904. The accommodations are basic but clean and comfortable; all rooms have private bathrooms. Best of all is the location, in the heart of town and immediately next door to the epicenter of Banff nightlife. Budget travelers who aren't into the hostel scene will find a lot to like here.

137 Banff Ave., Banff, AB, T0L 0C0. ✆ **800/344-4232** or 403/762-2202. Fax 403/762-0876. 21 units. C$129–C$159 (US$80–US$99) double. AE, MC, V. Limited free parking. **Amenities:** Restaurant, bar. *In room:* TV, coffeemaker.

**Mountain Home Bed & Breakfast** ★ If you're looking for a bit of historic charm coupled with modern comforts, this excellent B&B may be it. It was originally built as a tourist lodge in the 1940s, then served as a private home for years before being restored and turned back into a guesthouse. The present decor manages to be evocative without being too fussy. The bedrooms are airy and nicely furnished with quality furniture and antiques; all have an en suite bathroom and telephone. Especially nice is the cozy Rundle Room, with its own slate fireplace. Breakfast is a full cooked meal with homemade baked goods. Downtown Banff is just a 2-minute walk away.

129 Muskrat St. (P.O. Box 272), Banff, AB, T0L 0C0. ✆ **403/762-3889.** Fax 403/762-3254. www.mountainhomebb.com. 3 units. C$150 (US$93) double. Extra person $20 (US$12). Rates include full breakfast. MC, V. *In room:* TV/VCR w/pay movies, dataport, hair dryer, iron.

**Pension Tannenhof** *Value* This rambling historic home in a quiet neighborhood an eight minute stroll from downtown has a curious story. Built during World War II by a Calgary businessman with 10 children, the structure is the result of an elaborate adaptation of two preexisting cabins. During the war, no new construction was allowed, so the owner "remodeled" by building around the cabins, eventually tearing them down from the inside. Most rooms are quite large and simply furnished. In a separate chalet at the back of the inn are two king suites, each with a fireplace and jetted tub. Pension Tannenhof is excellent value and a good place to stay if you want clean, unfussy accommodations.

121 Cave Ave. (P.O. Box 1914), Banff, AB, T0L 0C0. ✆ **877/999-5011** or 403/762-4636. Fax 403/762-5660. www.pensiontannenhof.com. 10 units. C$95–C$180 (US$59–US$112) double. Extra person C$20 (US$12). Rates include full cooked breakfast. AE, MC, V. **Amenities:** Jacuzzi; sauna; coin-op laundry; use of "the world's oldest barbecue"—made of dinosaur bones. *In room:* TV.

**Red Carpet Inn** *Value* A handsome brick building with a balcony along the top floors, the Red Carpet Inn is located along the long, hotel-lined street leading to downtown. Well maintained and more than adequately furnished, this is one of the best deals in Banff. Guest rooms are furnished with easy chairs and desks. There's no restaurant, but there's an excellent one right next door. The entire facility is shipshape and very clean—just the thing if you don't want to spend a fortune.

425 Banff Ave., Banff, AB, T0L 0C0. ✆ **800/563-4609** or 403/762-4184. Fax 403/762-4894. 52 units. C$125–C$150 (US$78–US$93) double. AE, MC, V. **Amenities:** Jacuzzi in winter only. *In room:* A/C, TV, dataport, fridge, coffeemaker, hair dryer, iron.

**Rocky Mountain B&B** *Kids* A former boardinghouse converted into a B&B, this pleasant and rambling inn offers comfortable, clean, and cozy rooms and a location just a few minutes from downtown. Accommodations have a mix of private and shared bathrooms. Four units have kitchenettes. Families are welcome.

223 Otter St. (Box 2528), Banff, AB, T0L 0C0. ✆ and fax **403/762-4811.** www.bbcanada.com/3120.html. 10 units. From C$95 (US$59) double. Extra person C$15 (US$9). Rates include breakfast. MC, V. Closed Dec 1–April 30. *In room:* TV.

**Woodside Cottage** If you'd like a private room but you're on a budget, this charming B&B accommodation—a private main floor suite with two twin beds, en suite bathroom, and library—might be just the place. Originally built by a noted local artist, the Woodside is a heritage bungalow with a stone-columned porch just a couple minutes stroll from downtown Banff. Children are welcome here.

132 Otter St. (Box 227), Banff, AB, T0L 0C0. ✆ **403/762-2441.** 1 suite. C$85 (US$53). Rates include continental breakfast. No credit cards. *In room:* TV, fridge.

### Inexpensive

**Banff International Hostel** With a mix of two-, four-, and six-bed rooms, this new hostel is the most pleasant budget lodging in Banff. Couple and family rooms are available. Facilities include a recreation room, kitchen, laundry, and lounge with fireplace. Meals are available at the Cafe Alpenglow. Reserve at least a month in advance for summer stays.

On Tunnel Mountain Rd., 1.5km (1 mile) west of Banff (P.O. Box 1358), Banff, AB, T0L 0C0. ✆ **403/762-4122.** Fax 403/762-3441. www.hostellingintl.ca/alberta. 214 beds. C$21.50 (US$13) members, C$25 (US$16) nonmembers. Private rooms available. MC, V. **Amenities:** Restaurant; access to health club across the street; bike rental; activities desk; coin-op laundry.

**Banff Y Mountain Lodge (YWCA)** *Value* The YWCA is a bright, modern building with good amenities, just across the Bow River bridge from downtown. The Y welcomes both genders—singles, couples, and family groups—with accommodations in private or dorm rooms. Some units have private bathrooms. On site are a guest laundry and an assembly room with a TV.

102 Spray Ave., (P.O. Box 520), Banff, AB, T0L 0C0. ✆ **800/813-4138** or 403/762-3560. Fax 403/760-3202. www.ymountainlodge.com. 53 beds, 7 private rooms. C$20–C$22 (US$12–US$14) bunk in dorm room (sleeping bag required), C$55–C$99 (US$34–US$61) double. MC, V. Free parking. **Amenities:** Restaurant; coin-op laundry.

## WHERE TO DINE

Food is generally good in Banff, although you pay handsomely for what you get. The difference in price between a simply okay meal in a theme restaurant and a nice meal in a classy dining room can be quite small. Service is often indifferent, as many restaurant staff members have become used to waiting on the in-and-out-in-a-hurry tour-bus crowds. An abundance of eateries line Banff Avenue, and most hotels have at least one dining room. The following recommendations are just the beginning of what's available in a very concentrated area.

### Expensive

**Buffalo Mountain Lodge** ★★ NEW CANADIAN One of the most pleasing restaurants in Banff, the dining room at the Buffalo Mountain Lodge occupies half of the lodge's soaring, three-story lobby, set in a quiet wooded location just outside town. As satisfying as all this is to the eye and the spirit, the food here is even more notable. The chef brings together the best of regional ingredients—Alberta beef, lamb, pheasant, venison, trout, and B.C. salmon—and prepares each in a seasonally changing, contemporary style. The fireplace-dominated lobby bar is a lovely place to come for an intimate cocktail.

1.5km (1 mile) west of Banff on Tunnel Mountain Rd. ✆ **403/762-2400.** www.crmr.com. Reservations recommended on weekends. Main courses C$19–C$33 (US$12–US$20). AE, DC, ER, MC, V. Daily 6–10pm.

**Grizzly House** FONDUE Grizzly House has nothing to do with bears except a rustic log-cabin atmosphere. The specialty here is fondue—from cheese to hot chocolate, and everything in between, including seafood, rattlesnake, frogs' legs, alligator, and buffalo fondue. Steaks and game dishes are the Grizzly's other specialty. The setting is frontier Banff, not the Swiss shtick you might expect from a fondue palace, and the fare is excellent.

207 Banff Ave. ✆ **403/762-4055.** Fax 403/762-4359. Reservations appreciated. A la carte fondue for 2 C$30–C$48 (US$19–US$30). AE, MC, V. Daily 11:30am–midnight.

**Ristorante Classico** INTERNATIONAL This dining room boasts the best views in Banff and a four-star rating that will appeal to the serious gastronome. The artfully prepared and aggressively flavored dishes, which feature fresh seafood, veal, fowl, and up-to-the-minute ingredients, are almost as impressive as the view. The cuisine invokes the classic traditions of France and Italy, while optimizing the regional ingredients of Canada. The menu features a mix of updated favorites along with more inventive dishes. Unusual combinations include rosehip & lavender smoked Atlantic salmon, macadamia nut crusted lamb rack on sweet pepper and peach couscous, and loin of Arctic caribou with candied endive and sour cherry pan juices.

In the Rimrock Resort Hotel, 5km (3 miles) south of Banff on Mountain Ave. ✆ **403/762-3356.** Reservations required. 3-course table d'hôte C$75 (US$47). AE, DC, DISC, MC, V. Tues–Sun 6–10pm.

**Saltlik** ★ STEAKS While most eateries in Banff are content to evoke mountain lodges or Swiss chalets, this new entry is all urban chic: minimalist steel, concrete and glass. The concept works, due in no small part to the fold-away glass walls that open to let in the incongruously natural beauty of the mountains. Steaks and meats are the specialty, fast-cooked in a 675°C (1,200°F) infrared oven, with a handful of grilled fish, rotisserie chicken and seafood entrees to round out the menu. Very stylish and upscale, the Saltlik is the restaurant of the moment in Banff.

221 Bear St, ✆ **403/760-2467.** Reservations recommended. Main courses C$12–C$25 (US$7–US$16). MC, V. Daily 11am–11pm.

### Moderate

**Balkan Restaurant** GREEK You'll find this airy blue-and-white dining room up a flight of stairs, with windows overlooking the street below. The fare consists of reliable Hellenic favorites, well prepared and served with a flourish; pasta and steaks are available as well. The Greek platter for two consists of a small mountain of beef souvlaki, ribs, moussaka, lamb chops, tomatoes, and salad. If you're dining alone, you can't do better than the lagos stifado (rabbit stew) with onions and red wine.

120 Banff Ave. ✆ **403/762-3454.** Main courses C$9–C$21 (US$6–US$13). AE, MC, V. Daily 11am–11pm.

**Coyotes Deli & Grill** ★ SOUTHWEST/MEDITERRANEAN One of the few places in Banff where you can find lighter, healthier food, Coyote's is an attractive bistro-like restaurant with excellent contemporary southwestern cuisine. There's a broad selection of vegetarian dishes, as well as fresh fish, grilled meats, and multiethnic dishes prepared with an eye to spices and full flavors. There's also a deli, where you can get the makings for a picnic and head to the park. This is a very popular place, so go early or make reservations if you don't want to stand in line.

206 Caribou St. ✆ **403/762-3963.** Reservations recommended. Main courses C$14–C$22 (US$9–US$14). AE, DC, MC, V. Daily 7:30am–11pm.

**Giorgio's Trattoria** ITALIAN Giorgio's is a cozy eatery dimly lit by low-hanging lamps. Divided into a counter section and table area (both comfortable), it serves authentic old-country specialties at eminently reasonable prices.

Wonderful crisp rolls—a delicacy in themselves—come with your meal. Don't miss the gnocchi alla piemontese (potato dumplings in meat sauce) or the Sicilian cassata (candied fruit ice cream).

219 Banff Ave. ✆ **403/762-5114.** Reservations accepted for groups of 8 or more. Pasta courses C$12–C$15 (US$7–US$9); pizza C$12–C$17 (US$7–US$11). MC, V. Daily 4:30–10pm.

**Magpie & Stump Restaurant & Cantina** ★ MEXICAN The false-fronted Magpie & Stump doesn't really match up architecturally with the rest of smart downtown Banff—and neither does the food nor atmosphere, thank goodness. The food here is traditional Mexican and Tex Mex, done up with style and heft: Someone in the kitchen sure knows how to handle a tortilla. This isn't high cuisine, just well prepared favorites like enchiladas, tamales, tacos, and the like. Barbecued ribs and chicken are also delicious. Meals are well priced compared to those elsewhere in town, and you won't leave hungry. The interior looks like a dark and cozy English pub, except for the buffalo heads and cactus plants everywhere—along with a lot of southwest kitsch. The Cantina is a good place for a lively late-night drink, as the town's young summer waitstaff likes to crowd in here to unwind with an after-shift beverage—usually a beer served in a jam jar.

203 Caribou St. ✆ **403/762-4067.** Reservations accepted for groups of 10 or more. Main courses C$8–C$18 (US$5–US$11). AE, ER, MC, V. Daily noon–2am.

**St. James Gate Irish Pub** IRISH The St. James Gate is owned by Guinness, a company that knows a thing or two about Irish pubs. Newly created to resemble a traditional draught house, this lively pub also offers an extensive menu of bar meals to accompany its selection of beers and ales. Halibut-fish-and-chips are a specialty, as are traditional meat pies and sandwiches. Full meals are available as well. This is a lively place, and in the Irish tradition, you never know when a table full of dislocated Finnians will break into a heartfelt ballad or two.

207 Wolf St. ✆ **403/762-9355.** Reservations not accepted. Main courses C$10–C$17 (US$7–US$11). MC, V. Food service available Mon–Fri 11am–2pm, Sat–Sun 10am–2pm.

### Inexpensive

If you're really on a budget, you'll probably get used to the deli case at Safeway, at Martin and Elk streets, as even inexpensive food is costly here. Other favorites for cheap and quick food include **Evelyn's Coffee Bar,** 201 Banff Ave. (✆ **403/762-0352**), for great home-baked muffins and rolls. The **Jump Start Coffee and Sandwich Place,** 206 Buffalo St. (✆ **403/762-0332**), offers sandwiches, soup, salads, pastries, and picnics to go. For all-day and all-night pizza, head to **Aardvark Pizza,** 304a Caribou St., (✆ **403/762-5500**), open daily to 4am.

**Bruno's Cafe and Grill** CANADIAN Named for Bruno Engler, a famed outdoor guide and photographer, Bruno's serves burgers, pizza, wraps, and hearty Canadian-style entrees—all best washed down with locally brewed draught beer. This cozy and casual little joint is open late, a rarity in Banff.

304 Caribou St. ✆ **403/762-8115.** Reservations not accepted. Main courses C$8–C$15 (US$5–US$9). Daily 7am–1pm. MC, V.

**Cafe Alpenglow** INTERNATIONAL You don't usually associate hostels with good food, but the Banff Hostel is different than most. This inexpensive little cafe has no dishes over C$10 (US$6)—yet you won't get hungry from the table. The menu features wraps, sandwiches, soups and other healthy, inexpensive food with youthful flair; it's got a patio and a liquor license, too.

The Banff International Hostel, 1.5km (1 mile) northeast on Tunnel Mountain Road. ✆ **403/762-4122.** Reservations not accepted. Main courses C$6–C$10 (US$3.70–US$6). Daily 7am–9pm. AE, V.

**Melissa's Restaurant and Bar** CANADIAN Banff's original hostelries weren't all as grand as the Banff Springs Hotel. There was also the Homestead Inn, established in the 1910s, with its much-loved restaurant, Melissa's. The original hotel has been replaced with a more modern structure, but the old log cabin that houses Melissa's remains. The food has been updated a bit in the last century, but old-fashioned, traditionally Canadian foods still dominate the menu. Breakfasts are famed, especially the apple hot cakes. Lunch and dinner menus feature burgers, sandwiches, local trout and steaks.

218 Lynx St. ✆ **403/762-5511**. Reservations recommended. Main courses C$8–C$25 (US$5–US$16). AE, MC, V.

### BANFF AFTER DARK

Most of Banff's larger hotels and restaurants offer some form of nightly entertainment. However, for a more lively selection, head to downtown's Banff Avenue.

One of the best spots is, the legendary **Wild Bill's Saloon,** 203 Banff Ave. (✆ **403/762-0333**), where you can watch tourists in cowboy hats learning to line dance. Alt-Rock bands dominate on Monday and Tuesday evenings, Wednesday to Saturday, it's all country rock, all the time. The venerable **Rose and Crown Pub,** 202 Banff Ave. (✆ **403/762-2121**), used to be the only place to hear live music in Banff. It's still one of the best. Bands range from Celtic to folk to rock. In summer, sit on the rooftop bar and watch the stars. Popular with foreign tourists, **The Barbary Coast,** 119 Banff Ave. (✆ **403/762-4616**), is a California-style bar and restaurant that features live music among the potted plants. Bands range from '80s cover bands to light jazz.

It took the ultra-cool cocktail lounge format a while to reach Banff, but here it is: **Aurora,** 110 Banff Ave. (✆ **403/760-5300**). Dance nightly to DJ-spun rock while sipping something delicious in a martini glass. Banff's most popular dance club, **Outabounds,** 137 Banff Ave. (✆ **403/762-8434**), is in the basement of the old King Eddy Hotel. DJs spin the tunes while young whitewater guides chat and dance with impressionable young tourists. Thursday night is ladies night.

## LAKE LOUISE ★★★

Deep-green Lake Louise, 56km (35 miles) northwest of Banff and surrounded by snowcapped mountains, is one of the most famed beauty spots in a park renowned for its scenery. The village in the valley below the lake has developed into a resort destination in its own right. Lake Louise boasts the largest ski area in Canada and easy hiking access to the remote high country along the Continental Divide.

The lake may be spectacular, but probably as many people wind up the road to Lake Louise to see its most famous resort, the Chateau Lake Louise. Built by the Canadian Pacific Railroad, the Chateau is, along with the Banff Springs Hotel, one of the most celebrated hotels in Canada. More than just a lodging, this storybook castle—perched a mile high in the Rockies—is the center of recreation, dining, shopping, and entertainment for the Lake Louise area.

In case you were wondering, there's a reason the water in Lake Louise is so green: The stream water that tumbles into the lake is filled with minerals, ground by the glaciers that hang above the lake. Sunlight refracts off the glacial "flour," creating vivid colors. You'll want to at least stroll around the shore and gawk at the glaciers and the massive Chateau. The gentle **Lakeshore Trail** follows the northern shore to the end of Lake Louise. If you're looking for more exercise and even better views, continue on the trail as it begins to climb. Now called the **Plain of Six Glaciers Trail** ★, it passes a teahouse 5km (3 miles) from the Chateau, and is open in summer only, on its way to a tremendous viewpoint over Victoria Glacier and Lake Louise.

## SEEING THE SIGHTS

The **Lake Louise Summer Sightseeing Lift** (✆ **403/522-3555**) offers a 10-minute ride up to the Whitehorn Lodge, midway up the Lake Louise Ski Area. From here, the views of Lake Louise and the mountains along the Continental Divide are magnificent. Hikers can follow one of many trails into alpine meadows, or join a free naturalist-led walk to explore the delicate ecosystem. The restaurant at the Whitehorn Lodge is much better than you'd expect at a ski area, and specially priced ride-and-dine tickets are available for those who would like to have a meal at 2,100m (7,000 ft.); the Canadian BBQ buffet is especially fun. The round-trip costs C$16.95 (US$11) for adults, C$14.95 (US$9) for seniors and students, and C$8.95 (US$6) for children ages 6 to 15. The lift operates from early June to mid-September.

To many visitors, **Moraine Lake** ★★ is even more beautiful than Lake Louise, its more famous twin. Ten spire-like peaks, each over 3,000m (10,000 ft.) high, rise precipitously from the shores of this tiny gem-blue lake. It's an unforgettable sight, and definitely worth the short 13km (8-mile) drive from Lake Louise. A trail follows the lake's north shore to the mountain cliffs. There's a lodge offering meals. If the panorama looks familiar, you might recognize it from the back of a Canadian $20 bill.

## WHERE TO STAY

**The Fairmont Chateau Lake Louise** ★ The Chateau Lake Louise is one of the best-loved hotels in North America—and one of the most expensive. If you want to splurge on only one place in the Canadian Rockies, make it this one—you won't be sorry. This massive, formal structure is blue-roofed and turreted, furnished with Edwardian sumptuousness and alpine charm. Built in stages over the course of a century by the Canadian Pacific Railroad, the entire hotel was remodeled and upgraded in 1990, and now stays open year-round. The cavernous grand lobby, with its curious figurative chandeliers, gives way to a sitting room filled with overstuffed chairs and couches; these and other common areas overlook the Chateau's gardens and the deep blue-green lake in its glacier-hung cirque. The guest rooms' marble-tiled bathrooms, crystal barware, and comfy down duvets are indicative of the attention to detail and luxury you can expect here. The Chateau can sometimes feel like Grand Central Station—so many guests and so many visitors crowding into the hotel. But the guest rooms are truly sumptuous and the service highly professional.

Lake Louise, AB, T0L 1E0. ✆ **800/441-1414** or 403/522-3511. Fax 403/522-3834. www.fairmont.com. 513 units. High season C$587–C$787 (US$364–US$488) double, C$790–C$979 (US$490–US$607) suite. Rates vary depending on whether you want a view of the lake or mountains. Off-season rates and packages available. Children under 17 stay free in parents' room. AE, DC, DISC, MC, V. Parking C$9 (US$6) per day. **Amenities:** 9 restaurants in high season, including the exquisite Edelweiss Room and the jolly Walliser Stube Wine Bar (see "Where to Dine," below), 2 bars; indoor pool; health club; Jacuzzi; sauna; exercise room; bike and canoe rental; concierge; tour desk; business center; shopping arcade; salon; 24-hour room service; massage; babysitting; laundry service; same-day dry cleaning; concierge-level rooms. *In room:* A/C, TV, dataport, minibar, coffeemaker, hair dryer, iron.

**Deer Lodge** ★ The Chateau Lake Louise isn't the only historic lodge here. Built in the 1920s, the original Deer Lodge was a teahouse for the early mountaineers who came to the area to hike (the original tearoom is now the very handsome and rustic Mount Fairview Dining Room, offering Northwest cuisine). Although Lake Louise itself is a short stroll away, the charming Deer Lodge features a sense of privacy and solitude that the busy Chateau can't offer. Choose from three types of accommodations: cozy rooms in the original lodge, larger rooms in the newer Tower Wing, and Heritage Rooms, the largest rooms in the newest wing. All units have feather duvets and handsome mountain-style furniture. The Caribou Lounge is open for drinks and three meals daily. Other facilities include a rooftop hot tub, billiards table, and a TV and VCR area. If you're looking for a quiet Rockies getaway, choose this over the Chateau.

109 Lake Louise Dr., Lake Louise (P.O. Box 1598), Banff, AB, T0L 0C0. ✆ **800/661-1595** or 403/522-3747. Fax 403/522-4222. www.crmr.com. 73 units. C$150–C$220 (US$93–US$136) double. AE, MC, V. **Amenities:** Restaurant, lounge; roof-top Jacuzzi; sauna; coin-op laundry; dry cleaning service. *In room:* TV.

**Lake Louise Inn** The Lake Louise Inn stands in a wooded 3ha (8-acre) estate at the base of the moraine, 7 driving minutes from the fabled lake You'll stay in a room with forest all around and snowcapped mountains peering over the trees outside your window. The inn consists of five different buildings—a central lodge with pool, whirlpool, steam room, restaurant, bar, and lounge, and four additional lodging units. There are five different room types, starting with standard units with double beds. The superior queen and executive rooms in Building Five are the newest and nicest, with pine-railed balconies and sitting areas. For families, the superior lofts are capable of sleeping up to eight, with two bathrooms, full kitchen, living room and fireplace, and two separate bedrooms and a fold-out couch—just the ticket for a big group.

210 Village Rd. (P.O. Box 209), Lake Louise, AB, T0L 1E0. ✆ **800/661-9237** or 403/522-3791. Fax 403/522-2018. www.lakelouiseinn.com. 232 units. High season C$165–C$375 (US$102–US$233) double. AE, DC, MC, V. Free parking. **Amenities:** Restaurant, bar; pool; Jacuzzi; sauna; business center; coin-op laundry. *In room:* TV, dataport, fridge, microwave, coffeemaker, hair dryer.

**Moraine Lake Lodge** The only lodging at beautiful Moraine Lake is this handsome lakeside lodge. The original building houses eight basic rooms, each with two double beds. In the newer Wenkchemna Wing are six rooms with queen beds and fireplaces. The cabins contain either one king or two twin beds, plus a sunken seating area with fireplace. One suite is available as well, with a fireplace, Jacuzzi, king bed, and views over the lake. All accommodations are simply but nicely furnished with pine furniture. The dining room is open for three meals daily and serves excellent Northwest cuisine. Room rates include use of canoes rentals and naturalist presentations.

8 miles (13km) south of Lake Louise at Moraine Lake (Box 70), Banff, AB, T0L 0C0. ✆ **403/522-3733.** Fax 403/522-3719. www.morainelake.com. 33 units. C$395–C$450 (US$245–US$279) double, C$500 (US$310) suite, C$490 (US$304) cabin. AE, MC, V. **Amenities:** Restaurant, bar; canoe rental; concierge. *In room:* Hair dryer.

**Post Hotel** ★★ Discreetly elegant and beautifully furnished, this wonderful log hotel with a distinctive red roof began its life in 1942 as a humble ski lodge. Between 1988 and 1993, new owners completely rebuilt the old lodge, transforming it into one of the most luxurious getaways in the Canadian Rockies; in fact, the Post Hotel is one of only two properties in western Canada that has been admitted into the French network Relais et Châteaux. The entire lodge is built of traditional log-and-beam construction, preserving the rustic flavor of the old structure and of its mountain setting. The public rooms are lovely, from the renowned dining room (preserved intact from the original hotel) to the arched, two-story, wood-paneled library (complete with rolling track ladders and river-stone fireplace).

Accommodations throughout are beautifully furnished with rustic pine pieces and rich upholstery. Most units have stone fireplaces, balconies, and whirlpool tubs. Due to the rambling nature of the property, there are a bewildering 14 different layouts available. Families will like the "N" rooms, as each has a separate bedroom with queen bed, a loft with queen and twin beds, a fireplace, and balconies. The "F" units are fantastic, featuring a huge tiled bathroom with both shower and Jacuzzi, a separate bedroom, a large balcony, and a sitting area with couch, river-stone fireplace, and daybed. Amenities include a notably attractive glass-encased pool meeting facility. Hospitality and service here are top-notch.

P.O. Box 69, Lake Louise, AB, T0L 1E0. ✆ **800/661-1586** or 403/522-3989. Fax 403/522-3966. www.posthotel.com. 98 units. High season C$340–C$374 (US$211–US$232) double, C$450–C$600 (US$279–US$372) suite, C$475–C$660 (US$295–US$409) cabin. AE, MC, V. Closed Nov. **Amenities:** Sublime restaurant (see "Where to Dine," below), 2 bars; indoor pool; Jacuzzi; sauna; massage; babysitting; laundry service; dry cleaning. *In room:* TV/VCR, hair dryer, iron.

## WHERE TO DINE

**Lake Louise Station** PIZZA/STEAKS This handsome and historic log building served as the Lake Louise train station for nearly a century, before rail service ceased in the 1980s. Guests now dine in the old waiting room, or enjoy a quiet drink in the old ticketing lobby. Two dining cars sit on the sidings beside the station and are open for fine dining in the evening. Excellent steaks and grilled meat are the specialties here.

200 Sentinel Rd. ✆ **403/522-2600.** Reservations recommended on weekends. Pizzas C$15 (US$9); steaks and seafood C$14–C$22 (US$9–US$14). AE, MC, V. Daily 11:30am–midnight.

**Post Hotel Dining Room** ★★ INTERNATIONAL Let's face it: Your trip through the Canadian Rockies is costing you a lot more than you planned. But don't start economizing on food just yet because the Post Hotel offers some of the finest dining in Western Canada. The food was famous long before the rebuilding and renovation of the old hotel, but in recent years, the restaurant has maintained such a degree of excellence that it has won the highly prized endorsement of the French Relais et Châteaux organization. Guests dine in a long, rustic room with wood beams and windows looking out onto glaciered peaks. The menu focuses on full-flavored meat and fish preparations. For an appetizer, you might try Pacific marlin carpaccio with heirloom tomato tartar and three mustard sauces, or buffalo striploin with blackberry maple syrup butter and corn fritters. Desserts are equally imaginative. Service is excellent, as is the very impressive wine list: with 25,000 bottles in the cellar, there are even some good values discreetly hidden in the mostly French selection.

In the Post Hotel, Lake Louise. ✆ **403/522-3989.** www.posthotel.com. Reservations required. Main courses C$30–C$42 (US$19–US$26). AE, MC, V. Daily 7–11am, 11:30am–2pm, and 5–10pm.

**Walliser Stube Wine Bar** ★ SWISS While the Chateau Lake Louise operates four major restaurants, including the formal Edelweiss Room, the most fun and relaxing place to eat is the Walliser Stube, a small dining room that serves excellent Swiss-style food and some of the best fondue ever. The back dining room is called the Library, and is indeed lined with tall and imposing wood cases and rolling library ladders. Happily, the cases are filled with wine, not books. A meal in the Walliser Stube is an evening's worth of eating and drinking, as the best foods—a variety of fondues and raclettes—make for convivial and communal dining experiences. The cheese fondue, C$33 (US$20) for two, is fabulous; forget the stringy glutinous experience you had in the 1970s and give it another chance. Raclettes are another communal operation, involving heat lamps that melt chunks of cheese until bubbly; the aromatic, molten result is spread on bread. It's all great fun in a great atmosphere—go with friends and you'll have a blast.

In Chateau Lake Louise. ✆ **403/522-1817.** Reservations required. Main courses C$17.50–C$29 (US$11–US$18); fondues for two C$33–C$45 (US$20–US$28). AE, DISC, MC, V. Daily 5–11:30pm.

## THE ICEFIELDS PARKWAY ★★★

Between Lake Louise and Jasper winds one of the most spectacular mountain roads in the world. Called the Icefields Parkway, the road climbs through three deep river valleys, beneath soaring, glacier-notched mountains, and past dozens of hornlike peaks shrouded with permanent snowfields. Capping this 287km (178-mile) route is the **Columbia Icefields,** a massive dome of glacial ice and snow straddling the top of the continent. From this mighty cache of ice—the largest nonpolar ice cap in the world—flow the Columbia, the Athabasca, and the North Saskatchewan rivers.

Although you can drive the Icefields Parkway in 3 hours, plan to take enough time to stop at eerily green lakes, hike to a waterfall, and take an excursion up onto the Columbia Icefields. There's also a good chance that you'll see wildlife: ambling bighorn sheep, mountain goats, elks with huge shovel antlers, and mama bears with cubs—all guaranteed to halt traffic and set cameras clicking.

After Lake Louise, the highway divides: Highway 1 continues west toward Golden, British Columbia, while Highway 93 (the Icefields Parkway) continues north along the Bow River. **Bow Lake,** the river's source, glimmers below enormous **Crowfoot Glacier;** when the glacier was named, a third "toe" was more in evidence, lending a resemblance to a bird's claw. Roadside viewpoints look across the lake at the glacier. **Num-Ti-Jah Lodge,** on the shores of Bow Lake, is a good place to stop for a bite to eat and to take some photographs.

The road mounts Bow Summit and drops into the North Saskatchewan River drainage. Stop at the **Peyto Lake Viewpoint** and hike up a short but steep trail to glimpse this startling blue-green body of water. The North Saskatchewan River collects its tributaries at the little community of Saskatchewan River Crossing; thousands of miles later, the Bow and Saskatchewan rivers will join and flow east through Lake Winnipeg to Hudson Bay.

The parkway then begins to climb up in earnest toward the Sunwapta Pass. Here, in the shadows of 3,490m (11,450-foot) **Mount Athabasca,** the icy tendrils of the **Columbia Icefields** come into view. However impressive these glaciers may seem from the road, they're nothing compared to the massive amounts of centuries-old ice and snow hidden by mountain peaks; the Columbia Icefields cover nearly 518km$^2$ (200 sq. miles) and are more than 760m (2,500 ft.) thick. From the parkway, the closest fingers of the ice field are **Athabasca Glacier,** which fills the horizon to the west of the **Columbia Icefields Centre** (✆ **780/852-7032**), a newly re-built lodge with a restaurant open from 8am to 10pm and double rooms starting at C$185 (US$115). The **Icefields Information Centre** (✆ **780/852-7030**), a park service office that answers questions about the area, stands beside the lodge. It's open May 1 to June 14, daily from 9am to

5pm; June 15 to September 7, daily from 9am to 6pm; and September 8 to October 15, daily from 9am to 5pm. It is closed October 15 to May 1.

From the **Brewster Snocoach Tours** ticket office (© **403/762-6735**), specially designed buses with balloon tires take visitors out onto the face of the glacier. The 90-minute excursion includes a chance to hike the surface of Athabasca Glacier. The Snocoach Tour is C$28 (US$17) for adults and C$14 (US$9) for children. If you don't have the time for the tour, you can drive to the toe of the glacier and walk up onto its surface. Use extreme caution when on the glacier; tumbling into a crevasse can result in broken limbs or even death.

From the Columbia Icefields, the parkway descends steeply into the Athabasca River drainage. From the parking area for **Sunwapta Falls,** travelers can choose to crowd around the chain-link fence and peer at this turbulent falls, or take the half-hour hike to equally impressive but less crowded Lower Sunwapta Falls. **Athabasca Falls,** farther north along the parkway, is another must-see. Here, the wide and powerful Athabasca River constricts into a roaring torrent before dropping 25m (82 ft.) into a narrow canyon. A mist-covered bridge crosses the chasm just beyond the falls; a series of trails lead to more viewpoints. The parkway continues along the Athabasca River, through a landscape of meadows and lakes, before entering the Jasper Townsite.

Facilities are few along the parkway. Hikers and bikers will be pleased to know that there are rustic hostels at Mosquito Creek, Rampart Creek, Hilda Creek, Beauty Creek, Athabasca Falls, and Mount Edith Cavell. Reservations for all Icefields Parkway hostels can be made by calling © **403/439-3215.** A shuttle runs between the Calgary International Hostel and hostels in Banff, Lake Louise, and along the Icefields Parkway to Jasper. You must have reservations at the destination hostel to use the service. Call © **403/283-5551** for more information.

## 8 Jasper National Park: Canada's Largest Mountain Park ★★

Jasper, now Canada's largest mountain park, was established in 1907. Slightly less busy than Banff to the south, Jasper Park attracts a much more outdoors-oriented crowd, with hiking, biking, climbing, horseback riding, and rafting the main activities. Sure, there is shopping and fine dining in Jasper, but it's not the focus of activity, as in Banff. Travelers seem a bit more determined and rugged-looking, as if they've just stumbled in from a long-distance hiking trail or off the face of a rock—certainly there's no shortage of outdoor recreation here.

For more information on the park, contact **Jasper National Park,** P.O. Box 10, Jasper, AB, T0E 1E0 (© **780/852-6176;** www.parkscanada. gc.ca).

### SPORTS & OUTDOOR ACTIVITIES IN THE PARK

The **Jasper Adventure Centre,** 604 Connaught Dr. (© **800/565-7547** in western Canada, or 780/852-5595; www.jasperadventurecentre.com) is a clearinghouse of local outfitters and guides. White-water rafting and canoeing trips, horseback rides, guided hikes, and other activities can be arranged out of this office, which is open June 1 to October 1, daily from 9am to 9pm.

A number of shops rent most of the equipment you'll need. Mountain bikes, canoes and rafts, tents, fishing gear, and skis are available for rent from **On-Line Sport and Tackle,** 600 Patricia St. (© **780/852-3630**) which can also set you up on guided rafting and fishing trips. Snowboards, cross-country ski equipment, and more bikes are available from **Freewheel Cycle,** 618 Patricia St. (© **780/852-3898**).

# Jasper Town & Jasper National Park

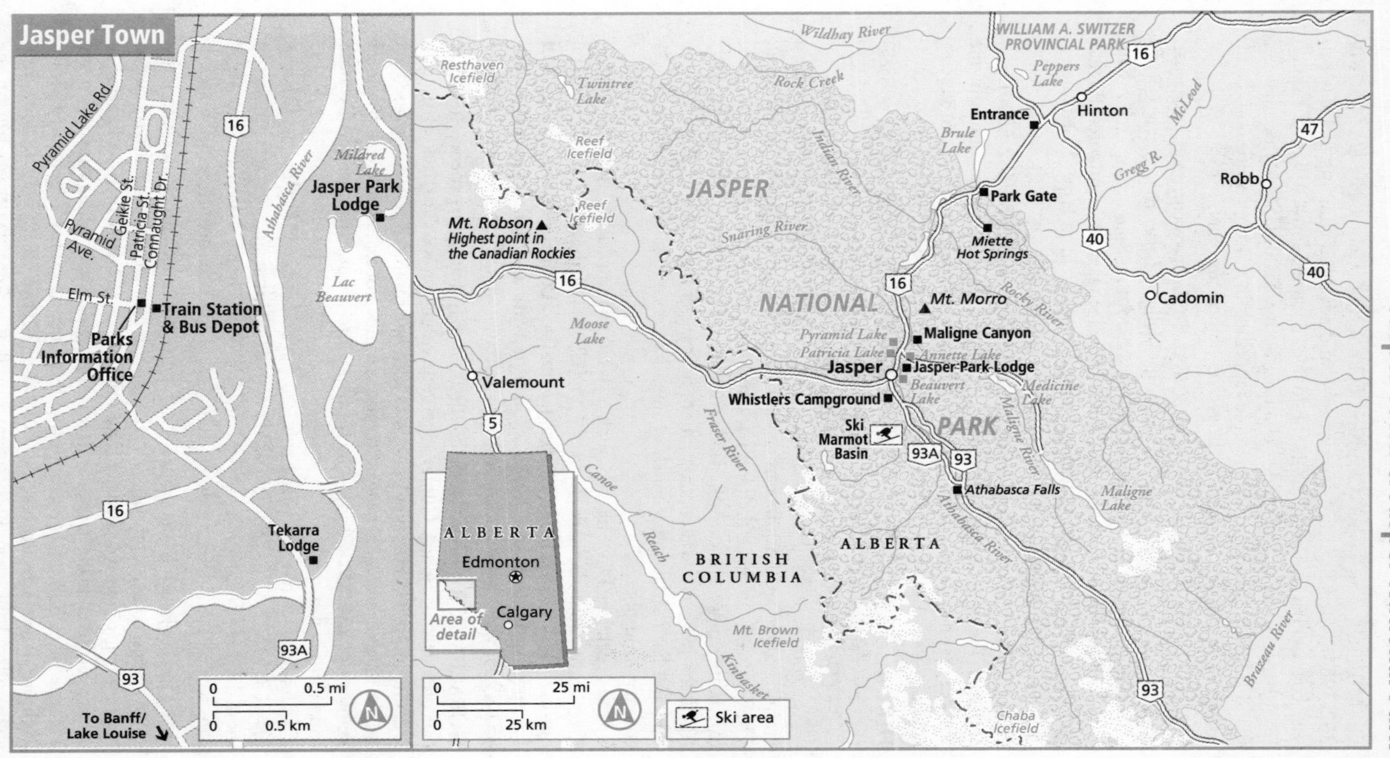

**CLIMBING** The **Jasper Climbing School,** 806 Connaught Dr. (**© 780/852-3964**), offers beginner, intermediate, and advanced climbing in 1-day private courses. Basics are taught at the foot of Mount Morro, 19km (12 miles) from Jasper. The personal guided climbing fee is C$250 (US$155) per day. For C$30 (US$19), beginners can sample rappelling in a 3-hour workshop. Food, transport, and accommodations (in private homes) are extra.

**FISHING** **Currie's Guiding** (**© 780/852-5650;** www.curriesguidingjasper.com), conducts fishing trips to beautiful Maligne Lake; the cost is C$149 (US$92) per person (minimum of two persons) for an 8-hour day. Tackle, bait, boat, and lunch are included. Ask about special single and group rates. Patricia and Pyramid lakes, north of Jasper, are more convenient to Jasper-based anglers who fancy trying their luck at trout fishing.

**GOLF** The 18-hole course at **Jasper Park Lodge** ★ (**© 780/852-6090**), east of Jasper Townsite, is one of the most popular and challenging courses in the Rockies, with 73 sand traps and other, more natural hazards—like visiting wildlife. *Score Magazine* ranked this the best golf course in Alberta.

**HIKING** Overnight and long-distance hikers will find an abundance of backcountry trails around Jasper, reaching into some of the most spectacular scenery in the Canadian Rockies. Day hikers will have fewer, but still good, choices.

The complex of trails around **Maligne Canyon** ★ makes a good choice for a group, as there are a number of access points (across six different footbridges). The less keen can make the loop back and meet fellow hikers (after getting the car) farther down the canyon. Trails ring park-like Beauvert and Annette lakes (the latter is wheelchair accessible), both near Jasper Park Lodge. Likewise, Pyramid and Patricia lakes just north of town have loop trails but more of a backcountry atmosphere.

The brochure "Day Hikers' Guide to Jasper National Park" details dozens of hikes throughout the park. It costs C$1 (US60¢) at the visitor center. Several outfitters lead guided hikes; contact **Jasper Park Lodge Mountaineering and Interpretive Hiking** (**© 780/852-3301**) or **Walk and Talks Jasper** (**© 780/852-4945;** www.walksntalks.com) for a selection of half- and full-day hikes.

**HORSEBACK RIDING** One of the most exhilarating experiences the park can offer is trail riding. Guides take your riding prowess (or lack of it) into account and select trails slow enough to keep you mounted. The horses used are steady, reliable animals not given to sudden antics. For a short ride, call **Pyramid Stables** (**© 780/852-7433**), which offers 1- to 3-hour trips around Pyramid and Patricia lakes.

Long-distance trail rides take you into the backcountry. **Skyline Trail Rides** (**© 888/582-7787** or 780/852-4215; www.skylinetrail.com) offers a number of short day trips costing roughly C$25 (US$16) per hour, as well as 3- to 4-day trips to a remote, albeit modernized, lodge. Sleigh rides are offered in winter.

**RAFTING** Jasper is the jumping-off point for float and white-water trips down several rivers. A raft trip is a good option for that inevitable drizzly day, as you're going to get wet anyway. The mild rapids (Class II to III) of the wide Athabasca River make a good introductory trip, while wilder runs down the Maligne River (Class III) will appeal to those needing something to brag about. **Maligne River Adventures** (**© 780/852-3370;** fax 780/852-3390; www.mra.ab.ca) offers trips down both rivers, as well as a 3-day wilderness trip on the Kakwa River (Class IV-plus).

Trips generally include most equipment and transportation. Jasper is loaded with rafting outfitters; a stroll along the main streets of town reveals a half-dozen options. Or just ask your hotel concierge for advice and help booking a trip.

**SKIING** Jasper's downhill ski area is **Ski Marmot Basin** (**© 780/852-3816;** www.skimarmot.com), located 19km (12 miles) west of Jasper on Highway 93. Marmot is generally underrated as a ski resort; it doesn't get the crowds of Banff, nor does it get the infamous Chinook winds. The resort has 52 runs and seven lifts, and rarely any lines. Lift tickets start at C$44 (US$27).

## GETTING AROUND THE PARK

Some of the principle outfitters and guides also offer transportation to outlying park beauty spots. Organized tours of the park's major sites—notably the Athabasca snowfields (C$83/US$51) and a Maligne Lake cruise (C$63/US$39)—are offered by **Brewster** (**© 780/852-3332;** www.brewster.ca) and **Maligne Tours** (**© 780/852-3370;** www.malignelake.com).

**Beyond the Beaten Path** (**© 780/852-5650;** www.jasperbeyondthebeatenpath.com) also offers excursions to these popular destinations, as well as trips to Miette Hot Springs (C$45/US$28) and more intimate sightseeing, photography, wildlife viewing, and picnic options. In addition, the company offers a shuttle service for hikers and rafting parties.

## JASPER TOWNSITE

Jasper isn't Banff, and to listen to most residents of Jasper, that's just fine with them. Born as a railroad division point, Jasper Townsite lacks its southern neighbor's glitz and slightly precious air of an internationalized alpine fantasyland. Instead, it gives off a lived-in, community-oriented feel that's largely lacking in Banff. The streets are thronged with avid young hikers and mountain bikers rather than the shopping hordes. Chances are, the people you meet in town will be a little muddy or wet, as if they've just gotten in from the river or the mountain. Chances are they have.

However, development is rapidly approaching: New nightclubs, restaurants, and shops geared toward tourists are springing up along Patricia Street, and that sound you hear in the distance is the thunder of tour buses.

### ESSENTIALS

**GETTING THERE** Jasper is on the Yellowhead Highway System, linking it with Vancouver, Prince George, and Edmonton—and is therefore an important transportation hub. The town is 287km (178 miles) northwest of Banff.

**VIA Rail** connects Jasper to Vancouver and Edmonton with three trains weekly; the train station (**© 780/852-4102**) is at the town center, along Connaught Street. The train tracks run due north before they start the long easterly sweep that leads to Edmonton. Also headquartered at the train station is the **Greyhound** bus station (**© 780/852-3926**) and **Brewster Transportation** (**© 780/852-3332**), which offers express service to Banff, as well as a large number of sightseeing excursions.

**VISITOR INFORMATION** For information on the townsite, contact **Jasper Tourism and Commerce,** P.O. Box 98, Jasper, AB, T0E 1E0 (**© 780/852-3858;** fax 780/852-4932; www.jaspercanadianrockies.com).

**TOWN LAYOUT** Jasper Townsite is much smaller than Banff. The main street, **Connaught Drive,** runs alongside the Canadian National Railway tracks, and is the address of the majority of Jasper's hotels. Patricia Street, a block west, is quickly becoming the boutique street, with new shops and cafes springing up. Right in the center of town, surrounded by delightful shady gardens, is the **Parks Information Offices** (✆ **780/852-6146**). The post office is at the corner of Patricia and Elm streets. At the northern end of Connaught and Geike streets, a half-kilometer (¼ mile) from downtown, is another complex of hotels.

**GETTING AROUND** For a rental car, contact **National,** 607 Connaught Dr. (✆ **780/852-1117**). Call a taxi at ✆ **780/852-5558** or 780/852-3600.

## EXPLORING JASPER & ENVIRONS

Just northeast of Jasper, off the Jasper Park Lodge access road, the Maligne River drops from its high mountain valley to cut an astounding canyon into a steep limestone face on its way to meet the Athabasca River. The chasm of **Maligne Canyon** is up to 46m (150 ft.) deep at points, yet only 3m (10 ft.) across; the river tumbles through the canyon in a series of powerful waterfalls. A sometimes-steep trail follows the canyon down the mountainside, bridging the gorge six times. Interpretive signs describe the geology. In summer, a teahouse operates at the top of the canyon.

An incredibly blue mountain lake buttressed by a ring of high-flying peaks, **Maligne Lake** is 45 minutes east of Jasper, and is one of the park's great beauty spots. Maligne is the largest glacier-fed lake in the Rockies, and the second largest in the world. The native Canadians, who called the lake Chaba Imne, had a superstitious awe of the region. White settlers didn't discover Maligne until 1908.

Today, droves of tour buses go to the "hidden lake," and the area is a popular destination for hikers, anglers, trail riders, and rafters. No matter what else they do, most visitors take a **boat cruise to Spirit Island,** at the head of the lake. The 90-minute cruise leaves from below the Maligne Lake Lodge, an attractive summer-only facility with a restaurant, bar, and gift shop (but no lodging). Cruise tickets cost C$35 (US$22) for adults, C$29 (US$18) for seniors, and C$17.50 (US$11) for kids.

Maligne Lake waters are alive with rainbow and eastern brook trout, and the Maligne Lake Boathouse is stocked with licenses, tackle, bait, and boats. Guided **fishing** trips include equipment, lunch, and hotel transportation, with half-day excursions starting at C$185 (US$115). You can rent a boat, canoe, or sea kayak to ply the waters. Morning and afternoon horseback rides up the Bald Hills depart from the Chalet at Maligne Lake; the cost is C$55 (US$34).

All facilities at Maligne Lake, including lake cruises, fishing, trail rides, and a white-water raft outfitter that offers trips down three Jasper Park rivers, are operated by **Maligne Tours** (www.malignelake.com). Offices are located at the lake, next to the lodge in Jasper at 626 Connaught Dr. (✆ **780/852-3370**) and at the Jasper Park Lodge (✆ **780/852-4779**). Maligne Tours also operates a shuttle bus between Jasper and the lake.

Downstream from Maligne Lake, the Maligne River flows into **Medicine Lake.** This large body of water appears regularly every spring, grows 8km (5 miles) long and 18m (60 ft.) deep, and then vanishes in fall, leaving only a dry gravel bed through the winter. The reason for this annual wonder is a system of underground drainage caves. The local Indians believed that spirits were responsible for the lake's annual disappearance, hence the name.

**Jasper Tramway** Canada's longest and highest aerial tramway tour starts at the foot of Whistler's Mountain, 6km (4 miles) south of Jasper off Highway 93.

Each car takes 30 passengers (plus baby carriages, wheelchairs, and the family dog) and hoists them 2km (1¼ miles) up to the 2,250m (7,400-foot) summit in a breathtaking sky ride. At the upper terminal, you'll step out into alpine tundra, the region above the tree line where some flowers take 25 years to blossom. A wonderful picnic area carpeted with mountain grass is alive with squirrels. You'll also see the "whistlers"—actually hoary marmots—that the mountain is named for. Combo tickets that include meals at the upper terminal's Treeline Restaurant are also available.

© **780/852-3093.** www.jaspertramway.com. Tickets C$17.75 (US$11) adults, C$9 (US$6) children. Lifts operate daily from 8:30am–10pm June 1–Labour Day, call for off season rates. Closed mid-October to April. Cars depart every 10–15 minutes.

**Miette Hot Springs** The hot mineral water pools are only one reason to make the side trip to Miette Hot Springs. The drive is also one of the best wildlife-viewing routes in the park. Watch for elk, deer, coyotes, and moose en route. The springs can be enjoyed in a beautiful swimming pool or in two soaker pools, surrounded by forest and an imposing mountain backdrop. Campgrounds and an attractive lodge with refreshments are nearby.

37 miles (60km) northeast of Jasper off Hwy. 16. © **780/866-3939.** Admission C$6 (US$3.70) adult, C$5 (US$3.10) children and seniors, C$17 (US$11) family. Open daily 8:30am–10:30pm June 22–Sept 9, daily 10:30am–9pm May 11–June 21 and Sept 10–Oct 8.

## SHOPPING

Weather can be unpredictable in Jasper. If it's raining, you can while away an afternoon in the town's shops and boutiques. The arcade at the Jasper Park Lodge, called the **Beauvert Promenade,** has a number of excellent clothing and gift shops. In Jasper itself, **Patricia Street** contains most of the high-quality choices. A number of galleries feature Inuit and native Arts and Crafts: Check out **Our Native Land,** 601 Patricia St. (© **780/852-5592**).

## WHERE TO STAY

As in Banff, there's a marked difference in rates between high season and the rest of the year, so if you can avoid the June-to-September crush, you may save up to 50%. All prices listed below are for high season. Call for off-season rates, as they usually follow a complex price structure. Reserve well in advance if possible. If you can't find a room, or don't want to bother with the details, contact **Rocky Mountain Reservations** (© **877/902-9455** or 780/852-9455; fax 780/852-9425; www.rockymountainreservations.com), which offers a free booking service for Jasper accommodations and activities.

If you find the prices too astronomical in Jasper, or just can't find a room, consider staying east of the park near Hinton (see below).

### Very Expensive

**Royal Canadian Lodge** ★ Usually considered Jasper Townsite's best hotel, this refined lodge provides some of the best staff and service in town. The grounds are beautifully landscaped, with colorful floral patches scattered throughout the courtyards. Guest rooms come with all the amenities you'd expect at a four-star lodging. If anything, the rooms are a tad over-decorated—considering the dramatic views from every window, you don't need the slightly boudoir-y upholstery and wall coverings. The noted **Beauvallon Dining Room** is just off the lobby (see "Where to Dine," later).

96 Geikie St., Jasper, AB, T0E 1E0. © **800/661-1225** or 780/852-5644. Fax 780/852-4860. www.charltonresorts.com. 119 units. C$315 (US$195) double, C$390–C$415 (US$242–US$257) suite. AE, DC, DISC,

MC, V. Parking C$5 (US$3.10) a day. **Amenities:** Restaurant, bar; indoor pool; Jacuzzi; concierge; room service; babysitting; laundry service; same-day dry cleaning. *In room:* A/C, TV, dataport, coffeemaker, hair dryer.

**The Fairmont Jasper Park Lodge** *Kids* Jasper's most exclusive lodging, the Jasper Park Lodge was built by the Canadian Pacific Railroad and has the same air of luxury and gentility as their other properties, but with a more woodsy feel—sort of like an upscale summer camp. The hotel's wooded, elk-inhabited grounds are located along Lac Beauvert, about 8km (5 miles) east of Jasper proper. The central lodge's amazing, lofty great room offers huge fireplaces to snuggle by. The accommodations are all extremely comfortable, though a bit hard to characterize, as there are a wide variety of cabins, lodge rooms, chalets, and cottages available—all from different eras, all set amid the forest, and all within easy walking distance of the beautiful central lodge. Since the rooms vary so much, it's a good idea to call and find out what suits your budget, needs, and group size. Families or groups can opt for one of the wonderful enormous housekeeping cabins, some of which have up to eight bedrooms. Dining options include the famed four-star **Edith Cavell** and the **Moose's Nook Northern Grill** (see "Where to Dine" later); the **Tent City Lounge** is one of Jasper's youthful hangouts.

P.O. Box 40, Jasper, AB, T0E 1E0. ✆ **800/465-7547** in Alberta, 800/441-1414 elsewhere in North America, or 780/852-3301. Fax 780/852-5107. www.fairmont.com. 446 units. C$159–C$499 (US$99–US$309) double, C$299–C$749 (US$185–US$464) suite, from C$1,850 (US$1,147) cabin. AE, DC, DISC, MC, V. Free parking. **Amenities:** 5 restaurants, 4 lounges; year-round outdoor heated pool; one of Canada's finest golf courses; 4 tennis courts; health club and spa; exercise room; canoe; paddleboat and bike rentals; children's center; concierge; tour desk; business center; shopping arcade; 24-hour room service; babysitting; laundry service; same-day dry cleaning; horseback riding. *In room:* TV w/pay movies, dataport, minibar, coffeemaker, hair dryer, iron.

## Expensive

**Amethyst Lodge** ★ If you're sick of the faux-alpine look prevalent in the Canadian Rockies, then you may be ready for the Amethyst Lodge, a comfortable and unabashed motor inn. All rooms come with two double or two queen beds; half of the rooms have balconies. The Amethyst is more central to downtown Jasper than most lodgings. On site are a large restaurant and lounge, where afternoon tea is served daily.

200 Connaught Dr. (P.O. Box 1200), Jasper, AB, T0E 1E0. ✆ **888/852-7737** or 780/852-3394. Fax 780/852-5198. www.mtn-park-lodges.com. 97 units. C$202 (US$125) double. AE, DC, MC, V. **Amenities:** Restaurant, lounge; Jacuzzi; coin-op laundry; dry cleaning service. *In room:* A/C, TV, dataport, hair dryer.

**Jasper Inn Alpine Resort** ★ *Kids* The Jasper Inn, on the northern end of town but set back off the main road, is one of the nicest lodgings in the area. Rooms are available in four different buildings, and in many different size and bed configurations. If you're looking for good value, ignore the standard and efficiency units (which are perfectly nice rooms, mind you); instead, fork over C$10 (US$6) more and reserve a spacious one-bedroom suite with a fireplace and full kitchen. Even nicer are the extra-spacious rooms in the separate Maligne Suites building, which come with enormous bathrooms, fireplaces, wet bars, Jacuzzis, and balconies. (The top of the line is Elke Sommers's former room; ask for it by name.) Also available are two-bedroom chalet-style rooms, which can sleep up to seven. With the full kitchen, balcony, fireplace, and loads of room, these are perfect for families.

98 Geikie St. (P.O. Box 879), Jasper, AB, T0E 1E0. ✆ **800/661-1933** or 780/852-4461. Fax 780/852-5916. www.jasperinn.com. 143 units. C$212–C$218 (US$131–US$135) double, C$225–C$413 (US$140–US$256)

suite. Extra person C$10 (US$6). Children 16 and under stay free in parents' room. AE, DC, MC, V. Free parking. **Amenities:** The Inn Restaurant in a garden-like atrium; small indoor pool; Jacuzzi; sauna; babysitting; coin-op and laundry service. *In room:* TV, dataport, fridge, microwave, hair dryer.

**Lobstick Lodge** ★ *Kids* The newly renovated Lobstick Lodge is a longtime favorite for the discerning traveler with an eye to value, with the largest standard units in Jasper. Even more impressive are the huge kitchen units, which come with a full-size fridge, four-burner stove, and microwave, plus double and twin beds and a foldout couch. These are perfect for families and go fast—reserve early. The upstairs meeting room has great views; when it's not in use, guests can play cards or lounge here.

96 Geikie St. (P.O. Box 1200), Jasper, AB, T0E 1E0. ✆ **888/852-7737** or 780/852-4431. Fax 780/852-4142. www.mtn-park-lodges.com. 139 units. C$202 (US$125) double, C$215 (US$133) kitchenette unit. Children under 15 stay free in parents' room. AE, DC, MC, V. Free parking. **Amenities:** Restaurant, lounge; indoor pool; 3 outdoor Jacuzzis. *In room:* TV, dataport, coffeemaker, hair dryer.

**Marmot Lodge** ★ At the northern end of Jasper's main street, the Marmot Lodge offers very pleasant rooms in three buildings, each with different types of accommodations. One building contains kitchen units with fireplaces, popular with families. The building facing the street offers smaller, less expensive rooms with two single beds or one queen bed, while the third building features very large deluxe rooms. All have been decorated with a Native American theme; some have tapestry-like weavings on the walls. All rooms are comfortable according to a relaxing, unfussy aesthetic that's restful after a day of non-stop sightseeing.

86 Connaught Dr., Jasper, AB, T0E 1E0. ✆ **800/661-6521** or 780/852-4471. Fax 780/852-3280. 107 units. C$183–C$205 (US$113–US$127) double, C$217–C$227 (US$135–US$141) kitchen unit. Children under 15 stay free in parents' room. AE, DC, MC, V. **Amenities:** Restaurant, lounge; indoor pool; Jacuzzi; sauna barbecue patio. *In room:* A/C (some rooms), TV w/pay movies, coffeemaker, hair dryer.

**Sawridge Hotel Jasper** ★ The three-story lobby of this hotel is large and airy, opening onto a long central atrium lit with skylights, where you'll find the award-winning dining room, a jungle of plants, a large pool and hot tub. The one-bedroom guest rooms face this atrium, while the two-queen-bedded rooms overlook the town and offer balconies as well. The entire hotel has recently been redecorated with a casual rustic theme, and all units are very comfortable furnished with fine furniture. The Sawridge, on the northern edge of Jasper, is unique in that it's owned by the Sawridge Cree Indian Band.

82 Connaught Dr., Jasper, AB, T0E 1E0. ✆ **800/661-6427** or 780/852-5111. Fax 780/852-5942. 154 units. C$219–C$259 (US$136–US$161) double, C$300–C$390 (US$186–US$242) suite. AE, MC, V. **Amenities:** Restaurant, lounge; indoor pool; Jacuzzi; spa; sauna; massage; business center; coin-op and laundry service. *In room:* A/C, TV, dataport, fridge, coffeemaker, hair dryer.

### Moderate

In high season, it seems that nearly half the dwellings in Jasper let rooms, B&B-style; contact **Jasper Home Accommodation Association,** P.O. Box 758, Jasper, AB, T0E 1E0 (www.bbcanada.com/jhaa.html), for a full list. B&Bs listed with the local visitor association have little signs in front; if you arrive early enough in the day, you can comb the streets looking for a likely suspect. Note that B&Bs here are much less grand than those in Banff, and less expensive as well. Double-occupancy accommodations are in the C$50 to C$75 (US$31–US$47) range at most homes. You'll need to pay cash for most. There's no central booking agency in Jasper, so contact your host directly.

**Athabasca Hotel** *Value* This hotel's lobby is like a hunting lodge, with a stone fireplace, rows of trophy heads of deer and elk, and a great bar with its own huge fireplace. A gray-stone corner building with a homey, old-fashioned air, the Athabasca was built in 1929 as a destination hotel. Each guest room offers a mountain view, although only half have private bathrooms. The rooms are of fair size, the furnishings simple and tasteful. The Athabasca has an attractive dining room and a small and trim coffee shop. The place is really quite pleasant—it's the very image of venerable Canadian charm—and one of the few good values in Jasper.

510 Patricia St., Jasper, AB, T0E 1E0. ✆ **877/542-8422** or 780/852-3386. Fax 780/852-4955. www.athabascahotel.com. 61 units (39 with private bathroom). C$145 (US$90) double with private bathroom, C$89 (US$55) double with shared bathroom. AE, DC, MC, V. **Amenities:** Restaurant, 2 bars; concierge; room service (7am–11pm). *In room:* TV, dataport, hair dryer.

**Becker's Chalets** ★ This attractive log-cabin resort offers a variety of lodging options in freestanding chalets, set in a glade of trees along the Athabasca River. While the resort dates from the 1940s and retains the feel and atmosphere of an old-fashioned mountain retreat, most of the chalets have been built in the last ten years, and thus are thoroughly modernized. Accommodations come with river-stone fireplaces and full kitchens. **Becker's Gourmet Restaurant,** open for breakfast and dinner, is one of Jasper's best (see "Where to Dine," below).

Hwy. 95, 3 miles (5km) south of Jasper (P.O. Box 579), Jasper, AB, T0E 1E0. ✆ **780/852-3779.** Fax 780/852-7202. www.beckerchalets.com. 118 chalets. C$85–C$155 (US$53–US$96) 1-bedroom cabin, C$145–C$215 (US$90–US$133) 2-bedroom cabin, C$185–C$350 (US$115–US$217) 3-bedroom cabin. AE, MC, V. **Amenities:** Restaurant; babysitting; coin-op laundry; playground. *In room:* TV, fridge, coffeemaker, hair dryer, no phone.

**Tekarra Lodge** ★ This charming log-cabin resort is just east of Jasper, situated above the confluence of the Miette and Athabasca rivers. Accommodations are in the lodge or in freestanding cabins (with kitchenette or full kitchen) that can sleep from two to seven people. The cabins are rustic looking and nicely furnished, but it's the location that really sets Tekarra Lodge apart. Just far enough from the bustle of Jasper, off a quiet road in the forest, it offers the kind of venerable charm that you dream of in a mountain cabin resort. One of Jasper's best restaurants is located in the lodge, making this a great place for a family seeking solitude and access to good food.

1.5km (1 mile) east of Jasper off Hwy. 93A (P.O. Box 669), Jasper AB, T0E 1E0. ✆ **888/404-4540** or 780/852-3058. Fax 780/852-4636. www.tekarralodge.com. 52 units. C$154 (US$95) lodge room; C$154–C$214 (US$95–US$133) cabin double. 2-night minimum for cabins in summer. Extra person C$10 (US$6). Rates for lodge rooms include continental breakfast. AE, DC, MC, V. **Amenities:** Restaurant, bar; bike rental; coin-op laundry. *In room:* kitchen, coffeemaker, hair dryer, no phone.

### Inexpensive

Two Hostelling International **hostels,** both reachable at P.O. Box 387, Jasper, AB, T0E 1E0 (✆ **780/852-3215;** www.hihostels.ca/alberta), are the best alternatives for the budget traveler. Advance reservations are strongly advised in summer. The 80-bed **Jasper International Hostel,** on Skytram Road 6km (4 miles) west of Jasper, charges C$18 (US$11) for members and C$23 (US$14) for nonmembers. The closest hostel to Jasper, it's open year-round. Two family rooms, a barbecue area, indoor plumbing, hot showers, and bike rentals are available. In winter, ask about ski packages. The **Maligne Canyon Hostel,** off Maligne Lake Road 18km (11 miles) east of Jasper, sleeps 24; rates are C$13 (US$8) for members and C$18 (US$11) for nonmembers. This convenient hostel is just above the astonishing Maligne Canyon. Facilities include a self-catering kitchen and dining area.

### In & Around Hinton

Just east of the park gate in and near Hinton are a number of options that offer high-quality accommodations at significantly lower prices than you'll find in Jasper. Downtown Jasper is a 30- to 45-minute drive away from the choices listed below.

Hinton has a number of motel complexes with standard, no-nonsense rooms. The **Best Western Motor Inn,** 828 Carmichael Lane (✆ **800/220-7870** in Canada, or 780/865-7777), has 42 air-conditioned rooms, most with kitchenettes. The **Black Bear Inn,** 571 Gregg Ave. (✆ **888/817-2888** or 780/817-2000), features an exercise room, hot tub, and restaurant. The **Crestwood Hotel,** 678 Carmichael Lane (✆ **800/262-9428** or 780/865-4001), has a pool and restaurant. Doubles at these motels cost between C$89 and C$105 (US$55–US$65).

**Mountain Splendour Bed & Breakfast** The spacious rooms at this large, modern home are outfitted with private bathrooms, tables and chairs, and English-theme decor. The largest of the three rooms is the English Garden Suite, a comfortable space with a private deck, fireplace, and large bathroom with Jacuzzi, separate shower, and cathedral ceilings. Guests can lounge by the fireplace or watch TV in the light, airy living room, which has picture windows framing a view of Jasper Park.

P.O. Box 6544, 17 Folding Mountain Village, Jasper East, AB, T7V 1X8. ✆ **780/866-2116.** Fax 780/866-2117. 3 units. C$105–C$150 (US$65–US$93) double. Rates include breakfast. MC, V. **Amenities:** Jacuzzi. *In room:* TV, hair dryer, iron.

**Overlander Mountain Lodge** ★ *Value* The Overlander is a historic lodge on the edge of Jasper Park. The original lodge building houses a rustic and evocative dining room and bar with tremendous views of the Rockies, plus cozy guest rooms with queen or twin beds. A newer wing features rooms with gas fireplaces, queen beds, and jetted tubs. The fourplex cabins have sitting rooms and separate bedrooms. Most of the chalets, which are scattered in the forest behind the lodge, contain a fireplace or wood-burning stove, full kitchen, washer/dryer, and patio. Accommodations throughout have private bathrooms and are handsomely furnished with rustic furniture. The dining room serves good Northwest cuisine, with specialties of rack of lamb, venison, and fish. The Overlander's staff is friendly and helpful. This property offers excellent value and makes a charming base for exploring the park.

Half a mile (1km) from Jasper Park East Gate (Box 6118), Hinton, AB, T7V 1X5. ✆ **780/866-2330.** Fax 780/866-2332. www.overlandermountainlodge.com. 29 units. C$165–C$185 (US$102–US$115) lodge room, C$125 (US$78) cabin room, C$275 (US$171) 2-bedroom chalet, C$325 (US$202) 4-bedroom chalet. AE, MC, V. **Amenities:** Restaurant, lounge. *In room:* Coffeemaker, hair dryer, no phone.

**Suite Dreams B&B** A modern, wheelchair-accessible home built as a B&B, Suite Dreams offers large, comfortable rooms with lots of natural light in a quiet, forested setting. Each room is decorated according to a horticultural theme and features art from several generations of the owner's talented family. All units have private bathrooms, and one can sleep up to four. The spacious living room has a fireplace. The backyard features 100 yards of golf greens. The hostess is happy to make specialty breakfasts for guests with dietary restrictions.

Box 6145 (Lot 3134 Maskuta Estates), Hinton, AB, T7V 1X5. ✆ **780/865-8855.** Fax 780/865-2199. www.suitedream.com. 3 units. From C$80 (US$50) double. Extra person C$20 (US$12). Rates include full breakfast. MC, V. **Amenities:** Golf greens. *In room:* TV/VCR, fridge.

**Wyndswept Bed & Breakfast** This excellent B&B has a hostess who will make you feel like family. The main-floor guest rooms have private bathrooms, robes, hair dryers, handmade soaps, kettles, and other extras. The suite, which gives out onto a deck, measures 110m$^2$ (1,200 sq. ft.) and has a full kitchen, large bathroom, and sitting area; it can sleep up to five. Guests have access to a computer and fax machine. Breakfast is delicious and substantial—there's even a dessert course. Chances are good you'll see wildlife while here: Bears, coyotes, wolves, and deer have all been spotted from the deck.

4km (2½ miles) east of Jasper Park gates (Box 2683), Hinton, AB, T7V 1Y2. ✆ **780/866-3950.** Fax 780/866-3951. www.wyndswept.com. 3 units. C$95 (US$59) double. Extra person C$35 (US$22). MC, V. *In room:* A/C, TV, dataport, coffeemaker, hair dryer, iron.

### A Local Guest Ranch

**Black Cat Guest Ranch** This venerable and historic wilderness retreat was established in 1935 by the Brewsters. The ranch boasts a superb mountain setting just outside the park boundaries in the foothills, with the Rockies filling up the western horizon. The rustic two-story lodge, built in 1978—guests don't stay in the original old cabins—offers 16 unfussy units, each with private bathroom, large windows, and an unspoiled view of the crags in Jasper Park across a pasture filled with horses and chattering birds. There's a large central fireplace room with couches, easy chairs, and game tables scattered about. Lodging rates include three home-cooked meals, served family-style by the friendly, welcoming staff. Activities include hiking, horseback riding (C$20/US$12 per hour for guided trips), canoe rentals, murder-mystery weekends, and fishing. The ranch staff will meet your train or bus at Hinton.

35 miles (56km) northeast of Jasper. P.O. Box 6267, Hinton, AB, T7V 1X6 ✆ **800/859-6840** or 780/865-3084. Fax 780/865-1924. www.blackcatranch.ab.ca. C$85 (US$53) per person, based on double occupancy. MC, V. **Amenities:** Large outdoor hot tub.

## CAMPING

There are 10 campgrounds in Jasper National Park. You need a special permit to camp anywhere in the parks outside the regular campgrounds—a regulation necessary due to fire hazards. Contact the parks information office (✆ **780/852-6176**) for permits. The campgrounds range from completely unserviced sites to those providing water, power, sewer connections, laundry facilities, gas, and groceries. The closest to Jasper Townsite is the Whistlers, up the road toward the gondola, providing a total of some 700 campsites.

## WHERE TO DINE

### Expensive

**Beauvallon Dining Room** ★ NEW CANADIAN Offering one of the most ambitious menus in Jasper, the Beauvallon specializes in innovative yet classically European preparations of Canadian meats, fish, and game. The menu changes seasonally, but usually features a broad selection of unusual and highly Canadian ingredients. Pan seared caribou loin is served with ice wine marinated figs, and West Coast salmon Cordon Blue comes wrapped in calamari bacon and stuffed with Boursin cheese. Local duck, beef and pork also receive inventive treatment, and there are always unusual vegetarian dishes to tempt the non-meat eater.

Service is excellent, and the dining room is cozy. The wine list is extensive and well priced.

In the Royal Canadian Lodge Jasper, 96 Geike St. ✆ **780/852-5644.** www.charltonresorts.com. Reservations recommended. Main courses C$20–C$40 (US$12–US$25); table d'hôte C$44 (US$27); Sun brunch C$18 (US$11) adults, C$14 (US$9) seniors and youths. AE, DC, MC, V. Daily 6:30am–1pm and 5:30–10:30pm.

**Becker's Gourmet Restaurant** ★ FRENCH/CANADIAN Although the name's not very elegant, it's highly descriptive. This high-quality, inventive restaurant serves what could only be termed gourmet food, at Becker's Chalets, one of the nicest log-cabin resorts in Jasper. The dining room is an intimate log-and-glass affair that overlooks the Athabasca River. The menu reads like a novel: four-nut crusted lamb chops, chèvre Mornay sauce and dill on grilled chicken breast, and grilled venison loin with Saskatoon berry compote. This restaurant observes the mandate to serve what's fresh and local, without turning the menu into a list of endangered game animals. Given the science experiments cum food preparations found on many Canadian Rockies' menus, the Gourmet Restaurant's frequent allusions to French cuisine seen almost reassuring.

Hwy. 93, 3 miles (5km) south of Jasper. ✆ **780/852-3779.** Reservations required. Main courses C$12–C$25 (US$7–US$16). MC, V. Daily 8am–2pm and 5:30–10pm.

**Moose's Nook Northern Grill** ★ CANADIAN This atmospheric restaurant off the great room of the Jasper Park Lodge features "Canadiana" specialties. With equal parts tradition and innovation, the Moose's Nook offers hearty presentations of native meats, fish, and game. Pheasant breast is grilled and served with a compote of local Saskatoonberry, while buffalo steak is prepared with a wild-mushroom, shallot, and whiskey sauce. Lighter appetites will enjoy the seafood hot pot and vegetarian cabbage rolls. The charming, wood-beamed room could double as a hunting lodge.

In the Fairmont Jasper Park Lodge, 8km (5 miles) east of Jasper. ✆ **780/852-6052.** Reservations recommended. Main courses C$18–$33 (US$11–US$20). AE, DISC, MC, V. Daily 6–10pm.

## Moderate

**Andy's Bistro** ★ CONTINENTAL/CANADIAN Andy's Bistro is a cozy and resourceful little restaurant operated by chef-owner Andy Allenbach, a Swiss-born chef and entrepreneur. The dining room looks like a wine cellar, and indeed the wine list (and the port and Scotch selection) is noteworthy. The food is classic Continental with a sprinkling of New World specialties thrown in for spice. Starters feature baked Brie Jubilee—with sour cherry sauce—and black olive toast. Main courses range from pork tenderloin Calvados (with sautéed apples) to ostrich schnitzel with white Zinfandel and stone-ground mustard sauce. Even though the menu might seem high-brow, the atmosphere is casual and friendly—one communal table for ten is saved for first-come, first served diners. Stop in at Andy's, savor lamb chops with wild mushrooms and goats cheese, and make a table full of new friends.

606 Patricia St. ✆ **780/852-4559.** Reservations recommended. Main courses C$17–C$29 (US$11–US$18). MC, V. Mid-May to mid-Oct daily 5–11pm, mid-Oct to mid-May Tues–Sat 5–11pm.

**Denjiro Japanese Restaurant** JAPANESE Denjiro's is a slice of Japan, complete with sushi bar, karaoke lounge, intimate ozashiki tables, shoeless patrons, soft Asian mood music, and service that's both fast and impeccable. The place has a studied simplicity that goes well with the traditional Japanese fare served: sukiyaki, sashimi, tempura, and teriyaki.

410 Connaught Dr. ✆ **780/852-3780.** Most items C$8–C$19 (US$5–US$12). AE, MC, V. Mid-May to mid-Oct daily noon–10pm, mid-Oct to mid-May 5pm–10pm.

**Fiddle River Seafood** ★ SEAFOOD This rustic-looking retreat has panoramic windows facing the Jasper railroad station and the mountains beyond. The specialty here is fresh fish, though a number of pasta dishes and red-meat entrees will complicate your decision-making process. While there are plenty of good selections on the menu, Fiddle River offers as many daily specials (presented at the table on an easel-propped blackboard). At least 8 or 10 fresh fish and seafood specials are featured, including oysters and several preparations of Pacific salmon, such as pan-seared Steelhead salmon filet with a honey, lime and tarragon butter sauce. For "landlubbers" as the menu denotes the non-fish eaters, there are also excellent steaks: a peppered rib eye is served with blue cheese demiglace. The wine list is short but interesting.

620 Connaught Dr. ✆ **780/852-3032.** Reservations required. Main courses C$15–C$28 (US$9–US$17). AE, MC, V. Daily 5pm–midnight.

**Something Else** INTERNATIONAL/PIZZA Something Else is accurately named: Folded together here are a good Greek restaurant and a pizza parlor, to which a high-quality Canadian-style restaurant has been added. Stir in a Creole bistro. In short, if you're with a group that can't decide where to eat, this is the place to go. Prime Alberta steaks, fiery Louisiana jambalaya and mesquite chicken, Greek saganaki and moussaka, an array of 21 pizzas—no matter what you choose, it's all well prepared and fresh, and the welcome is friendly.

621 Patricia St. ✆ **780/852-3850.** Reservations not needed. Main courses C$12–C$23 (US$7–US$14). AE, DC, MC, V. Daily 11am–11pm.

**Tekarra Lodge Restaurant** STEAK/INTERNATIONAL Located at the confluence of the Miette and Athabasca rivers, this longtime locals' favorite offers excellent Greek-influenced food, as well as steaks and other intriguing dishes like pan-seared chicken with roast grapes. Lighter dishes such as specialty stir-fries and pasta are also available. The charming lodge dining room is one of Jasper's hidden gems; the service is friendly, and the fireplace-dominated room intimate.

Hwy. 93A, 1.5km (1 mile) east of Jasper (call for directions). ✆ **780/852-3058.** Reservations recommended on weekends. Main courses C$13–C$23 (US$8–US$14). AE, DC, MC, V. Daily 5–11pm.

### Inexpensive

For muffins and sandwiches, coffee, desserts, soups, and salads, go to **Soft Rock Cafe,** 622 Connaught Dr. (✆ **780/852-5850**), in the Connaught Square Mall. You can log onto the Web or check your e-mail at one of its computers. Another casual spot is **Spooner's Coffee Bar,** upstairs at 610 Patricia St. (✆ **780/852-4046**), with a juice bar, coffee drinks, burritos, soups, sandwiches, and other deli items.

**Jasper Pizza Place** PIZZA One of Jasper's most popular eateries, the redesigned Pizza Place agreeably combines the features of an upscale boutique pizzeria with a traditional Canadian bar. The pizzas are baked in a wood-fired oven, and come in some very unusual—some would say unlikely—combinations. If you're not quite ready for the sourcream and Dijon-mustard pizza or the escargot pizza, then maybe the smoked salmon, caper, and black-olive version will please. Standard-issue pizzas are also available, as are sandwiches and a mammoth helping of lasagna for C$10 (US$6). The bar side of things is lively, with pool tables and a crowd of summer resort workers on display.

402 Connaught Dr. ✆ **780/852-3225.** Reservations not accepted. Pizza C$7–C$13 (US$4.35–US$8). MC, V. Daily 11am–11pm.

**Mountain Foods Café** *Value* DELI This small deli and cafeteria is bright and friendly, and just the antidote to the stodgy food pervasive in much of the park. Most meals are light and healthy—salads, soups, and quick ethnic dishes; specialties include burrito wraps, sandwich melts, and breakfast scrambles. The deli case is filled with items available to go. Nothing here costs much over C$7 (US$4.35). Beer and wine are served.

606 Connaught Dr. ✆ **780/852-4050.** Main courses C$5–C$10 (US$3.10–US$6). MC, V. Daily 8am–10pm.

### JASPER AFTER DARK

Nearly all of Jasper's nightlife can be found in the bars and lounges of the hotels, motels, and inns.

**O'Shea's,** Athabasca Hotel, 510 Patricia St. (✆ **780/852-3386**), is a longtime favorite party den, usually just called the Atha'B, or simply The B. It caters to a young clientele with its changing lineup of Top 40 bands, dance floor, and movies shown on the large-screen TV. O'Shea's is in action Monday to Saturday to 2am. If it's a straightforward and straight-head party scene that you're looking for, consider the **D'ed Dog Bar and Grill,** 404 Connaught Dr. (✆ **780/852-3351**). This is where the young river and hiking guides who work in Jasper every summer gather to compare exploits by shouting above the din of country rock. Jasper's hottest club for music, **Pete's Night Club,** upstairs at 614 Patricia St. (✆ **780/852-6262**), presents live alternative and blues bands.

It's a little bit anomalous—Jasper's most exclusive and expensive hotel providing shelter for one of Jasper's most popular twenty-something hangouts. **Tent City,** is a youthful gathering place in the bowels of the Jasper Park Lodge, where you'll find billiards, loud music, and a preponderance of the JPL's 650 employees.

You may think of most basement bars as dank and airless, but this lively billiard and drinks club has one advantage over most Canadian bars: it's nonsmoking. The pleasant **Downstream Bar,** 620 Conaught Dr. (✆ **780/852-9449**), is a friendly place for a late evening drink, and you won't feel out of place if you're not 25 and totally tan.

## 9 Edmonton: Capital of Alberta ★

Edmonton grew in spurts, following a boom-and-bust pattern as exciting as it was unreliable. During World War II, the boom came in the form of the Alaska Highway, with Edmonton as the material base and temporary home of 50,000 American troops and construction workers.

The ultimate boom, however, gushed from the ground in February 1947, when a drill at Leduc, 40km (25 miles) southwest of the city, sent a fountain of crude oil soaring skyward. Some 10,000 other wells followed, all within a 160km (100-mile) radius of the city. In their wake came the petrochemical industry and the major refining and supply conglomerates. In 20 years, the population of the city quadrupled, its skyline mushroomed with glass-and-concrete office towers, a rapid-transit system was created, and a C$150-million (US$93-million) civic center rose. Edmonton had become what it is today—the oil capital of Canada.

## ESSENTIALS

**GETTING THERE** **By Plane** **Edmonton International Airport** (✆ **800/268-7134;** www.edmontonairports.com) is served by **Air Canada** (✆ 800/372-9500) and **Northwest** (✆ 800/447-4747), among other airlines. The airport lies 29km (18 miles) south of the city on Highway 2, about 45 minutes away. By cab, the trip costs about C$35 (US$22); by Airporter bus, C$11 (US$7).

**By Train** The **VIA Rail** (✆ **800/561-8630** or 780/422-6032; www.viarail.ca) station is at 104th Avenue and 100th Street.

**By Bus** **Greyhound** (✆ **780/413-8747;** www.greyhound.ca) buses link Edmonton to points in Canada and the United States from the depot at 10324 103rd St.

**By Car** Edmonton straddles the Yellowhead Highway, western Canada's new east-west interprovincial highway. Just west of Edmonton, the Yellowhead is linked to the Alaska Highway. The city is 515km (320 miles) north of the U.S. border, 283km (176 miles) north of Calgary.

**VISITOR INFORMATION** Contact **Edmonton Tourism,** 9797 Jasper Ave. NW, Edmonton, AB, T5J 1N9 (✆ **800/463-4667** or 780/496-8400; www.tourism.ede.org). There are also visitor centers located at City Hall and at Gateway Park, both open from 9am to 6pm, and on the Calgary Trail at the southern edge of the city, open from 9am to 9pm.

**CITY LAYOUT** The winding **North Saskatchewan River** flows right through the heart of the city, dividing it into roughly equal halves. Most of this steep-banked valley has been turned into public parklands.

The street numbering system begins at the corner of 100th Street and 100th Avenue, which means that downtown addresses have five digits and that suburban homes often have smaller addresses than businesses in the very center of town. Edmonton's main street is **Jasper Avenue** (actually 101st Avenue), running north of the river. The "A" designations you'll notice for certain streets and avenues downtown add to the confusion: They're essentially old service alleys between major streets, many of which are now pedestrian areas with sidewalk cafes.

At 97th Street, on Jasper Avenue, rises the massive pink **Canada Place,** the only completely planned government complex of its kind in Canada. Across the street is the **Edmonton Convention Centre,** which stair-steps down the hillside to the river.

Beneath the downtown core stretches a network of pedestrian walkways—called **Pedways**—connecting hotels, restaurants, and shopping malls with the library, City Hall, and the Citadel Theatre. These Pedways not only avoid the surface traffic, but are also climate-controlled.

At the northern approach to the High Level Bridge, surrounded by parkland, stand the buildings of the **Alberta Legislature.** Across the bridge, to the west, stretches the vast campus of the **University of Alberta.** Just to the east is **Old Strathcona,** a bustling neighborhood of cafes, galleries, and hip shops that's now a haven for Edmonton's more alternative population. The main arterial through Old Strathcona is Whyte Avenue, or 82nd Avenue. Running south from here in a straight line is 104th Street, which becomes the Calgary Trail and leads to the airport.

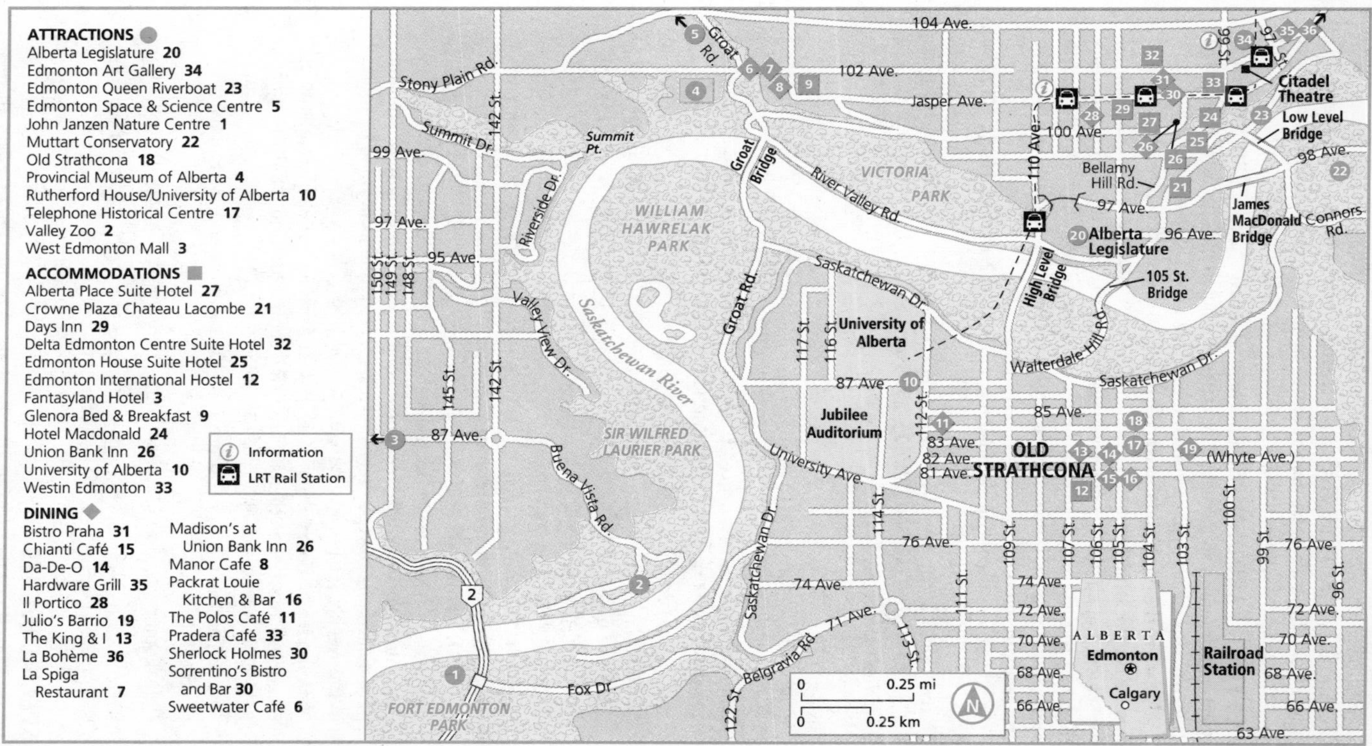
ATTRACTIONS
Alberta Legislature 20
Edmonton Art Gallery 34
Edmonton Queen Riverboat 23
Edmonton Space & Science Centre 5
John Janzen Nature Centre 1
Muttart Conservatory 22
Old Strathcona 18
Provincial Museum of Alberta 4
Rutherford House/University of Alberta 10
Telephone Historical Centre 17
Valley Zoo 2
West Edmonton Mall 3
ACCOMMODATIONS
Alberta Place Suite Hotel 27
Crowne Plaza Chateau Lacombe 21
Days Inn 29
Delta Edmonton Centre Suite Hotel 32
Edmonton House Suite Hotel 25
Edmonton International Hostel 12
Fantasyland Hotel 3
Glenora Bed & Breakfast 9
Hotel Macdonald 24
Union Bank Inn 26
University of Alberta 10
Westin Edmonton 33
DINING
Bistro Praha 31
Chianti Café 15
Da-De-O 14
Hardware Grill 35
Il Portico 28
Julio's Barrio 19
The King & I 13
La Bohème 36
La Spiga Restaurant 7
Madison's at Union Bank Inn 26
Manor Cafe 8
Packrat Louie Kitchen & Bar 16
The Polos Café 11
Pradera Café 33
Sherlock Holmes 30
Sorrentino's Bistro and Bar 30
Sweetwater Café 6
Information
LRT Rail Station
104 Ave.
102 Ave.
Jasper Ave.
100 Ave.
110 Ave.
Stony Plain Rd.
Groat Rd.
Summit Dr.
Summit Pt.
99 Ave.
97 Ave.
95 Ave.
Riverside Dr.
Valley View Dr.
Buena Vista Rd.
87 Ave.
150 St.
149 St.
148 St.
145 St.
142 St.
WILLIAM HAWRELAK PARK
Saskatchewan River
SIR WILFRED LAURIER PARK
FORT EDMONTON PARK
Fox Dr.
Groat Bridge
River Valley Rd.
VICTORIA PARK
Saskatchewan Dr.
University of Alberta
117 St.
116 St.
Jubilee Auditorium
112 St.
University Ave.
114 St.
111 St.
113 St.
71 Ave.
Belgravia Rd.
122 St.
74 Ave.
76 Ave.
85 Ave.
83 Ave.
82 Ave.
81 Ave.
OLD STRATHCONA
(Whyte Ave.)
109 St.
107 St.
106 St.
105 St.
104 St.
103 St.
100 St.
99 St.
96 St.
72 Ave.
70 Ave.
68 Ave.
66 Ave.
63 Ave.
ALBERTA
Edmonton
Calgary
Railroad Station
0 0.25 mi
0 0.25 km
High Level Bridge
Walterdale Hill Rd.
105 St. Bridge
Alberta Legislature
96 Ave.
Bellamy Hill Rd.
James MacDonald Bridge
Connors Rd.
98 Ave.
Low Level Bridge
Citadel Theatre
97 St.

West of downtown Edmonton, Jasper Avenue shifts and twists to eventually become Stony Plain Road, which passes near **West Edmonton Mall,** the world's largest shopping and entertainment center, before merging with Highway 16 on its way to Jasper National Park.

**GETTING AROUND** **Edmonton Transit** (© **780/496-1611;** www.gov.edmonton.ab.ca/transit) operates the buses and the LRT (Light Rail Transit). This electric rail service connects downtown Edmonton with Northlands Park to the north and the University of Alberta to the south. The LRT and buses have the same fares: C$1.75 (US$1.10) for adults and C$1.25 (US80¢) for seniors and children; a day pass goes for C$6 (US$3.70). You can transfer from one to the other at any station on the same ticket. On weekdays 9am to 3pm, downtown LRT travel is free between Churchill, Central, Bay, Corona, and Grandin stations.

In addition to the following downtown locations, **National,** 10133 100A St. NW., (© 780/422-6097;); **Budget,** 10016 106th St. (© 780/448-2000); and **Hertz,** 10815 Jasper Ave. (© 780/423-3431), each has a bureau at the airport.

Call **CO-OP Taxi** (© **780/425-2525** or 780/425-8310) for a ride in a driver/owner-operated cab.

## *FAST FACTS:* Edmonton

*American Express* The office at 10180 101st St., at 102nd Avenue (© **780/421-0608;** LRT: Corona), is open Monday to Friday from 9am to 5pm.

*Area Code* Edmonton's area code is © **780.**

*Doctors* If you need nonemergency medical care while in Edmonton, check the phone book for the closest branch of **Medicentre,** which offers walk-in medical services daily.

*Emergency* For fire, medical, or crime emergencies, dial © **911.**

*Hospitals* The closest hospital with emergency service to downtown Edmonton is the **Royal Alexandra Hospital,** 10240 Kingsway Ave. (© **780/477-4111;** bus: 9).

*Newspapers* The *Edmonton Journal* (www.edmontonjournal.com) and *Edmonton Sun* (www.fyiedmonton.com/htdocs/edmsun.shtml) are the local daily papers. Arts, entertainment, and nightlife listings can be found in the weekly *See* (www.greatwest.ca/see).

*Pharmacies* **Shoppers Drug Mart** has more than a dozen locations in Edmonton, most open till midnight. One central location is 8210 109th St. (© **780/433-2424;** bus 6).

*Post Office* The main post office is at 103A Avenue and 99th Street (LRT: Churchill).

*Time* Edmonton is on Mountain Time, the same as Calgary, Denver, and Phoenix.

## SPECIAL EVENTS

While **Klondike Days** (see box) is Edmonton's most famous event, there are other occasions to entice you to this city. The citywide **Jazz City International**

**Music Festival** (✆ **780/432-7166;** www.discoveredmonton.com/JazzCity) takes over most music venues in Edmonton during the last week of June and first week of July.

The **Edmonton Folk Music Festival** (✆ **780/429-1899;** www.efmf.ab.ca) is the largest folk-music festival in North America. Held in mid-August, it brings in musicians from around the world, from the Celtic north to Indonesia, plus major rock stars playing "unplugged." All concerts are held outdoors.

For 10 days in mid-August, Old Strathcona is transformed into a series of stages for the renowned **Fringe Theatre Festival** (✆ **780/448-9000;** www.fringe.alberta.com/fta). Only Edinburgh's fringe festival is larger than Edmonton's—more than 60 troupes attend from around the world.

## EXPLORING THE CITY

### THE TOP ATTRACTIONS

**Old Strathcona** ★★ This historic district used to be a separate township, but was amalgamated with Edmonton in 1912 and still contains some of the best-preserved landmarks in the city. It's best seen on foot, guided by the brochures given out at the **Old Strathcona Foundation,** 10324 82nd Ave., fourth floor (✆ **780/433-5866**). It's easy to spend an afternoon here, just wandering the shops, sitting at street-side cafes, and people watching. This is hipster-central for Edmonton, where students, artists, and the city's alternative community come to hang out. Be sure to stop by the **Old Strathcona Farmers Market** (✆ **780/439-1844**), at 83rd Avenue and 103rd Street, an open-air market with fresh produce, baked goods, and local crafts. It's open Saturday year-round, plus Tuesday and Thursday afternoons in summer.

Around 82nd Ave., between 103rd and 105th sts. Bus: 46 from downtown.

**Provincial Museum of Alberta** ★★ *Kids* Expertly laid out, this 18,500m$^2$ (200,000-sq.-foot) modern museum displays Alberta's natural and human history in three permanent galleries. The Habitat Groups show wildlife in astonishingly lifelike dioramas; these picture windows into Alberta's diverse ecosystems are sure to captivate the kids and have adults marveling at the trompe-l'oeil paint job. The redesigned Aboriginal Peoples Gallery tells the 11,000-year story of Alberta's native inhabitants, incorporating artifacts, film, interactive media, and native interpreters; it's one of Canada's foremost exhibits on native culture. The Natural History Gallery has fossils, minerals, and a live-bug room.

12845 102nd Ave. ✆ **780/453-9100.** Fax 780/454-6629. www.pma.edmonton.ab.ca. Admission C$8 (US$5) adults, C$6.50 (US$4) seniors, C$4.50 (US$2.80) children, C$20 (US$12) families; children under 7 free; Tues are half-price. Daily 9am–5pm. Bus: 1.

**West Edmonton Mall** You won't find many shopping malls mentioned in this book, but the West Edmonton Mall is something else. Although it contains 800 stores and services, including 90 eateries, it looks and sounds more like a large slice of Disneyland that has somehow broken loose and drifted north. The locals modestly call it the "Eighth Wonder of the World." More theme park than mall, it encompasses 480,000m$^2$ (5.2 million sq. ft.), and houses the world's largest indoor amusement park, including a titanic roller coaster, bungee-jumping platform, and enclosed wave-lake, complete with beach and enough artificial waves to ride a surfboard on. It has walk-through bird aviaries, a huge ice-skating palace, 19 (count them, 19) movie theaters, a lagoon with

## Edmonton's Klondike Days

The gold rush that sent an army of prospectors heading for the Yukon in 1898 put Edmonton "on the map," as they say. Although the actual goldfields lay 2,400km (1,500 miles) to the north, this little settlement became a giant supply store, resting place, and "recreation" ground for thousands of men who stopped here before tackling the hazards of the Klondike Trail, which led overland to Dawson City in the Yukon. Edmonton's population quickly doubled in size, and its merchants, saloonkeepers, and ladies of easy virtue grew rich in the process.

Since 1962, Edmonton has commemorated the event with one of the greatest and most colorful extravaganzas staged in Canada. The Klondike Days are held annually in late July, with street festivities and the great Klondike Days Exposition at Northlands Park lasting 10 days.

Locals and visitors dress up in period costumes, street corners blossom with impromptu stages featuring anything from country bands to cancan girls, stagecoaches rattle through the streets, and parades and floats wind from block to block.

The 16,000-seat Coliseum holds nightly spectacles of rock, pop, variety, or western entertainment. Northlands Park turns into Klondike Village, complete with the Chilkoot Gold Mine, Silver Slipper Saloon, and gambling casino—legal for this occasion only. The Walterdale Playhouse drops serious stage endeavors for a moment and puts on hilarious melodramas with mustachioed villains to hiss and dashing heroes to cheer.

Immense "Klondike breakfasts" are served in the open air, marching bands compete in the streets, and down the North Saskatchewan River float more than 100 of the weirdest-looking home-built rafts ever seen, competing in the "World Championship Sourdough River Raft Race."

For more information, contact **Klondike Days** (© **888/800-PARK** or 780/471-7210; www.klondikedays.com).

performing dolphins, and several absolutely fabulous adventure rides (one of them by submarine to the "ocean floor"). In the middle of it all, an immense fountain with 19 computer-controlled jets weaves and dances in a musical performance.

Of course, you can shop here, too, and some of Edmonton's most popular restaurants are located in the mall. On Saturdays at 2pm, you can even tour the rooms at the mall's excellent "theme" hotel, called Fantasyland. Roll your eyes all you want, but do go. You have to see the West Edmonton Mall to believe it.
8882 170th St. © **800/661-8890** or 780/444-5200. www.westedmontonmall.com. Bus: 10

**Fort Edmonton Park** ★ *Kids* Fort Edmonton Park is a complex of townscapes that reconstruct various eras of Edmonton's history. Perhaps most interesting is the complete reconstruction of the old Fort Edmonton fur trading post from the turn of the 18th century. This vast wooden structure is a warren of rooms and activities: Blacksmiths, bakers, and other docents ply their trades. On 1885 Street, you'll see Frontier Edmonton, complete with blacksmith, saloon, general store, and Jasper House Hotel, which serves hearty pioneer meals. On 1920 Street, sip an old-fashioned ice-cream soda at Bill's confectionery. You can ride streetcar no. 1, a stagecoach, or a steam locomotive between the various streets. As an open-air museum, the park is very impressive; the variety of activities and services here make this a great family destination.

On Whitemud Dr. at Fox Dr. ✆ **780/496-8787.** www.gov.edmonton.ab.ca/fort. Admission C$7.25 (US$4.50) adults, C$5.25 (US$3.25) seniors and youths, C$3.75 (US$2.30) children, C$22 (US$14) families. Open mid-May to late June Mon–Fri 10am–4pm, Sat–Sun 10am–6pm; late June to early Sept daily 10am–6pm. LRT to University Station, then bus 32.

**Muttart Conservatory** The conservatory, in four pavilions that look like I. M. Pei pyramids, houses one of the finest floral displays in North America. Each pyramid contains a different climatic zone—the tropical one has an 5.5m (18-foot) waterfall. The Arid Pavilion has desert air and shows flowering cacti and their relatives. The temperate zone includes a cross section of plants from this global region. The fourth pyramid features changing ornamental displays of plants and blossoms; an orchid greenhouse has newly opened. For good measure, there's also the Treehouse Cafe.

Off James MacDonald Bridge at 98th Ave. and 96A St. ✆ **780/496-8755.** www.gov.Edmonton.ab.ca/muttart. Admission C$5 (US$3.10) adults, C$4 (US$2.50) seniors/youths, C$2.50 (US$1.55) children. Mon–Fri 9am–6pm, Sat–Sun and holidays 11am–6pm. Bus: 51.

**Edmonton Queen Riverboat** Moored just outside the convention center, this riverboat plies the North Saskatchewan River as it runs through the city's many parks. A number of packages are offered, usually the cruise itself or a meal package that includes lunch or dinner.

9734 98th Ave. ✆ **780/424-2628.** Cruise only C$15 (US$9); meal packages C$50 (US$31). Call for hours. Bus: 12, 45.

## MORE ATTRACTIONS

**Alberta Legislature Building** The Alberta Legislature rises on the site of the early trading post from which the city grew. Surrounded by lovingly manicured lawns, formal gardens, and greenhouses, it overlooks the river valley. The seat of Alberta's government was completed in 1912; it's a stately Edwardian structure open to the public throughout the year. Free conducted tours tell you about the functions of provincial lawmaking: who does what, where, and for how long.

109th St. and 97th Ave. ✆ **780/427-7362.** www.assembly.ab.ca. Free tours daily every hour 9am–4pm, Sat–Sun and holidays noon–5pm. LRT: Grandin.

**Edmonton Art Gallery** The Edmonton Art Gallery occupies a stately building in the heart of downtown, east of City Hall. The interior, however, is state-of-the-art modern, subtly lit, and expertly arranged. Exhibits consist partly of contemporary Canadian art, partly of international contemporary art, partly of changing works on tour from every corner of the globe. The Gallery shop sells an eclectic array of items, from art books to handmade yo-yos.

2 Sir Winston Churchill Sq. ✆ **780/422-6223.** www.eag.org. Admission C$5 (US$3.10) adults, C$3 (US$1.85) seniors/students C$2 (US$1.20) children 6–12; children under 6 free. Mon–Wed 10:30am–5pm, Thurs–Fri 10:30am–8pm, Sat–Sun and holidays 11am–5pm. LRT: Churchill.

**Rutherford House** The home of Alberta's first premier, Alexander Rutherford, this lovingly preserved Edwardian gleams with polished silver- and gilt-framed oils. Around 1915, this mansion was the magnet for the social elite of the province: Today, guides dressed in period costumes convey some of the spirit of the times. There's also a charming restaurant/tearoom, the **Arbour** (✆ **780/422-2697**), open daily from 11:30am to 4pm.

11153 Saskatchewan Dr., on the campus of the University of Alberta. ✆ **780/427-3995.** Admission C$3 (US$1.85) adults, C$2 (US$1.20) seniors/youths, C$8 (US$5) families. Summer daily 9am–5pm; winter Tues–Sun noon–5pm. LRT: University.

**Telephone Historical Centre** North America's largest museum devoted to the history of telecommunications is located in the 1912 Telephone Exchange Building. Multimedia displays tell the history of words over wire and hints at what your modem will get up to next.

10437 83rd Ave. ✆ **780/433-1010.** www.telephonehistoricalcentre.com. Admission C$3 (US$1.85) adults, C$2 (US$1.20) children, C$5 (US$3.10) families. Tues–Fri 10am–4pm, Sat noon–4pm. Bus: 44.

## ESPECIALLY FOR KIDS

**Odyssium** ★ *Kids* This is one of the most advanced facilities of its kind in the world. It contains, among other wonders, an **IMAX theater** (✆ **780/493-4250**), the largest planetarium theater in Canada, high-tech exhibits (including a virtual-reality showcase and a display on robotics), and an observatory open on clear afternoons and evenings. New exhibits include a journey through the human body (including the Gallery of the Gross!) and Mystery Avenue, where young sleuths can collect clues at a crime scene, then analyze them at a crime lab.

11211 142nd St., Coronation Park. ✆ **780/451-3344.** www.odyssium.com. Admission C$9.95 (US$6) adults, C$7.95 (US$5) seniors/youths, C$6.95 (US$4.30) children 3–12, C$38.95 (US$24) families. Summer daily 10am–9pm, winter Sun–Thurs and holidays 10am–5pm, Fri–Sat 10am–9pm. Bus: 17 or 22. Free parking.

**Valley Zoo** *Kids* In this charming combination of reality and fantasy, real live animals mingle with fairy-tale creations. More than 500 animals and birds are neighbors to the Three Little Pigs, Humpty Dumpty, and the inhabitants of Noah's Ark.

In Laurier Park, 13315 Buena Vista Rd. ✆ **780/496-6911.** Admission C$5.75 (US$3.55) adults, C$4.25 (US$2.65) seniors/youths, C$3.25 (US$2) children under 13, C$18 (US$11) families. Summer daily 9:30am–8pm; winter daily 9:30am–4pm. Bus: 12.

## SHOPPING

There are more shops per capita in Edmonton than in any other city in Canada. Go for it! See "The Top Attractions," above, for the **West Edmonton Mall.**

**DOWNTOWN** Most of downtown's shops are in a few large mall complexes; all are linked by the Pedway system, which gives pedestrians protection from summer heat and winter cold. **Edmonton Centre** has 140 stores and shares the block with the Hudson's Bay Company. **Eaton Centre** contains over 100 stores, including the flagship Eatons. All face 102nd Avenue, between 103rd and 100th streets.

**OLD STRATHCONA** If you don't like mall shopping, then wandering the galleries and boutiques along **Whyte Avenue** might be more your style. About the only part of Edmonton that retains any historic structures, Old Strathcona is trend-central for students and bohemians. Shop for antiques, gifts, books, and crafts. Be sure to stop by the **Farmers Market** at 103rd Street and 102nd Avenue.

**HIGH STREET** This small district, which runs from 102nd to 109th avenues along 124th Street, has Edmonton's greatest concentration of art galleries, housewares shops, boutiques, and bookstores. It has great restaurants, too.

## WHERE TO STAY

For B&Bs, try **Alberta and Pacific Bed and Breakfast** (✆ **604/944-1793;** fax 604/552-1659) or the **Alberta Bed and Breakfast Association** (www.bbalberta.com). Note that accommodations are scarce during Klondike Days.

### EXPENSIVE

**Delta Edmonton Centre Suite Hotel** ★ This all-suite establishment forms part of the upscale Eaton Centre in the heart of downtown. Without having to stir out of doors, you can access 140 shops in the mall, plus movie theaters and an indoor putting green. Four other malls are connected to the hotel via Pedway. Three-quarters of the windows look into the mall, so you can stand behind the tinted one-way glass (in your pajamas, if you like) and watch the shopping action outside. Most units are deluxe executive suites, each with a large sitting area (with TV and wet bar) and separate bedroom (with another TV and a plate-glass wall looking into the mall). If you need lots of room, or have work to do in Edmonton, these very spacious rooms are just the ticket. The entire hotel was renovated in 2001.

Eaton Centre, 10222 102nd St., Edmonton, AB, T5J 4C5. ✆ **780/429-3900.** Fax 780/428-1566. www.deltahotels.com. 169 units. C$132–C$250 (US$82–US$155) standard business suite, C$218 (US$135) deluxe executive suite. Ask about summer family discounts, weekend packages, and special rates for business travelers. AE, DC, MC, V. Parking C$10 (US$6) per day; valet parking C$13 (US$8) per day. **Amenities:** Restaurant, bar; exercise room; Jacuzzi; sauna; children's center; concierge; business center; limited room service; babysitting; coin-op laundry and laundry service; same-day dry cleaning. *In room:* A/C, TV w/pay movies, dataport, iron, minibar, coffeemaker, hair dryer.

**Fantasyland Hotel** ★ From the outside, this solemn tower at the end of the huge West Ed Mall reveals little of the wildly decorated rooms found within. Fantasyland is a cross between a hotel and Las Vegas: It contains a total of 116 themed rooms decorated in nine different styles (as well as 238 large, well-furnished regular rooms). Theme rooms aren't just a matter of subtle touches; these units are exceedingly clever, very comfortable, and way over the top. Take the Truck Room: Your bed is located in the back end of a real pickup, the pickup's bench seats fold down into a child's bed, and the lights on the vanity are real stoplights. In the Igloo Room, a round bed is encased in a shell that looks like ice blocks; statues of sled dogs keep you company, and the walls are painted with amazingly lifelike arctic murals. The dogsleds even become beds for children. The themes continue, through the Canadian Rail Room (train berths for beds), the African Room, and more. All theme rooms come with immense four-person Jacuzzis and plenty of amenities. The hotel offers tours of the different theme types on Saturdays at 2pm.

It's not all fantasy here, though. The non-theme rooms are divided into superior rooms, with either a king or two queen beds, and executive rooms, with a king bed and Jacuzzi. The hotel's restaurant is quite good; of course, you have all-weather access to the world's largest mall and its many eateries as well.

17700 87th Ave., Edmonton, AB, T5T 4V4. ✆ **800/737-3783** or 780/444-3000. Fax 780/444-3294. www.fantasylandhotel.com. 355 units. C$175–C$305 (US$109–US$189) double. Extra person C$10 (US$6). Weekend and off-season packages available. AE, MC, V. Free parking. **Amenities:** Restaurant, bar; exercise room; concierge; 24-hour room service; babysitting; laundry service; same-day dry cleaning. *In room:* A/C, TV w/pay movies, fax, dataport, fridge, coffeemaker, hair dryer, iron.

**Hotel Macdonald** ★★★ From the outside, with its limestone facade and gargoyles, the Mac looks like a feudal château—right down to the kilted staff. High ceilings and crystal chandeliers grace the lobby. The Library Bar resembles an Edwardian gentlemen's club, while the Harvest Room offers panoramic views of the valley as well as a garden terrace for summer dining.

The palatial Hotel Macdonald opened in 1915. After a long and colorful career, it was bought by the Canadian Pacific chain in 1988. What ensued was a masterwork of sensitive renovation and restoration. The guest rooms were completely rebuilt to modern luxury standards, while retaining all of their original charm. Signature elements like the deep tubs, brass doorplates, and paneled doors were kept intact, while important additions like new plumbing were installed. Rooms are beautifully furnished with amazingly comfortable beds, luxurious upholstery, feather duvets and pillows, and a bin for recyclables—a thoughtful touch. Even pets, which are welcome, get special treatment: a gift bag of treats and a map of pet-friendly parks. Needless to say, there aren't many hotels like this in Edmonton, or in Canada for that matter.

10065 100th St., Edmonton, AB, T5J 0N6. ✆ **800/441-1414** or 780/424-5181. Fax 780/429-6481. www.fairmont.com. 198 units. High season C$249–C$269 (US$154–US$167) deluxe standard room, C$289–C$309 (US$179–US$192) premier suite, C$369–C$389 (US$229–US$241) executive suite, C$429–C$449 (US$266–US$278) specialty suite. Weekend and off-season discounts available. AE, DC, DISC, MC, V. Parking C$15 (US$9) per day. **Amenities:** Restaurant, lounge; indoor pool; health club and spa; concierge; business center; 24-hour room service; babysitting; laundry service; same-day dry cleaning; concierge-level rooms. *In room:* A/C, TV/VCR w/pay movies, dataport, minibar, coffeemaker, hair dryer, iron.

**Westin Edmonton** ★ Located in the heart of the downtown shopping and entertainment district, this modern hotel offers some of the city's largest rooms. Although the lobby is a bit austere, the guest rooms are very comfortably furnished. For an extra C$20 (US$13), business travelers can request a Westin Guest Office room, which comes with a printer and fax. Guests frequent one of two restaurants, including Pradera, one of Edmonton's most inventive establishments (see "Where to Dine," below).

10135 100th St., Edmonton, AB, T5J 0N7. ✆ **800/228-3000** or 780/426-3636. Fax 780/428-1454. www.westin.ab.ca. 413 units. From C$225 (US$140) double. AE, DC, DISC, MC, V. Parking C$14 (US$9) per day, valet parking C$17 (US$11) per day. **Amenities:** 2 restaurants, lounge; indoor pool; exercise room; Jacuzzi; sauna; concierge; business center; room service; babysitting; laundry service. *In room:* A/C, TV, dataport, minibar, fridge, coffeemaker, hair dryer, iron.

### MODERATE

**Alberta Place Suite Hotel** This downtown apartment hotel is an excellent choice for travelers who need extra space or for families who want full cooking facilities. The apartments, of various sizes, are very well furnished and comfortable. The hotel is located half a block from public transport, and is within easy walking distance of most business and government centers.

10049 103rd St., Edmonton, AB, T5J 2W7. ✆ **800/661-3982** or 780/423-1565. Fax 780/426-6260. www.albertaplace.com. 86 units. C$123–C$158 (US$76–US$98) double. Extra person C$8 (US$5). Children 16 and under stay free in parents' room. AE, DC, MC, V. Free parking. **Amenities:** Indoor pool; exercise room; Jacuzzi; sauna; coin-op laundry. *In room:* A/C, TV, dataport, fridge, coffeemaker, hair dryer.

**Crowne Plaza Chateau Lacombe** Centrally located downtown, the Crowne Plaza, a round 24-story tower sitting on the edge of a cliff overlooking the North Saskatchewan River, possesses some of the city's best views. The unusual design blends well with the dramatic skyline, yet it's instantly recognizable from afar—a perfect landmark. The nicely furnished rooms and suites aren't huge, though the wedge-shaped design necessitates that they are broadest toward the windows, where you'll spend time looking over the city. Two private executive floors, nonsmoking floors, and wheelchair-accessible rooms are available.

10111 Bellamy Hill, Edmonton, AB, T5J 1N7. ✆ **800/661-8801** or 780/428-6611. Fax 780/425-6564. www.chateaulacombe.com. 307 units. C$139 (US$86) double, C$185–C$350 (US$115–US$217) suite. Extra person C$15 (US$9). Weekend packages available. AE, DC, MC, V. Parking C$8 (US$5) per day. **Amenities:** Revolving restaurant, lounge; exercise room; business center; room service; babysitting; laundry service; nonsmoking rooms. *In room:* A/C, TV, dataport, coffeemaker, hair dryer, iron.

**Edmonton House Suite Hotel** ★ This is a great alternative to pricier downtown hotels: The rooms are big and well decorated, and you don't have to pay stiff parking fees. With a great location right above the North Saskatchewan River, the all-suite hotel has one of the best views in Edmonton. Each suite comes with a full kitchen and dining area, bedroom, separate sitting area with foldout couch, balcony, and two phones. Edmonton House is within easy walking distance of most downtown office areas and to public transport.

10205 100th Ave., Edmonton, AB, T5J 4B5. ✆ **800/661-6562** or 780/420-4000. Fax 780/420-4008. www.edmontonhouse.com. 305 units. C$165 (US$102) 1-bedroom suite. Extra person C$15 (US$9). Weekend packages and weekly/monthly rates available. AE, DC, MC, V. Free parking. **Amenities:** Restaurant, lounge; indoor pool; exercise room; business center; room service. *In room:* TV, dataport, kitchens, fridge, microwave, coffeemaker, hair dryer, iron.

**Glenora Bed & Breakfast** ★ Located in the heart of the High Street district, just west of downtown, the Glenora occupies the upper floors of a 1912 heritage boardinghouse. There's an array of room types, from simple units with a mix of shared and private bathrooms to studios, suites, and rooms that are best thought of as apartments, with full kitchens. All are pleasantly furnished with period antiques and rich designer fabrics. A deluxe continental breakfast is served.

12327 102nd Ave. NW, Edmonton, AB, T5N 0I8. ✆ **780/488-6766.** Fax 780/488-5168. www.glenorabnb.com. 18 units. C$70–C$140 (US$43–US$87) double. Rates include breakfast. AE, MC, V. **Amenities:** Restaurant, bar; access to nearby health club; coin-op laundry. *In room:* TV/VCR, dataport, minibar, coffeemaker, hair dryer, iron.

**Union Bank Inn** ★★ If you're weary of anonymous corporate hotels, this is a wonderful choice. The stylish Union Bank, built in 1910, now houses an elegant restaurant and intimate boutique hotel. The owner asked Edmonton's top interior designers to each design a room. The results are charming, with each unique guest room displaying its own style, colors, furniture, and fabrics. All units, however, have the same amenities, including fireplaces, voice mail, feather duvets, and nice toiletries. Joining the original inn are 14 rooms in a new addition—each equally idiosyncratic and uniquely designed. The older rooms vary in layout and aren't incredibly big; if you're in town with work to do, ask for one of the newer and larger units. Service is very friendly and professional. The restaurant/bar, Madison's, is a great place to meet friends (see "Where to Dine," below).

10053 Jasper Ave., Edmonton, AB, T5J 1S5. ✆ **780/423-3600.** Fax 780/423-4623. www.unionbankinn.com. 34 units. C$129–C$259 (US$80–US$161) double. Rates include full breakfast. AE, DC, MC, V. Free parking. **Amenities:** Restaurant, bar; exercise room; access to nearby health club; business center; room service; same-day dry cleaning. *In room:* A/C, TV, dataport, fridge, hair dryer, iron.

### INEXPENSIVE

**Days Inn** *Value* For the price, this is one of downtown Edmonton's best deals. Located just 5 minutes from the city center, the motor inn has everything you need for a pleasant stay, including comfortably furnished rooms and easy access to public transport. If all you need for a night or two is a clean and basic room in a convenient location, this is a top choice.

10041 106th St., Edmonton, AB, T5J 1G3. ✆ **800/267-2191** or 780/423-1925. Fax 780/424-5302. www.daysinn.com. 76 units. C$59–C$89 (US$37–US$55) double. Children 11 and under stay free in parents' room. Senior, AAA, and corporate discounts available. AE, DC, DISC, MC, V. Free parking. **Amenities:** Restaurant, bar; limited room service; babysitting; coin-op laundry; same-day dry cleaning. *In room:* A/C, TV, dataport, coffeemaker, hair dryer, iron.

**Edmonton International Hostel** Well-located near the university in the lively Old Strathcona neighborhood, this pleasant hostel has shared kitchen facilities and spacious common rooms. Some family rooms are available and check in is 3pm.

10647 81st Ave. ✆ **780/988-6836.** Fax 780/988-8698. www.hihostels.ca. 88 beds. Members C$18–C$23 (US$11–US$14), nonmembers C$20–C$25 (US$12–US$16).MC, V. **Amenities:** Self-catering kitchen; coin-op laundry; bike rental.

**University of Alberta** In summer, 1,200 dormitory rooms in Lister Hall at the University of Alberta are thrown open to visitors. Most are standard bathroom-down-the-hall dorm rooms for C$30 (US$19). Available year-round are guest suites, which are two-bed dorms that share a bathroom with only one other suite, costing C$40 (US$25). The university is right on the LRT line and not far from trendy Old Strathcona.

87th Avenue and 116th Street. ✆ **780/492-4281.** Fax 780/492-7032. www.hfs.ualberta.ca. C$30–C$40 (US$19–US$25). MC, V. Parking C$3 (US$1.85) per day. **Amenities:** Food service nearby; coin-up laundry.

## WHERE TO DINE

Edmonton has a vigorous dining scene, with lots of hip new eateries joining traditional steak and seafood restaurants. In general, fine dining is found downtown and on High Street, close to the centers of politics and business. Over in Old Strathcona, south of the river, are trendy—and less expensive—cafes and bistros.

### DOWNTOWN

#### Expensive

**Hardware Grill** ★★ NEW CANADIAN Housed in a historic building that was once Edmonton's original hardware store, this is easily one of the city's most exciting restaurants. The building may be historic, but there's nothing antique about the dining room. Postmodern without being stark, the room is edged with glass partitions, with exposed pipes and ducts painted a smoky rose. The menu here reflects new cooking styles and regional ingredients. There are as many appetizers as entree selections, making it tempting to graze through a series of smaller dishes. Bison carpaccio is served with Quebec Migneron cheese, wild-mushroom ragout spills over grilled polenta, and duck "pastrami" comes with summer greens and Saskatoon berries. But it's hard to resist entrees like grilled lamb loin with pea-mint sauce, house-made duck sausage, or braised buffalo ribs with black coffee barbecue sauce. The wine list is extensive.

9698 Jasper Ave. ✆ **780/423-0969.** www.hardwaregrill.com. Reservations suggested. Main courses C$24–C$37 (US$15–US$23). AE, DC, MC, V. Mon–Fri 11:30am–2pm; Mon–Thurs 5–9:30pm, Fri–Sat 5–10pm. Closed first week of July.

**La Bohème** FRENCH La Bohème consists of two small, lace-curtained dining rooms in a historic building northeast of downtown (at the turn of the 20th century, this structure was a luxury apartment building—the upper floors are now available as B&B accommodations). The cuisine is French, of course, and so is the wine selection, with a particular accent on Rhône Valley vintages. There's a wide selection of appetizers and light dishes, including a number of intriguing salads. The entrees are hearty, classically French preparations of lamb, chicken, and seafood. The restaurant also features daily changing vegetarian entrees. Desserts are outstanding.

6427 112th Ave. ✆ **780/474-5693.** Reservations required. Main courses C$15–C$29 (US$9–US$18). AE, MC, V. Mon–Sat 11am–3pm, Sun 11am–3:30pm; daily 5–11pm.

**Madison's at Union Bank Inn** ★ NEW CANADIAN One of the loveliest dining rooms and casual cocktail bars in Edmonton is Madison's. Once an early-20th-century bank, the formal architectural details remain, but they share the light and airy space with modern art, avant-garde furniture, and excellent food. The menu is up-to-date, with grilled and roast fish and meats, pasta dishes, interesting salads (one special featured rose petals, baby lettuce, and shaved white chocolate), and several daily specials. Many entrees boast an international touch, such as prawns with cilantro and tequila lime cream served over pasta.

10053 Jasper Ave. ✆ **780/423-3600.** Reservations suggested. Main courses C$14–C$27 (US$9–US$17). AE, MC, V. Mon–Thurs 7–10am, 11am–2pm, 5–10pm; Fri 7–10am, 11am–2pm, 5–11pm; Sat 5–11pm; Sun 5–8pm.

**Pradera Cafe & Lounge** ★ INTERNATIONAL One of downtown's most inventive restaurants is Pradera, featuring creative fusion cooking. The menu free-associates across several cuisines, notably French, Italian, and Canadian, to arrive at new dishes that succeed at being more than just the sum of their parts. Ostrich medallions are served with a chive and local mushroom sauce, salmon is pan-seared with peppercorns and mustard seeds, and raviolis come stuffed with veal and truffled fennel. Service is excellent.

In the Westin Edmonton, 10135 100th St. ✆ **780/426-3636.** Fax 780/428-1454. Reservations recommended. Main courses C$18–C$30 (US$11–US$19). AE, DC, DISC, MC, V. Mon–Fri 6:30am–2pm, Sat–Sun 7am–2pm; daily 5–11pm.

**Sorrentino's Bistro and Bar** ITALIAN This upscale branch of a local chain of Italian restaurants is a good addition to the downtown scene. The coolly sophisticated dining room and bar—flanked by the Havana Room, where Cuban cigars are available with port and single-malt Scotch—is a popular meeting place for the captains of the city's business and social life. The food is excellent: You can't do better than a plate from the daily appetizer table, which features grilled vegetables, salads, and marinated anchovies. Entrees range from risotto to wood-fired pizza to imaginative choices like tournedos of salmon and scallops, veal and chicken dishes, and several rotisserie specials.

10162 100th St. ✆ **780/424-7500.** www.sorrentinos.com. Reservations suggested. Main courses C$23–C$35 (US$14–US$22). AE, DC, MC, V. Mon–Fri 11:30am–2:30pm, and 5–11pm; Sat 5–11pm.

### Moderate & Inexpensive

**Bistro Praha** CENTRAL EUROPEAN Bistro Praha is one of several side-by-side casual restaurants—all with summer street-side seating—that take up the single block of 100A Street. It's also the best of these restaurants, and features a charming, wood-paneled interior, a mural-covered wall, and very good Eastern European cooking. The menu offers a wide selection of light dishes, convenient for a quick meal or mid-afternoon snack. The entrees center on schnitzels, as well as a wonderful roast goose with sauerkraut. Desserts tend toward fancy, imposing confections like Sacher torte. The clientele here is mainly young, stylish, and cosmopolitan. Service is friendly and relaxed.

10168 100A St. ✆ **780/424-4218.** Reservations recommended on weekends. Main courses C$13–C$18 (US$8–US$11). AE, DC, MC, V. Daily 11:30am–2am.

**Il Portico** ★★ ITALIAN One of the most popular Italian restaurants in town, Il Portico has a wide menu of well-prepared traditional but updated dishes. With excellent selections of grilled meats, pastas, and pizza, it's one of those rare restaurants where you want to try everything. The Caesar salad will remind you how wonderful these salads can be. Service is impeccable, and the wine list one of the best in the city: Remarkably, the staff will open any bottle on the list (except reserve bottles) if you buy a half-liter. The dining room is nicely informal but classy, and in summer there's a lowly Tuscan-style courtyard for al fresco dining.

10012 107th St. ✆ **780/424-0707.** Reservations recommended on weekends. Main courses C$13–C$27 (US$8–US$17). AE, DC, DISC, MC, V. Mon–Fri 11:30am–2pm; Mon–Sat 5:30–11pm.

**Sherlock Holmes** ENGLISH The Sherlock Holmes is a tremendously popular English-style pub with local and regional beers on tap (as well as Guinness) and a very good bar menu. The pub is housed in a charming building with a picket fence around the outdoor patio. The menu has a few traditional English dishes—fish-and-chips, steak-and-kidney pie—but there's a strong emphasis on new pub grub like chicken-breast sandwiches, beef curry, burgers, and salads. There are two other Sherlock Holmeses in Edmonton, one in the West Edmonton Mall and the other in Old Strathcona at 10341 82nd Ave.

10012 101A Ave. ✆ **780/426-7784.** www.thesherlockhomes.com. Main courses C$7–C$13 (US$4.35–US$8). AE, MC, V. Mon–Sat 11:30am–2am, Sun noon–8pm.

## HIGH STREET

**La Spiga Restaurant** ★ ITALIAN La Spiga, located along High Street's gallery row, offers nouveau Italian cooking with an emphasis on fresh, stylish ingredients and unusual tastes and textures. The rack of lamb is marinated in fresh herbs and grappa, while the prawns and scallops are paired with a white-wine lemon sauce and served over angel-hair pasta. The dining room is casual and comfortable, and the service laid-back but astute.

10133 125th St. ✆ **780/482-3100.** Fax 780/488-3225. Reservations recommended on weekends. Main courses C$13–C$23 (US$8–US$14). AE, DC, MC, V. Mon–Fri 11:30am–2pm; Mon–Sat 5–11pm.

**Manor Cafe** ★ INTERNATIONAL Housed in a stately mansion overlooking a park, the Manor Cafe offers one of the most fashionable outdoor dining patios in Edmonton. This longtime Edmonton favorite offers international cuisine, ranging from Italian pastas—Manor Pasta with chicken, spinach, goat cheese and tomato gin cream sauce is the signature dish—to a delicious Moroccan curry to fire-roasted jerk chicken. The food is eclectic, but always delicious.

10109 125th St. ✆ **780/482-7577.** Fax 780/488-7763. www.manorcafe.com. Reservations recommended on weekends. Main courses C$10–C$18 (US$6–US$11). AE, MC, V. Sun–Thurs 11am–11pm, Fri–Sat 11am–midnight.

**Sweetwater Cafe** INTERNATIONAL/SOUTHWESTERN Here's a bright and lively bistro with good, inexpensive food; in summer, you can sit on the charming outdoor deck in the back, thankfully far from the roar of traffic. The food is international but leans towards the southwestern—sandwiches are served in tortillas, and there are several types of quesadillas.

12427 102nd Ave. ✆ **780/488-1959.** Main courses C$5–C$12 (US$3.10–US$7). AE, MC, V. Mon–Thurs 11am–10pm, Fri 11am–midnight, Sat 9am–midnight, Sun 10am–5pm.

## OLD STRATHCONA

**Chianti Cafe** ITALIAN Chianti is a rarity among Italian restaurants: very good and very inexpensive. Pasta dishes begin at C$7 (US$4.50) and run to C$12 (US$7) for fettuccine with scallops, smoked salmon, curry, and garlic; even veal dishes (more than a dozen are offered!) and seafood specials barely top C$15 (US$9). Chianti is located in a handsomely remodeled post-office building; the restaurant isn't a secret, so it can be a busy and fairly crowded experience.

10501 82nd Ave. ✆ **780/439-9829.** Reservations required. Main courses C$7–C$15 (US$4.35–US$9). AE, DC, DISC, MC, V. Sun–Thurs 11am–11pm, Fri–Sat 11am–midnight.

**Da-De-O** CAJUN/SOUTHERN This New Orleans–style diner is authentic right down to the low-tech, juke-box-at-your-table music system. The food is top-notch, with good and goopy po' boy sandwiches, fresh oysters, and five kinds of jambalaya. Especially good is the Louisiana Linguine, with crawfish and clams in basil cream. Relax in a vinyl booth, listen to Billie Holiday, and graze through some crab fritters.

10548A 82nd Ave. ✆ **780/433-0930.** Main courses C$6–C$15 (US$3.70–US$9).AE, MC, V. Mon–Wed 11:30am–11pm, Thurs–Sat 11:30am–midnight, Sun 10am–10pm.

**Julio's Barrio** MEXICAN If you like Mexican food, it's worth a detour to Julio's—in Canada, South of the Border cooking normally takes on quite a different meaning. This Mexican restaurant and watering hole is a great place to snack on several light dishes while quaffing drinks with friends. The food ranges from enchiladas and nachos to sizzling shrimp fajitas. The atmosphere is youthful, high energy, and minimalist-hip: no kitschy piñatas or scratchy recordings of marimba bands here.

10450 82nd Ave. ✆ **780/431-0774.** Main courses C$9–C$19 (US$6–US$12). AE, MC, V. Mon–Wed 11:45am–11pm, Thurs 11:45am–midnight, Fri–Sat noon–1am, Sun noon–11pm.

**The King & I** ★ THAI This is the place for excellent, zesty Thai food, which can be a real treat after the beef-rich cooking of western Canada. Many dishes are vegetarian, almost a novelty in Alberta. Various curries, ranging from mild to sizzling, and rice and noodle dishes are the house specialties. For a real treat, try the lobster in curry sauce with asparagus.

8208 107th St. ✆ **780/433-2222.** Main courses C$12–C$25 (US$7–US$16). AE, MC, V. Mon–Thurs 11:30am–10:30pm, Fri 11:30am–11:30pm, Sat 4:30–11:30pm.

**Packrat Louie Kitchen & Bar** ★★ ITALIAN Bright and lively, this very popular bistro has a somewhat unlikely name, given that it's one of the best casual Italian trattorie in Edmonton. Menu choices range from specialty pizzas to fine entree salads to grilled meats, chicken, and pasta. Most dishes cast an eye toward light or healthy preparations without sacrificing complexity. A grilled chicken breast comes with an arresting mélange of puréed spinach and red bell pepper; grilled lamb chops are garnished simply with plenty of fresh tomatoes, feta cheese, and polenta.

10335 83rd Ave. ✆ **780/433-0123.** Reservations recommended on weekends. Main courses C$8–C$21 (US$5–US$13). MC, V. Tues–Sat 11:30am–11:30pm.

**Polos Café** ★★ ITALIAN/CHINESE/FUSION The Polo in question is Marco Polo, the first European to travel between Italy and China, and the namesake and inspiration for this exciting restaurant. The menu brings together classic Italian and Chinese cooking in a new cuisine loftily hailed as "Orie-ital." And it works: The food here is always delicious. Grilled salmon comes with macadamia nut aioli; Italian pasta and Shanghai noodles are tossed together with a variety of Sino-Italian sauces; pork tenderloin is served with a coconut milk/merlot reduction. The dining room has art-hung mauve walls, cool pools of light, and eager diners. Polos is definitely worth a visit.

8405 112th St. ✆ **780/432-1371.** Reservations suggested. Main courses C$10–C$24 (US$6–US$15). AE, DC, MC, V. Mon–Fri 11am–2:30pm; Mon–Thurs 5–10pm, Fri–Sat 5pm–midnight.

## EDMONTON AFTER DARK

Tickets to most events are available through **Ticketmaster** (✆ **780/451-8000**). For listings of current happenings, check the Friday arts section of the *Edmonton Journal* (www.edmontonjournal.com) or the alternative weekly *See* (www.greatwest.ca/see).

**THE PERFORMING ARTS** A masterpiece of theatrical architecture, the **Citadel Theatre,** 9828 101A Ave. (✆ **780/426-4811;** www.citadeltheatre.com), looks like a gigantic greenhouse and takes up the entire city block adjacent to Sir Winston Churchill Square. It houses five different theaters, workshops and classrooms, a restaurant, and a magnificent indoor garden with a waterfall. The Citadel is one of the largest, busiest theaters in Canada.

Home to the **Edmonton Opera** (✆ **780/424-4040;** www. edmontonopera.com) and the **Alberta Ballet** (✆ **780/428-6839;** www.albertaballet.com), the **Northern Alberta Jubilee Auditorium,** 11455 87th Ave. (✆ **780/ 427-2760;** fax 780/422-3750; www.jubileeauditorium. com), also plays host to traveling dance troupes, Broadway shows, and other acts that require a large stage and excellent acoustics.

**THE CLUB & BAR SCENE** The flashy, upscale country-and-western scene is the name of the game in Edmonton, with new places opening up all the time. However, the hottest country dance bar in town is still the **Cook County Saloon,** 8010 103rd St. (✆ **780/432-2665**).

An Edmonton institution, the **Sidetrack Café** ★, 10333 112th St. (✆ **780/421-1326**), is a hold-over from the '60s, when live music was a way of life. This venerable club on the wrong side of the tracks sees a real variety of bands, from Australian rock to West Coast punk to progressive jazz. For something uniquely Edmonton without the twang, be sure to check out the versatile Sidetrack Café.

It may not look like much (and that's usually a good sign) but the popular **Blues on Whyte,** 10329 82nd Ave. (✆ **780/439-5058**), in the vintage Commercial Hotel in Old Strathcona is Edmonton's best blues club.

The university-area club **Rev,** 10032 102nd St. (✆ **780/424-2745**), is the premier spot for the alternative-music scene. Most bands are local, though national bands also appear here on tour.

Looking for Edmonton's gay and lesbian scene? Start your investigation of the city's lively gay life at **The Roost,** 10345 104th St. (✆ **780/426-3150**), with dancing and cocktails.

## SIDE TRIPS FROM EDMONTON

**Elk Island National Park** ★ One of Canada's most compact and prettiest national parks, Elk Island protects one of Canada's most endangered ecosystems and is the home and roaming ground to North America's largest and smallest mammals—the wood buffalo and the pygmy shrew (a tiny creature half the size of a mouse but with the disposition of a tiger). The park has hiking trails, campgrounds, golf courses, a lake, and a sandy beach.

On the Yellowhead Hwy., 32km (20 miles) east of Edmonton. © **780/992-5790.** www.parcscanada.gc.ca. Admission C$4 (US$2.50) adults, C$3 (US$1.85) seniors, C$2 (US$1.20) youths, or C$8 (US$5) per group.

**Ukrainian Cultural Heritage Village** ★ This open-air museum has 30 restored historic buildings arranged in an authentic setting; the adjacent fields and pastures are planted and harvested according to period techniques. You'll learn what life was like for Ukrainian pioneers in the 1892-to-1930 era through costumed interpreters who re-create the daily activities of the period. The village and interpretive center are definitely worth the drive, especially in midsummer, when you can watch horse-drawn wagons gathering hay and harvesting grain.

25 minutes east of Edmonton on Yellowhead Hwy. 16 © **780/662-3640.** hssuchv@oanet.com It's open daily: May 15 to early September 10am to 6pm and mid-September to mid-October 10am to 4pm. Admission is C$6.50 (US$4) adults, C$5.50 (US$3.40) seniors, and C$3 (US$1.85) children; children under 6 are free, C$15 (US$9) family.

**Reynolds Alberta Museum** Located 40 minutes south of Edmonton off Highway 2, the Reynolds Alberta is a science-and-technology museum with specialties in transport, industry, and agricultural engineering. The collection of vintage cars and period farm equipment is especially impressive, and there are hands-on activities to keep children busy. Adjoining the museum is Canada's Aviation Hall of Fame, with a hangar full of vintage airplanes.

© **800/661-4726** or 780/352-5855. Admission is C$9 (US$6) adults, C$7 (US$4.35) seniors, C$5 (US$3.10) youths 7–17, or C$20 (US$12) families. June–early September, daily 9am–5pm; mid-September to May, Tues–Sun 9am–5pm.

15

# Vancouver

*by Shawn Blore*

If you really want to understand **Vancouver,** stand at the edge of the Inner Harbour (the prow of the Canada Place pavilion makes a good vantage point) and look up: past the float planes taking off over Stanley Park, around the container terminals, over the tony waterfront high rises, and then up the steep green slopes of the north-shore mountains to the twin snowy peaks of the Lions. All this—well, 90% of it anyway—is the result of a unique collaboration between God and the Canadian Pacific Railway (CPR).

It was the Almighty—or Nature (depending on your point of view)—who raised up the Coast range and then sent a glacier slicing along its foot, simultaneously carving out a deep trench and piling up a tall moraine of rock and sand. When the ice retreated, water from the Pacific flowed in and the moraine became a peninsula, flanked on one side by a deep natural harbor and on the other by a river of glacial meltwater. Some 10,000 years later, a CPR surveyor came by; took in the peninsula, the harbor, and the river; and decided he'd found the perfect spot for the railway's new Pacific terminus. He kept it quiet until the company had bought up most of the land around town, and then the railway moved in and set up shop. The city of Vancouver was born.

The resulting boom was pretty small. Though the port did a good business shipping out grain and sawmills and salmon canneries sprang up, the city was too far from the rest of North America for any serious manufacturing. Vancouver became a town of sailors, lumberjacks, and fishers. Cheap draught was a staple; gambling and whoring were the major service industries. And so it remained until the 1980s, when Vancouver decided to host Expo '86, a stunning success. The world came to visit, including many people from the newly emerging tiger economies of Hong Kong, Taiwan, and Malaysia. They looked at the mountains, the ocean, and the price of local real estate and were amazed. Many people moved here and settled new neighborhoods. On the Fraser river delta, the bedroom community of Richmond became a city, with a population more than half Chinese. In older neighborhoods, prices went ballistic, doubling and tripling overnight. And on the railyard-turned-Expo site, 40 new high-rise condo towers began to rise.

Unlike previous immigrants, these newcomers didn't worry about finding work; they made their own, founding financial services, software, international education, engineering, and architectural consulting businesses. A film industry sprang up. Vancouver became a postmodern town of Jags, Beemers, cell phones, and shining residential towers. The newcomers brought a love of dining out, so the steak house and the ubiquitous "Chinese and Canadian" diner gave way to a thousand little places offering sushi and Szechuan, tapas and bami, and, inevitably, fusion.

Working indoors, Vancouverites fell in love with the outdoor activities like mountain biking, windsurfing, kayaking, rock climbing, parasailing, snowboarding, and back-country skiing. When they mastered all these, they began experimenting with new sports, and strange summer-winter combinations were born: skiing-kayaking, mountain-biking snowboarding, and snowshoe-paragliding.

Splints and scrapes aside, folks seemed happy with the new state of affairs. And the rest of the world seemed to agree. *Outside* magazine voted Vancouver one of the 10 best cities in the world to live in. *Condé Nast Traveler* called it one of the 10 best cities to visit. And the World Council of Cities ranked it second only to Geneva for quality of life. Heady stuff, particularly for a spot that less than 20 years ago was derided as the world's biggest mill town. But then again, God—and the Canadian Pacific Railway—works in mysterious ways.

## 1 Essentials

### GETTING THERE

**BY PLANE** **Vancouver International Airport** (www.yvr.ca) is 13km (8 miles) south of downtown on uninhabited Sea Island. Daily direct flights between major U.S. cities and Vancouver are provided by **Air Canada** (© 800/661-3936), **United Airlines** (© 800/241-6522), **American Airlines** (© 800/433-7300), **Continental** (© 800/231-0856), and **Northwest Airlines** (© 800/447-4747). **Tourist Information Kiosks** on Levels 2 and 3 of the Main and International terminals (© **604/276-6101**) are open daily 6:30am to 11:30pm.

**Parking** is available at the airport for both loading passengers and long-term stays (© **604/276-6106**). **Courtesy buses** to the airport hotels are available, and a **shuttle bus** links the Main and International terminals to the South Terminal, where smaller and private aircraft are docked. Drivers heading into Vancouver take the Arthur Laing Bridge, which leads directly into Granville Street, the most direct route to downtown.

The pale-green **YVR Airporter** (© **604/946-8866**) provides bus service to downtown Vancouver's major hotels. It leaves from Level 2 of the Main Terminal every 15 minutes daily 6:30am to 10:30pm and every 30 minutes 10:30pm to 12:15am. The 30-minute ride whisks you up the delta through central Vancouver before taking the Granville Street Bridge into downtown. The one-way fare is C$10 (US$6) for adults, C$8 (US$5) for seniors, and C$5 (US$3.10) for children. The round-trip fare is C$17 (US$11) for adults, C$16 (US$10) for seniors, and C$10 (US$6) for children. Bus service back to the airport leaves from selected downtown hotels every half an hour 5:35am to 10:55pm. Scheduled pickups serve the Bus Station, Four Seasons, Hotel Vancouver, Waterfront Centre Hotel, Georgian Court, Sutton Place, Landmark, and others.

Getting to and from the airport with public transit is a pain. The buses are slow, and you have to transfer at least once to get downtown. The hassle probably isn't worth the savings, but **bus 100** stops at both terminals. At the Granville/West 71st Street stop, get off and transfer to **bus 8** to downtown Vancouver. BC Transit fares are C$1.50 (US95¢) during off-peak hours and C$2.25 (US$1.40) during weekdays up to 6:30pm. But transfers are free in any direction within a 90-minute period.

The average **taxi** fare from the airport to a downtown Vancouver hotel is about C$25 (US$16) plus tip. Nearly 400 taxis service the airport. Most major **car-rental firms** have airport counters and shuttles. Make advance reservations

# Greater Vancouver

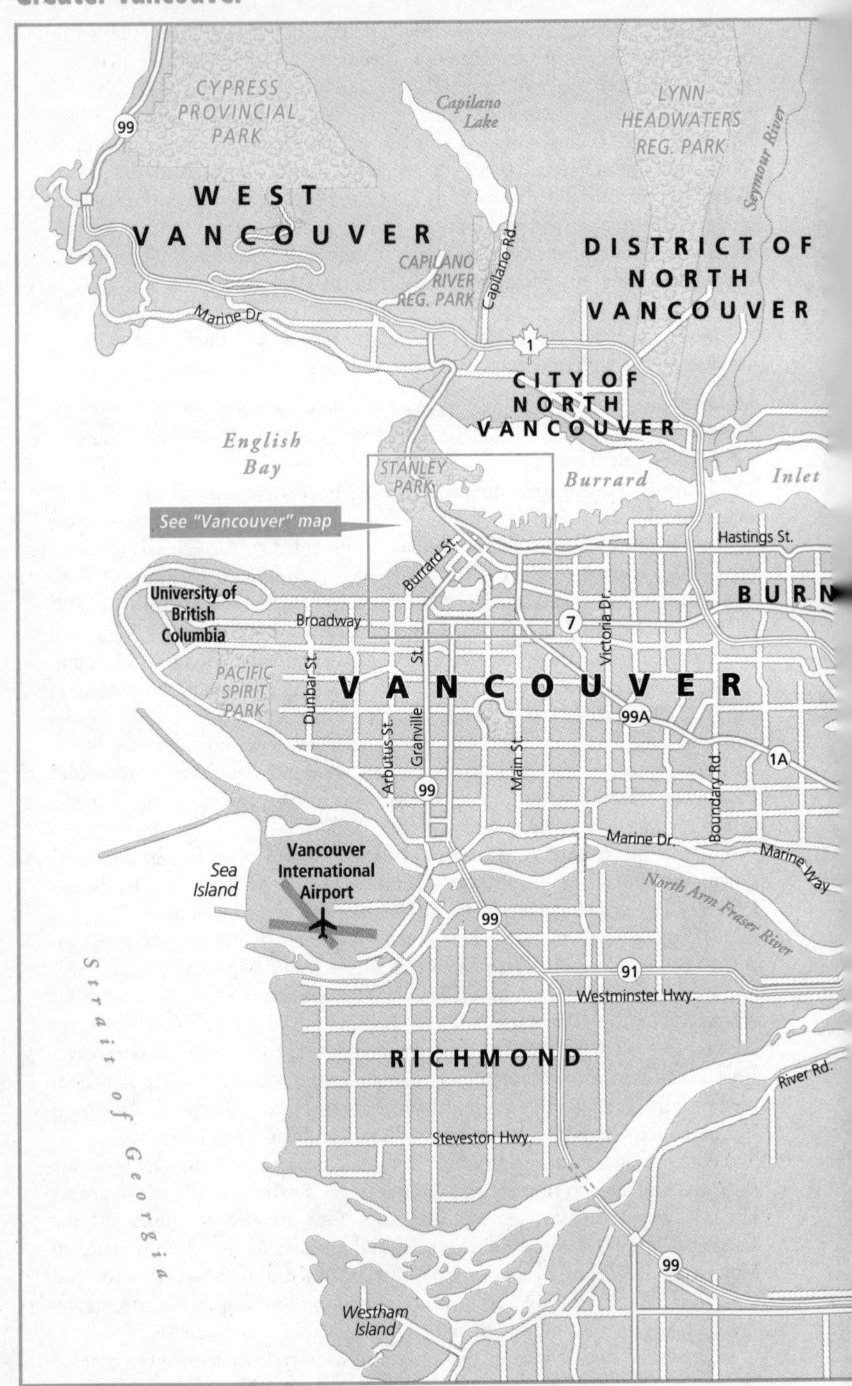

CYPRESS PROVINCIAL PARK
Capilano Lake
LYNN HEADWATERS REG. PARK
Seymour River
99
WEST VANCOUVER
CAPILANO RIVER REG. PARK
Capilano Rd.
DISTRICT OF NORTH VANCOUVER
Marine Dr.
1
CITY OF NORTH VANCOUVER
English Bay
STANLEY PARK
Burrard
Inlet
See "Vancouver" map
Hastings St.
Burrard St.
University of British Columbia
BURN
Broadway
7
Victoria Dr.
Dunbar St.
St.
PACIFIC SPIRIT PARK
VANCOUVER
99A
Arbutus St.
Granville
Main St.
1A
Boundary Rd.
99
Marine Dr.
Marine Way
Sea Island
Vancouver International Airport
North Arm Fraser River
99
91
Westminster Hwy.
Strait of Georgia
RICHMOND
River Rd.
Steveston Hwy.
99
Westham Island

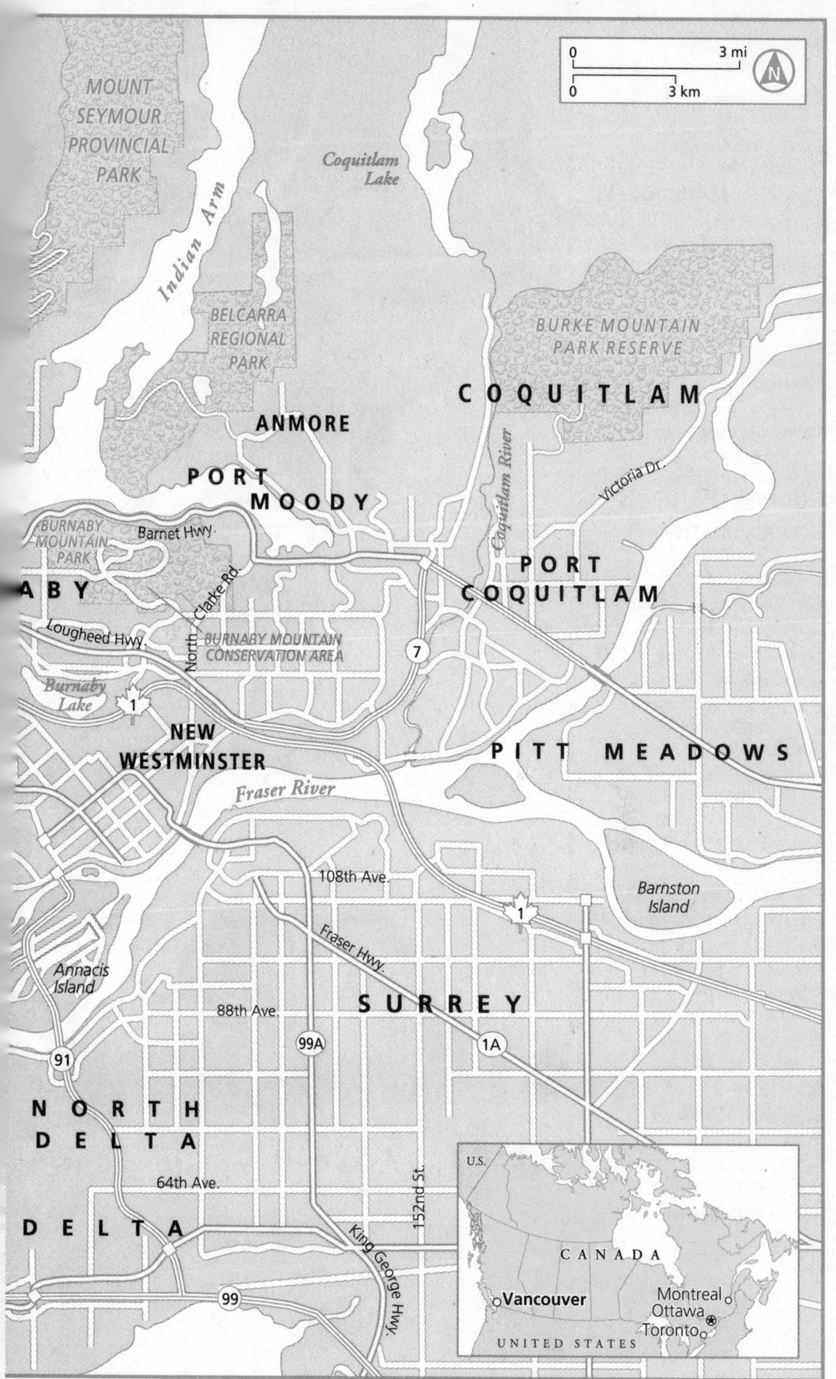

0
3 mi
0
3 km
N
MOUNT SEYMOUR PROVINCIAL PARK
Coquitlam Lake
Indian Arm
BELCARRA REGIONAL PARK
BURKE MOUNTAIN PARK RESERVE
COQUITLAM
ANMORE
PORT MOODY
Coquitlam River
Victoria Dr.
BURNABY MOUNTAIN PARK
Barnet Hwy.
PORT COQUITLAM
ABY
North Clarke Rd.
Lougheed Hwy.
BURNABY MOUNTAIN CONSERVATION AREA
7
Burnaby Lake
1
NEW WESTMINSTER
PITT MEADOWS
Fraser River
108th Ave.
Barnston Island
1
Fraser Hwy.
Annacis Island
88th Ave.
SURREY
99A
1A
91
NORTH DELTA
64th Ave.
152nd St.
DELTA
King George Hwy.
99
U.S.
CANADA
Vancouver
Montreal
Ottawa
Toronto
UNITED STATES

# Vancouver

**ATTRACTIONS** ●

Canadian Craft Museum **28**
Capilano Suspension Bridge & Park **1**
Dr. Sun Yat-sen Classical Garden **44**
Museum of Anthropology **15**
Science World British Columbia **40**
Stanley Park's Children's Farm **4**
Stanley Park's Miniature Railway **3**
Vancouver Aquarium Marine Science Centre **2**
Vancouver Art Gallery **27**
Vancouver Centennial Police Museum **45**
Vancouver Maritime Museum **14**

**ACCOMMODATIONS** ■

Barclay House in the West End **10**
Best Western Downtown Vancouver **33**
Fairmont Hotel Vancouver **25**
Granville Island Hotel **21**
Hostelling International Vancouver Downtown Hostel **12**
Howard Johnson Hotel **32**
Johnson Heritage House Bed & Breakfast **20**
Kenya Court Ocean Front Guest House **16**
Pacific Palisades Hotel **23**
Pan-Pacific Hotel Vancouver **24**
Penny Farthing Inn **18**
Rosedale on Robson Suite Hotel **41**
Rosellen Suites **3**
Sheraton Wall Centre Vancouver **30**
Sylvia Hotel **6**
West End Guest House **9**
Westin Bayshore Resort & Marina **4**
Westin Grand **42**
YMCA Hotel/Residence **40**

STANLEY PARK
Beaver Lake
Lost Lagoon
Coal
Lagoon Dr.
W. Georgia St.
Alberni St.
Robson St.
Haro St.
Barclay St.
Nelson St.
Comox St.
Chilco St.
Gilford St.
Denman St.
Pendrell St.
Beach Ave.
ENGLISH BAY BEACH
Bidwell St.
Cardero St.
Nicola St.
Broughton St.
Jervis St.
Burnaby St.
Davie St.
Harwood St.
Pacific St.
Beach Ave.
WEST
English Bay
SUNSET BEACH PARK
Ogden Ave.
Whyte Ave.
VANIER PARK
Vancouver Museum
KITSILANO BEACH PARK
Burrard Bridge
Granville Bridge
Granville Island
Cartwright St.
Cornwall Ave.
W. 1st Ave.
KITSILANO
W. 3rd Ave.
W. 5th Ave.
W. 7th Ave.
W. Broadway

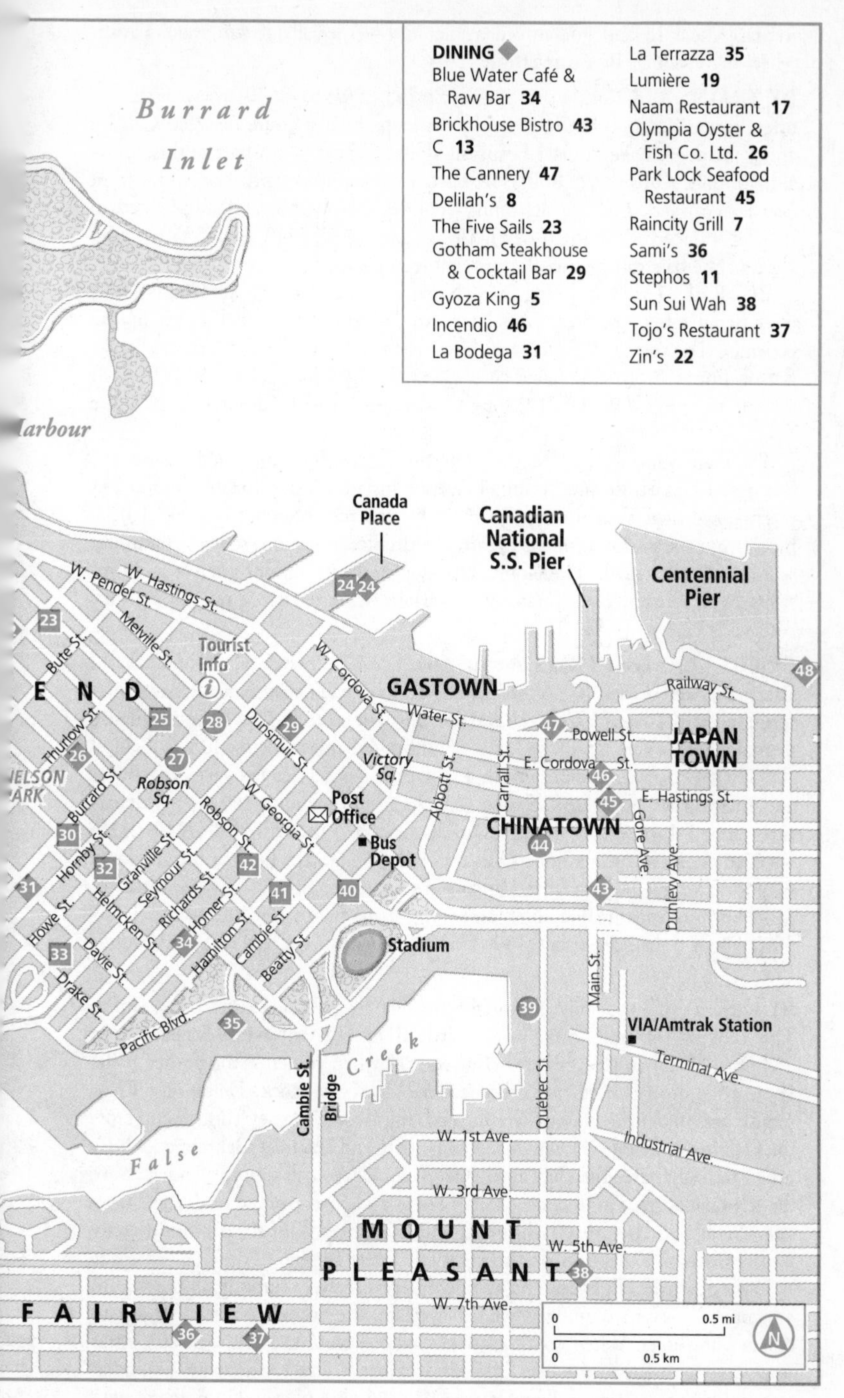
DINING
Blue Water Café & Raw Bar 34
Brickhouse Bistro 43
C 13
The Cannery 47
Delilah's 8
The Five Sails 23
Gotham Steakhouse & Cocktail Bar 29
Gyoza King 5
Incendio 46
La Bodega 31
La Terrazza 35
Lumière 19
Naam Restaurant 17
Olympia Oyster & Fish Co. Ltd. 26
Park Lock Seafood Restaurant 45
Raincity Grill 7
Sami's 36
Stephos 11
Sun Sui Wah 38
Tojo's Restaurant 37
Zin's 22
Burrard Inlet
Harbour
Canada Place
Canadian National S.S. Pier
Centennial Pier
W. Hastings St.
W. Pender St.
Melville St.
Bute St.
Tourist Info
END
Thurlow St.
Burrard St.
Robson Sq.
Dunsmuir St.
W. Cordova St.
GASTOWN
Water St.
Railway St.
Powell St.
JAPAN TOWN
E. Cordova St.
Victory Sq.
Abbott St.
Carrall St.
E. Hastings St.
Post Office
Bus Depot
CHINATOWN
Gore Ave.
Dunlevy Ave.
Robson St.
W. Georgia St.
Hornby St.
Granville St.
Seymour St.
Richards St.
Homer St.
Hamilton St.
Cambie St.
Beatty St.
Howe St.
Helmcken St.
Davie St.
Drake St.
Stadium
Main St.
VIA/Amtrak Station
Terminal Ave.
Pacific Blvd.
Creek
Cambie St. Bridge
Québec St.
W. 1st Ave.
Industrial Ave.
False
W. 3rd Ave.
MOUNT PLEASANT
W. 5th Ave.
W. 7th Ave.
FAIRVIEW
0
0.5 mi
0
0.5 km
N

for fast check-in and guaranteed availability—especially if you want a four-wheel-drive vehicle or a convertible.

**BY TRAIN** **VIA Rail,** 1150 Station St. (✆ **800/561-8630;** www.viarail.ca), offers service from Toronto, traveling on a spectacular route between Calgary and Vancouver. Lake Louise's beautiful alpine scenery is just part of this enjoyable journey. **Amtrak** (✆ **800/USA-RAIL;** www.amtrak.com) has service from Seattle, Portland, Los Angeles, and San Diego. Non-U.S. and non-Canadian travelers can buy a 15- to 30-day USA Railpass for US$440 to US$550 at peak season. The pass can be used for rail connections to Vancouver.

**BC Rail,** 1311 W. First St., North Vancouver (✆ **604/631-3500;** www.bcrail.com), connects Vancouver to Whistler and other cities in the province. The trip to Whistler is 2½ hours each way, and the fare includes breakfast or dinner. A one-way ticket costs C$33 (US$20) for adults, C$29 (US$18) for seniors, and C$19 (US$12) for children ages 2 to 12. Children under 2 are free.

The main Vancouver rail station, **Pacific Central Station,** is at 1150 Station St., near Main Street and Terminal Avenue just south of Chinatown. You can reach downtown Vancouver from there by cab for about C$5 (US$3.10). A block from the station is the **SkyTrain's Main Street Station,** so within minutes you can be downtown. The Granville and Waterfront stations are two and four stops away, respectively. A one-zone SkyTrain ticket (covering the city of Vancouver) is C$1.75 (US$1.10).

**BY BUS** **Greyhound Bus Lines** (✆ **604/482-8747;** www.greyhound.ca) and **Pacific Coach Lines** (✆ **604/662-8074;** www.pacificcoach.com) have their terminals at the **Pacific Central Station,** 1150 Station St. Greyhound Canada's **Canada Pass** offers 15 or 30 days of unlimited travel for C$405 to C$480 (US$251–US$298). Pacific Coach Lines provides service between Vancouver and Victoria at C$26 (US$16) one-way per adult, including ferry; daily departures are 5:45am to 7:45pm. **Quick Coach Lines** (✆ **604/940-4428;** www.quickcoach.com) connects Vancouver to the Seattle-Tacoma International Airport. The bus leaving from Vancouver's Sandman Inn, 180 W. Georgia St., picks up from most major hotels and stops at the Vancouver International Airport. The 4-hour ride costs C$39 (US$24) one-way or C$70 (US$43) round-trip.

**BY CAR** You'll probably be driving into Vancouver along one of two routes. The 226km (140-mile) drive from Seattle along **U.S. Interstate 5** takes about 2½ hours. The road changes into **Highway 99** when you cross the border at the Peace Arch. You'll drive through the cities of White Rock, Delta, and Richmond; pass under the Fraser River through the George Massey Tunnel; and cross the Oak Street Bridge. The highway ends there and becomes Oak Street, a busy urban thoroughfare. Turn left onto 70th Avenue. (A small sign suspended above the left lane at the intersection of Oak Street and 70th Avenue reads CITY CENTRE.) Six blocks later, turn right onto Granville Street. This street heads directly into downtown Vancouver on the Granville Street Bridge.

**Trans-Canada Highway 1** is a limited-access freeway running all the way to Vancouver's eastern boundary, where it crosses the Second Narrows bridge to North Vancouver. When coming on Highway 1 from the east, exit at Cassiar Street and turn left at the first light onto Hastings Street (Highway 7A), adjacent to Exhibition Park. Follow Hastings Street 6.5km (4 miles) into downtown.

When coming to Vancouver from Whistler or parts north, take exit 13 (the sign says TAYLOR WAY, BRIDGE TO VANCOUVER) and cross the Lions Gate Bridge into Vancouver's West End.

**BY SHIP & FERRY** The **Canada Place** cruise-ship terminal at the base of Burrard Street (✆ **604/665-9085**) is a city landmark. Topped by five eye-catching white Teflon sails, Canada Place pier juts out into the Burrard Inlet and is at the edge of the downtown financial district. **Princess Cruises, Holland America, Royal Caribbean, Crystal Cruises, Norwegian Cruise Lines, World Explorer Majesty Cruise Line, Hanseatic, Seabourn,** and **Carnival Cruise lines** dock at Canada Place and the nearby Ballantyne Pier to board passengers headed for Alaska via British Columbia's Inside Passage. Public-transit buses and taxis greet new arrivals, but you can also easily walk to many major hotels, like the Pan-Pacific, Waterfront Centre, and Hotel Vancouver.

**BC Ferries** (✆ **888/223-3779;** www.bcferries.bc.ca) has three routes between Vancouver and the Island. The one-way fare is C$9.50 (US$6) for adults, C$4.75 (US$2.95) for children ages 5 to 11, and C$33.50 (US$21) per car. Children under 5 are free. The most direct route to Victoria is the **Tsawwassen-Swartz Bay ferry,** running every 2 hours daily 7am to 9pm. The Tsawwassen terminal is about 19km (12 miles) south of Vancouver. Take Highway 17 from Tsawwassen until it merges with Highway 99 just before the George Massey Tunnel, then follow the driving directions to Vancouver given in "By Car," above. The **Mid-Island Express** operates between Tsawwassen and Duke Point, just south of Nanaimo. The 2-hour crossing runs six times daily 5:30am to 11pm. The **Horseshoe Bay-Nanaimo ferry** has eight daily sailings, leaving Horseshoe Bay near West Vancouver and arriving 95 minutes later in Nanaimo. To reach Vancouver from Horseshoe Bay, take the Trans-Canada Highway (Highways 1 and 99) east and then take Exit 13 (Taylor Way) to the Lions Gate Bridge and downtown Vancouver's West End.

## VISITOR INFORMATION

**TOURIST OFFICES** The **Vancouver Tourist Info Centre,** 200 Burrard St. (✆ **604/683-2000;** www.tourismvancouver.com; bus: 22), is your best source for details about Vancouver and the North Shore. May to Labor Day, it's open daily 8am to 6pm; the rest of the year, hours are Monday to Friday 8:30am to 5:30pm and Saturday 9am to 5pm. If you plan to see more of this beautiful province, contact **Super Natural British Columbia** (✆ **800/HELLO-BC** or 604/435-5622; www.travel.bc.ca).

Some of the best sites out there are Tourism BC (**www.hellobc.com**), Super Natural British Columbia (**www.travel.bc.ca**), Tourism Vancouver (**www.tourismvancouver.com**), Environment Canada (**www.weatheroffice.com**), BC Transit (**www.bctransit.com**), BC Ferries (**www.bcferries.com**), and *Vancouver* magazine (**www.vanmag.com**).

## CITY LAYOUT

Think of Vancouver's downtown peninsula as being like an upraised thumb on the mitten-shaped Vancouver mainland. Stanley Park, the West End, Yaletown, and Vancouver's business-and-financial center are on the "thumb," bordered to the west by English Bay, to the north by Burrard Inlet, and to the south by False Creek. The mainland part of the city, the "mitten," is mostly residential, with a sprinkling of businesses along main arteries. Both the mainland and the peninsula are covered by a simple rectilinear street pattern.

On the downtown peninsula are four key east-west streets. **Robson Street** starts at B.C. Place Stadium on Beatty Street, flows through the West End's touristy shopping district, and ends at Stanley Park's Lost Lagoon on Lagoon Drive. **Georgia Street**—far more efficient for drivers than the pedestrian-oriented Robson—runs from the Georgia Viaduct on downtown's eastern edge through Vancouver's commercial core and carries on through Stanley Park and over the Lions Gate Bridge to the North Shore. Three blocks north of Georgia is **Hastings Street,** which begins in the West End, runs east through downtown, and skirts Gastown's southern border as it heads east to the Trans-Canada Highway. **Davie Street** starts at Pacific Boulevard near the Cambie Street Bridge, travels through Yaletown into the West End's more residential shopping district, and ends at English Bay Beach.

Three **north–south downtown streets** will get you everywhere you want to go in and out of downtown. Two blocks east of Stanley Park is **Denman Street,** which runs from West Georgia Street at Coal Harbour to Beach Avenue at English Bay Beach. This main West End thoroughfare is where the locals go to dine out. It's also the shortest north-south route between the two ends of the Stanley Park Seawall. Eight blocks east of Denman is **Burrard Street,** which starts near the Canada Place Pier, runs south through downtown, crosses the Burrard Street Bridge, and then forks. One branch, still **Burrard Street,** continues south and intersects **West 4th Avenue** and **Broadway** before terminating at **West 16th Avenue** on the borders of Shaughnessy. The other branch becomes **Cornwall Avenue,** which heads due west through Kitsilano, changing its name two more times to **Point Grey Road** and then **Northwest Marine Drive** before entering the University of British Columbia campus.

**Granville Street** starts near the Waterfront Station on Burrard Inlet and runs the entire length of downtown, crosses over the Granville Bridge to Vancouver's West Side, and continues south across the breadth of the city before crossing the Arthur-Laing Bridge to **Vancouver International Airport.**

On the mainland portion of Vancouver, the city's east-west roads are successively numbered from 1st Avenue at the downtown bridges to 77th Avenue by the banks of the Fraser River. By far the most important east-west route is **Broadway** (formerly 9th Avenue), which starts a few blocks from the University of British Columbia and extends across the length of the city to the border with neighboring Burnaby, where it becomes the Lougheed Highway. In Kitsilano, **West 4th Avenue** is also an important east-west shopping-and-commercial corridor. Intersecting with Broadway at various points are a number of important north-south commercial streets, each of which defines a particular neighborhood. The most significant are (west to east) **Macdonald Street** in Kitsilano, then **Granville Street, Cambie Street, Main Street,** and **Commercial Drive.**

The Vancouver Tourist Info Centre (see "Visitor Information," above) and most hotels can provide you with detailed downtown maps. A good all-around metropolitan area map is the **Rand McNally Vancouver city map,** available for C$3 (US$1.85) at the Vancouver Airport Tourism Centre kiosk. If you're an auto-club member, the Canadian Automobile Association (CAA) map is also good. It's not for sale but is free to both AAA and CAA members and is available at AAA offices across North America. **International Travel Maps and Books,** 552 Seymour St. (✆ **604/687-3320**), has the city's most extensive selection of Vancouver and British Columbia maps and specialty guidebooks.

### Tips Finding an Address

In many Vancouver addresses, the suite or room number precedes the building number. For instance, 100-1250 Robson St. is Suite 100 at 1250 Robson St.

In downtown Vancouver, Chinatown's **Carrall Street** is the east-west axis from which streets are numbered and designated. Westward, numbers increase progressively to Stanley Park; eastward, numbers increase heading toward Commercial Drive. For example, 400 West Pender would be about 4 blocks from Carrall Street heading toward downtown; 400 East Pender would be 4 blocks on the opposite side of Carrall Street. Off the peninsula, the system works the same, but **Ontario Street** is the east-west axis. All east-west roads are avenues (like 4th Avenue), while streets (Main Street) run exclusively north-south.

## NEIGHBORHOODS IN BRIEF

When figuring out what's where in Vancouver, keep in mind that this is a city where property is king and the word *west* has such positive connotations folks have gone to great lengths to associate it with their particular patch of real estate. Thus there's the **West End,** the **West Side,** and **West Vancouver,** which improbably enough is located immediately beside **North Vancouver.** The West End is a high-rise residential neighborhood on the downtown peninsula. The West Side is one-half of Vancouver, from Ontario Street west to the University of British Columbia. (The more working-class **East Side** covers the city's mainland portion, from Ontario Street east to Boundary Road.) The tony West Vancouver is a city to itself on the far side of Burrard Inlet. Together with its more middle-class neighbor North Vancouver, it forms an area called the **North Shore.**

**DOWNTOWN** Vancouver's commercial-and-office core runs from Nelson Street north to the harbor, with Homer Street as the eastern edge and a more ragged boundary running roughly along Burrard Street forming the western border. The truly prime office space is on or near Georgia Street. Hotels stick mostly to the northern third of downtown, clustering especially thickly near the water's edge, but restaurants are sprinkled throughout. Walking is a good bet for transport downtown, day and night. Unlike in many North American cities, lots of people live in and around Vancouver's central business district, so the area is always populated.

**THE WEST END** A fascinating neighborhood of high-rise condos mixed with Edwardian homes, the West End has within its borders all the necessities of life: great cafes and nightclubs, many and varied bookshops, and some of the city's best restaurants. The Pacific Ocean laps against the West End on two sides, in the form of Burrard Inlet to the north and English Bay to the south, while on the western edge spreads Stanley Park. Burrard Street forms the West End's eastern border.

**GASTOWN** The city's oldest section, Gastown was named after Vancouver's first settler, riverboat skipper/saloon keeper Jack Deighton, nicknamed "Gassy" thanks to his longwinded habits of speech. It was rebuilt in brick after the 1886 fire wiped out the original wooden city. Gastown's cobblestone streets and late Victorian architecture make it well worth a visit, despite an infestation of curio shops and souvenir stands. It lies east of downtown, in the 6 square blocks between Water and Hastings streets and Cambie and Columbia streets.

**CHINATOWN** South of Hastings Street, between Gore and Carrall streets to the east and west and Keefer Street to the south, Chinatown isn't large but is intense. Fishmongers stand calling out their wares in Cantonese before a shop filled with crabs, eels, geoducks, and bullfrogs. Women haggle over produce, while their husbands hunt for deer antler or dried seahorse at a traditional Chinese apothecary. And inside any one of a dozen restaurants, you'll find an entire extended family sitting at a single big round table, consuming half a dozen plates of succulent Cantonese cooking.

**YALETOWN** Vancouver's former warehouse district, Yaletown is below Granville Street and above Pacific Boulevard, from Davie Street over to Smithe Street. It has long since been converted to an area of apartment lofts, nightclubs, restaurants, high-end furniture shops, and a fledgling multimedia biz. In recent years the area has finally come into its own.

**GRANVILLE ISLAND** On a peninsula on False Creek, this former industrial site is now a fun and fascinating mix of urban markets, craft fairs, artisan workshops, theaters, cafes, offices, parks, and restaurants.

**KITSILANO** In the 1960s, Kitsilano was Canada's Haight-Asbury, a slightly seedy enclave of coffeehouses, head shops, and long-haired hippies. Today, Kits is one of Vancouver's most popular neighborhoods, with a mix of affordable apartments and heritage homes, funky shops, great restaurants, and pleasant walkable streets. And there's Kits beach. Roughly speaking, Alma Street and Burrard Street form Kitsilano's east and west boundaries, with West 16th Avenue to the south and the ocean to the north.

**RICHMOND** Twenty years ago, Richmond was mostly farmland, with a bit of sleepy suburb. Now it has become Asia West, an agglomeration of shopping malls geared to the new (read rich, educated, and successful) Chinese immigrants. Malls like the Aberdeen Mall and the Yao Han Centre will make you feel as if you've just stepped into Singapore.

**COMMERCIAL DRIVE** Every immigrant group that ever passed through the city has left its mark on "The Drive," as Vancouverites call it. Combine those influences with the indigenous culture of left-wing activism and ongoing "yuppification," and the result is a peculiar but endearing mix: the Italian cafe next to the Marxist bookstore across from the vegetarian deli that has taken to selling really expensive yeast-free Tuscan bread.

**PUNJABI MARKET** Most of the businesses catering to Vancouver's sizable Punjabi population are found on a 4-block stretch of Main Street, from 48th up to 52nd avenues. The area is at its best during business hours, when the fragrant scent of spices wafts out from food stalls and Hindi pop songs blare out from hidden speakers. Shopping here is like sipping from the distilled essence of the Indian subcontinent.

**THE NORTH SHORE (NORTH VANCOUVER & WEST VANCOUVER)** The most impressive thing about the North Shore is its mountain range. Huge and wild, the mountains are responsible for much of Vancouver's reputation for compelling physical beauty. The cities themselves, however, aren't without their charms. West Vancouver offers some fine waterfront restaurants, particularly in the Dundarave area. North Vancouver's Lonsdale Quay Market—where the SeaBus docks—makes a pleasant afternoon's outing.

## 2 Getting Around

### BY PUBLIC TRANSPORTATION

**Translink/BC Transit** (© **604/521-0400;** www.translink.bc.ca) system includes electric buses, SeaBus catamaran ferries, and the magnetic-rail SkyTrain. It's an ecologically friendly, highly reliable, and inexpensive system that allows you to get everywhere, including the beaches and ski slopes. Regular service on the main routes runs daily 5am to 2am, with less frequent "Owl" service operating on several downtown and suburban routes to 4:20am.

Schedules and routes are available at the Vancouver Tourist Info Centre, at many major hotels, online, and on buses. Pick up a copy of ***Discover Vancouver on Transit*** at the Vancouver Tourist Info Centre (see "Visitor Information," above). This publication gives transit routes for many city neighborhoods, landmarks, and attractions, including numerous Victoria sites.

**Fares** are the same for the bus, SeaBus, and SkyTrain. One-way, all-zone fares are C$1.75 (US$1.10) after 6:30pm on weekdays and all day on weekends and holidays. At other times, a one-zone fare costs C$1.75 (US$1.10) and covers the entire city of Vancouver. A two-zone fare—C$2.50 (US$1.55)—is required to travel to nearby suburbs such as Richmond or North Vancouver, while a three-zone fare—C$3.50 (US$2.20)—is required for travel to the far-off edge city of Surrey. Free transfers are available on boarding and are good for travel in any direction and for the SkyTrain and SeaBus, but they do have a 90-minute expiration. DayPasses, which are good on all public transit, are C$7 (US$4.35) for adults and C$5 (US$3.10) for seniors, students, and children. Tickets and passes are available at the Vancouver Tourist Info Centre, both SeaBus terminals, convenience stores, drugstores, credit unions, and other outlets displaying the "FareDealer" symbol.

The **SkyTrain** is a computerized magnetic-rail train servicing 20 stations along its 35-minute trip from downtown Vancouver east to Surrey through Burnaby and New Westminster. The **SeaBus** catamaran ferries annually take more than 700,000 passengers, cyclists, and wheelchair riders on a scenic 12-minute commute between downtown's Waterfront Station and North Vancouver's Lonsdale Quay. Weekdays, a SeaBus leaves each stop every 15 minutes 6:15am to 6:30pm, then every 30 minutes to 1am. SeaBuses depart on Saturdays every half hour 6:30am to 12:30pm, then every 15 minutes to 7:15pm, then every half hour to 1am. On Sundays and holidays, runs depart every half hour 8:30am to 11pm.

### BY TAXI

Cab fares are quite reasonable, starting at C$2.30 (US$1.45) and increasing at a rate of C$1.25 (US80¢) per kilometer, plus C30¢ (US20¢) per minute at stoplights. In the downtown area, you can expect to travel for less than C$6 (US$3.70) plus tip. The typical fare for the 13km (8-mile) drive from downtown to the airport is C$25 (US$16).

### Tips Key Bus Routes

Keep these routes in mind as you tour the city by bus: **no. 5** (Robson Street), **no. 22** (Kitsilano beach to downtown), **no. 50** (Granville Island), **nos. 35** and **135** (to Stanley Park bus loop), **no. 240** (North Vancouver), **no. 250** (West Vancouver–Horseshoe Bay), and **nos. 4** and **10** (UBC–Exhibition Park via Granville Street downtown). In summer, the Vancouver Parks Board operates a bus route through Stanley Park.

Taxis are easy to find in front of major hotels, but flagging one can be tricky. Most drivers are usually on radio calls. But thanks to built-in satellite positioning systems, if you call for a taxi, it usually arrives faster than if go out and hail one. Call for a pickup from **Black Top** at ✆ **604/731-1111, Yellow Cab** at ✆ **604/681-1111,** or **MacLure's** at ✆ **604/731-9211. AirLimo** at ✆ **604 /273-1331** offers flat-rate stretch limousine service. AirLimo charges C$29 (US$19) per trip to the airport (not per person), plus tax and tip. The drivers accept all major credit cards.

## BY CAR

Vancouver's driving laws are similar to those of much of the United States. You may turn right on red after coming to a full stop, seat belts are mandatory, children under 5 must be in a child seat, and motorcyclists must wear helmets. (The only exception is the flashing green light, which in BC isn't a left turn signal but a sign to proceed with caution.) Gas is sold by the liter, averaging around C60¢ (US40¢). This may seem inexpensive until you consider that a gallon of gas is about C$2.70 (US$1.70). Speeds and distances are posted in kilometers.

You won't need a car to explore the city, but you may want one to explore the environs or continue on elsewhere in Canada. If you're over 25 and have a major credit card, you can rent a vehicle from **Avis,** 757 Hornby St. (✆ **800/879-2847** or 604/606-2847; bus: 22); **Budget,** 450 W. Georgia St. (✆ **800/527-0700,** 800/268-8900, or 604/668-7000; bus: 15); **Enterprise,** 585 Smithe St. (✆ **800/736-8222** or 604/688-5500; bus: 15); **Hertz Canada,** 1128 Seymour St. (✆ **800/263-0600,** or 604/688-2411; bus: 4); **National/Tilden,** 1130 W. Georgia St. (✆ **800/387-4747** or 604/685-6111; bus: 22); and **Thrifty,** 1015 Burrard St. or 1400 Robson St. (✆ **800/367-2277** or 604/606-1666; bus: 22). These firms all have counters and shuttle service at the airport as well.

All major downtown hotels have guest **parking;** rates vary from free to C$20 (US$12) per day. There's public parking at **Robson Square** (enter at Smithe and Howe streets), the **Pacific Centre** (Howe and Dunsmuir streets), and **The Bay** department store (Richards near Dunsmuir Street). You'll also find **parking lots** at Thurlow and Georgia streets, Thurlow and Alberni streets, and Robson and Seymour streets.

Metered **street parking** isn't impossible to come by, but it may take a trip or three around the block to find a spot. Rules are posted on the street and invariably are strictly enforced. Unmetered parking on side streets is often subject to neighborhood residency requirements. Check the signs. If you park in such an area without the appropriate sticker on your windshield, you'll get ticketed, then towed. If your car is towed away or if you need a towing service and aren't a member of AAA, call **Unitow** (✆ **604/251-1255**) or **Busters** (✆ **604/685-8181**).

Members of the American Automobile Association (AAA) can get assistance from the **Canadian Automobile Association (CAA),** 999 W. Broadway, Vancouver (© **604/268-5600,** or for road service 604/293-2222; bus: 9).

## BY BICYCLE

Vancouver is decidedly bicycle friendly. There are plenty of places to rent a bike along Robson Street and Denman Street near Stanley Park. A trip around the **Stanley Park seawall** ★ is one of Vancouver's premier sightseeing experiences, enjoyed by thousands of visitors every year. Bike routes are designated throughout the city. Paved paths crisscross though parks and along beaches. Helmets are mandatory and riding on sidewalks is illegal except on designated bike paths.

**Cycling BC** (© **604/737-3034**) accommodates cyclists on the SkyTrain and buses by providing "Bike & Ride" lockers at all "Park & Ride" parking lots. The department also dispenses loads of information about events, bike touring, and cycle insurance. Many downtown parking lots and garages also have no-fee bike racks.

You can take a bike on the SeaBus anytime free. All the West Vancouver blue buses (including the bus to the Horseshoe Bay ferry terminal) can carry two bikes free, first come, first served. In Vancouver, only a limited number of suburban routes allow bikes on the bus, and space is limited. Bikes aren't allowed on the Skytrain or in the George Massey Tunnel, but a tunnel shuttle operates four times daily mid-May to September to transport you across the Fraser; May 1 to Victoria Day (the third weekend of May), the service operates on weekends only.

## BY FERRY

Crossing False Creek to Vanier Park or Granville Island on one of the blue mini-ferries is cheap and fun. The **Aquabus** docks at the foot of Howe Street. It takes you either to Granville Island's public market or east along False Creek to Science World and Stamps Landing. The **Granville Island Ferry** docks at Sunset Beach below the Burrard Street Bridge and the Aquatic Centre and goes to Granville Island and Vanier Park. Ferries to Granville Island leave every 5 minutes 7am to 10pm; those to Vanier Park, every 15 minutes 10am to 8pm. One-way fares for both companies on all routes are $2.50 (US$1.55) for adults and C1.25 (US80¢) for seniors and children.

## *FAST FACTS:* Vancouver

*American Express* The office at 666 Burrard St. (© **604/669-2813;** bus: 22), is open Monday to Friday 8am to 5:30pm and Saturday 10am to 4pm.

*Area Codes* The area code for Vancouver and the rest of the British Columbia Lower Mainland is **604.** Note that ten-digit dialing was recently introduced in the Vancouver area. All calls, whether long-distance or not, must be preceded by the "604" area code. The area code for all other parts of British Columbia, including Victoria, Vancouver Island, and the BC Interior, is **250.**

*Consulates* The **U.S. Consulate** is at 1095 W. Pender St. (© **604/685-4311;** bus: 35). The **British Consulate** is at 800-1111 Melville St. (© **604/683-4421;** bus: 35). The **Australian Consulate** is at 1225-888 Dunsmuir St. (© **604/684-1177;** bus: 5). Check the yellow pages for other countries.

*Currency Exchange* Banks and ATMs have a better exchange rate than most foreign exchange bureaus (the latter charge transaction and service fees).

*Dentists* Most major hotels have a dentist on call. The **Vancouver Centre Dental Clinic,** Vancouver Centre Mall, 11-650 W. Georgia St. (✆ **604/682-1601;** bus: 4), is an option. You must make an appointment. The clinic is open Monday to Saturday with varying hours somewhere between 8:30am and 6pm.

*Doctors* Hotels usually have a doctor on call. The **Vancouver Medical Clinics,** Bentall Centre, 1055 Dunsmuir St. (✆ **604/683-8138;** bus: 22), is a drop-in clinic open Monday to Friday 8am to 5pm. Another drop-in medical center, **Carepoint Medical Centre,** 1175 Denman St. (✆ **604/681-5338;** bus: 5), is open daily 9am to 9pm. See also "Emergencies," below.

*Drugstores* **Shopper's Drug Mart,** 1125 Davie St. (✆ **604/685-6445;** bus: 6), is open 24 hours. Several Safeway supermarkets have late-night pharmacies, including the one at the corner of Robson and Denman streets, which is open to midnight.

*Emergencies* Dial ✆ **911** for fire, police, ambulance, and poison control.

*Hospitals* **St. Paul's Hospital,** 1081 Burrard St. (✆ **604/682-2344;** bus: 22), is the closest facility to downtown and the West End. West Side Vancouver hospitals include **Vancouver General Hospital Health and Sciences Centre,** 855 W. 12th Ave. (✆ **604/875-4111;** bus: 9, 17), and **British Columbia's Children's Hospital,** 4480 Oak St. (✆ **604/875-2345;** bus: 17). In North Vancouver, there's **Lions Gate Hospital,** 231 E. 15th St. (✆ **604/988-3131;** bus: 250).

*Internet Access* There's free Internet access at the **Vancouver Public Library Central Branch,** 350 W. Georgia St. (✆ **604/331-4000;** bus: 5), open Monday to Thursday 10am to 8pm, Friday and Saturday 10am to 6pm, and Sunday 1 to 5pm. Downtown, there's **Roberto's Internet Café,** 311 West Pender, (✆ **604/683-6500**). In Kitsilano there's also **Dakoda's Internet Cafe,** 1602 Yew St. (✆ **604/731-5616;** bus: 22), a pleasant small cafe in the pub/restaurant zone across from Kits Beach; it's open Monday to Friday 7am to 10pm and Saturday and Sunday 7:30am to 10pm. **Webster's Internet Cafe,** 340 Robson St. (✆ **604/915-9327;** bus: 5), is across from the main public library and is open daily 9am to 11pm.

*Liquor & Wine* The legal drinking age in British Columbia is 19. Spirits are sold only in government liquor stores, but you can buy beer and wine from specially licensed, privately owned stores and pubs. There are 22 LCBC (Liquor Control of British Columbia) stores scattered throughout Vancouver. Most are open Monday to Saturday 10am to 6pm, but some are open to 11pm. Call the **Liquor Distribution Branch** at ✆ **604/252-3000** for location details.

*Newspapers/Magazines* The two local papers are the *Vancouver Sun* (Mon–Sat mornings) and *The Province* (Sun–Fri mornings). The free weekly entertainment paper *The Georgia Straight* comes out Thursday. The monthly *Vancouver* magazine is a glossy attitude-filled guide to the city's cultural scene, available on newsstands.

*Police* For emergencies, dial ✆ **911.** Otherwise, the **Vancouver City Police** can be reached at ✆ **604/717-3535.**

*Post Office* The **main post office,** 349 W. Georgia St., at Homer Street (Bus: 17), is open Monday to Friday 8am to 5:30pm. Postal outlets are located in souvenir stores and drugstores displaying the red-and-white Canada Post emblem.

*Safety* Overall, Vancouver is a safe city; violent-crime rates are quite low. However, property crimes and crimes of opportunity (such as items being stolen from unlocked cars) do occur with troubling frequency, particularly downtown. Vancouver's Downtown East Side, between Gastown and Chinatown, is a troubled neighborhood and should be avoided at night.

*Taxes* Hotel rooms are subject to a 10% tax. The provincial sales tax (PST) is 7% (excluding food, restaurant meals, and children's clothing). For specific questions, call the **B.C. Consumer Taxation Branch** at ✆ **604/660-4500.** Most goods and services are subject to a 7% federal goods and services tax (GST). You can get a refund on short-stay accommodations and all shopping purchases that total at least C$100 (US$67). (This refund doesn't apply to car rentals, parking, restaurant meals, room service, tobacco, or alcohol). Hotels and the Info Centres can give you application forms. Save your receipts. For details on the GST, call ✆ **800/561-6990.**

*Time Zone* Vancouver is in the Pacific time zone, as are Seattle and San Francisco. Daylight saving time applies April to October.

## 3 Where to Stay

The past few years have seen a lot of activity in the Vancouver hotel business. Lots of new rooms have opened up, some in the high end, and a lot more in the moderate-to-budget range. Most of the hotels are in the downtown/Yaletown area, or else in the West End. Both neighborhoods are close to major sites and services. Remember that quoted prices don't include the 10% **provincial accommodations tax** or the 7% **goods and services tax (GST).** Non-Canadian residents can get a GST rebate on short-stay accommodations by filling out the Tax Refund Application.

Reservations are highly recommended from June to September and over the holidays. If you arrive without a reservation or have trouble finding a room, call **Super Natural British Columbia's Discover British Columbia** hot line (✆ **800/663-6000**) or **Tourism Vancouver's** hot line (✆ **604/683-2000**). Specializing in last-minute bookings, either organization can make arrangements using its large daily listing of hotels, hostels, and B&Bs.

### DOWNTOWN & YALETOWN

All downtown hotels are within 5 to 10 minutes' walking distance of shops, restaurants, and attractions. Hotels in this area lean more toward luxurious than modest, a state of affairs reflected in their prices.

#### VERY EXPENSIVE

**Fairmont Hotel Vancouver** ★★ Thanks to a recent C$75-million (US$47-million) renovation, the grande dame of Vancouver's hotels has been restored beyond her former glory. A landmark in the city since it first opened its doors

### Tips Bed & Breakfast Registries

If you prefer to stay in a B&B, **Born Free Bed & Breakfast of BC,** 4390 Frances St., Burnaby, BC V5C ZR3 (✆ **800/488-1941** or 604/298-8815; www.vancouverbandb.bc.ca), specializes in matching guests to establishments that best suit their needs.

in 1939, the hotel has been completely brought up to 21st century standards. Rooms are spacious, with a sitting area, modern lighting and ample desks; bathrooms gleam with marble floors and sinks. The decorations evoke an elegance of days gone by. The courtyard suites provide spacious accommodations with a large luxuriously furnished living room, separated from the bedroom with French glass doors. A number of rooms have been adapted for wheelchair access and facilities for those with a hearing impairment. For those who like to be pampered, the hotel just inaugurated its state-of-the art spa facilities.

900 W. Georgia St., Vancouver, BC V6C 2W6. ✆ **800/866-5577** or 604/684-3131. Fax 604/662-1929. www.fairmont.com. 556 units. High season C$259–C$489 (US$161–US$303) double; C$419–C$1,899 (US$260–US$1,177) suite. Low season from C$179 (US$111) double; from C$339 (US$210) suite. Children under 18 stay free in parents' room. AE, DC, DISC, MC, V. Parking C$19 (US$12). Small pets are welcome for a C$25 (US$16) charge. **Amenities:** 2 restaurants (a brasserie and a west coast grill), bar; indoor pool; health club; excellent spa; Jacuzzi; sauna; concierge; car rental; tour desk; business center; shopping arcade; salon; 24-hr. room service; massage; babysitting; laundry service; same-day dry cleaning; nonsmoking rooms; Entree Gold concierge level. *In room:* A/C, TV w/pay movies, dataport, minibar, coffeemaker, hair dryer, iron.

**Pan-Pacific Hotel Vancouver** ★★ Since its completion in 1986, this luxury hotel atop the Vancouver Convention Centre has become perhaps the key landmark on the Vancouver waterfront; Canada Place and the cruise-ship terminal are at your door step. If you're taking an Alaskan cruise, this is the place to stay. Guests rooms are located from the ninth floor, above a huge glass atrium of a lobby that seems to invite the mountains and the harbor right in. Superior rooms face toward the city and offer a partial waterfront view. For the best views, book a deluxe room, and you can wake up to see the sun glinting on the mountains of the North Shore and the floatplanes drifting in with a morning tide of commuters from parts west and north. All rooms are very spacious, with a wide hallway entrance, large closet, and elegant maple wood furniture. Huge picture windows add to the brightness. Bathrooms are particularly spacious and don't scrimp on luxury.

300–999 Canada Place, Vancouver, BC V6C 3B5. ✆ **800/937-1515** in the U.S., or 604/662-8111. Fax 604/685-8690. www.panpac.com. 504 units. May–Oct C$465–C$545 (US$288–US$338) double. Nov–Apr C$380–C$430 (US$236–US$267) double. C$565–C$3,000 (US$235–US$1,860) suite year-round. AE, DC, DISC, MC, V. Parking C$21 (US$13). **Amenities:** 3 restaurants, bar; outdoor heated pool; squash courts; outstanding health club (C$15/US$9); spa; Jacuzzi; sauna; concierge; tour desk; car rental; business center; shopping arcade; 24-hour room service; massage; babysitting; laundry service; same-day dry cleaning; nonsmoking floors. *In room:* A/C, TV w/pay movies, dataport and high-speed Internet, minibar, coffeemaker, hair dryer, iron, safe.

**The Sheraton Vancouver Wall Centre Hotel** ★★★ The tallest—and the largest—hotel in the city, the Wall Centre is hard to miss. Look for the towering two-tone oval spire, the result of a strange compromise between city hall—which wanted the tower to have clear glass—and the developer, who preferred his glass aviator-shades black. Completed in May 2001, the Wall Centre is development mogul Peter Wall's personal tribute to everything he's ever liked in the world's finest accommodations. The opulent decor would not look out of place in a modern-art gallery, from the lobby's gold-leaf staircase, custom-designed furniture, and handblown glass chandeliers, to the half-dozen peepholes on each guest room door. All guest rooms—each with stunning floor-to-ceiling windows—are elegantly appointed with blond-wood furnishings, luxury bathrooms, heated floors, and king-size or double beds with down duvets and Egyptian cotton sheets.

1088 Burrard St., Vancouver, BC V6Z 2R9. ✆ **800/325-3535** or 604/331-1000. Fax 604/331-1000. www.sheratonvancouver.com. 735 units. Oct 23–May 14 C$129–C$249 (US$80–US$154) double; C$179–C$399 (US$111–US$210) suite. May 15–Oct 22 C$199–C$399 (US$123–US$247) double; C$249–C$549 (US$154–US$340) suite. Crystal Club upgrade C$25–C$40 (US$16–US$25). Valet parking C$19 (US$12). **Amenities:** 2 restaurants, 2 bars; indoor pool; state-of-the-art health club; spa; Jacuzzi; sauna; concierge; tour desk; car-rental desk; business center; salon; 24-hour room service; babysitting; same-day laundry and dry cleaning; nonsmoking rooms; executive level rooms. *In room:* A/C, TV w/pay movies, dataport, minibar, coffeemaker, hair dryer, iron, safe.

**The Westin Grand** ★★★ The luxurious Westin Grand opened in April 1999, right next to Vancouver's new Broadway-style music hall, the Ford Centre for the Performing Arts. The location was considered a key selling feature—the building itself was shaped to look like a grand piano. The Grand is also across from the public library and within easy walking distance of Yaletown, GM Place, and the Robson shopping area. The spacious suites are brightened by the natural light pouring in through the floor-to-ceiling windows, a nice foil to the somber mahogany furniture and earth tones decor. Sitting rooms come with a kitchenette tucked away behind the blond-wood cabinet doors, and bedrooms have either queen or king beds. Rooms for travelers with disabilities are available.

433 Robson St., Vancouver, BC V6B 6L9. ✆ **888/680-9393** or 604/602-1999. Fax 604/647-2502. www.westingrandvancouver.com. 207 suites. May 16–Oct 14 C$199–C$429 (US$123–US$266) suite. Oct 15–May 15 C$149–C$299 (US$92–US$185) suite. Up to 2 children under 17 stay free in parents' room. AE, DC, DISC, MC, V. Self-parking C$15 (US$9); valet parking C$19 (US$12). **Amenities:** Restaurant; outdoor pool; excellent health club; Jacuzzi; sauna; children's program; concierge; business center; 24-hour room service; babysitting; laundry service; dry cleaning; nonsmoking rooms; executive rooms. *In room:* A/C, TV w/pay movies, dataport, kitchen, minibar, coffeemaker, hair dryer, iron, safe.

## MODERATE

**Best Western Downtown Vancouver** The Best Western is located on Granville and Drake, a 5-block walk from the theater area on Granville Street at the south end of downtown. Of the 143 rooms, 32 have full kitchens, available for an additional C$20 to C$25 (US$12–US$16). All rooms are comfortable, and some rooms have harbor views. The corner rooms are a bit smaller than the rest, but they do have more light. This hotel is not overflowing with facilities, but the rooms are well furnished and the location is convenient. A complimentary deluxe continental breakfast is served in the breakfast lounge in the lobby.

718 Drake St., Vancouver, BC V6Z 2W6. ✆ **888/669-9888** or 604/660-9888. Fax 604/669-3440. www.bestwesterndowntown.com. 143 units. C$139–C$209 (US$86–US$130) double; C$280–C$350 (US$174–US$217) penthouse. AE, DC, DISC, MC, V. Parking C$5 (US$3.10). **Amenities:** Restaurant; rooftop exercise room; Jacuzzi; sauna; game room; tour desk; shuttle service to downtown; babysitting; laundry service; nonsmoking rooms; corporate rooms. *In room:* A/C, TV/VCR, dataport, coffeemaker, hair dryer, iron, safe.

**Rosedale on Robson Suite Hotel** ★★ *Kids* Located directly across the street from Library Square, the Rosedale provides excellent value for the money, particularly when it comes to the amenities. All rooms are one- or two-bedroom suites and feature separate living rooms with a pull-out couch and full kitchenettes. Complimentary hot and cold drinks and baked goods are served in the morning. Very family friendly, the Rosedale offers designated two-bedroom family suites. The kids bedrooms are furnished with bunk beds and decorated in either a sports or Barbie theme; they contain a large toy chest and blackboards with crayons to keep little ones busy. On Saturday night, the Rosedale staff puts on a movie or craft night to take the little ones off their parents' hands for a while. The sun deck and patio area also include a child's play area and sandbox. Even the family dog or cat is welcome to check in.

838 Hamilton (at Robson St.), Vancouver, BC V6B 6A2. ✆ **800/661-8870** or 604/689-8033. Fax 604/689-4426. www.rosedaleonrobson.com. 275 units. May–Sept C$205–C$285 (US$127–US$177) suite. Oct–Apr C$125–C$185 (US$78–US$115) suite. Additional adult C$20 (US$12). AE, DC, DISC, MC, V. Parking C$8 (US$5). **Amenities:** Restaurant (NY deli); indoor lap pool; exercise room; Jacuzzi; sauna; steam room; concierge; tour desk; car-rental desk; business center; limited room service; massage; babysitting; laundry service; same-day dry cleaning; nonsmoking rooms; executive-level rooms. *In room:* A/C, TV w/pay movies, fax, dataport, kitchen, coffeemaker, hair dryer, iron.

### INEXPENSIVE

**The Howard Johnson Hotel** *Finds* Yet another sign of south Granville's rapid gentrification, this formerly down-at-the-heels hotel was bought, gutted, renovated, and reopened in 1998 with an eye to the budget-conscious traveler. Hallways are decorated with photographs of Vancouver's early days, while the rooms themselves are comfortably if simply furnished. Some rooms have mini-kitchenettes, and the suites provide sofa beds, convenient for those traveling with children. A continental breakfast is served in the lounge on the mezzanine.

1176 Granville St., Vancouver, BC V6Z 1L8. ✆ **888/654-6336** or 604/688-8701. Fax 604/688-8335. www.hojovancouver.com. May 1–Oct 15 C$129–C$149 (US$80–US$92) double; C$149–C$169 (US$92–US$105) suite. Oct 16–Apr 30 C$69–C$89 (US$43–US$55) double; C$99–C$119 (US$61–US$74) suite. Children under 17 stay free in parents' room. Rates include a continental breakfast. AE, DC, MC, V. Parking C$8 (US$5). **Amenities:** Restaurant (Italian), bar; access to nearby health club; concierge; tour desk; babysitting; laundry service; same-day dry cleaning; nonsmoking rooms; executive-level rooms. *In room:* A/C, TV w/pay movies, dataport, fridge, coffeemaker, hair dryer, iron, safe.

**The YWCA Hotel/Residence** ★★ *Value* Built in 1995, this attractive residence is next door to the Georgian Court Hotel. It's an excellent choice for male and female travelers as well as families with limited budgets. Bedrooms are simply furnished; some have TVs. There are quite a few reasonably priced restaurants nearby (but none in-house). All guest rooms do have mini-refrigerators, and three communal kitchens are available for guests' use. (There are a number of small grocery stores nearby, as well as a Save-On Foods Supermarket a 10-minute walk west on Davie Street.) There also are three TV lounges, a coin laundry, and free access to the best gym in town at the nearby co-ed YWCA Fitness Centre.

733 Beatty St., Vancouver, BC V6B 2M4. ✆ **800/663-1424** or 604/895-5830. Fax 604/681-2550. www.ywcahotel.com. 155 units, 53 with bathroom. C$68–C$88 (US$42–US$55) double with shared bathroom, C$74–C$112 (US$46–US$69) double with private bathroom. Weekly, monthly, group, and off-season discounts available. AE, MC, V. Parking C$5 (US$3.10) per day. **Amenities:** Access to YWCA facility; coin laundry; nonsmoking rooms. *In room:* A/C, TV in some rooms, dataport, fridge, hair dryer.

## THE WEST END

### EXPENSIVE

**Pacific Palisades Hotel** ★★★ *Finds* Walk into the Pacific Palisades lobby and you know right away that this is not just another boring hotel. Bold and bright colors, whimsically shaped glass chandeliers, and a sleek metal fireplace give the hotel a contemporary modern look. Watch your step for Pal the robotic dog who likes to sniff out newcomers by the check-in desk. Guest rooms are spread out over two towers; both have recently undergone extensive renovations, and the revamped rooms are fabulous. Rooms are spacious with large wall-to-wall windows. Even bigger are the one-bedroom suites, which boast large living/dining rooms. All suites have balconies and can easily accommodate four adults. A couple of other perks are the complimentary afternoon wine tasting and the best minibar items in town (everyone's a sucker for animal crackers and licorice).

1277 Robson St., Vancouver, BC V6E 1C4. ✆ **800/663-1815** or 604/688-0461. Fax 604/688-4374. www.pacificpalisadeshotel.com. 233 units. May 1–Oct 15 C$275 (US$171) double; C$325 (US$202) suite. Oct 16–Apr 30 C$200 (US$124) double; C$250 (US$155) suite. Full kitchens C$10 (US$6) extra. AE, DC, DISC, MC, V. Parking C$15 (US$9). **Amenities:** Restaurant (see Zin's in "Where to Dine," later), bar; indoor lap pool; basketball court; excellent health club; spa; Jacuzzi; sauna; bike rentals; concierge; tour desk; business center; 24-hour room service; massage; babysitting; coin laundry and laundry service; same-day dry cleaning; nonsmoking rooms. *In room:* A/C, TV, dataport, kitchenette, minibar, fridge, coffeemaker, hair dryer, iron.

**Westin Bayshore Resort & Marina** ★★★ *Kids* Thanks to a C$50-million (US$31-million) renovation, this venerable '60s resort hotel looks better than ever. The lobby has been completely redesigned to show off the surrounding park and mountains; achieving much the same thing are two new restaurants and a coffee bar, one of which has a huge outdoor deck overlooking the harbor. Perched on the water's edge overlooking Stanley Park's eastern entrance, the Bayshore is still just a short stroll along the seawall from the Canada Place Pier and downtown, and the neighborhood just keeps getting better. Rooms in the original 1961 building have been completely refurbished with classic-looking decor and modern gadgets such as high-speed Internet, two phone lines, and comfortable lighting. In the newer tower, the rooms are spacious and bright; all come with balconies and large windows. Both towers offer unobstructed views of the harbor's dazzling array of sailboats, luxury yachts, and floatplanes. This family-friendly hotel provides children with their own welcome package upon check-in and organizes Super Saturdays, a behind-the-scenes tour and movie night for the young ones, giving the parents the night off.

1601 Bayshore Dr., Vancouver, BC V6G 2V4. ✆ **800/228-3000** or 604/682-3377. Fax 604/687-3102. www.westinbayshore.com. 510 units. Mid-Apr to Oct C$289 (US$179) double; C$450–C$700 (US$279–US$434) suite. Nov to mid-Apr C$195 (US$118) double; C$370–C$420 (US$229–US$260) suite. Children under 19 stay free in parents' room. AE, DC, MC, V. Self-parking C$10 (US$6); valet parking C$15 (US$9). **Amenities:** 2 restaurants, bar; indoor and magnificent outdoor pool with mountain view; health club; Jacuzzi; sauna; watersports rental; children's programs; concierge; tour desk; car rental; business center; shopping arcade; 24-hour room service; massage; babysitting; laundry service; same-day dry cleaning; nonsmoking rooms. *In room:* A/C, TV w/pay movies, dataport, minibar, coffeemaker, hair dryer, iron.

## MODERATE

**Barclay House in the West End** ★★ *Finds* Barclay House in the West End is located just one block from the heritage Barclay Square, on one of the West End's quiet maple-lined streets. Open as a bed-and-breakfast since 1999, this beautiful house built in 1904 by Thomas Hunter, a local developer, can be a destination on its own. The elegant parlors and dining rooms are perfect for lounging on a rainy afternoon, sipping a glass of complimentary sherry before venturing out for dinner in the trendy West End. On a summer day, the front porch with its comfortable chairs makes for a great spot to read a book. All rooms are beautifully furnished in Victorian style; a number of the pieces are family heirlooms. The modern conveniences such as CD players, TV/VCRs, and luxurious bathrooms blend in perfectly. The Penthouse offers skylights, a cozy fireplace, and a romantic claw-foot tub, and the south room contains a queen-size brass bed and an elegant sitting room overlooking the front of the house.

1351 Barclay St., Vancouver, BC V6E 1H6. © **800/971-1351** or 604/605-1351. Fax 604/605-1382. www.barclayhouse.com. 5 units. C$145–C$225 (US$90–US$140) double. MC, V. Free parking. **Amenities:** Access to nearby fitness center; nonsmoking rooms. *In room:* TV/VCR w/pay movies, extensive video library, hair dryer.

**Rosellen Suites** ★★ *Kids* Staying at the Rosellen is like having your own apartment in the West End. Stanley Park and the seawall are within a few blocks and busy Denman Street with its many restaurants and shops is just three blocks east. Converted into a hotel to meet the demand for rooms during the 1986 Expo, the Rosellen has remained a favorite among travelers, with a high rate of repeat guests. The hotel offers a no-frills stay; the lobby is only open during office hours, and guests receive their own key. The largest apartment is known as the director's suite, with two bedrooms, a large dining room, a spacious kitchen, and more storage room than you know what to do with. The remaining apartments are certainly smaller than this mammoth one, but none of them really skimp on size. The one-bedroom suites sleep four people comfortably, and all units come with fully equipped kitchens, making them a great option for families.

102–2030 Barclay St., Vancouver, BC V6G 1L5. © **888/317-6648** or 604/689-4807. Fax 604/684-3327. www.rosellensuites.com. 30 units. June–Aug C$159–C$199 (US$99–US$123) 1-bedroom apt; C$199–C$299 (US$123–US$185) 2-bedroom apt; C$399 (US$247) penthouse. Sept–May C$105–C$119 (US$65–US$74) 1-bedroom apt; C$125–C$229 (US$78–US$142) 2-bedroom apt; C$325 (US$202) penthouse. Minimum 3-night stay. Rates include up to 4 people in a 1-bedroom apt and 6 in a 2-bedroom apt. Cots and cribs free. AE, DC, DISC, MC, V. Limited parking in the rear of the building C$5 (US$3.10); reserve when booking room. Pets are welcome. **Amenities:** Access to nearby health club; coin laundry; nonsmoking rooms. *In room:* TV, dataport, modern kitchen, coffeemaker, hair dryer, iron.

**West End Guest House** ★★ *Finds* A beautiful heritage home built in 1906, the West End Guest House is a fine example of what the neighborhood looked like up until the early '50s, before the concrete towers and condos replaced the original Edwardian homes. This is a wonderful respite from the hustle and bustle of the West End. The seven guest rooms are beautifully furnished and offer the ultimate in bed-time luxury: feather mattresses, down duvets, and your very own resident stuffed animal. Particularly indulgent is the Grand Queen Suite, an attic-level bedroom with skylights, brass bed, fireplace, sitting area, and claw-foot bathtub. Owner Evan Penner pampers his guests with a scrumptious breakfast and serves iced tea and sherry in the afternoon. Throughout the day, guests have access to the porch kitchen stocked with home-baked munchies and refreshments. If you ask nicely, Penner will even crank up the gramophone.

1362 Haro St., Vancouver, BC V6E 1G2. © **604/681-2889.** Fax 604/688-8812. www.westendguesthouse.com. 7 units. C$145–C$240 (US$90–US$149) double. Rates include full breakfast. AE, DISC, MC, V. Free valet parking. **Amenities:** Complimentary bikes; concierge; business center; laundry service; nonsmoking rooms. *In room:* TV/VCR, fax, dataport, hair dryer, iron.

### INEXPENSIVE

**Hostelling International Vancouver Downtown Hostel** Located in a converted nunnery, this new and modern hostel is an extremely convenient base of operations from which to explore downtown. The beach is a few blocks south;

downtown is a 10-minute walk north. Most beds are in quad dorms, with a limited number of doubles and triples available. Except for two rooms with a private bathroom, all bathroom facilities are shared. Rooms and facilities are accessible for disabled travelers. There are common cooking facilities, as well as a rooftop patio and game room. The hostel gets extremely busy in the summertime, so book ahead. Many organized activities and tours can be booked at the hostel. There's free shuttle service to the bus/train station and Jericho Beach. There is no curfew here.

1114 Burnaby St. (at Thurlow St.), Vancouver, BC V6E 1P1. © **888/203-4302** or 604/684-4565. Fax 604/684-4540. www.hihostels.bc.ca. 239 beds in 4-person units; some double and triple units. Beds C$20 (US$12) IYHA members, C$24 (US$15) nonmembers; doubles C$55 (US$34) members, C$64 (US$40) nonmembers; triples C$70 (US$43) members, C$86 (US$53) nonmembers. Annual adult membership C$37 (US$23). MC, V. Limited free parking. **Amenities:** Bike rental; activities desk; coin laundry. *In room:* No phone.

**Sylvia Hotel** Built in 1912 when the West End was relatively unpopulated, the Sylvia is on the shores of English Bay just a few blocks from Stanley Park. One of Vancouver's oldest hotels, the gray-stone, ivy-wreathed Sylvia resembles a mansion. The lobby sets up high expectations with its beautiful stain-glass windows, marble staircase, red carpets, and overstuffed chairs. Alas, the elegance does not carry over to the rooms, which are rather plainly furnished with slightly mismatched furniture. The best rooms are located on the higher floors facing English Bay; views of the water get better in the winter when the tall trees lining the beach lose their leaves. The suites have fully equipped kitchens and are large enough for families. Sixteen rooms in the 12-year-old low-rise annex have individual heating but offer less atmosphere.

1154 Gilford St., Vancouver, BC V6G 2P6. © **604/681-9321.** Fax 604/682-3551. www.sylviahotel.com. 118 units. Apr–Sept C$75–C$135 (US$47–US$84) double. Oct–Mar C$75–C$100 (US$47–US$62) double. Children under 18 stay free in parents' room. AE, DC, MC, V. Parking C$7 (US$4.35). **Amenities:** Restaurant, bar; concierge; limited room service; dry cleaning; nonsmoking rooms. *In room:* TV, dataport, hair dryer.

## THE WEST SIDE

### EXPENSIVE

**Granville Island Hotel** ★ *Finds* The Granville Island Hotel offers a unique waterfront setting on the east end of Granville Island, in the heart of some of the city's most interesting galleries and theatres, and just a short stroll from the cornucopia that is the Granville Island food market. The hotel's rooms are spacious with large bathrooms and soaker tubs. The rooms on the third floor come with vaulted ceilings and balconies. Flanked on one side by the waters of False Creek and the seawall and island on the other, it is almost impossible to not have a good view. Ultimately prime views, however, are to be had in one of the Penthouse suites, located in the new wing opened in September 2001. Most rooms also have a microwave (or one can be requested from housekeeping) to warm up any goodies you bring back from the market.

1253 Johnston St., Vancouver, BC V6H 3R9. © **800/663-1840** or 604/683-7373. Fax 604/683-3061. www.granvilleislandhotel.com. 85 units. C$229 (US$142) double. Off-season discounts available. AE, DC, DISC, MC, V. Parking C$6 (US$3.70). Pets welcome. **Amenities:** Restaurant, brew pub; access to nearby health club and tennis courts; small exercise room; Jacuzzi; bike rental; concierge; tour desk; car-rental desk; business center; limited room service; massage; babysitting; laundry; same-day dry cleaning; nonsmoking rooms. *In room:* A/C, TV w/pay movies, fax, dataport, minibar, coffeemaker, hair dryer, iron.

### MODERATE

**Kenya Court Ocean Front Guest House** ★ *Finds* Every room in this apartment building at Kitsilano Beach has an unobstructed waterfront view of

Vanier Park, English Bay, downtown Vancouver, and the Coast Mountains. This architectural landmark is an ideal launching pad for strolls around Granville Island, Vanier Park, the Maritime Museum, the Vancouver Museum, and other Kitsilano sights. An outdoor pool, tennis courts, and jogging trails are nearby. Run by a retired doctor and his wife (Dr. and Mrs. Williams), the Kenya Court has the feel of a bed-and-breakfast. Each guest suite—with a living room, bathroom, separate bedroom, and full kitchen—is a large converted apartment that's been tastefully furnished. A full breakfast (including eggs and bacon) is served in a glass solarium up on the rooftop, where there's a spectacular view of English Bay.

2230 Cornwall Ave., Vancouver, BC V6K 1B5, ✆ **604/738-7085.** H&dwilliams@telus.net. 4 units. C$135–C$165 (US$84–US$102) double. Extra person C$50 (US$31). No credit cards. Garage or street parking. **Amenities:** All nonsmoking rooms. *In room:* TV, kitchen, fridge, coffeemaker, hair dryer, iron.

## INEXPENSIVE

**Johnson Heritage House Bed & Breakfast** ★★ *Finds* Innkeeper Ron Johnson is a collector. Antique phonographs, coffee grinders, wooden giraffes, hobby horses, Indonesian stone sculpture—all these and countless other objects are on display in various nooks and crannies of this old Craftsman home in Vancouver's quiet Kerrisdale neighborhood (a 15-minute drive from the Vancouver airport and about a 10-minute drive to downtown). The Garden room downstairs is quiet and self-contained, with big bright windows looking out on a garden full of raspberries and blueberries. Upstairs the small but cozy Sunshine room (shower only) offers a balcony with a view of the back garden, while the larger Mountain View room offers an excellent view of the Lions and the other peaks of the North Shore. And though the private bathroom for the Mountain View is across the hall, it comes with a giant 2-person, 7-million pound (ok, it's heavy anyway) claw-foot tub. Best of all is the Carousel room. It's large and bright, with a big four-poster brass bed, a slate fireplace, and a generous size bathroom. A full breakfast is served in the spacious dining room that looks out onto the tree-shaded garden. Guests are also provided with a little sight-seeing booklet, specially prepared by Ron.

2278 W. 34th Ave., Vancouver, BC V6M 1G6. ✆ **604/266-4175.** Fax 604/266-4175. www.johnsons-inn-vancouver.com. 4 units. C$115–C$180 (US$71–US$112) double. Rates include full breakfast. No credit cards. Free parking. *In room:* TV/VCR, dataport w/high-speed Internet access, hair dryer.

**Penny Farthing Inn** Built in 1912, this landmark house on a quiet residential street is filled with antiques and stained glass. There's a common room with a fireplace, and in the backyard an English-country-style garden. All guest rooms are decorated with lovely pine furniture. On the top floor, Abigail's Suite is bright and self-contained with nice views from both front and back. Bettina's Room features a fireplace and a small balcony. Sophie's Room, though smaller, has a nice porch with two wicker chairs. Lucinda's Room—with a private bathroom across the hall—offers the best value of the four. Coffee and a selection of teas and hot chocolate are always on hand for guests. Fix a cuppa and watch the resident cats at play while you relax.

2855 W. Sixth Ave., Vancouver, BC V6K 1X2. ✆ **866/739-9002** or 604/739-9002. Fax 604/739-9004. www.pennyfarthinginn.com. 4 units. May–Oct C$115 (US$71) double; C$170 (US$105) suite. Nov–Apr C$95 (US$59) double; C$145 (US$90) suite. Rates include full breakfast. No credit cards. Street parking. **Amenities:** Free bikes; business center; nonsmoking rooms. *In room:* TV/VCR, fax, dataport, fridge, coffeemaker, hair dryer, CD player.

## THE NORTH SHORE (NORTH VANCOUVER & WEST VANCOUVER)

### EXPENSIVE

**Lonsdale Quay Hotel** ★ Directly across the Burrard Inlet from the Canada Place Pier, the Lonsdale Quay Hotel is at the water's edge above the Lonsdale Quay Market at the SeaBus terminal. An escalator rises from the midst of the market's food, crafts, and souvenir stalls to the front desk on the third floor. The rooms are simply furnished and tastefully decorated, without the grandeur or luxurious touches of comparably priced downtown hotels. Nevertheless, the hotel has unique and fabulous harbor and city views, is only 15 minutes by bus or car from Grouse Mountain Ski Resort and Capilano Regional Park, and provides easy access to the BC Rail and ferry terminals.

123 Carrie Cates Court, North Vancouver, BC V6M 3K7. ✆ **800/836-6111** or 604/986-6111. Fax 604/986-8782. www.lonsdalequayhotel.com. 83 units. High season C$125–C$225 (US$78–US$140) double or twin; C$350 (US$217) suite. Low season C$90–C$165 (US$56–US$102) double or twin; C$250 (US$155) suite. Extra person C$25 (US$16). Senior discount available. AE, DC, DISC, MC, V. Parking C$7 (US$4.35); free on weekends and holidays. SeaBus: Lonsdale Quay. **Amenities:** 2 restaurants; small exercise room; spa; bike rental; children's play area; concierge; tour desk; shopping arcade; limited room service; massage; babysitting; laundry service; same-day dry cleaning; nonsmoking hotel; executive-level rooms. *In room:* A/C, TV, fax, dataport, minibar, coffeemaker, hair dryer, iron.

### MODERATE

**Beachside Bed & Breakfast** ★★ *Finds* As promised by the name, the Beachside sits on its own private little beach on the shores of English Bay, with a sweeping view of Stanley Park, the Lion's Gate Bridge, and the tall skyline of downtown Vancouver. The upstairs common area of this split-level house—reserved exclusively for guests—features wall-to-ceiling windows and binoculars for gazing at the seals and bald eagles and (on rare occasions) killer whales that swim by. There's also a fireplace, VCR and videos, and lots of good books should the ocean view lose its appeal. Downstairs are two beachfront rooms featuring floor-to-ceiling windows facing out toward the ocean. The Seaside room features a jetted tub for two in a somewhat small but very private bathroom, while the Oceanfront room has a private Jacuzzi big enough for six friends and their pet sea lion (it's big!). Located out back, the smallest and least expensive of the rooms—Diane's Room—features a small patio but lacks an ocean view.

4208 Evergreen Ave., West Vancouver, B.C. V7V 1H1. ✆ **800/563-3311** or 604/922-7773. www.beach.bc.ca. 3 units. C$150–C$250 (US$93–US$155) double. Extra person C$30 (US$19). Rates include full breakfast. MC, V. Free parking. Bus: 250, 251, 252, 253. **Amenities:** Beachside Jacuzzi; nonsmoking hotel. *In room:* TV/VCR, fridge, coffeemaker, hair dryer, iron.

## 4 Where to Dine

Vancouverites do seem to dine out more than residents of any other Canadian city. Outstanding meals are available in all price ranges and in many different cuisines, from Caribbean to Mongolian and Japanese. Even better, over the past few years Vancouverites have come to expect top quality, and yet they absolutely refuse to pay the kind of top dollar restaurant-goers pay in New York or San Francisco. For discerning diners from elsewhere, Vancouver is a steal.

The cuisine buzzword here is West Coast. Justifiable pride in local produce, game, and seafood is combined with innovation and creativity. More restaurants are shifting to seasonal, even monthly, menus, giving their chefs greater freedom.

Once less than palatable, British Columbian wines have improved to the point that local vintners are now winning international acclaim.

## DOWNTOWN & YALETOWN

### VERY EXPENSIVE

**C** ★★★ SEAFOOD/WEST COAST It's become almost habit to quietly backhand the conspicuous consumption of the '80s generation—what's forgotten is just how well they consumed. C brings it all back, in a room done up in brilliant shades of Miami white, with the decor itself providing a little postindustrial commentary. Look for pale-green bread baskets made from cut sheets of heavy-gauge rubber, footrests upholstered with truck-tire retreads, and faux vinyl siding in the washrooms. Beyond the decor, however, C re-creates the '80s through the sheer indulgent quality with which they serve fish. C's taster box—a kind of small wooden high-rise of appetizers—includes salmon gravlax cured in Saskatoon berry tea, artichoke carpaccio, abalone tempura, and grilled garlic squid. A variety of seafood main courses are available, but for the ultimate dining experience, let chef Robert Clark show off (he's dying to), and order the seven-course sampling menu. Savor the exquisite cuisine as you watch the sun go down over the marina.

1600 Howe St. ✆ **604/681-1164.** www.crestaurant.com. Reservations recommended. Main courses C$21–C$32 (US$13–US$20). AE, DC, MC, V. Daily for dinner 5:30–11pm; lunch Mon–Fri 11:30am–2:30pm and Sun 11am–2:30pm. Valet parking C$7 (US$4.35). Bus: 1, 2.

**The Five Sails** ★★ WEST COAST The Five Sails's view of Coal Harbour, the Lions Gate Bridge, and the Coast Mountains is as spectacular as the food. Where for a number of years the Five Sails served up its own interpretation of West Coast or Pacific Northwest cuisine, chef Jean-Yves Benoit and his right hand maitre d' and spouse, Minna, have turned the ship around and set sail for the Old World. Look for appetizers that combine pasta with seafood, like the Dungeness crab ravioli served with a basil flan and tomato emulsion. As a hotel restaurant, Five Sails does cover the bases with chicken, steak, and vegetarian dishes; but ask Minna for suggestions, and she will quickly point out the signature French cuisine. The Marseille bouillabaisse, thick with seafood, is worth a try and so is the grilled halibut with sautéed morel mushrooms, shallot confit, and finished with a rich veal jus. The wine selection leans slightly toward British Columbian selections and highlights a different winery every month.

999 Canada Place Way, in the Pan-Pacific Hotel. ✆ **604/891-2892.** Reservations recommended. Main courses C$25–C$38 (US$16–US$24); tasting menu C$55–C$65 (US$34–US$40). AE, DC, MC, V. Daily 6–10pm. SkyTrain: Waterfront.

**Gotham Steakhouse and Cocktail Bar** ★★ STEAK Vegetarians beware: Gotham means meat. Okay, potatoes and a bit of seafood, but that's it. The room is of ambitious proportions—a 12m (40-ft.) high timber ceiling divided down the middle with a cocktail bar on one side, a dining room on the other, and a patio with fireplace balancing things out. Furnishings are aggressively masculine. The wine list is encyclopedic. And then there's the food. The deep-fried calamari appetizer was a light and tasty revelation. Jumbo shrimp were sumo-size. And the steaks—these were incredible: a porterhouse cut the size of a catcher's mitt, a petit filet mignon as tall as half a bread loaf. The meat just melts away on your tongue. Better to pass on the forgettable veggie side dishes entirely and spend the money on another glass of French merlot. The service is impeccable.

615 Seymour St. ✆ **604/605-8282.** Fax 604/605-8285. www.gothamsteakhouse.com. Reservations recommended. Main courses C$27–C$49 (US$17–US$30). AE, DC, MC, V. Mon–Fri 11:30am–2:30pm; daily 5–11pm (cocktail bar somewhat later). Bus: 4, 7.

## EXPENSIVE

**Blue Water Café and Raw Bar** ★★★ SEAFOOD If you had to describe the Blue Water Café in one word it would be *fresh:* fresh seafood and a fresh concept. The raw bar serves up sushi, oysters, sashimi, and a range of Asian inspired seafood dishes. We started off with "sushi" rolls of scallops and thinly sliced cucumbers wrapped in smoked salmon. For the main courses we tried a lightly seared yellow fin tuna in a citrus-pepper crust which came served on a bed of yellow beans, seasoned with herb and basil infused oil. When in season, order the diver-caught sea scallops, plainly grilled and served with sautéed zucchini, pancetta, and arugula in a maple chive dressing. Since opening in the fall of 2000, the Blue Water has become one of Vancouver's hottest restaurants, a place to see and be seen. Reservations are recommended on weekends, but it is just as much fun to wait at the bar, watching sushi-maestro Max Katsuno at work while you chill your cocktail on the world's only (so far) fully refrigerated bar top.

1095 Hamilton St., Yaletown. ✆ **604/688-8078.** www.bluewatercafe.net. Reservations recommended. Main courses C$17–C$30.50 (US$11–US$19). AE, DC, MC, V. Daily 11am–1am, light menu 3–5pm and 11pm–1am. Bus 2.

**La Terrazza** ★★ ITALIAN Located on the edge of Yaletown, La Terrazza's sleek, modern exterior contrasts sharply with the warm bustling dining room inside. The kitchen is in the capable hands of Neapolitan chef Gennaro Iorio. No fusion or complicated culinary acrobatics on his menu. On the contrary, many dishes stand out for their simplicity. The menu changes with the seasons, and a tasting menu with matching wines highlights a different culinary region of Italy every month. One of the more intriguing appetizers is the bocconcini cheese, wrapped in prosciutto and raddicchio, grilled and drizzled with strawberry vinaigrette. Main courses include various pasta dishes, but following the chef's recommendation, we tried the roasted guinea hen and duck breast with frangelico brandy; both were outstanding (though the duck breast was the hands-down favorite). The wine list is extensive, offering selections from all over the world. Save room for dessert, particularly the white cheesecake baked in phyllo pastry topped with sour cherries and fruit coulis.

1088 Cambie St. ✆ **604/899-4449.** www.laterrazza.ca. Reservations recommended. Main courses C$16–C$30 (US$10–US$19). AE, DC, MC, V. Mon–Thurs 5–11pm, Fri–Sat 5pm–midnight, Sun 5–10pm. Bus: 2.

## MODERATE

**La Bodega** ★★ *Value* TAPAS This warm, dark Spanish bar has a dozen or so tables and some great little romantic corners. Expect authentic Spanish tapas—garlic prawns, ceviche, marinated mushrooms, pan-fried squid, and good black olives. Specials on the blackboard regularly include *conejo* (rabbit with tomatoes and peppers), quail, and B.C. scallops. All of it comes with lots of crusty bread for soaking up the wonderful garlicky goo. La Bodega has a good selection of Portuguese and Spanish wines and the best sangria in town.

1277 Howe St. ✆ **604/684-8815.** Reservations accepted. Tapas C$3.95–C$7.95 (US$2.45–US$4.90); main courses C$11.25–C$17.95 (US$7–US$11). AE, DC, MC, V. Mon–Fri 4:30–midnight, Sat 5pm–midnight, Sun 5–11pm. Bus: 4, 7.

## INEXPENSIVE

**Olympia Oyster & Fish Co. Ltd.** *Finds* FISH & CHIPS This hole in the wall of a restaurant, just off Vancouver's trendiest shopping street, serves up the city's best fish-and-chips. On any given day you'll find West End residents, German tourists, and well-heeled shoppers toting their "daily catch" from Mexx or

Banana Republic vying for counter space. There are only a few tables and a window-seat counter, plus three sidewalk tables (weather permitting), but the fish is always fresh and flaky and can be grilled if you prefer. You can choose sole, halibut, or cod, which may be combined with oysters or prawns. If you want to take home smoked salmon, the staff will wrap it up or ship it if you prefer.

820 Thurlow St. ✆ **604/685-0716.** Main courses C$6–C$10 (US$3.70–US$6). AE, MC, V. Mon–Fri 10am–8pm, Sat 10am–7pm, Sun 11am–7pm. Bus: 5.

## GASTOWN & CHINATOWN

### EXPENSIVE

**The Cannery** ★ SEAFOOD At least some of the pleasure of eating at The Cannery comes from simply finding the place. Hop over the railway tracks and thread your way past container terminals and fish packing plants until you're sure you're lost, and then with a last turn the road opens onto a brightly lit parking lot and there it is—a great ex-warehouse of a building hanging out over the waters of Burrard Inlet. The building itself—its beam-laded warehouse interior, loaded with old nets and seafaring memorabilia—is another hefty portion of The Cannery's charm. As for the view, it's simply stunning, one of the best in Vancouver. You'll find good, solid, traditional seafood here, often alder-grilled, with ever-changing specials to complement the salmon and halibut basics. Chefs Frederic Couton and Jacques Wan have been getting more inventive of late, but when an institution is 27 years old and still going strong, no one's ever *too* keen to rock the boat. The wine list is stellar, and the desserts are wonderfully inventive.

2205 Commissioner St., near Victoria Dr. ✆ **604/254-9606.** www.canneryseafood.com. Reservations recommended. Main courses C$17–C$27 (US$11–US$17). AE, DC, DISC, MC, V. Mon–Fri 11:30am–2:30pm; Mon–Sat 5:30–10:30pm, Sun 5:30–9:30pm. Closed Dec 24–26. Bus: 7 to Victoria Dr. From downtown, head east on Hastings St., turn left on Victoria Dr. (2 blocks past Commercial Dr.), then right on Commissioner St.

### MODERATE

**Park Lock Seafood Restaurant** *Kids* CHINESE/DIM SUM If you've never done dim sum, this traditional dining room in the very heart of Chinatown is the place to give it a try. From 8am to 3pm daily, waitresses wheel little carts loaded with Chinese delicacies past white-linen-covered tables. When you see something you like, you grab it. The final bill is based upon how many little dishes are left on your table. Dishes include spring rolls, *hargow* and *shumai* (steamed shrimp, beef, or pork dumplings), prawns wrapped in fresh white noodles, small steamed buns, sticky rice cooked in banana leaves, curried squid, and lots more. Parties of four or more are best—that way you get to try each other's food.

544 Main St. (at E. Pender St., on the second floor). ✆ **604/688-1581.** Reservations recommended. Main courses C$10–C$35 (US$6–US$22); dim sum dishes C$2.50–C$3.25 (US$1.55–US$2). AE, MC, V. Daily 8am–3pm; Tues–Sun 5–10pm. Bus: 19, 22.

### INEXPENSIVE

**Incendio** ★ *Finds* PIZZA If you're looking for something casual and local that won't be full of other people reading downtown maps, this little Gastown hideaway is sublime. The 22 pizza combinations are served on fresh, crispy crusts baked in an old wood-fired oven. Pastas are homemade, and you're encouraged to mix and match—try the mussels with spinach fettuccine, capers, and tomatoes in lime butter. The wine list is decent and the beer list is inspired. And now, there's a patio. Sunday night features all-you-can-eat pizza for C$8 (US$5).

103 Columbia St. ✆ **604/688-8694.** Incendio@imag.net. Main courses C$8–C$12 (US$5–US$7). AE, MC, V. Mon–Thu 11:30am–3pm and 5–10pm, Fri 11:30am–3pm and 5–11pm, Sat 5–11pm, and Sun 4:30–10pm. Closed Dec 23–Jan 3. Bus: 1, 8.

## THE WEST END

### EXPENSIVE

**Delilah's** ★★ CONTINENTAL Walk down the steps from the Denman Place Mall and you've entered Delilah's French bordello of a room—red velvet chaise longues, little private corner rooms, cherubim cavorting on the ceiling, and wall-mounted lamps with glass shades. First order of business is a martini—Delilah's forte, and the fuel firing the laughter and conversation all around. The two-page martini list comes with everything from the basic Boston Tea Partini (Citron vodka and iced tea in a glass with sugared rim and lemon wedge) to the ultimate in Southern excess, the Miranda (pineapple, vodka, and fresh floating fruit). The staff are brisk and helpful and run to the Miranda side—flamboyant, friendly, and over the top. The menu is seafood heavy, which Delilah's does well, sticking to freshness and simple sauces such as the seared jumbo scallops with saffron risotto or grilled swordfish with a sun-dried cherry-cranberry compote. The chef gets in a bit over his head with land-based fare, so go with the flow and order something from the sea.

1789 Comox St. ✆ **604/687-3424.** Reservations accepted for parties of 6 or more. Fixed-price menu C$23–C$32.50 (US$14–US$20). AE, DC, MC, V. Daily 5:30pm–midnight. Bus: 5 to Denman St.

**Raincity Grill** ★★ WEST COAST Raincity's room is long and low and hugs the shoreline, the better to let the evening sun pour in. With the location—by English Bay Beach—and the spacious patio, you wonder if the owner didn't have to kill for the spot. Then you realize he's paying off the view with volume—they do pack them in at Raincity, making dinner more of a social occasion than you may have wished. Ah, but the view, and the food. Raincity's forte is local ingredients, West Coast style. That means appetizers of barbecued quail with a sage and goat-cheese polenta, crispy jumbo spot prawns, or a salad of smoked steelhead. Entrees include grilled Fraser Valley free-range chicken and fresh-caught spring salmon. And then there's the award-winning wine list. It's huge and, in keeping with the restaurant's theme, it sticks pretty close to home. Better yet, most varieties are available by the glass.

1193 Denman St. ✆ **604/685-7337.** www.raincitygrill.com. Reservations recommended. Main courses C$18–C$34 (US$11–US$21). AE, DC, MC, V. Mon–Fri 11:30am–2:30pm, Sat–Sun 10:30am–2:30pm; daily 5–10:30pm. Bus: 1, 5.

### MODERATE

**Zin's** ★ CASUAL Located on Vancouver's Robson-street fashion heartland, Zin's made quite a splash when it opened thanks to its creation of a new concept: taste tripping. The latest trend in Vancouver dining, Zin's takes you on a food trip around the globe, dish by dish. Unlike fusion, where flavors from all over the world were mushed together on one plate, with taste tripping, the global dishes arrive chastely one after the other. Zin's chef may start you off with a grilled naan bread and mint tomato chutney or maybe a pure and unadulterated spicy Thai soup. For the main course you could go for a French goat cheese fondue (served with baguettes for dipping), or a Malaysian *laksa* seafood stew in coconut broth. For your safety and dining comfort, Zin's chef maintains the integrity of each cuisine and the quality of each dish throughout the culinary voyage. For casual dining the wine list is one of the best, with close to 50 wines by the glass.

1277 Robson St. ✆ **604/408-1700.** www.zin-restaurant.com. Main courses C$11–C$17 (US$7–US$11). AE, DC, MC, V. Mon–Wed 7am–midnight, Thu–Sat 7am–1am, Sun 8am–11pm.

### INEXPENSIVE

**Gyoza King** JAPANESE Gyoza King features an entire menu of *gyoza*—succulent Japanese dumplings filled with prawns, pork, vegetables, and other combinations—as well as Japanese noodles and staples like *katsu-don* (pork cutlet over rice) and *o-den* (a rich, hearty soup). This is the gathering spot for hordes of young Japanese visitors looking for cheap eats that still taste close to home cooking. Seating is divided among Western-style tables, the bar (where you can watch the chef in action), and the Japanese-style front table, which is reserved for larger groups if the restaurant is busy. The staff is very courteous and happy to explain the dishes if you're not familiar with Japanese cuisine.

1508 Robson St. ✆ **604/669-8278.** Main courses C$6–C$13 (US$3.70–US$8). AE, MC, V. Sat–Sun 11:30am–3pm; Mon–Sat 5:30pm–2am, Sun 5:30pm–midnight. Bus: 5.

**Stephos** *Value* GREEK A fixture on the Davie Street dining scene, Stephos has been packing them in since Zorba was a boy. The cuisine is simple Greek fare at its finest and cheapest. Customers line up outside to wait up to 30 minutes for a seat amid Greek travel posters, potted ivy, and whitewashed walls (the average wait is about 10 to 15 minutes). Once inside, the staff will never rush you out the door. Order pita and dip (hummus, spicy eggplant, or garlic spread) while you peruse the menu. An interesting appetizer is the Avgolemono soup, a delicately flavored chicken broth with egg and lemon, accompanied by a plate of piping hot pita bread. When choosing a main course, keep in mind that portions are huge. The roasted lamb, lamb chops, fried calamari, and a variety of souvlakis are served with rice, roast potatoes, and Greek salad. The beef, lamb, or chicken pita come in slightly smaller portions served with fries and *tzatziki* (garlic sauce).

1124 Davie St. ✆ **604/683-2555.** Reservations accepted for parties of 5 or more. Main courses C$4.25–C$10 (US$2.65–US$6). AE, MC, V. Daily 11:30am–11:30pm. Bus: 5.

## THE WEST SIDE

### VERY EXPENSIVE

**Lumière** ★★★ FRENCH The success of this French dining experiment in the heart of Kitsilano has turned chef Rob Feenie into a hot commodity. He now regularly jets off to New York to teach folks back east how to do it right. And how's that? Preparation and presentation are immaculately French, while ingredients are resolutely local, which makes for interesting surprises—fresh local ginger with the veal, or raspberries in the foie gras. Lumière's tasting menus are a series of 8 or 10 delightful plates that change with the season, perfectly matched to a local wine vintage (not included in the fixed price) and gorgeously presented. Diners simply choose one of the four tasting menus (one menu is vegetarian) and then sit back and let the pilots in Lumière's kitchen take them on a culinary journey they won't forget. If you can afford it, it's a voyage you shouldn't miss.

2551 W. Broadway. ✆ **604/739-8185.** Reservations recommended. Tasting menu (8 courses) C$60–C$100 (US$37–US$62). AE, DC, MC, V. Tues–Sun 5:30–9:30pm. Bus: 9, 10.

**Tojo's Restaurant** ★★ JAPANESE I had never met Hideki Tojo, or even tried his cooking, until one afternoon at Vancouver's first-ever sumo wrestling demonstration, when a diminutive man on the tatami mat next to me lifted up a bento box and proffered a tray of delicate sushi rolls. As two thunderous giants eyed each other in the ring, I picked out a piece with fresh salmon and popped it in my mouth. Incredible. A thousand pounds of screaming human flesh were smashing each other in the ring, but my attention was entirely captured by the exquisite flavors exploding in my mouth. Back in Tojo's modest sushi bar, the ever-changing menu offers such specialties as sea urchin on the half shell, herring roe, lobster claws, tuna, crab, and asparagus. I'd like to say I've since become a regular, but at the prices Tojo charges for his creations, regulars are either film stars or fully mortgaged for the next seven generations. Still, if you don't mind splurging and you want the very best, Tojo is your man.

202–777 W. Broadway. ✆ **604/872-8050.** Reservations recommended. Full dinners C$23–C$100 (US$14–US$62). AE, DC, MC, V. Mon–Sat 5–10:30pm. Closed Christmas week. Bus: 9.

## MODERATE

**Sami's** ★★ *Finds* INDIAN Always in the running for best Indian food in Vancouver, Sami's is still going strong. Briefly there were two, when Sami's opened a downtown location, but this restaurant has now left the warm nest of chef Sami Lalji and gone off in its own direction. This means that those wanting to try the original fabulous East-meets-West South Asian cooking will have to make the trip out to a strip mall off West Broadway again. True, the food is worth the journey, offering inventive and delicious dishes—try the Mumbai-blackened New York steak set atop spiked mashers with blueberry coriander jus—that won't put a large hole in your wallet. Service is efficient and knowledgeable. Expect a line.

986 W. Broadway. ✆ **604/736-8330.** Reservations not accepted. Main courses C$12 (US$7). DC, MC, V. Mon–Sat 11:30am–2:30pm; daily 5pm–11pm. Bus: 9.

**The SandBar** ★★ CASUAL Fridays and Saturdays the bar and patio become refuges for 20-something singles and rebounding baby boomers out on the prowl. Those who are not ready to tear into the pickup scene can actually sink their teeth into a number of fairly decent tapas. The mussels and clams come wonderfully steamed, positively demanding that one sop up the juices with some warm bits of bread. Shrimp and pork pot stickers or dumplings provide the Asian component of a menu that spans the globe. Mexican-inspired fishcakes are served with a pineapple salsa, while fish taquitos come with a chipotle dip sauce. The menu also offers a number of main courses, including cedar-planked grilled salmon and a daily pasta special that in season may feature fresh B.C. scallops in a light tomato sauce. In summer the patio on the third floor is fabulous for lazing about in the warm sunshine, while come fall or winter it's a good spot to cuddle up beneath a heat lamp in the big leather chair.

1535 Johnston St., Granville Island, ✆ **604/669-9030.** www.mysandbar.com. Reservations not accepted for patio. Tapas C$5.75–C$11.75 (US$3.55–US$7); main courses C$10–C$20 (US$6–US$12). AE, MC, V. Daily 11am–midnight; kitchen may close at 10:30pm. Bus 50 to Granville Island.

## INEXPENSIVE

**The Naam Restaurant** ★ *Kids* VEGETARIAN Back in the sixties, when Kitsilano was Canada's hippie haven, the Naam was tie-dye central. Things have changed a tad since then, but Vancouver's oldest vegetarian and natural-food restaurant retains a pleasant granola feel. The decor is simple, earnest, and welcoming: well-worn wooden tables and chairs, plants, an assortment of local art, and a fabulous garden patio. The brazenly healthy fare ranges from all vegetarian burgers, enchiladas, and burritos to tofu terriyaki, Thai noodles, and a variety of pita pizzas. The sesame spice fries are a Vancouver institution. And though the Naam is not quite vegan, they do cater to the anti-egg-and-cheese crowd with specialties like the macrobiotic Dragon Bowl of brown rice, tofu, peanut sauce, sprouts, and steamed vegetables. The only real trick is to arrive well before you're actually hungry. Serving staff will invariably disappear on an extended search for personal fulfillment at some point during your meal.

2724 W. Fourth Ave. ✆ **604/738-7151.** www.thenaam.com. Reservations accepted on weekdays only. Main courses C$4.95–C$10 (US$3–US$6). AE, MC, V. Daily 24 hours. Live music every night 7–10pm. Bus: 4, 22.

## THE EAST SIDE

### EXPENSIVE

**Sun Sui Wah** ★★ *Kids* CHINESE/DIM SUM/SEAFOOD One of the most elegant and sophisticated Chinese restaurants in town, the award-winning Sun Sui Wah is well known for its seafood. Fresh and varied, the catch of the day can include fresh crab, rock cod, geoduck, scallops, abalone, oyster, prawns, and more. Pick your own from the tank or order from the menu if you don't like to meet your food eye-to-eye before it's cooked. The staff is quite helpful for those unfamiliar with the cuisine. Dim sum is a treat, with the emphasis on seafood. Just point and choose. For land lovers and vegetarians, there are plenty of other choices, though they are missing out on one of the best seafood feasts in town.

3888 Main St. ✆ **604/872-8822.** www.sunsuiwah.com. Also in Richmond: 102 Alderbridge Place, 4940 No. 3 Rd. (✆ **604/273-8208**). Reservations accepted. Main courses C$11–C$50 (US$7–US$31). AE, DC, MC, V. Daily 10:30am–3pm and 5–10:30pm. Bus: 3.

### MODERATE

**The Brickhouse Bistro** ★★ *Value* BISTRO There were once two partners who opened a bar in a slightly seedy part of town. It ought to do well, they reasoned, for there are many with money who have recently bought condos, and right now they have nowhere to drink. And do well it did. Encouraged, the partners refurbished the room above their bar, and opened a bistro—a casual, funky place. They hired a chef capable of cooking simple but superior food, dishes like New Zealand rib eye in Madeira jus or specials of fresh fish. To lure customers, the partners kept prices very low. A selection of B.C. wines was also available, at two-thirds the price charged by other bistros. Word of the cuisine and ambience has spread far and wide, so that dinner on a weekend is a pleasant social affair. But the Brickhouse is still a tasty steal.

730 Main St. ✆ **604/689-8645.** Reservations accepted. Main courses C$10–C$16 (US$6–US$10). MC, V. Tues–Thurs 6pm–midnight, Fri–Sat 6pm–1am. Bus: 3.

## THE NORTH SHORE

### EXPENSIVE

**The Beach House at Dundarave Pier** ★★ WEST COAST Set on a dramatic waterfront location, the House offers a panoramic view of English Bay. Those on the heated patio also get sunshine, but they miss out on the rich interior of this restored 1912 teahouse. The food is consistently good—innovative, but not so experimental that it leaves the staid West Van burghers gasping for breath. Appetizers include soft-shell crab with salt-and-fire jelly; grilled scallops with baby spinach, crispy onions, and red-pepper cream; and grilled portobello mushroom with Okanagan Valley goat cheese. Entrees have included garlic-crusted rack of lamb with honey balsamic glaze and baked striped sea bass with basil mousse and rock prawns. The wine list is award winning.

150 25th St., West Vancouver. ✆ **604/922-1414.** www.beachhousewestvan.com. Reservations recommended. Main courses C$12–C$16 (US$7–US$10) lunch, C$17–C$29 (US$11–US$18) dinner. AE, DC, MC, V. Mon–Sat 11am–3pm, Sun brunch 10:30am–3pm; Sun–Thurs 5–10pm, Fri–Sat 5–11pm. Light appetizers served 3–5pm. Bus: 255 to Ambleside Pier.

**The Salmon House on the Hill** ★ WEST COAST/SEAFOOD High above West Vancouver, The Salmon House offers a spectacular view of the city and Burrard Inlet. The rough-hewn cedar walls are adorned with a growing collection of indigenous West Coast art. Chef Dan Atkinson's menu reflects his extensive research into local ingredients and First Nations cuisine. An alderwood-fired grill dominates the kitchen, lending a delicious flavor to many of the dishes. To start, we recommend the Salmon House Sampler, featuring smoked and candied salmon, accompanied by fresh salsas, chutneys, and relishes. Entrees include alder-grilled British Columbia salmon with a pernod bread stuffing, a Japanese style sesame crusted tuna in a mustard and wasabi sauce, and a rum and maple syrup marinated salmon topped with a vanilla bean and pineapple salsa. Desserts bear little resemblance to early First Nations cuisine: mocha torte with pecan-toffee crust, blueberry tiramisu. The wine list earned an award of excellence from *Wine Spectator.*

2229 Folkstone Way, West Vancouver. ✆ **604/926-3212.** www.salmonhouse.com. Reservations recommended for dinner. Lunch main courses C$11.25–C$15 (US$7–US$9); dinner main courses C$17.50–C$30 (US$11–US$19). AE, DC, MC, V. Mon–Sat 11:30am–2:30pm, Sun brunch 11am–2:30pm; Sun–Thurs 5–10pm, Fri–Sat 5–10:30pm. Bus: 251 to Queens St.

## 5 Exploring Vancouver

A city perched on the edge of a great wilderness, Vancouver offers unmatched opportunities for exploring the outdoors. Paradoxically, within the city limits Vancouver is intensely urban. There are sidewalk cafes to match those in Paris and shopping streets that rival London's. The forest of downtown residential high-rises looks somewhat like New York, while the buzz and movement of Chinatown reminds you of San Francisco or Canton. Comparisons with other places soon begin to pall, however, as you come to realize that Vancouver is entirely its own creation: a self-confident, sparklingly beautiful city, like no place else on earth.

### THE TOP ATTRACTIONS

#### DOWNTOWN & THE WEST END

**The Canadian Craft Museum** ★ Hidden behind the Cathedral Place building at the edge of a beautiful outdoor courtyard, the Canadian Craft Museum presents a small but impressive collection of Canadian and international crafts in glass, wood, metal, clay, and fiber. It will appeal to modern art lovers and anyone who devours interior design and architectural magazines.

639 Hornby St. ✆ **604/687-8266.** Craftmus@direct.ca. Admission C$5 (US$3.10) adults, C$3 (US$1.85) seniors and students, free for children under 12. Thurs 5–9pm admission is by donation. Mon–Wed and Fri–Sat 10am–5pm, Thurs 10am–9pm, Sun and holidays noon–5pm. Closed Tues Sept–May. SkyTrain: Granville. Bus: 3

**Vancouver Aquarium Marine Science Centre** ★★★ Kids One of North America's largest and best, the Vancouver Aquarium houses more than 8,000 marine species, most in meticulously re-created environments. In the icy-blue Arctic Canada exhibit, you can see beluga whales whistling and blowing water at unwary onlookers. Human-size freshwater fish inhabit the Amazon Rain Forest gallery, while overhead, an hourly rainstorm is unleashed in an atrium that houses three-toed sloths, brilliant blue and green poison tree frogs, and piranhas. On the Marine Mammal Deck, there are sea otters, Steller sea lions, beluga whales, and a Pacific white-sided dolphin. During regularly scheduled shows, the staff explain marine mammal behavior while working with these impressive creatures.

Stanley Park. © **604/659-FISH.** www.vanaqua.org. Admission C$14.50 (US$9) adults; C$12 (US$7) seniors, students, and youths 13–18; C$9 (US$6) children 4–12; free for children under 4. Late June–Labour Day daily 9:30am–7pm; Labour Day–late June daily 10am–5:30pm. Bus: 135; "Around the Park" shuttle bus June–Sept only. Parking C$5 (US$3.10) summer, C$3 (US$1.85) winter.

**Vancouver Art Gallery** ★★ The VAG is an excellent stop for anyone who wants to see what sets Canadian and West Coast art apart from the rest of the world. There is an impressive collection of paintings by B.C. native Emily Carr, as well as examples of a unique Canadian art style created during the 1920s by members of the "Group of Seven," who included Vancouver painter Fred Varley. On the contemporary side, the VAG hosts rotating exhibits of sculpture, graphics, photography, and video art, some from B.C. artists, many from around the world. Geared to younger audiences, the Annex Gallery offers rotating presentations of visually exciting educational exhibits.

750 Hornby St. © **604/662-4719** or 604/662-4700. www.vanartgallery.bc.ca. Admission C$10 (US$6) adults and seniors, C$6 (US$3.70) students and youths, C$30 (US$19) family, free for children 12 and under. Thurs 5–9pm by donation. Mon–Wed and Fri–Sun 10am–5:30pm, Thurs 10am–9pm. Closed on Mondays and Tuesdays in fall and winter. SkyTrain: Granville. Bus: 3.

## THE WEST SIDE

**H.R. MacMillan Space Centre** *Kids* Housed in the same building as the Vancouver Museum, the space center and observatory has hands-on displays and exhibits that will delight budding astronomy buffs and their parents. You can try your hand at designing a spacecraft, maneuver a lunar robot, or punch a button and a get a punchy video explanation of the Apollo 17 manned-satellite engine that stands before you. Most exciting of all perhaps is the Virtual Voyages Simulator, which takes you on a voyage to Mars or a collision course with an oncoming comet. The StarTheatre shows movies—many of them for children—on an overhead dome. And on selected nights, you can shoot the moon through a half-meter telescope for C$10 (US$6) per camera (© **604/736-2655**).

1100 Chestnut St., in Vanier Park. © **604/738-STAR.** www.hrmacmillanspacecentre.com. Admission C$12.75 (US$8) adults, C$9.75 (US$6) seniors and youths 11–18, C$8.75 (US$5) children 5–10, C$5 (US$3.10) children under 5, C$40 (US$25) families (up to 5, maximum 2 adults). Additional Virtual Voyages experiences C$5 (US$3.10) each. Sept–June Tues–Sun 10am–5pm, daily in July and Aug. Closed Dec 25. Bus: 22.

**Museum of Anthropology** ★★★ This isn't just any old museum. In 1976, architect Arthur Erickson re-created a classic Native post-and-beam structure out of modern concrete and glass to house one of the world's finest collections

---

### *Moments* 360 Degrees of Vancouver

The most popular (and most touristy) spot from which to view **Vancouver's skyline** is high atop the space needle observation deck at the **Lookout!, Harbour Centre Tower,** 555 W. Hastings St. (© **604/689-0421**). It's a great place for first-time visitors who want a panorama of the city. The glass-encased Skylift whisks you up 166 meters (553 ft.) to the rooftop deck in less than a minute. The 360° view is remarkable. (Yes, that is Mt. Baker looming above the southeastern horizon.) Skylift admission is C$9 (US$6) for adults, C$8 (US$5) for seniors, C$6 (US$3.70) for students, and C$25 (US$16) for families. It's open daily in summer from 8:30am to 10:30pm and in winter from 9am to 9pm.

---

of West Coast Native art. Haida artist Bill Reid's masterpiece, *The Raven and the First Men,* is worth the price of admission all by itself. The huge carving in glowing yellow cedar depicts a Haida creation myth, in which Raven—the trickster—coaxes humanity out into the world from its birthplace in a clamshell. Some of Reid's fabulous creations in gold and silver are also on display. Intriguingly, curators have recently begun salting contemporary Native artworks in among the old masterpieces—a sign that West Coast artistic traditions are alive and well. Don't forget to take a walk around the grounds behind the museum. Ten hand-carved totem poles stand in attendance along with contemporary carvings on the outdoor longhouse facades.

6393 NW Marine Dr. ✆ **604/822-3825.** www.moa.ubc.ca. Admission C$7 (US$4.35) adults, C$5 (US$3.10) seniors, C$4 (US$2.50) students and children 6–18, C$20 (US$12) families, free for children under 6. Free Tues after 5pm. Late May–early Sept Wed–Mon 10am–5pm, Tues 10am–9pm; Early Sept–late May Wed–Sun 11am–5pm, Tues 11am–9pm. Closed Dec 25–26. Bus: 4, 10, or 99.

**Science World British Columbia** ★ *Kids* Science World is impossible to miss. It's in the big blinking geodesic dome on the eastern end of False Creek. Inside, it's a hands-on scientific discovery center where you and your kids can light up a plasma ball, walk through a 160m² (1,700-sq. ft.) maze, walk through the interior of a camera, create a cyclone, watch a zucchini explode as it's charged with 80,000 volts, and create music with a giant synthesizer. In the OMNIMAX Theatre—a huge projecting screen equipped with Surround-Sound—you can take a death-defying flight through the Grand Canyon and perform other spine-tingling feats.

1455 Quebec St. ✆ **604/443-7443.** www.scienceworld.bc.ca. Admission C$19.75 (US$12) adults, C$12.25 (US$8) seniors, students, and children, free for children under 4. Combination tickets available for OMNIMAX film. Mon–Fri 10am–5pm, Sat–Sun and holidays 10am–6pm. SkyTrain: Main Street–Science World.

**Vancouver Museum** Established in 1894, the Vancouver Museum is dedicated to amassing evidence of the city's history, from its days as a Native settlement and European outpost to the city's early 20th-century maturation into a modern urban center. The exhibits allow visitors to walk through the steerage deck of a 19th-century passenger ship, peek into a Hudson's Bay Company frontier trading post, or take a seat in an 1880s Canadian-Pacific Railway passenger car. Re-creations of Victorian and Edwardian rooms show how early Vancouverites decorated their homes. Rotating exhibits include a display of the museum's collection of neon signage from the 1940s and 1950s.

1100 Chestnut St. ✆ **604/736-4431.** www.vanmuseum.bc.ca. Admission C$8 (US$5) adults, C$6 (US$3.70) youths. Group rates available. Fri–Wed 10am–5pm, Thurs 10am–9pm. Closed Mon Sept–June. Bus: 22, then walk 3 blocks south on Cornwall Ave. Boat: Granville Island Ferry to Heritage Harbour.

## GASTOWN & CHINATOWN

**The Dr. Sun Yat-sen Classical Chinese Garden** ★ This small reproduction of a Classical Chinese Scholar's garden truly is a remarkable place, but to get the full effect you have to take the guided tour. An untrained eye will insist on seeing only gaggles of tourists wandering round a pretty pond surrounded by bamboo and funny shaped rocks. The engaging guides, however, can explain that the garden is based on the yin-yang principle, or the idea of harmony through dynamic opposition. Chinese designers constantly place contrasting elements in juxtaposition. Soft moving water flows across solid stone; smooth swaying bamboo grows around gnarled immovable rocks; dark pebbles are placed next to light pebbles in the floor. Moving with the guide, you discover the yin-yang principle applies to larger elements in a more complex fashion as well. When the guide ended her tour in a little courtyard outside the scholar's study, the entire audience burst into applause.

578 Carrall St. ✆ **604/689-7133.** www.vancouverchinesegarden.com. C$7.50 (US$4.65) adults, C$6 (US$3.70) seniors, C$5 (US$3.10) children and students. Free guided tour included. Daily May 1–June 14 10am–6pm, June 15–Aug 31 9:30am–7pm, Sept 1–Sept 30 10am–6pm, and Oct 1–April 30 10am–4:30pm. Bus: 19 and 22.

**Vancouver Centennial Police Museum** A bizarre, macabre, and utterly delightful little place, the Police Museum is dedicated to memorializing some of the best crimes and crime-stoppers in the city's short but colorful history. Housed in the old Vancouver Coroner's Court—where actor Errol Flynn was autopsied after dropping dead in the arms of a 17-year-old girl—the museum features photos, text, and vintage equipment from files and evidence rooms of Vancouver's finest.

240 E. Cordova St. ✆ **604/665-3346.** www.city.vancouver.bc.ca/police/museum. Admission C$6 (US$3.70) adults, C$4 (US$2.50) students and seniors, free for children under 6. Year-round Mon–Fri 9am–3pm; May 1–Aug 31 also Sat 10am–3pm. Bus: 4 or 7.

### NORTH VANCOUVER & WEST VANCOUVER

**Capilano Suspension Bridge & Park** *Overrated* Vancouver's first and oldest tourist trap (built in 1889), this attraction still works—mostly because there's still something inherently thrilling about standing on a narrow, shaky walkway, 69m (230 ft.) above the canyon floor, held up by nothing but a pair of tiny cables. In addition to the bridge, there's a **carving centre,** a pair of restaurants, and a gift shop.

3735 Capilano Rd., North Vancouver. ✆ **604/985-7474.** www.capbridge.com. Admission C$13 (US$8) adults, C$10.75 (US$7) seniors, C$8 (US$5) students, C$3.75 (US$2.35) children 6–12, free for children under 6. Winter discounts available. May–Sept daily 8:30am–dusk, Oct–Apr daily 9am–5pm. Closed Dec 25. Bus: 246 from downtown Vancouver, 236 from Lonsdale Quay SeaBus terminal.

**Grouse Mountain Resort** ★★ Once a small local ski hill, Grouse has been slowly developing itself into a year-round mountain recreation park, offering impressive views and instantaneous access to the North Shore mountains. Located only a 20-minute drive from downtown, the SkyRide gondola transports you to the mountain's 1,110m (3,700-ft.) summit in about 10 minutes. At the top, there's a bar, restaurant, large-screen theatre, ski and snowboard area, hiking and snowshoeing trails, skating pond, children's snow park, interpretive forest trails, logger sports show, helicopter tours, mountain bike trails, and a Native feast house. Some of these are free with your SkyRide ticket—most aren't—but the view is free and one of the best around.

6400 Nancy Greene Way, North Vancouver. ✆ **604/984-0661.** www.grousemountain.com. SkyRide C$18.95 (US$12) adults, C$16.95 (US$11) seniors, C$13.95 (US$9) youths, C$7 (US$4.35) children 6–12, free for children under 6. SkyRide free with advance Observatory Restaurant reservation. Daily 9am–10pm. SeaBus: Lonsdale Quay, then transfer to bus 236.

## VANCOUVER'S PLAZAS & PARKS

### OUTDOOR PLAZAS

Unlike many a city, Vancouver's great urban gathering places stand not at the center but on the periphery; the two **seawalls,** one at one end of Denman street by **English Bay,** the other at the other end of Denman by **Coal Harbour,** are the West Coast equivalent of an Italian piazza, the places where Vancouverites go to stroll and be seen. On warm sunny days, they're packed.

## PARKS & GARDENS

For general information about Vancouver's parks, call ✆ **604/257-8400.**

**Stanley Park** is a 400ha (1,000-acre) rain forest near the busy West End. It's named after the same Lord Stanley whose name is synonymous with professional hockey success—the Stanley Cup. The park is filled with towering western red cedar trees, placid lagoons, walking trails, manicured lawns, and flower gardens. Stanley Park houses the Vancouver Aquarium, a petting zoo, three restaurants, a handful of snack bars, cricket greens, a pool, a miniature railway, and a water park. It also boasts abundant wildlife, including beavers, coyotes, bald eagles, raccoons, geese, ducks, and skunks, as well as pristine natural settings and amazing marine views.

In Chinatown, the **Dr. Sun-Yat-sen Classical Garden** is a small, tranquil oasis in the heart of the city (see entry above). On the West Side, **Queen Elizabeth Park** at Cambie Street and West 33rd Avenue sits atop a 150m (500-ft.) high extinct volcano and is the highest urban Vancouver vantage point south of downtown, offering panoramic views in all directions. It's Vancouver's most popular location for wedding-photo sessions, with well-manicured gardens and a profusion of colorful flora. The **Bloedel Conservatory** (✆ **604/257-8570**) stands next to the park's huge sunken garden, an amazing reclamation of an abandoned rock quarry. A 40m (140-ft.) high domed structure with a commanding 360° view, the conservatory houses a tropical rain forest with more than 100 plant species, as well as free-flying tropical birds. Admission is C$3 (US$1.85) for adults and C$1.50 (US95¢) for seniors/children.

Nearby is the **VanDusen Botanical Garden,** 5251 Oak St., at 37th Avenue (✆ **604/878-9274**). Formerly the Shaughnessy Golf Course, the 22ha (55-acre) formal garden features rolling lawns, lakes, Elizabethan hedge mazes, and marble sculptures. Admission is C$6 (US$3.70) for adults, C$2.75 (US$1.70) for seniors/students/children, and C$11 (US$7) for families. Off-season admission is usually less. The garden opens daily at 10am but closes between 6 and 8pm, depending on the time of year.

The University of British Columbia campus incorporates a number of parks and gardens. Established nearly a century ago, the **UBC Botanical Garden,** 6250 Stadium Rd., Gate 8 (✆ **604/822-9666**), has 30ha (70 acres) of formal alpine, herb, and exotic plantings. Nearby is the **Nitobe Memorial Garden,** 6565 NW Marine Dr., Gate 4 (✆ **604/822-6038**), a traditional Japanese garden. March 7 to October 4, both are open daily 10am to 6pm; October 5 to March 6, the Botanical Garden is open daily during daylight hours and the Nitobe Memorial Garden is open Monday to Friday about 10am to 2:30pm. Admission to the Botanical Garden is C$4.50 (US$2.80) for adults and C$1.75 (US$1.10) for seniors; admission for Nitobe Memorial Garden is C$2.50 (US$1.55) for adults and C$1.50 (US95¢) for seniors. A dual pass for both is C$6 (US$3.70) for adults. Out near UBC, Pacific Spirit Park (usually called the Endowment Lands) comprises 760ha (1,885 acres) of temperate rain forest, marshes, and beaches and includes nearly 35km (22 miles) of trails suitable for hiking, riding, mountain biking, and beachcombing.

Across the Lions Gate Bridge are six provincial parks that delight outdoor enthusiasts year-round. The publicly maintained **Capilano River Regional Park,** 4500 Capilano Rd. (✆ **604/666-1790**), surrounds the Capilano Suspension Bridge and Park. Hikers can follow the river for 7km (4½ miles) down the well-maintained Capilano trails to the Burrard Inlet and the Lions Gate Bridge, or 1.5km (1 mile) upstream to Cleveland Dam, which serves as the launching point for whitewater kayakers and canoeists. The **Capilano Salmon Hatchery,** on Capilano Road (✆ **604/666-1790**), is on the river's east bank about .5km (¼ mile) below the Cleveland Dam. Approximately 2 million coho and Chinook salmon are hatched annually in glass-fronted tanks connected to the river by a series of channels. Admission is free, and the hatchery is open daily 8am to 7pm (to 4pm in winter).

## ESPECIALLY FOR KIDS

Pick up copies of the free monthly newspapers ***BC Parent,*** 4479 W. 10th Ave. (✆ **604/221-0366;** www.bcparent.com), and ***West Coast Families,*** 81551 Johnston St. (✆ **604/689-1331**). *West Coast Families'* centerfold "Fun in the City" and event calendar list everything currently going on, including IMAX and Omnimax shows and free children's programs. Both publications are available at Granville Island's Kids Only Market and at neighborhood community centers throughout the city.

Stanley Park offers a number of attractions for children. The **Stanley Park's Children's Farm** (✆ **604/257-8530**) has peacocks, rabbits, calves, donkeys, and Shetland ponies. Next to the petting zoo is **Stanley Park's Miniature Railway** (✆ **604/257-8531**). The diminutive steam locomotive with passenger cars runs on a circuit through the woods, carrying nearly as many passengers annually as all the Alaska-bound cruise ships combined. Also in Stanley Park, the **Vancouver Aquarium** has sea otters, sea lions, whales, and numerous other marine creatures, as well as many exhibits geared toward children.

Right in town, **Science World** is a hands-on kids' museum where budding scientists can get their hands into everything. **Granville Island's Kids Only Market,** 1496 Cartwright St. (✆ **604/689-8447**), offers playrooms and 21 shops filled with toys, books, records, clothes, and food. Kids will also love taking the Aquabus or Granville Island Ferry to get there. Also on Granville Island is the **Water Park and Adventure Playground** where kids can really let loose with movable water guns and sprinklers. They can also have fun on the water slides or in the wading pool. The facilities are open in summer daily 10am to 6pm. Admission is free.

Across Burrard Inlet on the North Shore, **Maplewood Farm,** 405 Seymour River Place, North Vancouver (✆ **604/929-5610**), has more than 200 barnyard animals living on its 2ha (5-acre) farm, open daily year-round. The farm also offers pony rides. Three-quarters of an hour east of the city, the **Greater Vancouver Zoological Center,** 5048-264th St., Aldergrove (✆ **604/856-6825**), is a lush 50ha (120-acre) farm filled with lions, tigers, jaguars, ostriches, elephants, buffalo, elk, antelope, zebras, giraffes, a rhino, hippos, and camels. And the **Burnaby Heritage Village and Carousel,** 6501 Deer Lake Ave., Burnaby (✆ **604/293-6501**), is a 3.5ha (9-acre) re-creation of the Victorian era. You can walk along boardwalk streets among costumed townspeople, watch a blacksmith pounding horseshoes, shop in a general store, ride a vintage carousel, and visit an ice-cream parlor that's been at the same location since the early 1900s.

## SPECIAL EVENTS & FESTIVALS

The first event of the year is the annual New Year's Day **Polar Bear Swim** at English Bay Beach; thousands of hardy citizens show up in elaborate costumes to take a dip in the icy waters of English Bay. On the second Sunday in January, the **Annual Bald Eagle Count** takes place in Brackendale. The count starts at the **Brackendale Art Gallery** (✆ **604/898-3333**).

In late February, the **Chinese New Year** is celebrated with 2 weeks of firecrackers, dancing dragon parades, and other festivities. The **Vancouver Playhouse International Wine Festival** (www.winefest.bc.sympatico.ca) in March or April is a major wine-tasting event featuring the latest international vintages. Each winery sets up a booth where you may try as many varieties as you like. The **Vancouver Sun Run** (www.sunrun.com), in April, is Canada's biggest 10K race, featuring 17,000 runners, joggers, and walkers who race through 10 scenic kilometers (6¼ miles). The run starts and finishes at B.C. Place Stadium.

The June **International Children's Festival** (✆ **640/708-5655;** www.vancouverchildrensfestival.com) features plays and music; it's held in Vanier Park on False Creek. The **VanDusen Flower and Garden Show,** at the VanDusen Botanical Garden, 5251 Oak St. (✆ **604/878-9274**), is Vancouver's premier flora gala. The late June **Alcan Dragon Boat Festival** features more than 150 local and international teams racing huge dragon boats. Four stages of music, dance, and Chinese acrobatics also take place as part of the events at the **Plaza of Nations** (✆ **604/688-2382**).

During the July **Vancouver International Jazz Festival** (✆ **604/872-5200;** www.jazzvancouver.com), more than 800 international jazz and blues players perform at 25 venues around town. Running July to September, the **Bard on the Beach Shakespeare Festival** in Vanier Park (✆ **604/739-0559**) presents Shakespeare's plays in a tent overlooking English Bay. On **Canada Day,** July 1, Canada Place Pier hosts an all-day celebration including music and dance and an evening fireworks display over the harbor to top off the entertainment. The second or third weekend in July brings the **Vancouver Folk Music Festival** (✆ **604/602-9798;** www.thefestival.redpoint.ws). International folk music is played outdoors at Jericho Beach Park. During the **HSBC Power Smart Celebration of Light** ★★★ (www.celebration-of-light.com), three international fireworks companies compete for a coveted title by launching their best displays timed to explode in time to accompanying music over English Bay Beach. Don't miss the grand finale on the fourth night.

Mid-August to Labour Day, the **Pacific National Exhibition** (✆ **604/253-2311;** www.pne.bc.ca) offers everything from big-name entertainment to a demolition derby, livestock demonstrations, logger sports competitions, fashion shows, and North America's finest all-wooden roller coaster. On the Labour Day weekend, the **Molson Indy** (✆ **604/684-4639;** www.molsonindy.com) roars around the streets of False Creek, attracting more than 500,000 spectators. Later in September, the Vancouver's **Fringe Festival** (✆ **604/257-0350;** www.vancouverfringe.com) highlights the best of Vancouver's independent theater.

Every October, the **Vancouver International Film Festival** (✆ **604/685-0260;** www.viff.org) features 250 new works, revivals, and retrospectives, representing filmmakers from 40 countries. All December, the **Christmas Carol Ship Parade** lights up Vancouver Harbour, as harbor cruise ships decorated with colorful Christmas lights sail around English Bay, while on-board guests sip cider and sing Christmas Carols.

## OUTDOOR ACTIVITIES

Just about every imaginable sport has a world-class outlet within the Vancouver city limits. Downhill and cross-country skiing, snowshoeing, sea kayaking, fly-fishing, diving, hiking, paragliding, and mountain biking are just a few of the options. Activities that can't really be practiced in metropolitan Vancouver, but can be done close by, include rock climbing, river rafting, and heli-skiing.

**BEACHES** A great place for viewing sunsets, **English Bay Beach** lies at the end of Davie Street off Denman Street and Beach Avenue. South of English Bay Beach near the Burrard Street Bridge and the Vancouver Aquatic Centre is **Sunset Beach.** On Stanley Park's western rim, **Second Beach** is a quick stroll north from English Bay Beach. A playground, a snack bar, and an immense heated freshwater pool make this a convenient spot for families. Farther along the seawall lies secluded **Third Beach,** due north of Stanley Park Drive. At **Kitsilano Beach,** along Ogden Street, a heated saltwater pool is open in summer for people who don't enjoy the rather-bracing ocean temperatures. Farther west along Point Grey Road is **Jericho Beach,** followed by **Locarno Beach** and **Spanish Banks.** Below UBC's Museum of Anthropology, **Wreck Beach** is Vancouver's immensely popular nude beach. At the northern foot of the Lions Gate Bridge, **Ambleside Park** is a popular North Shore spot.

**BICYCLING & MOUNTAIN BIKING** Helmets are legally required for cyclists, both off-road and on. Marked cycle lanes traverse Vancouver, including the cross-town Off-Broadway route, the Adanac route, and the Ontario route. One of the city's most scenic cycle paths has been extended and now runs all the way from Canada Place Pier to Pacific Spirit Park. Cycling maps are available at most bicycle retailers and rental outlets.

Local mountain bikers love the cross-country ski trails on **Hollyburn Mountain** in Cypress Provincial Park. Mount Seymour's very steep **Good Samaritan Trail** connects to the Baden-Powell Trail and the Bridle Path near Mount Seymour Road. Closer to downtown, both **Pacific Spirit Park** and **Burnaby Mountain** offer excellent beginner and intermediate off-road trails.

Rentals run around C$4 (US$2.50) for a one-speed "Cruiser" to C$10 (US$6) for a top-of-the-line mountain bike per hour or C$15 to C$40 (US$9–US$25) per day. Bikes, helmets, locks, and child trailers are available by the hour or day at **Spokes Bicycle Rentals & Espresso Bar,** 1798 W. Georgia St. (✆ **604/688-5141;** bus: 23, 35). **Bayshore Bicycle and Rollerblade Rentals,** 745 Denman St. (✆ **604/688-2453;** bus: 5), and 1601 W. Georgia St. (✆ **604/689-5071;** bus: 23, 35), rents 21-speed mountain bikes, bike carriers, tandems, city bikes, and kids' bikes.

**BOATING** You can find rentals of 4.5m to 5m (15-ft.–17-ft.) powerboats for as little as a few hours or up to several weeks at **Stanley Park Boat Rentals Ltd.,** Coal Harbor Marina (✆ **604/682-6257;** bus: 23, 35). **Granville Island Boat Rentals, Ltd.,** 1696 Duranleau St., Granville Island (✆ **604/682-6287;** bus: 50), features hourly, daily, and weekly rentals of 4.5m to 6m (15-ft.–19-ft.) speedboats and also offers sportfishing, cruising, and sightseeing charters. Rates on all the above begin at around C$30 (US$19) per hour and C$135 (US$84) per day for a sport boat that holds four. **Delta Charters,** 3500 Cessna Dr., Richmond (✆ **800/661-7762** or 604/273-4211; bus: 100), has weekly and monthly rates for 10m to 18m (32-ft.–58-ft.) powered craft. Prices begin around C$1,400 (US$868) per week for a boat sleeping four.

**CANOEING & KAYAKING** Both placid, urban False Creek and the incredibly beautiful 30km (19-mile) North Vancouver fjord known as Indian Arm have launching points you can reach by car or bus. Rentals range from C$7 (US$4.35) per hour to C$32 (US$20) per day for kayaks and about C$25 (US$16) per day for canoes. Customized tours range from C$70 to C$110 (US$43–US$68) per person. **Adventure Fitness,** 1510 Duranleau St. on Granville Island (✆ **604/687-1528;** bus: 50), rents canoes and kayaks, offers lessons, and has a cool showroom filled with outdoor gear. In North Vancouver, **Deep Cove Canoe and Kayak Rentals,** Deep Cove (✆ **604/929-2268;** bus: 240), offers an easy starting point for anyone planning an Indian Arm run. It offers hourly and daily rentals of canoes and kayaks, as well as lessons and customized tours. **Lotus Land Tours,** 2005-1251 Cardero St. (✆ **800/528-3531** or 604/684-4922; bus: 5), runs guided kayak tours on Indian Arm, complete with transportation to and from Vancouver, a barbecue salmon lunch, and incredible scenery. One-day tours cost C$130 (US$81).

**DIVING** BC's underwater scenery is stunning, but the water is chilly. Most local divers use dry suits. Cates Park in Deep Cove, Whytecliff Park and Porteau Cover near Horseshoe Bay, and Lighthouse Park are nearby dive spots. The **Diving Locker,** 2745 W. 4th Ave. (✆ **604/736-2681;** bus: 4), rents equipment and offers courses and lots of free advice. Rentals cost around C$50 (US$31) per day or C$63 (US$39) with a second tank included; hiring a dive master to accompany you costs about C$60 (US$37) per dive, and a seat on a weekend dive boat runs about C$69 (US$43) per dive.

**ECOTOURS** **Rockwood Adventures,** 1330 Fulton Ave. (✆ **604/926-7705**), offers guided hikes of the north shore rain forest, complete with a trained naturalist and a gourmet lunch. Tours cover Capilano Canyon, Bowen Island, or Lighthouse Park and cost C$75 (US$47). Pickups are at major hotels downtown.

**FISHING** Five species of salmon, rainbow and Dolly Varden trout, steelhead, and even sturgeon abound in the local waters. To fish, you need a nonresident saltwater or freshwater license. **Hanson's Fishing Outfitters,** 102-580 Hornby St. (✆ **604/684-8988** or 684-8998; bus: 22), and **Granville Island Boat Rentals,** 1696 Duranleau St. (✆ **604/682-6287;** bus: 50), are outstanding outfitters as well as sources for tackle and licenses. Licenses for freshwater fishing are C$16 (US$10) for 1 day or C$32 (US$20) for 8 days. Saltwater fishing licenses cost C$8 (US$5) for 1 day, C$20 (US$12) for 3 days, and C$39 (US$24) for 5 days.

**Bonnie Lee Fishing Charters, Ltd.,** on the dock at the entrance to Granville Island, (mailing address: 744 W. King Edward Ave., Vancouver, BC V5Z 2C8; ✆ **604/290-7447;** bus: 50), is another reputable outfitter. **Corcovado Yacht Charters, Ltd.,** 1696 Duranleau St., Granville Island (✆ **604/669-7907;** bus: 50), has competitive rates. The *Vancouver Sun* prints a daily fishing report in the B section that details which fish are in season and where they can be found.

**GOLF** This is a year-round Vancouver sport. The public **University Golf Club,** 5185 University Blvd. (✆ **604/224-1818;** bus: 4), is a great 5,998m (6,560-yd.), par-71 course with a clubhouse, a pro shop, locker rooms, a bar and grill, a sports lounge, and a 280-car parking lot. Or call **A-1 Last Minute Golf Hot Line** (✆ **800/684-6344** or 604/878-1833) for substantial discounts and short-notice tee times at more than 30 Vancouver-area courses.

**HIKING** Good trail maps are available from the **Greater Vancouver Regional Parks District** (✆ **604/432-6350**) and from **International Travel Maps and Books,** 552 Seymour St. (✆ **604/687-3320;** bus: 4), which also stocks guidebooks and topographical maps. If you're looking for a challenge without the time commitment, hike the aptly named Grouse Grind from the bottom of Grouse Mountain to the top, then buy a one-way ticket down on the Grouse Mountain SkyRide gondola. The one-way fare is C$5 (US$3.10) per person.

Lynn Canyon Park, Lynn Headwaters Regional Park, Capilano River Regional Park, Mount Seymour Provincial Park, Pacific Spirit Park, and Cypress Provincial Park have good easy-to-challenging trails that wind up through stands of Douglas fir and cedar and contain a few serious switchbacks. Pay attention to the trail warnings posted at the parks; some have bear habitats. Golden Ears, in Golden Ears Provincial Park, and The Lions, in West Vancouver, are for seriously fit hikers.

**ICE SKATING** November to early April, Robson Square has free skating on a covered rink directly under Robson Street between Howe and Hornby streets (Bus: 5). Rentals are available in the adjacent concourse. The **West End Community Centre,** 870 Denman St. (✆ **604/257-8333;** bus: 5), also rents skates at its enclosed rink, open October to March. The enormous **Ice Sports Centre,** 6501 Sprott, Burnaby (✆ **604/291-0626;** bus: 110), is the Vancouver Canucks' official practice facility. It has eight rinks, is open year-round, and offers lessons and rentals.

**IN-LINE SKATING** You'll find locals rolling along beach paths, streets, park paths, and promenades. If you didn't bring a pair of blades, try **Bayshore Bicycle and Rollerblade Rentals,** 745 Denman St. (✆ **604/688-2453;** bus: 23, 35). Rentals generally run C$5 (US$3.10) per hour, with a 2-hour minimum, or C$15 (US$9) per day or overnight.

**JOGGING** You'll find fellow runners traversing Stanley Park's **Seawall Promenade,** where the scenery is spectacular and cars aren't allowed.

**RAFTING** A 2½-hour drive from Vancouver on the wild Nahatlatch River, **Reo Rafting,** 355-535 Thurlow St., Vancouver (✆ **800/736-7238;** www.reorafting.com; bus: 4), offers some of the best guided white-water trips in the province at a reasonable price. One-day packages including breakfast, lunch, all your gear, and 4 to 5 hours on the river start at C$99 (US$61). Multi-day trips and group packages are also available.

**SAILING** **Cooper Boating Center,** 1620 Duranleau St. (✆ **604/687-4110;** bus: 50), offers cruises, boat rentals, and sail instruction packages on 6.5m to 14m (21-ft.–46-ft.) boats. Prices vary widely, from C$150 (US$93) for a 3-hour lesson to C$4,000 (US$2,480) or more for a week charter.

**SKIING & SNOWBOARDING** It seldom snows in the city's downtown and central areas, but Vancouverites can ski before work and after dinner at the three ski resorts in the North Shore mountains.

The **Grouse Mountain Resort,** 6400 Nancy Greene Way, North Vancouver (✆ **604/984-0661;** snow report 604/986-6262; bus: 241), has four chairs, two beginner tows, and two T-bars to take you to 22 alpine runs. There's also a 90mn (300-ft.) half pipe for snowboarders. Full-day lift tickets are C$29 (US$18) for adults, C$22 (US$14) for youths ages 13 to 18, and C$16 (US$10) for children ages 7 to 12; children under 7 are free. **Mount Seymour Provincial Park,** 1700 Mt. Seymour Rd., North Vancouver (✆ **604/986-2261;** snow report 604/986-3999), has the area's highest base elevation; it's accessible via four chairs and a tow. Lift tickets are C$18 (US$11) for adults/children. A shuttle bus to Mt. Seymour departs daily from Rogers Avenue in Lonsdale Quay (accessible via SeaBus). On weekdays, the bus departs at 3:30 and 5:30pm, with return trips leaving at 4:30, 6:30, 8:30, and 10pm. On weekends and holidays, departures are at 8:30am, 10:30am, 12:30pm, 3pm, and 5pm, with return trips at

11:30am, 1:30pm, 4pm, 6pm, 8pm, and 10pm. The trip takes about 50 minutes one-way. Round-trip fares are C$7 (US$4.35) for adults and C$5 (US$3.10) for students/youth/seniors; one-way fares are C$4 (US$2.50) for adults and C$3 (US$1.85) for students/youth/seniors. **Cypress Bowl,** 1610 Mt. Seymour Rd. (✆ **604/926-5612;** snow report 604/419-7669), has the area's longest vertical drop at 533m (1,750 ft.), challenging ski and snowboard runs, and 16km (10 miles) of track-set cross-country skiing trails. Full-day lift tickets are C$35 (US$22) for adults, C$29 (US$18) for youths ages 13 to 18, C$17 (US$11) for children ages 5 to 12, and C$2 (US$1.20) for children under 5. A shuttle bus to Cypress departs daily from Lonsdale Quay (accessible via SeaBus). Departures are every 2 hours 7:15am to 5:15pm. The bus returns from the Cypress alpine area every 2 hours 12:15pm to 10:15pm, with the last departure at 11pm. A round-trip costs C$7 (US$4.35) for adults and C$5 (US$3.10) for youths; a one-way trip is C$5 (US$3.10) for adults and $C3 (US$1.85) for youths.

**SWIMMING** Vancouver's mid-summer saltwater temperature rarely exceeds 18°C (65°F). Some swimmers opt for fresh- and saltwater pools at city beaches (see "Beaches," above). Others take to indoor pools, including the **Vancouver Aquatic Centre,** 1050 Beach Ave. at the foot of Thurlow Street (✆ **604/665-3424;** bus: 22); the **YWCA fitness center,** 535 Hornby St. (✆ **604/895-5777;** bus: 22); and **UBC's Aquatic Centre,** 2075 Wesbrook Mall (✆ **604/822-4521;** bus: 4, 7, or 10).

**TENNIS** Vancouver maintains 180 outdoor hard courts that have a 1-hour limit and accommodate patrons on a first-come, first-served basis 8am to dusk. With the exception of the Beach Avenue courts, which charge a nominal fee, all city courts are free. Stanley Park has four courts near Lost Lagoon and 17 courts near the Beach Avenue entrance, next to the Fish House Restaurant. Queen Elizabeth Park's 18 courts service the central Vancouver area, and Kitsilano Beach Park's 10 courts service the beach area between Vanier Park and the UBC campus (Bus: 22). You can play at night at the **Langara Campus of Vancouver Community College,** West 49th Avenue between Main and Cambie streets (Bus: 15). The **UBC Coast Club,** Thunderbird Boulevard (✆ **604/822-2505;** bus: 4), has 10 outdoor and 4 indoor courts. Indoor courts are C$10 (US$6) per hour, plus C$3 (US$1.85) per person; outdoor courts are C$3 (US$1.85) per person.

**WILDLIFE-WATCHING** During winter, thousands of **bald eagles** line the banks of Indian Arm fjord and the Squamish, Cheakamus, and Mamquam rivers to feed on spawning salmon. The official January 1994 eagle count in Brackendale (a small community near Squamish) recorded 3,700—the largest number ever seen in North America. The annual **summer salmon runs** attract more than bald eagles. Tourists also flock to coastal streams and rivers to watch the waters turn red with leaping coho and sockeye. The salmon are plentiful at the Capilano Salmon Hatchery (see "Parks & Gardens," earlier), Adams River, Goldstream Provincial Park, and numerous other fresh waters.

Along the Fraser River delta, more than 250 **bird species** migrate to or perennially inhabit the George C. Reifel Sanctuary's wetland reserve. Nearby Richmond Nature Park has educational displays for young and first-time birders plus a boardwalk-encircled duck pond. Stanley Park and Pacific Spirit Park are both home to a heron rookery. You can see these large birds nesting just outside the

Vancouver Aquarium. Ravens, dozens of species of waterfowl, raccoons, skunks, beavers, and even coyotes are also full-time residents.

**WINDSURFING** Windsurfing isn't allowed at the mouth of False Creek near Granville Island, but you can bring a board to Jericho and English Bay beaches or rent one there. Equipment sales, rentals (including wet suits), and instruction can be found at **Windsure Windsurfing School,** 1300 Discovery St., at Jericho Beach (✆ **604/224-0615;** bus: 4). Rentals start at C$17 (US$11) per hour.

## SPECTATOR SPORTS

You can get schedule information on all major events at the **Vancouver Tourist Info Centre,** 200 Burrard St. (✆ **604/683-2000;** bus: 22).

**FOOTBALL** The Canadian Football League's **B.C. Lions** (✆ **604/930-5466;** www.cfl.ca/CFLBC/) play in the 60,000-seat B.C. Place Stadium, 777 Pacific Blvd. S. (Bus: 2). Tickets are C$25 to C$47 (US$16–US$29).

**HOCKEY** The National Hockey League's **Vancouver Canucks** play at General Motors Place, 800 Griffith Way (✆ **604/899-4600;** event hotline 604/899-7444; www.canucks.com; bus: 2). Tickets are C$26 to C$95 (US$16–US$59).

**HORSE RACING** Mid-April to October, thoroughbreds run at **Hastings Park Racecourse,** Exhibition Park, East Hastings and Cassiar streets (✆ **604/254-1631;** www.hastingspark.com; bus: 10).

**SOCCER** The USL's **Vancouver Whitecaps,** formerly the 86ers, as well as the women's **Vancouver Breakers** (✆ **604/930-5466;** www.prowavesoccer.com) play at Swangard Stadium, at Boundary Road and Kingsway in Burnaby (✆ **604/435-7121;** bus: 19). Admission is normally C$15 to C$25 (US$9–US$16).

# 6 Shopping

## THE SHOPPING SCENE

Blessed with a climate that seems semitropical in comparison to that of the rest of Canada, Vancouverites tend to do their shopping on the street, browsing from one window to the next on the lookout for something new. **Robson Street** is the spot for high-end fashions. The 10-block stretch of **Granville Street** from 6th Avenue up to 16th Avenue is were Vancouver's old-money comes to shop for classic men's and women's fashions, housewares, and furniture. **Water Street** in **Gastown** features knickknacks, antiques, cutting-edge furniture, First Nations art, and funky basement retro shops. **Main Street** from 19th Avenue to 27th Avenue means antiques and lots of them. **Granville Island,** a rehabilitated industrial site beneath the Granville Street Bridge, is one of the best places to pick up salmon and other seafood. It's also a great place to browse for crafts and gifts.

## SHOPPING A TO Z

**ANTIQUES** The **Vancouver Antique Centre,** 422 Richards St. (✆ **604/669-7444;** bus: 20), contains 15 shops, specializing in everything from china, glass, Orientalia, and jewelry to military objects, sports, toys, and watches. **Uno Langmann Ltd.,** 2117 Granville St. (✆ **604/736-8825;** bus: 4), caters to upscale shoppers, specializing in European and North American paintings, furniture, and silver.

**BOOKS** Since 1957, the locally owned chain **Duthie Books,** 2239 W. 4th Ave., Kitsilano (✆ **604/732-5344;** bus: 4), has been synonymous with good books in Vancouver. On Granville Island, **Blackberry Books,** 1663 Duranleau St. (✆ **604/685-4113;** bus: 50), stocks books about art, architecture, and fine cuisine, as well as a wide variety of more general categories. **Chapters,** 788 Robson St. (✆ **604/682-4066;** bus: 5), is pleasant and well planned, with little nooks and comfy benches in which to browse at length; there are other locations around town. **Little Sister's Book & Art Emporium,** 1238 Davie St. (✆ **604/669-1753;** bus: 1), is the West End bookstore with the largest selection of lesbian, gay, bisexual, and transgender books, videos, and magazines. **International Travel Maps,** 552 Seymour St. (✆ **604/687-3320;** bus: 4), has the best selection of travel books, maps, charts, and globes.

**DEPARTMENT STORES** From the establishment of its early trading posts during the 1670s to its modern coast-to-coast chain, **The Bay** (Hudson's Bay Company), 674 Granville St. (✆ **604/681-6211;** bus: 4), has built its reputation on quality goods. You can still buy a Hudson's Bay woolen "point" blanket (the colorful stripes originally represented how many beaver pelts each blanket was worth in trade), but you'll also find wares from Tommy Hilfiger, Polo, DKNY, Ellen Tracy, Anne Klein II, and Liz Claiborne.

**FASHION** International designer outlets in Vancouver include **Chanel Boutique,** 103-755 Burrard St. (✆ **604/682-0522;** bus: 22); **Salvatore Ferragamo,** 918 Robson St. (✆ **604/669-4495;** bus: 5); **Gianni Versace Boutique,** 757 W. Hastings St. (✆ **604/683-1131;** bus: 4); **Versace's Versus,** 1008 W. Georgia St. (✆ **604/688-8938;** bus: 22); **Polo/Ralph Lauren,** The Landing, 375 Water St. (✆ **604/682-7656;** bus: 1); and **Plaza Escada,** Sinclair Centre, 757 W. Hastings St. (✆ **604/688-8558;** bus: 4).

For something uniquely West Coast, don't miss the one-of-a-kind First Nations designs of **Dorothy Grant,** 250-757 W. Hastings St. (✆ **604/681-0201;** bus: 4). Grant's exquisitely detailed Haida motifs are appliquéd onto coats, leather vests, jackets, caps, and accessories. The clothes are gorgeous and collectible. **Dream,** 311 W. Cordova (✆ **604/683-7326;** bus: 1), is one of the few places to find the early collections of local designers. **Zonda Nellis Design Ltd.,** 2203 Granville St. (✆ **604/736-5668;** bus: 4), offers imaginative hand-woven separates, sweaters, vests, soft knits, and a new line of hand-painted silks.

**FIRST NATIONS ART** You'll find First Nations art in abundance. **Images for a Canadian Heritage,** 164 Water St. (✆ **604/685-7046;** bus: 1), is a government-licensed First Nations art gallery, featuring traditional and contemporary works. The **Leona Lattimer Gallery,** 1590 W. 2nd Ave. (✆ **604/732-4556;** bus: 4), presents museum-quality displays of ceremonial masks, totem poles, argillite sculptures, and gold and silver jewelry, at a more affordable price than galleries downtown.

**FOOD** At **Chocolate Arts,** 2037 W. 4th Ave. (✆ **604/739-0475;** bus: 4), the works are of such exquisite craftsmanship that they're sometimes a wrench to eat. Look for the all-chocolate diorama in the window—it changes every month or so. **Murchie's Tea & Coffee,** 970 Robson St. (✆ **604/669-0783;** bus: 5), is a Vancouver institution. You'll find everything from Jamaican Blue Mountain and Kona coffees to Lapsing, Souchong, and Kemun teas. **The Lobsterman,** 1807 Mast Tower Rd. (✆ **604/687-4531;** bus: 50), is one of the city's best spots to pick up seafood. Salmon and other seafood can be packed for air travel. And the **Salmon Village,** 779 Thurlow St. (✆ **604/685-3378;** bus: 4), specializes in salmon of all varieties.

**GIFTS** For a good range of basic souvenirs, try **Canadian Impressions** at the Station, 601 Cordova St. (✆ **604/681-3507;** bus: 1). The store carries lumberjack shirts, Cowichan sweaters, T-shirts, and other trinkets.

**JEWELRY** Opened in 1879, **Henry Birk & Sons Ltd.,** 698 W. Hastings St. (✆ **604/669-3333;** bus: 7), has a long tradition of designing and creating beautiful jewelry and watches and selling jewelry to international designers. On Granville Island, **The Raven and the Bear,** 1528 Duranleau St. (✆ **604/669-3990;** bus: 50), is a great spot to shop for West Coast native jewelry.

**MALLS & SHOPPING CENTERS** The **Pacific Centre Mall,** 700 W. Georgia St. (✆ **604/688-7236;** bus: 7), is a 3-block complex containing 200 shops and services, including Godiva, Benetton, Crabtree & Evelyn, and Eddie Bauer. For more upscale shopping, try the **Sinclair Centre,** 757 W. Hastings St. (✆ **604/659-1009;** bus: 7), which houses elite shops like Armani, Leone, and Dorothy Grant, as well as smaller boutiques, art galleries, and a food court.

**SPORTING GOODS** Everything you'll ever need for the outdoors is at **Mountain Equipment Co-op,** 130 W. Broadway (✆ **604/872-7858;** bus: 9).

**TOYS** The **Kids Only Market,** Cartwright St., Granville Island (✆ **604/689-8447;** bus: 50), is a 24-shop complex that sells toys, games, computer software, and books for kids.

**WINE** In addition to carrying a full range of British Columbian wines, **Marquis Wine Cellars,** 1034 Davie St. (✆ **604/684-0445** or 604/685-2246; bus: 1), has a large international selection, plus a very knowledgeable staff.

## 7 Vancouver After Dark

For an overview of Vancouver's nightlife, pick up a copy of the weekly tabloid *The Georgia Straight,* the glossy *Vancouver* magazine, or *Xtra! West,* the free gay-and-lesbian biweekly tabloid. The **Vancouver Cultural Alliance Arts Hot Line** (✆ **604/684-2787;** www.allianceforarts.com) is a great source for all performing arts, music, theater, literary events, art films, and dance, including where and how to get tickets. **Ticketmaster** (Vancouver Ticket Centre), 1304 Hornby St. (✆ **604/280-3311;** www.ticketmaster.ca; bus: 4), has 40 outlets in the greater Vancouver area. With a credit card, you can buy tickets over the phone and pick them up at the venue.

Three major Vancouver theaters regularly host touring performances: the **Orpheum Theatre,** 801 Granville St. (✆ **604/665-3050;** bus: 7); the **Queen Elizabeth Theatre,** 600 Hamilton St. (✆ **604/665-3050;** bus: 5); and the **Vancouver Playhouse** (same number). They share a website at www.city.vancouver.bc.ca.

In a converted early 1900s church, the **Vancouver East Cultural Centre** (the "Cultch" to locals), 1895 Venables St. (✆ **604/254-9578;** www.vecc.bc.ca; bus: 20), hosts avant-garde theater productions, children's programs, and art exhibits.

### THE PERFORMING ARTS

Theater isn't only an indoor pastime here. There's an annual summertime Shakespeare series called **Bard on the Beach,** in Vanier Park (✆ **604/737-0625;** bus 22). You can also bring a picnic dinner to Stanley Park and watch **Theatre Under the Stars** (✆ **604/687-0174;** www.tuts.bc.ca; bus: 35), which features popular musicals and light comedies. For more original fare, don't miss Vancouver's **Fringe Festival** (✆ **604/257-0350;** www.vancouverfringe.com).

The Fringe features more than 500 innovative and original shows each September, all costing under C$10 (US$6).

The **Arts Club Theatre Company** (✆ **604/687-1644;** www.artsclub.com) presents live theater in two venues, the Granville Island Stage at the Arts Club Theatre, 1585 Johnston St. (Bus: 50), and the Stanley Theatre, 2750 Granville St. (Bus: 8). Housed in Vancouver's Firehall No. 1, the **Firehall Arts Centre,** 280 E. Cordova St. (✆ 604/689-0926; www.firehall.org; bus: 4), is home to three cutting-edge companies: the Firehall Theatre Company, Touchstone Theatre, and Axis Mime. Expect experimental and challenging plays.

**OPERA** The **Vancouver Opera,** 500-845 Cambie St. (✆ **604/683-0222;** www.vanopera.bc.ca; bus: 17), alternates between obscure or new works and older, more popular favorites. English super-titles projected above the stage help audiences follow the dialogue of the lavish productions.

**CLASSICAL MUSIC** The extremely active **Vancouver Symphony,** 601 Smithe St. (✆ **604/876-3434;** www.vancouversymphony.ca; bus: 7), presents a number of series: great classical works, light classics, modern classics and ethnic works, popular and show tunes, and music geared toward school-age children. The traveling summer concert series takes the orchestra from White Rock to the top of Whistler Mountain.

**DANCE** For fans of modern and original dance, the time to be here is early July, when the **Dancing on the Edge Festival** (✆ **604/689-0691**) presents 60 to 80 envelope-pushing original pieces over a 10-day period. **Ballet British Columbia,** 502-68 Water St. (✆ **604/732-5003;** www.balletbc.com; bus: 4), is a young company that strives to present innovative works. For more about other festivals and dance companies around the city, call the **Dance Centre** (✆ **604/606-6400**).

## COMEDY & LIVE-MUSIC CLUBS

Performers with the **Vancouver TheatreSports League** (✆ **604/687-1644;** www.vtspl.com) rely on a basic plot supplemented by audience suggestions the actors take and improvise on, often to hilarious results. Performances are in the **Arts Club Theatre,** 1585 Johnston St., Granville Island (Bus: 50), with shows costing C$13 (US$8) weekends and C$6 (US$3.70) weeknights. **Yuk Yuk's Komedy Kabaret,** Plaza of Nations, 750 Pacific Blvd. (✆ **604/687-5233;** bus: 2), presents a constantly changing lineup of leading Canadian and American stand-up comics; the cover is C$10 (US$6).

Cover at the functional **Starfish Room,** 1055 Homer St. (✆ **604/682-4171;** bus: 7), ranges from C$3 to C$30 (US$1.85–US$19), depending on the act. Bands vary from jazz and blues to Celtic, lounge, funk, and even punk. For folk, the **WISE Hall,** 1882 Adanac (✆ **604/254-5858;** bus: 20), is the place to be, with a cover running C$5 to C$15 (US$3.10–US$9). And for blues, go to the smoky, sudsy old **Yale Hotel,** 1300 Granville St. (✆ **604/681-9253;** bus: 4), with a Thursday-to-Saturday cover of C$5 to C$12 (US$3.10–US$7).

## BARS, PUBS & LOUNGES

The **Atlantic Trap and Gill,** 612 Davie St. (✆ **604/806-6393;** bus 4), is an east-coast sea shanty of a place, where the regulars know the words to every song. **Fred's Tavern,** 1006 Granville St. (✆ **604/605-4350;** bus: 4), features a steady stream of simulcast sports, but for some reason those in the beautiful young crowd are mostly interested in each other. Called a diamond in the rough, the

**Brickhouse Bar,** 730 Main St. (✆ **604/689-8645;** bus: 8), is a great bar in the slowly gentrifying neighborhood around Main and Terminal. The **Shark Club Bar and Grill,** 180 W. Georgia St. (✆ **604/687-4275;** bus: 5), is the city's premier sports bar. If you're looking for a brew pub, **Steamworks Pub & Brewery,** 375 Water St. (✆ **604/689-2739;** bus: 7), is your best bet. Choose from a dozen in-house beers, from dark Australian-style ales to light, refreshing wheat lagers. The **Yaletown Brewing Company,** 1111 Mainland St. (✆ **604/688-0039;** bus: 2), also offers good home-brewed fare.

View junkies will think they've died and gone to heaven at **Cloud Nine,** 1400 Robson St., on the 42nd floor of the Empire Landmark Hotel (✆ **604/687-0511;** bus: 5). This sleek hotel-top lounge rotates six degrees a minute, offering an ever-changing and always-fabulous view of the city. The **Georgia Street Bar and Grill,** 801 W. Georgia St. (✆ **604/602-0994;** bus: 22), is a pleasant street-front lounge with great weekend jazz combos.

## DANCE CLUBS

You get two venues for the price of one at Gastown's **The Purple Onion,** 15 Water St. (✆ **604/602-9442;** bus: 4). The Club room is a dance floor pure and simple; in the Lounge a house band squeals out funky danceable jazz for a slightly older crowd. The cover runs C$5 to C$7 (US$3.10–US$4.35). The dance-oriented **Richards on Richards,** 1036 Richards St. (✆ **604/687-6794;** bus: 7), has been packing 'em in for close to 2 decades, and the cover is C$5 to C$40 (US$3.10–US$25). **Sonar,** 66 Water St. (✆ **604/683-6695;** bus: 4), is Vancouver's purest hip-hop house joint; it was named one of world's top-20 nightclubs by Britain's *Ministry* magazine. The cover runs C$5 to C$9 (US$3.10–US$6). And at the **Stone Temple Cabaret,** 1082 Granville St. (✆ **604/488-1333;** bus: 7), it's disco pure and simple. The moderate-size dance floor in the front room features lights, smoke, booming bass, and an early 20s collegiate crowd. The cover is C$5 to C$20 (US$3.10–US$12).

## GAY & LESBIAN BARS

Open Monday to Saturday noon to 6pm, the **Gay & Lesbian Centre,** 2-1170 Bute St. (✆ **604/684-6869;** bus: 1), has information on the current hot spots, but it's probably easier just to pick up a free copy of *Xtra West!,* available in most downtown cafes. On the Web, check out **www.gayvancouver.net**.

Billed as a "neighborhood club," **Homers,** 1249 Howe St. (✆ **604/689-2444;** bus: 4), has a relaxed atmosphere, a few billiards tables, and a great pub menu. The **Dufferin Pub,** 900 Seymour St. (✆ **604/683-4251;** bus: 7), is home to the city's glitziest drag show, Buff at the Duff. The rest of the time (and before, during, and after many of the shows) the DJs play a mix of sounds to keep you grooving. **The Odyssey,** 1251 Howe St. (✆ **604/689-5256;** bus: 4), is the hippest, and most happening gay/mixed dance bar in town, with a cover of C$3 to C$5 (US$1.85–US$3.10). The **Heritage House Hotel,** 455 Abbott St. (✆ **604/685-7777;** bus: 4), is home to two gay bars, **Charlie's Lounge** and the slightly seedy **Chuck's Pub,** and one lesbian locale, the **Lotus Cabaret.** Cover at the Lotus is C$4 to C$7 (US$2.50–US$4.35). The Lotus offers a big bar, little alcoves for sitting, an adequate dance floor, and an upbeat atmosphere. The crowd is normally mixed, but on Fridays it's women only.

## CASINOS

There's no alcohol and there are no floor shows, but on the other hand, you haven't really lived until you've sat down for some serious gambling with a room full of Far Eastern big shots trying to re-create the huge night they had in Happy Valley or Macau. At the **Gateway Casino,** 611 Main St., third floor (**© 604/688-9412;** bus: 3), you can play pai gow poker, blackjack, roulette, and sic bo mini bac, and let it ride. It's open noon to 2am, with a C$500 (US$310) maximum bet. Similar games are on offer at the **Great Canadian Casino,** 1133 W. Hastings St. (**© 604/682-8145;** bus: 23), and the **Royal Diamond Casino,** 750 Pacific Blvd., in the Plaza of Nations (**© 604/685-2340;** bus: 2).

# 16

# Victoria & British Columbia

*by Shawn Blore & Bill McRae*

**British Columbia** runs the length of Canada's west coast, from the Washington border to the Alaskan panhandle. Roughly 947,800 (588,935 sq. miles), it's more than twice the size of California, though the population (3.7 million) is roughly a quarter of Los Angeles's. Most residents live in the greater Vancouver and **Victoria** areas in the southwest, along a coast dotted with beachfront communities, modern cities, and belts of rich farmland. But just a few hours' drive to the north on any of BC's mostly two-lane highways, the communities are tiny, the sparse population is scattered, and the land is alternately towering forest, fields of stumps left by timber harvests, and high alpine wilderness. Between these extremes are the areas covered in this chapter.

British Columbia's outstanding feature is its variety of scenery, climates, and cultures. The rough-hewn mountains of the Cariboo and Chilcotin regions are topped with glaciers running off into hidden lakes. Alpine meadows, buried under snow all winter, burst forth with a profusion of blossoms every summer. The rugged fjords fjord and misty islands along the coast from the Queen Charlotte Islands to Howe Sound are home to the world's only resident population of orcas, most of the world's remaining old-growth temperate rain forests, and some of North America's earliest human settlements. The arid Okanagan Valley is filled with fruit trees and surrounded by vineyards and wineries on the hillsides, and it boasts sagebrush and sand deserts. And hundreds of lakes, sheltered beaches, and majestic mountains stretch across the province, separating each region from the others yet interlacing them all.

## 1 Exploring the Province

There's more to British Columbia than Vancouver's urban bustle. In fact, the other Vancouver—**Vancouver Island**—is 90 minutes from the city by ferry. On Vancouver Island is the province's capital, **Victoria.** It's a lovely seaport city that's proud of its English roots, lavish Victorian gardens, and picturesque port. It's also the ideal place to begin exploring the entire island, which stretches more than 450km (279 miles) from Victoria to the northwest tip of Cape Scott.

You can reach most Vancouver Island destinations via the Island Highway. From Victoria, which is Mile 0, to Nanaimo, it's part of the coast-to-coast Trans-Canada Highway (Highway 1). At Nanaimo, the Trans-Canada crosses the ferry to the mainland, and the route up the island becomes Highway 19 until it arrives at its northern terminus in Port Hardy.

The raging beauty of the Pacific Ocean on the west coast entices photographers, hikers, kayakers, naturalists, and divers to explore **Pacific Rim National Park, Long Beach,** and the neighboring towns of **Ucluelet** and **Tofino.** Thousands arrive between March and May to see as many as 20,000 **Pacific gray**

**whales** pass close to shore as they migrate north to their summer feeding grounds in the Arctic Circle. More than 200 **shipwrecks** have occurred off the shores in the past 2 centuries, luring even more travelers to this eerily beautiful underwater world. And the park's world-famous **West Coast Trail** beckons an international collection of intrepid backpackers and "extreme" hikers to brave the 10-day hike over the rugged rescue trail—established after the survivors of a shipwreck in the early 1900s died from exposure on the beach because there was no land access route for the rescuers.

On east-central Vancouver Island, the towns of Parksville, Qualicum Beach, Courtenay, and Comox are famous for their warm sandy beaches and for their numerous championship golf courses. Campbell River—the "Salmon Fishing Capital of the World"—is dominated by fishing resorts, while just-offshore Quadra Island has one of the world's best museums of Native art. The waters along the island's northeast coast near **Port McNeil** are home to two species of orca whales: residents, which feed on salmon and live in the area consistently, and transients, which feed on seals and other marine mammals and move annually from **Johnstone Strait** to the open Pacific. In this vicinity are also two tiny unique communities: the native-Indian town of **Alert Bay,** on Cormorant Island, and **Telegraph Cove,** a boardwalk community on pilings above the rocky shore.

The Island Highway's final port of call, **Port Hardy** is the starting point for the **Inside Passage ferry cruise** up the northern coast. The ferry carries passengers bound for Prince Rupert, where it meets the ferries to the **Queen Charlotte Islands.**

Since 1966, BC Ferries has operated the **Inside Passage ferry** between Port Hardy on Vancouver Island and Prince Rupert. This rugged, thickly forested mainland coastline is the highlight of the Vancouver-to-Alaska cruises. It's also the ancestral home of native-Indian tribes who intrigued late–19th-century American photographer Edward Curtis so much he spent more than a decade photographing and filming the people, their villages, and their potlatch feasts.

The ferry system also connects Prince Rupert to the remote **Queen Charlotte Islands,** the ancestral home of the Haida tribe and the location of a UNESCO World Heritage Site, **Haida Gwaii.** The remains of untouched Haida villages, abandoned more than 400 years ago, stand amid a thick rain forest of old-growth Sitka spruce. Cedar totem poles, sculptures, funerary boxes, and long-houses are all that remains of the culture that flourished there for nearly 10,000 years—and inspired Victoria-born artist Emily Carr's now-famous paintings and drawings, which you can see at the Vancouver Art Gallery.

Between Lillooet and Prince George in the Fraser River Valley, you'll discover that the Canadian Wild West hasn't changed too much in the past century. This is **Cariboo Country,** the scene of the 1860s Cariboo Gold Rush. The town of **Lillooet,** "Mile 0" of the Old Cariboo Highway, was the starting point of a 402km (250-mile) journey taken by prospectors and settlers who sought their fortunes in the northern Cariboo goldfields. The gold-rich town of **Barkerville** sprang up after a British prospector named Billy Barker struck it rich on Williams Creek. But gold isn't the only thing that attracts thousands to this area year-round. Cross-country skiers and snowmobilers explore the creekside paths during the winter.

It's only a 121km (75-mile) drive from Vancouver—to North America's most popular ski resort—the glacial peaks of **Whistler and Blackcomb mountains.**

## Southern British Columbia

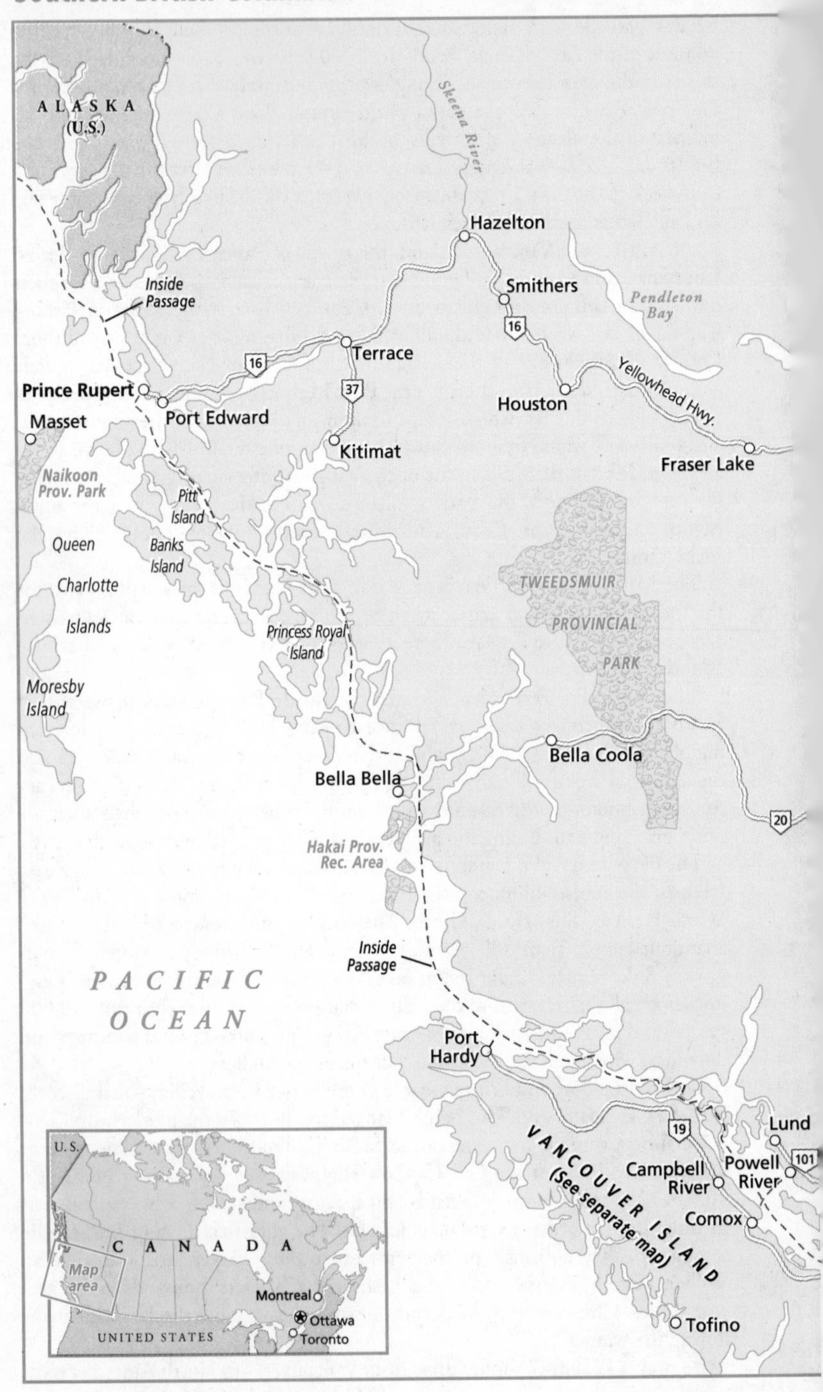

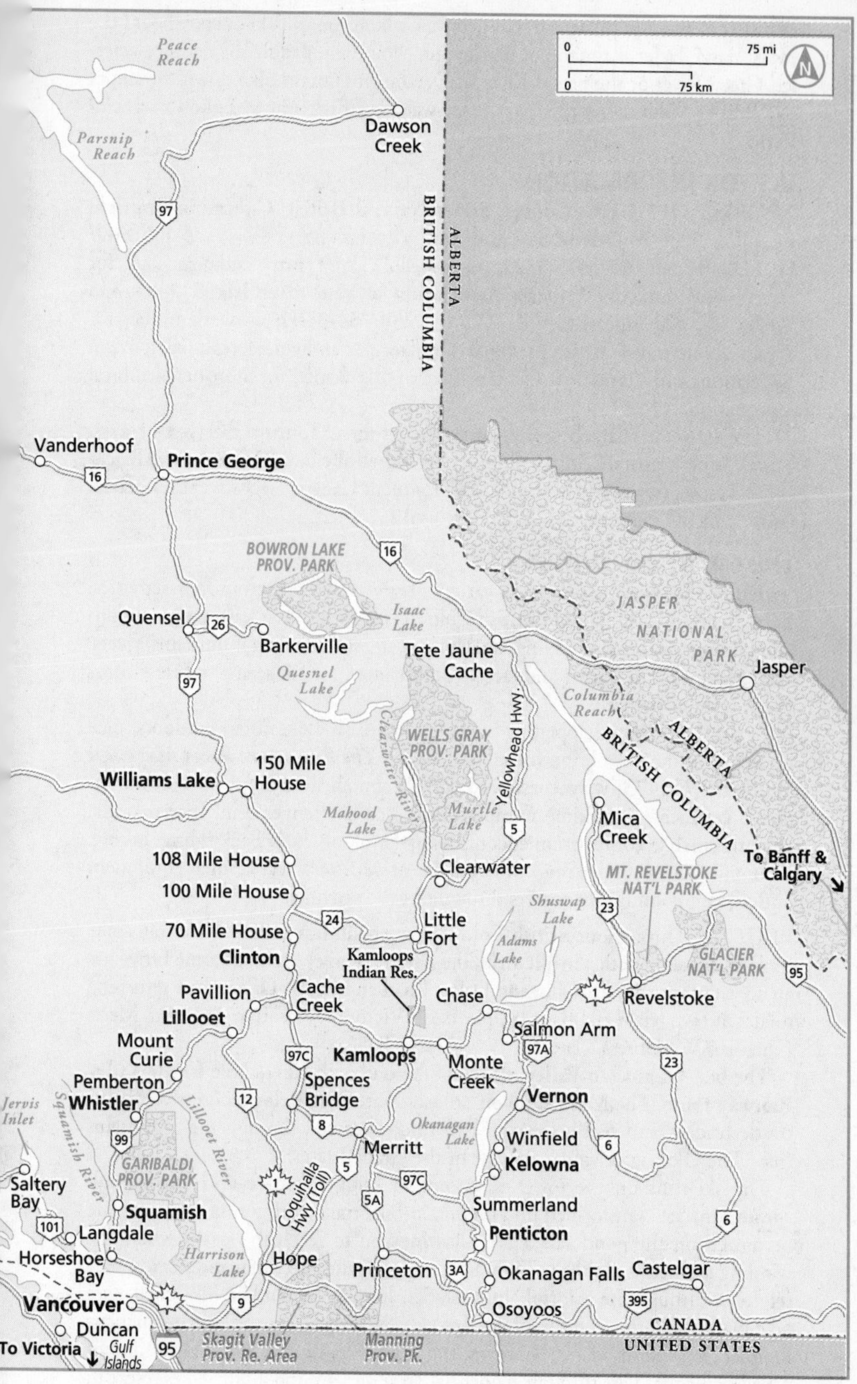

0
75 mi
0
75 km
N
Peace Reach
Parsnip Reach
Dawson Creek
ALBERTA
BRITISH COLUMBIA
97
Vanderhoof
16
Prince George
BOWRON LAKE PROV. PARK
16
Isaac Lake
Quensel
26
Barkerville
Tete Jaune Cache
JASPER NATIONAL PARK
Jasper
Quesnel Lake
97
Clearwater River
WELLS GRAY PROV. PARK
Yellowhead Hwy.
Columbia Reach
ALBERTA
BRITISH COLUMBIA
150 Mile House
Williams Lake
Mahood Lake
Murtle Lake
5
Mica Creek
To Banff & Calgary
108 Mile House
Clearwater
MT. REVELSTOKE NAT'L PARK
100 Mile House
Shuswap Lake
23
24
Little Fort
70 Mile House
Adams Lake
GLACIER NAT'L PARK
Clinton
Kamloops Indian Res.
95
Pavillion
Cache Creek
Chase
1
Revelstoke
Lillooet
Salmon Arm
97A
Mount Curie
97C
Kamloops
Monte Creek
23
Pemberton
Spences Bridge
Vernon
Whistler
Lillooet River
12
Jervis Inlet
Squamish River
8
Okanagan Lake
99
Merritt
Winfield
6
GARIBALDI PROV. PARK
1
5
Kelowna
Saltery Bay
Coquihalla Hwy (Toll)
97C
5A
Summerland
Squamish
6
101
Langdale
Penticton
Horseshoe Bay
Harrison Lake
Hope
Princeton
3A
Okanagan Falls
Castelgar
Vancouver
1
9
395
Osoyoos
Duncan
CANADA
To Victoria
Gulf Islands
95
Skagit Valley Prov. Re. Area
Manning Prov. Pk.
UNITED STATES

Whistler is also a popular summer getaway, where you can ski or snowboard the Horstman Glacier at the top of Blackcomb Mountain, paddle the raging glacier-fed Green River or the placid River of Dreams, mountain bike down the slopes of Whistler Mountain, or fish in the icy waters of **Birkenhead Lake Provincial Park.**

## VISITOR INFORMATION

**TOURIST OFFICES** Contact **Super Natural British Columbia–Tourism BC,** Box 9830 Stn. Prov. Government, Victoria, BC V8W 9W5 (© **800/HELLO-BC** or 604/435-5622; www.hellobc.com; http://snbc-res.com for reservations), and the **Tourism Association of Vancouver Island,** (203–335 Wesley St., Nanaimo, BC V9R 2T5 (© **250/754-3500;** www.islands.bc) for details about travel in the province. Contact the individual regional tourism associations and Visitor Info Centres listed in this chapter for more detailed local information.

Here are some of the best sites currently out there: Tourism BC (**www.travel.bc.ca**), Super Natural British Columbia (**www.hellobc.com**), Whistler and Blackcomb Resorts (**www.whistler.net**), Environment Canada (**www.weather office.com**), and BC Ferries (**www.bcferries.com**).

## THE GREAT OUTDOORS

It's hard to believe the province's variety of sports and other outdoor activities. Even the most cosmopolitan British Columbians spend their leisure time mountain biking, windsurfing, skiing, or hiking in the surrounding mountains, rivers, and meadows. The varied and largely uninhabited terrain seems to lure visitors to get close to nature.

To find out what's happening in the great British Columbian outdoors, pick up a copy of the free bimonthly tabloid ***Coast: The Adventure Sport Magazine*** (© **604/876-1473;** www.coastmag.com). It contains the latest info on mountain-bike races, kayaking competitions, eco-challenges (an international pentathlon-style competition encompassing kayaking, horseback riding, hiking, mountain biking, and skiing). It's available at outfitters, recreational-equipment outlets, and community centers throughout the province.

**BIKING** Throughout British Columbia are countless marked mountain-bike trails and cycling paths. In **Victoria,** the 13km (8-mile) Scenic Marine Drive has an adjacent paved path following Dallas Road and Beach Drive, then returning to downtown via Oak Bay Avenue (see "Victoria: Victorian England Meets Canadian Wilderness," later).

The best **Okanagan Valley** off-road bike trail is the incredible **Kettle Valley Railway** route. The **Myra Canyon** railway route near Kelowna crosses over 18 trestle bridges and passes through two tunnels carved through the mountains (see "The Okanagan Valley: A Taste of the Grape," later).

The ski runs on the lower elevations of both **Whistler and Blackcomb Mountains** are transformed into mountain-bike trails during summer. Bikes are permitted on the gondola ski lift, allowing you to reach the peaks where the winding marked trails begin. From here, experts, intermediates, and novices barrel down through the colorful alpine slopes. June to September, bike challenges take place regularly on both mountains (see "Whistler: One of North America's Premier Ski Resorts," later). In town, the **Valley Trail** offers 20km (12 miles) of paved paths that pass through residential areas and around alpine lakes. Next to the Chateau Whistler Golf Course, the **Lost Lake Trails** feature numerous unpaved alternative routes that fan out from the main lakeside trail (see "Whistler: One of North America's Premier Ski Resorts," later).

**BOATING & SAILING** While you're in **Victoria,** take a leisurely cruise south to Sooke Harbour or up the Strait of Georgia in a rental boat or a skippered vessel. There are many outfitters at the **Brentwood Bay** and **Oak Bay Marinas** (see "Victoria: Victorian England Meets Canadian Wilderness," later).

On the **Gulf Islands,** you can take the wheel of a 48m (30-ft.) sailing craft or enjoy a skippered cruise on a power catamaran around the Gulf Islands. The remote **Queen Charlotte Islands** offer a world of marine beauty you can best discover by taking a guided cruise on a skippered schooner. The crews are familiar with the history and lore of the mysterious waters surrounding the home of the Haida Native-Indian tribe (see "The Inside Passage: Prince Rupert & the Queen Charlotte Islands," later). On the mainland, more than a dozen **Okanagan Valley** lakes lure boaters, houseboaters, and watersports enthusiasts. Whether you're into waterskiing, fishing, jet skiing, house-, or pleasure boating, local marinas offer full-service rentals (see "The Okanagan Valley: A Taste of the Grape," later).

**CAMPING** British Columbia's national parks, provincial parks, marine parks, and private campgrounds are generally filled during summer weekends. Most areas are first-come, first-served, so stake your claim early in the afternoon (for weekends, arrive by Thurs). However, March 1 to September 15, you can book a campsite up to 3 months in advance by contacting **Discover Camping** (**© 800/689-9025** in North America or 604/689-9025; www.discover camping.ca). It's open Monday to Friday 7am to 9pm and Saturday and Sunday 9am to 5pm. There's a nonrefundable service fee of C$6 (US$3.70), and reservations can be confirmed only with MasterCard or Visa.

The provincial park campgrounds charge C$9 to C$19 (US$6–US$12) per site. There's a 2-week maximum for individual campsite stays. Facilities vary from rustic (walk-in or water-access) to basic (pit toilets and little else) to luxurious (hot showers, flush toilets, and sani-stations). All provincial drive-in campgrounds offer precut-wood piles, grill-equipped fire pits, bear-proof garbage cans, pumped well water, and well-maintained security. The rustic wilderness campgrounds provide minimal services—a covered shelter or simply a cleared patch of ground and little else.

**CANOEING & KAYAKING** You'll quickly discover why sea kayakers rate **Vancouver Island's west coast** one of the world's best places to paddle. Novice and intermediate paddlers launch from the passenger ferry MV *Lady Rose* into the sheltered waters of **Barkley Sound.** Surf kayakers are drawn to the tidal swells that crash along the shores of **Long Beach,** part of Pacific Rim National Park. And the **Broken Island Group's** many islands offer paddlers an excellent site for overnight expeditions amid the rugged beauty of the outer coast.

In **Whistler,** paddlers are treated to an exhilarating stretch of glacial waters that runs behind the village itself. Some savvy kayakers and canoeists call it the "River of Dreams" (see "Whistler: One of North America's Premier Ski Resorts," later).

**CLIMBING & SPELUNKING** Off Valleyview Road, east of Penticton in the Okanagan Valley, **Skaha Bluffs** has more than 400 bolted routes set in place. For info about organized climbing trips throughout the province, contact the

## Three Trips of a Lifetime

Each of the following trips, within striking distance of Vancouver and Victoria, takes you to a place like no other on earth.

**KAYAKING CLAYOQUOT SOUND** ★★ In 1993, environmentalists from across the province and around the world arrived in British Columbia to protect this pristine fjord on the West Coast of Vancouver Island. More than 1,000 were arrested before the government and logging companies gave in and agreed to leave Clayoquot (pronounced *kla*-kwat) Sound's temperate old-growth rain forest intact. This trip involves paddling a kayak for 4 or 5 days through the protected waters of the sound, from the funky former fishing village of Tofino to a natural hot-springs bath near a native village of the Hesquiaat people. Along the way, you'll see thousand-year-old trees, glaciers, whales, and bald eagles.

Three companies in Tofino can set you up with a kayak: **Pacific Kayak,** 606 Campbell St. (✆ **250/725-3232;** www.tofino-bc.com/pacifickayak); the **Tofino Sea Kayaking Company,** 320 Main St. (✆ **800/863-4664;** www.tofino-kayaking.com); and **Remote Passages,** 71 Wharf St. (✆ **800/666-9833** or 250/725-3330; www.remotepassages.com). Sea kayaking isn't hard, and the great advantage of a trip on Clayoquot Sound is that it's entirely in sheltered inshore waters, though the scenery and the feeling are those of being in a wide-open wilderness. If you're tentative about kayaking on your own, many companies, like the three above, can set you up on a guided trip.

The preferred route leaves Tofino and travels for 2 or 3 days through the protected waters of Clayoquot Sound up to the natural Hot Springs Cove. From there you can fly back—strapping your kayak to the floats of the plane—or retrace your route to Tofino. Whichever way you go, save some time and money for a memorable meal at the Pointe Restaurant in the Wickaninnish Inn (see "Where to Stay," later in this chapter); after a week in the wilderness, the food here will seem sublime.

**SAILING THROUGH THE GREAT BEAR RAIN FOREST** ★★★ If you look at a map of British Columbia, you'll see, about halfway up the west coast, an incredibly convoluted region of mountains, fjords, bays, channels, rivers, and inlets. There are next to no roads here—the geography's too

**Federation of Mountain Clubs of BC,** 1367 W. Broadway, Vancouver, BC V6H 4A9 (✆ **604/737-3053**).

**FISHING** Numerous fishing packages depart from the **Victoria** docks, where charters run to the southern island's best catch-and-release spots for salmon, halibut, cutthroat, and lingcod. About 134km (83 miles) north of Victoria, **Elk & Beaver Lakes Provincial Park**'s Beaver Lake is stocked with steelhead, rainbow trout, kokanee, Dolly Varden char, and smallmouth bass. Year-round sportfishing for salmon, steelhead, trout, Dolly Varden char, halibut, cod, and snapper lures anglers to the waters near **Port Alberni** and **Barkley Sound.** Nearby **Long Beach** is great for bottom fishing (see "Vancouver Island's West Coast: Pacific Rim National Park, Tofino & Ucluelet," later).

intense. Thanks to that isolation, this is also one of the last places in the world where grizzly bears are still found in large numbers, not to mention salmon, large trees, killer whales, otters, and porpoises. But to get there, you'll need a boat. And if you have to take a boat, why not take a 100-year-old fully rigged 28m (92-ft.) sailing schooner?

Run by an ex-pilot turned naturalist and sailor, **Maple Leaf Adventures,** 2087 Indian Crescent, Duncan, BC V9L 5L9 (© **888/599-5323** or 250/715-0906; fax 250/715-0912; www.cowichan.com/business/mla), runs a number of trips to this magic area. Owner Brian Falconer is extremely knowledgeable and normally brings along a trained naturalist to explain the fauna (especially the whales, dolphins, and grizzlies). The trips vary from 4 days to 2 weeks and from C$1,250 to C$2,500 (US$775–US$1,550), covering territory from the mid-coast to the Queen Charlotte Islands (Haida Gwaii) to the coasts of Alaska. All include gourmet meals (more than you could ever eat) and comfortable but not luxurious accommodation aboard Brian's beautiful schooner, the *Maple Leaf.*

**HORSE TREKKING ON THE CHILCOTIN PLATEAU** ★★ The high plateau country of the BC interior boasts some of the most impressive scenery around. Soaring peaks rise above deep valleys, and mountain meadows come alive with flowers that bloom for just a few weeks in high summer. The advantage to taking in this territory on horseback are that the horse's feet get sore, not yours; if you come across a grizzly, you've got some height on him; and horses can carry far more and far better food.

While dude ranches abound in both Canada and the States, there's one key difference to certain British Columbia outfits. It's called a guide-outfitter tenure—one company is granted exclusive rights to run guided tours through that section of wilderness. In BC, the territories are typically 5,000km$^2$ (1,900 sq. miles), all high-country wilderness where you likely won't meet another horse team. One of the guide-outfitters closest to Vancouver is the **Chilcotin Holidays Guest Ranch,** Gun Creek Road, Gold Bridge, BC V0K 1P0 (© **250/238-2274;** www.chilcotinholidays.com). Their trips run 4 to 7 days, cost C$600 to C$900 (US$372–US$558), and involve encounters with wildflowers, bighorn sheep, grizzlies, and wolves.

On Vancouver Island's east coast, **Campbell River** is the home of **Painter's Lodge.** A favorite Hollywood getaway for over 50 years, it has entertained Bob Hope, John Wayne (who was a frequent guest), and Goldie Hawn (see "Vancouver Island's East Coast: Parksville to Campbell River & Quadra Island," later). The **Queen Charlotte Islands** were only recently opened to sport fishermen, and the fish stories about 70-pound tyee salmon and 125-pound halibut emanating from these misty shores are true. **Langara Island and Naden Harbour on Graham Island** are perfect salmon-fishing spots where anglers commonly release catches under 30 pounds as they aim for the big fish (see "The Inside Passage: Prince Rupert & the Queen Charlotte Islands," later).

The desert-like **Okanagan Valley** summers are far too hot for fish and fishermen, but for the region's **Okanagan, Kalamalka, and Skaha Lakes,** spring and fall are bountiful seasons. The best summer fishing centers around the small hillside lakes surrounding the valley. These spots brim with trout, steelhead, Dolly Varden char, and smallmouth bass (see "The Okanagan Valley: A Taste of the Grape," later in this chapter). Sportfishing is the best reason to visit the **Cariboo Country lakes,** about 250 of which are accessible by road. Some lakes are nestled at altitudes as high as 6,000 feet and can be reached by booking a guided floatplane trip (see "Cariboo Country to Prince George," later).

Whistler's **Green River** and nearby **Birkenhead Lake Provincial Park** have runs of steelhead, rainbow trout, Dolly Varden char, cutthroat, and salmon that attract sport anglers from around the world (see "Whistler: One of North America's Premier Ski Resorts," later).

**GOLFING** Considering **Victoria**'s British heritage and its lush rolling landscape, it's no wonder golf is a popular pastime. The three local courses offer terrain—minus thistles—similar to Scotland's, too (see "Victoria: Victorian England Meets Canadian Wilderness," below).

There are also a number of outstanding layouts in central **Vancouver Island,** including an 18-hole course designed by golf legend Les Furber. The **Morningstar** championship course is in Parksville. The **Storey Creek Golf Club** in Campbell River also has a challenging course design and great scenic views (see "Vancouver Island's East Coast: Parksville to Campbell River & Quadra Island," later). There are 9- and 18-hole golf courses in the **Okanagan Valley,** including the **Gallagher's Canyon Golf & Country Club** in Kelowna and **Predator Ridge** in Vernon (see "The Okanagan Valley: A Taste of the Grape," later). Visitors to **Whistler** can tee off at the **Chateau Whistler Golf Course,** at the base of Blackcomb Mountain, or at the **Nicklaus North** golf course on the shore of Green Lake (see "Whistler: One of North America's Premier Ski Resorts," later).

**HIKING** Among the best short nature walks on Vancouver Island, the lush temperate rain forest of **Goldstream Provincial Park** offers hikes through centuries-old stands of Douglas fir (see "A Side Trip from Victoria: Goldstream Provincial Park," later). On Vancouver Island's west coast, the world-famous **West Coast Trail** ★ is considered by many seasoned hikers the challenge of a lifetime. The boardwalked **South Beach Trail** near Tofino provides a contemplative stroll through a Sitka-spruce temperate rain forest, as does the **Big Cedar Trail** on Meares Island. The trails following **Long Beach** allow hikers a close-up glimpse of the marine life that inhabits the tidal pools in the park's many quiet coves (see "Vancouver Island's West Coast: Pacific Rim National Park, Tofino & Ucluelet," later). At Whistler, **Lost Lake Trails**' 30km (19 miles) of marked trails around creeks, beaver dams, blueberry patches, and lush cedars are ideal for biking, Nordic skiing, or just quiet strolling and picnicking. The **Ancient Cedars** area of Cougar Mountain above Whistler's Emerald Estates is an awe-inspiring grove of towering old-growth cedars and Douglas firs.

Whistlers' **Singing Pass Trail** is a 4-hour moderately difficult hike winding from the top of Whistler Mountain down to the village via the Fitzsimmons Valley. North of Whistler, **Nairn Falls Provincial Park** features a gentle 1.5km (1-mile) trail leading to a stupendous view of the icy-cold Green River as it plunges 60m (196 ft.) over a rocky cliff into a narrow gorge. There's also an incredible view of Mount Currie peaking over the treetops.

**HORSEBACK RIDING** Besides booking a trip to one of the **Cariboo Country guest ranches** (see "Cariboo Country to Prince George," later), you can take an afternoon ride along a wooded trail near Victoria's Buck Mountain.

In Whistler, there are riding trails along the Green River, across the Pemberton Valley, and even up on Blackcomb Mountain itself (see "Whistler: One of North America's Premier Ski Resorts," later).

**RAFTING** Whistler's **Green River** offers novices small rapids and views of snowcapped mountains for their first rafting runs (see "Whistler: One of North America's Premier Ski Resorts," later). The Chilco-Chilcotin-Fraser river system near Williams Lake has some of the most challenging whitewater in the province (see "Cariboo Country to Prince George," later).

**SKIING & SNOWBOARDING** Cross-country and powder skiing are the **Okanagan Valley's** main winter attractions. **Big White Ski Resort** gets an annual average of 18 feet of powder and has more than 20km (12 miles) of cross-country trails. **Apex Resort** maintains 56 downhill runs and extensive cross-country trails. And **Silver Star Mountain Ski Resort & Cross-Country Centre** offers cross-country skiers 93km (58 miles) of trails (including 6.5km/4 miles lit for night skiing), plus 50km (31 miles) of trails in the adjacent Silver Star Provincial Park. The ski-in/ski-out resort resembles a 19th-century mining town. For off-piste fanatics, some of Canada's most extreme verticals are here among the resort's 72 downhill runs. Nearby **Crystal Mountain** caters to intermediate and novice downhill skiers and snowboarders (see "The Okanagan Valley: A Taste of the Grape," later).

**Whistler Mountain,** with a 1,525m (5,006-ft.) vertical and 100 marked runs, is the cream of the province's ski resorts. **Blackcomb Mountain,** which shares its base with Whistler, has a 1,600m (5,280-ft.) vertical and also has 100 marked runs. Dual-mountain passes are available. **Helicopter skiing** makes another 100-plus runs accessible on nearby glaciers. **Lost Lakes Trails** are converted into miles of groomed cross-country trails, as are the **Valley Trail System, Singing Pass,** and **Ancient Cedars** (see "Whistler: One of North America's Premier Ski Resorts," below).

**WILDLIFE WATCHING** Whether you're in search of the 20,000 **Pacific gray whales** that migrate to **Vancouver Island's** west coast (see "Vancouver Island's West Coast: Pacific Rim National Park, Tofino & Ucluelet," later), or the thousands of **bald eagles** ★ in Goldstream Provincial Park (see "A Side Trip from Victoria," below), there are land-based observation points and numerous knowledgeable outfitters who can guide you to the best nature and bird-spotting areas the island has to offer.

If you take the ferry cruise up the **Inside Passage,** you have a great opportunity to spot **orcas, Dall porpoises, salmon, bald eagles,** and **sea lions.** While on the Queen Charlotte Islands, you can observe **peregrine falcons, Sitka deer, horned puffins, Cassin's auklets, Steller's sea lions,** and the world's largest **black bears** (see "The Inside Passage: Prince Rupert & the Queen Charlotte Islands," later).

## 2 Victoria: Victorian England Meets Canadian Wilderness ★★★

In an Arcadian parkland of oak and fir at the edge of a natural harbor, **Victoria** spent the better part of the 20th century in a reverie, looking back to its glorious past as an outpost of England at the height of the Empire. It was a booming colonial city in the 19th century, but Victoria's lot began to fade soon after Vancouver was established in the 1880s. When its economy finally crashed early in the 20th century, shocked Victorians realized they were looking at a future with nothing much to live on but some fabulous Tudor and Victorian architecture, a beautiful natural setting, and a carefully cultivated sense of Englishness. So they decided to market that.

So successful was the sales job that the Victorians themselves began to believe they inhabited a little patch of England. They began growing elaborate rose gardens, which flourished in the mild Pacific climate, and cultivated a taste for afternoon tea with jam and scones. For decades, the reverie continued unabated. But the Victorians proved flexible enough to accommodate some changes as well. Early on, it was discovered that few in the world shared the English taste for cooking; so, Victoria's restaurants branched out into seafood and ethnic and fusion cuisines. And lately, as visitors have shown themselves more interested in exploring the natural world, Victoria has quietly added whale-watching and mountain-biking trips to its traditional tours on London-style double-decker buses. The result, at century's end, is that Victoria is the only city in the world where you can zoom out on a zodiac in the morning to see a pod of killer whales and make it back in time for a lovely afternoon tea with all the trimmings.

## ESSENTIALS

**GETTING THERE By Plane Victoria International Airport** (**© 250/953-7500;** www.cyyj.ca) is near the Sidney ferry terminal, 17 miles (27km) north of Victoria off the Patricia Bay Highway (Highway 17). **Air Canada** (**© 888/247-2262**) offers direct connections from Seattle, Vancouver, and other western cities. Provincial commuter airlines, including floatplanes that land in Victoria's Inner Harbour and helicopters, service the city as well. They include Air Canada affiliate **Air BC** (**© 888/247-2262** or 604/688-5515), **Harbour Air** (**© 604/688-1277**), **Pacific Spirit Air** (**© 800/665-2359**), **Kenmore Air** (**© 800/543-9595**), and **Helijet Airways** (**© 250/382-6222** in Victoria, or 604/273-1414 in Vancouver).

The airport **bus service,** operated by AKAL Airport (**© 250/386-2526**), makes the 45-minute trip into town every 30 minutes 4:30am to midnight; the fare is C$13 (US$8) one-way and C$23 (US$14) round-trip. A cab ride from the airport into downtown Victoria takes about half an hour and costs about C$40 (US$25) plus tip. **Empress Cabs** and **Blue Bird Cabs** make airport runs. Several **car-rental firms** have desks at the airport, including **Avis** (**© 250/656-6033**), **Hertz** (**© 250/656-2312**), and **Tilden** (**© 250/656-2541**).

**By Train** Travelers on the Horseshoe Bay–Nanaimo ferry can board a train that winds down the Cowichan River Valley through Goldstream Provincial Park into Victoria. The VIA Rail's **E&N Railiner** leaves Courtenay (about 210km/130 miles northwest of Victoria) at 1:15pm daily and arrives in Nanaimo at about 3:07pm and in Victoria at 5:45pm. The Victoria **E&N Station,** 450 Pandora Ave. (**© 800/561-8630** in Canada), is near the Johnson Street Bridge. The one-way fare from Nanaimo to Victoria is C$20 (US$12) for adults, C$18 (US$11) for seniors/students, and C$12 (US$7) for youths.

**By Bus Pacific Coach Lines** (**© 800/661-1725** in Canada, or 604/662-8074; www.pacificcoach.com) operates bus service between Vancouver and Victoria. The 4-hour trip from the Pacific Central Station, 1150 Terminal Ave. in Vancouver, to the Victoria Depot, 710 Douglas St., includes passage on the Tsawwassen–Swartz Bay ferry. The adult fare is C$26 (US$16) one-way, including the ferry, with daily departures from 5:45am to 7:45pm.

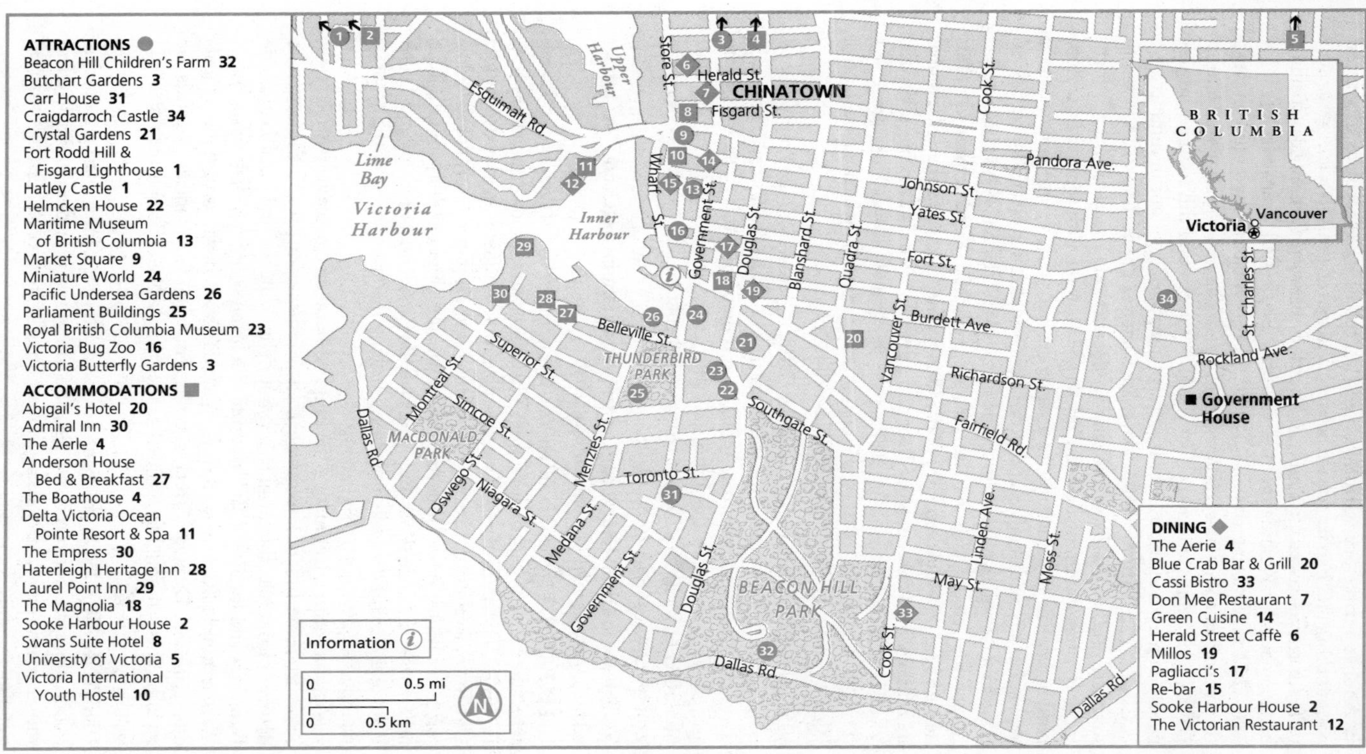
ATTRACTIONS
Beacon Hill Children's Farm 32
Butchart Gardens 3
Carr House 31
Craigdarroch Castle 34
Crystal Gardens 21
Fort Rodd Hill & Fisgard Lighthouse 1
Hatley Castle 1
Helmcken House 22
Maritime Museum of British Columbia 13
Market Square 9
Miniature World 24
Pacific Undersea Gardens 26
Parliament Buildings 25
Royal British Columbia Museum 23
Victoria Bug Zoo 16
Victoria Butterfly Gardens 3
ACCOMMODATIONS
Abigail's Hotel 20
Admiral Inn 30
The Aerle 4
Anderson House Bed & Breakfast 27
The Boathouse 4
Delta Victoria Ocean Pointe Resort & Spa 11
The Empress 30
Haterleigh Heritage Inn 28
Laurel Point Inn 29
The Magnolia 18
Sooke Harbour House 2
Swans Suite Hotel 8
University of Victoria 5
Victoria International Youth Hostel 10
DINING
The Aerie 4
Blue Crab Bar & Grill 20
Cassi Bistro 33
Don Mee Restaurant 7
Green Cuisine 14
Herald Street Caffè 6
Millos 19
Pagliacci's 17
Re-bar 15
Sooke Harbour House 2
The Victorian Restaurant 12
BRITISH COLUMBIA
Vancouver
Victoria
CHINATOWN
Store St.
Herald St.
Fisgard St.
Wharf St.
Government St.
Douglas St.
Blanshard St.
Quadra St.
Vancouver St.
Cook St.
Pandora Ave.
Johnson St.
Yates St.
Fort St.
Burdett Ave.
Richardson St.
Fairfield Rd.
Rockland Ave.
St. Charles St.
Government House
Esquimalt Rd.
Upper Harbour
Lime Bay
Victoria Harbour
Inner Harbour
Belleville St.
Superior St.
Montreal St.
Simcoe St.
Menzies St.
Toronto St.
Southgate St.
Oswego St.
Niagara St.
Medana St.
Dallas Rd.
Linden Ave.
May St.
Moss St.
THUNDERBIRD PARK
MACDONALD PARK
BEACON HILL PARK
Information
0 0.5 mi
0 0.5 km
N

**By Ship & Ferry** See "Getting There," in chapter 15, "Vancouver," for information about **BC Ferries** service between Vancouver and Victoria.

Three ferry services offer daily connections between Port Angeles, Bellingham, or Seattle, Washington, and Victoria. **Black Ball Transport** (✆ **250/386-2202** in Victoria, or 360/457-4491 in Port Angeles; www.northolympic.com/coho/) operates between Port Angeles and Victoria, with one-way fares at C$11 (US$7) for adults and C$44 (US$27) for cars and drivers. The crossing takes 1½ hours, and there are at least two sailings per day (four in summer).

**Clipper Navigation,** 1000A Wharf St., Victoria (✆ **800/888-2535** in North America, or 250/382-8100 in Victoria), operates the *Victoria Clipper,* a high-speed catamaran running between Seattle and Victoria, with some sailings stopping in the San Juan Islands. It's a passenger-only service, and sailing time is about 3 hours with daily sailings. One-way adult fares are C$85 to C$106 (US$53–US$66). A round-trip is C$140 to C$177 (US$87–US$110).

June to October, Victoria San Juan Cruises's **MV *Victoria Star*** (✆ **800/443-4552** in North America, or 360/738-8099) departs the Fairhaven Terminal in Bellingham, Washington, at 9am and arrives in Victoria at noon. It departs Victoria at 5pm, arriving in Bellingham at 8pm. One-way fares are C$65 (US$40). It costs C$137 (US$85) round-trip for an adult which includes a free salmon dinner on the return Victoria–Bellingham run.

**VISITOR INFORMATION** **Tourist Office** Across from the Empress hotel is the **Tourism Victoria Visitor Info Centre,** 812 Wharf St. (✆ **250/953-2033;** www.tourismvictoria.com; bus 5, 30). If you didn't reserve a room before you arrived, you can go to this office or call its reservations hot line at ✆ **800/663-3883** or 250/953-2022 for last-minute bookings. The center is open daily 9am to 5pm (summer to 8pm).

Visit **www.tourismvictoria.com**, **www.victoriashomepage.com**, or **http://victoriabc.com** for additional information.

**CITY LAYOUT** Victoria is on the southeastern tip of Vancouver Island, across the Strait of Juan de Fuca from Washington state's snow-capped Olympic Peninsula. The areas of most interest to visitors, including the **downtown** and **Old Town,** lie along the eastern edge of the **Inner Harbour.** (North of the Johnson Street Bridge is the **Upper Harbour,** which is almost entirely industrial.) A little farther east, the **Ross Bay** and **Oak Bay** residential areas around Dallas Road and Beach Drive reach the beaches along the open waters of the Strait of Juan de Fuca.

Victoria's central landmark is the **Empress hotel** on Government Street, right across from the Inner Harbour wharf. If you turn your back to the hotel, the downtown and Old Town will be on your right, while the provincial **Legislative Buildings** and the **Royal BC Museum** will be on your immediate left.

**Government Street** goes through Victoria's main downtown shopping-and-dining district. **Douglas Street,** running parallel to Government Street, is the main business thoroughfare as well as the road to Nanaimo and the rest of the island.

**GETTING AROUND** **By Foot** Strolling along the Inner Harbour's pedestrian walkways and streets is very pleasant. The terrain is predominantly flat, and with few exceptions, Victoria's points of interest are accessible in less than 30 minutes on foot.

**By Bus** The **Victoria Regional Transit System (BC Transit),** 520 Gorge Rd. (✆ **250/382-6161;** http://transitbc.com), operates 40 bus routes through greater Victoria, as well as the nearby towns of Sooke and Sidney. Regular service on the main routes runs 6am to just past midnight. Schedules and routes are available at the Tourism Victoria Visitor Info Centre. Fares are calculated on a per-zone basis. One-way single-zone fares are C$1.75 (US$1.10) for adults and C$1.10 (US70¢) for seniors/children ages 5 to 13; two zones are C$2.50 (US$1.55) and C$1.75 (US$1.10), respectively. Transfers are good for travel in one direction only with no stops. A **DayPass** (C$5.5/US$3.40 adults, C$4/US$2.50 seniors/children 5–13) covers unlimited travel throughout the day. You can buy passes at the Tourism Victoria Visitor Info Centre, as well as in convenience stores and ticket outlets displaying the FareDealer symbol.

**By Ferry** Crossing the Inner, Upper, and Victoria Harbors by one of the 12-passenger blue **Victoria Harbour Ferries** (✆ **250/708-0201**) is cheap and fun. During the high summer season, ferries to the Empress hotel, Coast Harborside Hotel, and Ocean Pointe Resort Hotel run about every 15 minutes 9am to 9pm. Off-season, the ferries run only on sunny weekends 11am to 6pm. The cost is C$3 (US$1.85) for adults and C$1.50 (US95¢) for children.

**By Car** Make sure your hotel has parking. Metered **street parking** is hard to come by in the downtown area, and rules are strictly enforced. Unmetered parking on side streets is rare. All major downtown hotels have guest parking; rates vary from free to C$20 (US$12) per day. There are parking lots at **View Street** between Douglas and Blanshard streets; **Johnson Street** off Blanshard Street; **Yates Street** north of Bastion Square; and **the Bay** on Fisgard at Blanshard Street. Car-rental agencies in Victoria include **ABC,** 2507 Government St. (✆ **800/464-6464** or 250/388-3153; Bus: 31); **Avis,** 1001 Douglas St. (✆ **800/879-2847** or 250/386-8468; Bus: 5); **Budget,** 757 Douglas St. (✆ **800/268-8900** or 250/253-5300; Bus: 5); **Hertz Canada,** 102-907 Fort St. (✆ **800/263-0600** or 250/388-4411; Bus: 11); and **Tilden International,** 767 Douglas St. (✆ **800/387-4747** or 250/386-1213; Bus: 11). Car rentals cost about C$25 to C$45 (US$16–US$28) per day for a compact to midsize vehicle. Remember that it's always cheaper to arrange the rental before you leave home.

**By Bicycle** There are bike lanes throughout the city and paved paths along parks and beaches. Bikes and child trailers are available by the hour or day at **Cycle BC** rentals, 747 Douglas St. (year-round) or 950 Wharf St. (May–Oct) (✆ **250/885-2453**). Rentals run C$6 (US$3.70) per hour and C$20 (US$12) per day, helmets and locks included.

**By Taxi** Within the downtown area, you can expect to travel for less than C$6 (US$3.70) plus tip. It's best to call for a cab; drivers don't always stop on city streets for flag-downs, especially when it's raining. Call for a pickup from **Empress Cabs** at ✆ **250/381-2222** or **Blue Bird Cabs** at ✆ **250/382-8294.**

**SPECIAL EVENTS & FESTIVALS** So many flowers bloom during the temperate month of February in Victoria and the surrounding area that the city holds an annual **Flower Count** (✆ **250/383-7191**). In April, the city hosts the **TerrifVic Dixieland Jazz Party** (✆ **250/953-2011**) with bands from around the world playing swing, Dixieland, honky-tonk, and fusion. Toward the end of May, thousands of yachts sail into Victoria Harbor during the **Swiftsure Yacht Race** (✆ **250/953-2033**). In June, the **Jazz Fest International** (✆ **250/388-4423**) brings jazz, swing, bebop, fusion, and improv artists from around the world. The **Folkfest,** a free 8-day world-beat music festival, takes place at the end of June.

The provincial capital celebrates **Canada Day** (July 1) with events centered around the Inner Harbour, including music, food, and fireworks. The August **First Peoples Festival** (✆ **250/384-3211**) highlights the culture and heritage of the Pacific Northwest First Nations tribes. In November, the **Great Canadian Beer Festival** (✆ **250/952-0360**) features samples from the province's best microbreweries. And Victoria rings in the New Year with **First Night** (✆ **250/380-1211**), a family-oriented New Year's Eve celebration with free performances at many downtown venues.

## FAST FACTS

*American Express* The office at 1203 Douglas St. (✆ **250/385-8731;** bus: 5) is open Monday to Friday 8:30am to 5:30pm and Saturday 10am to 4pm.

*Area Code* The telephone area code for all Vancouver Island, including Victoria and most of British Columbia, is **250.**

*Dentist* Most major hotels have a dentist on call. **Cresta Dental Centre,** 3170 Tillicum Rd. at Burnside Street (✆ **250/384-7711;** bus: 21), in the Tillicum Mall, is open Monday 8am to 5pm, Tuesday to Friday 8am to 9pm, Saturday 9am to 5pm, and Sunday noon to 5pm.

*Doctor* Hotels usually have a doctor on call. The **James Bay Treatment Center,** 100–230 Menzies St. (✆ **250/388-9934;** bus: 5), a medical facility, is open Monday to Friday 9am to 6pm and Saturday and statutory holidays 10am to 4pm.

*Emergencies* Dial ✆ **911** for fire, police, ambulance, and poison control.

*Hospitals* Local hospitals include the **Royal Jubilee Hospital,** 1900 Fort St. (✆ **250/370-8000;** emergency 250/370-8212; bus: 11), and **Victoria General Hospital,** 1 Hospital Way (✆ **250/727-4212;** emergency 250/727-4181; bus: 22).

*Police* Dial ✆ **911.** The **Victoria City Police** can also be reached by calling ✆ **250/995-7654.** The **Royal Canadian Mounted Police** can be reached at ✆ **250/380-6261.**

*Safety* Crime rates are quite low in Victoria, but transients panhandle throughout the downtown and Old Town areas. As in any city, stay alert to prevent crimes of opportunity.

*Time Zone* Victoria is in the Pacific time zone, as are Vancouver, Seattle, and San Francisco.

## SEEING THE SIGHTS

### THE TOP ATTRACTIONS

**British Columbia Aviation Museum** ★ A must for plane buffs, or for anyone with an interest in the history of flight. Located adjacent to Victoria International Airport, this small hanger is crammed to bursting with a score of original, rebuilt, and replica airplanes. The collection ranges from the first Canadian-designed craft ever to fly (a bizarre kite-like contraption) to World War I–

intage Nieuports and Tiger Moths, to floatplanes and Spitfires and slightly more modern water bombers and helicopters. Thursdays you can watch the all-volunteer crew in the restoration hanger working to bring these old craft back to life. Other days, the museum is staffed by a crew of knowledgeable volunteer guides who take pride in explaining the displays. Allow 1 hour.

1910 Norseman Rd., Sidney. ✆ **250/655-3300.** www.bcam.net. Admission C$5 (US$3.10) adults, C$4 (US$2.50) seniors, C$3 (US$1.85) students, children under 12 free. V. Summer daily 10am–4pm; winter daily 11am–3pm. Closed Dec 25. Bus: Airport.

**Butchart Gardens** ★★★ These internationally acclaimed gardens were born after Robert Butchart exhausted the limestone quarry near his Tod Inlet home. His wife, Jenny, gradually landscaped the deserted eyesore into the resplendent Sunken Garden, opening it to the public in 1904. A Rose Garden, Italian Garden, and Japanese Garden were added. As the fame of the 20ha (50-acre) gardens grew, the Butcharts also transformed their house into an attraction. The gardens—still in the family—now display more than a million plants throughout the year. As impressive as the numbers, is the sheer perfection of each garden—not a blade out of place, each flower the same height, and all blooming at the same time. Gardeners will be amazed.

Evenings in summer, the gardens are beautifully illuminated with a variety of softly colored lights. June to September, musical entertainment is provided free on Monday to Saturday evenings. You can even watch fireworks displays on Saturdays in July and August. A very good lunch, dinner, and afternoon tea are offered in the Dining Room Restaurant in the historic residence; afternoon and high teas are also served in the Italian Garden (reservations strongly recommended). Allow 2 to 3 hours.

800 Benvenuto Ave., Brentwood Bay. ✆ **250/652-4422;** dining reservations 250/652-8222. www.butchartgardens.com. Admission C$19.25 (US$12) adults, C$9.50 (US$6) youths 13–17, C$2 (US$1.20) children 5–12, free for children under 5. Spring, fall, and winter discounts. Gates open daily 9am–sundown (call for seasonal closing time). Visitors can remain in gardens for 1 hour after gate closes. AE, DISC, MC. Bus: 75 or the Gray Line shuttle from the Victoria Bus Station. C$4 (US$2.50) one-way. Shuttle departure times vary seasonally. Call ✆ 250/388-5248 for exact times. Take Blanshard St. (Hwy. 17) north toward the ferry terminal in Saanich, then turn left on Keating Crossroads, which leads directly to the gardens—about 20 min. from downtown Victoria. It's impossible to miss if you follow the trail of billboards.

**Fort Rodd Hill & Fisgard Lighthouse National Historic Site** Perched on an outcrop of volcanic rock, the Fisgard Lighthouse has guided ships toward Victoria's sheltered harbor since 1873. The light no longer has a keeper (the beacon has long been automated), but the site itself has been restored to its 1873 appearance. Two floors worth of exhibits in the light keepers' house recount stories of the lighthouse, its keepers, and the terrible shipwrecks that gave this coastline its ominous moniker "the graveyard of the Pacific."

Adjoining the lighthouse, Fort Rodd Hill is a preserved 1890s coastal artillery fort that—though in more than half a century it never fired a shot in anger—still sports camouflaged searchlights, underground magazines, and its original guns. Audiovisual exhibits bring the fort to life with the voices and faces of the men who served at the outpost. Displays of artifacts, room re-creations, and historic film footage add to the experience. It's so close to the lighthouse that concussion from the guns once blew out all the lighthouse's windows. Allow 1 to 2 hours.

603 Fort Rodd Hill Rd. ✆ **250/478-5849.** www.parkscanada.pch.gc.ca. Admission C$3 (US$1.85) adults, C$2.25 (US$1.40) seniors, C$1.50 (US95¢) children 6–16, C$7.50 (US$4.65) families, children under 6 free. Mar–Oct daily 10am–5:30pm; Nov–Feb daily 9am–4:30pm. No public transit.

**Maritime Museum of British Columbia** Housed in the former provincial courthouse, this museum is dedicated to recalling BC's rich maritime heritage. The displays do a good job of illustrating maritime history, from the early explorers to the fur trading and whaling era to the days of grand ocean liners and military conflict. There's also an impressive collection of ship models and paraphernalia—uniforms, weapons, gear—along with photographs and journals. The museum also shows films in its Vice Admiralty Theatre. Allow 1 to 2 hours.

28 Bastion Sq. ✆ **250/385-4222.** www.mmbc.bc.ca. Admission C$6 (US$3.70) adults, C$5 (US$3.10) seniors, C$3 (US$1.85) students, C$2 (US$1.20) children 6–11, C$15 (US$9) families, children under 6 free. Daily 9am–4:30pm. Closed Dec 25. Bus: 5 to View St.

**Miniature World** *Kids* It sounds cheesy—hundreds of dolls and miniatures and scenes from old fairy tales. And Miniature World's case isn't helped by its brochure, which features photos of "Brady Bunch" clones in 1950s fashions grinning like idiots as they loom over yet another diorama. And yet Miniature World—inside The Empress hotel (the entrance is around the corner)—is actually kind of cool. You walk in and you're plunged into darkness, except for a moon, some planets, and a tiny spaceship flying up to rendezvous with an orbiting mother ship. This is the most up-to-date display. Farther in are re-creations of battle scenes, fancy 18th-century dress balls, a miniature CPR railway running all the way across a miniature Canada, a three-ring circus and midway, and scenes from Mother Goose and Charles Dickens's stories. Better yet, most of these displays do something. The train moves at the punch of a button; the circus rides whirl around and light up as simulated darkness falls. Allow 1 hour.

649 Humboldt St. ✆ **250/385-9731.** www.miniatureworld.com. Admission C$9 (US$6) adults, C$7 (US$4.35) youths, C$6 (US$3.70) children, children under 4 free. AE, MC, V. Summer daily 8:30am–9pm; winter daily 9am–5pm. Bus: 5, 27, 28, or 30.

**Pacific Undersea Gardens** *Kids* A gently sloping stairway leads down to this unique marine observatory's glass-enclosed viewing area, where you can observe the Inner Harbour's marine life up close. Some 5,000 creatures feed, play, hunt, and court in these protected waters. Sharks, wolf eels, poisonous stonefish, sea anemones, starfish, sturgeon, and salmon are just a few of the organisms that make their homes here. One of the harbor's star attractions is a remarkably photogenic huge octopus (reputedly the largest in captivity). Injured seals and orphaned seal pups are cared for in holding pens alongside the observatory as part of a provincial marine-mammal rescue program. The gardens are a great spot for kids or any budding marine biologist. Allow 1 hour.

490 Belleville St. ✆ **250/382-5717.** www.pacificunderseagardens.com. Admission C$7.50 (US$4.65) adults, C$6.50 (US$4) seniors, C$5 (US$3.10) youths 12–17, C$3.50 (US$2.20) children 5–11,children under 5 free. MC, V. Sept–June daily 10am–5pm; July–Aug daily 10am–7pm. Bus: 5, 27, 28, or 30.

**Parliament Buildings (Provincial Legislature)** ★ Designed by 25-year-old Francis Rattenbury and built between 1893 and 1898 at a cost of nearly C$1,000,000 (US$620,000), the Parliament Buildings (also called the Legislature) are architectural gems. The 40-minute tour comes across at times like an eighth-grade civics lesson, but it's worth it to see the fine mosaics, marble, woodwork, and stained glass. And if you see a harried-looking man surrounded by a pack of mini-cam crews, it's likely just another BC premier getting hounded out of office by the aggressive and hostile media. Politics is a blood sport in BC.

501 Belleville St. ✆ **250/387-3046.** www.protocol.gov.bc.ca. Free admission. Late May–Labour Day daily 9am–5pm; Sept–late May 9am–5pm Mon–Fri. Tours offered every 20 min. in summer, hourly in winter; check for exact times due to school group bookings. No tours noon–1pm.

**Royal British Columbia Museum** ★★★ *Kids* One of the world's best regional museums, the Royal BC features natural history dioramas indistinguishable from the real thing (except the grizzly bear won't rip your face off). The museum's mandate is to present the land and the people of coastal British Columbia. The second-floor Natural History Gallery shows the coastal flora, fauna, and geography from the Ice Age to the present; it includes dioramas of a temperate rain forest, a seacoast, an underground ecology of giant bugs, and (particularly appealing to kids) a live tidal pool with sea stars and anemones. The third-floor Modern History Gallery presents the recent past, including historically faithful re-creations of Victoria's downtown and Chinatown. On the same floor, the **First Peoples Gallery** ★ is an incredible showpiece of Native art that also houses many artifacts showing day-to-day Native life, a full-size re-creation of a longhouse, and many smaller village scenes. The museum also has an IMAX theater showing an ever-changing variety of large-screen movies. On the way out (or in), be sure to stop by Thunderbird Park, beside the museum, where a cedar longhouse (Mungo Martin House, named after a famous Kwakiutl artist) houses a workshop where Native carvers work on new totem poles. To see and experience everything allow 3 to 4 hours.

675 Belleville St. ✆ **888/447-7977** or 250/387-3701. www.royalbcmuseum.bc.ca. Admission C$9 (US$6) adults, C$6 (US$3.70) seniors/students/children, C$24 (US$15) families, children under 6 free. Higher rates sometimes in effect for traveling exhibits. AE, MC, V. Daily 9am–5pm. Closed Dec 25 and Jan 1. Bus: 5, 28, or 30.

**Royal London Wax Museum** *Overrated* See the same royal family you already get too much of on television. See other, older royals of even less significance. See their family pets. These sights are all courtesy of Madame Tussaud's 200-year-old wax technology. There's also the chamber of horrors, which rates well below a *Buffy the Vampire Slayer* episode on the scariness scale. Still not thrilled? The management seems to suspect as much; they've started taking liberties with their wax figures' figures. Look especially for the Princess Diana dummy with the Pamela Anderson implants.

470 Belleville St. ✆ **250/388-4461.** www.waxworld.com. Admission C$8.50 (US$5) adults, C$7.50 (US$4.65) seniors, C$4 (US$2.50) children. AE, MC, V. June–Sept 9am–7pm; Oct–May 9am–5pm. Bus: 5, 27, 28, or 30.

**Victoria Butterfly Gardens** ★ *Kids* This is a great spot for kids, nature buffs, or anyone who just likes butterflies. Hundreds of exotic colorful butterflies flutter freely through this lush tropical greenhouse. You're provided with an ID chart and set free to roam around. Species present range from the tiny Central American Julia (a brilliant orange butterfly about 8cm/3 inches across) to the Southeast Asian Giant Atlas Moth (mottled brown and red, with a wingspan approaching 30cm/12 inches). Other butterflies are brilliant blue, yellow, or a mix of colors and patterns. Naturalists are on hand to explain butterfly biology, and there's a display where you can see the beautiful creatures emerge from their cocoons. Allow 1 hour.

1461 Benvenuto Ave. (P.O. Box 190), Brentwood Bay. ✆ **877/722-0272** or 250/652-3822. www.butterflygardens.com. Admission C$8 (US$5) adults, C$7 (US$4.35) students/seniors, C$4.50 (US$2.80) children 5–12, children under 5 free. DC, MC, V. Mar 1–May 13 and Oct daily 9:30am–4:30pm; May 14–Sept 30 daily 9am–5:30pm. Closed in winter. Bus: 75.

## ARCHITECTURAL HIGHLIGHTS & HISTORIC HOMES

For an excellent guide to many of Victoria's buildings, as well as short biographies of its most significant architects, pick up ***Exploring Victoria's Architecture,*** by

Martin Segger and Douglas Franklin. You'll find copies in **Munro's Books,** 1008 Government St. (✆ **604/382-2464;** bus: 5, 30).

Perhaps the most intriguing downtown edifice isn't a building at all but a work of art. The walls of **Fort Victoria,** which once covered much of downtown, have been demarcated in the sidewalk with bricks bearing the names of original settlers and fur traders. Look in the sidewalk on Government Street at the corner of Fort Street.

Most of the retail establishments in Victoria's Old Town area are housed in 19th-century shipping warehouses that have been carefully restored. You can take a **self-guided tour** of these buildings, most of which were erected between the 1870s and 1890s and whose history is recounted on easy-to-read outdoor plaques. The majority of the restored buildings are between Douglas and Johnson Streets from Wharf Street to Government Street. The most impressive structure once contained a number of shipping offices and warehouses but is now the home of a 45-shop complex known as **Market Square,** 560 Johnson St./255 Market Sq. (✆ **250/386-2441;** bus: 6).

What do you do when you're the richest man in British Columbia, when you've clawed and scraped and bullied your way up from indentured servant to coal baron and merchant prince? You build a castle, of course. So in the 1880s, Scottish magnate Robert Dunsmuir built **Craigdarroch Castle** ★, 1050 Joan Crescent (✆ **250/592-5323;** bus: 11, 14). The 39-room Highland-style castle is topped with stone turrets and chimneys and filled with the opulent Victorian splendor you'd expect to read about in a romance novel. You're provided with a self-tour booklet, and for those with the urge to know more, there are volunteer docents on every floor. Admission is C$8 (US$5) for adults, C$5 (US$3.10) for students, C$2 (US$1.20) for children ages 6 to 12; and free for children under 6. It's open daily: June 15 to August 9am to 7pm and September to June 14 10am to 4:30pm.

Dunsmuir's son, James, built his own palatial home, **Hatley Castle,** off Highway 14 in Colwood. The younger Dunsmuir reportedly commissioned architect Samuel Maclure with the words "Money doesn't matter; just build what I want." The bill, in 1908, came to over C$1 million (over US$620,000). The grounds of the castle, now home to **Royal Roads University,** feature extensive floral gardens and are open to the public free of charge (✆ **250/391-2511;** bus: 50 to Western Exchange, then bus 56).

To get a taste of how upper-middle-class Victorians lived, visit the **Carr House,** 207 Government St. (✆ **250/383-5843;** bus: 5, 30), where painter Emily Carr was born in 1871. An artistic pioneer, Carr broke free of then-dominant European conventions about art to create a vibrant painting style all her own. Many of her works depict rugged west coast landscapes or people or scenes from native villages along the coast. Carr was also an accomplished writer, and her most popular book, *Klee Wyck,* tells of her travels among west coast natives. **Helmcken House,** 675 Belleville St. (✆ **250/386-0021;** bus: 5, 30), was the residence of a pioneer doctor who settled in the area during the 1850s; it still contains the original imported British furnishings and his medicine chest. **Craigflower Farmhouse,** 110 Island Highway (✆ **250/383-4621;** bus: 14), in the View Royal district, was built in 1856 by a Scottish settler who brought many of his furnishings from the old country. The Carr House, Helmcken House, and Craigflower Farmhouse are open in summer, Thursday to Monday 11am to 5pm. Admission is C$5 (US$3.10) for adults, C$4 (US$2.50) for students/seniors, C$3 (US$1.85) for children ages 6 to 12, and free for children under 6.

## PARKS & GARDENS

The 62ha (154-acre) **Beacon Hill Park** (Bus: 11) stretches from Southgate Street to Dallas Road between Douglas and Cook Streets. Stands of indigenous Garry oaks (found only on Vancouver Island, Hornby Island, and Salt Spring Island) and manicured lawns are interspersed with floral gardens and ponds. Hike up Beacon Hill to get a clear view of the Strait of Georgia, Haro Strait, and Washington's Olympic Mountains. The children's farm (below), aviary, tennis courts, lawn-bowling green, putting green, cricket pitch, wading pool, playground, and picnic area make this a wonderful place to spend a few hours with the family.

**Government House,** the official residence of the Lieutenant Governor, is at 1401 Rockland Ave. (Bus: 1), in the Fairfield residential district. The house itself is closed to the public (and not worth touring anyway), but the formal gardens are open and well worth a wander. Round back, the hillside of Garry oaks is one of the last places to see what the area's natural fauna would've looked like before European settlers arrived. At the front, the rose garden is sumptuous.

Victoria has an indoor garden that first opened as a huge saltwater pool in 1925 (Olympic swimmer and *Tarzan* star Johnny Weismuller competed here) and was converted into a big-band dance hall during World War II. The **Crystal Garden,** 731 Douglas St. (© **250/953-8800;** bus: 5, 30), is filled with rare and exotic tropical flora and fauna and is open daily 10am to 5:30pm (later in summer). Admission is C$8 (US$5) for adults, C$7 (US$4.35) for seniors, C$4 (US$2.50) for children ages 5 to 16, and free for children under 5. Family and group discounts are available.

## ESPECIALLY FOR KIDS

Nature's the thing for kids in Victoria. At the **Beacon Hill Children's Farm,** Circle Drive, Beacon Hill Park (© **250/381-2532;** bus: 11), kids can ride ponies; pet goats, rabbits, and other barnyard animals; and even cool off in the wading pool. Mid-March to September, the farm is open daily 10am to 5pm. Admission is by donation.

For a new take on an old concept, visit the **Victoria Butterfly Gardens** (see above). The **Crystal Gardens** (© **250/381-1277;** bus: 5, 11, 30), behind the Empress hotel, also has butterflies, as well as macaws and pelicans. Closer to town and two shades creepier than the Butterfly Gardens is the **Victoria Bug Zoo,** 1107 Wharf St. (© **250/384-BUGS;** bus: 6), home to praying mantises and giant African cockroaches, along with knowledgeable guides who can bring the bugs out and let you or your kids handle and touch them. Admission is C$6 (US$3.70) for adults, C$4 (US$2.50) for children ages 3 to 16, and free to children 2 and under. Kids also love the creatures at the **Pacific Undersea Gardens** (see above), or the live tidal pools at the **Royal British Columbia Museum** (see above). For a different experience, check out the animated miniatures at the **Miniature Museum** (see above).

## ORGANIZED TOURS

**BUS TOURS** **Gray Line of Victoria,** 700 Douglas St. (© **250/388-5248;** www.victoriatours.com; bus: 5, 11, 30), conducts tours of Victoria and Butchart Gardens. The 1½-hour "Grand City Tour" costs C$18 (US$11) for adults and

C$9 (US$6) for children ages 6 to 12. Mid-May to June tours depart every 30 minutes 9:30am to 7pm; December to mid-March, there are daily departures at 11:30am and 1:30pm. The same company operates a **trolley service** every 40 minutes 9:30am to 5:30pm on a circuit of 35 hotels, attractions, shops, and restaurants. A day pass, which allows you to stop and reboard at the destinations of your choice throughout the day, costs C$7 (US$4.35) for adults and C$4 (US$2.50) for children.

**SPECIALTY TOURS** For C$12 (US$7), **Victoria Harbour Ferries,** 922 Old Esquimalt Rd. (✆ **250/708-0201**), offers a terrific 45-minute tour of the Inner and Outer Harbors. A 50-minute tour of the Gorge opposite the Johnson Street Bridge, where tidal falls reverse with each change of the tide, costs C$14 (US$9) for adults, C$12 (US$7) for seniors, and C$7 (US$4.35) for children. Tours depart from seven stops around the Inner Harbour every 15 minutes daily 10am to 10pm. To get a bird's-eye view of Victoria, take a 30-minute tour with **Harbour Air Seaplanes,** 1234 Wharf St. (✆ **250/361-6786;** bus: 6). Rates are C$72 (US$45) per person; flights depart at 10am, noon, and 4pm.

**Heritage Tours and Daimler Limousine Service,** 713 Bexhill Rd. (✆ **250/474-4332**), will pick you up and guide you through the city, Butchart Gardens, and Craigdarroch Castle in a six-passenger Daimler limo. Rates start at C$65 (US$40) per hour per vehicle (not per person). The bicycle-rickshaws operated by **Kabuki Kabs,** 15-950 Government St. (✆ **250/385-4243**), usually "park" in front of the Empress hotel, and a tour is C$1 (US60¢) per minute for a two-person cab and C$1.50 (US95¢) per minute for a four-person cab.

**Tallyho Horse Drawn Tours,** 2044 Milton St. (✆ **250/383-5067**), has conducted tours of Victoria in horse-drawn carriages since 1903. Excursions start at the corner of Belleville and Menzies streets; fares are C$14 (US$9) for adults, C$9 (US$6) for students, and C$6 (US$3.70) for children ages 17 and under. Family discounts are available. Tours operate every 30 minutes daily 9am to 10pm in summer (10am–5:30pm in late March, Apr, May, and Sept). Tallyho also offers private tours (maximum six people) at C$35 (US$22) for 15 minutes and C$60 (US$37) for 30 minutes.

For a pleasant and informative summer-evening stroll, join a guided walk through downtown and Old Town. The **Old Cemetery Society of Victoria,** Box 40115, Victoria, BC V8W 3R8 (✆ **250/598-8870**), presents **Lantern Tours in the Old Burying Ground,** which begin at the Cherry Bank Hotel, 845 Burdett St. (Bus: 5), at 9pm nightly in July and August. On Sundays at 2pm, the tour leaves from Bagga Pasta, in the Fairfield Plaza, 1516 Fairfield Rd. (Bus: 1), across from the cemetery gate. Both tours are C$5 (US$3.10) per person or C$12 (US$7) per family. The Society also offers individual tours of the Ross Bay Cemetery; cost is by donation. Phone for times and information; group tours of the Ross Bay Cemetery are also available for C$35 (US$22).

**Discover the Past** (✆ **250/ 384-6698;** www.discoverthepast.com) organizes two year-round walks: Ghostly Walks explores Victoria's haunted Old Town, Chinatown, and historic waterfront, and the Neighbourhood Discovery Walk is a tour through Victoria's many distinct neighborhoods. Both combine interesting local history as well as natural history, architecture, archaeology and urban legends to bring the city's character to life. The cost is C$10 (US$6) for adults, C$8 (US$5) for seniors/students, C$6 (US$3.70) for children, and C$25 (US$16) for families. Call ahead for times and locations.

**Victoria's Haunted Walk & Other Tours,** 185-911 Yates St., Victoria, BC V8V 4Y9 (✆ **250/361-2619**), introduces you to some of the city's nefarious ghosts and spirits. June to September, tours lasting 1½ hours begin nightly at 7 and 9pm at the Tourism Victoria Info Centre on the Inner Harbour. Cost is C$8 (US$5) for adults and C$7 (US$4.35) for students/seniors; children under 12 are free.

## OUTDOOR ACTIVITIES

Specialized rental outfitters are listed with each activity below, but **Sports Rent,** 3084 Blanshard St. (✆ **250/385-7368;** www.sportsrentbc.com; bus: 30, 31), is a general-equipment and water-sport rental outlet to keep in mind if you forget to pack something.

**BIKING** The 13km (8-mile) **Scenic Marine Drive** bike path begins at Dallas Road and Douglas Street, at the base of Beacon Hill Park. The paved path follows the walkway along the beaches, winds up through the residential district on Beach Drive, and eventually turns left and heads south toward downtown Victoria on Oak Bay Avenue. The **Inner Harbour pedestrian path** has a bike lane for cyclists who want to take a leisurely ride around the entire city seawall. The new **Galloping Goose Trail** runs from Victoria west through Colwood and Sooke all the way up to Leechtown. If you don't want to cycle the whole thing, there are numerous places to park along the way, as well as several places where the trail intersects with public transit. Call **BC Transit** (✆ **250/382-6161**) to find out which bus routes take bikes.

Bikes, helmets, locks, and child trailers are available by the hour or day at **Cycle BC** rentals, 747 Douglas St. (year-round) or 950 Wharf St. (May–Oct) (✆ **250/885-2453**). Rentals run C$6 (US$3.70) per hour and C$20 (US$12) per day, helmets and locks included.

**BOATING** You can book boat rentals and charters of a few hours to a couple of weeks at **Brentwood Inn Resort Boat Rentals,** 7176 Brentwood Dr., Brentwood Bay (✆ **250/652-3151;** bus: 75). There are also a number of independent charter companies docked at the **Oak Bay Marina,** 1327 Beach Dr. (✆ **250/598-3369;** bus: 2) For example, the **Horizon Yacht Centre** (✆ **250/595-2628**) offers sailboat charters, lessons, and navigational tips geared toward familiarizing you with the surrounding waters. The **Marine Adventure Centre** (✆ **250/995-2211**), on the floatplane docks in the Inner Harbour, can arrange boat charters and almost anything else marine related. Skippered charters in the area run about C$600 (US$372) per day, and boat rentals average C$125 (US$78) for a couple of hours. If you're taking the wheel yourself, don't forget to check the **marine forecast** (✆ **250/656-7515**) before casting off.

**CANOEING & KAYAKING** **Ocean River Sports,** 1437 Store St., Victoria, BC V8W 3J6 (✆ **250/381-4233;** www.oceanriver.com; bus: 6), can equip you with everything from single-kayak, double-kayak, and canoe rentals to life jackets, tents, and dry-storage camping gear. Rental for a single kayak is C$14 (US$9) per hour and C$42 (US$26) per day. If you're a little tentative about renting a boat on your own, Ocean River also runs guided tours on the harbor and on the sheltered waters near Sidney, in sight of the Gulf Islands. Tours start at C$55 (US$34) for a 3-hour novice lesson and paddle. Sundown tours are especially popular.

**FISHING** If you're looking to do saltwater fishing, **Adam's Fishing Charters** (✆ **250/370-2326**) and the **Marine Adventure Centre** (✆ **250/995-2211**) in Victoria are good places to look for a charter (see also "Boating," above). To fish, you need a nonresident saltwater or freshwater license. Licenses for freshwater fishing cost C$16 (US$10) for 1 day for those who live outside the province. Saltwater fishing licenses cost C$6 (US$3.70) for 1 day for those who live outside the province, plus a surcharge of C$6 (US$3.70) for salmon fishing. **Robinson's Sporting Goods Ltd.,** 1307 Broad St. (© **250/385-3429;** bus: 1, 5, 11, 30), is a reliable source for information, recommendations, lures, licenses, and gear.

**GOLF** The **Cedar Hill Municipal Golf Course,** 1400 Derby Rd. (© **250/595-3103;** bus: 24), is an 18-hole public course 3.5km (2 miles) from downtown Victoria; daytime greens fees are C$30 (US$19) and twilight fees C$26 (US$16). The **Cordova Bay Golf Course,** 5333 Cordova Bay Rd. (© **250/658-4075;** bus: 75), is northeast of downtown. Designed by Bill Robinson, the 18-hole course features 66 sand traps and some tight fairways. Greens fees are C$45 (US$28) Monday to Thursday and C$48 (US$30) Friday to Sunday and holidays. The **Olympic View Golf Club,** 643 Latoria Rd. (© **250/474-3673;** www.sunnygolf.com/ov/ov.html; bus: 50 to CanWest Exchange, then bus 54), is one of the top-35 golf courses in Canada. Amid 12 lakes and a pair of waterfalls, this 18-hole, 5,865m (6,414-yd.) course is open daily, with greens fees C$49 (US$30) Monday to Thursday and C$55 (US$34) Friday to Sunday and holidays. You can also call the **A-1 Last Minute Golf Hotline** (© **800/684-6344** or 604/878-1833) for substantial discounts and short-notice tee times at courses around the area.

**HIKING** For groups of 10 or more who want to learn more about the surrounding flora and fauna, book a naturalist-guided tour of the island's rain forests and seashore with **Coastal Connections Interpretive Nature Hikes** (© **250/480-9560**) or **Nature Calls** (© **877/361-HIKE**). Tours cost C$60 to C$110 (US$37–US$68), transport included, and go to **Botanical Beach, East Sooke Park,** or the **Carmanah Valley.**

**WATERSPORTS** The **Crystal Pool & Fitness Centre,** 2275 Quadra St. (© **250/380-7946;** schedule 250/380-4636; bus: 6), is Victoria's main aquatic facility. The 50m (165-ft.) lap pool, children's pool, diving pool, sauna, whirlpool, and steam, weight, and aerobics rooms are open daily 6am to midnight. Drop-in admission is C$4.20 (US$2.60) for adults, C$3.15 (US$1.95) for seniors/students, and C$2.10 (US$1.30) for children ages 6 to 12. **Beaver Lake** in Elk and Beaver Lake Regional Park (Bus: 70, 75) has lifeguards on duty, as well as picnicking facilities along the shore. **All Fun Recreation Park,** 650 Hordon Rd. (© **250/474-4546** or 250/474-3184; bus: 52), operates a 1km (½-mile) water-slide complex that's ideal for cooling off on hot summer days. It's open daily 11am to 7pm in season, and full-day passes are C$16 (US$10) for sliders over 6 years old (non-sliders get in for C$6/US$3.70); after 3pm admission drops to C$12 (US$7) for sliders and C$5 (US$3.10) for non-sliders.

**Windsurfers** skim along the Inner Harbour and Elk Lake when the breezes are right. Though there are no specific facilities, French Beach, off Sooke Road on the way to Sooke Harbour, is a popular local windsurfing spot. **Ocean Wind Water Sports Rentals,** 5411 Hamsterly Rd. (© **250/658-8171;** bus: 70, 75), rents nearly every form of popular watersports gear, including parasails.

**WHALE-WATCHING** The waters surrounding the southern tip of Vancouver Island teem with **orcas** ★ (killer whales), harbor seals, sea lions, bald eagles, and harbour and Dahl's porpoises. **Victoria Marine Adventures,** 950 Wharf (© **250/995-2211;** bus: 6), is just one of many outfits offering whale-watching tours in both Zodiacs and covered boats. Fares are C$75 (US$47) for adults and C$49 (US$30) for children. March to October, **Pride of Victoria Cruises,** Oak Bay Beach Hotel, 1175 Beach Dr. (✆ **250/592-3474;** bus: 1), offers daily 3½-hour whale-watching charters on a fully equipped 14m (45-ft.) catamaran that can handle up to eight passengers. A picnic-style lunch is served. Fares are C$79 (US$49) for adults and C$39 ($24) for children; lunch is C$6 (US$3.70) per person in summer.

## SHOPPING

Victoria has dozens of little specialty shops that appeal to every taste and whim, and because the city is built to such a pedestrian scale, you can wander from place to place seeking out whatever treasure it is you're after. Nearly all the areas below are within a short walk of the Empress hotel.

**ANTIQUES** Many of the best stores are in **Antiques Row,** a 3-block stretch on Fort Street between Blanshard and Cook streets. Though farthest from downtown, **Faith Grant's Connoisseur Shop Ltd.,** 1156 Fort St. (✆ **250/383-0121;** bus: 1, 10), is also the best. Other shops on the row that are worth poking your nose into are **Jeffries and Co. Silversmiths,** 1026 Fort St. (✆ **250/383-8315;** bus: 1, 10); **Romanoff & Company Antiques,** 837 Fort St. (✆ **250/480-1543;** bus: 1, 10); and for furniture fans **Charles Baird Antiques,** 1044A Fort St. (✆ **250/384-8809;** bus: 1, 10).

**ARTS & CRAFTS** **Cowichan Trading Ltd.,** 1328 Government St. (✆ **250/383-0321;** bus: 1, 5, 30), sells a mix of T-shirts and gewgaws in addition to fine Cowichan sweaters, masks, and fine silver jewelry.

**BOOKS** All bookstores should look as good as **Munro's Book Store,** 1108 Government St. (✆ **250/382-2464;** bus: 1, 5, 30), with its mile-high ceiling and wall murals. All bookstores should also stock more than 35,000 titles, including an excellent selection of books about Victoria.

**CAMERAS** Come to **Lens and Shutter,** 615 Fort St. (✆ **250/383-7443**), for all your camera needs—film, filters, lenses, cameras, or just advice.

**A DEPARTMENT STORE & SHOPPING MALL** **The Bay (Hudson's Bay Company),** 1701 Douglas St. (✆ **250/385-1311;** bus: 5), sells camping and sports equipment, Hudson's Bay woolen point blankets, and fashions by Tommy Hilfiger, Polo, DKNY, and Liz Claiborne. Right in the center of town, the **Victoria Eaton Centre,** between Government and Douglas streets (✆ **250/382-7141;** bus: 1, 5, 30), is a full modern shopping mall disguised as a block of heritage buildings. Inside are three floors of shops and boutiques.

**FASHION** **A Wear,** 1205 Government St. (✆ **250/382-9327**), lives in a large airy space in a converted heritage building and sells a large collection of fashionable threads for younger men and women.

More classic clothing lines are to be found at **W.&J. Wilson's Clothiers,** 1221 Government St. (✆ **250/383-7177;** bus: 1, 5, 30), Canada's oldest family-run clothing store. **Prescott & Andrews,** 909 Government St. (✆ **250/953-7788;** bus: 1, 5, 30), is the place to pick up a sweater. For men's fashions, try **British Importers,** 1125 Government St. (✆ **250/386-1496;** bus: 1, 5, 30).

**JEWELRY** Ian MacDonald of **MacDonald Jewelry,** 618 View St. (✆ **250/382-4113;** bus: 1, 2), designs and crafts all his own jewelry, which makes for some interesting creations. At the **Jade Tree,** 606 Humboldt St. (✆ **250/388-4326;** bus: 1, 5, 30), you'll find jewelry crafted from British Columbia jade into necklaces, bracelets, and other items.

**NATIVE ART** All the coastal tribes are represented in the **Alcheringa Gallery,** 665 Fort St. (✆ **250/383-8224;** bus: 1, 2), along with a significant collection of pieces from Papua New Guinea. Presentation is museum quality, with prices to match. **Hill's Indian Crafts,** 1008 Government St. ✆ **250/385-3911;** bus: 1, 5, 30), features exquisite traditional native art, including wooden masks and carvings, Haida argillite, and silver jewelry.

**OUTDOOR CLOTHES & EQUIPMENT** **Ocean River Sports,** 1437 Store St. (✆ **250/381-4233;** bus: 6), is the place to go to arrange a sea-kayak tour. It's also a good spot for outdoor clothing and camping knickknacks.

## WHERE TO STAY

Reservations are absolutely essential in Victoria from May to September. If you arrive without a reservation and have trouble finding a room, **Tourism Victoria** (✆ **800/663-3883** or 250/382-1131) can make reservations for you at hotels, inns, and B&Bs.

### INNER HARBOUR

#### Very Expensive

**Delta Victoria Ocean Pointe Resort and Spa** ★★ On the Inner Harbour's north shore, the luxurious modern "OPR" (as the staff call it) offers commanding views of downtown, the legislature, and The Empress. Other great pluses are the things you expect in a top property—fancy giveaway stuff in the bathrooms, fluffy robes, and large beds with fine linen. In a city with a fetish for floral prints, the OPR's decor is refreshingly modern—polished woods and solid muted colors and not a lot of bric-a-brac. The Inner Harbour rooms offer the best views, many with floor-to-ceiling windows; rooms facing the Outer Harbour top that with floor-to-ceiling bay windows. In the grand lobby, that floor-to-ceiling theme is repeated with windows two stories tall, facing downtown. The Spa is one of the best in Victoria and accommodation/spa packages are available; check the website for specials. The Victorian Restaurant is highly recommended (see "Where to Dine," later).

45 Songhees Rd., Victoria, BC V9A 6T3. ✆ **800/667-4677** or 250/360-2999. Fax 250/360-1041. www.oprhotel.com. 250 units. Apr 16–May 31 C$322–C$574 (US$200–US$356) double. June 1–Oct 11 C$448–C$736 (US$278–US$456) double. Oct 12–Dec 31 C$340–C$448 (US$211–US$278) double. Jan 1–Apr 15 C$295–C$403 (US$183–US$250) double. Promotional rates available all seasons. Children under 17 stay free in parents' room. Wheelchair-accessible units available. AE, DC, MC, V. Underground valet parking C$9 (US$6). Bus: 24 to Colville. Pets under 30 lb. allowed. **Amenities:** 2 restaurants, bar; indoor pool; 2 lighted tennis courts; health club; spa; Jacuzzi; sauna; watersports rental; bike rental; concierge; business center; shopping arcade; 24-hour room service; in-room massage; babysitting; same-day dry cleaning; nonsmoking rooms; executive level rooms. *In room:* A/C, TV/VCR w/pay movies, fax, dataport, minibar, coffeemaker, hair dryer, iron, safe.

**The Empress** ★★ Francis Rattenbury's 1908 harborside creation is such a joy to look at, The Empress should probably charge for the view. When you see it, you'll know immediately that you absolutely *have* to stay there. However, you should know before you throw down the credit card that, with 90 different configurations, not all rooms are created equal. Some deluxe rooms and all Entree Gold rooms are a dream (or a Merchant/Ivory film), with large beds, wide windows, high ceilings, and abundant natural light. Entree Gold rooms also include private check-in, concierge, breakfast in the private lounge, and extras like CD players and TVs in the bathrooms. Many of the other rooms—despite a C$4-million (US$2.5-million) renovation in 1996—are built to the "cozy" standards of 1908. And the fact that they come with down duvets, ceiling fans, and minibars doesn't make them any bigger. If you can afford an Entree Gold or deluxe room—go for it. If you can't, it may be better to admire The Empress from afar or confine your relationship to afternoon visits.

721 Government St., Victoria, BC V8W 1W5. ✆ **800/866-5577** or 250/384-8111. Fax 250/381-4334. www.fairmont.com. 460 units. May–Oct C$295–C$490 (US$185–US$304) double. Nov–Apr C$200–C$395 (US$124–US$245) double. Year-round C$425–C$1,500 (US$264–US$930) suite. Wheelchair-accessible units available. AE, DC, DISC, MC, V. Underground valet parking C$17 (US$11). Bus: 5. Small pets allowed for C$50 (US$31). **Amenities:** 3 restaurants, bar; indoor pool; health club; Jacuzzi; sauna; concierge; car rental; business center; shopping arcade; 24-hour room service; in-room massage; babysitting; laundry service; same-day dry cleaning service; nonsmoking rooms; executive level rooms. *In room:* A/C, TV w/pay movies, dataport, minibar, hair dryer, iron.

## Expensive

**The Haterleigh Heritage Inn** ★★★ Haterleigh owner and innkeeper Paul Kelly is a font of information, on Victoria in general and on this lovingly restored 1901 home in particular. With his wife, Elizabeth, he runs this exceptional B&B that captures the essence of Victoria's romance with a combination of antique furniture, stunning stained-glass windows, and attentive personal service. The spacious rooms boast high arched ceilings, large windows, sitting areas, and enormous bathrooms, some with Jacuzzi tubs. On the top floor, the new and somewhat cozy Angel's Reach room features a big four-poster bed. The second-floor Secret Garden room has a small balcony with stunning views of the Olympic mountain range. The Day Dreams room downstairs is the dedicated honeymoon suite, but truth be told, all the suites make for wonderful romantic weekends. Bathrooms come with terry robes, candles, and plastic champagne flutes. A full gourmet breakfast is served family style at 8:30am sharp. Paul likes it that way because it gives guests a chance to meet and chat. There's complimentary sherry in the drawing room each evening.

243 Kingston St., Victoria, BC V8V 1V5. ✆ **250/384-9995.** Fax 250/384-1935. www.haterleigh.com. 7 units. C$213–C$327 (US$132–US$203) double. Rates include full breakfast. MC, V. Free parking. Bus: 30 to Superior and Montreal sts. **Amenities:** Jacuzzi; nonsmoking rooms.

**Laurel Point Inn** ★★ The original owners were deeply enamored of Japan, so the lobby and hotel design reflect Japanese artistic principals: elegant simplicity, blond-wood surfaces, and the subtle integration of light, water, and stone. That sense of Eastern suave is heightened as you pass the little gurgling fountains on your way to the elevator; in your room, you'll find a crisp cotton kimono laid out—something to slip into before stepping onto the private terrace, with a panoramic view of the harbor and the hills. The hotel, occupying most of a promontory jutting out into the Inner Harbour, consists of a new south wing and the original north wing. Rooms in the north wing are better than many in town. The south wing is where you want to be: All the rooms here are suites, featuring blond wood with black marble accents, shoji-style sliding doors, Asian artworks, and deep tubs and floor-to-ceiling glassed-in showers in the bathrooms.

680 Montreal St., Victoria, BC V8V 1Z8. ✆ **800/663-7667** or 250/386-8721. Fax 250/386-9547. www.laurelpoint.com. 200 units. Nov–April C$129 (US$80) double; C$179 (US$111) junior suite; C$229 (US$142) one-bedroom suite; C$289 (US$179) full suite. May C$239 (US$148) double; C$289 (US$179) junior suite; C$339 (US$210) one-bedroom suite; C$479 (US$297) full suite. June–Oct C$259 (US$161) double; C$309 (US$192) junior suite; C$359 (US$223) one-bedroom suite; C$499 (US$309) full suite. Seasonal discounts available. Children under 12 stay free in parents' room. Wheelchair-accessible units available. AE, DC, DISC, MC, V. Valet parking. Bus: 30 to Montreal and Superior sts. Pets accepted for C$25 (US$16). **Amenities:** Restaurant, bar; indoor pool; complimentary access to YMCA facilities; Jacuzzi; sauna; concierge; business center; 24-hour room service; babysitting; same-day dry cleaning; nonsmoking hotel. *In room:* A/C, TV w/pay movies, dataport, coffeemaker, hair dryer, iron.

### Moderate

**Admiral Inn** ★★ Value The family-operated Admiral is in an attractive building on the Inner Harbour, near the Washington-bound ferry terminal and close to restaurants and shopping. The combination of comfortable rooms and reasonable rates attracts young couples, families, seniors, and other travelers in search of a harbor view at a price that doesn't break the bank. Rooms are pleasant and comfortably furnished, with balconies or terraces. Suites come with full kitchens. Some units can sleep up to six (on two double beds and a double sofa bed). The owners provide sightseeing advice as well as extras like free bicycles and an Internet terminal in the lobby.

257 Belleville St., Victoria, BC V8V 1X3. ✆ **888/823-6472.** ✆/Fax 250/388-6267. www.admiral.bc.ca. 29 units. May–Sept C$155–C$199 (US$96–US$123) double; C$169–C$215 (US$105–US$133) suite. Oct–Apr C$99–C$119 (US$62–US$74) double; C$109–C$129 (US$68–US$80) suite. Extra person C$10 (US$6). Children under 12 stay free in parents' room. Rates include continental breakfast. Senior, weekly, and off-season discounts available. AE, DISC, MC, V. Free parking. Bus: 5 to Belleville and Government sts. Pets welcome. **Amenities:** Free bikes; tour desk; business center; coin laundry; same-day dry cleaning; nonsmoking rooms. *In room:* A/C, TV, kitchenette or kitchen, coffeemaker, hair dryer, iron.

**Andersen House Bed & Breakfast** ★★ The art and furnishings in Andersen House are drawn from the whole of the old British Empire and a good section of the modern world beyond. The 1891 house has the high ceilings, stained-glass windows, and ornate fireplaces typical of the Queen Anne style, but the art and decorations are far more eclectic: hand-knotted Persian rugs, raku sculptures, large cubist-inspired oils, and carved-wood African masks. Each room has a unique style: The sun-drenched Casablanca room on the top floor, for example, boasts Persian rugs, a four-poster queen bed, and a lovely boxed window seat. All rooms have private entrances and come with books and CD players and CDs; some feature soaker tubs. The Andersens have also recently opened Baybreeze Manor, a restored 1885 farmhouse a 15-minute drive from downtown. The three farmhouse units feature hardwood floors, fireplaces, queen beds, and Jacuzzi tubs, as well as free bicycle, canoe, and kayak usage and easy access to Cadboro Beach.

301 Kingston St., Victoria, BC V8V 1V5. ✆ **250/388-4565.** Fax 250/721-3938. www.andersenhouse.com. 4 units, 3 manor units. June–Sept C$195–C$250 (US$121–US$155) double (up to 40% discount Oct-May); C$250 (US$155) manor unit. Off-season C$115–C$195 (US$71–US$121) manor unit. Rates include breakfast. MC, V. Some free off-street parking. Bus: 30 to Superior and Oswego sts. Children under 12 not accepted. **Amenities:** Jacuzzi; nonsmoking rooms. *In room:* TV/VCR, fridge, coffeemaker, hair dryer, iron.

## DOWNTOWN & OLD TOWN

### Expensive

**Abigail's Hotel** ★★★ The most serious existential problem you'll face here is determining at exactly what point you slipped from semi-sensuous luxury into full decadent indulgence. It could be when you first entered your room and saw the fresh flowers in crystal vases or came across the marble fireplace with wood in place. More likely, it's when you slipped into the double Jacuzzi in your marble bathroom or nestled into your four-poster canopied bed. In a Tudor mansion just east of downtown, Abigail's began life in the 1920s as a luxury apartment house before being converted to a boutique hotel. In the original building, some of the 16 rooms are bright and sunny and beautifully furnished, with pedestal sinks and goose-down comforters. Others boast soaker tubs and double-sided fireplaces, so you can relax in the tub by the light of the fire. The six Celebration Suites in the Coach House addition are the apogee of indulgence. Abigail's chef prepares a multicourse gourmet breakfast, served in the sunny breakfast room.

906 McClure St., Victoria, BC V8V 3E7. ✆ **800/561-6565** or 250/388-5363. Fax 250/388-7787. www.abigailshotel.com. 22 units. C$219–C$329 (US$136–US$204) double. Rates include full breakfast. Winter discounts up to 40%. AE, MC, V. Free parking. Bus: 1 to Cook and McClure sts. Children under 10 not accepted. **Amenities:** Concierge; tour desk; same-day dry cleaning; nonsmoking rooms.

**The Magnolia** ★★ A new boutique hotel in the center of Victoria, the Magnolia offers a taste of luxury at a reasonable price. The tiny lobby, with a fireplace, a chandelier, and overstuffed chairs, immediately conveys a sense of quality. Room decor manages to be classic without feeling frumpy, from the two-poster beds with high-quality linen and down duvets to the bathrooms with walk-in showers and deep tubs. Windows extend floor to ceiling, providing excellent harbor views from some rooms. The needs of business travelers are also kept in mind: work desks are well lit and large enough to spread your work out. Two phone lines run to every room, and the phone itself is cordless. The top-floor Diamond Suite features a sitting room with fireplace. The hotel also boasts a microbrewery and a full day spa—not necessarily to be enjoyed in that order.

623 Courtney St., Victoria, BC V8W 1B8. ✆ **877/624-6654** or 250/381-0999. Fax 250/381-0988. www.magnoliahotel.com. 66 units. June 1–Oct 15 C$239–C$279 (US$148–US$173) double; C$399–C$419 (US$247–US$260) suite. Oct 16–Apr 15 C$169–C$209 (US$105–US$130) double; C$249–C$269 (US$154–US$167) suite. Apr 16–May 31 C$209–C$229 (US$130–US$142) double; C$289–C$309 (US$179–US$192) suite. Rates include continental breakfast. AE, DC, MC, V. Valet parking C$10 (US$6). Bus: 5 to Courtney St. **Amenities:** Restaurant, bar; access to nearby health club; spa; concierge; salon; limited room service; massage; laundry service; same-day dry cleaning; executive rooms. *In room:* A/C, TV w/pay movies, dataport, minibar, fridge, coffeemaker, hair dryer, iron.

**Swans Suite Hotel** ★★ *Kids* This heritage building was abandoned for years until 1988, when Victoria renaissance man Michael Williams turned it into a hotel, restaurant, brewpub, and nightclub all in one. Just by the Johnson Street Bridge, it's one of Old Town's best-loved buildings. Like any great inn, Swans is small, friendly, and charming. Suites are large. Many are split-level, featuring open lofts and huge exposed beams. All come with fully equipped kitchens, dining areas, living rooms, and queen-size beds. The two-bedroom suites have the space and feel of little town houses; they're great for families, accommodating up to six comfortably. Swans also works for business travelers—it's one of the few hotels in town with dual dataports. The original Pacific Northwest artwork is a little disappointing—high-quality stuff, but not nearly up to the pieces hung in the bar and restaurant. Williams, alas, passed on in 2001, leaving most of his substantial holding—Swans included—to the University of Victoria.

506 Pandora Ave., Victoria, BC V8W 1N6. ✆ **800/668-7926** or 250/361-3310. Fax 250/361-3491. www.swanshotel.com. 30 suites. C$159–C$249 (US$99–US$154) suite. Off-season discounts available. AE, DC, DISC, MC, V. Parking C$8 (US$5). Bus: 23 or 24 to Pandora Ave. **Amenities:** Restaurant, brew pub; limited room service; laundry service; dry cleaning; nonsmoking hotel. *In room:* TV; kitchen; coffeemaker; hair dryer; iron.

### Inexpensive

**Victoria International Youth Hostel** The location is perfect—right in the heart of Old Town. In addition, this hostel has all the usual accoutrements, including two kitchens (stocked with utensils), a dining room, a TV lounge with VCR, a game room, a common room, a library, laundry facilities, an indoor bicycle lockup, 24-hour security, and hot showers. The dorms are on the large side (16 to a room), showers are shared and segregated by gender, and a couple of family rooms are available (one of which has a private toilet). There's an extensive ride board, and a large collection of outfitter and tour information. The front door is locked at 2:30am, but you can make arrangements to get in later.

516 Yates St., Victoria, BC V8W 1K8. ✆ **250/385-4511.** Fax 250/385-3232. www.hihostels.bc.ca. 104 beds. International Youth Hostel members C$17 (US$11), nonmembers C$20 (US$12). Wheelchair-accessible unit available. MC, V. Parking on street. Bus: 70 from Swartz Bay ferry terminal. **Amenities:** Game room; tour desk; laundry facilities.

## OUTSIDE THE CENTRAL AREA

### Expensive

**The Aerie** ★★ On a forested mountain slope by a fjord about half an hour from town, this Mediterranean-inspired villa was designed, built, and decorated by Maria Schuster, an Austrian hotelier with extravagant tastes and no shortage of self-confidence. The initial result was perhaps a tad over the top, so in recent years Schuster has been quietly stripping away some of the leopard skin and white leather furnishings. In its current configuration the Aerie is no longer overwhelming, just spectacular. In particular, the view over Finlayson Inlet—seen from your room, the indoor pool, the outdoor whirlpool, or the dining room—is quite simply stunning. Inside, the Aerie offers six room configurations: All include big comfortable beds, and all but the standard rooms include a soaker tub for two. As you move into the master and residence suites you get private decks and fireplaces. Dining is an integral part of the Aerie experience, and the restaurant (see "Where to Dine," below) is among the best in all Victoria.

600 Ebedora Lane (P.O. Box 108), Malahat, BC V0R 2L0. ✆ **250/743-7115.** Fax 250/743-4766. www.aerie.bc.ca. 24 units. Apr 6–May 17 C$235–C$295 (US$146–US$183) double; C$345–C$455 (US$214–US$282) suite. May 18–Oct 31 C$285–C$325 (US$177–US$202) double; C$375–C$495 (US$233–US$307) suite. Nov 1–Apr 5 C$185–C$230 (US$115–US$143) double; C$285–C$350 (US$177–US$217) suite. Rates include 7am breakfast hamper at your door and full breakfast later. Accommodation and dinner packages available. AE, DC, MC, V. Free parking. Take Hwy. 1 to the Spectacle Lake turnoff; take the first right and follow the winding driveway up. **Amenities:** Excellent restaurant, bar; indoor pool; indoor and outdoor whirlpools; tennis courts; small weight room; full spa; concierge; tour desk; 24-hour room service; massage; laundry; dry cleaning; non-smoking rooms. *In room:* A/C, TV, dataport, minibar, coffeemaker, hair dryer, iron.

**The Boathouse** ★★ *Finds* It's a short row (or a 25-min. walk) to Butchart Gardens from this secluded red cottage in Brentwood Bay, a converted boathouse set on pilings over Saanich Inlet. The only passersby you're likely to encounter are seals, bald eagles, otters, herons, and raccoons, plus the occasional floatplane flying in. The cottage is at the end of a very long flight of stairs behind the owner's home. Inside are a new queen bed, a dining table, a kitchen area with a small refrigerator and toaster oven, an electric heater, and a reading alcove with a stunning view all the way up Finlayson Arm. Toilet and shower facilities are in a separate bathhouse. All the makings for a delicious continental breakfast are provided, plus free coffee and newspaper delivery. Just below the boathouse is a floating dock—which doubles as a great sundeck—moored to which is a small dinghy reserved for the exclusive use of guests. There can perhaps be nothing more stylish than pulling up to the Butchart Gardens dock in your own private watercraft.

746 Sea Dr., RR 1, Victoria, BC VM8 1B1. ✆ **250/652-9370.** www.members.home.net/boathouse. 1 unit. C$175 (US$109) double. Rate includes continental breakfast. AE, MC, V. Free parking. Closed mid-Oct to Apr 1. Bus: 75 to Wallace Dr. and Benvenuto Ave. No children. *In room:* Fridge, coffeemaker, hair dryer, iron.

**Sooke Harbour House** ★★★ This little (but expanding) inn/restaurant, at the end of a sand spit about 30km (19 miles) west of Victoria, has earned an international reputation thanks to the care lavished on the guests and rooms by owners Frederique and Sinclair Philip. Frederique looks after the rooms, sumptuously furnishing and decorating each according to a particular Northwest theme. The Herb Garden room, looking out over a garden of fragrant herbs and edible flowers, is done in pale shades of mint and parsley. The large split-level Thunderbird room is a veritable celebration of First Nations culture, with books, carvings, totems, and masks, including one of a huge Thunderbird. Thanks to some clever architecture, all rooms are awash in natural light and have fabulous ocean views. In addition, all boast wood-burning fireplaces and sitting areas, all but one have sun decks, and most have Jacuzzis or soaker tubs. The other half of the Harbour House's reputation comes from the outstanding cooking of Sinclair Philip (see "Where to Dine," below).

1528 Whiffen Spit Rd., Sooke, BC V0S 1N0. ✆ **250/642-3421.** Fax 250/628-6988. www.sookeharbourhouse.com. 28 units. May–June and Oct C$280–C$490 (US$174–US$304) double. July–Sept C$299–C$555 (US$185–US$344) double. Nov–Apr C$230–C$355 (US$147–US$220) Mon–Fri double; C$255–C$455 (US$158–US$282) weekend double. Rates include full breakfast and picnic lunch (no picnic lunch weekdays Nov–April). MC, V. Free parking. Pets accepted C$20 (US$12) per day. Take the Island Hwy. (Hwy. 1) to the Sooke/Colwood turnoff (Junction Hwy. 14). Follow Hwy. 14 to Sooke. About 1.5km (1 mile) past the town's only traffic light, turn left onto Whiffen Spit Rd. **Amenities:** Restaurant, golf course; access to nearby health club; spa; limited room service; massage; babysitting; laundry service; nonsmoking rooms. *In room:* Dataport, fridge, coffeemaker, hair dryer, iron.

### Inexpensive

**University of Victoria Housing, Food, and Conference Services** *Value*

One of the best deals going is found at the University of Victoria, when classes aren't in session and summer visitors are welcomed. All rooms have single or twin beds and basic furnishings, and there are bathrooms, pay phones, and TV lounges on every floor. Linens, towels, and soap are provided. The suites are an extremely good value—each has four bedrooms, a kitchen, a living room, and 1½ bathrooms. The disadvantage, of course, is that the U. Vic. campus is a painfully long way from everywhere—the city center is about a half-hour drive away. For C$5 (US$3.10) extra per day, however, you can make use of the many on-campus athletic facilities. Each of the 28 buildings has a coin laundry.

P.O. Box 1700, Sinclair at Finerty Rd., Victoria, BC V8W 2Y2. ✆ **250/721-8395.** Fax 250/721-8930. www.hfcs.uvic.ca/uvichfcs.htm. 898 units. MC, V. May–Aug C$38 (US$24) single; C$50 (US$31) twin; C$146 (US$91) suite. Discounts available for longer stays. Room rates include full breakfast and taxes; suite rates include taxes. Parking C$5 (US$3.10). Closed Sept–Apr. Bus: 4 or 14 to University of Victoria. **Amenities:** Indoor pool; athletic facilities for C$5/US$3.10 a day; coin laundry; nonsmoking rooms.

## WHERE TO DINE

Though early Victoria settlers were intent on re-creating a little patch of the old country on their wild western island, the one thing they were never tempted to import was British cooking. Thankfully. Instead, following the traditional Canadian norm, each little immigrant group imported its own cuisine, so now Victoria is a cornucopia of culinary styles. With more than 700 restaurants, there's something for every taste and wallet.

But with all this variety, the one thing you're unlikely to find is a lot of late-night dining. Victorians time their meal to the setting of the sun. Try for a seat at 7pm and the restaurant will be packed. Try at 9pm and it'll be empty. Try at 10pm and it'll be closed, especially on weekdays. Reservations are strongly recommended for prime sunset seating in summer.

## INNER HARBOUR & OLD TOWN

### Expensive

**The Blue Crab Bar and Grill** ★★ SEAFOOD Victoria's best seafood spot, the Blue Crab combines fresh ingredients, inventive recipes, and beautiful presentation. It also has a killer view—floatplanes slip in and out while you're dining, little ferries chug across the harbor, and the sun sets slowly over the Sooke Hills. After you've had a chance to check out the understated elegance of the room and perhaps choose from the extensive selection of excellent BC wines, peruse the chalkboard of daily seafood specials. What's on the board is entirely dependent on what came in on the boats or floatplanes that day—salmon, spotted prawns, and crab (in season) are strong possibilities. Occasionally, little Salt Spring Island lambs are on offer. The chef is particularly fond of unusual combinations: sea bass with taro root, grapefruit, and blood orange or foie gras with raspberries. And how about house-smoked chicken sausage in portobello-mushroom broth or tenderloin with Indonesian *pindasaus* (peanut sauce)? The service is deft, smart, and obliging.

146 Kingston St., in the Coast Hotel. ✆ **250/480-1999.** Reservations recommended. Main courses C$20–C$30 (US$12–US$19). AE, DC, MC, V. Daily 6:30am–10:30pm. Bus 30 to Erie St.

**The Victorian Restaurant** ★ WEST COAST One of the only good bets when it comes to waterfront dining in Victoria is this elegant restaurant in the Ocean Pointe Resort. The views are tremendous, and in recent years the food has begun to win some recognition, including awards from *Wine Spectator* and *Western Living* magazines. In culinary terms, the chef takes few risks, sticking to fresh ingredients with a slight emphasis on seafood but enough lamb, steak, and veggie dishes to cover all the bases. The service is polished, and the wine list one of the better ones in town.

45 Songhees Rd., in the Ocean Pointe Resort. ✆ **250/360-2999.** www.oprhotel.com. Reservations recommended. Main courses C$14–C$29 (US$9–US$18). AE, MC, V. Daily 11am–10:30pm. Bus: 24 to Colville.

### Moderate

**Cassis Bistro** ★★ BISTRO If you've got the time, the pretty neighborhood of Cook Street Village is worth a stroll, but if you've only come for the food, this cozy candlelit bistro is exactly the right place. Chef and owner John Hall describes the menu as eclectic Italian, which means dishes from the whole boot plus borrowings here and there from Asia and France. Recent highlights on this ever-changing menu have included ling cod filet, lightly seared and served with *shimjii* mushrooms; smoked tuna ravioli in a miso jus; and a braised Gulf Island halibut on a bed of spinach and finely sliced pancetta in a rich game stock. Being partial to duck I was an easy pushover for the Fraser Valley duck breast served on a bed of warm goat cheese crouton. Pickled bing cherries added just that exquisite hint of sweetness to the tender duck breast. And if you thought Hall was passionate about food, just get him going on the topic of wine. He's especially good at pairing up his dishes with a local BC wine.

253 Cook St. ✆ **250/384-1932.** Reservations recommended. Main courses C$23–C$27 (US$14–US$17). MC, V. Daily 5:30–9:30pm; Sun brunch 10am–2pm.

**Herald Street Caffe** ★ PASTA/WEST COAST An old warehouse on the far side of Chinatown, this cafe sizzles from midweek onward with the sound of diners young and old. The room is large and has walls painted a warm red and covered with an ever-changing display of local art. This is a fun place to dine and

### *Moments* Tea for Two

Afternoon tea at the **Fairmont Empress** hotel, 721 Government St. (✆ **250/384-8111;** bus: 5, 30), is undoubtedly the best in town, served in the Palm Court or in the Lobby Lounge, both of which are beautifully ornate and luxurious. Tea runs C$46 (US$29) (C$32/US$20 Nov–Mar) per person, with seatings at 12:30, 2, 3:30, and 5pm. The **Point Ellice House,** an old villa at 2616 Pleasant St. on the Gorge waterway just outside downtown (✆ **250/380-6506;** bus: 14), also makes a fine destination for afternoon tea, especially on a sunny day, when tea is served on the lawn. Tea runs C$17 (US$11), including admission to the grounds, and seatings are at 12:30, 2, and 3:30pm. Reservations are required. The **Butchart Gardens Dining Room Restaurant,** 800 Benvenuto Ave. (✆ **250/652-4422;** bus: 75), offers the impeccably groomed gardens as a backdrop to a memorable tea experience that runs C$25 (US$16). June to August, seatings are noon to 7pm; September to May, seatings are noon to 5pm.

drink. The menu comes with a list of more than 20 martinis, and for oenophiles, the wine list offers French and Canadian labels, along with a good selection of BC reds and whites. The cuisine is sophisticated without going too far over the top. Appetizers may include barbecued duck in phyllo pastry with apple-current chutney or oysters in cornmeal crust on a nest of new potatoes. The entrees include many clever seafood dishes, as well as free-range chicken, duck and lamb dishes, and a whole page of pastas. Portions are generous and the service is knowledgeable and helpful, particularly when it comes to wine pairings. Don't miss the Boca Negra (a chocolate cake with rich chocolate bourbon sauce and fresh raspberries) for dessert.

546 Herald St. ✆ **250/381-1441.** Reservations required. Main courses C$17–C$27.95 (US$11–US$17). AE, DC, MC, V. Wed–Fri 11:30am–2:30pm, Sat–Sun brunch 11am–3pm; Sun–Thurs 5:30–10pm, Fri–Sat 5:30pm–midnight. Bus: 5.

**Millos** ★★ *Kids* GREEK Millos isn't hard to find—look for the blue-and-white windmill behind The Empress or listen for the hand clapping and plate breaking as diners get into the swing of things. Flaming *saganaki* (a sharp cheese sautéed in olive oil and flambéed with Greek brandy), grilled halibut souvlaki, baby back ribs, and succulent grilled salmon are a few of the menu items at this lively five-level restaurant. Kids get their own menu. Folk dancers and belly dancers highlight the entertainment on Friday and Saturday nights, and the waitstaff are remarkably warm and entertaining at all times.

716 Burdett Ave. ✆ **250/382-4422.** Reservations recommended. Main courses C$10–C$28 (US$6–US$17), with most dishes costing around C$15 (US$9). AE, DC, MC, V. Mon–Sat 11am–11pm, Sun 4–11pm. Bus: 5.

**Pagliacci's** ★★ ITALIAN Victoria's night owls used to come here when Pagliacci's was one of the few places to offer late night dining. Though the evening scene has improved since expatriate New Yorker Howie Siegal opened the restaurant in 1979, Pagliacci's can still boast an un-Victorian kind of big city buzz and energy. Tables jostle against one another as guests ogle each other's food and eavesdrop on conversations, while Howie works the room, dispensing a word or two to long-lost friends, many of whom he's just met. The menu is southern Italian—veal parmigiana, tortellini, and 19 or 20 other a la carte pastas, all fresh and made by hand, many quite inventive. The service isn't fast, but when you're having this much fun, who cares? Grab some wine, munch some focaccia, and enjoy the atmosphere. Sunday to Wednesday there's live jazz, swing, blues, or Celtic starting at 8:30pm. On Sunday, there's a very good brunch.

1011 Broad St. ✆ **250/386-1662.** Reservations not accepted. Main courses C$11–C$19 (US$6–US$12). AE, MC, V. Sun–Thurs 11:30am–10pm, Fri–Sat 11:30am–midnight, light menu 3–5:30pm.

## Inexpensive

**Don Mee Restaurant** ★ CHINESE Since the 1920s, elegant Don Mee's has been serving Victoria's best dim sum, chop suey, and chow mein, along with piquant Szechuan seafood dishes and delectable Cantonese sizzling platters. You can't miss this second-story restaurant—a huge neon Chinese lantern looms above the small doorway. A gold-leaf laughing Buddha greets you at the foot of the stairs leading up to the huge dining room, where, if it's lunchtime, you'll find many Chinese-Canadian businesspeople munching away. The dinner specials are particularly good deals if you want to sample lots of everything on the menu.

538 Fisgard St. ✆ **250/383-1032.** Reservations accepted. Main courses C$9–C$14 (US$6–US$9); 4-course dinner from C$14 (US$9). AE, DC, MC, V. Sun–Thu 11am–10pm, Fri–Sat 11am–midnight. Bus: 5.

**Green Cuisine** *Value* VEGETARIAN In addition to being undeniably healthy, Victoria's only fully vegan enclave is remarkably tasty, with a self-serve salad bar, hot buffet, dessert bar, and full bakery. Available dishes range from Moroccan chickpea and vegetable soup to pasta primavera salad to pumpkin tofu cheesecake, not to mention a wide selection of freshly baked breads (made with natural sweeteners and fresh-ground organic flour). Green cuisine also has a large selection of freshly squeezed organic juices, smoothies and shakes, and organic coffees and teas. And for the sake of the truly discriminating diner, the ingredients for every dish are carefully listed. The atmosphere is casual—bordering on cafeteria—but comfortable. And for healthy-dessert hounds, order the wheat-free chocolate raspberry cake. If you like the food, check out the website, which features monthly recipes from the restaurant.

560 Johnson St., in Market Sq. ✆ **250/385-1809.** www.greencuisine.com. Main courses C$3.95–C$10 (US$2.50–US$6). AE, MC, V. Daily 10am–8pm.

**Re-bar** ★★ *Kids* VEGETARIAN Even if you're not hungry, it's worth dropping in for a juice blend—say grapefruit, banana, melon, and pear with bee pollen or blue-green algae for added oomph. If you're hungry, then rejoice: Re-bar is the city's premier dispenser of vegetarian comfort food. Disturbingly wholesome as that may sound, Re-bar is not only tasty, but fun, and a great spot to take the kids for brunch or breakfast. The room—in the basement of an 1890s heritage building—is pastel-tinted funky, with loads of cake tins glued to the walls. The service is friendly and casual. The food tends to the simple and wholesome, including a vegetable-and-almond patty with red onions, sprouts, and fresh tomato salsa on a multigrain kaiser roll, as well as quesadillas, omelettes, and crisp salads with toasted pine nuts, feta cheese, fresh vegetables, and sun-dried tomato vinaigrette. Juices are still the crown jewels, with over 80 blends on the menu. And if the one you want isn't there, they'll make it anyway.

50 Bastion Sq. ✆ **250/361-9223.** Main courses C$7–C$14 (US$4.35–US$9). AE, MC, V. Mon–Thurs 8:30am–9pm, Fri–Sat 8:30am–10pm, Sun 8:30am–3:30pm. Bus: 5.

## OUTSIDE THE CENTRAL AREA

### Expensive

**The Aerie** ★★ FRENCH The dining room of this red-tile villa boasts panoramic windows overlooking Finlayson Inlet, the Straight of Georgia, and on a clear day even the Olympic Peninsula mountains. The room itself is bright and decorated with a gold-leaf ceiling, crystal chandeliers, and a large open-hearth fireplace. Views and luxury aside, most people come for chef Christophe Letard's cooking. His creations combine West Coast freshness with unmistakably French accents. You might start your culinary event with a seared wild sockeye served with a green asparagus salad. Another fish favorite is the peppercorn crusted lingcod accompanied by steamed young fennel and garlic shoots in a gooseberry and red currant beurre blanc. Sauces are light. The fish, plus inventive twists on Sooke rabbit and duck breast, might be followed by a plate of local goat cheeses. For dessert, the spiced local raspberries served with star anise and fennel ice cream are outstanding.

600 Ebedora Lane, Malahat. ✆ **250/743-7115.** www.aerie.bc.ca. Reservations required. Main courses C$27–C$35 (US$17–US$22); 7-course set menu C$95 (US$59), C$155 (US$96) with wine pairings. AE, DC, MC, V. Daily noon–1:30pm and 6–9:30pm. Free parking. Take Hwy. 1 to the Spectacle Lake turnoff; take the first right and follow the winding driveway.

**Sooke Harbour House** ★★★ WEST COAST In a rambling white house on a bluff on the edge of the Pacific, this small restaurant/hotel offers spectacular waterfront views, a relaxed atmosphere, and what could be the best food in all Canada. Chef/proprietor Sinclair Philip is both a talented innovator and a stickler for details. The result is an ever-changing menu in which each of the dishes is prepared with care, imagination, and flair. The ingredients are resolutely local (many come from the inn's own organic herb garden or from the ocean at the Harbour House's doorstep). On any given night, dishes might include seared scallops with sea asparagus (harvested from the sand spit below the inn), nori rolls with gooseneck barnacles in mustard broth, or chinook salmon with red wine/gooseberry sauce. The presentation is always interesting—often with edible flowers—while the service is knowledgeable and professional. The wine cellar is extensive (one of the best in Canada), and the pairings for Philips' culinary creations are particularly well chosen.

1528 Whiffen Spit Rd., Sooke. ✆ **250/642-3421.** www.sookeharbourhouse.com. Reservations required. Main courses C$29–C$36 (US$18–US$22). DISC, MC, V. Daily 5–9pm. Take the Island Hwy. to the Sooke/Colwood turnoff (Junction Hwy. 14). Continue on Hwy. 14 to Sooke. About a mile past the town's only traffic light, turn left onto Whiffen Spit Rd.

## VICTORIA AFTER DARK

Victoria is never going to set the world on fire, but taken together, the U Vic. students, tourists, and a small but dedicated cadre of Victoria revelers form a critical mass large enough to keep a number of small but steady reactions going in various parts of the city. You just have to know where to look. ***Monday*** magazine (www.monday.com) has a listings section with near-comprehensive coverage of what's happening in town.

You can buy tickets and get schedules from the **Tourism Victoria Travel Visitor Centre,** 812 Wharf St. (✆ **800/663-3883** or 250/382-1131; bus: 5, 30), open daily 9am to 5pm (summer to 9pm). Another source of theater and event info is the **CHEK-by-phone** line at ✆ **250/389-6460.**

**THE PERFORMING ARTS** The **Royal Theatre,** 805 Broughton St. (✆ **250/361-0820;** box office 250/386-6121; www.rmts.bc.ca; bus: 5, 30), hosts events like Victoria Symphony concerts, dance recitals, and touring stage plays. The box office is at the **McPherson Playhouse,** 3 Centennial Sq., at Pandora Avenue and Government Street (✆ **250/386-6121.** Bus: 5, 30), which is also home to Victoria's Pacific Opera and the Victoria Operatic Society. The box office is open Monday to Saturday 9:30am to 5:30pm.

The **Belfry Theatre,** 1291 Gladstone St. (✆ **250/385-6815;** www.belfry.bc.ca; bus: 1, 2), is a nationally acclaimed theatrical group that stages four productions October to April and a summer show in August. The **Victoria Fringe Festival** (✆ **888/FRINGE2** or 250/383-2663; www.victoriafringe.com) presents short, inexpensive original fare at six venues from late August to mid-September.

The **Pacific Opera Victoria,** 1316B Government St. (✆ **250/385-0222;** www.pov.bc.ca; box office 250/386-6121; bus: 5, 30), presents productions in October, February, and April. Performances are normally at the McPherson Playhouse and Royal Theatre. **The Victoria Operatic Society,** 798 Fairview Rd. (✆ **250/381-1021**), stages old-time Broadway musicals and other popular fare year-round at the McPherson Playhouse.

The **Victoria Symphony Orchestra,** 846 Broughton St. (✆ **250/385-9771;** www.vos.bc.ca; bus: 5, 30), kicks off its season on the first Sunday of August with Symphony Splash, a free concert performed on a barge in the Inner Harbour. Regular performances begin in October and last to May.

**LIVE-MUSIC CLUBS** **Legends,** 919 Douglas St. (✆ **250/383-7137;** bus: 5, 30), is the live-music venue below street level in the Strathcona Hotel. It covers the gamut from afro-pop to blues to zydeco. **The Lucky Bar,** 517 Yates St. ✆ **250/382-5825** is currently the hottest spot in Victoria. This low cavernous space has a pleasantly grungy feel like Seattle's Pioneer Square. The Bar features DJs on Wednesdays, rockabilly on Thursdays, and a lot of good bands (and sometimes DJs) on weekends. **Steamers,** 570 Yates St. (✆ **250/381-4340;** bus: 5, 30), is the city's premium blues bar. Cover hovers around C$5 (US$3.10).

**LOUNGES, BARS & PUBS** A truly unique experience, the **Bengal Lounge** in the Empress hotel, 721 Government St. (✆ **250/384-8111;** bus: 5, 30), is one of the last outposts of the old empire, except the martinis are ice cold and jazz plays in the background (on weekends it's live in the foreground). **Rick's Lounge,** in the Ocean Pointe Resort, 45 Songhees Rd. (✆ **250/360-2999;** bus: 6 or harbor ferry), is without doubt the best place to watch as the last light of day fades.

The **Harbour Canoe Club,** 450 Swift St. (✆ **250/361-1940;** bus: 6), is one of the most pleasant spots going to hoist a pint after a long day's sightseeing. **Big Bad John's,** 919 Douglas St., in the Strathcona Hotel (✆ **250/383-7137;** bus: 5, 30), is Victoria's only hillbilly bar—a low, dark warren of a place, with inches of discarded peanut shells on the plank floor and a crowd of drunk and happy rowdies. Overlooking Victoria Harbour on the west side of the Songhees Point Development, **Spinnaker's Brew Pub,** 308 Catherine St. (✆ **250/386-BREW** or 250/386-2739; bus: 6 or harbor ferry), has one of the best views and some of the best beer in town.

**DANCE CLUBS** Most dance clubs are open Monday to Saturday to 2am and Sunday to midnight. The **Ice House,** 1961 Douglas St., in the Horizon West Hotel (✆ **250/382-2111;** bus: 5, 30), is the place if house is your thing. Don't let the name of **The Blues House,** 1417 Government St. (✆ **250/386-1717;** bus: 5 to Douglas and Fisgard St.) fool you. It's actually an all-DJ dance spot, featuring everything from house to trip funk to retro-1970s and 1980s nights. The cover is around C$5 (US$3.10). The **One Lounge,** 1318 Broad St. (✆ **250/384-3557**), spins Top 40 dance tracks for a late twenties to early thirties crowd. The format ('70s and '80s retro) depends on the night of the week. There is a C$5 (US$3.10) cover on weekends.

**GAY & LESBIAN BARS** **Hush,** 1325 Government St. (✆ **250/385-0566;** bus: 5), the new gay-yet-straight-friendly space (crowd is about 50/50) features top-end touring DJs, hosted by Brent Carmichael, the 40-something granddaddy of Victoria DJs. There is a C$5 (US$3.10) cover on weekends.

**Friends of Dorothy's Cafe,** 615 Johnson St. (✆ **250/381-2277;** bus: 1, 2, 5), used to play *The Wizard of Oz* continuously, but now they just make do with Dorothy memorabilia. The staff are slightly outré and the crowd is fun-loving at this little cafe/hangout. **BJ's Lounge,** 642 Johnson St. (✆ **250/388-0505;** bus: 1, 2, 5), has a full menu and lounge decor.

**A CASINO** At the **Great Canadian Casino,** 3075 Douglas St. (✆ **250/389-1136;** bus: 30), there are no floor shows, no alcohol, no dancing girls in glittering bikinis—just blackjack, roulette, sic bo, red dog (diamond dog), and Caribbean stud poker. Admission is free, and it's open daily noon to 3am.

## 3 A Side Trip from Victoria: Goldstream Provincial Park

The tranquil arboreal setting of Goldstream Provincial Park overflowed with prospectors during the 1860s gold-rush days. Trails take you past abandoned mine shafts and tunnels, as well as 600-year-old stands of towering Douglas fir, lodge pole pine, red cedar, indigenous yew, and arbutus trees. The **Gold Mine Trail** leads to Niagara Creek and the abandoned mine that was operated by Lt. Peter Leech, a Royal Engineer who discovered gold in the creek in 1858. The **Goldstream Trail** leads to the salmon spawning areas. (You might also catch sight of mink and river otters racing along this path.)

The park is 20km (12 miles) west of downtown Victoria along Highway 1; the drive takes about half an hour. For general information on this and all the other provincial parks on the South Island, contact **BC Parks** at ✆ **250/391-2300.** Throughout the year, Goldstream Park's **Freeman King Visitor Centre** (✆ **250/478-9414**) offers guided walks, talks, displays, and programs geared toward kids but interesting for adults too. It's open daily 9:30am to 6pm.

Three species of salmon (chum, Chinook, and steelhead) make **annual salmon runs** up the Goldstream River in October, November, December, and February. You can easily observe this natural wonder along the riverbanks. For details, contact the park's **Freeman King Visitor Centre** at ✆ **250/478-9414**.

## 4 Vancouver Island's West Coast: Pacific Rim National Park ★, Tofino & Ucluelet

Vancouver Island's west coast is a magnificent area of old-growth forests, stunning fjords (called sounds in local parlance), rocky coasts, and long sandy beaches. And though **Pacific Rim National Park** was established back in 1971 as Canada's first marine park, it wasn't until 1993—when thousands of environmentalists gathered to protest the clear-cutting of old-growth forests in Clayoquot Sound—that the area really exploded into the people's consciousness. Tourism here has never looked back.

## Vancouver Island

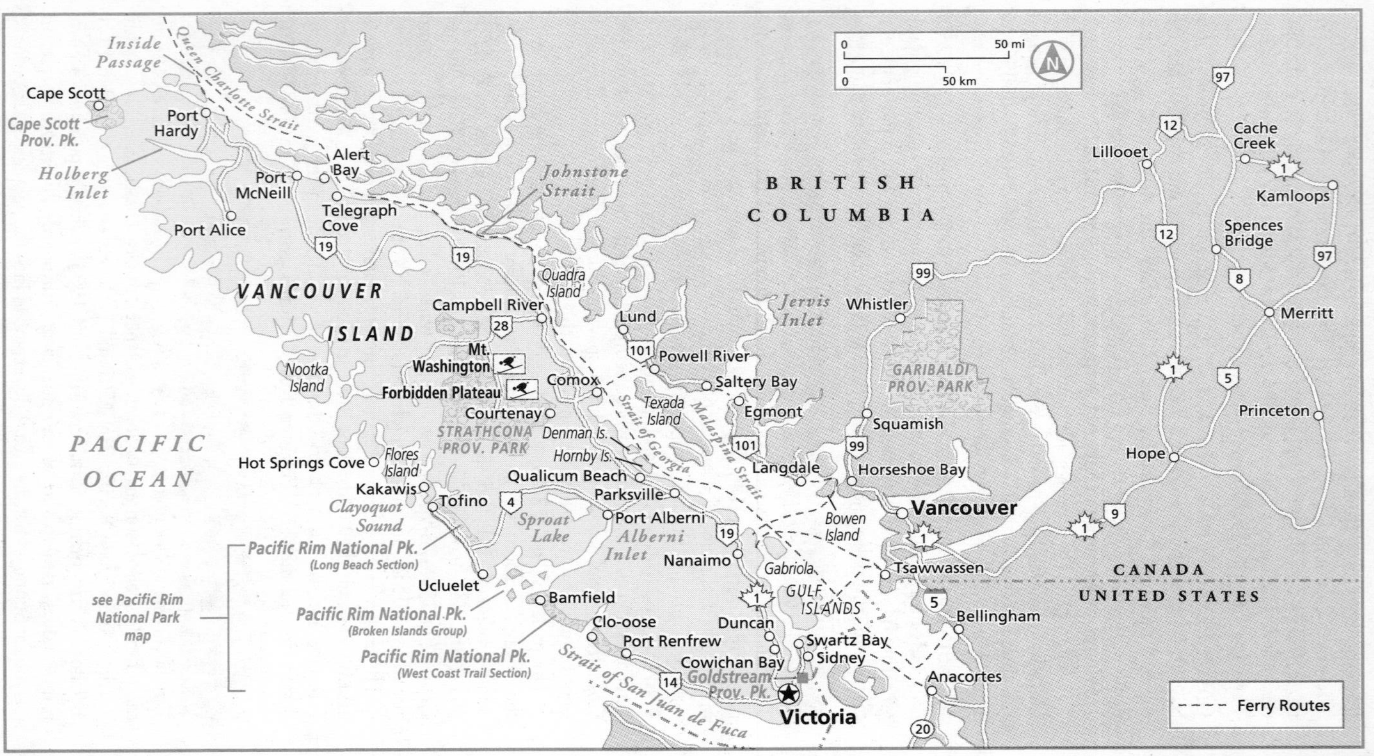

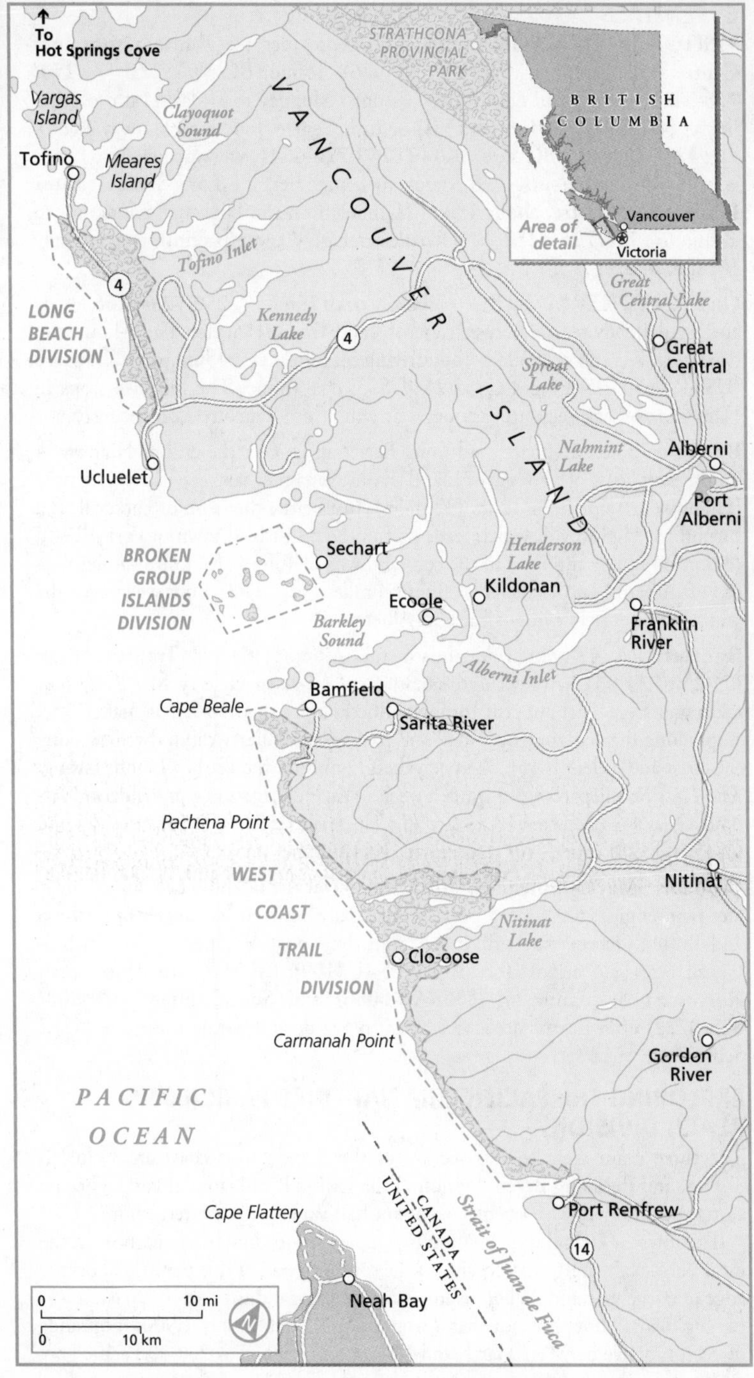
To Hot Springs Cove
Vargas Island
Clayoquot Sound
Tofino
Meares Island
STRATHCONA PROVINCIAL PARK
VANCOUVER ISLAND
BRITISH COLUMBIA
Vancouver
Area of detail
Victoria
Tofino Inlet
4
LONG BEACH DIVISION
Kennedy Lake
Great Central Lake
Great Central
Sproat Lake
Nahmint Lake
Alberni
Ucluelet
Port Alberni
BROKEN GROUP ISLANDS DIVISION
Sechart
Henderson Lake
Kildonan
Ecoole
Franklin River
Barkley Sound
Alberni Inlet
Bamfield
Cape Beale
Sarita River
Pachena Point
WEST COAST TRAIL DIVISION
Nitinat
Nitinat Lake
Clo-oose
Carmanah Point
Gordon River
PACIFIC OCEAN
CANADA
UNITED STATES
Strait of Juan de Fuca
Cape Flattery
Port Renfrew
14
Neah Bay
0
10 mi
0
10 km

## ESSENTIALS

**VISITOR INFORMATION** March to September, the **Tofino Visitor Info Centre,** 380 Campbell St. (P.O. Box 476), Tofino, BC V0R 2Z0 (✆ **250/725-3414;** www.island.net/~tofino), is open Monday to Friday 11am to 5pm. July to September, the **Ucluelet Visitor Info Centre,** Junction Highway 4 (P.O. Box 428), Ucluelet, BC V0R 3A0 (✆ **250/726-4641;** www.uclueletinfo.com), is open the same hours. Mid-March to September, the **Long Beach Visitor Information Centre,** about 1.5km (1 mile) from the Highway 4 junction to Tofino (✆ **250/726-4212;** http://parkscan.harbour.com/pacrim), is open daily 10am to 6pm.

**GETTING THERE** **By Bus** **Island Coach Lines** (✆ **250/724-1266**) operates regular daily service between Victoria and Tofino/Ucluelet. The 7-hour trip, departing Victoria at 7:30am and arriving in Tofino at 2:45pm, costs C$49.50 (US$31) to Ucluelet and C$52.25 (US$32) to Tofino. The bus also stops in Nanaimo and can pick up passengers arriving from Vancouver on the ferry.

**By Car** Tofino, Ucluelet, and Long Beach all lie near the end of Highway 4 on the west coast of Vancouver Island. From Nanaimo, take the Island Highway (Highway 19) north for 52km (32 miles). Just before the town of Parksville is a turnoff for Highway 4, which leads first to the mid-island town of Port Alberni (38km/24 miles) and then to the coastal towns of Tofino (135km/84 miles west of Port Alberni) and Ucluelet (103km/64 miles west). The road is well paved the whole way but gets windy after Port Alberni.

**By Ferry** A 4½-hour ride aboard the **Alberni Marine Transportation** (✆ **250/723-8313;** www.ladyrosemarine.com) passenger ferry MV *Lady Rose* takes you from Port Alberni through Alberni Inlet to Ucluelet. It makes brief stops along the way to deliver mail and packages to solitary cabin dwellers along the coast and to let off or pick up kayakers bound for the Broken Islands Group. The *Lady Rose* departs three times a week to each destination from Alberni Harbour Quay's Angle Street. The fare to Ucluelet is C$23 (US$14) one-way and C$45 (US$28) round-trip. The service is in summer only.

**By Plane** May to September, **North Vancouver Air** (✆ **800/228-6608**) operates twin-engine, turbo-prop plane service daily between Vancouver or Victoria and Tofino; October to April, it runs four times a week. One-way fare, including all taxes and airport fees, is C$175 (U$109); flying time is 45 minutes. **Northwest Seaplanes** (✆ **800/690-0086**) and **Sound Flight** (✆ **800/825-0722**) offer floatplane service between Seattle and Tofino mid-June to late September.

## EXPLORING THE PACIFIC RIM NATIONAL PARK (LONG BEACH DIVISION)

The three main areas to this section of the island's west coast are Ucluelet, Tofino, and the Long Beach division of the Pacific Rim National Park. They lie along the outer edge of a peninsula about half-way up the western shore.

The town of **Ucluelet** (pronounced you-*clue*-let, meaning "safe harbor" in the local Nuu-chah-nulth dialect) sits on the southern end of this peninsula, on the edge of Barkely Sound. When fishing was the major industry on the coast, it was the big town. Though it now has a winter population of only 1,900, thousands of visitors arrive between March and May to see as many as 20,000 Pacific gray whales pass close to the shore as they migrate north to their summer feeding grounds in the Arctic Circle. At the moment, the town has a beautiful location

**Fun Fact** **A Whale of a Festival**

About 20,000 Pacific gray whales migrate to this area annually. During the second week of March, the **Pacific Rim Whale Festival** (**✆ 250/726-4641**; www.island.net/~whalef/) is held in Tofino and Ucluelet. Live crab races, the Gumboot Golf Tournament, guided whale-watching hikes, and a Native Indian festival are just a few of the events celebrating the annual whale migration.

and a couple of fine B&Bs but has yet to develop the range of restaurants and activities Tofino offers. On the plus side, Ucluelet is cheaper, just as close to Long Beach, and much less busy.

About a 15-minute drive north is **Long Beach** ★, part of the Pacific Rim National Park group. The beach is more than 16km (10 miles) long, broken here and there by rocky headlands and bordered by tremendous groves of cedar and Sitka spruce. The beach is popular with countless species of birds and marine life and lately also with wet-suited surfers.

At the far-northern tip of the peninsula, **Tofino** (pop. 1,300) borders on beautiful Clayoquot Sound and is the center of the west coast eco-tourism business. It's a schizophrenic kind of town: Half is composed of eco-tourism outfitters, nature lovers, activists, and serious granolas; the other half is composed of loggers and fishers. Conflict was common in the early years, but recently the two sides seem to have learned how to get along. Hikers and beachcombers come to Tofino simply for the scenery, while others use it as a base from which to explore Clayoquot Sound.

## OUTDOOR PURSUITS

**FISHING** Sportfishing for salmon, steelhead, rainbow trout, Dolly Varden char, halibut, cod, and snapper is excellent off the west coast of Vancouver Island. **Chinook Charters,** 450 Campbell St., Tofino (**✆ 800/665-3646** or 250/725-3431; www.chinookcharters.com), organizes fishing charters throughout the Clayoquot Sound area. Fishing starts in March or April and goes to December. The company supplies all the gear, a guide, and a boat. Prices start at a minimum of C$85 (U$53) per hour, with a minimum of 4 hours. A 10-hour fishing trip for four people on an 8m (25-ft.) boat costs C$750 (US$465).

**GUIDED NATURE HIKES** Owned/operated by Bill McIntyre, former chief naturalist of the Pacific Rim National Park, the **Long Beach Nature Tour Co.** (**✆ 250/726-7099;** fax 250726-4282; www.oceansedge.bc.ca) offers guided beach walks, storm watching, land-based whale-watching tours, and rain-forest tours customized to suit your group's needs. Also excellent are the tours offered by wildlife author Adrienne Mason of **Raincoast Communications** (**✆ 250/725-2878;** amason@port.island.net). A local naturalist/science writer, she can accommodate various group sizes and will greatly enhance your knowledge of the rainforest ecology and local flora and fauna.

**HIKING** In and around **Long Beach,** numerous marked trails a one to 3.5km long (½ mile–2 miles) take you through the thick temperate rain forest edging the shore. The **Gold Mine Trail** (about 3.5km/2 miles long) near Florencia Bay still has a few artifacts from the days when a gold-mining operation flourished here. The partially boardwalked **South Beach Trail** (less than

## Walking the Wild Side: A Glimpse of First Nations Life

Clayoquot Sound is the traditional home of the Nuu-chah-nulth peoples. Accessed via water taxi, the **Walk the Wild Side Trail** (✆ **888/670-9586**) runs along the south side of Flores Island to the village of Ahousat. There's a fee for walking the trail, as well as the cost of the water taxi; the booking line above is supposed to arrange both. Some who have done the trail have reported incredible experiences and afterward were invited by elders to come to the village to celebrate a potlatch. Others have paid their money only to be foisted off on 12- and 13-year-old native boys more interested in playing with their two-way radios than looking at nature. So it's a toss-up. Keep an open mind and the spirit of adventure and you might be rewarded.

1.5km/1 mile long) leads through the moss-draped rain forest onto small quiet coves like Lismer Beach and South Beach, where you can see abundant life in the rocky tidal pools. The **Big Cedar Trail** (✆ **250/725-3233**) on Meares Island is a 3.5km (2-mile) boardwalk path built in 1993 to protect the old-growth temperate rain forest. Maintained by the Tla-o-qui-aht Native Indian Band, the trail has a long staircase leading up to the Hanging Garden Tree, the province's fourth-largest western red cedar.

**KAYAKING** Perhaps the quintessential Clayoquot experience, and certainly one of the most fun, is to slip into a kayak and paddle out into the Sound. For beginners, half-day tours to Meares Island (usually with the chance to do a little hiking) are an especially good bet. For rentals, lessons, and tours, try **Pacific Kayak,** 606 Campbell St., at Jamie's Whaling Station (✆ **250/725-3232;** www.tofino-bc.com/pacifickayak). The **Tofino Sea-Kayaking Company,** 320 Main St., Tofino (✆ **800/863-4664** or 250/725-4222; www.tofino-kayaking.com), offers kayaking packages ranging from 4-hour paddles around Meares Island (from C$52/US$32 per person) to weeklong paddling and camping expeditions. Instruction by experienced guides makes even your first kayaking experience a comfortable, safe, and enjoyable one.

**STORM-WATCHING** Watching the winter storms behind big glass windows has become very popular in Tofino over the past year or so. For a slight twist on this, try the outdoor storm-watching tours offered by the **Long Beach Nature Tour Co.** (✆ **250/726-7099;** fax 250/726-4282; www.oceansedge.bc.ca). Owner Bill McIntyre, former chief naturalist of the Pacific Rim National Park, can explain how storms work and where to stand so you can get close without getting swept away.

**WHALE-WATCHING, BIRDING & MORE** A number of outfitters conducts tours through this region inhabited by gray whales, bald eagles, porpoises, orcas, seals, and sea lions. **Chinook Charters,** 450 Campbell St., Tofino, BC V0R 2Z0 (✆ **800/665-3646** or 250/725-3431; www.chinookcharters.com), offers whale-watching trips in Clayoquot Sound on 8m (25-ft.) Zodiac boats. The company also conducts trips to Hot Springs Cove on its 10m (32-ft.) Chinook Key. March to October, **Jamie's Whaling Station,** 606 Campbell St.,

Tofino, BC V0R 2Z0 (© **800/667-9913** or 250/725-3919;), uses a glass-bottomed 20m (65-ft.) power cruiser as well as a fleet of Zodiacs for tours to watch the gray whales. A combined Hot Springs Cove and whale-watching trip aboard a 10m (32-ft.) cruiser can be booked year-round. Fares for both companies' expeditions generally start at C$75 (US$47) per person for a 3-hour tour; customized trips can run as high as C$200 (US$124) per person for a full day.

March to November, **Remote Passages,** Meares Landing, 71 Wharf St., Tofino, BC V0R 2Z0 (© **800/666-9833** or 250/725-3330; www.remotepassages.com), runs daily 2½-hour whale-watching tours in Clayoquot Sound on Zodiac boats, costing C$50 (US$31) for adults and C$35 (US$22) for children under 12. The company also conducts a 7-hour whale-watching/hot springs trip at C$75 (US$47) for adults and C$50 (US$31) for children under 12. Reservations are recommended.

For land-based bird watching, contact local naturalist/science writer Adrienne Mason of **Rainforest Communications** (© **250/725-2878**). She knows the area and can customize a tour depending on your needs.

**Hot Springs Cove,** accessible only by water, is a natural hot spring about 67km (41 miles) north of Tofino. Take a water taxi, sail, canoe, or kayak up to Clayoquot Sound to enjoy swimming in the steaming pools and bracing waterfalls. A number of kayak outfitters and boat charters offer trips to the springs.

## RAINY DAY ACTIVITIES

You can browse books at the **Wildside Booksellers and Espresso Bar,** Main Street (© **250/745-4222**), or get a massage or salt glow at the **Ancient Cedars Spa** at the Wickaninnish (© **250/725-3100**).

You can also check out the galleries. The **Eagle Aerie Gallery,** 350 Campbell St. (© **250/725-3235**), constructed in the style of a Native Indian Longhouse, features the innovative work of Tsimshian artist Roy Henry Vickers. The **House of Himwitsa,** 300 Main St. (© **250/725-2017**), is also owned/operated by Native Indians. The quality and craftsmanship of the shop's artwork, masks, baskets, totems, gold and silver jewelry, and apparel are excellent. The **Island Folk Artisans Gallery,** 120 4th St. (© **250/725-3130**), represents mainly art from Vancouver Island artists. The themes are often trees, wildlife, and crafts made out of wood or seashells, a lasting memory of your trip. You can find the new age side of Tofino in the **Reflecting Spirit Gallery,** 441 Campbell St. (© **250/725-4229**), which offers medicine wheels, rocks, and crystals, as well as a great selection of native art, carvings, wood crafts, and pottery.

## WHERE TO STAY

The 94 campsites on the bluff at **Green Point** are maintained by the Pacific Rim National Park (© **250/726-7721**). The grounds are full every day in July and August, and the average wait for a site is 1 to 2 days. Leave your name at the ranger station when you arrive to be placed on the list. You're rewarded for your patience with a magnificent ocean view, pit toilets, fire pits, pumped well water, and free firewood (no showers or hookups). Sites in July and August are C$14 to C$20 (US$9–US$12) and in the shoulder season C$12 to C$18 (US$8–U$11). The campground is closed October to March.

The **Bella Pacifica Resort & Campground,** 3.5km (2 miles) south of Tofino on the Pacific Rim Highway (P.O. Box 413), Tofino, BC V0R 2Z0 (© **250/725-3400;** www.bellapacifica.com), is privately owned and has 165 campsites from which you can walk to Mackenzie Beach or take the resort's private nature trails to Templar Beach. Flush toilets, hot showers, water, laundry, ice, fire pits, firewood, and full and partial hookups are available. Rates are C$18 to C$36 (US$11–US$22) per two-person campsite. Reserve at least a month in advance for a summer weekend.

## IN UCLUELET

**Ocean's Edge B&B** This remarkable little B&B sits on its own tiny peninsula jutting out into the Pacific, with only a thicket of interwoven hemlocks sheltering it from the wind and the surf of the ocean, which roars up surge channels on either side. Rooms are pleasant and spotless, without being opulent. The real attractions are the scenery and the wildlife, which abound. Owners Bill and Susan McIntyre installed a skylight in the kitchen so breakfasting guests could keep an eye on the pair of bald eagles and their chicks nesting in a 200-year-old Sitka spruce in the driveway. The former chief naturalist of Pacific Rim National Parks, host Bill McIntyre, is a font of information and also does nature tours.

855 Barkley Crescent, Box 557, Ucluelet, BC V0R 3A0. ✆ **250/726-7099.** Fax 250/726-7090. www.oceansedge.bc.ca. 3 units. C$105–C$120 (US$65–US$74) double. Breakfast included. MC, V. 2-night minimum on long weekends, holidays, and high season. No children permitted. **Amenities:** Nonsmoking facility. *In room:* Binoculars.

**A Snug Harbour Inn** A beautiful cliff top B&B overlooking its own little bay, A Snug Harbour Inn makes the most of its location. There are several large viewing decks (one with a hot tub), and guests can make use of a monster-size telescope to watch the sea lions on the reef just offshore. The inn is luxurious—the rooms are spacious, with queen- or king-size beds, opulent bathrooms, and jetted tubs. The heart-shaped tub with a waterfall may be a bit over the top, but who's complaining? Owner Skip Rowland had the inn built by a shipwright, and the craftsmanship shows. The nautical theme is carried out in the decor. If you visit during the winter storm season and the wind blows full gale force, Skip will put either a C$50 (US$31) bill under your pillow or provide a chilled bottle of champagne for your storm-viewing pleasure.

460 Marine Dr., Box 367, Ucluelet, BC V0R 3A0. ✆ **888/936-5222** or 250/726-2686. www.awesomeview.com. 4 units. May–Sept C$200–C$280 (US$124–US$174) double; Oct–Apr C$180–C$200 (US$112–US$124) double. Breakfast included. MC, V. **Amenities:** Jacuzzi; nonsmoking rooms. *In room:* Fridge, coffeemaker, hair dryer.

## IN TOFINO

**The Clayoquot Wilderness Resort** ★ The latest in absolute luxury in the area, the Clayoquot Wilderness Resort (CWR) floats alone in splendid isolation on Quoit Bay, about a half-hour boat ride from Tofino. Guests are encouraged to use the lodge as base camp for exploring the natural beauty of the sound. The CWR has set up a number of forest trails nearby and also runs trips out to Hot Springs Cove, as well as horseback riding excursions and mountain-biking trips. (Most of these activities are charged separately.) There are also spots to fly-fish or simply laze in the sun. Meals, prepared by noted West Coast chef Timothy May, are included and served up with a view of Clayoquot Sound. A luxurious spa and wellness center opened in June 2001. Surrounded by lush rain forest, the spa offers a range of treatments; weather permitting, massages can be done outside on the cedar deck. For the ultimate pampered outdoor experience try the Outpost camp, located a short boat ride away from the resort on the Bedwell River. Ten luxurious prospector tents, decorated with handmade Adirondack furniture, Persian carpets, and period accessories, welcome the guests for an adult camping experience. Gourmet food and wine plus a range of activities such as horseback riding, sailing, kayaking, and fishing are included in the Outpost package (2-night minimum stay, May–Sept only).

P.O. Box 130, Tofino, BC V0R 2Z0. ✆ **888/333-5405** in North America or 250/725-2688. Fax 250/726-8558. www.wildretreat.com. 16 units, 10 camps. March 15–Nov 30 C$269–C$489 (US$167–US$303) per person in double accommodation. Outpost camp May 24–Sept 30 C$575 (US$357) per person, includes all activities, meals, and transfer to and from Tofino. AE, MC, V. Parking provided in Tofino. **Amenities:** Restaurant, bar; spa; Jacuzzi; sauna; watersports equipment; tour desk; massage; nonsmoking rooms. *In room:* TV/VCR, hair dryer, iron.

**The Inn at Tough City** This is possibly Tofino's nicest small inn and certainly the quirkiest. Built in 1996 from salvaged and recycled material, it's filled with antiques, stained glass, and bric-a-brac. The rooms are spacious, and several feature soaker tubs, fireplaces, or both. Crazy Ron and Johanna are the innkeepers.

350 Main St., P.O. Box 8, Tofino, BC V0R 2Z0. ✆ **877/725-2021** or 250/725-2021. Fax 250/725-2088. www.alberni.net/toughcity. 6 units. Mar 1–Feb 28 C$75–C$175 (US$47–US$109) double. MC, V. **Amenities:** Laundry service; nonsmoking rooms. *In room:* TV.

**Middle Beach Lodge** This beautiful lodge/resort complex is on a headland overlooking the ocean. The rustic look was accomplished by using largely recycled beams, and the result is very pleasant. Accommodations range from simple lodge rooms to cabins with waterside decks, soaker tubs, gas fireplaces, and kitchenettes. All guests have access to a lofty common room overlooking the ocean. It's a good place to pour a coffee or something stronger and look out over the waves crashing in.

P.O. Box 100, Tofino, BC V0R 2Z0. ✆ **250/725-2900.** Fax 250/725-2901. www.middlebeach.com. 13 units, 19 cabins. C$110–C$165 (US$68–US$102) double; C$165–C$275 (US$102–US$171) suite; C$175–C$370 (US$109–US$229) single cabin; C$160–C$295 (US$99–US$183) duplex cabin; C$110–C$210 (US$68–US$130) triplex cabin; C$125–C$195 (US$78–US$121) sixplex suite. AE, MC, V. **Amenities:** Exercise room; tour desk; laundry service; nonsmoking facility. *In room:* TV/VCR, kitchenette, coffeemaker.

**Red Crow Guest House** While the Wickaninnish and other coastal lodges show you the wild, stormy side of the coast, the Red Crow displays a kinder, subtler beauty. By the sheltered waters of Clayoquot Sound, this pleasant Cape Cod cottage looks like it could be set on a lake in Michigan or northern Ontario. That is, until you paddle 15m (50 ft.) out in a canoe or rowboat (free for guests) and see the glaciers. Oh, and twice a day the water disappears completely with the tide. Rooms here are large and pleasant, with queen beds and 1920s-style furnishings. On the lower level of the large house, they have their own porch and look out on a fabulous view of the sound.

Box 37, 1084 Pacific Rim Hwy., Tofino, BC V0R 2Z0. ✆ and fax **250/725-2275.** www.bbhost.com/redcrowtofino. 3 units. C$115–C$160 (US$71–US$99) double. Extra person C$20 (US$12). V. *In room:* Fridge, coffeemaker.

**The Wickaninnish Inn** ★★★ No matter which room you book in this beautiful new cedar, stone, and glass lodge, you'll wake to a magnificent view of the untamed Pacific. The inn is on a rocky promontory, surrounded by an old-growth spruce and cedar rain forest and the sprawling sands of Chesterman Beach. You do have to make some choices: select king- or queen-size beds and decide whether you want a room with an ocean view from the tub. Rustic driftwood, richly printed textiles, and local artwork highlight the rooms, each of which features a fireplace, down duvet, soaker tub, and private balcony. Winter storm-watching packages have become so popular that the inn is as busy in winter as it is in summer. The Pointe Restaurant (see "Where to Dine," below) and On-the-Rocks Bar offers an oceanfront view. The staff can arrange whale-watching, golfing, fishing, and diving packages. No-Stress Express packages include air transport and accommodations.

Osprey Lane at Chesterman Beach, P.O. Box 250, Tofino, BC V0R 2Z0. ✆ **800/333-4604** in North America or 250/725-3100. Fax 250/725-3110. www.wickinn.com. 46 units. Mar–FebC$230–C$420 (US$143–US$260) double. Special packages available year-round. Wheelchair-accessible units available. AE, DC, MC, V. Drive 5km (3 miles) south of Tofino toward Chesterman Beach to Osprey Lane. **Amenities:** Restaurant, bar; spa; concierge; in-room massage; babysitting; nonsmoking facility. *In room:* TV, dataport, minibar, coffeemaker, hair dryer, iron.

## WHERE TO DINE

### IN UCLUELET

Fine dining is only just beginning in this coast town, as urban refugees with a flair for cooking arrive and try to make a go of it. The **Matterson Teahouse and Garden,** 1682 Peninsula Road (✆ **250/726-2200**), is a great spot for lunch; sandwiches, salads, and a great chowder are served in the cute dining room. Somewhat less ambitious but still good is the **Eagle's Nest Marine Pub,** 140 Bay St. (✆ **250/726-7515**), open Monday to Saturday 10am to midnight and Sunday 10am to 10pm.

### IN TOFINO

If you're just looking for a cup of java and a snack, it's hard to beat the **Coffee Pod,** 151 Fourth St. (✆ **250/725-4246**), a laid-back, semi-granola kind of place at the entrance to town. The Pod, open 7am to 6pm, (check for seasonal hours) also does an excellent breakfast. Main courses are C$7 to C$10 (US$4.35–US$6). The **Common Loaf Bakeshop,** 180 First St. (✆ **250/725-3915**), open 8am to 9pm, is locally famous as the gathering place for granola lovers, hippies, and other reprobates back when such things mattered in Tofino. At the "far" end of town, the Loaf does baked goods really well and a healthy lunch or dinner can be had for C$6 to C$9 (US$3.70–US$6). Liquids include herbal teas, coffee, juices, and wine and beer.

**The Pointe Restaurant** ★★★ PACIFIC NORTHWEST This restaurant is perched on the water's edge at Chesterman Beach, where a 280° view of the roaring Pacific is the backdrop to a dining experience that can only be described as pure Pacific Northwest. Top chef Jim Garraway applies his talents to an array of local ingredients, including Dungeness crab, spotted prawns, halibut, salmon, quail, lamb, and rabbit. His signature version of bouillabaisse, Wickaninnish Potlatch, is a chunky, fragrant blend of soft and firm fish, shellfish, and vegetables simmered in a thick seafood broth. Other offerings include delectable appetizers like goat-cheese tarts and shaved fennel salad, and entrees like grilled lamb chops with new potatoes, fresh artichokes, and sea asparagus. Garraway's signature dessert—a double-chocolate mashed-potato brioche—is superb when accompanied by a glass of raspberry wine.

The Wickaninnish Inn, Osprey Lane at Chesterman Beach. ✆ **250/725-3100.** Reservations required. Main courses C$29–C$32 (US$18–US$20). MC, V. Daily 8am–2:30pm, 2–5pm (snacks), 5–9:30pm.

**The RainCoast Cafe** WEST COAST This cozy restaurant, just off the main street, has developed a deserved reputation for some of the best—and best value—seafood and vegetarian dishes in town. To start off, try the popular RainCoast salad—smoked salmon, sautéed mushrooms, and chèvre cheese on a bed of greens, with maple balsamic vinaigrette. Fresh fish is a big part of the cuisine, and the menu is supplemented by a catch-of-the-day special. Mainstays include seafood and Asian style noodle dishes, such as the prawns, scallops, and clams served on soba noodles with toasted cashew and miso sauce.

120 Fourth St. © 250/725-2215. www.raincoastcafe.com. Main courses C$12–C$24 (US$7–US$15). AE, MC, V. Daily 11:30am–3pm and 5–10pm; in the winter dinner only.

## 5 Vancouver Island's East Coast: Parksville to Campbell River & Quadra Island

Vancouver Island's east coast is lined with long sandy beaches, world-class golf courses, and fishing resorts. Parksville and neighboring Qualicum Beach are longtime favorites for family vacations. With miles of beach for the kids and six local golf courses for the parents, these twinned towns are the perfect base for a relaxing vacation. Comox and Courtenay, 61km (38 miles) north, are another set of inter-grown beach towns with access to great sea kayaking and tours to fossil digs. Campbell River (pop. 29,000), 46km (29 miles) farther north, is by far the most famous salmon fishing center in British Columbia, with many long-established fishing resorts that have hosted everyone from the Shah of Iran to John Wayne to Goldie Hawn. A short ferry ride across Discovery Channel from Campbell River is Quadra Island, a mountainous island with one of the best First Nations museums in Canada.

### ESSENTIALS

**VISITOR INFORMATION** For information on Qualicum Beach, contact **Qualicum Beach Visitor Information Centre,** 2711 W. Island Highway, Qualicum Beach, BC, V9K 2C4 (© **250/752-9532;** fax 250/752-2923; www.qualicum.bc.ca). The **Parksville Visitor Information Centre** is at 1275 E. Island Highway (P.O. Box 99), Parksville, BC, V9P 2G3 (© **250/248-3613;** fax 250/248-5210; www.chamber.parksville.bc.ca). For more information on the Comox/Courtenay area, contact the **Comox Valley Visitor Info Centre,** 2040 Cliffe Ave., Courtenay, BC, V9N 2L3 (© **888/357-4471** or 250/334-3234; www.tourism-comox-valley.bc.ca). The **Campbell River Visitor Info Centre** is at 1235 Shopper's Row, Campbell River, BC V9W 2C7 (© **250/287-4636;** www.campbellriverchamber.ca/vic.html), or mail to Box 400, Campbell River, BC V9W 5B6.

**GETTING THERE** **By Plane** The **Campbell River and District Regional Airport,** located south of Campbell River off Jubilee Parkway, has regularly scheduled flights on commuter planes to and from Vancouver and Seattle. **Air Canada** (© **888/247-2262**) hosts flights on Air BC from Vancouver to Campbell River. **Pacific Coastal Airlines** (© **800/663-2872**; www.pacific-coastal.com) also flies here.

Harbor-to-harbor service between Vancouver and Campbell River is available late June to Labour Day via **Air Rainbow** (© **250/287-8371**; www.air-rainbow.com). You can also fly from Seattle's Lake Washington or Lake Union to Campbell River harbor mid-May to late September on **Kenmore Air** (© 800/543-9595; www.kenmoreair.com).

**Comox Valley Regional Airport,** north of Comox off Ryan Road, has daily scheduled flights to and from Vancouver. You can book flights through **Air Canada** (see above) for service to Comox on its subsidiary **Air BC**. The airport is also served by **Pacific Coastal Airlines** (see above) and **WestJet** (© **877/952-4638**; www.westjet.com).

**By Train** The **E&N Railiner** operates daily between Courtenay and Victoria, with stops in Parksville and Qualicum Beach.

**By Bus** **Laidlaw Coach Lines** (✆ **250/385-4411**) operates four buses daily with service to and from Victoria and Port Hardy via Nanaimo, with stops in Parksville, Qualicum Bay, Courtenay, and Campbell River. One-way fare from Nanaimo to Campbell River is C$30 (US$19).

**By Ferry** **BC Ferries** (✆ **888/724-5223** or 604/444-2890; www.bcferries.bc.ca) operates a 75-minute crossing from Powell River on the mainland to Little River, just north of Comox to Powell River. The one-way passenger fare is C$8 (US$5) per passenger and C$25 (US$16) per vehicle.

**By Car** From Nanaimo, the Island Highway (Highway 19) links Parksville, Courtenay, and Campbell River with points north. Campbell River is 52km (32 miles) north of Courtenay and 266km (165 miles) north of Victoria.

## EXPLORING THE EAST COAST

**Parksville** (pop. 9,576) and **Qualicum Beach** (pop. 6,874) are near the most popular beaches on Vancouver Island: Spending a week on the beach here is a family tradition for many longtime residents. Parksville claims to have the warmest ocean-water beaches in all Canada. **Rathtrevor Beach Provincial Park** is a popular place for swimming and sunbathing.

Facing each other across the Courtenay River Estuary, the twin towns **Comox** (pop. 11,847) and **Courtenay** (pop. 18,420) provide a bit of urban polish to a region rich in beaches, outdoor recreation, and dramatic land- and seascapes. The highlight of the **Courtenay District Museum & Paleontology Centre,** 207 4th St. (✆ **250/334-0686;** www.courtenaymuseum.ca), is a 12m (39-ft.) cast skeleton of an elasmosaur, a crocodile-like Cretaceous marine reptile. July and August, the museum leads 3-hour **fossil tours** of its paleontology lab and to a local fossil dig; C$15 (US$9) adults, C$12 (US$7) seniors and students, C$7.50 (US$4.65) children, or C$45 (US$28) per family. Call ahead for reservations. Admission to the museum alone is C$3 (US$1.85) adults and C$2.50 (US$1.55) seniors and children 12 and over. Summer hours are Monday to Saturday 10am to 5pm and Sunday 12 to 4pm. Winter hours are Tuesday to Saturday 10am to 5pm.

**The Museum at Campbell River,** 470 Island Highway ✆ **250/287-3103.** www.crmuseum.ca, is worth seeking out. This large and captivating museum is devoted to carvings and artifacts from the local First Nations tribes; especially fine is the display of contemporary carved wooden masks. Also compelling is the sound-and-light presentation *The Treasures of Siwidi,* which uses masks to retell an ancient native Indian myth. Another gallery houses a replica of a pioneer-era cabin and a collection of photos and tools from the early days of Vancouver Island logging. The 30-seat theater offers a couple of short films; one, *War of the Land Canoes,* is a 1914 documentary shot in local native villages. The gift shop is one of the best places in Campbell River to buy authentic native art and jewelry. The museum is open mid-May to September daily 10am to 5pm; and October to mid-May Tuesday Sunday noon to 5pm. Admission is C$5 (US$3.10) adults, C$3.75 (US$2.35) seniors and students, C$12 (US$7) family, free for children under 6.

**Quadra Island** sits right across Discovery Channel from Campbell River. The main reason to make the 10-minute ferry passage (C$4.50/US$2.80 per passenger, C$12/US$7 per vehicle) is to visit the excellent **Kwakiutl Museum and Cultural Center** ★, WeiWai Road in Cape Mudge Village

(**© 250/285-3733**), www.island.net/~kmccchin). The museum has one of the world's best collections of artifacts, ceremonial masks, and tribal costumes once used by the Cape Mudge Band in elaborate potlatch ceremonies. The Canadian government outlawed the potlatch in 1922 as part of a short-lived enforced-assimilation policy. During this time, the artifacts in the Kwakiutl Museum were removed to museums and private collections in eastern Canada and England, where they were preserved and cataloged. The collection was repatriated to the Cape Mudge Band in the early 1990s, when the tribe built the present spectacular museum. From June through September the museum is open Monday through Saturday from 10am to 4:30pm and Sunday from noon to 4:30pm. The rest of the year it's open Tuesday to Saturday 10am to 4:30pm. Admission is C$3 (US$1.85) adults, C$2 (US$1.20) seniors and students, C$1 (US60¢) children 6 to 12, children under 6 free. The road to the museum is not well marked. From the ferry, take Cape Mudge Road south about 5km (3 miles); watch for signs for WeWay Road and a hand-painted sign saying museum.

## SPORTS & OUTDOOR ACTIVITIES

**DIVING** The decommissioned **HMCS *Columbia*** was sunk in 1996 near the sea-life-rich waters of Seymour Narrows off the Quadra Island's west coast. For information on diving to this artificial reef and on other diving sites (with enticing names like Row and Be Damned, Whisky Point, Copper Cliffs, and Steep Island) in the Campbell River area, contact **Beaver Aquatics** (**© 250/287-7652;** www.connected.bc.ca/~baquatics).

**FISHING** Between Quadra Island and Campbell River, the broad Strait of Georgia squeezes down to a narrow mile-wide passage called Discovery Channel. All the salmon that entered the Strait of Juan de Fuca near Victoria to spawn in northerly rivers funnel down into this tight constriction, a churning waterway with 4m (13-ft.) tides.

However, fishing isn't what it once was in Campbell River, when tyee and coho salmon regularly tipped the scales at 34kg (75 pounds). Some salmon runs are now catch-and-release only, while others are open for limited catches; many fishing trips are now billed as much as wildlife adventures as hunting-and-gathering expeditions.

If you'd like to get out onto the waters and fish, be sure to call ahead and talk to an outfitter or the tourist center to find out what fish are running during your visit and if the seasons have been opened. Because of plummeting numbers of salmon and of recent treaties with the United States, the next few years will see even more greatly restricted fishing seasons in the waters off Vancouver Island. Don't be disappointed if there's no salmon fishing when you visit or if the salmon you hook is catch-and-release only. For one thing, there are other fish in the sea: Not all types of salmon are as threatened as the coho and tyee, and fishing is also good for halibut and other bottom fish. And if you really just want to get out on the water and have an adventure, consider a wildlife-viewing boat tour, offered by many fishing outfitters.

There are dozens of fishing guides in the Campbell River area, with a range of services that extend from basic to pure extravagance. Expect to pay around C$70 (US$43) per hour for 4 to 5 hours of fishing with a no-frills outfitter. A flashier trip on a luxury cruiser can cost more than C$120 (US$74) per hour. The most famous guides are associated with the Painter's Lodge and its sister property, April Point Lodge. A few smaller fishing-guide operations include **Destiny Sportfishing**, 2653 Vargo Rd. (**© 250/286-9610**; www.destinyguide.bc.ca); **CR Fishing**

**Village**, 260 Island Highway (✆ **250/287-3630**); and **Larry Craig Salmon Charters**, 47 S. McLean St. (✆ **250/287-2592**. You can also check out the Info Centre's directory to fishing guides at www.campbellrivertourism.bc.ca/member/fishi.html.

Most hotels in Campbell River also offer fishing/lodging packages; ask when you reserve.

**GOLF** Greens fees at the following courses are C$35 to C$45 (US$22–US$28) for 18 holes. For more information, check out the Web site at **www.golfvancouverisland.com**.

There are six courses in the Parksville–Qualicum Beach area, and more than a dozen within an hour's drive. Here are two favorites: The **Eagle Crest Golf Club,** 2035 Island Highway (✆ **250/752-6311**), is a 18-hole, par-71 course with an emphasis on shot making and accuracy; and the public **Morningstar Golf Club,** 525 Lowry's Rd. (✆ **250/248-8161**), is an 18-hole, 6,417m (7,018-yd.) course with a par-72 rating.

One of the finest courses on Vancouver Island is the brand-new **Crown Isle Resort & Golf Community,** 339 Clubhouse Dr., Courtenay (✆ **888/338-8439** or 250/703-5050; www.crownisle.com). This lavish 18-hole links-style championship golf course has already hosted the Canadian Tour and Canadian Junior Men's Tournament. Because it was carved out of a dense forest, you may see wildlife grazing on the fairway and roughs at the **Storey Creek Golf Club,** Campbell River (✆ **250/923-3673**). Gentle creeks and ponds also wind through this course.

**KAYAKING** With the Courtenay Estuary and Hornby, Tree, and Denman islands an easy paddle away, sea kayaking is very popular in this area. **Comox Valley Kayaks**, 2020 Cliffe Ave., Courtenay (✆ **888/545-5595** or 250/334-2628; www.comoxvalleykayaks.com), offers rentals, lessons, and tours. A 3-hour introductory lesson is C$40 (US$25). A day trip to Tree Island goes for C$70 (US$43). Rentals start at C$20 (US$12) for 2 hours. **Tree Island Kayaking** (✆ **250/339-0580**; www.island.net/~tree) offers lessons (C$35/US$22), natural-history tours, and rentals. If you take a lesson you get a 50% discount off your first rental.

**SKIING** With the Courtenay Estuary and Hornby, Tree, and Denman islands an easy paddle away, sea kayaking is very popular in this area. **Comox Valley Kayaks**, 2020 Cliffe Ave., Courtenay (✆ **888/545-5595** or 250/334-2628; www.comoxvalleykayaks.com), offers rentals, lessons, and tours. A 3-hour introductory lesson is C$40 (US$25). A day trip to Tree Island goes for C$70 (US$43). Rentals start at C$20 (US$12) for 2 hours. **Tree Island Kayaking** (✆ **250/339-0580**; www.island.net/~tree) offers lessons (C$35/US$22), natural-history tours, and rentals. If you take a lesson you get a 50% discount off your first rental.

## WHERE TO STAY

### IN PARKSVILLE & QUALICUM BEACH

**Bahari B&B** ★ Bed-and-breakfasts come in all shapes and styles, but Bahari is unique for its attention to detail and its artistically exquisite sure-handedness. Decorated with a delicate Asian influence that's more Pacific Rim elegant than the usual clutter that typifies many B&Bs, this property could easily take pride of place in *Architectural Digest.* Each unit is uniquely outfitted. All rooms have original artwork, balconies, robes, and complimentary sherry. Guests are welcome in the sitting room, with its open staircase and incredible wood carvings, and in the more intimate TV room and library, with leather couches and fireplace. Follow the paths to the beach, frequented by seals and eagles, or soak in the hot tub perched above the beach, where you can watch ships ply the waters of the Georgia Strait.

In addition to the B&B rooms is a 1,200-sq.-foot, two-bedroom apartment, with one queen and two twin beds, fireplace, balcony, and kitchen. Kids are allowed in the apartment, which is separated from the main house by a breezeway. The apartment is available either with breakfast or without (self-catering), for a lower rate.

5101 Island Hwy., Qualicum Beach, BC, V9K 1Z1. ✆ **877/752-9278** or 250/752-9278. Fax 250/752-9038. www.baharibandb.com. 5 units. Feb–May (Spring) and Oct–Nov (Fall) C$85–C$135 (US$55–US$88), June–Sept (high season) C$125–C$185 (US$78–US$115) double; Spring and Fall C$120–C$190 (US$74–US$118), high season C$180–C$260 (US$112–US$161) 2-bedroom apt. High season 2-night minimum stay in apt. Single person deducts C$20 (US$12) per day. Add C$35 ($US22) per person per day. Breakfast included in rates. Weekly rates and packages available. AE, MC, V. Children accepted in apt; B&B guests must be 16 or older. **Amenities:** Golf course nearby; Jacuzzi; free laundry facilities; nonsmoking rooms; apartment rooms. *In room:* TV, hair dryer.

**Hollyford Guest Cottage** ★★ Hollyford Guest Cottage is a marvelous choice if you value the chance to admire fascinating objects and antiques. Bedrooms are large and stylish, and the hosts charming and thoughtful, but what really makes the Hollyford stand out is its fascinating collection of antiques and Canadiana. The lounge's carved black-walnut sideboard—rumored to have been designed for the Banff Springs Hotel—is simply amazing. You'll also see collections of early western Canadian landscape paintings, Native American jewelry, Inuit art, and an homage to the Mounties, complete with a full regalia uniform of red serge.

Each newly constructed, fully soundproofed guest room has heated floors, quality new and antique furniture, a small garden patio, a fireplace, a beautifully tiled bathroom with deep soaker tub, Aveda toiletries, and handmade local soaps. For the full breakfast served in the original dining room, your hosts will bring out the antique china, Waterford crystal, and silver from the glory days of the Canadian Pacific Railway. If you want to get a little exercise and see the local scenery, the hosts will also loan you one or both of their bicycles. *Note:* Smoking is not permitted.

106 Hoylake Rd. E. (at Memorial Ave.), Qualicum Beach, BC, V9K 1L7. ✆ **877/224-6559** or 250/752-8101. Fax 250/752-8102. www.hollyford.ca. 3 units. June–Sept C$165 (US$102) double. Oct–May C$135 (US$84) double. Rates include full breakfast and refreshment sideboard. Rates may vary during off-season. 3-night specials available. MC, V. Children must be 12 or older. **Amenities:** Golf course nearby; laundry service; same-day dry cleaning; nonsmoking rooms. *In room:* TV/VCR, hair dryer.

**Tigh-Na-Mara Resort Hotel** ★★ *Kids* This time-honored log-cabin resort just keeps getting better. Established in the 1940s on a forested waterfront beach (near Rathtrevor Beach Provincial Park), Tigh-Na-Mara has expanded over the years: more cottages, lodge-style rooms, and beautifully furnished condo-style suites with stunning ocean views, all log-built. Accommodation types include studio and one-bedroom lodge rooms, plus one- and two-bedroom cottages. If you're traveling with a group, the duplex cottages can be converted into a series of rooms large enough to sleep eight. The new ocean-side condo units all have views as well as balconies or patios. All rooms and cottages at Tigh-Na-Mara have fireplaces and full bathrooms, and almost all have a kitchen. The cottages are comfortably lived-in and homey, while the condos are new and lavish. New units are being added and older ones constantly renovated. The resort is also adding a new spa and health club and renovating its restaurant as this book goes to press.

Families will especially appreciate the lengthy list of supervised child-friendly activities (many of them free), such as swimming lessons, and small amenities like video rentals and babysitting (for a fee). Or, in season, take the family down to the water to try your hand at shellfishing (allowed on the resort's beach). The restaurant in the log-and-stone lodge serves an eclectic version of Northwest cuisine. There's a full children's menu, adjacent lounge, and Friday barbecues and dances in summer.

1095 E. Island Hwy., Parksville, BC, V9P 2E5. ✆ **800/663-7373** or 250/248-2072. Fax 250/248-4140. www.tigh-na-mara.com. 210 units. July–Aug C$109–C$249 (US$68–US$154) double. Rates vary throughout the year. Extra person C$5–C$10 (US$3.10–US$6). Weekly rates available. Varying minimum stays apply in mid-summer, on holidays, and weekends. AE, DC, MC, V. Free parking. One pet allowed per cottage Sept–June, add C$2 (US$1.20) per day. **Amenities:** Restaurant, bar; indoor pool; golf courses nearby; unlit tennis court; access to health club; sauna; paddle boats; bike rental; children's programs; concierge; tour/activities desk (summer); car-rental desk; business center; in-room massage; babysitting; coin-op laundry; laundry service; dry cleaning; nonsmoking rooms. *In room:* TV, fridge, coffeemaker.

## IN COURTENAY

**Kingfisher Oceanside Resort and Spa** ★★ Located 7km (4½ miles) south of Courtenay, this long-established resort has modernized with an added bank of beachfront suites and a classy spa. The older motel units are large, nicely furnished rooms with balconies or patios, most with views of the pool and the Strait of Georgia. The newer one-bedroom suites are splendid, each with a full kitchen, two TVs, fireplace, and balcony that juts out over the beach; most suites have a two-person whirlpool tub in addition to a full bathroom with heated tile floors. Our favorite is no. 401, on the end of the building, with banks of windows on two sides. Two rooms are available for people with disabilities.

The **Kingfisher restaurant** is one of the best places to eat in Courtenay. The spa offers a wide selection of treatments and body work. Trained technicians offer thalassotherapy baths and wraps, massage, reiki, and facials. Guests also have access to a steam cave. *Note:* Smoking is not permitted,

4330 Island Hwy. S, Courtenay, BC, V9N 9R9. ✆ **800/663-7929** or 250/338-1323. Fax 250/338-0058. www.kingfisherspa.com. 64 units. C$129 (US$80) double, C$170 (US$105) suite. Extra person C$10 (US$6). Golf, ski, fishing, spa, and women's wellness packages available. Senior discounts available. AE, DC, DISC, MC, V. Free parking. Pets allowed in 3 rooms, add C$7 (US$4.35). **Amenities:** Restaurant; outdoor pool; golf course nearby; unlit tennis court; exercise room; spa; Jacuzzi; sauna; canoe and kayak rentals; activities desk; courtesy limo; business center; 24-hour room service; massage; babysitting; coin-op laundry; laundry service; dry cleaning; nonsmoking rooms; executive-level rooms. *In room:* TV (suites w/VCR), dataport, fridge, coffeemaker, hair dryer.

## IN CAMPBELL RIVER

**Hotel Bachmair Suite Hotel** *Value* This hotel on the southern edge of town offers very large and beautifully furnished rooms at moderate prices. Accommodations range from standard hotel rooms to two-bedroom suites; one of the penthouse suites can sleep eight. The suites all come with large bedrooms, kitchens, sitting rooms, and dining areas. Furnishings are exquisite: leather couches, fine carpeting, and hand-painted armoires. Kitchens are fully equipped with china, utensils, and appliances. Most units have balconies and views of Discovery Passage. The hotel itself—wrapped in carved-wooden-rail balconies lined by flower boxes—is handsome in the Bavarian style so favored in Canada.

492 S. Island Hwy., Campbell River, BC V9W 1A5. ✆ **888/923-2849** or 250/923-2848. Fax 250/923-2849. www.hotelbachmair.com. 23 units. C$89–$140 (US$55–$87) double. Extra person C$10 (US$6). Off-season

rates available. Fishing charters arranged. AE, DC, MC, V. Free parking. Pets allowed, add C$5 (US$3.0) per night. **Amenities:** Restaurant, bar next door; golf course nearby; in-room massage; babysitting; coin-op laundry; laundry service; nonsmoking rooms. *In room:* TV, dataport, kitchen, fridge, coffeemaker, hair dryer.

**Painter's Lodge Holiday & Fishing Resort** ★ This resort has been a favorite fishing hideaway for film stars such as John Wayne, Bob Hope, Goldie Hawn, and Kurt Russell. Once you see the awe-inspiring wooded coastal location, you'll understand why. Built in 1924 on a point overlooking the Discovery Passage, the lodge retains a rustic grandeur, with spacious rooms and suites decorated in natural wood and pastels. Four secluded, self-contained cottages nestled near the lodge are also available for rent. Guests can enjoy all three meals and cocktails in the **Legends Dining Room,** Tyee Pub (offering burgers and pub food), and Fireside Lounge. Amenities include guided fishing trips, and jogging and hiking trails around the grounds. The Painter's Lodge is also popular and well-equipped for business conferences. Wheelchair accessible rooms are available. *Note:* It is requested that guests smoke outside. Common areas are nonsmoking.

1625 McDonald Rd., Box 460, Campbell River, BC V9W 5C1. © **800/663-7090** or 250/286-1102. Fax 250/286-0158. www.painterslodge.com. 94 units. C$184–C$479 (US$114–US$297) double, C$152–C$363 (US$94–US$225) cottage. Extra person C$15 (US$9). Off-season discounts available. AE, DC, MC, V. Closed Nov–Mar. **Amenities:** Restaurant, pub, and lounge; golf course nearby; 2 unlit tennis courts; heated outdoor pool; exercise room; Jacuzzi; bicycle; scooter; and kayak rentals; children's center; tour and activities desk; car rental desk; courtesy limo; in-room massage; babysitting; laundry service; same day dry cleaning; executive-level rooms. *In room:* TV, coffeemaker, hair dryer.

## 6 The Inside Passage: Prince Rupert & the Queen Charlotte Islands

The ferry cruise along British Columbia's **Inside Passage** ★ combines the best scenic elements of Norway's rocky fjords, New Zealand's majestic South Island, Chile's Patagonian range, and Nova Scotia's wild coastline. Once nearly inaccessible, this rugged 491km (304-mile) stretch of Pacific coast is now served by two BC Ferry lines. The **Inside Passage ferry** operates between **Port Hardy** on Vancouver Island and **Prince Rupert** on the mainland. Also departing from Port Hardy, the Discovery Coast's ***Queen of Prince Rupert*** connects with small, mostly First Nations communities along the fjords and islands of the central BC coast, including Namu, Bella Bella, Shearwater, Ocean Falls, and Klemtu.

The BC Ferries system also connects Prince Rupert to the remote **Queen Charlotte Islands,** the ancestral home of the Haida tribe. The misty archipelago known as **Haida Gwaii** has been designated as a UNESCO World Heritage Site and is managed by the Gwaii Haanas Reserve. Amid the lush old-growth Sitka spruce in this temperate rain forest are the remains of untouched Haida villages abandoned over 400 years ago.

### ESSENTIALS

**VISITOR INFORMATION** The **Prince Rupert Visitor Info Centre,** Ste 215, Cow Bay Rd., Prince Rupert, BC V8J 1A2 (© **800/667-1994** in Canada, or 250/624-5637; fax 250/627-0992; www.tourismprincerupert.com), is on the waterfront about 2km (1¼ miles) from Highway 16; now the pickup and drop-off point for the airport. It's open year-round, Monday to Saturday 8am to 4pm, Monday to Friday 5:30 to 9pm, and Sunday 8 to 11am and 5:30 to 9pm (all day in the summer). The **Queen Charlotte Islands Visitor Info Centre,** 3220 Wharf St. (Box 189), Queen Charlotte, BC V0T 1S0 (© **250/559-8316;**

www.qcinfo.com), is open May to September daily 8am to 8pm. For more information, contact **Gwaii Haanas,** Box 37, Queen Charlotte City, BC V0T 1S0 (© **250/559-8818;** http://parkscan.harbour.com/gwaii), or the Queen Charlotte Islands Visitor Info Centre (© **250/559-8316;** www.qcinfo.com).

**GETTING THERE By Plane Air Canada** (© **888/247-2262**), through its regional subsidiaries, provides service between Vancouver and the Prince Rupert Airport, located east of the city off Highway 16. A new small, regional airline, **Hawk Air** (© **866/429-5247** or 800/487-1216; www.hawkair.net), is also offering daily service from Vancouver to Prince Rupert.

**Air Canada** also provides scheduled daily flights to the Sandspit Airport on northern Moresby Island. The small carrier **Montair** (© **888/666-8247** or 604/946-6688) flies several days a week from Vancouver to Masset, on Graham Island (flights depart either Vancouver International South Terminal or Boundary Bay; ask for a preference when making reservations). **Harbour Air** (© **800/689-4234** or 250/627-1341 in Prince Rupert; www.harbour-air.com) has scheduled seaplane flights daily from Prince Rupert to Masset and a few times weekly to Sandspit and Queen Charlotte City, and they also offer charters and flight-seeing tours. Many other charter seaplane companies offer transport around the islands as well as flight-seeing trips.

**By Train VIA Rail** (© **888/VIA-RAIL** or 800/561-8630; www.viarail.ca) departs from Prince Rupert on Wednesday, Friday, and Sunday at 8am and arrives in Prince George at 8:10pm. The train follows the same route as the Yellowhead Highway along the scenic Skeena River valley. At Prince George, travelers can continue east into Alberta and beyond or southwest to Vancouver.

**By Ferry** ★ **BC Ferries**'s (© **888/223-3779** or 250/386-3431; www.bcferries.bc.ca) MV *Queen of the North* makes the daytime crossing from Port Hardy through the Inside Passage to Prince Rupert in 15 hours. Humpback whales, orcas, Dall porpoises, salmon, bald eagles, and sea lions line the route past the relatively uninhabited coast and around countless forested islands.

June to mid-October, the 125m (410-ft.) *Queen of the North* ferry crosses every other day, leaving Port Hardy at 7:30am and arriving in *Prince Rupert* at 10:30pm. The *Queen of Prince Rupert* travels the Discovery Coast, the name given to the central BC coastline, stopping at Bella Coola, Ocean Falls, Shearwater, McLoughlin Bay, and Klemtu. Both ferries briefly encounter open ocean before passing behind Calvert Island and entering Fitz Hugh Sound.

The ferries carry up to 750 passengers and 157 vehicles. You can wander around the ferry and lounge on inside and outside deck seating or rest in a private dayroom or overnight cabin. On board you'll find buffet-style dining, a cafeteria, a snack bar, a playroom, a business center, and a gift shop.

Mid-summer one-way fares between Prince Rupert and Port Hardy are C$99 (US$61) per car passenger or walk-on, C$233 (US$144) for a normal-size vehicle. A car with two passengers adds up to C$431 (US$267). Reservations are mandatory. The ship's cabins rent for between C$50 and C$60 (US$31–US$37), for day use.

In summer, the Discovery Coast's ***Queen of Prince Rupert*** has two direct ferry runs on Tuesday and Thursday to Bella Coola, plus a Saturday-departing circular run that goes north to Klemtu before returning to Port Hardy via Bella Coola. These trips depart from Port Hardy at 9:30am; the Tuesday and Saturday departures require a night on the boat. In high season, fares between Port

Hardy and Bella Coola are C$102.50 (US$64) per adult passenger and C$205 (US$127) for a car.

From Prince Rupert, you can continue north to Skagway, Alaska, on the **Alaska Marine Highway System ferry** (✆ **800/642-0066**), which docks at the same terminal. Or you can travel to the Queen Charlotte Islands on the **Prince Rupert–Skidegate ferry,** which leaves Prince Rupert late in the morning and arrives about 6½ hours later at Skidegate in the Queen Charlotte Islands. The one-way high season tickets are C$25 (US$16) for a passenger and C$93 (US$58) for most passenger vehicles.

**By Car** The 1,518km (941-mile) drive from Vancouver to Prince Rupert begins on the Sea-to-Sky Highway (**Highway 99**), which intersects the Cariboo Highway (Highway 97) after passing through Whistler, Pemberton, and Lillooet. The town of Prince George is 812km (503 miles) north of Vancouver. At this central junction, head east for 745km (462 miles) on the Yellowhead Highway (Highway 16).

**GETTING AROUND** In the Queen Charlotte Islands, the island-to-island **Skidegate–Alliford Bay ferry** operates 12 daily sailings between the main islands. The fare is C$4.50 (US$3) each way or C$12 (US$8) per vehicle. **Budget** (✆ **250/559-4675**), **Rustic Car Rentals** (✆ **250/559-4641**), **Tilden** (✆ **250/626-3318**), and **Thrifty** (✆ **250/559-8050**) have car-rental offices on the islands.

**SPECIAL EVENTS** During the second week in June, Prince Rupert hosts **Seafest** (✆ **250/624-9118**), which features a fishing derby, parades, games, food booths, the annual blessing of the fleet, and bathtub races.

## EXPLORING PRINCE RUPERT

**Prince Rupert** gets more than 18 hours of sunlight a day during summer. And despite its northerly location, this coastal city of 17,700 residents enjoys a mild climate most of the year. Mountain biking, cross-country skiing, fishing, kayaking, hiking, and camping are just a few of the region's popular activities. And northern British Columbia's rich native-Indian heritage has been preserved in its museums and archaeological sites.

**Museum of Northern British Columbia** This recently renovated museum displays artifacts created by the Tsimshian, Nisga'a, and Haida First Nations (among others), who have inhabited this area for more than 10,000 years. There are also artifacts and photographs from Prince Rupert's 19th-century European settlement. In summer, the museum sponsors a number of special programs, ranging from 2-hour archaeological boat tours of the harbor (which allow you to see the area's many active dig sites at ancestral villages that date back more than 5,000 years) to walking tours of the city. The excellent gift shop is one of the best places in town to buy native art. Also sponsored by the museum is the **Carving Shed,** a working studio located a block away on Market Place. Native carvers use the space to work on their art; visitors are welcome, but are encouraged to be discreet while the carvers concentrate. Save your ticket to the museum, as it will get you in free to *The Prince Rupert Story,* a 1-hour dramatization and slide show in the auditorium.

100 First Ave. ✆ **250/624-3207.** Fax 250/627-8009. www.museumofnorthernbc.com. Admission C$5 (US$3.10) adults, C$2 (US$1.20) students, C$1 (US60¢) children 6–11, C$10 (US$6) per family. MC, V. Parking available on street. Summer Mon–Sat 9am–8pm, Sun 9am–5pm; winter Mon–Sat 10am–5pm.

**North Pacific Cannery Museum** ★ Salmon canning was one of the region's original industries, back when the salmon run up the Skeena River was one of the greatest in North America. The province's oldest working salmon-cannery village, built on the waterfront of Inverness Passage in 1889, was home to hundreds of First Nations, Japanese, Chinese, and European workers and their families. Every summer, fishing fleets dropped off their catches at the cannery, where the salmon was packed and shipped out to world markets. This company-owned community reached its apex from 1910 to 1950, when the work force numbered 400 and the community grew to about 1,200; the cannery has been closed since 1968.

Now a National Historic Site, the North Pacific Cannery Village Museum complex includes the cannery building, various administration buildings and residences, the company store, a hotel, and a dining hall—a total of over 25 structures linked by a long boardwalk (the land is so steep here that most of the houses were built on wharves). Workers were segregated by race: the Chinese, Japanese, and Native Canadian workers had their own micro-neighborhoods along the boardwalk, all overseen by the European bosses. Guided tours of the cannery complex, offered on the hour, provide a very interesting glimpse into a forgotten way of life.

The **boardinghouse** is now open for B&B accommodations as the **Waterfront Inn**, with doubles going for C$45 (US$28); the **Cannery Café** and **Forge Broiler Bar** are open during museum hours, and the **Salmon House Restaurant** (✆ **250/628-3273**) is open 11am to 7pm, year round.

20km (12 miles) south of Prince Rupert in Port Edward. Mailing address: Box 1104, Prince Edward, BC, V0V 1G0. ✆ **250/628-3538.** http://district.portedward.bc.ca/northpacific. Admission C$8 (US$5) adults, C$7.50 (US$4.65) seniors and students, C$5.50 (US$3.40) children 6 and over, free for children under 6. May 1–Sept 30 daily 9am–6pm. Call for off-season hours. Take the Port Edward turnoff on Hwy. 16 and drive 5km (3 miles) past Port Edward on Skeena Drive.

## OUTDOOR ACTIVITIES

**HIKING & BIKING** **Far West Sports,** 212 Third Ave. W. (✆ **250/624-2568**), is one of the best sources for information about hiking and mountain-biking trails and directions. The area experiences annual as well as seasonal changes in trail conditions, and some hiking and backcountry ski areas are too challenging for beginners. This outfitter can supply clothing and equipment for camping, climbing, and skiing.

**KAYAKING & CANOEING** The waters surrounding Prince Rupert are tricky, and rough tidal swells and strong currents are common. **Eco Trek Adventures** (✆ **250/624-8311;** www.citytel.net/ecotreks) offers guided half-day trips (C$47/US$29) and 2-day expeditions to the grizzly sanctuary (C$595/US$369), among numerous other options. Single kayak rentals start at C$25 (US$16) for 2 hours or C$35 (US$22) for a half day.

## WHERE TO STAY

One and a half kilometers (1 mile) from the ferry terminal, the **Park Avenue Campground,** 1750 Park Ave. (✆ **250/624-5861;** fax 250/627-8009; mailing address: Box 612, Prince Rupert, BC V8J 4J5), has 97 full-hookup and tenting sites. Facilities include a laundry, hot showers, flush toilets, a playground, a mail drop, and pay phones. Make reservations in advance during summer because this campground is the best in the area. Rates are C$14 to C$19 (US$9–US$12) per campsite.

**Coast Prince Rupert Hotel** Right downtown, the Coast Prince Rupert offers views of the harbor and mountains from just about every room. Accommodations are large and comfortable, with refrigerators and minibars available by request. Friendly service and good dining options make this a fine lodging choice. Amenities include Charlie Hays Restaurant, which serves fresh local seafood; horse-race betting in the Turf Lounge; dancing at Bogey's Cabaret; a beer-and-wine store; and staff-arranged guided charter fishing boats in summer. 118 Sixth St., Prince Rupert, BC V8J 3L7. © **800/663-1144** or 250/624-6711. Fax 250/624-3288. www.coasthotels.com. 92 units. C$105–C$110 (US$65–US$68) double. Extra person C$10 (US$6). Family plan, corporate and off-season rates, and senior and AAA discounts available. AE, DC, DISC, MC, V. **Amenities:** Restaurant, lounge, club; golf course nearby; guest passes to health club; room service 6am–8pm; laundry service; same day dry cleaning; nonsmoking rooms; executive-level rooms. *In room:* A/C, TV w/movie channel, dataport, coffeemaker, hair dryer, iron.

**Crest Hotel** ★ If you're looking for one package that offers the best views, good dining, and beautifully furnished rooms, then you're looking for the Crest. Situated on the bluff's edge overlooking Tuck Inlet, Metlakata Pass, and the busy Prince Rupert harbor, the Crest is one of the finest hotels in northern British Columbia. The views are fabulous and the rooms nicely furnished, though in a style more 1980s than 21st century. The wood-paneled lobby and common rooms are gracious and opulent. The staff will happily set you up with fishing charters and sealife-viewing trips.

The coffee shop is open for three meals daily. The **Waterfront Restaurant,** with incredible views and patio dining, is one of the best places to eat. With a heated deck, Charley's Lounge has the city's best year-round view from a bar stool.

222 First Ave. W., Prince Rupert, BC, V8J 3P6. © **800/663-8150** or 250/624-6771. Fax 250/627-7666. www.cresthotel.bc.ca. 102 units. C$145–C$165 (US$90–US$102) rm double. C$179–C$249 (US$111–US$154) suite double. AE, MC, V. Free parking. Small pets allowed, add C$10 (US$6). **Amenities:** Restaurant, bar; golf course nearby; health club; Jacuzzi; sauna; room service (7am–10pm); dry cleaning; nonsmoking rooms; executive-level rooms. *In room:* TV w/pay movies, dataport, coffeemaker, hair dryer, iron.

## WHERE TO DINE

For 60 years, **Smile's Seafood Cafe,** 113 Cow Bay Rd. (© **250/624-3072**), has served seafood in every shape and form, from oyster burgers and seafood salads to heaping platters of fried fish. In the historic Cow Bay district, this small place is always busy during summer, but it's worth the wait. Main courses are C$7 to C$23 (US$4.35–US$14). It's open daily: summer 10am to 10pm and the rest of the year 11am to 9pm.

Right next door is **Breakers Pub** (© **250/624-5990**), a popular local pub with a harbor view and tasty fare like fish-and-chips, barbecued ribs, and stir-fries. It's open Monday to Saturday noon to 2am and Sunday noon to midnight.

## EXPLORING THE QUEEN CHARLOTTE ISLANDS

The misty and mysterious Queen Charlotte Islands inspired 19th-century painter Emily Carr to document her impressions of the towering carved-cedar totem poles and longhouses at the abandoned village of **Ninstints on Anthony Island.** The islands still lure artists, writers, and photographers wishing to experience their haunting beauty.

On **South Moresby Island,** you'll discover an array of rare fauna and flora, including horned puffins, Cassin's auklets, waterfowl raptors, gray whales, harbor seals, Steller's sea lions, and the world's largest black bears—all framed by moss-covered Sitka spruces, western hemlocks, and red cedars.

Graham Island's **Naikoon Provincial Park** is a 73,000ha (180,000-acre) wildlife reserve where whales can be spotted from the beaches, peregrine falcons fly overhead, and Sitka deer silently observe you as you walk along trails through the dense temperate rain forest. And just outside the town of Masset, the **Delkatla Wildlife Sanctuary** is a birder's paradise. It's the first landfall for the 113 migrating species of bird life that use the Pacific Flyway.

## GWAII HAANAS: THE LAND WHERE TIME STOOD STILL

**Ninstints** on Anthony Island is an ancient native-Indian village revered as sacred ground by the modern-day Haida tribe. According to local legends, the Haida people were created on this island by the "Raven who captured the Sun" after he brought the life-giving light to the dark, ice-encrusted earth. Cedar totem poles and longhouses stand in mute testament to a culture that flourished here for nearly 10,000 years. An epidemic spread by European explorers in the 1890s wiped out 90% of the Kunghit Haida tribe. The village was abandoned in 1900.

The island and the surrounding area are a designated UNESCO World Heritage Site called **Gwaii Haanas** (also known as South Moresby National Park Marine Reserve). Gwaii Haanas is accessible only by sea kayak and sailboat. For permission to enter the area, contact the **Haida Gwaii Watchmen** (© **250/559-8225**; mailing address: Box 609, Skidegate, Haida Gwaii, BC V0T 1S0), who act as site guardians and area hosts. Their office is at Second Beach, just north of Skidegate Landing on Highway 16.

### TOURS & EXCURSIONS

Longtime sea-kayak outfitter **Ecosummer Expeditions** (© **800/465-8884** or 250/674-0102; www.ecosummer.com) offers 1- and 2-week trips to Gwaii Haanas, with prices starting at C$1,495 (US$927). **Pacific Rim Paddling Company** (© **250/384-6103**; www.islandnet.com/~prp) has both 7- and 14-day kayak trips to the park, with prices from C$1,395 (US$865).

Sailing into Qwaii Haanas is another popular option, and most sailboat operators also have kayaks aboard for the use of guests. Sailing into Gwaii Haanas is another popular option, and most sailboat operators also have kayaks aboard for guests' use. **Bluewater Adventures** (© **888/877-1770** or 604/980-3800; www.bluewateradventures.ca) offers several 9- or 10-day tours of the park each year on its 20m (68-ft.) ketch, starting at C$2,500 (US$1,550). **Ocean Light II Adventures** (© **604/328-5339**; www.oceanlight2.bc.ca) offers 8-day Haida Gwaii sailings on a 22m (71-ft.) boat for C$2,560 (US$1,587).

### WHERE TO DINE & STAY

After a long day of exploration, stop in at **Daddy Cool's Neighbourhood Pub,** Collison Avenue at Main Street, Masset (© **250/626-3210**), for a pint and a fish tale or two. It's open Monday to Saturday noon to 2am and Sunday noon to midnight. The **Sandpiper Restaurant,** Collison Avenue at Orr Street in Masset (© **250/626-3672**), serves hearty portions of seafood, steaks, pasta dishes, sandwiches, and salads. **Oceana**, at 3119 3rd Ave. in Queen Charlotte City (© **250/559-8683**) offers both Chinese and Continental cuisine, and is open for lunch and dinner.

**Dorothy & Mike's Guest House** The atmosphere here has an island flavor: A large deck overlooks the Skidegate Inlet, while a serene garden surrounds the house. The warm, cozy guest rooms are filled with local art and antiques; one suite comes with a full kitchen and all three have private entrances. All guests have access to a common area with an entertainment center and reading library. The inn is within walking distance of the ocean, restaurants, and shopping.

3127 Second Ave. (Box 595), Queen Charlotte City, BC V0T 1S0. © **250/559-8439.** Fax 250/559-8439. www.qcislands.net/doromike. 8 units (4 with shared bathroom). May–Sept C$60 (US$37) double with shared bathroom, C$75 (US$47) double with private bathroom. Rates include breakfast. Off season rates available. MC, V. Drive 3.5km (2 miles) away from the Skidegate ferry terminal on Second Ave. *In room:* TV, no phone.

**Spruce Point Lodging** This rustic inn, overlooking the Hecate Strait, features rooms with private entrances as well as excellent views. Each unit has a fridge and a choice of either private shower or tub. Some rooms even have full kitchen facilities, and all have complimentary tea and coffee service. The shared balcony is used as a guest lounge. Your friendly hosts can arrange kayaking packages to the surrounding islands. *Note:* The inn prefers guests to smoke only on outside decks.

609 Sixth Ave., Queen Charlotte City (on Graham Island), BC V0T 1S0. © **250/559-8234.** www.qcislands.net/sprpoint. 7 units. C$65 (US$40) double. Kitchen unit C$10 (US$6) extra. Rates include full breakfast. MC, V. Drive about 15 minutes west on the main road away from the Skidegate ferry terminal, then turn left at Sam & Shirley's Grocery (the corner store). *In room:* TV, fridge, coffeemaker.

## 7 Cariboo Country to Prince George

North of Lillooet and south of Prince George along Highway 97, the Canadian Wild West hasn't changed much in the past century. This is **Cariboo Country,** a vast landscape that changes from alpine meadows and thick forests of Douglas fir and lodgepole pine to rolling prairies and granite-walled arid canyons as it encounters the gigantic glacial peaks of Coastal Mountains.

The **Sea-to-Sky Highway (Highway 99)** ★ from Vancouver through Whistler and the Cayoosh Valley eventually descends into the town of **Lillooet,** which was Mile 0 of the Old Cariboo Highway during the gold-rush days of the 1860s. Prospectors and settlers made their way north up what's now called the **Cariboo Gold Trail** (Highway 97).

Highway 97 follows the gold-rush trail through **70 Mile House, 100 Mile House, 108 Mile House, 150 Mile House, Williams Lake,** and **Quesnel,** to the gold-rich town of **Barkerville.** Many of these towns were named after the mile-marking roadhouses patronized by prospectors and settlers headed north to the goldfields.

### ESSENTIALS

**VISITOR INFORMATION** Contact the **Cariboo Chilcotin Coast Tourist Association,** 266 Oliver St., Williams Lake, BC V2G 1M1 (© **800/663-5885** or 250/392-2226; www.cariboocountry.org). For info on Prince George, contact the **Prince George Visitor Info Centre,** 1198 Victoria St., Prince George, BC V2L 2L2 (© **800/668-7646** or 250/562-3700; fax 250/563-3584; www.tourismpg.bc.ca).

**GETTING THERE By Plane Air Canada** (© **888/247-2262**), through regional subsidiaries, provides service to Prince George several times daily.

**By Train BC Rail**'s (© **604/984-5246;** www.bcrail.com/bcr/) *Cariboo Prospector* departs from the North Vancouver train station three times a week at 7am. The first section of the route (Vancouver to Lillooet) is extraordinarily scenic. The train continues north to 100 Mile House, Williams Lake, and Quesnel and terminates in Prince George. Prince George is a transfer point onto the mainline transcontinental VIA Rail system.

**Tips A Visual Treat**

Whether you travel by train or by car, the trip from Whistler to Cariboo Country is a visually exhilarating experience.

**By Bus** **Greyhound** buses (✆ **800/661-8747;** www.greyhound.ca) travel from Vancouver through the Cariboo to Prince George via Highway 1 and Highway 97, passing through 100 Mile House, Williams Lake, and Quesnel. Greyhound also has two buses daily among Prince George, Jasper, and Edmonton.

**By Car** The shortest and most scenic route to the Cariboo from Vancouver is along Highway 99 past Whistler to Lillooet and continuing to Highway 97 and turning north to 100 Mile House and points north. From Vancouver to Quesnel is 600km (372 miles). If you want to bypass dramatic but slow-speed Highway 99 and head straight up to the central Cariboo district, you can also take the Highway 1 expressway east from Vancouver and jump onto Highway 97 at Merritt.

## LILLOOET TO 100 MILE HOUSE

There's nothing subtle about the physical setting of **Lillooet** (pop. 2,058). To the west, the soaring glaciated peaks of the Coast Mountains are *right there,* filling up half the sky. To the east rise the steep desert walls of the Fountain Range, stained with rusty red and ochre. Cleaving the two mountain ranges is the massive and roaring Fraser River. From the Coast Range peaks immediately behind Lillooet to the surging river is a drop of nearly 2,700m (9,000 ft.), making an incredibly dramatic backdrop for a town.

Lillooet was Mile 0 of the 1860s **Cariboo Gold Rush Trail.** In 1858, a trail was established from the Fraser Valley goldfields in the south to the town of Lillooet. At the big bend on Main Street, a cairn marks MILE 0 of the original Cariboo Wagon Road.

From Lillooet, Highway 99 heads north along the Fraser River Canyon, affording lots more dramatic vistas before turning east to its junction with Highway 97. Immediately before the junction is the **Hat Creek Ranch** (✆ **800/782-0922** or 250/457-9722), built in 1861 as an inn for gold miners headed north during the Cariboo gold rush. The only extant roadhouse from this period, the Hat Creek remained a stagecoach inn until 1916. The grounds boast more than 20 restored period buildings, including a blacksmith shop, an 1894 barn, a wash house, and a stable. You can stroll the ranch grounds year-round; however, regular visitor services and guided tours are offered mid-May to Labour Day daily 10am to 6pm.

Named for the roadhouse inn that marked the hundredth mile north of Lillooet in the days of the Cariboo gold rush, **100 Mile House** (pop.1,978) is an attractive ranching community at the heart of a vast recreational paradise. There are thousands of lakes in the valleys ringing the town, and canoeing, fishing, and boating are popular activities. In winter, the gently rolling landscape, combined with heavy snowfalls, make 100 Mile House a major cross-country ski destination. Eight miles north of 100 Mile House is, naturally enough, **108 Mile Ranch,** another old-time community that sprung up during the Cariboo gold rush.

## WHERE TO STAY & DINE

### NEAR LILLOOET

**Tyax Mountain Lake Resort** Just outside the town of Gold Bridge, Tyaughton Lake is the perfect alpine setting for a romantic vacation. On its shores stands this huge log lodge, which offers guests luxurious accommodations and a host of activities, ranging from fly-out fishing and heli-skiing trips to barbecues on the lake. Guest rooms are comfortably furnished with queen-size beds. The resort restaurant serves Pacific Northwest cuisine.

Tyaughton Lake Rd., Gold Bridge, BC, V0K 1P0. ✆ **250/238-2221.** Fax 250/238-2528. www.tyax.com. 29 lodge rms, 5 chalets, 18 campsites. May and Oct–Dec C$124 (US$77) lodge double; C$258 (US$160) chalet quad. July–Sept C$144 (US$89) lodge double, C$298 (US$185) chalet quad, C$28 (US$17) campsite double. Extra person add C$20 (US$12) per night in lodge and chalet quad; add C$9 (US$6) per night in campsite. AE, MC, V. Free parking. Drive 2 hr. (92km/57 miles) from Lillooet on Hwy. 40 to Tyaughton Lake Rd. Follow signs to the resort. Pets allowed in chalets and campground. **Amenities:** Restaurant, bar; golf course nearby; unlit tennis court; exercise room; Jacuzzi; sauna; watersports equipment rentals; bike rentals; children's programs; tour/activities desk; business center; shopping arcade; coin-op laundry; nonsmoking rooms. *In room:* TV, dataport, hair dryer.

### NEAR 100 MILE HOUSE

**Best Western 108 Resort** ★ This upscale hotel and resort centers on its fantastic golf course, although even if you're not a duffer, there's a lot to like here. Other activities here include horseback riding, mountain biking and canoeing. In winter the golf course is transformed into a vast undulating cross-country center. Guest rooms are large and beautifully furnished, all with balconies that overlook either the golf course or a small lake. Golf, cross-country skiing, and horseback riding packages are available.

13km (8 miles) north of 100 Mile House. 4618 Telqua Dr., Box 2, 108 Mile Ranch, BC, V0K 2Z0. ✆ **800/667-5233** or 250/791-5211. Fax 250/791-6537. www.108resort.com. 62 units and 11 campsites. C$130–C$160 (US$81–US$99) double. Extra person C$10 (US$8). Campsites C$20 (US$12) per vehicle with a C$5 (US$3.10) charge for electricity. Off-season rates and packages available. AE, MC, V. **Amenities:** Restaurant (good Northwest cuisine), bar; indoor pool; Jacuzzi; sauna; bike and canoe rentals; stables. *In room:* A/C, TV, dataport, kitchenettes (some rooms), coffeemaker, hair dryer.

**Ramada Limited** The area's newest hotel, the Ramada has large, well-furnished rooms in a variety of configurations and styles. In addition to standard hotel rooms are suites with Jacuzzi tubs, fireplace and balcony, plus family suites with full kitchens. Complimentary continental breakfast is served. All in all, a very good value.

917 Alder Rd (Hwy 97), 100 Mils House, BC, V0K 2E0. ✆ **877/395-2777** or 250/395-2777. Fax: 250/395-2037. 36 units. From C$79 (US$49) double. Kitchens C$10 (US$6) extra. AE, MC, V. **Amenities:** Jacuzzi; sauna; coin-op laundry. *In room:* A/C, TV, dataport, coffeemaker.

## "ROUGHING IT" AT A GUEST RANCH

**Big Bar Guest Ranch** A long-time favorite for horse-focused family vacations, the Big Bar is a comfortable all-in-one destination with lots of recreational and lodging options. The centerpiece of the property is the **Harrison House,** a hand-hewn log home built by pioneers in the early 1900s. Summer outdoor activities here include horseback riding and pack trips, plus you can canoe, fish, hike, pan for gold, bike and go for buggy rides. In winter, the ranch remains open for cross-country skiing, snowshoeing, snowmobiling, ice-fishing and dog-sledding. All accommodations have private bathrooms. Lodge rooms all include three meals daily; some lodge rooms have an additional two-person sleeping loft. All cabins have full kitchens; rates do not include meals.

If you're looking for a comfortable and friendly place to take the family and enjoy the open air, this is one of the top spots in the Cariboo. In addition to the comfortable, no-fuss lodge rooms and cabins with fireplaces, there are teepees that sleep four (with bathrooms nearby), and a six-bedroom lodge (call for rates).

54km (35 miles) northwest of Clinton off Highway 97. P.O. Box 27, Jesmond, BC, V0K 1K0. © **250/459-2333.** Fax 250/459-2400. www.bigbarranch.com. 17 units. C$214 (U.S.$133) double in lodge rooms, including meals; extra person C$97 (US$60) adult, C$64 (US$40) child; C$149 (US$92) double in cabins (no meals included); teepees C$81 (US$50) double including meals. Campsites also available. MC, V. **Amenities:** Restaurant, lounge; Jacuzzi; game room; play ground; loads of outdoor activities. *In room:* No phones.

**Cariboo Lodge Resort** There's been a log lodge on this site for well over a century—the original Cariboo Lodge was built to serve the trading and social needs of frontier trappers and miners. Times have changed, and so has the Cariboo Lodge. This modern log resort hotel is built of local spruce and cedar, and with comfortable rooms and good facilities, the lodge makes a perfect destination for exploring central BC. The lodge makes it easy to get outdoors and enjoy yourself. The proprietors will organize horseback rides, whitewater rafting trips, fishing expeditions, mountain-biking tours and in winter, cross-country ski trips. Rooms are large and nicely, simply furnished—without the Old West clutter you'd normally expect in a lodge resort.

Box 459, Clinton, BC, V0K 1K0. © **877/459-7992** or 250/459-7992. www.cariboolodgebc.com. 23 units. C$80 (US$50) double. MC, V. **Amenities:** Family restaurant, Western pub. *In room:* A/C, TV, fridge, coffeemaker.

**Hills Health & Guest Ranch** This full-service spa and guest ranch combo offers guests a full complement of beauty and health treatments as well as outdoor activities such as horseback riding, hayrides, guided hiking trips, and cross-country skiing on more than 167km (100 miles) of private trails. The large guest rooms feature ranch-style natural pine decor. Also available are self-contained three bedroom chalet accommodations with kitchens and full bathrooms. There are 10 campsites on this amazing property as well, going for C$20 (US$12).

The spa offers a large variety of treatments, classes and programs, including weight loss and exercise classes, wellness workshops, massage, wraps, facials, reflexology, and body packs. Within the vast spa building are hydrotherapy pools, aerobics gym, exercise room, dry saunas and 15 treatment rooms. Ranch and recreational activities are as wide-ranging, from mountain bike touring to wildlife viewing to downhill skiing on the ranch's own ski area. Most of the spa and recreational options are combined into multi-day package holidays.

Hwy. 97, 108 Mile Ranch, P.O. Box 26, BC, V0K 2Z0 © **250/791-5225.** Fax 250/791-6384. www.grt-net.com/thehills. 46 units. C$119–C$160 (US$74–US$99) double. All-inclusive packages available. AE, DISC, MC, V. **Amenities:** 2 restaurants (cowboy favorites and spa cuisine, fondue and hot rock cooking), lounge; indoor pool; full-service spa; nearby golf course; bike and ski rental; game room; salon; massage. *In room:* A/C, TV, dataport.

## WILLIAMS LAKE TO BARKERVILLE

Unabashedly a ranch town, **Williams Lake** (pop. 11,398) is known across the West for its large hell's-a-poppin' rodeo, the **Williams Lake Stampede,** held the first weekend of July. Begun in the 1920s as an amusement for area cowboys, the stampede has grown into a 4-day festival. Rodeo cowboys from across Canada and the western United States gather here to compete for prizes in excess of C$80,000 (US$49,600). For more information, contact the Williams Lake Stampede, P.O. Box 4076, Williams Lake, BC V2G 2V2 (© **250/398-8388;**

www.imagehouse.com/rodeo). For tickets, call ✆ **800/717-6336.** Reserved seats are C$13 (US$8) adults and C$8 (US$5) seniors/children.

Williams Lake is also the Highway 20 gateway to the **Chilcotin,** the mountainous coastal area to the west. The Chilko-Chilcotin-Fraser river system running east from the Coast Mountains is a major whitewater-rafting destination, though not for the faint of heart—Lava Canyon on the Chilko River drops 1,500 feet in just 15 miles, with almost continuous Class IV rapids. **Chilko River Expeditions,** P.O. Box 4723, Williams Lake, BC V2G 2V7 (✆ **800-967-7238** or 250/398-6711; fax 250/398-8269; www.chilkoriverexpeditions.com;), leads a variety of trips on the three rivers, including a 1-day trip on the Chilcotin for C$93 (US$58) adults.

Highway 20 continues through a wild and rugged land of lakes and towering glacier-hung mountains on its way to **Bella Coola,** a native village on a Pacific inlet. From here, BC Ferries Discovery Coast service connects to **Port Hardy** on Vancouver Island, making this an increasingly popular sightseeing loop (see "The Inside Passage: Prince Rupert & the Queen Charlotte Islands," earlier).

Like most other towns throughout the Cariboo District, **Quesnel** (pop. 8,588) was founded during the gold-rush years in the 1860s. After the long overland journey from Lillooet, the prospectors turned east and followed the Quesnel River to the gold fields near Barkerville and Wells. From Quesnel on Highway 26 east, drive 87km (58 miles) deep into the moss-covered forests of the Cariboo Mountains, where moose, black bears, and deer are often seen on the road. At the end of the paved road is **Barkerville** ★, one of the most intact ghost towns in Canada.

The 1860 Cariboo Gold Rush was the reason thousands of miners made their way to this boom town on the banks of Williams Creek. Barkerville was founded after a British immigrant, Billy Barker, discovered one of the region's richest gold deposits 50 feet below the water line in the summer of 1862. The town sprang up practically overnight—and died almost as quickly when the gold ran out.

May to Labour Day, the "townspeople" dress in period costumes and bring Barkerville back to life. You can pan for gold outside the general store, learn about the big strikes and the miners' lives from the local miners, take a stagecoach ride, or attend a criminal trial. The Theatre Royal actors perform dramatic productions in the town hall. You can have a root beer at the town saloon or a meal in the Chinatown section.

Two-day admission to the town is C$8 (US$5) adults, C$6.25 (US$3.90) seniors, C$4.75 (U.S.$2.95) youths 13 to 17, and C$2.25 (US$1.40) children. Barkerville is open year-round, daily from dawn to dusk. For information, contact **Barkerville Historic Town,** Box 19, Barkerville, BC, V0K 1B0 (✆ **250/994-3332;** www.heritage.gov.bc.ca/bark/bark.htm)

## WHERE TO STAY & DINE

There are three campgrounds in **Barkerville Provincial Park,** Highway 26, Barkerville (✆ **250/398-1414;** mailing address: 181 1st Ave. N., Williams Lake, BC V2G 1Y8), all open year-round. They cost C$12 to C$15 (US$7 to US$9). **Lowhee Campground** is the best and closest to the park entrance.

**Fraser Inn** The Fraser Inn overlooks Williams Lake from its hillside perch north of town along Highway 97. Large and modern, the Fraser offers a level of facilities not usually found in small ranch towns, plus a good steak-house restaurant, the **Great Cariboo Steak Company**. Rooms are comfortably furnished and most have great views over the valley and lake. Kitchen units available.

285 Donald Rd., Williams Lake, BC, V2G 4K4. © **888/452-6789** or 888/331-8863 (in the US) or 250/398-7055. Fax 250/398-8269. www.Fraserinn.com. 75 units. C$69–C$95 (US$43–US$59) double. Kitchen C$10 (US$6) extra. Extra person C$7–C$10 (US$4.35–US$6). AE, MC, V. Pets accepted. **Amenities:** Restaurant, bar; Jacuzzi; sauna; exercise room; beer and wine store. *In room:* A/C, TV, minibar, coffeemaker.

**The Wells Hotel** Established in 1933, the 15 historic rooms at this restored hotel is filled with lovely antique furnishings and offers amenities that you'll truly appreciate after a day of hiking, canoeing, skiing, or gold panning: fine dining, a frothy cappuccino, and a soothing hot tub. Guest rooms are tastefully refurbished and decorated with antiques and local artwork. Some units have private bathrooms and/or fireplaces. The hotel added another 23 rooms in a new wing in 1999; these preserve the flavor of the older hotel but allow for more space and modern luxuries. Continental breakfast included in all rates.

Pooley St. (Box 39), Wells, BC, V0K 2R0. © **800/860-2299** in Canada, or 250/994-3427. Fax 250/994-3494. www.wellshotel.com. 40 units, 24 with private bathroom. C$70–C$120 (US$43–US$74) double. Rates include breakfast. AE, MC, V. **Amenities:** 3 restaurants, including the Pooley Street Café with fine dining, pub; Jacuzzi; bike rental; massage.

## PRINCE GEORGE

The largest city in northern BC, **Prince George** (pop. 77,996) is a natural base for exploring the sites and recreation of the province's north central region, filled with forested mountains, lakes, and mighty rivers.

There has been settlement at the junction of the Fraser and the Nechako rivers for millennia, because the two river systems were as much a transportation corridor for the early First Nations people as for the European settlers who came later. What really put Prince George on the map was the building of the Grand Trunk Railroad, Canada's northerly transcontinental rail route, which passed through here in 1914.

Prince George is rightly proud of its parks, many of them linked by the Heritage Rivers trail system. **Fort George Park** is the site of the original fur trading post that established the city. On the grounds is a First Nations Burial Ground, a working miniature railway, and the original Fort George rail station. Also in the park, the outstanding **Fraser Fort George Regional Museum** (© **250/562-1612**) details the region's long history, starting with excellent exhibits on the customs and lifestyle of the native Carrier people and moving on through the region's fur-trading and logging past. Admission is C$7 (US$4.35) adults, C$6 (US$3.70) seniors, C$4.50 (US$2.80) children under 12, and C$10 (US$6) families. Fort George Park is on the Fraser River end of 20th Avenue.

### WHERE TO STAY & DINE

**Coast Inn of the North** ★ One of the best of British Columbia's Coast chain of hotels is right in the thick of things in downtown Prince George. The guest rooms here are very nicely furnished; ask for a corner room and you'll get a balcony.

770 Brunswick St., Prince George, BC, V2L 2C2. © **800/663-1144** or 250/563-0121. Fax 250/563-1948. www.coasthotels.com. 155 units. C$89–C$165 (US$55–US$102) double. Extra person C$10 (US$6). Family plan, corporate and off-season rates, and senior and AAA discounts available. AE, MC, V. Free parking with engine heater plug-ins. **Amenities:** 3 restaurants (Japanese, Continental, Canadian), pub, dance club; indoor pool; fitness center; Jacuzzi; sauna; shopping arcade; 24-hour room service; nonsmoking rooms; executive-level rooms. *In room:* A/C, TV, dataport, minibar.

## 8 Whistler: One of North America's Premier Ski Resorts ★

The premier ski resort in North America, according to Ski and Snow Country magazines, the **Whistler/Blackcomb complex** ★ boasts more vertical, more lifts, and more varied ski terrain than any other on the continent. In winter, you can choose from downhill skiing, backcountry skiing, cross-country skiing, heli-skiing, snowboarding, snowmobiling, sleigh riding, and more. In summer there are rafting, hiking, golfing, and horseback riding.

And then there's **Whistler Village,** a resort town of 40,000 beds, arranged around a central village street in a compact-enough fashion you can park your car and remain a pedestrian for the duration of your stay.

### ESSENTIALS

**VISITOR INFORMATION** The **Whistler Visitor Info Centre,** 2097 Lake Placid Rd., Whistler, BC V0N 1B0 (✆ **604/932-5528;** www.whistlerchamber ofcommerce.com), is open daily 9am to 5pm. An **information kiosk** on Village Gate Boulevard at the entry to Whistler Village is open mid-May to early September during the same hours. **Tourism Whistler** is at the Whistler Conference Centre at 4010 Whistler Way, Whistler, BC V0N 1B0, open week-days 9am to 5pm (✆ **604/932-3928;** www.tourismwhistler.com). This office can assist you with event tickets and last-minute accommodations bookings, and can also provide general information.

**GETTING THERE** **By Car** Whistler is about a 2-hour drive from Vancouver along Highway 99, also called the Sea to Sky Highway. The drive is spectacular, winding along the edge of Howe Sound before climbing up through the mountains. Parking at the mountain is free for day skiers.

**By Bus** **Whistler Express,** 8695 Barnard St., Vancouver (✆ **604/266-5386** in Vancouver; 604/905-0041 in Whistler; www.perimeterbus.com), operates bus service from Vancouver International Airport to the Whistler Bus Loop. Buses depart five times daily in the summer and eight times in winter. The trip takes about 3 hours; round-trip fares are C$106 (US$66) for adults in summer and C$110 (US$68) in winter and C$60 (US$39) for children in summer and C$68 (US$42) in winter; children under 5 are free. Reservations are required year-round. **Greyhound,** Pacific Central Station, 1150 Station St., Vancouver (✆ **604/662-8051** in Vancouver; 604/482-8747 in Whistler; www.grey hound.ca), operates service from the Vancouver Bus Depot to the Whistler Bus Loop. The trip takes about 2½ hours; one-way fares are C$20 (US$12) for adults and C$10 (US$6) for children ages 5 to 12.

**By Train** **BC Rail** (✆ **604/984-5246;** www.bcrail.com) operates the *Cariboo Prospector* throughout the year. It leaves the North Vancouver train terminal daily at 7am and reaches the Whistler train station at 10:35am. The same train leaves Whistler at 6:10pm and returns to the North Vancouver train terminal at 8:45pm. The 2½-hour trip includes breakfast or dinner. A one-way ticket is C$39 (US$24) for adults, C$19 (US$12) for seniors and children ages 2 to 12, and C$11 (US$7) for children under 2.

**GETTING AROUND** The walk between the Whistler Mountain (Whistler Village) and Blackcomb Mountain (Upper Village) resorts takes about 5 minutes.

**By Bus** A year-round **public transit service** (✆ **604/932-4020**) operates on frequent daily schedules from the Tamarisk district and the BC Rail Station to the neighboring districts of Nester's Village, Alpine Meadows, and Emerald

Estates. Bus service from the Village to Village North and Upper Village accommodation is free. For other routes, one-way fares are C$1.50 (US95¢) for adults and C$1.25 (US80¢) for seniors/students.

**By Taxi** The village's taxis operate around the clock. Taxi tours, golf-course transfers, and airport transport are also offered by **Airport Limousine Service** (✆ **604/273-1331**), **Whistler Taxi** (✆ **604/938-3333**), and **Sea to Sky Taxi** (✆ **604/932-3333**).

**By Car** Rental cars are available from **Budget** at the Holiday Inn Sunspree, 4295 Blackcomb Way (✆ **604/932-1236**), and from **Thrifty** in the Listel Whistler Hotel, 4121 Village Green (✆ **604/938-0302**).

**SPECIAL EVENTS** Dozens of downhill ski competitions are held December to May. They include the **Whistler Snowboard World Cup** (Dec), **Owens-Corning World Freestyle Competition** (Jan), **Power Bar Peak to Valley Race** (Feb), **Kokanee Fantastic Downhill Race** (Mar), and **World Ski & Snowboard Festival** (Apr). Mountain bikers compete in the **Power Bar Garibaldi Gruel** (Sept) and the **Cheakamus Challenge Fall Classic Mountain Bike Race** (Sept).

During the third week in July, the villages host **Whistler's Roots Weekend** (✆ **604/932-2394**). Down in the villages and up on the mountains, you'll hear the sounds of Celtic, zydeco, bluegrass, folk, and world-beat music at free and ticketed events. The **Whistler Summit Concert Series** (✆ **604/932-3434**) is held during August weekends. The mountains provide a stunning backdrop for the on-mountain concerts.

The **Alpine Wine Festival** (✆ **604/932-3434**) takes place on the mountaintop during the first weekend in September and features wine tastings and other events that highlight North America's finest vintages. And the second weekend in September ushers in the **Whistler Jazz & Blues Festival** (✆ **604/932-2394**), featuring live performances in the village squares and the surrounding clubs. **Cornucopia** (✆ **604/932-3434**) is Whistler's premier wine-and-food festival. Held the second week in September, the opening gala showcases 50 top wineries from the Pacific region.

## WINTER ACTIVITIES

**CROSS-COUNTRY SKIING** The 30km (19 miles) of easy to very difficult marked trails at **Lost Lake** start a block away from the Blackcomb Mountain parking lot. Passes are C$8 (US$5); a 1-hour cross-country lesson runs about C$35 (US$22) and can be booked at the same station where you purchase your trail pass. The **Valley Trail System** in the village becomes a well-marked cross-country ski trail during winter.

**DOWNHILL SKIING** The **Whistler/Blackcomb Mountains,** 4545 Blackcomb Way, Whistler, BC V0N 1B4 (✆ **604/932-3434;** snow report 604/687-1032; www.whistler-blackcomb.com), are now jointly operated by Intrawest, so your pass gives access to both ski areas.

**Whistler Mountain** has 1,525m (5,006 ft.) of vertical and 100 marked runs that are serviced by a high-speed gondola and eight high-speed chair lifts, plus four other lifts and tows. There are cafeterias and gift shops on the peak, as well as a fully licensed restaurant. **Blackcomb Mountain** has 1,610m (5,280 ft.) of vertical and 100 marked runs that are serviced by nine high-speed chair lifts, plus three other lifts and tows. The cafeteria and gift shop aren't far from the peak. Both mountains also have bowls and glade skiing, with Blackcomb offering glacier skiing well into August.

During winter, daily lift tickets for both mountains are C$61 to C$63 (US$38–US$39) for adults, C$52 to C$54 (US$32–US$33) for youths/seniors, and C$31 to C$32 (US$19–US$20) for children. Lifts are open 8:30am to 3:30pm (to 4:30pm mid-Mar to closing, depending on weather and conditions). Whistler/Blackcomb offers ski lessons and guides for all levels and interests. (For skiers looking to try snowboarding, a rental package and a half-day lesson is a particularly attractive option.) Phone **Guest Relations** at © **604/932-3434** for details. **Summit Ski** (© **604/938-6225** or 604/932-6225), at various locations, including the Delta Whistler Resort and Market Pavilion, rents high-performance and regular skis, snowboards, cross-country skis, and snowshoes.

**HELI-SKIING** **Whistler Heli-Skiing** (© **888/HELISKI** or 604/932-4105; www.heliskiwhistler.com), is one of the more established operators. A three-run day, with 2,400m to 3,000m (8,000 ft.–10,000 ft.) of vertical helicopter lift, costs C$560 (US$347) per person. A four-run day for expert skiers and riders only, with 3,000m to 3,600m (10,000 ft–12,000 ft.) of vertical helicopter lift, costs C$630 (US$391) per person, including a guide and lunch.

**SLEIGH RIDING** For a sleigh ride with horses, contact **Blackcomb Horse-drawn Sleigh Rides,** 103-4338 Main St., Whistler, BC V0N 1B4 (© **604/932-7631;** www.whistlerweb.net/resort/sleighrides). In winter, tours go out every evening and cost C$45 (US$28) for adults and C$25 (US$16) for children under 12.

**SNOWMOBILING** The year-round ATV/snowmobile tours offered by **Canadian Snowmobile Adventures Ltd.,** Carleton Lodge (© **604/938-1616;** www.canadiansnowmobile.com), are a unique way to take to the Whistler Mountain trails. Exploring the Fitzsimmons Creek watershed, a 2-hour tour costs C$99 (US$61) for a driver and C$69 (US$43) for a passenger. **Blackcomb Snowmobile** (© **604/905-7002**) offers 4- to 8-hour guided snowmobile tours on Blackcomb Mountain. The Fresh Tracks tour, including breakfast, costs C$169 (US$105) per person, with two people for a 4-hour tour, or C$259 (US$161) per person with two people for an all-day Braelorne Back Country tour, lunch included.

**SNOWSHOEING** **Outdoor Adventures@Whistler,** P.O. Box 1054, Whistler, BC V0N 1B0 (© **604/932-0647;** www.adventureswhistler.com), has guided tours for novices at C$39 (US$24) for 1½ hours. A 4-hour tour to a ghost town costs C$69 (US$43), including lunch. If you want to just rent the snowshoes and find your own way around, rentals are C$15 (US$9) per day.

## SUMMER ACTIVITIES

**BIKING** Some of the best mountain-bike trails in the village are on Whistler and Blackcomb Mountains. Lift tickets at both mountains are C$19 to C$30 (US$12–US$19) per day, and discounted season mountain-bike passes are available. You can rent a mountain bike from **Blackcomb Ski & Sports,** Blackcomb Mountain Day Lodge, Upper Village (© **604/938-7788**); **Trax & Trails,** Chateau Whistler Hotel, 4599 Chateau Blvd., Upper Village (© **604/938-2017**); and from the **Whistler Bike Company,** Delta Whistler Resort, 4050 Whistler Way, Whistler Village (©**604/938-9511**). Prices range from C$10 (US$6) per hour to C$30 to C$65 (US$19–US$40) per day.

**CANOEING & KAYAKING** The 3-hour River of Golden Dreams Kayak & Canoe Tour offered by **Whistler Sailing & Water Sports Center Ltd.,** P.O. Box

1130, Whistler, BC V0N 1B0 (✆ **604/932-7245**), is a great way to get acquainted with an exhilarating stretch of racing glacial water that runs between Green Lake and Alta Lake behind the village of Whistler. Packages range from C$29 (US$18) per person unguided to C$40 (US$25) per person unguided for a kayak or canoe.

**FISHING** Spring runs of steelhead, rainbow trout, and Dolly Varden char; summer runs of cutthroat and salmon; and fall runs of coho salmon attract anglers from around the world to the many glacier-fed lakes and rivers in the area and to **Birkenhead Lake Provincial Park,** 44 miles (67km) north of Pemberton. Bring your favorite fly rod and don't forget to buy a fishing license when you arrive. **Whistler Backcountry Adventures,** 36-4314 Main St., Whistler (✆ **888/932-3532** or 604/932-3532; www.whistlerriver.com), and **Sea-to-Sky Reel Adventures** (✆ **604/894-6928**), offer half-day and full-day catch-and-release fishing trips in the surrounding glacier rivers. Rates are C$125 to C$185 (US$78–US$115) per person, based on two people, which includes all fishing gear, round-trip transport to/from the Whistler Village Bus Loop, and a snack or lunch.

**GOLF** Robert Trent Jones's **Chateau Whistler Golf Club,** at the base of Blackcomb Mountain (✆ **604/938-2092,** pro shop 604/938-2095), is an 18-hole, par-72 course. Greens fees are C$130 to C$205 (US$81–US$127), which includes power-cart rental. A multiple-award-winning golf course, **Nicklaus North at Whistler** (✆ **604/938-9898**) is a 5-minute drive north of the village on the shores of Green Lake. The par-71 course's mountain views are spectacular. Greens fees are C$100 to C$125 (US$62–US$78). The **Whistler Golf Club** (✆ **800/376-1777** or 604/932-4544), designed by Arnold Palmer, features nine lakes, two creeks, and magnificent vistas. In addition to the 18-hole, par-72 course, the club offers a driving range, putting green, sand bunker, and pitching area. Greens fees are C$125 to C$205 (US$78–US$127).

The **A-1 Last Minute Golf Hotline** (✆ **800/684-6344** or 604/878-1833) can arrange a next-day tee time at Whistler golf courses. Savings can be as much as 40% on next-day, last-minute tee times. No membership is necessary. Call between 3 and 9pm for the next day or before noon for the same day.

**HIKING** There are numerous easy hiking trails in and around Whistler. You can take a lift up to Whistler and Blackcomb Mountains' trails during summer, but you have a number of other choices as well. The **Lost Lake Trail** starts at the northern end of the Day Skier Parking Lot at Blackcomb. The 30km (19 miles) of marked trails that wind around creeks, beaver dams, blueberry patches, and lush cedar groves are ideal for biking, cross-country skiing, or just strolling and picnicking.

The **Valley Trail System** is a well-marked paved trail connecting parts of Whistler. The trail starts on the west side of Highway 99 adjacent to the Whistler Golf Course and winds through quiet residential areas, as well as golf courses and parks. Garibaldi Provincial Park's **Singing Pass Trail** is a 4-hour hike of moderate difficulty. The fun way to experience this trail is to take the Whistler Mountain gondola to the top and walk down the well-marked path that ends in the village.

**Nairn Falls Provincial Park** is about 33km (21 miles) north of Whistler on Highway 99. It features a 1.5km (1-mile) long trail leading you to a stupendous view of the icy-cold Green River as it plunges 60m (196 ft.) over a rocky cliff into a narrow gorge on its way downstream. On Highway 99 north of Mount

Currie, **Joffre Lakes Provincial Park** is an intermediate-level hike leading past several brilliant-blue glacial lakes up to the very foot of a glacier. The **Ancient Cedars** area of Cougar Mountain is an awe-inspiring grove of towering cedars and Douglas firs. Some of the trees are over 1,000 years old and measure 2.5m (9 ft.) in diameter.

**HORSEBACK RIDING** **Whistler River Adventures** (see "Jet Boating," below) offers 2-hour (C$49/US$30) and 5-hour (C$109/US$68) trail rides along the Green River, through the forest, and across the Pemberton Valley from its 4ha (10-acre) riverside facility in nearby Pemberton. The 5-hour ride goes up into the mountains and includes lunch.

**JET BOATING** **Whistler River Adventures,** Whistler Mountain Village Gondola Base (© **888/932-3532** or 604/932-3532; fax 604/932-3559; www.whistlerriver.com), takes guests up the Green River just below Nairn Falls, where moose, deer, and bear sightings are common in the sheer-granite canyon. The Lillooet River tour goes past ancient petroglyphs, fishing sites, and the tiny Native village of Skookumchuk. Tours range from 1-hour-long trips for C$75 (US$47) to 6-hour cruises for C$135 (US$84).

**RAFTING** **Whistler River Adventures** (see "Jet Boating," above) offers 2-hour and full-day round-trip rafting runs down the Green, Elaho, or Squamish River. They include equipment and ground transport for C$61 to C$135 (US$38–US$84). The full-day trip includes a salmon barbecue lunch. The company also conducts 3-hour round-trip jet-boat tours on the Green river for C$75 (US$47) per person, which includes ground transport and a wet suit.

**TENNIS** The **Whistler Racquet & Golf Resort,** 4500 Northland Blvd. (© **604/932-1991;** www.whistlertennis.com), features three covered courts, seven outdoor courts, and a practice cage, all open to drop-in visitors. Indoor courts are C$24 (US$15) per hour and outdoor courts are C$14 (US$9) per hour. Adult and junior tennis camps are offered during summer. Camp prices range from C$250 to C$365 (US$155–US$226) for a 3-day camp; kids camps cost C$40 (US$25) per day drop-in or C$150 (US$93) for a 5-day camp. The **Mountain Spa & Tennis Club,** Delta Whistler Resort, Whistler Village (© **604/938-2044**), and the **Chateau Whistler Resort,** Chateau Whistler Hotel, Upper Village (© **604/938-8000**), also offer courts to drop-in players. Prices run C$10 (US$6) per hour per court, with racquet rentals at C$5 (US$3.10) per hour.

There are **free public courts** at Myrtle Public School, Alpha Lake Park, Meadow Park, Millar's Pond, Brio, Blackcomb Benchlands, White Gold, and Emerald Park. Call © **604/938-PARK** for details.

## EXPLORING THE TOWN

**SEEING THE SIGHTS** To learn more about Whistler's heritage, flora, and fauna, visit the **Whistler Museum & Archives Society,** 4329 Main St., off Northlands Boulevard (© **604/932-2019**). June to Labour Day, the museum is open daily 10am to 4pm; call ahead for winter opening hours. Admission is C$1 (US60¢) for adults and is free for children under 18.

The **Whistler Inuit Gallery,** 4599 Chateau Blvd. (© **604/938-3366**), on the lower concourse of the Chateau Whistler Resort, specializes in Inuit, West Coast, and contemporary artists. **Gallery Row** in the Delta Whistler Resort consists of three galleries: the **Whistler Village Art Gallery** (© **604/938-3001**), the **Northern Lights Gallery** (© **604/932-2890**), and the **Adele Campbell**

**Gallery** (✆ **604/938-0887**). Their collections include fine art, sculpture, and glass.

Departing from the Whistler train station on Lake Placid Road at 8am, **BC Rail's *Whistler Explorer*** (✆ **604/984-5246;** www.bcrail.com/bcr/) takes an 8½-hour round-trip ramble through Pemberton Valley before arriving at Kelly Lake, adjacent to the historic Cariboo Gold Rush Trail. After a 1-hour strolling break, you reboard the train, returning to Whistler at 5:30pm. The round-trip fare is C$139 (US$86) for adults/seniors/children over 12 and C$99 (US$61) for children ages 2 to 12.

Whistler Village and the Upper Village, near the base of the mountains, sponsor **daily activities** tailored for active kids of all ages. There are mountain-bike races, an in-line skating park, a trapeze, a trampoline, wall-climbing lessons, summer skiing, snowboarding, and snowshoeing. There's even a first-run multiplex movie theater.

Based at Blackcomb Mountain, the **Dave Murray Summer Ski Camp,** P.O. Box 98, Whistler, BC V0N 1B0 (✆ **604/932-5765;** www.skiandsnowboard.com), is North America's longest-running summer ski camp. Junior programs cost about C$1,475 (US$915) per week mid-June to mid-July. The packages include food, lodging, and lift passes, as well as tennis, trapeze, and mountain-biking options.

**SHOPPING** The **Whistler Marketplace,** in the center of Whistler Village, and the area surrounding the **Blackcomb Mountain lift** brim with clothing, jewelry, craft, specialty, gift, and equipment shops open daily 10am to 6pm. The **Horstman Trading Company** (✆ **604/938-7725**), beside the Chateau Whistler at the base of Blackcomb, carries men's and women's casual wear to suit seasonal activities, from swimwear and footwear to polar-fleece vests and nylon jacket shells. The **Escape Route** (✆ **604/938-3228**), at Whistler Marketplace and Crystal Lodge, has a great line of outdoor clothing and equipment.

**GETTING THE SPA TREATMENT** The **Spa at Chateau Whistler Resort** (✆ **604/938-2086**) is considered the best in Whistler. Open daily 8am to 9pm, it offers massage therapy, aromatherapy, skincare, body wraps, and steam baths. The **Whistler Body Wrap,** 210 St. Andrews House, next to the Keg in the Village (✆ **604/932-4710**), can nurture you with shiatsu massage, facials, pedicures or manicures, waxings, sun beds, and aromatherapy. The therapists at **Whistler Physiotherapy** (✆ **604/932-4001** or 604/938-9001) have a lot of experience with the typical ski, board, and hiking injuries. There are two locations: 339-4370 Lorimer Rd., at Marketplace, and 202-2011 Innsbruck Dr., next to Boston Pizza in Creekside.

## WHERE TO STAY

South of Whistler on the Sea to Sky corridor is the very popular **Alice Lake Provincial Park.** You can reserve spots for Alice Lake by calling **Discover Camping** at ✆ **800/689-9025.** About 27km (17 miles) north of Whistler, the well-maintained campground at **Nairn Falls,** Highway 99 (✆ **604/898-3678**), is more adult-oriented, with pit toilets, pumped well water, fire pits, and firewood, but no showers. Prices for the 88 campsites are C$15 (US$9), on a first-come, first-served basis.

The 85 campsites at **Birkenhead Lake Provincial Park,** off Portage Road, Birken (✆ **604/898-3678**), fill up very quickly during summer. To reserve a spot, call **Discover Camping** at ✆ **800/689-9025.** Boat launches, great fishing, and well-maintained tent and RV sites make this an angler's paradise. Campsites are C$12 (US$7).

Prices for Whistler's studios, one- to five-bedroom fully furnished condos, town houses, and chalets are C$90 to C$1,400 (US$56–US$868). **Whistler Central Reservations** (© **800/944-7853** or 604/664-5625; fax 604/938-5758; www.whistler-resort.com) has more than 2,000 rental units to choose from and can book a wide range of accommodations in the Whistler area, from B&Bs to hotel rooms or condos. Other booking agencies are **Whistler Chalets and Accommodations Ltd.**, 4360 Lorimer Rd., Whistler, BC V0N 1B0 (© **800/663-7711** in Canada, or 604/932-6699; www.whistlerchalets.com), and **Rainbow Retreats Accommodations Ltd.**, 2129 Lake Placid Rd., Whistler, BC V0N 1B0 (© **604/932-2343;** www.rainbowretreats.com). Reservations for peak winter periods should be made by September.

## IN THE VILLAGE

**The Fairmont Chateau Whistler** ★★ The one exception to the everything's-the-same-in-Whistler rule, the Chateau Whistler is outstanding. The Former Canadian Pacific hotel chain, now part of Fairmont, spared little expense in re-creating the look and feel of an old-time country retreat at the foot of Blackcomb Mountain. Massive wooden beams support an airy peaked roof in the lobby, while in the hillside Mallard Bar, double-sided stone fireplaces cast a cozy glow on the couches and leather armchairs. The rooms and suites feature double, queen-, and king-size beds, duvets, and soaker tubs. Gold service guests can have breakfast or relax après-ski in a private lounge with the feel of a Victorian library. All guests can use the heated outdoor pool and Jacuzzis, which look out over the base of the ski hill.

4599 Chateau Blvd., Whistler, BC V0N 1B4. © **800/441-1414** in the U.S., 800/606-8244 in Canada, or 604/938-8000. Fax 604/938-2099. www.fairmont.com. 558 units. Winter C$385–C$435 (US$239–US$270) double; C$570–C$1,200 (US$353–US$744) suite. Summer C$299–C$335 (US$185–US$208) double; C$425–C$1,000 (US$264–US$620) suite. Wheelchair-accessible units available. AE, MC, V. Underground valet parking C$22 (US$14). Pets are welcome. **Amenities:** 2 restaurants, bar; 2 heated outdoor pools; 2 tennis courts (no night play); health club; outstanding spa facility; Jacuzzi; children's programs; concierge; tour desk; business center; 24-hour room service; shopping arcade; in-room massage; babysitting; coin laundry; laundry service; same-day dry cleaning; nonsmoking rooms; concierge-level rooms. *In room:* A/C, TV w/pay movies, dataport, minibar, coffeemaker, hair dryer, iron, safe.

**The Pan Pacific Lodge Whistler** ★ The Pan-Pacific's furnishings and appointments are top-notch, and the kitchenettes (in all suites) contain the cutlery and equipment required to cook up a gourmet meal. With sofa beds and fold-down Murphy beds, the studio suites are fine for couples, while the one- and two-bedroom suites allow a bit more space for larger groups or families with kids. Comfortable as the rooms are, however, the true advantage to the Pan Pacific is its location at the foot of the Whistler Mountain gondola. Not only can you ski right to your hotel, but thanks to a large heated outdoor pool and Jacuzzi deck, you can sit at the end of the day sipping a glass of wine, gazing up at the snowy slopes, and marvel at the ameliorative effects of warm water on aching muscles.

4320 Sundial Crescent, Whistler, BC V0N 1B4. © **888/905-9995** or 604/905-2999. Fax 604/905-2995. www.panpacific.com. 121 units. High season Nov 22–April 30 C$409–C$599 (US$254–US$371) studio; C$509–C$759 (US$316–US$471) 1-bedroom suite; C$709–C$959 (US$440–US$595) 2-bedroom suite. Low season May–Nov 21 C$309–C$409 (US$192–US$254) studio; C$359–C$509 (US$223–US$316) 1-bedroom suite; C$409–C$709 (US$254–US$440) 2-bedroom suite. Wheelchair-accessible units available. AE, MC, V.

Underground valet parking C$15 (US$9). **Amenities:** Restaurant, pub; heated outdoor pool; fitness center; Jacuzzis; steam room; concierge; limited room service; laundry. *In room:* A/C, TV, dataport, kitchen, minibar, fridge, coffeemaker, hair dryer, iron, safe.

**The Westin Resort and Spa Whistler** ★★★ A latecomer to the Whistler hotel scene, the Westin Resort snapped up the best piece of property in town and squeezed itself onto the mountainside at the bottom part of the main ski run into the village. Both the Whistler and Blackcomb gondolas are within a few hundred yards from your doorstep. The hotel is built in the style of a mountain chalet with lots of local stone finishings such as granite and basalt and cedar timbers. All 419 suites offer full kitchens. The beds, Westin's signature Heavenly Beds, are indeed divine. Start with a custom-designed brand-name mattress, add a down blanket, then three layers of heavy cotton sheets, and top it off with a down duvet and the best pillows money can buy. To get you going in the morning, little luxuries include a ski valet service and (no more cold toes!) a boot warming service. That is certainly one of the reasons why in the short period since the Westin opened in 2000, it already grabbed a couple of top awards, including best ski resort hotel in North America by the readers of *Condé Nast Traveler.*

4090 Whistler Way, Whistler, BC V0N 1B4. ✆ **800/WESTIN-1** or 604/905-5000. Fax 604/ 905-5589. www.westinwhistler.net. 419 units. April 16–Nov 23 C$159–C$469 (US$99–US$291) junior suite; C$249–C$589 (US$154–US$365) 1-bedroom suite; C$409–C$1,049 (US$254–US$650) 2-bedroom suite. Nov 24–April 15 C$199–C$569 (US$123–US$353) junior suite; C$319–C$689 (US$198–US$427) 1-bedroom suite; C$519–C$1,499 (US$322–US$929) 2-bedroom suite. Children 17 and under stay free in parents' room. AE, DC, DISC, MC, V. Parking C$21 (US$13). **Amenities:** Restaurant, bar; indoor and outdoor pool; nearby golf course; nearby tennis courts; outstanding health club; top-notch spa; indoor and outdoor Jacuzzi; sauna; nearby watersports rental; bike rental; children's program; concierge; business center; shopping arcade; salon; 24-hour room service; massage; babysitting; laundry; dry cleaning; nonsmoking facility. *In room:* TV w/pay movies, dataport, kitchen, fridge, coffeemaker, hair dryer, iron, safe.

## OUTSIDE THE VILLAGE

**Cedar Springs Bed & Breakfast Lodge** Guests at this charming modern lodge have a choice of king-, queen-, or twin-size beds in comfortably modern yet understated surroundings. The honeymoon suite boasts a fireplace and balcony. The guest sitting room has a TV, VCR, and video library. A sauna and hot tub on the sun deck overlooking the gardens add to the pampering after a day of play. A gourmet breakfast is served by the fireplace in the dining room, and guests are welcome to enjoy afternoon tea. Owners Joann and Jackie Rhode can provide box lunches and special-occasion dinners at this cozy hideaway. A complimentary shuttle service takes you to the ski lifts, and additional public transit is available to and from the Village.

8106 Cedar Springs Rd., Whistler, BC V0N 1B8. ✆ **800/727-7547** or 604/938-8007. Fax 604/938-8023. www.whistlerbb.com. 8 units, 6 with bathroom. C$85–C$239 (US$53–US$148) double; C$130–C$279 (US$81–US$173) suite. Rates include full breakfast. MC, V. Take Hwy. 99 north toward Pemberton 2½ miles (4km) past Whistler Village. Turn left onto Alpine Way, go a block to Rainbow Dr., and turn left; go a block to Camino St. and turn left. The lodge is a block down at the corner of Camino and Cedar Springs Rd. **Amenities:** Jacuzzi; sauna; game room; courtesy car to ski slopes; nonsmoking rooms. *In room:* TV, hair dryer, no phone.

**Durlacher Hof Pension Inn** ★★ *Finds* This lovely inn boasts both an authentic Austrian feel and a sociable atmosphere. Both are the result of the exceptional care and service shown by owners Peter and Erika Durlacher. Guests are greeted by name at the entranceway, provided with slippers, and then given a tour of the two-story chalet-style property. The rooms (on the second floor) vary in size from comfortable to quite spacious and come with goose-down duvets and Ralph Lauren linens on extra long twin- or queen-size beds, private bathrooms (some with jetted tubs) with deluxe toiletries, and incredible mountain views from private balconies. Better still is the downstairs lounge, with a welcoming fireplace and complementary après-ski appetizers baked by Erika (these are delectable enough that guests are drawn from all over the inn to snack, share stories, and strategize on ways to obtain Erika's recipes). For much the same reason, many guests seem to linger over the complimentary (and substantial) hot breakfast.

7055 Nesters Rd. Whistler, BC V0N 1B7. ✆ **877/932-1924** or 604/932-1924. Fax 604/938-1980. www.durlacherhof.com. 8 units. Dec 18–Mar 31 C$150–C$265 (US$151–US$164) double. June 19–Sept 30 C$120–C$205 (US$74–US$127) double. Extra person C$35 (US$22). Discounts for spring and fall available. Rates include full breakfast and afternoon tea. 1 wheelchair-accessible unit available. MC, V. Free parking. Take Hwy. 99 about a half-mile (1km) north of Whistler Village to Nester's Rd. Turn left and the inn is immediately on the right. **Amenities:** Jacuzzi; sauna; concierge; tour desk; laundry service; dry cleaning; nonsmoking rooms. *In room:* TV, hair dryer.

**Hostelling International Whistler** *Value* One of the few inexpensive spots in Whistler, the hostel also happens to have one of the nicest locations: on the south edge of Alta Lake, with a dining room, deck, and lawn looking over the lake to Whistler Mountain. Inside, the hostel is extremely pleasant; there's a lounge with a wood-burning stove, a common kitchen, a piano, Ping-Pong tables, and a sauna, as well as a drying room for ski gear and storage for bikes, boards, and skis. In the summer, guests have use of a barbecue, canoe, and rowboat. As with all hostels, most rooms and facilities are shared. Beds at the hostel book up very early. Book by September at the latest for the winter ski season.

5678 Alta Lake Rd., Whistler, BC V0N 1B5. ✆ **604/932-5492.** Fax 604/932-4687. www.hihostels.bc.ca. 33 beds in 4- to 8-bed dorms. C$19.50 (US$12) IYHA members, C$23.50 (US$15) nonmembers; annual adult membership C$27 (US$17). Family and group memberships available. MC, V. Free parking. **Amenities:** Sauna; watersports equipment; bike rental; nonsmoking facility.

## WHERE TO DINE

Whistler literally overflows with dining spots. A quick meal for gourmets on the go can be found at **Chef Bernard's,** 4573 Chateau Blvd., Whistler Village (✆ **604/932-7051**). It serves full breakfasts, soups, salads, and sandwiches, as well as hot entrees for C$4.95 to C$8 (US$3.10–US$5); it's open daily 7am to 9pm. **Ingrid's Village Café,** just off the Village Square (✆ **604/932-7000**), is another locals' favorite, for both quality and price. A large bowl of Ingrid's clam chowder costs just C$4.50 (US$2.80), while a veggie burger comes in at C$5 (US$3.10). It's open daily 8am to 6pm.

The **Citta Bistro,** in the Whistler Village Square (✆ **604/932-4177**), serves thin-crust pizzas like the Californian herb, topped with spiced chicken breast, sun-dried tomatoes, fresh pesto, and mozzarella, as well as gourmet burgers like the Citta Extraordinaire, topped with bacon, cheddar, and garlic mushrooms. Main courses are C$7 to C$11 (US$4.35–US$7), and it's open daily noon to midnight. The **Dubh Linn Gate Irish Lounge/Bar** in the Pan Pacific hotel offers solid pub grub and the atmosphere of the Emerald Isle; it's open Monday to Saturday 10am to midnight and Sunday 10am to 10pm. Brand new to Whistler but long known in Vancouver for its quality beef is **Hy's Steakhouse,** 4308 Main St. (✆ **604/905-5555**), open daily 4pm to midnight.

**Araxi Restaurant & Bar** ★ ITALIAN/WEST COAST Frequently awarded for its wine list, as well as voted "Best Restaurant in Whistler" in 1998 and 1999 by readers of *Vancouver* magazine, this is one of the top places to dine. And thanks to a major renovation, Araxi now has storage enough for its 12,000-bottle inventory of fine BC and foreign wines. Outside, the heated patio seats

80 people amid barrels of flowers, while inside, the artwork, antiques, and terracotta tiles give it a subtle Italian ambience. The menu, however, is less Italian and more West Coast. The locally caught trout is smoked in the Araxi kitchen. Various soups and salads are made from scratch with fresh ingredients like Pemberton sheep cheese and Okanagan tomatoes. Main courses include seafood such as ahi tuna, salmon filet, and scallops. For meat lovers, the menu offers rack of lamb, tenderloin, and alder-smoked pork loin. And considering the near encyclopedic length of Araxi's famous wine list, don't hesitate to ask sommelier Chris Van Nus for suggestions.

4222 Village Sq. © **604/932-4540.** www.araxi.com. Main courses C$24.50–C$36 (US$15–US$22). AE, MC, V. Mid-May to Oct daily 11am–10:30pm; during ski season daily 5pm–10pm.

**Caramba! Restaurant** MEDITERRANEAN The room is bright and filled with the pleasant buzz of nattering diners. The kitchen is open, and the smells wafting out hint tantalizingly of fennel, artichoke, and pasta. Caramba! is casual dining, but its Mediterranean-influenced menu offers fresh ingredients, prepared with a great deal of pizzazz. Try the pasta, free-range chicken, or roasted pork loin. Better still, if you're feeling especially good about your dining companions, order a pizza or two; a plate of grilled calamari; some hot spinach, cheese, and artichoke-and-shallot dip; and a plate of sliced prosciutto and bullfighters toast (savory toasted Spanish bread with herbs).

12–4314 Main St., Town Plaza. © **604/938-1879.** Main courses C$11–C$17 (US$7–US$11). AE, MC, V. Daily 11:30am–10:30pm.

**Rimrock Cafe and Oyster Bar** ★★ SEAFOOD Upstairs in a long narrow room with a high ceiling and a great stone fireplace at one end, Rimrock is very much like a Viking mead hall of old. It's not the atmosphere, however, that causes people to hop in a cab and make the C$5 (US$3.10) journey out from Whistler Village. What draws folks in is the food. The first order of business should be a plate of oysters. Chef Rolf Gunther serves them up half a dozen ways, from raw with champagne to cooked in hell (broiled with fresh chilies). For my money, though, the signature Rimrock oyster is still the best: broiled with béchamel sauce and smoked salmon. Other appetizers are lightly seared ahi tuna or Québec foie gras with portobello mushrooms. Main dishes are equally seafood-oriented and inventive. Look for lobster and scallops in light tarragon sauce on a bed of Capellini pasta or swordfish broiled with pecans, almonds, pistachios, and a mild red Thai curry. The accompanying wine list has a number of fine vintages from BC, California, New Zealand, and Australia.

2117 Whistler Rd. © 877/932-5589 or 604/932-5565. www.rimrockwhistler.com. Main courses C$24–C$40 (US$15–US$25). AE, MC, V. Daily 11:30am–11:30pm.

## WHISTLER AFTER DARK

For a town of just 8,000, Whistler has a more-than-respectable nightlife scene. You'll find concert listings in the ***Pique,*** a free local paper available at cafes and food stores. **Tommy Africa's,** underneath the Pharmasave at the entrance to the Main Village (© **604/932-6090**), and the dark and cavernous **Maxx Fish,** in the Village Square below the Amsterdam Cafe (© **604/932-1904**), cater to the 18- to 22-year-old crowd; you'll find lots of beat and not much light. The crowd at **Garfinkel's,** at the entrance to Village North (© **604/932-2323**), is similar, though the cutoff age can reach as high as 26 or 27. The **Boot Pub,** Nancy Green Drive just off Highway 99 (© **604/932-3338**), is crammed with young Australian ski-lift operators. **Buffalo Bills,** across from the Whistler Gondola

(✆ **604/932-6613**), and the **Savage Beagle,** opposite Starbucks in the Village (✆ **604/938-3337**), cater to the 30-something crowd. Bills is bigger, with a pool table, a video ski machine, and a smallish dance floor. The Beagle has a fabulous selection of beer and bar drinks, with a pleasant little pub upstairs and a house-oriented dance floor below.

## 9 The Okanagan Valley: A Taste of the Grape ★★

The arid **Okanagan Valley** with its long chain of lakes is the ideal destination for fresh-watersports enthusiasts, golfers, skiers, and wine lovers. The climate is hot and dry during the summer high season (when, one local told me, the valley's population increases five-fold from its winter average of about 35,000).

Ranches and small towns have flourished here for more than a century; the region's **fruit orchards and vineyards** will make you feel as if you've been transported to the Spanish countryside. Summer visitors get the pick of the fruit crop at insider prices from the many fruit stands that line Highway 97. Be sure to stop for a pint of cherries, a basket of apples, homemade jams, and other goodies.

An Okanagan region chardonnay won gold medals in 1994 at international competitions held in London and Paris. And more than three dozen other wineries produce vintages that are following right on its heels. Despite this coveted honor, the valley has received little international publicity. Most visitors are Canadian, and the valley isn't yet a major tour-bus destination. Get here before they do.

Many Canadian retirees have chosen **Penticton** as their home because it has relatively mild winters and dry, desert-like summers. It's also a favorite destination for younger visitors, drawn by boating, waterskiing, sportfishing, and windsurfing on 128km (79-mile) long Lake Okanagan.

Remember to bring your camera when you head out on the lake. If you spot its legendary underwater resident, **Ogopogo,** take a picture. The shy monster (depicted in ancient petroglyphs found in the valley as a snakelike beast with a horselike head) is said to be a distant cousin of Scotland's Loch Ness monster.

The town of **Kelowna** in the central valley is the hub of the BC winemaking industry and the valley's largest city. And the town of **Vernon** is a favorite destination for cross-country and powder skiers, who flock to the northern valley's top resort—**Silver Star Mountain.**

### ESSENTIALS

**VISITOR INFORMATION** The **Penticton Visitor Info Centre** is at 888 Westminster Ave. W., Penticton, BC, V2A 8R2 (✆ **800/663-5052** or 250/493-4055; www.penticton.org). The **Kelowna Visitor Info Centre** is at 544 Harvey Ave., Kelowna, BC, V1Y 6C9 (✆ **800/663-4345** or 250/861-1515; www.bcyellowpages.com/advert/k/kcc).

**GETTING THERE By Plane Air BC** (✆ **800/667-3721**) has frequent daily commuter flights from Calgary and Vancouver to Penticton and Kelowna. **Horizon Air** (✆ **800/547-9308**) offers service from Seattle. **WestJet** (✆ **800/538-5696;** www.westjet.com) operates flights from Vancouver, Victoria, Calgary, and Edmonton.

**By Car** The 395km (245-mile) drive from Vancouver to Penticton via the Trans-Canada Highway (Highway 1) and Highway 3 rambles through rich delta farmlands and the forested mountains of Manning Provincial Park and the Similkameen River region before descending into the Okanagan Valley's antelope-brush and sagebrush desert. For a more direct route to the valley, take the Trans-Canada Highway to the Coquihalla Toll Highway (C$10/US$6) via Merritt and Hope. Using this expressway allows drivers to make the journey from Kelowna to Vancouver in 4 hours.

**SPECIAL EVENTS** Colorful balloons meet to fly the valley's air thermals during the first and second weeks in February at Vernon's **Annual Winter Carnival & Hot Air Balloon Festival** (© **250/545-2236**). Indoor and outdoor events like arts and crafts exhibits, food stands, and live musical entertainment take place at locations throughout the city.

Be the first to taste the valley's best chardonnay, pinot noir, merlot, and ice wines at the **Okanagan Wine Festival** (© **250/861-6654;** www.owfs.com), during the first and second weeks in October at wineries and restaurants throughout Penticton.

## TASTING THE FRUITS OF THE VINEYARDS

British Columbia has a long history of producing wines, ranging from mediocre to really, truly bad. A missionary, Father Pandosy, planted apple trees and vineyards in 1859 and produced sacramental wines for the valley's mission. Other monastery wineries cropped up, but none of them worried about the quality of their bottlings, because they were subsidized by the BC government.

In the 1980s, the government threatened to pull its support of the industry unless it could produce an internationally competitive product. The vintners listened. Root stock was imported from France and Germany. European-trained master vintners were hired to oversee the development of the vines and the wine-making process. The climate and soil conditions turned out to be some of the best in the world for wine making, and today, British Columbian wines are winning international gold medals. Competitively priced, about C$7 to C$50 (US$4.35–US$31) per bottle, they represent some great bargains in well-balanced chardonnays, pinot blancs, and gewürztraminers; full-bodied merlots, pinot noirs, and cabernets; and dessert ice wines that surpass the best muscat d'or.

Because U.S. visitors are allowed to bring back 1 liter (33.8 oz.) of wine per person without paying extra duty, Americans can bring a bottle of their favorite selection back home if they've visited Canada for more than 24 hours. Travelers from the United Kingdom can take back up to 2 liters of still wine without paying duty.

The valley's more than 36 vineyards and wineries conduct free tours and wine tastings throughout the year. Here are a few favorite stops:

The town of **Okanagan Falls** is 20km (12 miles) south of Penticton along Highway 97. Adjacent to a wilderness area and bird sanctuary overlooking Vaseaux Lake, **Blue Mountain Vineyards & Cellars,** Allendale Road (© **250/497-8244;** www.bluemountainwinery.com), offers tours by appointment and operates a wine shop and tasting room. Near Oliver, **Tinhorn Creek Vineyards,** Road 7 (© **888/846-4676**, www.tinhorn.com), is one of the top Okanagan wineries. Self-guided tours allow you to linger; guided tours can be arranged by appointment. Specialties include gewürztraminer, pinot gris, chardonnay, pinot noir, cabernet franc, merlot, and ice wine. Also near Oliver, the **Hester Creek Estate Winery,** Road 8 (© **250/498-4435;** www.hestercreek.com), has a wine boutique open daily 10am to 5pm, and tours of the wine-making area are available by appointment; especially nice here is the grapevine-shaded patio that invites picnickers. The superior growing conditions at Hester Creek produce intense fruit flavors that make the wines from here some of the best in all BC.

In and around **Kelowna** are some of the biggest names in British Columbia's wine-making industry. **Calona Wines,** 1125 Richter St., Kelowna, BC V1Y 2K6 (✆ **250/762-3332**), conducts tours through western Canada's oldest (since 1932) and largest winery. Many antique wine-making machines are on display alongside the state-of-the-art equipment the winery now uses. May to September, tours are given daily on the hour 11am to 5pm. The wine shop is open daily, May to September 10am to 7pm and October to April 10am to 5pm. At **Summerhill Estate Winery,** 4870 Chute Lake Rd., Kelowna, BC V1W 4M3 (✆ **800/667-3538** in Canada, or 250/764-8000), the wine shop and tasting room are open daily 10am to 6pm year-round.

Another experience worth savoring even if you're not an oenophile is the **Quail's Gate Estate,** 3303 Boucherie Rd., Kelowna, BC V1Z 2H3 (✆ **250/769-4451**). If ice wines (made with grapes that have been allowed to stay on the vine through several frosts, dehydrating them and intensifying the sugars) are your favorite dessert potable, you'll want to taste the vintages here. May 30 to late June, tours are conducted daily at 11am, 1pm, and 3pm; from the last weekend in June to Labour Day, they're given daily on the hour 11am to 4pm. The wine shop and tasting room are housed in the restored log home of the Allison family, pioneers who arrived in the valley during the 1870s. The shop is filled with historic regional artifacts. It's open daily: May 30 to Labour Day 10am to 6pm and the rest of the year 10am to 5pm.

The neighboring town of **Westbank** is home to **Mission Hill Wines,** 1730 Mission Hill Rd., Westbank, BC V4T 2E4 (✆ **250/768-7611;** www.missionhillwinery.com), established in 1981. July and August, tours are given daily on the hour 10am to 5pm; the rest of the year, tours are Saturday and Sunday on the hour 10am to 5pm. July and August, the wine shop is open daily 9am to 7pm; the rest of the year, it's open Saturday and Sunday 10am to 5pm.

Located 43km (27 miles) north of Penticton, the **Hainle Vineyards Estate Winery,** 5355 Trepanier Bench Rd. (✆ **250/767-2525;** www.hainle.com), was the first Okanagan winery to produce ice wine. May to October, the wine shop is open Tuesday to Sunday 10am to 5pm; November to April, it's open for tastings Thursday to Sunday noon to 5pm. **Amphora,** the winery's bistro, is open Tuesday to Sunday noon to 3pm.

North of Penticton along Highway 97 is another wine-producing area, where you'll find the **Sumac Ridge Estate Winery,** 17403 Highway 97 (✆ **250/494-0451;** www.sumacridge.com). May to mid-October, winery tours are daily 10am to 4pm on the hour. Besides operating a wine shop and tasting room, the winery features a fine dining room, the Cellar Door Bistro.

## SPORTS & OUTDOOR ACTIVITIES

**BIKING** The best **Okanagan Valley** off-road bike trail is the old **Kettle Valley** railway route. The tracks and ties have been removed, making way for some incredibly scenic biking. The **Myra Canyon** railway route between Kelowna and Penticton crosses over 18 trestle bridges, and passes through two tunnels were carved through the mountains. **Sun Country Cycle,** 533 Main St. (✆ **250/493-0686**), has bike rentals and lots of friendly advice.

**BOATING & WATERSPORTS** The Okanagan Valley's numerous local marinas offer full-service boat rentals. **Okanagan Boat Charters,** 291 Front St., Penticton (✆ **250/492-5099**), rents houseboats with fully equipped kitchens that can accommodate up to 10 people. Prices for a weeklong rental begins at C$1,295 (US$864). The **Marina on Okanagan Lake,** 291 Front St., Penticton

(© **250/492-2628**), rents ski-boats, Tigersharks (similar to Jet-Skis or Sea-Doos), fishing boats, and tackle.

**GOLF** The greens fees throughout the Okanagan Valley range from C$37 to C$105 (US$20 to US$57) and are a good value not only because of the beautiful locations but also for the quality of service you'll find at each club. Les Furber's **Gallagher's Canyon Golf and Country Club,** 4320 McCulloch Rd., Kelowna (© **250/861-4240**), has an 18-hole course that features a hole overlooking the precipice of a gaping canyon and another that's perched on the brink of a ravine. It also has a 9-hole course, a midlength course, and a new double-ended learning center. Resting high on a wooded ridge between two lakes, Les Furber's **Predator Ridge,** 360 Commonage Rd., Vernon (© **250/542-3436**), has hosted the BC Open Championship in recent years. The par-5 fourth hole can be played only over a huge mid-fairway lake; it's a challenge even for seasoned pros.

**A-1 Last Minute Golf Hotline** (© **800/684-6344** or 604/878-1833) can arrange a next-day tee time at local golf courses. Savings can be as much as 40% on next-day, last-minute tee times. No membership is necessary. Call between 3 and 9pm for the next day or before noon for the same day.

**SKIING** Cross-country and powder skiing are the Okanagan Valley's main winter attractions. Intermediate and expert downhill skiers frequent the **Apex Resort,** Green Mountain Road, Penticton (© **800/387-2739,** 250/492-2880, 250/292-8111, or 250/492-2929, ext. 2000 for snow report), where 56 runs are serviced by one quad chair, one triple chair, one T-bar, and one beginner tow/platter. The 52km (32 miles) of cross-country ski trails are well marked and well groomed, offering both flat stretches and hilly ascents. Facilities include an ice rink, snow golf, sleigh rides, casino nights, and racing competitions.

Only a 15-minute drive from Westbank, **Crystal Mountain Resorts Ltd.** (© **250/768-5189,** or 250/768-3753 for snow report; mailing address: Box 26044, Westbank, BC V4T 2J9), has a range of ski programs for all types of skiers, specializing in clinics for children, women, and seniors. This friendly family-oriented resort lets you ski free on your birthday as one of its regular promotions. The resort's 20 runs are 80% intermediate-to-novice grade and are serviced by one double chair and two T-bars. The runs are equipped for day and night skiing. There's also a half pipe for snowboarders. Lift tickets start at C$29 (US$18) adults and C$20 (US$12) juniors. Half-day and nighttime discounts are available.

If you yearn for hip-deep dry powder, then head to **Big White Ski Resort,** Parkinson Way, Kelowna (© **250/765-3101,** or 250/765-SNOW for snow report, or 250/765-8888 for lodge reservations). The resort spreads over a broad mountain, featuring long, wide runs. Skiers cruise open bowls and tree-lined glades. There's an annual average of 5.5m (18 ft.) of fluffy powder, so it's no wonder the resort's 57 runs are so popular. There are three high-speed quad chairs, one fixed-grip quad, one triple quad, one double chair, one T-bar, one beginner tow, and one platter lift. The resort also offers more than 40km (25 miles) of groomed cross-country ski trails, a recreational racing program, and night skiing 5 nights a week.

## WHERE TO STAY

The **BC Provincial Parks Service/Okanagan District** (© **250/494-6500**) maintains a number of provincial campgrounds in this area. They're open April to October, and fees are C$12 to C$19 (US$7–US$12) per night. There are 41 campsites at **Haynes Point Provincial Park** in Osoyoos, which has flush toilets, a boat launch, and visitor programs. This campground is popular with naturalists interested in hiking the "pocket desert." **Vaseaux Lake Provincial Park,** near Okanagan Falls, offers 12 campsites and great wildlife-viewing opportunities; deer, antelope, and even a number of California bighorn sheep live in the surrounding hills. And **Okanagan Lake Provincial Park** has 168 campsites nestled amid 10,000 imported trees. Facilities include free hot showers, flush toilets, a sani-station, and a boat launch.

## IN PENTICTON

**Penticton Lakeside Resort Convention Centre & Casino** Set on the water's edge, the Penticton Lakeside Resort has its own stretch of sandy Lake Okanagan beachfront, where guests can sunbathe or stroll along the adjacent pier. The deluxe suites feature Jacuzzis, and the lakeside rooms are highly recommended for their view. All rooms have been recently redecorated and are smartly furnished with quality furniture; all rooms have balconies. The menus at the Okanagan Surf N' Turf Company Restaurant and the Barking Parrot Bar & Patio feature locally grown ingredients. Other facilities include a extensive pool and health club facility, tennis courts, volleyball area and casino.

21 W. Lakeshore Dr., Penticton, BC, V2A 7M5. ✆ **800/663-9400** or 250/493-8221. Fax 250/493-0607. www.rpbhotels.com. 204 units. C$155 (US$96) double; C$159–C$205 (US$99–US$127) suite. AE, DC, DISC, MC, V. Free parking. When you arrive in town, follow the signs to Main St. Lakeshore Dr. is at the north end of Main St. Pets accepted with C$20 (US$12) fee. **Amenities:** Restaurant, lounge; indoor pool; Jacuzzi; sauna; health club; watersports equipment rental; children's center; concierge; tour desk; business center; 24-hour room service; babysitting; same-day dry cleaning. *In room:* A/C, TV/VCR w/pay movies, dataport, coffeemaker, hair dryer, iron.

## IN KELOWNA

**Grand Okanagan Lakefront Resort & Conference Centre** This elegant lakeshore resort sits on 10ha (25 acres) of beach and parkland; its atmosphere is reminiscent of Miami Beach in the 1920s. The atrium lobby of the modern hotel has a fountain with a sculpted dolphin as its centerpiece. The rooms are spacious and regally outfitted with opulent furniture and upholstery, with views from every window. This is an ideal location for visitors who want to feel pampered in sophisticated surroundings while maintaining easy access to the waterfront. The restaurant and lounge overlook the resort's private marina, where guests can moor their small boats. Motorized swans and boats sized for kids offer fun for children in a protected waterway.

1310 Water St., Kelowna, BC, V1Y 9P3. ✆ **800/465-4651** or 250/763-4500. Fax 250/763-4565. www.grandokanagan.com. 320 units. C$179–C$279 (US$111–US$173) double; C$290–C$499 (US$180–US$309) suite or condo. Extra person C$15 (US$9). Off-season discounts available. AE, DC, MC, V. From Vancouver, On Hwy. 97, cross the Lake Okanagan Bridge. At the first set of lights, turn left onto Abbott St. At the second set of lights, turn onto Water St. **Amenities:** 3 restaurants, pub, lounge; indoor/outdoor pool; health club with spa; watersports equipment rentals; concierge; business center; shopping arcade; salon; 24-hour room service; laundry service; same-day dry cleaning. *In room:* A/C, TV, dataports, coffeemaker, hair dryer, iron.

**Hotel Eldorado** This is one of the most charming places to stay in Kelowna if you like historic inns. One of Kelowna's oldest hotels (from 1926), the Eldorado was floated down the lake from its original location to its present site on the water's edge south of downtown. It has been fully restored and is now decorated with a unique mix of antiques. All rooms are individually decorated, and there's a wide mix of floor plans and layouts. The third-floor guest rooms with views of the lake are the largest and quietest. Some rooms also feature lakeside balconies. On the premises are a boardwalk cafe, lounge, and dining room. The staff can arrange boat moorage, boat rentals, and waterskiing lessons.

500 Cook Rd. (at Lakeshore Rd.), Kelowna, BC, V1W 3G9. ✆ **250/763-7500.** Fax 250/861-4779. www.sunnyokanagan.com/el. 20 units. C$139–C$179 (US$86–US$111) double. AE, DC, MC, V. Free parking. From downtown follow Pandosy Rd. south 1.5km (1 mile). Turn right on Cook Rd. **Amenities:** Fine dining restaurant, boardwalk cafe, bar; Jacuzzi; marina. *In room:* A/C, TV.

## WHERE TO DINE

### IN & AROUND PENTICTON

**Cellar Door Bistro** CONTINENTAL The microbrewery boom got us used to eating in breweries; now we have restaurants in wineries. This excellent, attractive choice is hidden inside the Sumac Ridge Estate Winery in Summerland, just north of Penticton. The menu changes monthly to emphasize what's fresh. The cuisine has a hearty country-French finesse, such as a savory mushroom tart, roast duck breast with chantrelle mushroom-studded potatoes, and Chardonnay-poached salmon. The dishes are paired with wines from Sumac Ridge.

17403 Hwy. 97, Summerland, 17km (10 miles) north of Penticton. ✆ **250/494-3316.** www.cellardoorbistro.com. Reservations recommended. Main courses C$16–C$26 (US$10–US$16). AE, MC, V. Tues–Sat 11:30–2:30pm; Tues–Sat 5–9pm.

### IN KELOWNA

**de Montreuil** ★★ CONTEMPORARY CANADIAN This low-key, high-performance restaurant produces the Okanagan's most exciting cooking. The menu is simply divided into four sections: Appetizers, Bowls, Salads, and Main Plates. You can order à la carte or, better yet, follow the simple pricing system in which any two-course meal (main course plus appetizer, salad, or soup) is C$30 (US$19), a three-course meal is C$36 (US$22), and a four-course meal is C$41 (US$25). The menu changes weekly, but expect everything to be fresh and filled with hearty earthiness. As an appetizer, try pan-seared goose liver with fiddleheads and morel mushroom risotto. A couscous salad is served with asparagus spears and fresh apricots, then drizzled with orange ginger dressing. For an entree, choose roast free-range chicken with red curry and coconut yogurt sauce. An impressive wine list and friendly, sophisticated staff make de Montreuil even more noteworthy.

368 Bernard Ave. ✆ **250/860-5508.** Reservations recommended. Main courses C$18–C$24 (US$11–US$15). AE, DC, MC, V. Mon–Fri 11:30am–2pm, Daily 5:30pm–10pm.

**Fresco** ★★ NEW CANADIAN This coolly sophisticated restaurant is the newest dining hot spot in Kelowna. The cooking focuses on fresh regional cuisine, while keeping the preparations relatively unfussy—as these things go with this class of cutting edge cooking. The open kitchen overlooks a studied casual dining room; service is top-notch and the wine list celebrates the vintages of the Okanagan Valley. Start a meal with a chilled salad of citrus-marinated scallops, cucumber, radish and pepper, and move on to a main dish of baked root vegetable torte, or seared Pacific tuna. Fresco's chef/owner Rod Butters has cooked at some of western Canada's top restaurants; this is his first solo venture. Stop by and see what's cooking.

1560 Water St. ✆ **250/868-8805.** Reservations recommended. Main courses C$19–C$32 (US$12–US$20). Tues–Sat 5:30–10pm.

17

# The Yukon, the Northwest Territories & Nunavut: The Great Northern Wilderness

*by Bill McRae*

The **Far North** of Canada is one of North America's last great wilderness areas. The Yukon, the Northwest Territories, Nunavut, and the far north of British Columbia are home to the (Aboriginal) Inuit and northern First Nations peoples like the Dene, vast herds of wildlife, and thousands of square miles of tundra and stunted subarctic forest. For centuries, names like the Klondike, Hudson's Bay, and the Northwest Passage have conjured up powerful images of rugged determination in an untamed and harsh wilderness. For an area so little visited and so distant, the North has long played an integral role in the history and imagination of the Western world.

Yet the North has been changing rapidly, creating a whole pattern of paradoxes. The Arctic is a hotbed of mineral, oil, gas, and diamond exploration. Jobs and schools have brought Aboriginal peoples from their hunting camps to town, where they live in prefabs instead of igloos and drive trucks and snowmobiles out to their trap lines. Still, much of the money they spend in supermarkets they earn using ancestral hunting and artisan skills, and for many, life remains based on the pursuit of migrating game animals and marine creatures.

Native or Aboriginal Canadians—including **First Nations** peoples (Indians), the **Inuit,** and the **Métis,** offspring of white and First Nations couples—make up the majority of the North's population. All of Canada's Aboriginal peoples were originally nomadic, traveling enormous distances in pursuit of migrating game animals. Today nearly all First Nations people have permanent homes in settlements, but many of them spend part of the year in remote tent camps hunting, fishing, and trapping. And though the Inuit no longer live in igloos, these snow houses are still built as temporary shelters when the occasion arises.

Survival is the key word for Native Canadians. They learned to survive in conditions that seem unimaginably harsh to more southerly peoples, relying on skills and technologies that become more wondrous the better you know them. Early white explorers quickly learned that in order to stay alive they had to adopt those skills and technologies as best they could. Those who refused to "go native" rarely survived in the great Canadian north.

Norse merchants and explorers traveling from Greenland may have been the first non-Native visitors to the Canadian North, as long as 800 years ago, but the first non-Native known to have penetrated the region was **Martin Frobisher.** His written account of meeting the Inuit, over 400 years old, is the earliest on record. At about the same time, European whalers, hunting whales for their oil, were occasionally forced ashore by storms or shipwrecks and depended on Inuit hospitality for survival. This almost-legendary hospitality, extended to any stranger who came to them, remains an outstanding characteristic of the Inuit. Whites began to move into the Canadian Arctic in greater number during the "fur rush" of the late 18th century. In the wake of the fur hunters and traders came Roman Catholic and Anglican missionaries, who built churches and opened schools.

For most of its recorded history, the Far North was governed from afar, first by Great Britain, then by the Hudson's Bay Company, and from 1867 by the new Canadian government in Ottawa. At that time the Northwest Territories included all of the Yukon, Saskatchewan, Alberta, and huge parts of other provinces. Then, in 1896, **gold** was discovered on Bonanza Creek in the midwestern Yukon region of Klondike. Tens of thousands of people flocked to the Yukon in a matter of months, giving birth to Dawson City in Klondike, **Whitehorse** (later the capital) in south-central Yukon, and a dozen other tent communities, many of which eventually went bust along with the gold veins. The Yukon gold rush was the greatest in history; prospectors washed more than C$500,000 (US$310,000) in gold out of the gravel banks along the Klondike before industrial mining moved in, to reap in the millions. With its new wealth and population, the Yukon split off from the rest of the Northwest Territories in 1898.

The rest of the Northwest Territories didn't receive its own elected government until 1967, when the center of government was moved from Ottawa to the new territorial capital of **Yellowknife** and a representative assembly was elected. In 1999, the eastern section of the Northwest Territories, almost 2 million km$^2$ (about 775,000 sq. miles), became a separate and autonomous territory, known as **Nunavut** (meaning "our land" in the Inuit language of Inuktitut), with its capital of **Iqaluit** (formerly Frobisher Bay) on Baffin Island. The rest of the pre-Nunavut Northwest Territories—1,172,000km$^2$) (452,500 sq. miles) of land that contains the drainage of the Mackenzie River, a sizeable portion of Arctic coast, the Great Slave and Great Bear lakes, and a few arctic island territories—has retained the Northwest Territories name.

## 1 Exploring the North

The Arctic isn't like any other place. That observation may seem elementary, but even a well-prepared first-timer will experience many things here to startle—and perhaps offend—the senses.

No matter where you start from, the Arctic is a long way away. By far the easiest way to get there is by plane. Whitehorse, Yellowknife, and Iqaluit all have airports with daily service from major Canadian cities. Each of these towns is a center for a network of smaller airlines with regularly scheduled flights to yet smaller communities; here you'll also find charter services to take you to incredibly out-of-the-way destinations.

### VISITOR INFORMATION

For information, write **Tourism Yukon,** P.O. Box 2703, Whitehorse, YT Y1A 2C6 (✆ **867/667-5340;** fax 867/667-3546; www.touryukon.com). Be sure to ask for a copy of the official vacation guide *Yukon: Canada's True North.*

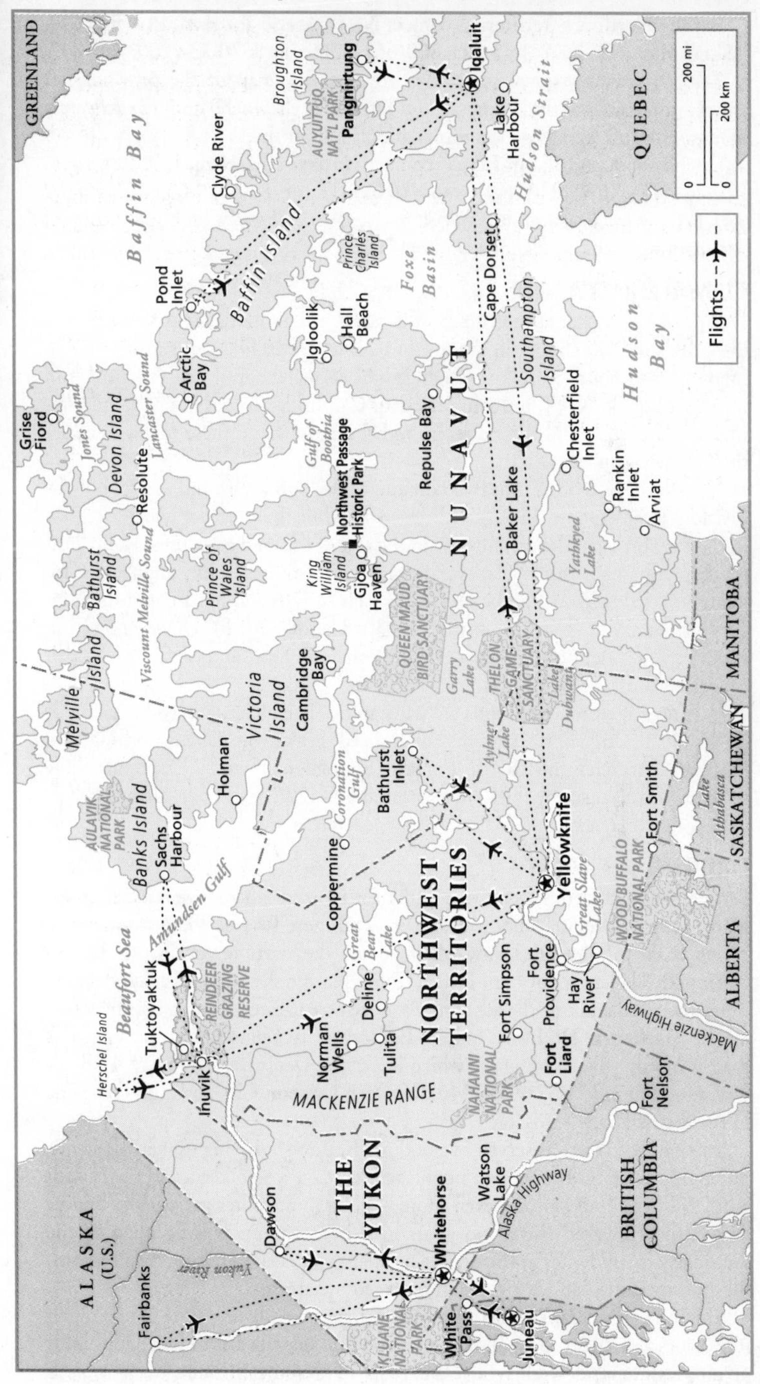
GREENLAND
Baffin Bay
Broughton Island
AUYUITTUQ NAT'L PARK
Pangnirtung
Iqaluit
Lake Harbour
Hudson Strait
QUEBEC
Clyde River
Baffin Island
Pond Inlet
Prince Charles Island
Foxe Basin
Cape Dorset
Igloolik
Hall Beach
Arctic Bay
Southampton Island
Hudson Bay
Grise Fiord
Jones Sound
Devon Island
Lancaster Sound
Resolute
Gulf of Boothia
Northwest Passage Historic Park
Repulse Bay
NUNAVUT
Chesterfield Inlet
Baker Lake
Rankin Inlet
Arviat
Yathkyed Lake
Bathurst Island
Viscount Melville Sound
Prince of Wales Island
King William Island
Gjoa Haven
QUEEN MAUD BIRD SANCTUARY
THELON GAME SANCTUARY
Garry Lake
Lake Dubawnt
MANITOBA
Melville Island
Victoria Island
Cambridge Bay
Aylmer Lake
Holman
AULAVIK NATIONAL PARK
Banks Island
Sachs Harbour
Coronation Gulf
Bathurst Inlet
Coppermine
Yellowknife
Fort Smith
Lake Athabasca
SASKATCHEWAN
WOOD BUFFALO NATIONAL PARK
Great Slave Lake
Amundsen Gulf
Beaufort Sea
Tuktoyaktuk
REINDEER GRAZING RESERVE
Herschel Island
Inuvik
Great Bear Lake
Deline
Norman Wells
Tulita
NORTHWEST TERRITORIES
Fort Simpson
Fort Providence
Hay River
ALBERTA
Mackenzie Highway
MACKENZIE RANGE
NAHANNI NATIONAL PARK
Fort Liard
Fort Nelson
ALASKA (U.S.)
Fairbanks
Yukon River
Dawson
THE YUKON
Whitehorse
Watson Lake
Alaska Highway
BRITISH COLUMBIA
KLUANE NATIONAL PARK
White Pass
Juneau
Flights
0 200 mi
0 200 km

For the Northwest Territories, contact **NWT Arctic Tourism,** P.O. Box 610, Yellowknife, NT X1A 2N5 (© **800/661-0788** or 867/873-7200; fax 867/873-4059; www.nwttravel.nt.ca). Ask for the free map of the province (it's almost impossible to find a map of the Territories elsewhere) and *The Explorers' Guide,* with full listings of accommodations and outfitters.

For Nunavut and Baffin Island, contact **Nunavut Tourism,** P.O. Box 1450, Iqaluit, NT X0A 0H0 (© **866/NUNAVUT** or 867/979-6551; fax 867/979-1261; www.nunatour.nt.ca). Ask for the *Arctic Traveller,* with full listings of destinations, accommodations, and outfitters.

## CLIMATE & SEASONS

During summer, the farther north you travel, the more daylight you get. Yellowknife and Whitehorse, in the south, bask under 20 hours of sunshine a day, followed by 4 hours of milky twilight bright enough to read a newspaper by. In northern Inuvik, NWT, or Iqaluktuuttiaq (Cambridge Bay), Nunavut, the summer sun shines around the clock. In midwinter, however, these towns don't see the northern sun rise at all.

The North is divided into two climatic zones: **sub arctic** and **arctic,** but the division doesn't follow the Arctic Circle. And while there are permanent ice caps in the far-northern islands, summer in the rest of the land gets considerably hotter than you might think. The average high temperatures in July and August for many subarctic regions can be in the 20s Celsius (70s and 80s F), and the mercury has been known to climb into the 30s Celsius (90s F). However, even in summer you should bring a warm sweater or ski jacket—and don't forget a pair of really sturdy shoes or boots.

In winter, weather conditions are truly arctic. The mercury may dip as low as 50°C (60°F) for short periods. You'll need heavily insulated clothing and footwear to travel during this time of year. Spring is an increasingly popular time to visit, with clear sunny skies, highs around 5°C (20°F), and days already longer than seems reasonable.

## DRIVING THE NORTH

Setting out to drive the back roads of the Far North has a strange fascination for many people, most of whom own RVs. The most famous route through the North is the **Alaska Highway,** which linked the wartime continental United States with Alaska via northern British Columbia and the Yukon. Today the route is mostly paved and isn't the adventure it once was. Off-road enthusiasts may prefer the **Mackenzie Highway,** linking **Edmonton** to **Yellowknife.** But even this road is mostly paved nowadays, which leaves the **Dempster Highway** ★ (highway information © **867/979-2040**), between **Dawson City** and **Inuvik,** as one of the few real back roads left.

Much of the North is served by good roads, though driving up here demands different preparations than you might be used to. It's a good idea to travel with a full 20l (5-gallon) gas can, even though along most routes gas stations appear frequently. However, there's no guarantee these stations will be open in the evenings, on Sunday, or at the precise moment you need to fill up. By all means, fill up every time you see a gas station in remote areas.

In summer, dust can be a serious nuisance, particularly on gravel roads. When it becomes a problem, close all windows and turn on your heater fan. This builds up air pressure inside your vehicle and helps to keep the dust out. Keep cameras in plastic bags for protection.

It's a good idea to attach a bug or gravel screen and plastic headlight guards to your vehicle. And it's absolutely essential that your windshield wipers are operative and your washer reservoir full. In the Yukon (outside of Whitehorse), the law requires that all automobiles drive with their headlights on; it's a good idea while traveling on any gravel road.

April and May are the spring slush months, when mud and water may render some road sections hazardous. The winter months, December to March, require a lot of special driving preparations; winter isn't a good time to plan a road trip to the North.

## SHOPPING FOR NATIVE ARTS & CRAFTS

The handiwork of the Dene and Inuit people is absolutely unique. Some of it has utility value—you won't get finer, more painstakingly stitched cold-weather clothing anywhere in the world.

The Baffin Island, Nunavut, communities are famous worldwide for their **stone, bone,** and **ivory carvings.** Inuit artists also produce noted weavings, prints, and etchings with native themes; clothing articles made of sealskin are also common. The Dene produce caribou-skin moccasins and clothing, often with beaded decoration.

Most Arts and Crafts articles are handled through community cooperatives, thus avoiding the cut of the middleman. Official documentation will guarantee that a piece is a genuine Native-Canadian object. Don't hesitate to ask retailers where a particular object comes from, what it's made of, and who made it. They'll be glad to tell you and frequently will point out where the artist lives and works. In the eastern Arctic particularly, artists will often approach tourists in the streets or in bars and restaurants, seeking to sell their goods. While these articles may lack the official paperwork, the price is often right; use your judgment when deciding to buy.

Before investing in Native art, make sure you know what the **import restrictions** are in your home country. In many countries, it's illegal to bring in articles containing parts of marine mammals (this includes walrus or narwhal ivory, as well as whale bones or polar-bear fur). Sealskin products are commonly prohibited. Consult a customs office to find out what restrictions are in place.

## FOOD, DRINK & ACCOMMODATIONS

Northerners traditionally lived off the land by hunting and fishing (many still do), and Arctic specialties have now worked their way onto many fine dining menus. **Caribou** and **musk ox** appear on almost all menus in the North and offer a different taste and texture for meat eaters. Good caribou, sometimes dressed in sauces made from local berries (wild blueberries or Saskatoon berries) tastes like mild venison and is usually cheaper than beef or lamb in the North. Musk ox is rather stronger tasting, with a chewy texture, and is often served with wild mushrooms. **Arctic char** is a mild pink-fleshed fish, rather like salmon but coarser grained and less oily. You won't find the mainstays of the Inuit diet—seal and whale meat—on most restaurant menus, but in outlying communities you won't have to look hard to find someone able to feed you some ***maktaaq*** (whale blubber and skin) or ***igunaq*** (aged, fermented meat, of walrus or seal). **Bannocks,** a type of baking-powder biscuit, and so-called **Eskimo doughnuts,** a cousin of Indian fry bread, are popular snacks to feed tourists. You'll have to decide how appetizing you find the delicacy known as **Eskimo ice cream** (***akutuq***), a mousse-like concoction made of whipped animal fats (caribou fat and seal oil, for instance) and berries.

**Tips** **Warning: Get Thee to an Outfitter**

Outdoor enthusiasts in many parts of the world can simply arrive at a destination and put together a recreational trip when they get there. That isn't the case in the North. If you want to get out onto the land, the water, or the glacier, you'll need to have the assistance of an outfitter or a local tour provider. There are no roads to speak of here, so you'll need help simply to get wherever you're going. This usually involves a boat or an airplane trip. Sports-equipment rental is all but unheard of, and it's very foolish to head out into the wilds (which start at the edge of the village) without the advice and guidance of someone who knows the terrain, weather, and other general conditions. For all these reasons—and for the entree you'll get into the community—you should hire an outfitter. You'll end up saving money, time, and frustration.

Vegetarians aren't going to find much to eat in the North. The traditional Arctic diet doesn't include much in the way of fruits or vegetables, and green stuff that's been air-freighted in is pretty sad-looking by the time it reaches the table. *Bring your own dietary supplements if you have a restricted diet.*

No matter what you eat in the North, it's going to be expensive. In towns like Yellowknife, Inuvik, and Iqaluit, a normal entree at a decent hotel restaurant will cost at least C$25 (US$16); at outlying villages, where hotels offer full board, a sandwich with fries will run C$20 (US$12). Chances are excellent that, for the money, your food will be very pedestrian in quality. In most towns, the grocery-store chain The Northern shelters a few fast-food outlets, usually the only other dining option.

**Alcohol** is banned or highly restricted in most Native communities. Some towns are completely dry: no one, not even visitors in the privacy of their hotel rooms, is allowed to possess or consume alcohol. In some locales, RCMP officers will check the baggage of incoming travelers and confiscate alcohol. In other communities, alcohol is legal but regulated to such a degree the casual visitor will find it impossible to get hold of a drink. In other communities, alcohol is available in hotel bars or restaurants but not in stores (or even by room service). Alcohol is a major social problem in the North, so by all means respect the local laws regulating alcohol consumption.

**Accommodations** are the most expensive day-to-day outlay in the North. Almost every community, no matter how small, will have a hotel, but prices are very high. You can save some money with B&Bs or homestays, which also have the advantage of introducing you to the locals.

## THE GREAT OUTDOORS

**SEASONAL TRAVEL** Hiking and naturalist trips are popular in late July, August, and early September. The ice is off the ocean, allowing access by boat to otherwise-remote areas. Auyuittuq National Park, with its famed long-distance hiking and rock climbing, is popular with experienced recreationists. Float trips on the Soper River in Katannilik Park are popular with those seeking adventures that are a bit softer. Naturalist-led hikes out onto the tundra make great day trips. The South Nahanni River, in Nahanni National Park, is popular for week-long raft or canoe trips below the massive 96m (316-ft.) Virginia Falls.

While it may seem natural to plan a trip to the Arctic in summer, the Far North is a year-round destination. Late-winter dog-sledding trips out into the frozen wilderness are popular with adventurous souls. In May and June from Pond Inlet, dogsled or snow-machine trips visit the edge of the ice floe, where wildlife viewing is superb. And in the dead of winter, there is the 24-hour darkness and the northern lights that lure people north.

**MOSQUITOES, DEERFLIES & OTHER CRITTERS** During summer especially, two of the most commonly heard sounds in the North are the rhythmic buzzing of winged biting insects and the cursing of their human victims. **Insect repellent** is a necessity, as is having a place you can get away from the mosquitoes for a while. Some hikers wear expedition hats or head nets to ward off the worst attacks. Mosquitoes can go through light fabric, which is why it's better to wear sturdy clothes even on the hottest days. Wasps, hornets, and other stinging insects are common. If you're allergic, be ready with your serum.

**CANOEING & DOG-SLEDDING** If you want to see the land as early explorers and Natives did, try exploring the North via these two traditional methods. The following outfitters usually offer recreation in more than one part of the North or different recreational pursuits depending on the season.

**Canoeing** The early French-Canadian trappers, or ***voyageurs,*** explored the North—particularly the Yukon—by canoe, and outfitters now offer multi-day expeditions down the region's wide powerful rivers. A good place to go for advice and some advice on guided tours on Yukon and Northwest Territories rivers is the **Canadian Recreational Canoeing Association,** P.O. Box 398, 446 Main St. W., Merrickville, ON K0G 1N0 (© **888/252-6292** or 613/269-2910; fax 613/269-2908; www.crca.ca). **Kanoe People,** P.O. Box 5152, Whitehorse, YT Y1A 4S3 (© **867/668-4899;** fax 867/668-4891; www.kanoepeople.com), offers both custom and guided canoe trips on Yukon rivers and lakes. River trips pass historic mining ghost towns and Native-Canadian villages. A guided trip on the Yukon goes for 8 days and costs C$1,596 (US$990), and one on the Telsin lasts 10 days at C$1,649 (US$1,022). Bring your own sleeping bag, pad, and small personal gear (including fishing tackle) of choice; everything else—including camping equipment, food, and transportation from Whitehorse—is included.

In southern Baffin Island, the Soper River, flowing past innumerable waterfalls in Katannilik Park, is the most famous canoeing river. **NorthWinds Arctic Adventures,** P.O. Box 888, Iqaluit, NT X0A 0H0 (© **800/549-0551** or 867/979-0551; fax 867/979-0573; www.northwinds-arctic.com), offers 12-day raft trips down the beautiful Soper—gentle enough for family groups—starting at C$3,300 (US$2,046). **Wanapeiti Canoe,** 338 Caves Rd., R.R. #2, Warsaw, ON K0L 3A0 (© **888/781-0411;** www.wanapiteicanoe.com), offers many arctic and sub arctic Canadian river trips by canoe, including excursions on the Soper, Nahanni, and Coppermine. A 10-day trip on the Soper costs C$2,995 (US$1,857).

**Dog-Sledding** An even more indigenous mode of transport in the north is travel by dogsled. While few people run dogs as their sole means of getting around any longer, the sport of dog-sledding is hugely popular, and dog-sledding trips to otherwise-snowbound backcountry destinations make a great early-spring adventure. **NorthWinds Arctic Adventures** (see above) offers a variety of dogsled trips ranging from 7 to 16 days and costing C$2,650

(US$1,643) to as much as C$12,000 (US$7,440), depending on the size of tour groups. Several trips are on **Baffin Island** ★, but others venture into the extreme north, including northern Quttinirpaaq (Ellesmere Island) and the North Pole.

In the Yukon, **Uncommon Journeys,** P.O. Box 20621, Whitehorse, YT Y1A 7A2 (© **867/668-2255;** fax 867/668-2254; www.uncommonyukon.com), offers 7- and 10-day guided backcountry dog-sledding trips out into the northern wilderness. Seven-day trips start at C$2,650 (US$1,643).

**WILDLIFE** It's easy to confuse **caribou** with European reindeer, as the two look very much alike and, in fact, are generally classified as the same species. But while reindeer are mostly domesticated animals, caribou are wild, and still travel in huge migrating herds that stretch to the horizon, sometimes numbering 100,000 or more. Caribou form the major food and clothing supply for many Native Canadians, whose lives cycle around the movements of the herds.

The mighty **musk ox** is indigenous to the Arctic. About 12,000 of them live on the northern islands. Immense and prehistoric looking, the bulls weigh up to 590kg (1,300 pounds). They appear even larger because they carry a mountain of shaggy hair. Underneath the coarse outer coat, musk oxen have a silky-soft layer of underwool, called ***qiviut*** in Inuit. One pound of qiviut can be spun into a 40-strand thread 40km (25 miles) long! As light as it is soft, a sweater made from the stuff will keep its wearer warm in subzero weather. And it doesn't shrink when wet. Qiviut is extremely expensive. Once spun, it can sell for as much as C$90 (US$56) an ounce.

The monarch of the Arctic, the **polar bear** roams the coast and the shores of Hudson Bay; you'll have to travel quite a way over mighty tough country to see one in its habitat. Weighing up to 658kg (1,450 lb.), they're the largest land predators in North America. **Grizzly bears** are found in the boreal forests and river basins. Both animals are very dangerous; if you encounter them, give them a wide berth. The North is full of other animals much easier to observe than the bears. In the wooded regions, you'll come across **wolves** and **wolverines** (harmless to humans, despite the legends about them), **mink, lynx, otter, ptarmigan,** and **beaver.** The sleek and beautiful white or brown **Arctic foxes** live in ice regions as well as beneath the tree line and near settlements.

Mid-July to late August, **seals, walruses, narwhals,** and **bowhead** and **beluga whales** are in their breeding grounds off the coast of Baffin Island and in Hudson Bay. And in the endless skies above there are **eagles, hawks, owls, razor-billed auks,** and **ivory gulls.**

## 2 The Alaska Highway: On to the Last Frontier ★

Constructed as a military freight road during World War II to link Alaska to the Lower 48, the **Alaska Highway** (a.k.a. the Alcan Highway) is now a popular tourist route to the Last Frontier. Now as much a phenomenon as a road, it has become something of a pilgrimage route. The vast majority of people who make the trip are recent retirees, who take their newly purchased RVs and head up north—it's a rite of passage.

Strictly speaking, the Alaska Highway starts at the Mile 1 marker in **Dawson Creek,** on the eastern edge of **British Columbia,** and travels northwest for 2,242km (1,390 miles) to **Delta Junction, Alaska,** passing through the Yukon along the way. The **Richardson Highway** (Alaska Route 4) covers the additional 158km (98 miles) from Delta Junction to **Fairbanks.** Even a decade ago, much of the talk of the Alaska Highway had to do with conditions of the road itself where the really torn-up sections were. Other problems included making it through soupy roads during freak rain and snowstorms, and how to make it between far-flung gas pumps. However, for the road's 50th anniversary in 1992, the final stretches were paved.

You should consider several things before setting out to drive this road. First, it's a very ***long*** road. Popular wisdom states that if you drive straight out, it's a 3-day drive between Fairbanks and Dawson Creek. If you're in that big of a hurry to get to Fairbanks, consider flying as much of the road is winding, slow-moving RV traffic is heavy, and a considerable amount of the road is under reconstruction every summer. If you try to keep yourself to a 3-day schedule, you're going to be miserable.

Summer is the only opportunity to upgrade or repair the road, so construction crews really go to it; depend on lengthy delays and some very rugged detours. Visitor centers along the way get faxes of daily construction schedules and conditions, so stop and ask about any delays. Or, to get website links and phone numbers for the latest information on Alaska Highway road conditions, see **www.themilepost.com/road_report.html**. In the Yukon, call toll-free ✆ **877/456-7623** (outside the Yukon, call ✆ 867/456-7623) for **24-hour highway information.**

While gasoline availability isn't the problem it once was, there are a couple of things to remember. Gas prices can be substantially higher than in, say, Edmonton or Calgary. While there's gasoline at most of the little communities that appear on the provincial road map, most close early in the evening, and some outfits are less than friendly. There are 24-hour gas stations and plenty of motel rooms at Dawson City, Fort St. John, Fort Nelson, Watson Lake, and Whitehorse.

Try to be patient when driving the Alaska Highway. During the high season, the entire route is one long caravan of RVs. Many people have their car in tow, a boat on the roof, and several bikes chained to the spare tire. Thus encumbered, they lumber up the highway at top speeds of 70kmph (43 mph).

## DRIVING THE ALASKA HIGHWAY

The route begins (or ends) at **Dawson Creek** in British Columbia and before long crosses the Peace River and passes through **Fort St. John.** There are ample tourist facilities along this stretch of the highway. It continues north, parallel to the Rockies. The forests thin, with pointy spruce trees replacing pine and fir trees. Wildlife-viewing is good; you can often see moose from the road.

From Fort St. John to **Fort Nelson,** there are gas stations and cafes every 65km to 81km (40 miles–50 miles), though lodging options are pretty dubious. At Fort Nelson, the Alaska Highway turns west and heads into the Canadian Rockies; from here, too, graveled **Liard Highway** (BC Highway 77; NT Highway 7) continues north to Fort Liard and Fort Simpson, the gateway to **Nahanni National Park.** Fort Nelson is thick with motels and gas stations; hours from any other major service center, this is a good place to spend the night.

The stretch of the Alaskan Highway through the Rockies is mostly narrow and winding; you can pretty much depend on finding a construction crew working along this portion. The Rockies are relatively modest mountains in this area, not as rugged or scenic as they are farther south in Jasper Park. Once over the Continental Divide, the Alaska Highway follows tributaries of the Liard River through **Stone Mountain Provincial Park** and **Muncho Lake Provincial Park.** Attractive rustic lodges and cabin resorts are scattered along the road for accommodations; this is also a good place to find a campsite.

At the town of **Liard River,** be sure to stop and stretch your legs or go for a soak at **Liard Hot Springs.** The provincial parks department maintains two nice soaking pools in the deep forest; the boardwalk out into the mineral water marsh is pleasant even if you don't have time for a dip. As you get closer to **Watson Lake** in the Yukon, you'll notice that mom-and-pop gas stations along the road will advertise they have cheaper gas than in Watson Lake. Believe them and fill up: Watson Lake is an unappealing town whose extortionately priced gasoline is probably its only memorable feature. If you don't plan your trip well, you may end up spending the night here.

The long road between Watson Lake and **Whitehorse** travels through rolling hills and forest to **Teslin and Atlin lakes,** where the landscape becomes more mountainous and the gray clouds of the Gulf of Alaska's weather systems hang menacingly in the western horizon. Whitehorse is the largest town along the route of the Alaska Highway, and unless you're in a great hurry, plan to spend at least a day here. You'll want to wash the dust off the car at the very least and eat a decent meal before another day of driving on the way to Alaska.

Hope for good weather as you leave Whitehorse, since the trip past **Kluane National Park** is one of the most beautiful parts of the entire route. The two highest peaks of Canada straddle the horizon, while glaciers push down mountain valleys. The road edges by lovely Kluane Lake before passing Beaver Creek and crossing over into Alaska. From the border crossing to Fairbanks is another 481km (298 miles).

A number of guidebooks deal exhaustively with driving the Alaska Highway; particularly good is the mile-by-mile classic, the annual ***Alaska Milepost*** (www.themilepost.com).

## 3 Whitehorse: Capital of the Yukon ★

Once part of the Northwest Territories, the Yukon is now a separate territory bordering on British Columbia in the south and Alaska in the west. Compared with the old Northwest Territories, it's a mere midget in size, but with 483,450km$^2$ (186,660 sq. miles), it's immense by most other standards.

The entire territory has a population of only 31,000—over half of them (23,000) living in **Whitehorse.** The capital of the Yukon is a late arrival on the scene. It was established only in the spring of 1900, fully 2 years after the stampeders had swarmed into Dawson City. But Whitehorse, on the banks of the Yukon River, is the logical hub of the Territory, and it became the capital in 1953 after Dawson fizzled out along with the gold.

### ESSENTIALS

**GETTING THERE** **Whitehorse Airport** (© **867/667-8440**) on a rise above the city, is served by **Air Canada** (© **888/247-2262**) from Vancouver. **Canada 3000** (© **888/300-0669**) also flies from Calgary or Vancouver to Whitehorse May to October. **Air North** (© **800/661-0407** in Canada or 800/764-0407 from the U.S.) flies round-trip from Juneau, Alaska. Their Klondike Explorer Pass allows you to travel over a 21-day period to many Yukon and Alaska destinations for C$650 (US$403). **Cab fare** to downtown Whitehorse from the airport is around C$12 (US$7). Whitehorse is 458km (284 miles) southeast of Beaver Creek (the Alaskan border).

**VISITOR INFORMATION** **Tourist office** Your first stop should be the **Yukon Visitor Reception Centre,** 2nd and Hanson streets (© **867/667-3084**).

The third week in May to the third week in September, the center is open daily 8am to 8pm; winter hours are Monday to Friday 9am to 4:30pm. A bounty of information can be found at the city's official website, **www.city.whitehorse.yk.ca**, as well as at **www.yukoninfo.com** and **www.touryukon.com**.

**GETTING AROUND** Public transit is handled by **Whitehorse Transit** (✆ **867/668-7433**); fare is C$1.50 (US95¢). Car rental is available from **National Tilden/Norcan** (✆ **800/661-0445** in western Canada or 867/668-2137, or 800/CAR-RENT in the U.S.), **Avis** (✆ **800/354-2847** or 867/667-2847), **Budget** (✆ **800/858-5377** or 867/667-6200), and **Sears** (✆ **800/268-8900** or 867/667-6220). If you need a taxi, try **Yellow Cabs** (✆ **867/668-4811**), **Global Taxi** (✆ **867/633-5300**), **Fifth Avenue Taxi** (✆ **867/667-4111**), or **Yukon Taxi** (✆ **867/633-7657**).

**SPECIAL EVENTS** February is a happening month in Whitehorse. One of the top dogsled races in North America, the **Yukon Quest** (www.yukonquest.org) begins in Whitehorse and runs to Fairbanks. The town is filled with hundreds of yapping dogs and avid mushers, eager to vie for the C$100,000 (US$62,000) top prize. Making even more noise is the **Frostbite Music Festival** (www.frostbitefest.com), which attracts musicians and entertainers from across Canada. Immediately afterward is the **Yukon Sourdough Rendezvous** (http://rendezvous.yukon.net), a midwinter festival commemorating the days of the gold rush with various old-fashioned competitions, like dog pulls, fiddling and costume contests, and a "mad trapper" competition.

For a short time every spring, thousands of migrating tundra and trumpeter swans descend on the Whitehorse region's waterways, and the town commemorates the spectacle of flocks returning from the south in mid-April with a birding event, the **Celebration of Swans** (www.taiga.net/swans/celebration_of_swans.html). In early summer, Whitehorse hosts the **Yukon International Storytelling Festival** (www.yukonstory.com), the third largest event of its kind in the world. The festival highlights ancient stories of First Nations and Native circumpolar peoples, but features traditional stories from all over the world. Many stories are performed theatrically, with song, music, and dance. In late summer, the folks who put on the Sourdough Rendezvous host what is billed as the longest and toughest bathtub race in the world, dubbed the **Yukon River Bathtub Race** (www.tubrace.com). Contestants travel a grueling 782km (486 miles) from Whitehorse to Dawson City, just in time to join in that town's **Discovery Days Festival.**

## EXPLORING WHITEHORSE

**Yukon Transportation Museum** ★ *Kids* This fascinating museum presents the development of travel, from dogsled to railway to bush plane, through to the building of the Alaska Highway. You'll come away with a new appreciation of how adventurous and arduous it once was to travel to the Yukon. The exhibits and vintage photos on travel by dogsled are especially interesting. There's also a replica of the historic aircraft *Queen of the Yukon,* the sister aircraft of *The Spirit of St. Louis.* A film details the building of the White Pass Railroad from Skagway to Whitehorse, and a model recreation of that railway features a replica of downtown Whitehorse in the 1920s and '30s. Step outside the museum and you'll see its DC3 weathervane, the world's largest, at the entrance of the Whitehorse airport.

Adjacent to Whitehorse Airport and the Beringia Centre (see below), 30 Electra Crescent; Mile 917 on the Alaska Hwy. ✆ **867/668-4792.** Admission C$4.25 (US$2.65) adults, C$3.25 (US$2) seniors/students, C$2 (US$1.20) children 6–12, C$9 (US$6) families, children 5 and under enter free. Mid-May to mid-Sept daily 10am–6pm.

**SS Klondike** Take a tour of the largest of the 250 riverboats that chugged up and down the Yukon River between 1929 and 1955, primarily as a cargo transport. Actually, the one on view was built in 1936 to replace the first *Klondike,* which ran aground. The *Klondike* is now permanently dry-docked beside the river, and is a designated national historic site. The boat has been restored to its late 1930s glory.

Anchored at the Robert Campbell Bridge. ✆ **867/667-4511** (summer and gift shop number) or 867/667-3910 in the off season. Admission C$4 (US$2.50) adults, C$3.50 (US$2.15) seniors, C$2.50 (US$1.55) students, and C$10 (US$6) families. Tours on the half hour: May 15–June 11 daily 9am–6pm; June 12–Aug 21daily 9am–7:30pm; Aug 22–Sept 8 daily 9am–6pm; Sept 9–Sept 15 daily 9am–3pm.

**MacBride Museum** ★ Covering half a city block, this log-cabin museum is crammed with relics from the gold-rush era and has a large display of Yukon wildlife and minerals, all lovingly arranged by a nonprofit society. Within the museum compound you'll find Sam McGee's Cabin (read Robert Service's poem on the cremation of same) and the old Whitehorse Telegraph Office. The MacBride has four galleries, open-air exhibits, and a gift shop.

First Ave. at Wood St. ✆ **867/667-2709.** www.macbridemuseum.com. Admission C$4 (US$2.50) adults, C$3.50 (US$2.15) seniors, children under 6 free. Mid-May to Labour Day (Sept 3) daily 10am–6pm; Winter Thurs–Sat noon–4pm.

**Yukon Arts Centre** ★ This is the hub of visual and performance arts in Whitehorse and the Yukon. The gallery hosts 10 to 17 rotating exhibits yearly, featuring both regional and international artists, photographers, and themes. It also offers workshops, lectures, and children's programs. You can see world-class, local and touring theatrical, musical, and dance performances year round in the center's 424-seat theater.

Yukon Place at Yukon College, off Range Rd. N; NW of downtown. ✆ **867/667-8575.** www.yukonartscentre.org. Admission by donation. Gallery hours: Jun–Aug Mon–Wed and Fri 11am–5pm, Thurs 11am–9pm, Sat–Sun noon–5pm; Sept–Aug Tue–Fri 11am–5pm, Sat–Sun 1pm–4pm, 3rd Thurs monthly 11pm–9pm. Call or visit website for performance calendar.

**Yukon Beringia Interpretive Centre** *Kids* During the last ice age, a land bridge joined Asia to Alaska and the Yukon, forming a subcontinent known as Beringia. This museum presents the archaeological and paleontological past of Beringia, with exhibits, multimedia displays, and films on its prehistoric people, animals, plants, and ecosystems. Bordered on all sides by glaciers, Beringia was once home to woolly mammoths and other fascinating Pleistocene-era animals, as well as to cave-dwelling humans.

Adjacent to the Yukon Transportation Museum, on Electra Crescent.; Mile 917 on the Alaska Hwy. ✆ **867/667-8855.** www.beringia.com. C$6 (US$3.70) adults, C$7 (US$4.35) combo ticket w/Yukon Transportation Museum, C$5 (US$3.10) seniors, C$4 (US$2.50) students, children 5 and under free. Mid-May to mid-Sept daily; May and Sept 9am–6pm; June–Aug 8:30am–7pm.

**Old Log Church** The first resident priest of Whitehorse arrived in 1900, and the town immediately proceeded to build a log church and rectory to house him and his services. They're now the only buildings of that time still in use in town. The Old Log Church was once the Anglican cathedral for the diocese—the only wooden cathedral in the world—and it now contains artifacts on the history of all the Yukon's churches. (On the next block over are two "log skyscrapers"—old two- and three-story log cabins used as apartments and offices).

Elliott St. at Third Ave. ✆ **867/668-2555.** Admission C$2.50 (US$1.55) adults, C$2 (US$1.20) seniors, C$1 (US60¢) children 6–12, C$6 (US$3.70) families; children under 6 free. Mid-May to mid-Sept daily 10am–6pm.

**Takhini Hot Springs** A swimming pool fed by natural hot springs and surrounded by rolling hills and hiking trails, the developed Takhini Hot Springs might be just what you need after days on the Alaska Highway. After swimming, you can refresh yourself at the restaurant. Depending on the season, camping, horseback riding, hiking, cross-country skiing, and wagon or sleigh rides are also available.

Off of the N Klondike Hwy. (10 Hotsprings Rd.), 27km (17 miles) north of Whitehorse. ✆ **867/633-2706.** www.takhinihotsprings.yk.ca. Admission C$5.50 (US$3.40) adults, C$5 (US$3.10) seniors/students, C$4 (US$2.50) children under 5. June–Aug daily 8am–10pm; Oct–April Thurs–Fri 6pm–10pm, Sat–Sun and holidays noon–10pm. Call for May and Sept hours as well as campground rates.

**Whitehorse Fishway** Narrowly bounded by high basalt walls and once one of the roughest sections of the Yukon River, Miles Canyon is now the site of a hydroelectric dam and the world's longest wooden fish ladder. The native chinook salmon that migrate past Whitehorse use the fishway to bypass the dam, on their way to completing one of the longest fish migrations in the world. Mid-July to mid-August you can view these magnificent fish through windows looking in on the ladder. Interpretive displays and an upper viewing deck show you the entire process by which the dam has ceased to be an obstruction to the salmon migration.

At the end of Nisutlin Dr., in suburban Riverdale. Free admission. Fishladder open late June–early Sept daily 8:30am–8:30pm.

## TOURS & EXCURSIONS

**HISTORICAL WALKING TOURS** The **Yukon Historical and Museums Association,** Donnenworth House, 3126 Third Ave., next to Le Page Park and behind the T.C. Richard's Bldg. (✆ **867/667-4704;** www.yukonalaska.com/yhma), offers Whitehorse Heritage Buildings Walking Tours in June, July, and August. Monday through Saturday, the hour-long tours are at 9am, 11am, 1pm, and 3pm and cost C$2 (US$1.20). They pass many of the gold-rush-era structures and historic sites, and are a good introduction to the town.

**WILDLIFE TOURS** North of Whitehorse 26km (16 miles), the **Yukon Game Farm and Wildlife Preserve,** Box 20411, Mile 5, Takhini Hot Springs Rd., Whitehorse, YK Y1A 7A2, one mile east of the Takhini Hot Springs (✆ **867/633-2922;** www.yukongamefarm.com), manages populations of many different indigenous animal species for breeding and conservation purposes, and is open for public viewing. The preserve covers hundreds of acres of forests, marshes, and meadows, and features such animals as bison, moose, musk ox, elk, mountain goats, and rare peregrine falcons. Much local wildlife also frequents the preserve. The preserve offers its own tours year-round; call ahead for hours, admission fees, and further details. **Gray Line Yukon/Holland America Lines-Westours** also runs group 2-hour tours between mid-May and mid-September, costing C$21 (US$13) for adults. Book through Gray Line, Steele St. and Second Ave., in the Westmark Hotel (✆ **867/668-3225, ext. 4701;** www.yukonweb.com/tourism/westours).

**RIVER CRUISES** The **MV *Schwatka*** (✆ **867/668-4716** for reservations; www.landair.ca) is a river craft that cruises the Yukon River through the famous

Miles Canyon. This stretch—once the most hazardous section of water in the Territory—is now dammed and tamed, though it still offers fascinating wilderness scenery. The cruise takes 2 hours, accompanied by narration telling the story of the old "wild river" times. Adults pay C$21 (US$13), children are half price. Trips are offered June to August. The boat leaves 5km (3 miles) south of Whitehorse; follow the signs for Miles Canyon.

A more authentic river experience is offered by the ***Emerald May,*** a steel pontoon raft that closely duplicates (but this one is completely safe and motorized) the style of boat used by the original 98ers, the gold-rush prospectors who stormed through the Yukon on their way to the Klondike in 1898. Instead of shooting dangerous rapids, today's trips focus on wildlife viewing and historic sites. Excursions are offered by **Taste of 98 Tours** (© **867/633-4767;** www.yukonweb.com/tourism/tasteof98) and leave daily from the log cabin on First Avenue (at Main St.), across from the MacBride Museum. Tickets are C$50 (US$31) with a maximum of 11 people per group for each 3-hour tour (available up to 3 times daily). Chartered outings are also available, the cost depending on length and services provided. Tours run June to August daily, with charters available through September.

**Gray Line** also offers a combination tour of Whitehorse and a cruise across Lake Schwatka and up the Yukon River through Miles Canyon. This 7-hour tour operates June to early August, and departs at 9am daily from the Westmark Hotel (Second Ave. and Steele St.). Contact Gray Line (see above) for reservations.

## SHOPPING

The **Yukon Gallery,** 2093 Second Ave. (© **867/667-2391;** www.yukongallery.ca), is Whitehorse's best commercial visual-arts gallery, featuring a large show space devoted to Yukon and regional artists. There's an extensive display of paintings and prints, as well as some ceramics and Northern crafts, like moose-hair tufting. **Northern Images,** 311 Jarvis St. (© **867/668-5739**), is the best gallery in the Yukon for native-Canadian art, in particular Inuit carvings and native masks. **Mac's Fireweed Books,** 203 Main St. (© **867/668-2434** or 800/661-0508; www.yukonbooks.com), is the best bookstore in town, specializing in Yukon-related books and "Arcticana," as well as rare texts and antiquarian paraphernalia.

## SPORTS & OUTDOOR ACTIVITIES

**CANOEING** The rivers of the Yukon were once navigated only by Native canoeists, and the Yukon's swift-flowing wide rivers still make for great canoe trips. In addition to their multi-day expeditions (see "The Great Outdoors" earlier), **Kanoe People** (© **867/668-4899;** www.kanoepeople.com) offers a variety of planned, self-guided day-trips on the Yukon River for C$65 to C$95 (US$40–US$59) per person. It also rents canoes, sea kayaks, and other equipment by the day or week. For day rentals at C$25 (US$16) for canoes or C$30 (US$19) for kayaks, as well as a selection of easy day canoe trips, contact **Up North,** (© **867/667-7905;** www.upnorth.yk.ca), on the Yukon River across from the MacBride Museum (86 Wickstrom Rd.). You can also rent a canoe for a day and shoot the once-harrowing 40km (25-mile) Miles Canyon—C$45 (US$28) pays for two shuttles and the canoe rental. Other day-trips on the Yukon and a 3-day trip on the Takhini are also offered.

**HIKING** During July and August the **Yukon Conservation Society,** 302 Hawkins St. (© **867/667-5678**), offers free guided nature walks in the Whitehorse area. Contact them weekdays between 10am and 2pm for details. Hikes are given Monday to Friday, and on most days several destinations are offered, including the **Whitehorse Rapids Dam** and **Miles Canyon.** Most walks are only a couple of hours long. You must get yourself to the departure point for any hike, and be sure to bring comfortable shoes and insect repellent.

If you're looking for a nice hike on your own, Miles Canyon is a good option. Cross the Second Avenue Bridge and follow the riverside path past the dam and up to the canyon. Here the Yukon River cuts a narrow passage through the underlying basalt. Though not very deep, the canyon greatly constricts the river, forming rapids that were once the object of dread to the greenhorn 98ers in their homemade boats. (The name Whitehorse is said to refer to the pre-dam rapids, the foamy currents of which resembled a stampede of horses' manes). A footbridge crosses the river 3km (2 miles) up the canyon, leading to both the Miles Canyon Road (where you might arrange a pickup) and a series of footpaths on the opposite side of the canyon.

**HORSEBACK RIDING** The **White Horse Riding Stable** (✆ **867/663-3086;** www.yukonweb.com/tourism/whrs) is 8km (5 miles) south of Whitehorse, just before the Miles Canyon turnoff (Alaska Hwy Mile 912.5). The stable's open 9am to 7pm daily from May to early September, and riding costs C$20 (US$12) per hour.

## WHERE TO STAY

There are a great number of campgrounds in and around Whitehorse; they represent the best alternative for travelers watching their money.

Tenters will like the **Robert Service Campground,** South Access Road (✆ **867/668-6678** or 867/668-3721), close to downtown and free of RVs. There are 48 unserviced tent sites, plus fire pits, washrooms, showers, and a picnic area. The rate is C$11 (US$7) per tent. Just north of Whitehorse on the Dawson City road are a number of lakeside territorial parks with campgrounds. At Lake Laberge Park, you can camp "on the marge of Lake Lebarge" with the creatively spelled verses of Robert Service filling your thoughts.

Whitehorse has more than 20 hotels, motels, and chalets in and around the downtown area, including a couple opposite the airport. This is far more than you'd expect in a place its size, and the standards come up to big-city levels in every respect.

### EXPENSIVE

**Edgewater Hotel** ★ At the end of Main Street, overlooking the Yukon River, this small vintage hotel has a distinct old-fashioned charm of its own. The lobby and guest rooms are cozy, and there's a well-appointed lounge. The rooms are newly renovated, in soft pastel colors, and equipped with extra-long beds. More expensive rooms have kitchenette facilities.

101 Main St., Whitehorse, YT Y1A 2A7. ✆ **867/667-2572** or toll-free 877/484-3334. Fax 867/668-3014. www.edgewaterhotel.yk.ca. 30 units. C$119–C$179 (US$74–US$111) double; C$239–C$299 (US$148–US$185) suite. Discounts for seniors and AAA/CAA members. AE, DC, MC, V. Free parking. **Amenities:** 2 restaurants (seafood and steaks, Italian). *In room:* A/C, TV, dataport, kitchenette, coffeemaker, hair dryer, iron.

**Westmark Whitehorse Hotel** ★ Centrally located in downtown Whitehorse, this national chain location has one of the busiest lobbies in town—the Gray Line/Holland America/Westours tour booking office is located here—nicely fitted with armchairs and settees. There's a small arcade alongside, housing a gift shop, barber, and hairdresser, plus a travel agency. The spacious guest rooms, including rooms for travelers with disabilities, are well furnished and decorated. The hotel's lounge hosts one of Whitehorse's popular musical revues, the *Frantic Follies.* The conference facilities are among the best in the Yukon.

201 Wood St., Whitehorse, YT Y1A 3T3. ✆ **800/544-0970** or 867/668-4700. Fax 867/668-2789. www.westmarkhotels.com. 181 units. C$125 (US$78) double. Children under 12 stay free in parents' room. AE, DC, MC, V. Free parking. **Amenities:** Restaurant, lounge with performances; guest laundry. *In room:* TV.

## MODERATE

**Best Western Gold Rush Inn** ★ Modern, but with a Wild West motif, the Gold Rush Inn is one of the most comfortable and central lodgings in Whitehorse, within easy walking distance of attractions and shopping. All of the guest rooms are recently remodeled. Some suites come with Jacuzzis and all have kitchenettes.

411 Main St., Whitehorse, YT Y1A 2B6. ✆ **800/661-0539** in the Yukon or northern BC, 800/764-7604 in Alaska, or 867/668-4500. Fax 867/668-7432. www.goldrushinn.com. 101 units. C$155 (US$96) double, C$165–185 (US$102–115) suite. Weekend specials. Senior and AAA/CAA discounts. Children under 12 stay free in parents' room. AE, DC, DISC, MC, V. Free parking. Pets may be allowed. **Amenities:** Restaurant, tavern w/entertainment, salon; laundry services. *In room:* A/C, TV w/free and pay movies, fridge, coffeemaker, hair dryer.

**Hawkins House** ★ All guest rooms have balconies in this modern but stylishly retro Victorian home. Rooms are decorated according to theme, but tastefully so: The Fireweed Room has rustic pine furniture à la Klondike, while the Fleur de Lys Room recalls Belle Epoque France. For business travelers, they have worktables and computer jacks and fax service available. Breakfast is available for C$7 (US$4.35). The proprietors also offer weekly vacation apartment rentals in an adjacent building.

303 Hawkins St., Whitehorse, YT Y1A 1X5. ✆ and fax **867/668-7638.** www.hawkinshouse.yk.ca. 5 units. Winter C$99 (US$61), spring and fall $109–C$119 (US$68–US$74), summer C$149 (US$92) double. AE, DC, MC, V. Free on-site parking. **Amenities:** Jacuzzi; laundry service. *In room:* TV/VCR, fridge, coffeemaker.

**River View Hotel** *Value* One of the oldest establishments in the Yukon, completely rebuilt in 1970, the River View breathes territorial tradition. Don't judge by the rather plain exterior; guest rooms are large and fully modern and represent a good deal in an otherwise expensive town. The lobby is crowded with Old Yukon memorabilia, from hand-cranked phones to moose antlers, but also offers Internet access (for a fee) for business travelers. You can't beat the location either: It's on the Yukon River, across from the MacBride Museum, and only 1 block from Main Street.

102 Wood St., Whitehorse, YT Y1A 2E3. ✆ **867/667-7801.** Fax 867/668-6075. www.riverview.ca. 53 units. Fall–winter C$79–$89 (US$49–$55), spring–summer C$109–$119 (US$68–$74) double. Extra person C$10 (US$6) each. DC, DISC, MC, V. Heated underground parking C$5 (US$3.10). Airport service C$5 (US$3.10) each way. Pets allowed. **Amenities:** Restaurant, lounge w/entertainment; room service; coin-op laundry; nonsmoking rooms; pet rooms. *In room:* TV, coffeemaker, hair dryer.

# WHERE TO DINE

Food is generally more expensive in Whitehorse than in the provinces, and this goes for wine as well. Be happy you didn't come during the gold rush, when a meal of beans, stewed apples, bread, and coffee could cost US$5—the equivalent of as much as US$100 today!

## EXPENSIVE

**Cellar Dining Room** ★ CANADIAN This plush lower-level place has a big local reputation. You'll enjoy whatever you order, but expect to pay top dollar. Pasta dishes start at C$19 (US$12). You can't go wrong selecting king crab, lobster, or prawns, and there's also an excellent prime rib (C$29/US$18). Dress casually, but not too casually. For good food—including steaks and prime rib—at a cheaper price point, eat at the Gallery, just upstairs from the Cellar.

In the Edgewater Hotel, 101 Main St. ✆ **867/667-2572.** www.edgewaterhotel.yk.ca. Reservations recommended. Main courses C$19–C$40 (US$12–US$25). AE, DC, MC, V. Mon–Fri 11:30am–1:30pm; daily 5–10pm.

**Panda's** ★ INTERNATIONAL Panda's is possibly the finest and certainly the most romantic restaurant in the Yukon. The decor is a mix of restrained elegance enlivened by traditional Klondike touches, and the service is smoothly discreet. This is one of the few places in town to offer daily specials apart from the regular menu. Many dishes are classic European, like beef Wellington or Wiener schnitzel, but Panda's also offers a variety of fresh seafood entrees, featuring local fish in season.

212 Main St. ✆ **867/667-2632.** Reservations recommended. Main courses C$18–C$45 (US$11–US$28). AE, DC, MC, V. Tue–Fri 11:30am–1:30pm; Mon–Sat 5–10pm (July–Aug also Sun 5–10pm).

## MODERATE

**China Garden Restaurant** *Value* CHINESE If you're looking for a moderately priced copious lunch, try the Asian buffet, served Monday to Friday 11:30am to 2pm for C$9.50 (US$6). China Garden also serves full dinners daily from its extensive menu.

309 Jarvis St. (✆ **867/668-2899.** Main courses C$8.75–C$16.75 (US$5–$10) and up. Mon–Fri 11:30am–10:30pm. Sat–Sun 4:30–10:30pm.

**No Pop Sandwich Shop** ★ COFFEE SHOP/SANDWICHES Whitehorse's hip "alternative" eating spot is No Pop, part bakery, part espresso shop, and part evening bistro. The baked goods are especially notable (try a raisin cinnamon roll) and the midday sandwiches are meaty and happily retro. At night, the extensive sandwich menu is available, as well as a number of daily changing special entrees, usually featuring fresh fish. On Sunday, this is the place for brunch, with omelettes and crêpes leading the menu.

312 Steele St. (1 block off Main St. on the corner of Steele and 4th Ave.). ✆ **867/668-3227.** Sandwiches C$4–C$7 (US$2.50–US$4.35); dinner main courses C$10–C$15 (US$6–US$9). MC, V. Mon–Thurs 9am–8:30pm, Fri 9am–9pm, Sat 10am–8pm, Sun 10am–3pm.

## INEXPENSIVE

**Midnight Sun Coffee Roastery** COFFEE BAR/PASTRIES/SANDWICHES If you're looking for a European/bohemian-style cafe atmosphere in Whitehorse, check out the Midnight Sun Coffee Roastery. They specialize in fresh-roasted coffees—made in an antique roaster on the premises—as well as freshly baked muffins, croissants, cookies, pastries, and breakfast and lunch sandwiches. The cafe has a warm atmosphere of local wood & stonework, decorated with the works of local artists. Stay in touch while you sip your coffee using the cafe's Internet terminal.

4168-C 4th Ave. (at Black St.). ✆ **867/633-4563.** www.midnight-sun-coffee.com. Sandwiches C$5.50 (US$3.40). Mon–Fri, 7am–6pm; Sat 8am–6pm; Sun 9am–5pm.

**Pasta Palace** *Value* ITALIAN/EUROPEAN/TAPAS This is one of the few inexpensive restaurants in Whitehorse where you don't feel you're eating on a budget. The best thing about the menu is the extensive selection of tapas and appetizers, available throughout the day. The selection includes bruschettas, salads, and satays, all between C$5 and C$6 (US$3.10 to US$3.70). Full entrees are also good bargains, with full-flavored pasta dishes starting at C$8 (US$5.20) and steaks, chops, and kebobs topping out at C$11 (US$7), and a full seafood platter at C$18.95 (US$12). Everything is à la carte, but you can still have a full meal and get change back from C$12 (US$7). The dining room isn't fancy, but service is prompt and friendly.

209 Main St. (near 2nd Ave.). ✆ **867/667-6888.** Main courses C$8–C$18.95 (US$5–US$12). MC, V. Daily 10am–10pm.

## WHITEHORSE AFTER DARK

The top-of-the-bill attraction in Whitehorse is the **Frantic Follies**★ (✆ **867/668-2042;** fax 867/633-4363; http://vaudeville.yk.net), a singing, dancing, clowning, and declaiming gold-rush revue that has become famous throughout the North. The show is an entertaining mélange of skits; music-hall drollery; whooping, high-kicking, garter-flashing cancan dancers; sentimental ballads; and deadpan corn, interspersed with rolling recitations of Robert Service's poetry. Shows take place nightly at the **Westmark Whitehorse Hotel,** 201 Wood St. Tickets are C$19 (US$12) for adults and C$9.50 (US$6) for children.

# 4 Kluane National Park ★★

Tucked into the southwestern corner of the Yukon, a 2-hour drive from Whitehorse, these 22,015km$^2$ (8,500 sq. miles) of glaciers, marshes, mountains, and sand dunes are unsettled and virtually untouched. Bordering on Alaska in the west, **Kluane National Park** contains **Mount Logan** and **Mount St. Elias,** respectively the second- and third-highest peaks in North America.

The park also contains an astonishing variety of **wildlife.** Large numbers of moose, wolves, red foxes, wolverines, lynx, otters, and beavers abound, plus black bears in the forested areas and lots of grizzlies in the major river valleys.

Designated as a **UNESCO World Heritage Site,** Kluane Park lies 158km (98 miles) west of Whitehorse—take the Alaska Highway to Haines Junction. There, just outside the park's boundaries, you'll find the **Visitor Reception Centre,** open year-round (✆ **867/634-7250**). The center has information on hiking trails and canoe routes and shows an award-winning audiovisual presentation on the park. Admission to the park is free.

## OUTDOOR ADVENTURES

Because this park is largely undeveloped and is preserved as a wilderness, casual exploration of Kluane is limited to a few day-hiking trails and to aerial sightseeing trips on small aircraft and helicopters.

The shortest hike up to one of Kluane's glaciers follows the **Slims East Trail,** leaving from south of the **Sheep Mountain Information Centre** (NW of the Haines Junction Visitor Centre). To reach Kaskawulsh Glacier and return will take at least 3 days, but this is an unforgettable hike into very remote and dramatic country. If you're interested in exploring the backcountry, you'll need to be in good shape and have experience with mountaineering techniques.

Day hikers have a few options, mostly near Haines Junction and south along Haines Road. Stop at lovely **Kathleen Lake,** where there's an easy interpreted hike or else a longer trail along the lake's south bank. Stop at the visitor center for more information on hikes in Kluane, or see.

## KLUANE AREA OUTFITTERS

The vast expanse of ice and rock in the wilderness heart of Kluane is well beyond the striking range of the average outdoor enthusiast. The area's white-water rafting is world-class but likewise not for the uninitiated. The Tatshenshini and Alsek rivers are famous for cold and wild white-water that flows through magnificent mountain and glacier scenery. Some raft trips pass through iceberg-filled lakes just below huge glaciers!

To explore this part of Kluane, contact an outfitter. **Ecosummer Expeditions,** 936 Peace Portal Dr., #240, Blaine, WA 98231 (✆ **800/465-8884** or 250/674-0102; www.ecosummer.com), takes guided backpacking, mountaineering, and white-water rafting parties to Kluane National Park. Individual trips can feature trekking or rafting, while others combine the two in one trip. Trekking expeditions include a 9-day naturalist tour in the St. Elias Mountains and an 8-day expedition around the Donjek and Lowell Glaciers (C$1,650/US$1,023). Rafting trips include an 11-day trip down the Alsek and Tatshenshini for C$2,895 (US$1,795) and a 6-day through the Alsek Valley for C$1,795 (US$1,113).

Also offering white-water trips is **Tatshenshini Expediting,** 1602 Alder St., Whitehorse, YT Y1A 3W8 (✆ **867/633-2742;** www.tatshenshiniyukon.com). Trips range from a 1-day run down the Tatshenshini at C$100 (US$62) to an 11-day trip down the Tatshenshini from Dalton Post and down the Alsek River to the Pacific at C$2,500 (US$1,550). Four- and six-day trips down the Alsek are also available. Call ahead because trip offerings vary from year to year and fill up fast.

### AERIAL SIGHTSEEING

Purists may object, but the only way the average person is going to have a chance to see the backcountry of Kluane Park is by airplane or helicopter. The most popular trips are flown by **Trans North Helicopters** (✆ **867/668-2177** or 600/700-1034; www.tntaheli.com). Their offerings range from C$90 (US$56) per person for 25 minutes in the air to C$350 (US$217) per person for a 90-minute ride. Short trips provide a panorama of Kluane Lake and the foothills of the park; longer trips explore the glaciers. Some trips offer the option of being dropped off for a hike. **Sifton Air** (✆ **867/634-2916;** www.kluaneglaciertours.com) has five airplane flights over the park; the shortest takes 40 minutes to fly over the Kaskawulsh Glacier for C$90 (US$56) per person; the longest trip, C$200 (US$124) per person, covers much more of the park over 2 hours.

## 5 The Chilkoot Trail & White Pass

South of Whitehorse, massive ranges of glacier-chewed peaks rise up to ring the Gulf of Alaska; stormy waters reach far inland as fjords and enormous glaciers spill into the sea (the famed Glacier Bay is here). This spectacularly scenic region is also the site of the **Chilkoot Trail,** which in 1898 saw 100,000 gold-rush stampeders struggle up its steep slopes. Another high mountain pass was transcribed in 1900 by the White Pass and Yukon Railroad on its way to the goldfields; excursion trains now run on these rails, considered a marvel of engineering.

To see these sites, most people embark on long-distance hiking trails, rail excursions, or cruise boats. Happily, two highways edge through this spectacular landscape; if you use the **Alaska Marine Highway ferries** (✆ **800/642-0066;** www.dot.state.ak.us/external/amhs) this trip can be made as a loop from either Whitehorse or Haines Junction. Because the ferries keep an irregular schedule, you'll need to call to find out what the sailing times are on the day you plan to make the trip.

### THE CHILKOOT TRAIL

In 1896, word of the great gold strikes on the Klondike reached the outside world, and nearly 100,000 people set out for the Yukon to seek their fortunes.

There was no organized transportation into the Yukon, so the stampeders resorted to the most expedient methods. The **Chilkoot Trail,** long an Indian trail through one of the few glacier-free passes in the Gulf of Alaska, became the primary overland route to the Yukon River, Whitehorse, and the goldfields near Dawson City.

The ascent of the Chilkoot became the stuff of legend, and pictures of men and women clambering up the steep snowfields to Chilkoot Summit are one of the enduring images of the stampeder spirit. The North Western Mounted Police demanded that anyone entering the Yukon carry a ton of provisions (literally); there were no supplies in the newly born gold camps on the Klondike, and malnutrition and lack of proper shelter were major problems. People were forced to make up to 30 trips up the trail in order to transport all their goods into Canada. Once past the RCMP station at Chilkoot Summit, the stampeders then had to build some sort of boat or barge to ferry their belongings across Bennett Lake and down the Yukon River.

Today, the Chilkoot Trail is a national historic park jointly administered by the Canadian and U.S. parks departments. The original trail is open year-round to hikers who wish to experience the route of the stampeders. The route also passes through marvelous glacier-carved valleys, coastal rain forest, boreal forest, and alpine tundra.

However, the Chilkoot Trail is as challenging today as it was 100 years ago. Though the trail is only a total of 53km (33 miles) in length, the vertical elevation gain is nearly 1,128m (3,700 ft.) and much of the path is very rocky. Weather, even in high summer, can be extremely changeable, making this always-formidable trail sometimes a dangerous one.

Most people make the trip from **Dyea,** 15km (9 miles) north of Skagway in Alaska over the Chilkoot Summit (the U.S.-Canadian border) to **Bennett** in northwest British Columbia, in 4 days. Many shuttles and taxis run from Skagway to Dyea. The third day of the hike is the hardest, with a steep ascent to the pass and a 12km (7½-mile) distance between campsites. At Bennett, there's no road or boat access; from the end of the trail, you'll need to make another 6km (4-mile) hike out along the rail tracks to Highway 2 near Fraser, British Columbia (the least expensive option), or you can ride the **White Pass and Yukon Railway** (**© 800/343-7373;** www.whitepassrailroad.com) from Bennett out to Fraser for US$30 (C$48) or down to Skagway for US$65 (C$105)—and there's a US$15 (C$24) surcharge for tickets purchased in Bennett, so plan ahead. Remember to take identification with you on this hike—you're crossing an international border.

The Chilkoot Trail isn't a casual hike; you'll need to plan and provision for your trip carefully. And it isn't a wilderness hike, because between 75 and 100 people start the trail daily. Remember that the trail is preserved as a historic park; leave artifacts of the gold-rush days—the trail is strewn with boots, stoves, and other effluvia of the stampeders—as you found them.

Permits are also required to make the hike. The U.S. and Canadian parks authorities cooperate to administer these permits, and they can be obtained on either side of the border. Only 50 hikers are allowed per day, and 42 of the permits may be reserved for C$10 (C$6) each—the other 8 are held for last minute hikers. The permits cost C$35 (US$22) for adults and C$17.50 (US$11) for youths ages 6 to 17.

For details on the Chilkoot Trail, contact the **Klondike Gold Rush National Historic Park,** P.O. Box 517, Skagway, AK 99840 (**© 907/983-2921;**

www.nps.gov/klgo/chilkoot.htm), or the **Canadian Parks Service,** Suite 200–300 Main St., Whitehorse, YT Y1A 2B5 (© **800/661-0486;** http://parkscan.harbour.com/ct).

## WHITE PASS & THE YUKON ROUTE

In 1898, engineers began the task of excavating a route up to **White Pass.** Considered a marvel of engineering, the track edged around sheer cliffs on long trestles and tunneled through banks of granite. The train effectively ended traffic on the Chilkoot Trail, just to the north.

The White Pass and Yukon Route railroad now operates between Skagway, Alaska, and Bennett, British Columbia. Several trips are available on the historic line. Trains travel twice daily from Skagway to the summit of White Pass, a 3-hour return journey costs US$82 (C$132) for adults. Roughly twice a month, a train makes an 8-hour round-trip from Skagway to Lake Bennett, the end of the Chilkoot Trail, costing US$128 (C$206) for adults; hikers on the Chilkoot Trail can catch this train on its downhill run for a reduced price (see Chilkoot Trail section above). Connections between Fraser and Whitehorse via motor coach are available daily. Prices for children ages 3 to 12 on all rides are half the adult fare, and infants ride free.

The White Pass and Yukon excursion trains operate mid-May to the last weekend of September. Advance reservations are suggested; for details, contact the **White Pass and Yukon Route,** P.O. Box 435, Skagway, AK 99840 (© **800/343-7373;** www.whitepassrailroad.com).

# 6 Dawson City: An Authentic Gold-Rush Town ★★

**Dawson City** is as much of a paradox as it is a community today. Once the biggest Canadian city west of Winnipeg, with a population of 30,000, it withered to practically a ghost town after the stampeders stopped stampeding. In 1953 the seat of territorial government was shifted to Whitehorse, which might've spelled the end of Dawson—but didn't. For now, every summer the influx of tourists more than matches the stream of gold rushers in its heyday. The reason for this is the remarkable preservation and restoration work done by Parks Canada. Dawson today is the nearest thing to an authentic gold-rush town the world has to offer.

However, Dawson City is more than just a gold-rush theme park; it's a real town with 2,000 year-round residents, many still working as miners (and many as sourdough wannabes). The citizens still like to party, stay up late, and tell tall tales to strangers, much as they did 100 years ago.

## ESSENTIALS

**GETTING THERE** From Whitehorse you can catch an **Air North** plane for the 1-hour hop (© **800/764-0407** from the U.S. or 800/661-0407 in Canada). You can also fly round-trip from Fairbanks, Alaska.

If you're driving from Alaska, from Chicken take the unpaved **Taylor Highway** across the border, where it becomes the **Top of the World Highway,** completing the trip to Dawson. The **Klondike Highway** runs from Skagway, Alaska, to Whitehorse, and from there north to Dawson City via Carmacks and Stewart Crossing. Skagway is a port for the Alaska Marine Highway ferries system (© **800/642-0066;** www.dot.state.ak.us/external/amhs). The 537km (333 miles) from Whitehorse to Dawson City is a very long and tiring drive, even though the road is fine.

**VISITOR INFORMATION** **Tourist office** The **Visitor Reception Centre,** Front and King streets (✆ **867/993-5566**), provides details on all historic sights and attractions; the national park service also maintains an information desk here. It's open mid-May to mid-September daily 9am to 8pm. Walking tours of Dawson City, led by highly knowledgeable guides, depart from the center daily in summer, costing C$5 (US$3.10).

A good website to visit for info on Dawson City is **www.dawsoncity.com.** Additional info can be found at **www.touryukon.com.**

**SPECIAL EVENTS** **Discovery Days** in mid-August commemorates the finding of the Klondike gold a century ago with dancing, music, parades, and canoe races. Contestants from Whitehorse's Yukon River Bathtub Race pull into Dawson during this festival. In mid-July the city hosts the **Dawson City Music Festival** (www.dcmf.com), featuring rock, folk, jazz, blues, world-beat, and traditional music from across Canada and beyond. Dawson also hosts a variety of winter events. In late February and early March, the **Trek over the Top** (www.trekoverthetop.com) features snowmobile races from Tok, Alaska, to Dawson City, and vice-versa, via the Top of the World Highway. In mid-March, the **Percy De Wolfe Memorial Race and Mail Run,** a 336km (210-mile) dogsled race from Dawson City to Eagle, Alaska, commemorates the route of historic Dawson mail carrier Percy De Wolfe.

## EXPLORING DAWSON CITY & ENVIRONS

All of Dawson City and much of the surrounding area is preserved as a National Historic Site, and it's easy to spend a day wandering the boardwalks, looking at the old buildings, shopping the boutiques, and exploring vintage watering holes. About half of the buildings in the town are historic; the rest are artful contemporary reconstructions. **Klondike National Historic Sites** (✆ **867/993-7200** or 867/993-7237; http://parkscan.harbour.com/khs) preserves eight buildings and sites in and around Dawson City. The Parks Service fees are usually C$5 (US$3.10) for adults for a guided tour, for most of its sites and services. However, you can get a season (mid-May to mid-Sept) pass to all the Park Service's Dawson City sites for C$15 (US$9). For current Parks Canada program information and tickets, head over to the local Visitor Reception Centre.

Between the town and the mighty Yukon River are a **series of dikes** channeling the once-devastating floodwaters. A path follows the dikes and makes for a nice stroll. The **SS *Keno,*** a Yukon riverboat, is berthed along the dikes (next to the Canadian Imperial Bank of Commerce on Front St.). Built in Whitehorse in 1922, it was one of the last riverboats to travel on the Yukon—there were once more than 200 of them.

**Dawson City Museum** ★ In the grand old Territorial Administration building, this excellent museum should be your first stop on a tour of Dawson City. Well-curated displays explain the geology and paleontology of the area (this region was on the main migratory path between Asia and North America during the last ice age), as well as the history of the native Hän peoples. The focus, of course, is the gold rush, and the museum explains various mining techniques; one of the galleries is dedicated to demonstrating the day-to-day life of early-1900s Dawson City. Various tours and programs are offered on the hour, including two video presentations. Costumed docents are on hand to answer questions and recount episodes of history. On the grounds are early rail steam engines that served in the mines.

Fifth Ave. at Minto Park. ✆ **867/993-5291.** http://users.yknet.yk.ca/dcpages/Museum.html. Admission C$5 (US$3.10) adults, C$4 (US$2.50) students/seniors, C$12 (US$7) families, free for small children. Mid-May to Mid-Sept daily 10am–6pm. MC, V.

**Robert Service Cabin** Poet Robert Service lived in this two-room log cabin from 1909 to 1912. Backed up against the steep cliffs edging Dawson City, Service's modest cabin today plays host to a string of pilgrims who come to hear an actor recite some of the most famous verses in the authentic milieu. In this cabin, Service composed his third and final volume of *Songs of a Rolling Stone,* plus a middling-awful novel entitled *The Trail of Ninety-eight.* Oddly enough, the bard of the gold rush neither took part in nor even saw the actual stampede. Born in England, he didn't arrive in Dawson until 1907—as a bank teller—when the rush was well and truly over. He got most of his plots by listening to old prospectors in the saloons, but the atmosphere he soaked in at the same time was genuine enough—and his imagination did the rest.

Eighth Ave. ✆ **867/993-7200.** http://parkscan.harbour.com/khs/robert.htm. Admission C$5 (US$3.10) adults, C$2.50 (US$1.55) children. Mid-May to Sept daily 9am–5pm; recitals daily at 10am and 3pm.

**Jack London's Cabin and Interpretive Centre** American adventure writer Jack London lived in the Yukon less than a year—he left in June 1898 after a bout with scurvy—but his writings immortalized the North, particularly the animal stories like *The Call of the Wild, White Fang,* and *The Son of Wolf.* The cabin, a replica, contains more than 60 photos, documents, newspaper articles and other London memorabilia. Yukon author Dick North, who was instrumental in the creation of the historic site, serves as an interpreter at the center.

Eighth Ave. ✆ **867/993-5575.** Admission C$2 (US$1.20). Mid-May to Mid-Sept daily 10am–5pm; recitations daily.

**Bonanza Creek** The original Yukon gold strike and some of the richest pay dirt in the world were found on **Bonanza Creek,** an otherwise-insignificant tributary flowing north into the Klondike River. A century's worth of mining has left the streambed piled into an orderly chaos of gravel heaps, the result of massive dredges. The national park service has preserved and interpreted a number of old prospecting sites; however, most of the land along Bonanza Creek is owned privately, so don't trespass, and by no means should you casually gold-pan.

The **Discovery Claim,** about 16km (10 miles) up Bonanza Creek Road, is the spot, now marked by a National Historic Sites cairn, where George Carmack, Skookum Jim, and Tagish Charlie found the gold that unleashed the Klondike Stampede in 1896. They staked out the first four claims (the fourth partner, Bob Henderson, wasn't present). Within a week, Bonanza and Eldorado creeks had been staked out from end to end, but none of the later claims matched the wealth of the first. Just over 12km (7½ miles) up Bonanza Creek, Parks Canada has preserved **Dredge no. 4** (✆ **867/993-7200;** http://parkscan.harbour.com/khs), one of the largest gold dredges ever used in North America; it's open June through early to mid-September daily 9am to 5pm, with tours offered hourly to 4pm at C$5 (US$3.10) for adults or C$2.50 (US$1.55) for youths ages 12 and under. Dredges—which augured up the permafrost, washed out the fine gravel, and sifted out the residual gold—were used after placer miners had panned out the easily accessible gold along the creek. Dredge no. 4 began operation in 1913 and could dig and sift 13,800m$^3$ (18,000 cubic yd.) in 24 hours, thus doing the work of an army of prospectors. You can do some free panning yourself at Claim 6, 14km (9 miles) up Bonanza Road. Bring your own pan (BYOP)!

The next drainage up from Bonanza Creek is **Bear Creek,** which became the headquarters for the dredge gold mining that dominated the Klondike area from 1905 to 1965, after the bloom went off placer mining. Parks Canada has developed a 65-building interpretive site that explores the history of industrial mining, including a dredge, a hydraulic monitor, and a gold mill, where the gold nuggets were cleaned, melted down, and cast into bullion. The turnoff for **Bear Creek Historic Mining Camp** is about 11km (7 miles) south of Dawson City, off the Klondike Highway. The site is open dawn to dusk from June through the first week of September, and two tours of the gold mill are given daily, at 1:30 and 2:30pm, costing C$5 (US$3.25).

Head west on Bonanza Creek Rd., about 2km (1¼ miles) south of Dawson City.

## THE KLONDIKE GOLD RUSH

The Klondike gold rush began with a wild war whoop from the throats of three men—two First Nations Canadians and one white—that broke the silence of Bonanza Creek on the morning of August 17, 1896: "Gold!" they screamed, "Gold, gold, gold!" That cry rang through the Yukon, crossed to Alaska, and rippled down into the United States. Soon the whole world echoed with it, and people as far away as China and Australia began selling their household goods and homes to scrape together the fare to a place few of them had ever heard of before.

Some 100,000 men and women from every corner of the globe set out on the Klondike Stampede, descending on a territory populated by a few hundred souls. Tens of thousands came by the Chilkoot Pass from Alaska—the shortest route but also the toughest. Canadian law required each stampeder to carry 909kg (2,000 pounds) of provisions up over the 914m (3,000-ft.) summit. Sometimes it took 30 or more trips up a 45° slope to get all the baggage over, and the entire trail—with only one pack—takes about 3½ days to hike. Many collapsed on the way, but the rest slogged on—on to the Klondike and the untold riches to be found there.

The riches were real enough. The Klondike fields proved to be the richest ever found anywhere. Klondike stampeders were netting C$300 to C$400 (US$186–US$248) in a single pan (and gold was then valued at around C$15/US$9 an ounce)! What's more, unlike some gold that lies embedded in veins of hard rock, the Klondike gold came in dust or nugget forms buried in creek beds. This placer gold, as it's called, didn't have to be milled—it was already in an almost-pure state!

The trouble was that most of the clerks who dropped their pens and butchers who shed their aprons to join the rush came too late. By the time they had completed the backbreaking trip, all the profitable claims along the Klondike creeks had been staked out and were defended by grim men with guns in their fists.

Almost overnight, Dawson boomed into a roaring, bustling, gambling, whoring metropolis of 30,000 people, thousands of them living in tents. And here gathered those who made fortunes from the rush without ever handling a pan: the supply merchants, saloonkeepers, dance-hall girls, and cardsharks. There were also some oddly peripheral characters: A bank teller named Robert Service who listened to the tall tales of prospectors and set them to verse (he never panned gold himself). And a stocky 21-year-old former sailor from San Francisco who adopted a big mongrel dog in Dawson, then went home and wrote about him a book that sold half a million copies. The book was *The Call of the Wild;* the sailor, Jack London.

By 1903, more than C$500 million (US$310 million) in gold had been shipped south from the Klondike, and the rush petered out. A handful of millionaires bought mansions in Seattle, tens of thousands went home with empty pockets, and thousands more lay dead in unmarked graves along the Yukon River. Dawson—"City" no longer—became a dreaming backwater haunted by 30,000 ghosts.

## TOURS & EXCURSIONS

From June to early September the national park service offers C$5 (US$3.10) **daily walking tours** of Dawson City; check for hours and sign up for the tour at the **Visitor Reception Centre,** at Front and King streets (✆ **867/993-5566**). **Gold City Tours** (✆ **867/993-5175**) offers a 3½-hour minibus tour of Dawson City and the Bonanza goldfields, as well as a late-evening trip up to Midnight Dome for a midnight-sun panorama of the area. The office is on Front Street, across from the riverboat *Keno.*

The ***Yukon Queen II*** is a "fast cat" catamaran that can carry 104 passengers over the 173km (108-mile) stretch of river from Dawson City to Eagle, Alaska. Tickets include meals; mid-May to mid-September, the two-day, round-trip and same-day, one-way journeys run daily. Adults pay C$210 (US$130) round-trip and C$125 (US$78) one-way; if you take the round-trip, you'll have to make arrangements to stay in Eagle or fly back. Book the boat trip and return flights through **Gray Line Yukon/Yukon Queen River Cruises** on Front Street (1st Ave.) near the visitor center (✆ **867/993-5599**); tickets go quickly, so try to reserve well in advance. If you want to stay overnight in Eagle, you'll have to make arrangements separately.

## WHERE TO STAY

There are about a dozen hotels, motels, and B&Bs in Dawson City. Most are well appointed, but none are particularly cheap. Only the Eldorado and Downtown hotels and a couple of the B&Bs remain open year-round.

### EXPENSIVE

**Downtown Hotel** ★ One of Dawson City's originals, the Downtown has been completely rebuilt, refurbished, and updated with all modern facilities, yet it preserves a real Western-style atmosphere. The Jack London Grill and Sourdough Saloon look right out of the gold-rush era; they're definitely worth a visit.

Second Ave. and Queen St., Dawson City, YT Y0B 1G0. ✆ **867/993-5346.** Fax 867/993-5076. www.downtown.yk.net. 59 units. C$124 (US$77) double. Senior discount offered. Children under 6 stay free with parents. AE, DC, DISC, MC, V. Transportation available for those with disabilities. **Amenities:** Restaurant, lounge; Jacuzzi; courtesy limo; winter plug-ins available for car head-bolt heaters. *In room:* TV w/pay movies, coffeemaker.

**Eldorado Hotel** ★ Another vintage hotel made over and modernized, the Eldorado offers guest rooms in its original building or in an adjacent modern motel unit. Some rooms feature kitchenettes.

Third Ave. and Princess St., Dawson City, YT Y0B 1G0. ✆ **800/764-3536** or 867/993-5451. Fax 867/993-5256. www.eldoradohotel.ca. 52 units. C$129 (US$80) double. Senior discounts available. Children under 12 stay free with parents. AE, DC, DISC, MC, V. **Amenities:** Restaurant, lounge; courtesy airport pickup; coin-op washers and dryers; executive-level suites; winter plug-ins available. *In room:* TV, coffeemaker.

**Westmark Inn** ★ The Westmark only looks old; on the inside, it reveals itself to be a modern hotel. Facilities include a Laundromat, a cafe with a courtyard deck, a gift shop, and a traditional cocktail lounge.

Fifth Ave. and Harper St., Dawson City, YT Y0B 1G0. ✆ **800/544-0970** or 867/993-5542 (summer only). www.westmarkhotels.com. 131 units. C$169 (US$105) double. AE, MC, V. Free Parking. Closed mid-Sept to mid-May. **Amenities:** Restaurant, lounge; laundromat; nonsmoking rooms; handicapped accessible. *In room:* TV.

## MODERATE

**Dawson City B&B** This nicely decorated, large home fronted by two stories of decks is on the outskirts of Dawson City, beside Gateway Park and overlooking the Klondike and Yukon rivers; with excellent views. The grounds are very attractively gardened. Rooms are ample sized, very clean, and simply but attractively furnished. Breakfasts are bounteous. Smoking is not permitted inside the house.

451 Craig St., Dawson City, YT Y0B 1G0. ✆ **867/993-5649.** Fax 867/993-5648. www.dawsonbb.com. 7 units, 3 with bathroom. C$99–C$119 (US$61–US$74) double. Winter C$10 (US$6) less. Senior and AAA/CAA discounts. DC, MC, V. Free parking. **Amenities:** Budget car rentals; courtesy pickup; free bicycles and fishing rods. *In room:* TV.

**Dawson City Bunkhouse** One of the few good lodging values in town, this handsome hotel looks Old West but is brand new. Guest rooms are small but bright and clean; the beds come with Hudson's Bay Company wool blankets. The cheapest rooms have their own toilets, but showers are down the landing. Only the queen (sleeps three) and king (sleeps four) suites have private bathrooms.

Front and Princess sts., Dawson City, YT Y0B 1G0. ✆ **867/993-6164.** Fax 867/993-6051. bunkhouse@yknet.yk.ca. 32 units, 20 with bathroom. C$55–C$95 (US$34–US$59) double. Senior discounts available. MC, V. Free parking. Closed mid-Sept to mid-May. *In room:* No phone.

**Triple J Motel** Right across from Diamond Tooth Gertie's Casino, the Triple J offers nice self-contained cabins and hotel-style rooms for decent rates at a good location. The décor harkens back to the hotel's past—it opened in the 1970s—but rooms are sizable and clean. Almost all the cabins come with a complete kitchenette, fully stocked with pots, dishes, and cutlery. All units have private bathrooms, and some cabins are wheelchair accessible. Also on site are a lounge and TJ's Steakhouse restaurant. Courtesy pick-up from the airport is available.

Fifth Ave. and Queen St., Box 359, Dawson City, YT Y0B 1G0. ✆ **800/764-3555** or 867/993-5323. Fax 867/993-5030. www.triplejhotel.com. 47 units (20 cabins, 27 rms). C$109–$119 (US$68–$74) double. Additional person add C$10 (US$6) per day. Senior citizen and corporate discounts available. Children under 12 stay free in parents' room. AE, MC, V. Closed early Sept–May. Pets allowed, add C$10 (US$7). **Amenities:** Restaurant, lounge; courtesy limo; coin-op laundry; nonsmoking rooms; executive-level rooms. *In room:* TV, coffeemaker.

## WHERE TO DINE

Food is generally good in Dawson City and, considering the isolation and transport costs, not too expensive. The hotels have good dining rooms and are open for three meals a day. Many restaurants close in winter or keep shorter hours. The **River West Food & Health,** Front and Queen Streets (✆ **867/993-6339**), is a health-food shop and cafe that's a good place to get a decent cup of coffee and order sandwiches either to eat in or take out for picnics. It's open daily in the summer 8am to 7pm, and mid-September to April 8:30 am to 5:30pm. Sandwiches run C$4 to C$5 (US$2.50–US$3.10), with a cup of soup an extra C$2 (US$1.20).

**Amica's** ★ PASTA/PIZZA/STEAKS With a focus on Italian and Greek cuisine, Amica's offers some of Dawson City's best dining year-round. For starters, the menu offers a wide variety of salads and such appetizers as spanakopita, baby calamari with onions and tzatziki dip, white-wine steamed mussels, and escargots.

Entrees include baked fresh halibut or salmon, souvlakis, and a sizeable selection of pastas, steaks, and homemade pizzas. A variety of sandwiches and focaccia round out the menu for the lunchtime crowd.

401 Craig St. (4th Ave. and Craig St.). © **867/993-6800.** Main courses C$14–C$23 (US$9–US$14). MC, V. Summer Daily 11am–11pm. Sept–May Mon–Fri 11am–2pm and daily 5–10pm.

**Klondike Kate's Restaurant** CANADIAN This friendly and informal cafe is near the theaters and casino and serves tasty, uncomplicated meals from a small but dependable menu. The atmosphere is Old Dawson, and weather permitting, there's dining on the veranda.

At the corner of Third Ave. and King St. © **867/993-6527.** Main courses C$5–C$25 (US$3.10–US$16). MC, V. April–Sept daily 6:30am–11pm.

## DAWSON CITY AFTER DARK

Dawson City is still full of honky-tonks and saloons, and most have some form of nightly live music. On warm summer evenings all the doors are thrown open and you can sample the music by strolling through town on the boardwalks; the music is far better than you'd expect for a town of 2,000 people. A couple of favorites: Both the lounge bar and the pub at the **Midnight Sun** (© **867/993-5495**), at Third Avenue and Queen Street, have live bands nightly. The tavern at the **Westminster Hotel,** between Queen and Princess on Third, often features traditional Yukon fiddlers, as well as other local and touring musical acts.

Canada's only legal gambling casino north of the 60th parallel, **Diamond Tooth Gertie's,** Fourth and Queen streets (© **867/993-5575**), has an authentic gold-rush decor, from the shirt-sleeved honky-tonk pianist to the wooden floorboards. The games include blackjack, roulette, 21, red dog, and poker, as well as slot machines; the minimum stakes are low, and the ambiance is friendly rather than tense. There's a maximum set limit of C$100 (US$62) per hand. The three nightly floor shows combine Can Can dancing, throaty siren songs, and ragtime piano. May to September, Gertie's is open daily 7pm to 2am, and admission is C$6 (US$3.70). An interesting side-note: gambling revenues from Gertie's support historic preservation in the Klondike.

Built at the height of the stampede by "Arizona Charlie" Meadows, the original **Palace Grand Theatre,** King Street (© **867/993-6217**), had its slam-bang gala premier in July 1899. Now totally rebuilt according to the original plans, it serves as a showcase for the *Gaslight Follies,* a spoof musical-comedy revue. Performances are given nightly mid-June to mid-September (two performances nightly on weekends through mid-August), with tickets at C$15 to C$17 (US$9 to US$11) for adults and C$7.50 (US$4.65) for children under 12.

# 7 The Top of the World Highway

The scenic **Top of the World Highway** links Dawson City to Tetlin Junction in Alaska. After the free Yukon River ferry crossing at Dawson City (depending on weather conditions, open mid-May through mid-October), this 282km (175-mile) road, a good portion of it unpaved, rapidly climbs above the tree line where it follows meandering ridge tops—hence the name. The views are wondrous: Bare green mountains undulate for hundreds of miles into the distance; looking down, you can see clouds floating in deep valley clefts.

After 106km (66 miles), the road crosses the U.S.-Canadian border; the border crossing is open in summer only (generally the same season as the Dawson City ferry), 8am to 8pm Pacific time (note that the time in Alaska is an hour earlier). There are no rest rooms, services, or currency exchange at the border. The quality of the road deteriorates on the Alaska side.

The free ferry at Dawson City can get very backed up in high season; delays up to 3 hours are possible. Peak traffic in mid-summer is from 7am to 11am and 4pm to 7pm. Commercial and local traffic have priority and don't have to wait in line. The Top of the World Highway isn't maintained during winter; it's generally free of snow April to mid-October.

## 8 North on the Dempster Highway

East of Dawson City 40km (25 miles), the famed **Dempster Highway** ★ heads north 735km (456 miles) to Inuvik, Northwest Territories, on the Mackenzie River near the Arctic Ocean. The most northerly public road in Canada, the Dempster is another of those highways that exudes a strange appeal to RV travelers; locals in Inuvik refer to these tourists as "end of the roaders." It's a beautiful drive, especially early in the fall, when frost brings out the color in tiny tundra plants and migrating wildlife is more easily seen. The Dempster passes through a wide variety of landscapes, from tundra plains to rugged volcanic mountains; in fact, between Highway 2 and Inuvik the Dempster crosses the Continental Divide three times. **North Fork Pass** in the Ogilvie Mountains, with the knife-edged gray peaks of Tombstone Mountain incising the horizon to the west, is especially stirring. The Dempster crosses the Arctic Circle—one of only two roads in Canada to do so—at Mile 252.

The Dempster is a gravel road open year-round. It's in good shape in most sections, though very dusty; allow 12 hours to make the drive between Inuvik and Dawson City. There are services at three points only: Eagle Plains, Fort McPherson, and Arctic Red River. Don't depend on gas or food outside of standard daytime business hours. At the Peel and the Mackenzie rivers are free ferry crossings in summer; in winter, vehicles simply cross on the ice. For 2 weeks, during the spring thaw and the fall freeze up, through-traffic on the Dempster ceases. For details on ferries and road conditions, call ✆ **877/456-7623** in the Yukon or **800/661-0752** in the Yukon or NWT. For more on Inuvik, see "The Arctic North: Getting Away from It All," earlier.

## 9 Yellowknife: Capital of the Northwest Territories ★

The capital of the Northwest Territories and the most northerly city in Canada, **Yellowknife** lies on the north shore of Great Slave Lake. The site was originally occupied by the Dogrib and Yellowknife (Chipewyan) Dene peoples, and whites didn't settle there until 1934, following the discovery of gold on the lakeshores.

This first **gold boom** petered out in the 1940s, and Yellowknife dwindled nearly to a ghost town in its wake. But in 1945 came a second gold rush that put the place permanently on the map. The local landmarks are the two operating gold mines flanking Yellowknife: **Miramar Con** and **Giant Yellowknife.**

Most of the old gold-boom vestiges are gone—the bordellos, gambling dens, log-cabin banks, and never-closing bars are merely memories now. But the original **Old Town** is there, a crazy tangle of wooden shacks hugging the lakeshore rocks, surrounded by bush-pilot operations that fly sturdy little planes—on floats in summer, on skis in winter.

Yellowknife is a vibrant, youthful place. A significant portion of the white population of Yellowknife consists of people in their late 20s and 30s. Yellowknife attracts young people just out of college looking for high-paying public-sector jobs, wilderness recreation, and the adventure of living in the Arctic. However, after a few years, many of them head back south to warmer climes. Yellowknife is also the center for a number of outlying native communities, which roots the city in a more long-standing traditional culture.

People are very friendly and outgoing and seem genuinely glad to see you. The party scene here is just about what you'd expect in a town surrounded by Native villages and filled with miners and young bureaucrats. There's a more dynamic nightlife here than the size of the population could possibly justify.

## ESSENTIALS

**GETTING THERE** **Yellowknife Airport** is 5km (3 miles) northeast of the town. **First Air** (✆ **800/267-1247** or 613/688-2635), flies direct to Yellowknife from Edmonton and Vancouver. **Air Canada** (✆ **888/247-2262**) has flights from Calgary through Edmonton. **Canadian North** (✆ **800/661-1505**) provides daily flights from Ottawa.

If you're driving from Edmonton, take Highway 16 to Grimshaw. From there the **Mackenzie Highway** leads to the Northwest Territories border, 475km (295 miles) north, and on to Yellowknife via Fort Providence. The total distance from Edmonton is 1,524km (945 miles). Most of the road is now paved, and the entire road should be by summer of 2003.

**VISITOR INFORMATION** For information about the territory in general or Yellowknife in particular, contact one of the following: the **Northern Frontier Regional Visitors Centre,** No. 4, 4807 49th St., Yellowknife, NT X1A 3T5 (✆ **877/881-4262** or 867/873-4262; fax 867/873-3654; www.northern frontier.com); or **NWT Arctic Tourism,** P.O. Box 610, Yellowknife, NT X1A 2N5 (✆ **800/661-0788** or 867/873-7200; fax 867/873-0294; www.nwttravel.nt.ca).

A useful phone number for motorists is the **ferry information line** at ✆ **800/661-0750** (NWT only), which lets you know the status of the various car ferries along the Dempster and Mackenzie highways. At breakup and freeze-up time, there's usually a month's time when the ferries can't operate and the ice isn't yet thick enough to drive on.

**CITY LAYOUT** The city's expanding urban center, **New Town**—a busy hub of modern hotels, shopping centers, office blocks, and government buildings—spreads above the town's historic birthplace, called **Old Town.** Together the two towns count about 18,000 inhabitants, by far the largest community in the Territories.

Most of New Town lies between rock-lined Frame Lake and Yellowknife Bay on Great Slave Lake. The main street in this part of town is **Franklin Avenue,** also called **50th Avenue.** Oddly, early town planners decided to start the young town's numbering system at the junction of 50th Avenue and 50th Street; even though the downtown area is only 10 blocks square, the street addresses give the illusion of a much larger city.

The junction of 48th Street and Franklin (50th) Avenue is pretty much the center of town. A block south are the post office and a number of enclosed shopping arcades (very practical up here, where winter temperatures would otherwise discourage shopping). Turn north and travel half a mile to Old Town and **Latham Island,** which stick out into Yellowknife Bay. This is still a bustling center for boats, floatplanes, B&Bs, and food and drink.

South of Frame Lake is the modern residential area, and just west is the airport. If you follow 48th Street out of town without turning onto the Mackenzie Highway, the street turns into the **Ingraham Trail,** a bush road heading out toward a series of lakes with fishing and boating access, hiking trails, and a couple of campgrounds. This is the main recreational playground for Yellowknifers, who love to canoe or kayak from lake to lake or all the way back to town.

**GETTING AROUND** Monday to Saturday, **Yellowknife City Transit** (contact Cardinal Coach Lines ✆ **867/873-4693,** or City Hall ✆ 867/920-5685) loops through Yellowknife once an hour—sometimes with a bus available every half-hour—with stops at the airport and throughout downtown. The fares are C$2 (US$1.20) for adults, C$1.50 (US95¢) for youth ages 5 to 18, and children under 5 are free; and tickets are available at City Hall and at various local shops.

For car rentals, **Budget** (✆ **800/527-0700** in the U.S., 800/472-3325 in Canada, or 867/873-3366) and **National/Tilden** (✆ **800/CAR-RENT** or 867/920-2970) have offices at the airport. **Rent-A-Relic,** 356 Old Airport Rd. (✆ **867/873-3400**), offers older models at substantial savings—and they'll pick you up and drop you off at the airport. At all these operations, the number of cars available during summer is rather limited and the demand very high. Budget and National also have downtown locations, so those are options for when the airport locations are rented out. You may have to settle for what's to be had rather than what you want. Try to book ahead as far as possible.

Taxis are pretty cheap in Yellowknife; call **City Cabs** (✆ **867/873-4444**) or **YK Cabs** (✆ **867/873-8888**) for a lift. A ride to the airport costs about C$10 (US$6).

**SPECIAL EVENTS** The **Caribou Carnival,** in late March, is a burst of spring fever after a very long, very frigid winter (one of the fever symptoms consists of the delusion that winter is over). For a solid week Yellowknife is thronged with parades, igloo-building contests, and Inuit wrestling. The competition highlight is the Canadian Championship Dog Derby, a 3-day, 240km (149-mile) dogsled race. The **Festival of the Midnight Sun** is an arts festival in mid-July. There are a one-act play competition, various arts workshops (including lessons in native beading and carving), and fine art on display all over town. Also in mid-July, the **Folk on the Rocks Music Festival** (www.folkontherocks.com) features a mix of northern (Arctic) and southern Canadian folk, rock, blues, and other genres, plus Native musical performances. The festival takes place on the shore of Long Lake, about 2km (1¼ miles) east of the Yellowknife Airport.

## EXPLORING YELLOWKNIFE

Stop by the **Northern Frontier Regional Visitor Centre** (✆ **877/881-4262** or 867/873-4262; www.northernfrontier.com), on 49th Street (just north of 49th Ave.) on the west edge of town, to see a number of exhibits explaining the major points of local history, ecology, and native culture. You'll want to put the kids on the "bush flight" elevator, which simulates a flight over Great Slave Lake while slowly rising to the second floor. The center also has a video library and information on parks and outdoor activities. Also pick up a free parking pass, enabling you to escape the parking meters. It's open May to August daily 8:30am to 6pm, and the rest of the year Monday to Friday 8:30am to 5:30pm and weekends noon to 4pm.

The **Prince of Wales Northern Heritage Centre** ★, on the shore of Frame Lake (✆ **867/873-7551;** www.pwnhc.learnnet.nt.ca), is a museum in a class all its own. You'll learn the history, background, and characteristics of the Dene and Inuit peoples, the Métis, and pioneer whites through dioramas; artifacts; and talking, reciting, and singing slide presentations. It depicts the human struggle with an environment so incredibly harsh that survival alone seems an accomplishment. Admission is free. June to August, it's open daily 10:30am to 5:30pm; September to May, it's open Tuesday to Friday 10:30am to 5pm and on weekends noon to 5pm.

Rising above Old Town, the **Bush Pilot's Monument** is a stone pillar paying tribute to the little band of airmen who opened up the Far North. The surrounding cluster of shacks and cottages is the original Yellowknife, built on the shores of a narrow peninsula jutting into Great Slave Lake. It's not exactly a pretty place, but definitely intriguing. Sprinkled along the inlets are half a dozen bush-pilot operations, minuscule airlines flying charter planes as well as scheduled routes to outlying areas. The little floatplanes shunt around like taxis, and you can watch a landing or takeoff every hour of the day. Off the tip of the Old Town peninsula lies **Latham Island,** which you can reach by a causeway. The island has a small native-Canadian community, a few luxury homes, and a number of B&Bs.

## TOURS & EXCURSIONS

**Raven Tours** (✆ **867/873-4776;** fax 867/873-4856; www.raventours.yk.com) offers a 3-hour city tour, exploring the sights, culture, history, and ecology of Yellowknife. Raven also offers a number of more specialized trips, particularly during the winter, including dog-sledding, snowmobiling, and wildlife tours, plus excursions just outside the city to view the Aurora Borealis. Yellowknife is on the 60th parallel which, at its longitude, places it directly within an oval-shaped range at which the aurora appears most often and vividly. Tours generally run 4 hours in length and include a meal of local foods, photography tips, and an astronomy lesson.

For natural-history tours of the Yellowknife area, with an emphasis on subarctic ecology, bird-watching, and geology, contact **Cygnus Ecotours** (✆ **867/873-4782;** cygnus@internorth.com). Some tours focus on the ecosystem near town, while others journey out along the Ingraham Trail to more distant lakes; hikes to Cameron Falls are also available. Offered mid-May through mid-October, trips are usually either a half or full day, and Cygnus provides binoculars, field guides, some food, and other necessities. Prices range from $C30 to C$75 (US$19–US$47) per person.

Cruise Canada's Arctic in the **MS *Norweta,*** a modern diesel-engine craft equipped with radar, owned by NWT Marine Group, 17 England Crescent, Yellowknife X1A 3N5 (✆ **867/873-2489;** www.denendeh.com/norweta), also booked by Mack Travel in Hay River (✆ **877/874-6001** or 867/874-6001; www.macktravel.ca). When docked in Yellowknife, a few day excursions and dinner cruises are available on the *Norweta.* Call ahead to make reservations and to make sure the boat is available. Twice a summer, the *Norweta* conducts 9-day cruises to Inuvik, up the mighty Mackenzie River, costing C$3,995 to C$5,395 (US$2,477–US$3,345). The boat also offers week-long tour packages including a 5-day cruise on the Great Slave Lake, costing C$1,995 to C$3,395 (US$1,237–US$2,105).

## SHOPPING

Yellowknife is a principal retail outlet for Northern artwork and craft items, as well as for the specialized clothing the climate demands. Some of it is so handsome that sheer vanity will make you wear it in more southerly temperatures.

**Northern Images,** 4801 Franklin Ave. (✆ **867/873-5944**), features authentic Native-Canadian (Inuit and Dene) articles: apparel and carvings, graphic prints, silver jewelry, ornamental moose-hair tuftings, and porcupine quill work. Proceeds from sales go directly to Native artisans.

**Gallery of the Midnight Sun,** 5005 Bryson Dr. (✆ **867/873-8065;** www.gallerymidnightsun.com), has a great selection of northern sculptures (mainly Inuit stone carvings), and also sells a variety of apparel, paintings, and Arctic crafts. To browse an excellent selection of paintings and other artworks by northern artists of all cultural backgrounds, visit **Birchwood Gallery,** #26-4910 50th Ave. (✆ **867/873-4050;** www.birchwoodgallery.com).

**Trapper's Cabin,** 4 Lessard Dr., Latham Island (✆ **867/873-3020**), is the nearest thing to an old-time frontier store Yellowknife can offer, though it stocks mostly souvenirs and gift items. You can drop in not just to buy goods, but to have coffee and snacks, listen to gossip, and collect information from the knowledgeable staff.

## SPORTS & OUTDOOR ACTIVITIES

The town is ringed by hiking trails: some gentle, some pretty rugged. Most convenient for a short hike or a jog is the 9km (5½-mile) trail around **Frame Lake,** accessible from the Northern Heritage Centre, the Prince of Wales Heritage Centre, and other points.

The other major focus of recreation in the Yellowknife area is the **Ingraham Trail,** a paved and then gravel road starting just northwest of town and winding east over 73km (45 miles) to Tibbet Lake. En route lie a string of lakes, mostly linked by the Cameron River, making this prime canoe and kayak country. Ingraham Trail also crosses by several territorial parks, two waterfalls, the Giant Mine, and waterfowl habitat, plus lots of picnic sites, camping spots, boat rentals, and fishing spots.

One of the largest lakes along the trail is **Prelude Lake,** 32km (20 miles) east of town; it's a wonderful setting for scenic boating and trout, pike, and Arctic-grayling fishing. For boat rentals, you might check out **Overlander Sports** (✆ **867/873-2474;** www.overlandersports.com). For other rental providers, contact the visitor center (✆ **877/881-4262** or 867/873-4262; www.northernfrontier.com).

**CANOEING & KAYAKING** When you fly into Yellowknife, you'll notice that about half the land surface is composed of lakes, so it's no wonder that canoeing and kayaking are really popular here. **Narwal Northern Adventures,** 101-5103 51st Ave. (✆ **867/873-6443;** www.ssmicro.com/~narwal), offers canoe and kayak rentals and instruction, and can provide guided tours of Great Slave and Prelude lakes. A daylong rental from Narwal is around C$30 (US$19). The Northern Frontier Regional Visitor Centre offers maps of seven canoe paths through the maze of lakes, islands, and streams along the Ingraham Trail; with a few short portages, it's possible to float just about all the way from Prelude Lake to Yellowknife, about a 5-day journey.

**FISHING TRIPS** Traditionally, fishing has been the main reason to visit the Yellowknife and the Great Slave Lake area. Lake trout, Arctic grayling, northern pike, and whitefish grow to storied size in these Northern lakes; the pristine water conditions and general lack of anglers mean fishing isn't just good, it's great. Both **Bluefish Services** (✆ **867/873-4818**) and **Barbara Ann Charters** (✆ **867/873-9913;** www.fishingcharter.com/greatslavelake) offer fishing trips on Great Slave Lake directly from town, but most serious anglers fly in floatplanes to fishing lodges, either on Great Slave or on more remote lakes, for a wilderness fishing trip.

One of the best of the lodge outfitters on Great Slave Lake is the **Frontier Fishing Lodge** (© **780/465-6843;** www.frontierfishing.ab.ca). A 3-day all-inclusive guided fishing trip will cost around C$1,450 (US$899). Nearly two dozen fishing-lodge outfitters operate in the Yellowknife area; contact the visitor center or consult the *Explorers' Guide* for a complete listing.

**HIKING** The most popular hike along the **Ingraham Trail** is to **Cameron River Falls.** The well-signed trail head is 48km (30 miles) east of Yellowknife. Although not a long hike—allow 1½ hours for the round-trip—the trail to the falls is hilly. An easier trail is the **Prelude Lake Nature Trail,** winding along Prelude Lake through wildlife habitat. The 90-minute hike begins and ends at the lakeside campground. Closer to Yellowknife, the **Prospectors Trail** at Fred Henne Park is an interpreted trail through gold-bearing rock outcroppings; signs tell the story of Yellowknife's rich geology.

## WHERE TO STAY

The campground most convenient to Yellowknife is **Fred Henne Park** (© **867/920-2472,** for information on all territorial parks), just east of the airport on Long Lake. Both RVs and tents are welcome; there are showers, kitchen shelters, potable water, camp stoves, and electrical outlets, but no RV hookups. At **Prelude Lake Territorial Park,** 29km (18 miles) east of Yellowknife, there are 28 rustic campsites, with no facilities beyond running water and firewood. **Reid Lake Territorial Park,** 61km (38 miles) east of Yellowknife, is near the opposite end of the Ingraham Trail, and is the starting point for popular canoe trips on the Cameron River. Reid Lake also has 28 campsites with running water and firewood. All three territorial park campsites are open mid-May to mid-September and charge the same fees: C$10, C$15, or C$20 (US$6, US$9, or US$12). Although the parks don't take reservations, and get very busy during the summer, the park service will do everything possible to not turn anyone away.

### EXPENSIVE

**Chateau Nova** ★ Archival photos of Yellowknife's days of yore grace the walls of one of the town's newest hotels, which offers excellent amenities in a pleasant location right downtown. Guest rooms are large and comfortable, and suites include a kitchenette, queen sleeper sofa in addition to a queen bed, and a Jacuzzi tub.

Franklin Ave. between 44th and 45th sts. Box 250, Yellowknife, NT X1A 2N2. © **877/839-1236** or 867/873-9700. Fax 867/873-9702. www.chateaunova.com. 61 units. C$150–$180 (US$93–$112) double. Additional person add C$15 (US$9). Children under 12 stay free in parents' room. AE, DC, DISC, MC, V. **Amenities:** Restaurant, lounge; exercise room; Jacuzzi; sauna; courtesy limo; business center; room service (7am–10:30pm); laundry service; same-day dry cleaning; nonsmoking rooms; executive-level rooms. *In room:* A/C, TV/VCR, dataport, iron, coffeemaker, hair dryer.

**Explorer Regency International Hotel** ★★ The Explorer is a commanding snow-white structure overlooking both the city and a profusion of rock-lined lakes. It has long been Yellowknife's premier hotel—Queen Elizabeth herself has stayed here. Guest rooms are spacious and uncluttered, all with writing desks and tables. A newly added and welcome amenity for business travelers is high-speed wireless Internet access. A wheelchair-accessible room is also available. Barkley's Eats & Drinks is one of the Territories' finest restaurants (see "Where to Dine," below), and the Explorer also has a second restaurant featuring Japanese cuisine.

4825–49th Ave., Yellowknife, NT X1A 2R3. ✆ **800/661-0892** in Canada, or 867/873-3531. Fax 867/873-2789. www.explorerhotel.nt.ca. 128 units. C$184 (US$114) double; from C$225 (US$140) suite. AE, DC, MC, V. Free parking with winter plug-ins available for car head-bolt heaters. **Amenities:** 2 restaurants; exercise room; concierge; tour and activities desk; airport limo (C$4/US$2.50); room service (6:30am–11pm); same-day dry cleaning; nonsmoking rooms; executive-level rooms. *In room:* TV, dataport, coffeemaker, hair dryer.

**Yellowknife Inn** ★ This inn is right in the center of Yellowknife and has recently been completely refurbished and updated. The new lobby is joined to a large shopping-and-dining complex, the Centre Square Mall, making this the place to stay in winter. Guest rooms are fair-sized, some with minibars, and offer amenities that have won an International Hospitality award. The walls are decorated with Inuit art. Guests receive a pass to local fitness facilities. The hotel will also store extra luggage or equipment if you're off to a secondary destination for a while.

5010 49th St., Yellowknife, NT X1A 2N4. ✆ **800/661-0580** or 867/873-2601. Fax 867/873-2602. 130 units. www.yellowknifeinn.com. C$150 (US$93) double; C$165 (US$102) suite. Rates include breakfast. AE, DC, MC, V. Free parking. **Amenities:** Restaurant, lounge; courtesy limo; laundry services; nonsmoking rooms; executive suites. *In room:* TV, dataport, coffeemaker.

### MODERATE

**Captain Ron's** Located on Latham Island on the shores of Great Slave Lake, Captain Ron's is reached by causeway. It's a cozy and picturesque place with four guest rooms and a reading lounge with a fireplace and TV. Each room has a double bed, radio, and picture windows to take in the lake view.

8 Lessard Dr., Yellowknife, NT X1A 2G5. ✆ **867/873-3746.** 4 units, none with bathroom. C$98 (US$61) double. Rates include breakfast. V. *In room:* No phone.

**Igloo Inn** An attractive two-story wood structure, the Igloo sits at the bottom of the hill road leading to Old Town. Complimentary coffee and morning pastries are served in its breakfast room. Thirty-three of the units have pleasantly spacious kitchenettes stocked with electric ranges and all the necessary utensils. Altogether, it's a great value for your money. Jerry's Café, on site, serves all three meals and can provide room service.

4115 Franklin Ave. (P.O. Box 596), Yellowknife, NT X1A 2N4. ✆ **867/873-8511.** Fax 867/873-5547. igloo inn@internorth.com. 44 units. C$99 (US$61) double. Senior discounts and corporate rates available. AE, DC, MC, V. Free parking with plug-ins. **Amenities:** Restaurant; room service (9am–9pm); nonsmoking rooms. *In room:* TV.

### INEXPENSIVE

**Eva and Eric's B&B** Near the airport, Eva and Eric Henderson have four rooms available for nonsmokers. There are a shared lounge with a color TV, a shared bathroom, a kitchen for guests, a library, and Northern foods for breakfast (if requested). The Hendersons are some of the nicest and most welcoming people around; you'll enjoy staying here.

114 Knutsen Ave., Yellowknife, NT X1A 2Y4. ✆ **867/873-5779.** Fax 867/873-6160. 4 units, none with bathroom. C$70 (US$43) double. Rates include breakfast. No goods-and-services tax (GST) added to room rates. No credit cards. **Amenities:** Laundry services; nonsmoking rooms.

## WHERE TO DINE

### EXPENSIVE

**Barkley's Eats & Drinks** ★ INTERNATIONAL/NORTHERN Barkley's offers some of the best Northern cooking in the Northwest Territories. The menu lists a number of game dishes peculiar to the region (caribou and musk ox) but prepared with French sauces and finesse. Other dishes—steaks, pasta, and seafood—have a more international provenance.

In the Explorer Regency International Hotel, 4825 49th Ave. ✆ **867/873-3531, ext. 7121.** Reservations recommended. Main courses C$10–C$25 (US$6–US$16). AE, DC, MC, V. Mon–Sat 6am–2pm and 5pm–10pm, with lunch buffet 11:30am–2pm; Sun 7am–10pm, with brunch 10am–2pm. Lounge Mon–Sat 11am–11:30pm.

**The Office** ★ CANADIAN/NORTHERN This sophisticated retreat sports an elegant decor and paintings by local artists. House specialties include Northern fare, like the frozen thinly sliced Arctic char and various cuts of caribou. Otherwise the menu is top-grade Anglo: roast rack of lamb, beef tenderloin with Yorkshire pudding, great steaks, and a large selection of seafood and pastas. The steak sandwich and chicken in pita bread are popular among the lunchtime crowd.

4915–50th St. ✆ **867/873-3750.** odining@ssimicro.com. Reservations recommended. Main courses C$21–C$40 (US$13–US$25). AE, DC, MC, V. Daily 11am–2pm and 4:30–10pm.

## MODERATE

**L'Attitudes Restaurant & Bistro** INTERNATIONAL/NORTHERN L'Attitudes is one of Yellowknife's newest and most attractive restaurants and reflects its youth with lighter, more eclectic offerings. The menu ranges from boutique pizzas to pasta, barbecued ribs, and chicken and on to intriguing Northern specialties like rack of caribou with rosemary mint sauce. If you're more interested in grazing through several dishes, there's a snack menu, with salads and nibbles available all day; you can also caffeinate on espresso drinks. There are more vegetarian selections here than anywhere else in Yellowknife.

Center Square Mall, 5010 49th St. ✆ **867/920-7880.** Pizza C$10–C$12 (US$6–US$7); pasta C$12–C$15 (US$7–US$9); main courses C$12–C$26 (US$7–US$16). MC, V. Daily 7:30am–8pm.

**Wildcat Café** ★ NORTHERN The Wildcat Café is a tourist site as much as an eatery. A squat log cabin with a deliberately grizzled frontier look, it's actually refurbished in the image of the 1930s original. The atmospheric interior is reminiscent of Yellowknife in its pioneer days, and the cafe has been photographed, filmed, painted, and caricatured often enough to give it star quality. The menu focuses on local products like caribou and lake fish, in addition to steaks. Seating is along long benches, and you'll probably end up sharing your table with other diners.

3904 Wiley Rd., Old Town. ✆ **867/873-8850.** Reservations not accepted. Main courses C$7–C$17 (US$4.35–US$11). MC, V. June–early Sept, usually daily; call for hours. Closed in winter.

## INEXPENSIVE

The **Heritage Café** at the **Northern Heritage Centre,** on Frame Lake (✆ **867/873-7551;** www.pwnhc.learnnet.nt.ca/visit/cafe.html), has a good selection of inexpensive lunch items; this is a fine place to go for soups, salads, sandwiches, and pasta dishes, whether or not you plan on visiting the museum. It's open Tuesday to Friday 11am to 4pm and Sunday noon to 4pm. For a good and inexpensive bowl of body-warming nourishment, try some pho (beef noodle soup) at the **Vietnamese Noodle House,** 4601–50th Ave. (✆ **867/873-3399**), in a log cabin with the **Country Corner** store, just north of downtown. It's open daily 8am to 10pm. Brand-name fast food is present in Yellowknife, and for people on a tight budget, this is probably the way to avoid the otherwise rather high cost of dining. All the downtown shopping arcades have inexpensive food outlets as well.

## YELLOWKNIFE AFTER DARK

By and large, people in Yellowknife aren't scared of a drink, and nightlife revolves around bars and pubs. Increasingly, there's a music scene in Yellowknife; a number of local bands have developed national followings.

Officially called Bad Sam's, the **Gold Range Tavern,** in the Gold Range Hotel, 5010–50th St. (✆ **867/873-4441**), is better known by its local nickname—"Strange Range." The Range is an occasionally rip-roaring tavern that attracts the whole gamut of local and visiting characters in search of some after-dinner whoopee. You don't come here for a quiet evening, but you can't say you've seen Yellowknife if you haven't seen the Strange Range.

The pleasant **Black Knight Pub,** 4910–49th St. (✆ **867/920-4041**), has a selection of about 15 beers on tap, with an emphasis on English and Irish brews, as well as the largest selection of scotches in town (somewhere around 120!). It's open 11am until 2am, every day but Sunday.

If you're in the mood for some music, **Gallery,** Franklin Avenue near 50th Street (✆ **867/873-2651**), offers nightly top-40 and jazz tunes on two floors, plus a full bar. Most of the music is spun by DJs, but every other weekend the club has live jazz bands downstairs.

## 10 Nahanni National Park ★★★

A breathtaking, unspoiled wilderness of 4,766km² (1,840 sq. miles) in the southwest corner of the Territories, Nahanni National Park is accessible only by foot, motorboat, canoe, or charter aircraft. The park preserves 295km (183 miles) of the South Nahanni River. One of the wildest rivers in North America, the South Nahanni claws its path through the rugged Mackenzie Mountains, at one point charging over incredible Virginia Falls, twice as high as Niagara at 105m (344 ft.) and carrying more water. Below the falls, the river surges through one of the continent's deepest gorges, with canyon walls up to 1,333m (4,373 ft.) high.

**White-water rafting** from Virginia Falls through the canyon is the most popular, but not the only, white-water trip in the park. The trip from the falls (you'll need to fly in, because this is park has no road) to the usual takeout point takes 6 days or more, depending on the amount of time spent hiking or relaxing en route. The best white-water in the park is actually far above the falls, beginning at Moose Ponds and continuing to Rabbitkettle Lake, near an impressive hot-springs formation.

A number of outfitters are licensed to run the South Nahanni River. For a full listing and for details about the park, contact **Nahanni National Park,** Box 348, Fort Simpson, NT X0E 0N0 (✆ **867/695-3151;** http://parkscanada.pch.gc.ca/parks/nwtw/nahanni). As an example, **Nahanni River Adventures,** P.O. Box 31203, Whitehorse, YT Y1A 5P7 (✆ **800/297-6927** or 867/668-3180; fax 867/668-3056; www.nahanni.com), operates 7- and 12-day trips from the falls through the canyon with either canoes or inflatable rafts starting at C$3,165 (US$1,962).

A number of charter airlines offer access to Nahanni. **Deh Cho Air** (✆ **867/770-4103;** www.dehchoair.com), operating out of Fort Liard, offers fly-in and road pick-up packages for self-guided wilderness adventurers, as well as flight-seeing tours and day-trips to Virginia Falls. **Wolverine Air** (✆ **867/695-2263;** www.wolverineair.com), in Fort Simpson, offers charter drop-offs to various park destinations or sightseeing day-trips to the falls; a 3-hour flying-only tour costs C$700 (US$434) for up to 5 people, while a 5½-hour flying tour with a stopover at the falls costs C$900 (US$558) for up to 3 people.

## 11 The Arctic North: Getting Away from it All

Canada's **Arctic North** is one of the world's most remote and uninhabited areas, but one that holds many rewards for the traveler willing to get off the beaten path. Arctic landscapes can be breathtaking including the 72km-wide (45-mile-wide) wildlife-filled delta of the **Mackenzie River** and the awesome fjords and glaciers of **Baffin Island.** In many areas, traditional First Nation or Inuit villages retain age-old hunting and fishing ways but welcome respectful visitors to their communities. The **artwork** of the North is famous worldwide; in almost every community, artists engage in weaving, print-making, or stone, ivory, and bone carving. Locally produced artwork is available from community co-ops, galleries, or from the artists themselves.

Traveling the wilds of the Canadian Arctic is a great adventure, but frankly it isn't for everyone. Most likely the Arctic isn't like anywhere you've ever traveled before, and while that may be exciting, there are some realities of Arctic travel you need to be aware of before you start making plans.

**PRICES** The Arctic is an *expensive* place to travel. Airfare is very high (many tourists travel here on frequent-flier miles, one of the few ways to get around the steep ticket prices). While almost every little community has a serviceable hotel/restaurant, room prices are shockingly high; a hostel-style rustic room with full board costs as much as a decent room in Paris. Food costs are equally high (remember that all your food was air-freighted in) and the quality is poor. And don't plan on having a drink anywhere except Inuvik or Iqaluit, where you'll spend C$5 (US$3.10) for a bottle for beer.

**FLYING IN THE BUSH** Except for the Dempster Highway to Inuvik, there's no road access to any point in the Arctic. *All public transportation is by airplane.* To reach the most interesting points in the North, you'll need to fly on floatplanes, tiny commuter planes, and aircraft that years ago passed out of use in the rest of the world. Of course, all aircraft in the Arctic are regularly inspected and regulated for safety, but if you have phobias about flying, you might find the combination of rattling aircraft and changeable flying conditions unpleasant.

**CULTURE SHOCK** The Arctic is the homeland of the Inuit. Travelers are made welcome in nearly all Native villages, but it must be stressed that these communities aren't set up as holiday camps for southern visitors. Most people aren't English speakers; except for the local hotel, there may not be public areas open for non-natives. You're definitely a guest here; while people are friendly and will greet you, you'll probably feel very much an outsider.

The Inuit are hunters: On long summer nights, you'll go to sleep to the sound of hunters shooting seals along the ice floes. Chances are good you'll see people butchering seals or whales along the beaches. You may be lucky enough to visit an Inuit village during a traditional feast. All the meat, including haunches of caribou, entire seals, and slabs of whale, will be consumed raw. And the Arctic isn't a pristine place; garbage and carcasses litter the shoreline and town pathways. Don't come to the North expecting to find a sanitized feel-good atmosphere.

If these realities are a problem for you, then you should reconsider a trip here. If not, then traveling to a traditional Inuit village under a 24-hour summer sun to partake of native hospitality is a great adventure; this is surely one of the last truly traditional cultures and unexploited areas left in North America.

## INUVIK: END OF THE ROAD

**Inuvik,** 771km (478 miles) from Dawson City, is the town at the end of the long Dempster Highway—the most northerly road in Canada—and the most-visited center in the western Arctic. Because of its year-round road access and frequent flights from Yellowknife, Inuvik is becoming a tourist destination in itself and is the departure point for many tours out to more far-flung destinations. However, don't come looking for history: The town was built by the Canadian government in the 1950s and improved on by the oil boom in the 1970s. While there's not much charm to the town beyond its many-colored housing blocks, it does have lots of comforts and facilities: good hotels and restaurants, hospitals, schools, banks (and ATMs), shops, a Laundromat, and one traffic light. All this 2° north of the Arctic Circle!

Inuvik is on the Mackenzie River, one of the largest rivers in the world. Here, about 129km (80 miles) from its debouchment into the Arctic Ocean, the Mackenzie flows into its vast delta, 88km (55 miles) long and 65km (40 miles) wide. This incredible waterway, where the river fans out into a maze containing thousands of lakes, dozens of channels, and mile after mile of marsh, is a rich preserve of wildlife, especially waterfowl and aquatic mammals. Inuvik is also right at the northern edge of the taiga, near the beginning of the tundra, making this region a transition zone for a number of the larger Northern animals.

The town is home to a population of 3,500, composed of near-equal parts of **Inuvialuit,** the Inuit people of the western Arctic; of **Gwich'in,** a Dene tribe from south of the Mackenzie River delta; and of more recent white settlers, many of whom work at public-sector jobs.

### ESSENTIALS

**GETTING THERE** The drive from Dawson City along the Dempster usually takes 12 hours, and most people make the drive in 1 day (remember, in summer, there's no end of daylight). It's best to drive the road after July 1, when the spring mud has dried up. Three flights a week link Inuvik to Whitehorse on **Air North** (© **867/668-2228** or, in Canada **800/661-0407;** in the U.S. **800/764-0407**). From Yellowknife, **First Air** (© **800/267-1247** or 613/688-2635), and **Canadian North** (© **800/661-1505**) also fly three times a week.

**VISITOR INFORMATION** For more information about Inuvik and the surrounding area, contact **NWT Arctic Tourism,** P.O. Box 610, Yellowknife, NT X1A 2N5 (© **800/661-0788** or 867/873-7200; fax 867/873-0294; www.nwttravel.nt.ca).

**WEATHER** Weather can change rapidly in Inuvik. In summer, a frigid morning, with the winds and rains barreling off the Arctic Ocean, can change to a very warm and muggy afternoon in seemingly minutes. (Yes, it does get hot up here.) During summer, there's nearly a month when the sun doesn't set at all, and 6 months when there's only a short dusk at night. Correspondingly, there are about 3 weeks in winter when the sun doesn't rise.

**SPECIAL EVENTS** July is festival season in Inuvik. The **Great Northern Arts Festival** (© **867-777-3536;** www.greatart.nt.ca), the third week of July, is a celebration of the visual and performing arts, with most regional artists displaying works for sale; artists also give workshops on traditional craft techniques. The last week of July, Inuvik hosts the **Northern Games,** a celebration of traditional native sports and competitions, including drumming, dancing, high-kicking, craft displays, and the unique "Good Woman" contest, in which Inuit women show their amazing skill at seal and muskrat skinning, bannock baking, sewing, and other abilities that traditionally made a "good woman."

## WHAT TO SEE IN INUVIK

The most famous landmark in Inuvik is **Our Lady of Victory Church,** a large round structure with a glistening dome, usually referred to as the Igloo Church. You should definitely stop at the **Western Arctic Visitor Centre** (✆ **867/777-4727**) on the south end of town. Exhibits provide a good overview of the human and natural history of the area and of recreation and sightseeing options. June 15 to Labour Day, it's open 10am to 5pm.

Several art and gift shops offer local Inuit and Indian carvings and crafts; probably the best is **Northern Images,** 4801 Franklin Ave. (✆ **867/777-2786**). Don't miss the **Boreal Bookstore,** 181 Mackenzie Rd. (✆ **867/777-3748**), for a great selection of books on all things Northern.

## EXPLORING OUTSIDE INUVIK

The best of the local tour operators is **Arctic Nature Tours,** P.O. Box 1530, Inuvik, NT X0E 0T0 (✆ **867/777-3300;** www.arcticnaturetours.com). This Inuvialuit-owned business offers trips to all the following destinations. The **Arctic Tour Company,** P.O. Box 325, Tuktoyaktuk, NT X0E 1C0 (✆ **867/977-2230;** fax 867/977-2276; www.auroranet.nt.ca/atc), also offers tours to many of the same destinations, plus an imposing list of more specialized tours, all with native guides. However, because minimum numbers are necessary for all tours, don't count on specific trips to run while you're visiting.

**TUKTOYAKTUK** On the shores of the Beaufort Sea, 161km (100 miles) south of the permanent polar ice cap in the Arctic Ocean and popularly known as "Tuk," this little native town is reached by a short flight from Inuvik (in winter, the frozen Mackenzie River becomes an "ice road" linking the two towns by vehicle). Most tour operators in Inuvik offer half-day tours of Tuk (including the flight) for around C$160 (US$99), focusing on the curious "pingos" (volcano-like formations made of buckled ice that occur only here and in one location in Siberia) and the Inuvialuit culture. Stops are made at the workshops of stone carvers and other artisans, and you'll get the chance to stick your toe in the Arctic Ocean. Though there are a couple of hotels in Tuk, there's really no reason to spend more than a couple of hours up here; even as Arctic towns go, Tuk is pretty desolate.

**MACKENZIE DELTA TRIPS** When the Mackenzie River meets the Arctic Ocean, it forms an enormous basin filled with a multitude of lakes, river channels, and marshlands. River trips on the mazelike delta are fascinating: One popular trip visits a fishing camp for tea, bannock, and conversations with local fishers who prepare Arctic char by age-old methods; the cost is C$65 (US$40). Other river tours include a dinner or a midnight-sun champagne cruise. (You can also arrange to fly to Tuk and return by boat to Inuvik up the Mackenzie River.)

**HERSCHEL ISLAND** This island, 241km (149 miles) northwest of Inuvik, sits just off the northern shores of the Yukon in the Beaufort Sea. Long a base for native hunters and fishers, in the late 1800s Herschel Island became a camp for American and then Hudson's Bay Company whalers. Today, it's a territorial park, preserving both the historic whaling camp and abundant tundra plant- and wildlife (including Arctic fox, caribou, grizzly bear, and many shorebirds).

Tours of the island are generally offered only in July and August, when the Arctic ice floes move away from the island sufficiently to allow floatplanes to land in **Pauline Cove,** near the old whaling settlement. This is a great trip to an otherwise completely isolated environment. A day trip to the island, costing C$285 (US$177), includes a brief tour of the whaling station and a chance to explore the tundra landscape and Arctic shoreline. On the flight to the island, there's a good chance of seeing musk ox, nesting Arctic swans, caribou, and grizzly bear. Camping expeditions to the island can be arranged.

### WHERE TO STAY & DINE

Right in Inuvik is **Happy Valley Campground,** operated by the territorial parks department, with showers and electrical hookups. Between Inuvik and the airport is the similarly appointed **Chuk Campground.** The camping fee for both is C$12 to C$15 (US$7–US$9).

Rooms are expensive in Inuvik. It's not cheap to operate a hotel up here, and realistically, you're not likely to drive on to the next town looking for better prices. However, the following accommodations are fully modern and quite pleasant.

**Finto Motor Inn** ★ The newest and quietest place to stay in Inuvik is the Finto Motor Inn, a large wood-sided building on the southern edge of town. Guest rooms are good-sized and nicely furnished; many are recently updated and have kitchenettes. This is where most government people stay when they come up for business. The **Peppermill Restaurant** (✆ **867/777-2999**) offers gourmet renditions of local game and fishes, in addition to traditional steaks and other meats. The Sunday brunch is a major social event in Inuvik. In summer, a dinner theater with a good local history schtick operates from the hotel.

288 Mackenzie Rd. (P.O. Box 1925), Inuvik, NWT X0E 0T0. ✆ **867/777-2647.** Fax 867/777-3442. www.inuvikhotels.com. 39 units. C$174 (US$108) standard double, C$204 (US$126) kitchenette double. Senior rates available. AE, MC, V. **Amenities:** Restaurant, lounge; laundry; conference facilities; nonsmoking rooms. *In room:* A/C, TV, dataports.

**Mackenzie Hotel** In the town center, the Mackenzie is the oldest of Inuvik's hotels (it was built in the early 1960s). Guest rooms are large and nicely furnished, each with a couch, a couple of chairs, a desk, and a full-sized closet. On weekends, ask for a room away from the bar entrance and parking area. The staff is friendly and welcoming. The **Green Briar Dining Room,** probably the best restaurant in Inuvik, offers a wide selection of northern game and mainstream dishes; many main courses are under C$20 (US$12).

P.O. Box 1618, Inuvik, NWT X0E 0T0. ✆ **867/777-2861.** Fax 867/777-3317. www.inuvikhotels.com. 35 units. C$164 (US$102) double. AE, DC, MC, V. **Amenities:** 2 restaurants, 2 bars; laundry facilities. *In room:* TV.

**Robertson's B&B** This small, homey B&B has a handy location near downtown. Breakfast is an informal make-it-yourself affair, in keeping with the relaxed atmosphere here. The very accommodating Robertsons welcome children, as long as it's arranged in advance.

41 Mackenzie Rd. (P.O. Box 2356), Inuvik, NT X0E 0T0. (✆ **867/777-3111.** Fax 867/777-3112. robertbb@permafrost.com, 2 units with shared bathroom. C$70–C$80 (US$43–US$50) double. Rates include breakfast. MC, V. **Amenities:** Full office facilities available to guests; laundry room.

## BAFFIN ISLAND: ADVENTURE & INUIT ART

One of the most remote and uninhabited areas in North America, rugged and beautiful **Baffin Island** is an excellent destination for the traveler willing to spend some time and money for an adventure vacation; it's also a great place if your mission is to find high-quality Inuit Arts and Crafts.

It's easy to spend a day or two exploring the galleries and museums of Iqaluit, but if you've come this far, you definitely should continue on to yet more remote and traditional communities. Iqaluit is the population and governmental center of Baffin, but far more scenic and culturally significant destinations are just a short plane ride away. The coast of Baffin Island is heavily incised with fjords flanked by towering glacier-hung mountains. Life in the villages remains based on traditional hunting and fishing, though some of the smallest Baffin communities have developed worldwide reputations as producers of museum-quality carvings, prints, and weavings.

Though Baffin is the fifth-largest island in the world, it has a population of only 15,000. However, it's the largest population and cultural center—and capital—of the territory of **Nunavut,** which split off from the rest of the Northwest Territories in 1999.

**NorthWinds Arctic Adventures** ★, P.O. Box 888, Iqaluit, NU X0A 0H0 (✆ **800/549-0551** or 867/979-0551; fax 867/979-0573; www.northwinds-arctic.com), is Baffin Island's leading adventure-tour operator. A specialty of NorthWinds is its **dog-sledding expeditions** ★. The 7-day Arctic Odyssey tour (C$2,650/US$1,643) involves 5 days on the sea ice amid the amazing fjords of the Baffin coast; all members of the party (which is limited to 4 people) get a chance to drive the dogs. NorthWinds also offers a 12-day traverse of southern Baffin Island to Lake Harbour at C$4,500 (US$2,790). In summer, it leads hiking expeditions—10 and 13 days, costing C$2,500 and C$3,300 (US$1,550 and US$2,046)—into Auyuittuq National Park.

## ESSENTIALS

**GETTING THERE** Iqaluit, 2,266km (1,511 miles) from Yellowknife, is the major transport hub on Baffin and is linked to the rest of Canada by flights from Montréal, Ottawa, Winnipeg, and Yellowknife on **First Air** (✆ **800/267-1247**) and **Canadian North** (✆ **800/661-1505**). Flights are very expensive. To make the airfare more affordable, consider using frequent-flier miles.

Because there are no roads linking communities here, travel between small villages is also by plane. First Air is the major local carrier, centering out of Iqaluit; a bevy of smaller providers fill in the gaps.

**VISITOR INFORMATION** For information about Baffin Island communities, contact **Nunavut Tourism,** P.O. Box 1450, Iqaluit, NU X0A 0H0 (✆ **866/686-2888** or 867/979-6551; fax 867/979-1261; www.nunatour.nt.ca). Any serious traveler should get hold of ***The Nunavut Handbook,*** an excellent government-sponsored guide loaded with information on Nunavut's land, wildlife, history, people, culture, and practical tips for travelers. The handbook is available from local bookstores, and an on-line version is posted at **www.arctic-travel.com**.

You might also look at the NWT Arctic Tourism homepage at **www.nwttravel.nt.ca**.

**SPECIAL EVENTS** A festival of spring, **Toonik Tyme** is held the last week of April, featuring igloo building, ice sculpture, dogsled racing, and reputedly the toughest snowmobile race in the world. Cultural activities include Inuit dancing and singing, an arts fair, and traditional competitions like harpoon throwing, whip cracking, and high kicking.

On July 9, Nunavut celebrates its recent accession to territorial status with **Nunavut Day,** with festivities in every community. At this new celebration, traditional events might include bicycle races, running races, a tea-boiling contest, and other games of skill. The Elders play an important part in this celebration.

## IQALUIT: GATEWAY TO BAFFIN ISLAND

On the southern end of the island, **Iqaluit** (pronounced "ee-ka-*loo*-eet") is the major town on Baffin and like most Inuit settlements is quite young; it grew up alongside a U.S. Air Force airstrip built here in 1942. The rambling village overlooking Frobisher Bay now boasts a rapidly growing population of more than 4,400 and is a hodgepodge of weather-proofed government and civic buildings (the futuristic grade school looks like an ice-cube tray lying on its side) and wind-beaten public housing.

For a small town, there's a lot of activity here, with children roaring down the steep, rocky hills on mountain bikes; planes roaring; and husky pups yelping for attention. As in all Arctic towns, at any given time in summer, the entire population seems to be strolling somewhere. Even though no roads link Iqaluit to anywhere else, everyone seems to have at least one vehicle to drive endlessly around the town's labyrinth of dusty paths. There are no street addresses, because there are few roads organized enough to bother calling streets.

### What to See in Town

Begin at the **Unikkaarvik Visitor/Information Centre** (**✆ 867/979-4636;** www.nunavuttourism.com), overlooking the bay, with a friendly staff to answer questions and a series of displays on local native culture, natural history, and local art. There's even an igloo to explore. June 1 to Labour Day, the center is open daily 10am to 5pm; the rest of the year, it's open Monday to Friday the same hours.

Next door is the **Nunatta Sunakkutaangit Museum** (**✆ 867/979-5537**), housed in an old Hudson's Bay Company building. The collection of Arctic Arts and Crafts here is excellent; this is a good place to observe the stylized beauty of native carvings. It's open Tuesday to Sunday 1 to 5pm. The **Government of Nunavut Building,** at Iqaluit's "four corners," also has a good display of Northern art in the lobby.

If you are not planning to go any farther afield in Baffin, you may wish to catch a taxi or walk 30 minutes out to **Sylvia Grinnell Park** and take a hike on the tundra. The park is only 5km (3 miles) from Iqaluit but is on the other side of the ridge from town; it's a relatively quiet and protected place to see wildflowers and walk along an Arctic river. Another good **hiking trail** runs from Iqaluit to the "suburb" of Apex, following the beach and headland above Frobisher Bay. The trail begins near the Iqaluit cemetery; watch for the "inuksuks" (manlike stone cairns) marking the trail. In Apex, note the *qammaq*, a traditional sod hut used by local women as a gathering place.

Iqaluit is the primary center for **Baffin Island art.** Local galleries carry works from communities around the island; ask at the visitor center for a map of Arts and Crafts locations if you're interested in buying; prices here can be at least half of what they are down south.

### Where to Stay

Camping is permitted at **Sylvia Grinnell Park** (see above), but the amenities are spare. Don't expect to find anything fancier than a pit toilet and a few tent platforms. Bring your own water, or come prepared to filter the river water.

**Discovery Lodge Hotel** ★ About halfway between town and the airport, the Discovery Lodge is a newer hotel with nicely furnished, good-sized guest rooms and an inviting public sitting area. All rooms come with two beds (some are specially designed wedge-shaped beds meant to save space). This place in general is better maintained than most Arctic hotels; for many travelers who've been to the

North before, the fact that there's no public bar in the hotel will be a plus. The restaurant is good (you can have a drink with a meal); it's one of the more formal places to eat in Iqaluit.

P.O. Box 387, Iqaluit, NU X0A 0H0. © **867/979-4433.** Fax 867/979-6591. www.arctic-travel.com/DIS/covery.html. 53 units. C$156 (US$97) double; C$245 (US$152) suite. AE, DC, MC, V. **Amenities:** Restaurant; free airport shuttle; laundry service; nonsmoking rooms. *In room:* TV.

**Frobisher Inn** High above the town, the "Frobe," as it's known by regulars, is in the same complex of buildings that houses the regional government offices, a small shopping arcade, and the municipal pool. Guest rooms are well heated and pleasantly furnished and decorated, each with a desk, a dresser, and two chairs. The views on the bay side are quite panoramic. There's a very lively bar as well as an excellent restaurant, with a mix of French and Northern choices.

P.O. Box 610, Iqaluit, NU X0A 0H0. © **867/979-2222.** Fax 867/979-0427. www.frobisherinn.com. 95 units. C$170–185 (US$105–115) double. AE, MC, V. **Amenities:** Restaurant, bar; room service; laundry service; complimentary shuttle bus; nonsmoking rooms. *In room:* TV, coffeemaker, hair dryer.

**Pearson's Arctic Home Stay** ★ Here at Iqaluit's premier B&B, you get to stay with the town's former mayor in a lovely home filled with Inuit carving and artifacts. The rooms are simply decorated but comfortable; one has a foldout bed.

P.O. Box 449, Iqaluit, NU X0A 0H0. © **867/979-6408.** Fax 867/979-4888. 3 units (can sleep up to 8), none with private bathroom. C$150 (US$93) per person. Rates include breakfast. No credit cards. *In room:* No phone.

## PANGNIRTUNG & AUYUITTUQ NATIONAL PARK

Called "Pang" by Territorians, **Pangnirtung** is at the heart of one of the most scenic areas in Nunavut. Located on a deep, mountain-flanked fjord, Pang is the jumping off point for 21,497km² (8,300-sq.-mile) Auyuittuq National Park, often referred to as "the Switzerland of the Arctic." Pang is served by daily flights from Iqaluit on First Air.

Pang itself is a lovely little village of 1,200 people, with a postcard view up the narrow fjord to the glaciered peaks of Auyuittuq. The local population is very friendly and outgoing, which isn't the case in some other Inuit villages. The **Angmarlik Interpretive Centre** (© **867/473-8737**) is definitely worth a stop, with well-presented displays on local Inuit history and culture. June 15 to Labour Day, it's open daily 10am to 5pm. June to mid-September, it's open Monday to Saturday 9am to 9pm, Sunday 1 to 9pm. During the rest of the year, hours are Monday to Friday 8:30am to 5pm. Across the street are print and weaving shops, where you can visit local artisans.

Most people go to Pang to reach **Auyuittuq National Park,** 31km (19 miles) farther up Pangnirtung Fjord. *Auyuittuq* (pronounced "ow-you-*ee*-tuk") means "the land that never melts" and refers to 5,698km² (2,200-sq. mile) Penny Ice Cap, which covers the high plateaus of the park, and the glaciers that edge down into the lower valleys and cling to the towering granite peaks. The landscapes are extremely dramatic: Cliffs rise from the milky-green sea, terminating in hornlike glacier-draped peaks 2,333m (7,654 ft.) high; in fact, the world's longest uninterrupted cliff face (over 1km/½ mile of sheer rock) is in the park. Auyuittuq is largely the province of long-distance hikers and rock climbers; if you're looking for an adventurous walking holiday in magnificent scenery, this might be it. The best time to visit is July to mid-August, when the days are long and afternoons bring short-sleeve weather. You'll need to hire an outfitter with a boat to take you to the park trail head; costs are C$85 to C$100 (US$53–US$62). For details, contact the Auyuittuq Park Superintendent, P.O. Box 353, Pangnirtung, NU X0A 0R0 (✆ **867/473-8828;** fax 867/473-8612; http://parkscanada.pch.gc.ca/parks/Nunavut/Auyuittuq).

**OUTFITTERS** The best of the local outfitters is **Joavee Alivaktuk,** a personable Pang native with 25 years of experience as a professional guide. Joavee provides boat service to Auyuittuq for C$95 (US$59) and operates day trips to Kekerten Historic Park for C$150 (US$93), Arctic char–fishing trips, and whale-watching trips into Cumberland Sound. Contact **Alivaktuk Outfitting** at P.O. Box 3, Pangnirtung, NU X0A 0R0 (✆ and fax **867/473-8721**). Information about other outfitters is available at the Angmarlik Interpretive Centre.

### Where to Stay & Dine

In summer there's a free campground on the edge of Pang.

**Auyuittuq Lodge** The only year-round place to stay and eat in Pang, the Auyuitutuq is more a hostel than a hotel. There are 25 clean, cheerful rooms, each with two twin beds; the bathroom is down the hall. Meals are served family-style in the pleasant guest lounge and at set times only. Those who are not guests are welcome for meals; reservations are requested.

P.O. Box 53, Pangnirtung, NU X0A 0R0. ✆ **867/473-8955.** Fax 867/473-8611. pang.lodge@nunanet.com. 25 units. C$135 (US$84) per person, full board C$200 (US$124) per person. MC, V. **Amenities:** Restaurant; nonsmoking rooms.

## POND INLET

In many ways, the best reason to make the trip to **Pond Inlet** on Baffin's northern shore is simply to see the landscape. On a clear day, the flight from Iqaluit up to Pond is simply astounding: hundreds of miles of knife-edged mountains, massive ice caps (remnants of the ice fields that once covered all North America), glacier-choked valleys, and deep fjords flooded by the sea. It's an epic landscape—in all the country, perhaps only the Canadian Rockies can match the eastern coast of Baffin Island for sheer scenic drama.

Pond Inlet sits on **Eclipse Sound,** near the top of Baffin Island in the heart of this rugged beauty. Opposite the town is **Bylot Island,** a wildlife refuge and part of Sirmilik (North Baffin) National Park. Its craggy peaks rear 2,167m (7,109 ft.) straight up from the sea; from its central ice caps, two massive glaciers pour down into the sound directly across from town.

Considering the amazing scenery in the area, Pond Inlet is relatively untouristy. The peak tourist season is May and June, when local outfitters offer trips out to the edge of the ice floes, the point where the ice of the protected bays meets the open water of the Arctic Ocean. In spring this is where you find much of the Arctic's **wildlife** ★: seals, walruses, bird life, polar bears, narwhals, and other species converge here to feed, often on one another. A wildlife-viewing trip out to the floe edge (by snowmobile or dogsled) requires at least 3 days, with 5-day trips advised for maximum viewing opportunities. Other recreation opportunities open up in August, when the ice clears out of Eclipse Sound. Bird-watching boat trips out to Bylot Island are offered (the rare ivory gull nests here), as well as narwhal-watching trips in the fjords. Hill walking to glaciered peaks, sea kayaking in fjords, and superlative Arctic char fishing are also popular summer activities. It's best to allow several days in Pond Inlet if you're coming for summer trips; the weather is very changeable this far north. First Air flies into Pond Inlet 5 days a week from Iqaluit.

**OUTFITTERS** Two outfitters operate out of Pond Inlet. The local **Toonoonik Sahoonik Co-op,** General Delivery, Pond Inlet, NU X0A 0S0

(✆ **867/ 899-8366;** fax 867/899-8364; www.pondtours.ca), offers a variety of trips throughout the year. **Polar Sea Adventures,** P.O. Box 60, Pond Inlet, NU X0A 0C0 (✆ **867/899-8870,** or 613/241-2865 Oct–Mar; fax 867/899-8817; www.polarseaadventures.com), is operated by Scottish-born John Henderson and offers naturalist-guided floe-edge trips and guided hiking and boat trips in summer; Polar Sea is the best contact for sea kayaking or narwhal-watching trips on Milne Inlet.

### Where to Stay & Dine

**Sauniq Hotel** The Toonoonik Co-op operates Pond Inlet's only hotel. It's not fancy, but it is quite comfortable by northern standards. Be sure to sign up for full board, and spend some time in the sitting room chatting with the other guests.

General Delivery, Pond Inlet, NU X0A 0S0 ✆ **867/899-8928.** Fax 867/899-8770. 17 units. C$230 (US$143) double, including full board. AE, MC, V. **Amenities:** Restaurant; laundry facilities. *In room:* TV, no phone.

## KIMMIRUT (LAKE HARBOUR): STONE CARVERS & KATANNILIK TERRITORIAL PARK

The center for Baffin Island's famed stone-carving industry, **Kimmirut,** or **Lake Harbour,** is located along a rocky harbor, directly south of Iqaluit on the southern shore of Baffin Island. First Air flies to Kimmirut from Igaluit about C$300 (US$186).

While many people make the trip to this dynamic picturesque community to visit the workshops of world-renowned carvers, there are other reasons to make the trip. **Katannilik Territorial Park** is a preserve of Arctic wildlife and lush tundra vegetation and offers access to Soper River. The Soper, a Canadian Heritage River, is famed for its many waterfalls in side valleys and for its long-distance float and canoe trips.

Many people visit Katannilik Territorial Park for a less demanding version of rugged Auyuittuq National Park farther north. Wildlife viewing is good, and hiking trails wind through the park. Canoeing or kayaking the Soper River is a popular 3-day trip that's full of adventure but still suitable for a family. For more information on the park, contact the Katannilik Park Manager, Lake Harbour, NU X0A 0N0 (✆ **867/939-2084;** fax 867/939-2406; www.nunavutparks.com/katannilik). For information on canoe rentals and guided trips through Katannilik Park, contact NorthWinds (see above).

To watch local artists at work, visit the **carving studio** ★ across from the tourist office. For a selection of local carvings, go to the co-op store.

### Where to Stay & Dine

**Kimik Co-op Hotel** This simple hotel, upstairs from the co-op store, can be a surprisingly busy place, so it's wise to reserve a room well in advance. If you can, book a room overlooking Glasgow Inlet, where it's possible to see an occasional whale.

General Delivery, Kimmirut, NU X0A 0N0. ✆ **867/939-2093.** Fax 867/939-2005. 8 units. C$185–225 (US$115–140). Rates include all meals. AE, MC, V. **Amenities:** Restaurant. *In room:* TV, no phone.

## OTHER ARCTIC DESTINATIONS

**BATHURST INLET** One of the most notable Arctic lodges, **Bathurst Inlet Lodge** was founded in 1969 for naturalists and those interested in the Arctic's natural history and ecology. The lodge is at the mouth of the Burnside River, in a rugged landscape of tundra and rocky cliffs, housed in the historic buildings of a former Oblate mission and the old Hudson's Bay Company trading post.

The lodge provides custom quotes and can make arrangements to suit your individual needs, such as fly-ins, fishing, hiking, cross-country skiing, or dog-teaming; flight-seeing, caribou-viewing, wildlife photography; and use of a wilderness cabin in any season, including winter, with rentals by the day, week, month, or year.

For more details, contact **Bathurst Inlet Lodge,** P.O. Box 820, Yellowknife, NT X1A 2N6 (✆ **867/873-2595;** fax 867/920-4263; www.bathurstinletlodge.com).

**QUTTINIRPAAQ (Ellesmere Island) National Park Reserve** A good part of the intrigue of **Ellesmere Island** is its absolute remoteness. A preserve of rugged glacier-choked mountains, ice fields, mountain lakes and fjords, and Arctic wildlife, Ellesmere Island National Park is the most northerly point in Canada. During the short summer, experienced hikers and mountaineers make their way to this wilderness area to explore some of the most isolated and inaccessible land in the world.

Getting to Ellesmere is neither easy nor cheap. From Resolute Bay (served by regularly scheduled flights on Air North and First Air), park visitors must charter a private airplane for the 960km (595-mile) flight farther north. There are no facilities or improvements in the park itself, so you must be prepared for extremes of weather and physical endurance. The most common activity is hiking from Lake Hazen at the center of the park to Tanquary Fjord in the southwest corner. This 129km (80-mile) trek crosses rugged tundra moorland, as well as several glaciers, and demands fords of major rivers. Needless to say, Ellesmere Island Park isn't for the uninitiated.

For more information and an up-to-date listing of outfitters who run trips into the park, contact **Parks Canada,** P.O. Box 353, Pangnirtung, NU X0A 0R0 (✆ **867/473-8828;** fax 867/473-8612; You can visit the website devoted to Canada's territorial and national parks at **www.parcscanada.gc.ca**.

# Appendix: Canada in Depth

*by Bill McRae*

Canada's sheer amount of elbow space can make you dizzy. At 6.1 million km$^2$ (3.8 million sq. miles), 322,000km$^2$ (200,000 sq. miles) more than the United States, this colossal expanse contains only 29 million people—nearly 10 million fewer than the state of California alone. Most of the population is clustered in a relatively narrow southern belt that boasts all the nation's large cities and nearly all its industries. The silent Yukon, Northwest Territories, and Nunavut—where 55,000 people dot 2.4 million km$^2$ (1.5 million sq. miles)—remain a frontier, stretching to the Arctic shores and embracing thousands of lakes no one has ever charted, counted, or named.

It's impossible to easily categorize this land or its people—just when you think you know Canada, you discover another place, another temperament, a hidden side.

## 1 History 101

### THE FOUNDING OF NEW FRANCE

The Vikings landed in Canada more than 1,000 years ago, but the French were the first Europeans to get a toehold in the country. In 1608, Samuel de Champlain established a settlement on the cliffs overlooking the St. Lawrence River—today's Québec City. This was exactly a year after the Virginia Company founded Jamestown. Hundreds of miles of unexplored wilderness lay between the embryo colonies, but they were inexorably set on a collision course.

The early stages of the struggle for the new continent were explorations, and there the French outdid the English. Their fur traders, navigators, soldiers, and missionaries opened up not only Canada but also most of the United States. At least 35 of the 50 United States were either discovered, mapped, or settled by the French. Gradually, they staked out an immense colonial empire that, in patches and minus recognized borders, stretched

### Dateline

- **1608** Samuel de Champlain founds the settlement of Kebec—today's Québec City.
- **1642** The French colony of Ville-Marie established, later renamed Montréal.
- **1759** The British defeat the French at the Plains of Abraham. Québec City falls.
- **1763** All "New France" (Canada) ceded to the British.
- **1775** American Revolutionary forces capture Montréal but are repulsed at Québec City.
- **1813** Americans blow up Fort York (Toronto) in the War of 1812.
- **1841** The Act of Union creates the United Provinces of Canada.
- **1855** Ottawa becomes Canada's capital.
- **1869** The Hudson's Bay Company sells Rupert's Land to Canada. It becomes the Province of Alberta.
- **1873** The Northwest Mounted Police (the Mounties) are created.
- **1875** The West Coast community of Gastown is incorporated as the city of Vancouver. The Northwest Mounted

*continues*

from Hudson Bay in the Arctic to the Gulf of Mexico. Christened New France, it was run on an ancient seigniorial system, whereby settlers were granted land by the Crown in return for military service.

The military obligation was essential, for the colony knew hardly a moment of peace during its existence. New France blocked the path of western expansion by England's seaboard colonies with a string of forts that lined the Ohio-Mississippi Valley. The Anglo-Americans were determined to break through, and so the frontier clashes crackled and flared, with the native tribes participating ferociously. These miniature wars were nightmares of savagery, waged with knives and tomahawks as much as with muskets and cannons, characterized by raids and counter-raids, burning villages, and massacred women and children.

The French retaliated in kind. They converted the Abenaki tribe to Christianity and encouraged them to raid deep into New England territory, where, in 1704, they totally destroyed the town of Deerfield, Massachusetts. The Americans answered with a punitive blitz expedition by the famous green-clad Roger's Rangers, who wiped out the main Abenaki village and slaughtered half its population.

By far the most dreaded of the tribes was the Iroquois, who played the same role in the Canadian east as the Sioux (another French label) played in the American West. Astute politicians, the Iroquois learned to play the English against the French and vice versa, lending their scalping knives first to one side, then to the other. It took more than a century before they finally succumbed to the whites' smallpox, firewater, and gunpowder—in that order.

Police build the log fort that will develop into the city of Calgary.

- 1885 Under Louis Riel, the Métis rebel in western Saskatchewan.
- 1887 The Transcontinental Railroad reaches Vancouver, connecting Canada from ocean to ocean.
- 1896 The Klondike gold rush brings 100,000 people swarming into the Yukon.
- 1914 Canada enters World War I alongside Britain. Some 60,000 Canadians die in combat.
- 1920 The Northwest Territories separate from the Yukon.
- 1930 Depression and mass unemployment hit Canada.
- 1939 Canada enters World War II with Britain.
- 1947 Huge oil deposits are discovered at Leduc, southwest of Edmonton. The Alberta oil boom begins.
- 1959 The opening of the St. Lawrence Seaway turns Toronto into a major seaport.
- 1967 Montréal hosts the World Expo.
- 1968 The Parti Québecois is founded by René Lévesque. The separatist movement begins.
- 1970 Cabinet Minister Pierre Laporte is kidnapped and murdered. The War Measures Act is imposed on Québec Province.
- 1976 Montréal becomes the site of the Olympic Games.
- 1988 Calgary hosts the Winter Olympics.
- 1989 The Canada-U.S. Free Trade Agreement eliminates all tariffs on goods of national origin moving between the two countries.
- 1993 The Conservative party is swept out of power in elections.
- 1995 Québec votes narrowly to remain in Canada.
- 1997 Jean Chrétien is reelected prime minister.
- 1999 Nunavut severs itself from the rump Northwest Territories to become a self-governed territory and Inuit homeland.
- 2002 Canadian figure skaters Jamie Sale and David Pelletier win Olympic gold, breaking 40-year Russian dominance.

## 2 The Fall of Québec

There were only about 65,000 French settlers in the colony, but they more than held their own against the million Anglo-Americans, first and foremost because they were natural forest fighters—one Canadian trapper could stalemate six redcoats in the woods. Mainly, however, it was because they made friends with the local tribes whenever possible. The majority of tribes sided with the French and made the English pay a terrible price for their blindness.

Even before French and English interests in the New World came to the point of armed struggle in the Seven Years' War, the British had largely taken control of Acadia, though its lush forests and farmlands were dotted with French settlements. The governors knew there would be war, so, suspicious of Acadia's French-speaking inhabitants, they decided on a bold and ruthless plan: All Acadians who wouldn't openly pledge allegiance to the British sovereign would be deported. The order came in 1755, and French-speaking families throughout the province were forcibly moved from their homes, many resettling in the French territory of Louisiana, where their Cajun language and culture are still alive today. To replace the Acadians, shiploads of Scottish and Irish settlers arrived from the British Isles, and the province soon acquired the name Nova Scotia—New Scotland.

When the final round of fighting began in 1754, it opened with a series of shattering English debacles. The French had a brilliant commander, the Marquis de Montcalm, exactly the kind of unorthodox tactician needed for the fluid semi-guerrilla warfare of the American wilderness. Britain's proud General Braddock rode into a French-Indian ambush that killed him and scattered his army. Montcalm led an expedition against Fort Oswego that wiped out the stronghold and turned Lake Ontario into a French waterway. The following summer he repeated the feat with Fort William Henry, at the head of Lake George, which fell amid ghastly scenes of massacre, later immortalized by James Fenimore Cooper in *The Last of the Mohicans.* Middle New York now lay wide open to raids, and England's hold on America seemed to be slipping.

Then, like a cornered boxer bouncing from the ropes, the British came back with a devastating right-left-right that not only saved their colonies but also won them the entire continent. The first punches were against Fort Duquesne, in Pennsylvania, and against the Fortress of Louisbourg, on Cape Breton, both of which they took after bloody sieges. Then, where least expected, came the ultimate haymaker, aimed straight at the enemy's solar plexus—Québec.

In June 1759, a British fleet nosed its way from the Atlantic down the St. Lawrence River. In charge of the troops on board was the youngest general in the army, 32-year-old James Wolfe, whose military record was remarkable and whose behavior was so eccentric he had the reputation of being "mad as a March hare." The struggle for Québec dragged on until September, when Wolfe, near desperation, played his final card. He couldn't storm those gallantly defended fortress walls, though the British guns had shelled the town to rubble. Wolfe therefore loaded 5,000 men into boats and rowed upriver to a cove behind the city. Then they silently climbed the towering cliff face in the darkness, and when morning came Wolfe had his army squarely astride Montcalm's supply lines. Now the French had to come out of their stronghold and fight in the open.

## 3 A Confederation of Provinces

Canada has always been a loosely linked country, a confederation of provinces, not a union of states. Canadians are quick to tell you theirs is a "cultural mosaic" of people, not a "melting pot." These factors account in great part for two of Canada's most striking characteristics: its cultural vitality and its habits of mistrust and contention.

### THE FIRST SCALPERS

According to some historians, the English introduced scalping to North America by offering a cash bounty for each French scalp the native braves brought in.

The British formed their famous "thin red line" across the bush-studded Plains of Abraham, just west of the city. Montcalm advanced on them with five regiments, all in step, and in the next quarter of an hour the fate of Canada was decided. The redcoats stood like statues as the French drew closer—100 yards, 60 yards, 40 yards. Then a command rang out, and (in such perfect unison it sounded like a single thunderclap) the English muskets crashed. The redcoats advanced four measured paces, halted, fired, advanced another four paces with robot precision—halted, fired again. Then it was all over.

The plain was covered with the fallen French. Montcalm lay mortally wounded, and the rest of his troops fled helter-skelter. Among the British casualties was Wolfe himself. With two bullets through his body, he lived just long enough to hear that he'd won. Montcalm died a few hours after him. Today, overlooking the boardwalk of Québec, you'll find a unique memorial to these men—a statue commemorating both the victor and vanquished of the same battle.

### THE U.S. INVASION

The capture of Québec determined the war and left Britain ruler of all North America down to the Mexican border. Yet, oddly enough, this victory generated Britain's worst defeat. For if the French had held Canada, the British government would certainly have been more careful in its treatment of the American colonists. As it was, the British felt cocksure and decided to make the colonists themselves pay for the outrageous costs of the French and Indian Wars. The taxes slapped on all imports—especially tea—infuriated the colonists to the point of open rebellion against the Crown.

But if the British misjudged the temper of the colonists, the Americans were equally wrong about the mood of the Canadians. Washington felt sure the French in the north would join the American Revolution or at least not resist an invasion of American soldiers. He was terribly mistaken on both counts. The French had little love for either of the English-speaking antagonists. But they were staunch Royalists and devout Catholics, with no sympathy for the "godless" republicans from the south. Only a handful changed sides, and most French Canadians fought grimly shoulder to shoulder with their erstwhile enemies.

Thirty-eight years later, in the War of 1812, another U.S. army marched up the banks of the Richelieu River where it flows from Lake Champlain to the St. Lawrence. And once again the French Canadians stuck by the British and flung back the invaders. The war ended in a draw, but with surprisingly happy results. Britain and the young United States agreed to demilitarize the Great Lakes and to extend their mutual border along the 49th parallel to the Rockies.

### LOYALISTS & IMMIGRANTS

One of the side effects of the American Revolution was an influx of English-speaking newcomers for Canada. About 50,000 Americans who had remained faithful to George III, the United Empire Loyalists, migrated to Canada because they were given rough treatment in the States. They settled mostly in Nova Scotia and began to populate the almost-empty shores of what's now New Brunswick.

After the Napoleonic Wars, a regular tide of immigrants came from England, which was going through the early and cruelest stages of the Industrial Revolution. They were fleeing from the hideously bleak factory towns, from workhouses, starvation wages, and impoverished Scottish farms. Even the unknown perils of the New World seemed preferable to these blessings of the Dickens era. By 1850, more than half a million immigrants had arrived, pushing Canada's population above 2 million. The population centers began to shift westward, away from the old seaboard colonies in the east, opening up the territories eventually called Ontario, Manitoba, and Saskatchewan.

With increased population came the demand for confederation, largely because the various colony borders hampered trade. Britain complied rather promptly. In 1867, Parliament passed an act creating a federal union out of the colonies of Upper and Lower Canada, Nova Scotia, and New Brunswick. British Columbia hesitated over whether to remain separate, join the United States, or merge with Canada, but finally voted itself in. Remote Newfoundland hesitated longest of all—it remained a distinct colony until 1949, when it became Canada's 10th province.

## THE METIS REBELLION

Geographically, Canada stretched from the Atlantic to the Pacific, but in reality most of the immense region in between lay beyond the rule of Ottawa, the nation's capital. The endless prairies and forest lands of the West and Northwest were inhabited by about 40,000 people, more than half of them nomadic tribes pushed there by the waves of white settlers. They lived by hunting, fishing, and trapping, depending largely on buffalo for food, clothing, and shelter. As the once-enormous herds began to dwindle, life grew increasingly hard for the nomads. Adding to their troubles were whiskey traders peddling poisonous rotgut for furs and packs of outlaws who took what they wanted at gunpoint.

Ordinary law officers were nearly useless. In 1873, the federal government created a quite extraordinary force: the Northwest Mounted Police, now called the Royal Canadian Mounted Police (and now rarely mounted). The scarlet-coated Mounties earned a legendary reputation for toughness, fairness, and the ability to hunt down wrongdoers. And unlike their American counterparts, they usually brought in prisoners alive.

But even the Mounties couldn't handle the desperate uprising that shook western Saskatchewan in 1885. As the railroad relentlessly pushed across the prairies and the buffalo vanished, the people known as the Métis felt they had to fight for their existence. The Métis, offspring of French trappers and native women, were superb hunters and trackers. The westward expansion had driven them from Manitoba to the banks of the Saskatchewan River, where some 6,000 of them now made their last stand against iron rails and wooden farmhouses. They had a charismatic leader in Louis Riel, a man educated enough to teach school and mad enough to think God wanted him to found a new religion.

With Riel's rebels rose their natural allies, the Plains tribes, under chiefs Pound-maker and Big Bear. Together, they were a formidable force. The Métis attacked the Mounted Police at Duck Lake, cut the telegraph wires, and proclaimed an independent republic. Their allies stormed the town of Battleford, then captured and burned Fort Pitt. The alarmed administration in Ottawa sent an army marching westward under General Middleton, equipped with artillery and Gatling machine guns. The Métis checked them briefly at Fish Creek but had to fall back on their main village of Batoche. There the last battle of the west took place—long lines of redcoats charging with fixed bayonets, the Métis fighting from house to house, from rifle pits and crude trenches, so short of ammunition they had to shoot lead buttons instead of bullets.

Batoche fell (you can still see the bullet marks on the houses there), and the rebellion was completely crushed shortly afterward. Louis Riel was tried for treason and murder. Though any court today probably would've found him insane, the Canadian authorities hanged him.

### RAILROADS, WHEAT & WAR

The reason the army was able to crush Riel's rebellion so quickly was also the reason for its outbreak: the Canadian Pacific Railway. The railroad was more than a marvel of engineering—it formed a steel band holding the country together, enabling Canada to live up to its motto, *A Mari Usque ad Mare* ("From Sea to Sea").

Though the free-roaming prairie people hated the iron horse, railroads were vital to Canada's survival as a nation. They had to be pushed through, against all opposition, because the isolated provinces threatened to drift into the orbit of the United States. Without the western provinces, the Dominion would cease to exist. As one journalist of the time put it: "The whistle of a locomotive is the true cradle song and anthem of our country." As the country's transportation system developed, the central provinces emerged as one of the world's biggest breadbaskets. In a single decade, wheat production zoomed from 56 million bushels to more than 200 million, putting Canada on a par with the United States and Russia as a granary.

And despite the bitterness engendered by Riel's execution, in the following year Canada elected its first prime minister of French heritage. Sir Wilfrid Laurier had one foot in each ethnic camp and proved to be a superlative leader—according to some, the best his country ever produced. His term of office (1896–1911) was a period in which Canada flexed its muscles like a young giant and looked forward to unlimited growth and a century of peaceful prosperity—just like an equally optimistic American neighbor to the south.

With the onset of World War I, the Dominion went to war allied with Britain and likewise tried to fight it on a volunteer basis. It didn't work. The tall, healthy Canadians, together with the Australians, formed the shock troops of the British Empire and earned that honor with torrents of blood. The entire western front in France was littered with Canadian bones. The flow of volunteers became a trickle, and in 1917 the Dominion was forced to introduce conscription. The measure ran into violent opposition from the French-speaking minority, who saw conscription as a device to thin out their numbers.

The draft law went through, but it strained the nation's unity almost to the breaking point. The results were ghastly. More than 60,000 Canadians fell in battle, a terrible bloodletting for a country of 250,000. (In World War II, by contrast, Canada lost 40,000 from a population of 11.5 million.)

## 4 Toward World Power

Between the world wars, the fortunes of Canada more or less reflected those of the United States, except that Canada was never foolish enough to join the "noble experiment" of Prohibition. Some of its citizens, in fact, waxed rich on the lucrative bootlegging trade across the border.

But the Great Depression, coupled with disastrous droughts in the western provinces, hit all the harder in Canada. There was no equivalent of Roosevelt's New Deal in the Dominion. The country staggered along from one financial crisis to the next until the outbreak of World War II totally transformed the situation. The war provided the boost Canada needed to join the ranks of the major industrial nations. And the surge of postwar immigration provided the numbers required to work the new industries. From 1941 to 1974, Canada doubled in population and increased its gross national product nearly tenfold.

With the discovery of huge uranium deposits in Ontario and Saskatchewan, Canada was in the position to add nuclear energy to its power resources. And the opening of the St. Lawrence Seaway turned Toronto—more than 1,600km (1,000 miles) from the nearest ocean—into a major seaport. All these achievements propelled Canada into its present position: a powerhouse of manufacturing and trading, with a standard of living to match that of the United States. But, simultaneously, old ghosts were raising their heads again.

## TROUBLE IN QUEBEC

As an ethnic enclave, the French Canadians had won their battle for survival with flying colors. From their original 65,000 settlers, they had grown to more than 6 million, without receiving reinforcements from overseas. They had preserved and increased their presence by means of large families, rigid cultural cohesion, and the unifying influence of their Catholic faith. But they had fallen far behind the English-speaking majority economically and politically. Few of them held top positions in industry or finance, and they enjoyed relatively little say in national matters.

What rankled most with them was that Canada never recognized French as a second national language. In other words, the French were expected to be bilingual if they wanted good careers, but the English-speakers got along nicely with just their own tongue. On a general cultural basis too, the country overwhelmingly reflected Anglo-Saxon attitudes rather than an Anglo-French mixture.

By the early 1960s, this discontent led to a dramatic radicalization of Québecois politics. A new separatist movement arose that regarded Québec not as simply 1 of 10 provinces but as *l'état du Québec,* a distinct state that might, if it chose, break away from the country. The most extreme faction, the Front de Liberation du Québec (FLQ), was frankly revolutionary and terrorist. It backed its demands with bombs, arson, and murder, culminating in the kidnap-killing of Cabinet Minister Pierre Laporte in October 1970.

The Ottawa government, under Prime Minister Pierre Trudeau, imposed the War Measures Act and moved 10,000 troops into the province. The police used their exceptional powers under the act to break up civil disorders, arrest hundreds of suspects, and catch the murderers of Laporte. And in the 1973 provincial elections, the separatists were badly defeated, winning only 6 seats from a total of 110.

The crisis eventually calmed down. In some ways, its effects were beneficial. The federal government redoubled its efforts to remove the worst grievances of the French Canadians. Federal funds flowed to French schools outside Québec (nearly half the schoolchildren of New Brunswick, for example, are French-speaking). French Canadians were appointed to senior positions. Most important, all provinces were asked to make French an official language, which entailed making signs, government forms, transportation schedules, and other printed matter bilingual. Civil servants had to bone up on French to pass their exams, and the business world began to stipulate bilingualism for men and women aiming at executive positions. All these measures were already afoot before the turmoil began, but there's no doubt that bloodshed helped to accelerate them.

## UNION OR SEPARATION?

Ever since the violent crisis, Canadian politicians of all hues have been trying to patch up some sort of compromise that would enable their country to remain united. They appeared close to success when they formulated the so-called Meech Lake Accord in the 1980s. Québec's premier set up a commission to study ways to change the province's constitutional relationship with Ottawa's federal government. This aroused the ire of other provinces, which failed to see why Québec should be granted a "special" position in Canada. During this time, the separatist Parti Québecois rallied its forces and staged a political comeback. The Meech Lake agreement became too unwieldy to pass muster, and an alliance of French Canadians, native Canadian groups, western Canadian libertarians—and the province of New Brunswick—drove a stake through the heart of the accord. So the proposals, memorandums, and referendums go on and on; each one vetoed by the other camp and none coming closer to a solution.

The rift between Québec's French and English speakers—and between Québec and the other provinces—is today wider than ever. To make the situation even more complex, the only population segment in Québec that's growing is that of non-English- and non-French-speaking immigrants. Winning over the immigrant vote is suddenly big political business in Québec.

In October 1995, Québec again faced a referendum asking whether the French-speaking province should separate from the rest of Canada, and suddenly Canada teetered on the brink of splitting apart. The vote went in favor of the pro-unity camp by a razor-thin margin, but the issue was hardly resolved: In all likelihood, it lives to be reborn as another referendum. Meanwhile, as public officials debate separatism, Québec's younger generation is voting with its feet. Many of its brightest and best are heading west, particularly to more prosperous British Columbia and Alberta. However, these western provinces—no lovers of Ottawa—themselves dream of loosening the federal laws binding them to eastern Canada.

By now, most Canadians are heartily tired of the Québec debate, though nobody seems to have a clear idea how to end it. Some say secession is the only way out; others favor the Swiss formula of biculturalism and bilingualism. For Québec, the breakaway advocated by Francophone hotheads could spell economic disaster. Most of Canada's industrial and financial power is in the English-speaking provinces. An independent Québec would be a poor country. But all Canada would be poorer by losing the special flavor and rich cultural heritage imparted by the presence of La Belle Province.

# 5 Onward Into the Millennium: The Creation of Nunavut & More

Elements of the Canadian economy are still adapting to the landmark Free Trade Agreement concluded with the States in 1989. While free trade hasn't done much to revive the smokestack industries that once were the engines of eastern Canada, the agreement, combined with the weak dollar, has actually been good for much of Canada's huge agricultural heartland. However, the globalization of

## Canada's Cultural Mosaic

Canada has sought "unity through diversity" as a national ideal, and its people are even more diverse than its scenery. In the eastern province of Québec live 6 million French Canadians, whose motto, Je me souviens ("I remember"), has kept them "more French than France" through 2 centuries of Anglo domination. They've transformed Canada into a bilingual country where everything official—including parking tickets and airline passes—comes in two tongues.

The English-speaking majority of the populace is a mosaic rather than a block. Two massive waves of immigration—one before 1914, the other between 1945 and 1972—poured 6.5 million assorted Europeans and Americans into the country, providing muscles and skills, as well as a kaleidoscope of cultures. The 1990s saw another wave of immigration—largely from Asia and particularly from Hong Kong—that has transformed the economics and politics of British Columbia. Thus, Nova Scotia is as Scottish as haggis and kilts, Vancouver has the largest Chinese population outside Asia, the plains of Manitoba are sprinkled with the onion-shaped domes of Ukrainian churches, and Ontario offers Italian street markets and a theater festival featuring the works of Shakespeare at, yes, Stratford.

You can attend a native-Canadian tribal assembly, a Chinese New Year dragon parade, an Inuit spring celebration, a German Bierfest, a Highland gathering, or a Slavic folk dance. There are group settlements on the prairies where the working parlance is Danish, Czech, or Hungarian, and entire villages speak Icelandic.

trade is transforming the Canadian economy in ways that produce confusion and hostility in the average citizen. Many Canadians are deeply ambivalent about being so closely linked to their powerful southern neighbor, and the trade agreement (and U.S. culture in general) often gets the blame for everything that's going wrong with Canada. At the same time, the reality of the joined Canadian and U.S. economies—85% of Canada's trade is with its southern neighbor—has started a dialogue in Jean Chrétien's center-left cabinet about linking the Canadian and U.S. dollars, a move many heralded as the beginning of the end of an independent Canada.

Public interest in protecting the environment runs high, as reflected in public policy. Recycling is commonplace, and communities across the country have made great strides in balancing economic interests with environmental goals. On Vancouver Island, for example, environmentalists and timber companies agreed in 1995 on forestry standards that satisfy both parties. When salmon fishing boats blockaded an Alaska ferry in Prince Rupert in 1997, the issue for the Canadians was perceived as overfishing by Americans. Salmon have been reduced to an endangered species in much of the Pacific Northwest, and the Canadians consequently don't think much of U.S. fisheries policies.

In 1999, the huge Northern Territories divided in two. The eastern half, which takes in Baffin Island, the land around Hudson's Bay, and most of the

Arctic islands, is now called Nunavut and essentially functions as an Inuit homeland. The rump Northwest Territories officially retains the territory's old name, though many refer to the region as the Western Arctic.

The success of the Nunavut negotiations has emboldened other native groups to settle their own land claims with the Canadian government. While many of the claims in northern Canada can be settled by transferring government land and money to native groups, those in southern Canada are more complex. Some tribes assert a prior claim to land currently owned by non-Indians; in other areas, native groups refuse to abide by environmental laws that seek to protect endangered runs of salmon. The situation in a number of communities has moved beyond protests and threats to armed encounters and road barricades. The path seems set for more and increasingly hostile confrontations between official Canada and its native peoples.

Canada is challenged internally on many fronts, with social and economic forces working to fragment a cohesive sense of national identity. Whether the long-standing cultural and political institutions that have guided the country successfully for so many years will survive is a question that'll be answered in the very near future.

# Index

# NOTES

## FROMMER'S® COMPLETE TRAVEL GUIDES

Alaska
Alaska Cruises & Ports of Call
Amsterdam
Argentina & Chile
Arizona
Atlanta
Australia
Austria
Bahamas
Barcelona, Madrid & Seville
Beijing
Belgium, Holland & Luxembourg
Bermuda
Boston
Brazil
British Columbia & the Canadian Rockies
Budapest & the Best of Hungary
California
Canada
Cancún, Cozumel & the Yucatán
Cape Cod, Nantucket & Martha's Vineyard
Caribbean
Caribbean Cruises & Ports of Call
Caribbean Ports of Call
Carolinas & Georgia
Chicago
China
Colorado
Costa Rica
Denmark
Denver, Boulder & Colorado Springs
England
Europe
European Cruises & Ports of Call
Florida
France
Germany
Great Britain
Greece
Greek Islands
Hawaii
Hong Kong
Honolulu, Waikiki & Oahu
Ireland
Israel
Italy
Jamaica
Japan
Las Vegas
London
Los Angeles
Maryland & Delaware
Maui
Mexico
Montana & Wyoming
Montréal & Québec City
Munich & the Bavarian Alps
Nashville & Memphis
Nepal
New England
New Mexico
New Orleans
New York City
New Zealand
Northern Italy
Nova Scotia, New Brunswick & Prince Edward Island
Oregon
Paris
Philadelphia & the Amish Country
Portugal
Prague & the Best of the Czech Republic
Provence & the Riviera
Puerto Rico
Rome
San Antonio & Austin
San Diego
San Francisco
Santa Fe, Taos & Albuquerqu
Scandinavia
Scotland
Seattle & Portland
Shanghai
Singapore & Malaysia
South Africa
South America
South Florida
South Pacific
Southeast Asia
Spain
Sweden
Switzerland
Texas
Thailand
Tokyo
Toronto
Tuscany & Umbria
USA
Utah
Vancouver & Victoria
Vermont, New Hampshire & Maine
Vienna & the Danube Valley
Virgin Islands
Virginia
Walt Disney World & Orlando
Washington, D.C.
Washington State

## FROMMER'S® DOLLAR-A-DAY GUIDES

Australia from $50 a Day
California from $70 a Day
Caribbean from $70 a Day
England from $75 a Day
Europe from $70 a Day
Florida from $70 a Day
Hawaii from $80 a Day
Ireland from $60 a Day
Italy from $70 a Day
London from $85 a Day
New York from $90 a Day
Paris from $80 a Day
San Francisco from $70 a Day
Washington, D.C. from $80 a Da

## FROMMER'S® PORTABLE GUIDES

Acapulco, Ixtapa & Zihuatanejo
Amsterdam
Aruba
Australia's Great Barrier Reef
Bahamas
Baja & Los Cabos
Berlin
Boston
California Wine Country
Cancún
Charleston & Savannah
Chicago
Disneyland
Dublin
Florence
Frankfurt
Hawaii: The Big Island
Hong Kong
Houston
Las Vegas
London
Los Angeles
Maine Coast
Maui
Miami
New Orleans
New York City
Paris
Phoenix & Scottsdale
Portland
Puerto Rico
Puerto Vallarta, Manzanillo & Guadalajara
Rio de Janeiro
San Diego
San Francisco
Seattle
Sydney
Tampa & St. Petersburg
Vancouver
Venice
Virgin Islands
Washington, D.C.

## FROMMER'S® NATIONAL PARK GUIDES

Banff & Jasper
Family Vacations in the National Parks
Grand Canyon
National Parks of the American West
Rocky Mountain
Yellowstone & Grand Teton
Yosemite & Sequoia/ Kings Canyon
Zion & Bryce Canyon

## Frommer's® Memorable Walks

Chicago
London
New York
Paris
San Francisco

## Frommer's® Great Outdoor Guides

Arizona & New Mexico
New England
Northern California
Southern New England
Vermont & New Hampshire

## Suzy Gershman's Born to Shop Guides

Born to Shop: France
Born to Shop: Hong Kong, Shanghai & Beijing
Born to Shop: Italy
Born to Shop: London
Born to Shop: New York
Born to Shop: Paris

## Frommer's® Irreverent Guides

Amsterdam
Boston
Chicago
Las Vegas
London
Los Angeles
Manhattan
New Orleans
Paris
Rome
San Francisco
Seattle & Portland
Vancouver
Walt Disney World
Washington, D.C.

## Frommer's® Best-Loved Driving Tours

Britain
California
Florida
France
Germany
Ireland
Italy
New England
Northern Italy
Scotland
Spain
Tuscany & Umbria

## Hanging Out™ Guides

Hanging Out in England
Hanging Out in Europe
Hanging Out in France
Hanging Out in Ireland
Hanging Out in Italy
Hanging Out in Spain

## The Unofficial Guides®

Bed & Breakfasts and Country Inns in:
- California
- Great Lakes States
- Mid-Atlantic
- New England
- Northwest
- Rockies
- Southeast
- Southwest

Best RV & Tent Campgrounds in:
- California & the West
- Florida & the Southeast
- Great Lakes States
- Mid-Atlantic
- Northeast
- Northwest & Central Plains
- Southwest & South Central Plains
- U.S.A.

Beyond Disney
Branson, Missouri
California with Kids
Chicago
Cruises
Disneyland
Florida with Kids
Golf Vacations in the Eastern U.S.
Great Smoky & Blue Ridge Region
Inside Disney
Hawaii
Las Vegas
London
Mid-Atlantic with Kids
Mini Las Vegas
Mini-Mickey
New England and New York with Kids
New Orleans
New York City
Paris
San Francisco
Skiing in the West
Southeast with Kids
Walt Disney World
Walt Disney World for Grown-ups
Walt Disney World with Kids
Washington, D.C.
World's Best Diving Vacations

## Special-Interest Titles

Frommer's Adventure Guide to Australia & New Zealand
Frommer's Adventure Guide to Central America
Frommer's Adventure Guide to India & Pakistan
Frommer's Adventure Guide to South America
Frommer's Adventure Guide to Southeast Asia
Frommer's Adventure Guide to Southern Africa
Frommer's Britain's Best Bed & Breakfasts and Country Inns
Frommer's Caribbean Hideaways
Frommer's Exploring America by RV
Frommer's Fly Safe, Fly Smart
Frommer's France's Best Bed & Breakfasts and Country Inns
Frommer's Gay & Lesbian Europe
Frommer's Italy's Best Bed & Breakfasts and Country Inns
Frommer's New York City with Kids
Frommer's Ottawa with Kids
Frommer's Road Atlas Britain
Frommer's Road Atlas Europe
Frommer's Road Atlas France
Frommer's Toronto with Kids
Frommer's Vancouver with Kids
Frommer's Washington, D.C., with Kids
Israel Past & Present
The New York Times' Guide to Unforgettable Weekends
Places Rated Almanac
Retirement Places Rated

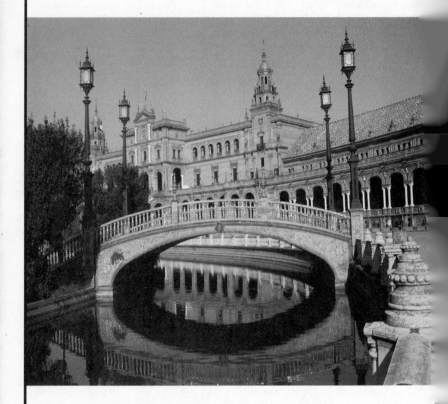